HANDBOOK TO THE GRAMMAR
OF THE GREEK TESTAMENT

HANDBOOK TO THE GRAMMAR OF THE GREEK TESTAMENT

TOGETHER WITH COMPLETE VOCABULARY,
AND AN EXAMINATION OF THE CHIEF
NEW TESTAMENT SYNONYMS

BY THE
REV. SAMUEL G. GREEN, D.D.
AUTHOR OF "A HANDBOOK TO OLD TESTAMENT HEBREW"
"A HANDBOOK OF CHURCH HISTORY" ETC.

*ILLUSTRATED BY
NUMEROUS EXAMPLES
AND COMMENTS*

REVISED AND IMPROVED EDITION

WIPF & STOCK · Eugene, Oregon

Wipf and Stock Publishers
199 W 8th Ave, Suite 3
Eugene, OR 97401

Handbook to the Grammar of the Greek New Testament
Together with Complete Vocabulary,
and an Examination of the Chief New Testament Synonyms
By Green, Samuel G.
ISBN 13: 978-1-5326-7108-1
Publication date 9/25/2018
Previously published by Fleming H. Revell Company, 1904

PREFACE.

(SEE ALSO NOTE TO REVISED EDITION, *p.* xi.)

THAT a knowledge of the New Testament in its original tongue is a thing to be desired by intelligent Christians none will question. Such desire has probably been largely quickened by the appearance of the Revised Version. No book can be thoroughly known in a translation only; and the Bible, although " the most translatable of books," is no exception.

Many, who would gladly undertake the study, are deterred by the manifold and unquestionable difficulties of the Greek language. It seems worth while to ask whether this obstacle cannot, in some measure, be removed.

Undoubtedly, the Greek of the New Testament, as a later dialect of an elaborate and polished language, can most effectively be studied through the medium of the elder forms of the tongue. This method, accordingly, is in general chosen; and the historians and orators, the philosophers and poets of Greece, have led the way to the Evangelists and the Apostles.

Yet many persons have no opportunity for studies so extended and difficult. Are they, therefore, to be forbidden all access, save through translators, critics, and interpreters, to the words of the Divine revelation?

In attempting to reply, we note that the Greek of Scripture is, for most purposes, a language complete in itself. Its forms and rules are definite, its usages in general precise. Its peculiarities, though best approached from the classic side, may be reached by a shorter way, and be almost as well comprehended.

Many circumstances, again, facilitate the special study of the New Testament tongue. The language of orators and philosophers had descended to men of simpler mind and less artificial speech. Comparing the Sacred Volume with Greek literature generally, we find a smaller vocabulary, fewer grammatical forms, less intricate etymological rules, with scantier lists of exceptions, and a far less elaborate syntax; while the student has the advantage of being confined for the time to one limited, but intensely interesting, field.

The following pages are then intended as a sufficient guide to Biblical Greek for English students, that is, for those who have not studied the classical languages. It may also be of service to those who have made some progress in classical studies, but who wish to concentrate their chief regards upon the language and syntax of the New Testament.

The plan of the volume, and the method recommended for its study, are sufficiently set forth in the Introduction. To specify all the sources, English and German, from which valuable aid has been derived, would be unnecessary. Winer's comprehensive work (translated into English, with large and valuable additions, by the Rev. Dr. Moulton, of Cambridge) has of course been consulted throughout. Scarcely less useful have been the researches and discussions of the late Dr. Donaldson. The New Testament Grammars of the Rev. W. Webster, and of the Rev. T. S. Green, have afforded some very valuable hints. On Greek Testament Lexicography, it will suffice to name the *Clavis Novi Testamenti* by Dr. C. L. W. Grimm, now translated into English, with additions, by Dr. J. H. Thayer; also Cremer's *New Testament Lexicon*, translated by the Rev. W. Urwick, M.A.

The first Edition of the work was carefully revised in MS. by the Rev. Dr. Jacob, late Head Master of Christ's Hospital, author of the *Bromsgrove Greek Grammar*, and other classical works; and, in the proof sheets, by the Rev. R. B. Girdlestone, M.A., and by the late Rev. T. G. Rooke, B.A., afterwards President of Rawdon College. To the important suggestions of those gentlemen the volume owes very much. It is commended to attentive students of the New Testament, in the hope that it may lead not a few to the better understanding, and therefore to the higher appreciation of the Divine oracles.

INTRODUCTION.

THE following work so far differs from other manuals of the Greek language, both in its method and in the persons for whom it is intended, that some preliminary words on the plan by which its several parts should be studied will not be out of place.

On ORTHOGRAPHY, the sections should be thoroughly mastered, not only for the sake of facility in reading, but because most of the difficulties and so-called irregularities in the inflection of substantives, adjectives, and verbs depend on letter-changes, of which the rules are comparatively few, and really simple. To know these laws at the outset is to be provided with a key to varieties and intricacies which might otherwise prove hopelessly bewildering. It will be advisable that no student should advance beyond this portion of the work before being able to read the lessons on pages 10, 11 with fluency, and accurately to transliterate the paragraph on page 12. Great attention should be paid at this stage to pronunciation, especially to the distinction between the long and short vowels; and those who may be studying the work by themselves are strongly recommended to take an opportunity of reading a chapter or two in Greek to some scholar who can criticise and correct their mistakes.

In ETYMOLOGY, the forms must be carefully and completely learned. Everything in the student's further progress depends upon this. It is believed that the systematic and progressive plan on which the substantives and verbs, as the groundwork of the whole, have been discussed, will but lightly burden the memory, while the judgment will be kept constantly at work. The chief point to be noted is the place and power of the STEM in Greek words. The first and second declensions of SUBSTANTIVES will be seen to be mainly reducible to the same law; the third declension, instead of perplexing the learner by countless varieties, will exhibit one normal form. The inflection of ADJECTIVES will appear but a repetition of that of the Substantives; while the PRONOUNS only slightly differ. Of the VERBS, the terminations should in the first instance be carefully studied. The first Paradigm exhibits the simplest way in which these terminations are combined with the verbal root; those that follow being but variations on the same model, according to the character of the Stem. The Verbs in μι, called here "the Second Conjugation," are classified in a way which, it is believed, will give no serious difficulty to the student.

The EXERCISES up to this point are simply for practice in declension and conjugation, consisting almost exclusively of words occurring in the "Sermon on the Mount:" they are fair specimens of the ordinary vocabulary of the language; and the learner is strongly recommended to write them out in all their forms, not neglecting the accents, which, by the help of the rules given under the several heads, will present but little difficulty.

A stock of words will thus have been acquired, with a knowledge of forms of inflection quite sufficient for ordinary cases. Some chapters of greater difficulty follow (§§ 93—99 inclusive), treating of the Verbs, tense by tense, and exhibiting the chief variations and anomalies in particular words. These sections may be omitted on a first study of the volume, but it will be important to read them carefully afterwards. The aim has been, so to classify the verbal forms that the apparent irregularities may be seen to be, in general, exemplifications of some more extended rule; and without trespassing on the more extended field of classical literature, to leave no word in the New Testament without the means of ready analysis and explanation.

The Exercises which succeed these sections are for still further test. Here for the first time some easy sentences are introduced for translation. Logically, these should no doubt have been deferred until some rules of Syntax had been laid down; but the interest and utility of such Exercises may be held a sufficient defence of the irregularities, especially as they contain scarcely any usages but such as are already familiar to those who have grammatically studied any language. Here the Vocabulary will be found necessary.

The chapters on the indeclinable Parts of Speech (§§ 118—138 inclusive) call for no remark. Their complete discussion belongs to Syntax: but it was held necessary to the completeness of the Etymology to give at least a general view of their formation and meaning. So far as they extend, these sections should be closely studied.

The reader will then be prepared for the SYNTAX, the study of the intermediate chapters being postponed, if preferred, to a subsequent stage. These sections (§§ 139—159 inclusive), on the different Languages of which the New Testament contains the trace, and on New Testament Proper Names, will suggest topics of interesting inquiry, which, in a manual like the present, could be pursued only for a very little way.

The SYNTAX embodies the simplest laws of concord, government, and the connection of sentences, as well as others of a more special and less obvious kind. The doctrines of the Article, of the Preposition, and of the Tenses, have received careful attention, as throwing light on many obscure or misunderstood passages. The arrangement of the Syntax has been adopted with a view to the learner's convenience, and for the most part follows the order of the parts of speech.

The student is specially and strongly recommended to study the order of the whole work, and especially of this part, in the ANALYTICAL TABLE OF CONTENTS. To this Table much care has been devoted, in the hope that it might be convenient, not only for ordinary reference, but as an outline and *conspectus* of the volume; suggesting at one view the leading principles of the language, and especially useful in recapitulatory examinations.

The sentences from the Greek Testament, so numerous in this division of the work, are intended partly to exemplify the rules to which they are appended, the illustrative words being printed in a thicker type; partly also to form together a series of Preparatory Reading Lessons or *Primer*, introductory to the Sacred Volume. The student is therefore earnestly counselled to study these sentences in order. Most of them, of course, belong to the easier parts of New Testament Scripture; others again are more difficult and unusual in their structure; while in very many will be discovered shades or specialties of meaning which the English Version does not exhibit, and which perhaps no translation could reproduce. The study, therefore, of these sentences will be an introduction to Biblical exegesis, which may prepare not a few readers for more extended inquiries.

A brief discussion of the chief New Testament SYNONYMS, and a VOCABULARY to the whole New Testament, complete the plan of the work.

This HANDBOOK claims, be it remembered, to be an Introduction only. By its means, a not inadequate beginning may be made in what is surely the noblest of studies. Its aim is to familiarise many readers, who else had despaired of the possibility, with the words of CHRIST and of His Apostles. Should its purpose in any way be accomplished, it will give access also to those criticisms by which expositors in our own land and age, as in others, have so variously and nobly illustrated the "living oracles." The labour followed by such rewards will have been well spent: and readers of the New Testament in its own tongue, whether they advance or not to that high critical discernment which only the few attain, will have found in the acquisition a pure and life-long joy.

NOTE TO REVISED EDITION.

THE experience of many years, and the numerous testimonies received to the value of the HANDBOOK, have warranted the Editor in re-issuing the work in the same general form as heretofore. The whole, however, has undergone a very close and careful revision, results of which appear on almost every page. The frequent references to the REVISED NEW TESTAMENT VERSION of 1881 are indicated by the letters R. V. Improvements have also been made in the size of the page, and the emphasising of points of importance by thick type, that the eye may aid the mind.

In the former editions the Greek Testament quotations were made in general from the Received Text; the various readings of Griesbach, Lachmann, Tischendorf, and Tregelles, being occasionally given. In order to secure the advantage of a modern critical text, without discussions that often convey no real help to the learner, the passages are now mostly cited from the Greek Testament of Drs. WESTCOTT and HORT, 1881, while cases of important divergence from the Received Text are always noted. The Editor begs to acknowledge the courtesy and kindness of Messrs. Macmillan in permitting the free use of this Text; and to add that a school edition has been published, with lists of

NOTE TO REVISED EDITION.

various readings, and a sufficient critical apparatus for learners. The letters W. H. indicate the references to this work. It should be added that its *orthography* has not been implicitly followed, in the many cases where it differs from that of ordinary Greek.

The VOCABULARY has been entirely reconstructed, and is printed on a new plan, which it is hoped will greatly add to the usefulness of this important part of the work.

The Editor would only add, that the revision of this HANDBOOK has been mainly the work of his son, the Rev. S. Walter Green, M.A., New Testament Professor in Regent's Park College, London. Both are much indebted to T. Osborne, Esq., of Stroud, for his suggestions on the former edition; and to the Rev. S. Newth, D.D., late Principal of New College, London, and member of the New Testament Revision Company, for corrections and additions in the Vocabulary.

SAMUEL G. GREEN.

ANALYTICAL TABLE OF CONTENTS.

PART I.

ORTHOGRAPHY.

SECT. PAGE
1. **THE ALPHABET.** Names, forms, and numeral values of the letters 1
2. Notes on the Alphabet 2
3. THE VOWELS : (a) their pronunciation, long and short 2
    (b) The diphthongs (regularly *long*) 2
    (c) The "breathings" of initial vowels 3
    (d) The "breathings" of initial ρ 3
    (e) The lengthening of vowels in inflection 3
    (f) The contraction of vowels. **Table.**
    Exercise 1. Vowel Contractions 4
    (g) Diæresis 4
    (h) Hiatus, and the ways of avoiding it—
        1. The *nu* suffixed (ν ἐφελκυστικόν) 4
        2. Elision (apostrophe). 4
        3. Crasis 4
4. THE CONSONANTS 5
    (a) Division into mutes and liquids 5
    (b) Classification of mutes 5
    (c) The sibilant σ, and its combinations 5
    (d) Rules of consonant combination—
        1. Labials or gutturals, with σ 6
        2. Labials or gutturals, with a dental 6
        3. Dentals before σ 6
        4. Mutes before μ 6
        5. Combinations of ν with other consonants 6
        6. A sharp mute before an aspirated vowel 6
        7. Consecutive syllables not to begin with an aspirate . . . 6
        8. Consonants that may be final 6
    Exercise 2. On the Combinations of Consonants . 6
5. Changes of Consonants by assimilation, duplication, transposition, omission, or insertion 7

xiv ANALYTICAL TABLE OF CONTENTS.

SECT.   PAGE
6. **THE ACCENTS** 7
   (*a*) Use of the accents 7
   (*b*) The different accents 7
   (*c*) Rules of accentuation 8
   (*d, e*) Enclitics and Proclitics. 8
7. On the transference of Greek words into English . . . 9
   Latin the usual medium. 9
   Equivalents of κ, υ, αι, οι, ει, ου, initial I and 'P 9
8. **Punctuation** 10
   Marks of pause, interrogation, quotation, and for "etc." . . . 10
   Reading Lessons—
   1. Acts ii. 1–13 10
   2. Rom. iv. 1–16 11
   3. Matt. v. 1–16, in Roman characters 12

PART II.

ETYMOLOGY.

CHAPTER I.—INTRODUCTION.

9. The "Parts of Speech" 14
10. **THE ROOT and STEM** 14
   Pure and (impure) liquid or mute stems. 14
   (The stem to be marked by thick letters) 14

CHAPTER II.—THE NOUN OR SUBSTANTIVE.

11. **GENDER, NUMBER, and CASE** 15
   General significance of the Cases 15
12, 13. THE DEFINITE ARTICLE and Indefinite Pronoun 15
   Types of Substantive and Adjective Declension 16
14. Characteristics of all Declensions of Nouns 16
   (*a*) Neuter Nominatives and Accusatives alike 16
      Their plural termination always α. 16
   (*b*) The Dative Singular in ι ("iota subscript") 16
   (*c*) The Genitive Plural in ων 16
   (*d*) Masculine like the Neuter in Genitive and Dative . . . 16
15. Rules for determining the GENDER of Nouns 17
   (*a*) *Masculine :* names of males, rivers, winds 17
   (*b*) *Feminine :* names of females, trees, countries, islands, and abstract
       nouns 17

ETYMOLOGY. XV

SECT.		PAGE
15.	(c) *Neuter:* diminutives, indeclinables, and the verbal noun (infinitive)	17
	(Note on common and epicœne words)	17
16.	**DECLENSION OF NOUNS SUBSTANTIVE**	17
	Three leading types	17
	Illustrations: πύλη, ἄνθρωπος, παῖς	18
	Resemblances between the first and second	18
	The A and O Declensions (parisyllabic)	19
	The Separable Declension (imparisyllabic)	19
17.	THE FIRST DECLENSION (A)	19
18.	Feminine Paradigms (ἡμέρα, δόξα, τιμή, σκία), and Remarks	19
19.	Masculine Paradigms (μαθητής, νεανίας), and Remarks	20
	Exercise 3. Nouns of the First Declension	21
20.	Irregular forms of the First Declension	21
21.	THE SECOND DECLENSION (O)	22
22.	Masculine (λόγος) and Feminine (ὁδός) Paradigms, and Remarks	22
23.	Neuter Paradigm (σῦκον), and Remarks	23
24.	Paradigm of Contracted Nouns in oo-, εo-, νοῦς, οστοῦν ('Απολλώς)	23
25.	Declension of 'Ιησοῦς	24
	Exercise 4. Nouns of the Second Declension	24
26.	THE THIRD DECLENSION (imparisyllabic)	24
	Importance of knowing the Stem	25
27.	General Paradigm: αἰών, ῥῆμα	25
28.	Terminations of this Declension	25
29.	Paradigms of Third Declension	26
	1. Ἄραψ, κῆρυξ, ἰχθύς, πόλις	26
	2. ποιμήν, λέων, αἰδώς, πατήρ, ἀνήρ	27
	3. βασιλεύς, βοῦς	28
	4. γένος	29
	5. Referred to § 27	29
	Exercise 5. Nouns of the Third Declension	29
30.	Rules for the Nominative	30
	1. s added to the stem	30
	2. The stem lengthened	30
	3. Digammated stems (ευ-, αυ-, ου-)	31
	4. Neuter stems in ες- (ος)	31
	5. Stem unchanged	31
31.	Irregular Nouns of the Third Declension	32
32.	SUBSTANTIVES OF VARIABLE DECLENSION	32
	(a) Interchanges between the second and third	32
	(b) The word σάββατον, *Sabbath*	32
	(c) Proper names, especially *Moses, Jerusalem*	33
	Hebrew indeclinables	33
	Exercise 6. Promiscuous List of Nouns	33

xvi   ANALYTICAL TABLE OF CONTENTS.

CHAPTER III.—ADJECTIVES.

SECT. | | PAGE
33. **THREE FORMS**, correspondent with substantive declensions . . 34
34. FIRST FORM 34
     Paradigms of ἀγαθός, δίκαιος, μικρός, and Remarks 34
35. Contracted Adjectives, χρυσοῦς ; Remarks 35
36. SECOND FORM 36
     General Remarks 36
37. Paradigms of ὀξύς, πᾶς, ἑκών 36
38. Participles of this class (declension of ἑστώς) 37
39. Adjectives of double form : μέγας, πολύς 38
40. THIRD FORM 39
     General Remarks 39
41. Paradigms of ἀληθής, σώφρων 39
    COMPARISON OF ADJECTIVES 40
42. FIRST METHOD 40
    Comparison of πιστός, ἀληθής, σοφός, νέος 40
43. SECOND METHOD 41
    Comparison of ταχύς, αἰσχρός, καλός, μέγας 41
44. Declension of comparatives in -ίων (μείζων) 41
45. Irregular and alternative comparisons 42
    ἀγαθός, κακός, μικρός, πολύς 42
46. DEFECTIVE COMPARATIVES AND SUPERLATIVES 42
47. EMPHATIC METHODS OF COMPARISON 42
    Exercise 7. Adjectives for Practice 43
    NUMERALS 44
48. THE CARDINAL NUMBERS 44
    (a) Signs of numeration 44
    (b) Disused letters as numeral signs 44
    (c) Composite numerical expressions 44
49. Declension of the cardinal numbers 44
    εἷς, δύο, τρεῖς, τέσσαρες 44
50. THE ORDINAL NUMBERS 45
51. **Table of Cardinals and Ordinals,** and Remark . . . 45
52. DISTRIBUTIVE NUMBERS 47
    Exercise 8. Numbers: Numerical symbols, and phrases for translation 47

CHAPTER IV.—PRONOUNS.

53. **PERSONAL PRONOUNS** 49
    1. SUBSTANTIVE-PERSONAL (" personal ") 49
       First person, ἐγώ, ἡμεῖς ; second, σύ, ὑμεῖς 49
54.   Third person, by αὐτός, ἡ, ό 49

ETYMOLOGY. xvii

SECT.		PAGE
55.	2. REFLEXIVE	49
	First person, ἐμαυτοῦ ; second, σεαυτοῦ	50
	Third, ἑαυτοῦ (αὑτοῦ)	50
56.	3. ADJECTIVE-PERSONAL (possessive)	50
	(a) ἐμός, ἡμέτερος, σός, ὑμέτερος	50
	(b, c) Genitive of the personal pronouns as possessives . . .	50
57.	DEMONSTRATIVE PRONOUNS	51
	Framed upon the model of the Article	51
	(a, b, c, d) ὅδε, οὗτος, ἐκεῖνος, ὁ αὐτός	51
	(e) τοιοῦτος, τοσοῦτος, τοσοῦτοι, τηλικοῦτος	52
58.	THE RELATIVE PRONOUN	52
	(a, b) ὅς, ἥ, ὅ ; (c, d) ὅστις, ὅσπερ, ὅσγε	52
	(e) Relatives of quality, quantity, number, degree	53
59.	INTERROGATIVE PRONOUNS	53
	(a) The simple Interrogative, τίς ; τί ;	53
	(b) Correlatives of quality, quantity, number, degree	53
	(c) Direct interrogatives in indirect construction	53
	(d) Interrogatives properly indirect	53
60.	INDEFINITE PRONOUNS	54
	(a, b) The ordinary Indefinite, τις, and negative compound . .	54
	(c) The old Indefinite, ὁ δεῖνα	54
61.	DISTRIBUTIVE PRONOUNS	54
	(a) ἄλλος, (b) ἕτερος, (c) ἀλλήλων, (d) ἕκαστος	54
62.	Table of Correlative Pronouns	54

CHAPTER V.—THE VERB.

63.	THE VOICES	55
	Four things predicated by the Verb	55
	Threefold modification of the verbal stem	55
	Active, Middle, Passive	55
64.	THE MOODS	55
	Four Modes or Moods	55
	1. The INDICATIVE, and its use.	55
	2. The IMPERATIVE	55
	3. The SUBJUNCTIVE	55
	4. The OPTATIVE (properly a division of the Subjunctive) . . .	56
	5. *Interrogative Forms*	56
	6. The INFINITIVE, } Participials	56
	7. The PARTICIPLES, }	
65.	THE TENSES	56
	Time and State jointly expressed	56
	Nine *possible* Tenses. Scheme	57

b

SECT.		PAGE
65.	Seven *actual* Tenses (in common use, six)	57
	"Principal" and "Historical" Tenses	57
	Arrangement of Tenses. Tenses of λύω	57
66.	**NUMBERS and PERSONS**	57
67.	THE TWO CONJUGATIONS	58
	Remark on the Greek and English typical forms	58
68.	THE VERBAL STEM—How ascertained: affixes and suffixes	58
69.	AUGMENT AND REDUPLICATION	58
	(*a*) *Augment* in the historical tenses, indicative	58
	1. The syllabic augment—with initial consonants	58
	2. The temporal augment—with initial vowels	58
	(*b*) *Reduplication* in the perfect tenses throughout	58
	An initial consonant repeated, with ε	59
	An initial vowel lengthened (like temporal augment)	59
	(*c*) Augment and reduplication in compound verbs	59
70.	INFLECTIONAL TERMINATIONS	59
	(*a*) Denoting voice, mood, tense, number, and person	59
	(*b*) Personal endings originally fragments of pronouns	59
	Normal forms	59
71.	TENSE-CHARACTERISTICS (consonant)	60
	Active Future and First Aorist, σ	60
	,, Perfect and Pluperfect, κ	60
	Passive Future and First Aorist, θ	60
72.	MODAL VOWELS	60
	Subjunctive—lengthened indicative vowels	60
	Optative—diphthongal forms	60
73.	VERBAL ADJECTIVES	61
74.	PARADIGM OF THE FIRST CONJUGATION : pure uncontracted	61
	πιστεύω. Principal parts	61
	Conjugation throughout	62
75.	All other forms variations of this type	70
	Exercise 9. On pure, uncontracted Verbs	70
76.	Verbs of the pure uncontracted class	70
77.	Possible stem-endings	71
	Pure, mute, and liquid verbs	71
78.	PURE VERBS. Special Rules	71
	(*a*) The stem-vowels	71
	(*b*) Contraction with α, ε, or ο	71
	(*c*) Contraction confined to Present and Imperfect Tenses	71
	(*d*) Peculiarities of contraction. Compare § 3, *f*	71
79.	PARADIGMS of τιμάω, φιλέω, δηλόω, Present and Imperfect	72
80.	Note on remaining Tenses	75
	Exercise 10. On pure, contracted Verbs	75
81.	MUTE VERBS. Special Rules	75
82.	Stem unaffected by a following vowel	76

ETYMOLOGY. xix

SECT.		PAGE
83.	(*a*) Tense-characteristics (§ 71) and terminations beginning with a consonant modify the stem	76
	(*b*) Rules of modification	76
	1. As caused by -σ after the verbal stem	76
	2. ,, by -θ ,, ,,	76
	3. ,, by -τ ,, ,,	76
	4. ,, by -μ ,, ,,	76
	5. ,, by -σθ ,, ,,	77
	6. ,, by -ντ ,, ,,	77
	7. ,, by -κ ,, ,,	77
84.	PARADIGMS OF THE MUTE VERBS. Remarks (*a*, *b*, *c*)	77
	Conjugation of τρίβω, ἄγω, πείθω	78
85.	Modification of the Present (and Imperfect)	81
	(*a*) The stem of the Present not always the stem of the Verb	82
	1. Labial verbal stems, that add τ	82
	2. Guttural verbal stems, that change the stem-consonant to σσ or ζ	82
	3. Dental verbal stems, that change the stem-consonant to ζ	82
	(*b*) All other tenses formed from the verbal stem	82
	(*c*) Vowels changed to diphthongs in short stem-syllables	83
	Here the Future and Perfect formed from the Present stem	83
86.	The *Secondary Tenses* of modified Verbs	83
	In these Tenses, the simple verbal stem always appears	83
87.	THE SECOND AORIST.	83
	Conjugated like the Imperfect Indicative (in other moods as Present)	83
	Illustrations from φυγ- (φεύγω), τυπ- (τύπτω)	83
	Note on Accentuation	83
	Active, Middle, and Passive	84
88.	THE SECOND FUTURE (Passive).	84
	Illustration from τυπ- (τύπτω).	84
89.	THE SECOND PERFECT (Active).	85
	Illustration from πραγ- (πράσσω)	85
90.	*General Rules for the Second Tenses*	85
	1. In what verbs they do not occur	85
	2, 3. Seldom found in First Tenses in the same verb, except in Passive	85
	4. First and Second Perfects, Active	85
	Exercise 11. On mute Verbs.	85
91.	LIQUID VERBS. Special Rules.	86
	(*a*) Present stem mostly modified	86
	(*b*) Future Active and Middle, contracted	86
	(*c*) First Aorist Active and Middle	86
	(*d*) Perfect Active, variations.	87
	(*e*) Perfect Passive, variations	87
92.	PARADIGMS OF LIQUID VERBS.	87
	ἀγγέλλω, κρίνω, αἴρω	87
	Exercise 12. On liquid Verbs	91

ANALYTICAL TABLE OF CONTENTS.

SECT.		PAGE
93.	NOTES ON THE TENSES. [*These Sections, to the close of § 99, dealing chiefly with minute variations and seeming irregularities in particular verbs, may be omitted in the first study of the book.*]	92
94.	THE PRESENT AND IMPERFECT. I. *The Present*	92
	1–4. Details of modification, as § 85	92
	5. Modifications of pure and impure stems by ν, νε, αν	93
	6. Alternative stems, consonant and ε-	93
	7. Inchoative forms in σκ- or ισκ-	93
	8. Reduplicated stems	94
	II. *The Imperfect*	94
	Peculiarities of Augment	94
	Double ρ-. Double augment. Attic augment in η-	94
95.	THE SECOND AORIST, Active and Middle	94
	Contains the simple verbal stem	94
	(Reduplicated Second Aorist. Change of short stem-vowel)	94
	The Vowel Aorist, as of Second Conjugation	94
96.	THE FUTURE, Active and Middle	95
	(*a*) Lengthening or otherwise of pure stems	95
	(*b*) The Attic Future of Verbs in ιδ- (ιζω)	95
	(*c*) The digammated future of verbs in εϝ- (εω)	96
	(*d*) Future in middle form, with active meaning	96
97.	THE FIRST AORIST, Active and Middle	96
	(*a*) Connection of Aorist with Future stem	96
	(1) In pure and mute; (2) in liquid verbs	96
	(*b*) Peculiarities of Augment	97
	Note on Accentuation	97
98.	THE AORISTS AND FUTURES PASSIVE	98
	(*a*) Modified like the Perfect Passive	98
	(*b*) Vowel stem-endings, lengthened, shortened, or with σ	98
	(*c*) Transposition of vowel and liquid in short roots	98
	(*d*) Change of a weak vowel into α	98
	(*e*) First and Second Tenses seldom in the same verb	98
	Notes on Irregularities of Augment, and on Accentuation	98
99.	PERFECT AND PLUPERFECT	99
	(*a*) Variations in reduplication	99
	1. ἐ- before a double consonant	99
	2. εἴληφα from λαβ- (λαμβάνω)	99
	3. Double reduplication and augment	99
	4. Pluperfect generally omits augment	99
	(*b*) Third person plural Perfect active in -αν	99
	(*c*) The Second Perfect active : its special sense	99
	(*d*) The Perfect passive : its peculiarities	100
	(*e*) The Future Perfect passive (or mid.)	100
	Note on accentuation	100
100.	**DEPONENT VERBS**	100

ETYMOLOGY.

SECT.		PAGE
100.	Active and Passive, as determined by the Aorist	100
101.	**IMPERSONAL VERBS**	101
	Their use	101
	List and usual forms of the chief Impersonals	101
102.	**DEFECTIVE VERBS**.	101
	Originally caused by redundancy	101
103.	PRINCIPAL DEFECTIVE VERBS AND THEIR PARADIGMS	102
	αἱρέω, ἔρχομαι, ἐσθίω, ὁράω, τρέχω, φέρω, εἶπον	102
	Exercise 13. On the Defective Verbs	104
104.	**THE SECOND CONJUGATION,** or Verbs in -μι . . .	104
	The chief peculiarity of these Verbs	104
	Future, First Aorist, and Perfect like Verbs in -ω . . .	104
105.	Modifications of the Verbal Stem	105
	(a) Vowel of a pure stem lengthened	105
	(b) Reduplication prefixed	105
	(c) The syllable -νυ- (-ννυ-) affixed	105
	Two classes thus formed	105
106.	FIRST CLASS—Paradigms in two divisions	105
	First Division—regular forms	105
107.	PARADIGMS of ἵστημι, τίθημι, δίδωμι	106
108.	Remarks on the Paradigms	114
	1. First Aorist Active, with -κ- (τίθημι, δίδωμι) . . .	114
	2. Peculiarities in augment of ἵστημι	114
	3. Active Aorist of ἵστημι—their difference	114
	4. The verb στήκω	114
109.	**List of Verbs in this division**	114
	A-stems : a. Active ; b. Deponent	114
	E-stems : Deponent only	115
110.	Second Division—Stems ἐσ- (εἰμί), ἰ-(εἶμι), ἑ-(ἵημι). . . .	115
	CONJUGATION of εἰμί (εἶναι), to be	116
111.	,, εἶμι (ἰέναι), to go	117
112.	,, ἵημι in its compound ἀφίημι	118
113.	SECOND CLASS—Verbs in -νυμι or -ννυμι	120
	Remarks	120
114.	Paradigms of δείκνυμι and ζώννυμι	121
115.	Remarks on Paradigms	124
116.	New Testament Verbs like δείκνυμι	124
117.	New Testament Verbs like ζώννυμι	125
	A-stems. E-stems. O-stems	125
	Exercise 14. On the Verbs in -μι	126
	Exercise 15. General, on the Verbs (from 2 Thess.) . .	126
	Exercise 16. Short Sentences.	127
	i. The Beatitudes	127
	ii. Parts of John i.	128
	iii. Selected Sentences	129

CHAPTER VI.—PREPOSITIONS.

118. **THE THREE CASES**: general relations of place, etc. . . . 131
Prepositions extend these relations indefinitely 131
They may govern the *Genitive, Dative,* or *Accusative;* one, two, or all 131
119. PREPOSITIONS GOVERNING THE GENITIVE ONLY, ἀντί, ἀπό, ἐκ (ἐξ), πρό 131
120. PREPOSITIONS GOVERNING THE DATIVE ONLY, ἐν, σύν 132
121. PREPOSITIONS GOVERNING THE ACCUSATIVE ONLY, ἀνά, εἰς . . . 132
122. PREPOSITIONS GOVERNING THE GENITIVE AND ACCUSATIVE, διά, κατά, μετά, περί, ὑπέρ, ὑπό 132
123. PREPOSITIONS GOVERNING THE GENITIVE, DATIVE, AND ACCUSATIVE, ἐπί, παρά, πρός 132
124. **Synoptical Table of the Prepositions** 133
125. Note on the various meanings of the Prepositions 134

CHAPTER VII.—ADVERBS.

126. ADVERBS IN THEIR ORIGINAL FORM, FROM SUBSTANTIVES . . . 135
(*a*) As an Accusative Noun, Adjective, or Pronoun 135
(*b*) As a Dative ,, ,, . . . 135
(*c*) As a Genitive ,, ,, . . . 135
(*d*) As a Preposition, with its Case 135
(*e*) Old Case-endings in -θεν, -θι, and -δε 135
127. ADVERBS FROM ADJECTIVES (in -ως) 135
128. Comparison of Adverbs 136
129. PRONOMINAL ADVERBS. **Table, with Correlatives** . . 136
130. NUMERAL ADVERBS (in -ις, -κις, or -ακις) 137
131. ADVERBS FROM VERBS 137
Ancient verbal forms, δεῦρο, δεῦτε 137
Derivatives from Verbs in -ίζω 138
132. ADVERBS FROM PREPOSITIONS (or in -ω) 138
133. PREPOSITIVE ADVERBS ("improper Prepositions"). **List** . . 138
134. NEGATIVE ADVERBS, οὐ and μή 139

CHAPTER VIII.—CONJUNCTIONS AND OTHER PARTICLES.

135. Meaning of the word *Particles* 140
136. Classification of Conjunctive Particles 140
1. Conjunctions of ANNEXATION 140
2. ,, COMPARISON 140
3. ,, DISJUNCTION 140
4. ,, ANTITHESIS 141
5. ,, CONDITION 141

ETYMOLOGY. xxiii

SECT.		PAGE
136.	6. Conjunctions of CAUSE	141
	7. ,, INFERENCE	141
	8. ,, INTENTION or RESULT	141
137.	(a) Particles of EMPHASIS, γέ, δή, -περ, -τοι	141
	(b) Particles of INTERROGATION, εἰ, ἤ, ἆρα	141
138.	INTERJECTIONS	141
	(a) Natural instinctive sounds	141
	(b) The Interjection ἴδε, ἰδού, behold!	142

CHAPTER IX.—ON THE FORMATION OF WORDS.

[*Chapters IX., X., XI., XII., may be omitted in the first reading of the book.*]

139. 1. **ROOTS**, with primary, secondary, tertiary, etc., formations . . 143
 2. Classes of Words 143
 3. Modification of Stem-endings 144
140. Classes of SUBSTANTIVES 144
 (a) *First Declension* 144
  1. Masculine, in -της 144
  2. Feminine, in -ία, -οσύνη 144
 (b) *Second Declension* 144
  1. Masculine, in -μός 144
  2. Neuter, in -τρον, -ιον (-άριον, -ίδιον) 144
  3. Masculine and Feminine Diminutives, -ισκος, -ίσκη . . 145
 (c) *Third Declension* 145
  1. Masculine, -εύς, -τήρ, -τωρ 145
  2 Feminine, -σις, -της 145
  3. Neuter, -μα, -ος 145
141. **Scheme of Terminations of Derivative Nouns** . . 145
142. Classes of ADJECTIVES 146
 1. *First Form* 146
  (a) In -ιc;, (-ιᾶ), -ιον 146
  (b) In -ικός, -ή, -ον 147
  (c) In -ἰνος, -ή, -όν 147
   (So -εος, contr., -ους, -ουν) 147
  (d) In -ρός, -ρά, -ρόν 147
  (e) In -(σ)ἰμος, -ον 147
  (f) Verbals in -τός and -τέος 147
 2. *Second and Third Forms* 147
  (a) In -ης, -ες 147
  (b) In -μων, -μον 147
143. **Scheme of Terminations of Derivative Adjectives** . . 148
144. Classes of VERBS 148
 (a) Verbs from subst. or adj. roots ("denominative") . . . 148
 Their principal terminations 148

xxiv ANALYTICAL TABLE OF CONTENTS.

SECT. PAGE
144. (b) Verbs from verbal stems—"Inceptives," "Frequentatives" (or
emphatic), "Causatives," etc. 149
145. General Remark on Derivation 149

CHAPTER X.—ON THE FORMATION OF COMPOUND WORDS.

146. "Parathetic" and "Synthetic" Compounds 150
147. PARATHETIC COMPOUNDS 150
   The former element a Particle 150
   (a) Significance of the *Preposition* in Composition . . . 151
   (b) ,, Adverbs ,, . . . 151
   (c) ,, Inseparable Particles in Composition . . 151
   (a, Compound Nouns and Adjectives generally from Verbs) . . 152
   (b, c, Adverbs and Inseparable Particles not found with Verbs,
   except ά-) 152
   (d, Combination of Prepositions) 152
148. SYNTHETIC COMPOUNDS 152
   The former element a Noun or Verb 152
   Connective vowels -o-, -ι- 152
   Compound Verbs usually from Compound Nouns 152
   The chief significance in the latter element 153
   Illustrations 153
149. **Derivation and Composition illustrated** by the Variations
   and Combinations in the New Testament of the root κρι, verbal stem
   κριν-, *to separate, to judge* 153

CHAPTER XI.—FOREIGN WORDS IN NEW TESTAMENT GREEK.

150. **Languages of Palestine:** HEBREW 155
   What was the "Hebrew tongue" in New Testament times? . . 155
   Question as to St. Matthew's Gospel 155
151. The introduction of GREEK 155
   Various influences contributing to this 155
   Greek the usual language of our Lord 156
   The Dialect of Galilee 156
   Difference of New Testament writers in style 156
152. Infusion of LATIN 156
   Influences contributory to this 156
   Classes of words derived from Latin 156
153. **Aramaic (Hebrew) Words and Phrases** . . . 156
   (a) Assimilated words 157
   (b) Indeclinable words 157
   1. Proper Names 157
   2. Common Nouns 157
   3. Special Phrases 158

SYNTAX. xxv

SECT.		PAGE
154.	**Latin Words**	. 158
	(a) Names of Coins	. 158
	(b) Judicial terms	. 159
	(c) Military terms	. 159
	(d) Political terms	. 159
	(e) Articles of Dress	. 159
	(f) General terms	. 159

CHAPTER XII.—NEW TESTAMENT PROPER NAMES.

155.	These Names from the three languages (Chapter XI.)	. 160
156.	HEBREW NAMES	. 160
	(a) Indeclinable Hebrew forms	. 160
	(b) Indeclinable and assimilated	. 160
	(c) Assimilated, Hebrew, *-ah*; Greek, *-as*	. 161
	(d) Later forms, Hebrew, *-a*; Greek, *-âs*	. 161
157.	DOUBLE NAMES	. 161
	(a) Greek the *translation* of the Hebrew	. 161
	(b) ,, *vocal imitation* ,,	. 161
	(c) Name and Surname	. 161
	1. The latter being *characteristic*	. 161
	2. ,, *patronymic*	. 161
	3. ,, *local*	. 161
	(d) Different names of the same man among Jews and Greeks	. 162
158.	GREEK NAMES	. 162
	(a) Pure Greek—"The Seven"	. 162
	(b) Contracted forms	. 162
159.	LATIN NAMES	. 162
	(a) In connection with Rome	. 162
	(b) Names of the Emperors	. 163
	(c) The name of "Paul"	. 163
	(d) Contractions, "*Luke*," "*Silas*," etc.	. 163

PART III.

SYNTAX.

CHAPTER I.—CONSTRUCTION OF THE SIMPLE SENTENCE.

160.	A knowledge of the general laws of Grammar necessary	. 164
161.	The SENTENCE—as consisting of Propositions	. 164
162.	The PROPOSITION—Subject and Predicate	. 164
163.	The SUBJECT—a Substantive or its equivalent	. 164

b 2

ANALYTICAL TABLE OF CONTENTS.

SECT.		PAGE
164.	The PREDICATE—a Substantive, Adjective, or equivalent	164
165.	The COPULA—a tense of the verb "to be"	164
166.	Omission of the Copula	165
167.	The VERBAL PREDICATE	165
168.	The Substantive verb as Predicate	165
169.	Omission of the Pronominal Subject	166
	Its insertion for emphasis. Examples	166
170.	Omitted in third person plural, "generalised assertion"	166
171.	Omitted in third person singular, "impersonals"	166
172.	The Nominative the case of the Subject	167
	THE FIRST CONCORD	167
173.	Exceptions, (1) Neuter plural Nominative with singular Verb	167
174.	Variations in this idiom, a, b, c, d	167
175.	(2) "Rational Concord." Collective singular Subject with plural Verb, a, b	168
176.	Combined Nominatives, a, b	169
177.	Agreement of substantival Predicate with the Subject	170
	Law of Apposition	170
178.	Agreement of adjective Predicate with the Subject	170
	THE SECOND CONCORD	170
179.	"Rational Concord," (1) Collective singular Subject with plural Adjective	170
180.	(2) Masculine or Feminine Subject with Neuter Adjective	171
181.	*Rule for Copulative Verbs*	171
182.	Complements of the simple Sentence	171
183.	Extension of the Subject	171
184.	„ Substantival Predicate	172
185.	„ Adjective-Predicate	172
186.	„ Verbal Predicate	172
187.	Accessory Clauses	172
188.	Co-ordinate	172
189.	Subordinate	172
190.	Methods of introducing subordinate Clauses	172
191.	Difficulties in the resolution of Sentences—illustrated	173
192.	*Rule for the resolution of Compound Sentences*	173

CHAPTER II.—THE ARTICLE.

	Construction of the Article	174
193.	Employed with Substantives; by the Second Concord	174
194.	Originally a Demonstrative Pronoun	174
195.	Shown by its often standing alone	174
196.	By its being followed by a Genitive	175
197.	Or by a Preposition and its Case	175
198.	By its construction with Adverbs	175

SYNTAX

SECT.		PAGE
199.	The Article with ADJECTIVES	176
200.	With PARTICIPLES	176
	Often equivalent to a Relative and Verb	176
201.	With the INFINITIVE, in all the Cases	177
	Note on the verbal in -*ing* (Lat., *gerund*) . . .	177
202.	With PHRASES OR SENTENCES	177
203.	With PRONOUNS. (See § 220)	177
204.	*Substantivised Words or Phrases*	178
	Significance of the Article: its insertion or omission . .	178
205.	The Article strictly definite	178
206.	The Article marks the *Subject*	178
207.	Definition of the Predicate by the Article	179
208.	(The Article may be omitted before words already defined) . .	179
209.	Use of the Article *with Monadic Substantives*	179
210.	*For individual emphasis*	180
211.	*In collective expressions*	180
212.	*To make renewed mention*	181
	(This sometimes *implicit*)	181
213.	Passages where the Article, omitted in the A.V., should be supplied from the original	181
214.	The Article with ABSTRACT SUBSTANTIVES, *a, b, c* . . .	183
215.	The Article as an UNEMPHATIC POSSESSIVE	185
216.	The Article with PROPER NAMES	185
217.	With the **Divine Names**	186
	(*a*) Θεός, *God*	186
	(*b*) Κύριος, *Lord*	187
	(*c*) υἱὸς Θεοῦ, *Son of God*	187
	(*d*) Ἰησοῦς, *Jesus*	188
	(*e*) Χριστός, *Anointed, Christ*	188
	(*f*) Πνεῦμα (ἅγιον), *Holy Spirit*	189
218.	*Monadic Nouns* (as Proper Names) without the Article . .	190
219.	*Prepositional Phrases* without the Article	190
220.	The Article with DEMONSTRATIVE PRONOUNS	191
221.	Omitted with ἕκαστος, τοσοῦτος	192
222.	The Article with αὐτός, *the same*	192
223.	With POSSESSIVE PRONOUNS	192
224.	With πᾶς, πάντες, *all*	192
225.	With ὅλος, *whole*	194
226.	With ἄλλος, ἕτερος, *other*	194
227.	With πολύ, *much*; πολλοί, *many*	194
228.	With the Nominative for Vocative	195
229.	The Article *separated from its Substantive* by qualifying words .	196
	(*a*) A Preposition with its Case	196
	(*b*) An Adverb	196
230.	*Repeated after its Substantive for emphasis*	196
	(*b*) Sometimes where no Article precedes	197

xxviii ANALYTICAL TABLE OF CONTENTS.

SECT.   PAGE
231. The Article with PARTICIPLES 197
232. The Article in Enumerations 198
      (a) Combined Enumeration 198
      (b) Separate Enumeration 198
233. The Omission of the Article marks Indefiniteness 199
234. The Article with νόμος, law—illustrations 200

CHAPTER III.—THE NOUN SUBSTANTIVE.

235. **NUMBER** 202
     Singular and Plural used as in other languages 202
236. Singular Nouns for a whole class 202
237. Nouns predicated of several individuals (as σῶμα, καρδία) . . 202
238. Abstract Substantives in the Plural 202
239. The Plural, by a speaker of himself 202
240. Plural to denote a single agent or object 203
     (a) As viewing it in its constituent parts 203
     (b) As generalising the statement, (1), (2) 204
     CASE 205
     THE NOMINATIVE AND VOCATIVE 205
241. Nominative as Subject and Predicate 205
242. The Suspended Nominative 205
243. The Elliptical Nominative 206
     (a) After ἰδού, behold ! 206
     (b) ,, ὄνομα, name 206
     (c) The phrase, ὁ ὢν καὶ ὁ ἦν καὶ ὁ ἐρχόμενος . . . 206
244. Nominative for Vocative : an elliptical usage 206
245. The Vocative, with and without ὦ 207
     THE GENITIVE 207
246. Primarily signifying motion from 207
247.   Modifications, 1–7 207
248. I. Genitive **of origin** 208
     After Substantives, to denote the source or author . . . 208
249.   After Verbs of sense or mental affection 208
          (a) Of sense, as hearing, taste, touch 208
          (b) Of affection, as desire, caring for, despising . . 209
          (c) Of remembrance and forgetting 210
250.   After Verbs of accusation, condemnation, etc. . . . 210
251.   After Verbs and Adjectives of plenty, want, fulness, etc. . 210
252. II. Genitive of **separation** or **ablation** 210
     After Verbs of removal, difference, hindrance, etc. . . . 210
253. Genitive of comparison 211
      After Verbs 211
      After Adjectives in the Comparative Degree 211

SYNTAX. xxix

SECT.		PAGE
254.	III. Genitive of **Possession**	212
	After Substantives "the Possessive Case"	212
255.	The Genitive Personal Pronouns so used	212
256.	Words of kindred, etc., omitted before Possessive, 1—7	212
257.	Attributive Possessive Genitive	213
258.	Special Possessive phrases	213
259.	The Genitive of Apposition	214
260.	POSITION OF THE GENITIVE	215
	(a) Generally *after* the governing Substantive	215
	(b) Instances where the Genitive *precedes*	215
261.	IV. Genitive of **Partition**	215
262.	After Partitive *Adjectives*	216
	Pronouns	216
	Numerals	216
	Superlatives	216
263.	After Verbs of *partaking*	216
264.	After Verbs of *taking hold of, attaining*, etc.	216
	Different usage of Active and Middle	217
265.	After *Adverbs of time*	217
266.	Partitive Phrases of Time or Place	217
267.	Partitive Genitive after Verb *to be*	217
268.	V. Genitive of **Object**	218
	May be expressed by various Prepositions: Illustrations	218
269.	Phrases that may be Possessive or Objective	218
270.	VI. Genitive of **Relation**	219
	In respect of, as shown by the context: Illustrations	219
271.	After *Adjectives*, generally	220
272.	Specially after Adjectives of *worthiness, fitness*, etc.	220
273.	Genitive of *price, penalty*, etc.	221
274.	Genitives of different relations with the same Substantive	221
275.	VII. The **Genitive Absolute**	221
	Originally *causal*	222
	THE DATIVE	222
276.	Primarily signifying *juxtaposition*	222
	Modifications, 1—4	222
277.	I. Dative of **Association**	223
	(a) After Verbs of *intercourse, companionship*, etc.	223
	(b) After Verbs and Adjectives of *likeness, fitness*, etc.	223
	(c) After the Substantive Verb: to express *property*	223
	Verb sometimes omitted	223
278.	II. Dative of **Transmission**	223
	(a) After Verbs of *giving* (Indirect Object)	223
	(b) ,, *information, command*, etc.	224
	(c) ,, *succour, assistance*, etc.	224
	(d) ,, *mental affection, obedience, faith*	224
	Distinction from Genitive	224

SECT.		PAGE
279.	III. Dative of **Reference**	225
	May be expressed in English by *for* (or *against*)	225
280.	IV. Dative of **Accessory Circumstance**	226
	(*a*) Expressing the *modes of an action*	226
	(*b*) Sometimes repeating the notion of the Verb (Hebraism) .	226
	(*c*) Dative of *cause* or *motive*.	226
	(*d*) ,, *instrument*	227
	Dative after χράομαι, *to use*	227
	(*e*) Dative of *agent* (rare)	227
	(*f*) ,, *sphere*, that in which a quality inheres . .	228
	(*g*) ,, *time*	228
	(1) A space of time: *for*—(2) A point of time: *at, on*	228
281.	THE ACCUSATIVE	229
	Primarily signifying *motion towards*	229
	Hence used as the **Object of Transitive Verbs** . . .	229
	(*a*) Verbs intransitive in English, transitive in Greek . .	229
	(*b*) The same Verbs sometimes transitive and intransitive. .	230
	(*c*) Especially those denoting faculty	230
	(*d*) The direct Object omitted after certain Verbs . . .	230
282.	The *internal Object* of Verbs, or "cognate Accusative" . .	230
283.	Accusative of *Definition*	231
	Dative of Accessory more common	231
284.	The *Double Accusative*, "nearer" and "remoter Object" . .	231
285.	The Accusative as **Subject of Infinitive Verbs** . . .	232
	To be rendered as Nominative with *that*	232
	Generally different from the Subject of the principal Verb .	233
	Accusative with the substantivised Infinitive	233
286.	Accusative of **Time** and **Space**.	233
	(*a*) Space: *Distance*	233
	(*b*) Time: (1) a *Point*; (2) *Duration*	233
287.	The Accusative in *Elliptical*, or unusual constructions . .	234
288.	**THE CASES WITH PREPOSITIONS** . . .	234
	Two elements to be considered, the *Preposition* and the *Case* .	234
	Variety of combinations hence resulting	234
289.	*Interchangeable* Prepositions: not identical	235
290.	Note on the correspondence of words in different languages .	235
	Table of Prepositions	236
	PREPOSITIONS WITH THE GENITIVE ONLY	236
291.	ἀντί, *over against*: opposition as an equivalent . . .	236
	Hence, *instead of, for*; adverbial phrase, ἀνθ' ὧν . .	236
292.	ἀπό, *from the exterior*	236
	Hence, (1) *from*; (2) *of*; (3) *on account of*; (4) elliptical use;	
	(5) use with Adverbs.	236
293.	ἐκ, ἐξ, *from the interior*	237
	Hence, (1) *out of*; (2) *from*; (3) *by*; (4) made *of*; (5) *belonging to*;	
	(6) springing *from*; (7) temporal use	**237**

SYNTAX. xxxi

SECT.		PAGE
294.	πρό, *in front of*	238
	Hence, *before* in (1) time ; (2) place ; (3) degree	238
	PREPOSITIONS WITH THE DATIVE ONLY	239
295.	ἐν, *in*	239
	Hence, (1) *in*, of place ; (2) *among* ; (3) "the ἐν of investiture ;" (4) *in* "the sphere ;" (5) special uses, *by* ; (6) adverbial phrases ; (7) temporal use ; (8) "constructio prægnans". . . .	239
296.	σύν, *in conjunction with* (co-operation)	241
	Hence, *with, together with* (beside)	241
	PREPOSITIONS WITH THE ACCUSATIVE ONLY . . .	242
297.	ἀνά, *up to, up by*	242
	Only in special phrases in the New Testament	242
298.	εἰς, *to the interior*	242
	Hence (1) of place, *into* ; (2) *unto, to* ; (3) *towards*, against ; (4) *in order to, for* ; (5) *into*, a state ; (6) *for, as*, of equivalence ; (7) of time, *during*, or *up to* ; (8) "constructio prægnans" . .	242
	PREPOSITIONS WITH THE GENITIVE AND ACCUSATIVE . . .	245
299.	διά, *through*	245
	α. Genitive : (1) *through*, of place ; (2) of agency ; (3) of time, *during* or *after*	246
	β. Accusative : *on account of*	247
300.	κατά, *down*	248
	α. Genitive : (1) *down from* ; (2) *against* ; (3) *by* ; (4) *throughout*, as Accusative	248
	β. Accusative : (1) *throughout* ; (2) *over against* ; (3) *at the time of* ; (4) distributive use ; (5) *according to* ; (6) adverbial phrases	248
301.	μετά, *in association with*	250
	α. Genitive : (1) *with, among* ; (2) *together with* ; (3) "with and on behalf of"	250
	β. Accusative : *after* (beyond)	250
302.	περί, *around*	250
	α. Genitive : *about, concerning*	250
	β. Accusative : (1) *around* ; (2) *about*, of time ; (3) *about*, in reference to	251
303.	ὑπέρ, *over*	251
	α. Genitive : (1) *on behalf of* ; (2) *for the sake of* ; (3) *in reference to*	251
	β. Accusative : *beyond, above*	253
304.	ὑπό, *under*	253
	α. Genitive : *by*, of the Agent	253
	β. Accusative : (1) *under* ; (2) *close upon*	253
	PREPOSITIONS WITH THE GENITIVE, DATIVE, AND ACCUSATIVE .	254
305.	ἐπί, *upon*	254
	α. Genitive : (1) *on*, of basis ; (2) *over*, of superintendence ; (3) *upon*, fig. ; (4) *before* ; (5) *in the time of* ; (6) "constructio prægnans".	254

xxxii ANALYTICAL TABLE OF CONTENTS.

SECT. PAGE
305. (ἐπί) β. Dative : (1) on, of basis; (2) over, of superintendence ; (3) upon,
fig. ; (4) in addition to ; (5) "constructio prægnans " . . 255
γ. Accusative : (1) upon, motion implied ; (2) over ; (3) to (for,
against) ; (4) with regard to ; (5) up to, of quantity ; (6) during,
of time 256
306. παρά, beside 258
α. Genitive : from, of persons only 258
β. Dative : (1) with, near ; (2) in the esteem or power of . . . 258
γ. Accusative : (1) by, near ; (2) contrary to ; (3) above ; (4)
consequence 259
307. πρός, towards 259
α. Genitive : conducive to 259
β. Dative : near 260
γ. Accusative : (1) to ; (2) with ; (3) mental direction ; (4) estimate ;
(5) intention 260
ON THE INTERCHANGE OF CERTAIN PREPOSITIONS 261
308. Mutual approach in meaning ; real distinction 261
309. Interchange of διά with ἐκ, ἀπό, ἐν (εἰς, ἐπί, κατά) 261
310. Interchange of ἐκ and ἀπό 262
311. ,, ἐν and the simple Dative 263
312. ,, εἰς with πρός, ἐπί, and Dative (also ἐν) . . . 263
Note on 2 Cor. iv. 17 264
313. ,, περί with διά and ὑπέρ 265
314. Repetition or otherwise of Prepositions governing several words . 265
Note on Verbs compounded with Prepositions 266

CHAPTER IV. ADJECTIVES.

315. **SECOND CONCORD,** re-stated 267
316. Omission of Substantives 267
Occasional ambiguities 267
List of Substantives frequently omitted 267
317. " Rational Concord " in Number and Gender 268
318. Adjectives referring to several Substantives 269
319. Adjectives in adverbial relations 269
The Degrees of Comparison 270
THE COMPARATIVE 270
320. Followed by a Genitive of Object 270
321. Or by ἤ, than, as a Conjunction 270
Employed in special cases 1, 2, 3 270
Omitted before Numerals after more, less 271
(μᾶλλον) ἤ after the Positive, sometimes after a Substantive or Verb. 271
322. Comparative strengthened by ὑπέρ or παρά 272
Emphatic Comparatives, as in § 47 272

SYNTAX.   xxxiii

SECT.		PAGE
323.	Comparative without expressed Object	272
	(1) Where the context supplies it	272
	(2) Where the Comparative is a familiar phrase	272
	(3) Where the Object may be supplied mentally	272
	THE SUPERLATIVE	273
324.	General significance	273
325.	Emphatic Superlatives	274
	Followed by πάντων, preceded by ὡς, ὅτι	274
326.	Use of πρῶτος	274
327.	Hebraistic Superlatives	274
	(1) By Preposition ἐν after simple Adjective	274
	(2) By Adjective repeated in the Genitive	274
	Other so-called Hebraisms to be rejected	275
	The Numerals	275
328.	Special uses of the Cardinal εἷς, one	275
	(1) As an Indefinite Pronoun (Indefinite Article)	275
	(2) For the Correlatives, one ... other	275
	(3) Its proper Negative combined with the Predicate	275
	(4) Ordinal first instead of it	276
329.	Adverbial Particles with Numerals	276
330.	Omission of Names of Quantity after Numerals	276
331.	The Ordinals in Enumerations.	276

CHAPTER V.—THE PRONOUNS.

	The Personal Pronouns	277
332.	Subject to the rules for Substantives	277
	Omission of Pronominal Subject	277
333.	Possessive Genitive of Pronouns instead of the Adjective	277
	Possessive Adjective Pronoun instead of the Genitive	277
334.	Redundant or repeated Personal Pronoun	278
335.	Use of αὐτός, self, in apposition	278
	As a Nominative, always emphatic	278
	[The reflexive ἑαυτοῦ for the Second Person	279
	,, ἑαυτῶν for First and Second]	279
	"Rational Concord," with αὐτός—Gender—Number	279
	The Possessive Pronouns	280
336.	Their various uses exemplified	280
	In apposition with a Genitive Substantive	280
337.	Unemphatic Possessive Pronouns by the Article	280
	Emphatic Possessive Pronouns by ἴδιος, own	280
	The Demonstrative Pronouns.	281
338.	Use of οὗτος, this (near), and ἐκεῖνος, that	281
339.	Use of ὅδε, this (here)	281

xxxiv ANALYTICAL TABLE OF CONTENTS.

SECT.		PAGE
340.	Exceptions to the ordinary use of οὗτος, ἐκεῖνος.	281
	ἐκεῖνος, the *Emphatic Demonstrative* .	282
341.	Emphatic (or redundant) Demonstrative Constructions	282
342.	Special uses of τοῦτο, ταῦτα	282
	The Relative Pronoun	283
343.	Agreement of the Relative. **THE THIRD CONCORD**	283
344.	A clause as Neuter Antecedent	283
345.	"Rational Concord" with the Relative—Gender—Number	283
346.	*Attraction*	284
	(a) Attraction of the Relative to the Predicate	284
	(b) Attraction of the Relative to the Antecedent	284
	Inverse Attraction (transposed Antecedent)	285
347.	Demonstrative Antecedent omitted .	285
348.	αὐτός complementary to the Relative (a Hebraism)	286
349.	The *Compound Relative*, ὅστις, strictly Indefinite	286
	But also *explicative*, and *logical*	287
	Used often with Proper Names	287
	The Interrogative and Indefinite Pronouns	287
350.	Various uses of the Interrogative, τίς ;	287
	(1) Simply, with or without a Substantive	287
	(2) Elliptically, as ἵνα τί; *why ?*	287
	(3) Adverbially, *how !*	288
	(4) In alternative questions	288
351.	The Interrogative in indirect questions	288
352.	Transition from the Interrogative to the Indefinite .	288
	Uses of the Indefinite, τις	289
	(1) Simply, with or without a Substantive	289
	(2) Emphatically, *somebody !*	289
	(3) As "a kind of"	289
	(4) "Some" approximately with numbers	290
	(5) In alternative expressions .	290
	(6) [Negatives of τις, *i.e.*, οὐδείς, μηδείς]	290

CHAPTER VI.—THE VERB.

	VOICE	291
353.	Voice : the distinction in *form* and *significance*	291
354.	THE ACTIVE VOICE	291
	Intransitives used as Transitives	291
	Variations in meaning according to form (ἵστημι)	292
	Special use of ἔχω	292
355.	THE MIDDLE VOICE : its three senses	292
	1. *Reflexive* (the "Accusative Middle") .	292
	But Pronouns generally employed with Active .	292

SYNTAX.

SECT.		PAGE
355.	2. *Appropriative* (the "Dative Middle").	293
	The direct Object of the Active retained	293
	3. *Causative* (nearly resembling the Passive)	293
	This meaning sometimes becomes reciprocal	294
356.	THE PASSIVE VOICE	294
	Its Subject. The primary or secondary Object of the Active	294
	(In the latter case, the primary Object remains in the Acc.)	295
357.	Agent after Passive Verbs	295
358.	Frequent difficulty of distinguishing Passive and Middle	295
	THE MOODS AND TENSES	296
359.	Significance of the *Moods*	296
	The **Indicative**—Declarative and Interrogative	296
360.	The *Tenses*. The six employed (the three others essential to completeness) "Historical" and "principal" Tenses	296
361.	THE PRESENT TENSE	297
	General meaning, and Illustrations	297
	(a) A state as now existing, a process	297
	(b) An habitual or usual act	297
	(c) Past time, in vivid narration (the Historical Present)	297
	(d) Certain futurity	298
362.	THE IMPERFECT TENSE	298
	General meaning, with Illustrations	298
	(a) An act unfinished at a past time.	298
	(b) An act statedly repeated	298
	(c) To be distinguished from the Aorist	299
	(d) An inchoative act	300
	(e) Potential sense from the Inchoative	300
	(f) The "resolved Imperfect"	301
363.	THE FUTURE TENSE	301
	General meaning, with Illustrations	301
	(a) Indefinite futurity	301
	(b) Command, especially in prohibitions	301
	(c) General truths or maxims, "Ethical Future"	302
	(d) Future with οὐ μή (see § 377)	302
	(e) The "resolved Future," or Future Imperfect	302
	(f) The Future Auxiliary, μέλλω	302
	Use of θέλω, *to will*, emphatic; with Examples	302
364.	THE AORIST TENSES	303
	General meaning, with Illustrations	303
	(a) The absolutely past, "Preterite"	303
	Distinction between Aorist, Imperfect, and Perfect.	303
	(b) The Aorist, as Pluperfect	304
	(c) The "Epistolary Aorist"	304
	(d) Sometimes equivalent to our Present Indicative	305
	(e) Marking the completeness of an act	305

SECT.		PAGE
365.	THE PERFECT TENSE	305
	General meaning, and Illustrations	305
	(a) A completed action, or one whose consequences remain	305
	(b) Distinction between the Perfect and Aorist	305
366.	THE PLUPERFECT TENSE	306
	Rare in the New Testament: an act repeated in the past	306
367.	The "Perfect Present," and corresponding Pluperfect	306
368.	INTERROGATIVE FORMS	307
	With or without interrogative words	307
	Elliptic questions	308
369.	Peculiar forms of affirmative reply	308
370.	Negative questions	308
	(a) With οὐ; (b) with μή; (c) with μήτι	308
	The Imperative Mood	309
371.	Used for command or entreaty	309
	μή its proper negative Adverb	309
372.	Employed in simple permission	309
373.	Tenses of the Imperative	309
	(a) The Present—generality, continuity, repetition	309
	(b) The Aorist—instantaneousness, completeness	310
	(c) The Perfect (very rare)	310
	Contrast between Present and Aorist illustrated	310
374.	**The Subjunctive Mood**	311
	Always really dependent. Elliptical forms	311
375.	The Subjunctive in independent sentences	311
	1. As a hortatory Imperative—First Person	311
	2. As the Imperative in prohibitions	311
376.	3. In questioning or doubt, "Deliberative Subjunctive"	312
377.	4. In strong denial (Aorist), with οὐ μή	312
	5. For the Future Perfect (Aorist)	313
378.	**The Optative Mood**	313
	Always really dependent	313
	The Optative in independent sentences	313
	1. To express a wish	313
	So with μή (μὴ γένοιτο!)	313
	2. With ἄν for Potential	314
	THE MOODS IN DEPENDENT CLAUSES	314
379.	Different kinds of Subordinate Clauses	314
380.	Mood and Tense in such Clauses	314
	The Subjunctive after words compounded with ἄν	314
381.	OBJECT SENTENCES	314
	ὅτι with the Indicative	315
382.	(a) Direct quotation: Pleonastic ὅτι	315
	(b) Indirect quotation: "Oratio obliqua"	315

SYNTAX. xxxvii

SECT.		PAGE
382.	(c) Indirect interrogation	315
	Use of the Indicative, the Subjunctive, and the Optative . .	315
	(d) Object and Objective Sentence after some Verbs	317
383.	CONDITIONAL SENTENCES	317
	The "Protasis" and "Apodosis"	317
	Four forms of the Conditional Sentence	317
	α. The supposition of a *fact* (εἰ, Indicative)	317
	β. The supposition of a *possibility* (ἐάν, Subjunctive) . . .	318
	γ. Entire *uncertainty* (εἰ, Optative)	318
	δ. A condition *unfulfilled* (εἰ, Indicative past ... ἄν, Indicative past)	319
384.	INTENTIONAL CLAUSES : expressive of purpose or design	320
	The Intentional Particles (ἵνα, ὅπως, μή)	320
	(a) With the Subjunctive, to express intention	320
	(Distinction between Intentional and Object Sentences) . . .	320
	Does ἵνα ever mean *so that?*	321
	Passages relating to Scripture prophecy	321
	The negative intentional particle	322
	(b) With the Indicative Future (infrequent), conveying emphasis, force	323
	An *apparent* Indicative Present in Intentional Sentences . .	323
385.	**The Infinitive**	324
	(a) Properly a Verbal Substantive	324
	(b) Negative Adverbs with the Infinitive	324
	(c) The Infinitive governs the same cases as the Verb	324
386.	*Tenses of the Infinitive*	324
	Present, Aorist, Future, Perfect	324
387.	*Subject of the Infinitive* (compare § 285).	325
388.	The Infinitive *as Subject* (substantivised)	325
389.	The Infinitive *as Object*	325
	(a) After Verbs denoting faculty, act, assertion, etc. . .	325
	(b) To denote intention or result	326
	(1) After a Verb	326
	(2) After a Substantive	326
	(3) After an Adjective	326
390.	The Infinitive *in oblique cases* (as Lat., gerund) . . .	326
	(a) Genitive, with τοῦ	326
	(1) After Substantives	326
	(2) After Verbs	327
	(3) To express design	327
	(b) Dative, with τῷ, to express cause	327
	(c) With Prepositions (τοῦ, τῷ, τό)	327
	Illustrations : διά, εἰς, ἐν, μετά, πρό, πρός, ἀντί . .	328
391.	Infinitive of *result*, with ὥστε (so Indicative)	328
392.	Infinitive *as Imperative*	329

SECT.		PAGE
93.	**The Participles**	329
	Properly verbal Adjectives	329
	Negatives with the Participles	330
	Subject of a Participle (Genitive Absolute)	330
94.	PREDICATIVE uses of Participles	330
	1. *After the Substantive Verb:* "the resolved Tenses"	330
	2. *Complementary* to the verbal Predicate	331
	3. *Adjuncts* to the verbal Predicate	332
	(*a*) Modal	332
	(*b*) Temporal	332
	(1) Contemporaneous (Present Participle)	332
	(2) Preceding (Aorist Participle)	332
	(3) Succeeding (Future Participle)	333
	(*c*) *Relations* of cause, condition, etc.	333
	(*d*) *Intensive* (Hebraistic)	333
	A Predicative Participle may be modified by ὡς	333
95.	ATTRIBUTIVE use of Participles	334
	Epithetic (like Adjectives)	334
96.	With the Article : like the Relative and a Finite Verb	334
	The Temporal reference sometimes lost	335
	Usual force of the Present Tense	335
97.	Participles in *broken constructions*	335
	Anacolouthon (compare § 412)	336

CHAPTER VII.—ADVERBS.

98.	Their general use	337
99.	Adverbial phrases	337
	(*a*) A Substantive with or without Preposition	337
	(*b*) An Adjective	337
	(*c*) A Participle	337
	(*d*) The combination of two Verbs	338
100.	Adverbs as *Prepositions* (see § 133)	338
	Combinations of Adverbs	338
101.	The *Negative Adverbs*, οὐ and μή	338
	Combinations of Negatives	339
	Comparison sometimes expressed as denial	339

CHAPTER VIII.—CONJUNCTIONS.

102.	Rule for words connected by Conjunctions	340
103.	Conjunctions OF ANNEXATION : especially καί, *and*	340

SYNTAX.

SECT.		PAGE
403.	Special uses of καί	340
	(a) For rhetorical emphasis	340
	(b) In the enumeration of particulars (with τε)	340
	(c) Marking points of transition	341
	(d) Explanatory : "καί epexegetic"	341
	(e) As *also, even*	341
	Frequently in comparisons, and in the rising climax	342
404.	Conjunctions of ANTITHESIS : especially ἀλλά, δέ	342
	1. ἀλλά, *but*, marks opposition, interruption, transition	342
	(1) To throw emphasis on its clauses	343
	(2) In the Apodosis of a Conditional Sentence, *yet*	343
	(3) After a negative, ἀλλ' ἤ, *except*	343
	2. δέ, *but*, unemphatic adversative	344
	Often may be rendered, *and, then, now*, etc.	344
	καί ... δέ, *yea ... moreover*	344
	Antithesis with μέν ... δέ	344
	μέν occasionally without δέ (three cases)	345
405.	The Disjunctives : especially ἤ, εἴτε	345
	ἤ ... ἤ, ἤτοι ... ἤ, εἴτε ... εἴτε	345
	ἤ καί, *or even*	345
	ἤ "interrogative"	346
406.	The Inferential Conjunctions : especially ἄρα, οὖν	346
	Their distinction. Slighter meanings	346
	Other Inferential Particles	346
407.	The Causal Conjunctions : especially γάρ	347
	(a) Relative Conjunctions, as ὅτι, *because*	347
	(b) The Demonstrative Causal γάρ, *for*	347
	Introduces a direct reason	347
	Or the reason of some fact implied	347
	(c) Sometimes refers to a suggested thought	347
	(d) The combination καὶ γάρ, its two senses	348
408.	Asyndeton : or the omission of Conjunctions	348
	(a) Of the Copulative	348
	(b) Of καί, Epexegetic	348
	(c) Of the Antithetic	349
	(d) Of the Causal Particle	349

CHAPTER IX.—ON SOME PECULIARITIES IN THE STRUCTURE OF SENTENCES.

409.	The Arrangement of Words	350
	(a) General rules	350
	(b, c) Emphasis gained by variety of arrangement	350

xl ANALYTICAL TABLE OF CONTENTS.

SECT.		PAGE
410.	SPECIAL FORMS OF ELLIPSIS.	351
	1. Aposiopēsis	351
	2. Zeugma	351
	Inartificial collocation of Clauses	351
411.	APPARENT REDUNDANCY	352
	(a) For special emphasis; frequently; in three ways	352
	(b) Object and Object-sentence (see § 382)	352
412.	ANACOLOUTHON	352
	(Not to be hastily assumed)	352
	(a) Transition from indirect to direct speech	352
	(b) Transition from a Participle to a Finite Verb	353
	(c) Nominative Participles standing alone (see § 397)	353
	(d) A sudden change of structure	353
	(e) The non-completion of a Compound Sentence	353
413.	ATTENTION TO SOUND AND RHYTHM	354
	(a) Paronomasia	354
	Simple alliteration	354
	Alliteration associated with kindred meanings	354
	(b) Parallelisms, after the manner of Hebrew	354
	Christian hymns	354
	Rhythmic constructions in passages of strong emotion	354
	"Chiasmus"	355
	(c) (1) Quotations of Greek poetry in the New Testament	355
	(2) Metrical lines apparently unconsciously introduced	356

ANALYTICAL EXERCISE ON 2 THESSALONIANS 357
ON SOME NEW TESTAMENT SYNONYMS 369
    Introductory Remarks 369
    List of Words illustrated 371
    I. Verbs in ordinary use 374
    II. Words chiefly expressive of moral quality 377
    III. Theological and Ecclesiastical Words 380
    IV. Miscellaneous 383
VOCABULARY 387

PART I.

ORTHOGRAPHY.

1. The Greek Alphabet contains twenty-four letters, arranged and named as follows:—

Name.	Capital.	Small.	Sound.	Numerical value.
Alpha	A	α	a	1
Beta	B	β or ϐ	b	2
Gamma	Γ	γ sometimes ɼ	g (hard)	3
Delta	Δ	δ	d	4
Epsĭlon	E	ε	e (short)	5
Zeta	Z	ζ or ʓ	z	7
Eta	H	η	e (long)	8
Theta	Θ	θ or ϑ	th	9
Iōta	I	ι	i	10
Kappa	K	κ	k	20
Lambda	Λ	λ	l	30
Mu	M	μ	m	40
Nu	N	ν	n	50
Xi	Ξ	ξ	x	60
Omĭcron	O	ο	o (short)	70
Pi	Π	π sometimes ϖ	p	80
Rho	P	ρ or ϱ	r	100
Sigma	Σ	σ final ς	s	200
Tau	T	τ sometimes ɫ	t	300
Upsĭlon	Υ	υ	u	400
Phi	Φ	φ	ph	500
Chi	X	χ	ch (guttural)	600
Psi	Ψ	ψ	ps	700
Omĕga	Ω	ω	o (long)	800

NOTES ON THE ALPHABET.

2. *a.* The word **Alphabet** is derived from the names of the first two letters, *alpha, beta.* The forms of the Greek letters, which, it will be seen, greatly resemble those of our own language (the Roman letter), were originally modified from the Phœnician.

b. The second forms of certain letters are used interchangeably with the first, but less frequently. Those of *gamma* and *tau* are almost obsolete. The final **s**, besides being **always employed at the end of words**, is often placed in the middle of compound terms when a part of the compound ends with *sigma*. Thus, προςφερω.

c. For an explanation of the numeral use of letters, and especially of omissions in the list, see § 48.

THE VOWELS.

3. The vowels are α, ε, η, ι, ο, υ, ω.

a. In this country they are generally **pronounced according to the English sounds.** The Continental pronunciation of α, η, ι, is undoubtedly the more strictly correct; but the matter is of little practical importance. Absolute conformity to the ancient mode is unattainable, and it is most convenient to adopt the method of pronunciation current among scholars of our own country.

η and ω are long vowels. Care must be taken to distinguish them from the short ε and ο. Thus, μεν is pronounced like the English *men ;* μην, like *mean.* In τον, the ο is pronounced as in *on;* in των, as in *own;* α, ι, υ, may be either long or short.

b. **The diphthongs** are αι, αυ, ει, ευ, οι, ου, pronounced as in English; also ᾳ, ῃ, ῳ (or, with capitals, Αι, Ηι, Ωι), where the ι occurs with a long vowel, and is *not pronounced*, being, therefore, written underneath the vowel (excepting in the case of capitals), and called **iota subscript.** It will be important to note this in the declension of nouns and the conjugation of verbs.

ηυ is pronounced like ευ, *eu;* and υι like *wi*.

c. Every vowel, when standing as the first letter of a word, has what

§ 3, f.] THE VOWELS. 3

is called a **breathing** over it, written as an apostrophe, either turned outwards, as ('), or inwards, as (ʽ). The former is termed the **soft breathing**, and shows that the vowel is simply to have its own sound, the latter the **hard breathing**, and is equivalent to the English *h* aspirated. To note the latter is most necessary for correct pronunciation. Thus, ὁ, ἡ must be pronounced *ho, hē*.

The initial υ is always aspirated. So, ὑπερ, *huper*.

d. At the beginning of a word, the consonant (or semivowel) ρ always takes the aspirate, becoming *rh*. When two ρ's come together in the middle of a word, the aspirate and soft breathing are successively employed. Thus, ῥεω, *rheō;* ἄῤῥητος, *arrhetos*. When a word begins with a diphthong, the breathing is placed upon the second letter: αὐτόν, *auton;* αὑτόν, *hauton*.

e. In the lengthening of vowels for purposes of inflection or derivation, ᾰ becomes ᾱ, or more generally η; ε becomes η, or ει; ῐ, ῠ, become respectively ῑ, ῡ; ο becomes ω, or ου.

f. **Two vowels, or a vowel and a diphthong, occurring together in different syllables are often contracted into one,** according to the following Table:—

followed by...	α	ε	η	ο	ω	αι	ει	ῃ	οι	ῳ	ου
α becomes	α	α	α	ω	ω	ᾳ	ᾳ	ᾳ	ῳ	ῳ	ω
ε "	α or η	ει	η	ου	ω	ῃ	ει	ῃ	οι	ῳ	ου
ο "	ω	ου	ω	ου	ω	ῳ	οι[1]	οι	οι	ῳ	ου

The left perpendicular line in this table gives the former vowel in each combination, the upper horizontal line the latter, and the result of the contraction will easily be found. Thus, εο gives ου; αε, long *a*; and so of the rest. It must be noted that where the letter σ occurs in inflection between two short vowels, it is generally dropped, and contraction takes place according to the table.

It will be observed by inspection of the table that an *o* sound always preponderates in contraction with the other vowels; that an *a* sound, when first, prevails over an *e* sound following it, and *vice versâ*. Some special and exceptional methods of contraction will be found noticed in ETYMOLOGY.

---

[1] Or ου, when the ει is the contraction of εε, as in the infinitive of contracted verbs in *o*.

VOWELS—CONTRACTIONS—HIATUS.   [§ 3, ƒ.

Exercise 1.—Vowel Contractions.

Write the contracted forms of τιμαω, τιμαεις, τιμαει, τιμαομεν, τιμαετε, φιλεω, φιλεεις, φιλεει, φιλεομεν, φιλεετε, δηλοω, δηλοεις, δηλοει, δηλοομεν, δηλοετε, φιλεῃς, τιμαοι, δηλοητε, νοος, νοου, γενεος, αιδοα, ὀρεα, βασιλεες, μειζοα.

g. **Diæresis** is the opposite of contraction, and is expressed by two dots (¨) over the second of two vowels which are to be **separately pronounced.** Thus, Καϊναν, *Ca-i-nan,* not Cai-nan.

h. **Hiatus, and the ways of avoiding it.**—The hiatus (*i.e.* yawning) caused by the meeting of vowels at the end of one word and the beginning of the next is often prevented by one or other of the following ways :—

(1.) The νῦ ἐφελκυστικόν, or *nu-suffixed.* This **ν** is added to datives plural ending in ι, and to the third persons of verbs ending in ε or ι, when the following word begins with a vowel, or at the end of a sentence. These words will be marked in declension and conjugation by a bracketed (ν); thus, αἰῶσι(ν), ἐπίστευσε(ν). In a similar manner, οὕτω, μέχρι, and ἄχρι, as a rule add **s** when followed by a vowel. In the last two words, however, the New Testament text is not by any means uniform ; and on all three the best MSS. greatly differ.

The negative οὐ becomes οὐκ when the next word begins with a vowel,[1] and the preposition ἐκ becomes ἐξ.

(2.) *Elision marked by an apostrophe.*—The following words lose their final vowel before an initial vowel in the next word : the prepositions ἀπό, διά, ἐπί, παρά, μετά, and the conjunction ἀλλά ; with (occasionally) the particle δέ and its negative compound οὐδέ ; also (before ὧν) the preposition ἀντί. When the initial vowel is aspirated, π, τ, become φ, θ (see § 4, *b*). Thus, ἀπὸ αὐτῶν becomes ἀπ' αὐτῶν, and ἀπὸ ἑαυτῶν, ἀφ' ἑαυτῶν ; so for μετὰ ἀλλήλων, μετ' ἀλλήλων, but for μετὰ ἡμῶν, μεθ' ἡμῶν ; and for ἀντὶ ὧν, ἀνθ' ὧν.

This elision was, in classical Greek poets, used much more frequently in words ending in α, ε, ι, ο.

(3.) *Crasis.*—An hiatus is sometimes prevented by a Crasis (lit. a *"mixing"*), or the union of the two words ; the vowels forming a long vowel, or diphthong. This takes place but rarely, and only when the former word is very short and closely connected with the latter. The breathing of the vowel in the second word is retained, to mark the fusion, and is then called a *Coronis.* Thus, for

---
[1] Compare § 4, *d,* 6.

τὰ αὐτά, *the same things*, ταὐτά is sometimes written; for καὶ ἐγώ, *and I*, κἀγώ; for τὸ ἐναντίον, *the contrary*, τοὐναντίον; and once for τὸ ὄνομα, *the name*, τοὔνομα (Matt. xxvii. 57).

The Consonants.

4. *a.* As in the orthography of other languages, the four consonants, λ, μ, ν, ρ, are termed *liquids;* the nine consonants, β, γ, δ, π, κ, τ, φ, χ, θ, are *mutes*.

b. The mutes may be evidently arranged according to the organs of speech specially concerned in their formation.

Thus π, β, φ, are *labials* (*p*-sounds);

κ, γ, χ, are *gutturals* (*k*-sounds);

τ, δ, θ, are *dentals* (*t*-sounds).

Each of these divisions has, it is also plain, a sharp, a flat, and an aspirate consonant. Hence the highly important classification of the following Table:—

	Sharp.	Flat.	Aspirate.	
Labials...	π	β	φ	*p*-sounds.
Gutturals..	κ	γ	χ	*k*-sounds.
Dentals...	τ	δ	θ	*t*-sounds.

The guttural γ is pronounced, before a *k*-sound or ξ, like the nasal *ng*. Thus, ἄγγελος, ang-gelos (the second γ, as always, being *hard*); ἄγκυρα, ang-kura.

c. σ is the simple sibilant, which, in combination with a *p*-sound, gives ψ=πσ, βσ, or φσ; in combination with a *k*-sound gives ξ=κσ, γσ, χσ; in combination with δ gives ζ=δσ; these three, ζ, ξ, ψ, being double letters.

d. **The following eight rules** must be carefully observed, as they relate to the changes which are imposed by the necessities of orthography on the conjugation and declension of words, and will explain much hereafter that would otherwise be found very perplexing.

1. As above, a labial followed by σ becomes ψ; a guttural followed by σ becomes ξ.
2. A labial or guttural before a dental must be of the same order, *i.e.* must be changed, if not already so, into a sharp, flat, or aspirate, according to the nature of the dental.
3. A dental followed by σ disappears.
4. Before the letter μ a *labial* becomes μ; a *guttural* becomes γ; a *dental* becomes σ.
5. The letter ν becomes μ before *labials;* γ before *gutturals;* before a *liquid* is changed into the same liquid; and before σ or ζ is dropped.

The combination of ν with a dental and the sibilant, as ντσ, becomes simply σ, with compensation by the lengthening of the preceding vowel; ε becoming ει, and ο, ου. Thus,

γιγαντσι	becomes	γιγᾶσι;
ἐλμινθσι	,,	ἐλμῖσι;
τυφθεντσι	,,	τυφθεισι;
τυπτοντσι	,,	τυπτουσι.

6. **A sharp mute before an aspirated vowel** is changed into the corresponding aspirate. Sometimes this change will take place when the mute occurs at the end of one word, and the vowel at the beginning of the next. Thus, ἀφ' ὧν for ἀπ' ὧν; οὐχ ὁράω for οὐκ ὁράω.
7. When two consecutive syllables of the same word begin with an aspirate, the former often loses its aspiration. Thus, θριχος is changed into τριχος; and ἐχω into ἐχω. But affixes generally lose their aspiration in preference to the stem, whether they are placed first or last; as, τι-θε-τι for θι-θε-θι, where the last syllable is a mere adjunct to the root.
8. No consonant can end a Greek word, except ν, ρ, σ, ξ, ψ; the last two being compounds of s. The preposition ἐκ before a consonant, and the negative adverb οὐκ before a vowel, are apparent exceptions; but, having no accent, they may be counted as parts of the following words.

Exercise 2.—On the Combination of Consonants.

Rule 1.—Write down the proper forms of γραφσει, τυπσω, λεγσον, ἐχσω, στρεφσεις, τριβσομεν, λεγσας, πεμπσον.

2. Of πειθσω, ἐλπιδσεις, ἀδσοντες, ἀνυτσει.

3. Of τετριβται, γεγραφται, λελεγται, βεβρεχται, ἐτριβθην, πλεκθηναι, λεγθηναι, ἐπεμπθην.

4. Of τετριβμαι, γεγραφμαι, βεβρεχμαι, πεπειθμαι, ἠνυτμαι, πεπλεκμαι.

5. Of παντπολυς, συνφημι, συνγνωμη, συνχαιρω, συνζυγος, συνστρατιωτης; also of παντς, λυοντσι, λυθεντσιν.

5. Some other **changes of consonants** may be noticed, though they do not so invariably conform to general rules as the preceding.

1. *Assimilation.*—The labials π, β, φ before μ, and ν before the other liquids, are regularly assimilated to the following letters; *i.e.* changed into the same letter (see § 4, *d*, 5). Sometimes a latter consonant is assimilated to a former one; as, ὄλλυμι for ὀλ-νυμι.

2. *Duplication.*—The letter ρ is regularly doubled when a vowel is placed before it. Thus, ἀπο-ρίπτω becomes ἀπορρίπτω.

Sometimes λ is doubled, to compensate for the loss of a vowel; as, μᾶλλον for μαλιον, ἀγγέλλω for ἀγγελεω. In comparatives and in verbs, σσ or ττ is sometimes put for a guttural κ, γ, χ with a following vowel; as, ἧσσον for ἡκιον, ταράσσω for ταραχεω. In some words, ζ appears instead of σσ; as, μείζων for μεγιων.

3. *Transposition.*—A vowel with a liquid is often transposed; as, θνήσκω for θαν-σκω.

4. *Omission.*—Any consonants which make a harsh sound may be omitted in the formation or inflection of words.

5. *Insertion.*—Sometimes, though rarely, a consonant is inserted to assist the sound; as, from ἀνήρ, gen. (ἄνερος, ἀν-ρος) ἀνδρός; so, ἄνθρωπος is from ἀνὴρ ὤψ, making ἀν-ρωπος, and, with θ inserted, ἄνθρωπος.

THE ACCENTS.

6. *a.* Every Greek word, except the proclitics and enclitics, which will be noticed under their respective parts of speech, **has an accent expressed on one of its last three syllables.** The accents are employed in writing, but mostly disregarded in pronunciation. Their use was to mark a certain stress (or "rising" or "falling" inflection) on the syllables where they are placed. It is said that they were invented by Greek grammarians, as a guide to foreigners in pronouncing the language. Some linguists of our own day have endeavoured to reinstate them as helps in this respect, but without much success.

b. The accents are the **acute** (′), the **grave** (`), and the **circumflex** (^).

The accent is marked upon a vowel, and in diphthongs upon the latter vowel; as, αὐτός, οὕτως. The acute and grave are placed *after* the breathing, and the circumflex over it; as, ὅς, οὗτος. The acute on the last syllable becomes grave, unless the word ends a sentence; except τίς, the interrogative, which always keeps its acute. Every unaccented syllable is said to have the *grave tone;* but the grave accent is not marked, except where it stands for a final acute.

c. Words are called, with reference to accent—**Oxytone** (lit. *sharp-toned*), when the acute is on the last syllable, as ἐλπίς; **Paroxytone**, when the acute is on the penultima (last but one), as οὕτως; **Proparoxytone**, when the acute is on the antepenultima (last but two), as φίλιος; **Perispomenon** (lit. *drawn-out*), when the circumflex is on the last syllable, as αὐτοῦ; **Properispomenon**, when on the penultima, as οὗτος. The circumflex cannot be farther back than the penultima, nor the acute than the antepenultima.

If the last syllable of the word contains a long vowel, the acute accent must be on the last or last but one, the circumflex only on the last. Should, therefore, the final syllable of a proparoxytone be lengthened by declension, the accent is thrown forward, *i.e.* the word becomes paroxytone; thus, ἄνθρωπος, ἀνθρώπων. But if the final syllable of a properispomenon is lengthened, the accent is changed to the acute, *i.e.* the word becomes paroxytone; thus, λιβερτῖνος, λιβερτίνων.

It should be observed that the circumflex accent is always the result of *contraction*, *i.e.* of an acute and grave (´ ˋ)—not of a grave and acute (ˋ ´)—as will be shown under Etymology.

d. **Enclitics** are words which merge their accent into the word immediately preceding, which word is affected as follows:—A proparoxytone or properispomenon takes an acute accent on the last syllable also; thus, ἄνθρωπός τις, οἶκός τις. An oxytone that would otherwise (see above) take the grave accent retains the acute; thus, μαθητής τις. Paroxytones and perispomena show no alteration.

e. **Proclitics** lose their accent in the words following. In an emphatic position, a proclitic becomes oxytone. Thus, οὐ with a verb is *not;* οὔ alone, *no!* A proclitic followed by an enclitic is also oxytoned; as, οὔ τις. The two may be written as one word.

Special rules of accentuation will be given under the sections of Etymology The learner is recommended to accentuate from the first, in writing Greek;

§ 7.] ORTHOGRAPHY, GREEK AND ENGLISH. 9

especially as the accent of very many words can only be known by acquaintance with the words themselves, and if neglected at first, will be extremely difficult to acquire afterwards.

ON THE TRANSFERENCE OF GREEK WORDS INTO ENGLISH.

7. Most proper names, and some few other words, are *literally* transcribed from the one language into the other. The medium of transference is almost always the Latin, and therefore the orthography conforms to Latin rules. For the most part, the Greek letters are represented by the equivalents given (§ 1). The following exceptions must, however, be noted :—

κ is always *c*, the letter *k* not being found in the usual Roman alphabet. Where the *c* would be soft in ordinary English pronunciation, it is *generally* so in Greek names, as Κυρήνη, *Cyrene*. In some words of infrequent use, good speakers sometimes deviate from this rule, saying, *e.g.* A*k*éldama, not A*s*éldama.

The vowel υ is represented by *y*, as Συρία, *Syria*.

The diphthong αι becomes *æ*, as Καῖσαρ, *Cæsar*. Occasionally, the diphthong is made simply *e ;* so, Αἴγυπτ(ος), *Egypt;* Τρύφαινα, *Tryphena*.

The diphthong οι becomes *æ*, as Φοίβη, *Phœbe ;* sometimes, as above, only *e :* thus, Φοινίκη, *Phenice.*

The diphthong ει becomes *ē* or *ī*, as Λαοδίκεια, *Laodicēa ;* Θυάτειρα, *Thyatīra :* sometimes (in practice) *ĭ*, as Σελεύκεια, *Seleucia*. But the *i* ought really to be long, or long *e ;* so *Attalia*.

The diphthong ου appears as *u*, as Λουκᾶς, *Luke ;* or, before a vowel, as *v*, as Σιλουανός, *Silvanus.*

The initial Ι before a vowel becomes *J*, as Ἰούδας, *Judas*.

The initial Ρ, always aspirated in Greek (§ 3, *d*), is *generally* without the aspirate in English. Thus, Ῥαββί, *Rabbi*. But Ῥήγιον, *Rhegium ;* Ῥόδη, *Rhoda ;* and Ῥόδος, *Rhodes*, are exceptions, being original Greek words.

> Changes in the terminations of these transferred words belong to Etymology. No rule can be given but usage why some should have their endings changed, while others are exactly transcribed. Occasionally, the same word appears in two forms. Thus, *Marcus* and *Mark, Lucas* and *Luke*. The learner is recommended to read carefully parts of the New Testament where many proper names occur, comparing the English with the Greek. No better portion for the purpose could be found than Romans xvi.

PUNCTUATION.

8. Four marks of punctuation are used for the division of sentences: the comma, the colon, the period, and the note of interrogation.
The comma (,) and the period (.) are like our own.

> In modern typography it is very usual not to begin new sentences with capital letters; reserving these for proper names, for the commencement of quotations, and for the beginning of paragraphs.

The colon (sometimes called semicolon) is expressed by a point above the line, thus (·).

Interrogation is marked by a sign, after the question, resembling our semicolon (;).

Inverted commas, as marks of quotation, are sometimes, though rarely, employed in printed Greek.

The Greek equivalent for etc., *et cœtera*, is in the initials κ. τ. λ., for καὶ τὰ λοιπά, *and the rest*.

The following sentence exhibits the different marks of punctuation (John ix. 40) :—

Καὶ εἶπαν αὐτῷ, Μὴ καὶ ἡμεῖς τυφλοί ἐσμεν; εἶπεν αὐτοῖς (ὁ) Ἰησοῦς, Εἰ τυφλοὶ ἦτε, οὐκ ἂν εἴχετε ἁμαρτίαν. νῦν δὲ λέγετε ὅτι, Βλέπομεν· ἡ ἁμαρτία ὑμῶν μένει.

READING LESSONS.

I. Acts ii. 1–13.

Write the following in Roman letters, carefully inserting the initial aspirate wherever it occurs, and discriminating between the long and the short *o* and *e*, as in Lesson III. below :—

Καὶ ἐν τῷ συμπληροῦσθαι τὴν[1] ἡμέραν τῆς πεντηκοστῆς,
2 ἦσαν πάντες ὁμοῦ ἐπὶ τὸ αὐτό,[2] καὶ ἐγένετο ἄφνω ἐκ τοῦ οὐρανοῦ ἦχος ὥσπερ φερομένης πνοῆς βιαίας καὶ ἐπλήρωσεν
3 ὅλον τὸν οἶκον οὗ ἦσαν καθήμενοι, καὶ ὤφθησαν αὐτοῖς διαμεριζόμεναι γλῶσσαι ὡσεὶ πυρός, καὶ ἐκάθισεν ἐφ᾿ ἕνα ἕκαστον
4 αὐτῶν, καὶ ἐπλήσθησαν πάντες πνεύματος ἁγίου, καὶ ἤρξαντο λαλεῖν ἑτέραις γλώσσαις καθὼς τὸ πνεῦμα ἐδίδου ἀποφθέγ-

---

[1] According to what rule is the accent on the final syllable made *grave*?
[2] Why does this accent remain *acute*?

§§ 1-8.] READING LESSONS. 11

5 γεσθαι αὐτοῖς. Ἦσαν δὲ (ἐν) Ἰερουσαλὴμ κατοικοῦντες
  Ἰουδαῖοι, ἄνδρες εὐλαβεῖς ἀπὸ παντὸς ἔθνους τῶν ὑπὸ τὸν
6 οὐρανόν· γενομένης δὲ τῆς φωνῆς ταύτης συνῆλθε τὸ πλῆθος
  καὶ συνεχύθη, ὅτι ἤκουον εἷς ἕκαστος τῇ ἰδίᾳ διαλέκτῳ
7 λαλούντων αὐτῶν· ἐξίσταντο δὲ καὶ ἐθαύμαζον λέγοντες, Οὐχὶ
8 ἰδοὺ πάντες οὗτοί[1] εἰσιν οἱ λαλοῦντες Γαλιλαῖοι; καὶ πῶς
  ἡμεῖς ἀκούομεν ἕκαστος τῇ ἰδίᾳ διαλέκτῳ ἡμῶν ἐν ᾗ ἐγεννήθη;
9 μεν; Πάρθοι καὶ Μῆδοι καὶ Ἐλαμεῖται, καὶ οἱ κατοικοῦντες
  τὴν Μεσοποταμίαν, Ἰουδαίαν τε καὶ Καππαδοκίαν, Πόντον
10 καὶ τὴν Ἀσίαν, Φρυγίαν τε καὶ Παμφυλίαν, Αἴγυπτον, καὶ τὰ
   μέρη τῆς Λιβύης τῆς κατὰ Κυρήνην, καὶ οἱ ἐπιδημοῦντες
11 Ῥωμαῖοι, Ἰουδαῖοί[1] τε καὶ προσήλυτοι, Κρῆτες καὶ Ἄραβες,
   ἀκούομεν λαλούντων αὐτῶν ταῖς ἡμετέραις γλώσσαις τὰ με-
12 γαλεῖα τοῦ Θεοῦ. ἐξίσταντο δὲ πάντες καὶ διηποροῦντο, ἄλλος
   πρὸς ἄλλον λέγοντες, Τί θέλει τοῦτο εἶναι; ἕτεροι δὲ
13 διαχλευάζοντες ἔλεγον ὅτι, Γλεύκους μεμεστωμένοι εἰσίν.

II. ROMANS iv. 1–16.

Read the following, carefully attending to the *punctuation*, which in this passage is marked with unusual decisiveness:—

   Τί οὖν ἐροῦμεν Ἀβραὰμ τὸν προπάτορα ἡμῶν κατὰ σάρκα;
2 εἰ γὰρ Ἀβραὰμ ἐξ ἔργων ἐδικαιώθη, ἔχει καύχημα· ἀλλ᾽
3 οὐ πρὸς θεόν, τί γὰρ ἡ γραφὴ λέγει; 'Ἐπίστευσεν δὲ
   'Ἀβραὰμ τῷ θεῷ, καὶ ἐλογίσθη αὐτῷ εἰς δικαιοσύνην.'
4 τῷ δὲ ἐργαζομένῳ ὁ μισθὸς οὐ λογίζεται κατὰ χάριν ἀλλὰ
5 κατὰ ὀφείλημα· τῷ δὲ μὴ ἐργαζομένῳ, πιστεύοντι δὲ ἐπὶ
   τὸν δικαιοῦντα τὸν ἀσεβῆ, λογίζεται ἡ πίστις αὐτοῦ εἰς
6 δικαιοσύνην, καθάπερ καὶ Δαυεὶδ λέγει τὸν μακαρισμὸν
   τοῦ ἀνθρώπου ᾧ ὁ θεὸς λογίζεται δικαιοσύνην χωρὶς ἔργων,
7 'Μακάριοι ὧν ἀφέθησαν αἱ ἀνομίαι καὶ ὧν ἐπεκαλύφθησαν
8 'αἱ ἁμαρτίαι, μακάριος ἀνὴρ (οὗ) οὐ μὴ λογίσηται Κύριος
9 'ἁμαρτίαν.' ὁ μακαρισμὸς οὖν οὗτος ἐπὶ τὴν περιτομὴν
   ἢ καὶ ἐπὶ τὴν ἀκροβυστίαν; λέγομεν γάρ, 'Ἐλογίσθη τῷ
10 'Ἀβραὰμ ἡ πίστις εἰς δικαιοσύνην.' πῶς οὖν ἐλογίσθη;

---
[1] Why has this word *two* accents?

ἐν περιτομῇ ὄντι ἢ ἐν ἀκροβυστίᾳ; οὐκ ἐν περιτομῇ
11 ἀλλ' ἐν ἀκροβυστίᾳ· καὶ 'σημεῖον' ἔλαβεν 'περιτομῆς,'
σφραγῖδα τῆς δικαιοσύνης τῆς πίστεως τῆς ἐν 'τῇ ἀκροβυστίᾳ,' εἰς τὸ εἶναι αὐτὸν πατέρα πάντων τῶν πιστευόντων
δι' ἀκροβυστίας, εἰς τὸ λογισθῆναι αὐτοῖς (τὴν) δικαιοσύνην,
12 καὶ πατέρα περιτομῆς τοῖς οὐκ ἐκ περιτομῆς μόνον ἀλλὰ
(καὶ τοῖς) στοιχοῦσιν τοῖς ἴχνεσιν τῆς ἐν ἀκροβυστίᾳ
13 πίστεως τοῦ πατρὸς ἡμῶν Ἀβραάμ. Οὐ γὰρ διὰ νόμου
ἡ ἐπαγγελία τῷ Ἀβραὰμ ἢ τῷ σπέρματι αὐτοῦ, τὸ κληρο-
νόμον αὐτὸν εἶναι κόσμου, ἀλλὰ διὰ δικαιοσύνης πίστεως·
14 εἰ γὰρ οἱ ἐκ νόμου κληρονόμοι, κεκένωται ἡ πίστις καὶ
15 κατήργηται ἡ ἐπαγγελία. ὁ γὰρ νόμος ὀργὴν κατεργάζεται,
16 οὗ δὲ οὐκ ἔστιν νόμος, οὐδὲ παράβασις. Διὰ τοῦτο ἐκ
πίστεως, ἵνα κατὰ χάριν.

The quotation marks (inverted commas) introduced in verses 3, 7, 8, are used, as is the practice in some editions of the Greek Testament, to indicate a citation from the ancient Scriptures.

III. MATTHEW v. 1–16.

Write the following in Greek characters, punctuating the sentences, inserting the soft and aspirate "*breathings*," but not attempting accentuation. The usual marks (¯) and (˘) discriminate the long and the short vowels. In the diphthongs, the short *o* and *e* are to be used. Where an iota is to be *subscribed*, the vowel is italicised ; thus, *ō* = ῳ.

1 Idōn dĕ tous ŏchlous anĕbē eis tŏ ŏrŏs; kai kathisantŏs autou
2 prosēlthan (autō) hoi mathētai autou; kai anoixas tŏ stŏma autou
3 ĕdidaskĕn autous lĕgōn, Makarioi hoi ptōchoi tō pneumati, hŏti autōn
4 ĕstin hē basileia tōn ouranōn. makarioi hoi pĕnthountĕs, hŏti autoi
5 paraklēthēsŏntai. makarioi hoi praeis, hŏti autoi klērŏnŏmēsousi tēn
6 gēn. makarioi hoi peinōntĕs kai dipsōntĕs tēn dikaiŏsunēn, hŏti
7 autoi chŏrtasthēsŏntai. makarioi hoi ĕlĕĕmŏnĕs, hŏti autoi ĕlĕēthē-
8 sŏntai. makarioi hoi katharoi tē kardia, hŏti autoi tŏn theŏn
9 ŏpsŏntai. makarioi hoi eirēnŏpoioi, hŏti (autoi) huioi theou
10 klēthēsontai. makarioi hoi dĕdiōgmĕnoi hĕnĕkĕn dikaiŏsunēs, hŏti
11 autōn ĕstin hē basileia tōn ouranōn. makarioi ĕstĕ hŏtan ŏneidisōsin
humas kai diōxōsin kai eipōsin pan pŏnērŏn kath' humōn pseudŏmĕnoi

12 hĕnĕkĕn ĕmou ; chairĕtĕ kai agalliasthĕ, hŏti hŏ misthŏs humōn pŏlus ĕn tois ouranois; houtōs gar ĕdiōxan tous prŏphētas tous prŏ humōn.
13   Humeis ĕstĕ tŏ halas tēs gēs ; ĕan dĕ tŏ halas mōranthē, ĕn tini halisthēsĕtai ? eis oudĕn ischuei ĕti ei mē blēthĕn ĕxō katapateisthai
14 hupŏ tōn anthrōpōn. humeis ĕstĕ tŏ phōs tou kŏsmou, ou dunatai
15 pŏlis krubēnai ĕpanō ŏrous keimĕnē ; oudĕ kaiousi luchnŏn kai tithĕasin autŏn hupŏ tŏn mŏdiŏn all' ĕpi tēn luchnian, kai lampei
16 pasin tois ĕn tē oikia. houtōs lampsatō tŏ phōs humōn ĕmprŏsthĕn tōn anthrōpōn, hŏpōs idōsin humōn ta kala ĕrga kai doxasōsin tŏn. patĕra humōn tŏn ĕn tois ouranois.

The Greek Testament will furnish many other exercises, which should be repeated until the learner can read the language with perfect facility. A little care and time now devoted to this point, even before the meaning of a single word is understood, will very greatly contribute to future progress.

PART II.

ETYMOLOGY.

Chapter I. INTRODUCTION.

9. ETYMOLOGY treats of the **classification**, the **derivation**, and the **inflection** of words.

a. The *parts of speech* in Greek, and in all other languages, are substantially the same.

b. More important than any others are the *Noun* and the *Verb*. These, as the necessary elements of a sentence, will first be treated of, in their various inflections. With the Noun are closely connected the *Article*, the *Adjective*, and the *Pronoun*. The Verb also has its noun, the *Infinitive*, and its adjective, the *Participle*. Of these two the latter only is inflected.

10. The elementary part of every word is called its **STEM**, as every inflection presupposes it, and branches from it.

The *Root* of a word is its yet simpler element in the same or another language. With this, practical grammar has comparatively little to do; but to know the stem is of the utmost importance in the analysis of any word. Throughout the Etymology the *stem* will be marked by *thick letters*, with a hyphen indicating the (general) incompleteness of the stem until some letter or syllable be added by way of inflection.

The last letter of a stem is called the *stem-ending*. If the letter is a vowel, the stem is called "vowel," or *pure*. So a stem ending with a liquid is called a *liquid* stem ; ending with a mute, a *mute* stem. Liquid and mute stems are sometimes called *impure*.

Chapter II. THE NOUN, or SUBSTANTIVE.

11. Nouns have **three genders**, *Masculine, Feminine,* and *Neuter;* also **three numbers**, *Singular, Dual,* and *Plural.* The dual number denotes two, or a pair of anything; but as it is not found in the Greek Testament, it will not be noticed in the forms of declension given.

There are **five cases**: the *Nominative,* or case of the Subject; the *Genitive,* or Possessive; the *Dative,* or Conjunctive; the *Accusative,* or Objective; the *Vocative,* employed in direct address.

Strictly speaking, the Nominative and Vocative are not *cases:* the word implying dependence. Of the three true cases, often called *oblique*,[1] the Genitive originally signifies *motion from,* then, more generally, separation; the Dative, *rest in,* hence conjunction with; the Accusative, *motion towards,* hence denoting simply the object of the transitive verb. This general description of the three cases, for the further illustration of which see SYNTAX, will explain most of their uses.

> In the paradigms of Nouns Substantive, a convenient English rendering of the Genitive is by the preposition *of,* and of the Dative by *to.* It must, however, be remembered that these words are used for the sake of distinction merely, and not as intimating that such are the most correct or usual renderings.

12. Before proceeding to the inflection of Nouns, it will be convenient to give the **Definite Article** in its numbers, genders, and cases. This must be thoroughly committed to memory.

There is no indefinite article in Greek, the nearest equivalent being the *indefinite pronoun* τις, *any.*[2] This is also subjoined, chiefly for the reason that the two words together furnish a model, nearly complete, of the declension of ALL SUBSTANTIVES AND ADJECTIVES.

---

[1] *Oblique,* or slanting, from the habit among old grammarians of expressing the forms of the noun by a diagram, the nominative being an upright stem, from which the cases branched at different angles.

[2] Or the numeral εἷς, *one.*

Definite Article, *the*. Stem. m. n. το-, fem. τα-

	SINGULAR.			PLURAL.		
	M.	F.	N.	M.	F.	N.
N.	ὁ	ἡ	τό	οἱ	αἱ	τά
G.	τοῦ	τῆς	τοῦ	τῶν	τῶν	τῶν
D.	τῷ	τῇ	τῷ	τοῖς	ταῖς	τοῖς
A.	τόν	τήν	τό	τούς	τάς	τά

Accentuation.—The nominative, masculine and feminine, singular and plural, is *proclitic;* the genitive and dative of both numbers are *perispomena;* the rest *oxytone.*

13.   Indefinite Pronoun: *any, a certain, a.*   Stem, τῐν-

	SINGULAR.		PLURAL.	
	M. and F.	N.	M. and F.	N.
N.	τις	τι	τινες	τινα
G.	τινος	τινος	τινων	τινων
D.	τινι	τινι	τισι	τισι
A.	τινα	τι	τινας	τινα

Accentuation.—The word is generally *enclitic,* as here given; the accent being regarded as transferred to the previous word (§ 6, *d*). When accented, the forms are *oxytone,* except the genitive plural, which is *perispomenon.* Thus, τινός, τισί, τινῶν.

14. A comparison of the two forms now given will show four particulars, applicable to all nouns, adjectives, and pronouns; and, therefore, at the outset, important to remember.

a. **Neuters have but one form in each number for the nominative and accusative.** Perhaps this might have arisen from things without life being regarded as *objects only.* Neuters plural, nominative and accusative, always end in α (*short*), except when contracted, as τείχη for τείχεα (Heb. xi. 30).

b. **The dative singular always ends in ι**; though, where the letter preceding is a long vowel, the iota is *subscript* (§ 3, *b*).

c. **The genitive plural always ends in ων.**

d. **Masculine and neuter forms are always alike in the genitive and dative.**

Gender of Substantives. General Rules.

15. Many names of inanimate objects are of the masculine or feminine gender. This fact, no doubt, arose from the habit of personification, common in early ages. The English, indeed, is the only great language in which *masculine* and *feminine*, with almost undeviating strictness, denote *male* and *female*. The French idiom, in the opposite extreme, entirely rejects the neuter.

Considerable difficulty, therefore, is felt by beginners in determining the gender of many nouns. In some cases, it will be necessary to consult the Lexicon; in others, the termination of the word will be a guide, as is shown under the several declensions.

The following rules, however, are of general application :—

a. The names of *males* are Masculine;[1] so of *rivers* and *winds*, which were regarded by the early Greeks as gods.

b. The names of *females* are Feminine;[1] so also of *trees, countries, islands*, most *towns*, and *abstract* terms.

c. Diminutives in **-ον** are Neuter, even though the names of persons. To the class of neuters also belongs the *verbal substantive*, or infinitive verb, with *indeclinable* nouns generally.

Declension of Nouns Substantive.

16. There are **three leading types of inflection**, under one or other of which all declinable nouns may be classified. These are called the **Three Declensions**, and, as has been stated, the model of each may be traced in the Article and the Indefinite Pronoun.

The *First Declension* corresponds with the feminine of the article, ἡ. The *Second Declension* corresponds with the masculine or neuter of the article, ὁ, τό. The *Third Declension* corresponds with the form of the indefinite pronoun, τις, τι.

A model of each declension is here given.

---

[1] The generic names of animals are sometimes *common*, i.e. of either masc. or fem. gender, according to circumstances (so also παῖς, *child*); more frequently *epicoene*, i.e. of one gender, used indifferently for both sexes. Thus, in Greek, *wolf* is always masc., *fox* always fem., even in Luke xiii. 32.

First Declension.

πύλη, *a gate.* Stem, πυλα-

SINGULAR.
- N. πύλη, a gate (*subj.*)
- G. πύλης, of a gate
- D. πύλῃ, to a gate
- A. πύλην, a gate (*obj.*)
- V. πύλη, O gate !

PLURAL.
- πύλαι, gates (*subj.*)
- πυλῶν, of gates
- πύλαις, to gates
- πύλας, gates (*obj.*)
- πύλαι, O gates !

Second Declension.

ἄνθρωπος, *a man.* Stem, ἀνθρωπο-

SINGULAR.
- N. ἄνθρωπος, a man (*subj.*)
- G. ἀνθρώπου, of a man
- D. ἀνθρώπῳ, to a man
- A. ἄνθρωπον, a man (*obj.*)
- V. ἄνθρωπε, O man !

PLURAL.
- ἄνθρωποι, men (*subj.*)
- ἀνθρώπων, of men
- ἀνθρώποις, to men
- ἀνθρώπους, men (*obj.*)
- ἄνθρωποι, O men !

Accentuation.—The reason why the place of the accent varies in the genitive and dative is explained, § 6, c.

Third Declension.

παῖς, *a child, boy, servant.* Stem, παιδ-

(Accent of this word irregular.)

SINGULAR.
- N. παῖς, a child (*subj.*)
- G. παιδός, of a child
- D. παιδί, to a child
- A. παῖδα, a child (*obj.*)
- V. παῖ, O child !

PLURAL.
- παῖδες, children (*subj.*)
- παίδων, of children
- παῖσι, to children
- παῖδας, children (*obj.*)
- παῖδες, O children !

These three paradigms having been committed to memory, the several declensions, with their rules of formation, their analogies and variations, may now be more particularly discussed.

A certain likeness will, on examination, be detected between the *First* and *Second*, especially in the plural number. The plural terminations may be set side by side, thus:—

§ 18.] THE FIRST AND SECOND DECLENSIONS.

	First Declension,		Second Declension,	
N. and V.		-αι		-οι
G.	”	-ων	”	-ων
D.	”	-αις	”	-οις
A.	”	-ας	”	-ους

In the former, the predominant vowel is evidently α; in the latter, ο. So in the singular, the first declension in the dative has η (for α lengthened, § 3, e); the second, ω (for ο lengthened). In the accusative, the first has αν, or ην; the second, ον.

The two may accordingly be discriminated as the **A** declension and the **O** declension; a distinction which the further examination of their structure makes yet more plain.

Both, again, are distinguished from the *third* by **admitting the termination which marks the case into the last syllable of the word**; while the latter **adds the termination as a distinct syllable.**

The First and Second Declensions are, on account of this last peculiarity, called the *Inseparable*, or *Parisyllabic*; the Third, the *Separable*, or *Imparisyllabic* declension.

All three admit, however, of many variations, as will now be shown in detail.

17. FIRST (INSEPARABLE), OR A-DECLENSION.

This declension includes both masculine and feminine nouns. **The stem invariably ends in α.** As the feminine has already been given as containing the typical form, that may be placed first.

18.   FEMININE PARADIGMS.   First Declension.

ἡμέρα, day.
Stem, ἡμερα-

	SINGULAR.	PLURAL.
N.	ἡμέρα	ἡμέραι
G.	ἡμέρας	ἡμερῶν
D.	ἡμέρᾳ	ἡμέραις
A.	ἡμέραν	ἡμέρας
V.	ἡμέρα	ἡμέραι

δόξα, opinion.
Stem, δοξα-

	SINGULAR.	PLURAL.
N.	δόξα	δόξαι
G.	δόξης	δοξῶν
D.	δόξῃ	δόξαις
A.	δόξαν	δόξας
V.	δόξα	δόξαι

THE FIRST DECLENSION.

τιμή, honour.
Stem, τιμα-

	SINGULAR.	PLURAL.
N.	τιμή	τιμαί
G.	τιμῆς	τιμῶν
D.	τιμῇ	τιμαῖς
A.	τιμήν	τιμάς
V.	τιμή	τιμαί

σκιά, shadow.
Stem, σκια-

	SINGULAR.	PLURAL.
N.	σκιά	σκιαί
G.	σκιᾶς	σκιῶν
D.	σκιᾷ	σκιαῖς
A.	σκιάν	σκιάς
V.	σκιά	σκιαί

REMARKS.

a. The stem-ending **α** becomes **η** in the nominative and accusative singular whenever *preceded by a consonant;* except by the liquid **ρ**, the double consonants, or **σ**, sometimes **ν** preceded by a diphthong or long vowel. In these cases, the **α** remains, *long* after **ρ**, *short* in the other cases. Preceded by a vowel, the **α** remains, generally *long*. Thus we have the nominatives ἐντολή, συναγωγή, ψυχή; but θύρᾱ, δόξᾰ, γλῶσσᾰ, βασίλισσᾰ, λέαινᾰ, σκιᾱ́, βασιλείᾱ, ἀλήθειᾰ.

b. In the genitive and dative singular, the stem-ending **α**, when not preceded by a vowel or **ρ**, becomes **η**. After a vowel or **ρ**, it remains. Thus, N. δόξα; G. δόξης; D. δόξῃ; but ἡμέρα, ἡμέρας, ἡμέρᾳ, and σκιά, σκιᾶς, σκιᾷ.

c. The plural terminations in all forms of this declension are exactly alike, the **α** in **-ας** of the accusative being *long* (contracted for **-ανς**).

d. Accentuation.—Whatever syllable is accented in the nominative retains the accent throughout, so long as the laws in § 6, c, permit. The only *apparent* exception is in the genitive plural, which in this declension is always *perispomenon*. This, however, is accounted for by its being a contraction of **-άων**. Oxytone words become perispomenon in the genitive and dative of both numbers. For purposes of accentuation, the termination **αι** in the plural nominative is considered short.

19. MASCULINE PARADIGMS. First Declension.

μαθητής, *disciple.*
Stem, μαθητα-

	SINGULAR.	PLURAL.
N.	μαθητής	μαθηταί
G	μαθητοῦ	μαθητῶν
D.	μαθητῇ	μαθηταῖς
A.	μαθητήν	μαθητάς
V.	μαθητά	μαθηταί

νεανίας, *a youth.*
Stem, νεανια-

	SINGULAR.	PLURAL.
N.	νεανίας	νεανίαι
G	νεανίου	νεανιῶν
D.	νεανίᾳ	νεανίαις
A.	νεανίαν	νεανίας
V.	νεανία	νεανίαι

REMARKS.

a. All masculine nouns of the first declension form the nominative from the stem by adding ς, lengthening α into η after all consonants except the liquid ρ, and retaining α after vowels and ρ. The vowel of the nominative is retained in the dat. and acc. sing.

b. The genitive singular of all masculine nouns of this declension ends in ου, originally αο. The vocative gives the simple stem. Other cases conform entirely to the feminine type.

c. Accentuation.—The remarks under the feminine paradigms are applicable to masculine also.

Exercise 3.—Nouns of the First Declension, for Practice.
(Selected from the "Sermon on the Mount.")

1. MASCULINE.

κριτής, judge
ὀφειλέτης, debtor
προφήτης, prophet
τελώνης, tax-gatherer, "publican"
ὑπηρέτης, attendant, servant

2. FEMININE.

βασιλεία, kingdom
δικαιοσύνη, righteousness
ἐντολή, commandment
ζωή, life
θύρα, gate
κεφαλή, head
λυχνία, lampstand
οἰκία, house
πέτρα, rock
ψυχή, soul, natural life

The learner should commit these words to memory, with their meanings, and should then write them down in different numbers and cases, with and without the corresponding articles, until all the forms are mastered. So with the other Exercises.

IRREGULAR FORMS OF THE FIRST DECLENSION.

20. *a.* Masculine proper names in ας of this declension form the genitive in α, *excepting when preceded by a vowel*. Thus, Ἰωνᾶς, *Jonah*, gen. Ἰωνᾶ; Κηφᾶς, *Cephas*, gen. Κηφᾶ; Βαρνάβας, gen. Βαρνάβα; Ἰούδας, *Judah* or *Judas*, gen. Ἰούδα. The accent of the genitive corresponds with that of the nominative. But Ἀνδρέας, *Andrew*, makes Ἀνδρέου; Ἡσαΐας, *Isaiah*, Ἡσαΐου. These names are from the Hebrew, with the exception of Ἀνδρέας.

b. In Acts v. 1, we find Σαπφείρῃ, dative of the proper name *Sapphira;* and in Acts x. 1, σπείρης is used as the genitive of σπεῖρα, *cohort*—in both instances contrary to the rule in § 19, *a*. Similar variations from the regular form are found in good MSS. in the case of other substantives.

21. SECOND (INSEPARABLE), OR O-DECLENSION.

This declension contains masculine, feminine, and neuter nouns. The **stem invariably ends in o,** to which **-s** is added to form masculine and feminine nominatives, and **-v** to form the neuter.

22. MASCULINE AND FEMININE PARADIGMS. Second Declension.

λόγος, *word,* masc.
Stem, λογο-

ὁδός, *way,* fem.
Stem, ὁδο-

	SINGULAR.	PLURAL.	SINGULAR.	PLURAL.
N.	λόγος	λόγοι	ὁδός	ὁδοί
G.	λόγου	λόγων	ὁδοῦ	ὁδῶν
D.	λόγῳ	λόγοις	ὁδῷ	ὁδοῖς
A.	λόγον	λόγους	ὁδόν	ὁδούς
V.	λόγε	λόγοι	ὁδέ	ὁδοί

REMARKS.

a. As before noticed, this paradigm corresponds with that of the first declension, **o-** being substituted for **a-**. The differences are, that in the nominative singular the stem-vowel is not lengthened, and that the vocative singular changes this vowel into **ε**. In the accusative plural, the termination **-ous** is for **-ovs** (§ 4, *d*, 5), as in the first declension **-ās** is for **-avs**; in each case, **s** being added to the accusative singular.

b. Accentuation.—The remarks on the first declension are mostly applicable. The syllable accented in the nominative retains the accent throughout, wherever possible; oxytones becoming perispomena in the genitive and dative of both numbers. The genitive plural of other nouns is not, as in the first declension, perispomenon. In the nominative plural, the termination οι is treated with reference to the accent as a short syllable.

23. NEUTER PARADIGM. Second Declension.

σῦκον, *fig-tree.* Stem, συκο-

SINGULAR.	PLURAL.
N. σῦκον	σῦκα
G. σύκου	σύκων
D. σύκῳ	σύκοις
A. σῦκον	σῦκα
V. σῦκον	σῦκα

REMARKS.

The only difference between this paradigm and that of the masculine and feminine is that already stated, § 14, *a*. The accusative of all neuters is the same form with the nominative and vocative; and in the plural these cases end in ă.

Accentuation. — For the accentual changes in the declension of σῦκον, see § 6, *c*.

24. PARADIGM OF CONTRACTED NOUNS. Second Declension.

Nouns of this declension whose stem-vowel o- is preceded by ε or o, *generally* suffer contraction, according to the scheme in § 3, *f*. Thus, νόος, *mind*, becomes νοῦς; ὀστέον, *bone*, ὀστοῦν. The contracted forms of these words are not invariably employed in the Septuagint or New Testament. On νοῦς, see Variable Nouns, § 32, *a*.

To this head may also be referred some nouns in -ως, like the proper names, Ἀπολλώς, Κῶς.

νόος, *mind*, m. Stem, νοο-

SINGULAR.	PLURAL.
N. (νόος) νοῦς	(νόοι) νοῖ
G. (νόου) νοῦ	(νόων) νῶν
D. (νόῳ) νῷ	(νόοις) νοῖς
A. (νόον) νοῦν	(νόους) νοῦς
V. (νόε) νοῦ	(νόοι) νοῖ

ὀστέον, *bone*, n. Stem, ὀστεο-

SINGULAR.	PLURAL.
(ὀστέον) ὀστοῦν	(ὀστέα) ὀστᾶ
(ὀστέου) ὀστοῦ	(ὀστέων) ὀστῶν
(ὀστέῳ) ὀστῷ	(ὀστέοις) ὀστοῖς
(ὀστέον) ὀστοῦν	(ὀστέα) ὀστᾶ
(ὀστέον) ὀστοῦν	(ὀστέα) ὀστᾶ

Ἀπολλώς, *Apollos.*

N. Ἀπολλώς
G. Ἀπολλώ
D. Ἀπολλῷ
A. Ἀπολλών, or Ἀπολλώ (irreg.)
V. Ἀπολλώ

25. The word Ἰησοῦς, JESUS, is thus declined:—

N. Ἰησοῦς   A. Ἰησοῦν
G. Ἰησοῦ   V. Ἰησοῦ
D. Ἰησοῦ

Exercise 4.—Nouns of the Second Declension, for Practice.
(Selected from the "Sermon on the Mount.")

1. MASCULINE.

ἀδελφός, brother   λύκος, wolf
ἐχθρός, enemy   νόμος, law
ἄνθρωπος, man   ὀφθαλμός, eye
ἥλιος, sun   ποταμός, river

2. FEMININE.

ἄμμος, sand   δοκός, beam

3. NEUTER.

δῶρον, gift   κρίνον, lily
ἔργον, work   πρόβατον, sheep
μέτρον, measure   τέκνον, child

26. THIRD (OR SEPARABLE) DECLENSION.

Nouns in this declension are masculine, feminine, or neuter. The **stem** may end in **any consonant** (except μ, and the double consonants ζ, ξ, ψ), and in the **vowels** ι and υ. These varieties necessitate the giving of several paradigms, although all are reducible to a simple form, already illustrated in the indefinite pronoun τις, and shown in the two nouns declined below.

§ 28.] THE THIRD DECLENSION. 25

The **one essential thing**, in this declension especially, **is to know the stem**, which may end in a consonant (*impure*, mute or liquid), or in a vowel (*pure*). From this the nominative, as well as every other case, is derived; but the stem-ending is better seen in the genitive, which, in Vocabularies and Lexicons, is therefore given with the nominative.

The termination of the genitive singular in this declension is always **os**. Take this away, and the remaining part of the word is the stem.

27. GENERAL PARADIGM OF THE THIRD DECLENSION.

	M. or F.		N.	
	αἰών, *age, duration,* masc.		ῥῆμα, *word.*	
	Stem, αἰων-		Stem, ῥημᾰτ-	
	SINGULAR.	PLURAL.	SINGULAR.	PLURAL.
N.	αἰών	αἰῶνες	ῥῆμα	ῥήματα
G.	αἰῶνος	αἰώνων	ῥήματος	ῥημάτων
D.	αἰῶνι	αἰῶσι(ν)	ῥήματι	ῥήμασι(ν)
A.	αἰῶνα	αἰῶνας	ῥῆμα	ῥήματα
V.	αἰών	αἰῶνες	ῥῆμα	ῥήματα

Accentuation.—The accented syllable of the nominative, as in other nouns, retains the accent throughout, wherever possible. For a special rule respecting monosyllables, see § 29. In the above paradigm, αἰών in the nominative is written for αἰῶν.

TERMINATIONS OF THE THIRD DECLENSION.

28. These paradigms are essentially alike in termination, setting aside the invariable differences between neuter and other forms (§ 14, *a*).

We thus find that the terminations of the third declension are, in the SINGULAR—

Genitive, **os,** appended to the stem.

Dative, **ι,** also appended to the stem.

Accusative, ă. This, however, is *really a substitute for ν*, which we find in the first and second declensions, and which in pure stems often appears in the third also.

Vocative, the stem, subject to necessary modifications (§ 4, *d*, 8), or like the nominative.

In the PLURAL—

Nominative, ες, appended to the stem.

Genitive, ων, appended to the stem.

Dative, σι, added to the stem, with necessary modifications (§ 4, *d*, 1, 5) On the νῦ ἐφελκυστικόν, see § 3, *h*, 1.

Accusative, ᾰs, the ᾰ *short*, or s added to the accusative singular. Compare the First and Second Declensions, § 22, *a*.

Vocative, like the nominative.

TABLE OF TERMINATIONS.

	SINGULAR.	PLURAL.
N.	s, or none	ες, α
G.	ος	ων
D.	ι	σι
A.	α, ν	as, α
V.	as Nom.	ες, α

29. PARADIGMS OF THIRD DECLENSION (see § 30).

I. The letter s affixed to the stem.

    a. CONSONANT STEMS (*mute*), **labial** and **guttural**.

Ἄραψ, *Arabian*, masc.   κῆρυξ, *herald*, masc.

    Stem, Ἀράβ-   Stem, κηρῡκ-

	SINGULAR.	PLURAL.	SINGULAR.	PLURAL.
N.	Ἄραψ	Ἄραβες	κῆρυξ	κήρυκες
G.	Ἄραβος	Ἀράβων	κήρυκος	κηρύκων
D.	Ἄραβι	Ἄραψι(ν)	κήρυκι	κήρυξι(ν)
A.	Ἄραβα	Ἄραβας	κήρυκα	κήρυκας
V.	Ἄραψ	Ἄραβες	κῆρυξ	κήρυκες

§ 29.]   THIRD DECLENSION—PARADIGMS.

For example of **a dental stem** (neuter), see Introductory Paradigm of the Declensions, § 16. The feminine noun χάρις (χαριτ-), *favour*, makes acc. χάριν; κλείς, *key*, fem. (κλειδ-) has acc. sing. κλεῖδα; acc. plur. by syncope and contraction, κλεῖς (Rev. i. 18); but also κλεῖδας (Matt. xvi. 19).

b. Vowel Stems.

ἰχθύς, *fish*, masc.
Stem, ἰχθυ-

SINGULAR.	PLURAL.
N. ἰχθύς	ἰχθύες
G. ἰχθύος	ἰχθύων
D. ἰχθύϊ	ἰχθύσι (ν)
A. ἰχθύν	(ἰχθύας) ἰχθῦς
V. ἰχθύ	ἰχθύες

πόλις, *city*, fem.
Stem, πολι-

SINGULAR.	PLURAL.
πόλις	(πόλεες) πόλεις
πόλεως (Attic gen.)	πόλεων
(πόλεϊ) πόλει	πόλεσι(ν)
πόλιν	(πόλεας) πόλεις
πόλι	(πόλεες) πόλεις

REMARKS.

Stems in -ι, and some in -υ, change to -ε before the case-endings (§ 37, note).

One neuter noun, σίναπι, *mustard* (singular only), is declined like πόλις, excepting that the accusative is, of course, like the nom.

Accentuation.—For accentual purposes, the genitive termination, -εως or -εων, in these nouns, is considered as *one syllable*, and does not, therefore, require the acute accent to be thrown forward.

II. The vowel of the last syllable stem lengthened.

ποιμήν, *shepherd*, masc.
Stem, ποιμεν-

SINGULAR.	PLURAL.
N. ποιμήν	ποιμένες
G. ποιμένος	ποιμένων
D. ποιμένι	ποιμέσι(ν)
A. ποιμένα	ποιμένας
V. ποιμήν	ποιμένες

λέων, *lion*, masc.
Stem, λεοντ-

SINGULAR.	PLURAL.
λέων	λέοντες
λέοντος	λεόντων
λέοντι	λέουσι(ν)
λέοντα	λέοντας
λέων	λέοντες

αἰδώς, *modesty*, fem. Stem, αἰδοσ-

SINGULAR ONLY.
N. αἰδώς
G. (αἰδό(σ)ος) αἰδοῦς
D. (αἰδό(σ)ι) αἰδοῖ
A. (αἰδό(σ)α) αἰδῶ
V. αἰδώς

Syncopated Nouns of this Form.

πατήρ, *father*.

Stem, πατερ-

	SINGULAR.	PLURAL.
N.	πατήρ	πατέρες
G.	πατρός	πατέρων
D.	πατρί	πατράσι(ν)
A.	πατέρα	πατέρας
V.	πάτερ	πατέρες

ἀνήρ, *man*.

Stem, ἀνερ-

	SINGULAR.	PLURAL.
N.	ἀνήρ	ἄνδρες
G.	ἀνδρός	ἀνδρῶν
D.	ἀνδρί	ἀνδράσι(ν)
A.	ἄνδρα	ἄνδρας
V.	ἄνερ	ἄνδρες

REMARKS.

The syncopation takes place in the G. and D. sing. and D. plur.

To this class belong μήτηρ, *mother*; θυγάτηρ, *daughter*; γαστήρ, *belly*. ἀστήρ, *star*, has ἀστράσι(ν) in the dative plural, but is not syncopated in any other case.

Accentuation.—These words are paroxytone in the cases that retain ε, and throughout the plural (excepting ἀνήρ, which is irregular). The syncopated cases of the singular are oxytone, and the vocative throws back its accent as far as possible.

III. **Nouns in -αυς, -ευς, -ους, with original digamma.**

βασιλεύς, *king*, masc.   Stem, βασιλεϝ-

	SINGULAR.	PLURAL.
N.	βασιλεύς	(βασιλέες) βασιλεῖς
G.	βασιλέως	βασιλέων
D.	(βασιλέϊ) βασιλεῖ	βασιλεῦσι(ν)
A.	βασιλέα	βασιλέας, βασιλεῖς
V.	βασιλεῦ	(βασιλέες) βασιλεῖς

§ 29.] THE THIRD DECLENSION.

βοῦς, *ox*, masc.   Stem, βοϝ-

	SINGULAR.	PLURAL.
N.	βοῦς	βόες
G.	βοός	βοῶν
D.	βοΐ	βουσί(ν)
A.	βοῦν	(βόας) βοῦς
V.	βοῦ	βόες

REMARKS.

Nouns in -ευς form the accusative singular in -εα (the α *long*); those in -αυς and -ους take ν.

Accentuation.—Nouns in -ευς are all oxytone in the nominative singular, and perispomenon in the vocative.

IV. Neuter nouns in -ος, from the stem-ending -ες.

γένος, *race*.   Stem, γενες-

	SINGULAR.	PLURAL.
N.	γένος	(γένε(σ)α) γένη
G.	(γένε(σ)ος) γένους	γενέων and γενῶν
D.	(γένε(σ)ι) γένει	γένεσι(ν)
A.	γένος	(γένε(σ)α) γένη
V.	γένος	(γένε(σ)α) γένη

V. The simple stem as nominative.
See αἰών and ῥῆμα, already given, § 27.

Exercise 5.—Nouns of the Third Declension, for Practice.

(Selected from the "Sermon on the Mount.")

⁎⁎* The learner should assign each noun to its proper class.

MASCULINE.

γραμματεύς, -έως, scribe
χιτών, -ῶνος, vest, inner garment

ὀδούς, ὀδόντος, tooth
ὄφις, ὀφέως, snake

FEMININE.

δύναμις, -εως, power
θρίξ, τριχός, hair

κρίσις, -εως, judgment
χείρ, χειρός, hand, *dat. plur* χερσί

Neuter.

ἔθνος, -ους, nation | ὄρος, -ους, mountain
θέλημα, -ατος, will | πῦρ, πυρός, fire
ὄνομα, -ατος, name | φῶς, φωτός, light

30. A careful inspection of the paradigms of § 29 yields the following **rules of the third declension.**

First Rule.—The most usual termination of the nominative singular is **s** added to the stem in accordance with the orthographic law, § 4, *c.*
Thus—(1) A *labial* stem makes the nominative in **ψ**.

Examples.

Ἄραψ, *Arabian,*   from   αραβ-,   gen. ἄραβος
Αἰθίοψ, *Ethiopian,*   ,,   αιθιοπ-,   gen. αἰθίοπος

(2) A *guttural* stem makes the nominative in **ξ**.

Examples.

φλόξ, *flame,*   from   φλογ-,   gen. φλογός
κῆρυξ, *herald,*   ,,   κηρυκ-,   gen. κήρυκος
νύξ, *night,*   ,,   νυκτ-,   gen. νυκτός
θρίξ, *hair,*   ,,   θριχ-,   gen. τριχός (§ 4, *d*, 7)

(3) A *dental* stem drops the stem-termination before **s**.

Examples.

παῖς, *child,*   from   παιδ-,   gen. παιδός
ὄρνις, *bird,*   ,,   ὀρνιθ-,   gen. ὄρνιθος
χάρις, *favour,*   ,,   χαριτ-,   gen. χάριτος
ὀδούς, *tooth,*   ,,   ὀδοντ-,   gen. ὀδόντος (§ 4, *d*, 5)

(4) *Vowel* stems add **s** simply.

Examples.

πόλις, *city,*   from   πολι-,   gen. πόλεως, for πόλιος
ἰχθύς, *fish,*   ,,   ἰχθυ-,   gen. ἰχθύος

Second Rule.—**Stems ending in ν and ντ** (*generally*), **in ρ** (*almost always*), **and in s** (*invariably*, except in neuters), form the nominative by **lengthening the vowel** preceding the termination.

§ 30.] VARIETIES IN THE THIRD DECLENSION. 31

EXAMPLES.

ποιμήν, *shepherd*,   from   ποιμεν-,   gen. ποιμένος
λέων, *lion*,   „   λεοντ-,   gen. λέοντος
ῥήτωρ, *orator*,   „   ῥητορ-,   gen. ῥήτορος
αἰδώς, *modesty*,   „   αἰδος-,   (gen. αἰδόσος)

The genitive of this last word is contracted by dropping the s between two short vowels, and combining them; αἰδόος, αἰδοῦς. (See § 3, *f*, Table and Note.)

Certain nouns with the stem-ending ρ preceded by ε are *syncopated*, *i.e.* omit this vowel in some of their cases. One, ἀνήρ, *man*, ανερ-, in omitting ε, inserts the letter δ between ν and ρ. (See § 5, 5.) The dative plural of these nouns also adds α after ρ. (See the Paradigms.)

Third Rule.—**Stems in ευ, αυ, ου,** while adding **s** in the nominative singular, according to the first rule, **drop the υ** in the genitive singular and other cases, thus forming an *apparent* exception to the rule that the genitive gives the stem by taking away the termination **ος**. **The irregularity is only apparent,** as the υ of the stem is in reality the old consonant *v* (written in Greek ϝ, and called, from its shape, *digamma*), which originally belonged to the genitive, like the other consonant stem-endings. Thus, βοῦς, *ox*, βοϝ-, gen. βοϝος, now written βοός. Some of the cases of these nouns are also contracted, as the paradigm will show. Stems in ευ take a special form of the genitive singular, called the "Attic Genitive," ending in εως.

Fourth Rule.—**Neuter stems in ες** change this termination in the nominative into **-ος**; in other cases **they drop the s of the stem**, and suffer contraction by § 3, *f*.

EXAMPLE.—ὄρος, *mountain*, ὀρες-, gen. (ὄρεσος, ὄρεος) ὄρους, nominative and accusative plural (ὄρεσα, ὄρεα) ὄρη. (See Paradigm.)

Fifth Rule.—**Other neuter nouns,** together with those masculines and feminines which have liquid stems preceded by a long vowel, **retain the stem in the nominative unchanged,** save by the general orthographic law. Thus, αἰών, ῥῆμα, already given. The latter becomes ῥῆμα from ῥηματ-, according to § 4, *d*, 8.

Accentuation.—Monosyllabic neuters are oxytone in all their dissyllabic forms, except the genitive plural, which is perispomenon. Masculine and feminine monosyllables accent the penultimate in the accusative singular and nominative and accusative plural; in other cases follow the rule of neuters.

Irregular Nouns of the Third Declension.

31. These are irregular chiefly in the *nominative*. Thus, γυνή, *woman*, takes gen. γυναικός, and forms all its cases from the stem γυναικ- the vocative being γύναι by § 4, *d*, 8.

γόνυ, *knee*, is declined regularly as from the stem γονατ- (neuter), gen. γόνατος, nom. plur. γόνατα, etc.

κύων, *dog* (masculine, also feminine in singular), is declined as from κυν-, gen. κυνός, etc.; but voc. sing. κύον, dat. plur. κυσί(ν).

μάρτυς, *witness* (masculine), is from the stem μαρτυρ-, which it follows throughout, except in dat. plur. μάρτυσι(ν).

ὕδωρ, *water*, is declined regularly as from the neuter stem ὑδατ-, gen. ὕδατος, nom. plur. ὕδατα, etc.

Some neuter stems in -ατ- form the nominative by changing the τ into s, instead of dropping it. Thus, κερατ-, *horn*, nom. sing. κέρας, nom. plur. κέρατα, gen. κεράτων; κρεατ, *flesh*, nom. sing. κρέας, nom. plur. κρέα, by syncope from κρέατα; τερατ-, *prodigy*, nom. sing. τέρας, nom. plur. τέρατα, dat. τέρασι(ν).

The accusative plural form, ἄρνας, *lambs*, is once found (Luke x. 3), and may be referred to the stem ἀρεν-, nom. sing. ἄρην, the ε dropped in inflection by syncope.

In one passage, the name of the Greek deity *Zeus* is found (nom. Ζεύς) gen. Διός, acc. Δία (Acts xiv. 12, 13).

Nouns of Variable Declension in the New Testament.

32. *a.* A few substantives in -ος are found with forms both of the *second* declension and of the *third* (neuter stem -ες like γένος). Thus, πλοῦτος, *wealth*, is properly masculine of the second, but is found in good MSS. neuter of the third. νοῦς, *mind* (see § 24), second declension, occasionally takes a genitive and dative as of the third declension; νοός, νοΐ (Rom. vii. 25; 1 Cor. i. 10, xiv. 15). So, πλοός (Acts xxvii. 9) for πλοῦ.

b. The word σάββατον, *sabbath*, is a regular noun, second declension, neuter, except in the dative plural, which in the New Testament is σάββασι (as if from σαββατ-, σάββα). But the Septuagint has also σαββάτοις (1 Chron. xxiii. 31).

§ 32.] NOUNS OF VARIABLE DECLENSION.

c. In *proper names* much irregularity exists. Μωσῆς (or Μωυσῆς), *Moses*, is thus declined:—

    G. Μωσέως
    D. Μωσεῖ, or Μωσῇ
    A. Μωσέα, or Μωσῆν
    V. Μωσῆ (LXX.)

The name of *Jerusalem* is found in a threefold form: (1) Ἱερουσαλήμ, *indeclinable*, a transcript of the Hebrew word; (2) Ἱεροσόλυμα, neuter plural, second declension; (3) Ἱεροσόλυμα, feminine singular (Matt. ii. 3, only). Many proper names analogous in form to nominatives of the different declensions are indeclinable. So, Κανᾶ, Βηθσαιδά, Βηθφαγή, Γολγοθᾶ, Ῥαμᾶ, Ἀαρών, Συμεών, Κεδρών, Ἱεριχῶ. To this class may be referred the indeclinable neuters, πάσχα, *passover;* σίκερα, *strong drink* (Luke i. 15). The last two are, in fact, but adaptations of Hebrew words. ἰῶτα, *jot* (Matt. v. 18), ἄλφα and ὦ μέγα (Rev. i. 8), the names of Greek letters, are also treated as neuter nouns without inflection.

Exercise 6.—Promiscuous List of Nouns, for Practice.

_{*} The genitive case is given, to show the declension and the stem. Learners should, wherever possible, infer the gender from the form.

ἀετός, οῦ, m. *eagle*
αἷμα, ατος, *blood*
ἄνθος, ους, *flower*
ἀρνίον, ου, *lamb*
βουλή, ῆς, *counsel*
γονεύς, έος, *parent*
δάκρυ, υος, *tear*
δένδρον, ου, *tree*
διδάσκαλος, ου, *teacher*
ἐλπίς, ίδος, f. *hope*
ἑορτή, ῆς, *festival*
Ἡρώδης, ου, *Herod*

θυγάτηρ, τρός, *daughter*
κακία, ας, *vice*
κιθάρα, ας, *harp*
μάστιξ, ιγος, f. *scourge*
μέρος, ους, *part*
ὄφις, εως, m. *serpent*
πολίτης, ου, *citizen*
πόνος, ου, m. *labour*
πρᾶγμα, ατος, *thing*
σάλπιγξ, ιγγος, *trumpet*
στόμα, ατος, *mouth*
ὥρα, ας, *hour*

Chapter III. ADJECTIVES.

33. Adjectives in Greek **follow precisely the inflection of substantives.** Every declension, almost every form, reappears, but in different combinations.

In respect of form, adjectives are divided into three classes:—
  1. Those which combine the first and second declensions.
  2. Those which combine the first and third.
  3. Those which follow exclusively the type of the third.

In the first two, the form of the first declension is feminine.

34. First Form. PARADIGMS. (Stems, o- m. a- f. o- n.)

ἀγαθο-, -α-, *good.*

	SINGULAR.			PLURAL.	
M.	F.	N.	M.	F.	N.
N. ἀγαθός	ἀγαθή	ἀγαθόν	ἀγαθοί	ἀγαθαί	ἀγαθά
G. ἀγαθοῦ	ἀγαθῆς	ἀγαθοῦ	ἀγαθῶν	ἀγαθῶν	ἀγαθῶν
D. ἀγαθῷ	ἀγαθῇ	ἀγαθῷ	ἀγαθοῖς	ἀγαθαῖς	ἀγαθοῖς
A. ἀγαθόν	ἀγαθήν	ἀγαθόν	ἀγαθούς	ἀγαθάς	ἀγαθά
V. ἀγαθέ	ἀγαθή	ἀγαθόν	ἀγαθοί	ἀγαθαί	ἀγαθά

All participles in **-μενος** are declined like ἀγαθός.

δικαιο-, -α-, *just.*

N. δίκαιος	δικαία	δίκαιον	δίκαιοι	δίκαιαι	δίκαια
G. δικαίου	δικαίας	δικαίου	δικαίων	δικαίων	δικαίων
D. δικαίῳ	δικαίᾳ	δικαίῳ	δικαίοις	δικαίαις	δικαίοις
A. δίκαιον	δικαίαν	δίκαιον	δικαίους	δικαίας	δίκαια
V. δίκαιε	δικαία	δίκαιον	δίκαιοι	δίκαιαι	δίκαια

μικρο-, -α-, *little.*

N. μικρός	μικρά	μικρόν	μικροί	μικραί	μικρά
G. μικροῦ	μικρᾶς	μικροῦ	μικρῶν	μικρῶν	μικρῶν
D. μικρῷ	μικρᾷ	μικρῷ	μικροῖς	μικραῖς	μικροῖς
A. μικρόν	μικράν	μικρόν	μικρούς	μικράς	μικρά
V. μικρέ	μικρά	μικρόν	μικροί	μικραί	μικρά

ADJECTIVES—FIRST FORM.

REMARKS.

a. The feminine singular of these adjectives, as will be seen in the above paradigms, is formed in strict analogy with the usage of the first declension. The rule is, that where the masculine has -os preceded by a vowel or ρ, the feminine ends in ᾱ, which vowel is preserved through all the cases of the singular. os preceded by a consonant becomes η, which also runs through the singular.

b. Several adjectives belonging to this first form employ the masculine terminations for the feminine also, conforming thus *throughout* to the second declension. This is especially the case with polysyllables and compound words. But as there is no definite rule to distinguish these **adjectives of two terminations** from those of three, it will be necessary in doubtful cases to consult the Vocabulary or Lexicon.

c. Accentuation.—The rules in § 18 are strictly observed. Note, however, that the feminine plural is not, like that of the first declension, necessarily perispomenon, but, like the other cases, follows the stem of the word. Thus, from δίκαιος, f. pl. gen. δικαίων (the accent being thrown one syllable forward by the terminal long syllable—§ 6, *c*) ; but μικρός makes μικρῶν.

CONTRACTED ADJECTIVES OF THE FIRST FORM.

35. Adjectives in εο- and οο- belong to this class. The explanations given with contracted substantives (§ 24), and the scheme in § 3 *f*, will sufficiently show the reason of each contraction.

χρυσεο-, -α-, *golden.* By contraction, χρυσοῦς (εος), -ῆ (έη), -οῦν (εον).

	SINGULAR.			PLURAL.		
	M.	F.	N.	M.	F.	N.
N.	χρυσοῦς	χρυσῆ	χρυσοῦν	χρυσοῖ	χρυσαῖ	χρυσᾶ
G.	χρυσοῦ	χρυσῆς	χρυσοῦ	χρυσῶν	χρυσῶν	χρυσῶν
D.	χρυσῷ	χρυσῇ	χρυσῷ	χρυσοῖς	χρυσαῖς	χρυσοῖς
A.	χρυσοῦν	χρυσῆν	χρυσοῦν	χρυσοῦς	χρυσᾶς	χρυσᾶ
V.	χρύσεε	χρυσῆ	χρυσοῦν	χρυσοῖ	χρυσαῖ	χρυσᾶ

ADJECTIVES—SECOND FORM. [§ 35, a.

REMARKS.

a. ἀργύρεος, *silver* (adjective), occurs in N.T. in two forms : acc. plur. ἀργυροῦς, neut. nom. and acc. plur. ἀργυρᾶ.

b. These adjectives occur very infrequently. It will be observed that the feminine of χρύσεος is formed irregularly ; as -ος preceded by a vowel, according to rule, requires -α. The adjective στερεός, εά, εόν, *firm*, is declined without contraction.

c. Accentuation.—The final syllable in these adjectives, when contracted, is circumflexed throughout. Thus we have not only ἁπλοῦς from ἁπλόος, *simple* (regular, see § 6, *c*), but χρυσοῦς from χρύσεος, and ἀργυροῦς from ἀργύρεος, anomalous.

36. Second Form. GENERAL REMARKS.

Masculine.—The nominative is formed from the stem, according to the methods of the third declension. Thus, ὀξυ- gives nom. masc. ὀξύς, *sharp* (§ 29, *first rule*, 4) ; παντ- becomes πᾶς, *all* (§§ 29, *first rule*, 3 ; 4, *d*, 5) ; and ἑκοντ- gives ἑκών, *willing* (§§ 29, *second rule ;* 4, *d*, 8).

Feminine.—The nominative always ends in ἄ ; the other cases in the singular follow the model of the first declension (§ 18, *a*). The stem-ending υ becomes -εια, as ὀξύς, ὀξεῖα ; ντ- becomes -σα, as πᾶς, πᾶσα, and ἑκών, ἑκοῦσα. But stems in -ν- insert an ι before that consonant, as μέλας, *black*, μελαν-, f. μέλαινα ; and οτ- (originally Ϝοτ) becomes -υια. Thus, λελυκώς (participle), *having loosened*, λελυκοτ-, f. λελυκυῖα.

Neuter.—The neuter nominative contains the simple stem, altered only by the general euphonic rules ; as, ὀξύ, πᾶν, ἑκόν, μέλαν, λελυκός.

37. PARADIGMS OF THE SECOND FORM.

ὀξυ-, -εια-, *sharp.*

| | SINGULAR. | | | PLURAL. | |
	M.	F.	N.	M.	F.	N.
N.	ὀξύς	ὀξεῖα	ὀξύ	ὀξεῖς	ὀξεῖαι	ὀξέα
G.	ὀξέος	ὀξείας	ὀξέος	ὀξέων	ὀξειῶν	ὀξέων
D.	ὀξεῖ	ὀξείᾳ	ὀξεῖ	ὀξέσι(ν)	ὀξείαις	ὀξέσι(ν)
A.	ὀξύν	ὀξεῖαν	ὀξύ	ὀξεῖς	ὀξείας	ὀξέα
V.	ὀξύ	ὀξεῖα	ὀξύ	ὀξεῖς	ὀξεῖαι	ὀξέα

§ 38.] ADJECTIVES—SECOND FORM. 37

Note.—The stem-ending **υ** becomes **ε** in the genitive and dative singular, and throughout the plural : έϊ, dative singular, being contracted into εῖ; and έες, έας, in the plural, into εῖς. But έος, genitive singular, and έα in the neuter plural, are uncontracted. A very few substantives also change **υ** into **ε**; the only instance in the New Testament being πηχῶν (John xxi. 8 ; Rev. xxi. 17) for πηχέων, from πῆχυς, *cubit*.

παντ-, -ασα-, *all, every.*

	SINGULAR.			PLURAL.	
	M.	F.	N.	M.	F.	N.
N.	πᾶς	πᾶσα	πᾶν	πάντες	πᾶσαι	πάντα
G.	παντός	πάσης	παντός	πάντων	πασῶν	πάντων
D.	παντί	πάσῃ	παντί	πᾶσι(ν)	πάσαις	πᾶσι(ν)
A.	πάντα	πᾶσαν	πᾶν	πάντας	πάσας	πάντα
V.	πᾶς	πᾶσα	πᾶν	πάντες	πᾶσαι	πάντα

Participles in -ας are similarly declined (stem, αντ-) as λύσας, *having loosed*. The participial stem-ending **εντ-** makes, nom. -είς, -εῖσα, -έν, gen. έντος, είσης, έντος, etc. ; as βουλευθείς, *having been counselled*.

ἑκοντ-, -ουσα-, *willing.*

	SINGULAR.			PLURAL.	
	M.	F.	N.	M.	F.	N.
N.	ἑκών	ἑκοῦσα	ἑκόν	ἑκόντες	ἑκοῦσαι	ἑκόντα
G.	ἑκόντος	ἑκούσης	ἑκόντος	ἑκόντων	ἑκουσῶν	ἑκόντων
D.	ἑκόντι	ἑκούσῃ	ἑκόντι	ἑκοῦσι(ν)	ἑκούσαις	ἑκοῦσι(ν)
A.	ἑκόντα	ἑκοῦσαν	ἑκόν	ἑκόντας	ἑκούσας	ἑκόντα
V.	ἑκών	ἑκοῦσα	ἑκόν	ἑκόντες	ἑκοῦσαι	ἑκόντα

Participles in -ων, -ουσα, -ον, are declined on this model.

38. The declension of adjectives like μέλας, μέλαινα, μέλαν, *black*, gen. μέλανος, μελαίνης, μέλανος, dat. plur. m. and n. μέλασι(ν), and of participles like λελυκώς, λελυκυῖα, λελυκός, *having loosened*, gen. λελυκότος, λελυκυίας, λελυκότος, will not now present any difficulty. One participle, ἑστηκώς, *having stood*, from the verb ἵστημι, takes the alternative form, ἑστώς, the result of syncope and contraction, and is thus declined:—

IRREGULAR ADJECTIVES—SECOND FORM. [§ 38.

	SINGULAR.			PLURAL.		
	M.	F.	N.	M.	F.	N.
N.	ἑστώς	ἑστῶσα	ἑστός	ἑστῶτες	ἑστῶσαι	ἑστῶτα
G.	ἑστῶτος	ἑστώσης	ἑστῶτος	ἑστώτων	ἑστωσῶν	ἑστώτων
D.	ἑστῶτι	ἑστώσῃ	ἑστῶτι	ἑστῶσι(ν)	ἑστώσαις	ἑστῶσι(ν)
A.	ἑστῶτα	ἑστῶσαν	ἑστός	ἑστῶτας	ἑστώσας	ἑστῶτα

The contraction is from ἑσταώς. (See § 3, ƒ.)

Accentuation.—Oxytones circumflex the feminine. Adjectives of the second class otherwise follow the ordinary rules. It will be observed that in the genitive and dative singular, masculine and neuter, πᾶς takes oxytone forms, otherwise accenting the stem-syllable throughout.

39. Two adjectives of common occurrence are irregular in the singular masculine and neuter, owing to a combination of forms. Their declension is as follows :—

1. μεγα- (μεγαλο-, μεγαλα-), *great*.

Sing.	M.	F.	N.
N.	μέγας	μεγάλη	μέγα
G.	μεγάλου	μεγάλης	μεγάλου
D.	μεγάλῳ	μεγάλῃ	μεγάλῳ
A.	μέγαν	μεγάλην	μέγα

Plural regular, as if from μεγάλος.

2. πολυ- (πολλο-, πολλα-), *many*.

Sing.	M.	F.	N.
N.	πολύς	πολλή	πολύ
G.	πολλοῦ	πολλῆς	πολλοῦ
D.	πολλῷ	πολλῇ	πολλῷ
A.	πολύν	πολλήν	πολύ

Plural regular, as if from πολλός.

Third Form. General Remarks.

40. Adjectives of this class being **altogether of the third declension**, have no special form for the feminine, and are, therefore, of **two terminations** or (sometimes) of only one. (Compare τις, § 13.)

For the most part, the declension of these adjectives is without peculiarity. It should be noted that an adjective in -ων (nominative singular) may be from one or other of the stem-endings οντ and ον. If from the latter, it belongs to the third class. Thus, ἑκών, from ἑκοντ-, has three terminations; but σώφρων, from σωφρον-, only two.

By far the largest and most important class of adjectives in this division are those in -ης, neut. -ες, where the stem-ending ες is not changed into ος in the nominative and accusative singular, as in the corresponding class of substantives (§ 29, iv.), but where similar contractions take place in the other cases.

41.   Paradigms of the Third Form.

ἀληθες-, *true.*

SINGULAR.

	M. and F.	N.
N.	ἀληθής	ἀληθές
G.	(ἀληθέος) ἀληθοῦς	ἀληθοῦς
D.	(ἀληθέϊ) ἀληθεῖ	ἀληθεῖ
A.	(ἀληθέα) ἀληθῆ	ἀληθές
V.	ἀληθές	ἀληθές

PLURAL.

	M. and F.	N.
N.	(ἀληθέες) ἀληθεῖς	(ἀληθέα) ἀληθῆ
G.	(ἀληθέων) ἀληθῶν	ἀληθῶν
D.	ἀληθέσι(ν)	ἀληθέσι(ν)
A.	(ἀληθέας) ἀληθεῖς	(ἀληθέα) ἀληθῆ
V.	(ἀληθέες) ἀληθεῖς	(ἀληθέα) ἀληθῆ

σωφρον-, *sober-minded.*

SINGULAR.		PLURAL.	
M. and F.	N.	M. and F.	N.
N. σώφρων	σῶφρον	σώφρονες	σώφρονα
G. σώφρονος	σώφρονος	σωφρόνων	σωφρόνων
D. σώφρονι	σώφρονι	σώφροσι	σώφροσι
A. σώφρονα	σῶφρον	σώφρονας	σώφρονα
V. σῶφρον	σῶφρον	σώφρονες	σώφρονα

To this class belong **comparatives in ων**. (See § 44.)

COMPARISON OF ADJECTIVES.

42 There are two regular methods of forming the Greek comparative and superlative.

The first and most usual is by adding to the stem of the positive the further stem-ending **τερο-** for the comparative, **τατο-** for the superlative. These forms are then **declined exactly like the first form of adjectives** (§ 34).

Thus, from πιστός, *faithful*, stem **πιστο-**, we have—

Comparative, nom. sing. πιστότερος, πιστοτέρα, πιστότερον.
Superlative, nom. sing. πιστότατος, πιστοτάτη, πιστότατον.

From ἀληθής, *true*, stem **ἀληθες-**

Comparative, ἀληθέστερος, ἀληθεστέρα, ἀληθέστερον.
Superlative, ἀληθέστατος, ἀληθεστάτη, ἀληθέστατον.

Adjectives of the first class which have a short syllable before the stem-ending **ο-** *change this vowel into* **ω.**

Thus, σοφός, *wise*, makes—

Comparative, σοφώτερος, σοφωτέρα, σοφώτερον.
Superlative, σοφώτατος, σοφωτάτη, σοφώτατον.

From νέος, *new*, we have, in like manner—

Comparative, νεώτερος, νεωτέρα, νεώτερον.
Superlative, νεώτατος, νεωτάτη, νεώτατον.

Accentuation.—Comparatives and superlatives of this form are always proparoxytone, except when the final syllable is long; then paroxytone. In other words, the accent is thrown back as far as possible.

§ 44.] ADJECTIVES—COMPARISON. 41

43. The second form of comparison is by adding, generally to an *abbreviated* form of the positive stem, -ῑων (stem-ending ιον-for the comparative, and -ιστος (stem-ending ιστο-) for the superlative.

EXAMPLES.

ταχύς,	swift,	ταχίων,[1]	τάχιστος
αἰσχρός,	disgraceful,	αἰσχίων,	αἴσχιστος
καλός,	fair	καλλίων	κάλλιστος
μέγας,	great,	μείζων (for μεγίων),	μέγιστος

Accentuation.—In these, as in other comparative and superlative forms, the accent is thrown back as far as possible.

PARADIGM OF COMPARATIVES IN -ιων OR -ων.

44. These follow the third form of adjectives (see σώφρων, § 41), but are *sometimes* contracted by the omission of the **ν** before **α** or **ε**, and the combination of this vowel with the **ο** of the stem. This contraction is, however, infrequent in the New Testament.

μείζων, μεῖζον, *greater.*

SINGULAR.

	M. and F.	N.
N.	μείζων	μεῖζον
G.	μείζονος	μείζονος
D.	μείζονι	μείζονι
A.	μείζονα or μείζω	μεῖζον
V.	μεῖζον	μεῖζον

PLURAL.

	M. and F.	N.
N.	μείζονες or μείζους	μείζονα or μείζω
G.	μειζόνων	μειζόνων
D.	μείζοσι(ν)	μείζοσι(ν)
A.	μείζονας or μείζους	μείζονα or μείζω
V.	μείζονες or μείζους	μείζονα or μείζω

---

[1] See John xx. 4 (τάχειον). In classic Greek, θάττων is the form generally used.

45. To this form of comparison belong several **irregular comparatives and superlatives**, of which the following list will suffice :—

ἀγαθός, *good*,	comp.	βελτίων,	sup.	βέλτιστος
	,,	κρείσσων,	,,	κράτιστος
κακός, *bad*,	,,	κακίων,	,,	κάκιστος
	,,	χείρων,	,,	χείριστος
μικρός, *little*	,,	μικρότερος (regular)		
	,,	ἐλάσσων,	,,	ἐλάχιστος
	,,	ἥσσων,	,,	ἥκιστος
πολύς, *many*,	,,	πλείων or πλέων	,,	πλεῖστος

Some adjectives, it will be seen from the above, have an **alternative comparison**, having recourse to different roots for the purpose. The respective forms are now interchangeable, or nearly so. For shades of difference between them, see Vocabulary and the chapter on Synonyms.

46. The following comparatives and superlatives have no answering positives :—

(From ἄνω, adv. *up*) ἀνώτερος, *upper;* ἀνώτατος, *topmost*
(From κάτω, adv. *down*) κατώτερος, *lower;* κατώτατος, *lowest*
(From ἔσω, adv. *within*) ἐσώτερος, *inner;* ἐσώτατος, *inmost*
(From πρό, prep. *before*) πρότερος, *former;* πρῶτος, *first*

Many of these forms are but seldom used.

Emphasis in Comparison.

47. (*a*) An emphatic comparative is made by the adverb μᾶλλον, *more.* So Mark ix. 42, καλόν ἐστιν αὐτῷ μᾶλλον, " it is far better for him." The same adverb is sometimes prefixed to a comparative, as in Mark vii. 36, μᾶλλον περισσότερον, " much (lit. *more*) the more abundantly." In Phil. i. 23, yet another adverb of intensity is affixed to μᾶλλον with the comparative, πολλῷ μᾶλλον κρεῖσσον (lit. " by much the more better ").

§ 47.] ADJECTIVES—COMPARISON—EXERCISE.

Compare "most unkindest cut of all" in Shakspeare (Julius Cæsar, iii. 2). So Psa. ix. 2 (Prayer Book version), "O Thou Most Highest."

(*b*) Another form of securing emphasis is by affixing a comparative termination to a comparative or superlative form. Thus, from μείζων, *greater* (iii. John, 4), μειζοτέραν οὐκ ἔχω χαράν, "I have no *greater* (*more greater*) joy ;" and from ἐλάχιστος, *least* (Eph. iii. 8), τῷ ἐλαχιστοτέρῳ πάντων τῶν ἁγίων, well rendered in E. V., "*less than the least* of all saints."

Exercise 7.—Additional Adjectives, for Practice.

(Selected from the "Sermon on the Mount.")

First Form.

ἅγιος, holy
ἄδικος, unjust
ἀρχαῖος, ancient
καθαρός, pure
πονηρός, wicked

πτωχός, poor, pauper
στενός, narrow
τέλειος, full-grown, perfect
φανερός, evident
φρόνιμος, prudent

Second Form.

ἅπας, ἅπασα, ἅπαν, all, altogether
μέλας, μέλαινα, μέλαν, black
πλατύς, πλατεῖα, πλατύ, broad

Third Form.

ἅρπαξ, -αγος, rapacious | ἐλεήμων, -ονος, merciful

In practising with these forms, they should be combined with the nouns of the previous Exercises. The adjectives should also be put into the different forms of the comparative and superlative. Almost countless combinations will thus result, by which the learner, either with or without the aid of an instructor, may become versed in these parts of speech.

NUMERALS.

The Cardinal Numbers.

48. (*a*) For the signs of the respective numbers, the letters of the Alphabet are used, according to the list in § 1. When a letter is employed numerically, an acute accent is appended. Thus, α', 1; β', 2, and so on. To express thousands, an accent is placed beneath: ͵α, 1,000; ͵β, 2,000; ͵ι, 10,000, etc.

(*b*) It will be seen that the places of some numbers are vacant, owing to letters having dropped, in very ancient times, out of the Greek Alphabet: the Digamma (Ϝ) having come between ε and ζ; while the space between π and ρ was occupied by Koppa (Ϙ), a guttural with a hard *k*-sound, the original of the Latin and English letter *q*. As the alphabet ends with ω', 800, another discarded letter, Sampi (Ϡ) was used for 900.[1] Three signs have therefore been added, as follows: ϛ' (the sign of a double consonant, *st*, used instead of Ϝ), 6; Ϙ', 90; Ϡ', 900.

(*c*) Combinations of tens and units, or of hundreds, tens, and units, are expressed, not as in our Arabic numeration, by the collocation of unit-signs, but by addition. Thus, ια', 11; ιβ', 12; κγ', 23; ρδ', 104; ͵αωξη', 1868; χξϛ' (Rev. xiii. 18), 666. In these expressions, the numeral accent is only written once, excepting with thousands.

49. The cardinal numbers, εἷς, *one;* δύο, *two;* τρεῖς, *three;* τέσσαρες, *four,* **are declined as follows.** The rest are indeclinable up to *two hundred,* which, with the other hundreds, follows the plural of the first form of adjectives in -οι, -αι, -α.

εἷς, μία, ἕν (stems ἑν-, μια-), *one.*

	M.	F.	N.		M.	F.	N.
N.	εἷς	μία	ἕν	D.	ἑνί	μιᾷ	ἑνί
G.	ἑνός	μιᾶς	ἑνός	A.	ἕνα	μίαν	ἕν

---

[1] Hebrew students will recollect that these are the places of *Vav, Qoph,* and *Shin* respectively.

§ 51.] NUMERALS. 45

Like εἷς are declined its compounds, οὐδείς, *no one* (absolutely), and μηδείς, *no one* (hypothetically). The accentuation of all three is irregular, as seen above.

δύο, *two.*

N. G.[1] and A. δύο | D. δυσί(ν)

τρεῖς, τρία, *three.*

	M. and F.	N.		M. and F.	N.
N.	τρεῖς	τρία	D.	τρισί(ν)	τρισί(ν)
G.	τριῶν	τριῶν	A.	τρεῖς	τρία

τέσσαρες, τέσσαρα, *four.*

	M. and F.	N.		M. and F.	N.
N.	τέσσαρες	τέσσαρα	D.	τέσσαρσι(ν)	τέσσαρσι(ν)
G.	τεσσάρων	τεσσάρων	A.	τέσσαρας	τέσσαρα

THE ORDINAL NUMBERS.

50. For *first*, the superlative form πρῶτος (§ 46) is used. The succeeding ordinals are derived from the stem of their cardinal numbers, and are declined like adjectives of the first form. Cardinal numbers are sometimes used instead of ordinals in reckoning the days of the week, etc. (See SYNTAX.)

51. TABLE OF CARDINALS AND ORDINALS.

	CARDINAL.		ORDINAL.
1,	εἷς, μία, ἕν	πρῶτος,	first
2,	δύο	δεύτερος,	second
3,	τρεῖς, τρία	τρίτος,	third
4,	τέσσαρες, τέσσαρα	τέταρτος,	fourth
5,	πέντε	πέμπτος,	fifth

---

[1] In classic Greek the gen. is δυοῖν or δυεῖν (dual forms). So also the dative, sometimes.

	CARDINAL.	ORDINAL.	
6,	ἕξ	ἕκτος,	sixth
7,	ἑπτά	ἕβδομος,	seventh
8,	ὀκτώ	ὄγδοος,	eighth
9,	ἐννέα	ἔννατος,	ninth
10,	δέκα	δέκατος,	tenth
11,	ἕνδεκα	ἑνδέκατος	etc.
12,	δώδεκα, or δεκαδύο (Acts xix. 7)	δωδέκατος	
13,	τρισκαίδεκα	τρισκαιδέκατος	
14,	τεσσαρεσκαίδεκα, or δεκατέσσαρες (Matt. i. 17)	τεσσαρακαιδέκατος	
15,	πεντεκαίδεκα, or δεκαπέντε (John xi. 18)	πεντεκαιδέκατος	
16,	ἑκκαίδεκα	ἑκκαιδέκατος	
17,	ἑπτακαίδεκα	ἑπτακαιδέκατος	
18,	ὀκτωκαίδεκα, or δέκα καὶ ὀκτώ (Luke xiii. 4)	ὀκτωκαιδέκατος	
19,	ἐννεακαίδεκα	ἐννεακαιδέκατος	
20,	εἴκοσι(ν)	εἰκοστός	
21,	εἴκοσι καὶ εἷς, μία, ἕν	εἰκοστὸς καὶ πρῶτος	
22,	εἴκοσι καὶ δύο	εἰκοστὸς καὶ δεύτερος	
30,	τριάκοντα	τριᾱκοστός	
40,	τεσσαράκοντα	τεσσαρᾰκοστός	
50,	πεντήκοντα	πεντηκοστός	
60,	ἑξήκοντα	ἑξηκοστός	
70,	ἑβδομήκοντα	ἑβδομηκοστός	
80,	ὀγδοήκοντα	ὀγδοηκοστός	
90,	ἐνενήκοντα	ἐνενηκοστός	
100,	ἑκατόν	ἑκατοστός	
200,	διᾱκόσιοι	διακοσιοστός	
300,	τριᾱκόσιοι	τριακοσιοστός	
400,	τετρᾱκόσιοι	τεσσαρακοσιοστός	
500,	πεντᾱκόσιοι	πεντακοσιοστός	

§ 52.] NUMERALS.

	CARDINAL.	ORDINAL
600,	ἑξάκοσιοι	ἑξακοσιοστός
700,	ἑπτάκοσιοι	ἑπτακοσιοστός
800,	ὀκτάκοσιοι	ὀκτακοσιοστός
900,	ἐνάκοσιοι	ἐνακοσιοστός
1,000,	χίλιοι	χιλιοστός
2,000,	δισχίλιοι	δισχιλιοστός
3,000,	τρισχίλιοι	τρισχιλιοστός
4,000,	τετρακισχίλιοι	τετρακισχιλιοστός
10,000,	μύριοι	μυριοστός

Remark.—In *compound* numbers, the **largest is placed first**,[1] and the smaller follow in order, **with or without the conjunction καὶ,** *and*. The smaller numbers are in many copies treated as enclitics, and attached to the larger as one word.

EXAMPLES.—Τεσσαράκοντα δύο, "forty-two" (Rev. xi. 2, xiii. 5); ἑκατὸν πεντήκοντα τριῶν, "of a hundred and fifty-three" (John xxi. 11); θρόνοι εἴκοσι τέσσαρες, "twenty-four thrones" (Rev. iv. 4); τεσσαράκοντα καὶ ἓξ ἔτεσιν, "for forty-six years" (John ii. 20); ἐτῶν ὀγδοήκοντα τεσσάρων, "of eighty-four years" (Luke ii. 37); δέκα καὶ ὀκτὼ ἔτη, "eighteen years" (Luke xiii. 16); τὰ ἐνενήκοντα ἐννέα, "the ninety-nine" (Matt. xviii. 12; Luke xv. 4).

DISTRIBUTIVE NUMBERS.

52. The distribution or repetition of a number is variously expressed. In Mark vi. 7, the simple cardinal is repeated : δύο δύο, "two and two ;" Luke x. 1, for the same thing, more classically employs a preposition, ἀνὰ δύο; Mark xiv. 19 combines another preposition with the cardinal : εἷς κατὰ εἷς, "one by one."

Exercise 8.—Numbers.

1. Interpret the following numerical symbols:—θ', ιη', κδ', μϛ', ριδ', τλβ', ΤϘΘ', νοέ, ωια', ζφμγ', βσκβ', ψν', χπζ'.

2. [*Vocabulary.*—ὥρα, -ας, *hour ;* ἡμέρα, -ας, *day ;* σάββατον, -ου (*lit.*

---

[1] The rule in classic Greek is to place the smaller number first with καί, or the larger without καί.

sabbath), *week*, sing. or plur. ; μήν, μηνός, m. *month ;* ἔτος, -ους, n. *year ;* πλείων, comp. adj. *more ;* καὶ, *and ;* ἤ, *or ;* ἐν (prep., proclitic), *in*, governing the dative.]

Translate the following :—

1. ἐν ἔτει πεντεκαιδεκάτῳ.
2. ἐν τῷ μηνὶ τῷ ἕκτῳ.
3. ἡ ὥρα ἡ δεκάτη.
4. ἐν τῷ ἑνὶ καὶ ἑξακοσιοστῷ ἔτει, ἐν τῷ δευτέρῳ μηνί.
5. ἡ μία (ἡμέρα) τῶν σαββάτων. (See John xx. 1, etc.)
6. ἡ πρώτη σαββάτου. (See Mark xvi. 9.)
7. τῇ τρίτῃ ἡμέρᾳ. Supply *on*, to express the force of the dative.
8. ἡμέραι πλείους ὀκτὼ ἢ δέκα. Supply *than*, after the comparative.
9. διακόσιοι ἑβδομήκοντα ἕξ.
10. ἔτη ὀγδοήκοντα τέσσαρα.

3. Render the following into Greek :—

1. Thirty years.
2. Eleven months.
3. In the fourth month, on the sixth day. (See 7, above.)
4. Twelve hours in the day.
5. On the first day of the week.[1]

---

[1] In what two ways might *first* and *week* respectively be expressed ? (See 5, 6, above.)

Chapter IV. PRONOUNS.

Personal Pronouns.

53. These are divided into (1) the simple substantive-pronoun (2) the reflexive, and (3) the adjective-personal or possessive.

The Substantive Pronouns of the first Two Persons.

First Person—		Second Person—	
SINGULAR.	PLURAL.	SINGULAR.	PLURAL.
N. ἐγώ, I	ἡμεῖς, we	σύ, thou	ὑμεῖς, you
G. ἐμοῦ or μου	ἡμῶν	σοῦ or σου	ὑμῶν
D. ἐμοί or μοι	ἡμῖν	σοί or σοι	ὑμῖν
A. ἐμέ or με	ἡμᾶς	σέ or σε	ὑμᾶς

Accentuation.—In the singular, genitive, dative, and accusative, the unemphatic pronoun is *enclitic*. (See § 6.)

54. For the **third personal pronoun**, *he, she, it*, the New Testament employs the three genders of the adjective-pronoun αὐτός, *self* (αὐτο-, -α-).

SINGULAR.			PLURAL.		
M.	F.	N.	M.	F.	N.
N. αὐτός	αὐτή	αὐτό	αὐτοί	αὐταί	αὐτά
G. αὐτοῦ	αὐτῆς	αὐτοῦ	αὐτῶν	αὐτῶν	αὐτῶν
D. αὐτῷ	αὐτῇ	αὐτῷ	αὐτοῖς	αὐταῖς	αὐτοῖς
A. αὐτόν	αὐτήν	αὐτό	αὐτούς	αὐτάς	αὐτά

The nominative of this pronoun, when used in the personal sense, is always emphatic.

Reflexive Pronouns.

55. These are formed by the combination of the personal pronouns with the oblique cases of αὐτός. In the singular, the two are written as one word.

PRONOUNS—REFLEXIVE AND POSSESSIVE. [§ 55.

SINGULAR.

G. ἐμαυτοῦ, -ῆς, *of myself*   σεαυτοῦ, -ῆς, *of thyself*
D. ἐμαυτῷ, -ῇ, *to myself*   σεαυτῷ, -ῇ, *to thyself*
A. ἐμαυτόν, -ήν, *myself* (obj.)   σεαυτόν, -ήν, *thyself* (obj.)

The plurals of these forms are written separately. Thus, ἡμῶν αὐτῶν, *of ourselves;* ὑμῖν αὐτοῖς, *to yourselves,* etc.

Third person (from the old stem, ἑ-, *him*), *of himself, herself, itself,* etc.—

| | SINGULAR. | | | PLURAL. | |
	M.	F.	N.	M.	F.	N.
G.	ἑαυτοῦ	ἑαυτῆς	ἑαυτοῦ	ἑαυτῶν	ἑαυτῶν	ἑαυτῶν
D.	ἑαυτῷ	ἑαυτῇ	ἑαυτῷ	ἑαυτοῖς	ἑαυταῖς	ἑαυτοῖς
A.	ἑαυτόν	ἑαυτήν	ἑαυτό	ἑαυτούς	ἑαυτάς	ἑαυτά

This reflexive pronoun is sometimes written without the ἑ, as αὐτοῦ, αὐτόν, etc., **and is only distinguished from the cases of αὐτός by the aspirate.**

Where there is no risk of ambiguity, this reflexive pronoun may be used for the first and second persons likewise. Thus, ἐν ἑαυτοῖς, "in ourselves" (Rom. viii. 23); τὴν ἑαυτῶν σωτηρίαν, "your own salvation" (Phil. ii. 12).

POSSESSIVE, OR ADJECTIVE-PERSONAL PRONOUNS.

56. (*a*) These are declined precisely like adjectives of the first form, and are as follows:—

First person,	ἐμός,	ἐμή,	ἐμόν,	*my*
"	ἡμέτερος,	ἡμετέρα,	ἡμέτερον,	*our*
Second person,	σός,	σή,	σόν,	*thy*
"	ὑμέτερος,	ὑμετέρα	ὑμέτερον,	*your*

(*b*) There is **no possessive pronoun** in the New Testament **for the third person** singular or plural, the genitive case of αὐτός or of ἑαυτοῦ being used instead. Thus, υἱὸς ἑαυτοῦ, or αὐτοῦ, *his own son, i.e.,* the son of the person who is subject of the sentence; υἱὸς αὐτοῦ, *his son, i.e.,* the son of another person. In Heb. i. 3, τῷ ῥήματι τῆς δυνάμεως αὐτοῦ is "by the word of His power," *i.e.*, that of God the Father; αὑτοῦ, the reading of some editors, would denote "of His own power," *i.e.*, that of Christ Himself. Again, 1 John iii. 3, τὴν ἐλπίδα ἐπ' αὐτῷ, " the hope in[1] Him," *i.e.*, in Christ, not αὑτῷ, which would have referred the hope to the subject of the sentence, " every one."

(*c*) The genitive cases of the other personal pronouns are also used most frequently with the force of the possessive.

DEMONSTRATIVE PRONOUNS.

57. The chief original demonstrative was the *article*, already given (§ 12), and all other demonstrative pronouns are formed upon its model.

They are—(*a*) ὅδε, ἥδε, τόδε, *this* (here)
(*b*) οὗτος, αὕτη, τοῦτο, *this* (near)
(*c*) ἐκεῖνος, ἐκείνη, ἐκεῖνο, *that* (yonder)
(*d*) ὁ αὐτός, ἡ αὐτή, τὸ αὐτό, *the same*

(*a*) ὅδε is simply the article declined with the enclitic δε.

(*b*) οὗτος is thus declined (stem, τουτο-):—

	SINGULAR.				PLURAL.	
	M.	F.	N.	M.	F.	N.
N.	οὗτος	αὕτη	τοῦτο	οὗτοι	αὗται	ταῦτα
G.	τούτου	ταύτης	τούτου	τούτων	τούτων	τούτων
D.	τούτῳ	ταύτῃ	τούτῳ	τούτοις	ταύταις	τούτοις
A.	τοῦτον	ταύτην	τοῦτο	τούτους	ταύτας	ταῦτα

Care must be taken to distinguish the feminine of the nominative singular and plural, αὕτη, αὗται, from the corresponding cases of αὐτός, viz., αὐτή, αὐταί.

(*c*) ἐκεῖνος is declined exactly like the article.

(*d*) ὁ αὐτός in all its cases is only αὐτός (§ 54), with the definite article prefixed. The neuter plural, nominative and accusative, is sometimes written ταὐτά, being distinguished by the coronis over the υ (§ 3, *h*, 3), as well as by the accent, from ταῦτα, *these*, neuter plural of οὗτος.

---

[1] The preposition employed in this passage further marks this meaning. See Revised Version: "this hope *set* on Him."

(e) The demonstrative pronouns of *quality, quantity* (number). and *degree* are declined like (b) preceding :—

Quality,	τοιοῦτος,	τοιαύτη,	τοιοῦτο,	*such*
Quantity,	τοσοῦτος,	τοσαύτη,	τοσοῦτο,	*so great* ⎱
Number,	τοσοῦτοι,	τοσαῦται,	τοσαῦτα,	*so many* ⎰
Degree,	τηλικοῦτος,	τηλικαύτη,	τηλικοῦτο,	*so very great*

The last-mentioned pronoun is found only in 2 Cor. i. 10; Heb. ii. 3, James iii. 4; Rev. xvi. 18.

THE RELATIVE PRONOUN.

58. (a) The relative ὅς, ἥ, ὅ, *who* or *which*, is thus declined :—

	SINGULAR.				PLURAL.	
	M.	F.	N.	M.	F.	N.
N.	ὅς	ἥ	ὅ	οἵ	αἵ	ἅ
G.	οὗ	ἧς	οὗ	ὧν	ὧν	ὧν
D.	ᾧ	ᾗ	ᾧ	οἷς	αἷς	οἷς
A.	ὅν	ἥν	ὅ	οὕς	ἅς	ἅ

(b) The similarity between this pronoun and the article will be seen at once. In the nominative singular feminine, and the nominative plural masculine and feminine, the only difference is that the article is *proclitic*. The stem of the relative is ὁ-, while that of the article is το-.

(c) An indefinite relative, *whoever, whatever*, is made by affixing the enclitic τις to ὅς, ἥ, ὅ. Both parts of the word are declined, as follows :—

	SINGULAR.				PLURAL.	
	M.	F.	N.	M.	F.	N.
N.	ὅστις	ἥτις	ὅ,τι	οἵτινες	αἵτινες	ἅτινα
G.	οὗτινος	ἧστινος	οὗτινος	ὧντινων	ὧντινων	ὧντινων
D.	ᾧτινι	ᾗτινι	ᾧτινι	οἷστισι	αἷστισι	οἷστισι
A.	ὅντινα	ἥντινα	ὅ,τι	οὕστινας	ἅστινας	ἅτινα

The neuter singular, nominative and accusative, is divided as above (sometimes by a space without the comma), to distinguish the word from the conjunction ὅτι, *that*.

The genitive masculine singular is sometimes written ὅτου, used in the New Testament only in the adverbial phrase ἕως ὅτου, *as long as, until* (Matt. v. 25, etc.).

§ 59, d.]   PRONOUNS—RELATIVE AND INTERROGATIVE.   53

(d) Sometimes the relative is declined with the particle -περ (marking emphatic identity), and means *the very one who*. Other indeclinable suffixes are often used, *e.g.*, ὅσγε (Rom. viii. 32), ὁσδηποτε. (See Syntax, on the Particles.) For the relative adverb οὗ, consult § 129.

(e) **Derivative relative pronouns** are employed to express *quality, quantity,* and *number*.

> Quality, οἷος, *such as*.
> Quantity, ὅσος, *so great as*.
> Number, ὅσοι, plural of ὅσος, *so many as*.

Also the relative of degree, ἡλίκος, *of what a size*, used only in two passages (Col. ii. 1 ; James iii. 5).

INTERROGATIVE PRONOUNS.

59. (a) The **simple interrogative** is τίς ; τί ; *who?* or *what?* The declension of this pronoun is identical with that of the indefinite τις (§ 13), except that in the interrogative the ι of the stem syllable is accented throughout, the dissyllabic forms being paroxytone.

For the adverbial interrogative form, μήτι, see § 134, *c*.

(b) **Other interrogative forms** are employed, *correlative* to the relative pronouns under § 58, *e*, and, like them, denoting *quality, quantity, number,* and *degree*. They all prefix the letter π- to the relative forms.

> Quality, ποῖος, *of what kind?*
> Quantity, πόσος, *how great?*
> Number, πόσοι, *how many?*
> Degree, πηλίκος, *how great?* used in the New Testament only *indirectly:* Gal. vi. 11, "with how large letters" (probably to mark emphasis) ; Heb. vii. 4.

(c) Direct interrogatives are often themselves used in the *indirect construction,* as John v. 13, "*He that was healed knew not who* (τίς) *it was.*"

(d) The properly indirect interrogatives prefix the letter ὁ- to the direct forms beginning with the letter π. ὁποῖος, *of what kind?* is the only one of these employed in the New Testament.

Indefinite Pronouns.

60. (a) The ordinary indefinite pronoun τις, *any, a certain one*, has been given, § 13. The genitive and dative singular are occasionally του, τῳ, enclitic.

(b) Compounds of this are οὔτις, μήτις, *no one*. For the distinction between them, see § 134, b, and compare under εἷς, § 49.

(c) The old indefinite pronoun δεῖνα, *such a one*, used with the article, is once found (Matt. xxvi. 18).

Distributive Pronouns.

61. These are mostly declined like adjectives, and are as follows :—

(a)   ἄλλος,   ἄλλη,   ἄλλο,   *another* (numerically)
Plur. ἄλλοι,   ἄλλαι, ἄλλοι, *others*
(b)   ἕτερος, ἑτέρα, ἕτερον, *other* (different)
Plur. ἕτεροι, ἕτεραι, ἕτερα, *others*

For the force of the article with these pronouns, see Syntax.

(c) ἀλλήλων, *of each other*, only used in the genitive, dative, and accusative plural.

(d) ἕκαστος, ἑκάστη, ἕκαστον, *each*, used only in the singular; with a doubtful exception, in Phil. ii. 4.

62. The number of the pronouns being so limited, it is unnecessary to give exercises for further practice. The foregoing forms and inflections must be very accurately committed to memory, and the distinctions between similar words carefully marked.

The following **Table of Correlative Pronouns** will be found useful as a summary :—

	Demonstrative.	Relative.	Interrogative.	Dependent Interrogative.	Indefinite.
Simple	οὗτος	ὅς	τίς	...	τις
Quality	τοιοῦτος	οἷος	ποῖος	ὁποῖος	...
Quantity	τοσοῦτος	ὅσος	πόσος	...	...
Degree	τηλικοῦτος	ἡλίκος	...	πηλίκος	...

Chapter V. THE VERB.

The Voices.

63. There are four principal things which verbs are employed to predicate concerning a given subject:—

1. Its state.
2. Its action upon an object.
3. Its action upon itself.
4. The action of the object upon it.

Hence arises a fourfold division of verbs: into *neuter* (or intransitive), *active* (or transitive), *reflexive*, and *passive*.

The Greek language employs a threefold modification of the verbal stem to express these varieties of meaning. The modifications, or "voices," are named as follows:—

The *Active* Voice, as λύω, *I loosen*.
The *Reflexive*, or *Middle* Voice, as λύομαι, *I loosen myself*.
The *Passive* Voice, as λύομαι, *I am loosened*.

Neuter verbs borrow the Active or the Middle form, as πάσχω, *I suffer;* βούλομαι, *I wish*.

The Moods.

64. The Greek verb has four modes, or moods:[1] the Indicative, Imperative, Subjunctive, and Infinitive.

1. The **Indicative** asserts absolutely, as ἔλυσα τὸν δέσμιον, *I loosened the prisoner*.

2. The **Imperative** commands, as λύετε τὸν δέσμιον, *loosen* (ye) *the prisoner !*

3. The **Subjunctive** asserts conditionally, as ὅταν λύσητε τὸν δέσμιον, *when you have loosened the prisoner*. A subjunctive clause, it is evident, requires another to complete its meaning; hence the name

---

[1] Compare "Handbook of the English Tongue," § 277.

of the mood, the "subjoined" mood. It is often also called the "**Conjunctive**."

4. A division of the Subjunctive is called the **Optative** Mood, because sometimes employed to express a wish, as in the frequent phrase, μὴ γένοιτο (rendered E. V. "God forbid "), *may it not be !* It is really the **subjunctive of the historical tenses.** Thus, in the phrase, *He asks if it be so*, the verb *be*, subjoined to the principal tense "asks" (present), would, in Greek, be subjunctive. *He asked if it were so*, would require *were* to be in the optative after the historical tense "asked" (aorist). For further detail, the Syntax must be consulted.

5. For the **Interrogative,** either the Indicative or the Subjunctive may be employed, according to the nature of the question. (See Syntax, §§ 368, 376.)

6. The **Infinitive** expresses the action or state denoted by the verb, as in itself an object of thought, as λύειν τὸν δέσμιον, *to loosen the prisoner*, *i.e.,* "the act of loosening him." The Infinitive, it is plain, partakes of the nature of a substantive, and is often called the **verbal noun**; being, moreover, employed as an uninflected singular neuter, with the article in all its cases. (See Syntax, §§ 201, 388, 390.)

7. To the Moods must be added the **Participles,** which are **verbal adjectives,** and **agree with substantives** expressed or understood, as ὁ δέσμιος λυθείς, *the prisoner, being loosened;* ὁ λελουμένος, *he who has been washed.*

As the Infinitive "partakes" the nature of the substantive, and the Participle that of the adjective, they are sometimes both called *participials*. It is, however, more common to distinguish them by the phrase "the infinitive verb," the remaining moods being known as "the finite verb."

Both the Infinitive and the Participles are used in **different tenses,** for which see the paradigm of the Verb.

The Tenses.

65. *a.* Time is *present, past,* and *future.* In each an action may be predicated as *indefinite* (*i.e.,* having regard to the *act* itself rather than to its completedness or otherwise), *imperfect* (*i.e.,* going on),

§ 66.]   TENSES, NUMBERS, AND PERSONS OF THE VERB.   57

or *perfect* (*i.e.*, finished). Hence **nine possible tenses**, of which the Greek language has **seven**, as follows:—

	Indefinite state.	Imperfect state.	Perfect state.
Present time ...	———(I write)	*Present* (I am writing)	*Perfect* (I have written)
Past time ...	*Aorist* (I wrote)	*Imperfect* (I was writing)	*Pluperfect* (I had written)
Future time ...	*Future* (I shall write)	——— (I shall be writing)	*Future-perfect*[1] (I shall have written)

b. More detailed exposition of these tenses, the names of which the table gives in italics, will be found in the Syntax, § 360, *seq.*, where it will also be explained how the meaning of the deficient tenses, the Present Indefinite and the Future Imperfect, is supplied.

The **Aorist** (ἀόριστος, *indefinite*) is properly an indefinite *past*, but it has other uses, which will also be afterwards explained.

c. Of the above, the Present, Perfect, Future, and Future-perfect are called **principal tenses**; the Imperfect, Aorist, and Pluperfect, **historical tenses.**

d. The tenses are usually arranged as follows:—

    1. Present,   λύω,   *I loosen.*
    2. Imperfect,   ἔλυον,   *I was loosening.*
    3. Future,   λύσω,   *I shall or will loosen.*
    4. Aorist,   ἔλυσα,   *I loosened.*
    5. Perfect,   λέλυκα,   *I have loosened.*
    6. Pluperfect,   (ἐ)λελύκειν, *I had loosened.*
    7. Future-perfect, found only in the passive or middle, λελύσομαι, *I shall have been loosened.*

NUMBERS AND PERSONS.

66. There are in the Greek verb three persons, corresponding with those in other languages, and three numbers, the singular, dual, and plural, of which the dual is not used in the New Testament. (See § 11.) Only the singular and plural, therefore, are given.

---

[1] Very rare. See *d*, 7.

CONJUGATIONS.

67. There are two principal forms of conjugation. In the most ancient, the first person singular, present indicative active of the verb has the termination μι; in the later, the termination ω. The latter being the easier, the more symmetrical, and embracing the far larger number of verbs, is usually given first, and is called the **First Conjugation.** The other is termed the **Second Conjugation,** or, more generally, "the verb in -μι."

REMARK.

The first person singular, present indicative active, is the form of the verb given in almost all Vocabularies and Lexicons, and is generally explained by the English infinitive. Thus, λύω, *to loosen;* more properly, *I am loosening.*

THE VERBAL STEM.

68. The chief thing necessary to be known in a verb is the *stem,* which is easily found by abstracting from any given verbal form the adjuncts of mood and tense. Thus, a glance over the forms of the verb "to loosen," in § 65, *d,* will at once disclose its stem, λυ-.

Additions to the stem are made either at its beginning or its end. An addition at the beginning is termed **augment** or **reduplication;** an addition at the end, the **inflectional termination.** The former belongs alike to the two conjugations; in the latter, the conjugations vary.

AUGMENT AND REDUPLICATION.

69. *a.* The **augment** characterises the **historical tenses** (§ 65, *c*) in the **indicative mood.**

(1) Verbs beginning with a consonant prefix the letter ἐ, called the **syllabic augment.** Thus, from λύω, imperfect ἔλυον, aorist ἔλυσα.

(2) Verbs beginning with a short vowel augment by lengthening it: ἀ- into η-, ε- into η- (in a few cases into ει-), ῐ- into ῑ-, ῠ- into ῡ-, and ο- into ω-. This is termed the **temporal augment.** Verbs beginning with the ("changeable") diphthongs αι, αυ, οι, are augmented by changing the former vowel. Thus, αι- becomes ῃ-, αυ- is changed to ηυ-, and οι- becomes ῳ-. Sometimes, also, ευ- is augmented into ηυ-. The other diphthongs and the long vowels are ("unchangeable," *i.e.*) incapable of augment.

b. The **reduplication,** *i.e.,* the repetition of the initial consonant of the stem with ε, belongs to those tenses which mark a completed action (the **perfect, pluperfect, and future-perfect**), and is **continued through all the moods**. It takes place, in general, only when a verb begins with a single consonant or a mute and a liquid. Thus λέ-λυκα, perf. from λύω; βε-βούλευκα, from βουλεύω; γέ-γραφα, from γράφω.

In verbs beginning with a vowel, only the Temporal Augment is employed in these tenses, but it is continued through all the moods. To distinguish this augment from that of the historical tenses, it is sometimes called the **improper reduplication.**

c. Verbs compounded with prepositions almost invariably take the augment or reduplication **after the preposition** and at the beginning of the proper verbal stem. Thus, from ἐκ-λύω, *to set free*, comes the Aorist ἐξέλυσα (ἐκ changed into ἐξ by § 3, *h*, 1), and from ἀπο-λύω, *to dismiss*, the Aorist is ἀπέλυσα, the ο disappearing by elision before the augment vowel (§ 3, *h*, 2). The prepositions περί and πρό, however, do not elide their vowels; and a few other exceptions will be noted in their place.

Inflectional Terminations.

70. *a.* As a verb is distinguished by voice, mood, tense, number, and person, **five different elements** will evidently concur in fixing the termination in any given case. Thus, if the phrase, *we were being loosened*, is to be translated into Greek, it will be necessary to fix "the personal ending" of the first person plural passive, the "tense-characteristic" of the imperfect, and the "modal vowel" of the indicative.

b. The **Personal endings** are no doubt the fragments of ancient personal pronouns, affixed to the verb;[1] but the original forms are in a great measure disused or lost. The attentive student will observe the recurrence of **-s** in the second person singular, and of **-μεν, -τε**, in the first and second persons plural, throughout the active. It will be seen, also, that in the active *principal* tenses the third person plural ends in **-σι** (**-σιν** before an initial vowel in the next word), and in the *historical* tenses in **-ν**. In the passive and middle, the normal forms are, for the *principal* tenses—Sing., -μαι, -σαι, -ται; Plur., -μεθα, -σθε, -νται; *historical* tenses— Sing., -μην, -σο, -το; Plur., -μεθα, -σθε, -ντο. Study of the Paradigms which follow will suggest other points of comparison.

---

[1] See Müller's "Lectures on the Science of Language," first series, especially p. 272, *seq.*

71. The **Tense-characteristics** most important to be noticed are the following:—

a. **The Future and (First) Aorist Active have -σ-.** So, from the verbal stem πιστευ- we have the **Future stem** πιστευσ-. When the verbal stem ends with a short vowel, it is generally lengthened in the Future: thus, from λυ- is formed λῡσ-; from τιμᾰ-, τιμησ- (see § 3, *e*); and from δηλο-, δηλωσ-.

b. **The Perfect and Pluperfect Active take -κ-.** Thus, πιστευ- (with the reduplication, § 69, *b*), makes πεπιστευκ-. Here also a final stem-vowel is usually lengthened; as from τιμᾰ-, τετιμηκ-, and from δηλο-, δεδηλωκ-. But λυ- makes λελῠκ-.

c. **The Future and (First) Aorist Passive take -θ-,** lengthening the vowel where lengthened in the Perfect Active. Thus, from the verbal stems already given, πιστευθ-, λῠθ-, τιμηθ-, δηλωθ-.

d. In the Perfect and Pluperfect Middle and Passive the normal forms (see § 70, *b*) are affixed to the verbal stem without any connecting letter.

> The successive paradigms will show how the tense-characteristics are modified by the consonants of the verbal stem.

72. The Modal Vowels will be sufficiently traced in the Paradigms. It will be especially noted how the Subjunctive throughout lengthens the vowels of the Indicative, and how the Optative abounds in diphthongal forms. In the third person plural it will also be seen that the Subjunctive takes the termination of the *principal* tenses, the Optative of the *historical*.

The Imperfect and Pluperfect tenses occur only in the Indicative Mood;[1] the Future, also, is absent from the Imperative and Subjunctive.

---

[1] It will be seen under Syntax, § 378, that the Optative mood really is the *historical Subjunctive*. Hence the Present and Perfect Optative are the Imperfect and Pluperfect Subjunctive. The ordinary names have, however, been retained to prevent unnecessary difficulty to the learner.

The Verbal Adjectives.

73. Many verbs have, in addition to their passive participles, a kind of participial adjective, to signify either *capability* or *duty*. The former is generally expressed by the termination -τός, -τή, -τόν, appended to the verbal stem; the latter by the termination -τέος, -τέα, -τέον. Thus, from λυ- may be formed λυτός, *capable of being loosened;* λυτέος, *that ought to be loosened.*

74. PARADIGM OF THE FIRST CONJUGATION, OR OF "THE VERB IN -ω."

The verb πιστεύω has been chosen as a model, because it is a characteristic word of the New Testament, and because all its forms contain the unaltered stem. The verb βουλεύω, *to advise*, employed by Kühner and others, only occurs in the New Testament in the middle voice; and λύω, *to loosen*, chosen by Professor Curtius and Principal Greenwood, though easy to conjugate, has the disadvantage of having the stem long in some forms, and short in others, although unaltered to the eye.

The learner will have little difficulty in discovering throughout the paradigm the *root* (πιστευ-), the *augment* or *reduplication*, the *connecting letter* (σ or κ), and the *termination*. As a help, however, the augment and terminations are printed in a darker type.

Stem, πιστευ-, *to believe* or *trust;* Mid., *to trust one's self* or *to confide;* Pass., *to be entrusted.*

a. Principal parts.

Present Indicative Active,	πιστεύω
Future ,, ,,	πιστεύσω
Perfect ,, ,,	πεπίστευκα
Perfect Indicative, Mid. and Pass.,	πεπίστευμαι
(First) Aorist Indicative Passive,	ἐπιστεύθην

To know these five parts thoroughly, with the addition, in many verbs, of the Second Aorist (§§ 86-88), is TO KNOW THE VERB.

THE VERB IN -ω : ACTIVE VOICE. [§ 74.

Active Voice.

INDICATIVE MOOD.

Present Tense. *I am believing.*

SINGULAR.	PLURAL.
πιστεύω	πιστεύομεν
πιστεύεις	πιστεύετε
πιστεύει	πιστεύουσι(ν)

Imperfect. *I was believing.*

SINGULAR.	PLURAL.
ἐπίστευον	ἐπιστεύομεν
ἐπίστευες	ἐπιστεύετε
ἐπίστευε(ν)	ἐπίστευον

Future. *I shall or will believe.*

SINGULAR.	PLURAL.
πιστεύσω	πιστεύσομεν
πιστεύσεις	πιστεύσετε
πιστεύσει	πιστεύσουσι(ν)

Aorist (First Aorist[1]). *I believed.*

SINGULAR.	PLURAL.
ἐπίστευσα	ἐπιστεύσαμεν
ἐπίστευσας	ἐπιστεύσατε
ἐπίστευσε(ν)	ἐπίστευσαν

Perfect. *I have believed.*

SINGULAR.	PLURAL.
πεπίστευκα	πεπιστεύκαμεν
πεπίστευκας	πεπιστεύκατε
πεπίστευκε(ν)	πεπιστεύκασι(ν)

Pluperfect.[2] *I had believed.*

SINGULAR.	PLURAL.
ἐπεπιστεύκειν	ἐπεπιστεύκειμεν
ἐπεπιστεύκεις	ἐπεπιστεύκειτε
ἐπεπιστεύκει	ἐπεπιστεύκε(ι)σαν

---

[1] See § 86.
[2] Augment generally omitted in N. T. in plupf. act. and pass.

THE VERB IN -ω: ACTIVE VOICE.

IMPERATIVE MOOD.

Present Tense. *Believe* (continuously).

SINGULAR.	PLURAL.
2nd pers. πίστευε	πιστεύετε
3rd pers. πιστευέτω	πιστευέτωσαν

Aorist. *Believe* (at once).

SINGULAR.	PLURAL.
πίστευσον	πιστεύσατε
πιστευσάτω	πιστευσάτωσαν

Perfect. *Have believed* (i.e., remain so).

SINGULAR.	PLURAL.
πεπίστευκε	πεπιστεύκετε
πεπιστευκέτω	πεπιστευκέτωσαν

SUBJUNCTIVE MOOD.

Present Tense. *I may believe.*

SINGULAR.	PLURAL.
πιστεύω	πιστεύωμεν
πιστεύῃς	πιστεύητε
πιστεύῃ	πιστεύωσι(ν)

Aorist. *I may believe, or shall have believed.*

SINGULAR.	PLURAL.
πιστεύσω	πιστεύσωμεν
πιστεύσῃς	πιστεύσητε
πιστεύσῃ	πιστεύσωσι(ν)

Perfect. *I may have believed.*

SINGULAR.	PLURAL.
πεπιστεύκω	πεπιστεύκωμεν
πεπιστεύκῃς	πεπιστεύκητε
πεπιστεύκῃ	πεπιστεύκωσι(ν)

OPTATIVE MOOD.

(*Or*, SUBJUNCTIVE OF HISTORICAL TENSES.)

Present (or Imperfect).   *I might believe.*

SINGULAR.	PLURAL.
πιστεύοιμι	πιστεύοιμεν
πιστεύοις	πιστεύοιτε
πιστεύοι	πιστεύοιεν

Future.   *I should believe.*

SINGULAR.	PLURAL.
πιστεύσοιμι	πιστεύσοιμεν
πιστεύσοις	πιστεύσοιτε
πιστεύσοι	πιστεύσοιεν

Aorist.   *I might or am to believe.*

SINGULAR.	PLURAL.
πιστεύσαιμι	πιστεύσαιμεν
πιστεύσαις	πιστεύσαιτε
πιστεύσαι	πιστεύσαιεν or -ειαν [1]

Perfect (or Pluperfect).   *I might have believed.*

SINGULAR.	PLURAL.
πεπιστεύκοιμι	πεπιστεύκοιμεν
πεπιστεύκοις	πεπιστεύκοιτε
πεπιστεύκοι	πεπιστεύκοιεν

INFINITIVE.

Present, πιστεύειν, *to believe (be believing).*
Future, πιστεύσειν, *to be about to believe.*
Aorist, πιστεῦσαι, *to believe.*
Perfect, πεπιστευκέναι, *to have believed.*

PARTICIPLES.

Present nom., πιστεύων, πιστεύουσα, πιστεῦον, *believing;* stems, πιστευοντ- (m. and n.), πιστευουσα- (f.).

Future nom., πιστεύσων, πιστεύσουσα, πιστεῦσον, *about to believe;* stems, πιστευσοντ- (m. and n.), πιστευσουσα- (f.).

---

[1] The form in -ειαν (Æolic) is found only once in N. T. (Acts xvii. 27).

§ 74.] THE VERB IN -ω: MIDDLE AND PASSIVE.

Aorist nom., πιστεύσας, πιστεύσᾱσα, πιστεῦσαν, *having believed* stems, πιστευσαντ- (m. and n.), πιστευσασα- (f.).

Perfect nom., πεπιστευκώς, πεπιστευκυῖα, πεπιστευκός, *having now believed;* stems, πεπιστευκοτ- (m. and n.), πεπιστευκυια- (f.).

Middle and Passive Voices—Forms common to both.

INDICATIVE MOOD.

Present Tense. *I am confiding (trusting myself), or am being entrusted.*[1]

SINGULAR.	PLURAL.
πιστεύομαι	πιστευόμεθα
πιστεύῃ [2]	πιστεύεσθε
πιστεύεται	πιστεύονται

Imperfect. *I was confiding, or was being entrusted.*

SINGULAR.	PLURAL.
ἐπιστευόμην	ἐπιστευόμεθα
ἐπιστεύου [3]	ἐπιστεύεσθε
ἐπιστεύετο	ἐπιστεύοντο

Perfect. *I have confided, or have been entrusted.*

SINGULAR.	PLURAL.
πεπίστευμαι	πεπιστεύμεθα
πεπίστευσαι	πεπίστευσθε
πεπίστευται	πεπίστευνται

Pluperfect. *I had confided, or had been entrusted.*

SINGULAR.	PLURAL.
ἐπεπιστεύμην	ἐπεπιστεύμεθα
ἐπεπίστευσο	ἐπεπίστευσθε
ἐπεπίστευτο	ἐπεπίστευντο

---

[1] The collocation *am being* is doubtlessly inelegant; but the true force of the tense could be given in no other way. The Greek language has no present indefinite.
[2] Contracted from -εσαι. The contraction into -ει is very rare.
[3] Contracted from -εσο.

THE VERB IN -ω: MIDDLE AND PASSIVE.

IMPERATIVE MOOD.

Present. *Confide, or be thou entrusted.*

SINGULAR.	PLURAL.
2nd pers. πιστεύου [1]	πιστεύεσθε
3rd pers. πιστευέσθω	πιστευέσθωσαν or -έσθων

Perfect. *Have confided, or have been entrusted (i.e., remain so).*

SINGULAR.	PLURAL.
πεπίστευσο	πεπίστευσθε
πεπιστεύσθω	πεπιστεύσθωσαν or -σθων

SUBJUNCTIVE MOOD.

Present. *I may confide, or be entrusted.*

SINGULAR.	PLURAL.
πιστεύωμαι	πιστευώμεθα
πιστεύῃ	πιστεύησθε
πιστεύηται	πιστεύωνται

Perfect. *I may have confided, or have been entrusted.*

SINGULAR.	PLURAL.
πεπιστευμένος ὦ [2]	πεπιστευμένοι ὦμεν
πεπιστευμένος ᾖς	πεπιστευμένοι ἦτε
πεπιστευμένος ᾖ	πεπιστευμένοι ὦσι(ν)

OPTATIVE MOOD.

(*Or,* SUBJUNCTIVE OF HISTORICAL TENSES.)

Present. *I might confide, or be entrusted.*

SINGULAR.	PLURAL.
πιστευοίμην	πιστευοίμεθα
πιστεύοιο	πιστεύοισθε
πιστεύοιτο	πιστεύοιντο

---

[1] Contracted from -εσο.
[2] These forms are made by the perfect participle, with the substantive verb "*to be*" as an auxiliary.

THE VERB IN -ω: MIDDLE.

Perfect. *I might have confided, or been entrusted.*

SINGULAR.	PLURAL.
πεπιστευμένος εἴην	πεπιστευμένοι εἴημεν
πεπιστευμένος εἴης	πεπιστευμένοι εἴητε
πεπιστευμένος εἴη	πεπιστευμένοι εἴησαν

INFINITIVE.

Present, πιστεύεσθαι, *to confide, or be entrusted.*
Perfect, πεπιστεῦσθαι, *to have confided, or have been entrusted.*

PARTICIPLES.

Present, πιστευόμενος, πιστευομένη, πιστευόμενον, *confiding, or being entrusted.*

Perfect, πεπιστευμένος, πεπιστευμένη, πεπιστευμένον, *having confided, or having been entrusted.*

Forms peculiar to the Middle.

INDICATIVE MOOD.

Future Tense. *I shall or will confide.*

SINGULAR.	PLURAL.
πιστεύσομαι	πιστευσόμεθα
πιστεύσῃ	πιστεύσεσθε
πιστεύσεται	πιστεύσονται

(First) Aorist. *I confided.*

SINGULAR.	PLURAL.
ἐπιστευσάμην	ἐπιστευσάμεθα
ἐπιστεύσω[1]	ἐπιστεύσασθε
ἐπιστεύσατο	ἐπιστεύσαντο

IMPERATIVE MOOD.

Aorist. *Confide* (at once).

SINGULAR.	PLURAL.
2nd pers. πίστευσαι	πιστεύσασθε
3rd pers. πιστευσάσθω	πιστευσάσθωσαν or -ἀσθων

---

[1] Contracted from -ασο.

SUBJUNCTIVE MOOD.

Aorist. *I may confide,* or *shall have confided.*

SINGULAR.	PLURAL
πιστεύσωμαι	πιστευσώμεθα
πιστεύσῃ	πιστεύσησθε
πιστεύσηται	πιστεύσωνται

OPTATIVE MOOD.
(*Or*, SUBJUNCTIVE OF HISTORICAL TENSES.)

Future. *I should confide.*

SINGULAR.	PLURAL.
πιστευσοίμην	πιστευσοίμεθα
πιστεύσοιο	πιστεύσοισθε
πιστεύσοιτο	πιστεύσοιντο

Aorist. *I might* or *am to confide.*

SINGULAR.	PLURAL.
πιστευσαίμην	πιστευσαίμεθα
πιστεύσαιο	πιστεύσαισθε
πιστεύσαιτο	πιστεύσαιντο

INFINITIVE.

Future, πιστεύσεσθαι, *to be about to confide.*
Aorist, πιστεύσασθαι, *to confide immediately.*

PARTICIPLES.

Future, πιστευσόμενος, πιστευσομένη, πιστευσόμενον, *about to confide.*
Aorist, πιστευσάμενος, πιστευσαμένη, πιστευσάμενον, *having confided.*

Forms peculiar to the Passive.

INDICATIVE MOOD.

(First) Future Tense. *I shall be entrusted.*

SINGULAR.	PLURAL.
πιστευθήσομαι	πιστευθησόμεθα
πιστευθήσῃ	πιστευθήσεσθε
πιστευθήσεται	πιστευθήσονται

(First) Aorist. *I was entrusted.*

SINGULAR.	PLURAL.
ἐπιστεύθην	ἐπιστεύθημεν
ἐπιστεύθης	ἐπιστεύθητε
ἐπιστεύθη	ἐπιστεύθησαν

IMPERATIVE MOOD.

Aorist. *Be thou entrusted* (at once).

SINGULAR.	PLURAL.
2nd pers. πιστεύθητι	πιστεύθητε
3rd pers. πιστευθήτω	πιστευθήτωσαν

SUBJUNCTIVE MOOD.

Aorist. *I may be* or *shall have been entrusted.*

SINGULAR.	PLURAL.
πιστευθῶ	πιστευθῶμεν
πιστευθῇς	πιστευθῆτε
πιστευθῇ	πιστευθῶσι(ν)

OPTATIVE MOOD.

Future. *I should be entrusted.*

SINGULAR.	PLURAL.
πιστευθησοίμην	πιστευθησοίμεθα
πιστευθήσοιο	πιστευθήσοισθε
πιστευθήσοιτο	πιστευθήσοιντο

Aorist. *I might be* or *am to be entrusted.*

SINGULAR.	PLURAL.
πιστευθείην	πιστευθείημεν
πιστευθείης	πιστευθείητε
πιστευθείη	πιστευθεῖεν

INFINITIVE.

Future, πιστευθήσεσθαι, *to be about to be entrusted.*
Aorist, πιστευθῆναι, *to be entrusted.*

PARTICIPLES.

Future, πιστευθησόμενος, -η, -ον, *about to be entrusted.*
Aorist, πιστευθείς, -εῖσα, -έν, *having been entrusted;* stem, πιστευθεντ- (m. and n.).

VERBAL ADJECTIVE.

πιστευτός, -τή, -τόν, *capable of entrusting,* or *of being entrusted;*
πιστευτέος, -τέα, -τέον, *that ought to be entrusted.*

75. The learner who has thoroughly mastered the different forms of πιστεύω now given is ready to encounter with comparative ease the manifold variations of verbs in -ω. First, however, let the following Exercises be written :—

Exercise 9.—On Pure Uncontracted Verbs.

1. Write out the whole of the regular verb βουλεύω: active, *to advise;* middle, *to deliberate, to advise oneself;* passive, *to be advised.*

2. [*Vocabulary of Verbs selected from the "Sermon on the Mount."*—ἀκούω, *to hear;* δουλεύω, *to serve;* λύω, *to loosen* (compound derivatives, ἀπολύω, *to put away;* καταλύω, *to abrogate*); νηστεύω, *to fast;* προφητεύω, *to prophesy;* φονεύω, *to murder.*]

Analyse and translate the following forms :—δουλεύειν, καταλῦσαι, λύσῃ, ἠκούσατε, φονεύσεις, φονεύσῃ, ἀπολύσῃ, ἀπολελυμένην, νηστεύητε, νηστεύοντες, προεφητεύσαμεν.

Also the following :—κατελύθη, ἀπολέλυται, νήστευσον, πεφονεύκασιν, λελυκέναι, καταλελυκώς, νηστεύσω, προφήτευσον, προφητεύουσαι, προφητεύητε, δεδουλεύκαμεν, δουλεύοντες, ἐδούλευσεν, δουλευέτωσαν, ἀπολυθέντες, ἀπολελύσθαι, ἀπελύοντο.

76. The verbs in the foregoing Exercise, as well as the conjugated verb πιστεύω, are all distinguished by a **vowel stem-ending,** which, in the great majority of cases, is the letter **υ** in a diphthongal or simple form. They are, therefore, called **pure verbs;** and inasmuch as the stem appears throughout without contraction or alteration, they are further termed **uncontracted.**

To the class of pure uncontracted verbs belong most with the stem-ending υ or ι, but no others. It is, therefore, necessary to see how the verbal terminations are to be adapted to other kinds of stem; and to do this *thoroughly* in the case of all regular verbs, little else is needed than the remembrance and application of the elementary laws of euphony, as stated in § 4.

> It must be noted by the learner that, when the terminations of the voices, moods, and tenses are once known, and a very few simple general rules of conjugation impressed on the memory, the acquisition of all the multifarious "classes" and "species" of verbs in -ω is a matter of euphony and nothing else.

77. Let us take the possible verbal stem-endings according to the alphabet. It will appear that the stem may terminate (1) in a vowel or (2) in a consonant; and that the consonant may be (1) a mute, (2) a liquid, or (3) a double letter. The last may be rejected from the account, as no verbal stems, in fact, do so terminate. We have, then, three main divisions: the **PURE** verbs, the **MUTE**, and the **LIQUID**.

78.   PURE VERBS.—SPECIAL RULES.

a. A verbal stem may end in α, ε, ι, ο, or υ; *i.e.*, in any short vowel. Those in ι and υ, the **uncontracted**, have been considered already.

b. From the rules and tables given under § 3, *f*, and the partial illustrations of them given in the nouns and adjectives, it has been seen that when α, ε, or ο precedes a vowel, long or short, it is generally contracted with it into one syllable. Hence, verbal stems ending in these vowels form a second class of pure verbs—viz., the **contracted**.

c. As, however, it appears from the paradigm that the last letter of the stem precedes a vowel only in the **Present** and **Imperfect** tenses, it follows that the **contraction will be confined to these parts of the verb**, and that there will be no deviation in other parts from the general form of πιστεύω.

d. For the **Table of Contractions**, see § 3, *f*. Note especially that with -ου the stem-vowel α- makes ω-, while ε- and ο- disappear before the diphthong. In the Infinitive, also, the combination -οειν becomes -ουν.

79. The following paradigms will now present no difficulty :—

    1. A-stem, τιμάω, *to honour.*
    2. E-stem, φιλέω, *to love.*
    3. O-stem, δηλόω, *to manifest.*

	Stem, τῑμα-	φῐλε-	δηλο-
		Active.	
		INDICATIVE—Present.	
-ω	τιμῶ	φιλῶ	δηλῶ
-εις	τιμᾷς	φιλεῖς	δηλοῖς
-ει	τιμᾷ	φιλεῖ	δηλοῖ
-ομεν	τιμῶμεν	φιλοῦμεν	δηλοῦμεν
-ετε	τιμᾶτε	φιλεῖτε	δηλοῦτε
-ουσι(ν)	τιμῶσι(ν)	φιλοῦσι(ν)	δηλοῦσι(ν)
		Imperfect.	
ἐ- . . -ον	ἐτίμων	ἐφίλουν	ἐδήλουν
-ες	ἐτίμας	ἐφίλεις	ἐδήλους
-ε	ἐτίμα	ἐφίλει	ἐδήλου
-ομεν	ἐτιμῶμεν	ἐφιλοῦμεν	ἐδηλοῦμεν
-ετε	ἐτιμᾶτε	ἐφιλεῖτε	ἐδηλοῦτε
-ον	ἐτίμων	ἐφίλουν	ἐδήλουν
		IMPERATIVE—Present.	
-ε	τίμα	φίλει	δήλου
-έτω	τιμάτω	φιλείτω	δηλούτω
-ετε	τιμᾶτε	φιλεῖτε	δηλοῦτε
-έτωσαν	τιμάτωσαν	φιλείτωσαν	δηλούτωσαν
		SUBJUNCTIVE—Present.	
-ω	τιμῶ	φιλῶ	δηλῶ
-ῃς	τιμᾷς	φιλῇς	δηλοῖς
-ῃ	τιμᾷ	φιλῇ	δηλοῖ
-ωμεν	τιμῶμεν	φιλῶμεν	δηλῶμεν
-ητε	τιμᾶτε	φιλῆτε	δηλῶτε
-ωσι(ν)	τιμῶσι(ν)	φιλῶσι(ν)	δηλῶσι(ν)

(Like the Indicative.)

§ 79.] CONTRACTED VERBS IN -ω : MIDDLE AND PASSIVE.

Stem, τῑμα-   φῐλε-   δηλο-

	OPTATIVE—Present.		
-οιμι	τιμῷμι or -ῴην	φιλοῖμι or -οίην	δηλοῖμι or -οίην[1]
-οις	τιμῷς or -ῴης	φιλοῖς or -οίης	δηλοῖς or -οίης
-οι	τιμῷ or -ῴη	φιλοῖ or -οίη	δηλοῖ or -οίη
-οιμεν	τιμῷμεν or -ῴημεν	φιλοῖμεν or -οίημεν	δηλοῖμεν or -οίημεν
-οιτε	τιμῷτε or -ῴητε	φιλοῖτε or -οίητε	δηλοῖτε or -οίητε
-οιεν	τιμῷεν	φιλοῖεν	δηλοῖεν
	INFINITIVE—Present.		
-ειν	τιμᾶν	φιλεῖν	δηλοῦν
	PARTICIPLE—Present.		
-ων	τιμῶν	φιλῶν	δηλῶν
f. -ουσα	τιμῶσα	φιλοῦσα	δηλοῦσα
n. -ον	τιμῶν	φιλοῦν	δηλοῦν
	Middle and Passive.		
	INDICATIVE—Present.		
-ομαι	τιμῶμαι	φιλοῦμαι	δηλοῦμαι
-ῃ, -ει	τιμᾷ	φιλῇ or -εῖ	δηλοῖ
-εται	τιμᾶται	φιλεῖται	δηλοῦται
-όμεθα	τιμώμεθα	φιλούμεθα	δηλούμεθα
-εσθε	τιμᾶσθε	φιλεῖσθε	δηλοῦσθε
-ονται	τιμῶνται	φιλοῦνται	δηλοῦνται
	INDICATIVE—Imperfect.		
ἐ- . . -όμην	ἐτιμώμην	ἐφιλούμην	ἐδηλούμην
-ου	ἐτιμῶ	ἐφιλοῦ	ἐδηλοῦ
-ετο	ἐτιμᾶτο	ἐφιλεῖτο	ἐδηλοῦτο
-όμεθα	ἐτιμώμεθα	ἐφιλούμεθα	ἐδηλούμεθα
-εσθε	ἐτιμᾶσθε	ἐφιλεῖσθε	ἐδηλοῦσθε
-οντο	ἐτιμῶντο	ἐφιλοῦντο	ἐδηλοῦντο

[1] The latter are the more usual terminations.

CONTRACTED VERBS IN -ω: MIDDLE AND PASSIVE. [§ 79.

Stem, τῑμα-   φῐλε-   δηλο-

IMPERATIVE—Present.

-ου	τιμῶ	φιλοῦ	δηλοῦ
-έσθω	τιμάσθω	φιλείσθω	δηλούσθω
-εσθε	τιμᾶσθε	φιλεῖσθε	δηλοῦσθε
-έσθωσαν	τιμάσθωσαν	φιλείσθωσαν	δηλούσθωσαν
or -ἔσθων	τιμάσθων	φιλείσθων	δηλούσθων

SUBJUNCTIVE—Present.

-ωμαι	τιμῶμαι	φιλῶμαι	δηλῶμαι
-ῃ	τιμᾷ	φιλῇ	δηλοῖ
-ηται	τιμᾶται	φιλῆται	δηλῶται
-ώμεθα	τιμώμεφα	φιλώμεθα	δηλώμεθα
-ησθε	τιμᾶσθε	φιλῆσθε	δηλῶσθε
-ωνται	τιμῶνται	φιλῶνται	δηλῶνται

Like the Indicative.

OPTATIVE—Present.

-οίμην	τιμῴμην	φιλοίμην	δηλοίμην
-οιο	τιμῷο	φιλοῖο	δηλοῖο
-οιτο	τιμῷτο	φιλοῖτο	δηλοῖτο
-οίμεθα	τιμώμεθα	φιλοίμεθα	δηλοίμεθα
-οισθε	τιμῷσθε	φιλοῖσθε	δηλοῖσθε
-οιντο	τιμῷντο	φιλοῖντο	δηλρῖντο

INFINITIVE—Present.

-εσθαι	τιμᾶσθαι	φιλεῖσθαι	δηλοῦσθαι

PARTICIPLE.

m. -όμενος	τιμώμενος	φιλούμενος	δηλούμενος
f. -ομένη	τιμωμένη	φιλουμένη	δηλουμένη
n. -όμενον	τιμώμενον	φιλούμενον	δηλούμενον

§ 81.]   MUTE VERBS: SPECIAL RULES.   75

Note on the Remaining Tenses.

80. These are **regularly formed.** The lengthening of the vowel before the future, aorist, and perfect tense-endings must be marked.

Principal tenses	of τιμάω,	of φιλέω,	of δηλόω—
Present active	τιμῶ	φιλῶ	δηλῶ
Future active	τιμήσω	φιλήσω	δηλώσω
Perfect active	τετίμηκα	πεφίληκα	δεδήλωκα
1st Aor. passive	ἐτιμήθην	ἐφιλήθην	ἐδηλώθην
Perf. mid. and pass.	τετίμημαι	πεφίλημαι	δεδήλωμαι

Exercise 10.—On pure Contracted Verbs.

[*Vocabulary of Verbs, selected from the "Sermon on the Mount."*—ἀγαπάω, *to love;* αἰτέω, *to ask;* διψάω, *to thirst;* θεάομαι, *to behold* (dep.[1]); θεμελιόω, *to found;* ζητέω, *to seek;* μετρέω, *to measure;* μισέω, *to hate;* οἰκοδομέω, *to build;* ὁμοιόω, *to liken;* πεινάω, *to hunger;* ποιέω, *to do, make.*]

Analyse and translate the following words:—πεινῶντες, διψῶντες, ποιεῖ, ἀγαπήσεις, μισήσεις, ἀγαπήσητε, ἀγαπῶντας, ποιῆσαι, ποιοῦσι, ποιεῖτε, ποιεῖν, θεαθῆναι, ποιῇς, αἰτῆσαι, ζητεῖτε, μετρεῖτε, αἰτήσῃ, αἰτοῦσιν (*dat. plur.*), ποιῶσιν, ποιοῦν, ὁμοιώσω, ᾠκοδόμησε, τεθεμελίωτο, ὁμοιωθήσεται.

Also the following:—θεάσασθαι, τεθέαται, ἠγάπησεν, ἀγαπᾷ, ἠγαπημένην, ἀγαπᾶν, αἰτεῖσθε, ᾐτοῦντο, ᾐτήσαντο, αἰτῶμεν, ἐζήτουν, ζητῶν, ζητείτω, ἐζητεῖτο, ὁμοιώθημεν, ἐπείνασα (see § 96, *a*), πεινᾷ, ἐδίψησα, διψᾷ.

Mute Verbs.—Special Rules.

81. The large class of **mute verbs** comes next in order—*i.e.*, verbs whose stem-ending (or "characteristic") is either a **labial, π, β, φ**; a **guttural, κ, γ, χ**; or a **dental, τ, δ, θ**. It will be convenient to retain

---

[1] *Deponent, i.e.,* middle *form* with *active* meaning: an active form not being used. See § 100.

the names of (§ 4, b) p-sounds (labials), k-sounds (gutturals), and t-sounds (dentals). The cross-division, into *sharp, flat,* and *aspirate,* must also be remembered.

82. Whenever, in the conjugation of a verb, the stem is followed immediately by a vowel, the mute stem-ending is unaffected. In the Present and Imperfect tenses, therefore, the mute verb precisely resembles πιστεύω.

83. *a.* Many tense forms, however, begin with a consonant: as those of the Future and First Aorist with -σ-, that of the Perfect with -κ-, that of the First Aorist passive with -θ-; while in the different parts of the Perfect middle and passive there occur four several consonants immediately following the stem, the terminations being -μαι, -σαι, -ται, -μεθα, -σθε, -νται. So with the Pluperfect.

b. The rules, therefore, in § 4, *d*, will be applied to modify the mute stem-endings.

1. Thus, with -σ (Fut. act., First Aorist act. and mid., Perf. mid. and pass., second person sing., and imper.)—

    π-, β-, φ-, become ψ.
    κ-, γ-, χ-, ,, ξ.
    τ-, δ-, θ-, *disappear.*

2. Before -θ (pass. Fut. and First Aor.)—

    π- and β- become φ.
    κ- and γ- ,, χ.
    τ-, δ-, θ-, ,, σ.

3. Before -τ (mid. and pass. Perf. ind., third person sing.)—

    β- and φ- become π.
    γ- and χ-, ,, κ.
    τ-, δ-, θ-, ,, σ.

4. Before -μ (mid. and pass. Perf., first person sing. and plur., and Perf. participle)—

    π-, β-, φ-, become μ.
    κ- and χ- ,, γ.
    τ-, δ-, θ-, ,, σ.

§ 84, c.] MUTE VERBS—THEIR CONJUGATION. 77

5. Terminations commencing with -σθ drop the σ after a consonant; the remaining θ affecting the mute according to rule. Thus, from τρῑβ-, τέ-τριβ-σθε (mid. and pass. Perf. ind., second person plur.) becomes first τέ-τριβ-θε, then τέτριφθε.

6. The combination -ντ in the terminations of the middle and passive Perfect (-νται) and Pluperfect (-ντο) is impracticable after a consonant. Hence the form is dropped altogether, and the perfect Participle, with the substantive verb, put in its stead, as in the Perf. subj. and opt. Thus, τρῑβ- would regularly give the combination (third person plur., Perf. mid. and pass.) τέ-τριβ-νται, which cannot be dealt with by any of the foregoing laws.[1] The compound form τετριμμένοι εἰσί(ν) is therefore employed.

7. There only remains the -κ- of the Perfect active. Before this letter the dentals τ-, δ-, θ-, are *dropped*. Thus, πέ-πειθ-κα becomes πέπεικα. But when the stem-ending is a labial or a guttural, the κ is *treated as an aspirate* or *hard breathing*, the mute being changed into its corresponding aspirate, and κ disappearing. So ἄγω gives ἦχα for ἦγ-κα = ἦγ-ἁ, and τρίβω gives τέ-τρῑ-φα, from τέ-τριβ-κα = τέ-τριβ-ἁ.

PARADIGMS OF THE MUTE VERBS.

84. *a.* To facilitate comparison, all the tenses are given. It has not, however, been thought necessary to go through all the numbers and persons, excepting in the Perf. mid. and pass.

b. It will be seen that the *sharp* labial, the *flat* guttural, and the *aspirate* dental have been selected. No difficulty will be found in applying the laws of inflection to mutes of the kindred classes.

c. The verb ἄγω, beginning with a vowel, takes the temporal augment instead of the reduplication in the Perfect tenses. See § 69, *b.*

---

[1] In the older Greek writers, the ν is sometimes replaced by the aspirate ἁ. Thus the word would become τετρίφαται; but this usage is not confined to mute verbs or to the Perfect tense.

MUTE VERBS—ACTIVE. [§ 84.

	LABIAL. *p*-sounds. Stem, τρῑβ-	GUTTURAL. *k*-sounds. ἀγ-	DENTAL. *t*-sounds. πειθ-
		Active.	
		INDICATIVE.	
Present, -ω	τρίβω, *I rub*	ἄγω, *I lead*	πείθω, *I persuade*
Imperf. ἐ- . . . -ον	ἔτριβον	ἦγον	ἔπειθον
Future, -σω	τρίψω	ἄξω	πείσω
1st Aor. ἐ- . . -σα	ἔτριψα	ἦξα	ἔπεισα
Perf. redup. -α [1]	τέτριφα	ἦχα	πέπεικα
Plup. redup. -ειν	(ἐ)τετρίφειν	ἤχειν	(ἐ)πεπείκειν
		IMPERATIVE.	
Present, -ε	τρῖβε	ἄγε	πεῖθε
1st Aor. -σον	τρῖψον	ἄξον	πεῖσον
Perf. redup. -ε	τέτριφε	ἦχε	πέπεικε
		SUBJUNCTIVE.	
Present, -ω	τρίβω	ἄγω	πείθω
1st Aor. -σω	τρίψω	ἄξω	πείσω
Perf. redup. -ω	τετρίφω	ἤχω	πεπείκω
		OPTATIVE.	
Present, -οιμι	τρίβοιμι	ἄγοιμι	πείθοιμι
Future, -σοιμι	τρίψοιμι	ἄξοιμι	πείσοιμι
1st Aor. -σαιμι	τρίψαιμι	ἄξαιμι	πείσαιμι
Perf. redup. -οιμι	τετρίφοιμι	ἤχοιμι	πεπείκοιμι
		INFINITIVE.	
Present, -ειν	τρίβειν	ἄγειν	πείθειν
Future, -σειν	τρίψειν	ἄξειν	πείσειν
1st Aor. -σαι	τρῖψαι	ἄξαι	πεῖσαι
Perfect, -έναι	τετριφέναι	ἠχέναι	πεπεικέναι

[1] In labials and gutturals. See § 83, *b*, **7.**

§ 84.] MUTE VERBS—ACTIVE, MIDDLE AND PASSIVE. 73

Stem, τρῐβ-   ἀγ-   πειθ-

PARTICIPLES.

Present, -ων	τρίβων	ἄγων	πείθων
Future, -σων	τρίψων	ἄξων	πείσων
1st Aor. -σας	τρίψας	ἄξας	πείσας
Perf. redup. -ώς	τετρῐφώς	ἠχώς	πεπεικώς

Middle and Passive.
INDICATIVE.

Present, -ομαι		τρίβομαι	ἄγομαι	πείθομαι
Imperf. ἐ- ... -όμην		ἐτριβόμην	ἠγόμην	ἐπειθόμην
Perf. redup.	-μαι	τέτριμμαι	ἦγμαι	πέπεισμαι
	-σαι	τέτριψαι	ἦξαι	πέπεισαι
	-ται	τέτριπται	ἦκται	πέπεισται
	-μεθα	τετρίμμεθα	ἤγμεθα	πεπείσμεθα
	-(σ)θε	τέτριφθε	ἦχθε	πέπεισθε
	-(νται)	τετριμμένοι εἰσί(ν)	ἠγμένοι εἰσί(ν)	πεπεισμένοι εἰσί(:)
Plup. (ἐ) redup.	-μην	(ἐ)τετρίμμην	ἤγμην	(ἐ)πεπείσμην
	-σο	(ἐ)τέτριψο	ἦξο	(ἐ)πέπεισο
	-το	(ἐ)τέτριπτο	ἦκτο	(ἐ)πέπειστο
	-μεθα	(ἐ)τετρίμμεθα	ἤγμεθα	(ἐ)πεπείσμεθα
	-(σ)θε	(ἐ)τέτριφθε	ἦχθε	(ἐ)πέπεισθε
	-(ντο)	τετριμμένοι ἦσαν	ἠγμένοι ἦσαν	πεπεισμένοι ἦσαν

IMPERATIVE.

Present, -ου		τρίβου	ἄγου	πείθου
Perf. redup.	-σο	τέτριψο	ἦξο	πέπεισο
	-(σ)θω	τετρίφθω	ἤχθω	πεπείσθω
	-(σ)θε	τέτριφθε	ἦχθε	πέπεισθε
	-(σ)θωσαν	τετρίφθωσαν, or τετρίφθων	ἤχθωσαν, or ἦχθων	πεπείσθωσαν, or πεπείσθων

SUBJUNCTIVE.

Present, -ωμαι	τρίβωμαι	ἄγωμαι	πείθωμαι
Perf. part. with ὦ	τετριμμένος ὦ	ἠγμένος ὦ	πεπεισμένος ὦ

MUTE VERBS—MIDDLE AND PASSIVE. [§ 84.

	Stem, τρῑβ-	ἀγ-	πειθ-
	OPTATIVE.		
Present, -οίμην	τριβοίμην	ἀγοίμην	πειθοίμην
Perf. part. with εἴην	τετριμμένος εἴην	ἠγμένος εἴην	πεπεισμένος εἴην
	INFINITIVE.		
Present, -εσθαι	τρίβεσθαι	ἄγεσθαι	πείθεσθαι
Perfect, -(σ)θαι	τετρῖφθαι	ἦχθαι	πεπεῖσθαι
	PARTICIPLES.		
Present, -όμενος	τριβόμενος	ἀγόμενος	πειθόμενος
Perf. redup. -μένος	τετριμμένος	ἠγμένος	πεπεισμένος
	Middle only.		
	INDICATIVE.		
Future, -σομαι	τρίψομαι	ἄξομαι	πείσομαι
1st Aor. ἐ- ... -σάμην	ἐτριψάμην	ἠξάμην	ἐπεισάμην
	IMPERATIVE.		
1st Aor. -σαι	τρῖψαι	ἄξαι	πεῖσαι
	SUBJUNCTIVE.		
1st Aor. -σωμαι	τρίψωμαι	ἄξωμαι	πείσωμαι
	OPTATIVE.		
Future, -σοίμην	τριψοίμην	ἀξοίμην	πεισοίμην
1st Aor. -σαίμην	τριψαίμην	ἀξαίμην	πεισαίμην
	INFINITIVE.		
Future, -σεσθαι	τρίψεσθαι	ἄξεσθαι	πείσεσθαι
1st Aor. -σασθαι	τρίψασθαι	ἄξασθαι	πείσασθαι
	PARTICIPLES.		
Future, -σόμενος	τριψόμενος	ἀξόμενος	πεισόμενος
1st Aor. -σάμενος	τριψάμενος	ἀξάμενος	πεισάμενος

§ 85.] MUTE VERBS—PASSIVE.

	Stem, τρῑβ-	ἀγ-	πειθ-
	Passive only.		
	INDICATIVE.		
Future, -θήσομαι	τριφθήσομαι	ἀχθήσομαι	πεισθήσομαι
1st Aor. ἐ- ... -θην	ἐτρίφθην	ἤχθην	ἐπείσθην
	IMPERATIVE.		
1st. Aor. -θητι	τρίφθητι	ἄχθητι	πείσθητι
	SUBJUNCTIVE.		
1st Aor. -θῶ	τριφθῶ	ἀχθῶ	πεισθῶ
	OPTATIVE.		
Future, -θησοίμην	τριφθησοίμην	ἀχθησοίμην	πεισθησοίμην
1st Aor. -θείην	τριφθείην	ἀχθείην	πεισθείην
	INFINITIVE.		
Future, -θήσεσθαι	τριφθήσεσθαι	ἀχθήσεσθαι	πεισθήσεσθαι
1st Aor. -θῆναι	τριφθῆναι	ἀχθῆναι	πεισθῆναι
	PARTICIPLES.		
Future, -θησόμενος	τριφθησόμενος	ἀχθησόμενος	πεισθησόμενος
1st Aor. -θείς	τριφθείς	ἀχθείς	πεισθείς
	VERBALS.		
-τός and -τέος	τριπτός	ἀκτός	πειστός
	τριπτέος	ἀκτέος	πειστέος

Note.—The Future Perfect, "Paulo-post Future" (see § 65, d, 7), is once found in the New Testament (rec. text): κεκράξονται (Luke xix. 40), from κράζω (stem κραγ-, § 85, a, 2, ii.). But as this is the only instance, the tense has not been given in the paradigm. (W. H. read κράξουσιν.)

85. Before treating of the remaining class of consonant-verbs, *i.e.*, those with a liquid stem-ending, it is necessary to notice a most important modification to which very many mute verbs, as well as those of other classes, are subjected.

82 MUTE VERBS: MODIFIED STEMS. [§ 85, *a*.

a. In the examples given, the stem appears full and unaltered in the Present tense. τρίβω is from the stem τριβ-, ἄγω from ἀγ-, and πείθω from πειθ-. There are, however, many verbs in which **the stem is modified** in the formation of the **Present**. It is therefore requisite to note two main points: first, *the stem of the Verb*, from which all the tenses are derived; and secondly, *the stem of the Present*, as found in Lexicons and Vocabularies.

1. **Labial stems** are modified by the introduction of -τ- before the termination. Thus:—stem τυπ-, *strike*, Present τύπτω; stem βλαβ-, *hurt*, Present βλάπτω (for βλάβ-τ-ω, § 4, *d*, 2); stem ῥιφ-, *throw*, Present ῥίπτω (for ῥίφ-τ-ω, § 4, *d*, 2).

2. **Guttural stems** are modified by changing the stem-ending—(i.) into -σσ-, or its equivalent -ττ-; thus from the stem ταγ-, *set in order*, we have Present τάσσω or τάττω: (ii.) into -ζ-, *e.g.*, stem κραγ-, *cry out*, Present κράζω.

3. **Dental stems** are modified by changing the stem-ending into -ζ-: thus, from the stem φραδ-, *tell*, comes the Present φράζω.

> It will be seen that, as the Present termination -ζω may be derived either from a guttural or a dental stem, a knowledge of the verb will be required before deciding to which of the two to refer it.[1]

b. The tenses of these "strengthened" verbs, as they are called, are formed from the *verbal stem*, according to the rules before given. Thus—

τύπτω,	to strike,	τυπ-	fut. τύψω	perf.	τέτυφα
βλάπτω,	to hurt,	βλαβ-	,, βλάψω	,,	βέβλαφα
ῥίπτω,	to throw,	ῥιφ-	,, ῥίψω	,,	ἔρῥιφα
τάσσω,	to arrange,	ταγ-	,, τάξω	,,	τέταχα
κράζω,	to cry,	κραγ-	,, κράξω	,,	κέκραχα
φράζω,	to tell,	φραδ-	,, φράσω	,,	πέφρακα

---

[1] The original modification of guttural and dental stems was probably by the insertion of a short vowel (ι or ε) after the characteristic. So, ταγ-, ταγίω, τάσσω; φραδ-, φραδέω, φράζω. The softening occasioned by the vowel may be compared with the effect of *i* upon *t* in the termination *-tion*.

c. Every class of mute verbs (as well as others, on which see hereafter) may receive modification by the insertion of a vowel in a short stem-syllable, so as to form a diphthong. Thus, φυγ-, *flee*, gives φεύγω, and λιπ-, *leave*, λείπω. Only, in this case, the Future and Perfect are formed from the stem of the Present, as λείπω, λείψω, λέλειφα.

86. The most important point connected with the modification of the stem is the introduction, into the verbs so characterised, of a set of "**secondary**" tenses, in which the unmodified stem appears. These tenses, except in special cases, are of precisely similar meaning to the corresponding "primary" tenses. For example, the difference between the First and the **Second Aorist** is a difference of form only. The same remark can hardly be applied so unreservedly to the First and **Second Perfect**; but the instances of different meaning belong rather to the Lexicon than to the Grammar, and will be explained in the Vocabulary.

<small>A few unmodified verbs, as ἔχω, have a Second Aorist, as will be afterwards noted. Occasionally, too, the Second Aorist differs in meaning from the First. The above rule, however, is general.</small>

SECOND AORIST.

87. *a.* The Second **Aorist Active** in the Indicative resembles the **Imperfect**, in the other moods the Present, except that the Imperfect is taken from the modified, the **Second Aorist from the original stem.**

Thus, from φεύγω (φυγ-), *to flee*—

Imperfect,   ἔφευγον, ἔφευγες, ἔφευγε(ν), ἐφεύγομεν, κ.τ.λ.
Second Aorist, ἔφυγον, ἔφυγες, ἔφυγε(ν), ἐφύγομεν, κ.τ.λ.

The augment and the terminations of the two tenses will be seen to be exactly alike.

In the moods after the Indicative, the Second Aorist drops the augment and follows the Present in termination, but accentuates the final syllable of the Infinitive (perispomenon) and Participle (oxytone).

With these explanations, the Second Aorist Active paradigm will present no difficulty.

τύπτω, to strike.   λείπω, to leave.

	Stem, τυπ-	λιπ-
Indicative,	ἔτυπον	ἔλιπον
Imperative,	τύπε	λίπε
Subjunctive,	τύπω	λίπω
Optative,	τύποιμι	λίποιμι
Infinitive,	τυπεῖν	λιπεῖν
Participle,	τυπών, -οῦσα, -όν	λιπών

b. The **Second Aorist Middle** follows exactly the same analogy. The Imperative, however, is perispomenon, the Infinitive paroxytone.

Indicative,	ἐτυπόμην	ἐλιπόμην
Imperative,	τυποῦ	λιποῦ
Subjunctive,	τύπωμαι	λίπωμαι
Optative,	τυποίμην	λιποίμην
Infinitive,	τυπέσθαι	λιπέσθαι
Participle,	τυπόμενος	λιπόμενος

c. **Second Aorist Passive.**—Here the mood and tense-endings are like those of the passive First Aorist, the difference being that the unmodified root is used instead of the aspirated form with -θ-. First Aorist, ἐτύφθην; Second Aorist, ἐτύπην. In the Imperative second person, -θι is found instead of -τι. One paradigm of this tense will suffice:—

Indicative,	ἐτύπην	Optative,	τυπείην
Imperative,	τύπηθι, τυπήτω	Infinitive,	τυπῆναι
Subjunctive,	τυπῶ	Part.	τυπείς, τυπεῖσα, τυπέν

SECOND FUTURE.

88. In the **Passive voice** there is a **Second Future** connected with the Second Aorist, exactly as the First Future is connected with the First Aorist. Thus, from τύπτω we have—First Aor. pass., ἐτύφθην;

§ 90.]   SECOND FUTURE AND SECOND PERFECT.   85

First Fut., τυφθήσομαι; Second Aor., ἐτύπην; Second Fut., τυπήσομαι. The paradigm is as follows :—

| Indicative, | τυπήσομαι | Infinitive, | τυπήσεσθαι |
| Optative, | τυπησοίμην | Participle, | τυπησόμενος |

SECOND PERFECT.

89. The **Second Perfect** belongs to the **Active voice only,** and is distinguished from the **ordinary** Perfect of mute verbs by having the **unmodified stem** without the aspirate. Thus: τύπτω (τυπ-), First Perf., τέτυφα; Second Perf., τέτυπα. The tense is of rare occurrence, and its special significance will have to be explained in individual cases. It occurs in some verbs that do not modify their stem. The **Second Pluperfect** accompanies it where found. One paradigm here also will be sufficient. Second Perfect of πράσσω (πραγ-), *to do* :—

Indicative,	πέπραγα	Optative,	πεπράγοιμι
„ Plup.	(ἐ)πεπράγειν	Imperative,	πέπραγε
Subjunctive,	πεπράγω	Infinitive,	πεπραγέναι
Participle,	πεπραγώς, -υῖα, -ός.

90.   GENERAL RULES FOR THE SECOND TENSES.

1. These do not occur in the pure verbs, or in verbs having a **dental, τ, δ, θ (ζ),** for their characteristic.

2. **The same verb very seldom takes both First and Second Aorist in the Active or Middle.**

3. The Passive may have both First and Second Aorist and Future.

4. When both First and Second Perfect active are found, the **former** is often **transitive,** the **latter intransitive.** πέπραχα, *I have done;* πέπραγα, *I have fared* (compare English, "How do you *do?*").

REMARK.—For the vowel-modifications of the second tenses, see the sections on Tense-formation, §§ 93—99.

Exercise 11.—On Mute Verbs.

[*Vocabulary, from the "Sermon on the Mount."*—(1) LABIAL STEMS: βλέπω, *to see;* ἀλείφω, *to anoint;* θλίβω, *to straiten;* κρύπτω, *to hide;* νίπτω, *to wash;* στρέφω, *to turn;* τρέφω (θρεφ-), *to nourish.*

(2) GUTTURAL STEMS: ἄγω, to lead; διώκω, to pursue; ἔχω (ἐχ), to have; λέγω, to say; προσεύχομαι, to pray (dep.). (3) DENTAL STEMS: ψεύδομαι, to lie (dep.); ὀνειδίζω, to reproach; δοξάζω, to glorify; νομίζω, to suppose; νήθω, to spin; ἁγιάζω, to hallow.]

Analyse and translate the following words:—δεδιωγμένοι, ὀνειδίσωσιν, διώξουσι, ψευδόμενοι, ἐδίωξαν, κρυβῆναι, δοξάσωσι, νομίσητε, ἔχει, στρέψον, προσεύχεσθε, διωκόντων, ἔχετε, βλέπων, προσεύχῃ, πρόσευξαι, προσευχόμενοι, ἁγιασθήτω, ἄλειψαι, νίψαι, βλέπων, κλέπτουσι, νήθει, λέγοντες, στράφεντες (see § 98, d), τεθλιμμένη.

Also the following: ἤλειψε, ἡγιασμένοι, ἁγιάσαι, ἐδίωκον, κεκρυμμένα, κρύψατε, εἶχον, ἕξω, ἔχον, ἐψεύσω, ψεύσασθαι, ἐθρέψαμεν, νίψῃς, ἔστρεψε, λεγόμενος, λεχθείς, προσηύχετο, προσευξάμενοι, θρέψω.

LIQUID VERBS.

91. Verbs with the stem-endings λ, μ, ν or ρ, present many variations from the foregoing models, which will be noticed in the sections on Tense-formation. It will be sufficient, as introductory to the paradigms, to observe—

a. The **stem** of these verbs is **generally modified in the Present**: e.g., stem ἀγγελ-, *announce*, Present act. ἀγγέλλω; φαν-, *appear*, Pres. φαίνω.

b. The **Future active originally ended in** -έσω, middle -έσομαι; but the σ being dropped (see a similar case in Nouns, § 30, iv.), two vowels are brought together, and **contraction ensues**. Thus, ἀγγελ-, Fut. (ἀγγελέ-σ-ω, ἀγγελέ-ω), ἀγγελῶ; middle (ἀγγελ-έ-σ-ομαι, ἀγγελ-έ-ομαι), ἀγγελοῦμαι. The Future active and middle of liquid verbs is therefore **declined like the Present of contracted pure verbs with stem-ending ε-**.

c. The **First Aorist** active and middle follows the Future in the omission of the σ, but **lengthens the vowel of the preceding syllable**. Thus:—

φαίνω	φᾰν-,	fut.	φανῶ	1st Aor.	ἔφηνα
ἀγγέλλω	ἀγγελ-,	,,	ἀγγελῶ	,,	ἤγγειλα
κρίνω	κρῐν-,	,,	κρινῶ	,,	ἔκρῑνα
σύρω	σῠρ-,	,,	συρῶ	,,	ἔσῡρα

d. In the **Perfect active**, as ν- and μ- cannot come before -κ, various expedients are adopted. κρίνω, *to judge,* κλίνω, *to bend,* πλύνω, *to wash,* drop the ν (κέκρικα, etc.). Other verbs, as φαίνω, adopt a Second Perfect, lengthening the vowel as in the Aorist (πέφηνα). Others, again, form the Perfect as from a pure root in ε-, as μένω, *to remain,* μεμένηκα, as if from μενέω.

e. In the **Perfect passive**, ν- is changed into σ- or into μ- before -μαι; thus, from φαν-, πέφασμαι instead of πέφαν-μαι, and from ξηραν-, ἐξήραμμαι instead of ἐξήραν-μαι. The three verbs which drop ν- before -κα in the Perfect active, lose it also in the Perfect and First Aorist passive. Thus, κέκριμαι, ἐκρίθην. Those verbs which assume a root in ε- for the Perfect active, construct the passive Perfect and First Aorist after the same analogy.

92. PARADIGMS.

Stem,	ἀγγελ-	κρῐν-	ἀρ-
Strengthened,	ἀγγελλ-	κρῑν-	αἰρ-

Active.
INDICATIVE.

Present,	ἀγγέλλω	κρίνω	αἴρω
Imperfect,	ἤγγελλον	ἔκρινον	ἦρον
Future sing.	ἀγγελῶ	κρινῶ	ἀρῶ
„ „	ἀγγελεῖς	κρινεῖς	ἀρεῖς
„ „	ἀγγελεῖ	κρινεῖ	ἀρεῖ
„ plur.	ἀγγελοῦμεν	κρινοῦμεν	ἀροῦμεν
„ „	ἀγγελεῖτε	κρινεῖτε	ἀρεῖτε
„ „	ἀγγελοῦσι(ν)	κρινοῦσι(ν)	ἀροῦσι(ν)
1st Aorist,	ἤγγειλα	ἔκρῑνα	ἦρα
Perfect,	ἤγγελκα	κέκρῐκα	ἦρκα
Pluperfect,	ἠγγέλκειν	(ἐ)κεκρίκειν	ἤρκειν
2nd Aorist,	ἤγγελον		ἦρον

LIQUID VERBS—PARADIGMS. [§ 92.

	Stem, ἀγγελ-	κρῖν-	ἀρ-
	Strengthened, ἀγγελλ-	κρῖν-	αἰρ-

IMPERATIVE.

Present,	ἄγγελλε	κρῖνε	αἶρε
1st Aorist,	ἄγγειλον	κρῖνον	ἆρον
Perfect,	ἤγγελκε	κεκρίκε	ἦρκε
2nd Aorist,	ἄγγελε		ἆρε

SUBJUNCTIVE.

Present,	ἀγγέλλω	κρίνω	αἴρω
1st Aorist,	ἀγγείλω	κρίνω	ἄρω
Perfect,	ἠγγέλκω	κεκρίκω	ἤρκω
2nd Aorist,	ἀγγέλω		ἄρω

OPTATIVE.

Present,	ἀγγέλλοιμι	κρίνοιμι	αἴροιμι
Future,	ἀγγελοῖμι or -οίην	κρινοῖμι or -οίην	ἀροῖμι or -οίη·
1st Aorist,	ἀγγείλαιμι	κρίναιμι	ἄραιμι
Perfect,	ἠγγέλκοιμι	κεκρίκοιμι	ἤρκοιμι
2nd Aorist,	ἀγγέλοιμι		ἄροιμι

INFINITIVE.

Present,	ἀγγέλλειν	κρίνειν	αἴρειν
Future,	ἀγγελεῖν	κρινεῖν	ἀρεῖν
1st Aorist,	ἀγγεῖλαι	κρῖναι	ἆραι
Perfect,	ἠγγελκέναι	κεκρικέναι	ἠρκέναι
2nd Aorist,	ἀγγελεῖν		ἀρεῖν

PARTICIPLES.

Present,	ἀγγέλλων	κρίνων	αἴρων
Future,	ἀγγελῶν	κρινῶν	ἀρῶν
1st Aorist,	ἀγγείλας	κρίνας	ἄρας
Perfect,	ἠγγελκώς	κεκρικώς	ἠρκώς
2nd Aorist,	ἀγγελών		ἀρών

§ 92.]   LIQUID VERBS—PARADIGMS.   89

Stem, ἀγγελ-   κρῐν-   ἀρ-
Strengthened, ἀγγελλ-   κρῑν-   αἰρ-

Middle and Passive.
INDICATIVE.

Present,	ἀγγέλλομαι	κρίνομαι	αἴρομαι
Imperfect,	ἠγγελλόμην	ἐκρινόμην	ἠρόμην
Perfect,	ἤγγελμαι	κέκρῐμαι	ἦρμαι
Pluperfect,	ἠγγέλμην	(ἐ)κεκρίμην	ἤρμην

IMPERATIVE.

Present,	ἀγγέλλου	κρίνου	αἴρου
Perfect,	ἤγγελσο, -θω κ.τ.λ.	κέκρισο, -σθω	ἦρσο, ἤρθω

SUBJUNCTIVE.

Present,	ἀγγέλλωμαι	κρίνωμαι	αἴρωμαι
Perfect,	ἠγγελμένος ὦ	κεκριμένος ὦ	ἠρμένος ὦ

OPTATIVE.

Present,	ἀγγελλοίμην	κρινοίμην	αἰροίμην
Perfect,	ἠγγελμένος εἴην	κεκριμένος εἴην	ἠρμένος εἴην

INFINITIVE.

Present,	ἀγγέλλεσθαι	κρίνεσθαι	αἴρεσθαι
Perfect,	ἠγγέλθαι	κεκρίσθαι	ἦρθαι

PARTICIPLES.

Present,	ἀγγελλόμενος	κρινόμενος	αἰρόμενος
Perfect,	ἠγγελμένος	κεκριμένος	ἠρμένος

Middle only.
INDICATIVE.

Future,	ἀγγελοῦμαι	κρινοῦμαι	ἀροῦμαι
1st Aorist,	ἠγγειλάμην	ἐκρινάμην	ἠράμην
2nd Aorist,	ἀγγελόμην		ἠρόμην

LIQUID VERBS—PARADIGMS.

	Stem,	ἀγγελ-	κριν-	ἀρ-
	Strengthened,	ἀγγελλ-	κρῑν-	αἰρ-

	IMPERATIVE.		
1st Aorist,	ἄγγειλαι	κρῖναι	ἆραι
2nd Aorist,	ἀγγελοῦ		ἀροῦ

	SUBJUNCTIVE.		
1st Aorist,	ἀγγείλωμαι	κρίνωμαι	ἄρωμαι
2nd Aorist,	ἀγγέλωμαι		ἄρωμαι

	OPTATIVE.		
Future,	ἀγγελοίμην	κρινοίμην	ἀροίμην
1st Aorist,	ἀγγειλαίμην	κριναίμην	ἀραίμην
2nd Aorist,	ἀγγελοίμην		ἀροίμην

	INFINITIVE.		
Future,	ἀγγελεῖσθαι	κρινεῖσθα	ἀρεῖσθαι
1st Aorist,	ἀγγείλασθαι	κρίνασθαι	ἄρασθαι
2nd Aorist,	ἀγγελέσθαι		ἀρέσθαι

	PARTICIPLES.		
Future,	ἀγγελούμενος	κρινούμενος	ἀρούμενος
1st Aorist,	ἀγγειλάμενος	κρινάμενος	ἀράμενος
2nd Aorist,	ἀγγελόμενος		ἀρόμενος

Passive only.

	INDICATIVE.		
1st Future,	ἀγγελθήσομαι	κριθήσομαι	ἀρθήσομαι
1st Aorist,	ἠγγέλθην	ἐκρίθην	ἤρθην
2nd Aorist,	ἠγγέλην		ἤρην
2nd Future,	ἀγγελήσομαι		ἀρήσομαι

	IMPERATIVE.		
1st Aorist,	ἀγγέλθητι	κρίθητι	ἄρθητι
2nd Aorist,	ἀγγέληθι		ἄρηθι

§ 92.] LIQUID VERBS.

	Stem, ἀγγελ- Strengthened, ἀγγελλ-	κρῐν- κρῑν-	ἀρ- αἰρ-
	SUBJUNCTIVE.		
1st Aorist,	ἀγγελθῶ	κριθῶ	ἀρθῶ
2nd Aorist,	ἀγγελῶ		ἀρῶ
	OPTATIVE.		
1st Future,	ἀγγελθησοίμην	κριθησοίμην	ἀρθησοίμην
1st Aorist,	ἀγγελθείην	κριθείην	ἀρθείην
2nd Aorist,	ἀγγελείην		ἀρείην
2nd Future,	ἀγγελησοίμην		ἀρησοίμην
	INFINITIVE.		
1st Future,	ἀγγελθήσεσθαι	κριθήσεσθαι	ἀρθήσεσθαι
1st Aorist,	ἀγγελθῆναι	κριθῆναι	ἀρθῆναι
2nd Aorist,	ἀγγελῆναι		ἀρῆναι
2nd Future,	ἀγγελήσεσθαι		ἀρήσεσθαι
	PARTICIPLES.		
1st Future,	ἀγγελθησόμενος	κριθησόμενος	ἀρθησόμενος
1st Aorist,	ἀγγελθείς	κριθείς	ἀρθείς
2nd Aorist,	ἀγγελείς		ἀρείς
2nd Future,	ἀγγελησόμενος		ἀρησόμενος
	VERBALS.		
	ἀγγελτός	κριτός	ἀρτός
	ἀγγελτέος	κριτέος	ἀρτέος

*** It is not to be supposed that all the above forms are actually in use. They are given as παραδείγματα, *examples*, of words that may occur.

Exercise 12.—On Liquid Verbs.

[*Vocabulary, from the "Sermon on the Mount."*—αὐξάνω, *to grow, to increase;* βάλλω, *to throw, cast;* θέλω, *to will* (augment with η, comp. § 94, II.); κρίνω, *to judge;* μωραίνω, *to corrupt;* σπείρω, *to sow;* φαίνω, *to show* (Second Aorist, passive or middle, *appear*); χαίρω, *to rejoice.*]

LIQUID VERBS. [§ 92.

Analyse and translate the following forms :—χαίρετε, μωρανθῇ, βληθῆναι (see § 98, c.), βληθήσῃ, βάλε, βληθῇ, θέλοντι, κριθῆναι, φανῇς, σπείρουσιν, αὐξάνει, βαλλόμενον, κριθῆτε, κριθήσεσθε, βάλητε, θέλητε.

Also the following :—θέλει, ἤθελον, ἠθέλησα, θέλοντες, κρίνει, κρινεῖ, κρίνατε, ἐμωράνθησαν, ἐμώρανεν, σπείρων, σπαρείς, ἐσπαρμένον, ἐφάνη, φαίνεσθε, φανεῖται, βάλε, βλήθητι, βάλλειν, βαλεῖν, βάλλω, βαλῶ.

NOTES ON THE TENSES.

93. The foregoing paradigms have fully given the **typical forms** of the First Conjugation, *i.e.*, of the great majority of verbs, and of most of the tenses in *all* verbs. Many minute variations must now be noticed, with apparent irregularities, which for the most part can themselves be reduced to rule, or explained by some early usage of the language.

Accentuation.—It may be repeated at the outset from § 73, that *verbal forms mostly retract the accent, i.e.*, throw it back as far as possible. Exceptions are noted below under the different Tenses. When the accent falls on the penultimate, *e.g.*, in dissyllables, a long vowel is circumflexed, in certain forms, as has been already shown.

THE PRESENT AND IMPERFECT: ACTIVE, MIDDLE, AND PASSIVE.

94. I. The PRESENT INDICATIVE ACTIVE, first person (the form usually given in Lexicons, Vocabularies, and Concordances[1]) contains the verbal stem, **often modified.**

The principal forms of modified stem are as follows :—

1. Labial stem-endings, strengthened by τ-. (See § 85, *a*, 1.)
2. Short stem-syllables lengthened. (See § 85, *c*.)
3. The euphonic σσ-, ττ-, for a guttural characteristic; ζ- for a dental, or occasionally for γ-. (See § 85, *a*, 2, 3.)
4. λλ- for the characteristic λ-. (See *note*, § 85.)

---

[1] Bruder's Concordance, 4to (Tauchnitz), gives the Present *Infinitive*.

§ 94.] ON TENSE-FORMATION. 93

5. The letter ν- affixed to the stem-syllable.
This may take place in different ways.

a. To a pure stem, simply affixed:
Thus, from φθα-, φθάνω, *to anticipate*.
from πι-, πίνω, *to drink*.

b. Two consonant stems follow this model:
from καμ-, κάμνω, *to be weary*.
from δακ-, δάκνω, *to bite*.

c. One affixes νε-, ἀφικ-, ἀφικνέομαι, *to arrive*.

d. To a pure stem lengthened, two verbs only:
from βα-, βαίνω, *to go*.
from ἐλα-, ἐλαύνω, *to drive*.

e. To a consonant stem, with connective α:
from ἁμαρτ-, ἁμαρτάνω, *to sin*.
from λαβ-, λαμβάνω, *to take*.

In the last-mentioned verb it will be seen that μ is also inserted in the stem-syllable. This is for -ν- (made μ before a labial, § 4, d, 5). So μανθάνω, *to learn*, from μαθ-, and other verbs. The stem appears in the Second Aorist, ἥμαρτον, ἔλαβον, ἔμαθον.

6. An alternative pure stem in ε-.

This appears generally in the Future, Aorist, and Perfect.

Thus, ἐχ- and σχε-, *to have*, ἔχω, ἕξω, or σχήσω, ἔσχηκα; Second Aor., ἔσχον.
θελ- and θελε- (also ἐθελ-), *to will*, θέλω, θελήσω, ἐθέλησα.
μεν- and μενε-, *to remain*, μένω, μεμένηκα.

Occasionally the ε-stem appears in the Pres. Thus, δοκ- and δοκε-, *to appear*, δοκῶ (δοκέω), δόξω, ἔδοξα.
Some of the verbs under 5, e, have a similar alternative stem. Thus, from ἁμαρτάνω we find ἁμαρτήσω, ἡμάρτηκα.

7. The *inchoative* form (so called because some verbs of this class denote the *beginning* of an action), in σκ- or ισκ-.

Pure stems add -σκ-, generally lengthening a short stem-vowel. So, θνα-, transposed from θαν-, *to die*, θνήσκω, ἔθανον, Perf. τέθνηκα.
Consonant stems add -ισκ-, and often, as in 6, have an alternative stem in ε-. Thus, εὑρ-, εὑρε-, *to find*, εὑρίσκω, εὑρήσω, εὕρηκα, εὗρον. πάσχω, *to suffer* (παθ-, with alternative stem, πενθ-), has Second Aor. ἔπαθον, Second Perf. πέπονθα. διδάσκω, *to teach*, originally from δα-, assumes a mute guttural stem: Fut., διδάξω; First Aor. pass., ἐδιδάχθην.
Verbs of this class are very various in form, as exhibited in the Lexicon or Vocabulary.

8. Reduplicated stems, the initial consonant repeated with ι.
Four verbs of this class are of very common occurrence.

a. γίνομαι (deponent intransitive), *to become,* stem γεν-, by reduplication γιγεν-, shortened into γιγν-, the second γ- being dropped for the sake of euphony; Impf., ἐγινόμην; Inf., γίνεσθαι; Second Aor., ἐγενόμην, γενέσθαι.

b. γινώσκω, *to become acquainted with, to know.* Stem γνο-, which becomes γνωσκ-, after the model of class 7; then by reduplication γιγνωσκ-, when γ- is dropped, as in the last instance; Fut., γνώσομαι; Perf., ἔγνωκα; Second Aor., ἔγνων (like second conjugation).

c. μιμνήσκομαι, *to remember* (deponent), from μνα-, μνήσομαι, ἐμνήσθην, μέμνημαι.

d. πίπτω, *to fall.* This is not a labial verb strengthened by τ-. Its root is πετ-, by reduplication πιπετ-. The weak vowel -ε- is then dropped, leaving πιπτ-. Second Aor., ἔπεσον, the σ- being softened from τ-; Fut., πεσοῦμαι; Perf., πέπτωκα. (Compare § 96, *d.*)

II. THE IMPERFECT TENSE **always follows the stem of the Present,** the Augment being prefixed.

For the Augment, consult § 69. After the Augment, an initial -ρ- is doubled, as from ῥύομαι; Impf., ἐῤῥυόμην; First Aor., ἐῤῥύσθην. A few verbs have the *Attic double augment* η instead of ε. Thus, μέλλω, *to be about to do* a thing, has ἔμελλον and ἤμελλον interchangeably. ὁράω, *to see,* has a double augment also: Impf., ἑώρων; Perf., ἑώρακα. (See further under the Aorist, § 97.)

THE SECOND AORIST, ACTIVE AND MIDDLE.

95. This is the **simplest of the Tenses** (see § 87), and in general contains **the exact verbal stem.** Hence it is **mainly found in verbs whose Present-stem is modified.** So Imperf., ἔτυπτον; Second Aor., ἔτυπον. In one verb, ἄγω, *to lead,* where the Present-stem is unmodified, the Second Aorist is distinguished from the Imperfect by a reduplication: Impf., ἦγον; Second Aor., ἤγαγον; Inf., ἀγαγεῖν.

Note.—Some short stem-syllables with ε- change this into α- in the Second Aorist, as from σπείρω, *to sow* (σπερ-), ἔσπαρον.

The Vowel Aorist.—A few pure stems (like the second conjugation, or " verbs in -μι") affix the tense-endings to the stem, with lengthened vowel, rejecting the usual modal vowel.

Thus, γινώσκω (γνο-, see § 94, 8, *b*), ἔγνων.
δύνω, *to set* (as the sun) (δυ-), ἔδυν.
βαίνω, *to go* (βα-), ἔβην.

For the conjugation of these forms, see paradigms of verbs in -μι.

Accentuation.—The Second Aorist active infinitive circumflexes the final syllable: τυπεῖν; in the participle accents the stem-syllable -οντ, with a circumflex on the fem. where possible: τυπών, τυποῦσα, τυπόν. In the middle the imperative is perispomenon, τυποῦ; the inf. paroxytone, τυπέσθαι.

The Future, Active and Middle.

96. For the relation between the Future stem and the simple stem of the verb, consult § 85, *b, c*.

a. In **pure stems**, the **vowel is lengthened** before the Future characteristic -σ-. The stem-endings α- and ε- become η- ; ο- becomes ω- ; ι- and υ- are made long. Thus, τιμάω, τιμήσω; φιλέω, φιλήσω; δηλόω, δηλώσω; λύω, λύσω.

Exceptions: (i.) α- becomes ᾱ- after a vowel or ρ. Thus:—

   ἐάω, *to permit,*   Fut. ἐάσομαι.
   ἰάομαι, *to heal,*   ,,   ἰάσομαι.
   πειράομαι, *to try,*   ,,   πειράσομαι.
  So, πεινάω, *to hunger,* ,,   πεινάσω.
   χαλάω, *to loosen,*   ,,   χαλάσω.

But χράομαι, *to use,* makes χρήσομαι.

(ii.) The following verbs do not lengthen their stem-endings for the Future[1]:—

  α-forms: γελάω, *to laugh,*   Fut. γελάσω.
      κλάω, *to break,*   ,   κλάσω.
  ε-forms: ἀρκέω, *to suffice,*   ,,   ἀρκέσω.
      ἐπαινέω, *to praise,*   ,,   ἐπαινέσω.
      καλέω, *to call,*   ,,   καλέσω.
      τελέω, *to finish,*   ,,   τελέσω.
      φορέω, *to carry,*   ,,   φορέσω.

b. Verbs in ίζω (stem ιδ-) *usually* **drop the** -σ- Future characteristic, replacing it by a **contraction** similar to that of the liquid verbs. This form is called the **Attic Future**.

---

[1] Some of these verbs are *regular* in classic Greek.

Thus: ἀφορίζω, *to separate*,   makes Fut. ἀφοριῶ.
ἐλπίζω, *to hope*,   „   ἐλπιῶ.
κομίζω, *to carry*,   „   κομιῶ, mid. κομιοῦμαι.
καθαρίζω, *to purify*,   „   καθαριῶ and καθαρίσω.
βαπτίζω, *to baptize*,   „   βαπτίσω only.
σαλπίζω, *to sound a trumpet*,   „   σαλπίσω only.[1]

But the verbs of this class which drop -σ- in the Future, resume it in the First Aorist; so far differing from the liquid verbs.

c. Three verbs in -έω, originally -έϝω, **show the digamma** (see § 29, iii.) **in inflection as ν**:—

πλέω, *to sail*,   Fut. πλεύσομαι.
πνέω, *to blow*,   „   πνεύσω.
ῥέω, *to flow*,   „   ῥεύσω.

Another digammated verb, χέω, *to pour*, omits the σ altogether, and conforms to the Attic Future, retaining, however, the ε before the circumflexed final: ἐκχεῶ, *I will pour forth* (Acts ii. 17).

In this class the First Aorist characteristic conforms to that of the Future. So ἔπνευσα. From ἐκχεῶ is formed First Aor. ἐξέχεα, uncontracted.

To the digammated verbs may be referred καίω, *to burn*, Fut. καύσω; κλαίω, *to weep*, Fut. κλαύσω and κλαύσομαι (Luke vi. 25; Rev. xviii. 9). (See *d*.)

d. Several active verbs of frequent occurrence have a **Future** in the **middle form**, still with **active meaning**; as—

ἀκούω, *to hear*,   Fut. ἀκούσομαι, or ἀκούσω.
ζάω, *to live*,   „   ζήσομαι, or ζήσω.
λαμβάνω, *to take*,   „   λήψομαι (from λαβ-, ληψ-).
θαυμάζω, *to wonder*,   „   θαυμάσομαι, once.
φεύγω, *to flee*,   „   φεύξομαι.
πίνω, *to drink*,   „   πίομαι, -εσαι, -εται (Luke xvii. 8).

THE FIRST AORIST, ACTIVE AND MIDDLE.

97. *a.* **Connection of the Aorist stem with that of the Future.**—
(1) In the **pure** and **mute** verbs, the σ of the Future is retained.
(2) In the liquid verbs, the Aorist lengthens a short vowel before the

---

[1] In classic Greek, σαλπίγξω, from stem σαλπιγγ-.

stem-ending. Thus, σπερ-, *to sow;* Fut., σπερῶ; First Aor., ἔσπειρα; and from ἀγγελ-, ἤγγειλα.

Verbs in αίνω, from the stem -ᾰν-, generally have ᾰ in the Future, ᾱ in the First Aorist. So, λευκαίνω, *to whiten;* Fut., λευκᾰνῶ; First Aor., ἐλεύκᾱνα. σημαίνω, *to signify;* First Aor. inf., σημᾶναι (Acts xxv. 27). Similarly, ἐπιφᾶναι (Luke i. 79), from ἐπι, φαίνω,[1] *to show, appear.* But κερδαίνω, *to gain,* Fut. κερδᾰνῶ, makes ἐκέρδησα, as from an alternative pure root, κερδα-.

b. Peculiarities of Augment.—The double augment is occasionally found: ἀνοίγω, *to open,* ἀνέῳξα, also ἤνοιξα. **Compound verbs prefix the augment to the verbal stem;** but where the compound has lost its force, or has usurped the place of the simple verb, the augment may precede the whole verb. Thus, from προφητεύω, ἐπροφήτευσα, instead of προεφήτευσα. The prefix εὐ, *well,* is sometimes augmented into ηὐ-, sometimes left unaltered. But a verbal stem after εὐ, beginning with α, ε, ο, is itself augmented. So, from εὐαγγελίζομαι, *to preach the Gospel,* we have εὐηγγελισάμην, not ηὐαγγελισάμην.

The root ἀγ-, *to break* (second conjugation, ἄγνυμι (with prefix κατα-, makes First Aor. κατέαξα (John xix. 32), instead of κάτηξα. But as the ε is found in the Future of the same verb (κατεάξει, Matt. xii. 20), and in the Second Aor. subj. pass. (κατεαγῶσι, John xix. 31), it may mark a collateral form of the verb, and not be intended as an augment.[2]

The Aorist augment of the verb αἴρω (see § 92) is variously printed ᾐ or ἤ. The latter is correct, as it is the *simple* stem which is lengthened.

Note.—Some verbs in the LXX. have a kind of compound Aorist tense ("Alexandrian"), like the First in termination, but like the Second in tense-form: *i.e.,* attaching First Aorist terminations to the simple verbal stem. So in classic Greek, ἤνεγκον or ἤνεγκα. (See § 103, 6.) An instance in the New Testament of the Alexandrian Aorist is Heb. ix. 12, εὑράμενος. Many others occur in the most ancient MSS., and have been adopted into critical editions, as ἔπεσαν (compare § 94, 8, *d*), and εἶπα in different numbers and persons; in imper., εἰπάτωσαν (Acts xxiv. 20).

Accentuation.—The active First Aor. Infinitive accents the penultima, circumflexing all diphthongs and long vowels, as φυλάξαι, πιστεῦσαι. The act. Optative third person sing. has an acute accent on the same syllable, the αι being here regarded as long, as πιστεύσαι. The same form again is found in the middle Imperative; the αι, as usual, being treated as short, and the accent thrown back, as πίστευσαι. Only in monosyllabic stems, where the accent must be on the penultima, a long vowel is circumflexed, as λῦσαι. To present the three cases at one view:—Act. Opt., 1st Aor., third pers. sing., πιστεύσαι λύσαι φυλάξαι.
Active, 1st Aorist, infinitive, πιστεῦσαι λῦσαι φυλάξαι.
Middle, 1st Aorist, imperative, πίστευσαι λῦσαι φύλαξαι.

---

[1] The classical First Aor. of φαίνω is ἔφηνα.
[2] Or it may be simply to distinguish the forms from those of κατάγω, *to lead down.*

THE AORISTS AND FUTURES PASSIVE.

98. *a.* The First Aorist, Future and Perfect (with the Pluperfect) Passive, have generally the **same modification of the verbal root.** Thus, from τιμα-, ἐτιμήθην, τετίμημαι; from λυ-, ἐλύθην, λυθήσομαι, λέλυμαι; and from πειθ-, ἐπείσθην, πεισθήσομαι, πέπεισμαι. To know one of these Tenses is, therefore, a help to the knowledge of the rest. But σώζω, *to save,* makes ἐσώθην and σέσωσμαι.

b. The **chief variation** in the stem-syllable of these tenses from the ordinary model is in the case of **pure verbs.** Usually, these **lengthen the vowel stem-ending.** In several verbs, however, the short vowel remains, as in ἐδέθην, ἐλύθην, and others. In many, again, the **letter σ is inserted** after the stem, as in ἐτελέσθην (Perf., τετέλεσμαι), ἐχαλάσθην (2 Cor. xi. 33), and from ῥύομαι, *to deliver,* ἐρύσθην (2 Tim. iv. 17). Thus, also, from ἀκούω, *to hear,* ἠκούσθην, ἀκουσθήσομαι, ἤκουσμαι.

c. The **transposition of a vowel and liquid,** in short monosyllabic roots, is very common in these tenses. Thus, βαλ-, *to throw,* becomes βλα-, and gives ἐβλήθην, βληθήσομαι, βέβλημαι. The root καλε-, *to call,* is treated as καλ-, κλα-; First Aor. Pass., ἐκλήθην; Fut., κληθήσομαι; Perf., κέκλημαι.

d. A **weak vowel in a short liquid stem is often changed into α.** This rule generally applies to the Perfects Active and Passive, and to the Aorists and Futures Passive (sometimes also to the Second Aorist Active: see § 95, *note*). Thus, from ἀποστέλλω, *to send forth* (στελ-), ἀπέσταλκα, ἀπέσταλμαι, ἀπεστάλην, ἀποσταλήσομαι. The verb πίνω, *to drink* (καταπίνω, *to swallow*), changes ι into ο. So we find πέπωκα, κατεπόθην, καταποθήσομαι.

e. The First Aorist and Future Passive are chiefly found in pure stems and derivative verbs; the Second in original consonant-verbs. Where, too, the First would give an inharmonious concurrence of letters, the Second will generally be employed. Both are seldom used in the same verb. But a verb that has the First Aorist in the Active may have the Second in the Passive, and *vice versâ.*

For the usage of particular verbs, consult the Vocabulary. πλήσσω, πληγ-, *to strike,* makes second Aor. ἐπλήγην; but in compounds η becomes α, as ἐξεπλάγησαν (Luke ii. 48); φύω, *to grow,* has the Second Aor. participle φυέν (Luke viii. 6, 8).

Irregularities of Augment in the Aorists Passive.—κατελήφθη, in many copies of John viii. 4; ἀπεκατεστάθη (ε after both prepositions): Matt. xii. 13. From ἀνοίγω

[§ 99, c.] ON TENSE-FORMATION. 99

(compare § 99, a, 3) we find ἠνοίχθην, ἀνεῴχθην, ἠνεῴχθην; and Second Aor. ἠνοίγην, with Second Future ἀνοιγήσομαι.

Accentuation.—The Aorists Passive circumflex the Subjunctive mood-vowel throughout, and the penultima of the Inf. -ῆναι. The participle accents the stem-syllable -εντ throughout, with a circumflex on the fem. wherever possible.

Thus: λυθείς,   λυθεῖσα,   λυθέν,
λυθέντος,   λυθείσης,   λυθέντος, κ.τ.λ.

THE PERFECT AND PLUPERFECT, ACTIVE, MIDDLE, AND PASSIVE.

99. *a.* For the **Reduplication**, see § 69. The **following variations** must be noted:—

1. A verb **beginning with two consonants**, other than a mute followed by a liquid, **or with a double consonant, takes** ε. Thus, στεφανόω, *to crown*, ἐστεφάνωκα, ἐστεφάνωμαι; ξηραίνω, *to wither*, ἐξήραμμαι. So when ν follows γ-, as from γνο-, ἔγνωκα.

2. The verb λάμβανω, λαβ-, takes εἰ- instead of the reduplication,[1] εἴληφα.

3. Some verbs beginning with α, ε, or ο take a **double reduplication** in the active.

ἀκούω, *to hear*, ἀκήκοα.
(ἐλυθ-), *to come*, ἐλήλυθα (see § 103, 2).

The verb ἀνοίγω (see §§ 97, 98) may have a double reduplication in the perf. pass., ἠνεῳγμένη (Rev. iv. 1).

4. The PLUPERFECT in the New Testament **generally omits the augment**, taking only the reduplication, as τεθεμελίωτο, *it had been founded* (Matt. vii. 25).

b. For the **termination of the Active Perfect third person plural**, many MSS. frequently give -αν, like the First Aor. In John xvii. 7 the rec. text reads ἔγνωκαν.

c. The SECOND PERFECT active takes the termination of the First without the characteristic -κ- or aspirate, and **often modifies a vowel** in the stem-syllable, preferring ο. Thus, λείπω, λέλοιπα, πάσχω (alternate stem, πενθ-), πέπονθα.

This tense is often intransitive; as from πείθω, *to persuade*, First Perf. πέπεικα, *I have persuaded;* but Second Perf. πέποιθα, *I have confidence, I fully believe*. To

---

[1] So in classic Greek some other verbs, as λαγχάνω, εἴληχα.

the class of Second Perfects belong the forms ἔοικα, *I am like* (ϝικ-); οἶδα, *I know* (ϝιδ-). (See § 103.)

When the **stem-ending of the verb is an aspirate**—mute, labial or guttural—the **Perfect** is in the **Second,** or unaltered, form: as from γραφ-, *to write,* γέγραφα.

d. Some peculiarities of the PERFECT PASSIVE have been noted under the head of the Aorist. Vowel changes in the stem-syllable are given in the Lexicon or Vocabulary. So, also, the insertion or otherwise of -σ- after a vowel stem-ending.

E.g., τρέφω, *to nourish* (θρεφ-), τέτροφα, τέθραμμαι. Again, θραύω, *to crush,* makes τέθραυσμαι (Luke iv. 18); but παύομαι, *to cease,* πέπαυμαι (1 Pet. iv. 1).

e. The FUTURE-PERFECT (passive in classic Greek; called often the Paulo-post Future) is but the middle Future reduplicated. Luke xix. 40 is the only instance in the New Testament: κεκράξονται, *will immediately cry out.* (But W. H. read κράξουσιν).

Accentuation.—The Perfect Infinitive accents the penultima -έναι. In the active participle the stem-syllable, masc. -οτ, fem. -υι, is accented all through, the latter circumflexed wherever possible.

λελυκώς, λελυκυῖα, λελυκός,
λελυκότος, λελυκυίας, λελυκότος.

In the middle and passive, the Infinitive accents the penult., circumflex on diphthongs and long vowels, βεβουλεῦσθαι, τετιμῆσθαι, τετύφθαι. The participle accents the penultima; as λελυμένος, λελυμένη, λελυμένον.

DEPONENT VERBS.

100. Deponent verbs **have no active voice, but may be either middle or passive in form. This is decided by the Aorist.**

Thus: δέχομαι, *to receive;* First Aor., ἐδεξάμην (middle).

βούλομαι, *to wish;* First Aor., ἐβουλήθην (passive).

αἰσθάνομαι, *to perceive;* Second Aor., ᾐσθόμην (middle).

Some verbs have **both Aorists,** middle and passive, with the same meaning: as ἀποκρίνομαι, *to answer;* First Aor., ἀπεκρινάμην and ἀπεκρίθην, *I answered.*

Deponent transitives often have each tense with its proper force.

Thus: ἰάομαι, *to heal;* ἰασάμην, *I healed;* ἰάθην, *I was healed.*

λογίζομαι, *to reckon;* ἐλογισάμην, *I reckoned;* ἐλογίσθην, *I was reckoned.*

§ 102.] IMPERSONAL AND DEFFCTIVE VERBS. 101

The verb γίγνομαι, or γίνομαι, *to become* (γεν-, see 94, 8, *a*), has the forms—Fut., γενήσομαι; First Aor., ἐγενήθην; Second Aor., ἐγενόμην; Perf., γέγονα (Second Perf.); rarely γεγένημαι.

IMPERSONAL VERBS.

101. Impersonal verbs are used only in the **Third Person singular**, and are generally rendered into English with the pronoun *it*.

For the grammatical construction of impersonals, see § 171.

The chief impersonal verbs are δεῖ, *it is necessary, one ought;* χρή, *it is expedient* or *fitting;* πρέπει, *it becomes;* δοκεῖ, *it seems;* μέλει, *it is a care*.

The following forms of these verbs almost all occur in the New Testament. The participle, it will be observed, is *neuter*. Some of the verbs are also found personally:—

Indic. Pres.	δεῖ,	χρή,	πρέπει,	δοκεῖ,	μέλει.
Imperf.	ἔδει,	ἐχρῆν,	ἔπρεπε(ν),	ἐδόκει,	...
First. Aor.	...	...	...	ἔδοξε(ν),	...
Subj.	δέῃ,	...	...	...	...
Inf.	δεῖν,	χρῆναι,	...	...	...
Part. Pres.	δέον,	...	πρέπον,	δοκοῦν,	...

From εἰμί, the substantive verb, is formed the impersonal ἔξεστι, *it is lawful;* part., ἔξον.

DEFECTIVE VERBS OF THE FIRST CONJUGATION.

102. The explanations given under the several Tenses have sufficiently accounted for most of the so-called "irregularities" in the conjugation of verbs in -ω.

Some verbs, however, of very frequent occurrence, are anomalous in another way.

The ancient Greek tongue, like all early languages, while destitute of words expressing the more complex ideas, had a redundancy of terms denoting some of the simplest actions. Hence arose many synonymous words, some of which, being evidently unnecessary, were afterwards dropped. But in several instances of two or three verbs with the same meaning, different tenses were discontinued in each, so that forms of distinct verbs had to be brought together to constitute a whole. Compare in English *go*, without a Preterite, and *went*, without a Present, except in some phrases, *wend*.

Occasionally, again, where the same tense of two synonymous verbs has been retained, it expresses two different shades of meaning.

103. The following are the principal verbs which thus derive their forms from different roots:—

1. αἱρέω, *to take* (in comp., καθαιρέω, *to take down;* προαιρέω, *to take beforehand*, etc.); Mid., αἱροῦμαι, *to choose;* Principal Tenses, αἱρήσω, αἱρήσομαι, ᾕρηκα, ᾕρημαι, ᾑρέθην, αἱρεθήσομαι. From stem ἑλ-: Second Aor. act., εἷλον; Inf., ἑλεῖν; mid., εἱλόμην; Inf., ἑλέσθαι.

2. ἔρχομαι, *to go, come;* Impf., ἠρχόμην. Other tenses from stem ἐλυθ-, lengthened into ἐλευθ- (Fut.), contracted into ἐλθ- (Second Aor.): Fut., ἐλεύσομαι; Perf., ἐλήλυθα; Plup., ἐληλύθειν; Second Aor., ἦλθον; in the several moods, ἔλθε, ἔλθω, ἔλθοιμι, ἐλθεῖν, ἐλθών. So, many compounds.

3. ἐσθίω, *to eat;* Impf., ἤσθιον; Second Aor. from φαγ-, ἔφαγον, φαγεῖν; Fut., φάγομαι, φάγεσαι, φάγεται, κ.τ.λ. So, κατεσθίω, *to devour*.

4. ὁράω, *to see;* Impf., ἑώρων; Perf., ἑώρακα. Tenses from stem ὀπ-, ὀπτ-: Fut., ὄψομαι, ὄψει, ὄψεται; First Aor. subj., ὄψωμαι (once, Luke xiii. 28); First Aor. pass., ὤφθην, ὀφθῆναι; First Fut. pass., ὀφθήσομαι. Tenses from Ϝιδ-: Second Aor., εἶδον, ἴδω, ἰδεῖν, ἰδών (ἰδού, an old Imperfect middle used as an interjection, *behold!*); Second Perf., *I know* (= *have seen*) οἶδα, οἶδας, οἶδε(ν), οἴδαμεν, οἴδατε, οἴδασι(ν) (in Imp., ἴσθι, ἴστε; Subj., εἰδῶ; Inf., εἰδέναι; Part., εἰδώς; Plup. ind., *I knew*, ᾔδειν); Fut., εἰδήσω, *shall know* (Heb. viii. 11).

5. τρέχω, *to run;* Second Aor. from δρεμ-, ἔδραμον; Fut., δραμοῦμαι (LXX.).

6. φέρω, *to bear;* Fut. from stem οἰ-, οἴσω. Tenses from ἐνεγκ- or ἐνεκ-: First Aor. act., ἤνεγκα; Second Aor., ἤνεγκον, ἐνεγκεῖν; First Aor. pass., ἠνέχθην; Perf., ἐνήνοχα, with double reduplication. Compare προσφέρω, εἰσφέρω, κ.τ.λ.

7. εἶπον; Second Aor., *I said* (supplies Present and Imperfect from φημί, second conjugation); stem, ἐπ-; First Aor., εἶπα. Tenses from ἐρ-: Fut., ἐρέω, ἐρῶ; Perf., εἴρηκα; Perf. pass., εἴρημαι. Tenses from ῥε-: First Aor. pass., ἐρρέθην or ἐρρήθην; Part., ῥηθείς.

SUMMARY OF DEFECTIVE VERBS.

	to take	to go, come	to eat	to see	to run	to bear	to say
IND.—Pres.	αἱρέω	ἔρχομαι	ἐσθίω	ὁράω	τρέχω	φέρω	(φημί)
Imperf.	...	ἠρχόμην	ἤσθιον	ἑώρων	...	ἔφερον	(ἔφην)
Future	αἱρήσω	ἐλεύσομαι	φάγομαι	ὄψομαι	δραμοῦμαι	οἴσω	ἐρῶ
1st Aor.	...	...	...	ὠψάμην	...	ἤνεγκα	εἶπα
Perfect	ᾕρηκα	ἐλήλυθα	...	ἑώρακα	...	ἐνήνοχα	εἴρηκα
Pluperf.	...	ἐληλύθειν	...	ἑωράκειν	...	...	...
2nd Aor.	εἷλον	ἦλθον	ἔφαγον	εἶδον	ἔδραμον	ἤνεγκον	εἶπον
2nd Perf.	(Special signif.)	...	...	οἶδα	...	...	...
Pluperf.	...	...	...	ᾔδειν	...	...	...
Future	...	...	...	εἰδήσω	...	...	...
INF.—Pres.	αἱρεῖν	ἔρχεσθαι	ἐσθίειν	ὁρᾶν	τρέχειν	φέρειν	(φάναι)
2nd Aor.	ἑλεῖν	ἐλθεῖν	φαγεῖν	ἰδεῖν	δραμεῖν	ἐνεγκεῖν	εἰπεῖν
2nd Perf.	...	...	...	εἰδέναι	...	...	...

Middle and Passive.

Middle.

	to take	to go, come	to eat	to see	to run	to bear	to say
IND.—Pres.	αἱροῦμαι	...	...	ὀπτάομαι	...	φέρομαι	εἴρημαι
Perfect	ᾕρημαι	...	...	...	...	...	...
IND.—Future	αἱρήσομαι	...	...	...	...	...	...
2nd Aor.	εἱλόμην	...	...	...	...	...	...
INF.—2nd Aor.	ἑλέσθαι	...	...	...	...	...	...

Passive.

	to take	to go, come	to eat	to see	to run	to bear	to say
IND.—1st Aor.	ᾑρέθην	...	...	ὤφθην	...	ἠνέχθην	{ ἐρρήθην / ἐρρέθην }
Future	αἱρεθήσομαι	...	...	ὀφθήσομαι	...	ἐνεχθήσομαι	

These forms are not all actually found in the New Testament, though most of them are. Other forms occur in Greek authors, and, if required, may easily be formed by the usual analogies.

Exercise 13.—On the Defective Verbs.

[The following forms, **which should be carefully analysed**, are all from the "Sermon on the Mount," and illustrate the frequency with which this class of verbs occurs.

In addition to the meanings of the verbs given in their paradigms, and unnecessary, therefore, to repeat, it must be noted that the prefix εἰς denotes *into;* ἐξ, *out of;* παρα, *by* or *aside* (παρέρχομαι, *to pass away*); and προς, *in addition to.* For further details, see § 147, *a*, and the Vocabulary.]

FORMS.—ὄψονται, ἴδωσιν, οἶδε, οἴδατε, εἴπωσι, ἐρρέθη, εἴπῃ, ἐρεῖς, ἐροῦσι, ἦλθον, παρέλθῃ, εἰσέλθητε, ἐλθών, ἐξέλθῃς, εἴσελθε, ἐλθέτω, εἰσέλθετε, εἰσερχόμενοι, εἰσελεύσεται, προσφέρῃς, πρόσφερε, εἰσενέγκῃς, ἔξελε, φάγητε, φάγωμεν.

THE SECOND CONJUGATION, OR VERBS IN -μι.

104. The chief peculiarity of the Second Conjugation is that the **Present** and **Imperfect** tenses, and in many verbs the **Second Aorist** active and middle, **affix the ancient terminations** (see § 70)[1] **to the stem, without a connecting vowel.** The mood-vowels, however, of the Subjunctive and Optative are retained. The old Infinitive ending, **-ναι,** reappears.

The other tenses conform to the paradigm of the First Conjugation, with occasional exceptions that will be noted in their place.

---

[1] These terminations are, in the Active, for the Present (as a *principal* tense), singular, -μι, -σι, -τι ; plural, -μεν, -τε, -νσι for the Imperfect and Second Aorist (as *historical*), singular, -ν, -s, -ν (generally dropped); plural, -μεν, -τε, -σαν. The ancient Imperative ending -θι also appears. In several cases the terminations are slightly modified, as the paradigms will show. The analogy to the *Aorists Passive* of the First Conjugation will be observed throughout, in form and accentuation.

Modifications of the Stem.

105. Verbs in -μι modify the verbal stem in one or more of three ways.

a. A pure stem **lengthens the vowel** in the active Indicative singular. Thus, from φα-, *say*, we have first person φη-μί; third person, φη-σί.

b. Most stems **prefix a reduplication** in the Present and Imperfect tenses. Thus, δο-, *give*, first becomes δω-, as above; then, δί-δω-μι. So, τίθημι, from θε-, *put*. The vowel preferred in this reduplication is ι. The root στα-, *place*, accordingly makes ἵστημι, and ἑ-, *send*, ἵημι. Sometimes the stem is reduplicated within itself (the *Attic reduplication*, see also § 109, *a*), as, from ὀνα-, *profit*, ὀνίνημι. In other cases, a nasal -ν- is inserted, modified before labials into -μ- ; thus, πρα-, *burn*, gives πίμπρημι.

c. Several verbs **add the syllable** -νυ- to the stem before the personal endings in the Present and Imperfect tenses. Pure stems take -ννυ-. Thus, δεικ-, *show*, gives δείκνυμι; and στρο-, *strew* or *spread* (with lengthened vowel, as above), στρώννυμι.

It is convenient, then, to mark **two chief classes of verbs in** -μι.

The **first** exhibits the simple lengthened stem, generally with reduplication preceding.

The **second** inserts -νυ- or -ννυ- between the stem and the personal endings.

Paradigms of the First Class.

106. These also fall into **two divisions**. The former exhibits the normal forms; the latter contains a few verbs, with short monosyllabic stems, somewhat irregular in their conjugation, and, from their importance, requiring separate treatment. To the latter class belongs the *substantive verb:* εἰμί, *I am;* εἶναι, *to be.*

107.   REGULAR FORMS, STEMS A-, E-, O-.

The tenses conjugated like those of verbs in -ω will be given at the end of the paradigms. The accent throughout is generally thrown back as far as possible. Exceptions will be noted.

ἵστημι, to place.   τίθημι, to put.   δίδωμι, to give.

Stem, στα-   θε-   δο-

	Active.		
	INDICATIVE.		
Present,	ἵστημι	τίθημι	δίδωμι
	ἵστης	τίθης	δίδως
	ἵστησι(ν)	τίθησι(ν)	δίδωσι(ν)
	ἵστᾰμεν	τίθεμεν	δίδομεν
	ἵστᾰτε	τίθετε	δίδοτε
	ἱστᾶσι(ν)	τιθέασι(ν)	διδόασι(ν)
Imperfect,	ἵστην	ἐτίθην	ἐδίδων
	ἵστης	ἐτίθης	ἐδίδως
	ἵστη	ἐτίθη or ἐτίθει[1]	ἐδίδω or ἐδίδου[2]
	ἵστᾰμεν	ἐτίθεμεν	ἐδίδομεν
	ἵστᾰτε	ἐτίθετε	ἐδίδοτε
	ἵστᾰσαν	ἐτίθεσαν[1]	ἐδίδοσαν
2nd Aorist,	ἔστην		
	ἔστης		
	ἔστη		
	ἔστημεν	ἔθεμεν	ἔδομεν
	ἔστητε	ἔθετε	ἔδοτε
	ἔστησαν	ἔθεσαν	ἔδοσαν

[1] 2 Cor. iii. 13, Acts iii. 2, have ἐτίθει, ἐτίθουν, as from forms of the First Conjugation contracted.

[2] Matt. xxvi. 26, etc.   As from a form of the First Conjugation contracted.

§ 107.]   VERBS IN -μι—FIRST CLASS—PARADIGMS.

	Stem, στα-	θε-	δο-
	IMPERATIVE.		
Present,	ἴστη for ἴσταθι	τίθει (for τίθετι)	δίδου (for δίδοθι)
	ἰστάτω	τιθέτω	διδότω
	ἴστατε	τίθετε	δίδοτε
	ἰστάτωσαν	τιθέτωσαν	διδότωσαν
2nd Aorist,	στῆθι or στά[1]	θές (for θέτι)	δός (for δόθι)
	στήτω	θέτω	δότω
	στήτε	θέτε	δότε
	στήτωσαν	θέτωσαν	δότωσαν
	SUBJUNCTIVE.		
Present,	ἰστῶ	τιθῶ	διδῶ
	ἰστῇς	τιθῇς	διδῷς
	ἰστῇ	τιθῇ	διδῷ
	ἰστῶμεν	τιθῶμεν	διδῶμεν
	ἰστῆτε	τιθῆτε	διδῶτε
	ἰστῶσι(ν)	τιθῶσι(ν)	διδῶσι(ν)
2nd Aorist,	στῶ, κ.τ.λ.	θῶ, κ.τ.λ.	δῶ, κ.τ.λ.
	like Pres.	like Pres.	like Pres.
	OPTATIVE.		
Present,	ἰσταίην	τιθείην	διδοίην
	ἰσταίης	τιθείης	διδοίης
	ἰσταίη	τιθείη	διδοίη
	ἰσταῖμεν	τιθεῖμεν	διδοῖμεν
	ἰσταῖτε	τιθεῖτε	διδοῖτε
	ἰσταῖεν	τιθεῖεν	διδοῖεν
2nd Aorist,	σταίην	θείην	δοίην or δῴην
	σταίης	θείης	δοίης or δῴης
	σταίη	θείη	δοίη or δῴη

[1] Only in compound verbs, as ἀνάστα (Acts xii. 7; Eph. v. 14), and similar words.

Stem, στα-   θε-   δο-

	OPTATIVE—*continued*.		
2nd Aorist,	σταίημεν	θείημεν	δοίημεν
	σταίητε	θείητε	δοίητε
	σταῖεν	θεῖεν	δοῖεν
	INFINITIVE.		
Present,	ἱστάναι	τιθέναι	διδόναι
2nd Aorist,	στῆναι	θεῖναι	δοῦναι
	PARTICIPLES.		
Present,	ἱστάς, -ᾶσα, -άν	τιθείς, -εῖσα, -έν	διδούς, -οῦσα, -όν
2nd Aorist,	στάς, -ᾶσα, -άν	θείς, -εῖσα, -έν	δούς, -οῦσα, -όν

Middle and Passive.

	INDICATIVE.		
Present,	ἵσταμαι	τίθεμαι	δίδομαι
	ἵστασαι	τίθεσαι or τίθῃ	δίδοσαι
	ἵσταται	τίθεται	δίδοται
	ἱστάμεθα	τιθέμεθα	διδόμεθα
	ἵστασθε	τίθεσθε	δίδοσθε
	ἵστανται	τίθενται	δίδονται
Imperfect,	ἱστάμην	ἐτιθέμην	ἐδιδόμην
	ἵστασο	ἐτίθεσο or ἐτίθου	ἐδίδοσο or ἐδίδου
	ἵστατο	ἐτίθετο	ἐδίδοτο
	ἱστάμεθα	ἐτιθέμεθα	ἐδιδόμεθα
	ἵστασθε	ἐτίθεσθε	ἐδίδοσθε
	ἵσταντο	ἐτίθεντο	ἐδίδοντο
	IMPERATIVE.		
Present,	ἵστασο or ἵστω	τίθεσο or τίθου	δίδοσο or δίδου
	ἱστάσθω	τιθέσθω	διδόσθω
	ἵστασθε	τίθεσθε	δίδοσθε
	ἱστάσθωσαν	τιθέσθωσαν	διδόσθωσαν

§ 107.]   VERBS IN -μι—FIRST CLASS—PARADIGMS.   109

	Stem. στα-	θε-	δο-
		SUBJUNCTIVE.	
Present,	ἱστῶμαι	τιθῶμαι	διδῶμαι
	ἱστῇ	τιθῇ	διδῷ
	ἱστῆται	τιθῆται	διδῶται
	ἱστώμεθα	τιθώμεθα	διδώμεθα
	ἱστῆσθε	τιθῆσθε	διδῶσθε
	ἱστῶνται	τιθῶνται	διδῶνται
		OPTATIVE.	
Present,	ἱσταίμην	τιθείμην	διδοίμην
	ἱσταῖο	τιθεῖο	διδοῖο
	ἱσταῖτο	τιθεῖτο	διδοῖτο
	ἱσταίμεθα	τιθείμεθα	διδοίμεθα
	ἱσταῖσθε	τιθεῖσθε	διδοῖσθε
	ἱσταῖντο	τιθεῖντο	διδοῖντο
		INFINITIVE.	
Present,	ἵστασθαι	τίθεσθαι	δίδοσθαι
		PARTICIPLES.	
Present,	ἱστάμενος	τιθέμενος	διδόμενος
		Middle only.	
		INDICATIVE.	
2nd Aorist,		ἐθέμην	ἐδόμην
		ἔθου (-εσο)	ἔδου (-οσο)
		ἔθετο	ἔδοτο
		ἐθέμεθα	ἐδόμεθα
		ἔθεσθε	ἔδοσθε
		ἔθεντο	ἔδοντο
		IMPERATIVE.	
2nd Aorist,		θοῦ (-εσο)	δοῦ (-οσο)
		θέσθω	δόσθω
		θέσθε	δόσθε
		θέσθωσαν	δόσθωσαν

VERBS IN -μι—FIRST CLASS—PARADIGMS. [§ 107.

	Stem, στα-	θε-	δο-
		SUBJUNCTIVE.	
2nd Aorist,		θῶμαι	δῶμαι
		θῇς	δῷ
		θῆται	δῶται
		θώμεθα	δώμεθα
		θῆσθε	δῶσθε
		θῶνται	δῶνται
		OPTATIVE.	
2nd Aorist,		θείμην	δοίμην
		θεῖο	δοῖο
		θεῖτο	δοῖτο
		θείμεθα	δοίμεθα
		θεῖσθε	δοῖσθε
		θεῖντο	δοῖντο
		INFINITIVE.	
2nd Aorist,		θέσθαι	δόσθαι
		PARTICIPLES.	
2nd Aorist,		θέμενος	δόμενος

Tenses after the Model of the First Conjugation.

Active.
INDICATIVE.

Future,	στήσω	θήσω	δώσω
1st Aorist,	ἔστησα	ἔθηκα	ἔδωκα
Perfect,	ἕστηκα	τέθεικα,	δέδωκα,
	ἕστηκας	κ.τ.λ.	κ.τ.λ.
	ἕστηκε(ν)		
	ἑστήκαμεν		
	or ἕσταμεν¹		

¹ This syncopated or shortened form is very usual. So in Perf. Inf. and Part.

§ 107.] VERBS IN -μι—FIRST CLASS—PARADIGMS.   111

Stem, στα-   θε-   δο-

	INDICATIVE—continued.		
Perfect,	ἑστήκατε or ἕστατε ἑστήκασι(ν) or ἕστασι(ν)		
Pluperfect,	εἱστήκειν or ἑστήκειν	(ἐ)τεθείκειν	(ἐ)δεδώκειν
	IMPERATIVE.		
1st Aorist,	στῆσον		
Perfect,	ἕστηκε	τέθεικε	δέδωκε
	SUBJUNCTIVE.		
1st Aorist,	στήσω		δώσω[1]
Perfect,	ἑστήκω	τεθείκω	δεδώκω
	OPTATIVE.		
Future,	στήσοιμι	θήσοιμι	δώσοιμι
1st Aorist,	στήσαιμι		
Perfect,	ἑστήκοιμι	τεθείκοιμι	δεδώκοιμι
	INFINITIVE.		
Future,	στήσειν	θήσειν	δώσειν
1st Aorist,	στῆσαι		
Perfect,	ἑστηκέναι or ἑστάναι	τεθεικέναι	δεδωκέναι
	PARTICIPLES.		
Future,	στήσων	θήσων	δώσων
1st Aorist,	στήσας		
Perfect,	ἑστηκώς,-υῖα,-ός τεθεικώς or ἑστώς, -ῶσα, -ός[2]		δεδωκώς

[1] See John xvii. 2; Rev. viii. 3, xiii. 16, in which passages the form δώσῃ occurs. W. H., however, read δώσει, fut. indic.
[2] See § 38. Some grammarians contend for the neuter form ἑστώς.

VERBS IN -μι—FIRST CLASS—PARADIGMS. [§ 107.

Stem, στα-   θε-   δο-

	Middle and Passive.		
	INDICATIVE.		
Perfect,	ἔσταμαι	τέθειμαι	δέδομαι
Pluperfect,	ἐστάμην	(ἐ)τεθείμην	(ἐ)δεδόμην
	SUBJUNCTIVE.		
Perfect,	ἐσταμένος ὦ	τεθειμένος ὦ	δεδομένος ὦ
	OPTATIVE.		
Perfect,	ἐσταμένος εἴην	τεθειμένος εἴην	δεδομένος εἴην
	INFINITIVE.		
Perfect,	ἐστάσθαι	τεθεῖσθαι	δεδόσθαι
	PARTICIPLES.		
Perfect,	ἐσταμένος	τεθειμένος	δεδομένος
	Middle only.		
	INDICATIVE.		
Future,	στήσομαι	θήσομαι	δώσομαι
1st Aorist,	ἐστησάμην		
	IMPERATIVE.		
1st Aorist,	στῆσαι		
	SUBJUNCTIVE.		
1st Aorist,	στήσωμαι		
	OPTATIVE.		
Future,	στησοίμην	θησοίμην	δωσοίμην
1st Aorist,	στησαίμην		
	INFINITIVE.		
Future,	στήσεσθαι	θήσεσθαι	δώσεσθαι
1st Aorist,	στήσασθαι		
	PARTICIPLES.		
Future,	στησόμενος	θησόμενος	δωσόμενος
1st Aorist,	στησάμενος		

§ 107.]   VERBS IN -μι—FIRST CLASS—PARADIGMS.   113

Stem, στα-   θε-   δο-

	Passive only.		
	INDICATIVE.		
Future,	σταθήσομαι	τεθήσομαι	δοθήσομαι
1st Aorist,	ἐστάθην	ἐτέθην	ἐδόθην
	IMPERATIVE.		
1st Aorist,	στάθητι	τέθητι	δόθητι
	SUBJUNCTIVE.		
1st Aorist,	σταθῶ	τεθῶ	δοθῶ
	OPTATIVE.		
Future,	σταθησοίμην	τεθησοίμην	δοθησοίμην
1st Aorist,	σταθείην	τεθείην	δοθείην
	INFINITIVE.		
Future,	σταθήσεσθαι	τεθήσεσθαι	δοθήσεσθαι
1st Aorist,	σταθῆναι	τεθῆναι	δοθῆναι
	PARTICIPLES.		
Future,	σταθησόμενος	τεθησόμενος	δοθησόμενος
1st Aorist,	σταθείς, -εῖσα, -έν	τεθείς, -εῖσα, -έν	δοθείς, -εῖσα, -έν
	VERBALS.		
	στατός	θετός	δοτός
	στατέος	θετέος	δοτέος

Note.—It will be observed that several Aorist forms are *omitted*, the alternative tense being in use. For example: in the Active Indicative of τίθημι and δίδωμι, the First Aorist is employed for the *singular*, the Second for the *plural*, while in the Middle throughout ἵστημι has the First, τίθημι and δίδωμι the Second. The Active First Aorist of ἵστημι is *transitive*, the Second Aorist *intransitive*, as will be shown hereafter.

I

Remarks on the Paradigms.

108. 1. The First Aorist Active of τίθημι and δίδωμι, and, as will be seen hereafter, of ἵημι also, takes -κ- instead of -σ- for tense-characteristic. This peculiarity is confined to these three verbs; and their First Aorist is found only in the Indicative mood.[1]

2. The Perfect tenses of ἵστημι, from the stem στα-, take the hard breathing, with ε- as an "improper reduplication:" ἕστηκα. The augmented tenses have ἐ-, as ἔστην; but the Imperfect retains ἱ-.

3. The First Aorist of ἵστημι is **transitive**, the Second **intransitive**, in meaning: ἔστησα, *I placed;* ἔστην, *I stood.*

4. A verb, στήκω (intransitive), *to stand,* of the First Conjugation, derived from the Perfect of στα-, is found in a few forms in the New Testament. It must be distinguished from the Perfect forms of ἵστημι.

Verbs belonging to this Class.

109. The number of verbs which conform to the above paradigms is very small. The principal are subjoined.

A-STEMS.—Like ἵστημι, are conjugated the following:—

a. 1. ὀνίνημι, *to benefit* (stem ὀνα-, with Attic reduplication), only once in the New Testament; Second Aorist, Optative, middle, ὀναίμην (Phile. 20), *may I have joy!*

2. πίμπρημι, *to burn* (stem πρα-, reduplicated, with μ), only once in the New Testament, Present Infinitive, passive, πίμπρασθαι (Acts xxviii. 6), *to be burned* or *inflamed.*

3. φημί, *to say* (stem φα-). The Present Indicative is usually enclitic, except second person singular, otherwise oxytone; third person singular, φησί(ν); plural, φασί(ν); Imperfect, ἔφην; third person singular, ἔφη. (See § 103, 7.)

---

[1] To this remark there is one exception if the reading δώσῃ (on which see note, p. 111) be genuine.

§ 110.] VERBS IN -μι—FIRST CLASS—REMARKS. 115

4. χρή, *it is fitting* (stem χρα-), impersonal. (See § 101.) Once in the New Testament (James iii. 10).

b. **Deponent Verbs.**—1. δύναμαι, *to be able* (stem δυνα-). Present Indicative, -μαι, -σαι (or in MSS., δύνῃ), -ται, κ.τ.λ.; Imperfect, ἐδυνάμην, or (with double augment) ἠδυνάμην; Present Subjunctive, δύνωμαι; Optative, δυναίμην; Infinitive, δύνασθαι; Participle, δυνάμενος; Verbal, δυνατός, *possible, capable;* Future, δυνήσομαι; First Aorist, ἐδυνήθην, or ἠδυνήθην (occasionally in MSS., ἠδυνάσθην).

2. ἐπίσταμαι, *to know*, or *to feel sure, i.e.*, "to take one's stand upon" (stem ἐπί, preposition, and -στα-, but without aspiration), only in Present in New Testament; Indicative, -μαι, -σαι, -ται, -μεθα, -σθε, -νται; Participle, ἐπιστάμενος.

3. κρέμαμαι, *to hang*, neuter (stem κρεμα-); Present Indicative, third person, κρέμαται; plural, κρέμανται; Participle, κρεμάμενος; First Aorist, ἐκρεμάσθην; Subjunctive, κρεμασθῶ; Participle, κρεμασθείς.

E-STEMS. Deponent Verbs.—1. ἧμαι, *to be seated* (stem ἑ-), properly a Perfect middle or passive, as from ἕω, *I set* or *seat;* ἕομαι, *I seat myself;* ἧμαι, *I have seated myself*, and so *am* now *sitting*. Only found in the New Testament compounded with the preposition κατά, *down*. κάθημαι, *I am sitting down*, second person, καθῇ, for καθῆσαι; Imperative, κάθου, for κάθησο; Infinitive, καθῆσθαι; Participle, καθήμενος; Imperfect Indicative, ἐκαθήμην, properly a Pluperfect.

2. κεῖμαι, *to lie down* (stem κει-), properly also a Perfect, "I have laid myself" or "have been laid down;" Infinitive, κεῖσθαι; Participle, κείμενος; Imperfect Indicative, ἐκείμην, -σο, -το.

110. The three stems, ἐσ-, ἑ-, and ἑ-, being marked by special peculiarities, must be placed alone. The first of the three is by far the most important, as the stem of **the substantive verb.** *esse, to be.* With the personal termination, -μι, the stem (ἐσ-μι) becomes εἰμί, *I am;* and with the Infinitive ending, -ναι, εἶναι, *to be.*

Several tenses are wanting in the conjugation of this verb, which is as follows:—

Stem, ἐσ-

INDICATIVE MOOD.
Present, am.

εἰμί	ἐσμέν
εἶ (for ἐσσί)	ἐστέ
ἐστί	εἰσί(ν)

Imperfect or Aorist, was.

ἦν or ἤμην	ἦμεν or ἤμεθα
ἦσθα	ἦτε
ἦν	ἦσαν

Future, shall be.

ἔσομαι	ἐσόμεθα
ἔσῃ	ἔσεσθε
ἔσται (for ἔσεται)	ἔσονται

IMPERATIVE MOOD.
Be thou.

ἴσθι	ἔστε
ἔστω or ἤτω	ἔστωσαν

SUBJUNCTIVE MOOD.
Present, may be.

ὦ	ὦμεν
ᾖς	ἦτε
ᾖ	ὦσι(ν)

OPTATIVE MOOD.
Present, might be.

εἴην	εἴημεν
εἴης	εἴητε
εἴη	εἴησαν

§ 111.]   VERBS IN -μι—FIRST CLASS—SPECIAL FORMS.   117

INFINITIVE.

Present, *to be*, εἶναι.   Future, *to be about to be*, ἔσεσθαι.

PARTICIPLES.

Present, *being*, ὤν, οὖσα, ὄν; gen. ὄντος, οὔσης, ὄντος, κ.τ.λ.
Future, *about to be*, ἐσόμενος, -η, -ον; gen. -ου, -ης, -ου, κ.τ.λ.

Note on Accentuation.—In the Present Indicative, with the exception of the second person singular, this verb is an enclitic, excepting (1) where it follows a paroxytone, when it retains its accent as above; and (2) in the third person, where it is a *predicate*, when it becomes paroxytone, as ἔστι Θεός, *there is a God*. It is also paroxytone after ὡς, οὐκ, εἰ καί, τοῦτ', ἀλλ'. Thus, οὐκ ἔστι, *it is not*; τοῦτ' ἔστι, *that is to say*.

111. Not unlike the substantive verb in conjugation, and therefore to be carefully distinguished from it, are the verbs εἶμι (stem ἰ-), *go*, and ἵημι (stem ἑ-), *send*. Neither of them is found in the New Testament,[1] except in composition. It will suffice to give a few forms of εἶμι, to show the differences between it and the substantive verb; while the most important compound of ἵημι is subjoined in full.

Forms of εἶμι, *to go* (stem ἰ-):—

IND.—Pres.	εἶμι	εἶ	εἶσι	ἴμεν	ἴτε	ἴασι(ν)
„ Imp.	ᾔειν	ᾔεις	ᾔει	ᾔειμεν	ᾔειτε	ᾔεσαν
IMPER.		ἴθι	ἴτω		ἴτε	ἴτωσαν
SUBJ.—Pres.	ἴω	ἴῃς	ἴῃ	ἴωμεν	ἴητε	ἴωσι(ν)
OPT.—Pres.	ἴοιμι	ἴοις	ἴοι	ἴοιμεν	ἴοιτε	ἴοιεν
INF.—Pres.	ἰέναι					
PART.—Pres.	ἰών	ἰοῦσα	ἰόν			

---

[1] Some MSS. read in John vii. 34, 36, for εἰμί, *I am*, εἶμι, *I* (*will*) *go*. This Present tense has in classic Greek a Future significance, equivalent to the English idiom, *I am going*.

VERBS IN -μι—FIRST CLASS. [§ 112.

CONJUGATION OF ἵημι, *to send*, IN ITS COMPOUND, ἀφίημι.

112. The stem is ἑ-, which, reduplicated, gives ἵημι. Prefixed is the preposition ἀπό, *from, away from;* the o being lost before ι by elision, and the π changed by the aspirate into φ.

Hence ἀφίημι, *to send away, let go* (permit), *forgive*.

The tenses which follow the analogy of the First Conjugation are included, so far as necessary, in the following paradigm, and will readily be traced.

Active.

INDICATIVE.

Pres., sing., ἀφίημι, -ίης or -εῖς,[1] -ίησι(ν)
  „ plur., -ίεμεν -ίετε -ιᾶσι(ν) or ἀφιοῦσι(ν)
Impf., sing.,[2] ἤφιον ἤφιες ἤφιε
Fut., ἀφήσω   1st Aor., ἄφηκα. (See § 108, 1.)
Perf., ἀφεῖκα   Pluperf., ἀφείκειν
2 Aor., sing., wanting. Plural, ἀφεῖμεν ἀφεῖτε ἀφεῖσαν

IMPERATIVE.

Pres., ἀφίει, ἀφιέτω   Plural, ἀφίετε, ἀφιέτωσαν
2 Aor., ἄφες, ἀφέτω   „ ἄφετε, ἀφέτωσαν

SUBJUNCTIVE.

Pres., ἀφιῶ, -ιῇς, -ιῇ   -ιῶμεν, -ιῆτε, -ιῶσι(ν)
2 Aor., ἀφῶ, -ῇς, -ῇ   -ῶμεν, -ῆτε, -ῶσι(ν)

OPTATIVE.

Pres., ἀφιείην, -ης, -η   ἀφιεῖμεν, -εῖτε, -εῖεν
2 Aor., ἀφείην, -ης, -η   ἀφεῖμεν, -εῖτε, -εῖεν

INFINITIVE.

Pres., ἀφιέναι   2 Aor., ἀφεῖναι

PARTICIPLES.

Pres., ἀφιείς, -εῖσα, -έν   2 Aor., ἀφείς, -εῖσα, -έν

---

[1] Rev. ii. 20, W. H.
[2] Preposition augmented. Plural wanting.

Middle and Passive.

INDICATIVE.

Pres., ἀφίεμαι, -σαι, -ται   Plural, ἀφιέμεθα, -σθε, -νται
Impf., ἀφιέμην, -σο, -το   „   ἀφιέμεθα, -σθε, -ντο
Perf., sing., ἀφεῖμαι   ἀφεῖσαι   ἀφεῖται
„ plur., ἀφείμεθα   ἀφεῖσθε   ἀφεῖνται or ἀφέωνται[1]
Plup., ἀφείμην   ἀφεῖσο   ἀφεῖτο, κ.τ.λ.

IMPERATIVE.

Pres., ἀφίεσο or ἀφίου   ἀφιέσθω, κ.τ.λ.

SUBJUNCTIVE.

Pres., ἀφιῶμαι, -ιῇ, -ιῆται, κ.τ.λ.   -ιώμεθα, -ιησθε, -ιωνται

OPTATIVE.

Pres., ἀφιοίμην or ἀφιείμην, -οῖο or -εῖο, -οῖτο or -εῖτο, κ.τ.λ.

INFINITIVE.

Pres., ἀφίεσθαι

PARTICIPLE.

Pres., ἀφιέμενος

Middle only.

INDICATIVE.

Fut., ἀφήσομαι   2 Aor., ἀφείμην, as Plup.

IMPERATIVE.

2 Aor., ἀφοῦ, ἀφέσθω   ἄφεσθε, ἀφέσθωσαν

SUBJUNCTIVE.

2 Aor., ἀφῶμαι, -ῇ, -ῆται, κ.τ.λ.

OPTATIVE.

Fut., ἀφησοίμην   2 Aor., ἀφοίμην, -οῖο, -οῖτο

INFINITIVE.

Fut., ἀφήσεσθαι   2 Aor., ἀφέσθαι

PARTICIPLES.

Fut., ἀφησόμενος   2 Aor., ἀφέμενος

---

[1] This is the more common form, and is taken from the Doric dialect.

Passive only.

INDICATIVE.
Fut., ἀφεθήσομαι   1 Aor., ἀφέθην

IMPERATIVE.
1 Aor., ἀφέθητι

SUBJUNCTIVE.
1 Aor., ἀφεθῶ

OPTATIVE.
Fut., ἀφεθησοίμην   1 Aor., ἀφεθείην

INFINITIVE.
Fut., ἀφεθήσεσθαι   1 Aor., ἀφεθῆναι

PARTICIPLES.
Fut., ἀφεθησόμενος   1 Aor., ἀφεθείς

VERBALS.
ἀφετός   ἀφετέος

SECOND CLASS. VERBS IN -νυμι OR -ννυμι.

113. 1. These verbs have no Second Aorist.[1]

2. Most of them have a kindred form of the First Conjugation, in -νύω or -ννύω. From this form are taken—*often*, the Indicative Present and Imperfect, with the Present Infinitive; *generally*, the Present Participle; and *always*, the Subjunctive and Optative moods. Thus, from δεικ-, *show*, we sometimes find the forms δεικνύω, -εις, -ει, δεικνύειν, δεικνύων; while the only Present Subjunctive recognised is δεικνύω, -ῃς, -ῃ; and the only Present Optative, δεικνύοιμι.

> In the paradigms, these forms of the First Conjugation are marked by a dagger (†).

3. All the tenses but the Present and Imperfect are formed from the stem (without -νν-). These are placed separately for comparison.

---

[1] With one exception, in classic Greek, σβέννυμι, *to quench*; Second Aor., ἔσβην.

114. Paradigms of δείκνυμι, *to show*, and ζώννυμι, *to gird*.

Stem (consonant), δεικ-   (vowel), ζο-

Active.

INDICATIVE.
Pres., δείκνῡμι or †δεικνύω   ζώννῡμι or †ζωννύω
       δείκνυς   δεικνύεις,   ζώννυς   ζωννύεις, κ.τ.λ.
       δείκνῡσι(ν)   κ.τ.λ.   ζώννῡσι(ν)
       δείκνῠμεν   ζώννῠμεν
       δείκνῠτε   ζώννῠτε
       δείκνῡσι(ν)   ζώννῡσι(ν)

Impf., ἐδείκνῡν or †ἐδείκνυον   ἐζώννῡν or †ἐζώννυον
       ἐδείκνῡς   ἐδείκνυες,   ἐζώννῡς   ἐζώννυες, κ.τ.λ.
       ἐδείκνῡ   κ.τ.λ.   ἐζώννῡ
       ἐδείκνῠμεν   ἐζώννῠμεν
       ἐδείκνῠτε   ἐζώννῠτε
       ἐδείκνῠσαν   ἐζώννῠσαν

IMPERATIVE.
Pres., δείκνῡ or δείκνυθι   ζώννῡ or ζώννυθι
       δεικνύτω   ζωννύτω
       δείκνῠτε   ζώννῠτε
       δεικνύτωσαν   ζωννύτωσαν

SUBJUNCTIVE.
Pres., †δεικνύω   †ζωννύω

OPTATIVE.
Pres., †δεικνύοιμι   †ζωννύοιμι

INFINITIVE.
Pres., δεικνύναι or †δεικνύειν   ζωννύναι or †ζωννύειν

PARTICIPLES.
Pres., δεικνύς, -ῦσα, or †δεικνύων ζωννύς, -ῦσα, or †ζωννύων

Stem, δεικ-   ζο-

Middle and Passive.

INDICATIVE.
Pres., δείκνῡμαι   δεικνύμεθα   ζώννῡμαι   ζωννύμεθα
        δείκνῠσαι   δείκνυσθε   ζώννῠσαι   ζώννυσθε
        δείκνῠται   δείκνυνται   ζώννῠται   ζώννυνται
Impf., ἐδεικνύμην ἐδεικνύμεθα ἐζωννύμην   ἐζωννύμεθα
        ἐδείκνῠσο   ἐδείκνυσθε   ἐζώννῠσο   ἐζώννυσθε
        ἐδείκνῠτο   ἐδείκνυντο   ἐζώννῠτο   ἐζώννυντο

IMPERATIVE.
Pres., δείκνῠσο   δείκνυσθε   ζώννῠσο   ζώννυσθε
        δεικνύσθω   δεικνύσθωσαν ζωννύσθω   ζωννύσθωσαν

SUBJUNCTIVE.
Pres., †δεικνύωμαι   †ζωννύωμαι

OPTATIVE.
Pres., †δεικνυοίμην   †ζωννυοίμην

INFINITIVE.
Pres., δείκνυσθαι or †δεικνύεσθαι   ζώννυσθαι or †ζωννύεσθαι

TENSES AFTER THE MODEL OF THE FIRST CONJUGATION.

INDICATIVE.   Active.
Fut.,   δείξω   ζώσω   1 Aor., ἔδειξα   ἔζωσα
Perf., δέδειχα   ἔζωκα   Plup., (ἐ)δεδείχειν ἐ(ι)ζώκειν

IMPERATIVE.
1 Aor., δεῖξον   ζῶσον

SUBJUNCTIVE.
1 Aor., δείξω   ζώσω   Perf., δεδείχω   ἐζώκω

OPTATIVE.
Fut.,   δείξοιμι   ζώσοιμι   1 Aor., δείξαιμι   ζώσαιμι
Perf., δεδείχοιμι   ἐζώκοιμι

§ 114.] VERBS IN -μι—SECOND CLASS.

Stem, δεικ-   ζο-

INFINITIVE.

Fut., δείξειν   ζώσειν   1 Aor., δεῖξαι   ζῶσαι
Perf., δεδειχέναι   ἐζωκέναι

Middle and Passive.

INDICATIVE.
Perf., δέδειγμαι ἔζωσμαι   Plup., ἐδεδείγμην ἐ(ι)ζώσμην

IMPERATIVE.
Perf., δέδειξο   δεδείχθω,   ἔζωσο   ἐζώσθω,
                  κ.τ.λ.   κ.τ.λ.

SUBJUNCTIVE.
Perf., δεδειγμένος ὦ   ἐζωσμένος ὦ

OPTATIVE.
Perf., δεδειγμένος εἴην   ἐζωσμένος εἴην

INFINITIVE.
Perf., δεδεῖχθαι   ἐζῶσθαι

Middle only.

INDICATIVE.
Fut., δείξομαι   ζώσομαι   1 Aor., ἐδειξάμην   ἐζωσάμην

IMPERATIVE.
1 Aor., δεῖξαι   ζῶσαι

SUBJUNCTIVE.
1 Aor., δείξωμαι   ζώσωμαι

OPTATIVE.
Fut., δειξοίμην ζωσοίμην   1 Aor., δειξαίμην   ζωσαίμην

INFINITIVE.
Fut., δείξεσθαι ζώσεσθαι   1 Aor., δείξασθαι   ζώσασθαι

PARTICIPLES.
Fut., δειξόμενος ζωσόμενος   1 Aor., δειξάμενος ζωσάμενος

VERBS IN -μι—SECOND CLASS. [§ 114.

Stem, δεικ- ζο-

Passive only.

INDICATIVE.
Fut., δειχθήσομαι ζωσθήσομαι 1 Aor., ἐδείχθην ἐζώσθην

IMPERATIVE.
1 Aor., δείχθητι ζώσθητι

SUBJUNCTIVE.
1 Aor., δειχθῶ ζωσθῶ

OPTATIVE.
Fut., δειχθησοίμην ζωσθησοίμην
1 Aor., δειχθείην ζωσθείην

INFINITIVE.
Fut., δειχθήσεσθαι ζωσθήσεσθαι
1 Aor., δειχθῆναι ζωσθῆναι

VERBALS.
δεικτός δεικτέος ζωστός ζωστέος

REMARKS ON THE PARADIGMS.

115. *a.* The quantity of the υ is marked in a sufficient number of cases to indicate the rest. Where, in the first class of verbs in -μι, the stem-vowel α, ε, or ο is made long, the υ of the second class is also lengthened. Thus, τίθημι, δείκνῡμι, but τίθεμεν, δείκνῠμεν.

b. Verbs of this class seldom occur in the New Testament, with the exception of δείκνυμι and ἀπόλλυμι. (See below.)

VERBS WITH CONSONANT-STEMS, LIKE δείκνυμι.

116. 1. μίγνυμι, *to mix* (stem, μιγ-), only found in the New Testament in forms like the First Conjugation. First Aorist, ἔμιξα; Perfect Passive, μέμιγμαι.

2. ὄλλυμι, *to destroy, to lose* (stem, ὀλ- or ὀλε-; hence ὄλ-νυμι and with the ν assimilated, ὄλλυμι), only found in the New Testament with

the prefixed preposition, ἀπό. Present Indicative, ἀπόλλυμι; Middle and Passive, ἀπόλλυμαι. Chiefly found in tenses derived from collateral stem ἀπολε-: Active Future, ἀπολέσω, once ἀπολῶ;[1] First Aorist, ἀπώλεσα; Perfect, with neuter meaning, *I perish* / ἀπόλωλα; Middle Future, ἀπολοῦμαι; Second Aorist, ἀπωλόμην; Present Participle, οἱ ἀπολλύμενοι often, *the perishing*.

3. ὄμνυμι, *to swear* (stem, ὀμ- or ὀμο-). The forms used in the New Testament are Present, as of First Conjugation, ὀμνύω, ὀμνύειν (but in Mark xiv. 71, W. H. read ὀμνύναι); First Aorist, ὤμοσα; Infinitive, ὀμόσαι, from ὀμό-.

4. ῥήγνυμι, *to tear* (stem, ῥαγ-). Present Passive Indicative, third person plural, ῥήγνυνται (Matt. ix. 17); but generally with forms as from ῥήσσω, ῥήξω.

Verbs with Vowel-stems, like ζώννυμι

117. 1. A-Stems.—κεράννυμι, *to mix* (stem, κερᾰ-). Only twice, First Aorist, ἐκέρασα (Rev. xviii. 6); Perfect Participle Passive, κεκερασμένος (Rev. xiv. 10).

2. E-Stems.—ἕννυμι, *to clothe* (stem, ϝε-), only found with the prefixed preposition, ἀμφί, *about*. Present Active Indicative, third person singular, ἀμφιέννυσι(ν) (Matt. vi. 30), and Perfect Passive Participle, with augment prefixed to the preposition, ἠμφιεσμένον (Matt. xi. 8; Luke vii. 25).

κορέννυμι, *to satisfy* (stem, κορε-). First Aorist Passive Participle, κορεσθείς (Acts xxvii. 38); Perfect Passive Participle, κεκορεσμένος (1 Cor. iv. 8).

σβέννυμι, *to extinguish* (stem, σβε-). Future Active, σβέσω; Future Passive, σβεσθήσομαι.

3. O-Stems.—ῥώννυμι, *to strengthen* (stem, ῥο-), found only in the Perfect Middle Imperative, ἔρρωσο; plural, ἔρρωσθε, *be strong!* *i.e.*, *Farewell!*

---

[1] 1 Cor. i. 19, from LXX.

στρώννυμι, *to strew* or *spread* (stem, στρο-). Present forms as from στρωννύω; First Aorist Active, ἔστρωσα; Perfect Participle Passive, ἐστρωμένος.

If the above verbs, with their significations, are now committed to memory, some trouble may be saved at subsequent stages.

Exercise 14.—On the Second Conjugation, or Verbs in -μι.

[The following examples of verbs in -μι occur in the "Sermon on the Mount," and are here presented for analysis. In addition to explanations already given (see Exercise 13, on the Defective Verbs), it must be noted that the prefix ἀπο- (*from, away from*) with the verb δίδωμι has the sense of *return: ἀποδίδωμι, to give back;* and ἐπι- with the same verb may be rendered *over;* ἀντι signifies *against*.]

FORMS.—ἐστιν, ἐστε, ἔσται, ἴσθι, εἶ, ἔστω, ἔσεσθε, ᾖ, ὄντα, ὄντες, τιθέασιν, προσθεῖναι, προστεθήσεται, ἀντιστῆναι, δός, δότω, δίδου, ἀποδῷς, παραδῷ, δῶτε, ἐπιδώσει, δοθήσεται, διδόναι, ἄφες, ἀφίεμεν, ἀφῆτε, ἀφήσει, δύνασαι, δύναται, δύνασθε, κειμένη, ἀπόληται, ὀμόσαι, ὀμόσῃς, ῥήξωσιν, ἀμφιέννυσιν.

Exercise 15.—General, upon the Verbs.

*** The learner should now be expert in tracing any verbal form to its stem. As a test of proficiency, the following list of verbs is subjoined, taken in order from the Second Epistle to the Thessalonians. Let the *stem, conjugation class, voice, mood, tense,* **and, when necessary, the** *number* **and** *person,* **of every one be written down**; if possible, without reference to any paradigm. Prefixes not belonging to the root are printed in thick type. The Vocabulary or Lexicon must be consulted for the meaning of the words.

CHAPTER I.

3. εὐχαριστεῖν, ὀφείλομεν, ὑπεραυξάνει, πλεονάζει. 4. καυχᾶσθαι (how do you distinguish in such a word between the First and Second Conjugations?), ἀνέχεσθε. 5. καταξιωθῆναι, πάσχετε. 6. ἀνταποδοῦναι, θλίβουσιν (Participle). 7. θλιβομένοις. 8. διδόντος, εἰδόσι, ὑπακούουσι

§ 117.]   EXERCISES.   127

(Participle). 9. τίσουσιν. 10. ἔλθῃ, ἐνδοξασθῆναι, θαυμασθῆναι, πιστεύουσιν (Participle), ἐπιστεύθη. 11. προσευχόμεθα, ἀξιώσῃ, πληρώσῃ. 12. ἐνδοξασθῇ.

CHAPTER II.

1. ἐρωτῶμεν. 2. σαλευθῆναι, θροεῖσθαι, ἐνέστηκεν. 3. ἐξαπατήσῃ, ἔλθῃ, ἀποκαλυφθῇ. 4. ἀντικείμενος, ὑπεραιρόμενος, λεγόμενον, καθίσαι, ἀποδεικνύντα. 5. μνημονεύετε, ἔλεγον. 6. κατέχον, οἴδατε, ἀποκαλυφθῆναι. 7. ἐνεργεῖται, κατέχων, γένηται. 8. ἀποκαλυφθήσεται, ἀναλώσει, καταργήσει. 10. ἀπολλυμένοις, ἐδέξαντο, σωθῆναι. 11. πέμψει, πιστεῦσαι (distinguish this from Optative forms, as in ver. 17). 12. κριθῶσι, πιστεύσαντες, εὐδοκήσαντες. 13. ὀφείλομεν, εὐχαριστεῖν, ἠγαπημένοι, εἵλετο (εἵλατο is read by W. H.; see § 97, note). 14. ἐκάλεσεν. 15. στήκετε (see § 108, 4), κρατεῖτε, ἐδιδάχθητε. 16. ἀγαπήσας, δούς. 17. παρακαλέσαι (Optative), στηρίξαι (Optative).

CHAPTER III.

1. προσεύχεσθε, τρέχῃ, δοξάζηται. 2. ῥυσθῶμεν. 3. στηρίξει, φυλάξει. 4. πεποίθαμεν, παραγγέλλομεν, ποιεῖτε, ποιήσετε. 5. κατευθῦναι (Optative). 6. στέλλεσθαι, περιπατοῦντος, παρέλαβε. 7. μιμεῖσθαι, ἠτακτήσαμεν (from ἀτακτέω). 8. ἐφάγομεν, ἐργαζόμενοι, ἐπιβαρῆσαι. 9. ἔχομεν, δῶμεν. 10. ἦμεν, παρηγγέλλομεν, θέλει, ἐργάζεσθαι, ἐσθίετω. 11. ἀκούομεν, ἐργαζομένους, περιεργαζομένους. 12. παρακαλοῦμεν, ἐσθίωσιν. 13. ἐκκακήσητε, καλοποιοῦντες. 14. ὑπακούει, σημειοῦσθε, συναναμίγνυσθε, ἐντραπῇ. 15. ἡγεῖσθε, νουθετεῖτε. 16. δῴη. 17. γράφω.

Exercise 16.—Short Sentences.

I. THE BEATITUDES (Matt. v. 3–10).

These and the following sentences are given **chiefly as practice in applying the rules of conjugation and declension.** As the clauses are complete in sense, they necessarily involve the principles of Syntax; but no difficulties in construction will be found. For the use of the Cases, see § 11. The references in the Notes to succeeding parts of the work will also be useful.

Observe that throughout the Beatitudes the substantive verb *are* must be supplied with the predicate, μακάριοι, *blessed.* (See § 166.) ὅτι is *because* (§ 136, 6).

1. Μακάριοι οἱ πτωχοὶ τῷ πνεύματι·[1] ὅτι αὐτῶν[2] ἐστὶν ἡ βασιλεία τῶν οὐρανῶν.
2. μακάριοι οἱ πενθοῦντες·[3] ὅτι αὐτοὶ παρακληθήσονται.
3. μακάριοι οἱ πραεῖς· ὅτι αὐτοὶ κληρονομήσουσι τὴν γῆν.
4. μακάριοι οἱ πεινῶντες καὶ διψῶντες[4] τὴν δικαιοσύνην· ὅτι αὐτοὶ χορτασθήσονται.
5. μακάριοι οἱ ἐλεήμονες· ὅτι αὐτοὶ ἐλεηθήσονται.
6. μακάριοι οἱ καθαροὶ τῇ καρδίᾳ· ὅτι αὐτοὶ τὸν Θεὸν ὄψονται.[5]
7. μακάριοι οἱ εἰρηνοποιοί· ὅτι αὐτοὶ υἱοὶ[6] Θεοῦ κληθήσονται.
8. μακάριοι οἱ δεδιωγμένοι ἕνεκεν[7] δικαιοσύνης· ὅτι αὐτῶν ἐστὶν ἡ βασιλεία τῶν οὐρανῶν.

II. From John I.

Prepositions.

ἀπό, with Gen., *from, of* (a place).
διά,   ,,   *by means of.*
ἐκ,   ,,   *out of.*
ἐν, with Dat., *in*, with plural, *among.*
παρά, with Gen., *from* (of persons).
πρός, with Acc., *unto, with* (§ 307, γ, 2).
Further details, Ch. VI., and Syntax.

Adverb used as Preposition.

χωρίς, with Gen., *without.*

Negative Adverbs.

οὐ, *not.*
οὐδέ, *not even.*

Conjunctions.

καί, *and* (§ 136, 1).
ὡς, *as* (§ 136, 2).

Verses 1–5.

Ἐν ἀρχῇ ἦν ὁ λόγος, καὶ ὁ λόγος ἦν πρὸς τὸν Θεόν, καὶ Θεὸς ἦν ὁ λόγος.[8] οὗτος ἦν ἐν ἀρχῇ πρὸς τὸν Θεόν. πάντα δι' αὐτοῦ ἐγένετο,[9] καὶ

---

[1] Dative: *in (the) spirit*, as hereafter explained, § 280, *f*. Compare τῇ καρδίᾳ, 6
[2] Of them = *theirs.*
[3] The mourning ones = *those who mourn*, § 200. Compare the Participles in sentences 4, 8.
[4] Hungering and thirsting *for* righteousness (acc.), § 281, *a.*
[5] See § 103, 4.
[6] Nominative after a copulative verb. See § 165, note.
[7] *For the sake of* (gen.), § 133.
[8] ὁ λόγος is the subject, § 206.
[9] Singular verb, with plural neuter nominative, § 173.

§ 117.]   EXERCISES.   129

χωρὶς αὐτοῦ ἐγένετο οὐδὲ ἓν ὃ γέγονεν. ἐν αὐτῷ ζωὴ ἦν, καὶ ἡ ζωὴ ἦν τὸ φῶς τῶν ἀνθρώπων, καὶ τὸ φῶς ἐν τῇ σκοτίᾳ φαίνει, καὶ ἡ σκοτία αὐτὸ οὐ κατέλαβεν.

Verse 14.

Καὶ ὁ λόγος σὰρξ ἐγένετο, καὶ ἐσκήνωσεν ἐν ἡμῖν (καὶ ἐθεασάμεθα τὴν δόξαν αὐτοῦ, δόξαν ὡς μονογενοῦς παρὰ πατρός·) πλήρης χάριτος καὶ ἀληθείας.

Verses 45, 46.

Εὑρίσκει Φίλιππος τὸν Ναθαναὴλ, καὶ λέγει αὐτῷ,[1] "Ὃν[2] ἔγραψε Μωυσῆς ἐν τῷ νόμῳ καὶ οἱ προφῆται[3] εὑρήκαμεν, Ἰησοῦν[4] υἱὸν τοῦ Ἰωσὴφ τὸν[5] ἀπὸ Ναζαρέτ. καὶ εἶπεν αὐτῷ[1] Ναθαναὴλ, Ἐκ Ναζαρὲτ δύναταί τι ἀγαθὸν εἶναι;[6] λέγει αὐτῷ[1] Φίλιππος, Ἔρχου καὶ ἴδε.

III. SELECTED SENTENCES.

Prepositions (additional).   *Conjunctions.*
εἰς, with Acc., *into.*   δέ, *but.*
ἐπί,   „   *to.*   ὅτι, *that.*
μετά, with Gen., *together with.*

1. Ἑτοιμάσατε[7] τὴν ὁδὸν Κυρίου.
2. Ἰησοῦ, ἐλέησόν[7] με.
3. Θάρσει,[7] ἔγειραι,[7] φωνεῖ σε.
4. Ἡ πίστις σου σέσωκέ σε.
5. Ἀφέωνταί σου αἱ ἁμαρτίαι.
6. Συνέδραμε[8] πρὸς αὐτοὺς πᾶς ὁ λαός.
7. Μετεκαλέσατο τοὺς πρεσβυτέρους τῆς ἐκκλησίας.
8. Μακάριόν ἐστι διδόναι μᾶλλον ἢ λαμβάνειν.
9. Καίσαρα[9] ἐπικέκλησαι, ἐπὶ Καίσαρα πορεύσῃ.

---

[1] *To him*, dative after the verb of *saying*, § 278, *b*.
[2] Understand *him* as antecedent: "him whom," § 347.
[3] Understand ἔγραψαν.
[4] (Namely) *Jesus*, in apposition (§ 177) with the antecedent (2) above.
[5] Simply refers to υἱόν (§ 230, *a*), not to be translated.
[6] The infinitive dependent on δύναται (§ 389, *a*), *can anything good be?*
[7] For the sense of the Aorist Imperative, and its distinction from the Present, § 373 may be consulted.
[8] See § 103 (5).
[9] *To* Cæsar: prep. implied in verb (§ 281, *a*). See ([4]) on the Beatitudes.

K

10. Ἀνάστηθι,¹ καὶ στῆθι¹ ἐπὶ τοὺς πόδας σου.
11. Ἡ πίστις ὑμῶν καταγγέλλεται ἐν ὅλῳ τῷ κόσμῳ.
12. Εὐφράνθητε,¹ ἔθνη, μετὰ τοῦ λαοῦ αὐτοῦ.
13. Ὡς σοφὸς ἀρχιτέκτων θεμέλιον τέθεικα, ἄλλος δὲ ἐποικοδομεῖ.
14. Φθείρουσιν ἤθη χρήσθ'² ὁμιλίαι κακαί.
15. Ἡ ἀγάπη τοῦ Χριστοῦ συνέχει ἡμᾶς.
16. Χωρήσατε¹ ἡμᾶς, οὐδένα ἠδικήσαμεν, οὐδένα ἐφθείραμεν, οὐδένα ἐπλεονεκτήσαμεν.
17. Πάντα δοκιμάζετε·¹ τὸ καλὸν κατέχετε·¹ ἀπὸ παντὸς εἴδους πονηροῦ³ ἀπέχεσθε.¹
18. Πιστὸς⁴ ὁ λόγος καὶ πάσης ἀποδοχῆς⁵ ἄξιος, ὅτι Χριστὸς Ἰησοῦς ἦλθεν εἰς τὸν κόσμον ἁμαρτωλοὺς σῶσαι.⁶
19. Ἠνοίγη ὁ ναὸς τῆς σκηνῆς τοῦ μαρτυρίου ἐν τῷ οὐρανῷ.

¹ For the sense of the Aorist Imperative, and its distinction from the Present, § 373 may be consulted.
² See § 3, h.
³ *From every form of evil*, 1 Thess. v. 22.
⁴ Understand ἐστι. Compare on the Beatitudes, prefixed note.
⁵ Genitive, by ἄξιος, *worthy of* (§ 272).
⁶ Infinitive, expressing *purpose*, as in English. (See § 339, h, 1.)

Chapter VI. PREPOSITIONS.

118. It was stated in § 11 that three forms of inflection, or "cases," in Nouns are used to denote three several relations of place: the Genitive implying *motion from*; the Dative, *rest in*, or *connection with*; and the Accusative, *motion towards*. The cases thus severally answer the questions, Whence? Where? Whither?

With this general distinction are connected very many other relations, which are expressed by the same three cases, with the aid of PREPOSITIONS.

To Syntax it belongs to exhibit the various meanings of the prepositions, and their place in sentences. For the present, it will suffice to give a list of the chief of them, with their general significations. This is necessary, partly because several adverbs (see § 132) are derived from prepositions; but chiefly because of the important place which prepositions hold in the composition of verbs. (See Chapter X.)

Prepositions may govern—
1. The Genitive only: *Whence?*
2. The Dative only: *Where?*
3. The Accusative only: *Whither?*
4. The Genitive and Accusative: *Whence? Whither?*
5. The Genitive, Dative, and Accusative: *Whence? Where? Whither?*

119. PREPOSITIONS GOVERNING THE GENITIVE ONLY.

ἀντί (opposition, equivalent), *over against, opposed to, instead of.*
ἀπό (motion from the exterior), *from, away from.*
ἐκ, ἐξ (motion from the interior), *from, out of.*
πρό, *before*, whether of time or place.

To these may be added most of the "improper" prepositions, as they are often called; being really adverbs with a prepositional government. (For a list of these, see § 133.)

120. Prepositions governing the Dative only.

ἐν, *in*, of time, place, or element; *among*.
σύν (union of co-operation; compare μετά), *with*.

121. Prepositions governing the Accusative only.

ἀνά (up in), used in the phrases ἀνὰ μέσον, *in the midst of;* ἀνὰ μέρος, *in turns* (1 Cor. xiv. 27).
εἰς (motion to the interior), *into, to, unto, with a view to.*

122. Prepositions governing the Genitive and Accusative.

διά, through. GEN. (through, as proceeding from), *through, by means of.* ACC. (through, as tending towards), *on account of, owing to.*

κατά, down. GEN. (down from: so, literally, 1 Cor. xi. 4), *against.* ACC. (down towards), *according to, throughout, during, over.*

μετά (union of locality; compare σύν). GEN., *together with, among.* ACC., *after.*

περί, around. GEN., *about, concerning, on behalf of;* once, *above* (3 John 2). ACC., *about, round about.*

ὑπέρ, over. GEN., *above, on behalf of, for.* ACC., *beyond.*

ὑπό, under. GEN., *by* (of the agent or efficient cause). ACC., *under, in the power of, close upon* (as Acts v. 21, *close upon morning,* i.e., "very early").

123. Prepositions governing the Genitive, Dative, and Accusative.

ἐπί (superposition). GEN., *upon* (as springing from), *over, in the presence of, in the time of.* DAT., *upon* (as resting on), *in addition to, on account of.* ACC., *up to* (used of place, number, aim), *over* (of time, place, extent).

παρά (juxtaposition). GEN. (from beside), *from,* used of persons, as ἀπό of places. DAT. (at the side of), *near, with,* of persons only, except

John xix. 25. Acc. (to, or along the side of), *beside, compared with, i.e.,* so as to be shown *beyond,* or *contrary to, instead of.*

πρός (in the direction of). GEN., *in favour of,* only in Acts xxvii. 34. DAT., *at, close by.* Acc., *towards, in reference to.*

124. Synoptical Table of the Prepositions.

The Prepositions are here exhibited in groups, both because their meaning may thus be more easily remembered, and because the comparison, both in meaning and form, suggests some interesting points of relationship. For further details the student may consult Goodwin's Greek Grammar (Macmillan). Only the general meaning of every preposition is given in the following table; and the initial capitals denote the cases governed. Cases found with certain prepositions in classic Greek, but not in the New Testament, are bracketed.

G.	ἀπό, in reference to the exterior, *from.*	
{ G.	ἐκ, in reference to the interior, *from,* proclitic.	
{ D.	ἐν, ,, ,, *in,* ,,	
{ A.	εἰς, ,, ,, *to,* ,,	
{ (D.) A.	ἀνά, *up;* opposite of κατά.	
{ G. A.	κατά, *down;* opposite of ἀνά.	
{ G. D. A.	ἐπί, superposition, *upon.*	
{ G. D. A.	παρά, juxtaposition, *beside.*	
{ G. D. A.	πρός, propinquity, *towards.*	
{ G. (D.) A.	περί, circumvention, entire; *around.*	
{ (G. D. A.)	ἀμφί, circumvention, partial; *about.*	
{ G. A.	ὑπέρ, over; *(super).*	
{ G. A.	ὑπό, under; *(sub).*	
{ G. A.	μετά, association, *with, after*	
{ D.	σύν, co-operation, *with.*	
{ G.	ἀντί, opposition, specific, *over against*	
{ G.	πρό, opposition, general, *in front of, before.*	
G. A.	διά, *through,* kindred with δύο, and regarding the object as divided into two parts.	

ἀμφί is not found in the New Testament, except in composition. In classic Greek its use is comparatively rare. With all three cases it means *about,* or *around.*

Accentuation.—The Prepositions are all oxytone except the proclitics, εἰς, ἐκ, ἐν.

125. For further details as to the meaning and use of the prepositions, see Chapter X., especially the Table, § 147, *a*; also Syntax.

In explanation of the very various significance which may belong to the same preposition, two points should be noted: (1) that its meaning will be necessarily modified by the signification of the verb that it may follow, and by that of the noun which it governs, as also by the case of the latter; and (2) that as all languages have a far smaller number of words than there are shades of thought to express, one word must often have many applications. Then, as no language is exactly parallel, word for word, with any other, the variations of meaning included under one Greek term, for instance, will not be the same as those embraced by the nearest English equivalent. Thus, ὑπέρ may often be translated *for ;* but the applications of the two words, though perhaps equally various, are very far from being identical.

Chapter VII. ADVERBS.

126. The simplest, and perhaps the original form of an Adverb, is **some case of a substantive, a pronoun, or an adjective agreeing with a noun understood**; fixed absolutely in that shape to express some quality, manner, place, or time.

a. The *Accusative* is very often thus employed, as ἀκμήν (Matt. xv. 16), *yet*, lit., "up to (this) point;" πέραν, *on the other side*. In like manner is used the accusative neuter of many adjectives, both singular and plural; often with the article: as, τὸ λοιπόν, *furthermore* (once, τοῦ λοιποῦ, Gal. vi. 17); τὰ πολλά, *for the most part*. So, possibly from obsolete adjectives, σήμερον, *to-day;* αὔριον, *to-morrow;* χθές, *yesterday*.

b. The *Dative* (sometimes in an obsolete form) is also frequently found: as ἰδίᾳ, *privately;* πεζῇ, *by land*. Here the iota subscript is often omitted: πάντη, *always* (Acts xxiv. 3, in some copies, πάντῃ); εἰκῇ, *without a cause*.

c. The *Genitive* occurs in αὐτοῦ, *there*, as well as in other forms which will be noticed immediately.

d. In some instances, *a preposition with its case* written as one word is used adverbially, as παραχρῆμα, *immediately*, lit., "along with the business;" ἐξαίφνης, *suddenly*, lit., "from a steep descent;" καθεξῆς, *in order*, lit., "according to a special course."

e. The older form of the language employed the terminations -θεν, -θι, and -δε as case-endings of nouns (Gen., Dat., Acc.), and when they became obsolete in ordinary declension, they were retained as adverbial terminations to denote *whence*, *where*, and *whither*. Thus: οὐρανόθεν, *from heaven;* παιδιόθεν, *from childhood* (Mark ix. 21); πέρυσι (the -σι standing for the older -θι), *last year* (2 Cor. viii. 10; ix. 2). These terminations are also found in adverbs derived from prepositions and other adverbs, on which see § 132.

Adverbs in -ως.

127. The most common form of adverbs is, however, that in -ως. This termination, which answers exactly in meaning to our final syllable -*ly*,[1] is affixed to adjective-**stems** of all forms, the stem-ending, where needful, being modified.

For example:
First form (§ 34), δίκαιος, *just*, **δικαιο-**; δικαίως, *justly*.
Second form (§ 37), πᾶς, *all*, **παντ-**; πάντως, *wholly*.
Third form (§ 41), ἀληθής, *true*, **ἀληθεσ-**; ἀληθῶς, *truly*.

Participles may also use this adverbial form, as ὄντως (from ὤν, stem ὀντ-), *really*.

Sometimes an adverb made from an adjective appears in two forms: as ταχύ and ταχέως, *quickly;* εὐθύς (probably a corrupt form of εὐθύ) and εὐθέως, *immediately*.

Comparison of Adverbs.

128. The comparative of adverbs is generally the **neuter singular** accusative of the corresponding adjective; the superlative, the **neuter plural**. Thus: ταχέως (or ταχύ), *quickly;* τάχιον, *more quickly* (John xx. 4);[2] τάχιστα, *most quickly* (Acts xvii. 15); εὖ, *well* (probably from ἐύς, an old equivalent of ἀγαθός); βελτίον, *better* (2 Tim. i. 18). Adverbs of other than adjective derivation conform to this model. So from ἄνω (see § 132) is found ἀνώτερον.

Some comparatives take the termination -ως, as περισσοτέρως, *more abundantly*.

An irregular comparative and superlative are μᾶλλον, *more;* μάλιστα, *most*. So, ἆσσον, *nearer* (Acts xxvii. 13), attributed to the adverb (in classic Greek) ἄγχι, *near;* superlative, ἄγχιστα.

Pronominal Adverbs, used also as Conjunctions.

129. Several adverbs are formed indirectly or directly from pronouns; and, like pronouns, are demonstrative, relative, interrogative, dependent interrogative, and indefinite (enclitic).

---

[1] It is possibly an old dative plural: -ως = -οις. The accentuation generally follows that of the genitive plural of the adjective; as δικαίων, δικαίως, ἀληθῶν, ἀληθῶς.
[2] But W. H. read τάχειον. Cf. § 43, note.

§ 131.] ADVERBS. 137

The following Table gives the chief pronominal adverbs found in the New Testament:—

	Demonstrative.	Relative.	Interrogative.	Dependent Interrogative.	Indefinite.
Time ...	τότε, then νῦν, νυνί, now	ὅτε, when ἡνίκα, when	πότε; when?	ὁπότε, when	ποτε, sometime
Place ...	αὐτοῦ, here ὧδε, here ἐκεῖ, ἐκεῖσε, there, thither ἐνθάδε, hither ἐντεῦθεν, hence, thence	οὗ, where ὅθεν, whence	ποῦ; where? πόθεν; whence?	ὁποῦ, where	που, somewhere
Manner	οὕτω(ς), thus, so	ὡς, as	πῶς; how?	ὅπως, how πότερον, whether	πω(ς), somehow

The correlatives in the above Table will be immediately perceived. For further details compare under Pronouns, especially § 62, and Syntax. οὕτω, *so*, becomes οὕτως before a vowel, and the indefinite πω is always πως, except in composition.

It will be observed that the scheme of adverbs is incomplete in the relative and interrogative divisions, by the omission of the (accusative) form *whither*. Classic Greek supplies the omission by the words οἷ, ποῖ; ὅποι, but these are not found in the New Testament, the genitive forms οὗ, ποῦ; ὁποῦ being used. Compare in English the tendency to say "*Where* are you going?" for "*Whither* are you going?"

Numeral Adverbs.

130. Numeral adverbs end in -ις, -κις, or -ακις, as δίς, *twice;* τρίς, *thrice;* ἑπτάκις, *seven times;* ἑβδομηκοντάκις, *seventy times* (Matt. xviii. 22); πολλάκις, *many times.* ἅπαξ, *once for all*, is exceptionally formed; ὁσάκις, *as often as* (1 Cor. xi. 25, 26), is from the relative.

Adverbs from Verbs.

131. Ancient verbal forms, used as adverbs, are δεῦρο, *hither*, with its plural, δεῦτε. These are generally employed as imperatives, "Come thou (or ye) *hither!"* The imperative ἄγε is also employed as a kind of adverb, *Go to!* (James iv. 13; v. 1).

Some verbs in -ίζω, expressing national peculiarity, form an adverb in -ιστί. Thus, from ἑλληνίζω, we find ἑλληνιστί, *in the Greek language;* similarly, ἑβραϊστί, *in the Hebrew language.*

Adverbs from Prepositions.

132. Many prepositions have a corresponding adverb in -ω (paroxytone). Thus, from ἀνά is formed ἄνω, *upwards;* and from κατά, κάτω, *downwards.* So, ἔσω, *within;* ἔξω, *without.* The termination -θεν is added to these adverbs also, with a genitive force; as ἄνωθεν, *from above;* ἔξωθεν, *from without.*

Once, a preposition without change is employed as an adverb (2 Cor. xi. 23), ὑπὲρ ἐγώ, *I (am) more.*[1]

Prepositive Adverbs, or Improper Prepositions.

133. Several adverbs may be used like prepositions to govern nouns, and are then termed "improper" or "spurious" prepositions. The following is an alphabetical list of the principal found in the New Testament:—

ἅμα, *together with.*
ἄνευ, *without.*
ἄχρι(ς), or μέχρι(ς), *until.*
ἐγγύς, *near* (in time or space).
ἔμπροσθεν, *before.*
ἐναντίον, *in front of, against.*
ἕνεκα (-εν), *for the sake of.*
ἐνώπιον, *before, in the presence of.*
ἔξω, *without.*
ἐπάνω, *above.*
ἔσω, *within.*
ἕως, *as far as.*
μέσον, *in the midst of* (Phil. ii. 15).
μεταξύ, *between.*

---

[1] So, πρός, *too,* often in classical Greek.

ὀπίσω, ὄπισθεν, *behind, after.*
ὀψέ, *at the end of* (Matt. xxviii. 1).
πλήν, *except.*
πλησίον, *near ;* παραπλησίον, *very near.*
ὑπερέκεινα, *beyond* (2 Cor. x. 16).
χάριν, *by favour of, for the sake of.*
χωρίς, *separated from, without.*

Some of the above, it is evident, are originally adverbial forms of adjectives and substantives. **All govern the Genitive,** except ἅμα (Matt. xiii. 29), and παραπλησίον (Phil. ii. 27),[1] which take the Dative; as does ἐγγύς sometimes.

NEGATIVE ADVERBS.

134. *a.* The negative adverbs are οὐ (before a vowel, οὐκ ; before an aspirated vowel, οὐχ), *not,* and μή, *not.*

Accentuation.—οὐ is proclitic, excepting where emphatic ; as οὔ, *No!* (John i. 21).

b. For an explanation of the difference between these two words, see Syntax. It must suffice now to say that οὐ denies facts, μή mental conceptions. The former is called the "categorical" or "objective" negative; the latter, the "conditional" or "subjective." Both words are used in composition with τις, τι (see § 60); also with the indefinite adverbs in the Table, § 129, as οὔπω, *not yet ;* μήποτε, *never in any case.*

c. μή is also used as an interrogative adverb, expecting the answer, *no;* and, in composition with the interrogative τίς, adds a kind of appeal to the hearers, as though enlisting their assent to the negative: thus, μήτι ἐγώ; (Mark xiv. 19), *Is it I?* i.e., "It is not I, is it?"

---

[1] But W. H. read παραπλήσιον θανάτου.

Chapter VIII. CONJUNCTIONS AND OTHER PARTICLES.

135. Besides the Conjunctions properly so called, used, as in other languages, to unite words and sentences, there are in Greek several indeclinable words, employed sometimes separately, often in combination with other words, for the purpose of emphasis. These cannot always be translated, the degree of emphasis being too slight for the words of less flexible languages to convey.

These indeclinable words, together with the conjunctions themselves (and sometimes the primitive adverbs), are generally called *Particles*.

It belongs to Syntax to discuss the place and power of the particles in a sentence. All, therefore, that is now necessary is, to classify the chief of them, and to indicate their general meaning.

Classification of the Conjunctive Particles.

136. The Conjunctions denote (1) annexation, (2) comparison, (3) disjunction, (4) antithesis, (5) condition, (6) reason, (7) inference, or (8) result. The relative forms of the adverbs (see § 129) are also really conjunctions.

1. *Annexation.*—The copulative conjunctions are καί, *and, also, even;* τε, *and, also.* The latter is generally subordinate : τε...καί, *both...and, not only...but;* sometimes καὶ...τε, or τε...τε. Very commonly, however, *both...and* is expressed by καὶ...καί, as in 1 Thess. ii. 14, 15, etc.

2. *Comparison.*—As conjunctions of comparison, the particles ὡς, *as;* ὥσπερ, *just as;* καθώς, *like as,* are used ; mostly in correlation with the adverb οὕτως, *so.* (Compare § 129, Table.)

3. *Disjunction.*—The disjunctive particles are ἤ, *or;* ἤ...ἤ, *either...or* (in general); ἤτοι...ἤ, *either...or* (as an exclusive alternative), εἴτε...εἴτε, *whether...whether.*

4. *Antithesis.*—The antithetic conjunctions are ἀλλά (originally neuter plural of ἄλλος) and δέ, both signifying *but.* The adversative sense is much stronger in the former than in the latter. With δέ the particle μέν often stands in the preceding sentence, and may be rendered *indeed,* or *on the one hand* (δέ, *on the other*), or, more frequently, may be left untranslated, marking simply that the two clauses stand in real or formal antithesis. Etymologically, μέν is (probably) "the first thing;" δέ, "the second thing:" the antithesis is, therefore, often very slight, a *distinction* rather than *opposition.*

5. *Condition.*—The conditional particles are εἰ, *if;* εἴγε, *if at least,* εἴπερ, *if at all;* ἐάν (εἰ ἄν), *if* (possibly). For the important rules as to their use with verbs, see Syntax.

6. *Cause.*—Particles expressive of a reason (causal) are, ὅτι, *that, because;* γάρ, *for;* διότι, *because;* ἐπεί (see § 407, *a*), *since.*

7. *Inference.*—The chief inferential particles are οὖν, *therefore;* τοίνυν, *then;* ἄρα, *consequently;* διό, *wherefore;* τοιγαροῦν, *accordingly.*

8. *Result.*—The "final" conjunctions are ἵνα, *in order that;* ὡς and ὅπως, *so that;* μή, *that not, lest.*

PARTICLES OF EMPHASIS AND INTERROGATION.

137. *a.* The chief emphatic particles are γε, *at least, indeed* (enclitic); and δή, *certainly, now.* To these may be added the enclitics περ, *very, verily,* and τοι, *certainly,* found in combination with other words, as ἐπειδήπερ (Luke i. 1), *since verily;* μέντοι, *however.*

b. As interrogative particles the following are employed: εἰ, *if,* used elliptically, "Tell us if—;" ἦ, simply denoting that a question is asked, and requiring no English equivalent save in the form of the sentence; and ἆρα (not to be confounded with ἄρα, § 136, 7), which makes the question emphatic (only in Luke xviii. 8; Acts viii. 30; Gal. ii. 17). For the interrogative adverbs, see § 129; and for the structure of interrogative sentences, consult the Syntax.

INTERJECTIONS.

138. *a.* An Interjection is generally but the transcript of a natural instinctive sound, and therefore scarcely ranks among the "parts of organised speech." Words of this kind in the New Testament are ὦ, *O!* *oh!* ἔα, *ah!* expressive of pain and terror (Luke iv. 34); οὐά, *ah!* expressing scorn and hatred (Mark xv. 29); οὐαί, *woe! alas!* often governing a dative; οὐαὶ ὑμῖν, *woe unto you! alas for you!*

b. The imperative form, ἴδε, *see,* is often treated interjectionally, but still more frequently the old imperative middle of the same verb is employed, accented as a particle: ἰδού, *lo! behold!*

Chapter IX. ON THE FORMATION OF WORDS.

139. 1. *Roots*.—Words of all kinds are derived from some Root. For the distinction between *root* and *stem*, see § 10. The root is that part which remains after taking away from a whole family of kindred words all the parts which are different in each. Thus **AK-** is the root of ἀκ-μή, ἄκ-ρος, ἄκ-ανθα.

The root expresses the leading idea, or general meaning, which runs through all the kindred words, though differently modified in each; thus, **AK-** expresses the general meaning of "sharpness" or "pointedness."

In the formation of words, some are derived directly from the root; as ἀκμή, from **AK-**. Others take as a ("secondary") root the stem of words already formed; as ἀκμάζω, from ἀκμή (ἀκμα-).

Hence we find **primary, secondary, tertiary,** etc., formations.[1] Thus:—

Primary.	Secondary.	Tertiary.
'AK-μή, *point*	'AKμ-άζω, *to flourish*.	
"AK-ρος, *pointed*	'AKρι-βής, *accurate*	'AKρίβε-ια, *accuracy*.
		'AKριβ-ῶς, *accurately*.

2. *Classes of Words*.—Without attempting here any extended statement of the methods and laws of derivation, it will be useful to specify some of the leading terminations which occur in the formation of Greek words. Each of these terminations has a particular force and meaning of its own, whatever be the root or stem to which it is joined: thus, κρι-τής, ζηλω-τής, κλέπ-της, πολί-της, have all the same termination, -της, and with the same meaning.

Classes of words may thus be formed, by arranging together those which have the same terminations, and marking their signification; and this may be done with words of all kinds—substantives, adjectives, pronouns, verbs, and particles.

---

[1] See, for greater detail, Goodwin's Greek Grammar, §§ 128—132.

3. *Modification of Stem-endings.*—The final vowel or consonant of the root or stem will be affected by the termination according to the general usages of the language, as illustrated especially in the inflections of the verbs. Thus, ποιη-τής, from ποιε- (compare § 96, *a*, etc.), and καλύπ-τω, κάλυμ-μα (see § 4, *d*, 4), from καλυφ- or καλυβ-.

Classes of Substantives.

140. a. First Declension.—1. *Masculine Nouns.*—The termination -της expresses a **male agent.** Thus, κρῑτής, *a judge;* ποιητής, *a maker, doer, poet.* Some nouns of this termination are formed from the root of simpler nouns : as πολίτης (πόλις), *citizen;* οἰκέτης (οἶκος), *domestic.*

Accentuation.—Dissyllables of this class, and polysyllables with short penultima, throw back the accent as far as possible, except κριτής. So ψεύστης, δεσπότης, ψεύσται, δέσποτα (voc.). The rest are oxytone, except πολίτης.

2. *Feminine Nouns.*—i. The termination -ῐα (paroxytone) expresses **quality.** Adjective stems in ες- or οο- give the forms (pro-paroxytone) -ειᾰ, -οιᾰ. So, σοφία, *wisdom* (σοφός); ἀλήθεια, *truth* (ἀληθής); εὔνοια, *good-will* (εὔνους). A few nouns in -είᾱ (paroxytone) are from verbal stems in -ευ, and denote **the result of action ;** as βασιλεία, *kingdom* (βασιλεύω); παιδεία, *instruction* (παιδεύω).

ii. Substantives in -οσύνη connected with adjective stems in ον-, rarely in ο-, also denote **quality ;** as σωφροσύνη, *prudence,* from σώφρων, stem ον- ; ἐλεημοσύνη, *compassion* (ἐλεήμων); δικαιοσύνη, *righteousness* (δίκαιος); ἁγιωσύνη, *holiness* (ἅγιος), the ο- becoming -ω, because of the short preceding syllable. (Compare § 42.)

b. Second Declension.—1. *Masculine Nouns.*—The termination -μός (oxytone) appended to verbal stems denotes **action ;** as from θύω (θυ-), *to rage,* θυμός, *passion.* Sometimes σ intervenes, as in δεσμός, *bond,* from δε-, δέω, *to bind;* or θ, as κλαυθμός, *lamentation,* from κλαϝ-, κλαίω, *to weep.* (See § 96, *c.*)

2. *Neuter Nouns.*—i. The ending -τρον, from verbal roots, denotes **instrument.** Thus, λυ-, λύω, *to release;* λύτρον, *ransom.*

ii. The termination -ιον, from substantive stems, is **diminutive :** as from παῖς (παιδ-), *a child;* παιδίον, *a little child.* To -ιον is sometimes prefixed the syllable αρ- or ιδ- : as παιδάριον, *a little boy;* κλινίδιον, *a*

§ 141.] WORD-FORMATION—SUBSTANTIVES. 145

little bed, from κλίνη, *a couch;* ἀσσάριον, *a farthing*, from Latin, *as.* (See § 154, *a.*)

Diminutives in -ιον must be distinguished from neuters of adjectives in -ιος, used as substantives: *e.g.*, ἱλαστήριον, *propitiatory*.

The masculine and feminine terminations -ισκος, -ισκη are also occasionally used as **diminutives**. Thus, νεανίας (stem α-), *a youth;* νεανίσκος, *a lad* So, παιδίσκη, *a damsel*.

Accentuation of Neuters.—Neuter nouns generally retract the accent. Diminutives in -ιον are, however, paroxytone, except when a short syllable precedes this termination.

c. Third Declension.—1. *Masculine Nouns.*—i. The suffix -εύς (oxytone), stem ἐ-, denotes an **agent**: as γραμματεύς, *a scribe*, from γραμματ-, γράμμα, *a letter*. (For the declension of these substantives, see § 30, iii.)

ii. The terminations -τήρ (oxytone) and -τωρ (paroxytone, stem τορ-) also signify an **agent**: as φωστήρ, *luminary*, from φῶς, *light;* ῥήτωρ, *an orator*, from ῥε- (in the obsolete verb ῥέω, *to speak*).

2. *Feminine Nouns.*—i. The ending -σις (gen. -σεως, stem σι-), from verbal stems, expresses **action**. Thus, δικαιο- (δικαιόω, *to justify*) gives δικαίωσις, *justification;* and πραγ- (πράσσω, *to do*), πρᾶξις, *action*. These nouns, a.very numerous class, retract the accent. (For their declension, see § 30, i. *b.*)

ii. The termination -της (gen. -τητος, stem τητ-) denotes **quality**, and is attached to adjective stems. Thus, ἴσος, *equal*, gives ἰσότης, *equality;* ἅγιος, *holy*, ἁγιότης, *holiness*. These also retract the accent.

3. *Neuter Nouns.*—i. The termination -μα (stem ματ-) denotes the **result of action**, and is affixed to verbal stems. Thus, πράσσω, πραγ-, gives πρᾶγμα, *a thing done, an action;* and the obsolete ῥέω, ῥε-, forms ῥῆμα, *a thing spoken, a word*.

ii. The ending -ος (from stem ἐς-, see § 30, iv.) denotes, from verbal stems, **result**; from adjective stems, **quality**. Thus, from ἰδ-, Second Aor. εἶδον, *I saw* (see § 103, 4), we have εἶδος, *an appearance;* and from βαθυ-, in βαθύς, *deep*, βάθος, *depth*.

141. The following scheme exhibits at one view **the principal terminations of derivative nouns**. The nominative and genitive endings

L

are given as in Lexicons and Vocabularies; but the stem and declension will easily be traced.

Signification.	Nom. and Gen. Terminations.		Gender.
Agent	-εύς,	-έως	M.
Do.	-της,	-του	M.
Do.	-τήρ,	-τῆρος	M.
Do.	-τωρ,	-τορος	M.
Instrument	-τρον,	-τρου	N.
Action	-μός[1]	-μοῦ	M.
Do.	-σις,	-σεως	F.
Result	-εία,	-είας	F.
Do.	-μα,	-ματος	N.
Do.	-ος,	-ους	N.
Quality	-της,	-τητος	F.
Do.	-ία,	-ίας	F.
Do.	-οσύνη,	-οσύνης	F.
Do.	-ος,	-ους	N.
Diminutive	-ιον,	-ίου	N.
Do.	-ισκος,	-ίσκου	M.
Do.	-ίσκη,	-ίσκης	F.

Classes of Adjectives.

142. 1. The most common derivative Adjectives are of the **First Form**, and the usual terminations are the following:—

a. From substantive roots, the ending -ιος (-ία[2]), -ιον, is **possessive,** *i.e.*, has the sense **of,** or **belonging to.** Thus, from οὐρανο-, οὐρανός, *heaven,* is derived οὐράνιος, *heavenly;* from τιμα-, τιμή, *honour,* τίμιος, *honourable, precious.* The ι of this termination sometimes forms a diphthong with a final stem vowel; so, from δίκη (δικα-), *justice,* comes δίκαιος, *just;* from ἀγορά, *market-place,* ἀγοραῖος, *public.* To this class also belong the

---

[1] Occasionally with prefix -θ or -σ.
[2] Some of these adjectives are "of two terminations." (See § 34, *b.*)

§ 142.] WORD-FORMATION—ADJECTIVES. 147

adjectives formed from the names of cities or countries, and denoting their inhabitants. Thus, Ἐφέσιος, *Ephesian* (Ἔφεσος); Ἰουδαῖος, *Jew* (Ἰουδαία).

Accentuation.—The diphthongal forms are *generally* properispomenon; the others are proparoxytone, *i.e.*, retract the accent.

b. The termination -ῐκός, -ή, -όν (oxytone), from verbal or substantive roots, marks **ability** or **fitness**: as κριτικός, *capable of judging* (κρίνω); βασιλικός, *royal* (βασιλεύς).

c. The ending -ῐνος, -η, -ον (proparoxytone), from substantive roots, expresses the **material** of which anything is made: as ξύλινος, *wooden* (ξύλον).

Note.—The same substantive stem may have a derivative of each of the two last-mentioned forms. Thus, from σαρκ- (σάρξ-), *flesh*, are formed σάρκινος, *made of flesh*, "fleshy;" and σαρκικός, *of the nature of flesh*, "fleshly." The former is only found in the received text of the New Testament in 2 Cor. iii. 3; but on the authority of MSS., many critics substitute it for the latter in Rom. vii. 14; 1 Cor. iii. 1; Heb. vii. 16 (so W. H.).

Sometimes the termination -εος (contr. -ους) denotes **material**: as ἀργύρεος, ἀργύρους *of silver* (ἄργυρος).

d. The termination -ρός, -ρά, -ρόν (oxytone) denotes the **complete possession** of a quality, like the English **-ful** or **-able**: as, from ἰσχυ-, ἰσχύς, *strength*, ἰσχυρός, *powerful*.

e. Adjectives ending in -ῐμος, -ον, -σῐμος, -ον (proparoxytone) are occasionally formed from verbal stems, and express **ability** or **fitness**: as δόκιμος, *receivable, current* (of coin); so, *approved*, from δεχ-, δέχομαι, *to receive;* χρήσιμος, *useful*, from χρα-, χράομαι, *to use.* Some proper names are of this class, as Ὀνήσιμος (lit. *profitable*, see Philem. vers. 10, 11).

f. The *verbals* in -τός and -τέος have already been noticed (§ 73, p. 61).

2. **Second and Third Forms.**—Here the derivative stem-endings -ες and -μον need only be noticed.

a. Adjectives in -ης (see § 41) are generally correlative to nouns in -ος (cf. § 140, *c.* 3, ii.), the stem of which, it will be remembered, is also in ες- (§ 30, iv.). So ψεῦδος, *falsehood;* ψευδής, *false.*

b. Adjectives in -μων, derived from verbal stems, attribute the action of the verb to the person: as ἐλεε-, ἐλεέω, *to pity;* ἐλεήμων, *compassionate.*

143. Scheme of Derivative Adjectives.

Signification.	Terminations of Nom. Sing.
Quality	-ης, -ες
Do. complete	-ρός, -ρά, -ρόν
Attribute, locality	-ιος (-αῖος, -εῖος, -οῖος) [-ια], -ιον
Property	-ικός, -ική, -ικόν
Material	-ινος, -ίνη, -ινον
Do.	(-εος) -οῦς [-έα], (-εον) -οῦν
Fitness	-(σ)ιμος, -(σ)ιμον
Attribute	-μων, -μον
Possibility (verbal)	-τός, -τή, -τόν
Obligation (verbal)	-τέος, -τέα, -τέον

Classes of Verbs.

144. *a.* Verbs from substantive or adjective roots ("**denominative verbs**") may signify the *being, doing,* or *causing* that which the noun imports. Verbs in -άω, -έω, -εύω, generally denote simply **state or action**; verbs in -όω, -αίνω, -ύνω, **causation**. Thus, δουλεύω, *I am a slave;* δουλόω, *I make a slave of another, I enslave.* The distinction is not always observed; for instance, πληθύνω may be either *I multiply,* transitive, or *I abound,* intransitive. Verbs in -ίζω often have the sense of **becoming** or acting that which the noun denotes. Thus, Ἰουδαῖος, *a Jew;* ἰουδαΐζω, *I act the Jew* (Gal. ii. 14).

The principal denominative verbal terminations are as follow:—

    -άω, as τιμάω, *to honour* (τιμή).
    -έω, ,, πολεμέω, *to make war* (πόλεμος).
    -όω, ,, δουλόω, *to enslave* (δοῦλος).
    -άζω, ,, ἐργάζομαι, *to work* (ἔργον).
    -ίζω, ,, ἐλπίζω, *to hope* (ἐλπίς).
    -αίνω, ,, λευκαίνω, *to whiten* (λευκός).
    -εύω, ,, βασιλεύω, *to reign* (βασιλεύς).
    -ύνω, ,, πληθύνω, *to abound, multiply* (πλῆθος).

§ 145.] WORD-FORMATION—VERBS. 149

b. Verbs from simpler verbal stems are **inceptives** in -σκω, as γηράσκω, *to grow old;* **frequentatives** or **emphatic verbs,** as βαπτίζω, *to baptise* (βάπτω); and **causatives,** as μεθύσκω, *to intoxicate* (μεθύω); γαμίζω or γαμίσκω, *to give in marriage* (γαμέω). To these, as anomalous derivatives from Perfects, may be added στήκω, *to stand,* from the Perfect ἕστηκα; and γρηγορέω, *to watch,* from ἐγρήγορα, the reduplicated Second Perfect of ἐγείρω.

GENERAL REMARK ON DERIVATION.

145. It often happens that the original of a derivative does not appear in the language in its simpler form; and still more frequently, that it is not found in the New Testament. On the other hand, the *actual* derived forms are far fewer than the *possible.* The copiousness and fertility of the Greek as a living language depended especially on the power which it possessed of expressing new thoughts and shades of thought by words framed according to strict analogy, and therefore competent to take their place at once without question in the vocabulary The language of science among ourselves—which, in fact, is borrowed from the Greek—furnishes an illustration of the same **power** to accompany, with equal step, the progress of knowledge and of thought.

Chapter X. ON THE FORMATION OF COMPOUND WORDS.

146. Compound words are either **parathetic** or **synthetic** in their formation.

In **parathetic**[1] compounds, both words retain their form and meaning, subject only to the laws of euphony. They are, therefore, merely *placed side by side*, as it were, though they are written as one word. This is the case with all verbs compounded with prepositions, as ἐκβάλλω, from ἐκ and βάλλω; ἀπέρχομαι, from ἀπό and ἔρχομαι; καθίστημι, from κατά and ἵστημι; συγχαίρω, from σύν and χαίρω. (The changes in the terminations of some of the above prepositions need no explanation.)

In **synthetic**[2] compounds, the former word, a noun or a verb, loses all inflection; while the latter often takes a form which it could not have had out of composition. The words are therefore *placed in close union*, and really make one word; as φιλόσοφος, from φίλος and σοφία.

Parathetic Compounds.

147. The former word of a **parathetic compound** is almost always in the New Testament a particle, *i.e.*, a preposition or an adverb; never a verb.

> The signification of many compounds can be satisfactorily ascertained only from the Lexicon, as the meaning of the prefix is often modified by that of the principal word.[3] It will, however, be helpful to the learner to have at one view the **chief significations of the particles used in composition.** The following table (*a*) should be compared with that in § 124; and a little thought will trace the connection in each case between the primitive significations (printed in *italics*) and the secondary meanings **that follow.**

---

[1] From παρά and θε- (τίθημι), "set side by side."

[2] From σύν and θε-, "*set together* or *com-posed.*"

[3] So in English: *e.g.*, the particle **over** varies its meaning in the words *overthrow, overtake, overrun, overtime, overbearing;* the fundamental signification being, however, discernible in all.

§ 147, c.]   WORD-FORMATION—COMPOUNDS.   151

a. The Prepositions, as used in Composition.

ἀμφι-, *round about.*
ἀνα-, *up,* back again.
ἀντι-, *instead of,* against, in return for.
ἀπο-, *away from,* dismission, completeness.
δια-, *through,* thorough, between.
εἰς-, *into.*
ἐκ- (ἐξ- before a vowel, ἐγ- before a guttural), *out of,* forth, utterly.
ἐν- (ἐμ- before a labial mute, or μ), *in,* upon, intrinsically.
ἐπι-, *upon,* to, in addition.
κατα-, *down,* downright, against.
μετα-, *with,* participation, change.
παρα-, *beside,* beyond, along.
περι-, *around,* over and above, excess.
προ-, *before,* forward.
προς-, *towards,* in addition to.
συν- (συμ- before a labial mute, or μ ; συγ- before a guttural), *with,* association, compression.
ὑπερ-, *above,* excess.
ὑπο-, *under,* concealment, repression.

b. Separable Particles (Adverbs) in Composition.

ἀ- (from ἅμα), *together,* as ἅπας (-ντ-), *all together.*
ἀρτι-, *lately,* only in ἀρτιγέννητος, *new-born* (1 Pet. ii. 2).
εὐ-, *well,* prosperously.
παλιν-, *again,* only in παλιγγενεσία, *regeneration* (Matt. xix. 28; Titus iii. 5).
παν-, *all* (from neuter of παντ-).
τηλε-, *afar off,* only in τηλαυγῶς, *distinctly* (Mark viii. 25).

c. Inseparable Particles in Composition.

ἀ- (from ἀνά), intensive : perhaps only in ἀτενίζω, *to gaze steadfastly.*
ἀ- or ἀν-, *not,* the usual negative prefix, answering to our *un-.*
δυς-, *hardly* or *ill,* like our *dis-, mis-,* or *un-.*
ἡμι-, *half* (Latin, *semi-*), only in ἡμιθανής, *half-dead,* and ἡμιώριον, *half an hour.*

The PREPOSITIONS (Table *a*), when used in the composition of nouns and adjectives, generally mark a *secondary* formation, *i.e.*, a derivation from a compound verb. Thus, ἀπόστολος, *apostle*, is not from ἀπό and στόλος, but from ἀποστέλλω, *to send forth;* so, ἀποστολή, *apostleship.* Again, from ἐκλέγομαι, *to choose out,* come ἐκλεκτός, *chosen, elect;* and ἐκλογή, *election.* Some such nouns and adjectives, however, are found without any corresponding compound verb.

The ADVERBS and INSEPARABLE PARTICLES (Tables *b, c*) (except ἀ- negative) are generally used with substantives and adjectives, not with verbs.

Two Prepositions may be combined in the formation of a word, the characteristic formative force of each being retained. Thus, καθίστημι, *to establish,* ἀποκαθίστημι, *to restore;* παρακαλέομαι, passive, *to be comforted,*[1] συμπαρακαλέομαι, *to be comforted together;* εἰσάγω, *to introduce,* παρεισάγω, *to introduce by the bye* (2 Pet. ii. 1). So παρεισῆλθεν (Rom. v. 20), *entered by the way.* Again, ἀντιλαμβάνομαι is *to help,* generally (lit., "to take hold of, over against"), but συναντιλαμβάνομαι is **to help by coming into association with** (as Luke x. 40; Rom. viii. 26).

SYNTHETIC COMPOUNDS.

148. In **synthetic compounds** the former word is a noun or a verb, never a particle.

When the former word is a noun, if its stem does not already end in -o, the vowel -o- is commonly added as a **connective,** when the latter word begins with a consonant, as from καρδία, καρδι-ο-γνώστης.

When the former word is a verb, the connecting vowel is usually -ι-, as from ἄρχω, ἀρχ-ι-συνάγωγος; but sometimes -o-, as ἐθελ-ο-θρησκεία. The form of a verbal noun is often employed, as from δείδω (δεῖσις), δεισιδαίμων.

Compound verbs of this class usually take their form from a compound noun; the verb thus appearing in a shape which it cannot have out of composition: as, εὐχαριστέω, *to give thanks,* from εὐχάριστος, not from εὖ and χαριστέω; φιλοτιμέομαι, *to be ambitious,* from φιλότιμος, not from φίλος and τιμέομαι.

---

[1] Literally, to be called to one's side: *i.e.*, for purposes of consolation, or, it might be, of exhortation or advocacy. Hence the word Παράκλητος has the threefold meaning of *Comforter, Exhorter, Advocate.* (See John xiv. 16, 26; 1 John ii. 1.)

In synthetic compounds the latter word generally has the leading significance, and is defined or modified by the former.

The following compounds illustrate the foregoing remarks:—

οἰκο-δεσπότης, *householder*.
κακ-οῦργος, *evildoer* (κακός ἔργον).
αἱματ-εκχυσία, *bloodshedding* (αἷμα, ἔκχυσις from ἐκ and χέ(F)ω).
καρδι-ο-γνώστης, *one who knows the heart*.
ἀρχ-ι-συνάγωγος, *ruler of the synagogue*.
μακρό-θυμος (adjective), μακροθυμία (substantive), *long-suffering*.
δωδεκά-φυλον (neuter-substantive), *ten tribes* (Acts xxvi. 7).
δευτερό-πρωτος, *second-first* (Luke vi. 1), probably "the *first sabbath* in the *second year* of the sabbatical cycle of seven years." See Wieseler's "Chronological Synopsis of the Four Gospels," II. ii. 4. Wieseler fixes the year as 782 A.U.C.[1]

ILLUSTRATION OF THE VARIETIES OF DERIVATION AND COMPOSITION.

149. The root κρι-, verbal stem κριν-, primary meaning *to separate*, may be taken as illustrating the variations and combinations of a Greek word.

First we have **simple derivatives**, formed as in Chapter IX.:—

κρίνω, to separate, or *judge*.
κρίσις, the process of separation, or *judgment*.
κρίμα, the act or result of judgment, *sentence*.
κριτήριον, a standard of judgment, or *tribunal*.
κριτής, a *judge*.
κριτικός (adjective), able to judge, a *discoverer* (Heb. iv. 12).

Next we note the **composition of the verb with different prepositions**:—

ανακρίνω, *to inquire, estimate*.
διακρίνω, *to distinguish, separate, decide;* middle, *to hesitate*.
ἐγκρίνω, *to judge*, or *reckon, among* (2 Cor. x. 12).
ἐπικρίνω, *to adjudge* (Luke xxiii. 24).

---

[1] But W. H. and the Revisers' Text omit the word altogether.

κατακρίνω, to give judgment against, *condemn*.
συγκρίνω, to judge together, *compare*.
ἀποκρίνομαι, *to answer*.
ἀνταποκρίνομαι, *to answer against* (Luke xiv. 6; Rom. ix. 20).
ὑποκρίνομαι, *to dissemble* (Luke xx. 20).
συνυποκρίνομαι, *to dissemble with any one* (Gal. ii. 13).

We may then note the various **compound substantives**, which may be compared with the corresponding verbs :—

ἀνάκρισις, an *examination* (Acts xxv. 26).
ἀπόκρισις, an *answer*.
διάκρισις, the act of distinguishing, *discernment*.
κατάκρισις, *condemnation*.
ὑπόκρισις, *dissimulation, hypocrisy*.
ἀπόκριμα, a *sentence*, as of death, or *response* (2 Cor. i. 9).
κατάκριμα, a *sentence of condemnation*.
πρόκριμα, a *prepossession, prejudice* (1 Tim. v. 21).
ὑποκριτής, lit. a stage-player, a *hypocrite*.

We now take a group of **negative compounds** :—

ἀδιάκριτος, not subject to distinction, *impartial* or *sincere* (James iii. 17).
ἀκατάκριτος, *uncondemned*.
ἀνυπόκριτος, *unfeigned*.

Finally, the New Testament contains three instances of the **composition of this root with nouns and pronouns** :—

αὐτοκατάκριτος, *self-condemned* (Titus iii. 11).
εἰλικρινής (perhaps from εἴλη, cognate with ἥλιος), judged of in the sunlight, *pure, sincere* (Phil. i. 10; 2 Pet. iii. 1).
εἰλικρίνεια (from the above), *sincerity*.

Many other compounds of this root exist, but these are all which the New Testament contains.

Chapter XI. FOREIGN WORDS IN NEW TESTAMENT GREEK.

Languages of Palestine.—Hebrew.

150. Two languages were spoken and understood in Palestine. The one, called in the New Testament "the Hebrew tongue" (Acts xxii. 2 ; xxvi. 14), was in reality a very considerable modification of the Old Testament Hebrew, and is generally now termed "the Syro-Chaldaic," or "**Aramaic**" (from *Aram*, the Hebrew word for Syria). This was the language of the people, and, to some uncertain extent,[1] remained in colloquial use until the destruction of Jerusalem.

Some critics believe that St. Matthew's Gospel was originally written in Aramaic, and that the book as it appears in the New Testament is a more or less literal translation. In this opinion we do not concur; but there can be no doubt that in the days of our Lord the ancient language was still most fondly cherished by the people. Expressions that fell from the Saviour's lips in moments of deep emotion, in the performance of signal miracles, in Gethsemane, and on the Cross, are carefully recorded; and other words of technical character, or religious association, or homely use, are also found in the native tongue of Israel.

Introduction of Greek.

151. But as a direct result of the conquests of Alexander the Great and his successors, the Greek tongue had been carried into almost all the countries of the civilised world, and had become the medium of commercial intercourse, the language of the courts, and, in fact, the universal literary tongue of the provinces afterwards absorbed in the Roman Empire. The natives of Alexandria and of Jerusalem, of Ephesus, and even of Rome, alike adopted it; everywhere with characteristic modifications, but substantially the same. Hence it had become a necessity to translate the Old Testament Scriptures into Greek ; and as this great

---

[1] See on the whole subject, Dr. Roberts' "Discussions on the Gospels."

work was executed by Alexandrian Jews, its language not only shows the influence of the Hebrew original, but contains special forms and peculiarities of expression indigenous to Egypt. This translation, or "the Septuagint,"[1] naturally became the basis of all subsequent Jewish Greek literature, and in particular of the New Testament, which, however, to the Egyptian superadds Palestinian influences. It was in the Greek of the Septuagint thus modified that, in all probability, our Lord and His apostles *generally* spoke. The dialect of Galilee (Matt. xxvi. 73) was not a corrupt Hebrew, but a provincial Greek.

The New Testament writers, it should be noted, differ considerably from one another in style. The Book of Revelation, for instance, is very unlike the writings of the Apostle Paul. All, again, vary greatly from classical models, both in vocabulary and syntax, exchanging the elaborate harmonies of Attic Greek for simpler constructions and homelier speech.

Infusion of Latin.

152. The Roman conquest and tenure of Palestine may be thought likely to have stamped some lasting traces on the language. Such traces undoubtedly appear in the New Testament; but, considering the might of the dominant people, these are marvellously few. The Romans could impose their laws, their polity, their military power, upon vanquished nations, but not their speech. Certainly, there are some Latin words in the New Testament; but these are almost wholly nouns denoting military rank or civil authority, coins, or articles of dress: a valuable historic testimony, were there none beside, how "the sceptre had departed from Judah, and a lawgiver from between his feet."

> By way of illustration to the foregoing remarks, **lists are here appended of the chief Aramaic** (or Syro-Chaldaic) **and Roman terms contained in the New Testament.**

Hebrew and Aramaic Words and Phrases.

153. The Hebrew root is in a few cases **assimilated** to the forms of the Greek language; but is oftener **simply transcribed** and used **without declension or conjugation.**

---

[1] That is "the Seventy" (often quoted as LXX.), from the traditional number of translators.

§ 153, b.] LATIN AND HEBREW IN THE NEW TESTAMENT. 157

a. **Assimilated words** are the following :—

Μεσσίας, MESSIAH, "the Anointed." This word occurs only in John i. 42, iv. 25; the Greek equivalent, Χριστός, from χρίω, *to anoint*, being everywhere else employed.

Φαρισαῖος, *Pharisee*, from a Hebrew word meaning *to separate*, and Σαδδουκαῖος, *Sadducee*, from another, meaning *to be righteous*, are of constant occurrence—"Separatists" and "Moralists."

μαμμωνᾶς (gen. -ᾶ, dat. -ᾷ), *mammon, riches* (Matt. vi. 24 ; Luke xvi. 9, 11, 13). Its derivation is uncertain; but there is no reason for supposing that it was anywhere the name of a false deity.

ἀῤῥαβών, -ῶνος, *a pledge*, or *earnest* (2 Cor. i. 22, v. 5).

On σάββατον, *sabbath*, see § 32, *b*.

γέεννα, -ης, from two words signifying *valley of Hinnom;* hence, metaphorically, for the place of future punishment (see 2 Kings xxiii. 10; Isa. xxx. 33; Jer. vii. 31).

b. **Indeclinable words** are more numerous.

i. The following may rank among **proper names**, on which class of words see further, § 156:—

Ἀκελδαμά, *field of blood* (Acts i. 19).

Βεελζεβούλ, *lord of dung* (Matt. xii. 24, etc.), perhaps a contemptuous turn to the name of the Ekronite god Beelzebub, "lord of flies" (see 2 Kings i. 2, 3). Hence "prince of the demons."

Βοανεργές, *Sons of thunder* (Mark iii. 17).

Γαββαθά, *the Pavement*, or *Tribunal* (John xix. 13).

Γολγοθά, *the Place of a skull*, or *of skulls* (Matt. xxvii. 33 ; Mark xv. 22 ; John xix. 17), called in Greek Κρανίον (Luke xxiii. 33), where our word *Calvary* is taken from the Vulgate.

Ῥεμφάν, probably the planet *Saturn* (Acts vii. 43, from Amos v. 26, LXX.).

ii. **Other Syro-Chaldaic nouns** are as follow :—

Ἀββᾶ, *Father*, in confidence, endearment, or entreaty (Mark xiv. 36 ; Rom. viii. 15 ; Gal. iv. 6).

κορβᾶν, *gift* (Mark vii. 11), κορβανᾶς (decl. Matt. xxvii. 6), *treasury*.

μάννα, lit. "what is this?" *manna* (Exod. xvi. 15 ; John vi. 31, 49, 58 ; Heb. ix. 4 : Rev. ii. 17).

μωρέ, *fool!* (Matt. v. 22) may be a Greek vocative (μωρός), but is more probably an Aramaic word of similar sound, denoting utter mental and moral worthlessness.

πάσχα, *Passover.*

ῥαββί, *my master!* lit. "my great one!" (Matt. xxiii. 7, etc.) So, ῥαββονί (Mark x. 51), and ῥαββουνί (John xx. 16).[1]

ῥακά, a term of contempt, from a Hebrew root signifying *emptiness,* or *vanity* (Matt. v. 22).

σαβαώθ, *hosts,* i.e., the hosts of heaven (Rom. ix. 29 ; Jas. v. 4).

σίκερα, *strong drink* (Luke i. 15).

χερουβίμ, *cherubim,* Hebrew plural of *cherub* (Heb. ix. 5).

c. Aramaic Phrases.

ἀλληλούϊα, *praise ye Jehovah!* (Rev. xix. 1, 3, 4, 6.)

ἀμήν, after ascriptions of praise, *so let it be;* before assertions, *verily.*

ἐφφαθά, *be opened!* (Mark vii. 34.)

Ἠλί, Ἠλί, λαμὰ σαβαχθανί; *My God, my God, why hast Thou forsaken me?* (Matt. xxvii. 46,) from Ps. xxii. 1; the last word being the Aramaic equivalent of the original Hebrew verb. Ἠλί is *my God,* from the Hebrew EL. Mark xv. 34 reads Ἐλωΐ.

μαραναθά, *The Lord cometh!* (1 Cor. xvi. 22.) (The word preceding, ἀνάθεμα, *accursed,* is pure Greek, and should be followed by a colon or period. W.H. write Μαρὰν ἀθά.)

ταλιθὰ κοῦμι, *maiden arise!* (Mark v. 41.)

ὡσαννά, *save now!* (Matt. xxi. 9 ; Mark xi. 9, 10; John xii. 13,) taken from Ps. cxviii. 25.

LATIN WORDS.

154. a. Names of Coins.—κοδράντης, "quadrans," *farthing* (Matt. v. 26 ; Mark xii. 42), the fourth part of the

ἀσσάριον, "as" (diminutive term), also rendered *farthing* in E.V. (Matt. x. 29 ; Luke xii. 6), the sixteenth part of the

δηνάριον, "denarius," rendered *penny* (as in Matt. xviii. 28, etc.), silver coin worth about $7\frac{1}{2}d$.

---

[1] W. H. read in both passages Ῥαββουνεί.

§ 154, f.] LATIN WORDS IN THE NEW TESTAMENT.

b. **Judicial.**—σικάριος, "sicarius," *assassin* (Acts xxi. 38).
φραγέλλιον, φραγελλόω, "flagellum, flagello," *scourge* (noun and verb) (John ii. 15 ; Matt. xxvii. 26 ; Mark xv. 15).

c. **Military.**—κεντυρίων, "centurio," *centurion* (Mark xv. 39, 44, 45). Elsewhere the Greek ἑκατόνταρχος (or -χης) is employed.
κουστωδία, "custodia," *guard* (Matt. xxvii. 65, 66 ; xxviii. 11).
λεγεών, "legio," *legion* (Matt. xxvi. 53 ; Mark v. 9, 15; Luke viii. 30).
πραιτώριον, "prætorium," *officer's* or *governor's quarters, palace* (Matt. xxvii. 27 ; Phil. i. 13, etc.).
σπεκουλάτωρ, "speculator," *member of the royal guard* (Mark vi. 27).

d. **Political.**—κῆνσος, "census," *tribute* (Matt. xvii. 25 ; xxii. 17).
κωλωνία, "colonia," *colony* (Acts xvi. 12).
λιβερτῖνοι, "libertini," *freedmen* (Acts vi. 9).

e. **Articles of Dress.**—λέντιον, "lenteum," *towel* (John xiii. 4, 5).
σιμικίνθιον, "semicinctium," *apron* (Acts xix. 12).
σουδάριον, "sudarium," *handkerchief* (Luke xix. 20, etc.).

f. **General.**—ζιζάνιον, "zizanium," *wild darnel*, "lolium" (Matt. xiii. 25–40).
κράββατος, "grabbatus," *mattress* or *small couch* (Mark ii. 4, etc.).
μάκελλον, "macellum," *shambles, meat-market* (1 Cor. x. 25).
μεμβράνη, "membrana," *parchment* (2 Tim. iv. 13).
μίλιον, "milliare," *mile* (Matt. v. 41).
μόδιος, "modius," a *measure* (about an English peck) (Matt. v. 15, etc.).
ξέστης, "sextus, sextarius," a *small measure* (about a pint and a half English), *pitcher* (Mark vii. 4).
ῥέδη, "rheda," *chariot* (Rev. xviii. 13).
ταβέρνη, "taberna," *tavern* (Acts xxviii. 15).
τίτλος, "titulus," *title, superscription* (John xix. 19, 20).
φόρον, "forum," part of the name *Appii Forum* (Acts xxviii. 15).
χάρτης, "charta," *paper* (2 John 12).

(For Latin Proper Names, see Chap. XII.)

Chapter XII. NEW TESTAMENT PROPER NAMES.

155. The personal names of the New Testament are in general derivative or composite words, originally with a specific meaning. They belong to three languages—Hebrew, Greek, and Latin (compare Chap. XI.)—a circumstance which causes some little difficulty and confusion, especially since the Hebrew names sometimes appear in the forms of the Greek declension, sometimes, as in their original shape, indeclinable. Our translators, too, have occasionally adopted various renderings of the same Greek name, and in many cases have made the New Testament English form different from that in the Old.

Hebrew Names.

156. *a.* The original indeclinable Hebrew forms may end in almost any letter; as, *e.g.*, Ἀβιούδ, Ἀβραάμ, Ἰσραήλ, Ἐλισάβετ, Ἰεφθαέ, Νῶε, Ἡσαῦ, Ἰεριχῶ. Such forms are *generally* oxytone. So, Ἐμμανουήλ, GOD WITH US.

b. The following names are found both in indeclinable and declinable forms:—

Ἰερουσαλήμ and Ἱεροσόλυμα, -ων,[1] *Jerusalem.*

Σαούλ and Σαῦλος, *Saul.*[2]

Ἰακώβ, *Jacob* (Old Testament), and Ἰάκωβος, *James* (New Testament).

Συμεών, *Simeon* (Old Testament), and Σίμων, -ωνος, *Simon*[3] (New Testament).

Λευΐ, *Levi* (Old Testament), and Λευΐς, *Levi* (Matthew, New Testament). (Compare § 32, *c.*)

---

[1] Once, Ἱεροσόλυμα appears as a feminine singular (Matt. ii. 3; so, perhaps, iii. 5).

[2] The Hebrew form occurs only in the accounts of Saul's conversion (Acts ix., xxii., xxvi.); except xiii. 21, where the reference is to the Old Testament king.

[3] Twice, however, the apostle bears the Old Testament name (Acts xv. 14; 2 Pet. i. 1).

§ 157, c.]   PROPER NAMES.   161

c. Hebrew names in -*ah* appear in the form -**as** (see § 20, a). Those in -*iah*, or -*jah*, a form of the name of the Supreme Being, JEHOVAH, are rendered into Greek by -ιας: as Ἡλίας, *Elijah;* Ἡσαίας, *Isaiah*. These, however, take a genitive in -ου. (Μεσσίας, *Anointed*, is of a different derivation.)

d. The circumflexed termination -ᾶς (gen. -ᾶ) marks some names belonging to the later Hebrew (or Aramaic): as Κηφᾶς, Βαραββᾶς. To these must be added, Ἰωνᾶς, *Jonah, Jonas,* or *Jona*.

More frequently, however, -ᾶς indicates the contraction of a Greek or Latin name, as shown §§ 158, b, 159, d.

DOUBLE NAMES.

157. a. When two names are applied to the same person, one is sometimes the Hebrew (or Aramaic) appellation, the other its translation into Greek. Thus, *Tabitha* (Hebrew) and *Dorcas* (Greek) both signify "gazelle;" *Thomas* (Hebrew) and *Didymus* (Greek) both stand for "twin." So also *Cephas* (Hebrew) is translated by *Peter*, "stone."

b. Some Greek names are mere vocal imitations of the Hebrew, the sound being imperfectly transferred. Thus, *Judah*, or *Judas*, becomes *Theudas* (Acts v. 36); while *Levi* may have given rise to the form *Lebbæus*. Some, again, have thought *Alphæus* (Matt. x. 3, etc.) and *Clopas* (John xix. 25) to be only two forms of the same Hebrew word. *Cleopas* (Luke xxiv. 18) is a different name from the latter. It is possible that *Paul*, Παῦλος, may in like manner have sprung from the Hebrew *Saul;* or it had a Latin origin. (See § 159, c.)

c. In many cases, again, where two names are borne, one is a *surname*, either (1) from some characteristic circumstance, as *Cephas* or *Peter* of Simon, and *Barnabas* of Joses; or (2) a patronymic formed by the Aramaic *Bar*, "son," as *Bar-jesus* (son of *Joshua*, Ἰησοῦς) of Elymas, and possibly *Bar-tolmai*, Βαρθολομαῖος, of Nathanael; or (3) a local appellation, as *Iscariot* (Hebrew, "a man of Kerioth," see Josh. xv. 25) and *Magdalene* (Greek, "a woman of Magdala"). Observe that *Canaanite* (R.V., Cananæan), properly "Kananite," Κανανίτης (Matt. x. 4; Mark iii. 18), is not a local name, but probably the Greek form of the Hebrew word for *zealot*, rendered (Luke vi. 15; Acts i. 13) Ζηλωτής.

d. When the name of the same person appears in a Græcised and a Hebrew style, the former would naturally be employed among the Gentiles and Hellenists; the latter among the Palestinian Jews. So *Saul* becomes *Paul* when he starts on his first missionary tour (Acts xiii. 9), and ever afterwards retains the name. (See § 159, *c.*)

Greek Names.

158. *a.* Pure Greek names are common, whether of Hellenists (*i.e.*, Greek-speaking or foreign Jews) or of Gentile converts. It has often been noticed that the names of all "the seven" (Acts vi.) are Greek. So throughout most of the Epistles. "Euodias," Εὐοδία (Phil. iv. 2), is a feminine form, and should have been rendered *Euodia* (R.V.).

b. Many Greek composite names are contracted into forms in -âς: as *Epaphroditus* into *Epaphras* (Col. i. 7; iv. 12); *Artemidorus* into *Artemas* (Titus iii. 12); *Nymphodorus* into *Nymphas* (Col. iv. 15); *Zenodorus* into *Zenas* (Titus iii. 13); *Olympiodorus* into *Olympas* (Rom. xvi. 15); *Hermodorus* into *Hermas* (Rom. xvi. 14). The termination *-dōrus* is from δῶρον, *gift;* and the former parts of these compounds are from the Greek mythology.

Other contractions are—*Parmenas,* for *Parmenides* (Acts vi. 5); *Demas,* probably for *Demetrius; Antipas,* for *Antipater; Apollos,* for *Apollonius.* Σώπατρος (Acts xx. 4) and Σωσίπατρος (Rom. xvi. 21) seem to be the same name in different forms.

Latin Names.

159. *a.* The Latin names occur chiefly where we might expect them, in letters written to or from Rome. The chief are *Cornelius, Aquila, Priscilla* or *Prisca, Caius* (i.e., *Gaius*), *Urban,*[1] *Rufus, Julia, Tertius, Quartus, Fortunatus, Marcus* or *Mark, Clement* (Κλήμης, -εντος), *Pudens, Claudia,* and perhaps *Linus* (2 Tim. iv. 21). Some have thought that the last-mentioned was a Briton, *Lin,* of the household of Caractacus.

---

[1] Rom. xvi. 9. This name is written in A.V. "Urbane," but it must be pronounced as a dissyllable. The R.V. has "Urbanus."

§ 159, d.] PROPER NAMES—LATIN. 163

b Three names of Roman Emperors are also found in the New Testament in a Latin form, *Augustus*, Αὐγούστος (Luke ii. 1; but the Greek equivalent, Σεβαστός, is found, referring to Nero, Acts xxv. 21, 25); *Tiberius*, Τιβέριος (Luke iii. 1); and *Claudius*, Κλαύδιος (as Acts xi. 28). The surname *Cæsar*, Καῖσαρ, is applied to Augustus (Luke ii. 1), to Tiberius (Luke iii. 1, etc.), to Claudius (Acts xi. 28), to Nero (Acts xxv. 8; Phil. iv. 22, etc.). Caligula is not mentioned.

c. If the word Παῦλος be not, as is most likely, an imperfect Greek transcript of the Hebrew name *Saul*, it must also be referred to the class of Latin words, as in Rome it was the name of a noble house. Some have thought that the apostle's family, on receiving the rights of Roman citizenship, had been adopted into this house; others, with even less likelihood, connect his assumption of the name with the conversion of Sergius *Paulus* (Acts xiii. 7–12).

d. Latin names, like Greek, may be contracted. Thus, *Luke*, Λοῦκας (rendered Lu*cas* in Philem. 24), is an abbreviated form of the Latin name Lu*canus*. Similarly, *Silvanus* (Σιλουανός) and *Silas* denote one person. *Amplias* (Rom. xvi. 8) is probably a contraction of the Roman name *Ampliatus*.

For the significance of these various names, the Lexicon may be consulted.

PART III.

SYNTAX.

CHAPTER I. CONSTRUCTION OF THE SIMPLE SENTENCE.

Subject—Copula—Predicate.

160. The laws of Universal Grammar, with regard to the construction and arrangement of Sentences, should be clearly borne in mind, that their special exemplifications in the Greek language may be understood. For the most part, it will be convenient to show the application of these laws under the heading of the parts of speech or forms of inflection severally affected by them. A brief summary may, however, first of all be given, with the essential rules of construction.

161. A SENTENCE, or "thought expressed in words," consists of one or more *Propositions*.

162. The essentials of a Proposition are, the SUBJECT and the PREDICATE.

163. The SUBJECT expresses the person or thing of which something is affirmed, desired, or asked, and must, therefore, be a noun substantive, or the equivalent of one.

> Equivalents to nouns substantive are (1) personal pronouns, or (2) substantivised expressions, for which see § 202.

164. The PREDICATE expresses that which is affirmed, denied, or asked respecting the subject; and in its simplest form it is (1) a noun substantive or its equivalent, or (2) an adjective or its equivalent.

> The equivalent of an adjective is a participle.

165. The simplest form of Proposition is that which connects Subject and Predicate by a tense of the substantive verb *to be*, called the **Copula**.

§ 168.] SUBJECT—COPULA—PREDICATE. 165

Acts xxiii. 6 : ἐγώ Φαρισαῖός εἰμι, *I am a Pharisee.*
Matt. xvi. 18 : σὺ εἶ Πέτρος, *thou art Peter.*
Matt. xiii. 38 : ὁ ἀγρός ἐστιν ὁ κόσμος, *the field is the world.*
Phil. iii. 3 : ἡμεῖς ἐσμεν ἡ περιτομή, *we are the circumcision.*
Acts xix. 15 : ὑμεῖς τίνες ἐστέ ; *who are ye ?*
Eph. v. 16 : αἱ ἡμέραι πονηραί εἰσι, *the days are evil.*
Luke v. 1 : αὐτὸς ἦν ἑστώς, *he was standing.*
Luke xxi. 24 : Ἰερουσαλὴμ ἔσται πατουμένη, *Jerusalem shall be trodden down.*

The verb εἰμί, *to be*, is the true copula ; but some other verbs admit a similar construction, such as ὑπάρχω, *to be essentially;* γίγνομαι, *to become;* φαίνομαι, *to appear;* καλοῦμαι, *to be called;* καθίσταμαι, *to be set down as* or *constituted.* These are called **Copulative Verbs**, as they agree with εἰμί in their construction, although in reality embodying part of the predicate. See § 181.

166. The **Copula is often omitted,** where ambiguity is not likely to arise from its absence.

Matt. v. 5 : μακάριοι οἱ πραεῖς, *blessed* (are) *the meek.*
2 Tim. ii. 11 : πιστὸς ὁ λόγος, *faithful* (is) *the word.*
Heb. xiii. 8 : Ἰησοῦς Χριστὸς ... ὁ αὐτός, *Jesus Christ* (is) *the same.*

For the way to distinguish between an attributive adjective and a predicate in such cases, see § 206.

167. The Copula and Predicate are most generally blended in a verb, which is then called the **Predicate.** Thus, ἐγὼ γράφω, *I write,* is very nearly equivalent to ἐγώ εἰμι γράφων, *I am writing.*

The careful student will observe that the term predicate is applied to the adjective and the verb in different senses. In the latter case it really means copula and predicate combined. An adjective or substantive predicate is sometimes called the "complement" of the verb with which it stands connected.

168. The substantive verb may become itself a Predicate, involving the notion of existence.

John viii. 58 : ... ἐγώ εἰμι, Before Abraham was, *I am.*
Rev. xxi. 1 : ἡ θάλασσα οὐκ ἔστιν[1] ἔτι, *the sea is no more.*

But the phrase, ἐγώ εἰμι, *it is I,* occurring in the Gospels (as Matt. xiv. 27 ; Mark vi. 50 ; John vi. 20, xviii. 5, 6, 8), may mean one of three things : ἐγώ being (1) subject or (2) predicate, or (3) the verb being predicate. (Cf. **Isa. xli. 4,** LXX.)

---

[1] For the accent see § 110, *note.*

169. The Subject, when a personal pronoun, is generally omitted, if no special emphasis or distinction is intended; the number and person of the verb itself showing its reference, § 332.

Thus, λέγω ὑμῖν (Matt. v. 18, 20; viii. 10, 11, etc.), *I say unto you*, is unemphatic; but in ἐγὼ λέγω ὑμῖν, *I say unto you* (v. 22, 28, 32, 34, 39, 44), our Lord pointedly contrasts His own teaching with that of the Rabbis. So (v. 21), οὐ φονεύσεις, *thou shalt not murder*. Had the reading been σὺ οὐ φ..., the meaning would have been "*thou*, in particular," shalt not. In Luke x. 23, 24 we read, "Blessed are the eyes which see the things that ye see" (βλέπετε, unemphatic): "for I tell you that many prophets and kings have desired to see those things which *ye* see" (ὑμεῖς βλέπετε, emphatic, by way of antithesis to "prophets and kings"). Again, σώσει is *he shall save;* αὐτὸς σώσει, *he* (emphatic, *and none other*) *shall save* (Matt. i. 21). See also Mark vi. 45, "until *he* (αὐτός) should send away the people," for no one else could do it. Observe also the repetition of αὐτοί, *they*, in the Beatitudes (Matt. v. 4–8).

> The emphasis conveyed by the insertion of the pronominal subject is often too subtle to be expressed by translation; but it is always worth noting. (See Acts iv. 20; 1 Cor. xv. 30, etc.) The emphatic ἐγώ (John xvi. 33; 1 Cor. ii. 1, 3) is very noticeable. So in many other passages.

170. The omitted Subject of the **third person plural** is often to be understood **generally**. Compare the English expressions, *They say*, etc.

Matt. v. 11: ὅταν ὀνειδίσωσιν ὑμᾶς καὶ διώξωσι, *when they reproach and persecute you;* i.e., men in general.

John xx. 2: ἦραν τὸν Κύριον, *they have taken away the Lord;* i.e., some persons have.

See also Matt. viii. 16, Mark x. 13, *they were bringing* (i.e., from time to time); Luke xvii. 23, John xv. 6 (A.V. "men," R.V. "they"), Acts iii. 2, etc.

171. Verbs in the **third person singular**, without a Subject expressed, frequently imply some necessary or conventionally understood Subject of their own.

1 Cor. xv. 52: σαλπίσει, lit., *he shall sound the trumpet*, a classical expression, implying ὁ σαλπιγκτής, *the trumpeter*, equivalent, as A.V., to *the trumpet shall sound*.

§ 174, a.]   SUBJECT AND PREDICATE.   167

To this head are to be referred **many so-called impersonals**: as βρέχει, *it rains* (in First Aorist, James v. 17). The Greeks originally understood and sometimes expressed Ζεύς, or Θεός, with all such words. "*He* rains, thunders," etc.; hence passing into the impersonal usage. Again φησί, λέγει, *he* or *it says;* once, εἴρηκε, *he* or *it hath said* (Heb. iv. 4); once, εἶπε, *he* or *it said* (1 Cor. xv. 27), are used as **formulas of quotation**: ἡ γραφή, *the Scripture*, to be supplied (compare Rom. iv. 3, etc.); or ὁ Θεός, *God* (see Matt. xix. 5).

See, for λέγει, 2 Cor. vi. 2, Gal. iii. 16, Eph. iv. 8, etc.; for φησί, 1 Cor. vi. 16, Heb. viii. 5.

Once, φησί seems to be used in the general sense, as plural, *they say* (2 Cor. x. 10); but many MSS. (W. H., marg.) there read φασί.

172. The Nominative is the case of the Subject, and the Subject and Predicate must correspond in number and person; whence the grammatical rule called the

First Concord. A Verb agrees with its nominative case in number and person.

For other uses of the Nominative, see §§ 242-244. All these are connected with its true use as Subject. It cannot be too strongly impressed upon the learner that the key to every proposition, however complicated, is in the nominative case and verb; that is, in the Subject and Predicate. To these all the other words are only adjuncts.

173. The great apparent exception to the First Concord is that **a Neuter Plural nominative often takes a singular verb.**

John ix. 3: ἵνα φανερωθῇ τὰ ἔργα τοῦ Θεοῦ, *that the works of God may be manifested.*

Acts i. 18: ἐξεχύθη πάντα τὰ σπλάγχνα αὐτοῦ, *all his bowels gushed out.*

2 Pet. ii. 20: γέγονεν τὰ ἔσχατα χείρονα, *the last things have become worse.*

So in many other passages.

The reason for this idiom is undoubtedly that, as neuters generally express things without life, the plural is regarded as one collective mass.

174. Variations in this idiom are as follow:—

a. When the neuter nominative plural denotes *animated* beings, the verb is commonly in the plural number.

Matt. x. 21 : ἐπαναστήσονται τέκνα ... καὶ θανατώσουσιν, *children shall rise up against ... and kill.*

James ii. 19 : τὰ δαιμόνια πιστεύουσιν καὶ φρίσσουσιν, *the demons believe and tremble.*

b. The usage, however, is by no means fixed. Thus, things without life are occasionally associated with a plural verb.

Luke xxiv. 11 : ἐφάνησαν ... τὰ ῥήματα, *the words appeared.*

John xix. 31 : ἵνα κατεαγῶσιν τὰ σκέλη, *that the legs might be broken.*

c. Living Subjects are also found with a singular verb.

1 John iii. 10 : φανερά ἐστιν τὰ τέκνα, κ.τ.λ., *the children* of God and those of the devil *are manifest.*

Luke viii. 30 : δαιμόνια πολλὰ εἰσῆλθεν, *many demons entered.*

d. In some passages the singular and plural seem used indiscriminately with the same Subjects.

John x. 4 : τὰ πρόβατα αὐτῷ ἀκολουθεῖ ὅτι οἴδασιν, κ.τ.λ., *the sheep follow him because they know* his voice.

Ver. 27 : τὰ πρόβατα ... ἀκούει (W. H., ἀκούουσιν) καὶ ἀκολουθοῦσί μοι, *the sheep hear* my voice *and follow me.*

1 Cor. x. 11 : ταῦτα πάντα συνέβαινον (W. H., -εν) ... ἐγράφη δε, *all these things happened,... and were written.*

> The uncertainty of the usage in this matter has been a fruitful source of various readings. It is often difficult, if not impossible, to decide whether the singular or the plural formed the original text.

175. *a.* When the Subject is a collective noun in the singular, denoting animate objects, the verb may be put in the plural number. This construction is known as **Rational Concord.**[1]

Matt. xxi. 8 : ὁ δὲ πλεῖστος ὄχλος ἔστρωσαν, κ.τ.λ., *the greater part of the multitude strewed* their (plural) garments in the way.

Luke xix. 37 : ἤρξαντο ἅπαν τὸ πλῆθος, κ.τ.λ., *all the multitude* of the disciples *began* to praise God, rejoicing (plur. masc.).

Rev. xviii. 4 : ἐξέλθετε, ὁ λαός μου, *Come forth, my people!*

---

[1] Constructio ad sensum, *or* Synesis.

§ 176, b.]   SUBJECT AND PREDICATE.   169

b. The Singular and Plural are combined in some passages.

John vi. 2 : ἠκολούθει ... ὄχλος πολύς ὅτι ἐθεώρουν, *a great multitude was following ... because they were seeing.*

Acts xv. 12 : ἐσίγησεν δὲ πᾶν τὸ πλῆθος καὶ ἤκουον, *the whole number became silent, and were listening.*

The singular, however, is the more usual construction.

176. *a.* When two or more nominatives, united by a copulative conjunction, form the Subject, the verb is generally in the plural.

If the nominatives are of different persons, the first is preferred to the second and third, the second to the third; that is, *I* (or *we*) *and you and he* are resolved into *we; you and he* into *you*.

Acts iii. 1 : Πέτρος δὲ καὶ Ἰωάνης ἀνέβαινον, *Peter and John were going up.*

John x. 30 : ἐγὼ καὶ ὁ πατήρ ἕν ἐσμεν, *I and my Father are one.*

1 Cor. ix. 6 : ἐγὼ καὶ Βαρνάβας οὐκ ἔχομεν, κ.τ.λ., *have not I and Barnabas* authority? etc.

1 Cor. xv. 50 : σὰρξ καὶ αἷμα ... οὐ δύνανται,[1] *flesh and blood cannot* inherit the kingdom of God.

b. The verb, however, often agrees with the nearest Subject.

In this case the Predicate is to be understood as repeated with the other Subjects, or that with which the verb agrees is thrown into prominence, the others being subordinate.

It should be observed that in this construction the Greek verb *usually* precedes the nominatives.

Acts xvi. 31 : σωθήσῃ σὺ καὶ ὁ οἶκός σου, *thou shalt be saved and thy house.*

1 Tim. vi. 4 : ἐξ ὧν γίνεται φθόνος, ἔρις, βλασφημίαι, κ.τ.λ., *from which comes envy, strife, railings,* etc.

In these two cases the verb is repeated in thought.

John ii. 12 : κατέβη ... αὐτὸς καὶ οἱ μαθηταὶ αὐτοῦ, *He went down* to Capernaum, *Himself and His disciples.*

Here the one Subject is thrown into prominence; and the construction is the common one when the principal Subject is placed nearest the verb. Compare Matt. xii. 3; Luke xxii. 14; John ii. 2, iv. 53, viii. 52, xviii. 15, xx. 3; Acts xxvi. 30; Philemon 23, 24, where the approved reading is ἀσπάζεται.

---

[1] W. H. read δύναται.

177. When the Predicate of a simple sentence is a noun or pronoun, united to the subject by the copula, it corresponds with the Subject by the **law of apposition,** viz. :—

A substantive employed to explain or describe another, under the same grammatical regimen, is put in the same case.

John xv. 1 : ὁ Πατήρ μου ὁ γεωργός ἐστι, *my Father is the husbandman.*

It is not necessary that the substantives should correspond in gender or number.

2 Cor. i. 14 : καύχημα ὑμῶν ἐσμεν, *we are your boast.*

2 Cor. iii. 3 : ἐστὲ ἐπιστολὴ Χριστοῦ, *ye are Christ's epistle.*

178. When the Predicate is an adjective, including adjective pronouns and participles, its agreement with the Subject comes under the **Second Concord,** viz. :—

Adjectives, pronouns, and participles agree with their substantives in gender, number, and case.

For further exemplification of this Concord, see Chapters IV., V., §§ 315, *sqq.*

In simple sentences the case is, of course, the nominative. The agreement in gender and number may be illustrated by the following :—

Matt. vii. 29 : ἦν διδάσκων, *he was teaching.*

Matt. xiii. 31, etc.: ὁμοία ἐστὶν ἡ βασιλεία, κ.τ.λ., *the kingdom* of heaven *is like,* etc.

Mark v. 9 : πολλοί ἐσμεν, *we are many.*

Luke xiv. 17 : ἔτοιμά ἐστι πάντα, *all things are ready.*

John iv. 11 : τὸ φρέαρ ἐστὶ βαθύ, *the well is deep.*

1 John v. 3 : αἱ ἐντολαὶ αὐτοῦ βαρεῖαι οὐκ εἰσίν, *His commandments are not grievous.*

Rev. vii. 14 : οὗτοί εἰσιν οἱ ἐρχόμενοι, κ.τ.λ., *these are they that are coming* out of the great tribulation.

179. When the Subject is a collective noun, the adjective Predicate is sometimes plural. (Compare § 173.)

John vii. 49 : ὁ ὄχλος οὗτος ... ἐπάρατοί εἰσιν, *this multitude are accursed.*

180. An adjective Predicate is occasionally generalised by being put in the neuter gender, though the Subject is masculine or feminine.

1 Cor. vi. 11 : ταῦτά τινες ἦτε, lit., *some of you were this* (these things).
1 Cor. vii. 19 : ἡ περιτομὴ οὐδέν ἐστι, *circumcision is nothing.*

181. The laws of apposition and concord, as above applied, may be re-stated in the form of the following rule :—

Copulative verbs require the Nominative case after as well as before them.

For the chief copulative verbs, see § 165, note.

John i. 14 : ὁ Λόγος ἐγένετο σάρξ, *the Word became flesh.*

Acts xvi. 3 : "Ελλην ὑπῆρχεν, *he was* (originally) *a Greek.*

2 Cor. xiii. 7 : ἵνα ἡμεῖς δόκιμοι φανῶμεν, *that we should appear approved,* or "be manifestly approved."

Matt. v. 9 : υἱοὶ Θεοῦ κληθήσονται, *they shall be called sons of God.*

Acts x. 32 : Σίμωνα, ὃς ἐπικαλεῖται Πέτρος, *Simon* (accusative), *who is surnamed Peter.*

Rom. v. 19 : ἁμαρτωλοὶ κατεστάθησαν οἱ πολλοί, δίκαιοι κατασταθήσονται οἱ πολλοί, *the many were made sinners, the many shall be made righteous.*

182. Hitherto the rules and examples given have been designed to show the main elements alone of the simple sentence. Other words, however, are very generally added to the Subject, to the Predicate, or to both, for the purpose of further explanation. These words are called the *complements* of the simple sentence, and are variously said to *complete,* to *extend,* or to *enlarge* the Subject or the Predicate, as the case may be.

183. The Subject, which is essentially a noun substantive, may be extended (1) by another noun in apposition, (2) by the qualifying force of adjectives, pronouns, or the article, (3) by dependent nouns, or (4) by prepositional phrases.

For *Apposition,* see § 177.
For *Adjectives,* see Chapter IV., §§ 315, *sqq.*
For *the Article,* see Chapter II., §§ 193, *sqq.*

For the *dependence* of nouns one upon another, and for *prepositional phrases*, see Chapter III.

184. The Predicate, when a noun, may be extended in the same manner as the Subject.

185. When an adjective is Predicate, it may be extended by dependent nouns, by adverbs, or by prepositional phrases.

186. Verbal Predicates may be variously extended. Any verb may be qualified by an adverb. Prepositional phrases may be employed in this connection also. Especially, the meaning of a verb transitive requires to be completed by the Object or Objects, direct or indirect.

For the *direct Object*, see § 281.

For *indirect Objects*, see on the Genitive and Dative cases, §§ 246, *sqq.*

187. The complements of a simple sentence cannot include a verb, as this would introduce a distinct predication. Verbal clauses, therefore, forming part of a period are termed *accessory clauses*, and a sentence with one or more accessory clauses besides the principal one is called a COMPOUND SENTENCE.

Accessory clauses, as related to the principal, are either co-ordinate or subordinate.

188. Co-ordinate accessory clauses are similar in construction to the principal, and are often connected with it and with one another by conjunctions. (See § 402, *sqq.*)

189. Subordinate clauses are dependent upon the principal or upon the accessory clauses, or upon single words or phrases in either.

It is plain that subordinate clauses may be co-ordinate with one another.

190. The methods of introducing subordinate clauses are very various. The chief are, (1) by the Relative Pronoun (§§ 343, 344), (2) by the use of the Participials (participle or infinitive) (§§ 385-396), and (3) by the Particles (§§ 383, 384).

Otherwise: subordinate clauses are **Substantival, Adjectival,** or **Adverbial.** A substantival clause expresses the subject or object of a verb, or stands in apposition, and usually employs the infinitive; an adjectival clause, qualifying a word or sentence, is introduced by a relative pronoun or conjunction, or employs a participle; and an adverbial clause is introduced by a conjunction, or employs a participle or the oblique case of a noun.

191. It is often difficult to determine whether a certain phrase is a complement of the Subject, or of the Predicate.

Many illustrations might be given from the Epistle to the Romans. For instance: ch. i. 17 (Hab. ii. 4), ὁ δίκαιος ἐκ πίστεως ζήσεται, lit., *the righteous* (man) *from faith shall live*. Are we to understand the prepositional phrase ἐκ πίστεως as the complement of the Subject ὁ δίκαιος, or of the Predicate ζήσεται? In other words, are we to translate "The righteous man from faith (he that is righteous, or justified by faith) shall live?" or, "The righteous man shall live from faith?"

Again, iv. 1: are we to attach the prepositional phrase, κατὰ σάρκα, *according to the flesh*, with the word προπάτορα, *forefather*, in apposition with *Abraham*, the Subject of the accessory clause, or to the Predicate *hath found?*—that is, does the Apostle ask, "What shall we say that Abraham, our father as pertaining to the flesh, hath found?" or, "What shall we say that Abraham our father hath found as pertaining to the flesh?"

The true connection of accessory clauses is also occasionally doubtful.

For instance, in Acts iii. 21, it may be fairly discussed whether the relative clause, *which God hath spoken by the mouth of all His holy prophets*, belongs to the word *times*, or to *all things*.

> Such questions of interpretation are not proposed for consideration here; their settlement must often depend not only on the laws of construction, but on the signification of individual words. Reference is made to them only to show the necessity, to a right interpretation of a passage, of distinctly analysing the parts of every compound sentence, and of assigning to each its right position. In our own language this is comparatively easy, as the order of the sentence in general indicates the mutual relation of its parts; in Greek, through the number and variety of the inflections, the order is of little importance to the *structure* of the sentence, though of much to its *emphasis*.

192. As hints for disentangling a compound sentence, the following may be valuable:—

Search first for the *predicate*, or thing affirmed—usually, of course, a verb,—then for the *subject*. These once fixed, every other verb will mark an *accessory clause*, which will have to be regarded apart. The remaining words, generally in close grouping with the Subject and Predicate, must be assigned to them respectively as their complements, according to the usages of the several parts of speech and forms of inflection. To these it is now necessary to turn, in order.

Chapter II. THE ARTICLE.

Latin, *Articulus;* Greek, ἄρθρον *(a joint).* Hence, *anarthrous,* " without an article."

Construction of the Article.

193. The Article, ὁ, ἡ, τό, *the* (see § 12), is usually employed, as in other languages, with nouns substantive. The Second Concord applies to this relation; **the article agrees with its noun in gender, number, and case.**

194. This general usage, however, admits of many variations, attributable to the fact that **the Article was originally a demonstrative pronoun.**[1]

Its demonstrative use is clearly seen in the Apostle Paul's quotation (Acts xvii. 28), τοῦ γὰρ καὶ γένος ἐσμέν, *we are his offspring.*

195. A remnant of the old demonstrative use is, that **the Article often stands without a noun expressed,** like our *this, that;* the sense of the phrase showing *who* or *what* is to be understood.

For example, the phrase ὁ μὲν ... ὁ δέ signifies *this ... that,* or *the one ... the other.*

Acts xiv. 4 : οἱ μὲν ἦσαν σὺν τοῖς Ἰουδαίοις, οἱ δὲ σύν τοῖς ἀποστόλοις, *some were with the Jews, others with the apostles.*

In Matt. xiii. 23 δέ is repeated: ὁ μὲν ἑκατόν, ὁ δὲ ἑξήκοντα, ὁ δὲ τριάκοντα, *some a hundred, some sixty, some thirty.*

See also Matt. xxii. 5 ; Mark xii. 5 ; Acts xvii. 32 ; Gal. iv. 22 ; Eph. iv. 11 ; Phil. i. 16, 17 ; Heb. vii. 20, 21.

---

[1] The student may be reminded that the English article *the,* the German *der,* the French *le,* are also original demonstratives. So in other languages.

§ 198.] THE ARTICLE AS DEMONSTRATIVE. 175

When ὁ δέ is used in narration, even without a preceding ὁ μέν, it always implies some other person previously mentioned, as—

Matt. ii. 5 : οἱ δὲ εἶπον, *and they said.*
Mark xiv. 61 : ὁ δὲ ἐσιώπα, *but he was silent.*
Acts xii. 15 : ἡ δὲ διϊσχυρίζετο, *but she steadfastly asserted.*
So in innumerable passages.

196. The Article, disconnected from a noun, **is often followed by a genitive.**

Matt. x. 2 : Ἰάκωβος ὁ τοῦ Ζεβεδαίου, *James the* (son) *of Zebedee.*

Mark xii. 17 : ἀπόδοτε τὰ Καίσαρος, *render the* (things or rights) *of Cæsar.*

Gal. v. 24 : οἱ τοῦ Χριστοῦ, *the* (servants or disciples) *of the Christ, i.e., of the Anointed one.*

2 Pet. ii. 22 : τὸ τῆς ἀληθοῦς παροιμίας, *the* (saying) *of the truthful proverb.*

The plural neuter τά is very frequently used in this construction, as in the second of the above instances. So τὰ τοῦ νόμου, *the things of the law;* τὰ τοῦ Πνεύματος, *the things of the Spirit;* τὰ ἑαυτῶν, *their own interests* (lit. the things of themselves), and so on.

197. Similarly, **the Article precedes a Preposition** with its case.

Matt. v. 15 : τοῖς ἐν τῇ οἰκίᾳ, *to those in the house.*
Mark i. 36 : Σίμων καὶ οἱ μετ' αὐτοῦ, *Simon and those with him.*
Luke ii. 39 : τὰ κατὰ τὸν νόμον, *the* (things) *according to the law.*
Eph. i. 10 : τὰ ἐν τοῖς οὐρανοῖς ... τὰ ἐπὶ τῆς γῆς, *the* (things) *in the heavens...the* (things) *on the earth.*
Acts xiii. 13 : οἱ περὶ Παῦλον, *those about Paul*, including himself (by a classic idiom), *i.e., Paul and his associates.*

Any of the prepositions may follow the Article; for their several significance, see Chapter II. § 288, etc.

198. A construction essentially similar is that of **the Article with Adverbs**, the noun being supplied in thought.

Instances of this are : τὸ νῦν, *the* (thing) *now: the present* (Matt. xxiv. 21 ; Luke v. 10) ; ἡ σήμερον, *to-day;* ἡ αὔριον, *the morrow* (feminine), as if from ἡμέρα, *day;* Matt. vi. 34; xxvii. 62). So, in many passages, ὁ πλησίον, *the* (man who is) *near, one's neighbour;* τὰ ἄνω, *the* (things) *above;* τὰ κάτω, *the* (things) *beneath;* οἱ ἔξω, *those* (people) *without;* τὰ ὀπίσω, *the* (things) *behind;* τὰ ἔμπροσθεν, *the* (things) *before,* etc.

199. The Article is frequently placed before Adjectives, the substantive being implied.

This construction belongs to all genders, and to both numbers. Instances of its occurrence are very frequent. Thus:—

Mark i. 24 : ὁ ἅγιος, *the Holy* (one).
Matt. vii. 6 : τὸ ἅγιον, *the holy* (thing).
Matt. xxiii. 15 : τὴν ξηράν, *the dry* (land).
Luke xvi. 25 : τὰ ἀγαθά, *the good* (things).
Eph. i. 3 : ἐν τοῖς ἐπουρανίοις, *in the heavenly* (places).
1 Thess. iv. 16 : οἱ νεκροὶ ἐν Χριστῷ, *the dead in Christ.*
Titus ii. 4 : ἵνα σωφρονίζωσι τὰς νέας, *that they may instruct the young* (women).

> Compare the ordinary English phrases, *the good, the great, the wise,* with the abstracts, *the true, the right, the beautiful.* In Greek, however, the usage is much more extended, and is exemplified also by anarthrous adjectives.

200. The Article is commonly also used before Participles; the sense again supplying the noun.

Matt. i. 22 : τὸ ῥηθέν, *the* (thing) *spoken.*
Matt. v. 4 : οἱ πενθοῦντες, *the* (persons) *mourning.*
Matt. xi. 3 : ὁ ἐρχόμενος, *the coming* (one).
Matt. xiii. 3 : ὁ σπείρων, *the* (man) *sowing, i.e.,* "a sower."
Matt. xxiii. 37 : τοὺς ἀπεσταλμένους, *the* (persons) *having been sent.*
2 Cor. ii. 15 : ἐν τοῖς σωζομένοις ... ἐν τοῖς ἀπολλυμένοις, *in the* (persons) *being saved ... in the* (persons) *perishing.*

> It will appear from these and other instances that **the most convenient way of translating the Article with the participle will often be by changing the phrase into a relative and finite verb.** Thus, in the last two examples, we idiomatically and accurately render, *those who have been sent,* and *those who are being saved...those who are perishing.*
>
> For further details on this frequent and important construction, see Chap. VI. § 396.

§ 203.] THE ARTICLE AS DEMONSTRATIVE. 177

201. **The Infinitive Mood** in all its tenses is treated as an indeclinable neuter substantive, and **is often thus qualified by the Article**, the phrase expressing the abstract notion of the verb. (See Chap. VI. §§ 388—390.)

Matt. xx. 23 : τὸ καθίσαι ἐκ δεξιῶν, *the sitting* (lit., "the to-sit") on my right hand.

Matt. xiii. 3 : τοῦ σπείρειν, (for the purpose) *of sowing.*

Matt. xiii. 4 : ἐν τῷ σπείρειν, *in the sowing.*

Mark xiv. 28 : μετὰ τὸ ἐγερθῆναι, *after the rising.*

Phil. i. 21 : τὸ ζῆν Χριστὸς ... τὸ ἀποθανεῖν κέρδος, *Living* (is) *Christ ... dying* (is) *gain.*

> This construction will be more fully illustrated under the head of the Infinitive. One caution here may not be out of place. The English form in *-ing* may be either an adjective or a substantive. Thus we may say, *a living man*, or *Living is enjoyment.* In the former case the word is a participle; in the latter an infinitive; and in rendering into or from Greek, the two must be carefully discriminated.

202. Sometimes, again, **whole phrases or sentences are qualified by a neuter Article**; especially quotations, before which some such word as *saying, proverb, command,* may be supplied, or expressions of a *question, problem,* or *difficulty.*

Quotations are as in Matt. xix. 18 : τὸ οὐ φονεύσεις, οὐ μοιχεύσεις, *the* (command) "*thou shalt do no murder, thou shalt not commit adultery.*"

> See also Luke xxii. 37; Rom. xiii. 9; Gal. iv. 25, τὸ Ἄγαρ, *the* (name) *Hagar;* Eph. iv. 9; Heb. xii. 27.

Expressions of the latter class are as in Luke i. 62 : τὸ τί ἂν θέλοι καλεῖσθαι, *the* (question) *what he would like* (him) *to be called.*

Luke ix. 46 : τὸ τίς ἂν εἴη μείζων, *the* (dispute) *who should be greater.*

Luke xxii. 4 : τὸ πῶς αὐτὸν παραδῷ, *the* (scheme) *how he might betray him.*

Rom. viii. 26 : τὸ τί προσευξώμεθα, *the* (manner) *how we should pray.*

> See likewise Luke xix. 48; Acts xxii. 30; 1 Thess. iv. 1, and a few other passages.

203. The employment of the Article with Pronouns is reserved for discussion in § 220.

204. Generally, an Infinitive, Participle, Adjective, or other word or phrase, qualified by the Article, is said to be *substantivised, i.e.*, made virtually a Noun, and treated similarly in the sentence.

SIGNIFICANCE OF THE ARTICLE: ITS INSERTION OR OMISSION.

205. The Article is strictly definite; and is used, as in other languages, **to mark a specific object of thought.**

Matt. vi. 22 : ὁ λύχνος τοῦ σώματός ἐστιν ὁ ὀφθαλμός, *the lamp of the body is the eye.*

206. Hence arises the *general* rule, that **in the simple sentence the Subject takes the article, the Predicate omits it.**

> The subject is definitely before the mind, the predicate generally denotes the class to which the subject is referred, or from which it is excluded, but the notion of the class is itself indeterminate.

Matt. xiii. 39 : οἱ δὲ θερισταὶ ἄγγελοί εἰσιν, *the reapers are angels.*

John iii. 6 : τὸ γεγεννημένον ἐκ τῆς σαρκὸς σάρξ ἐστιν, *that which is born of the flesh is flesh.*

John xvii. 17 : ὁ λόγος ὁ σὸς ἀλήθειά ἐστιν, *thy word is truth.*

John i. 1 : Θεὸς ἦν ὁ λόγος, *the Word was God.*

1 John iv. 8 : ὁ Θεὸς ἀγάπη ἐστίν, *God is love.*

The Copula being frequently omitted (§ 166), the presence or absence of the Article with a nominative adjective will often decide whether it is a Predicate or an attribute of the Subject. Thus, πιστὸς ὁ λόγος, 2 Tim. ii. 11, must be rendered *faithful is the word;* ὁ πιστὸς λόγος would have been *the faithful word.*

Matt. v. 5 : μακάριοι οἱ πραεῖς, *blessed* (are) *the meek.*

Rom. vii. 7 : ὁ νόμος ἁμαρτία ; *is the law sin?*

> From an examination of these examples, it will appear that the use of the Article with the Subject, and its omission with the Predicate, is no grammatical expedient, but arises from their respective definiteness. Had the article been employed with the Predicate in the above case, the sentences would have read thus: *The reapers are the angels,* the whole host ; *that which is born of the flesh is the flesh, i.e.,* is the part of human nature so denominated ; *Thy Word is the Truth,* and nothing else can be so described; *the Word was the entire Godhead,* and *God and Love are identical,* so that in fact Love is God ; *the blessed*

are the meek, and none others; *is the Law Sin?* (see on the Article with abstracts, § 214,) *i.e.*, are Sin and Law the same thing? The meaning of every proposition would thus have been materially altered.

207. When the Article is found with the Predicate, an essential identity with the Subject is asserted.[1]

John i. 4 : ἡ ζωὴ ἦν τὸ φῶς τῶν ἀνθρώπων, *the life was the light of men*, the only light.

2 Cor. iii. 17 : ὁ δὲ Κύριος τὸ πνεῦμά ἐστιν, *the Lord is the spirit*, to which the passage relates.

1 John iii. 4 : ἡ ἁμαρτία ἐστὶν ἡ ἀνομία, *sin is transgression of law ;* and conversely, transgression of law is sin.

> Personal and other pronouns are very frequently the Subject when the Predicate is thus defined. (Matt. v. 13, xvi. 16, xxvi. 26, 28 ; Acts xxi. 38, etc.)

208. When a word is defined by some other expression occurring with it, the Article may be omitted. So in English, we may say, "The house of my father," or "My father's house," the word *father's* in the latter phrase rendering *house* definite.

This most frequently occurs in Greek when the qualifying word, being a substantive, omits the Article.

Matt. i. 1 : βίβλος γενέσεως, *the book of the generation.*

1 Thess. iv. 15 : ἐν λόγῳ Κυρίου, *in the word of the Lord.*

But 1 Thess. i. 8 : ὁ λόγος τοῦ Κυρίου, *the word of the Lord.*

209. In the four following cases, the Article, in conformity with the general rule, marks definiteness.

(1) Monadic Nouns.—Objects of which there is but one of the kind, or only one of which is present to thought, are *usually* defined by the Article.

Thus, ὁ οὐρανός, *heaven ;* ἡ γῆ, *earth ;* ἡ θάλασσα, *the sea ;* ὁ μέγας βασιλεύς, *the great king.*

> Exceptions to this usage, and their reason, will be noted further on.

---

[1] This form of sentence answers to the affirmative proposition (in Sir W. Hamilton's Logic), in which the Predicate is "distributed."

210. (2) **Individual Emphasis.**—When some member of a class is singled out as bearing a distinctive character, the Article is employed.

Examples.—ἡ κρίσις, *the judgment*, *i.e.*, the final judgment, as Matt. xii. **41, 42**; Luke x. 14.

ἡ γραφή, αἱ γραφαί, *the writing*, *writings*, *i.e.*, the Holy Scriptures, as Matt. xxii. 29; John x. 35; Rom. iv. 3, xv. 4.

ἡ ἔρημος, *the desert*, *i.e.*, that of Judæa, Matt. xi. 7; or that of Sinai. John iii. 14, vi. 31; Acts vii. 30; and perhaps Matt. iv. 1.[1]

ὁ πειράζων, *the tempter* (participle, according to § 200), *i.e.*, Satan. Matt. iv. 3; 1 Thess. iii. 5.

ὁ ἐρχόμενος, *the coming one* (participle, present), *i.e.*, the Messiah Matt. xi. 3, xxi. 9, xxiii. 39; Heb. x. 37. Compare Rev. i. 4, 8, iv. 8.

211. (3) **Singular for Collective.**—A noun in the singular number with the Article occasionally stands for the whole class. Compare such English expressions as "he looked the king," "the good man is a law to himself."

Matt. xii. 35 : ὁ ἀγαθὸς ἄνθρωπος, *the good man*, denoting good men generally.

Matt. xii. 29 : τοῦ ἰσχυροῦ, *of the strong man*, any one who possesses that attribute.

Matt. xv. 11 : τὸν ἄνθρωπον, *the man*, whoever he may be.

Matt. xviii. 17 : ὁ ἐθνικὸς καὶ ὁ τελώνης, *the heathen man and the publican.*

Luke x. 7 : ὁ ἐργάτης, *the labourer*, generally.

2 Cor. xii. 12 : σημεῖα τοῦ ἀποστόλου, *signs of the apostle*, *i.e.*, of any rightful claimant of that character.

Gal. iv. 1 : ὁ κληρονόμος, *one who is heir.*

---

[1] Strong reasons have been assigned for the belief that "the wilderness" of our Lord's temptation was the same as that through which the Israelites journeyed to Canaan. See Mark i. 13, and compare our Lord's quotations with their original reference. Note also the parallels between our Lord's history and those of Moses and Elijah. *Webster and Wilkinson* on Matt. iv. 1 may be usefully consulted on these points.

James v. 6 : τὸν δίκαιον, *the righteous man*, generally.

> To this head also, perhaps, belongs John iii. 10, σὺ εἶ ὁ διδάσκαλος; *art thou the teacher?* i.e., is that the position to which thou hast been appointed? Or, as in the preceding instances, the word may mark a special emphasis, Nicodemus having in some eminent way the character of Rabbi.

212. (4) **Renewed Mention.**—A person or thing is often made definite by mention (without the Article) in a paragraph, the Article being employed in subsequent reference.

Matt. ii. 1 : *there came wise men*, μάγοι. Ver. 7, *Herod having called the wise men*, τοὺς μάγους.

Matt. xiii. 25 : *the enemy came and sowed tares*, ζιζάνια. Ver. 26, *then appeared the tares*, τὰ ζιζάνια.

> In like manner compare Luke ix. 16 with ver. 13 ; John iv. 43 with ver. 40 ; xx. 1 with xix. 41 ; Acts xi. 13 with x. 3, 22 ; James ii. 3 with ver. 2 ; 2 Thess. ii. 11, *the falsehood*, referring to ver. 9, (lit.) *wonders of* (in support of) *a falsehood*.

Sometimes the reference is *implicit*, the second expression, bearing the article, being equivalent to the former, though not identical.

Acts xx. 13 : ἐπὶ τὸ πλοῖον, *on board the ship*, implied in ver. 6, "we sailed away."

Heb. v. 4 : τὴν τιμήν, *the honour*, referring to the first verse, "that he may offer gifts and sacrifices."

1 Pet. ii. 7 : ἡ τιμὴ, κ.τ.λ., *the preciousness is for you who believe*, *i.e.*, that spoken of in the previous verse, "a corner-stone, elect, *precious*."

213. It is a remark of great importance (Winer) that "**it is utterly impossible that the Article should be omitted where it is decidedly necessary, or employed where it is quite superfluous or preposterous.**" "It would be a revolution of the laws of thought to express as definite that which is conceived indefinitely." Attention to this will add vividness and suggestiveness to many a passage in which our Authorised Version has failed to reproduce the force of the original. From a great number of texts to which this remark applies, the following may be selected. The Revised Version renders the force of the Article except in the cases indicated.

Matt. i. 23 (Isa. vii. 14): ἡ παρθένος, *the virgin*, *i.e.*, the personage so denominated.

Matt. v. 1: τὸ ὄρος, *the mountain* ; the high ground overlooking the spot. (See also Luke vi. 12.)

Matt. v. 15: τὸν μόδιον, τὴν λυχνίαν, *the modius, the lamp-stand*, recognised articles of furniture in every house.

Matt. xv. 26: τοῖς κυναρίοις, *to the little dogs*, *i.e.*, belonging to the household. (So Mark vii. 27.)

Matt. xvii. 24: τὰ δίδραχμα, *the half-shekels*, the well-known customary payment.

Matt. xxi. 12: τὰς περιστεράς, *the doves*, the accustomed offerings of the poor.

Matt. xxiii. 24: τὸν κώνωπα, τὴν κάμηλον, *the gnat, the camel*, of some popular fable or proverb.

Luke xii. 54: τὴν νεφέλην,[1] *the cloud*, "rising out of the west," of that peculiar character which foretells much rain. (1 Kings xviii. 44, 45.)

John iv. 22: ἡ σωτηρία, *the salvation*, expected by Israel. (R.V. *salvation*.)

John xiii. 5: τὸν νιπτῆρα, *the basin*, used on such occasions.

John xvi. 13: πᾶσαν τὴν ἀλήθειαν, *all the truth*, in reference to this particular subject. (Compare Mark v. 33.)

John xviii. 3: τὴν σπεῖραν, *the band*, on duty at the time.

John xxi. 3: τὸ πλοῖον, *the ship*, belonging to the disciples, or hired for their use.

Acts xvii. 1: ἡ συναγωγὴ τῶν Ἰουδαίων,[1] *the synagogue of the Jews*, *i.e.*, the chief or only synagogue of that particular district.

Acts xx. 9: ἐπὶ τῆς θυρίδος, *at the window*, or open lattice of the apartment.

Acts xxi. 38: τοὺς τετρακισχιλίους, *the four thousand*, the notorious band of desperadoes.

Acts xxiv. 23: τῷ ἑκατοντάρχῃ, *the centurion*, *i.e.*, the captain of the cavalry who had sole charge of the Apostle when the infantry (xxiii. 32) had returned to Jerusalem.

---

[1] Rev. Text and W. H. omit the article.

§ 214.] SIGNIFICANCE OF THE ARTICLE. 183

1 Cor. i. 21 : διὰ τῆς μωρίας τοῦ κηρύγματος, *by means of the foolishness of the proclamation, i.e.*, by the (so-called) folly of the preached Gospel.

1 Cor. iv. 5 : ὁ ἔπαινος, *the praise*, which is due, respectively, to each. (So R.V., *his praise*.)

1 Cor. v. 9 : ἐν τῇ ἐπιστολῇ, *in the letter*, referred to thus as well known by the Corinthians. Whether the Apostle speaks of the letter he is now writing, or of some previous one, is a question of interpretation. (Compare 2 Cor. vii. 8.)

1 Cor. x. 13 : τὴν ἔκβασιν, *the escape*, the appropriate means of deliverance.

1 Cor. xiv. 16 : τὸ Ἀμήν, *the Amen*, the appointed and usual response in Christian worship.

1 Cor. xv. 8 : ὡσπερεὶ τῷ ἐκτρώματι, *as to the one "born out of due time,"* the one Apostle specially bearing that character. (R.V. *one born*, etc.)

2 Thess. ii. 3 : ἡ ἀποστασία, *the falling away*, or *apostasy*, which the Thessalonians had been taught to expect.

1 Tim. vi. 12 : τὸν καλὸν ἀγῶνα τῆς πίστεως, *the good fight of the faith*, the Christian faith.

Heb. xi. 10 : τὴν τοὺς θεμελίους ἔχουσαν πόλιν, *the city which hath the foundations, i.e.*, the New Jerusalem.

Heb. xi. 35 : οὐ προσδεξάμενοι τὴν ἀπολύτρωσιν, *not accepting the deliverance*, proffered as the reward of apostasy.

James i. 11 : σὺν τῷ καύσωνι, *with the burning wind* from the east, fatal to vegetation. (Compare Matt. xx. 12 ; Jonah iv. 8 ; Luke xii. 55.)

Rev. ii. 10 : τὸν στέφανον τῆς ζωῆς, *the crown of the life*, the promised crown of the life immortal.

Rev. vii. 14 : ἐκ τῆς θλίψεως τῆς μεγάλης, *out of the great tribulation* (lit., the tribulation, the great one), the reference being to a special trial.

In ascriptions of praise, also, the Article is generally found. Thus, Rev. iv. 11, τὴν δόξαν καὶ τὴν τιμήν, *the glory and the honour* ; v. 12, 13 ; vii. 12.

214. Before abstract nouns the Article denotes that the conception is individualised, as an object of thought. It is often difficult to trace the distinction, and it may even be impossible to say in some instances whether the insertion or the omission of the Article before abstracts would give the better sense;[1] but there are many cases in which the difference is clearly marked. For example, the Article is employed:—

a. When the abstraction is personified.

1 Cor. xiii. 4 : ἡ ἀγάπη μακροθυμεῖ, κ.τ.λ., *Love suffereth long*, etc.

Acts xxviii. 4 : ὃν ἡ δίκη ζῆν οὐκ εἴασεν, *whom Justice permitted not to live*.

1 Cor. xi. 14 : οὐδὲ ἡ φύσις αὐτὴ διδάσκει; *doth not Nature itself teach?*

So when the abstract term is used for the whole mass of individuals.

Rom. xi. 7 : ἡ δὲ ἐκλογή, *the election*, i.e., the mass of the elect.

Phil. iii. 3 : ἡ περιτομή, *the circumcision*, i.e., the community of the circumcised.

b. When the abstraction is made a separate object of thought.

1 John iv. 10 : ἐν τούτῳ ἐστὶν ἡ ἀγάπη, *in this is love*, i.e., not merely "this is an act of love," but, herein Love in its very essence stands revealed.

1 Cor. xv. 21 : δι' ἀνθρώπου ὁ θάνατος, *by man* (came) *death*, the universal fact, apart from the consideration of special instances.

Matt. v. 6 : πεινῶντες καὶ διψῶντες τὴν δικαιοσύνην, *hungering and thirsting after righteousness*, as in itself a good to be obtained.

c. But where the abstract word expresses merely a quality of some further object of thought, the article is omitted.

Matt. v. 10 : οἱ δεδιωγμένοι ἕνεκεν δικαιοσύνης, *the persecuted for righteousness' sake*, such being an element in their character.

Rom. v. 13 : ἁμαρτία ἦν ἐν κόσμῳ, *sin was in the world*, i.e., as an attribute of human conduct; illustrating the more general assertion of verse 12, that *Sin*, in the abstract, ἡ ἁμαρτία, *entered into the world*.

1 Cor. xiii. 1 : ἐὰν ... ἀγάπην μὴ ἔχω, *If ... I have not love*, as a feature in my character.

<small>In determining the reason of the omission or the insertion of the Article before abstract nouns in any given case, it should be considered whether there is any</small>

---

[1] In fact, the subtlety of this distinction has given rise to a large number of various readings.

grammatical rule requiring it, apart from the meaning of the term. (See especially § 212.)

215. A definite attribute or property of an object is marked in Greek by the Article.

Thus, instead of saying, *He has large eyes*, the Greeks would say, *He has the eyes large*. But when the connection was only accidental, the Article would be omitted; thus, *He had a deep wound* would be expressed without the Article, unless the wound had been previously mentioned, when the case would come under § 212. The Article may, therefore, in such sentences as the following be rendered by the possessive pronoun.

Acts xxvi. 24: ὁ Φῆστος μεγάλῃ τῇ φωνῇ φησίν, *Festus says with his voice upraised*, or "with a loud voice," as A.V. So chap. xiv. 10.

1 Peter iv. 8: τὴν εἰς ἑαυτοὺς ἀγάπην ἐκτενῆ ἔχοντες, *having your love to one another fervent*.

Heb. vii. 24: ἀπαράβατον ἔχει τὴν ἱερωσύνην, R.V. *He hath his priesthood unchangeable*.

The Article, in effect, must often be rendered as an unemphatic possessive; the Greeks saying *the*, where we say *his, her, its, their*.

216. With proper names, the Article may or may not be employed. The only rule, probably, that can be safely laid down on the subject is that a name does not take the Article on its first mention, unless in the case of personages well known or specially distinguished. For the rest, the habit or taste of the writer seems to have decided his usage.[1]

It may, however, be noted that **indeclinable names in the oblique cases most frequently employ the Article.** Thus we find τοῦ, τῷ, τὸν, Ἰσραήλ. So also in the genealogies.

When a name is followed by some title or descriptive word, the Article is generally inserted. So, Μαρία ἡ Μαγδαληνή, *Mary the Magdalene;* Ἰούδας ὁ Ἰσκαριώτης, *Judas the Iscariot;* Σωσθένης ὁ ἀδελφός (1 Cor. i. 1), *Sosthenes the brother*.

Of geographical names, those of countries, generally feminine in α, almost always take the Article. The probable reason is that they

---

[1] Thus, in the Acts, the name of *Paul* almost always has the Article; that of *Peter* much more seldom, but still frequently. Both in the Gospels and the Acts the names of the other apostles usually omit the article.

were originally adjectives, agreeing with γῆ, *land.* Thus, ἡ Ἰουδαία, *Judæa,* properly "the Judæan land," or "land of the Jews." Αἴγυπτος, *Egypt,* is always used without the Article.

Names of cities greatly vary in their use, most generally omitting the Article after prepositions. Ἱερουσαλήμ (indecl.), Ἱεροσόλυμα (neut. plur.), *Jerusalem,* is almost always anarthrous.

217. The DIVINE NAMES appear to be somewhat irregular in their use or rejection of the Article.

a. **We find** Θεός, *God,* **almost interchangeably with** ὁ Θεός. It is certain, however, that an explanation may very commonly be found in the rules already given.

Apart from these, the general distinction seems to be that the name without the Article throws the stress rather upon the general conception of the Divine character—" One who is Omnipotent, All-holy, Infinite, etc."[1]—whereas the word with the Article (the *ordinary* use) specifies the *revealed Deity,* the God of the New Testament. Parts of the Epistles to the Corinthians may be taken by way of illustration :—

1 Cor. ii. 1 : *The testimony of God,* τοῦ Θεοῦ.

Ver. 7 : *We speak the wisdom of God,* Θεοῦ (without the Article), *i.e.,* the wisdom of an Infinite and Perfect being, as contrasted with the world's wisdom, *which God,* ὁ Θεός (the God revealed in the Gospel), *foreordained.*

Chap. iii. 6–9 : ὁ Θεὸς ηὔξανεν, (our) *God caused the seed to grow ... for we are God's fellow-workers, ye are God's husbandry, God's building.* In these three clauses the word is used without the Article, as though the Apostle reasoned, "It is a God for whom[2] we are labouring, a God who is moulding you, training you for Himself ;" resuming, then, in verse 10 with the Article, " *according to the grace of God,* τοῦ Θεοῦ, *which is given me.*"

Thus, again, 2 Cor. v. 18–21 : " All things are of God, (τοῦ Θεοῦ, *our God*) ... who hath given to us the ministry of reconciliation, that God,

---

[1] Compare a line of Dr. Watts's—
" This was compassion like *a God.*"

[2] Or, *with whom.*

(Θεός—all we can understand by that Name) was in Christ ... We are ambassadors, then, as though *this God*, (τοῦ Θεοῦ,) were beseeching ... Be ye reconciled to *this God*, (τῷ Θεῷ) ... Him who knew not sin, He made sin on our behalf, that we might become (δικαιοσύνη Θεοῦ,) *God's* righteousness, (*i.e.*, partakers of a Divine righteousness,) in Him."

b. **The name Κύριος,** *Lord,* **generally prefixes the Article.** The contrary usage, when not accounted for by ordinary rules, arises from this word having been adopted in the Septuagint as the Greek equivalent for the Hebrew name JEHOVAH. In the Gospels it usually signifies *God;* in the Epistles it commonly refers to *Christ*.[1] Instances of its occurrence without the article are (1) in direct renderings from the Old Testament, as 1 Cor. iii. 20, Κύριος γινώσκει τοὺς διαλογισμούς, κ.τ.λ., *Jehovah knows the thoughts,* etc. So 2 Tim. ii. 19 ; Heb. vii. 21, xiii. 6. In 1 Pet. i. 25 it is substituted for the other Hebrew Divine name (LXX., Θεοῦ); (2) after prepositions, as in the ordinary phrase, ἐν Κυρίῳ ; (3) preceding the appellation, Ἰησοῦς Χριστός, *Jesus Christ* (generally in the gen. case), as in the superscriptions (Rom. i. 7 ; 1 Cor. i. 3 ; Gal. i. 3). So in Eph. vi. 23, and strikingly Phil. iii. 20.

c. **The title υἱὸς Θεοῦ,** *a* or *the Son of God* (more emphatically, Θεοῦ υἱός, *God's Son*), **is found both with and without the Article.** The usual form is ὁ υἱὸς τοῦ Θεοῦ, *the Son of the* (revealed) *God* (comp. under Θεός). Υἱὸς τοῦ Θεοῦ occurs, as in the Tempter's interrogatory (Matt. iv. 3), where the supremacy of the revealed Deity is recognised, but the exclusive relationship of our Lord to the Father is at least left an open question ; while υἱὸς Θεοῦ expresses a view altogether less definite of our Lord's dignity. Thus, in their *first* confession, the disciples said, " Truly thou art *Son of God*," Θεοῦ υἱός. But afterwards Peter acknowledges, "Thou art *the* Son of *the* living God," ὁ υἱὸς τοῦ Θεοῦ, κ.τ.λ. (Matt. xvi. 16). The centurion amid the miracles of Calvary expresses a certain measure of faith : "Truly this man is Son of God," Θεοῦ υἱός, without an Article to either (Matt. xxvii. 54 ; Mark xv. 39 ; compare Luke xxiii. 47). But we read of Saul, the convert, how *he preached at once in the synagogues of Damascus that " this man is the Son of God,"* ὁ υἱὸς τοῦ Θεοῦ (Acts xi. 20).[2]

---

[1] *The* Name above every name, Phil. ii. 9, is Κύριος, JEHOVAH.

[2] *Apparent* exceptions to this course of remark occur—Luke i. 35 ; Rom. i. 4—which may be left to the thoughtful reader.

d. **The name Ἰησοῦς,** *Jesus,* **when used alone, in the Gospels and Acts, almost always has the Article.** The reason undoubtedly is that the word is strictly an appellative, being but the Greek form of the Hebrew for "Saviour." To the disciples, therefore, and the Evangelists, the significance of the word was ever present: *the Saviour.* When others employed the name, or it was used in converse with them, the Article might be omitted. See John vi. 24 (where for the moment the point of view taken is that of the spectators). So viii. 59 (and, in critical edd., xi. 51, xviii. 8);[1] Acts v. 30, xiii. 23, 33, and a few other passages. **When the name stands in apposition with others,** as Κύριος or Χριστός, **the Article is generally omitted.** In the Epistles this combination is most usual. The Apostle Paul, for instance, only has ὁ Ἰησοῦς alone four times, and Ἰησοῦς nine; his preference being for the appellative Χριστός, while his fervour adopts many variously-combined titles for the Lord his Saviour.[2]

e. **The employment of the Article with Χριστός,** "the Anointed One," *Christ,* **shows a remarkable difference between the Gospels and the Epistles.** Strictly speaking, the name is a verbal appellative, the Greek equivalent of the Hebrew word *Messiah,* "Anointed." Hence in our Lord's time it was customary and natural to speak of *the Christ.* This, accordingly, is the almost invariable form of speech in the Gospels and the Acts. Thus, Matt. ii. 4, we should read, "where *the Christ* is born;" Matt. xi. 2, "the works of *the Christ*," *i.e.,* such works as attested his possession of that character; Matt. xxii. 42, "what think ye of *the Christ?*" John xii. 34, "*the Christ* abideth for ever;" Acts xvii. 3, "that it behoved *the Christ* to suffer."

---

[1] So W. H.

[2] Mr. Rose, in his edition of "Middleton on the Greek Article," gives a list of the appellations used by St. Paul, with the number of times they respectively occur. They are—in the rec. text (but in some the readings vary)—

ὁ Ἰησοῦς	4 times.	ὁ Κύριος Ἰησοῦς	10 times.
Ἰησοῦς	9 ,,	Ἰησοῦς ὁ Κύριος	1 ,,
ὁ Χριστός	95 ,,	ὁ Κ. Ἰ. Χριστός	5 ,,
Χριστός	122 ,,	Κύριος Ἰ. Χ.	17 ,,
Ἰησοῦς ὁ Χριστός	1 ,,	ὁ Χ. Ἰ. ὁ Κύριος	1 ,,
ὁ Χριστὸς Ἰησοῦς (readings doubtful)	4 ,,	Χριστὸς Ἰ. Κ.	1 ,,
		Ἰ. Χ. ὁ Κ. ἡμῶν	3 ,,
Ἰησοῦς Χριστός	39 ,,	ὁ Κ. ἡμῶν Ἰ. Χ.	35 ,,
Χριστὸς Ἰησοῦς	58 ,,	Χ. Ἰ. ὁ Κ. ἡμων	9 ,,

Already, however, the tendency was at work which in later days changed this appellative into a recognised proper name. Traces of this may be seen in Matt. i. 1; Mark i. 1, ix. 41; Acts ii. 38; and in the Epistles of Paul the usage appears entirely reversed, the omission of the Article being the rule (in the forms Χριστός alone, Ἰησοῦς Χριστός, and Χριστὸς Ἰησοῦς), and its retention the exception. The descriptive title, "THE ANOINTED," has not been wholly lost, but the personal name of CHRIST has laid a yet deeper hold on the mind and heart of the Church. Sometimes, again, the Apostle employs one form in close repeated recurrence, as in Col. iii. 1–4 : " If ye be risen with *the Christ*, seek the things that are above, where *the Christ* sitteth ... your life is hid with *the Christ* ... when *the Christ* shall be manifested." Without the Article, we have the name thus recurrent in Phil. i. 18–23 : after speaking of those who preach *the Christ* out of envy and strife, the Apostle adds, as with a more personal love, " nevertheless *Christ* is preached "... uttering then his earnest hope " that *Christ* shall be magnified ... for me to live is *Christ* ... yet to depart and to be with *Christ* is far better."

> It is not asserted that the thoughtful reader will always discern the reason of the employment or the omission of the Article in connection with these sacred names. Often, however, unquestionably, most interesting and valuable suggestions will arise ; and the whole subject is worth the most painstaking investigation.[1]

f. **The name of the** *Holy Spirit*, Πνεῦμα ἅγιον, **requires the Article when He is spoken of in Himself;** but when the reference is to His operation, gifts, or manifestation in men, the Article is almost invariably omitted. In other words, "the Spirit" regarded *objectively* takes the Article, regarded *subjectively* is frequently anarthrous.

> Apparent exceptions to this rule are but instances of more general grammatical laws, as, for instance, when the term, although definite, follows a preposition or precedes a genitive.

Accordingly, when disciples of Christ are said to be *filled with the Spirit, to receive the Spirit, to walk in the Spirit,* the Article is omitted. See, *e.g.*, Luke i. 15, 41, 67, ii. 25, xi. 13 ; John iii. 5, xx. 22 ; Acts i. 5, ii. 4, iv. 8, vi. 3, viii. 15, 17 (the Article in 18 is a case of renewed mention),

---

[1] See a striking essay on "The Greek Testament" in the *Quarterly Review* for January, 1863.

xi. 16; Rom. viii. 9, ix. 1, xv. 13, 16; 1 Cor. ii. 4, 13, vii. 40; 2 Cor. iii. 3; Eph. v. 18, vi. 18; Col. i. 8; 2 Thess. ii. 13; 1 Pet. i. 2; 2 Pet. i. 21; Jude 19; Rev. i. 10, etc.

An instance of the force of the Article may be seen in John xiv. 17, 26, xv. 26, xvi. 13, in all of which passages we read τὸ Πνεῦμα. But when the Spirit is *imparted*, the Article disappears (xx. 22), λάβετε Πνεῦμα ἅγιον, "*Receive ye (the) Holy Ghost.*"

218. Some monadic nouns (see § 209), being regarded as proper names, **may be used with or without the Article.** Such are ἥλιος, *sun;* κόσμος, *world;* οὐρανός, οὐρανοί, *heaven* or *heavens;* γῆ, *earth,* or *land;* θάλασσα, *sea;* ἡμέρα, *day;* νύξ, *night;* ἐκκλησία, *church,* and some others. The Article, however, is most generally inserted.

219. Some prepositional phrases omit the Article; in most instances denoting time, place, or state. Compare the English expressions, *at home, on land, by day, in church.*

Examples.—ἀπ' ἀγροῦ, *from the country* (Mark xv. 21; Luke xxiii. 26); εἰς ἀγρόν, *into the country* (Mark xvi. 12); ἐν ἀγρῷ, *in the country* (Luke xv. 25).

ἐν ἀρχῇ, *in the beginning* (John i. 1, 2; Acts xi. 15); ἀπ' ἀρχῆς, *from the beginning* (Matt. xix. 4, 8; Luke i. 2; John viii. 44; 1 John i. 1, etc.); ἐξ ἀρχῆς, *from the beginning* (John xvi. 4).

ἐκ δεξιῶν...ἐξ ἀριστερῶν, *on* (lit., off) *the right...the left* (Mark x. 37; Luke xxiii. 33, etc.).

εἰς οἰκίαν, *into the house* (2 John 10).

ἐν ἐκκλησίᾳ, *in* (the) *church* (1 Cor. xiv. 19, 28, 35).

ἐπὶ πρόσωπον, *on the face* (1 Cor. xiv. 25).

ἀπὸ ἀνατολῶν, *from the East* (Matt. ii. 1, xxiv. 27); ἀπὸ δυσμῶν, *from the West* (Luke xii. 54; Rev. xxi. 13; both phrases combined, Matt. viii. 11; Luke xiii. 29); ἕως δυσμῶν, *unto the West* (Matt. xxiv. 27).

ἐκ νεκρῶν, *from the dead.* This phrase is of constant occurrence, as Matt. xvii. 9, etc. Occasionally, ἀπό is employed; very rarely the Article is found. Perhaps the omission is intended emphatically to mark the condition, "from *dead persons*"—those, indefinitely speaking, who are in that state.

Other instances of this idiom might be added. The student, however, must be cautioned against supposing that the preposition is *itself* a reason for the omission of the Article before a term intended to be taken as definite.[1]

220. Nouns defined by the demonstrative pronouns, οὗτος, *this,* **ἐκεῖνος,** *that,* **directly agreeing with them, take the Article, which always immediately precedes the noun;** the pronoun being placed indifferently, first or last. Thus we may have ὁ ἄνθρωπος οὗτος (Luke ii. 25), or οὗτος ὁ ἄνθρωπος (xiv. 30), *this man,* but never ὁ οὗτος ἄνθρωπος or οὗτος ἄνθρωπος, and scarcely ever ἄνθρωπος οὗτος.[2]

When the Article is omitted with the noun and demonstrative pronoun, the latter implies a predicate. Thus (Rom. ix. 8), οὐ... ταῦτα τέκνα τοῦ Θεοῦ, *these are not children of God.*

These rules apply for the most part to proper names, as Acts xix. 26, ὁ Παῦλος οὗτος, *this Paul;* Heb. vii. 1, οὗτος ὁ Μελχισεδέκ, *this Melchisedek;* John vi. 42, οὐχ οὗτός ἐστιν Ἰησοῦς, *Is this not Jesus?*[3] οὗτος after a name often implies contempt: Acts vii. 40; xix. 26.

The pronoun τοιοῦτος, τοιαύτη, τοιοῦτο, *such,* is found with the Article when the person or thing which is the subject of comparison is definitely before the writer's mind; the omission of the Article shows that the reference is more general, to quality or attribute.

Matt. xix. 14: τῶν τοιούτων, κ.τ.λ., *of such* (as these children) *is the kingdom of heaven.*

2 Cor. ii. 6: ἱκανὸν τῷ τοιούτῳ, *sufficient to such a man* (as the offender of whom I write).

Matt. ix. 6: ἐξουσίαν τοιαύτην, *such (kind of) power.*

John ix. 16: τοιαῦτα σημεῖα, *such (kind of) miracles.*

It is observable, however, that the two forms of expression, being separated by so slight a shade of difference, may often be used indifferently. The Article is *generally* omitted in the Gospels, *generally* inserted in the Epistles, except that to the Hebrews.

---

[1] See, for instance, Alford on Matt. i. 18, ἐκ πνεύματος ἁγίου. The Article is omitted, not on account of the preposition, but according to the distinction illustrated in § 217, *f.*

[2] The demonstrative ὅδε only once occurs in the adjective construction, and follows the same rule: James iv. 13, εἰς τήνδε τὴν πόλιν, *into this city.*

[3] The learner should be cautioned against rendering, "Is this Jesus not the son of Joseph?" which would have required ὁ Ἰησοῦς. The comma at *Jesus* in the R. V. conveys the proper stress.

221. The distributive pronominal adjective ἕκαστος, *each*, never takes the Article in the New Testament.

Before τοσοῦτος, *so much* (plur., *so many*), the Article is not found in the New Testament, with the exception of Rev. xviii. 17, ὁ τοσοῦτος πλοῦτος, *the wealth, which was so great.*

222. The Article prefixed to the pronoun αὐτός **gives it the meaning of** *the same.* (See § 57, *d.*)

2 Cor. iv. 13 : τὸ αὐτὸ πνεῦμα, *the same Spirit.*

But Rom. viii. 26 : αὐτὸ τὸ πνεῦμα, *the very Spirit*, the Spirit Himself.

<small>The New Testament MSS. often vary between the contracted plural ταὐτά and ταῦτα (plur. neut. of οὗτος). See Luke vi. 23, 26, xvii. 30; 1 Thess. ii. 14.</small>

223. *a.* **A possessive pronoun agreeing with a noun not a Predicate invariably takes the Article.**

John xvii. 10 : τὰ ἐμὰ πάντα σά ἐστιν καὶ τὰ σὰ ἐμά, *all* (things) *mine are thine, and thine are mine.*

Acts xxiv. 6 : κατὰ τὸν ἡμέτερον νόμον, *according to our law.*

John vii. 6 : ὁ καιρὸς ὁ ὑμέτερος, *your opportunity.*

b. The possessive sense is, however, generally given by the genitive of the personal pronoun; the article preceding the noun, as ὁ πατήρ μου, *my father;* οἱ πατέρες ὑμῶν, *your fathers.*

224. *a.* **The adjective** πᾶς, *all*, **in the singular number, without the Article, signifies** *every;* **with the Article, it means** *the whole of* the object which it qualifies. Thus, πᾶσα πόλις is *every city;* πᾶσα ἡ πόλις, or ἡ πᾶσα πόλις,[1] *the whole of the city.* ἡ πόλις πᾶσα would have a meaning slightly different—*the city, all of it,* "the city in every part." So with abstracts.

Luke iv. 13 : συντελέσας πάντα πειρασμόν, (the devil) *having ended every temptation, i.e.,* every form of temptation.

2 Cor. iv. 2 : πρὸς πᾶσαν συνείδησιν ἀνθρώπων, *to every conscience of men, i.e.,* to every variety of human conscience.

---

[1] A construction only twice found: Acts xx. 18, τὸν πάντα χρόνον; and 1 Tim. i. 16, τὴν πᾶσαν (W. H. ἅπασαν) μακροθυμίαν.

§ 224, b.]   SIGNIFICANCE OF THE ARTICLE.   193

Eph. iii. 15 : πᾶσα πατριά, κ.τ.λ., *every family in heaven and on earth.*

   Some critics have questioned this translation on the authority of chap. ii. 21, where they read πᾶσα οἰκοδομή, and render *the whole building.* This, however, is quite contrary to usage. The R.V. correctly renders *each several building.*

2 Tim. iii. 16 : πᾶσα γραφὴ θεόπνευστος, κ.τ.λ., *every writing* (*i.e.*, of those just mentioned, ver. 15) is *divinely inspired*,[1] etc., or *every divinely inspired writing* is *also profitable*,[2] etc.

   Luke ii. 10 : παντὶ τῷ λαῷ, *to all the people* of Israel.

     The phrase in chap. ii. 31 is different: "*before the face of all the peoples,*" *i.e.*, the nations of mankind.

1 Cor. xiii. 2 : ἐὰν ἔχω πᾶσαν τὴν πίστιν, κ.τ.λ., *if I have all the faith* requisite for such a task.

Col. i. 23 : ἐν πάσῃ τῇ κτίσει,[3] *in all creation*, R.V.; not "to every creature," as A.V. Compare ver. 15, πάσης κτίσεως, where the rendering is accurate, *of every creature.*

1 Tim. i. 16 : τὴν πᾶσαν μακροθυμίαν, *all the longsuffering* which belongs to the Divine character. R.V., *all his longsuffering.*

John v. 22 : τὴν κρίσιν πᾶσαν, κ.τ.λ., *the judgment* (of men), *all of it.* The Father has committed this wholly to the Son.

With proper names, as of countries, cities, etc., the Article after πᾶς may be omitted by § 216; the signification being still *the whole*. (Matt. ii. 3; Acts ii. 36.)

b. **The plural, πάντες, almost always has the Article when the substantive is expressed; almost always omits it when the substantive is implied.** The few exceptions to the former are chiefly when the noun is ἄνθρωποι, *men*.[4] The exceptions to the latter are where the idea is collective. Thus, πάντα is *all things*, severally; τὰ πάντα, *all things*, as constituting a whole.

   Phil. iv. 13 : πάντα ἰσχύω, *I can do all things.*

---

   [1] Middleton; R.V., marg.
   [2] Ellicott; R.V.
   [3] W. H. and Rev. Text omit the Article.
   [4] See also Acts xvii. 21, xix. 17; 1 Cor. x. 1; Heb. i. 6; 1 Pet. ii. 1

Col. i. 16: τὰ πάντα ἐν αὐτῷ, κ.τ.λ., *all things* were created *in Him* (Christ). See also 1 Tim. vi. 13; Heb. ii. 8, etc.

The usual position of the plural, πάντες, is before the Article and substantive. Twice (Acts xix. 7, xxvii. 37), with a special meaning, it stands between them: οἱ πάντες ἄνδρες, *the men in all;* αἱ πᾶσαι ψυχαί, *the souls* (persons) *in all.* Occasionally, employed after the Article and substantive, it takes a strong emphasis: as John xvii. 10, τὰ ἐμὰ πάντα σά ἐστι, *mine are all thine.*

225. The construction of ὅλος, *whole,* in respect of the Article, is similar to that of πᾶς. Generally the Article stands between it and its noun, as ὅλος ὁ κόσμος, *the whole world* (Rom. i. 8). Occasionally the noun and Article precede, with an added emphasis on ὅλος, as ὁ κόσμος ὅλος, *the world,* (yea,) *the whole* (of it) (Matt. xvi. 26).[1] A few times it is found without the Article, and its force is expressed by the English indefinite, as John vii. 23, ὅλον ἄνθρωπον, *a whole man* I have restored to health. The other instances are Acts xi. 26, xxi. 31 (before a proper name), xxviii. 30; Titus i. 11.

226. The employment of the Article with the adjective pronouns ἄλλος, *other* (numerically), and ἕτερος, *other* (properly implying some further distinction), is analogous to the English idiom.[2] Singular, *the other;* plural, *the others* (ἕτερος only once so used—Luke iv. 43).[3]

John xx. 3: ὁ ἄλλος μαθητής, *the other disciple.*

John xx. 25: οἱ ἄλλοι μαθηταί, *the other disciples.*

Matt. vi. 24: τὸν ἕτερον ἀγαπήσει, *the other* (master) *he will love.*

Luke iv. 43: ταῖς ἑτέραις πόλεσιν, *to the other cities.*

227. The Article with the neuter πολύ ("the much") is equivalent to "*the abundance*" (see 1 Pet. i. 3). More common, however, is its use with the plural, πολλοί, πολλαί, πολλά, *many,* to which it gives the

---

[1] The observant reader may trace the emphasis in the other passages where this order is found: Matt. xxvi. 59; Mark i. 33, viii. 36; Luke ix. 25, xi. 36; John iv. 53; Acts xix. 29, xxi. 30; Rom. xvi. 23; 1 Cor. xiv. 23; 1 John v. 19; Rev. iii. 10, xii. 9, xvi. 14.

[2] In classical Greek, ὁ ἄλλος means *the rest of.*

[3] Probably also Matt. xi. 16 (W. H.; Rev. Text).

§ 228.] SIGNIFICANCE OF THE ARTICLE. 195

significance of *the many, the generality*, the whole mass of the particular objects of thought. The only instances are the following :—

Matt. xxiv. 12 : ἡ ἀγάπη τῶν πολλῶν, *the love of the many* shall wax cold.

Luke vii. 47 : αἱ ἁμαρτίαι ... αἱ πολλαί, her *sins—the many, i.e., the whole of them*—are forgiven.

Acts xxvi. 24 : τὰ πολλὰ γράμματα, *the many letters ;* the mass, the quantity of thy learning.

Rom. xii. 5 : οἱ πολλοί, *the many* of us—the whole mass—are one body in Christ. (So 1 Cor. x. 17.)

1 Cor. x. 33 : τὸ τῶν πολλῶν, *the* (advantage) *of the many.*

2 Cor. ii. 17 : ὡς οἱ πολλοί, (we are not) *as the many.*

Rev. xvii. 1 : τῶν ὑδάτων τῶν πολλῶν, *of the many waters.*

> Rom. v. 15-19: This most important passage, containing this idiom, has been thus translated by the Revisers :—
>
> [We have noted by *italics* the Articles which the A.V. omits.]
>
> 15 But not as the trespass, so also is the free gift. For if by the trespass of *the* one *the* many died, much more did the grace of God, and the gift by the grace of *the* one man, Jesus Christ, abound unto *the* many.
>
> 16 And not as through one that sinned, so is the gift: for the judgment came of one unto condemnation, but the free gift came of many trespasses unto justification.
>
> 17 For if, by the trespass of *the* one, death reigned through *the* one ; much more shall they that receive *the* abundance of (*the*[1]) grace and of the gift of (*the*[1]) righteousness reign in life through *the* one, even Jesus Christ.
>
> 18 So then as through one trespass [the judgment came] unto all men to condemnation ; even so through one act of righteousness [the free gift came] unto all men to justification of life.
>
> 19 For as through *the* one man's disobedience *the* many were made sinners, even so through the obedience of *the* one shall *the* many be made righteous.

228. When the Nominative is used for the Vocative in direct address, the Article is prefixed. (For an explanation of the idiom, see § 244.)

Matt. xi. 26 : ναί, ὁ πατήρ, *even so, Father!*

Luke viii. 54 : ἡ παῖς, ἐγείρου, *Damsel, arise!*

---

[1] In the Greek, but not in R.V.

John xix. 3 : χαῖρε ὁ βασιλεύς, *hail, King !*
John xx. 28 : ὁ Κύριός μου καὶ ὁ Θεός μου, *my Lord and my God !*
Heb. i. 8 : ὁ θρόνος σου ὁ Θεός, *Thy throne, O God !* (See also ver. 9, and x. 7.)

229. The Article is often separated from its substantive by qualifying or explanatory words.

a. These are, generally, a preposition, with its case, other dependent words being sometimes added.

Matt. vii. 3 : τὴν δὲ ἐν τῷ σῷ ὀφθαλμῷ δοκόν, *but the beam in thine own eye.*

Luke xvi. 10 : ὁ ἐν ἐλαχίστῳ ἄδικος, *the* (man) *unjust in the least.*

1 Pet. i. 14 : ταῖς πρότερον ἐν τῇ ἀγνοίᾳ ὑμῶν ἐπιθυμίαις, *according to the former* (lit., formerly) *lusts in your ignorance.*

b. Adverbs also are often thus employed :—

2 Tim. iv. 10 : ἀγαπήσας τὸν νῦν αἰῶνα, *having loved the present* (lit., now) *world.*

230. *a.* **The Article is very frequently repeated after its noun, to introduce some attributive word or phrase.**

Clearly, this is a result of the original demonstrative force of the Article.

The phrase introduced may be an adjective or participle, a preposition with its case, or (rarely) an adverb.

The Article so employed gives the attributive a certain prominence or emphasis.

Matt. xvii. 5 : ὁ υἱός μου ὁ ἀγαπητός, *my beloved Son,* lit., *my Son, the beloved.*

Titus ii. 11 : ἡ χάρις τοῦ Θεοῦ ἡ[1] σωτήριος, *the grace of God that bringeth salvation,* lit., *the grace ... the salvation-bringing.*

Heb. xiii. 20 : τὸν ποιμένα τῶν προβάτων τὸν μέγαν, *the great Shepherd of the sheep.*

The absence of the Article before an attributive phrase is often significant. Thus, Rom. viii. 3 : κατέκρινε τὴν ἁμαρτίαν ἐν τῇ σαρκί, *He condemned sin in the flesh.* The phrase depends upon κατέκρινε. Had it been τὴν ἐν τῇ σαρκί, *in the flesh* would have qualified *sin.*

---

[1] W. H. omit the article.

§ 231.] EMPHATIC USE OF THE ARTICLE. 197

1 Pet. i. 25 : τὸ ῥῆμα τὸ εὐαγγελισθέν, *the word that was preached*, lit., the word, the spoken-as-glad-tidings.

Matt. v. 16 : τὸν Πατέρα ὑμῶν τὸν ἐν τοῖς οὐρανοῖς, *your Father in the heavens.*

Luke xx. 35 : τῆς ἀναστάσεως τῆς ἐκ νεκρῶν, *of the resurrection from the dead.*

Rev. xi. 2 : τὴν αὐλὴν τὴν ἔξωθεν, *the outer court.*

b. Occasionally, this emphatic form of expression is employed when the noun has no Article preceding.

Luke xxiii. 49 : γυναῖκες αἱ συνακολουθοῦσαι αὐτῷ, (there stood) *women, those who accompanied Him.*

John xiv. 27 : εἰρήνην τὴν ἐμὴν δίδωμι ὑμῖν, *peace,* (which is) *mine, I give to you.*

1 Tim. v. 3 : χήρας τίμα τὰς ὄντως χήρας, *honour widows, those who are widows indeed.*

Rom. ix. 30 : δικαιοσύνην δὲ τὴν ἐκ πίστεως, (he obtained) *righteousness, yea, that* (which is) *by faith.*

James i. 25 : εἰς νόμον τέλειον τὸν τῆς ἐλευθερίας, (whoso looketh) *into a perfect law, that of liberty.*

> In passages like these, the former clause contains the general description; the latter limits it to a particular case. See also Gal. ii. 20, iii. 21; 1 Pet. i. 10, "prophets, those who prophesied;" Jude 6, "Angels, (even) those, namely, that kept not their first estate."

231. The defining clause being frequently participial, it may be remarked, in anticipation of the account to be given of Participles (§§ 393–396), that with the Article the participle qualifies the noun, as a simple epithet, while without the Article it implies a predicate. Thus, ὁ Θεὸς ὁ ποιήσας τὸν κόσμον is, *God who made the world;* ὁ Θεὸς ποιήσας, κ.τ.λ., would be, *God having made,* or *when He had made,* etc. In 2 Pet. i. 18,[1] again, we render, not "the voice *which was borne* from heaven," but "the voice *as it* was borne."

> Sometimes it will be important to observe the force of the anarthrous participle.
> Thus, in a much controverted passage, 1 Pet. iii. 19, 20,[1] τοῖς ἐν φυλακῇ

---

[1] In these passages the R.V. is not exact.

πνεύμασι…ἀπειθήσασί ποτε, whatever be the true *interpretation*, the words must be translated, not "the spirits in prison who were once disobedient," but "the spirits in prison when once they disobeyed."

This usage will be further illustrated in the sections on Participles.

232. In the enumeration of several persons or things, joined by a connective particle, an Article *before the first only* intimates a connection between the whole, as forming one object of thought. This is termed "combined enumeration." The *repeated* Article, on the other hand, implies a separation, in themselves, or in the view taken of them.

Sometimes, however, the separation seems to be chiefly grammatical, different genders requiring the repeated Article.

a. **Combined enumeration.**—Eph. ii. 20 : ἐπὶ τῷ θεμελίῳ τῶν ἀποστόλων καὶ προφητῶν, *upon the foundation of the apostles and prophets*, all together constituting but one basis.

Eph. iii. 18 : τί τὸ πλάτος καὶ μῆκος καὶ βάθος καὶ ὕψος, *what (is) the breadth and length and depth and height*, one image of vast extension being before the mind.

Col. ii. 22 : τὰ ἐντάλματα καὶ διδασκαλίας τῶν ἀνθρώπων (obs. the different genders), *the commandments and teachings of men*, together constituting one system.

2 Pet. i. 10 : τὴν κλῆσιν καὶ ἐκλογήν, (your) *calling and election*, each mutually implying the other.

Matt. xvii. 1 : τὸν Πέτρον καὶ Ἰάκωβον καὶ Ἰωάννην, *Peter and James and John*, one inseparable group.

Titus ii. 13 : τὴν μακαρίαν ἐλπίδα καὶ ἐπιφάνειαν τῆς δόξης τοῦ μεγάλου Θεοῦ καὶ σωτῆρος ἡμῶν Ἰησοῦ Χριστοῦ; *the blessed hope and manifestation of the glory of our great God and Saviour Jesus Christ.*

Here are two cases of enumeration, each with a single article: (1) the "manifestation" is but another expression for the "hope;" and (2) the latter phrase may imply, on the above-stated principle, either that God (the Father) and Jesus Christ the Saviour are so inseparably conjoined that the glory of each is the same (R.V., marg.); or else, as the R.V. has it, and as Ellicott renders it in the translation above, that *God* in this passage is, like *Saviour*, an epithet of Christ. Comp. Eph. v. 5; 2 Thess. i. 12; 2 Pet. i. 1. See also the phrase, "*the God and Father of our Lord Jesus Christ*," Eph. i. 3; 1 Pet. i. 3; Rom. xv. 6; 2 Cor. i. 3, xi. 31 (1 Cor. xv. 24): not *God, even the Father*, etc.

b. **Separate enumeration.**—Luke xii. 11 : ἐπὶ τὰς συναγωγὰς καὶ τὰς ἀρχὰς καὶ τὰς ἐξουσίας, *to the synagogues, and the rulers, and the autho-*

rities, three different classes of tribunal. The reader may compare Mark xv. 1, where the elders and scribes are spoken of as constituting but one class, *i.e.*, in the Sanhedrin.

James iii. 11 : τὸ γλυκὺ καὶ τὸ πικρόν, *the sweet and the bitter*, from their very nature separate.

2 Thess. i. 8 : τοῖς μὴ εἰδόσι Θεόν, καὶ τοῖς μὴ ὑπακούουσι, κ.τ.λ., *to those who know not God, and to those who obey not the Gospel of our Lord Jesus Christ;* two distinct classes, incurring different degrees of punishment.

Heb. xi. 20 : εὐλόγησεν Ἰσαὰκ τὸν Ἰακὼβ καὶ τὸν Ἠσαῦ, *Isaac blessed Jacob and Esau*. Both received a blessing, but not together, and not the same.

> The same enumeration may be found in different places with and without the separating article. This arises from a difference in the writer's point of view in each particular case. So in 1 Thess. i. 7, the Apostle writes τῇ Μακεδονίᾳ καὶ τῇ Ἀχαΐᾳ ; but in ver. 8, τῇ Μακεδονίᾳ καὶ Ἀχαΐᾳ. In the former verse he seems to contemplate the *different* directions in which the influence of Thessalonian Christianity spread ; in the latter, the *uniform* spread of that influence.
>
> Such distinctions may be slight, but they are real, and must be noted for an accurate understanding of the Word of God.

233. The omission of the Article marks indefiniteness, which in translation may be represented by our Indefinite Article in the singular, and by the anarthrous plural. This point, also, has occasionally been neglected in the A.V., and generally (not always) observed by the R.V.

Matt. xii. 41, 42 : ἄνδρες Νινευῖται ... βασίλισσα νότου, *men of Nineveh ... a queen of the south.* (R.V., *the men, the queen.*)

Luke ii. 12 : εὑρήσετε βρέφος, *ye shall find a babe*, which shall be the sign that the promise is fulfilled.

Acts i. 7 : χρόνους ἢ καιρούς, *times or seasons*, generally.

Acts xvii. 23 : ἀγνώστῳ Θεῷ, *to an unknown God.*

Acts xxvi. 2, 7 : ἐγκαλοῦμαι ὑπὸ Ἰουδαίων, *I am accused by Jews;* that *they* should bring such a charge being the wonderful feature in the case. (R.V., *the Jews.*)

Rom. ii. 14 : ὅταν γὰρ ἔθνη, κ.τ.λ., *For when Gentiles* do the things contained in the law ; not *the* Gentiles, as though the case were ordinary.

1 Cor. iii. 10 : θεμέλιον ἔθηκα, *I laid a foundation.*

1 Cor. xiv. 4: ἐκκλησίαν οἰκοδομεῖ, *edifies an assembly*, antithetic to ἑαυτόν, *himself*. (R.V., *the church*.)

2 Cor. iii. 6: διακόνους καινῆς διαθήκης, *ministers of a new covenant*.

Gal. iv. 31: οὐκ ἐσμὲν παιδίσκης τέκνα, *we are not children of a bondwoman*.

Phil. iii. 5: Ἑβραῖος ἐξ Ἑβραίων, *a Hebrew of Hebrews*, i.e., of Hebrew parents.

1 Thess. iv. 16: ἐν φωνῇ ἀρχαγγέλου, *amid the voice of an archangel*. (R.V., *with the voice of the archangel*.)

Heb. i. 2: ἐλάλησεν ἡμῖν ἐν υἱῷ, God *spake to us by* (in) *a Son*, i.e., by one possessing that character, in contradistinction to the *prophets* of former ages.

234. **The use of the word νόμος deserves special attention.** With the Article, it invariably denotes the Mosaic law, except where its meaning is limited by accompanying words. Without the Article, in cases where the omission is not required by grammatical rule, the term appears to have a wider significance; sometimes referring to the Mosaic law as the type of law in general, and sometimes to law in the abstract, including every form of Divine command or moral obligation. In the following passages the R.V. generally has *the law* in the text, and *law* in the margin.

Rom. ii. 12: ὅσοι ἐν νόμῳ ἥμαρτον, κ.τ.λ., *as many as sinned under law shall be judged by law*.

Rom. ii. 23: ὃς ἐν νόμῳ καυχᾶσαι, κ.τ.λ., *who makest thy boast of law*, or of a law, *through breaking the law*, etc. (renewed mention).

Rom. ii. 25: ἐὰν νόμον πράσσῃς, *if thou keepest law*, i.e., if thou dost obey, in general; so the verse continues, *but if thou be a breaker of law*, etc.

Rom. iii. 20: ἐξ ἔργων νόμου, κ.τ.λ., *by deeds of law shall no flesh be justified ... for by law is the knowledge of sin*. The omission of the Article shows the truth to be universal, applicable to all men and to every form of law. Compare ver. 28, Gal. ii. 16, iii. 2, 5, 10, in all which passages the Article is consistently omitted.

A few passages further need only be mentioned.

Rom. iii. 31: "Do we make *law* void ?... yea, we establish *law*."

Rom. v. 20 : "there came in by the way *a law.*"
Rom. vii. 9 : "I was once alive *without law.*"
Rom. x. 4 : "Christ is the end *of law.*"
Rom. xiii. 10 : "love is the fulfilment *of law.*"
Gal. ii. 19 : "I *through law* died *to law* that I might live to God."
Gal. iii. 18 : "For if the inheritance is *of law*, it is no more of promise."
James iv. 11 : "He that speaketh evil of his brother, and judgeth his brother, speaketh evil *of law*, and judgeth *law;* but if thou judgest *law*, thou art not a doer *of law*, but a judge."

These passages, taken in connection with the numerous instances in which *the Law* is specifically spoken of, will illustrate the importance of a constant attention to the usage of Scripture in respect to the Article.

Chapter III. THE NOUN SUBSTANTIVE.

NUMBER.

235. The ordinary usage of the Singular and Plural needs no detailed illustration, but the following rules, explaining some peculiarities, must be noted.

236. A Masculine Singular Noun, with the Article, often represents a whole class.

> Instances have been given already, § 211. The omission of the Article in passages like Rom. i. 16, ii. 9, 10, Ἰουδαίῳ τε καὶ Ἕλληνι, *to both Jew and Greek*, is owing to the antithetic form. (See § 233.)

237. Some words, like σῶμα, *body*, καρδία, *heart*, when predicated of several individuals, are occasionally employed in the singular. The plural, however, is more common. Thus we read, τὸ σῶμα ὑμῶν and τὰ σώματα ὑμῶν, *your body* or *bodies;* ἡ καρδία or αἱ καρδίαι αὐτῶν, *their heart* or *hearts*.

> The word πρόσωπον, *face*, is always singular in such phrases as *they fell upon their face*, except in the Revelation, vii. 11, xi. 16.

238. Many abstract nouns are used in the plural, for repeated exemplifications of the quality denoted.

Mark vii. 22: πλεονεξίαι, πονηρίαι, *covetousnesses, wickednesses*.

James ii. 1: ἐν προσωπολημψίαις, *in regard* (regards) *to persons*.

2 Pet. iii. 11: ἐν ἁγίαις ἀναστροφαῖς καὶ εὐσεβείαις, lit., *in holy conducts and godlinesses*.

239. The plural is occasionally used, like the English rhetorical *we*, by a speaker of himself. See especially the passage 2 Cor. ii. 14—vii. 16, where the Apostle changes incessantly from singular to plural. The reason, however, may be that sometimes he is conscious of speaking on behalf of himself and his associates; sometimes, again, for himself alone. In any case the idiom in question is not a common one.

240. In some instances, where only one agent or object is actually meant, the plural is employed.

Strictly speaking, these cannot be called instances of the plural put for the singular, but arise, either (*a*) from the object being regarded in its constituent parts, or (*b*) from the writer having formed the conception generally, without limitation.

a. A familiar instance of the former kind is in the plural names of cities, as Ἀθῆναι, *Athens*, Κολοσσαί, *Colossæ*, where the words expressed in the first instance the several districts of the place, or the different tribes which formed its population. So, in Greek, Jerusalem is often Ἱεροσόλυμα (neut. plur.).

Analogous words are ἀνατολαί, *east;* δυσμαί, *west;*[1] τὰ δεξιά, *the right;* τὰ ἀριστερά or εὐώνυμα, *the left,* where some such word as *parts* may be supplied. These words are also found in the singular.

Some miscellaneous terms to be explained in a similar way are—

Luke xvi. 23: Λάζαρον ἐν τοῖς κόλποις αὐτοῦ, *Lazarus in his* (Abraham's) *bosom.* In ver. 22 the singular had been used.

John i. 13: οὐκ ἐξ αἱμάτων, *not of blood,* lit., *bloods*—a peculiar phrase, with a reference, perhaps, to both parents.[2]

Heb. ix. 12, etc.: εἰς τὰ ἅγια, *into the Sanctuary,* "the Holies," sometimes, as in ver. 3, ἅγια ἁγίων, *Holies of holies,*[3] suggesting that every spot and every object there was consecrated.

Names of festivals are sometimes plural: ἐγκαίνια, *feast of dedication* (John x. 22); ἄζυμα, *feast of unleavened bread* (Matt. xxvi. 17, etc.); γενέσια, *birthday feast* (Matt. xiv. 6; Mark vi. 21). So γάμοι, *marriage feast,* from the various observances and festivities accompanying.

αἰῶνες, *ages,* is plural, to mark the successive epochs of duration, especially of the Divine plan; the singular either referring to one such epoch, or including all as one mighty whole. Hence the phrase *for ever* may be represented either by εἰς τὸν αἰῶνα (Matt. xxi. 19; John vi. 51, 58; 1 Pet. i. 25, from Isa. xl. 8, etc.), or by εἰς τοὺς αἰῶνας (Luke i. 33; Rom. i. 25, ix. 5; Heb. xiii. 8, etc.); while the emphatic *for ever and ever* is expressed by εἰς τοὺς αἰῶνας τῶν αἰώνων, *to the ages of ages* (Heb. xiii. 21; 1 Pet. iv. 11; and Rev. *passim*). (See Vocabulary.)

---

[1] Or perhaps the plural in these words may denote *repetition.* The sun rises or sets there "again and again."

[2] Of the plural in this sense there is no other instance in the Scriptures, and only one in the classics. The plural of *blood* is often found in the LXX. (from the Hebrew), where violent bloodshedding is denoted.

[3] In this expression (not in the other), some would read ἁγία (fem.), as referring to a noun, like χώρα, *place.* This is, however, most unlikely.

204   THE NUMBERS OF NOUNS.   [§ 240, a.

οὐρανοί, *heavens*, is found with meaning indistinguishable from οὐράνος, *heaven*. The plural usage probably arose from the Hebrew, where the word is always plural: "the parts of the firmament." There is also "the third heaven." Matthew almost always has the plural; Luke, almost always the singular; Mark, most usually the singular; John, the singular always, except in Rev. xii. 12. The other parts of the New Testament vary between the two almost equally.

Other plurals of this kind will be sufficiently explained in the Vocabulary.

b. 1. In the second above-mentioned class may be included those cases where persons are said generally to do what was really done by one of their number. Thus, Matt. xxvi. 8, "*his disciples said*, To what purpose," etc.; while in John xii. 4 we read, "*one of his disciples, Judas.*" Compare Mark vii. 17 with Matt. xv. 15; Matt. xiv. 17 and Mark vi. 38 with John vi. 8, 9; Matt. xxiv. 1 with Mark xiii. 1; Matt. xxvii. 37 with John xix. 19; Matt. xxvii. 48 and Mark xv. 36 with John xix. 29. So in Luke xxii. 66, λέγοντες, when in all probability only one is meant. See also the same idiom in John xi. 8; Luke xx. 21, 39, xxiv. 5 (εἶπον); Matt. xv. 1, λέγοντες; xv. 12, λέγουσιν.[1]

These instances will help to explain apparent discrepancies. Thus it may be that only one of the crucified malefactors actually blasphemed, notwithstanding the plural in Matt. xxvii. 44; and the narrative of the cure of the blind men at Jericho (Matt. xx. 30–34; Mark x. 46–52; Luke xviii. 35–43) may possibly be harmonised in a similar way, although some expositors have thought that two different transactions of the kind then took place.[2]

2. Somewhat different from the above, yet related under the same head, are those cases in which a general statement suffices, although a particular one might also have been made.

John vi. 45; Acts xiii. 40: *the prophets* is a general reference, as when we quote from "the Bible" without specifying a particular part.

Matt. ii. 20: τεθνήκασιν οἱ ζητοῦντες, κ.τ.λ., *they are dead who seek*, etc., when Herod specifically is meant. (See Exodus iv. 19.)

Matt. ix. 8: τὸν δόντα ἐξουσίαν τοιαύτην τοῖς ἀνθρώποις, *who gave such power to men, i.e.,* as instanced in the case of Christ.

Rom. i. 4: ἐξ ἀναστάσεως νεκρῶν, *by the resurrection of the dead;* the

---

[1] Stuart's "New Testament Syntax."
[2] Lee on Inspiration, p. 393; Burgon's "Inspiration and Interpretation," p. 67. See, however, "Bible Handbook," part ii., § 148; Trench on the Miracles, p. 429.

context showing the reference to be to the one great illustration, in the case of Christ, of this general fact. It is, however, incorrect to interpret 1 Cor. xv. 29, on the authority of this passage, as referring to baptism "in the name of Him who was dead, *i.e.*, Christ."

Heb. ix. 23 : κρείττοσι θυσίαις, *with better sacrifices, i.e.*, whatever those sacrifices might be ; the question being, as it were, left open for a moment, although the aim was to show that in reality only *one* sacrifice could avail.

> For the use of singular adjectives, pronouns, etc., in agreement or apposition with plural nouns, or the contrary, see § 317.

CASE.

THE NOMINATIVE AND VOCATIVE.

241. The Nominative is properly the case of the Subject; hence also of the Predicate after copulative Verbs. See §§ 163–165.

242. In some passages a Nominative is found, unconnected with the grammatical structure of the sentence; calling attention, emphatically, to the thing or person spoken of. This is called a **Suspended Nominative** ("nominativus pendens").

Matt. xii. 36 : πᾶν ῥῆμα ἀργὸν ... ἀποδώσουσι περὶ αὐτοῦ λόγον, *every idle word ... they shall give account of it.*

Acts vii. 40 : ὁ Μωσῆς οὗτος ... οὐκ οἴδαμεν, κ.τ.λ., *this Moses ... we know not*, etc.

Rev. ii. 26 : ὁ νικῶν καὶ ὁ τηρῶν ... δώσω αὐτῷ ἐξουσίαν, *he that overcometh, and that keepeth ... to him I will give authority.* So iii. 12, 21.

So also Matt. x. 42 ; Luke xii. 10 ; John vii. 38, etc.

> A "suspended Nominative" is occasionally employed in expressions of time.
>
> Matt. xv. 32: ὅτι, ἤδη ἡμέραι τρεῖς, προσμένουσί μοι, *because they continue with Me now three days.* So Mark viii. 2.[1]
>
> Luke ix. 28: ἐγένετο ... ὡσεὶ ἡμέραι ὀκτώ, *it came to pass, about eight days* after the sayings.

---

[1] In both passages the ordinary text has ἡμέρας, the usual case in such construction. (See § 286.) But all critical editions give the Nominative.

Such cases may possibly be resolved into ellipsis, as, in the former instance, of the substantive verb; in the latter, of some such word as διάστημα, *interval*, the true Subject of ἐγένετο; and in apposition with ἡμέραι.

Some so-called "suspended Nominatives" are really instances of apposition. Thus (Mark vi. 40), πρασιαὶ πρασιαί, *rank by rank*, is in apposition with the Subject of ἀνέπεσον.[1]

In ver. 39, συμπόσια is in the Accusative in apposition with πάντας.

243. The Nominative is sometimes elliptically used, as in the cases following:—

a. The Nominative after the adverb ἰδού, *behold.*

Matt. iii. 17: ἰδού, φωνὴ ἐκ τῶν οὐρανῶν, *behold* (there was heard) *a voice out of the heavens.*

Heb. ii. 13: ἰδοὺ ἐγὼ καὶ τὰ παιδία, κ.τ.λ., *behold,* (here am) *I, and the children* which Thou gavest Me.

b. The word ὄνομα, introducing the name of a person or place, is generally found in the Dative, ὀνόματι, *by name.* (See § 280.) Occasionally, however, it occurs in the Nominative, with the name as predicate, and the copula omitted. So John i. 6, ἐγένετο ἄνθρωπος ... ὄνομα αὐτῷ Ἰωάννης, *there was a man ... his name* (was) *John.*

Luke xxiv. 13: εἰς κώμην ... ᾗ ὄνομα Ἐμμαούς, *to a village ... whose name* (was) *Emmaus.*

c. A peculiar Nominative phrase is used in the Revelation as an indeclinable noun, equivalent to the Hebrew name JEHOVAH (chap. i. 4), ἀπὸ ὁ ὢν καὶ ὁ ἦν καὶ ὁ ἐρχόμενος, *from Him who is, and who was, and who cometh.*

244. The use of the Nominative for the Vocative has been already noted, § 228, where see examples.

The usage is in fact elliptical, the true Vocative being in the personal pronoun, σύ or ὑμεῖς, omitted: *Thou ... who art !* or, *Ye ... who are !*

Matt. vii. 23: ἀποχωρεῖτε ... οἱ ἐργαζόμενοι τὴν ἀνομίαν, *depart,* (ye who are) *the workers of iniquity !*

Mark xiv. 36: ἀββᾶ ὁ πατήρ, *Abba,* (Thou who art) *the Father !*

So when the Nominative adjective is in apposition with the Vocative case.

---

[1] See Rev. T. S. Green's "Greek Testament Grammar," p. 86.

Rom. ii. 1 : ὦ ἄνθρωπε, πᾶς ὁ κρίνων, *O man!* (thou) *who judgest,* (I mean) *every one!*

> In Luke xii. 20 the Article is omitted, "Ἄφρων, and, accordingly, we must understand, not a direct address, as A.V., *Thou fool!* but an exclamation, "How foolish thou art!" A parallel instance is to be found in Rom. vii. 24 : ταλαίπωρος ἐγὼ ἄνθρωπος, *O wretched man that I am!* and xi. 33, ὦ βάθος πλούτου, *O the depth of the riches!*

245. With the Vocative proper, the interjection ὦ is employed, chiefly in vehement expressions.

Matt. xv. 28 : ὦ γύναι, μεγάλη σου ἡ πίστις, *O woman,* great is thy faith!

Acts xiii. 10 : ὦ πλήρης παντὸς δόλου, *O full of* all deceit!

Gal. iii. 1 : ὦ ἀνόητοι Γαλάται, *O foolish Galatians!*

> Sometimes, however, the interjection is employed (as in classical Greek) where no special vehemence is intended. So Acts i. 1, xviii. 14. But in such cases ὦ is more usually omitted (Luke xxii. 57; Acts i. 16, xiii. 15, xxvii. 25).

THE GENITIVE.

246. The Genitive Case (see § 11) **primarily signifies** *motion from,* **answering to our question,** *Whence?* From this general meaning arise many modifications, including the several notions expressed in English by the prepositions *of* or *from.*

247. These modifications may be classed under the following heads :[1]

   1. Origin.   4. Partition.
   2. Separation.   5. Object.
   3. Possession.   6. Relation.
     7. The Genitive Absolute.

The Genitive with Prepositions will be treated of hereafter. (See § 291, *sqq.*)

---

[1] These significations are again reduced, by Dr. Donaldson and others, to three:—

  1. Ablation.   2. Partition.   3. Relation.

The name of the case, γενική, designates it as expressive of the *genus* to which anything is referred, whether as belonging to it or classed under it (Max Müller); or, according to others, the source from which it is *generated,* or supposed to spring.

I. Origin.

248. The Genitive is often used after substantives, to mark the source or author.

1 Thess. i. 3 : μνημονεύοντες ὑμῶν τοῦ ἔργου **τῆς πίστεως** καὶ τοῦ κόπου **τῆς ἀγάπης** καὶ τῆς ὑπομονῆς **τῆς ἐλπίδος**, *remembering your work of faith, and labour of love, and endurance of hope, i.e.*, the work springing from faith, the labour prompted by love, the endurance sustained by hope.

2 Cor. xi. 26 : κινδύνοις **ποταμῶν**, κινδύνοις **λῃστῶν**, *in dangers of rivers, in dangers of robbers, i.e.*, occasioned by them.

Rom. iv. 13 : διὰ δικαιοσύνης **πίστεως**, *through the righteousness of faith.*

Rom. xv. 4 : διὰ τῆς παρακλήσεως **τῶν γραφῶν**, *through the comfort of the Scriptures.*

Col. i. 23 : ἀπὸ τῆς ἐλπίδος **τοῦ εὐαγγελίου**, *from the hope of the Gospel.*

Col. ii. 12 : διὰ τῆς πίστεως **τῆς ἐνεργείας** τοῦ Θεοῦ, *through the faith of the mighty working of God, i.e.*, mightily wrought by Him.

249. The Genitive, after many verbs expressive of sense or mental affections of various kinds, indicates the source from which the sensation or affection proceeds.

> The full force of the Genitive is evident also in these cases. Thus, to smell a flower, really means to receive a certain impression *from* the flower. Compare the ordinary phrase, to *taste of* different viands. In another use, the object of sense itself becomes subject of the verb, and its quality is expressed by the following Genitive, as *this rose smells of musk.*
>
> Again, to *recollect* is to remind myself *of* the object of thought; the influence being regarded as passing from the object to the person. In like manner may be explained the phrases denoting other mental affections.

a. **Verbs of Sense.** (1) ἀκούω, *to hear:*

Mark ix. 7 ; Luke ix. 35 : **αὐτοῦ** ἀκούετε, *hear him!*

John x. 3 : τὰ πρόβατα **τῆς φωνῆς** αὐτοῦ ἀκούει, *the sheep hear his voice.*

Luke xv. 25 : ἤκουσε **συμφωνίας** καὶ **χορῶν**, *he heard music and dancing.*

> It will be seen that this verb is construed with a **Genitive either of the person or the thing.** Generally, however, the thing is in the Accusative, as *the immediate object* (especially λόγον, λόγους, Matt. vii. 24, xiii. 20, etc.). When both are expressed together, the thing is in the Accusative, and the person in the Genitive (Acts i. 4); sometimes with a preposition (2 Cor. xii. 6 ; Acts x. 22).

The Genitive of the thing probably inclines to the partitive sense. Compare Acts ix. 7, where of Saul's companions it is said, ἀκούοντες τῆς φωνῆς, *hearing the voice,* with chap. xxii. 9, τὴν φωνὴν οὐκ ἤκουσαν, *they heard not the voice.* They heard of the voice, *i.e.,* its *sound,* but not *what it said.*

(2) **γεύομαι,** *to taste :*

Luke xiv. 24 : οὐδεὶς ... γεύσεταί μου τοῦ δείπνου, *no one shall taste of my supper.*

Mark ix. 1 : οὐ μὴ γεύσωνται θανάτου, *shall by no means taste of death.* So Luke ix. 27; John viii. 52; Heb. ii. 9.

In Heb. vi. 4, 5, the Genitive and Accusative are used in successive clauses, γευσαμένους τῆς δωρεᾶς, *having tasted of the gift;* γευσαμένους Θεοῦ ῥῆμα, *having tasted the word of God.*[1]

(3) **θιγγάνω,** *to touch:*

Heb. xii. 20 : κἂν θηρίον θίγῃ τοῦ ὄρους, *and even if a beast touch the mountain.* So xi. 28.

ψηλαφάω, *to handle, to touch closely,* governs the Accusative (Luke xxiv. 39; Acts xvii. 27; 1 John i. 1). "A (mount) that might be touched" (Heb. xii. 18), where this word is used, does not contradict v. 20, as it simply refers to the nature of the mountain, *palpable* or "material." (See R.V. marg.)

b. **Verbs expressive of mental affections; as desire, caring for, despising :**

Acts xx. 33 : ἀργυρίου ἢ χρυσίου ἢ ἱματισμοῦ οὐδενὸς ἐπεθύμησα, *I desired no one's silver or gold or raiment.*

Titus iii. 8 : ἵνα φροντίζωσι καλῶν ἔργων, *that they may be zealous of (careful to maintain,* R.V.) *good works.*

1 Tim. iii. 5 : πῶς ἐκκλησίας Θεοῦ ἐπιμελήσεται, *how shall he take care of the church of God ?*

Heb. xii. 5 : μὴ ὀλιγώρει παιδείας Κυρίου, *do not slight the chastisement of the Lord.*

---

[1] Mr. Jelf (Kühner's Greek Grammar) explains the difference simply as a variation in the mode of expression; the Accusative calling attention rather to the *action,* the Genitive to the *material,* as in English, "He eats some meat" (Gen.); "He eats meat" (Acc.). Bengel's view of this passage is more subtle. "'The gift,'" he says, "can be only partially received in this life; while 'the word' essentially belongs to us now." But see Alford's note, comparing the Accusative with that in John ii. 9.

c. **Verbs of remembrance and forgetting:**

Luke xvii. 32: μνημονεύετε **τῆς γυναικὸς Λώτ**; *remember Lot's wife.*

Heb. xii. 5: ἐκλέλησθε **τῆς παρακλήσεως**, *ye have entirely forgotten the exhortation.*

> Many grammarians prefer to class the Genitive after all these verbs under the head of "Partition." (See § 261, *sqq.*)

250. Verbs of accusing, condemning, etc., take a Genitive of the charge, *i.e.,* of the source of the accusation.

Acts xix. 40: ἐγκαλεῖσθαι **στάσεως**, *to be accused of sedition.*

The Genitive of the person is used after κατηγορέω, *to accuse,* lit., " to assert against one."

Matt. xii. 10: ἵνα κατηγορήσωσιν **αὐτοῦ**, *that they might accuse him.*

251. Adjectives and Verbs signifying plenty, want, fulness, and the like, are followed by a Genitive of that from which another is filled, etc.

John i. 14: πλήρης **χάριτος καὶ ἀληθείας**, *full of grace and truth.*

John xxi. 11: τὸ δίκτυον ... μεστὸν **ἰχθύων**, *the net ... full of fishes.*

Luke i. 53: πεινῶντας ἐνέπλησεν **ἀγαθῶν**, *He filled the hungry with good things.*

John ii. 7: γεμίσατε τὰς ὑδρίας **ὕδατος**, *fill the water-pots with water.*

Rom. iii. 23: πάντες...ὑστεροῦνται **τῆς δόξης** τοῦ Θεοῦ, *all...come short of the glory of God.*

James i. 5: εἴ τις ὑμῶν λείπεται σοφίας, *if any of you lacketh wisdom.*

> This Genitive is referred by some to the head of "Separation;" by others to "Partition."

II. *Separation,* or *Ablation.*

252. Verbs of separation, as those denoting removal, difference, hindrance, and the like, take a Genitive as the case of their secondary object. (See § 186.)

> Prepositions, however, are more generally inserted.

Acts xxvii. 43: ἐκώλυσεν αὐτοὺς **τοῦ βουλήματος**, *he restrained them from their purpose.*

Eph. ii. 12: ἀπηλλοτριωμένοι **τῆς πολιτείας** τοῦ Ἰσραήλ, *alienated from the commonwealth of Israel.*

1 Tim. i. 6 : ὧν τινες ἀστοχήσαντες, *from which some having gone wide in aim.*[1]

1 Pet. iv. 1 : πέπαυται ἁμαρτίας, *he hath ceased from sin.*

253. Under this head may be placed the important rule, that **the object of comparison is expressed by the Genitive,** whether after verbs, or, more usually, after adjectives in the comparative degree.

See on the Comparative, § 320. This Genitive, also, is one of Separation ; the two things compared being mentally set apart *from* each other. So in Latin, the Ablative case is employed.[2]

When the word *than* is expressed in Greek (by the conjunction ἤ), the things compared are put in apposition.

After Verbs implying comparison :

1 Cor. xv. 41 : ἀστὴρ γὰρ ἀστέρος διαφέρει, *for star differeth from star.*

The verb διαφέρω often implies superiority.

Matt. x. 31 : πολλῶν στρουθίων διαφέρετε ὑμεῖς, *ye are of more value than many sparrows.*

So, vi. 26, xii. 12; Luke xii. 7, 24; Gal. iv. 1, "is no better than a slave."

After Adjectives in the Comparative degree :

John xiii. 16 : οὐκ ἔστι δοῦλος μείζων τοῦ κυρίου αὐτοῦ, *a servant is not greater than his master.*

John xxi. 15 : ἀγαπᾷς με πλεῖον τούτων; *lovest thou me more than these ?*

1 Tim. v. 8 : ἔστιν ἀπίστου χείρων, *he is worse than an unbeliever.*

The subject of comparison is sometimes repeated by implication in the object.

Mark iv. 31 : μικρότερον ὂν πάντων τῶν σπερμάτων, *being less than all the seeds,* although itself a seed. So Matt. xiii. 32.

---

[1] Ellicott.
[2] The Hebrew language yet more clearly identifies comparison and separation, by its use of the preposition *from* with the simple adjective. Thus, "greater than he" would be expressed by the phrase, "great from him;" the Hebrews "conceiving pre-eminence as a taking out, a designating from the multitude" (Gesenius). So in Homer, ἐκ πάντων, *more than all.* In modern Greek the preposition ἀπό is used after the comparative.

1 Cor. xiii. 13 : μείζων δὲ τούτων ἡ ἀγάπη, *love is greater than these;* love, nevertheless, being one of the three.

A comparative and superlative are combined in Eph. iii. 8, so that the following Genitive may be referred to this rule or to the partitive construction : ἐμοὶ τῷ ἐλαχιστοτέρῳ πάντων ἁγίων, *to me, who am less than the least of all saints.*

III. *Possession.*

254. The most frequent use of the Genitive is as the Possessive case, generally with substantives.

Here also the fundamental meaning of the case as denoting *whence* is very apparent. From the notion of origination, by an easy transition, comes that of possession. Thus, "the sons of Zebedee" may be taken as "the sons *begotten by* Zebedee," or "the sons *belonging to* Zebedee;" "the kingdom of heaven" may mean "the kingdom *set up* by heavenly powers," or "the kingdom *governed by* these powers." So, again, the notion of "belonging to" attaches to the Genitive where that of "originated by" has disappeared.[1]

Mark i. 29 : ἦλθον εἰς τὴν οἰκίαν Σίμωνος καὶ Ἀνδρέου, *they came into the house of Simon and Andrew.*

Rom. i. 1 : Παῦλος δοῦλος Ἰησοῦ Χριστοῦ, *Paul, a servant of Jesus Christ.*

255. The Genitives of the personal pronouns are mostly employed in this sense instead of the possessive adjectival forms. So, ἡ θυγάτηρ μου, *my daughter;* οἱ μαθηταὶ αὐτοῦ, *his disciples.* (See § 333.)

256. Words denoting kindred, etc., are often omitted before a Possessive Genitive, especially when they would stand in apposition with a proper name. Sometimes the Article of the omitted noun is inserted. (See §§ 194, 196.)

1. υἱός. Matt. iv. 21 : Ἰάκωβον τὸν τοῦ Ζεβεδαίου, *James the (son) of Zebedee.*

John vi. 71 : τὸν Ἰούδαν Σίμωνος, *(the) Judas (son) of Simon.*

John xxi. 15, 16, 17 : Σίμων Ἰωνᾶ, *Simon (son) of Jonas.*

2. πατήρ. Acts vii. 16 : Ἐμμὸρ τοῦ Συχέμ, *of Hamor the (father) of Shechem.*

---

[1] Compare Müller's "Lectures on the Science of Language," vol. i., p. 105.

§ 258.]   THE POSSESSIVE GENITIVE.   213

3. **μήτηρ.** Luke xxiv. 10 : Μαρία ἡ Ἰακώβου, *Mary the (mother) of James.* So Mark xv. 47, xvi. 1.

4. **ἀδελφός.** Luke vi. 16 ; Acts i. 13 : Ἰούδας Ἰακώβου, *Judas (the brother) of James* (See Jude 1).

5. **γυνή.** Matt. i. 6 : ἐκ τῆς τοῦ Οὐρίου, *from the (wife) of Uriah.* So John xix. 25.

6. **οἴκειοι.** 1 Cor. i. 11 : ὑπὸ τῶν Χλόης, *by the (kinsfolk) of Chloe.*

7. **οἶκος or δῶμα.** Mark v. 35 : ἀπὸ τοῦ ἀρχισυναγώγου, *from (the house) of the ruler of the synagogue.* This is clear, as the ruler was himself with Jesus. So, perhaps, John xviii. 28.

Acts ii. 27, 31 : εἰς ᾅδου,[1] "thou wilt not abandon my soul" *to (the habitations) of Hades*—a classical phrase ; or, "to (the power) of the unseen world." In Ps. xvi. 10 some copies of the LXX. read ᾅδου, others ᾅδην.

> In Luke ii. 49, ἐν τοῖς τοῦ πατρός μου has been variously read, *in my Father's business* (A.V.), or *in my Father's house* (R.V.) (plural, as in John xix. 27, τὰ ἴδια). The former gives the wider significance : "among my Father's matters" (Alford). So all the versions of the English Hexapla, Luther, De Wette.

257. Attribute or quality is often expressed by the Possessive Genitive of an abstract substantive.

> In such cases the person or thing is spoken of as belonging to the virtue, vice, or other abstraction. The phrase may often be idiomatically rendered by turning the Genitive into an adjective. Thus, Luke xvi. 8, τὸν οἰκονόμον τῆς ἀδικίας, *the steward of injustice,* may be read *the unjust steward.* But such renderings lose the force of the original.

Rom. i. 26 : πάθη ἀτιμίας, *lusts of dishonour.*

Heb. ix. 10 : δικαιώματα σαρκός, *ordinances of flesh.*

James i. 25 : ἀκροατὴς ἐπιλησμονῆς, *a hearer of forgetfulness,* "a forgetful hearer."

James ii. 4 : κριταὶ διαλογισμῶν πονηρῶν, *judges of evil thoughts,* "evil-thinking judges."

258. To the strictly Possessive Genitive belong several phrases which have been otherwise interpreted—

---

[1] W. H. read ᾅδην.

2 Cor. iv. 6: τῆς γνώσεως τῆς δόξης τοῦ Θεοῦ, *of the knowledge of the glory of God*, i.e., the glory which belongs to God, and which He reveals in Christ; not, certainly, "the glorious God."

Eph. i. 6: εἰς ἔπαινον δόξης τῆς χάριτος αὐτοῦ, *to the praise of the glory of His grace*, i.e., the glory which characterises Divine grace; not "glorious praise" or "glorious grace."

Col. i. 11: κατὰ τὸ κράτος τῆς δόξης, *according to the might of His glory* (R.V.); "not 'His glorious power' (A.V., Beza, etc.), but 'the power which is the peculiar characteristic of His glory'; the Genitive belonging to the category of the Possessive Genitive" (Ellicott).

Heb. i. 3: τῷ ῥήματι τῆς δυνάμεως αὐτοῦ, *by the word of His power;* belonging to it, as its true utterance, "not," says Alford, "to be weakened into the comparatively unmeaning ' by His powerful word.'"

See also Rom. vii. 24; Col. i. 13; Rev. iii. 10.

259. The Genitive is occasionally used by way of apposition, as if with some such ellipsis as *consisting of*, or *bearing the name of*. Compare the English idiom, *the city of Jerusalem*, where Jerusalem is the city.

This rule is an exception to the ordinary construction. The usual idiom in Greek is *the city, Jerusalem.*

2 Pet. ii. 6: πόλεις Σοδόμων καὶ Γομόρρας, *(the) cities of Sodom and Gomorrah.*

John ii. 21: περὶ τοῦ ναοῦ τοῦ σώματος αὐτοῦ, *concerning the temple of his body.*

Rom. iv. 11: σημεῖον ἔλαβε περιτομῆς,[1] *he received the sign of circumcision.* So Acts iv. 22.

2 Cor. v. 1: ἡ οἰκία τοῦ σκήνους, *the house of our tabernacle.*

2 Cor. v. 5: τὸν ἀρραβῶνα τοῦ πνεύματος, *the earnest of the Spirit.* So chap. i. 22. Compare Rom. viii. 23.[2]

See also Eph. vi. 14–16; Heb. vi. 1; and many other passages.

The difficult phrase, Eph. iv. 9, εἰς τὰ κατώτερα μέρη τῆς γῆς, has by many interpreters been regarded as an instance of the Genitive of Apposition: "to the lower earth," "to earth beneath," contrasted with such phrases as "the height of heaven" (Isa. xiv. 14). See Bishop Ellicott's note, in which the opposite view (the descent into Hades) is maintained.

---

[1] W. H. marg. περιτομήν.

[2] "The firstfruits (of our inheritance) consisting of the Holy Spirit" (Dr. Vaughan on Rom. viii. 23. So Winer.).

Position of the Genitive.

260. *a.* The Genitive is usually placed after the governing noun.

When both nouns have the Article, each is usually preceded by its own. In classic Greek the Article of the governing noun usually stands first in the phrase; then the governed Article and Genitive; and lastly, the governing noun. This arrangement is very rarely followed in the New Testament: 1 Pet. iii. 20, ἡ τοῦ Θεοῦ μακροθυμία, *the longsuffering of God;* Heb. xii. 2, τὸν τῆς πίστεως ἀρχηγόν, *the author of the faith.* Occasionally the Article of the governing noun is repeated before the Genitive; also a classic idiom: 1 Cor. i. 18, ὁ λόγος ὁ τοῦ σταυροῦ, *the doctrine of the Cross.* For another arrangement, see § 196.

b. But the Genitive precedes—

1. When one Genitive belongs to more than one substantive—

Acts iii. 7: αὐτοῦ αἱ βάσεις καὶ τὰ σφυρά, *his feet and ankle-bones.*

2. When the word in the Genitive is emphatic. The emphasis may arise—

(*a*) From antithesis—

Phil. ii. 25: τὸν συστρατιώτην μου, ὑμῶν δὲ ἀπόστολον, *my fellow-soldier, but your messenger.* See also Eph. vi. 9; Heb. vii. 22, etc.

(*b*) From the Genitive containing the principal notion—

Rom. xi. 13: ἐθνῶν ἀπόστολος, *of the Gentiles an apostle.* See also 1 Cor. iii. 9; Titus i. 7; James i. 26, etc.

In Heb. vi. 2, βαπτισμῶν διδαχῆς,[1] it has been questioned which word is the governing one, *doctrine of baptisms,* or *baptisms of doctrine.* Winer favours the latter (Grammar, § xxx. 3, *note* 4).

IV. *Partition.*

261. Closely connected with the fundamental notion of the Genitive is that of participation. The part is taken *from* the whole.

1 Pet. i. 1: ἐκλεκτοῖς παρεπιδήμοις διασπορᾶς, *to elect sojourners of (the) dispersion.*

Matt. xv. 24: τὰ πρόβατα τὰ ἀπολωλότα οἴκου Ἰσραήλ, *the lost sheep of the house of Israel.*

262. This Genitive is most commonly found after (1) partitive adjectives, (2) the indefinite and interrogative pronouns, (3) the numerals, and (4) adjectives in the superlative degree.

---

[1] W. H. and R.V. marg. read διδαχήν.

1. Partitive Adjectives :

Matt. iii. 7 : πολλοὺς τῶν Φαρισαίων καὶ Σαδδουκαίων, *many of the Pharisees and Sadducees.*

Luke xix. 8 : τὰ ἡμίση τῶν ὑπαρχόντων, *the half* (halves) *of my goods.*

Acts xvii. 12 : ἀνδρῶν οὐκ ὀλίγοι, *of men not a few.*

Matt. xv. 37 : τὸ περισσεῦον τῶν κλασμάτων, *the remaining* (part) *of the broken pieces.*

2. Pronouns.

Matt. ix. 3 : τινὲς τῶν γραμματέων, *some of the Scribes.*

Acts v. 15 : ἐπισκιάσῃ τινὶ αὐτῶν, *might overshadow some one of them.*

Luke x. 36 : τίς τούτων; *who of these?*

3. Numerals—Cardinal, Ordinal, Negative :

Matt. v. 29 : ἓν τῶν μελῶν σου, *one of thy members.*

Acts x. 7 : φωνήσας δύο τῶν οἰκετῶν, *having called two of his house-servants.*

Rev. viii. 7 : τὸ τρίτον τῆς γῆς, *the third of the land.* So vers. 8–18.

Mark xi. 2 : οὐδεὶς ἀνθρώπων, lit., *no one of men.*

But the preposition ἐκ is more frequently used after numeral adjectives.

4. Superlatives :

1 Cor. xv. 9 : ὁ ἐλάχιστος τῶν ἀποστόλων, *the least of the apostles.*

263. Verbs of partaking are followed by a Genitive.

1 Cor. x. 21 : τραπέζης Κυρίου μετέχειν, *to partake of the table of the Lord.* Once this verb is found with ἐκ, ver. 17.

Heb. ii. 14 : τὰ παιδία κεκοινώνηκεν αἵματος καὶ σαρκός, *the children are partakers of flesh and blood.* This verb is found also with a Dative—Rom. xv. 27 ; 1 Tim. v. 22 ; 1 Pet. iv. 13 ; 2 John 11.

Heb. xii. 10 : μεταλαβεῖν τῆς ἁγιότητος αὐτοῦ, *to partake his holiness.*

264. So also verbs which signify to take hold of, to attain, when a part is implied.

Luke xx. 35 : τοῦ αἰῶνος ἐκείνου τυχεῖν, *to attain that world.*

Luke viii. 54 : κρατήσας τῆς χειρὸς αὐτῆς, *having taken hold of her hand.*

The strictly partitive sense is well illustrated by this verb. When the *whole* is grasped, κρατέω takes an Accusative, as in Matt. xiv. 3, etc.

§ 267.] THE PARTITIVE GENITIVE. 217

Some verbs of this class are followed in the Middle voice by a partitive Genitive, whereas in the Active they would take an Accusative.

Matt. vi. 24 : ἑνὸς ἀνθέξεται, *he will cleave to the one.*

Matt. xiv. 31 : ἐπελάβετο αὐτοῦ, *he took hold of him.*

> For the force of the Middle, see § 355. "Holding one's self by the given object" is implied.

265. Adverbs of time and numeral adverbs are followed by a partitive Genitive.

Matt. xxviii. 1 : ὀψὲ δὲ σαββάτων, *and at the end of the Sabbath.*

Heb. ix. 7 : ἅπαξ τοῦ ἐνιαυτοῦ, *once in the year.*

> So Luke xvii. 4, xviii. 12. Compare the English colloquialism, *late of an evening.*

266. Certain Genitive phrases are used, in the partitive sense, to denote time or place.

So Matt. ii. 14 : νυκτός, *by night;* Luke xviii. 7 : ἡμέρας καὶ νυκτός, *day and night;* Gal. vi. 17 : τοῦ λοιποῦ, *for the rest* (future); Luke v. 19 : ποίας (ὁδοῦ) εἰσενέγκωσιν αὐτόν, *by what (way) they might bring him in.*

> Prepositions are, however, more generally employed to define these relations.

267. The verb *to be* is often followed by a Genitive in the partitive sense.

Heb. x. 39 : ἡμεῖς δὲ οὐκ ἐσμὲν ὑποστολῆς... ἀλλὰ πίστεως, *but we are not of a desertion* (literally), *but of faith.*

Rom. ix. 9 : ἐπαγγελίας γὰρ ὁ λόγος οὗτος, *for this word was one of promise.*

> The Genitive in this connection may, however, have other significations, as, *e.g.*, that of Possession—
>
> 1 Cor. iii. 21 : πάντα ὑμῶν ἐστιν, *all things are yours.*
>
> 1 Cor. vi. 19 : οὐκ ἐστὲ ἑαυτῶν, *ye are not your own.*
>
> In general, the verb *to be*, followed by a Genitive, implies an ellipsis, such as *part, characteristic, property,* etc.

V. *Object.*

268. The Genitive case is often objectively employed,[1] **that is, it expresses the object of some feeling or action,** and may be rendered by various prepositions, as below.

The fundamental meaning of the Genitive is here also very apparent, the object of a sentiment being, in another view of it, the source or occasion of its existence. Thus, ἔχετε πίστιν Θεοῦ (Mark xi. 22), *have faith in (or towards) God*, really means, "have such faith as his character excites." Compare Col. ii. 12

Luke vi. 12 : ἐν τῇ προσευχῇ τοῦ Θεοῦ, *in prayer to God*.[2]

John ii. 17: ὁ ζῆλος τοῦ οἴκου σου, *the zeal concerning thy house*. Compare Titus ii. 14.

John xvii. 2: ἐξουσίαν πάσης σαρκός, *power* over *all flesh*. For similar constructions of ἐξουσία, see Matt. x. 1 ; Mark vi. 7 ; 1 Cor. ix. 12.

Acts iv. 9 : ἐπὶ εὐεργεσίᾳ ἀνθρώπου ἀσθενοῦς, *as to the benefit* conferred on *an impotent man*.

Heb. xi. 26 : τὸν ὀνειδισμὸν τοῦ Χριστοῦ, *the reproach* in connection with *the Christ* (as the hope of Israel).

1 Pet. ii. 19 : διὰ συνείδησιν Θεοῦ, *on account of conscience* toward *God*.

Rom. x. 2 : ζῆλον Θεοῦ ἔχουσιν, *they have a zeal* toward *God*.

2 Cor. x. 5 : εἰς τὴν ὑπακοὴν τοῦ Χριστοῦ, *to the obedience* rendered to *Christ*. But ὑπακοὴ πίστεως, Rom. i. 5, is *obedience* springing from *faith*.

Col. ii. 18 : θρησκείᾳ τῶν ἀγγέλων, *worship paid to angels*. (See Ellicott, *in loc.*)

269. Some phrases are susceptible of either a possessive (attributive, subjective) or an objective signification. Thus, ἡ ἀγάπη Θεοῦ, *the love of God*, may mean, the love which God possesses as His attribute, that which He bears to us, or that which is borne towards Him. A few important passages may be subjoined by way of illustration.

---

[1] Compare Angus's " Handbook of the English Tongue," § 384.

[2] Some, less naturally, interpret the phrase, *in the place of prayer* to God, comparing the passage with Acts xvi. 13 : "where we supposed there was *a place of prayer*." (R.V., reading ἐνομίζομεν προσευχὴν εἶναι with W. H. The A.V. has "where *prayer* was wont to be made," ἐνομίζετο προσευχὴ εἶναι).

§ 270.]   THE OBJECTIVE GENITIVE.   219

Passages with ἀγάπη and a *subjective* Genitive—
2 Cor. xiii. 14 : *the love of God ... be with you.*
Rom. viii. 35 : what shall separate us from the *love of Christ?* So ver. 39.
Eph. iii. 19: to know the *love of Christ*, which passeth knowledge.
2 Cor. v. 14: the *love of Christ* constraineth us. Not our love to Christ, but His love to us.

In the following the Genitive seems *objectively* used—
John v. 42 : ye have not the *love of God* in you. So 1 John ii. 15.
1 John ii. 5 : in him hath the *love of God* been perfected.
2 Thess. iii. 5 : the Lord direct your hearts into the *love of God.*

In Rom. v. 5, "the *love of God* hath been shed abroad in our hearts," Dr. Vaughan writes of the subjective and objective interpretations, that the two ideas may be included. See 1 John iv. 16, v. 3 : "the two are but opposite aspects of the same love ; the sense of God's love is not the cause only, but the essence of ours. 1 John iv. 19."

2 Cor. v. 11 : εἰδότες τὸν φόβον τοῦ Κυρίου, *knowing the fear of the Lord* (R.V.), generally taken as subjective, as A.V., "the terror of the Lord," belonging to Him as Judge ; but everywhere else the phrase is objective—fear, *i.e.*, reverence towards Him. So Alford renders here, *conscious* of the fear of the Lord ; but doubtfully. For other passages, see Acts ix. 31 ; Rom. iii. 18 ; 2 Cor. vii. 1 ; Eph. v. 21.

VI. *Relation.*

270. Closely connected with the objective use of the Genitive are cases where a more general relation is signified; some such prepositional phrase as *in respect of* being applicable, while the context shows the kind of relation intended.

This general way of expressing relation is often not so much ambiguous as comprehensive. Thus, in the frequent phrase, τὸ εὐαγγέλιον τοῦ Χριστοῦ, *the Gospel of Christ*, it is needless to ask whether the meaning be the Gospel from Christ as its author,[1] about Christ as its subject,[2] or in the prerogative of Christ as its administrator.[3] Each of these thoughts is but one element in the analysis of the phrase.

Mark i. 4 : βάπτισμα μετανοίας, a *baptism* which had reference to *repentance.*

---

[1] So *the Gospel of God*, Rom. i. 1, etc.
[2] Compare the phrase, *Gospel of the Kingdom*, Matt. iv. 23, ix. 35.
[3] In the language of the Apostle Paul, *my Gospel* is evidently the Gospel *entrusted to* and *preached* by me (Rom. ii. 16 ; xvi. 25; 2 Tim. ii. 8).

John v. 29 : ἀνάστασιν ζωῆς ... ἀνάστασιν κρίσεως, *resurrection* in order to *life* ... in order to *condemnation*.

John vii. 35 : τὴν διασπορὰν τῶν Ἑλλήνων, *the dispersion* (of the Jews) among *the Greeks* (Gentiles).

Rom. v. 18 : δικαίωσιν ζωῆς, *justification* in order to *life*.

Rom. vii. 2 : ἀπὸ τοῦ νόμου τοῦ ἀνδρός, *from the law of her husband, i.e., that which defines the relation*.[1]

Rom. viii. 36 : πρόβατα σφαγῆς, *sheep* doomed to *slaughter*.

Eph. iv. 16 : διὰ πάσης ἁφῆς τῆς ἐπιχορηγίας, *through every joint* (which is) for the purpose of *the supply*. See Ellicott, *in loc.*, who compares the phrase with τὰ σκεύη τῆς λειτουργίας, Heb. ix. 21, *the vessels of the ministering*.

Phil. iv. 9 : ὁ Θεὸς τῆς εἰρήνης, *the God* who bestows *peace ;* or perhaps a Genitive of quality.

> In most of these instances a preposition with its case would be an equally idiomatic usage.

271. The Genitive is also used after adjectives, as after nouns (§ 254), to denote various kinds of relation. Examples of this in the general sense are such as the following :—

Heb. v. 13 : ἄπειρος λόγου δικαιοσύνης, *without experience of the word of righteousness* (R.V.).

Heb. iii. 12 : καρδία πονηρὰ ἀπιστίας, *a heart wicked in respect to unbelief* (Winer).

James i. 13 : ἀπείραστος κακῶν, *unversed in things evil* (Alford. R.V. marg., *untried in evil*).

272. Adjectives, especially, signifying worthiness, fitness, or their opposites, take a following Genitive. So also their adverbs.

Matt. iii. 8 : καρπὸν ἄξιον τῆς μετανοίας, *fruit worthy of your repentance*.

Matt. x. 10 : ἄξιος ὁ ἐργάτης τῆς τροφῆς αὐτοῦ, *the workman is worthy of his maintenance*.

---

[1] See Winer, who quotes Old Testament parallels, Lev. vii. 1, xiv. 2, xv. 32; Numb vi. 13, 21.

§ 275.]   THE GENITIVE OF RELATION.   221

1 Cor. vi. 2 : ἀνάξιοί ἐστε κριτηρίων ἐλαχίστων; *are ye unworthy of* (incompetent for) *the least decisions?*

Rom. xvi. 2 : ἀξίως τῶν ἁγίων, *worthily of the saints* (R.V.).

See also Eph. iv. 1 ; Phil. i. 27; Col. i. 10 ; 1 Thess. ii. 12 ; 3 John 6.

273. So, in general, price, equivalent, penalty, and the like, are expressed by the Genitive.

Matt. x. 29 : οὐχὶ δύο στρούθια ἀσσαρίου πωλεῖται ; *are not two sparrows sold for a farthing?*

Rev. vi. 6 : χοῖνιξ σίτου δηναρίου καὶ τρεῖς χοίνικες κριθῶν δηναρίου, *a measure of wheat for a penny, and three measures of barley for a penny.*

274. In a few instances one noun governs two Genitives in different relations.

Acts v. 32 : ἡμεῖς ἐσμεν αὐτοῦ μάρτυρες τῶν ῥημάτων τούτων, *we are his* (possess.) *witnesses of* (remote obj.), or in respect to, *these things*.[1]

2 Cor. v. 1 : ἡ ἐπίγειος ἡμῶν οἰκία τοῦ σκήνους, *our* (possess.) *earthly house of the tabernacle* (appos.).

Phil. ii. 30 : τὸ ὑμῶν ὑστέρημα τῆς λειτουργίας, *your lack in respect of the service.*

2 Pet. iii. 2 : τῆς τῶν ἀποστόλων ὑμῶν ἐντολῆς τοῦ Κυρίου, *the commandment of the Lord* (orig.), *through* (remote obj.) *your apostles* (R.V.). The Text. Rec. has ἡμῶν, but even then the reading of A.V. is inadmissible.

The two Genitives in John vi. 1, ἡ θάλασσα τῆς Γαλιλαίας, τῆς Τιβεριάδος, are virtually in apposition, *the sea of Galilee* (as the Jews call it), *of Tiberias* (as the Gentiles), one name denoting the country, the other the city. So we might say, "the Lake of the Four Cantons, of Lucerne."

The dependence of successive Genitives *on each other* is frequent, as many foregoing examples will show.

VII. *The Genitive Absolute.*

275. A Genitive noun, in agreement with a participle expressed or understood, often occurs in a subordinate sentence absolutely, *i.e.,* **without immediate dependence on any other words.** The noun, in these cases, is to be translated first, without a preposition, then the

---

[1] But W. H. and Rev. Text omit αὐτοῦ, with (ἐν) αὐτῷ in marg.

participle. In idiomatic English, a conjunction must often be supplied, either temporal (*when*), causal (*since*), or concessive (*although*).

It will be observed that the Genitive in this construction must refer to some other than the Subject of the principal sentence.

Equivalent idioms are in English the nominative absolute, in Latin the ablative absolute.

Matt. i. 18 : μνηστευθείσης ... Μαρίας, *Mary having been betrothed.*

Matt. i. 20 : ταῦτα δὲ αὐτοῦ ἐνθυμηθέντος, *and he having reflected on these things, i.e.,* when he reflected.

Matt. ii. 1 : τοῦ Ἰησοῦ γεννηθέντος, *Jesus having been born, i.e.,* when Jesus was born.

Matt. ii. 13 : ἀναχωρησάντων δὲ αὐτῶν, *and they having returned, i.e.,* when they returned.

Matt. xvii. 9 : καταβαινόντων αὐτῶν ἐκ τοῦ ὄρους, *they descending from the mountain, i.e.,* while they were descending.

Heb. iv. 1 : καταλειπομένης ἐπαγγελίας, *a promise being* (still) *left.* (See Alford's note.)

The Genitive Absolute, says Dr. Donaldson, is originally **causal**, in conformity with the primary notion of the case. Hence arise, by way of analogy, its other uses as denoting accessories of **time, manner,** or **circumstance.** The tense of the participle greatly determines the force of the phrase. (See § 393.)

THE DATIVE.

276. In its primary local sense (see § 11), **the Dative implies juxtaposition.**[1] Hence the various modifications of its meaning, which may be classed as follows:—

1. Association.   3. Reference.
2. Transmission. 4. Accessory.

The Dative in a sentence is generally an indirect complement of the Predicate, or a "remote object." (See § 186.)

---

[1] The Greek Dative is therefore diametrically opposed to the Genitive. 1. The latter signifies separation, the former proximity. 2. The latter denotes subtraction, the former addition. 3. The latter expresses comparison of different things, the former equality, or sameness.—*Dr. Donaldson.*

I. Association.

277. *a.* **Verbs signifying intercourse, companionship, and the like, are often followed by a Dative.**

Matt. ix. 9 : ἀκολούθει μοι, *follow me.*
Luke xv. 15 : ἐκολλήθη ἑνὶ τῶν πολιτῶν, *he attached himself to one of the citizens.*
Acts xxiv. 26 : ὡμίλει αὐτῷ, *he conversed with him.*
Rom. vii. 2 : ἀνδρὶ δέδεται, *she is bound to her husband.*
James iv. 8 : ἐγγίσατε τῷ Θεῷ, καὶ ἐγγίσει ὑμῖν, *draw near to God, and He will draw near to you.*

b. **Likeness, fitness, equality, and their opposites, are marked by a Dative after adjectives, verbs, and participles.**

Matt. xxiii. 27 : παρομοιάζετε τάφοις κεκονιαμένοις, *ye resemble whited sepulchres.*
Luke xiii. 18 : τίνι ὁμοιώσω αὐτήν; *to what shall I liken it?*
James i. 6 : ἔοικε κλύδωνι θαλάσσης, *he is like a wave of the sea.*
Eph. v. 3 : καθὼς πρέπει ἁγίοις, *as it becometh saints.*
Matt. xx. 12 : ἴσους αὐτοὺς ἡμῖν ἐποίησας, *thou madest them equal with us.*

c. **After a substantive verb, the Dative often denotes possession or property.**

Matt. xviii. 12 : ἐὰν γένηταί τινι ἀνθρώπῳ ἑκατὸν πρόβατα, *if a man have* (if there be to any man) *a hundred sheep.*
Acts viii. 21 : οὐκ ἔστι σοι μερὶς οὐδὲ κλῆρος ἐν τῷ λόγῳ τούτῳ, *thou hast not* (there is not to thee) *part nor lot in this matter.*

The verb is sometimes omitted after a word of "association."

2 Cor. vi. 14 : τίς γὰρ μετοχὴ δικαιοσύνῃ καὶ ἀνομίᾳ; *for what fellowship have righteousness and lawlessness?*

II. Transmission.

278. *a.* **Verbs of giving, whether active or passive, are followed by a Dative of the person.**

After the active verb, the thing (Accusative) is the *direct*, the person (Dative) the *indirect* object. (See § 186.)

Matt. vii. 6 : μὴ δῶτε τὸ ἅγιον τοῖς κυσί, *give not that which is holy to the dogs.*

Matt. vii. 7 : αἰτεῖτε, καὶ δοθήσεται ὑμῖν, *ask, and it shall be given unto you.*

Rom. i. 11 : ἵνα τι μεταδῶ χάρισμα ὑμῖν πνευματικόν, *that I may impart to you some spiritual gift.*

Heb. ii. 5 : οὐ γὰρ ἀγγέλοις ὑπέταξε τὴν οἰκουμένην τὴν μέλλουσαν, *for not unto angels did he subject the world to come.*

b. **The Dative also indicates the receiver of information, tidings, command.**

So in the common λέγω ὑμῖν, *I say unto you.*

Matt. xiii. 3 : ἐλάλησεν αὐτοῖς πολλά, *he spake many things to them.*

1 Cor. v. 9 : ἔγραψα ὑμῖν ἐν τῇ ἐπιστολῇ, *I wrote unto you in my letter.*

Luke iv. 18 : εὐαγγελίσασθαι πτωχοῖς, *to preach glad tidings to the poor;* LXX., Isa. lxi. 1 (also with Accusative, Luke iii. 18, etc.).

Acts i. 2 : ἐντειλάμενος τοῖς ἀποστόλοις, *having given commandment to the apostles.*

But κελεύω, *to order,* governs the Accusative in the N.T.

c. **Words denoting assistance, succour, etc., are followed by a Dative.**

Matt. iv. 11 : καὶ διηκόνουν αὐτῷ, *and they ministered unto him.*

Matt. xv. 25 : Κύριε, βοήθει μοι, *Lord, help me!*

d. **The object of a mental affection, as esteem, anger, worship, etc., also obedience and faith, is often expressed by a Dative.**

The Genitive in a similar connection expresses the source of the feeling. (See § 249.)

But the construction with prepositions is generally preferred, as giving additional precision and emphasis.

Matt. vi. 25 : μὴ μεριμνᾶτε τῇ ψυχῇ, *care not for your life.* So Luke xii. 22. But with περί, Matt. vi. 28, Luke xii. 26 ; with ὑπέρ, 1 Cor. xii. 25 ; with Accusative, 1 Cor. vii. 32–34.

§ 279.] THE DATIVE OF TRANSMISSION. 225

Matt. v. 22 : ὁ ὀργιζόμενος τῷ ἀδελφῷ, *he who is angry with his brother.*[1] With ἐπί, Rev. xii. 17.

Gal. i. 10 : ζητῶ ἀνθρώποις ἀρέσκειν; *do I seek to please men ?*

Matt. ii. 2 : ἤλθομεν προσκυνῆσαι αὐτῷ, *we are come to worship him;* always with Dative in Matt., Mark, and Paul (except Matt. iv. 10, from LXX.), in other books with Dative or Accusative.

Matt. xxi. 25 : οὐκ ἐπιστεύσατε αὐτῷ ; *believed ye him not ?* also with ἐν and ἐπί (Dative), ἐπί and εἰς (Accusative).

Acts v. 36, 37 : ὅσοι ἐπείθοντο αὐτῷ, *as many as obeyed him.*

Rom. x. 16 : οὐ πάντες ὑπήκουσαν τῷ εὐαγγελίῳ, *they did not all obey the gospel.*

III. Reference.

279. The person or thing in respect of whom or which anything is done, whether to benefit or injure,[2] or in any other way, may be expressed by the Dative. This reference may generally be expressed in English by the preposition *for*.

Matt. iii. 16 : ἀνεῴχθησαν αὐτῷ οἱ οὐρανοί, *the heavens were opened for him.*

Matt. xvii. 4 : ποιήσω ὧδε τρεῖς σκηνάς, σοὶ μίαν καὶ Μωϋσεῖ μίαν καὶ Ἠλίᾳ μίαν, *let me make here three tabernacles, one for thee, and one for Moses, and one for Elijah.*

Rom. vi. 2 : οἵτινες ἀπεθάνομεν τῇ ἁμαρτίᾳ, *we who died to sin.*

2 Cor. v. 13 : εἴτε γὰρ ἐξέστημεν, Θεῷ, εἴτε σωφρονοῦμεν, ὑμῖν, *for whether we were beside ourselves, (it was) for God, whether we are sober, (it is) for you.*

James iii. 18 : καρπὸς ... σπείρεται τοῖς ποιοῦσιν εἰρήνην, *the fruit* of righteousness *is sown for them that make peace.*

Heb. iv. 9 : ἄρα ἀπολείπεται σαββατισμὸς τῷ λαῷ τοῦ Θεοῦ, *there remaineth therefore a sabbath rest for the people of God.*

Matt. xxiii. 31 : μαρτυρεῖτε ἑαυτοῖς, *ye bear witness against yourselves.* See also James v. 3 ; and compare 1 Cor. iv. 4.

---

[1] The following word εἰκῇ, *without a cause*, should probably be omitted. (W. H.? Rev. Text.)

[2] Latin, *Dativus commodi vel incommodi.*

Rom. vi. 20 : ἐλεύθεροι ἦτε τῇ δικαιοσύνῃ, *ye were free in regard to righteousness;* not simply "from righteousness," which would have required the Genitive.

To this use of the Dative may be attributed the phrase, τί ἐμοὶ καὶ σοί; *what have I to do with thee?* lit., what is for me and thee? *i.e.*, what have we in common? Mark v. 7 (Matt. viii. 29); John ii. 4, etc.

IV. *Accessory Circumstance.*

280. *a.* **The mode of an action is expressed by the Dative.**

Acts xi. 23: παρεκάλει πάντας τῇ προθέσει τῆς καρδίας προσμένειν τῷ Κυρίῳ, *he began exhorting all to cleave to the Lord with the purpose of the heart.*

1 Cor. x. 30: εἰ ἐγὼ χάριτι μετέχω, *if I partake with thankfulness.*

Phil. i. 18: παντὶ τρόπῳ, εἴτε προφάσει, εἴτε ἀληθείᾳ, Χριστὸς καταγγέλλεται, *in every way, whether in pretence or in truth, Christ is preached.*

See also Acts xv. 1; 2 Cor. iii. 18; Eph. v. 19, etc.

b. **A modal Dative sometimes emphatically repeats the notion of the verb.** See an analogous idiom with the Accusative (§ 282), and with the Predicate Participle (§ 394, 3, *d*). This Dative may have a qualifying adjective.

James v. 17: προσευχῇ προσηύξατο, *he prayed with prayer, i.e.,* he prayed earnestly.

Mark v. 42: ἐξέστησαν ἐκστάσει μεγάλῃ, *they were astonished with a great astonishment, i.e.,* were greatly astonished. See also 1 Pet. i. 8.

For other examples, see Matt. xv. 4; Luke xxii. 15; John iii. 29; Acts iv. 17, v. 28, xxiii. 14.

For modal Datives that have become actual Adverbs, see §§ 126, 399, *a*.

c. **The Dative is used to denote the cause or motive.**

Rom. iv. 20: οὐ διεκρίθη τῇ ἀπιστίᾳ ἀλλ' ἐνεδυναμώθη τῇ πίστει, *he hesitated not through unbelief, but was strengthened through faith.*

Gal. vi. 12: ἵνα μὴ τῷ σταυρῷ τοῦ Χριστοῦ διώκωνται, *that they may not be persecuted for the cross of Christ.*

1 Pet. iv. 12: μὴ ξενίζεσθε τῇ ἐν ὑμῖν πυρώσει, *be not surprised* (lit., "be not as strangers") *at the conflagration* (which has broken out) *among you.*

d. The Dative is also the case of the instrument.

Matt. iii. 12 : τὸ δὲ ἄχυρον κατακαύσει πυρὶ ἀσβέστῳ, *but the chaff he will burn with fire unquenchable.*

Acts xii. 2 : ἀνεῖλε δὲ Ἰάκωβον ... μαχαίρᾳ, *and he slew James with (the) sword.*

Rom. i. 29 : πεπληρωμένους πάσῃ ἀδικίᾳ, πονηρίᾳ, πλεονεξίᾳ, κακίᾳ, *being filled* (utterly engrossed) *by all unrighteousness, depravity, greed, malice.* "Filled *with*" would have required the Genitive. (See § 251.[1]) Comp. 2 Cor. vii. 4.

Eph. ii. 5, 8 : χάριτί ἐστε σεσωσμένοι, *by grace ye have been saved.* In Rom. viii. 24, τῇ γὰρ ἐλπίδι ἐσώθημεν may be rendered, *for we were saved by hope* (instrumental), or *in this hope* (modal).

2 Pet. i. 3 : τοῦ καλέσαντος ἡμᾶς ἰδίᾳ δόξῃ καὶ ἀρετῇ, *of him who called us by his own glory and virtue* (R.V.). The reading is that of Lachmann, Tischendorf, Rev. Text, and W. H. marg., but the Received Text gives the same meaning. "*To* glory and virtue" (A.V.) is manifestly incorrect. (See Alford's note.)

> See further 1 Cor. xv. 10; Eph. i. 13; Titus iii. 7; 1 Pet. i. 18; and many other passages.

Hence the verb χράομαι, *to use as an instrument,* is followed by a Dative.

2 Cor. iii. 12 : πολλῇ παρρησίᾳ χρώμεθα, *we employ much boldness.*

> So Acts xxvii. 3, 17; 1 Cor. ix. 12, 15; 2 Cor. i. 17; 1 Tim. i. 8, v. 23. In 1 Cor. vii. 31, the best MSS. (W. H.) read the Accusative, τὸν κόσμον.

e. From denoting the instrument, **the Dative sometimes appears to take the signification of the agent,** being used **after Passive verbs** where we might expect the more usual ὑπό with a Genitive (for which see § 304).

Luke xxiii. 15 : οὐδὲν ἄξιον θανάτου ἐστὶ πεπραγμένον αὐτῷ, *nothing worthy of death has been done by him.*

2 Cor. xii. 20 : κἀγὼ εὑρεθῶ ὑμῖν, *and I should be found by you.* Compare 2 Pet. iii. 14, and Rom. x. 20, from Isa. lxv. 1, LXX.

---

[1] In Eph. iii. 19, εἰς conveys a different notion again, "*that ye may be filled up to all the fulness of God.*"

Luke xxiv. 35: ὡς ἐγνώσθη αὐτοῖς, *how he was known by them*. Compare Phil. iv. 5.

The passive Aorist of ὁράω, *to see* (ὤφθην, see § 103, 4), is generally construed with the Dative, as 1 Tim. iii. 16, ὤφθη ἀγγέλοις, *he was seen by angels*. Here, however, the notion is rather that of *appearing to* (Luke xxiv. 34), so that the Dative is regular. And in some of the other instances a somewhat similar explanation may be given, as in the last: "*he was made known to them*."

In Matt. v. 21, ἐρρέθη τοῖς ἀρχαίοις, the R.V. rightly renders, *it was said to them of old time*, not "by them," as A.V.

f. **That in which a quality inheres, "the sphere," is expressed by the Dative.**

Matt. v. 3: οἱ πτωχοὶ τῷ πνεύματι, *the poor in spirit*. Ver. 8: οἱ καθαροὶ τῇ καρδίᾳ, *the pure in heart*.

Acts xiv. 8: ἀδύνατος τοῖς ποσίν, *impotent in his feet*.

1 Cor. vii. 34: ἵνα ᾖ ἁγία καὶ σώματι καὶ πνεύματι, *that she may be holy both in body and spirit*.

1 Cor. xiv. 20: μὴ παιδία γίνεσθε ταῖς φρεσίν ἀλλὰ τῇ κακίᾳ νηπιάζετε, *be not children in understanding, but be infants in malice* (Dative of mode).

Eph. ii. 3: ἤμεθα τέκνα φύσει ὀργῆς, *we were in nature children of wrath*.

This use of the Dative evidently springs from its original local import. The "local Dative" is not found in the New Testament, excepting (1) in the phrase *by the way*, or *ways*, ὁδῷ, ὁδοῖς, where the way is regarded as the *instrument*: James ii. 25; 2 Pet. ii. 15; and (2) connected with the figurative use of πορεύομαι, περιπατέω, *to walk*, as Acts ix. 31, xiv. 16; 2 Cor. xii. 18, etc.

g. **Accessories of time are marked by the Dative, as—**

(1) A space of time, *for*.

Acts xiii. 20: ὡς ἔτεσι τετρακοσίοις καὶ πεντήκοντα, *for about four hundred and fifty years*.

See also Luke viii. 29; John ii. 20; Acts viii. 11; Rom. xvi. 25.

The Accusative is more frequently used. (See § 286; also the Genitive under διά, § 299.)

(2) A point of time, *at, on*.

Mark vi. 21: Ἡρώδης τοῖς γενεσίοις αὐτοῦ δεῖπνον ἐποίησε, *Herod on his birthday made a banquet*.

§ 281, a.] THE ACCUSATIVE WITH TRANSITIVE VERBS.

Matt. xx. 19 : τῇ τρίτῃ ἡμέρᾳ ἐγερθήσεται, *on the third day he shall be raised*.

Luke xiv. 3 : εἰ ἔξεστι τῷ σαββάτῳ θεραπεύειν ; *is it lawful to heal on the Sabbath ?*

The preposition ἐν is frequently inserted for the same purpose. (See § 295, 7.)
But when only the time within which, not the point of time, is specified, the Genitive is used. (See § 266.)

THE ACCUSATIVE.

281. The Accusative primarily denotes that towards which motion is directed. Hence its use to complete the notion of the Predicate.[1]

The Accusative expresses the immediate Object of a transitive verb.

Matt. iv. 21 : εἶδεν ἄλλους δύο ἀδελφούς ... καὶ ἐκάλεσεν αὐτούς, *he saw other two brothers ... and he called them* (transitive active).

Acts i. 18 : ἐκτήσατο χωρίον, *he purchased a field* (transitive deponent).

a. It should be noted that **some verbs which in English are intransitive**, *i.e.*, complete in themselves as predicates, and which *extend* their meaning by the use of prepositions, **are transitive in Greek**, and therefore require an Accusative to *complete* their meaning.

Thus, English : " whosoever shall be ashamed *of* me and *of* my words."

Greek : ὃς ἐὰν ἐπαισχυνθῇ με καὶ τοὺς ἐμοὺς λόγους (Mark viii. 38). See also Rom. i. 16 ; 2 Tim. i. 8.

Acts xiv. 21 : εὐαγγελισάμενοί τε τὴν πόλιν ἐκείνην, καὶ μαθητεύσαντες ἱκανούς, *having both preached the Gospel in that city and made many disciples*, lit., "having evangelised that city and discipled many."

The two verbs in this passage, however, with some others, vary in their use. (See Vocabulary.)

---

[1] "The Accusative," says Dr. Donaldson, "has the following applications in Greek Syntax :—It denotes (*a*) motion to an object ; (*b*) distance in space ; (*c*) duration in time ; (*d*) the immediate object of a transitive verb ; (*e*) the more remote object of any verb, whether it has another Accusative or not ; (*f*) the Accusative of cognate signification, *i.e.*, the secondary predication by way of emphasis of that which is already predicated by the verb itself ; (*g*) an apposition to the object of the whole sentence ; (*h*) the subject of the objective sentence, when this is expressed in the infinitive mood."—*Greek Grammar*, p. 497.

b. Generally, the employment of the same verb in different places as transitive and neuter may be explained by change of meaning, or a variation in emphasis.

So 1 Cor. vi. 18 : φεύγετε τὴν πορνείαν, *flee fornication,* avoid it.

1 Cor. x. 14 : φεύγετε ἀπὸ τῆς εἰδωλολατρείας, *flee from idolatry,* make good your escape from it.

Matt. x. 28 : μὴ φοβηθῆτε ἀπὸ τῶν ἀποκτεινόντων τὸ σῶμα, κ.τ.λ. ... φοβεῖσθε δὲ μᾶλλον τὸν δυνάμενον, κ.τ.λ., *be not afraid of those who kill the body ... but the rather fear him who is able,* etc.

c. Some verbs, denoting the exercise of a faculty, may be read either transitively or intransitively, according to the nature of the expression. So in English we may say, "*I see,*" or "*I see you.*"

Matt. vi. 4 : ὁ βλέπων ἐν τῷ κρυπτῷ, *he that seeth in secret.*

Matt. vii. 3 : τί δὲ βλέπεις τὸ κάρφος ; *but why seest thou the splinter?*

Mark iv. 24 : βλέπετε τί ἀκούετε, *look to* (take heed) *what ye hear.*

In Mark viii. 15, xii. 38, βλέπετε ἀπό—lit., "look away from"—signifies *beware of.* But in Phil. iii. 2, βλέπετε τοὺς κύνας, κ.τ.λ., literally signifies "*look to the dogs, look to the evil-workers, look to the concision;*" caution being *implied.*[1]

d. The immediate Object is omitted after certain verbs, which are nevertheless strictly transitive ; as προσέχω, *to apply* (add τὸν νοῦν, the mind), *to give heed.*

Luke xvii. 3 : προσέχετε ἑαυτοῖς, *give heed to yourselves.*

With ἀπό, *to beware of,* lit., to give heed (so as to turn) from. Matt. vii. 15 : προσέχετε ἀπὸ τῶν ψευδοπροφητῶν, *beware of the false prophets.*

Other verbs similarly used are ἐπέχω (add τὸν νοῦν), *to observe,* Luke xiv. 7 ; Acts iii. 5 ; διατρίβω (add τὸν χρόνον), *to sojourn,* Acts xv. 35 ; ἐπιτίθημι (add τὰς χεῖρας), *to attack,* Acts xviii. 10.

282. Any verb, whether transitive or intransitive, may extend its meaning by a "**cognate Accusative.**" **This Accusative is always connected with the verb in signification, often in etymology.**

---

[1] Ellicott.

§ 284.] ACCUSATIVE OF DEFINITION. 231

For a similar use of the Dative, see § 280, *b* ; and of the Participle, § 394, 3, *d*.

Matt. ii. 10 : ἐχάρησαν χαρὰν μεγάλην, lit., *they rejoiced a great joy, i.e.,* " rejoiced greatly."

Luke ii. 8 : φυλάσσοντες φυλακὰς τῆς νυκτός, lit., *watching the watches of the night, i.e.,* keeping watch by night.

Col. ii. 19 : αὔξει τὴν αὔξησιν τοῦ Θεοῦ, *increaseth the increase of God, i.e.,* yields the increase given by God.

See also John vii. 24; 1 Tim. vi. 12; 1 Pet. iii. 14, etc.

Eph. iv. 8 : ᾐχμαλώτευσεν αἰχμαλωσίαν, *he led captive a captivity, i.e.,* a train of captives. Ps. lxviii. 18.[1]

283. An Accusative is often used by way of more exact definition of the Predicate.[2]

John vi. 10 : ἀνέπεσαν οἱ ἄνδρες, τὸν ἀριθμὸν ὡς πεντακισχίλιοι, *the men sat down, in number about five thousand.*

Phil. i. 11 : πεπληρωμένοι καρπὸν δικαιοσύνης, *filled with the fruit of righteousness.* So Col. i. 9. Compare under Genitive, § 251, and Dative, § 280, *d*. The Accusative strictly denotes the respect in which fulness is attained.

More generally, however, the Dative of accessory circumstance, § 280, is employed. In Acts xviii. 3, "*by their occupation* they were tent-makers," W. H. and Rev. Text read τῇ τέχνῃ, the Received Text τὴν τέχνην.

284. Many transitive verbs may have two objects, and be, therefore, followed by two Accusatives; generally of a person (" the

---

[1] This passage is rather an instance of a cognate external object, the abstract noun representing a multitude (Numb. xxxi. 12, LXX., " they brought the captivity "). So Ostervald's translation, " il a mené captive une grande multitude de captives ;" and De Wette's, " er führte Gefangene."

[2] This Accusative is often said to be governed by κατά, *in respect of*, understood. "It is only a variety of the cognate Accusative. It defines more exactly the act or state described by a verb or adjective by referring it to a particular object, or part affected. It is the Accusative of an *equivalent* notion—the part wherein the act or state consists."—*Dr. Jacob.*

external object") and a thing ("the internal object"). So **verbs of asking, teaching, clothing and unclothing, anointing,** with many others.

This Accusative of the "internal object" is analogous to the cognate accus. (See § 282.)

Matt. vii. 9 : ὃν αἰτήσει ὁ υἱὸς αὐτοῦ ἄρτον, *whom his son shall ask for a loaf.* (Occasionally the person with the prepp. παρά, ἀπό.)

John xiv. 26 : ἐκεῖνος ὑμᾶς διδάξει πάντα, *he will teach you all things.* (Once with Dative of person, Rev. ii. 14.)

Mark xv. 17 : ἐνδιδύσκουσιν αὐτὸν πορφύραν, *they clothe him in purple.* (The preposition ἐν sometimes found, as Matt. xi. 8.)

Heb. i. 9 : ἔχρισέ σε ... ἔλαιον ἀγαλλιάσεως, *he anointed thee with the oil of gladness,* Ps. xlv. 8, LXX. (But the Dative of material is sometimes used, Acts x. 38, and with ἀλείφω always.)

The Passive retains the Accusative of "the internal object."

Luke xvi. 19 : ἐνεδιδύσκετο πορφύραν καὶ βύσσον, *he was clothed with purple and fine linen.*

Acts xxviii. 20 : τὴν ἅλυσιν ταύτην περίκειμαι, *I am bound with this chain.* (See Heb. v. 2.)

2 Thess. ii. 15 : κρατεῖτε τὰς παραδόσεις ἃς ἐδιδάχθητε, *hold fast the instructions which ye were taught.*

1 Tim. vi. 5 : διεφθαρμένων ἀνθρώπων τὸν νοῦν, *of men corrupted in mind.*

The same remark applies to verbs which in the Active express "the remoter object" by the Dative.

1 Cor. ix. 17 : οἰκονομίαν πεπίστευμαι, *I have been entrusted with a stewardship.* So Rom. iii. 2; Gal. ii. 7; 1 Thess. ii. 4; 2 Thess. i. 10; 1 Tim. i. 11.

285. The Subject of an Infinitive Verb is put in the Accusative.

In translation, the Infinitive is generally to be rendered as a finite verb, and the Accusative as the nominative, with the conjunction *that* prefixed.

For the Infinitive, see § 387. It is really a verbal noun, and is used to complete the predication. The Accusative thus becomes an Accusative of definition[1] (§ 283).

1 Tim. ii. 8 : βούλομαι ... προσεύχεσθαι, "I wish for ... a praying;" βούλομαι προσεύχεσθαι τοὺς ἄνδρας, "I wish for a praying on the part of men," *I wish men to pray.*

---

[1] Compare Dr. Donaldson's Grammar, § 584.

§ 287.] THE ACCUSATIVE AND INFINITIVE.

Luke xxiv. 23 : οἳ λέγουσιν αὐτὸν ζῆν, *who say that he is alive.*
Acts xiv. 19 : νομίζοντες αὐτὸν τεθνηκέναι, *thinking that he was dead.*
1 Cor. vii. 10, 11 : παραγγέλλω ... γυναῖκα ἀπὸ ἀνδρὸς μὴ χωρισθῆναι ... καὶ ἄνδρα γυναῖκα μὴ ἀφιέναι, *I enjoin that a wife should not be separated from her husband, and that a man should not put away his wife.*
Luke i. 74 : τοῦ δοῦναι ἡμῖν ... ῥυσθέντας, λατρεύειν αὐτῷ, *to grant unto us that we being delivered* (ἡμᾶς implied in ῥυσθέντας) *should serve him.*

When the Subject of the Infinitive and of the principal verb is the same, it is not repeated except for emphasis, and adjectives, etc., in agreement with it are put in the nominative case.

Rom. xv. 24 : ἐλπίζω διαπορευόμενος θεάσασθαι ὑμᾶς, *I hope that when I pass through I shall see you.* See also 2 Cor. x. 2.

But Phil. iii. 13 : ἐγὼ ἐμαυτὸν οὐ λογίζομαι κατειληφέναι, *I do not reckon that I myself have attained.* So Rom. ii. 19 ; Luke xx. 20.

When the Infinitive is substantivised (see § 201) by the Article, the relations expressed by the Genitive after nouns are denoted by the Accusative.

Inf. gen., Acts xxiii. 15 : πρὸ τοῦ ἐγγίσαι αὐτόν, *before his approach.*
Inf. dat., Matt. xiii. 4 : ἐν τῷ σπείρειν αὐτόν, *in his sowing.* So xxvii. 12.
Inf. acc., Matt. xxvi. 32 : μετὰ τὸ ἐγερθῆναί με, *after I am raised.*

286. Relations of space and time are denoted by the Accusative.

a. Space.—Luke xxii. 41 : ἀπεσπάσθη ἀπ' αὐτῶν ὡσεὶ λίθου βολήν, *he withdrew from them about a stone's cast.*

John vi. 19 : ἐληλακότες οὖν ὡς σταδίους εἴκοσι πέντε ἢ τριάκοντα, *having therefore rowed about twenty-five or thirty stadia.*

b. Time.—(1) An (approximate) point of time—

Acts x. 3 : εἶδεν ... ὡσεὶ ὥραν ἐννάτην, *he saw, about the ninth hour.* W. H. read περί, which is the more usual construction. But see John iv. 52 ; Rev. iii. 3.

(2) Duration of time—

Luke xv. 29 : τοσαῦτα ἔτη δουλεύω σοι, *so many years am I serving thee.*

See also Matt. xx. 6; John i. 40, ii. 12, v. 5, xi. 6; Acts xiii. 21, etc.

287. The Accusative is sometimes found in elliptical or apparently irregular constructions.

Matt. iv. 15: ὁδὸν θαλάσσης, *the way of the sea*, stands apparently without government. The regimen is to be sought in its Old Testament connection, Isa. ix. 1, from which it is a citation.[1]

Luke xxiv. 47: ἀρξάμενον ἀπὸ Ἰερουσαλήμ, *beginning at* (from) *Jerusalem*, the Accusative neuter participle in apposition with the objective sentence. (W. H. and Rev. Text read ἀρξάμενοι.)

Acts xxvi. 3: γνώστην ὄντα σε, κ.τ.λ. The Accusatives here seem to stand without any dependence. A verb is probably to be understood from ἥγημαι, in the preceding verse: *especially as I regard thee as being acquainted*, etc.

Rom. viii. 3: τὸ ἀδύνατον τοῦ νόμου, *the impossibility of the law*. The phrase is either (1) a nominative absolute (nominativus pendens) (see § 242); (2) Accusative, in apposition to the object of the sentence,[2] or governed by ἐποίησεν understood; or (3) an anacolouthon (§ 412, *d.*)

1 Tim. ii. 6: τὸ μαρτύριον καιροῖς ἰδίοις, *the testimony to be set forth in its own seasons*, an Accusative, perhaps, in apposition with the preceding sentence.[3]

ON THE CASES AS USED WITH PREPOSITIONS.

288. Prepositions, as already stated (§ 118), govern the Genitive, Dative, or Accusative, and are auxiliary to the significance of these cases.

Sometimes a preposition is simply *emphatic*, *i.e.*, it is used where the case alone would have expressed the same meaning, although with less force. More frequently, however, it denotes a relation which the case of itself would be insufficient to specify.

Two points must be considered in relation to the prepositions: first, their own original force; and secondly, the significance of the case or cases to which they are severally applied.

Thus, παρά is *beside*, denoting—with the Genitive, *from* (from beside); with the Dative, *at* or *near* (by the side of); with the Accusative, *towards* or *along* (to or along the side of). From these meanings, again, others arise through the application of physical analogies to mental relations. Some prepositions from their meaning can govern only one case, as ἐκ, *out of* (Gen.); ἐν, *in* (Dat.); εἰς, *into* (Acc.). Others may govern two, as

---

[1] We often make similar quotations almost unconsciously: *e.g.*, "'Christ and Him crucified' is the theme of the faithful minister." *Him* in that sentence appears plainly ungrammatical until we turn to the connection, 1 Cor. ii. 2.

[2] Webster.

[3] Ellicott. The difficulty here is that the preceding sentence is *not objective*. It would seem better to take the Accusative as more directly dependent on δούς.

implying different directions of motion, but excluding the idea of rest, as κατά, *downwards;* with the Gen., *down from;* with the Acc., *down upon.* Others are found with all three cases.

Every preposition probably denoted at first a relation of *place.* (See the scheme in § 124.) Hence by an easy transition their reference to *time,* and their use for purely *mental relations.* It will be seen in the following sections that most prepositions have this threefold use.

289. Certain prepositions are very nearly allied in some of their significations. Hence it may be a matter of indifference which is employed, the same circumstance being regarded from slightly different points of view. Thus it might be said of a commission given to a servant, that the act was executed *by* him or *through* him. It will be seen, however, that there exists a real distinction in the notions, although they meet in one transaction. We could not, for instance, infer that the words *through* and *by* were synonymous, or that one was used for, or interchanged with, the other. Such mistakes, however, have often been made in New Testament criticism; and it is especially necessary, even where these important parts of speech appear most nearly alike in meaning, to observe their real distinction. (See further, § 308.)

290. No mistake is so common with learners as that of supposing that the words of one language must correspond individually to those of another. The fact is, that every word, as it were, fences off a particular enclosure from the great domain of thought; and each language has its own method of division. The ways in which the English and the Greek, for example, have mapped out the vast territory do not mutually correspond. Perhaps, therefore, no one word of the former claims a province that has its precise counterpart in the latter. Or, to adopt another illustration, the words of two languages do not run in equal parallel lines, thus:—

G. ——— ——— ——————— ——— ———
E. ——— ———— ——————— ——— ———

Were it so, translation would be easy work. Rather may they be represented thus:—

G. —— ————— ——— ———— ———— ——
E. ———— —— ——— ———— ———— ——

where in each language there are words that *overlap* those of the other, sometimes containing more meaning, sometimes less·; and a single word in one often including the significance or part of the significance of two or three in the other.

TABLE OF PREPOSITIONS.

One Case.	Two Cases.	Three Cases.
ἀντί, OVER AGAINST ⎫ ἀπό, FROM (exterior) ⎬ Gen. ἐκ, FROM (interior) ⎪ πρό, IN FRONT OF ⎭	διά, THROUGH ⎫ κατά, DOWN ⎪ μετά, WITH (association) ⎬ Gen. περί, AROUND ⎪ Acc. ὑπέρ, OVER ⎪ ὑπό, UNDER ⎭	ἐπί, UPON ⎫ Gen. παρά, BESIDE ⎬ Dat. πρός, TOWARDS ⎭ Acc.
ἐν, IN ⎫ Dat. σύν, WITH (co-operation) ⎭		
ἀνά, UP TO ⎫ Acc. εἰς, INTO ⎭		

Prepositions governing the Genitive only.

ἀντί, ἀπό, ἐκ, πρό.

291. ἀντί, OVER AGAINST,[1] containing the notion of opposition, **as an equivalent**: *instead of, for.*

Matt. v. 38 : ὀφθαλμὸν ἀντὶ ὀφθαλμοῦ, *an eye for an eye.*

Matt. xvii. 27 : δὸς αὐτοῖς ἀντὶ ἐμοῦ καὶ σοῦ, *give to them for thee and me.*

Matt. xx. 28 : λύτρον ἀντὶ πολλῶν, *a ransom for many.*

Heb. xii. 2 : ἀντὶ τῆς προκειμένης αὐτῷ χαρᾶς, *in return for the joy set before him.*

John i. 16 : ἐλάβομεν ... χάριν ἀντὶ χάριτος, *we received grace for grace*, i.e., grace within, as correspondent with grace without, the Divine gift being as the Divine source ; or (with most commentators), one measure of grace to succeed and replace another : " grace upon grace."[2]

> This preposition is employed with the neuter relative plural in the adverbial phrase, ἀνθ' ὧν (in return for which things) = *because*. (Luke i. 20, xii. 3, xix. 44; Acts xii. 23; 2 Thess. ii. 10.)

292. ἀπό, FROM THE EXTERIOR.

1. Separation, the preposition expressing removal, the governed noun showing the point of departure : *from.*

---

[1] The primal significance of each preposition will be shown by SMALL CAPITALS, the several applications of this by **thick type**.

[2] "Ununterbrochene, immer sich erneuernde Gnade."—*Winer.*

§ 293, 1.] PREPOSITIONS WITH THE GENITIVE, ἀπό, ἐκ.

Matt. i. 21: σώσει ... ἀπὸ τῶν ἁμαρτιῶν αὐτῶν, *he shall save ... from their sins*.

Matt. iii. 13: ἀπὸ τῆς Γαλιλαίας, *from Galilee*.

Matt. ix. 22: ἀπὸ τῆς ὥρας ἐκείνης, *from that hour*.

Matt. vi. 13: ῥῦσαι ἡμᾶς ἀπὸ τοῦ πονηροῦ, *deliver us from evil*, or, *the evil one*. Compare 2 Tim. iv. 18.

2. **Derivation, source, descent:** *from, of*.

Matt. vii. 16: ἀπὸ τριβόλων σῦκα, *figs from thistles*.

Matt. xi. 29: μάθετε ἀπ' ἐμοῦ, *learn of me*.

3. Hence, especially, **cause, occasion:** *from, on account of*.

Matt. xiv. 26: ἀπὸ τοῦ φόβου ἔκραξαν, *they cried out for fear*.

Matt. xviii. 7: οὐαὶ ... ἀπὸ τῶν σκανδάλων, *woe, on account of the offences!*

So, according to R.V., Heb. v. 7, εἰσακουσθεὶς ἀπὸ τῆς εὐλαβείας, *heard for his godly fear*. Some, however, understand "heard (and delivered) from his fear, *i.e.*, from the calamity which he apprehended.[1]

4. This preposition is sometimes used after transitive verbs elliptically, a word like *some* (as the real object of the verb) being understood.

John xxi. 10: ἐνέγκατε ἀπὸ τῶν ὀψαρίων, *bring of the fishes*.

Acts ii. 17: ἐκχεῶ ἀπὸ τοῦ πνεύματός μου, *I will pour out of my Spirit*.

5. ἀπό is frequently joined with adverbs, as ἀπὸ τότε, *from then*, Matt. iv. 17, etc.; ἀπ' ἄρτι, *henceforth*, Matt. xxiii. 39, etc.; ἀπὸ μακρόθεν, *from afar;* ἀπὸ ἄνωθεν, *from above;* ἀπὸ τοῦ νῦν, *from now*, etc. In all these cases, a substantive of place or time is really understood.

293. ἐκ, ἐξ, FROM THE INTERIOR (opposite to εἰς).

1. *Out of,* **locally.**

Matt. iii. 17: φωνὴ ἐκ τῶν οὐρανῶν, *a voice out of heaven*.

Matt. viii. 28: ἐκ τῶν μνημείων ἐξερχόμενοι, *coming out of the tombs*.

To this meaning may be assigned the phrase, ἐκ δεξιῶν, *on the right hand*, literally, "off from the right-hand parts" (Matt. xx. 21, etc.). But ἐν δεξιᾷ is also employed; see § 295, ἐν, 1.

---

[1] The verb εἰσακούω has a similarly extended meaning in Ps. cxviii. 5, LXX. But see Alford *in loc.*, who cites Luke xix. 3, xxiv. 41; John xxi. 6; Acts xii. 14, xx. 9, xxii. 11, as passages where ἀπὸ means *on account of*.

2. Originating in, as place, parentage, *from, of.*

Matt. iii. 9 : ἐκ τῶν λίθων τούτων, *of these stones.*

John iv. 7 : γυνὴ ἐκ τῆς Σαμαρείας, *a woman of Samaria.*

Phil. iii. 5 : Ἑβραῖος ἐξ Ἑβραίων, *a Hebrew of Hebrews,* i.e., of Hebrew descent.

3. Originating in, as the source, cause, or occasion, *from, by.*

Luke xvi. 9 : ποιήσατε ἑαυτοῖς φίλους ἐκ τοῦ μαμῶνα τῆς ἀδικίας, *make to yourselves friends by means of the mammon of unrighteousness* (R.V.), *i.e.,* by (the proper use of) your wealth.

Rom. v. 1 : δικαιωθέντες ἐκ πίστεως, *being justified by faith.* So in many passages.

1 Cor. ix. 14 : ἐκ τοῦ εὐαγγελίου ζῆν, *to live from the gospel.*

4. The material or mass from which anything is made or taken, *of.*

Matt. xxvii. 29 : στέφανον ἐξ ἀκανθῶν, *a crown of thorns.*

5. Belonging to a class, *of;* often with abstract nouns.

John xviii. 37 : ὁ ὢν ἐκ τῆς ἀληθείας, *he who is* (on the side) *of the truth.*

Rom. ii. 8 : οἱ ἐξ ἐριθείας, *they who are of a self-seeking spirit.*

Gal. iii. 9 ; Tit. i. 10 : οἱ ἐκ πίστεως · οἱ ἐκ περιτομῆς, *they who are of faith—of circumcision,* i.e., who range themselves under these opposite symbols. So Rom. iv. 14, οἱ ἐκ νόμου, *they who are of law,* etc.

This meaning is closely allied with (3).

6. Springing from : of the state of mind giving occasion to any action, *from, out of.*

2 Cor. ii. 4 : ἐκ πολλῆς θλίψεως ἔγραψα, *out of much affliction I wrote.*

1 Thess. ii. 3 : ἡ παράκλησις ἡμῶν οὐκ ἐκ πλάνης, οὐδὲ ἐξ ἀκαθαρσίας, *our exhortation was not from deceit nor from uncleanness.*

7. Used of **time,** *from,* the future being infolded in, and springing out of the present.

John vi. 66 : ἐκ τούτου, *from this time.*

Acts ix. 33 : ἐξ ἐτῶν ὀκτώ, *for eight years.*

294. πρό, IN FRONT OF.

1. *Before,* in respect of **place** or **person,**

§ 295, 2.]   PREPOSITIONS.   239

Acts xii. 6 : φύλακες πρὸ τῆς θύρας, *guards before the door.* So ch. xiv. 13; James v. 9.

Matt. xi. 10 : πρὸ προσώπου σου, *before thy face,* from LXX. So Mark i. 2; Luke i. 76, etc.

2. *Before,* in respect of **time.**

John xvii. 24 : πρὸ καταβολῆς κόσμου, *before the foundation of the world.*

1 Cor. iv. 5 : μὴ πρὸ καιροῦ τι κρίνετε, *judge nothing before the time.*

2 Cor. xii. 2 : πρὸ ἐτῶν δεκατεσσάρων, *fourteen years ago* (lit., before fourteen years, *i.e.,* counted backward from the present time). See also John xii. 1.

3. *Before,* by way of **superiority.**

Only in the phrase πρὸ πάντων, *before,* or *above all things.* Luke xxi. 12 ; Col. i. 17; James v. 12; 1 Pet. iv. 8.

Prepositions governing the Dative only.

ἐν, σύν.

295. ἐν, IN, correlative with εἰς and ἐκ.

1. Of **place,** *in;* so *within, on, at.*

Matt. ii. 1 : ἐν Βηθλεὲμ τῆς Ἰουδαίας, *in Bethlehem of Judæa.*

Matt. xx. 3 : ἐν τῇ ἀγορᾷ, *in the market-place.*

John xv. 4 : ἐν τῇ ἀμπέλῳ, *in the vine.*

Heb. i. 3 : ἐν δεξιᾷ τῆς μεγαλωσύνης, *on the right hand of the majesty.*[1]

Rev. iii. 21 : ἐν τῷ θρόνῳ μου, *on my throne.*

2. *Among,* with plurals or collective nouns.

Matt. ii. 6 : ἐν τοῖς ἡγεμόσιν Ἰούδα, *among the princes of Judah;* LXX., Micah v. 2.

Luke xiv. 31 : ἐν δέκα χιλιάσιν, *among ten thousands, i.e.,* attended by such a troop. See Jude 14; also Acts vii. 14.

Acts ii. 29 : ἐστὶν ἐν ἡμῖν ἄχρι τῆς ἡμέρας ταύτης, *it* (the sepulchre) *is among us unto this day.*

1 Pet. v. 1, 2 : πρεσβυτέρους τοὺς ἐν ὑμῖν ... τὸ ἐν ὑμῖν ποίμνιον, *the elders who are among you ... the little flock among you.*

---

[1] Compare the use of ἐκ, § 293, 1.

3. "**The ἐν of investiture**," *in* or *with;* as when we say, "The general came *in* his sword, the peers *in* their robes." The Greek of the New Testament extends this use of the preposition to accompaniments which do not literally invest.¹

1 Cor. iv. 21: ἐν ῥάβδῳ ἔλθω πρὸς ὑμᾶς; *am I to come to you with a rod?*

1 Cor. v. 8: μὴ ἐν ζύμῃ παλαιᾷ ... ἀλλ' ἐν ἀζύμοις, *not in the old leaven ...but in the unleavened.*

1 Tim. i. 18: ἵνα στρατεύῃ ἐν αὐταῖς, *that thou mayest fight in them* (prophesyings), *i.e.*, armed with them.

Heb. ix. 25: ὁ ἀρχιερεὺς εἰσέρχεται ... ἐν αἵματι ἀλλοτρίῳ, *the high priest enters ... in the blood of others.* Compare ch. x. 19 with xiii. 12.

So, perhaps, Eph. vi. 2: ἐντολὴ πρώτη ἐν ἐπαγγελίᾳ, *the first commandment in*, or *with promise.*

> To this notion of investiture that of action is sometimes superadded (Luke i. 51). Hence "**the ἐν instrumental.**"
>
> Luke xxii. 49: εἰ πατάξομεν ἐν μαχαίρᾳ; *shall we smite with the sword?* See § 368, *b.*
>
> See also Heb. xi. 37, and Rev. frequently, as ii. 16, vi. 8, xiii. 10, xiv. 15. In Matt. v. 13, Mark ix. 50, ἐν τίνι; may be rendered *wherewith?*

4. The **sphere** in which the subject is concerned, as dwelling or acting, *in.*

> So the phrases ἐν ἁμαρτίᾳ, *in sin;* ἐν πίστει, *in faith;* ἐν σοφίᾳ, *in wisdom;* ἐν ἀγάπῃ, *in love;* ἐν πνεύματι, *in spirit;* ἐν Πνεύματι, *in the Spirit* (217, *f*). Matt. xxii. 43; Rev. i. 10, etc.
>
> The frequent phrase, ἐν Χριστῷ (so ἐν Κυρίῳ, etc.), means, not simply attached to Christ as a follower, but *in Christ*, in the most intimate abiding fellowship.² So "Christ in you, me," Rom. viii. 10; Gal. i. 16; ii. 20, etc. A similar phrase is used of the revelation of God himself, "in us," 1 John iii. 24, iv. 13.
>
> 2 Cor. v. 19: Θεὸς ἦν ἐν Χριστῷ, κ.τ.λ., *God was in Christ reconciling*, etc.
>
> Eph. iv. 32: ὁ Θεὸς ἐν Χριστῷ ἐχαρίσατο ὑμῖν, *God in Christ forgave you.*
>
> See also Acts xvii. 31: *in a man whom he hath appointed.*

---

[1] A usage infrequent in classic Greek, and in the N.T. due to the influence of the Hebrew preposition בְּ, *in, with, by*, etc., for which the LXX. constantly uses ἐν.

[2] "Nicht blos *durch* Chr. *beneficio Christi*, sondern *in* Chr., in geistig kraftiger Gemeinschaft mit Chr."—*Winer.*

5. **In the power of,** *by.*

Matt. ix. 34: ἐν τῷ ἄρχοντι τῶν δαιμονίων, *by the prince of the demons.*

Matt. v. 34, 35: ἐν τῷ οὐρανῷ ... ἐν τῇ γῇ, *by heaven ... by earth.* So elsewhere in asseverations.

In Matt. iv. 4 some MSS. read ἐν παντὶ ῥήματι, *by every word* (W. H., ἐπὶ). Compare 1 Thess. iv. 15.

ἐν ἐμοί, 1 Cor. ix. 15, xiv. 11; Mark xiv. 6, may be rendered *in my case.*

6. This preposition with its case is often **equivalent to an adverb.** Compare (4) preceding. So we may render ἐν δυνάμει, *in power,* or *powerfully;* ἐν δόλῳ, *craftily;* ἐν τάχει, *speedily,* etc. In John xviii. 20, ἐν κρυπτῷ is *in secret, secretly,* different from ἐν τῷ κρυπτῷ, Matt. vi. 18.

7. **Of time,** *in.*

Matt. ii. 1: ἐν ἡμέραις Ἡρῴδου, *in the days of Herod.*

Matt. x. 15: ἐν ἡμέρᾳ κρίσεως, *in the day of judgment;* xii. 36, etc.

Often with the infinitive treated as a noun.

Matt. xiii. 4: ἐν τῷ σπείρειν αὐτόν, *while he was sowing.*

> With the relative pronoun, ἐν ᾧ, *whilst,* as Mark ii. 19; ἐν οἷς, *whilst,* as Luke xii. 1. The only difference between the singular and the plural is that the latter is more general.

8. *Constructio prægnans.*—This preposition seems occasionally to include the sense of εἰς, and so is used after verbs implying motion:— "*into,* so as to be *in.*"

Matt. xxvi. 23: ὁ ἐμβάψας ... ἐν τῷ τρυβλίῳ, *he who dipped ... in the dish.*

Luke xxiii. 53: ἔθηκεν αὐτὸ ἐν μνήματι λαξευτῷ, *he laid it in a rock-hewn sepulchre.*

Rom. ii. 5: θησαυρίζεις σεαυτῷ ὀργὴν ἐν ἡμέρᾳ ὀργῆς, *thou treasurest to thyself wrath* (to be poured forth) *in a day of wrath.*

296. II. **σύν,** CONJUNCTION WITH (union, or co-operation).

With, together with.

Matt. xxvi. 35: σὺν σοὶ ἀποθανεῖν, *to die with thee.*

242   PREPOSITIONS.   [§ 296.

Luke viii. 45 : Πέτρος καὶ οἱ σὺν αὐτῷ, *Peter and those with him.*

Not merely coexistence, but **association** is generally implied (see μετά). Hence, σύν is used of the fellowship of believers with Christ, etc. (Rom. vi. 8; Col. ii. 13, 20, iii. 3; 1 Thess. iv. 17, v. 10). There is the further suggestion of **co-operation** in such passages as 1 Cor. v. 4, xv. 10.

In Luke xxiv. 21, *together with* becomes nearly equal to *beside;* ἀλλά γε καὶ σὺν πᾶσι τούτοις, *Yea, and beside all this* (R.V.). Compare Neh. v. 18, LXX., "yet for all this" (A.V., R.V.).

Prepositions governing the Accusative only.

ἀνά, εἰς.

297. ἀνά, UP TO, or, UP BY.[1]

This preposition is of infrequent occurrence in the New Testament, and always has a special meaning, generally **distributive**.

1. ἀνὰ μέσον, *through the midst of*, Matt. xiii. 25 ; Mark vii. 31 ; *in the midst of*, Rev. vii. 17 ; *between*, 1 Cor. vi. 5.

2. ἀνὰ μέρος, *by turn*, 1 Cor. xiv. 27.

3. With numerals or measures of quantity or value, *apiece*, Matt. xx. 9, 10 ; ἀνὰ δηνάριον, *a denarius apiece*. Compare Mark vi. 40 ; Luke ix. 14, x. 1 (ἀνὰ δύο, *two by two*); John ii. 6 ; Rev. iv. 8.

4. In Rev. xxi. 21, ἀνὰ εἷς ἕκαστος, the preposition must be rendered as an adverb, *each one separately.*

298. εἰς, TO THE INTERIOR (opposite to ἐκ, and correlative with ἐν).[2]

1. Of **place**, *into;* so, figuratively, of a **state**.

Matt. ii. 11 : ἐλθόντες εἰς τὴν οἰκίαν, *having come into the house.*

Matt. v. 1 : ἀνέβη εἰς τὸ ὄρος, *he went up into the mountain.*

Matt. vi. 13 : μὴ εἰσενέγκῃς ἡμᾶς εἰς πειρασμόν, *lead us not into temptation.*

So with collective words.

---

[1] In some ancient Greek poets, with a Genitive and Dative.
[2] In Latin, the preposition *in* includes the notions of εἰς and ἐν, taking the Accusative and Ablative respectively ; and εἰς (really ἐνς), in fact, is only another form of ἐν, as ἐξ of ἐκ.

§ 298.]   PREPOSITIONS WITH THE ACCUSATIVE, εἰς.   243

Acts xxii. 21 : **εἰς ἔθνη ἐξαποστελῶ σε**, *I will send thee forth into* the community of *Gentiles*.

2. *Unto, to*, where the context or the nature of the case limits the movement to the exterior.

Matt. xvii. 27 : πορευθεὶς **εἰς θάλασσαν**, *having gone to the sea*.

John xi. 38 : ἔρχεται **εἰς τὸ μνημεῖον**, *he cometh to the tomb*. So xx. 1, 3, 4 (ver. 5, "he went not in").

Matt. vi. 26 : ἐμβλέψατε **εἰς τὰ πετεινά**, *look to the birds*.

Luke vi. 20 : ἐπάρας τοὺς ὀφθαλμοὺς **εἰς τοὺς μαθητάς**, *having raised his eyes to his disciples*.

Rev. x. 5 : ἦρε τὴν χεῖρα αὐτοῦ **εἰς τὸν οὐρανόν**, *he lifted his hand towards the heaven*.

3. The meaning *towards* is especially found in relation to **persons**, marking direction of thought, speech, etc. Sometimes this implies hostility, *against;* sometimes mere reference, *in regard to*.

Rom. xii. 16 : τὸ αὐτὸ **εἰς ἀλλήλους** φρονοῦντες, *being of the same mind one towards another*.

Luke xii. 10 : πᾶς ὃς ἐρεῖ λόγον **εἰς τὸν υἱὸν** τοῦ ἀνθρώπου, *every one who shall say a word against the Son of man*.

Acts ii. 25 : Δαβὶδ γὰρ λέγει **εἰς αὐτόν**, *for David says in reference to him*.

4. Towards, with respect to a certain **result**, *in order to, for*.

Matt. viii. 4, x. 18, etc.: **εἰς μαρτύριον** αὐτοῖς, *for a testimony to them*.

Matt. xxvi. 2 : παραδίδοται **εἰς τὸ σταυρωθῆναι**, *he is surrendered to be crucified*.

1 Cor. xi. 24 : τοῦτο ποιεῖτε **εἰς τὴν ἐμὴν ἀνάμνησιν**, *this do for the remembrance of me*.

2 Cor. ii. 12 : ἐλθὼν **εἰς τὴν Τρωάδα**, **εἰς τὸ εὐαγγέλιον**, *having come into Troas for* (the preaching of) *the gospel*.

5. *Into*, symbolically, as marking the entrance into a **state** or **sphere** (see under ἐν, 4).

So we enter **εἰς Χριστόν**, *into Christ*, actually by faith, symbolically by baptism, Christians being **ἐν Χριστῷ**, *in Christ*.

Rom. vi. 3, 4 : ὅσοι ἐβαπτίσθημεν **εἰς Χριστὸν Ἰησοῦν**, **εἰς τὸν θάνατον** αὐτοῦ ἐβαπτίσθημεν, *as many of us as were baptised into Christ Jesus, were baptised into his death*.

Compare Matt. xxviii. 19, "into the name," etc. ; Acts xix. 3 ; 1 Cor. i. 13, x. 2, xii. 13; Gal. iii. 27. So Acts ii. 38, εἰς τὴν ἄφεσιν ἁμαρτιῶν, *into the remission of sins*, or, according to some interpreters, as (4).

6. This preposition is used in some important passages to denote **equivalence**,[1] and may be rendered *for*, or *as*.

Matt. xix. 5 : ἔσονται...εἰς σάρκα μίαν, *they shall become one flesh*. So Mark x. 8 ; 1 Cor. vi. 16 ; Eph. v. 31 ; from LXX., Gen. ii. 24.

Matt. xxi. 42 : ἐγενήθη εἰς κεφαλὴν γωνίας, *it became the head of the corner*. So Mark xii. 10 ; Luke xx. 17 ; from LXX., Ps. cxviii. 22.

Compare Luke iii. 5 (from Isa. xl. 4), xiii. 19; John xvi. 20; Acts vii. 21, xiii. 22; Rom. xi. 9; 1 Cor. xiv. 22, xv. 45 (see Gen. ii. 7, LXX.); 2 Cor. vi. 18, viii. 14; Heb. i. 5; James v. 3.

Acts xix. 27 : τὸ ... ἱερὸν εἰς οὐδὲν λογισθῆναι, *the temple to be esteemed as nothing*.

Rom. ii. 26 : οὐχὶ ἡ ἀκροβυστία αὐτοῦ εἰς περιτομὴν λογισθήσεται; *shall not his uncircumcision be accounted as circumcision*?

Rom. ix. 8 : λογίζεται εἰς σπέρμα, *it is accounted for a seed*.

Rom. iv. 3, 5, 9, 22 ; Gal. iii. 6 : ἐλογίσθη αὐτῷ εἰς δικαιοσύνην, *it was accounted to him for righteousness*.

7. When referring to **time**, εἰς may mark either (*a*) the interval up to a certain point, *during;* or (*b*) the point itself, regarded as the object of some aim or purpose, *up to*, *for*.

a. Luke i. 50 : εἰς γενεὰς γενεῶν, or εἰς γενεὰς καὶ γενεάς (W. H.), *unto, during generations of* (or *and*) *generations*.

Matt. xxi. 19 : εἰς τὸν αἰῶνα, *for ever*, lit., "unto or during the age," John vi. 51, 58, "for ever." εἰς τοὺς αἰῶνας, lit., "unto the ages," "for ever," Rom. i. 25 ; 2 Cor. xi. 31. εἰς τοὺς αἰῶνας τῶν αἰώνων, *unto the ages of the ages*, "for ever and ever," Gal. i. 5 ; 1 Tim. i. 17. 2 Pet. iii. 18, εἰς ἡμέραν αἰῶνος, "to the day of eternity" (§ 259).

So in the adverbial phrases, εἰς τὸ μέλλον, *hereafter*, Luke xiii. 9 ; 1 Tim. vi. 19 ; εἰς τὸ διηνεκές, *continuously, perpetually*, Heb. x. 12.

---

[1] This answers to a common Hebrew use of the preposition ל (equivalent to εἰς) after copulative verbs.

b. Matt. vi. 34: μὴ οὖν μεριμνήσητε **εἰς τὴν αὔριον**, *be not therefore anxious for* (lit., "project not your anxieties into") *the morrow.*

Phil. i. 10: **εἰς ἡμέραν Χριστοῦ**, *unto the day of Christ.* So 2 Tim. i. 12. Eph. iv. 30 is slightly different, expressing more prominently the intent of the Spirit's "sealing."

Rev. ix. 15: ἡτοιμασμένοι **εἰς τὴν ὥραν καὶ ἡμέραν καὶ μῆνα καὶ ἐνιαυτόν**, *prepared for* (or unto) *the hour and day, and month and year, i.e.,* for the precise time appointed.

Acts xiii. 42: εἰς τὸ μεταξὺ σάββατον presents a little difficulty, as "*on* the next Sabbath" (A.V. and R.V.) seems rendering the preposition with undue licence. We must interpret either "for the next Sabbath"—the Gospel being regarded as a treasure reserved for that time (and perhaps, by *constructio prægnans* [see 8], *up to and on*)—or *during the intervening week* (A.V. marg.).

8. *Constructio prægnans.*—See under ἐν (8). As ἐν in a similar double construction implies the previous εἰς, so εἰς here implies the following ἐν.

Mark xiii. 16: ὁ **εἰς τὸν ἀγρὸν ὤν**,[1] "he who is into the field," *i.e.,* who has gone into the field and is in it. Matt. xxiv. 18 has ἐν.

Acts viii. 40: Φίλιππος εὑρέθη **εἰς Ἄζωτον**, *Philip was found* (to have been led) *to Azotus.*

Acts xxi. 13: ἀποθανεῖν **εἰς Ἱερουσαλήμ**, "to die into Jerusalem," *i.e.,* to go into Jerusalem and die there.

Heb. xi. 9: παρῴκησεν **εἰς γῆν**, "sojourned into the land," *i.e., travelled into the land and sojourned in it.*

In one passage, εἰς is apparently followed by a Genitive: Acts ii. 27, 31 (LXX., Ps. xvi. 10), εἰς ᾅδου,[2] *to Hades.* The phrase contains a classical ellipsis; οἰκίαν, *habitation,* being understood, and Hades being personified. "Thou wilt not abandon my soul to the realm of the Unseen."

Prepositions governing the Genitive and Accusative Cases.

διά, κατά, μετά, περί, ὑπέρ, ὑπό.[3]

299. διά, THROUGH, from the notion of separation, disjunction.

---

[1] W. H. and Rev. Text omit ὤν,—a reading which more vividly illustrates this construction.

[2] W. H. ᾅδην (see § 256, 7, *note*).

[3] In classic Greek, περί and ὑπό may take a Dative; also μετά in poets.

a. With the Genitive.

1. In reference to **place**: *through*, literally, *i.e.*, "through and from."

John iv. 4: ἔδει δὲ αὐτὸν διέρχεσθαι **διὰ τῆς Σαμαρείας**, *and he must needs go through Samaria*.

John xiv. 6: οὐδεὶς ἔρχεται πρὸς τὸν πατέρα εἰ μὴ **δι' ἐμοῦ**, *no one cometh to the Father but through me*—the Way.

1 Cor. iii. 15: σωθήσεται ... ὡς **διὰ τοῦ πυρός**, *he shall be saved as* (one who has passed) *through the fire*.

1 Cor. xiii. 12: βλέπομεν γὰρ ἄρτι **δι' ἐσόπτρου**, *for we see now through a mirror* (the image appearing to be on the opposite side).

2. In reference to **agency**: *through, by means of*.

Matt. i. 22: ῥηθὲν ὑπὸ Κυρίου **διὰ τοῦ προφήτου**, *spoken by the Lord through the prophet*. Here mark the distinction between ὑπό and διά, and compare ὑπό, § 304 (a).

1 Cor. iii. 5: διάκονοι **δι' ὧν** ἐπιστεύσατε, *ministers through whom ye believed*.

2 Thess. ii. 2: μήτε **διὰ πνεύματος**, μήτε **διὰ λόγου**, μήτε **δι' ἐπιστολῆς**, ὡς **δι' ἡμῶν**, *neither by spirit, nor by word, nor by letter as from us* (through us as the mediate authors).

Eph. i. 1, etc.: **διὰ θελήματος Θεοῦ**, *by the will of God*.

Eph. ii. 8, etc.: σεσωσμένοι **διὰ τῆς πίστεως**, *saved by faith*.

2 Cor. v. 10: τὰ **διὰ τοῦ σώματος**, *the things* (wrought) *by means of the body*.

3 John 13: οὐ θέλω **διὰ μέλανος καὶ καλάμου** γράφειν, *I do not wish to write with ink and pen*.

> This preposition is used, especially in such phrases as διὰ Ἰησοῦ Χριστοῦ, of Christ's mediatorial work in all its manifestations.[1] (Rom. ii. 16, v. 1; 2 Cor. i. 5; Gal. i. 1; Eph. i. 5; Phil. i. 11; Titus iii. 6.)
>
> Very rarely it seems to indicate the primary agent. 1 Cor. i. 9: πιστὸς ὁ Θεὸς δι' οὗ ἐκλήθητε, κ.τ.λ., *God is faithful, by* (R.V., *through*) *whom ye were called*, etc. Yet even here the proper force of διά is not lost. The Father is represented as acting on behalf of his Son, to bring Christians into fellowship with Him.

---

[1] Winer.

§ 299.]   διά, WITH THE GENITIVE AND ACCUSATIVE.   247

3. In reference to **time**, it marks the passage through an interval: (*a*) *during*, or (*b*) *after the lapse of*.

(*a*) Luke v. 5 : δι' ὅλης τῆς νυκτός, *all night*.

Heb. ii. 15 : διὰ παντὸς τοῦ ζῆν, *all through their life*.

The phrase διὰ (τῆς) νυκτός denotes *by night, i.e.,* during its lapse, no particular hour or hours being specified, Acts v. 19, xvi. 9, xvii. 10, xxiii. 31.   So Acts i. 3 : δι' ἡμερῶν τεσσαράκοντα, *at intervals during forty days*.

(*b*) Matt. xxvi. 61 ; Mark xiv. 58 : διὰ τριῶν ἡμερῶν, *three days afterwards*.

Gal. ii. 1 : διὰ δεκατεσσάρων ἐτῶν, *fourteen years after*. (Cf. 2 Cor. xii. 2.)

Compare Mark ii. 1 ; Acts xxiv. 17.

β. **With the Accusative.**

On account of: as in the frequent phrase διὰ τοῦτο, "on this account." So "because of," "for the sake of."

"**With the Genitive,** διὰ notes the instrument of an action; with the **Accusative,** its ground, *ratio*."[1]

Matt. x. 22, etc. : διὰ τὸ ὄνομά μου, *for my name's sake*.

Matt. xxiv. 12 : διὰ τὸ πληθυνθῆναι τὴν ἀνομίαν, *because of the abounding of the lawlessness*.

Eph. ii. 4 : διὰ τὴν πολλὴν ἀγάπην αὐτοῦ, *on account of his great love*.

John vi. 57 : ἐγὼ ζῶ διὰ τὸν πατέρα, *I live because of the Father, i.e.,* "because he liveth."

Heb. v. 12 : διὰ τὸν χρόνον, *on account of* (*i.e.*, considering) *the time that you have been Christians*.

Rom. viii. 11 : διὰ τὸ ἐνοικοῦν αὐτοῦ πνεῦμα, *on account of his indwelling Spirit*.

> The distinction between the Genitive and the Accusative should be marked in such passages as Rom. xii. 3, xv. 15. "I say to you," writes the Apostle in the former, διὰ τῆς χάριτος, *through the grace* given to me, *i.e.*, "the favour bestowed is the power by which I write;" but in the latter, διὰ τὴν χάριν, *on account of the grace* given me, "that I may worthily vindicate its bestowal."

---

[1] Winer.

An instance of a different kind is in Heb. ii. 10; δι' ὅν τὰ πάντα καὶ δι' οὗ τὰ πάντα, *for whom are all things and through whom are all things*, i.e., for his honour and by his agency. Compare also 1 Cor. xi. 9 and 12: διὰ τὴν γυναῖκα, *for the sake of the woman;* διὰ τῆς γυναικός, *by the woman,* i.e., in birth.

300. κατά, DOWN.

a. **With the Genitive**, " down from."

1. Literally, of **place**, *down.*

Matt. viii. 32 : ὥρμησε κατὰ τοῦ κρημνοῦ, *rushed down the steep.* Mark v. 13 ; Luke viii. 33.

1 Cor. xi. 4 : κατὰ κεφαλῆς ἔχων, *having* (something, *i.e.*, a veil, depending) *from the head.*

See also Mark xiv. 3; Acts xxvii. 14; 2 Cor. viii. 2.

2. Hence the more usual signification, *against, in opposition to* (the reverse of ὑπέρ, which see, § 303).

Mark xi. 25 : εἴ τι ἔχετε κατά τινος, *if ye have anything against any one.*

Acts xiv. 2 : ἐπήγειραν κατὰ τῶν ἀδελφῶν, *they raised up ... against the brethren.*

3. Occasionally in **asseverations**, *by.*

Matt. xxvi. 63 : ἐξορκίζω σε κατὰ τοῦ Θεοῦ, *I adjure thee by God.*

So Heb. vi. 13-16. 1 Cor. xv. 15 is probably to be referred to the same rule : " We have testified by God," though the rendering *against* might be admissible. " *Of* God," (A.V. and R.V.) is plainly incorrect.

4. As with the Accusative, *over, throughout,* a usage confined to Luke, and to the following passages :—

Luke iv. 14 : καθ' ὅλης τῆς περιχώρου, *through all the region round about.*

Luke xxiii. 5 ; Acts ix. 31, 42, x. 37.

β. **With the Accusative.**

1. *Throughout, among,* with singular or plural.

Luke viii. 39 : καθ' ὅλην τὴν πόλιν, *through the whole city.*

Acts viii. 1 : κατὰ τὰς χώρας τῆς Ἰουδαίας, *throughout the regions of Judæa.*

Acts xxvi. 3 : τῶν κατὰ Ἰουδαίους ἐθῶν, *of the customs among the Jews.*

§ 300.]   κατά, WITH THE ACCUSATIVE.   249

2. *Over against,* **locally.**

Luke ii. 31 : κατὰ πρόσωπον πάντων τῶν λαῶν, *before the face of all the peoples.*

So Acts ii. 10; Gal. ii. 11, iii. 1, etc.

3. In reference to **time,** *at* or *in,* "correspondent with," "at the period of" ("over against").

Matt. i. 20, etc.: κατ' ὄναρ, *in a dream.*

Acts xvi. 25 : κατὰ τὸ μεσονύκτιον, *at midnight.*

Rom. v. 6 : κατὰ καιρὸν, *in due time.*

4. Of place or time, **distributively,** *from one to another.*

Mark xiii. 8 : σεισμοὶ κατὰ τόπους, *earthquakes in divers places.*

Luke viii. 1 : διώδευε κατὰ πόλιν, *he was journeying from city to city.*

So κατ' ἔτος, *year by year,* Luke ii. 41 ; κατ' οἶκον, *at different houses,* Acts ii. 46, v. 42; κατὰ πᾶν σάββατον, *every Sabbath,* Acts xv. 21; καθ' ἡμέραν, *daily,* Matt. xxvi. 55, etc. (and the phrase καθ' εἷς, or καθεῖς, *one by one,* for εἷς καθ' ἕνα, Mark xiv. 19; John viii. 9; Rom. xii. 5).

5. From the meaning "over against" arises that of *according to,* in reference to some **standard of comparison,** stated or implied.

Matt. ix. 29 : κατὰ τὴν πίστιν ὑμῶν γενηθήτω, *according to your faith be it* unto you.

Luke ii. 39 : τὰ κατὰ τὸν νόμον Κυρίου, *the things according to the law of Jehovah.*

So in the phrases κατ' ἄνθρωπον, *as a man;* κατ' ἐμέ, *according to my ability or view;* κατὰ χάριν, *according to favour;* κατ' ἐξοχήν, *by way of pre-eminence,* Acts xxv. 23, etc. The phrase κατὰ Θεόν means, *in accordance with the character and will of God,* "divinely," as 2 Cor. vii. 9, 10, 11. Thus also, Rom. viii. 27, *He* (the Spirit) *divinely intercedes;*[1] Rom. xiv. 15, κατ' ἀγάπην, *according to love.*

- Heb. xi. 13: κατὰ πίστιν ἀπέθανον, *they died according to faith, i.e.,* in a way consistent with, corresponding to the spirit of faith; contented, though they had not seen the blessing.

6. Phrases like the foregoing often pass into an **adverbial** meaning.

Matt. xiv. 13, etc.: κατ' ἰδίαν, *alone.*

Acts xxviii. 16 : καθ' ἑαυτόν, *by himself.*

---

[1] Winer here prefers the rendering *before,* as (2) above, but, as it seems, without sufficient reason.

301. μετά, IN ASSOCIATION WITH (locally), distinguished from σύν, which implies *co-operation*, and is not necessarily local.

a. **With the Genitive,** "with and from," or separable connection.[1]

1. Of **persons,** *with,* amidst, among.

Matt. i. 23 : Ἐμμανουὴλ ... μεθ' ἡμῶν ὁ Θεός, *Emmanuel, God with us.*

Matt. xii. 3, etc.: οἱ μετ' αὐτοῦ, *those with him,* his companions.

So of two parties to a conversation or controversy.

John iv. 27 : μετὰ γυναικὸς ἐλάλει, *he was talking with a woman.*

See also Matt. xii. 41, 42, etc.

2. Of **attendant circumstances,** objects, states of mind (not instrumental), *together with.*

Matt. xxv. 4 : μετὰ τῶν λαμπάδων αὐτῶν, *with their lamps.*

Mark vi. 25 : εἰσελθοῦσα μετὰ σπουδῆς, *going in with haste.*

Heb. xii. 17 : μετὰ δακρύων ἐκζητήσας, *having sought with tears.*

1 Tim. iv. 14 : μετ' ἐπιθέσεως τῶν χειρῶν, *with* (not *by*) *the laying on of the hands.*

Matt. xxvii. 66 : μετὰ τῆς κουστωδίας, *together with the watch.*

3. The **object of a deed** of love, mercy, or the like, is sometimes spoken of, by this preposition, as associated with the agent.

Luke x. 37 : ὁ ποιήσας τὸ ἔλεος μετ' αὐτοῦ, *he who wrought the compassionate deed with him,* i.e., " who showed mercy towards him."

So in Acts xiv. 27, xv. 4 ; 1 John iv. 17.

β. **With the Accusative,** *after,* of **time** or **place.**

Matt. xxvi. 2 : μετὰ δύο ἡμέρας, *after two days.*

Luke v. 27, etc.: μετὰ ταῦτα, *after these things.*

Luke xxii. 20 : μετὰ τὸ δειπνῆσαι, *after supper;* 1 Cor. xi. 25.

Heb. ix. 3 : μετὰ τὸ δεύτερον καταπέτασμα, *beyond the second veil.*

302. περί, AROUND.

a. **With the Genitive,** " around and separate from."

About, concerning; chiefly as the **object of thought,** emotion, knowledge, discourse, etc.

---

[1] Donaldson. μετά is connected with μέσος, *midst.*

§ 303, a.]   περί, ὑπέρ.   251

Acts viii. 12 : εὐαγγελιζομένῳ περὶ τῆς βασιλείας τοῦ Θεοῦ (they believed Philip), *preaching concerning the kingdom of God.*

Matt. vi. 28 : περὶ ἐνδύματος τί μεριμνᾶτε; *why are ye anxious about raiment?*

Luke ii. 18 : ἐθαύμασαν περὶ τῶν λαληθέντων, *they wondered about the things that were spoken* (this verb more generally has ἐπί, "to wonder at").

Matt. ix. 36 : ἐσπλαγχνίσθη περὶ αὐτῶν, *he was compassionate about them* (also more generally with ἐπὶ, Dative or Accusative).

1 Thess. v. 25, etc. : προσεύχεσθε περὶ ἡμῶν, *pray for us.*

Rom. viii. 3 : ὁ Θεὸς τὸν ἑαυτοῦ υἱὸν πέμψας ... περὶ ἁμαρτίας, *God having sent his own Son ... for sin.* Compare Heb. x. 6, 8, 18, 26 ; 1 John ii. 2, iv. 10 ; also, perhaps, Gal. i. 4.[1] (See under ὑπέρ, § 303, a, 2.)

β. **With the Accusative,** "around and towards."

1. *Around,* of **place.**

Matt. viii. 18 : ἰδὼν ... ὄχλους περὶ αὐτόν, *seeing multitudes around him.*

Used of dress, etc., Matt. iii. 4 : περὶ τὴν ὀσφὺν αὐτοῦ, *about his loins.* So xviii. 6 ; Rev. xv. 6.

For the idiomatic expression, οἱ περὶ Παῦλον, see § 197.

2. *About,* of **time.**

Matt. xx. 3 : περὶ τρίτην ὥραν, *about the third hour.*

3. In reference to, *about,* of any **object of thought.**

Luke x. 40 : περιεσπᾶτο περὶ πολλὴν διακονίαν, *she was cumbered about much serving* (ver. 41).

1 Tim. i. 19 : περὶ τὴν πίστιν ἐναυάγησαν, *they made shipwreck in reference to the faith.*

See also Mark iv. 19; Acts xix. 25; 1 Tim. vi. 4, etc.

303. ὑπέρ, OVER.

a. **With the Genitive,** "over and separate from."

1. *On behalf of,* as though bending "over" to protect (the opposite of κατά). Of **persons.**

---

[1] W. H. read ὑπέρ with περί in marg.

Matt. v. 44 : προσεύχεσθε ὑπὲρ τῶν διωκόντων ὑμᾶς, *pray for*[1] *those who are persecuting you.*

Mark ix. 40 : ὃς γὰρ οὐκ ἔστι καθ' ἡμῶν ὑπὲρ ἡμῶν ἐστιν, *he who is not against us is for us.* Compare Rom. viii. 31.

2 Cor. v. 14, 15 : ὑπὲρ πάντων ἀπέθανεν, *he died for all.* So Rom. v. 6, 7, 8 ; Gal. ii. 20, iii. 13 ; Eph. v. 25 ; Heb. ii. 9 ; 1 Pet. ii. 21, etc.

Philemon 13 : ἵνα ὑπὲρ σοῦ μοι διακονῇ, *that he might minister to me for thee.*

As a service is often rendered *on behalf of* another by being offered *in his stead*, the notion of ὑπέρ may become interchangeable with that of ἀντί, as in the last passage. The distinction is, that ὑπέρ of itself leaves undetermined the way in which the service is performed, simply affirming the fact ; ἀντί, on the other hand, is definite. See Winer, § 47, *l*, n. 2.

2. Of **things,** *for their sake*, in various ways.

John xi. 4 : ὑπὲρ τῆς δόξης τοῦ Θεοῦ, *for the glory of God*, i.e., to promote it.

Rom. xv. 8 : ὑπὲρ ἀληθείας Θεοῦ, *for the truth of God*, i.e., to confirm his promises.

2 Cor. xii. 19 : ὑπὲρ τῆς ὑμῶν οἰκοδομῆς, *for your edification*, i.e., to minister to it.

Phil. ii. 13 : ὑπὲρ τῆς εὐδοκίας, *for* (his) *good pleasure*, i.e., to accomplish it.

Acts v. 41 : ὑπὲρ τοῦ ὀνόματος, *on behalf of the name* of Christ, i.e., to glorify it. Compare ix. 16 ; 3 John 7, etc.

1 Cor. xv. 3 : ἀπέθανεν ὑπὲρ τῶν ἁμαρτιῶν ἡμῶν, *he died for our sins*, i.e., to take them away. Compare Heb. v. 1, Gal. i. 4, etc. ; and see under περί, § 302, a.

3. *About,* "in reference to," simply ; the notion of benefit or service having disappeared.

2 Cor. viii. 23 : εἴτε ὑπὲρ Τίτου, *whether* (you inquire) *about Titus.*

2 Thess. ii. 1 : ὑπὲρ τῆς παρουσίας τοῦ Κυρίου, *in reference to the coming of the Lord.*

The passage, 1 Cor. xv. 29, βαπτιζόμενοι ὑπὲρ τῶν νεκρῶν, *baptised for*, or *on behalf of*, or *in reference to the dead*, possibly refers to some observance (perhaps local) in connection with the act of baptism, of which the trace is lost.

---

[1] More emphatic than περί in the same connection.

β. With the Accusative, " over and towards."

Beyond, above, used in comparison.

Matt. x. 24 : οὐκ ἔστι μαθητὴς ὑπὲρ τὸν διδάσκαλον, *a disciple is not above his teacher.*

2 Cor. i. 8 : ὑπὲρ δύναμιν ἐβαρήθημεν, *we were oppressed beyond our strength.*

So occasionally after a comparative adjective to add emphasis (Luke xvi. 8 ; Heb. iv. 12).

> Here, too, may be referred the use of ὑπέρ with adverbs, as 2 Cor. xi. 5, xii. 11, ὑπὲρ λίαν or ὑπερλίαν, *beyond measure;* also the "improper preposition" ὑπεράνω (from ἀνά), *up over,* governing the Genitive (Eph. i. 21, iv. 10; Heb. ix. 5). See under ὑπό, § 304, β, 1.

304. ὑπό, UNDER.

a. With the Genitive, "beneath and separate from."

This preposition marks that from which a fact, event, or action springs, *i.e.*, **the agent**; hence its meaning, *by,* especially after passive verbs.

Matt. iv. 1 : ἀνήχθη ὑπὸ τοῦ πνεύματος πειρασθῆναι ὑπὸ τοῦ διαβόλου, *he was led up by the Spirit to be tempted by the devil.*

Matt. v. 13 : καταπατεῖσθαι ὑπὸ τῶν ἀνθρώπων, *to be trodden under foot by men.*

> *Note.*—The **Agent** is signified by ὑπό.
> The **Instrument**, by the *Dative* alone.
> The **Minister** of another's will, by διά, *with the Genitive.*
> The **Motive** or **Cause**, by διά, *with the Accusative.*
> The **Occasion** may be signified by ἀπό.

β. With the Accusative, "under and towards."

1. *Under,* **locally** or **figuratively**.

Matt. v. 15 : τιθέασιν αὐτὸν ὑπὸ τὸν μόδιον, *they put it under the modius.*

Rom. vi. 14 : οὐ γάρ ἐστε ὑπὸ νόμον ἀλλ' ὑπὸ χάριν, *for ye are not under law, but under grace.*

In this sense, joined with the adverb κάτω (from κατά), ὑπό forms the "improper preposition" ὑποκάτω, *down under,* followed always by a Genitive, as Mark vi. 11, etc.

254   ὑπό, WITH ACCUSATIVE—ἐπί, WITH GENITIVE.   [§ 304, β.

2. *Close upon* ("under," as, *e.g.*, under a wall, hill, etc.), like the Latin *sub*, applied in the New Testament to **time** only, and in one passage—

Acts v. 21 : ὑπὸ τὸν ὄρθρον, *close upon the dawn*, "very early in the morning."

Prepositions governing the Genitive, Dative, and Accusative.

ἐπί, παρά, πρός.

305. ἐπί, UPON.

a. **With the Genitive,** "upon, and proceeding from," as, *e.g.*, a pillar upon the ground.

1. *On, upon,* **locally.**

Matt. vi. 10, etc. : ἐπὶ τῆς γῆς, *on the earth.*
Luke viii. 13 : οἱ δὲ ἐπὶ τῆς πέτρας, *and those upon the rock.*
John xix. 19 : ἐπὶ τοῦ σταυροῦ, *upon the cross.*
Acts xii. 21 : καθίσας ἐπὶ τοῦ βήματος, *sitting upon the throne* (lit., judgment-seat, tribunal). So xxv. 6. Compare Rev. iv. 9, 10, v. 13, vi. 16, etc. In Matt. xix. 28, ἐπί in this sense has both the Genitive and the Accusative.

2. *Over,* of **superintendence,** government, etc.

Acts vi. 3 : οὓς καταστήσομεν ἐπὶ τῆς χρείας ταύτης, *whom we will set over this business.*
Rom. ix. 5 : ὁ ὢν ἐπὶ πάντων, *who is over all*

3. **On the basis of,** figuratively, *upon.*

John vi. 2 : τὰ σημεῖα ἃ ἐποίει ἐπὶ τῶν ἀσθενούντων, *the miracles which he was working upon the afflicted.*

>Compare Gal. iii. 16, etc.
>
>Here, too, may be referred the phrase, ἐπ' ἀληθείας, *in truth* (Mark xii. 14; Luke iv. 25, etc.), *i.e.*, "on a basis of truth."

4. **In the presence of,** especially *before* a tribunal.

1 Cor. vi. 1 : κρίνεσθαι ἐπὶ τῶν ἀδίκων καὶ οὐχὶ ἐπὶ τῶν ἁγίων, *to be judged before the unrighteous, and not before the holy.*

>So Acts xxiii. 30, xxiv. 19, xxv. 9, 26, xxvi. 2; 1 Tim. vi. 13.

§ 305.] ἐπί, WITH THE GENITIVE AND DATIVE. 255

1 Tim. v. 19 : ἐπὶ δύο ἢ τριῶν μαρτύρων, *before two or three witnesses.* But see 2 Cor. xiii. 1 : ἐπὶ στόματος, κ.τ.λ., *upon the testimony* (mouth), where the preposition, from the LXX., denotes basis; as in (3), above.

5. **In the time of.**

Luke iii. 2 : ἐπὶ ἀρχιερέως Ἄννα, *in the high-priesthood of Annas* (R.V.) Acts xi. 28 : ἐπὶ Κλαυδίου, *in the days of Claudius.*

Matt. i. 11 : ἐπὶ τῆς μετοικεσίας Βαβυλῶνος, *at the time of the deportation to Babylon.*

Rom. i. 10 : ἐπὶ τῶν προσευχῶν μου, *at the time of my prayers;* 1 Thess. i. 2 ; Philemon 4.

1 Pet. i. 20 : ἐπ' ἐσχάτων τῶν χρόνων, *in the last times;* Heb. i. 2 ; 2 Pet. iii. 3; Jude 18 (W. H.).

In Mark xii. 26 ; ἐπὶ τοῦ βάτου, *at the Bush,* means, "at the Old Testament section entitled 'The Bush.'"

6. *Constructio prægnans.*—This preposition with the Genitive sometimes (see under ἐν, 8) implies the foregoing motion.

Matt. xxvi. 12 : βαλοῦσα ... τὸ μύρον τοῦτο ἐπὶ τοῦ σώματός μου, *having poured ... this ointment on my body.*

Mark xiv. 35 : ἔπιπτεν ἐπὶ τῆς γῆς, *he fell upon the ground.*

β. **With the Dative,** "resting upon."

1. *On, upon,* **locally**; like the Genitive, except that the point of view is different. (See α, 1, also γ, 1.)

Luke xix. 44 : οὐκ ἀφήσουσιν ... λίθον ἐπὶ λίθῳ,[1] *they will not leave ... stone resting upon stone.* See also chap. xxi. 6.

2. *Over,* of **superintendence,** etc. (See α, 2, also γ, 2.)

Luke xii. 44 : ἐπὶ τοῖς ὑπάρχουσι, *over the goods.*

3. *On* (at), as the **groundwork** of any fact or circumstance.

Matt. iv. 4 : οὐκ ἐπ' ἄρτῳ μόνῳ ζήσεται, *shall not live on bread alone.*

Luke v. 5 : ἐπὶ τῷ ῥήματί σου χαλάσω τὸ δίκτυον, *at thy word I will let down the net.*

---

[1] But W. H. read λίθον (cf. γ, 1). In Luke xxi. 6 the Dat. is undisputed, and the student will note that in the one case the verb is *active* (implying motion), in the other *passive.*

Acts xi. 19 : τῆς θλίψεως τῆς γενομένης ἐπὶ Στεφάνῳ, *the affliction that arose about Stephen.*

Mark ix. 37, etc.: ἐπὶ τῷ ὀνόματί μου, *in my name.* (Compare Matt. xxviii. 19 with Acts ii. 38.)

Rom. viii. 20 : ἐπ' ἐλπίδι, *in hope, i.e.,* "resting on the basis of a hope that," etc.

2 Cor. ix. 6 : ἐπ' εὐλογίαις, *on a groundwork of blessings, i.e.,* "bountifully."

1 Thess. iv. 7 : οὐ γὰρ ἐκάλεσεν ἡμᾶς ὁ Θεὸς ἐπὶ ἀκαθαρσίᾳ, *for God called us not on the ground of impurity,* or perhaps as (5). (R.V., *for uncleanness.*)

> So the phrase ἐφ' ᾧ, "on the condition being realised that," *wherefore, because* (Rom. v. 12, etc.).

4. Over and above, *in addition to;* as by one fact resting upon another.

Luke xvi. 26 : ἐπὶ πᾶσι τούτοις, *beside all these.*

2 Cor. vii. 13 : ἐπὶ τῇ παρακλήσει ἡμῶν, (W. H.) *in addition to our comfort.*

5. *Constructio prægnans.*—(See *a*, 6.) The force of the Accusative also is sometimes implied.

Matt. ix. 16 : οὐδεὶς ἐπιβάλλει ... ἐπὶ ἱματίῳ παλαιῷ, *no one putteth ... upon an old garment.*

γ. **With the Accusative,** "upon, by direction towards."

1. *Upon,* with motion implied.

Matt. v. 15 : τιθέασιν ἐπὶ τὴν λυχνίαν, *they put* (it) *upon the lampstand.*
Matt. vii. 24 : ᾠκοδόμησεν ἐπὶ τὴν πέτραν, *he built upon the rock.*
Matt. xiv. 29 : περιεπάτησεν ἐπὶ τὰ ὕδατα, *he walked upon the waters.*
Matt. xxiv. 2 : λίθος ἐπὶ λίθον. See the Dative in the same connection, β, 1, *note.* The notion there is of rest, simply ; here, perhaps, of downward pressure.

> So after the verb ἐλπίζω, *to hope;* ἐπί, with the Dat., 1 Tim. iv. 10 ; with the Acc., v. 5. In the one case, the hope is said to rest upon, as a fact ; in the other, to be placed upon, as an act. So after πείθω, 2 Cor. i. 9, compared with ii. 3. The difference is so **slight, that the** expressions are easily interchangeable.

§ 305.]   ἐπί, WITH THE ACCUSATIVE.   257

Constructio prægnans.—In Matt. xix. 28; 2 Cor. iii. 15, and some other passages.

2. *Over,* of authority, **superintendence.**

Luke i. 33: βασιλεύσει ἐπὶ τὸν οἶκον Ἰακώβ, *he shall reign over the house of Jacob.*

Heb. ii. 7: κατέστησας αὐτὸν ἐπὶ τὰ ἔργα, κ.τ.λ., *thou didst set him over the works of thy hands.*

> The three cases with this meaning seem "interchangeable," *i.e.*, the notions which they respectively express are so nearly allied that any of them may be employed without materially altering the sense. The Dative, however, and not the Accusative, is used when the preposition follows a verb of existence; the Accusative, and not the Dative, when the verb is transitive. The Examples (*a*, 2) show that the Genitive may be with either.

3. *To,* implying an **intention** (for, against).

Matt. iii. 7: ἐρχομένους ἐπὶ τὸ βάπτισμα, *coming for his baptism.*

Mark v. 21: συνήχθη ὄχλος πολὺς ἐπ' αὐτόν, *a great multitude was gathered together to him.*

So Luke xxiii. 48.

Matt. xxvi. 55: ὡς ἐπὶ λῃστὴν ἐξήλθατε; *are ye come out as against a robber?*

4. *Towards,* the direction of thought, feeling, speech.

Luke vi. 35; αὐτὸς χρηστός ἐστιν ἐπὶ τοὺς ἀχαρίστους καὶ πονηρούς, *he is kind to the unthankful and wicked.*

2 Cor. ii. 3: πεποιθὼς ἐπὶ πάντας ὑμᾶς, *having confidence with regard to you all.*

Mark ix. 12: γέγραπται ἐπὶ τὸν υἱὸν τοῦ ἀνθρώπου, *it is written with regard to the Son of man.*

Matt. xv. 32: σπλαγχνίζομαι ἐπὶ τὸν ὄχλον, *I have compassion on the multitude.* This verb and preposition are also found with the Dative (see β, 3); *i.e.*, the compassion may be conceived as *moving towards,* or as *resting on,* the multitude, Luke vii. 13. The verb has also περί (Gen.), *concerned about* the multitude, Matt. ix. 36.

5. Of **number** or quantity, *up to.*

Acts iv. 17: ἐπὶ πλεῖον, *to a further point,* "any further."

s

Rev. xxi. 16 : ἐπὶ σταδίους δώδεκα χιλιάδων, *to twelve thousands of stadia.*

Matt. xxv. 40, etc. : ἐφ᾽ ὅσον, *inasmuch as.* So of time, *as long as,* Matt. ix. 15, Rom. vii. 1.

With numeral adverbs, Acts x. 16, xi. 10. So in the compound adverb, ἐφάπαξ, *once for all,* at once (Rom. vi. 10; 1 Cor. xv. 6; Heb. vii. 27, ix. 12, x. 10).

6. Of **time,** *over, during, on.*

Luke x. 35 : ἐπὶ τὴν αὔριον, *in the course of the morrow.*
Luke xviii. 4 : οὐκ ἠθέλησεν ἐπὶ χρόνον, *he would not for a time.*
Acts xiii. 31 : ὤφθη ἐπὶ ἡμέρας πλείους, *he was seen during several days.*

So in the phrase, ἐπὶ τὸ αὐτό, *at the same place,* or *time,* "together" (Luke xvii. 35; Acts ii. 1; 1 Cor. vii. 5, etc.).

306. παρά, BESIDE (of juxtaposition).

α. **With the Genitive,** "beside and proceeding from."

With **persons only :** *from,* generally with the notion of something imparted.

Matt. ii. 4 : ἐπυνθάνετο παρ᾽ αὐτῶν, *he inquired of them.*
Phil. iv. 18 : δεξάμενος παρ᾽ Ἐπαφροδίτου τὰ παρ᾽ ὑμῶν, *having received of Epaphroditus the things from you.*
John xvi. 27 : παρὰ τοῦ πατρὸς ἐξῆλθον, *I came forth from the Father.* Compare John i. 14.
Matt. xxi. 42 : παρὰ Κυρίου ἐγένετο αὕτη, *this was from Jehovah* — "his doing," from LXX., Ps. cxviii. 23.
Mark iii. 21 : οἱ παρ᾽ αὐτοῦ, *those from him, i.e.,* from his home or family, his friends.

β. **With the Dative,** "beside and at."

1. *With, near,* of **persons** only, except John xix. 25.

John xiv. 17 : παρ᾽ ὑμῖν μένει, *he remains with you.*
Acts x. 6 : ξενίζεται παρά τινι Σίμωνι, *he lodges with one Simon.*
John xix. 25 : παρὰ τῷ σταυρῷ, *near the cross.*

2. *With,* in the estimation or power of,

§ 307.] παρά, WITH ACCUSATIVE—πρός, WITH GENITIVE. 259

Matt. xix. 26 : παρὰ ἀνθρώποις... ἀδύνατον, παρὰ δὲ Θεῷ πάντα δυνατά, *with men ... impossible ; but with God all things are possible.*
Rom. ii. 13 : δίκαιοι παρὰ τῷ Θεῷ, *just with God.*
Rom. xii. 16 : φρόνιμοι παρ' ἑαυτοῖς, *wise in your own esteem.*

γ. **With the Accusative,** " to or along the side of."

1. *By, near,* after verbs implying motion ; also rest by an extended object, as the sea.

Matt. xiii. 4 : ἔπεσε παρὰ τὴν ὁδόν, *it fell along the way,* or *path.*

Acts iv. 35 : ἐτίθουν παρὰ τοὺς πόδας τῶν ἀποστόλων, *they laid them at the apostles' feet.*

Acts x. 6 : ᾧ ἐστιν οἰκία παρὰ θάλασσαν, *whose house is by the seaside.*

2. Beside, as **not coinciding with,** hence *contrary to.*

Acts xviii. 13 : παρὰ νόμον, *contrary to law.*
Rom. i. 26 : παρὰ φύσιν, *contrary to nature.*
Rom. iv. 18 : παρ' ἐλπίδα, *contrary to hope.*
Rom. i. 25 : παρὰ τὸν κτίσαντα, *instead of the Creator;* or possibly, *rather than,* as (3) (R.V.).

3. Beside, with the notion of **comparison,** superiority, *above.*[1]

Luke xiii. 2 : ἁμαρτωλοὶ παρὰ πάντας, *sinners above all.*
Rom. xiv. 5 : κρίνει ἡμέραν παρ' ἡμέραν, *esteems day above day, i.e.,* one above another.
Heb. ix. 23 : κρείττοσι θυσίαις παρὰ ταύτας, *with better sacrifices than these.* So i. 4, iii. 3, xi. 4, xii. 24 ; Luke iii. 13.

4. From juxtaposition arises the notion of **consequence,**[2] in the phrase παρὰ τοῦτο, 1 Cor. xii. 15, 16, *therefore.*

307. πρός, TOWARDS.

a. **With Genitive,** "hitherwards."

Belonging to the part or character of,[3] *conducive to,* in one instance only—

---

[1] See ὑπέρ. The difference is, that ὑπέρ *affirms* superiority, παρά *institutes* comparison, and leaves the reader to *infer* superiority.
[2] So in Latin, *propter,* because of, from *prope,* near.
[3] So in classical Greek, πρὸς κακοῦ ἀνδρός.

Acts xxvii. 34 : τοῦτο γὰρ πρὸς τῆς ὑμετέρας σωτηρίας ὑπάρχει, *for this is for your health*.

β. With Dative, " resting in a direction towards."
Near, hard by—
Luke xix. 37 : πρὸς τῇ καταβάσει, *close to the descent.*
John xviii. 16 : πρὸς τῇ θύρᾳ ἔξω, *close to the door outside.*
John xx. 12 : ἕνα πρὸς τῇ κεφαλῇ καὶ ἕνα πρὸς τοῖς ποσίν, *one at the head and the other at the feet.*
Rev. i. 13 : πρὸς τοῖς μαστοῖς, *about the breast.*
    These are the only undoubted instances in the New Testament. W. H. and Rev. Text add Mark v. 11, John xx. 11, in the same sense.

γ. With the Accusative, " hitherwards."
1. *Unto,* of **literal direction.**
Matt. xi. 28 : δεῦτε πρός με, *come unto me.*
Matt. xxiii. 34 : ἀποστέλλω πρὸς ὑμᾶς προφήτας, *I send unto you prophets.*
Luke i. 19 : λαλῆσαι πρός σε, *to speak unto thee.*
1 Cor. xiii. 12 : πρόσωπον πρὸς πρόσωπον, *face to face.* 2 John 12 ; 3 John 14.

2. After the substantive verb (*constructio prægnans*), *with.*
Matt. xiii. 56 : οὐχὶ πᾶσαι πρὸς ἡμᾶς εἰσι; *are they not all with us?*
John i. 1 : ὁ λόγος ἦν πρὸς[1] τὸν Θεόν, THE WORD WAS WITH GOD.

3. Of **mental direction,** *towards, against.*
Luke xxiii. 12 : ἐν ἔχθρᾳ ὄντες πρὸς ἑαυτούς, *being in enmity towards themselves;* i.e., the one with the other.
1 Thess. v. 14 : μακροθυμεῖτε πρὸς πάντας, *be long-suffering towards all.*
Acts vi. 1 : γογγυσμὸς πρὸς τοὺς Ἑβραίους, *a murmuring against the Hebrews.*
Col. ii. 23 : οὐκ ἐν τιμῇ τινί πρὸς πλησμονὴν τῆς σαρκός, *not of any value against the indulgence of the flesh* (R.V.).

4. From the general notion of mental direction arises (i) that of **estimation** or proportion, *in consideration of.*
Matt. xix. 8 : πρὸς τὴν σκληροκαρδίαν ὑμῶν, *in consideration of the hardness of your hearts.*

---
[1] Very significant here as implying *motion* and *life.*

§ 309.] πρός, WITH THE ACCUSATIVE. 261

Luke xii. 47 : πρὸς τὸ θέλημα αὐτοῦ, *in consideration of* (in accordance with) *his will.*

Rom. viii. 18 : οὐκ ἄξια... πρὸς τὴν μέλλουσαν δόξαν ἀποκαλυφθῆναι, *unworthy* (of thought) ... *in consideration of the glory that is to be revealed.*

5. Also (ii.) that of **intention,** *in order to,* especially with the Infinitive.

1 Cor. x. 11 : ἐγράφη δὲ πρὸς νουθεσίαν ἡμῶν, *and they were written for our admonition.*

Matt. vi. 1 : πρὸς τὸ θεαθῆναι αὐτοῖς, *in order to be gazed at by them.*

ON THE INTERCHANGE OF CERTAIN PREPOSITIONS.

308. Although no two prepositions are synonymous, they often approach one another so nearly in meaning as to be apparently interchangeable. It is sometimes important to notice the distinction; at other times it appears to be of little or no importance.

Yet it is always safer to look for a real difference in meaning. Compare what has been said on the meaning of ἐπί in the government of the three cases. (See also § 289.)

Without entering into over-refined or needless details, it will be sufficient here to cite some of the principal instances of real or seeming interchange, with such brief explanations as may indicate the general principles on which these cases are to be judged.

309. διά, with the Genitive, is especially subject to these alternations of expression.

1. With ἐκ. Rom. iii. 30 : εἷς ὁ Θεός, ὃς δικαιώσει περιτομὴν ἐκ πίστεως, καὶ ἀκροβυστίαν διὰ τῆς πίστεως, *God is one, who will justify the circumcision by faith, and the uncircumcision by means of the* (same) *faith.* In the former case the source of the justification is more distinctly marked; in the latter, the means.

See also 2 Pet. iii. 5, etc.

2. With ἀπό. Gal. i. 1 : Παῦλος ἀπόστολος οὐκ ἀπ' ἀνθρώπων οὐδὲ δι' ἀνθρώπου, *Paul an apostle neither* (originally commissioned) *from men,*

nor through (the intervention of) *any man;* the latter particular being added to show how absolutely independent his designation had been even of human *instrumentality.* The ordination to the ministry, in general, is ἀπὸ Θεοῦ, but δι' ἀνθρώπων.

3. With ἐν. 2 Cor. iii. 11: εἰ γὰρ τὸ καταργούμενον διὰ δόξης, πολλῷ μᾶλλον τὸ μένον ἐν δόξῃ, *for if that which is being done away* (was) *by means of* (through the intervention of) *glory* (*i.e.*, a glorious display), *much more that which abideth* (is) *in glory.*

> Other instances are in Heb. xi. 2 (compare with 39); Rom. iv. 11, where ἐν ἀκροβυστίᾳ refers to that period in Abraham's life when, though in uncircumcision, he believed; but δι' ἀκροβυστίας being ruled by πιστευόντων, sets forth the possibility of men believing, through the state of uncircumcision, from age to age. Rom. v. 10. "For if, being enemies, we were reconciled to God through the (merits of the) death of his Son, much more we shall be saved by (his intercession, with the teaching of) his (resurrection) life." 1 John v. 6. In 1 Cor. i. 21 the distinction is plain: *in the wisdom of God, i.e.,* according to the wise appointment of Him who left mankind to make the effort, *the world by* (διά) *its wisdom, i.e.,* by the exercise of its reason, *knew not God* (including both failure and perversion).

4. In Romans xi. 36 the respective meaning of ἐκ, διά, εἰς (the starting-point, the course, the goal), are finely marked: ἐξ αὐτοῦ καὶ δι' αὐτοῦ καὶ εἰς αὐτὸν τὰ πάντα, all things are from him as their author, through him as their controller, to him as their end.

> See also 2 Cor. i. 16.

Eph. iv. 6 presents a somewhat different antithesis: ὁ ἐπὶ πάντων καὶ διὰ πάντων καὶ ἐν πᾶσιν, *who is over all and through all and in all.* 1 Cor. xii. 8, 9, has another combination: διὰ τοῦ πνεύματος ... κατὰ τὸ αὐτὸ πνεῦμα ... ἐν τῷ αὐτῷ πνεύματι,—" the word of wisdom is given *through the Spirit;* the word of knowledge *according to the same Spirit;* faith, *in the same Spirit*": the Spirit bestowing the gift according to His own love and might, while He himself becomes the element of the Christian life.

310. ἐκ and ἀπό may sometimes be interchanged without injury to the general sense; although the distinction is real.

Matt. vii. 16: μήτι συλλέγουσιν ἀπὸ ἀκανθῶν σταφυλάς; *surely they do not gather bunches of grapes from off thorns?*

§ 312.] INTERCHANGE OF PREPOSITIONS. 263

Luke vi. 44 : οὐ γὰρ ἐξ ἀκανθῶν συλλέγουσι σῦκα, *for they do not gather figs out of thorn-bushes.*
Heb. vii. 2 : δεκάτην ἀπὸ πάντων, *a tithe of all.* Ver. 4 : δεκάτην ... ἐκ τῶν ἀκροθινίων, *a tithe out of the spoils.*
1 Thess. ii. 6 : οὔτε ζητοῦντες ἐξ ἀνθρώπων δόξαν, οὔτε ἀφ' ὑμῶν οὔτε ἀπ' ἄλλων, *nor seeking glory from men, either of you or of others.*

See also John xi. 1. In these passages it is immaterial whether the phrase "*out of* a thing" or "*from* a thing" be employed; but in the following there is an evident distinction:—

John vii. 42 : ἐκ τοῦ σπέρματος Δαβὶδ καὶ ἀπὸ Βηθλεέμ, *out of the seed of David and from Bethlehem.*

2 Cor. iii. 5 : οὐχ ὅτι ἀφ' ἑαυτῶν ἱκανοί ἐσμεν λογίσασθαί τι ὡς ἐξ αὐτῶν, *not that we are sufficient of ourselves to think anything as from ourselves.*

311. ἐν is occasionally interchanged with a simple Dative.

So Col. ii. 13 : νεκροὶ ἐν[1] τοῖς παραπτώμασι, *dead in transgressions;* Eph. ii. 1 : νεκροὶ τοῖς παραπτώμασι. So Matt. vii. 2 : ἐν ᾧ μέτρῳ μετρεῖτε, *in what measure ye mete;* Luke vi. 38 : ᾧ γὰρ μέτρῳ μετρεῖτε, *with what measure ye mete.* Again, Luke iii. 16 : ὕδατι βαπτίζω, *I baptise with water;* so Acts i. 5, xi. 16 ; but ἐν ὕδατι, *in water,* Matt. iii. 11 ; John i. 26, 33. The expressions are evidently equivalent, however the act be understood.

The opposites ἐν and ἐκ may in some cases be used in the same connection. Thus, Matthew (xxii. 37) gives "the great commandment" as, Thou shalt love the Lord thy God *in* (ἐν) all thy heart, etc. ; Mark (xii. 30), *out of* (ἐξ) all thy heart; the love being regarded in one case as abiding in the heart, in the other as manifested by it. The LXX. (Deut. vi. 5) has ἐξ.

312. εἰς may often be interchanged with other forms of expression.

1. With πρός. Rom. iii. 25 : εἰς ἔνδειξιν ... ver. 26 : πρὸς τὴν ἔνδειξιν τῆς δικαιοσύνης αὐτοῦ, *in order to the manifestation...tending to the manifestation of his righteousness.* The former expression refers to a completed manifestation, the latter to one still in progress.

Philemon, ver. 5 : "thy love and thy faith," πρὸς[2] τὸν κύριον Ἰησοῦν

---
[1] But W. H. omit ἐν.
[2] W. H. read εἰς with πρὸς marg. The similarity of meaning between different prepositions has occasioned many various readings, transcribers having caught at the general sense without noting the finer shades of meaning.

καὶ εἰς πάντας τοὺς ἁγίους, *towards the Lord Jesus and unto all the saints.*

This seems nothing more than a variation in expression, although by some it is explained on the principle of reverted parallelism:

"thy love
and thy faith
towards the Lord Jesus
and to all the saints,"

i.e., love to the saints, and faith towards the Lord Jesus.

2. With ἐπί. These instances are very frequent, and need no special remark.

Matt. xxiv. 16 : φευγέτωσαν ἐπὶ[1] τὰ ὄρη, *let them flee up to the mountains.* Mark xiii. 14 : φευγέτωσαν εἰς τὰ ὄρη, *let them flee into the mountains.*

Rom. iii. 22 : δικαιοσύνη Θεοῦ ... εἰς πάντας καὶ ἐπὶ πάντας[2] τοὺς πιστεύοντας, *the righteousness of God unto all and upon all who believe*, *i.e.*, "*so communicated to as to abide upon.*"

3. Interchanged with a simple Dative.

Matt. v. 21, 22 : ἔνοχος τῇ κρίσει ... ἔνοχος εἰς τὴν γέενναν τοῦ πυρός, *liable to the judgment ... liable to* (up to the point of) *the Gehenna of fire.*

Rom. xi. 24 : ἐνεκεντρίσθης εἰς καλλιέλαιον ... ἐγκεντρισθήσονται τῇ ἰδίᾳ ἐλαίᾳ, *thou wast grafted into a good olive tree ... they shall be grafted on their own olive.*

4. The remarkable phrase, 2 Cor. iv. 17, in which εἰς is combined with κατά in one rhetorical expression, claims a reference here : καθ' ὑπερβολὴν εἰς ὑπερβολήν, A.V., "far more exceeding," R.V., "more and more exceedingly," literally, *according to abundance* (on a scale of vastness) *unto an abundance* (to the realisation of that which is immeasurable).

5. The many instances in which εἰς seems to be used for ἐν, and *vice versâ*, may be explained by *constructio prægnans*. (See § 295, 8.) The two prepositions are found in the same connection : Matt. iv. 18, compared with Mark i. 16 ; Mark xi. 8, with Matt. xxi. 8 ; Mark xiii. 16, with Matt. xxiv. 18.

---

[1] W. H. εἰς with ἐπί marg.
[2] W. H. omit καὶ ἐπὶ πάντας.

§ 314.]   INTERCHANGE OF PREPOSITIONS.   265

313. περί, *about* (with Genitive), may be substituted for a more definite preposition, and the converse, *e.g.*—

1. For διά (with Accusative). John x. 32: our Lord asks, διὰ ποῖον αὐτῶν ἔργον ἐμὲ λιθάζετε; *for which work of these do ye stone me?* The answer is, ver. 33: περὶ καλοῦ ἔργου οὐ λιθάζομέν σε ἀλλὰ περὶ βλασφημίας, *for a good work we stone thee not, but for blasphemy.*

2. For ὑπέρ. See under ὑπέρ and περί, §§ 302, 303.

Verbs signifying prayer, thanksgiving, etc., may be followed by either indifferently. *I pray about you,* περί, "you are the subject of my prayers;" or, *I pray for you,* ὑπέρ, "your welfare is the object of my prayers."

So in the many passages in respect of the death of Christ, which theological inquirers will do well to examine. In some, as in Gal. i. 4, the reading of good MSS. varies between ὑπέρ and περί.

314. A Preposition governing several words in one regimen is repeated before each of them if a distinction, severally, between them is to be marked; but if they are combined in one notion, the preposition is not repeated.

> This rule is analogous to that respecting the repetition of the article (§ 232). Yet the article is often repeated where the preposition is not.

Thus with the repeated preposition—

Matt. xxii. 37: ἐν ὅλῃ καρδίᾳ σου, καὶ ἐν ὅλῃ τῇ ψυχῇ σου, καὶ ἐν ὅλῃ τῇ διανοίᾳ σου, *with all thy heart, and with all thy soul, and with all thy understanding.* Compare Mark xii. 30 (ἐξ, see § 311, *note*).

> For other instances, see Mark vi. 4 (ἐν); Luke xxiv. 27 (ἀπό); 1 Thess. i. 5 (ἐν); John xx. 2 (πρός), etc.

With the preposition not repeated—

John iv. 23: ἐν πνεύματι καὶ ἀληθείᾳ, *in spirit and truth,* one state of mind, viewed under a twofold aspect. In like manner we interpret iii. 5, ἐξ ὕδατος καὶ πνεύματος, of one spiritual baptism, not of two things (as the outward and the inward). So Matt. iii. 11.

> For other instances, see Luke xxi. 26 (ἀπό); Phil. i. 15 (διά); and very frequently with proper names when closely connected, as Phil. i. 2, Acts vi. 9, etc.

Where the nouns after the preposition are connected by the disjunctive *or*, the preposition is always repeated; as also where they stand in antithesis. Acts iv. 7 : ἐν ποίᾳ δυνάμει ἢ ἐν ποίῳ ὀνόματι ἐποιήσατε τοῦτο ὑμεῖς; *in what power or in what name did ye this?* John vii. 22 : οὐχ ὅτι ἐκ τοῦ Μωυσέως ἐστίν, ἀλλ' ἐκ τῶν πατέρων, *not that it is from Moses, but from the fathers.* But where the antithesis is formed by two adjectives agreeing with the same noun, the preposition need not be repeated. 1 Pet. i. 23 : οὐκ ἐκ σπορᾶς φθαρτῆς, ἀλλὰ ἀφθάρτου, *not of corruptible, but of incorruptible seed.*

NOTE ON VERBS COMPOUNDED WITH PREPOSITIONS.

For the general meaning of the Prepositions in composition, see § 147. In most cases the preposition has a simple and evident force. The verb contains the general notion, the preposition indicates originally some space relation (§§ 124, 288); the compound verb expresses the general verbal notion limited to that definite space relation.

Thus, ἔρχομαι, *to come;* εἰσέρχομαι, *to come in, enter.* βαίνω, *to go;* παραβαίνω, *to go beside, transgress.* χαίρω, *to rejoice;* συγχαίρω, *to rejoice with.*

The prepositions ἀπό, ἐκ, κατά have often an *intensive* force.

As to the *cases* after compound verbs : (1) the Preposition may blend so intimately with the verb as to form a practically simple transitive verb governing the Accusative ; or (2) the Preposition may retain its distinct prepositional force, when the verb (*a*) is followed by the same preposition ; (*b*) is followed by a preposition of kindred meaning ; (*c*) is not followed by a preposition, but governs the case appropriate.

Examples : 1. ἀποδίδωμι, *to give away from* one's self, *bestow, pay back ;* followed like the simple δίδωμι by acc. of thing, dat. of person.

2. (a) ἐπιβάλλω (τὰς χεῖρας) ἐπί τινα, *to lay* (hands) *upon*, Matt. xxvi. 50.

(b) ἐκβάλλω ἀπό τινος, *to cast out from*, Mark xvi. 9 ; Acts xiii. 50 (generally with ἐκ).

(c) συμβάλλω τινι, *to dispute with*, Acts xvii. 18.

The usage of particular verbs must be gathered by observation.

§ 316.] ADJECTIVES—CONCORD. 267

CHAPTER IV. ADJECTIVES.

315. Adjectives, as also Participles and Adjective Pronouns, agree with their Substantives in Gender, Number, and Case (according to the Second Concord, § 178).

An adjective may be an Epithet (attribute) or a Predicate, the rule applying in both cases. For the adjective as predicate, see §§ 178-180.

316. Where the reference of the Adjective is plain, the Substantive is often omitted. Compare § 199.

Matt. xi. 5 : τυφλοὶ ἀναβλέπουσιν καὶ χωλοὶ περιπατοῦσιν, λεπροὶ καθαρίζονται καὶ κωφοὶ ἀκούουσιν, καὶ νεκροὶ ἐγείρονται καὶ πτωχοὶ εὐαγγελίζονται · *blind* (men) *are restored to sight and lame* (men) *walk, leprous* (men) *are cleansed and deaf* (men) *hear, and dead* (men) *are raised and destitute* (men) *have glad tidings brought to them.*

Rom. v. 7 : μόλις γὰρ ὑπὲρ δικαίου τις ἀποθανεῖται · ὑπὲρ γὰρ τοῦ ἀγαθοῦ τάχα τις καὶ τολμᾷ ἀποθανεῖν · *for scarcely for a righteous* (man) *will one die, for on behalf of the good* (man) *one perchance even dares to die.*

1 Cor. ii. 13 : πνευματικοῖς πνευματικὰ συγκρίνοντες, *putting together spirituals with spirituals, i.e.,* " attaching spiritual words to spiritual things " (Alford) ; or, " interpreting spiritual things by spiritual ;" or, " explaining spiritual things to spiritual men " (Stanley, R.V. marg.) ; or, " adapting spiritual language to spiritual matters " (Beza).

The last example shows how an occasional ambiguity will arise. In general, however, the application of the adjective will be perfectly plain.

Among the substantives most frequently omitted after Adjectives, beside the words for *man, woman, thing,* with the three genders respectively, are the following—

χείρ, *hand,* as ἡ δεξιά, " the right."

γῆ, *land,* as ἡ οἰκουμένη, the inhabited, " the world " (Rom. x. 18, etc.).

ἡμέρα, *day,* as τῇ ἐπιούσῃ, " on the morrow."

ὕδωρ, *water,* as ποτήριον ψυχροῦ, " a cup of cold " (Matt. x. 42 ; compare James iii. 11.)

Acts xix. 35 is peculiar: **τοῦ Διοπετοῦς,** *of that which fell from Zeus:* not "an image,"—probably a great meteoric stone.

For the neuter article, especially, as substantivising the Adjective, *i.e.*, making it an abstract noun, see § 199.

Matt. vi. 13: ῥῦσαι ἡμᾶς ἀπὸ **τοῦ πονηροῦ,** *deliver us from evil.* So chap. v. 37, 39; John xvii. 15.[1] Some with less appropriateness render "the evil one." In 1 John ii. 13, 14, the adjective (Accusative) is certainly masculine; in Rom. xii. 9 (Accusative), certainly neuter; but as the Genitive and Dative of both genders are alike, passages like Eph. vi. 16; 2 Thess. iii. 3; 1 John iii. 12, v. 19, can only be determined by the context.

In Matt. xix. 17 the best editors (W. H.) concur in the remarkable reading, τί με ἐρωτᾷς περὶ τοῦ ἀγαθοῦ; *why askest thou me concerning that which is good?* (R.V.) instead of *why callest thou me good?* In Mark x. 18, and Luke xviii. 19, the received reading stands without any variation.

317. The number and gender of adjectives, participles, and pronouns are often determined (according to Synesis, or Rational Concord) by the sense rather than the form of their substantives. Compare §§ 175, 179.

Acts iii. 11: συνέδραμε πᾶς ὁ λαὸς... **ἔκθαμβοι,** *all the people ran together, greatly wondering.*

Acts v. 16: συνήρχετο... **τὸ πλῆθος**... **φέροντες,** κ.τ.λ., *the multitude came together, bringing,* etc. So Luke xix. 37, etc.

Eph. iv. 17, 18: **τὰ ἔθνη** περιπατεῖ... **ἐσκοτωμένοι**... **ὄντες, ἀπηλλοτριωμένοι,** *the Gentiles walk... being darkened, estranged.*

Luke ii. 13: **πλῆθος στρατιᾶς** οὐρανίου, **αἰνούντων** τὸν Θεὸν καὶ **λεγόντων,** *a multitude of a heavenly host, praising God and saying.*

Rev. xi. 15: ἐγένοντο **φωναὶ μεγάλαι**... **λέγοντες,**[2] *there were great voices, saying.*

In Matt. xxi. 42, παρὰ Κυρίου ἐγένετο αὕτη καὶ ἔστι θαυμαστή, *this* (thing) *was from the Lord, and is wonderful,* the feminine gender is to be explained by the

---

[1] The R.V. in every instance takes the adjective as masc., rendering *the evil one* (Matt. v. 39, *him that is evil*) with *evil* in marg. For a discussion of the phrase in Matt, vi. 13, see pamphlet by Canon Cook *On the Revised Version of the Lord's Prayer.*

[2] W. H., Rev. Text (Received Text, λέγουσαι).

Hebrew idiom. That language, having no neuter, employs the feminine for abstract notions. See Ps. cxviii. 23 (LXX., cxvii.).

For Synesis with Pronouns, see §§ 335, 345.

318. An Adjective referring to two or more substantives, if an epithet, commonly agrees with the nearest, or is repeated before each; if a predicate, is properly in the plural number, and follows the rule, § 179.

Luke x. 1 : εἰς πᾶσαν πόλιν καὶ τόπον, *into every city and place* (different genders, agreeing with nearest).

James i. 17 : πᾶσα δόσις ἀγαθή καὶ πᾶν δώρημα τέλειον, *every good and every perfect gift.* So Mark xiii. 1 ; Acts iv. 7 (different genders, repeated).

Matt. ix. 35 : θεραπεύων πᾶσαν νόσον καὶ πᾶσαν μαλακίαν, *healing every* (kind of) *disease and every* (kind of) *infirmity* (same gender, repeated).

Matt. iv. 24 : ποικίλαις νόσοις καὶ βασάνοις, *with divers diseases and torments* (same gender, not repeated).

When two adjectives stand as epithets to one substantive, a conjunction generally stands between them. Thus, for "many other," the Greeks say, "many and other." This rule, however, is not invariable in the New Testament.

John xx. 30 : πολλὰ μὲν οὖν καὶ ἄλλα σημεῖα, *many other signs therefore.*

Acts xxv. 7 : πολλὰ καὶ βαρέα αἰτιώματα, *many heavy charges.*

See also Luke iii. 18 ; and on the contrary, Acts xv. 35 (substantive omitted).

319. An Adjective is often employed in Greek where the English idiom requires an Adverb.

Mark iv. 28 : αὐτομάτη ἡ γῆ καρποφορεῖ, *the earth yields fruit spontaneously.*

Luke ii. 2 : αὕτη ἀπογραφὴ πρώτη ἐγένετο, κ.τ.λ., *this enrolment was first made*[1] (compare John xx. 4).

For the adverbial use of adjective forms, see § 126.

---

[1] Other translations have been proposed to escape the chronological difficulty. Thus, "the enrolment first *took effect*, when," etc., it having been originated some years before ; or "the enrolment *was made before* Quirinus was governor" (compare πρῶτός μου, John i. 15). But Dr. Zumpt has recently shown the great probability of Quirinus having been governor of Syria at this early date, as well as A.D. 6, on the deposition of Archelaus. (See Smith's "Dictionary of the Bible," Art. "Cyrenius.") R.V. renders "this was the first enrolment made when Quirinus was governor of Syria."

THE DEGREES OF COMPARISON.

The Comparative.

320. An Adjective in the Comparative degree usually takes the object of comparison in the Genitive case. In English the conjunction *than* is to be supplied.

See § 253, with observations and examples.

The object, as expressed by the Genitive, sometimes corresponds, not with the precise subject of the comparison, but with the general notion of the sentence.

Matt. v. 20 : πλεῖον τῶν γραμματέων καὶ Φαρισαίων (your righteousness), lit., *more than the scribes and Pharisees.*

John v. 36 : ἐγὼ δὲ ἔχω τὴν μαρτυρίαν μείζω τοῦ Ἰωάννου, *the witness I have is greater than John.*

1 Cor. i. 25 : τὸ μωρὸν τοῦ Θεοῦ σοφώτερον τῶν ἀνθρώπων ἐστί, κ.τ.λ., *the foolishness of God is wiser than men,* etc.

> The beginner must beware of translating these genitives as possessives governed by an understood object of the comparative : "than John's (testimony)," "than men's (wisdom)," etc. This the construction will not admit. The form of expression is one of the utmost generality : "God's 'foolishness' is wiser," not only than men's wisdom, but "than men" themselves, with all that they are or can do. So of the other passages.[1]

321. The comparative particle ἤ, *than*, may also be employed; the object then being in the same case with the subject of comparison.

Luke ix. 13 : οὐκ εἰσὶν ἡμῖν πλεῖον ἢ ἄρτοι πέντε καὶ ἰχθύες δύο, *we have no more than five loaves and two fishes.*

1 Cor. xiv. 5 : μείζων ὁ προφητεύων ἢ ὁ λαλῶν γλώσσαις, *greater is he who prophesies than he who speaks with tongues.*

This particle is specially employed (1) after the comparative adverb μᾶλλον, *more.*

Acts iv. 19 : ὑμῶν ἀκούειν μᾶλλον ἢ τοῦ Θεοῦ, *to hear you rather than God.*

---

[1] Winer, § xxxv. 5.

§ 321.] ADJECTIVES—COMPARISON. 271

It may be hardly necessary to remind the learner that Θεοῦ is in the Genitive, not because it is the object of comparison, but because coupled by ἤ with ὑμῶν, Gen. after ἀκούειν, by § 249, a.

So Matt. xviii. 13 ; John xii. 43 (ἤπερ), etc. μᾶλλον ἤ may connect two adjectives, as 2 Tim. iii. 4, where a Greek classical idiom, of which there is no instance in the New Testament, would have admitted two comparatives.

(2) When the object of comparison is a clause.

Rom. xiii. 11 : ἐγγύτερον ... ἤ ὅτε ἐπιστεύσαμεν, *nearer* (our salvation) *than when we believed*.

(3) When a comparative governs, as an adjective, words other than its object.

Matt. x. 15 : ἀνεκτότερον ἔσται γῇ Σοδόμων ... ἤ τῇ πόλει ἐκείνῃ, *it shall be more tolerable for the land of Sodom* (Dative, by § 279) *than for that city*.

After πλείων, πλεῖον, *more,* and ἐλάττων, ἔλαττον, *less,* the particle may be omitted before numerals.

Acts xxiv. 11 : οὐ πλείους εἰσί μοι ἡμέραι δώδεκα, κ.τ.λ., lit., *there are to me no more days* (than) *twelve*. So iv. 22, xxiii. 13.

Matt. xxvi. 53 : πλείω δώδεκα λεγιῶνας, *more than twelve legions*.

In some of these passages the Received Text has ἤ.

A peculiar comparative is occasionally made by μᾶλλον after the positive.

Mark ix. 42 : καλόν ἐστιν αὐτῷ μᾶλλον, κ.τ.λ., *it is better for him*.

Acts xx. 35 : μακάριόν ἐστι μᾶλλον διδόναι ἤ λαμβάνειν, *it is more blessed to give than to receive*.

Sometimes μᾶλλον is omitted.

Matt. xviii. 8, 9 : καλόν σοί ἐστιν εἰσελθεῖν ... ἤ ... βληθῆναι, *it is better for thee to enter ... than ... to be cast*; lit., "*it is good ... rather than*." So Mark ix. 43–47. Compare also Luke xviii. 14 (rec., but W. H. read παρ' ἐκεῖνον ; § 306, γ, 3).

Hence also a comparative notion may be expressed by ἤ after a noun or verb.

Luke xv. 7 : χαρά ... ἐπὶ ἑνί ... ἤ ἐπὶ ἐνενήκοντα ἐννέα, *there shall be joy ... over one ...* (rather) *than over ninety-nine*.

Luke xvii. 2 : λυσιτελεῖ αὐτῷ ... ἤ ἵνα σκανδαλίσῃ, *it is profitable for him ...* (rather) *than that he should offend*.

272   ADJECTIVES—COMPARISON.   [§ 321.

1 Cor. xiv. 19 : θέλω πέντε λόγους τῷ νοΐ μου λαλῆσαι ... ἢ μυρίους λόγους ἐν γλώσσῃ, *I would* (rather) *speak five words with my understanding ... than ten thousand words in a tongue.*

322. For the Comparative as strengthened by the prepositions ὑπέρ and παρά, see §§ 303, 306.

Other emphatic modes of comparison are specified, § 47.

323. A Comparative is often found without any expressed object of comparison.

a. The object may be supplied by the context, as Acts xviii. 26 : ἀκριβέστερον αὐτῷ ἐξέθεντο τὴν ὁδόν τοῦ Θεοῦ, *they expounded to him the way of God more accurately, i.e.,* than he had known it before (ver. 25). Compare John xix. 11; Rom. xv. 15; 1 Cor. xii. 31; Phil. ii. 28; Heb. ii. 1, etc. So in correlative expressions, Rom. ix. 12 ; Heb. i. 4.

b. The Comparative may be a familiar phrase, as οἱ πλείονες, *the majority,* Acts xix. 32 ; 1 Cor. xv. 6 ; 2 Cor. ii. 6 (R.V., " the many ;" A.V., wrongly, " many"), etc.

c. The object is to be supplied mentally, according to the general sense of the passage.[1]

Matt. xviii. 1 : τίς ἄρα μείζων ἐστὶν ἐν τῇ βασιλείᾳ τῶν οὐρανῶν; *who then* (of us) *is greater* (than the rest) *in the kingdom of heaven?*

So Mark ix. 34 ; Luke ix. 46, xxii. 24. In Matt. xi. 11, ὁ μικρότερος may be rendered, *he that is less than all others, i.e.,* " he that is least," as A.V. (R.V., *he that is but little*), or *he that is less than John* (in fame and outward honour), *i.e.,* Christ himself; the sentiment being that of John i. 15.[2]

The following examples further illustrate this usage of the comparative :—

John xiii. 27 : *that thou doest, do more quickly,* τάχιον, *i.e.,* than thou seemest disposed to do.

Acts xvii. 21 : *to tell or to hear some newer thing,* τι καινότερον, than the last things that they had heard, " the later news."

Acts xvii. 22 : *ye men of Athens, I perceive that in all things ye are more addicted to worship,* δεισιδαιμονεστέρους, *i.e.,* than heathen nations

---

[1] See Winer, § 35, 4.
[2] This latter is the interpretation of many of the Fathers, but is disallowed by most modern critics. (See Alford's note.)

§ 324.] ADJECTIVES—COMPARISON. 273

generally (not merely, like them, worshipping recognised deities, but even the "unknown").[1]

Acts xxiv. 22: *the matters pertaining to the way* (the Christian doctrine) *more accurately*, ἀκριβέστερον, than to need detailed information.

Acts xxv. 10: *to the Jews I have done no wrong, as also thou knowest better*, κάλλιον, than thou choosest to confess. Alford compares our current phrase, *to know better*. So 2 Tim. i. 18, *better* even than I do.

Acts xxvii. 13: *they steered closer by Crete*, ἆσσον παρελέγοντο τὴν Κρήτην, i.e., than they had done before; ver. 8.

On Eph. iv. 9, see § 259.

Phil. i. 12: *rather*, μᾶλλον, *for the furtherance of the gospel* than for its hindrance as we feared.

1 Tim. iii. 14: *hoping to come unto thee more quickly*, τάχιον, than to make such injunctions needful. (W.H., ἐν τάχει.) Comp. Heb. xiii. 19, 23.

2 Tim. i. 17: *he sought me out more diligently*, σπουδαιότερον, than if I had not been in captivity. (W. H., σπουδαίως.)

2 Pet. i. 19: καὶ ἔχομεν βεβαιότερον τὸν προφητικὸν λόγον, lit., *and we have more sure the prophetic word*, i.e., we hold that word with a surer confidence even than before, inasmuch as we received a confirmation of its testimony "upon the holy mount."

2 Pet. ii. 11: *angels which are greater in power and might*, μείζονες, either greater than other angels,[2] as the archangel, Jude 9, or (with more probability) greater than these presumptuous, self-willed men.[3]

From the above explanations it will be seen that the Comparative in such cases is not to be explained as "put for the Superlative," or as expressing the notions of "too" or "very," but retains its true and proper force.

The Superlative.

324. The Superlative denotes the highest quality of any kind, and may be used when the objects of comparison are not explicitly intimated.

2 Pet. i. 4: τὰ τίμια καὶ μέγιστα ἐπαγγέλματα, *the precious and greatest promises*, or as A.V. happily, "exceeding great and precious."[4]

---

[1] "Too superstitious," therefore, misses the true meaning both of the word and the grammatical form; R.V. has *somewhat superstitious* (marg. *religious*).
[2] Huther. [3] Winer, Alford, R.V., etc.
[4] R.V. (*his precious and exceeding great promises*) well renders the force of the article, but unnecessarily transposes the adjectives.

In Luke i. 3 we read κράτιστε Θεόφιλε, *most excellent Theophilus;* in Acts xxiii. 26, xxiv. 3, the same title is applied to Felix, and in xxvi. 25 to Festus. It was simply a designation of rank.

325. For the **Superlative followed by a partitive Genitive,** see § 262. An emphatic Superlative is made by the addition of πάντων, Mark xii. 28, *the first commandment of all* (not πασῶν, as Received Text).

The particle ὡς (ὅτι, ὅπως), with a Superlative, means "in as great a degree as possible." Acts xvii. 15 : ἵνα ὡς τάχιστα ἔλθωσι πρὸς αὐτόν, *that they would come unto him as speedily as possible.*

326. The Superlative πρῶτος, *first,* may be used where but two things are compared.

Acts i. 1 : τὸν μὲν πρῶτον λόγον ἐποιησάμην, *the first* (former) *treatise I made.* So John xix. 32 ; 1 Cor. xiv. 30 ;[1] Heb. x. 9.

So the expression πρῶτός μου, *before me,* John i. 15, 30 ; πρῶτος ὑμῶν, *before you,* xv. 18. The Genitive is analogous to the Genitive after the Comparative. On Luke ii. 2 see note, § 319.

327. In Hebrew there are two principal ways of expressing the Superlative :—(i.) by the use of the preposition *in, among,* after the simple adjective, as Prov. xxx. 30, *a lion, strong among beasts, i.e.,* the strongest of beasts ;[2] (ii.) by the repetition of an adjective or noun in the Genitive relation, as in the common appellation of the holiest part of the Temple, *the holy of holies,* and Gen. ix. 25, *a servant of servants, i.e.,* utterly enslaved.[3]

The New Testament has instances of both these idioms :—(i.) Luke i. 42 : εὐλογημένη σὺ ἐν γυναιξί, *blessed art thou among women, i.e.,* most blessed. (ii.) Heb. ix. 3 : ἅγια ἁγίων, *the holy of holies.* Compare 1 Tim. vi. 15 ; Rev. xix. 16.

Neither of these constructions is confined to the Hebrew, although their occurrence in the New Testament may fairly be assigned to Hebrew influence.

---

[1] But perhaps here the mental comparison might be, not simply with the second speaker, but with the rest of the assembly.

[2] Compare the use of a Hebrew preposition to give the force of the comparative (§ 253).

[3] There is yet a third method, *i.e.,* the emphatic use of the adjective with the article, as Gen. ix. 24, *his son, the young, i.e.,* his youngest. But perhaps there is no example of this in the New Testament, though see Luke x. 42.

§ 327.]   ADJECTIVES—THE NUMERALS.   275

Other so-called Hebraisms must be rejected.[1] Thus, Acts vii. 20, ἀστεῖος τῷ Θεῷ, must not be rendered, as in A.V., R.V., "exceeding fair," but *beautiful before God,* in His eyes. Much less must the Divine name be taken as giving a simple superlative force in such passages as Luke i. 15; 2 Cor. i. 12 ; Col. ii. 19 ; Rev. xv. 2, etc.

NUMERALS.

328. The Cardinal εἷς, besides its ordinary use, is employed in the following ways :—

i. As an indefinite pronoun,[2] nearly equal to τις.

Matt. viii. 19 : εἷς γραμματεὺς εἶπεν αὐτῷ, *a scribe said to him.*

Matt. xxvi. 69 : προσῆλθεν αὐτῷ μία παιδίσκη, *there came to him a maid-servant.*

John vi. 9 : ἔστι παιδάριον ἓν ὧδε, *there is a lad here.* (W. H. omit ἕν.)

So Matt. xviii. 24, xix. 16 ; Mark x. 17, xii. 42 ; Rev. viii. 13, etc. Often with a Genitive following, as Matt. xvi. 14 ; Mark v. 22. Sometimes with ἐκ, as Matt. xxii. 35, xxvii. 48. Occasionally, εἷς τις combined, as Luke xxii. 50.

ii. For the correlatives, *one ... the other,* εἷς is sometimes employed in both clauses.

Matt. xx. 21 ; Mark x. 37 : εἷς ἐκ δεξιῶν καὶ εἷς ἐξ εὐωνύμων σου, *one on thy right hand, and the other on thy left.*

Matt. xxiv. 40, xxvii. 38; John xx. 12; Gal. iv. 22. But ἄλλος, ἕτερος, are more frequently used in the second clause, as Matt. vi. 24 ; Rev. xvii. 10.

iii. For *not one* (οὐδείς, μηδείς), the New Testament writers, following the Hebrew idiom, sometimes say *one ... not,* combining the negative with the predicate.

Matt. x. 29 : ἓν ἐξ αὐτῶν οὐ πεσεῖται, *one of them shall not fall, i.e.,* not one of them shall fall. So chap. v. 18 ; Luke xii. 6.

But the adjective πᾶς, *every,* is still more frequently employed in such expressions. Thus, "*everything is not ...*" means "*nothing is.*"

Luke i. 37 : οὐκ ἀδυνατήσει παρὰ τῷ Θεῷ[3] πᾶν ῥῆμα, *everything shall not be impossible with God, i.e.,* nothing shall be impossible.

---

[1] See Winer and others.

[2] The indefinite article in the European languages is but a form of the numeral "one." We say "a or an;" we should rather say "an or a," the longer being the original form, and an = Scottish *ane* = *one.* So French, *un*; German, *ein*, etc.

[3] W. H. read τοῦ Θεοῦ. So R.V., *no word from God shall be void of power.*

So Matt. xxiv. 22; Mark xiii. 20; John iii. 15, 16, vi. 39, xii. 46; Rom. iii. 20; 1 Cor. i. 29; Gal. ii. 16; 1 John ii. 21; Rev. xviii. 22. The idiom is frequent in Hebrew; "*forget not all his benefits*" (Ps. ciii. 2) of course means "forget not *any*." But when οὐ is connected with πᾶς, the meaning is simply *not all*. So Matt. vii. 21, οὐ πᾶς ὁ λέγων ... εἰσελεύσεται, *not every one ... shall enter*. Had the reading been πᾶς ὁ λέγων ... οὐκ εἰσελεύσεται, it would have meant "no one ... shall enter." See Matt. xix. 11; 1 Cor. xv. 39; Rom. x. 16: οὐ πάντες ὑπήκουσαν, *not all obeyed*. πάντες οὐχ ὑπήκουσαν would have been "they all disobeyed."

iv. Instead of the ordinal πρῶτος, the cardinal εἷς is used in the designation of the first day of the week (another Hebraism).

Matt. xxviii. 1: εἰς μίαν σαββάτων, lit., *towards the day one of the week*.

So Mark xvi. 2 (but ver. 9, πρώτῃ); Luke xxiv. 1; John xx. 1, 19; Acts xx. 7; 1 Cor. xvi. 2. In Titus iii. 10; Rev. vi. 1, 3, ix. 12, we find *one* and the *second* as correlatives.

329. The particles ὡς, ὡσεί, που, *about*, etc., are used with numerals *adverbially*, i.e., without affecting the case. Matt. xiv. 21; Mark v. 13; Rom. iv. 19, etc. So with ἐπάνω, *above*, which in other connections is followed by a Genitive.

1 Cor. xv. 6: ὤφθη ἐπάνω πεντακοσίοις ἀδελφοῖς, *he was seen by above five hundred brethren*. So Mark xiv. 5 (where the Genitive is that of price).

330. The names of measures and coins may be omitted after numeral designations. Acts xix. 19: ἀργυρίου μυριάδας πέντε (five myriads), *fifty thousands of silver*, i.e., δραχμῶν = denarii. Elsewhere the plural ἀργύρια (pieces of silver) is used, as Matt. xxvi. 16, etc.

331. The Greeks used the phrase "*himself third*," for "he and two others," αὐτὸς τρίτος. So αὐτὸς τέταρτος, *he and three others*, etc. Sometimes αὐτός was omitted. This idiom occurs once in the New Testament. 2 Pet. ii. 5: ὄγδοον Νῶε ... ἐφύλαξεν, *he preserved Noah, and seven others*.

The *Distributive Numerals* have been sufficiently explained, § 5.

Chapter V. PRONOUNS.

The Personal Pronouns.

332. The rules respecting the cases of nouns, and their employment with prepositions, for the most part apply to the personal and other substantive Pronouns also.

For the oblique cases of the third personal pronoun, in both numbers and all genders, forms of the adjective pronoun αὐτός are employed.

For the other uses of αὐτός, see § 335.

The Nominative of the personal pronoun, when the subject of a verb, is omitted, except where emphasis is required. (See § 169.)

333. The Genitive of the personal pronoun is very frequently used in a possessive sense; the adjective possessive pronoun being comparatively rare. (See § 255.)

Matt. vi. 9, 10 : Πάτερ ἡμῶν ὁ ἐν τοῖς οὐρανοῖς, ἁγιασθήτω τὸ ὄνομά σου, ἐλθάτω ἡ βασιλεία σου, κ.τ.λ., *Our Father which art in heaven, hallowed be thy name*, etc.

Matt. vii. 3 : τί δὲ βλέπεις τὸ κάρφος τὸ ἐν τῷ ὀφθαλμῷ τοῦ ἀδελφοῦ σου (personal pronoun), τὴν δὲ ἐν τῷ σῷ ὀφθαλμῷ (adjective possessive) δοκὸν οὐ κατανοεῖς; *and why seest thou the mote in the eye of thy brother, but discernest not the beam in thine own eye?*

The only possessive for the third person in the New Testament is the Genitive of αὐτός.

Conversely, an objective genitive may be expressed by the possessive adjective pronoun.

Luke xxii. 19 ; 1 Cor. xi. 25 : τοῦτο ποιεῖτε εἰς τὴν ἐμὴν ἀνάμνησιν, *this do for my remembrance, i.e.,* "for remembrance of me." So Rom. xi. 31, *through mercy shown to you;* xv. 4 ; 1 Cor. xv. 31, *by my glorying in you;* xvi. 17, *the lack of you.*

John xv. 9 : μείνατε ἐν τῇ ἀγάπῃ τῇ ἐμῇ, *abide in my love*, has sometimes been taken in a similar sense ; but it seems better to take the pronoun there as a true possessive. (Compare § 269.)

In one striking passage, Eph. iii. 18, there seems the omission of a genitive pronoun, "*what is the breadth?*" etc., *i.e.*, "of the love of Christ."[1]

334. Occasionally, in a lengthened sentence, a seemingly redundant personal pronoun is found.[2]

Matt. viii. 1 : καταβάντι δὲ αὐτῷ ἀπὸ τοῦ ὄρους ἠκολούθησαν αὐτῷ ὄχλοι πολλοί, *and when he had come down from the mountain, great multitudes followed him.*

Acts vii. 21 : ἐκτεθέντα δὲ αὐτὸν ἀνείλατο αὐτὸν ἡ θυγάτηρ Φαραώ, *and when he was cast out, the daughter of Pharaoh took him up.*

> Where the object of a verb is expressed in the nominative absolutely, for the sake of emphasis, its place in the sentence is supplied by a pronoun. (See § 242.)
> Rev. iii. 12 : ὁ νικῶν ποιήσω αὐτὸν στύλον, *he that overcometh, I will make him a pillar.*

335. As αὐτός properly means *very*, *self*, it is used in apposition with nouns of both numbers and of all cases and genders, as well as with the personal pronouns of the first and second persons. When employed in the nominative for the third person, it is always emphatic,[3] *i.e.*, not *he* **simply, but** *he himself*.

Rom. vii. 25 : αὐτὸς ἐγὼ ... δουλεύω, *I myself serve.*

John iv. 42 : αὐτοὶ γὰρ ἀκηκόαμεν, *for we ourselves have heard.*

1 Thess. iv. 9 : αὐτοὶ γὰρ ὑμεῖς θεοδίδακτοί ἐστε, *for ye yourselves are taught by God.*

(1) The reflexive pronoun of the third person may be used for that of the other persons where no ambiguity would be likely to occur.

---

[1] See Ellicott.
[2] W. H., however, in both passages cited read a Gen. Abs., καταβάντος δὲ αὐτοῦ, ἐκτεθέντος δὲ αὐτοῦ.
[3] See Winer.

§ 335 (3).] PRONOUNS—αὐτός. 279

a. **Singular** (never for ἐμαυτοῦ).
John xviii. 34 : ἀφ' ἑαυτοῦ¹ σὺ τοῦτο λέγεις; *sayest thou this of thyself?*
So in some other passages where the reading varies ; as in quotations of Lev. xix. 18 (Matt. xix. 19 ; Mark xii. 31; Luke x. 27 ; Rom. xiii. 9, where the approved reading is σεαυτόν).

b. **Plural** (more frequently).
2 Cor. iii. 1 : ἀρχόμεθα πάλιν ἑαυτοὺς συνιστάνειν; *are we beginning again to commend ourselves?*
2 Cor. xiii. 5 : ἑαυτοὺς πειράζετε ... ἑαυτοὺς δοκιμάζετε, *try yourselves ... test yourselves.*
So in the frequent phrase προσέχετε ἑαυτοῖς, or βλέπετε ἑαυτούς, *take heed to yourselves.* Luke xii. 1, xvii. 3, xxi. 34 ; Acts v. 35 : and Mark xiii. 9 ; 2 John 8.
For the use of αὐτός with the Article, see § 222.

(2) **In respect of gender and number, αὐτός often follows the rule of rational concord** (synesis). (See § 317, and for a similar usage with the relative pronoun, compare § 345.)

a. **Gender.**
Matt. xxviii. 19 : μαθητεύσατε πάντα τὰ ἔθνη, βαπτίζοντες αὐτούς, *disciple all the nations, baptising them.*
Col. ii. 15 : ἀπεκδυσάμενος τὰς ἀρχὰς καὶ τὰς ἐξουσίας ... θριαμβεύσας αὐτούς, *having stripped away from himself the principalities and the powers ... having triumphed over them.*
Mark v. 41 : κρατήσας τῆς χειρὸς τοῦ παιδίου, λέγει αὐτῇ, *having taken hold of the child's hand, he saith to her.*

b. **Number.**
Matt. i. 21 : σώσει τὸν λαὸν αὐτοῦ ἀπὸ τῶν ἁμαρτιῶν αὐτῶν, *he will save his people from their sins.*
3 John 9 : ἔγραψά τι τῇ ἐκκλησίᾳ, ἀλλ' ὁ φιλοπρωτεύων αὐτῶν Διοτρέφης, κ.τ.λ., *I wrote somewhat to the church, but Diotrephes who loves pre-eminence over them.*
So in reference to ὄχλος, πλῆθος, etc.

(3) This pronoun may also refer to a substantive implied in some previous word or phrase.

---

¹ W. H. have σεαυτοῦ even here—a reading not commonly accepted.

Matt. xix. 13 : οἱ δὲ μαθηταὶ ἐπετίμησαν **αὐτοῖς**, *but the disciples rebuked them*, i.e., those that brought the children ; Mark x. 13.

John viii. 44 : ψεύστης ἐστὶ καὶ ὁ πατὴρ **αὐτοῦ**, *he is a liar and the father of it*, i.e., of lying.

So Matt. iv. 23 ; Acts viii. 5; 2 Cor. v. 19, "*to them,*" i.e., the inhabitants of the world. Rom. ii. 26, the concrete implied in the abstract, ἀκροβυστία. Eph. v. 12, "by *those who walk in* the darkness," or (Ellicott) "*the children of* disobedience," ver. 6.

Possessive Pronouns.

336. On the possessive use of the Genitive of Personal Pronouns, and the employment of the Possessives as equivalent to the objective genitive, see § 333. **For the Article with possessive pronouns, see § 223.**

The various use of the Possessives as Adjectives, epithetic and predicative, may be exemplified by the following phrases :—

John v. 30 : ἡ κρίσις ἡ ἐμὴ δικαία ἐστίν, *my judgment is just.*

Rom. x. 1 : ἡ εὐδοκία τῆς ἐμῆς καρδίας, *the desire* (goodwill) *of my heart.*

Phil. iii. 9 : μὴ ἔχων ἐμὴν δικαιοσύνην τὴν ἐκ νόμου, *not having a righteousness of my own, which is from law.*

John xvii. 10 : τὰ ἐμὰ πάντα σά ἐστι, καὶ τὰ σὰ ἐμά, *mine are all thine, and thine are* (all) *mine.*

> The possessive adjective pronoun appears to have a greater emphasis than the genitive of the personal. Thus 1 John ii. 2, *he is the propitiation for our sins*, ἡμῶν, a general declaration; but in the next clause this is thrown into strong antithesis—*not for ours only, but*, etc. ; and here, accordingly, the adjective pronoun is employed, οὐ περὶ τῶν ἡμετέρων δὲ μόνον.

The genitive of a noun is sometimes found in apposition with the genitive notion in the possessive pronoun.

1 Cor. xvi. 21 : τῇ ἐμῇ χειρὶ Παύλου, *by my hand* (that is) *of me Paul.* Col. iv. 18; 2 Thess. iii. 17.

337. For a possessive pronoun, entirely unemphatic, the Article is often employed (see § 215), and on the other hand an emphatic possessive is expressed by the Adjective ἴδιος, *own*.

§ 340.] PRONOUNS—DEMONSTRATIVE. 281

John i. 41 : εὑρίσκει οὗτον πρῶτον τὸν ἀδελφὸν τὸν ἴδιον Σίμωνα, *this man findeth first his own brother Simon.*

See also Matt. ix. 1, xxv. 15 ; Luke vi. 44; John iv. 44, v. 18 : "*said that God was his own father ;*" Acts xx. 28 ; Gal. vi. 9 : "*its own season ;*" also 1 Tim. ii. 6 ; Titus i. 3 ; 2 Pet. i. 20, and many other passages.[1]

DEMONSTRATIVE PRONOUNS.

338. The demonstratives οὗτος, αὕτη, τοῦτο, *this* (the nearer, connected with the second person), and ἐκεῖνος, ἐκείνη, ἐκεῖνο, *that* (the more remote, connected with the third person), with the correlatives (see § 62), obey the laws of adjectival concord.

For the use of the demonstratives with the article, see § 220. οὗτος generally precedes its substantive, ἐκεῖνος follows ; but to this rule there are many exceptions.

Luke xviii. 14 : κατέβη **οὗτος** δεδικαιωμένος εἰς τὸν οἶκον αὐτοῦ παρ' ἐκεῖνον, *this man* (the latter) *went down justified to his house rather than that* (the former).

339. The demonstrative ὅδε, *this* ("this, here," connected with the first person), is found only Luke x. 39 ; James iv. 13 ; and in the phrase **τάδε λέγει**, *thus* (these things) *saith*, Acts xxi. 11, and the beginnings of the letters to the seven churches, Rev. ii., iii.

ὅδε marks a closer relation than οὗτος. In Greek narrative generally, ἔλεξε ταῦτα is, *he said this that precedes ;* ἔλεξε τάδε, *he said this that follows.*

There are a few other passages in which the Received Text has ὅδε, but where the best editors (so W. H.) adopt other readings, as Acts xv. 23 ; 2 Cor. xii. 19 ; Luke xvi. 25, where we should read, *here he is comforted* (R.V.).

340. In some passages, οὗτος seems to refer to the remoter subject.

Acts viii. 26 : **αὕτη ἐστὶν ἔρημος**, *it* (the *road*, not the *city* of Gaza,) *is desert.*

2 John 7 : **οὗτός ἐστιν ὁ πλάνος καὶ ὁ ἀντίχριστος**, *this is the deceiver and the antichrist, i.e.*, he who bears the character described at the commencement of the verse.

---

[1] Winer notes the following passages as without emphasis (but query?): Matt. xxii. 5, xxv. 14 ; Titus ii. 9 ; John i. 41 ; Eph. v. 22 ; Titus ii. 5 ; 1 Pet. iii. 1, 5.

So ἐκεῖνος may refer to the nearer.

John vii. 45 : καὶ εἶπον αὐτοῖς ἐκεῖνοι, *and they* (the chief priests and Pharisees just mentioned) *said to them*, the officers spoken of before.

> ἐκεῖνος is employed as an **emphatic demonstrative**, and sometimes on that account seems applied to the nearer antecedent. Thus 2 Cor. viii. 9 : *Ye know the grace of the Lord Jesus Christ, that for your sakes he became poor, rich as he was, that ye, through* HIS (ἐκείνου) *poverty might be enriched.* So Titus iii. 7. Compare Acts iii. 13.
>
> 2 Tim. ii. 26 is difficult : ἐζωγρημένοι ὑπ' αὐτοῦ, εἰς τὸ ἐκείνου θέλημα. The two pronouns can hardly refer to the same subject (compare iii. 9) ; and it seems best to connect the clause beginning with εἰς with ἀνανήψωσιν, taking ἐζωγρημένοι ὑπ' αὐτοῦ as parenthetical. Ellicott : *"and that they may return to soberness out of the snare of the devil (though holden captive by him) to do* HIS *will,"* i.e., God's. For other explanations, see Alford, Ellicott, etc. R.V. refers the αὐτοῦ back to "the Lord's servant " (ver. 24), and the ἐκείνου to God.

341. A Demonstrative often repeats the notion already expressed by a substantive. The pronoun thus occasionally seems redundant, but perhaps was always intended to convey some additional emphasis.

Matt. xiii. 20–23 : ὁ δὲ ... σπαρείς ... οὗτός ἐστιν, *that which was sown ... this is he*, etc.

> So x. 22, xiii. 38, xv. 11, xxvi. 23 ; John vi. 46 ; John i. 18, 33 (ἐκεῖνος), v. 11, x. 1, etc.
>
> 1 Cor. vi. 4, τούτους ; Rom. vii. 10 : compare Acts i. 22 ; 1 Cor. v. 5 ; 2 Cor. xii. 2.
>
> The Demonstrative itself may be repeated in a sentence. John vi. 42 : οὐχ οὗτός ἐστιν Ἰησοῦς ὁ υἱὸς Ἰωσήφ ... πῶς οὖν λέγει οὗτος ;[1] κ.τ.λ., *Is not this Jesus, the son of Joseph? ... how then saith this man ?* etc. (See also Acts vii. 35-38.)

342. A neuter singular Demonstrative sometimes stands as equivalent to a clause.

Acts xxiv. 14 : ὁμολογῶ δὲ τοῦτό σοι, ὅτι, κ.τ.λ., *but this I confess to thee, that,* etc.

> So xxvi. 16 ; Eph. iv. 17, etc.

The neuter plural may be employed for a single object of thought.

John xv. 17 : ταῦτα ἐντέλλομαι ὑμῖν, ἵνα ἀγαπᾶτε ἀλλήλους, *this I command you, that ye love one another.* (But see R.V. and § 384, *a*, 1.)

---

[1] But W. H. read πῶς νῦν λέγει ὅτι.

§ 345.] PRONOUNS—RELATIVE. 283

3 John 4 : μειζοτέραν τούτων οὐκ ἔχω χαράν (W. H., χάριν), *a more surpassing joy than this I have not.* Compare 1 Cor. vi. 11 : καὶ ταῦτά τινες ἦτε, *and this were some of you,* or " such in some degree were you." (See §§ 180, 352, iii.)

> In Heb. xi. 12, the phrase καὶ ταῦτα, κ.τ.λ., must be rendered, *and that, too, of him who was as good as dead.* Compare 1 Cor. vi. 8, Received Text.
>
> In Rom. xiii. 11; 1 Cor. vi. 6 ; Phil. i. 28 ; 3 John 5 (W. H.), καὶ τοῦτο is similarly *resumptive.*
>
> On Eph. ii. 8, τῇ γὰρ χάριτί ἐστε σεσωσμένοι διὰ πίστεως · καὶ τοῦτο οὐκ ἐξ ὑμῶν, κ.τ.λ., see § 403, *d.*
>
> For the ellipsis of the Demonstrative before the Relative, see § 347.

The Relative Pronoun.

343. The Relative Pronoun agrees with its Antecedent in gender, number, and person. This rule is termed the *Third Concord.*

> The clause in which the Relative stands is called the Relative Clause, and is Adjectival (see § 190), as qualifying the Antecedent.

The Case of the Relative is determined by the structure of its own clause.

Matt. ii. 9 : ὁ ἀστὴρ ὃν εἶδον ἐν τῇ ἀνατολῇ προῆγεν αὐτούς, *the star which they saw in the East, guided them forward.*

Rom. ii. 6 : τοῦ Θεοῦ, ὃς ἀποδώσει, κ.τ.λ., *of God, who will recompense,* etc.

344. A clause, or clauses, may form a neuter Antecedent to the Relative. So with the Demonstrative (see § 342).

Acts xi. 29, 30 : ὥρισαν ἕκαστος αὐτῶν εἰς διακονίαν πέμψαι τοῖς κατοικοῦσιν ἐν τῇ Ἰουδαίᾳ ἀδελφοῖς · ὃ καὶ ἐποίησαν, *they determined, each of them, to send to the brethren dwelling in Judæa for* (their) *relief ; which they also did.*

> See also Gal. ii. 10 ; Col. i. 29 ; Heb. v. 11, etc. ; and with plural relative, Acts xxiv. 18 (ἐν αἷς), xxvi. 12 ; Col. ii. 22.

345. Synesis, or rational concord, is very frequent with the Relative. (See § 317.)

a. Gender.

Acts xv. 17 : πάντα τὰ ἔθνη ἐφ' οὓς, κ.τ.λ., *all the Gentiles, upon whom*, etc. So xxvi. 17; Gal. iv. 19; 2 John 1.

b. Number.

Phil. ii. 15 : γενεᾶς σκολιᾶς καὶ διεστραμμένης, ἐν οἷς φαίνεσθε, κ.τ.λ., *of a crooked and perverted generation, among whom ye appear*, etc.

A plural may be implied in a singular phrase; hence sometimes a plural relative with a singular antecedent. Acts xv. 36 : κατὰ πόλιν πᾶσαν, ἐν αἷς, *through every city, in which* (*cities*). So 2 Peter iii. 1.

On the contrary, a singular may be implied in a plural phrase. Acts xxiv. 11; ἡμέραι δώδεκα ἀφ' ἧς, *twelve days from that on which* ; Phil. iii. 20 : οὐρανοῖς ... ἐξ οὗ. But here ἐξ οὗ may be adverbially taken, *whence*.

In John i. 42, ὅ agrees with ὄνομα, *name*, implied.

346. The Relative is often drawn, or "attracted," out of its proper gender or case by some other word.

Attraction is of two kinds.

a. Attraction of the Relative to the Predicate.—**The Relative Subject may take the gender of its own Predicate rather than that of the Antecedent.**

Mark xv. 16 : ἔσω τῆς αὐλῆς ὅ ἐστι πραιτώριον, *within the hall which is the Prætorium.*

Gal. iii. 16 : τῷ σπέρματί σου, ὅς ἐστι Χριστός, *to thy seed, which is Christ.*

Eph. vi. 17 : τὴν μάχαιραν τοῦ πνεύματος, ὅ ἐστι ῥῆμα Θεοῦ, *the sword of the Spirit, which is the word of God.*

Col. i. 27 : τοῦ μυστηρίου τούτου ... ὅς[1] ἐστι Χριστὸς ἐν ὑμῖν, κ.τ.λ., *of this mystery ... which is Christ in you*, etc. This text explains the meaning of 1 Tim. iii. 16, provided this reading be adopted; *confessedly great is the mystery of godliness*, ὅς[2] ἐφανερώθη ἐν σαρκί, κ.τ.λ., *who was manifested in flesh, i.e.*, the MYSTERY is CHRIST.

b. Attraction of the Relative to the Antecedent.—**A Relative which would properly, by the rules of its own clause, be in the Accusative case, may conform to a Genitive or Dative Antecedent.**

---

[1] W. H., ὅ with ὅς marg.
[2] So W. H., and R.V. (He who was manifested, etc.).

§ 347.] PRONOUNS—RELATIVE. 285

Luke iii. 19: περὶ πάντων ὧν ἐποίησε πονηρῶν, *for all the evil things which he did.*

John iv. 14: ἐκ τοῦ ὕδατος οὗ ἐγὼ δώσω αὐτῷ, *of the water which I will give to him.*

Acts i. 1: περὶ πάντων ὧν ἤρξατο ὁ Ἰησοῦς ποιεῖν τε καὶ διδάσκειν, *concerning all things which Jesus began both to do and to teach.*

Luke ii. 20: ἐπὶ πᾶσιν οἷς ἤκουσαν, *for all things which they heard.*

Acts ii. 22: δυνάμεσι καὶ τέρασι καὶ σημείοις, οἷς ἐποίησε, κ.τ.λ., *by mighty deeds and wonders, and signs which* (God) *wrought,* etc.

So in a great number of passages. The Relative is occasionally "attracted" out of other cases than the Accusative. See Acts i. 22; 2 Cor. i. 4.

Sometimes the Antecedent is put in the case of the Relative. This is called **inverse attraction.**

> In other words, the noun to which the Relative belongs is understood in the antecedent clause, and expressed in the relative, instead of being (as usual) expressed in the former and understood in the latter.

Mark vi. 16: ὃν ἐγὼ ἀπεκεφάλισα Ἰωάννην, οὗτος ἠγέρθη, *this John whom I beheaded is raised,* instead of ὃν ... οὗτος Ἰωάννης.

Rom. vi. 17: ὑπηκούσατε ... εἰς ὃν παρεδόθητε τύπον διδαχῆς, *ye obeyed the form of doctrine into which ye were delivered,* for ὑπηκ ... τῷ τύπῳ ... εἰς ὅν.

> See also Luke xii. 48; Acts xxi. 16, xxvi. 7; 1 Cor. x. 16, etc.; and the repeated quotation from Ps. cxviii. 22: λίθον ὃν ἀπεδοκίμασαν ... οὗτος ἐγενήθη, κ.τ.λ., Matt. xxi. 42; Mark xii. 10; Luke xx. 17; 1 Pet. ii. 7 (in this last passage W. H. have λίθος).

347. When the Antecedent would be a demonstrative pronoun, it is very often omitted, being implied in the Relative.

> So in English, for "he gave me *that which* I asked for," we say, "he gave me *what* I asked for;" the relative form "what" implying both words. But in Greek the same form is used whether the demonstrative antecedent is expressed or implied.

Matt. x. 27: ὃ λέγω ὑμῖν ἐν τῇ σκοτίᾳ ... καὶ ὃ εἰς τὸ οὖς ἀκούετε, *what I say to you in the darkness ... and what ye hear* (into, § 298, 8) *in the ear.*

The Relative and the implied Antecedent may be in different cases.

Luke vii. 47 : ᾧ δὲ ὀλίγον ἀφίεται, ὀλίγον ἀγαπᾷ, *but (he) to whom little is forgiven, loveth little.*

John iv. 18 : ὃν ἔχεις οὐκ ἔστι σου ἀνήρ, *(he) whom thou now hast is not thy husband.*

Heb. v. 8 : ἔμαθεν ἀφ᾽ ὧν ἔπαθε τὴν ὑπακοήν, *he learned obedience from those things which he suffered.*

348. The pronoun αὐτός is occasionally inserted in apposition with the Relative, as a kind of complement to it.

This is a Hebrew idiom; the relative in that language being indeclinable, and requiring to be complemented by a pronoun.

Matt. iii. 12 : οὗ τὸ πτύον ἐν τῇ χειρὶ **αὐτοῦ**, *whose fan is in his hand.*

Mark vii. 25 : ἧς εἶχε τὸ θυγάτριον **αὐτῆς** πνεῦμα ἀκάθαρτον, *whose little daughter had an unclean spirit.*

Acts xv. 17 : ἐφ᾽ οὓς ἐπικέκληται τὸ ὄνομά μου ἐπ᾽ **αὐτούς**, *upon whom my name has been called;* Amos ix. 12, LXX.

So also Mark i. 7; Luke iii. 16; 1 Pet. ii. 24 (not W. H.), etc.

349. The Compound Relative, ὅστις, is strictly indefinite. Thus, πᾶς ὃς ἀκούει, *every one who hears,* would denote "every one who is now hearing;" but πᾶς ὅστις ἀκούει, as Matt. vii. 24, is "every one, whoever he be that hears."

Matt. v. 39 : ὅστις ῥαπίζει ... ὅστις ἀγγαρεύσει, *whosoever smites ... whosoever shall impress.*

Luke x. 35 : ὅ,τι ἂν προσδαπανήσῃς, *whatsoever thou shalt have spent more* (for mood see § 380). John ii. 5, xiv. 13, xv. 16, etc.[1]

From the indefinite meaning of ὅστις arises a suggestion of *character, kind, reason,* **as marking the class to which this Relative is applied.**

For example, ὅστις, and not ὅς, is used in the following passages :—

Matt. vii. 15 : "beware of the false prophets, *who* come to you," *i.e.,* such as come.

Matt. vii. 24, 26 : "a wise man *who* built his house upon the rock, a foolish man *who* built his house upon the sand;" in each case the kind of man who did what is described.

---

[1] The instances of ὅ,τι, neuter, are very few; and there is much variation of reading, ὅτι, conj., being often preferred (as, *e.g.*, in 2 Cor. iii. 14).

§ 350, ii.]   PRONOUNS—RELATIVE: INTERROGATIVE.   287

Matt. xxv. 1 : "ten virgins *who* having taken their lamps went forth to meet the bridegroom," *i.e.*, who acted in accordance with their function.

In this way the compound Relative acquires a kind of logical force. Rom. vi. 2 : "we *who* died to sin, how shall we longer live therein?" *i.e.*, *inasmuch as we died*. Compare Phil. iv. 3.

With proper names, ὅστις is frequently preferred to ὅς. See Luke ii. 4, ix. 30, xxiii. 19; John viii. 53; Acts viii 15, xvi. 12 (on the attraction, see § 346), xvii. 10, xxviii. 18; Rom. xvi. 6, 12; Gal. iv. 26 ; 2 Tim. ii. 18. In all these passages there is an implied reference to character, position, calling.

INTERROGATIVE AND INDEFINITE PRONOUNS.

350. The interrogative pronoun τίς; τί; is used in various ways.

i. Simply, with or without a Substantive, or with an Adjective used substantively—

Nominative. Matt. iii. 7 : τίς ὑπέδειξεν ὑμῖν; *who warned you?*

Genitive. Matt. xxii. 20 : τίνος ἡ εἰκὼν αὕτη καὶ ἡ ἐπιγραφή; *whose is this image and superscription?*

Dative. Luke xii. 20 : ἃ δὲ ἡτοίμασας, τίνι ἔσται; *now the riches which thou didst amass, for whom shall they be?*

Accusative. Matt. v. 46, 47 : τίνα μισθὸν ἔχετε; ... τί περισσὸν ποιεῖτε; *what reward have ye? ... what do ye over and above?*

With Prepositions. Matt. v. 13 : ἐν τίνι ἁλισθήσεται; *wherewith shall it be salted?*

Matt. ix. 11 : διὰ τί[1] μετὰ τῶν τελωνῶν καὶ ἁμαρτωλῶν ἐσθίει; *wherefore eateth he with the publicans and sinners?* So Matt. xiv. 31 ; Mark xiv. 4; John xiii. 28.

ii. Elliptically, with ἵνα, *that* ("that what may happen?" or *wherefore?*)—

Matt. ix. 4 : ἵνα τί ἐνθυμεῖσθε πονηρά; *wherefore are ye imagining malignant things?*

1 Cor. x. 29 : ἵνα τί γὰρ ἡ ἐλευθερία μου κρίνεται; *for wherefore is my liberty judged?*

In quotations from the Old Testament, some editors (not W. H.) have ἱνατί; Matt. xxvii. 46 ; Acts iv. 25, vii. 26.

---

[1] Some editors (not W. H.) read διατί.

iii. Adverbially, neuter, τί; *why?* (or as an exclamation, *how!*) τί ὅτι; *how* (is it) *that ?*—

Matt. vi. 28: περὶ ἐνδύματος τί μεριμνᾶτε; *why are ye anxious about raiment ?*

So vii. 3, viii. 26, xvi. 8, etc.

Matt. vii. 14 (Lachmann, etc.): τί στενὴ ἡ πύλη! *how narrow is the gate!* But this rendering is doubtful, as well as the reading itself (W. H., ὅτι).

Luke ii. 49: τί ὅτι ἐζητεῖτέ με; *how* (is it) *that ye were seeking me ?*

See also Acts v. 4, 9.

iv. In alternative questions, where the classical idiom requires πότερος, α, ον; *whether of the two ?* the New Testament employs τίς—

Matt. ix. 5: τί γάρ ἐστιν εὐκοπώτερον; *for which of the two is easier ?*

Matt. xxi. 31: τίς ἐκ τῶν δύο ἐποίησε τὸ θέλημα τοῦ πατρός; *which of the two did the will of his father ?*

So xxiii. 17, 19, xxvii. 17, 21; 1 Cor. iv. 21; Phil. i. 22 (see § 382, c).

351. The simple interrogative, τίς, τί, is also used in indirect questions, and after verbs of knowing, thinking, etc., in objective sentences.

See § 382, d. The classic Greek idiom requires ὅστις, ὅ, τι, though not without frequent exceptions.

Matt. xx. 22: οὐκ οἴδατε τί αἰτεῖσθε, *ye know not what ye ask.*

Luke vi. 47: ὑποδείξω ὑμῖν τίνι ἐστὶν ὅμοιος· *I will shew you to whom he is like.*

John xviii. 21: ἐρώτησον τοὺς ἀκηκοότας τί ἐλάλησα αὐτοῖς· *ask those who have heard what I said to them.*

So in many other passages.

352. The transition from the interrogative to the indefinite pronoun can easily be traced. It comes to almost the same thing whether we say, "*What man* is there among you *who* will give his child a stone for bread ?" or, "Is there *any man* among you *who* will ?" etc.

Thus the only difference between the forms of the two is in accent and the position in the sentence.

The **indefinite**, τις, τι, may be used (i.) simply, with or without a Substantive expressed—

Luke i. 5: ἐγένετο ... ἱερεύς τις, *there was ... a certain priest.* So, very often, ἄνθρωπός τις, *a certain man.*

Luke xxii. 35: μή τινος ὑστερήσατε; *did ye lack anything ?*

Acts iii. 5: προσδοκῶν τι παρ' αὐτῶν λαβεῖν, *expecting to receive something from them.*

Luke xvii. 12: εἰσερχομένου αὐτοῦ εἴς τινα κώμην, *as he was entering into a certain village.*

Acts xv. 36: μετὰ δέ τινας ἡμέρας, *and after certain days.*

Phil. iii. 15: καὶ εἴ τι ἑτέρως φρονεῖτε, *and if in anything ye be otherwise minded* (for Acc., see § 283). So βραχύ τι, *for some short time,* Heb. ii. 7; μέρος τι, *in some part, partly,* 1 Cor. xi. 18.

With a Genitive following—

1 Cor. vi. 1: τολμᾷ τις ὑμῶν; *dares any one of you ?*

Acts iv. 32: τι τῶν ὑπαρχόντων αὐτῷ, *any of his goods.*

So v. 15, etc. With ἀπό, Luke xvi. 30; with ἐκ, Heb. iii. 13.

(ii.) Emphatically; "somebody important," "something great," "anything"—

Acts v. 36: λέγων εἶναί τινα ἑαυτόν, *saying that he was somebody.* Compare viii. 9.

Gal. vi. 3: εἰ γὰρ δοκεῖ τις εἶναί τι μηδὲν ὤν, φρεναπατᾷ ἑαυτόν, *for if any one thinks he is anything, being nothing, he deceives himself.*

See also 1 Cor. iii. 7; Gal. ii. 6 and (of things) 1 Cor. x. 19; Gal. vi. 15. Compare Heb. x. 27.

(iii.) " A kind of "—

James i. 18: εἰς τὸ εἶναι ἡμᾶς ἀπαρχήν τινα, *that we might be a kind of firstfruits.*

See also (in the opinion of some interpreters; not R.V.) 1 Cor. vi. 11, *such in some degree were you.*[1] But see § 342.

---

[1] Wahl.

(iv.) With numbers, "some," approximately (or perhaps simply redundant)—

Luke vii. 19: προσκαλεσάμενος δύο τινὰς τῶν μαθητῶν, *having called some two of his disciples.*

Acts xxiii. 23: προσκαλεσάμενος δύο τινὰς τῶν ἑκατονάρχων, *having called some two of the centurions.*

These are the only instances ; for the construction in Acts xix. 14 is different. For εἷς, *one,* instead of τις, and in conjunction with it, see § 328, i.

(v.) In alternative expressions we find both τινες ... τινες and τις ... ἕτερος—

Phil. i. 15: τινὲς μὲν καὶ διὰ φθόνον ... τινὲς δὲ καὶ δι' εὐδοκίαν, *some indeed even from envy ... but others also from goodwill.*

Compare Luke ix. 7, 8 ; 1 Tim. v. 24.

1 Cor. iii. 4: ὅταν γὰρ λέγῃ τις ... ἕτερος δέ, *for when one saith ... and another.*

(vi.) The negatives of τις are **οὐδείς, μηδείς**, *no one.* For their construction, and for the Hebraistic negative, οὐ πᾶς, see § 328, iii.

The compounds, οὔτις, μήτις, are not found in the New Testament. The latter, in John iv. 33 (Rec.) should be μή τις (W. H.). For the interrogative μήτι, see § 370.

Chapter VI. THE VERB.

VOICE.

353. The distinction of "voices," in respect of *form* (Active, Middle, and Passive), belongs to ETYMOLOGY. The Verb in SYNTAX is considered as transitive, intransitive, reflexive, or passive.

Transitive verbs may be of Active or Middle form. A transitive Active verb may in its middle voice retain the transitive meaning with certain modifications, or may become intransitive or reflexive. The passive sense is conveyed by the Passive form.

Intransitive, or "neuter" verbs, in like manner, may be Active or Middle in form.

THE ACTIVE VOICE.

354. An intransitive Active verb sometimes takes a transitive meaning.[1]

Matt. v. 45: τὸν ἥλιον αὐτοῦ ἀνατέλλει, *he causes his sun to arise;* ἀνατέλλω being generally *to arise*, as 2 Pet. i. 19, etc.

Matt. xxvii. 57: ἐμαθήτευσε (Rec.) is intransitive, *he was a disciple.* W. H., however, read ἐμαθητεύθη (though with ἐμαθήτευσε marg.); and elsewhere the verb is transitive, chap. xiii. 52, xxviii. 19; Acts xiv. 21.

αὐξάνω, *to grow*, is usually intransitive, Matt. vi. 28; but in 1 Cor. iii. 6, 7, 2 Cor. ix. 10, is transitive. The English verb is similarly used ("wheat grows;" "he grows wheat"). So of many others.

στρέφω, *to turn*, generally intransitive in the Middle, once in the Active also, Acts vii. 42.

---

[1] In the change of intransitive to transitive, we may often mark the influence of the Hebrew, which language attaches to neuter verbs a causative conjugation (Hiphil). In the LXX., both the neuter and the Hiphil are often rendered by the simple verb. So 1 Kings i. 43, ἐβασίλευσε, *he made* (Solomon) *king;* although βασιλεύω properly means *to be a king*.

Some verbs vary between the transitive and intransitive meaning, according to form. Thus, ἵστημι, a regularly transitive or causative verb, has (with some few others) an intransitive sense in the Perfect (with Pluperfect) and the Second Aorist. (See § 108, 3.) ἄγω, *to lead*, has imperative, ἄγε, *go ;* subjunctive, ἄγωμεν, *let us go*. The intransitive imperative only occurs in the New Testament interjectionally, *go to!* (James iv. 13, v. 1).

The verb ἔχω, *to have*, becomes neuter before an adverb, through the ellipsis of a pronominal object, "to *have one's self* in such a manner ;" hence "to *be* so," the adverb being often translated as an adjective. Matt. iv. 24 : τοὺς κακῶς ἔχοντας (those having *themselves* evilly), *those who were ill;* Mark v. 23 : τὸ θυγάτριόν μου ἐσχάτως ἔχει, *my little daughter is at an extremity*. So Acts xv. 36 : πῶς ἔχουσι, *how they do*. (See also John xi. 17 ; Acts vii. 1 ; 1 Pet. iv. 5, etc.). So in the participle, τὸ νῦν ἔχον, *the present time* (that which has *itself* now).

For variations in other verbs, see Vocabulary.

THE MIDDLE VOICE.

355. As compared with the Active Voice, the Middle generally expresses one of three things :—

    1. **Action upon one's self**: the *reflexive* sense.

    2. **Action for one's self**: the *appropriative* sense.

    3. **Action, as caused or permitted**: the *causative* sense.[1]

1. The *reflexive* sense of the Middle is comparatively rare ; reflexive pronouns being usually employed with the Active.

Act. Matt. viii. 25 : ἤγειραν αὐτόν, *they aroused him*.

Mid. Matt. xxvi. 46 : ἐγείρεσθε, ἄγωμεν, *rise, let us go*.

Act. 1 Pet. iii. 10 (LXX.) : παυσάτω τὴν γλῶσσαν ἀπὸ κακοῦ, *let him refrain his tongue from evil*.

Mid. 1 Cor. xiii. 8 : εἴτε γλῶσσαι, παύσονται, *whether* (there be) *tongues they shall cease*.

    See also Matt. xxvii. 5 ; Mark vii. 4 , Luke xiii. 29 ; 1 Pet. iv. 1. In this sense the Active is transitive, the Middle intransitive.

---

[1] Dr. Donaldson, § 432. (1) may be called the Accusative middle ; (2) the Dative middle. (See 2.)

§ 355.] THE VERB—ACTIVE AND MIDDLE VOICE. 293

2. As the reflexive sense is equivalent to the Active with the immediate pronominal Object (Acc.), so the *appropriative* sense corresponds with the Active and the remote Object (Dat.). Thus, Luke xvi. 9, ἑαυτοῖς ποιήσατε might have been fully expressed by the one word, ποιήσασθε.

Act. John xvi. 24: αἰτεῖτε καὶ λήψεσθε, *ask, and ye shall receive.*

Mid. Matt. xx. 22: οὐκ οἴδατε τί αἰτεῖσθε, *ye know not what ye ask* (for yourselves).

Act. Acts xxii. 20: φυλάσσων τὰ ἱμάτια, *watching the clothes* (of Stephen's murderers).

Mid. 2 Tim. iv. 15: ὃν καὶ σὺ φυλάσσου, *of whom do thou also beware,* i.e., watch him with a view to thy own safety.

Act. and Mid. 2 Pet. i. 10: σπουδάσατε βεβαίαν ὑμῶν τὴν κλῆσιν καὶ ἐκλογὴν ποιεῖσθαι· ταῦτα γὰρ ποιοῦντες, κ.τ.λ., *give diligence to make your calling and election sure* for yourselves; *for doing these things,* etc.

For other instances of the Middle of ποιέω, see Luke v. 33, xiii. 22; Acts i. 1, xx. 24, xxv. 17, xxvii. 18; Rom. i. 9, xiii. 14, xv. 26; Eph. iv. 16; Phil. i. 4; Heb. i. 3, and a few other passages.

In this sense, the Middle is transitive, retaining the direct object of the verb. Hence the difficulty of always distinguishing between the Active and the Middle signification; as *to perform an action,* and *to perform it for one's self,* are notions that may approach so as almost to coincide. Compare, for instance, παρεῖχε (Acts xvi. 16) with παρείχετο (xix. 24). The same object, ἐργασίαν, *gain,* follows in both cases. Demetrius had undoubtedly a more direct interest in his gains than the damsel in hers.

It is doubtful whether the Middle is ever to be taken as simply conveying an *intensive* force. Compare John i. 5, *the darkness comprehended it not* (act., κατέλαβεν), with Eph. iii. 18, *that ye may comprehend* (mid., καταλαβέσθαι) *with all saints, what is the breadth,* etc. The appropriative sense is here very decided. The careful student may note the middle verbs in Matt. xxi. 16 (Ps. viii. 3, LXX.); John xiii. 10 (compared with the rest of the passage); Matt. vi. 17; Luke x. 42; Acts ii. 39, v. 2, 13; ix. 39 (ἐπιδεικνύμεναι); Rom. iii. 25; Acts xx. 28; Gal. iv. 10; Eph. v. 16; Phil. i. 22; 2 Thess. iii. 14, and many other passages. In 1 Tim. iii. 13 the dative pronoun is added to the Middle verb.

3. The *causative* Middle expresses the interest of the Subject in the result, and yet implies a mediate agency: "to allow a thing to be done,"

"to have it done," "to provide for its being done." Here the Middle partakes more nearly of the nature of the Passive.[1]

Luke ii. 5 : ἀπογράψασθαι σὺν Μαριάμ, *to get enrolled with Mary*.

1 Cor. x. 2 : ἐβαπτίσαντο,[2] *they got baptised*. Compare Mark vii. 4, and especially Acts xxii. 16.

Hence, too, in some words a change of signification; both voices taking the accusative Object. ἀποδίδωμι, *to give off* or *away;* ἀποδίδομαι, mid., *to sell*, i.e., *give off* or *away for one's self*, i.e., to get money by the act. Compare Matt. xviii. 26-34 with Acts v. 8, vii. 9. δανείζω, *to borrow;* δανείζομαι, *to lend*, Matt. v. 42 ; Luke vi. 34, 35.

The causative meaning in some cases becomes *reciprocal :* "to do ... and cause others to do."

John ix. 22 : συνετέθειντο οἱ Ἰουδαῖοι, *the Jews had agreed amongst themselves*.

See also Matt. v. 40 and 1 Cor. vi. 1: κρίνεσθαι, *to contend at law;* Rom. iii. 4 : καὶ νικήσῃς ἐν τῷ κρίνεσθαί σε, *and that thou mayest overcome when thou comest into trial*, i.e., with the children of men ; the image being that of two parties to a suit—not, *when thou judgest*, as A.V., Ps. li. 4, nor *when thou art judged*, as in the New Testament quotation.[3]

For the special meanings of different verbs the Vocabulary must be consulted. The threefold division now given covers most of the relations of the Middle with the Active.

THE PASSIVE VOICE.

356. As in other languages, the *direct* Object of the Active verb becomes the Subject of the Passive.

But in Greek, the *remoter* Object of the Active may also become the Subject of the Passive.

Genitive. Acts xxii. 30 : κατηγορεῖται ὑπὸ τῶν Ἰουδαίων, *he is accused by the Jews* (for the gen. with κατηγορέω, see § 250).

Dative. Rom. iii. 2 : ἐπιστεύθησαν τὰ λόγια τοῦ Θεοῦ, *they were entrusted with the oracles of God*.

So 1 Cor. ix. 17; Gal. ii. 7 ; 1 Thess. ii. 4, etc.

---

[1] Lat., *curare;* Germ., *sich lassen*. So Winer, § xxxviii. 3
[2] W. H. have ἐβαπτίσθησαν in marg
[3] The R.V. retains A.V. in O.T. passage, but in Romans has correctly *when thou comest into judgment*.

§ 358.] THE VERB—PASSIVE VOICE. 295

Heb. xi. 2: ἐμαρτυρήθησαν οἱ πρεσβύτεροι, *the elders obtained a good report* (lit., were attested to).

So Acts xvi. 2, xxii. 12, etc.

Heb. viii. 5: καθὼς κεχρημάτισται Μωϋσῆς, *according as Moses has been divinely commanded.*

For the dative after the Active of such verbs, see § 278, a.

Where the Active governs two Accusatives (*person* and *thing*), **or a Dative of the** *person* **and an Accusative of the** *thing*, **the Passive may take also the Accusative of the thing.** (See § 284.)

2 Thess. ii. 15: κρατεῖτε τὰς παραδόσεις ἃς ἐδιδάχθητε, *hold fast the instructions which ye were taught.*

See also Mark xvi. 5; Acts xviii. 25, etc., for verbs of the former class.
For verbs of the latter class, note Rom. iii. 2, quoted above, with the connected passages.

357. After Passive verbs, the agent is marked by ὑπό with the Genitive; occasionally by other prepositions, as ἀπό, ἐκ, παρά, πρός; sometimes by the Dative without a preposition. (See §§ 280 e, 304.)

358. As many forms of the Middle and Passive are alike, it is sometimes difficult to decide which is intended. In considering this question, regard must chiefly be had to the usage of the particular verbs, and to the general construction of the sentence.

The following is a selection of instances:—

Matt. xi. 5: πτωχοὶ εὐαγγελίζονται, *poor men preach the gospel*, or *have the gospel preached to them.* The verb may be middle or passive,[1] but the sense of the passage seems decisively for the latter.

Rom. iii. 9: τί οὖν; προεχόμεθα; *what then? are we superior?* (mid.), or, *are we surpassed?* (pass.). The context requires the former meaning. Some, however (see Dr. Vaughan), prefer the passive, but render *are we preferred?* a sense without authority elsewhere. For other suggested renderings, see Alford's note. The R.V. has *are we in worse case than they?* with marg. *do we excuse ourselves?*

---

[1] For the middle, see Luke i. 19, ii. 10, iii. 18, iv. 18, 43, and many other passages; for the passive (with a personal subject), Heb. iv. 2, 6. The passive is also found, Luke xvi. 16; Gal. i. 11; 1 Pet. i. 25, iv. 6, the subject being that which was preached.

1 Cor. i. 2 : σὺν πᾶσι τοῖς ἐπικαλουμένοις τὸ ὄνομα τοῦ Κυρίου, *with all who call upon the name of the Lord*, or *who are called by the name*. The usage of the word clearly pronounces for the former. Compare Acts vii. 59, ix. 14, 21 ; Rom. x. 13 (Acts ii. 21), compared with ver. 14 ; 1 Pet. i. 17, etc. Acts xv. 17 (from LXX., Amos ix. 12) is quite different.

2 Cor. ii. 10 : καὶ γὰρ ἐγὼ ὃ κεχάρισμαι, εἴ τι κεχάρισμαι, δι' ὑμᾶς. Some render the verb here as pass., *I have been forgiven;* but χαρίζομαι nowhere else means "to be forgiven," and the ordinary rendering gives a sense harmonious with the context.

Eph. vi. 10 : ἐνδυναμοῦσθε ἐν Κυρίῳ. This verb is always passive in the New Testament : *"be strengthened."* (See Ellicott.)

THE MOODS AND TENSES.

359. The Indicative Mood is **objective**, describing that which *is;* the Subjunctive and Optative are **subjective**, describing that which is *conceived to be*. Hence the various uses of the three Moods in independent and subordinate sentences.

The Indicative.

The Indicative Mood is used in *declaration*, whether affirmative or negative, and in *interrogation*.

360. As the force of the Tenses will be best seen in the first instance by their use in the Indicative, an account of them is here introduced.

See the Table of Tenses, § 65. **Let it be remembered that Tense expresses both time and state.** Time is present, past, and future ; state is imperfect, perfect, and indefinite.

The Tenses to be considered are—

1. The present imperfect, or "Present."
2. The past imperfect, or "Imperfect."
3. The future indefinite, or "Future."
4. The past indefinite, or "Aorist."
5. The present perfect, or "Perfect."
6. The past perfect, or "Pluperfect."

§ 361, c.]   THE TENSES—PRESENT.   297

The future imperfect, the present indefinite, and the future perfect, are expressed in other ways.

The three past tenses are termed "**historical tenses**," the others "**principal tenses.**"

THE PRESENT TENSE.

361. *a.* **The present expresses a state or action as now existing**; as λέγω ὑμῖν, *I say unto you.*

Matt. iii. 10 : ἡ ἀξίνη πρὸς τὴν ῥίζαν τῶν δένδρων κεῖται, *the axe is lying at the root of the trees.*

John iii. 36 : ὁ πιστεύων εἰς τὸν υἱὸν ἔχει ζωὴν αἰώνιον, *he that believeth on the Son hath life eternal.*

Matt. xxv. 8 : αἱ λαμπάδες ἡμῶν σβέννυνται, *our lamps are going out* (R.V.); not "are gone out," as A.V.

Gal. i. 6 : θαυμάζω ὅτι οὕτω ταχέως μετατίθεσθε, *I marvel that ye are so soon changing.*

b. **It is also used to denote an habitual or usual act.**

Matt. vi. 2 : ὥσπερ οἱ ὑποκριταὶ ποιοῦσιν, *as the hypocrites do.*

Matt. vii. 8 : πᾶς ὁ αἰτῶν λαμβάνει, καὶ ὁ ζητῶν εὑρίσκει, *every one who asks receives, and he who seeks finds.*

c. **In vivid narration the Present is employed of past time (Historic Present).**

Matt. iii. 1 : ἐν δὲ ταῖς ἡμέραις ἐκείναις παραγίνεται Ἰωάννης, *and in those days cometh John.*

John i. 29 : τῇ ἐπαύριον βλέπει τὸν Ἰησοῦν ... καὶ λέγει, *on the next day he seeth Jesus, and saith.*

Sometimes the Historic Present is used with Aorists in the same narration.

Mark v. 14, 15 : ἔφυγον καὶ ἀπήγγειλαν ... καὶ ἦλθον ... καὶ ἔρχονται ... καὶ θεωροῦσι ... καὶ ἐφοβήθησαν, *they fled, and related ... and came ... and they come ... and behold ... and they feared.*

> Variations may here be noted in the comparison of different evangelists in the same narrative. Thus, Matt. xxi. 23, xxii. 23, we read, προσῆλθον, *they came to him;* Mark xi. 27, xii. 18, ἔρχονται, *they come.*[1] Compare also Matt. xxiv. 40 ; Luke xvii. 34.

---

[1] As a rule, the narrations of Mark are more vivid than those of the other evangelists.

d. **The Present is employed to express certain futurity**, as when we say, "To-morrow is Sunday."

Matt. xxvi. 2 : μετὰ δύο ἡμέρας τὸ πάσχα γίνεται, καὶ ὁ υἱὸς τοῦ ἀνθρώπου παραδίδοται, *after two days is the passover, and the Son of man is betrayed.*

Luke xix. 8 : τὰ ἡμίσιά μου τῶν ὑπαρχόντων κύριε τοῖς πτωχοῖς δίδωμι, *the half of my goods, Lord, I give to the poor;* not "I am in the habit of giving" now; but "I will give," immediately.

John xx. 17 : ἀναβαίνω, *I ascend.* Compare xvi. 16.

John xxi. 23 : ὅτι ὁ μαθητὴς ἐκεῖνος οὐκ ἀποθνήσκει, *that that disciple dieth not, i.e.,* is now and will be exempt from death.

1 Cor. xv. 26 : ἔσχατος ἐχθρὸς καταργεῖται ὁ θάνατος, *death the last enemy is destroyed,* or more lit., *is being destroyed.* In this case, and in some others, the notion of futurity is perhaps associated with that of the process now being conducted.

The verb ἔρχομαι, because of its meaning, carries with the present tense a future reference. So in English, "*I am coming.*" (See Luke xii. 54 ; 1 Cor. xiii. 11.) So Matt. xvii. 11 : Ἠλίας ἔρχεται, *Elijah is coming;* and especially John xiv. 3 : πάλιν ἔρχομαι καὶ παραλήψομαι ὑμᾶς, *I am coming again, and will receive you.* 1 Cor. xvi. 5 : Μακεδονίαν διέρχομαι must be rendered, *I* (am about to) *pass through Macedonia*, not "I am passing through," which would be contrary to fact. The participle of this verb, ὁ ἐρχόμενος, *the coming one,* is a frequent title of the Messiah (see § 210), and in the Revelation denotes the eternal self-existence of Deity, *who wast, and art, and art to come,* lit., "who comest."

On the other hand, the verb, ἥκω, in the present, has a perfect signification: *I am come.* Luke xv. 27 : ὁ ἀδελφός σου ἥκει, *thy brother is come ;* John ii. 4 ; Heb. x. 9 (not simply "Lo, I come," but *Lo, I am come*); 1 John v. 20.

The Imperfect Tense.

362. *a.* **The Imperfect expresses what was in progress at a definite past time**; as ἐκήρυσσε τὸ εὐαγγέλιον, *he was preaching the gospel ;* ἐβαπτίζοντο, *they were being baptised*

b. **Hence the Imperfect may refer to an action not continuous, but statedly repeated; also to anything customary.**

Acts iii. 2 : ὃν ἐτίθουν καθ' ἡμέραν, *whom they used to lay day by day.*

Mark xv. 6 : κατὰ δὲ ἑορτὴν ἀπέλυεν αὐτοῖς ἕνα δέσμιον, *and at each passover he used to release to them one prisoner.*

See also 1 Cor. xiii. 11

c. **The Imperfect should be carefully distinguished from the Aorist, or simple Past,** although the A.V. generally confuses the two tenses.[1] The R.V. is far more exact, and the use of the Parallel N.T. (A.V. and R.V.) will often suggest instructive references to the Greek.

So Luke xxiv. 32 : *was not our heart burning within us while he was talking with us by the way, and opening to us the scriptures ?*

Matt. ii. 4 : Herod *was inquiring* of the priests and scribes, not once for all, but repeatedly ; and when they had replied, he *ascertained* (Aorist, one act) of the Magi what they had seen.

Luke xiv. 7 : how they *were selecting* the chief seats.

John v. 16 : the Jews *were persecuting* Jesus, and *were seeking* to kill him, because he *was doing* (used to do) these things.

Acts xvi. 4 : as they *were going* through the cities they *were delivering* the decrees to the churches.

Matt. iv. 11 : ἄγγελοι προσῆλθον καὶ διηκόνουν αὐτῷ, *angels came and were ministering to him.*

Matt. xiii. 8 : *other seed fell* (ἔπεσεν) *upon the good ground, and was yielding* (ἐδίδου) *fruit.*

Matt. xxv. 5 : *they all fell asleep* (ἐνύσταξαν), *and were slumbering* (ἐκάθευδον).

Mark vii. 35 : *his ears were opened* (διηνοίχθησαν),[2] *and the bond of his tongue was loosed* (ἐλύθη), *and he was speaking* (ἐλάλει) *plainly.*

Luke viii. 23 : *a whirlwind came down* (κατέβη), *and they were filling* (συνεπληροῦντο) *and were in danger* (ἐκινδύνευον).

1 Cor. iii. 6 : *I planted, Apollos watered, God was giving the increase.* The transitory acts of human teachers are expressed by Aorists, the continual bestowal of Divine grace by the Imperfect. So, 1 Pet. ii. 23, 24, we have three Imperfects to denote continual and repeated acts ; but an Aorist to denote an act (" he bare our sins") once for all.

See further, Matt. xxi. 8-11; Mark xi. 18 ; John vii. 14, xi. 13, xx. 3-5 ;

---

[1] It may be noted, however, that the absence of any true Imperfect in English, and the necessity of employing a somewhat cumbrous circumlocution, often makes it difficult to render the Greek tense without loss of elegance, and has led to the loose employment of the English preterite.

[2] W. H. read ἠνοίγησαν.

Acts xi. 6 ; 1 Cor. x. 3, 4, xi. 23 (*the night on which he was being betrayed*); Gal. ii. 12 ; James ii. 22, and many other passages.

In parallel passages we occasionally find different tenses. Compare Matt. xix. 13 and Mark x. 13, where the one writer regards the action as momentary, the other as continuous. Some common verbs, as λέγω, are generally used in the Imperfect rather than in the Aorist.

d. **The Imperfect sometimes denotes an inchoative act,** *i.e.*, one begun, but not carried out.

Matt. iii. 14 : διεκώλυεν αὐτόν, *he was hindering him*, *i.e.*, was doing so until checked by our Lord's words.

Luke i. 59 : καὶ ἐκάλουν αὐτὸ ... Ζαχαρίαν, *and they began to call him Zacharias*.

Luke v. 6 : διερρήγνυτο δὲ τὸ δίκτυον αὐτῶν, *and their net was breaking*, began to give way.

Luke xxiv. 27 : διηρμήνευεν,[1] *began to interpret*, entered upon the explanation, rather than "expounded" all, as A.V.

Heb. xi. 17 : τὸν μονογενῆ προσέφερεν, *he was offering up his only begotten*, when the angel's voice arrested him.

e. From the inchoative sense arises a peculiar usage, in which **the Imperfect of verbs expressing desire seems to take a kind of** *potential* **sense :** *I was wishing*, *i.e.*, "I was on the point of wishing," nearly equivalent to "I could (almost) wish," "I should like."

Acts xxv. 22 : ἐβουλόμην καὶ αὐτὸς τοῦ ἀνθρώπου ἀκοῦσαι, *I should like also to hear the man myself.*

Sometimes the wish is one which cannot be carried out.

Gal. iv. 20 : ἤθελον δὲ παρεῖναι πρὸς ὑμᾶς ἄρτι, *I could wish to be present with you just now.*

Or there may be a moral impossibility in the way.

Rom. ix. 3 : ηὐχόμην γὰρ ἀνάθεμα εἶναι αὐτὸς ἐγὼ ἀπὸ τοῦ Χριστοῦ ὑπὲρ τῶν ἀδελφῶν μου, *I could even myself pray to be anathema from Christ on behalf of my brethren.*

> Some critics take this as a simple imperfect, referring to the apostle's unconverted state. "There was a time when even I myself (as you do now) begged to be anathema from Christ;" this being a parenthesis, and the words "on behalf of my brethren" being attached to verse 2. The exposition deserves

---

[1] W. H. and Rev. Text read διηρμήνευσεν.

attention as an attempt to evade a moral difficulty, but is a forced and improbable one.

f. **A compound (or "resolved") Imperfect** (imperf. of εἰμί, and pres. part. of the verb) **throws emphasis on the continuity of the action.** See instances in § 394, i. 1.

For the Imperfect in conditional expressions, see § 383.

The Future Tense.

363. *a.* **The Future expresses, in general, indefinite futurity**; as δώσω, *I will give;* and is employed **in prophecies, promises,** etc.

Matt. v. 5: αὐτοὶ παρακληθήσονται.[1] So in all the Beatitudes, save vers. 3, 10.

Phil. iii. 21: ὃς μετασχηματίσει τὸ σῶμα τῆς ταπεινώσεως ἡμῶν, *who will transform the body of our humiliation.*

Rom. vi. 14: ἁμαρτία γὰρ ὑμῶν οὐ κυριεύσει, *for sin shall not have dominion over you.* Not a command, but a promise.

2 John 3: ἔσται μεθ' ἡμῶν χάρις, *grace shall be with us,* as R.V.

In Matt. xxvii. 4, 24, Acts xviii. 15, the second person future has the force of a threat: "*you shall see to that.*" But compare next paragraph.

b. **Commands are often expressed by the Future second person** (by the third, if speaking of the person commanded).

Matt. i. 21: καλέσεις τὸ ὄνομα αὐτοῦ Ἰησοῦν, *thou shalt call his name Jesus.* Luke i. 13, 31.

So Matt. v. 48, xxii. 37, 39 (and parallels, as Rom. xiii. 9; Gal. v. 14); 1 Cor. v. 13, rec. text; W. H., etc., read imperative.

In 1 Tim. vi. 8 the expression of a resolution as to the future is indirectly a command: τούτοις ἀρκεσθησόμεθα, *we will be content with these things.*

Especially in prohibitions (from the Old Testament, but not only so).

Matt. vi. 5: οὐκ ἔσεσθε ὥσπερ οἱ ὑποκριταί, *ye shall not be as the hypocrites.*

So ch. iv. 7, v. 21, 27, 33; Acts xxiii. 5; Rom. vii. 7, etc.[2]

---

[1] So W. H. marg.; text κληρονομήσουσι.

[2] The difference between this and the classic idiom is, that in the latter the future, with οὐ, is the mildest form of prohibition. In Hebrew (and so in New Testament Greek) it is the special language of legislative authority, and is the idiom used in the Decalogue. So Winer.

c. **The Future sometimes denotes what is usual, and is employed in maxims, expressions of general truths, and the like ("ethical future").**

Eph. v. 31 : καταλείψει ἄνθρωπος πατέρα καὶ μητέρα, κ.τ.λ., *a man shall leave father and mother,* etc.

Gal. vi. 5 : ἕκαστος γὰρ τὸ ἴδιον φορτίον βαστάσει, *for each man shall bear his own load.*

So with a negative. Rom. iii. 20 : ἐξ ἔργων νόμου οὐ δικαιωθήσεται πᾶσα σάρξ, *by works of law shall no flesh be justified.*

d. **A strong negative is expressed by the Future with the double negative** οὐ μή. The Subjunctive, however, is more generally employed; and the idiom will be found explained, § 377.

Instances with the Future are, Matt. xvi. 22 : *this shall never be!* Mark xiv. 31 : *I will never deny thee!* Luke x. 19 : *nothing shall ever harm you.*

e. **A Future imperfect ("resolved future") is formed by the Future of the verb** εἰμί **with the Present participle.**

Luke i. 20 : ἔσῃ σιωπῶν, *thou shalt be silent.*

So Matt. x. 22, xxiv. 9 ; Mark xiii. 25 ; Luke v. 10, xvii. 35 ; 1 Cor. xiv. 9. (See § 394, 1.)

The *Future Perfect* has been sufficiently explained, § 101, i.

f. **Auxiliary Future Verbs** are μέλλω, *to be about to ;* and θέλω, *to will.* The former, which is scarcely ever represented in the A.V., gives emphasis to the notion that the thing *is to* happen, and hence is often used of fixed and appointed purpose.[1] The reader may study the following passages in which μέλλω occurs, noting especially the R.V.—

Matt. ii. 13, xvii. 12, 22, xx. 22, xxiv. 6 ; Mark xiii. 4 ; Luke vii. 2 (*was at the point of death*), ix. 31, 44, x. 1 ; John vi. 6, xiv. 22, xviii. 32 ; Acts v. 35 (*what ye are about to do*), xvii. 31 ; Rom. viii. 13 (*you are sure to die*) ; 1 Thess. iii. 4 ; Heb. xi. 8 (*which he was to receive*), and many other passages. τὸ μέλλον, part. neut., is "*the future.*" Once the verb is used in the sense of delay, τί μέλλεις ; *why tarriest thou?* Acts xxii. 16.

Still more important is it to mark the use of θέλω, as implying conscious volition. The English auxiliary, *will*, ought here to be read as emphatic.

---

[1] See Ellicott on 1 Thess. iii. 4.

Matt. v. 40 (*if any man wills to do so*), xi. 14, xvi. 24, 25 : *if any man wills to come after me ... for whosoever wills to save his life will* (future) *lose it ... but whosoever shall lose his life for my sake will find it* (simple futurity). So exactly Mark viii. 34, 35 ; Luke ix. 23, 24 ; John v. 6, 40, vii. 17 : *if any man wills to do his will, he shall know of the doctrine;* viii. 44 : *the lusts of your father ye choose to do;* Acts xvii. 18 : *what does this babbler want to say?* Rom. xiii. 3 ; 1 Cor. xiv. 35 : *if they wish to,* or, as in other passages, *if they would learn anything;* 1 Tim. v. 11 : *they want to marry;* James ii. 20 : *willest thou to know?* 3 John 13, etc.

The Aorist Tenses.

364. *a.* **The Aorist denotes what is absolutely past, and answers to the English Preterite,** as ἀνέβη εἰς τὸ ὄρος, *he went up into the mountain.*

The First and Second Aorists have precisely the same meaning, except in the few cases specified, §§ 100, 108, 3.

The distinction between the Aorist and the Imperfect is noted, § 362, *c*; between the Aorist and the Perfect, § 365, *b.*

When the *past* time is not strongly marked, **the English idiom often** includes a past act in a period reaching to the *present* time, and hence **uses the Perfect, where in Greek the Aorist is the usual tense.**

Luke i. 1 : ἐπειδήπερ πολλοὶ ἐπεχείρησαν ... ἔδοξε κἀμοί, *forasmuch as many undertook, it seemed good also to me* ("have undertaken," "it has seemed good").

Luke i. 19 : ἀπεστάλην λαλῆσαι πρὸς σέ, *I* (Gabriel) *was sent to speak unto thee* ("have been sent").

Luke ii. 48 : τέκνον, τί ἐποίησας ἡμῖν οὕτως; *child, why didst thou thus deal with us?* ("hast thou dealt").

Matt. xxiii. 2 : ἐπὶ τῆς Μωϋσέως καθέδρας ἐκάθισαν οἱ γραμματεῖς καὶ οἱ φαρισαῖοι, *the scribes and the Pharisees seated themselves in the chair of Moses* (not "sit," simply). "They found the seat virtually empty, and occupied it."[1]

---

[1] T. S. Green.

1 John iv. 8 : *he who loves not, never got a knowledge of* (ἔγνω) *God;* experimentally,—not having at any time known what love is.¹

See also Luke xiv. 18, 19 ; John viii. 29, xvii. 4 ; Rom. iii. 23, *all sinned, and so are coming short,* etc.; 1 Cor. vi. 11.

2 Cor. v. 15 : εἶς ὑπὲρ πάντων ἀπέθανεν· ἄρα οἱ πάντες ἀπέθανον· *one died for all, therefore all died.* Compare 2 Tim. ii. 11.

Phil. iii. 8 : *I suffered the loss of all things, i.e.,* at the crisis of his life, ver. 12. James i. 11 (a vivid, descriptive delineation). So ver. 24 (a Perfect interposed).

2 Pet. i. 14 : *knowing that the putting off of my tabernacle cometh swiftly, even as our Lord Jesus Christ signified unto me* (R.V.). By the "*hath* showed me" (of A.V.) we lose altogether the special allusion to an historic moment in the Apostle's life, to John xxi. 18, 19, which would at once have come out had ἐδήλωσέ μοι been rendered ²*showed me.*"²

b. In narration, an Aorist that starts from a time already past may be translated by the Pluperfect.

Matt. xxviii. 2 : σεισμὸς ἐγένετο μέγας, *there had been a great earthquake.*

Luke ii. 39 : ὡς ἐτέλεσαν πάντα, *when they had accomplished all things.*

See also Matt. xiv. 3 ; John vi. 22, xi. 30, xviii. 24 (?), etc.

c. **The Epistolary Aorist,** so called (as ἔγραψα), takes the reader's point of view, in which the writing of the letter is viewed as past. Our idiom requires us to take the writer's point of view, "*I have written.*"

Rom. xv. 15 ; 1 Pet. v. 12 (referring to the whole letter) ; 1 Cor. ix. 15 : 1 John ii. 21, and perhaps 1 Cor. v. 9, referring to a part of it.³ Gal. vi. 11, referring either to the whole or to part, according to the interpretation adopted.

But ἔγραψα has, in other cases, its ordinary Aorist force, referring to a former letter, "*I wrote,*" 2 Cor. ii. 3, 4, 9, vii. 12 ; probably 3 John 9 ; and perhaps 1 Cor. v. 9.

The word ἔπεμψα also exemplifies the Epistolary Aorist, "*I have sent,*" 1 Cor. iv. 17 ; 2 Cor. ix. 3 ; Eph. vi. 22 ; Rev. xxii. 16.

---

[1] Other passages in which ἔγνων has been regarded as standing for the Present may be explained in a similar way.

[2] Archbishop Trench on the Authorised Version of the New Testament, p. 146.

[3] See Ellicott on Gal. vi. 11.

§ 365, b.]   THE TENSES—PERFECT.   305

d. In classical Greek, the Aorist is frequently used to describe an act which has taken place in time past, and may take place at any time again. Here in English the Present is the usual tense. Accordingly, in the New Testament there are a few passages where the Aorist may best be translated by the Present.

Matt. iii. 17: ἐν ᾧ εὐδόκησα, *in whom I am well pleased,* i.e., "I was, and am." So in parallel passages.

Rom. viii. 30: ἐκάλεσε ... ἐδικαίωσε ... ἐδόξασε, *he calls ... justifies ... glorifies;* "he did, and does."[1]

e. **The completeness of an act is occasionally marked by the Aorist.**

John xiii. 31: νῦν ἐδοξάσθη ὁ υἱὸς τοῦ ἀνθρώπου, *now is the Son of man glorified;* the whole series of events being brought to a crisis.

1 Cor. vii. 28: *thou didst not ... she did not commit a sin.*

So in several of the parables: ὡμοιώθη, *is likened* (Matt. xiii. 24, xviii. 23, xxii. 2), "as if the mould had already received its shape, though the cast was yet to issue."[2]

Compare Luke i. 51-53; John viii. 29.

THE PERFECT AND PLUPERFECT TENSES.

365. *a.* **The Perfect denotes an action or event as now complete;** its point of view is, therefore, in the present, as ὁ γέγραφα, γέγραφα, *what I have written, I have written.* It denotes also a past act whose consequences remain, as γέγραπται, "it has been written, and abides;" *it is written.*[3]

b. **The distinction between the Aorist and Perfect is thus very marked.** Thus, τεθνήκασι (Matt. ii. 20), *they are dead;* ἔθανον (ἀπέθανον) would have been, *they died.* Compare Mark xv. 44. Even where either tense would be suitable, the proper force must be given to the one employed.

Matt. ix. 13: οὐ γὰρ ἦλθον καλέσαι δικαίους, *for I came not to call righteous persons.*

Luke v. 32: οὐκ ἐλήλυθα καλέσαι δικαίους, *I am not come,* etc.

---

[1] Alford interprets differently. See his note.
[2] T. S. Green.
[3] Luther, *steht geschrieben.*

In the following passages, among many others, the distinction of tenses is strikingly apparent:—

Mark iii. 26 : εἰ ὁ Σατανᾶς ἀνέστη ἐφ' ἑαυτὸν, καὶ μεμέρισται,[1] *for if Satan rose up against himself, and has become divided.*

Acts xxi. 28 : *he brought* (εἰσήγαγεν) *Greeks into the temple, and has profaned* (κεκοίνωκε) *this holy place ;* the single act, the abiding result.

1 Cor. xv. 4 : καὶ ὅτι ἐτάφη, καὶ ὅτι ἐγήγερται, *and that he was buried, and that he is risen again.* So all through this chapter. The simple historical fact is announced by the aorist, ἠγέρθη, Matt. xxviii. 6, 7 ; Mark xvi. 6 ; Luke xxiv. 6, 34 (John xxi. 14) ; Rom. vi. 4, etc. For the perf. part., see 2 Tim. ii. 8, compared with the aor. part., 2 Cor. v. 15.

Col. i. 16 : ὅτι ἐν αὐτῷ ἐκτίσθη τὰ πάντα ... τὰ πάντα δι' αὐτοῦ καὶ εἰς αὐτὸν ἔκτισται, *because in him were all things created ... all things have been created by him and for him.*

Col. iii. 3 : ἀπεθάνετε γάρ, καὶ ἡ ζωὴ ὑμῶν κέκρυπται ... *for ye died, and your life remains hidden.*

Rev. v. 7 : ἦλθε καὶ εἴληφε, *he came, and he hath taken the book* (which he still retains, as Lord of human destiny).

See also Luke iv. 18 ; John viii. 40 ; Heb. ii. 14 ; 1 John i. 1.

366. The Pluperfect, or Past Perfect, is but rarely used in the New Testament. It denotes that which was completed at some past time ; as, τεθεμελίωτο ἐπὶ τὴν πέτραν, *it had been founded on the rock.*

Acts xiv. 23 : παρέθεντο αὐτοὺς τῷ Κυρίῳ εἰς ὃν πεπιστεύκεισαν, *they commended them to the Lord, on whom they had believed.*

367. The Perfects of many verbs are used as Presents ; and correspondingly the Pluperfect takes a Past signification. This arises in each case from the simple meaning of the verb, as *coming into* a state : Perf., *being in* (having come into) that state.

So κτάομαι, *to gain ;* κέκτημαι, *to possess,* which does not, however, occur in the New Testament. See Luke xviii. 12: πάντα ὅσα κτῶμαι, not *of all that I possess,* but *of all that I gain*—the income, not the capital. So xxi. 19, "*ye shall win your souls*" (R.V.).

---

[1] But W. H. and Rev. Text read ἐμερίσθη.

For example, καθίζω, κάθημαι. Mark xi. 7: ἐκάθισεν, *he mounted.* Luke xviii. 35, etc.: ἐκάθητο, *he was sitting.* κοιμάομαι, *I fall asleep;* κεκοίμημαι, *I am asleep.* 1 Cor. xi. 30: κοιμῶνται ἱκανοί, *many are falling asleep.* John xi. 11: Λάζαρος ... κεκοίμηται, *Lazarus sleepeth.* οἶδα, *I have seen;* hence *I know.* (See § 103.)

ἵστημι and its compounds especially exhibit this "Present Perfect." ἕστηκα, *I stand,* as Acts xxvi. 6. So ἐνέστηκε, *is imminent,* 2 Thess. ii. 2; ἀνθέστηκε (trans.), *resisteth,* Rom. ix. 19, xiii. 2; ἐφέστηκε, *is at hand,* 2 Tim. iv. 6. From ἕστηκα comes a new Present (intrans.), στήκω, Rom. xiv. 4, etc.

For other words used in a similar sense, see Vocabulary.

Interrogative Forms.

368. The several tenses of the Indicative are employed interrogatively, each with its proper force. **The interrogative may be indicated by the appropriate pronouns or particles, or simply by the order of the words, or the general sense of the passage.**

a. With interrogative words—

Matt. xxv. 37: πότε σε εἴδομεν πεινῶντα; *when saw we thee hungry?*

John i. 19: σὺ τίς εἶ; *who art thou?*

John v. 47: πῶς τοῖς ἐμοῖς ῥήμασι πιστεύσετε; *how will ye believe my words?*

John xi. 34: ποῦ τεθείκατε αὐτόν; *where have ye laid him?*

Acts viii. 30: ἆρά γε γινώσκεις ἃ ἀναγινώσκεις; *understandest thou then what thou readest?*

Luke xviii. 8; Gal. ii. 17.

b. Without interrogative words—

Matt. ix. 28: πιστεύετε ὅτι δύναμαι τοῦτο ποιῆσαι; *believe ye that I am able to do this?*

Rom. vii. 7: ὁ νόμος ἁμαρτία; *is the law sin?*

So John xiii. 6; Acts xxi. 37; Rom. ii. 21-23.

Hence arises occasional ambiguity.

1 Cor. i. 13: μεμέρισται ὁ Χριστός; *is Christ divided?* (R.V., W. H. marg.). Lachmann reads this as an assertion: *Christ is divided, i.e.,* by your dissensions, which rend asunder his body (R.V. marg., W. H.).

Rom. viii. 33, 34. Many critics read this as a series of questions, not question and answer, as A.V. "Who shall lay anything to the charge of God's elect?

Shall God who justifieth? Who is he that condemneth? Is it Christ who died?" etc. (So R.V. marg. See Alford's note on the passage.)

An **elliptic question** is made by the use of the particle εἰ, *if*, some such phrase as *say*, or *tell us*, being understood. In this case the sentence is really dependent. (See § 383.)

Matt. xii. 10: εἰ ἔξεστι τοῖς σάββασι θεραπεύειν; *is it lawful to heal upon the sabbath?* (tell us if—).

Acts xix. 2: εἰ πνεῦμα ἅγιον ἐλάβετε πιστεύσαντες; *received ye the Holy Ghost when ye believed?*

So Acts vii. 1; xxi. 37; xxii. 25.

369. An affirmative answer is given, in a few passages, by the formula σὺ λέγεις, *thou sayest*, with or without addition: Matt. xxvii. 11; Luke xxii. 70; xxiii. 3; John xviii. 37. σὺ εἶπας, *thou didst say*, is similarly used, Matt. xxvi. 25, 64.

370. Negative questions are framed according to the answer expected.

a. οὐ presumes an affirmative reply.

Matt. vii. 22: οὐ τῷ σῷ ὀνόματι ἐπροφητεύσαμεν; *did we not prophesy in thy name?*

1 Cor. ix. 1: οὐκ εἰμὶ ἐλεύθερος; οὐκ εἰμὶ ἀπόστολος; κ.τ.λ., *am I not free? am I not an apostle?* etc.

Acts xiii. 10: οὐ παύσῃ διαστρέφων; *wilt thou not cease from perverting?* the affirmative answer being intimated as that which ought to be given. So Mark xiv. 60: *dost thou not answer anything?*

Once οὐκοῦν is found. John xviii. 37: *thou art not then a king, art thou?*

b. μή expects a negative answer.

Matt. vii. 9: μὴ λίθον ἐπιδώσει αὐτῷ; *will he give him a stone?*

Rom. ix. 14: μὴ ἀδικία παρὰ τῷ Θεῷ; *is there unrighteousness with God?*

c. μήτι suggests an emphatic negative.

Matt. vii. 16: μήτι συλλέγουσιν ἀπὸ ἀκανθῶν σταφυλὰς ἢ ἀπὸ τριβόλων σῦκα; *men do not gather grape-clusters of thorns, or figs of thistles, do they?*

§ 373, a.] THE IMPERATIVE MOOD. 309

Matt. xxvi. 22, 25 : μήτι ἐγώ εἰμι, Κύριε ; (from the disciples), μήτι ἐγώ εἰμι, ῥαββί ; (from Judas), *it is not I, is it, Lord?—is it, Rabbi?*

See also Mark iv. 21 ; John xviii. 35 ("*I a Jew!*").
It would sometimes appear as though dawning conviction would fortify resistance by a strong negative. So Matt. xii. 23 may be understood : μήτι οὗτός ἐστιν ὁ υἱὸς Δαβίδ ; *this is never the Son of David?*

THE IMPERATIVE MOOD.

371. The Imperative is used for command or entreaty.

Matt. v. 44 : ἀγαπᾶτε τοὺς ἐχθροὺς ὑμῶν, *love your enemies.*
Matt. viii. 25 : Κύριε, σῶσον, ἀπολλύμεθα, *Lord, save, we perish!*

The negative with imperative forms is always μή. (See § 375.)

John vi. 20 : ἐγώ εἰμι· μὴ φοβεῖσθε, *it is I, be not afraid.*

372. The form of command is sometimes employed where simple permission is intended.[1]

Matt. xxvi. 45 : καθεύδετε λοιπὸν καὶ ἀναπαύεσθε, *sleep on now, and take your rest.*[2]

See also 1 Cor. vii. 15, xiv. 38. "Rev. xxii. 11 is a challenge (*Aufforderung*): 'the fate of all is as good as already determined.'"

373. Of the Imperative *tenses*, the Present implies present continuance or repetition.

The Aorist expresses a command generally, or implies that the action is single or instantaneous.

The Perfect (very rare) **refers to an action complete in itself, yet continuous in its effect.** Its meaning coincides with that of the Present in verbs where the Perfect indicative has a present meaning.

a. The Present.

Matt. vii. 1 : μὴ κρίνετε, *judge not.*
1 Cor. ix. 24 : οὕτω τρέχετε ἵνα καταλάβητε, *so run that ye may obtain.*
1 Thess. v. 16–22 : πάντοτε χαίρετε, ἀδιαλείπτως προσεύχεσθε, ἐν παντὶ

---

[1] Winer, xliii. 1.
[2] Bengel. "Sleep, if you feel at liberty to do so ;" not in irony, not (as some) a question.

εὐχαριστεῖτε, κ.τ.λ., *rejoice evermore; pray without ceasing; in everything give thanks*, etc.

b. *The Aorist.*

Matt. vi. 6 : εἴσελθε εἰς τὸ ταμιεῖόν σου καὶ ... πρόσευξαι, *enter into thy chamber ... and pray.*

Matt. vi. 9–11 : in the Lord's Prayer, ἁγιασθήτω ... γενηθήτω ... δός ... ἄφες.

John xi. 44 : λύσατε αὐτόν, καὶ ἄφετε αὐτὸν ὑπάγειν, *loose him, and let him go.*

c. *The Perfect.*

Mark iv. 39 : σιώπα, πεφίμωσο, *peace! be still!*

The contrasted force of the Present and Aorist is shown where both are used in the same passage.

John v. 8 : ἆρον τὸν κράβαττόν σου καὶ περιπάτει, *take up thy bed and walk.*

Rom. vi. 13 : μηδὲ παριστάνετε τὰ μέλη ὑμῶν ὅπλα ἀδικίας τῇ ἁμαρτίᾳ, ἀλλὰ παραστήσατε ἑαυτοὺς τῷ Θεῷ, *yield not your members* (as the habit of your lives), *as instruments of unrighteousness, unto sin, but yield yourselves* (a single act, once for all) *unto God.*

> For the employment of the Future Indicative in commands and prohibitions, see § 363, b.
> For the similar use of the Subjunctive, especially in prohibitions, see § 375.
> The Infinitive may also be employed. (See § 392.)

In many instances the force of the Aorist and that of the Present seem nearly identical. The former is the more vigorous expression.

Matt. v. 16 : οὕτω λαμψάτω τὸ φῶς ὑμῶν, κ.τ.λ. Here the Present might have been employed:—"let your light beam continuously." The Aorist simply gives the general command, without the further thought of continuance.

John xiv. 15 : ἐὰν ἀγαπᾶτέ με, τὰς ἐντολὰς τὰς ἐμὰς τηρήσατε,[1] *if ye love me, keep my commandments :* adopt this as the law of your lives.

Rom. xv. 11 : αἰνεῖτε, πάντα τὰ ἔθνη, τὸν Κύριον, καὶ ἐπαινεσάτωσαν αὐτὸν πάντες οἱ λαοί, *praise the Lord, all the nations ; and let all the peoples burst into a song of praise to him.*

---

[1] W. H. and Rev. Text read τηρήσετε, *ye will keep.*

See also John ii. 8, 16 ; 1 Cor. xv. 34.

The consideration of such examples will bring to light many subtle beauties of expression, which no translation, perhaps, could accurately represent.

The Subjunctive Mood.

Subjunctives in Independent Clauses.

374. The Subjunctive, strictly speaking, cannot stand in an independent sentence. Where it appears to do so, there is in reality an ellipsis. Thus, ἴωμεν, *let us go*, is really a final clause (ἵνα understood) dependent on some implied verb or phrase. In such cases as the following, however, this distinction may be disregarded, and the sentences taken as to all intents and purposes independent.

> The tenses in the Subjunctive and Optative are distinguished as in § 373. Compare also § 386. The Present implies *continuity*, the Aorist *completion*.

375. The Subjunctive is used as a hortatory Imperative of the first person.

John xix. 24 : μὴ σχίσωμεν αὐτόν, ἀλλὰ λάχωμεν, *let us not rend it, but let us cast lots.*

Rom. v. 1 : εἰρήνην ἔχωμεν πρὸς τὸν Θεόν,[1] *let us have peace with God;* and ver. 2, 3 : καυχώμεθα, *let us glory.*

So 1 Cor. xv. 32 ; 1 Thess. v. 6.

The Subjunctive Aorist is used instead of the Imperative in prohibitions.[2]

---

[1] W. H., R.V. The MS. evidence for this reading is very strong ; indeed, in any ordinary case would be overwhelming. On internal grounds, however, Tischendorf and others prefer the rec. text, *we have peace*. In such a case, even the testimony of MSS. must be taken with great caution ; as it seems to have been a practice with some ancient transcribers to make Scripture, as they thought, more emphatic by turning a declaration or a promise into an exhortation. It could easily be done, as nothing more was needed than to change the ο of the indicative into the ω of the subjunctive. So John iv. 42, "let us believe ; " Rom. v. 10, " let us be saved ; " Rom. vi. 8, " let us believe ; " 1 Cor. xiv. 15, " let me pray ; " 1 Cor. xv. 49, " let us bear the image of the heavenly " (so W. H.) ; Heb. vi. 3, " this let us do ; " James iv. 13, " let us go,"etc.; and many similar passages. (See Alford's note on Rom. v. 1.)

[2] This is the regular classical idiom.

Matt. i. 20 : μὴ φοβηθῇς, *fear not.*
Matt. v. 17 : μὴ νομίσητε, *think not.*
Matt. vi. 2 : μὴ σαλπίσῃς, *sound not a trumpet.*

> This usage also depends upon the ellipsis of some phrase like "see," "take heed," etc., with ἵνα. In a few instances, a positive command is expressed by ἵνα with the subjunctive (Mark v. 23 ; 2 Cor. viii. 7 ; Eph. v. 33). For the complete phrase, see 1 Cor. xvi. 10 ; and with ellipsis of ἵνα, Matt. viii. 4.
> But the third person of the Aor. Imp. may be used with μή (Matt. vi. 3 ; Mark xiii. 16).

376. The Subjunctive is used in questions expressive of deliberation or doubt: thus, τί ποιῶμεν ; (John vi. 28) *what are we to do ?* but τί ποιοῦμεν ; (John xi. 47) *what are we doing ?* "what are we about?" and τί ποιήσει ; (Matt. xxi. 40) *what will he do ?*

Mark xii. 14 : δῶμεν ἢ μὴ δῶμεν ; *are we to give, or not to give ?*

Matt. xxvi. 54 : πῶς οὖν πληρωθῶσιν αἱ γραφαί, *how then should the scriptures be fulfilled ?*

1 Cor. xi. 22 : τί εἴπω ὑμῖν ; ἐπαινέσω ὑμᾶς ; *what am I to say to you ? am I to praise you ?*

> The second of these verbs might be the fut. indic., the connection only showing it to be aor. subj. As the two tenses are alike in the first pers. sing., it is often doubtful which is meant. So in the pres. of contracted verbs, τί ποιῶ ;

377. A strong denial is expressed by the Subjunctive Aorist with οὐ μή, as οὐ μή σε ἀνῶ, οὐδ' οὐ μή σε ἐγκαταλίπω (Heb. xiii. 5), *I will assuredly not leave thee, nor will I at all forsake thee.*

> This idiom arises from a combination of two phrases : μή, with the subjunctive elliptical, "fear *lest*" (see § 384) ; preceded by οὐ, with the word (understood) on which μή depends. "There is *not* any fear or possibility *lest I should.*"

Matt. v. 18 : ἰῶτα ἓν ἢ μία κεραία οὐ μὴ παρέλθῃ, *one iota* (the smallest letter of the alphabet), *or one tittle* (the fragment of a letter[1]) *shall by no means pass.*

Matt. v. 20 : οὐ μὴ εἰσέλθητε, *ye shall in no wise enter.*

Mark xiv. 25 : οὐκέτι οὐ μὴ πίω, *never will I drink at all.*[2]

---

[1] As, for instance, that which distinguishes A from Λ, or in Hebrew, ה from ח.
[2] The additional negative adds strength to the negation.

§ 378, a.] THE OPTATIVE MOOD. 313

See also Matt. xxiv. 2 ; Mark ix. 41 ; Luke vi. 37 (twice), xviii. 17, xxii. 67, 68 ; John vi. 37, viii. 51, x. 28, xiii. 8 ; Acts xxviii. 26 (twice, from the LXX.; so elsewhere); 1 Cor. viii. 13 ; 1 Thess. iv. 15 (*shall by no means precede*), v. 3 ; Heb. viii. 11, 12 (LXX.) ; 2 Pet. i. 10 ; Rev. xviii. 21-23 ; with many other passages. The study of these emphatic negatives of Scripture is fraught with interest.

In the following passages only (in the best MSS. and edd.), the future is found (see § 363, *d*) : Matt. xvi. 22, xxvi. 35 ; Mark xiv. 31 ; Luke x. 19 (W. H. marg. ἀδικήσῃ) ; John iv. 14, x. 5, xx. 25 (ambiguous).[1]

For the Aorist Subjunctive in a Future-perfect sense, see § 383, *β*.

THE OPTATIVE MOOD.

Optative in Independent Clauses.

378. a. The Optative is used in independent sentences to express a wish, as 2 Pet. i. 2 : χάρις ὑμῖν καὶ εἰρήνη πληθυνθείη, *grace and peace be multiplied unto you !*

As stated with regard to the Subjunctive (§ 374), the independence of the sentence is seeming only, a verbal notion on which the Optative depends being implied, as *desire, pray*. The Optative is in fact only another form of the Subjective mood, "the Subjunctive of the historical tenses." But this characteristic is almost lost in the New Testament, where the Optative is comparatively rare.

Rom. xv. 5 : ὁ δὲ Θεὸς ... δῴη ὑμῖν, *now may God grant unto you !*

Philemon 20 : ναί, ἀδελφέ, ἐγώ σου ὀναίμην ἐν Κυρίῳ, *yea, brother, let me have joy of thee in the Lord !*

So Acts viii. 20; 1 Thess. iii. 11, 12; 2 Thess. iii. 5, etc.

So with the negative, μή.

Mark xi. 14 : μηκέτι ... ἐκ σοῦ μηδεὶς καρπὸν φάγοι, *let no one ever eat fruit of thee.*

2 Tim. iv. 16 : μὴ αὐτοῖς λογισθείη, *may it not be laid to their charge !*

The formula μὴ γένοιτο, *may it not come to pass !* rendered in A.V. (and R.V., except Gal. vi. 14) " God forbid !" illustrates the same usage. Luke xx. 16 ; Rom. vi. 2, 15, vii. 13, etc.

---

[1] The future indic. with οὐ μή has no perceptible difference of meaning from that of the aor. subj. (*Madvig*, § 124, *a*, 3). Probably the future realises to the mind with greater vividness the possibility which is denied.

But a wish respecting something past is sometimes expressed by ὄφελον (really representing an old Second Aorist of a verb, *I ought*, and in classic Greek followed by an infinitive) used in the New Testament as a particle with the Indicative. 1 Cor. iv. 8; 2 Cor. xi. 1; Gal. v. 12; Rev. iii. 15.

b. **The particle ἄν gives a potential sense to the Optative, both in affirmations and in questions.**

Acts xxvi. 29 : εὐξαίμην ἂν τῷ Θεῷ, *I could wish to God.*

Acts viii. 31 : πῶς γὰρ ἂν δυναίμην; *nay, for how could I?*

The Moods in Dependent Clauses.

379. A Compound Sentence (see § 187) consists of co-ordinate clauses, or of a principal clause with subordinate (dependent) ones.

Subordinate clauses may be infinitive or participial, or they may be connected with the principal sentence by relatives or conjunctions.

For the Infinitive and Participle, see §§ 385-397. For the Relative, see §§ 343-349. For the Conjunctions uniting *co-ordinate* clauses, see §§ 403-407.

380. As a general rule, the moods and tenses in subordinate clauses are used as in principal ones.

It must be especially noted that relatives or conjunctions, with ἄν (ἐάν), the hypothetical particle, generally take the Subjunctive.

Matt. v. 19 : ὃς ἐὰν οὖν λύσῃ, *whosoever therefore shall break.*

Matt. v. 20 : ἐὰν (εἰ ἄν) μὴ περισσεύσῃ, *if it shall not surpass.*

Matt. vi. 2 : ὅταν (ὅτε ἄν) ποιῇς ἐλεημοσύνην, *when thou doest alms.* For ὅτε with Indicative, see Matt. vii. 28.

Matt. xvi. 28 : ἕως ἂν ἴδωσι, *until they shall have seen.*

So with many other passages.

But the Imperfect Indicative is occasionally found when a matter of fact is spoken of. Mark vi. 56; Acts ii. 45, iv. 35; 1 Cor. xii. 2.

The use of the moods in *object-sentences,* **in** *conditional sentences,* **and in** *intentional clauses,* **demands separate consideration.**

Object-Sentences.

381. When the dependent clause expresses the object of any of the senses, or the matter of knowledge, thought, belief, etc.,[1] it is

---

[1] That is, when it follows one of the "verba sentiendi et declarandi."

§ 382, c.] DEPENDENT CLAUSES—OBJECTIVE. 315

often introduced by ὅτι with the Indicative; although the Infinitive is more usual (§ 389, a).

Luke xvii. 15 : ἰδὼν ὅτι ἰάθη, *seeing that he was healed.*

Matt. ix. 28 : πιστεύετε ὅτι δύναμαι τοῦτο ποιῆσαι; *believe ye that I am able to do this?*

Mark v. 29 : ἔγνω ... ὅτι ἴαται, *she perceived that she is healed.* So John xi. 13, xx. 14.

When the verb in the principal clause is in *past* time, the subordinate verb may still be in *present* time (*Indicative*), or else may change to the *Optative.*

382. *a.* In the New Testament, quotation is generally direct, and is introduced without any conjunctive particle.

Matt. viii. 3 : ἥψατο αὐτοῦ, λέγων θέλω, καθαρίσθητι, *he touched him, saying, "I will, be thou clean."*

The particle ὅτι, however, is often used to introduce the quoted words, and is in this case not to be translated, as it answers exactly to our inverted commas (" ").

Matt. vii. 23 : ὁμολογήσω αὐτοῖς, ὅτι οὐδέποτε ἔγνων ὑμᾶς, *I will avow unto them, "I never knew you."*

Luke viii. 49 : ἔρχεταί τις παρὰ τοῦ ἀρχισυναγώγου λέγων, ὅτι τέθνηκεν ἡ θυγάτηρ σου, μηκέτι σκύλλε τὸν διδάσκαλον, *then cometh one from the house of the ruler of the synagogue, saying unto him, "Thy daughter is dead, trouble the Master no more."*

b. **In indirect quotation (oratio obliqua) the substance of the speech is given, not the words. Here, also, the Indicative is generally employed.**

Mark iii. 21 : ἔλεγον γὰρ ὅτι ἐξέστη, *for they said that he was beside himself.* It is, however, possible that the verb here is a direct quotation (Aorist, see § 364, *d*), *they said, "He is beside himself."*

Of the Optative in the *oratio obliqua*, so common in classic Greek, there is no example in the New Testament except in indirect interrogations, as in the following paragraph, *c*, γ.

c. **Indirect interrogations,** another form of the *oratio obliqua*, may be connected with the principal clause by interrogative pronouns or adverbs, or by the particle εἰ, *if, whether.*

In such clauses, either (1) the verb is precisely the same as in the corresponding direct interrogation, when : (a) the **Indicative** shows that the inquiry concerns matter of fact ; (β) the **Subjunctive** (§ 376) expresses objective possibility—what may or should take place—and always has respect to present or to future time ; or (2) when the principal verb is in a past tense, either (α) or (β) may become (γ) the **Optative**, denoting subjective possibility—that which may be conceived to exist—and referring especially to the past.

a. Mark xv. 44 : ἐθαύμασεν εἰ ἤδη τέθνηκε, *he wondered whether he were already dead.*

Acts xii. 18 : ἦν τάραχος οὐκ ὀλίγος ἐν τοῖς στρατιώταις τί ἄρα ὁ Πέτρος ἐγένετο, *there was no small stir among the soldiers—whatever had become of Peter.*

Acts x. 18 (Pres. after Imperf.): ἐπυνθάνοντο[1] εἰ Σίμων ... ἐνθάδε ξενίζεται, *they were asking whether Simon ... lodges here.*

Luke xxiii. 6 (Pres. after Aor.) : ἐπηρώτησεν εἰ ὁ ἄνθρωπος Γαλιλαῖός ἐστι, *he asked if the man is a Galilean.*

For the Future in the dependent clause, see Mark iii. 2 ; 1 Cor. vii. 16; Phil. i. 22.

β. Matt. vi. 25 : μὴ μεριμνᾶτε ... τί φάγητε ἢ τί πίητε, *be not anxious ... what you are to eat and what you are to drink.* Compare Luke xii. 22.

Luke xix. 48 : οὐχ ηὕρισκον τὸ τί ποιήσωσιν, *they found not what they should do.* Compare Mark xv. 24.

In Rom. viii. 26, the reading varies between προσευξώμεθα (rec., W. H., Lachmann) and προσευξόμεθα (Tischendorf).

γ. Luke i. 29 : διελογίζετο ποταπὸς εἴη ὁ ἀσπασμὸς οὗτος, *she was discussing with herself of what kind this salutation might be.*

Acts xvii. 11 : ἀνακρίνοντες τὰς γραφὰς εἰ ἔχοι ταῦτα οὕτως, *searching the scriptures if these things were so.*

Acts xvii. 27 : ζητεῖν τὸν Θεόν,[2] εἰ ἄρα γε ψηλαφήσειαν αὐτὸν καὶ εὕροιεν, *to seek God, if by any chance they might feel after him and find him.*

The Indicative and Optative constructions are combined in Acts xxi. 33 : ἐπυνθάνετο τίς ἂν εἴη καὶ τί ἐστι πεποιηκώς, *he asked who he might be, and*

---

[1] W. H. marg. ; text ἐπύθοντο.
[2] Unquestionably the true reading, not τὸν Κύριον, as rec.

what he had done. He must have done something, this was clear; but who he was seemed altogether uncertain.

d. **After verbs of perceiving, knowing, declaring, and the like, both an object and an objective sentence are often found.**

Luke xix. 3 : ἐζήτει ἰδεῖν τὸν Ἰησοῦν, τίς ἐστι, *he was seeking to see Jesus, who he was* (is).

1 Cor. iii. 20 : Κύριος γινώσκει τοὺς διαλογισμοὺς τῶν σοφῶν ὅτι εἰσὶ μάταιοι (LXX.), *Jehovah knoweth the reasonings of the wise, that they are vain.*

See also Mark xi. 32, xii. 34; John iv. 35, v. 42, vii. 27; Acts iii. 10, xv. 36; 2 Cor. xii. 3, 4, xiii. 5; 1 Thess. ii. 1, etc. Compare 1 Cor. xv. 12.

A similar construction is occasionally found with "intentional" clauses, as Col. iv. 17; Gal. iv. 11.

Conditional Sentences.

383. A conditional or "hypothetical" sentence contains two clauses, often called "**protasis**," or *condition*, and "**apodosis**," or *consequence*. The former expresses the condition; the latter, the thing conditioned. Of these two the protasis is really the dependent *clause*, though the apodosis contains the dependent *fact*.

Protasis (*condition*).	Apodosis (*consequence*).
α. If he speaks,	I always listen.
β. If he speak,	I will listen.
γ. If he should speak,	I should listen.
δ. { If he spoke,	I would listen.
{ If he had spoken,	I would have listened.

These four sentences illustrate four kinds of hypothesis—

α. The supposition of a **fact**.
β. ,, ,, of a **possibility**.
γ. ,, ,, of **uncertainty**.
δ. ,, ,, of **something unfulfilled**.

Hence arise four distinct forms—

a. **The conditional particle εἰ,** *if,* **with the Indicative, in the protasis, assumes the hypothesis as a fact. The apodosis may have the Indicative or Imperative.** [So the Subjunctive with οὐ μή, equivalent to future Indicative; or, in exhortations, equivalent to Imperative.]

Matt. iv. 3 : εἰ υἱὸς εἶ τοῦ Θεοῦ, εἰπέ, κ.τ.λ., *if thou art the Son of God, command*, etc., *i.e.*, assuming that thou art.

Acts xix. 39 : εἰ δέ τι περαιτέρω ἐπιζητεῖτε, ἐν τῇ ἐννόμῳ ἐκκλησίᾳ ἐπιλυθήσεται, *but if ye inquire anything further, it shall be determined in the legal assembly*.

1 Cor. xv. 16 : εἰ γὰρ νεκροὶ οὐκ ἐγείρονται, οὐδὲ Χριστὸς ἐγήγερται, *for if the dead arise not, neither has Christ arisen*.

Rom. iv. 2 : εἰ Ἀβραὰμ ἐξ ἔργων ἐδικαιώθη, ἔχει καύχημα, *if Abraham was justified by works* (assuming that he was so), *he hath a ground of boasting*.

> See also many other passages, *e.g.*, Matt. xix. 17; John vii. 4 (present, condition; imperative, consequence); Rom. viii. 25; 1 Cor. vi. 2 (pres. pres.); John v. 47 (pres. fut.); 2 Pet. ii. 20 (pres. perf.); Matt. xii. 26 (pres. aor.); Matt. xxvi. 33 (fut. fut.); Acts xvi. 15 (perf. imperf.); 2 Cor. v. 16 (perf. pres.); John xi. 12; Rom. vi. 5 (perf. fut.); 2 Cor. ii. 5 (perf. perf.), vii. 14 (perf. aor.); Rom. xi. 17, 18 (aor. imperf.); 1 John iv. 11 (aor. pres.); John xv. 20 (aor. fut.); Rom. v. 15 (aor. aor.). (1 Cor. viii. 13 has pres. ind. and aor. subj. with οὐ μή; Gal. v. 25, pres. ind., pres. subj.)

β. **Possibility, or uncertainty with the prospect of decision, is expressed by** ἐάν = εἰ ἄν (very rarely by εἰ alone[1]) **with the Subjunctive in the conditional clause, and the Indicative or Imperative in the apodosis.**

> The condition hence refers to future time. The Subj. Aor., with ἐάν, may be rendered in most cases by the Future Perfect.

Matt. xvii. 20 : ἐὰν ἔχητε πίστιν ὡς κόκκον σινάπεως, ἐρεῖτε, κ.τ.λ., *if ye have faith as a grain of mustard seed, ye shall say*, etc.

John iii. 3, 5 : ἐὰν μή τις γεννηθῇ ἄνωθεν, οὐ δύναται ἰδεῖν τὴν βασιλείαν τοῦ Θεοῦ, *excepting one shall have been born again,* (*or from above*), *he cannot see the kingdom of God*.

2 Tim. ii. 5 : ἐὰν δὲ καὶ ἀθλῇ τις, οὐ στεφανοῦται ἐὰν μὴ νομίμως ἀθλήσῃ, *and if any one strive in a contest, he is not crowned except he shall have striven according to rule*.

γ. **The Optative in a conditional sentence expresses entire uncertainty—a supposed case. Here the particle εἰ is always used.**

1 Cor. xiv. 10 : εἰ τύχοι, *if it should chance*. So xv. 37.

---

[1] See 1 Cor. xiv. 5; Phil. iii. 12 (Luke ix. 13), and a few various readings, as Rev. xi. 5.

§ 383, δ.] CONDITIONAL SENTENCES. 319

1 Pet. iii. 14 : εἰ καὶ πάσχοιτε διὰ δικαιοσύνην, μακάριοι, *if ye even should suffer for righteousness' sake, happy* (are ye). See ver. 17.

Acts xxiv. 19, xxvii. 39 : εἰ δύναιντο, *if* (by any possibility) *they could.*

δ. **When the condition is spoken of as unfulfilled, the Indicative is used in both clauses, with the particle εἰ in the protasis, and ἄν in the apodosis.**

1. The **Imperfect** (in the apodosis) with ἄν points to *present* time, "If this were so now (which it is not), this other thing *would be.*"

Luke vii. 39 : οὗτος, εἰ ἦν προφήτης, ἐγίνωσκεν ἂν τίς καὶ ποταπὴ ἡ γυνή, *this man, if he were a prophet, would know who and what the woman is.*

John v. 46 : εἰ γὰρ ἐπιστεύετε Μωϋσεῖ, ἐπιστεύετε ἂν ἐμοί, *for if ye believed Moses, ye would believe me.*

Heb. iv. 8 : εἰ γὰρ αὐτοὺς Ἰησοῦς κατέπαυσεν, οὐκ ἂν περὶ ἄλλης ἐλάλει, *for if Joshua had given them rest, he would not speak of another day.*

So (with Impf. in the protasis) John viii. 42, ix. 41 ; Acts xviii. 14 ; 1 Cor. xi. 31 ; Heb. xi. 15 (with Aor. in the protasis) ; Gal. iii. 21, etc. Sometimes ἄν is omitted. See John ix. 33, xv. 22, etc.

2. The **Aorist** with ἄν points to the *past*, "If this had been so then (which it was not), this other thing *would have been.*" Sometimes the **Pluperfect** is used, more emphatically, in the same sense.

John xiv. 28 : εἰ ἠγαπᾶτέ με, ἐχάρητε ἄν, *if ye loved me, ye would have rejoiced.* "Ye would rejoice" would have been expressed by ἐχαίρετε.

So with the Impf. in protasis : Luke xii. 39 ; John xviii. 30 ; Acts xviii. 14.

1 Cor. ii. 8 : εἰ γὰρ ἔγνωσαν, οὐκ ἂν τὸν Κύριον τῆς δόξης ἐσταύρωσαν, *for had they known, they would not have crucified the Lord of glory.*

So with the Aor. in protasis : Matt. xi. 21 ; Mark xiii. 20 ; Rom. ix. 29. (Matt. xii. 7 has plup.)

John xi. 21 : Κύριε, εἰ ἦς ὧδε, οὐκ ἂν ὁ ἀδελφός μου ἐτεθνήκει,[1] *Lord, if thou hadst been here, my brother would not have been dead.* Mary (ver. 32) uses the Aorist.

See 1 John ii. 19.

---

[1] W. H. and Rev. Text read ἀπέθανεν.

John xiv. 7: εἰ ἐγνώκειτέ με, καὶ τὸν πατέρα μου ἂν ᾔδειτε (W. H.), *if ye had known me, ye would have known my Father also.*

Intentional Clauses.

384. Intentional (final) clauses are those which express a purpose or design, following the particles ἵνα, *to the end that* (with emphasis on result); ὅπως, *in order that* (emphasis on method); μή, *(that) not,* or *lest.*

a. (1) **In intentional clauses, the Subjunctive is employed in its general meaning to signify objective possibility or intention.**[1]

Matt. xix. 13 : προσηνέχθησαν ... ἵνα τὰς χεῖρας ἐπιθῇ αὐτοῖς καὶ προσεύξηται, *they were brought ... that he might put his hands upon them and pray.*

Luke vi. 34 : δανείζουσιν ἵνα ἀπολάβωσιν, *they lend that they may receive back.*

Matt. ii. 8 : ἀπαγγείλατέ μοι, ὅπως κἀγὼ ἐλθὼν προσκυνήσω, *bring me back word, that I also may come and worship.*

Matt. vi. 16 : ἀφανίζουσι ... ὅπως φανῶσι, *they disfigure ... that they may appear.*

So in a great number of passages.

> The final intentional clause with a particle of design must be distinguished from the objective clause with ὅτι. So λέγω ὑμῖν ὅτι, *I say to you that*, introduces the *matter* of the communication ; but εἰπὸν ἵνα (Matt. iv. 3), *say that*, specifies the *purpose* of what is said, and therefore implies *command*. Now, after verbs expressive of desire, prayer, and the like, where the matter is coincident with the purpose, the final and the objective particles seem equally appropriate. As a matter of fact, however, it will be found that while hope has ὅτι, prayer has ἵνα, ὅπως. ἐλπίζω ὅτι, *I hope that, i.e.,* "such is the object presented to my hope;" εὔχομαι ἵνα, *I pray that, i.e.,* "such is the purpose to be secured by my prayer" (2 Cor. i. 13 ; Philemon 22 ; Phil. i. 9 ; 2 Thess. iii. 1, etc.) In 2 Thess. i. 11, 12, ἵνα marks the primary, and ὅπως the secondary result. In 1 Cor. xiv. 13, it is not meant that the disciple is to pray for the power to interpret, but that his gift of prayer is to be so exercised as to involve the power of interpretation. Again, 2 Cor. xiii. 7, the matter of the prayer is expressed by an infinitive clause ; the intention by two clauses with ἵνα.
>
> The Evangelist John often (with, occasionally, others of the New Testament writers) employs ἵνα as explanatory (*purport*, rather than *purpose*). Thus, xvii. 3 : "this is life eternal, that they should know thee," etc. So xv. 8 ; 1 John iii. 1,

---

[1] The distinction of classic Greek, that after a past tense a final clause generally has the Optative, does not hold in N.T.

etc. (often epexegetic of οὗτος); but in other passages the usual meaning of the particle may be taken, as 1 John iii. 1.

Compare Matt. x. 25; Luke xvii. 2; even Phil. ii. 2. ("Fill up my joy by being of the same mind."—*T. S. Green.*)

(2) It has been a question with grammarians whether ἵνα ever means merely *so that*, expressing *event* without any reference to *purpose*. The former presumed use of the particle has been called its eventual (or ecbatic) sense, the latter its final (or telic[1]). Most, however, now agree that (with the exception above noted) the final significance is generally discernible. 1 Thess. v. 4 has been cited as "losing the notion of finality in the eventual sense;" *ye are not in darkness, that the day should overtake you as a thief.* But it would seem appropriate enough to represent it as the intention of darkness that those surrounded with it should be suddenly surprised. Again, in John xii. 23, xvi. 2, 32, Meyer justly remarks, "that which shall happen in the ὥρα is regarded as the object of its coming." On Gal. v. 17, Bishop Lightfoot says, "ἵνα here seems to denote simply the result, whereas in classical writers it always expresses the purpose." But surely this is unnecessary. Bishop Ellicott renders, *to the end that ye may not* [R.V., *that ye may not*], not *so that ye cannot*, A.V.; but with the usual and proper telic force of ἵνα. "The object and end of the τὸ ἀντικεῖσθαι (the antagonism) on the part of each principle is to prevent a man doing what the other principle would lead him to do."

> For other passages in which the final sense has been questioned, but where Winer and most modern critics maintain it, see Luke ix. 45 (purposely hidden, as a part of the Divine plan); John iv. 36, vii. 23, ix. 2, xi. 15; Rom. ix. 11, xi. 31; 2 Cor. i. 9, v. 4; Eph. ii. 9, iii. 10. In these, and in many similar texts, sound criticism seems to require the meaning, not *so that it was*, but *in order that it might be*.[2]

The importance of the discussion is chiefly seen in relation to the passages which speak of a Divine purpose, in prophecy or otherwise. For instance, the words of Old Testament prediction, Isa. vi. 10, are quoted, Matt. xiii. 15; Mark iv. 12; Luke viii. 10; John xii. 40; Acts xxviii. 27 (Matt. and Acts have from the LXX. μήποτε, the rest

---

[1] ἵνα ἐκβατικόν (from ἐκβαίνω, *to issue from*); ἵνα τελικόν (from τέλος, *end*).

[2] Undoubtedly in the later forms of the language the *ecbatic* sense became established. Thus, in modern Greek the Infinitive itself has become superseded by a form of the verb with the particle νά for ἵνα.

ἵνα ... μή). Is the passage to be read, *in order that seeing they may not see*, etc., or, *so that seeing they see not*, or even, *because seeing they see not?* We believe that the former interpretation is the only one admissible. The blindness is represented as judicial—a punishment inflicted by God on disobedience and hardness of heart.

Again, in the phrase, ἵνα (ὅπως) πληρωθῇ, *that it* (the Old Testament prophecy) *might be fulfilled* (Matt. i. 22, ii. 15, 23, iv. 14, viii. 17, xii. 17, xiii. 35, xxi. 4, xxvi. 56; Mark xiv. 49; John xiii. 18, xv. 25, xvii. 12, xviii. 9, xix. 24, 36), are we to understand the statement to be that *so the words were fulfilled*, sometimes, as it would seem, by an accommodation of their meaning, or that the occurrence took place *in order that they might be* fulfilled? To answer this question fully, would lead into a discussion of the whole scope and meaning of prophecy. But, as a point of grammar, there seems every reason why the usual meaning of the telic particles should be retained. It is the expositor's business to translate in order to interpret; not to interpret in order to translate. In some cases, at least, the words quoted could not *primarily* have had the meaning attached to them in the New Testament; but in their original acceptation they fell into the line of the "increasing purpose" which runs through the ages, and so revealed their highest significance in Messiah's day. The true key to the passage is not to be found in a perverted use of the *particle*, but in an accurate comprehension of the *verb*.[1]

See, especially, the transaction recorded John xix. 28-30.

Acts iii. 19: μετανοήσατε οὖν καὶ ἐπιστρέψατε, πρὸς τὸ ἐξαλειφθῆναι ὑμῶν τὰς ἁμαρτίας, ὅπως ἂν ἔλθωσι καιροὶ ἀναψύξεως, κ.τ.λ., can only be translated, *repent ye, therefore, and turn again, that your sins may be blotted out, that so there may come seasons of refreshing*, etc. (R.V.). The meaning *when* (A.V.) cannot be sustained. Whatever be the special reference of καιροὶ ἀναψύξεως, they are set forth as the purposed result of the people's repentance, and denote in some way the blessings of Messiah's kingdom.

(3) As a negative final particle, standing alone after verbs expressing fear, caution, anxiety, μή has the force of ἵνα μή, ὅπως μή.

---

[1] See Olshausen on Matt. i. 22. Grotius, and those who have followed his criticisms, attach to the verb some such meaning as *consummated*.

§ 384 (3).] INTENTIONAL CLAUSES. 323

Matt. xviii. 10 : ὁρᾶτε μὴ καταφρονήσητε ἑνὸς τῶν μικρῶν τούτων, *see that ye do not despise one of these little ones.*
So 2 Cor. viii. 20 ; Gal. vi. 1 ; Heb. xii. 15, 16.

After verbs of fearing, μή may be translated *lest,* or *that.*

2 Cor. xii. 20, 21 : φοβοῦμαι γὰρ, μή πως ἐλθὼν οὐχ οἵους θέλω εὕρω ὑμᾶς, κ.τ.λ., *for I fear that when I come I shall not find you such as I desire,* etc.

Acts xxiii. 10, xxvii. 17.

b. **A particle of intention may be followed by an Indicative Future** (never with ὅπως).

The instances of this idiom are few, and most of them are contested readings. The Future, where admitted, must be taken as conveying the idea of duration more vividly than the Aorist Subjunctive.

Gal. ii. 4 : ἵνα ἡμᾶς καταδουλώσουσιν, *that they should enslave us.*

Rev. xxii. 14 : μακάριοι οἱ πλύνοντες τὰς στολὰς αὐτῶν, ἵνα ἔσται ἡ ἐξουσία αὐτῶν, κ.τ.λ., *blessed are they who wash their robes,*[1] *that theirs may be the access,* etc. In 1 Pet. iii. 1, Rev. xiv. 13, W. H. have Ind. Fut., the Received Text has Subj. Aor.

μή (ποτε) is found with the Indicative Future, Heb. iii. 12 : βλέπετε, ἀδελφοί, μή ποτε ἔσται ἔν τινι ὑμῶν καρδία πονηρὰ ἀπιστίας, *take heed, brethren, lest there should* (shall) *be in any one of you an evil heart of unbelief.* So Col. ii. 8.

The Indicative present or perfect after μή shows the ellipsis, not of ἵνα, but of ὅτι ; *i.e.,* the sentence is not *intentional,* but *objective.* Luke xi. 35 : "lest the light *is* darkness." Gal. iv. 11 : "lest I have laboured."

There are three passages in which the Indicative present seems to be used in intentional clauses:—

1 Cor. iv. 6 : ἵνα μὴ εἷς ὑπὲρ ἑνὸς φυσιοῦσθε κατὰ τοῦ ἑτέρου, *that ye be not puffed up one for another against yet another.*

Col. iv. 17 : ἵνα αὐτὴν πληροῖς, *that thou fulfil it* (the ministry).

Gal. iv. 17 : ἵνα αὐτοὺς ζηλοῦτε, *in order that ye may zealously affect them.*

It will, however, be noted that all these verbs are of the contracted conjugation in -όω ; and it is easier to suppose them examples of an irregularly formed Subjunctive than of a syntax so anomalous as an Indicative would be. ἵνα as an adverb of place, *where,* is not found either in LXX. or N.T.

---

[1] Note here the various reading, accepted by the best critics (W. H., R. V.).

The Infinitive.

385. *a.* **The Infinitive Mood is a Verbal Substantive, and expresses the abstract notion of the verb.**

Like the *verb* in other moods, it admits the modifications of tense and voice. It may have a subject, or may govern an object, near or remote ; and it is qualified by adverbs. Like a *substantive*, it may be the subject or object of a verb ; it is often defined by the article, and is employed in the different cases.

b. **The Negative Adverb with the Infinitive may be** οὐ or μή.

Since οὐ denies as matter of fact, μή as matter of thought, and since the Infinitive usually depends on some verb or clause implying thought, will, design, the latter will generally be the appropriate particle.

Matt. ii. 12 : χρηματισθέντες ... μὴ ἀνακάμψαι πρὸς Ἡρῴδην, *being divinely warned not to return to Herod.*

Matt. v. 34 : λέγω ὑμῖν μὴ ὀμόσαι ὅλως, *I enjoin you not to swear at all.*

So viii. 28, and many other passages. Where οὐ is found, it may generally be connected with the principal verb. (See John xxi. 25.)

c. **The Infinitive governs the same case as the other parts of the verb.**

Matt. vii. 11 : οἴδατε δόματα ἀγαθὰ διδόναι τοῖς τέκνοις ὑμῶν, *ye know how to give good gifts unto your children.*

Luke xx. 35 : οἱ δὲ καταξιωθέντες τοῦ αἰῶνος ἐκείνου τυχεῖν, καὶ τῆς ἀναστάσεως τῆς ἐκ νεκρῶν, *they who are deemed worthy to obtain that life and the resurrection from the dead.*

Compare the rules on the use of the cases after verbs.

386. The distinction between the **Tenses of the Infinitive** is analogous to that in the Imperative and Subjunctive. The Present marks *continuity;* the Aorist, *a single act;* the Future (very rare in the New Testament), *intention* or *futurity;* and the Perfect, *a completed act.*

Matt. xiv. 22 : ἠνάγκασε τοὺς μαθητὰς ἐμβῆναι ... καὶ προάγειν αὐτόν, *he made the disciples embark* (a single act), *and go before him* (continuous).

Acts xxvii. 10 : μέλλειν ἔσεσθαι τὸν πλοῦν, *that the voyage is going to be.*

Acts xxvi. 32 : ἀπολελύσθαι ἐδύνατο ὁ ἄνθρωπος οὗτος, *this man could have been set at liberty.*

§ 389, a.] THE INFINITIVE. 325

The Present Infinitive might more properly be called the Imperfect Infinitive, referring, like the Perfect, to *state* rather than to time. The time is fixed by the principal verb.

387. The Subject of the Infinitive, when expressed, is always in the Accusative Case.

For the explanation of this rule, with examples, see § 285.

But the Subject of the Infinitive, when the same with that of the preceding verb, is generally omitted, words agreeing with it being in the nominative.

Rom. xv. 24: ἐλπίζω διαπορευόμενος θεάσασθαι ὑμᾶς, *I hope to see you* (in) *passing through*.

2 Cor. x. 2: δέομαι δὲ τὸ μὴ παρὼν θαρρῆσαι, *but I pray that I may not* (when) *present be bold*.

388. The Infinitive, with or without the Article, may form the Subject of a sentence.

Rom. vii. 18: τὸ γὰρ θέλειν παράκειταί μοι, τὸ δὲ κατεργάζεσθαι τὸ καλὸν οὔ, *for to will is present with me, but to accomplish the good is not*.

Gal. vi. 14: ἐμοὶ δὲ μὴ γένοιτο καυχᾶσθαι, *but far be it from me to glory!*

Eph. v. 12: αἰσχρόν ἐστι καὶ λέγειν, *even to mention ... is disgraceful*.

A peculiar kind of extended subject is formed by the Infinitive with ἐγένετο, *it came to pass that...* Thus, Acts ix. 3: ἐγένετο αὐτὸν ἐγγίζειν τῇ Δαμασκῷ, *it came to pass that he was approaching Damascus*, lit., "his approach to Damascus occurred." So Mark ii. 23; Luke vi. 1, 6; Acts iv. 5, xvi. 16, etc. Acts xxii. 17 has a combination of construction: *it happened to me when I had returned* (μοι ὑποστρέψαντι) *to Jerusalem, and as I was praying* (προσευχομένου μου, gen. abs.) *in the temple, that I was* (γενέσθαι με) *in an ecstasy*, etc.

The Subject Infinitive may have its own Accusative Subject.

Matt. xvii. 4: καλόν ἐστιν ἡμᾶς ὧδε εἶναι, *it is good for us to be here*.

1 Cor. xi. 13: πρέπον ἐστὶ γυναῖκα ἀκατακάλυπτον τῷ Θεῷ προσεύχεσθαι; *is it becoming for a woman to pray to God uncovered?*

Matt. xviii. 8: καλόν σοί ἐστιν εἰσελθεῖν εἰς τὴν ζωὴν κυλλὸν ἢ χωλόν, *it is good for thee to enter into life maimed or halt*, the pronoun σε being understood from σοι before εἰσελθεῖν.

389. *a.* **The Infinitive regularly stands as the Object of verbs denoting a mental faculty, impression, or act**—such as *to be able*, *to hear, see, believe, know, wish, hope, endeavour,* etc.; **and an assertion of thought or will,** as *to say, announce, proclaim, command, forbid,* etc.[1]

In this connection also the Infinitive may have its own Subject, and may take or omit the Article.

Matt. vi. 24 : οὐδεὶς δύναται δυσὶ κυρίοις δουλεύειν, *no man is able to serve two masters.*

Rom. i. 22 : φάσκοντες εἶναι σοφοὶ ἐμωράνθησαν, *professing to be wise, they became fools.*

Phil. ii. 6 : οὐχ ἁρπαγμὸν ἡγήσατο τὸ εἶναι ἴσα Θεῷ, *he esteemed not his being on an equality with God an object of eager desire* (R.V., *a prize*).

Here the object Infinitive is defined by the article ; ἴσα Θ- is the predicate of the Infinitive in apposition with the subject (ἴσα is adverbial) ; and ἁρπαγμὸν is in predicative apposition with the Infinitive itself.

b. **The Infinitive may be employed, for the expression of intention or result,** as an adjunct (1) to a verbal predicate.

Matt. ii. 2 : ἤλθομεν προσκυνῆσαι αὐτῷ, *we came to worship him*

Matt. xx. 28 ; 1 Cor. i. 17 ; Rev. xvi. 9, etc.

(2). An Infinitive in this sense may depend upon a Substantive, as in the frequent phrase ὁ ἔχων ὦτα ἀκούειν, *he that hath ears to hear.* So Acts xiv. 5 ; Heb. xi. 15, etc.

(3) It may depend upon an Adjective, as Luke xv. 19 : οὐκέτι εἰμὶ ἄξιος κληθῆναι υἱός σου, *I am no longer worthy to be called thy son.*

So with δυνατός, Acts ii. 24 ; 2 Tim. i. 12 ; ἱκανός, Mark i. 7 ; ἐλεύθερος, 1 Cor. vii. 39 ; ἕτοιμος, Luke xxii. 33, etc. Once with ἄδικος, Heb. vi. 10, *God is not unjust to forget.*

390. The Infinitive with the oblique cases of the Article (substantivised, §§ 201, 204) is employed as follows :—

a. **Genitive.**

1. Dependent upon nouns—

Luke x. 19 : δέδωκα ὑμῖν τὴν ἐξουσίαν τοῦ πατεῖν, κ.τ.λ., *I have given to you the power of treading,* etc.

---

[1] "Verba sentiendi vel declarandi," etc.

§ 390, c.] THE INFINITIVE. 327

Acts xx. 3 : ἐγένετο γνώμης τοῦ ὑποστρέφειν, *he was of the intention of returning.*

Acts xxvii. 20 : ἐλπὶς πᾶσα τοῦ σώζεσθαι ἡμᾶς, *all hope of our being saved.*

> Acts xiv. 9; 2 Cor. viii. 11; Phil. iii. 21, etc. So with words signifying time (time *for*), Luke i. 57, ii. 6, 21, xxi. 22 ; 1 Pet. iv. 17; Rev. xiv. 15.

2. Dependent upon verbs that usually take a genitive—

Luke i. 9 : ἔλαχε τοῦ θυμιᾶσαι, *he had obtained the lot of sacrificing.*

2 Cor. i. 8 : ὥστε ἐξαπορηθῆναι ἡμᾶς καὶ τοῦ ζῆν, *so that we despaired even of life.*

> 1 Pet. iii. 10 (LXX.). So after adjectives, Luke xxiv. 25; Acts xxiii. 15. Especially, with verbs signifying hindrance, Luke iv. 42; Rom. xv. 22.

3. Expressive of design, like ἵνα with Subjunctive, or ἕνεκα with Genitive—

Matt. ii. 13 : μέλλει γὰρ Ἡρῴδης ζητεῖν τὸ παιδίον τοῦ ἀπολέσαι αὐτό, *for Herod will seek the young child to destroy it.*

> So Matt. iii. 13, xxi. 32, xxiv. 45; Luke xxiv. 29; Acts xiii. 47 (LXX.); Heb. x. 7 (LXX.), etc.

But sometimes the notion of design seems almost or entirely lost in that of result. See also under ἵνα (§ 384).

Acts vii. 19 : οὗτος ... ἐκάκωσεν τοὺς πατέρας τοῦ ποιεῖν τὰ βρέφη ἔκθετα αὐτῶν, *this man ... ill-treated our fathers, so that they caused their babes to be exposed.*

> Compare Acts iii. 12; Rom. i. 24, vii. 3.

b. **Dative.**

The Dative of Cause. (See § 280, *c.*)

2 Cor. ii. 13 : οὐκ ἔσχηκα ἄνεσιν ... τῷ μὴ εὑρεῖν με Τίτον τὸν ἀδελφόν μου, *I had no rest through my not having found Titus my brother.*

> In 1 Thess. iii. 3, τῷ (Rec.) should be τό (W. H.). The above instance is the only one.

c. **Genitive, Dative, or Accusative, with Prepositions.**

A few illustrations of this usage will be sufficient, as the Prepositions are taken in their ordinary meaning. (See §§ 288–307.)

328 THE INFINITIVE. [§ 390, c.

διά, with Genitive, "through."
Heb. ii. 15 : **διὰ παντὸς τοῦ ζῆν**, *through all their lifetime.*
διά, with Accusative, "on account of."
Matt. xiii. 5 : **διὰ τὸ μὴ ἔχειν βάθος** ... **διὰ τὸ μὴ ἔχειν ῥίζαν**, *on account of its having no depth ... on account of its having no root.*

    So, with acc. subject, Matt. xxiv. 12; Mark v. 4 ; Luke ii. 4, xi. 8, etc.

εἰς, "to the end that."
Matt. xx. 19 : **εἰς τὸ ἐμπαῖξαι καὶ μαστιγῶσαι καὶ σταυρῶσαι**, *to mock and scourge and crucify.*

    So Mark xiv. 55 ; Luke v. 17, with subject, etc. Both εἰς and πρός express purpose, but πρός the more emphatically.

ἐν, "in, during," especially of time.
Matt. xiii. 25 : **ἐν δὲ τῷ καθεύδειν τοὺς ἀνθρώπους**, *and while men slept.*

    So also Matt. xxvii. 12 ; Mark ii. 15 ; Luke i. 21, etc.

μετά, with Accusative, "after."
Matt. xxvi. 32 : **μετὰ δὲ τὸ ἐγερθῆναί με**, *but after I have risen.*

    So Luke xii. 5, xxii. 20 ; Acts i. 3, etc.

πρό, "before," opposed to μετά.
Matt. vi. 8 : **πρὸ τοῦ ὑμᾶς αἰτῆσαι αὐτόν**, *before ye ask him.*

    So Luke ii. 21, xxii. 15 ; John i. 48, etc.

πρός, with Accusative, "in order to."
Matt. vi. 1 : **πρὸς τὸ θεαθῆναι αὐτοῖς**, *in order to be gazed at by them.*

    So Matt. xiii. 30, xxvi. 12 ; Mark xiii. 22, etc. Once, *in reference to,* Luke xviii. 1.

Once ἀντί is found, James iv. 15, *instead of your saying;* and ἕνεκα, 2 Cor. vii. 12, *for the sake of your zeal being made manifest.* ἕως, "until," occurs with Gen. inf., Acts viii. 40, *until he came.*

391. To express result, the particle ὥστε is often prefixed to the Infinitive. It should be noted that ὥστε is properly *ecbatic,* as distinguished from *telic* particles. Compare § 384.

Matt. viii. 24 : **σεισμὸς μέγας ἐγένετο ... ὥστε τὸ πλοῖον καλύπτεσθαι**, *there arose a great storm, so that the vessel was being covered.*

Matt. xiii. 32 : **ὥστε ἐλθεῖν τὰ πετεινά**, *so that the birds came.*

§ 393.]   PARTICIPLES.   329

Luke ix. 52 : ὥστε¹ ἑτοιμάσαι αὐτῷ, *so as to make ready for him.*

Acts xvi. 26 : ὥστε σαλευθῆναι τὰ θεμέλια, *so that the foundations were shaken.*

So in a great number of passages. Twice only in N.T. is ὥστε foun[d] in this meaning with the Indicative; a construction common in classic Greek.

John iii. 16 : οὕτως γὰρ ἠγάπησεν ὁ Θεὸς τὸν κόσμον ὥστε τὸν υἱὸν τὸν μονογενῆ ἔδωκεν, κ.τ.λ., *God so loved the world that he gave his only-begotten Son,* etc.

So also Gal. ii. 13.

The proper distinction between the Infinitive and Indicative in this connection is, that the former expresses the result as the **natural and logical consequence** of what has been previously enunciated ; the latter states it simply as a **fact which occurs or has occurred.**[2]

392. In Phil. iii. 16 we find the Infinitive employed for the Imperative ; εἰς ὃ ἐφθάσαμεν, τῷ αὐτῷ στοιχεῖν, *whereto we have attained, in the same direction walk ye.*[3]

The use of χαίρειν in salutation is similar, "greeting," Acts xv. 23, xxiii. 26; James i. 1 (2 John 10, 11, suggests an ellipsis here). This habitual phrase reappears as a more decided Imperative, Rom. xii. 15, with an antithetic verb : χαίρειν μετὰ χαιρόντων, κλαίειν μετὰ κλαιόντων, *rejoice with the rejoicing, weep with the weeping.*

PARTICIPLES.

393. The Participles "partake" the nature of Verbs and of Adjectives.[4]

Like *verbs*, they have the modifications of Voice and Tense ; and may have an object, immediate or remote. Like *adjectives*, they agree with substantives, expressed or understood ; and are subject to the exceptional constructions of *Synesis*, or "rational concord."

On these points, therefore, nothing need be added to the rules already given.

---

[1] W. H. read ὡς.
[2] See Bishop Ellicott on Gal. ii. 13.
[3] Ellicott. The rest of the verse (Rec.) is omitted by the best critics.
[4] The Infinitive is the Verbal Substantive, the Participle the Verbal Adjective.

The **Tenses of the Participle** conform in meaning to those of the Indicative. Their various uses will be seen in the examples given under the following sections.

The **Negatives used with Participles** follow the general law. Thus, οὐκ εἰδότες, "not knowing," *as a matter of fact* (a class definite); μὴ εἰδότες, "not knowing," *as a matter of supposition* (a class indefinite), such ignorance being presumed as the ground of any further assertion respecting them. Compare Gal. iv. 8 with 1 Thess. iv. 5 ; 2 Thess. i. 8. As, however, the Participle is generally expressive of some condition, the negative employed is in most cases μή.

When a Participle has a Subject of its own in a separate clause, the construction is the **Genitive Absolute,** for which see § 275. The following rules give the use of Participles referring to the Subject or Object of another verb.

394. Participles (like Adjectives) are *predicative* or *attributive*. Their predicative uses may be classified as follows :—

1. **After the forms of the substantive verb, a Participle may be used as a simple or "primary" predicate.**

> This construction is confined to the present and perfect Participles. With the latter, certain parts of the verb *to be* make regular compound tense-forms, as the third person plur., perf. and plup. Passive. (See Paradigms.) The usage is extended, however, to the singular number and to other persons. Luke iv. 16 : οὗ ἦν τεθραμμένος, *where he had been brought up.* John iii. 28 : ἀπεσταλμένος εἰμί, *I have been sent.* With the present Participle, the substantive verb gives a *continuous* sense, forming what are called the "**resolved tenses.**" (See §§ 362, *e*, 363, *e*.)
>
> The resolved tense must be distinguished from the use of the Participle as secondary predicate. For example, 2 Cor. v. 19 is not to be read, *God was reconciling the world in Christ,* but *God was in Christ reconciling,* etc.

Luke xxiv. 32 : οὐχὶ ἡ καρδία ἡμῶν καιομένη ἦν ἐν ἡμῖν; *was not our heart burning within us?*

> Sometimes this construction appears very nearly equivalent to the simple verb, as Mark xiii. 25 (compare Matt. xxiv. 29). So Acts ii. 2 ; James i. 17, iii. 15. In other cases there is a greater stress upon the notion of state or duration :— Pres., Acts xxv. 10 ; Rev. i. 18 ; Matt. x. 26 ; Luke vi. 43 ; 2 Cor. ix. 12 ; Gal. iv. 24 (not "which things are *an allegory,*" but *are allegorised, i.e.,* susceptible of allegorical application, *contain an allegory,* R.V. ; ἅτινα being used, not ἅ, see § 349) ; Col. ii. 23 ; 1 Cor. xv. 19 ; 2 Cor. ii. 17. Impf., Matt. vii. 29, xix. 22 ; Mark i. 39 ; Luke i. 22, xv. 1, xxiii. 8 ; Acts xxi. 3 ; Gal. i. 22, 23. Fut., Matt. x. 22 ; Luke i. 20, v. 10, xxi. 24.

In Luke iii. 23, αὐτὸς ἦν ὁ Ἰησοῦς ἀρχόμενος ὡσεὶ ἐτῶν τριάκοντα, we must understand, *Jesus himself, when he began* (to teach), *was about thirty years of age* (R.V.) (for gen., see § 266), not "began to be about thirty" (A.V.).

2. Certain verbs, expressive of perception, or the conditions of an action, are complemented by a Participle, instead of an Infinitive.

If the verb is neuter or passive, the Participle agrees with the Subject; if active, with the Object.

Such verbs in the New Testament are—(1) neuter: παύομαι, τελέω (διαλείπω, ἐγκακέω), all variously signifying desistence from a thing; φαίνομαι, *to be manifest*, and λανθάνω, *to be secret*, in doing anything; (2) active: ἀκούω, γινώσκω, ὁράω, βλέπω, etc.

Luke v. 4 : ὡς ἐπαύσατο λαλῶν, *when he ceased speaking*.

Acts v. 42, vi. 13, xiii. 10, xx. 31, xxi. 32 ; Eph. i. 16 ; Col. i. 9 ; Heb. x. 2.

Matt. vi. 18 : μὴ φανῇς τοῖς ἀνθρώποις νηστεύων, *that thou appear not to men as fasting;* ver. 16.

Matt. xi. 1 : ὅτε ἐτέλεσεν ... διατάσσων, *when he made an end of commanding.*

Luke vii. 45 ; Gal. vi. 9 ; Matt. i. 18 (pass.).

Heb. xiii. 2 : ἔλαθόν τινες ξενίσαντες ἀγγέλους, *some unawares entertained* (were secret in entertaining) *angels*.[1]

Luke iv. 23 : ὅσα ἠκούσαμεν γενόμενα εἰς τὴν Καπερναούμ, *whatever things we heard of as done in Capernaum.*

Mark xiv. 58; Acts ii. 11, vii. 12 ; 2 Thess. iii. 11, etc.

Heb. xiii. 23 : γινώσκετε τὸν ἀδελφὸν ἡμῶν Τιμόθεον ἀπολελυμένον, *know that our brother Timothy has been liberated.*

Acts viii. 23 ; Heb. x. 25.

Some of these verbs may also be followed by an inf. or by a finite verb with ὅτι. Thus compare 2 Thess. iii. 11 with John xii. 18 and 34.

When the predicative Participle is used, the real Object of the verb is in the noun. In the infinitive construction, the Infinitive contains the Object, and ὅτι reduces the thing heard to the form of a proposition.

So 3 John 4 : ἀκούω τὰ ἐμὰ τέκνα ἐν τῇ ἀληθείᾳ περιπατοῦντα is, I hear of *my children*, that they walk in the truth.

---

[1] A very common classic idiom.

περιπατεῖν would have been, I hear of the *walking* of my children in the truth.

ὅτι περιπατοῦσιν would have meant, *the tidings* brought to me are these, *that*, etc.

Again : 1 John iv. 2 : ὁμολογεῖ Ἰησοῦν Χριστὸν ἐν σαρκὶ ἐληλυθότα, *confesses Jesus Christ come in the flesh* (not *who came*, which would have required τὸν ἐλ...). ἐληλυθέναι (W. H. marg.) would signify, *that Jesus Christ has come*. (Comp. 2 John 7.)

So with neuter verbs: ὅπως φανῶσι τοῖς ἀνθρώποις νηστεύοντες, *that they may appear unto men fasting*, i.e., the fasting was *real*. νηστεύειν would have implied that the fasting was only *apparent*. On the contrary, ἐπαιτεῖν αἰσχύνομαι (Luke xvi. 3) means, *I am ashamed to beg;* ἐπαιτῶν would have meant, I am ashamed *of begging*.[1]

3. A Participle without the Article, and in grammatical concord with the Subject of the verb, may stand as adjunct to the verbal Predicate.

These adjuncts may be of various kinds, as—

a. **Modal,** setting forth the manner in which the given action was performed.

Matt. v. 2 : ἐδίδασκεν αὐτοὺς λέγων, *he taught them, saying*.

Matt. xix. 22 : ἀπῆλθε λυπούμενος, *he went away sorrowful*.

Matt. xi. 25, etc. : ἀποκριθεὶς εἶπεν, *he said, having addressed himself to reply,* "he answered and said."

Matt. xxviii. 19; Acts iii. 8, xiii. 45 ; 1 Tim. i. 13. For the Aor. Part. marking the commencement of the action, see Acts i. 24 ; Rom. iv. 20.

b. **Temporal,** denoting (i.) a contemporaneous, (ii.) preceding, or (iii.) consequent fact.

(i.) Pres. Acts v. 4 : οὐχὶ μένον σοὶ ἔμενε; *while it remained did it not remain thine?*

Matt. vi. 7 ; Acts xxi. 28 ; 1 Tim. i. 3, *when I was on my way;*[2] Heb. xi. 21; Rom. xv. 25 (*ministering;* he had already entered on his errand of ministry); 1 Pet. i. 8, 9 (*while ye see not ... yet believe ... while* [also] *ye receive*).

(ii.) Aor. Acts ix. 39 : ἀναστὰς δὲ Πέτρος συνῆλθεν αὐτοῖς, *and Peter having arisen went with them,* i.e., "arose and went with them."

---

[1] See Rev. T. S. Green's "Greek Testament Grammar," p. 183.

[2] There is here a strong argument for an apostolic journey after Paul's Roman imprisonment, as no part of the history in the Acts corresponds with this mission of Timothy.

This use of the Aor. Part. is one of the most common idioms in the New Testament, and may be continually represented in translation by two verbs—the action of the one (the Participle) immediately preceding that of the other. Or we may render by some such preposition as *after, upon,* with the verbal noun; or by a temporal clause with *when.*

Acts iii. 3 : ὃς ἰδών ... ἠρώτα, *who saw ... and asked;* or, *on seeing ... asked;* or, *when he saw ... asked.*

So ver. 4, 7, 12, iv. 7, 8, 13 (*while beholding* [pres.] and *having ascertained*), 15, 18, 19, 21, 23, 36, 37, etc. In fact, there is scarcely any usage more common in the New Testament.

(iii.) Fut. Acts viii. 27 : ὃς ἐληλύθει προσκυνήσων. εἰς Ἱερουσαλήμ, *who had come to Jerusalem to worship.*

This idiom (the Fut. Part. to express a purpose) is rare in the New Testament. (See Acts xxiv. 11.)

c. A Participle often expresses some relation of cause, condition, etc., to the principal verb. This relation the general sense of the passage will show.

Causal. Acts iv. 21 : ἀπέλυσαν αὐτούς, μηδὲν εὑρίσκοντες, κ.τ.λ., *they released them, as they found nothing,* etc.

Concessive. Rom. i. 32 : οἵτινες τὸ δικαίωμα τοῦ Θεοῦ ἐπιγνόντες ... αὐτὰ ποιοῦσιν, κ.τ.λ., *who, though made aware of the righteous decree of God ... do these things,* etc.

Conditional. Rom. ii. 27 : καὶ κρινεῖ ἡ ἐκ φύσεως ἀκροβυστία τὸν νόμον τελοῦσα, κ.τ.λ., *and shall not that which naturally is uncircumcision, if it fulfil the law, judge thee,* etc.

Matt. vi. 27 (*by anxious care*); Rom. viii. 23 ; 2 Cor. v. 2 (*because we desire*).

d. **Intensive,** a Hebraism. (Compare § 280, *b.*) Like the cognate dative noun, a Participle of the same verb may be employed.

Heb. vi. 14 : εὐλογῶν εὐλογήσω σε, καὶ πληθύνων πληθυνῶ σε, *blessing I will bless thee, and multiplying I will multiply thee.* (LXX.; Gen. xxii. 17.)

So Matt. xiii. 14 ; Acts vii. 34.

A predicative Participle may be qualified by ὡς, *as, as if,* declaring the alleged ground of an assertion.

Luke xvi. 1 : διεβλήθη ... ὡς διασκορπίζων, κ.τ.λ., *he was accused, as though wasting,* etc.

Luke xxiii. 14 : προσηνέγκατέ μοι τὸν ἄνθρωπον τοῦτον ὡς ἀποστρέφοντα τὸν λαόν, *ye brought before me this man on the charge of perverting the people.*

    1 Cor. vii. 25.

    In like manner, the particles καίπερ, καίτοι, *although,* may be employed.

    Heb. v. 8 : καίπερ ὢν υἱός, *although he was a son.*

    So Heb. iv. 3, with gen. abs. ; vii. 5, ἐξεληλυθότας, in apposition with obj. ; 2 Pet. i. 12.

395. Participles as epithets are used like adjectives.

Acts xxi. 26 : τῇ ἐχομένῃ ἡμέρᾳ, *on the next day.*

1 Tim. i. 10 : εἴ τι ἕτερον τῇ ὑγιαινούσῃ διδασκαλίᾳ ἀντίκειται, *if anything else is opposed to the healthful teaching* (of the faith). For other instances of this participle, see vi. 3 ; 2 Tim. i. 13, iv. 3 ; Titus i. 9, ii. 1.

396. With the Article, the Participle is equivalent to the relative with the finite verb.

    It may thus stand in apposition with a noun in any relation to the sentence, or may be used alone, the substantive being understood.

Matt. i. 16 : Ἰησοῦς ὁ λεγόμενος Χριστός, *Jesus who is called Christ.*

Mark vi. 2 : ἡ σοφία ἡ δοθεῖσα τούτῳ, *the wisdom which is given unto this man.*

Luke xxi. 37 : τὸ ὄρος τὸ καλούμενον Ἐλαιῶν, *to the mount that is called "of Olives."*

1 Cor. ii. 7 : λαλοῦμεν Θεοῦ σοφίαν ... τὴν ἀποκεκρυμμένην, *we speak the wisdom of God ... that hath been hidden.*

1 Thess. ii. 15 : τῶν καὶ τὸν Κύριον ἀποκτεινάντων ... καὶ ἡμᾶς ἐκδιωξάντων καὶ Θεῷ μὴ ἀρεσκόντων, (of the Jews) *who both slew the Lord ... and drove us out, and do not please God.*

    By a comparison of examples, the distinction between the use of the Participle with and without the Article will be clearly seen. ὁ διδάσκων is *he who teaches ;* ὁ διδάξας, *he who taught ;* whereas διδάσκων alone would mean *while he was teaching,* and διδάξας, *when he had taught.*

The Participle and Article often form a substantive phrase. See §§ 200, 204 : ὁ σπείρων, *he who sows, a sower.*

§ 397.]   ATTRIBUTIVE PARTICIPLES.   335

In some cases the substantivised Participle appears to have lost all temporal reference.

Eph. iv. 28 : ὁ κλέπτων μηκέτι κλεπτέτω, *let him that stealeth steal no more*. Here ὁ κλέψας, *he who stole* (once), would be too weak in meaning, while ὁ κλέπτης would be too strong.[1]

So Heb. xi. 28. With an Object we find the same construction
Gal. i. 23 : ὁ διώκων ἡμᾶς ποτέ, *our former persecutor*.
1 Thess. i. 10 : Ἰησοῦν τὸν ῥυόμενον ἡμᾶς, *Jesus our deliverer*.

Winer quotes also Matt. xxvii. 40 ; John xii. 20 ; Acts iii. 2 ; Gal. ii. 2 ; Rom. v. 17 ; 1 Thess. v. 24 ; 1 Pet. i. 17. But in some of these passages there may well be a special reference to the time then present. So John xiii. 11 : he knew τὸν παραδιδόντα αὐτόν, *the man then betraying him, i.e.*, who was then at work for that purpose.

The Present may occasionally be explained according to § 361, *d*. Matt. xxvi. 28 : τοῦτό ἐστι τὸ αἷμά μου ... τὸ περὶ πολλῶν ἐκχυννόμενον, *this is my blood which is being shed (i.e.*, to be shed) *for many*. So διδόμενον, *being given*, Luke xxii. 19 ; κλώμενον, 1 Cor. xi. 24.

In other cases, the ordinary meaning of the Present is to be taken. Acts ii. 47 : "the Lord was adding daily to the church," τοὺς σωζομένους, *those who were being saved, i.e.*, in the course or way of salvation. 2 Cor. ii. 15 : "we are of Christ a sweet savour unto God, *in those who are being saved*, and *in the perishing*" (ἐν τοῖς σωζομένοις καὶ ἐν τοῖς ἀπολλυμένοις). 2 Cor. iii. 13 : "so that the children of Israel could not look to the end *of that which was vanishing away*" (τοῦ καταργουμένου), viz., the glory on the countenance of Moses.

397. In some cases a Participle seems to stand alone, the verb to which it is an adjunct being at a distance from it, or the construction of the sentence being broken.[2]

Rom. v. 11 : καυχώμενοι must be connected with σωθησόμεθα, ver. 9, *we shall be saved*—and not only that, but *saved with joyful consciousness of the blessing*.

1 Pet. ii. 18–iii. 7 : ὑποτασσόμενοι, ὑποτασσόμεναι, ἀγαθοποιοῦσαι, μὴ φοβούμεναι, συνοικοῦντες, are not for imperatives, as has been supposed, but are adjuncts to τιμήσατε, ii. 17 : *render due honour to all ... ye servants*

---

[1] Stier, Ellicott, Alford.
[2] See Winer's collection and explanation of instances, § 45, 6.

by subjection ... ye wives by subjection, well-doing, fearlessness, ye husbands by dwelling with them, etc.

2 Pet. i. 20 : γινώσκοντες continues the thought of προσέχοντες, dependent on καλῶς ποιεῖτε, ver. 19, *ye do well in taking heed, knowing this first*. So ch. iii. 3 ; read with μνησθῆναι, ver 2.

Instances of broken structure (anacolouthon, see § 412) may be found in Acts xxiv. 5 : *having found this man*, etc., *who also endeavoured to profane the temple, whom also we laid hold of*, instead of "we laid hold of him." 2 Cor. v. 6, 8 : *being confident—yea, we are confident and well pleased ;* the sentence, but for the parenthesis of ver. 7, being evidently intended as "we, being confident, are well pleased." 2 Cor. vii. 5, where θλιβόμενοι is really in apposition with the ἡμεῖς implied in ἡ σὰρξ ἡμῶν. Heb. viii. 10, where καί interrupts the structure of the sentence. Eph. iv. 1-3 ; Col. iii. 16, etc.

Chapter VII. ADVERBS.

398. Adverbs qualify verbs and adjectives as in other languages.

The rules for the formation of derivative Adverbs, with lists of the Adverbs most in use, are given, §§ 126–134.
The use of Adverbs with the Article is shown, § 198.

399. Adverbial phrases are very frequent in the New Testament, and are of various kinds.

a. **A substantive, with or without a preposition, may be adverbially used.** (Compare § 126.) The modal dative is adverbial (§ 280, *a*). So sometimes the accusative, as τὴν ἀρχήν, John viii. 25, *essentially* (Alford). Many phrases with κατά are adverbial (see § 300, 6). Special adverbial combinations are: ἀπὸ μέρους, *partially*, Rom. xi. 25; 2 Cor. i. 14, ii. 5. ἐκ μέρους, *individually*, 1 Cor. xii. 27; *partially*, 1 Cor. xiii. 9, 10, 12. κατὰ μέρος, *particularly*, Heb. ix. 5. ἀπὸ μιᾶς (γνώμης), "with one consent," *unanimously*, Luke xiv. 18. εἰς τὸ παντελές, "in any wise," Luke xiii. 11; "to the uttermost," Heb. vii. 25; *utterly*. ἐν ἀληθείᾳ, "in truth," *truly*, Matt. xxii. 16, etc. ἐν δικαιοσύνῃ, *righteously*, Acts xvii. 31. ἐν ἐκτενείᾳ, *instantly*, "in earnestness," Acts xxvi. 7. ἐπ' ἀληθείας, "of a truth," *truly*, Luke xxii. 59.

For the force of these and similar phrases, see under the respective prepositions.

James iv. 5: πρὸς φθόνον ἐπιποθεῖ τὸ πνεῦμα ὃ κατῴκισεν ἐν ἡμῖν.[1] This difficult passage should probably be rendered, *jealously does the Spirit which he placed in us desire* (us for his own, Alford). This adverbial force of the substantive with πρός is common in classical Greek, though elsewhere without parallel in the New Testament.

b. **For the adjective used adverbially,** see § 319.

c. **For adverbial notions conveyed by means of participles,** see § 394, 3.

---

[1] W. H. read interrogatively ἡμῖν; See R.V. and marg.

d. **An adverbial phrase is sometimes formed by a combination of two verbs.** So in the Old Testament often, "He added and spake," or, "He added to speak," for "He spake again," an idiom copied by the LXX. from the Hebrew.

Luke xx. 11, 12: προσέθετο πέμψαι, *he added to send;* where Mark xii. 4 reads πάλιν ἀπέστειλε, *he sent again.* Acts xii. 3: προσέθετο συλλαβεῖν, *he proceeded to apprehend,* or, "further apprehended." But Luke xix. 11, προσθεὶς εἶπεν is the participial construction, *he added and spake.*

> Some expositors have unnecessarily interpreted other verbal combinations as adverbial; *e.g.,* Luke vi. 48: ἔσκαψε καὶ ἐβάθυνε, "he digged deep" (A.V.), but rather, *he digged and went deep* (R.V.), the second verb being an advance upon the first. So Rom. x. 20: *Isaiah is very bold, and saith,* not "very boldly saith;" Col. ii. 5: *rejoicing* (over you) *and seeing,* not "seeing with joy" (comp. Ellicott's note); James iv. 2: *ye murder and envy,* not "envy murderously," or "murder enviously" (see Alford). So in many other passages.

400. For a list of the **Adverbs used as prepositions** governing cases, see § 133. These may enter into combination with other adverbs, as Matt. xi. 12: ἕως ἄρτι, *until now.* So John ii. 10, v. 17, etc. Matt. xvii. 17: ἕως πότε; *how long?* lit., "until when?" So Mark ix. 19; Luke ix. 41; John x. 24: *how long dost thou keep our minds in suspense?* (Alford). Matt. xviii. 21, 22: ἕως ἑπτάκις, κ.τ.λ., *until seven times,* etc. See also Matt. xxiv. 21: ἕως τοῦ νῦν; xxvii. 8: ἕως τῆς σήμερον. Mark xiv. 54: ἕως ἔσω. Luke xxiii. 5: ἕως ὧδε. Acts xxi. 5: ἕως ἔξω, etc. So Rom. i. 13: ἄχρι τοῦ δεῦρο, *until now,* lit., "until the (time) hitherto," viii. 22; 2 Cor. iii. 14, 15; Phil. i. 5.

> The use of the Article with the latter Adverb, however, renders it simply equivalent to a Substantive.

401. Repeated reference has already been made to the **distinction between the negative Adverbs** οὐ **and** μή. Generally speaking, οὐ denies as matter of fact, μή as matter of thought, supposition, etc. The former, therefore, is the *usual* negative with the Indicative mood, the latter the *usual* negative with the other parts of the verb. Deviations from this rule are to be explained by the primary sense of the two adverbs. Thus, John iii. 18: ὁ πιστεύων εἰς αὐτὸν οὐ κρίνεται, *he that believeth on him is not condemned* (the statement of a fact); ὁ δὲ μὴ πιστεύων, *but he that believeth not* (whoever he may be) *has already been condemned;* ὅτι μὴ

§ 401.] ADVERBS. 339

πεπίστευκεν, κ.τ.λ., *because he hath not believed* (according to the supposition made).

The same distinction applies to the compounds of οὐ and μή, as οὔδε, μήδε, οὐκέτι, μηκέτι, etc.

Two, or even three, negatives in the same clause do not contradict one another,[1] **but serve to strengthen the negation.**

Luke iv. 2 : οὐκ ἔφαγεν οὐδέν, *he ate not anything.*

Luke xxiii. 53 : οὗ οὐκ ἦν οὐδεὶς οὔπω κείμενος, *where no one at all had yet ever lain.* John xix. 41.

For special forms of strengthened negation, see §§ 363, d, 377. For the use of negatives in interrogations, see § 370.

When one of two contrasted statements is intended to *qualify* **the other, it is sometimes forcibly expressed as an actual** *denial.*

Thus, in Hosea vi. 6, the Hebrew reads, "I will have mercy *and not* sacrifice." The LXX. translates ἔλεος θέλω ἢ θυσίαν, "I will have mercy *rather than* sacrifice," so conveying the general meaning. Matt. ix. 13, in quoting the passage, returns to the Hebrew expression, καὶ οὐ θυσίαν. Compare Jeremiah vii. 22.

In this idiom the negatived thought, though not absolutely contradicted, is excluded from view, that its antithesis may make its full impression. Compare Matt. x. 20 ; Mark ix. 37 ; Luke x. 20 (omit μᾶλλον) ; John vii. 16,[2] xii. 44 ; Acts v. 4 ; 1 Thess. iv. 8, etc.

Only the context in such cases will show whether the negative is absolute or comparative. In some instances, where an exposition similar to the above has been adopted, the meaning of particular words has been mistaken. Thus, in John vi. 27, ἐργάζεσθε μὴ τὴν βρῶσιν τὴν ἀπολλυμένην, κ.τ.λ., "labour not for the meat that perisheth," etc., the verb ἐργάζεσθε does not mean "labour" generally, but *busy yourselves,* referring to the present excitement of the people. 1 Tim. v. 23 : μηκέτι ὑδροπότει is not "drink no longer water," but *be no longer a water-drinker,* the verb not being precisely equal to ὕδωρ πίνε, but pointing to the regular habit.[3]

---

[1] The usage is thus directly opposed to the English and Latin, where "two negatives make an affirmative."

[2] Winer holds, as it would appear without sufficient reason, that this passage and Matt. ix. 13 above intend absolute contradiction.

[3] Ellicott ; R. V.

Chapter VIII. CONJUNCTIONS.

402. For a classified list of the Conjunctions, see ETYMOLOGY, § 136.

Conjunctions are, with respect to their place in the sentence, either *prepositive*, *i.e.*, placed at the beginning of the clause, as καί, ἀλλά, ὅτι, or *postpositive, i.e.*, placed after some other word or words, as δέ, γάρ.

Words connected by Conjunctions are in the same grammatical regimen.

A clause connected with another by a Conjunction is either co-ordinate or subordinate. The rules for the chief kinds of subordinate clauses have been given, §§ 379–384. The following rules, therefore, imply Co-ordination.

CONJUNCTIONS OF ANNEXATION, καί, τε.

403. The proper copulative Conjunction, employed as in other languages, is καί, *and*.

Of the **special uses of** καί, the following may be enumerated.

a. Sometimes it appears to convey a kind of **rhetorical emphasis**.

Matt. iii. 14 : καὶ σὺ ἔρχῃ πρός με; *and comest thou unto me ?*

Matt. vi. 26 : καὶ ὁ πατὴρ ὑμῶν, κ.τ.λ., *and (yet) your heavenly Father feedeth them !*

John i. 10 : καὶ ὁ κόσμος αὐτὸν οὐκ ἔγνω, *and (yet) the world knew him not.*

> See Bruder's Concordance, p. 453, for an interesting collection of instances. The logical connection of the clauses being strongly apparent in their signification, it is sufficient to place the simple copulative between them, the reader's mind supplying the additional links.

b. In the **enumeration of particulars**, *both ... and* may be expressed by καί ... καί, by the postpositive τε with καί, or (rarely) by τε ... τε.

Acts ii. 29 : καὶ ἐτελεύτησε καὶ ἐτάφη, *he both died and was buried.*

Matt. xxii. 10 : συνήγαγον ... πονηρούς τε καὶ ἀγαθούς, *they collected ... both bad and good.*

§ 403, e.]   CONJUNCTIONS OF ANNEXATION.   341

Acts i. 1 : ὧν ἤρξατο Ἰησοῦς ποιεῖν τε καὶ διδάσκειν, *which Jesus began both to do and to teach.*

Acts xvii. 4 : τῶν τε σεβομένων Ἑλλήνων πλῆθος πολὺ γυναικῶν τε τῶν πρώτων οὐκ ὀλίγαι, *both a great multitude of the devout Greeks, and of the chief women not a few.*

John iv. 11 : οὔτε ἄντλημα ἔχεις καὶ τὸ φρέαρ ἐστὶ βαθύ, *thou both hast nothing to draw with, and the well is deep.* So 3 John 10.

> The difference[1] between καί and τε is that καί unites things strictly co-ordinate; τε annexes, often with implied relation or distinction. Hence it may sometimes be read as implying "and this as well as the other," with *ascensive* force, although generally it adds a less important particular.

c. The **points of transition** in a narrative are frequently marked by καί, rendered into English, for rhetorical variety, by *then, now,* etc.

Luke x. 29 : *and who is my neighbour?* Luke xviii. 26 : *and who can be saved?* John ix. 36 (W. H.) : *and who is he, Lord, that I should believe?* καί dramatically connects the question with what has just been said.

Matt. viii. 8. (See Mark iii. 13–26, viii. 10–18, and many other passages.)

d. This conjunction has also an **explanatory or "epexegetic" use**, repeating (in thought, or by the aid of a pronoun) something that has been said, in order to introduce some additional particular.

Eph. ii. 8 : τῇ γὰρ χάριτί ἐστε σεσωσμένοι διὰ πίστεως· καὶ τοῦτο οὐκ ἐξ ὑμῶν, Θεοῦ τὸ δῶρον· *for by grace have ye been saved through faith; and this not of yourselves, it (i.e., your being saved, is) the gift of God.* "You must not suppose, because your salvation was conditioned by your faith, that therefore you saved yourselves."[2]

Luke viii. 41 (pronoun and verb in the epexegetic clause), xxiii. 41; John i. 16 (neither verb nor pronoun); 1 Cor. i. 2, ii. 2, vi. 8 (read τοῦτο).

e. **Without direct connective force**, καί often takes the meaning of *also, even.*

---

[1] Winer. "καὶ conjungit, τε adjungit."—*Hermann.*
[2] Some still refer τοῦτο to πίστεως (quite allowable on the score of gender, by *synesis*); but this seems against the Apostle's argument. (See Ellicott, Eadie, Alford.)

Matt. v. 39 : στρέψον αὐτῷ καὶ τὴν ἄλλην, *turn to him also the other cheek.*

Mark i. 27: καὶ τοῖς πνεύμασι τοῖς ἀκαθάρτοις ἐπιτάσσει, *he lays his command even upon the unclean spirits.*

It is evident that the emphasis in such passages arises from the tacit connection and comparison with other objects of thought. The conjunction, therefore, is virtually still copulative.

This use of καί is frequent in **comparisons.**

Matt. vi. 10 : γενηθήτω τὸ θέλημά σου ὡς ἐν οὐρανῷ καὶ ἐπὶ γῆς, *thy will be done as in heaven so also upon earth.*

John vi. 57 : καθὼς ἀπέστειλέ με ὁ ζῶν πατήρ, κ.τ.λ., *as the living Father sent me,* etc. There are two following clauses with καί, either of which might supply the second member of comparison : " *so I live ... and,*" or (as A.V. and R.V.) " *and I live ... so.*"

Gal. i. 9 : ὡς προειρήκαμεν καὶ ἄρτι πάλιν λέγω, *as we have said before, so now also I say again.*

Hence the use of καί to introduce the apodosis after hypothetical and temporal clauses. Luke ii. 21 : *then also his name was called Jesus;* 2 Cor. ii. 2 : *for if I grieve you, then who is he that gladdens me?* often with ἰδού, *then behold!* as Matt. xxviii. 9 ; Acts i. 10, etc.

In the **rising climax**, οὐ μόνον is generally found in the former clause, ἀλλὰ καί in the latter.

Acts xxi. 13 : ἐγὼ γὰρ οὐ μόνον δεθῆναι ἀλλὰ καὶ ἀποθανεῖν ... ἑτοίμως ἔχω, *for I am ready not only to be bound, but also to die.*

Rom. xiii. 5 : οὐ μόνον διὰ τὴν ὀργὴν ἀλλὰ καὶ διὰ τὴν συνείδησιν, *not only on account of the wrath, but also on account of conscience.*

For the combination καὶ γάρ, see § 407, *d.*

Conjunctions of Antithesis, ἀλλά, δέ.

404. i. ἀλλά, *but* (emphatic as contrasted with δέ), is used to mark *opposition, interruption, transition.*

a. **Opposition**, simply. John xvi. 20 : ὑμεῖς λυπηθήσεσθε, ἀλλ' ἡ λύπη ὑμῶν εἰς χαρὰν γενήσεται, *ye shall grieve, but your grief shall be turned into joy.*

Frequently after negatives—

Matt. v. 17: οὐκ ἦλθον καταλῦσαι, ἀλλὰ πληρῶσαι, *I came not to destroy, but to fulfil.*

Rom. iii. 31 : μὴ γένοιτο · ἀλλὰ νόμον ἱστάνομεν, (W. H.) *assuredly not; but we establish law.*

b. **Interruption.** When a train of thought is broken, by some limitation, modification, correction.

John xii. 27 : πάτερ, σῶσόν με ἐκ τῆς ὥρας ταύτης · ἀλλὰ διὰ τοῦτο, κ.τ.λ., *Father, save me from this hour! but for this cause came I unto this hour.*

> Often in such connections the conjunction carries with it the force of *Nay*, especially after questions (Matt. xi. 8, 9 ; Luke vii. 25).

c. **Transition:** the point of contrast being that the succeeding phrase is a new subject, or the same in a different aspect; like our *Well, then; Moreover;* Luke vi. 27, xi. 42 ; Gal. ii. 14, etc.

Special uses of this conjunction are (1) **to throw emphasis on the following clause.**

John xvi. 2 : ἀποσυναγώγους ποιήσουσιν ὑμᾶς · ἀλλ' ἔρχεται ὥρα, κ.τ.λ., *they shall cast you out of the synagogues—yea, the hour cometh,* etc.

So with a negative—

Luke xxiii. 15 : οὐδὲν εὗρον ἐν τῷ ἀνθρώπῳ ... ἀλλ' οὐδὲ Ἡρῴδης, *I found no blame in the man ... no, nor yet Herod.*

(2) **In a conditional sentence,** ἀλλά may stand in the apodosis with the meaning *yet, nevertheless.*

1 Cor. ix. 2 : εἰ ἄλλοις οὐκ εἰμὶ ἀπόστολος, ἀλλά γε ὑμῖν εἰμί, *if I am not an apostle to others, yet at least I am so to you.* So Rom. vi. 5, etc.

(3) **After a negative** (expressed or implied), ἀλλ' ἤ means *other than, except, but rather.*

Luke xii. 51 : οὐχί, λέγω ὑμῖν, ἀλλ' ἢ διαμερισμόν · *I tell you, nay, but rather division.*

> In 2 Cor. i. 13 we find the combination ἄλλα ... ἀλλ' ἤ, *other things ... than.*
> For this idiom after a *virtual* negative, see 1 Cor. iii. 5 (Received Text), *who then is Paul and who is Apollos but ministers?* (ἀλλ' ἢ διάκονοι). But W. H. and Rev. Text omit ἀλλ' ἤ.

ii. δέ (postpositive) **is also most properly adversative, though less emphatic than** ἀλλά. It is to be carefully distinguished, on the other hand, from the copulatives καί, τε, with the latter of which it is, however, often interchanged in MSS.

Thus, the frequent phrase, ἐγὼ δὲ λέγω ὑμῖν, marks either a contrast with what has been said before, or an addition to it; the antithesis lying in the thought, "the foregoing is not all, *but* I add," etc.

It is generally difficult to exhibit the exact adversative force of this conjunction, and in translation it is often taken as a mere adjunctive. Thus, in the A.V. it is very frequently rendered *and*, or *then* (Matt. xix. 23), *now* (xxi. 18), *so* (xx. 8), or left entirely untranslated (xxviii. 1). The "δέ **resumptive**" is especially, perhaps unavoidably, so treated.

> A close attention to this particle in the innumerable instances of its occurrence will repay the student, who will often by its means mark an otherwise concealed antithesis. The following illustrations are from Winer:—
>
> Matt. xxi. 3: *but he will straightway send them*, i.e., not cavil or hesitate, but—.
>
> Acts xxiv. 17: *but* I pass on to another part of my history.
>
> 1 Cor. xiv. 1: *yet desire spiritual gifts*, notwithstanding the supremacy of love.
>
> 2 Cor. ii. 12: *but when I came to Troas;* δέ resumptive, from ver. 4.
>
> 1 Cor. xi. 2: *but I praise you*, even while I exhort, as ver. 1.
>
> Rom. iv. 3: *but Abraham believed God*, so far was he from being justified by works (James ii. 23).

καὶ ... δέ, together imply *yea ... moreover*, assuming what has been said, and passing on to something more.[1]

Matt. x. 18, xvi. 18 (*and not only so, but I say unto thee*); John vi. 51, viii. 16, 17, xv. 27; Acts iii. 24, xxii. 29; 2 Pet. i. 5; 1 John i. 3.

The full form of antithesis with μέν and δέ is frequent in the New Testament.[2] Compare § 136, *b*, 4.

Matt. ix. 37: ὁ μὲν θερισμὸς πολύς, οἱ δὲ ἐργάται ὀλίγοι, *the harvest is plenteous, but the labourers are few.*

Matt. xvi. 3, xx. 23, xxii. 8, xxiii. 27, 28, xxvi. 41, etc.

---

[1] See Alford, Matt. x. 18.
[2] Far less frequent, however, than in classic Greek.

§ 405.] THE DISJUNCTIVES. 345

Sometimes μέν is followed by the emphatic adversative ἀλλά : Mark ix. 12 ; Acts iv. 16 ; Rom. xiv. 20 ; also by πλήν, Luke xxii. 22 ; καί, Acts xxvi. 4, etc.

In several passages μέν is found without any antithetic particle. This is to be explained by an interrupted construction of the sentence, or by virtual antithesis. According to Winer, these cases may be classed in a threefold way :—

1. The suppressed parallel member of the antithesis is implied in the clause with μέν. Rom. x. 1 ; Col. ii. 23.

2. It is plainly indicated under another turn of expression. Rom. xi. 13.

3. The construction is entirely broken, and the parallel clause is to be supplied by the general sense of the sequel. Acts i. 1 ; Rom i. 8, iii. 2, vii. 12 ; 1 Cor. xi. 18, etc.

THE DISJUNCTIVES.

405. The disjunctives are ἤ, *or* (after a comparative, *than*) ; ἤ ... ἤ, *either ... or :* εἴτε ... εἴτε, *whether ... whether.* Once, ἤτοι ... ἤ, *whether ... or* (there being no other alternative), Rom. vi. 16.

Matt. v. 17 : μὴ νομίσητε ὅτι ἦλθον καταλῦσαι τὸν νόμον ἤ τοὺς προφήτας, *think not that I came to destroy the law or the prophets.*

Matt. xii. 33 : ἤ ποιήσατε τὸ δένδρον καλὸν ... ἤ ποιήσατε τὸ δένδρον σαπρόν, κ.τ.λ., *either make the tree good ... or make the tree corrupt,* etc.

Luke xx. 2 : ἐν ποίᾳ ἐξουσίᾳ ταῦτα ποιεῖς, ἤ τίς ἐστιν ὁ δούς σοι τὴν ἐξουσίαν ταύτην ; *in what authority doest thou these things, or who is he that gave thee this authority ?* Matt. xxi. 23 has καί. Either conjunction evidently gives equally good sense.

1 Cor. xi. 27 : ὅς ἂν ἐσθίῃ τὸν ἄρτον ἤ πίνῃ τὸ ποτήριον τοῦ Κυρίου, *whoever shall eat the bread or drink the cup of the Lord* (whichever he does, not by any means implying that he is not to do both). The previous verse has καί, which is also a var. read. here. (W. H., ἤ.)

1 Cor. x. 31 : εἴτε οὖν ἐσθίετε εἴτε πίνετε εἴτε τι ποιεῖτε, *whether then ye eat or drink, or do anything* (at all).

The combination ἤ καί, *or even*, occurs Luke xviii. 11 ; Rom. ii. 15 ; 2 Cor. i. 13.

The interrogative ἤ, so called, is no more than the disjunctive with the former clause understood.[1]

Rom. iii. 29 : ἤ Ἰουδαίων ὁ Θεὸς μόνον; οὐχὶ καὶ ἐθνῶν; *or is he the God of Jews only? not of Gentiles also?* Such, the Apostle suggests, is the alternative of denying the statement made, ver. 28.

> See Rom. vi. 3, vii. 1, etc. In 1 Cor. xiv. 36 the former ἤ is not correlative with the latter, but refers to the previous train of thought : *Or, was it that the word of God,* etc.? as must be supposed if you deny my authority in these matters.

INFERENTIAL CONJUNCTIONS.

406. The chief particles of inference are **οὖν**, *therefore*, postpositive, and **ἄρα**, *accordingly*, postpositive, or, with emphasis, prepositive.

> οὖν is properly the particle of formal inference, kindred to the participle of εἰμί, ὤν, ὄν (*quæ cum ita sint*). ἄρα, cognate with ἄρω, to fit, marks a correspondence in point of fact (*ergo*).

Matt. iii. 8 : ποιήσατε οὖν καρπὸν ἄξιον τῆς μετανοίας, *yield, therefore, fruit worthy of your repentance.*

Gal. ii. 21 : εἰ γὰρ διὰ νόμου δικαιοσύνη, ἄρα Χριστὸς δωρεὰν ἀπέθανεν, *for if righteousness is by law, then Christ died in vain.*

Both these particles, however, are often found with slighter meaning, as in our use of the words *Then, Well then,* in the continuance of narrative or speech. **ἄραγε** (Matt. vii. 20, xvii. 26 ; Acts xi. 18 ; xvii. 27) is emphatic. The combination, **ἄρα οὖν**, is found repeatedly in the Epistles of St. Paul, as Rom. v. 18 : *So, therefore,* the οὖν marking the logical inference, and the ἄρα intimating the harmony between premises and conclusion.

> For ἄρα interrogative, see 137, *b.*

Other inferential particles occasionally found are **μενοῦνγε,** *yes, indeed, but,* Luke xi. 28 ;[2] Rom. ix. 20, x. 18 ; **τοιγαροῦν,** *wherefore then,* 1 Thess. iv. 8 ; Heb. xii. 1 ; **τοίνυν** (*surely now*), *therefore,* Luke xx. 25 ; 1 Cor. ix. 26 ; Heb. xiii. 13.

---

[1] See Viger's "Greek Idioms," and Hartung, Partikellehre, *sub voc.* ἤ.
[2] W. H. and Rev. Text read μενοῦν, *yea rather.*

Causal Conjunctions, especially γάρ.

407. *a.* The causal conjunctions are *demonstrative* and *relative*. Of these the latter occur in subordinate clauses, the rules of which have already been given.

The relative causal particles are ὅτι, *because;* διότι, *because* (not in the Gospels or Rev.). Similarly used is ἐπεί (properly temporal, *when*), *since*, with its emphatic compounds ἐπειδή, *since now;* ἐπείπερ[1] (once, Rom. iii. 30), *since indeed;* and ἐπειδήπερ (only Luke i. 1), *forasmuch as.* (See § 137, *a.*)

For the relative phrases, with prepositions, used as conjunctions—*e.g.*, ἐφ' ᾧ, ἀνθ' ὧν—see under the Prepositions, §§ 305, 291.

b. The demonstrative causal conjunction, **γάρ**, always postpositive, is a contraction of **γὲ ἄρα**, "verily then;" hence, *in fact*, and, when the fact is given as a reason or explanation, *for.*

Matt. i. 21; ii. 2, 5, 6, 13, 20; iii. 2, 3, 9, 15, etc.

Generally, the explanation introduced by γάρ is also a direct reason. But this need not always be the case. See Matt. i. 18: "Mary, *as the fact was*, being betrothed." Mark v. 42: "She arose and walked, *for she was twelve years old;*" xvi. 4: "They saw that the stone was rolled away, *for it was very great*" (an explanation, not of the *fact* that it was rolled away, but of the *necessity* for this being done). Compare Ps. xxv. 11: "For thy name's sake, O Lord, pardon mine iniquity, *for it is great*" (the reason, not why pardon is to be *bestowed*, but why it is *sought*).

The student must beware of translating γάρ by such words as *but, although, yet peradventure,* etc.[2] Rom. v. 7 reads, *for scarcely on behalf of a righteous man will one die; for on behalf of the good man one even dares to die.* "The second *for*," says Alford, "is *exceptive*, and answers to 'I do not press this without exception,' understood." The good man and the righteous are not contrasted as *different* classes of persons, but the "good" (as the article also shows) are *classed under* the "righteous."

c. **In questions and answers especially, γάρ is often used in reference to the words or thought of the other party.**

Matt. xxvii. 23: τί γὰρ κακὸν ἐποίησε; *why, what evil hath he done?*
John vii. 41; Acts viii. 31, xix. 35 (*be calm! for what man is there?* etc.).

---

[1] W. H. and Rev. Text read εἴπερ, *if indeed.*
[2] See Winer, § 53, 10, 3.

John ix. 30 : ἐν τούτῳ γὰρ τὸ θαυμαστόν ἐστιν, *why, herein is the wonder!* In 1 Thess. ii. 20 the Apostle thus answers his own question : *yes, ye are our glory and our joy.*

d. In **the combination καὶ γάρ**, the true connective is generally καί, which resumes in thought the topic of the previous clause; while γάρ appends the explanation or the reason (Lat. *etenim*).

Matt. viii. 9 : καὶ γὰρ ἐγὼ ἄνθρωπός εἰμι, κ.τ.λ., *and (this I say) for I am a man under authority*, etc.

So Matt. xxvi. 73 ; Mark x. 45 ; Luke vi. 32, 34 ; John iv. 23 (*and [that,] because the Father,* etc.) ; Acts xix. 40 (*and [this advice I press,] seeing that,* etc.); 1 Cor. v. 7, xii. 13, 14 ; 2 Cor. v. 4, xiii. 4 ; 1 Thess. iv. 10 ; 2 Thess. iii. 10 ; Heb. v. 12, x. 34, etc. In these cases, καὶ γάρ must generally be rendered simply *for* (or *for, indeed*), except when it is desired by paraphrase to bring out its full meaning.

But sometimes **γάρ** is the connective, and καί belongs to the second clause, with the sense of *also, even* (γάρ, of course, being placed after it as a postpositive conjunction). (See Ellicott's note on 2 Thess. iii. 10.)

Rom. xi. 1 : καὶ γὰρ ἐγὼ Ἰσραηλίτης εἰμι, *for I also am an Israelite.*

Rom. xv. 3 : καὶ γὰρ ὁ Χριστὸς οὐχ ἑαυτῷ ἤρεσεν, *for even Christ pleased not himself.*

So perhaps Heb. xii. 29 : καὶ γὰρ ὁ Θεὸς ἡμῶν πῦρ καταναλίσκον, *for even our God is a consuming fire.*

ASYNDETON.

408. The omission of conjunctions, or *asyndeton*,[1] **often heightens the effect of a paragraph.**

a. The *copulative* may be omitted, as Gal. v. 22 : ὁ δὲ καρπὸς τοῦ πνεύματός ἐστιν ἀγάπη, χαρά, εἰρήνη, μακροθυμία, χρηστότης, ἀγαθωσύνη, πίστις, πραΰτης, ἐγκράτεια, *but the fruit of the Spirit is love, joy, peace, longsuffering, kindness, goodness, faith, meekness, self-control.*

b. **καί** *epexegetic* is sometimes dropped. Col. i. 14 : ἐν ᾧ ἔχομεν τὴν ἀπολύτρωσιν, τὴν ἄφεσιν τῶν ἁμαρτιῶν, *in whom we have the redemption, the remission of our sins.*

---

[1] ἀσύνδετον, from ἀ, *not*, and συνδέω, *to bind together.*

§ 408, c.]   CAUSAL CONJUNCTIONS.   349

c. The omission of the *antithetic* may be marked in passages like 1 Cor. xv. 42-44 :—

σπείρεται ἐν φθορᾷ, ἐγείρεται ἐν ἀφθαρσίᾳ.
σπείρεται ἐν ἀτιμίᾳ, ἐγείρεται ἐν δόξῃ.
σπείρεται ἐν ἀσθενείᾳ, ἐγείρεται ἐν δυνάμει.
σπείρεται σῶμα ψυχικόν, ἐγείρεται σῶμα πνευματικόν.

d. The *causal particle* is occasionally dropped. 2 Cor. xi. 30 : εἰ καυχᾶσθαι δεῖ, τὰ τῆς ἀσθενείας καυχήσομαι, (for) *if I must needs glory I will glory of the things that concern my weakness.* So, perhaps, Rev. xxii. 10, where the Rec. Text supplies ὅτι. (But W. H. and Rev. Text read ὁ καιρὸς γάρ.)

Chapter IX. ON SOME PECULIARITIES IN THE STRUCTURE OF SENTENCES.

409. *a.* **The arrangement of words in a sentence indicates the order of thought.** Hence, naturally, the Subject with the words connected takes the leading place, then the Predicate with its adjuncts. Words connected in sense are mostly kept together. The Object usually follows the governing verb; a Genitive or Dative, the word on which it depends; and an Adjective, the substantive with which it agrees (the *article* being repeated).

> The opposite constructions are emphatic, as--(1) When the Predicate stands first: see the Beatitudes, Matt. v. 3-11; also Matt. vii. 13-15; John i. 1, iv. 19, 24, vi. 60; Rom. viii. 18, *unworthy are the sufferings;* 2 Tim. ii. 11. (2) The Object before the verb: Luke xvi. 11, *the true riches who will entrust to you?* John ix. 31; Rom. xiv. 1, etc. (3) An oblique case before the governing noun: Rom. xi. 13, *of Gentiles an apostle;* Rom. xii. 19 (Heb. x. 30); 1 Cor. vii. 9; Heb. vi. 16; 1 Pet. iii. 21, etc. (4) An Adjective before its noun: Matt. vii. 13, *through the strait gate* (the emphasis being on the narrowness); 1 Tim. vi. 12, 14, where *good* (καλός) is repeatedly and strikingly emphatic; James iii. 5.
>
> The usual arrangement of Adverbs, Prepositions, and the Particles generally, has already been sufficiently illustrated.

b. **Since, in an inflected language like the Greek, it is unnecessary to indicate the grammatical dependence of words by their order, the arrangement of a sentence may be indefinitely varied for purposes of emphasis;** and there is, perhaps, not a paragraph in the New Testament in which the collocation of words does not indicate some subtle meaning or shade of thought, scarcely to be reproduced in the most accurate translation.

> Generally speaking, the emphatic positions are at the beginning and the end of a clause, especially the former.

c. **Constructions that apparently violate the simplicity of speech may generally also suggest some special emphasis.**

1 Cor. xiii. 1: *if with the tongues of men I speak, ... and of the angels.*

Heb. vii. 4: *to whom Abraham gave tithe of the spoils ... the patriarch,* *i.e.*, though he bore that sacred character.

§ 410 (2).]   PECULIARITIES OF CONSTRUCTION.   351

1 Pet. ii. 7 : *for you, then, is the preciousness .. who believe, i.e.*, on the condition that you are believers.

> See also Heb. ii. 9
> The displacement of a word or phrase, as in the above instances, for the sake of greater effect, is sometimes termed **Hyperbaton**, from ὑπερβαίνω.

410. Elliptical constructions are not infrequent. Many have already been noticed in their place; as the ellipsis of the Copula, § 166; of the Subject, § 169; of Substantives, §§ 256, 316. Two important elliptical forms of expression are the following:—

(1) **Aposiopēsis,** or expressive pause : some look or gesture, or the mind of the hearer, being supposed to supply the rest.

Luke xiii. 9 : κἂν μὲν ποιήσῃ καρπόν ... εἰ δὲ μήγε, κ.τ.λ., *and if it bear fruit ... but if not*, etc.

Acts xxiii. 9 : εἰ δὲ πνεῦμα ἐλάλησεν αὐτῷ, ἢ ἄγγελος ..., *but if a spirit spoke to him, or an angel ...* (The following words, *let us not fight against God,* are regarded by the best editors as an interpolation.)

> See also Luke xix. 42, xxii. 42 ; John vi. 62.

(2) **Zeugma:** a construction in which a verb is joined to two or more different objects, though only applicable in strictness to one.

1 Cor. iii. 2 : γάλα ὑμᾶς ἐπότισα, οὐ βρῶμα, *I gave you milk to drink, not meat.*

> See also Luke i. 64; Acts iv. 28; 1 Tim. iv. 3 (where the antithetic verb must be understood).

In accordance with the primitive simplicity of language, **the links between different clauses are sometimes omitted,** being left to the reader to supply in thought.

Thus, Rom. vi. 17 : *thanks be to God that ye were the servants of sin, but ye obeyed*, etc., *i.e.*, "that *although* ye were once the servants of sin, ye have now obeyed."

So 1 Tim. i. 13, 14 : *I obtained mercy, because I did it ignorantly in unbelief, but the grace of our Lord was exceeding abundant, i.e.,* " I obtained mercy, because (while I acted thus) the grace of the Lord abounded."

> Compare also Matt. xi. 25 ; John iii. 19.

411. *a.* **Some forms of expression are apparently redundant. In these cases a special emphasis may generally be marked.**

Instead, therefore, of assuming pleonasm, the careful student will note the emphatic meaning. Frequent cases are the following:—(1) Simple *repetition* of a phrase. Rom. viii. 15 : "ye *received* not the *spirit* of bondage, but ye *received* the *spirit* of adoption;" Col. i. 28 : "warning *every man*, and teaching *every man* in all wisdom, that we may present *every man* perfect in Christ Jesus ;" Heb. ii. 16 : "he *taketh* not *hold* of angels, but he *taketh hold* of the seed of Abraham." (2) Repetition in a *contrasted* form. John i. 20 : "he *confessed*, and *denied not ;*" Acts xviii. 9 : "*Speak*, and *be not silent ;*" Rom. ix. 1 (1 Tim. ii. 7): "I *speak the truth* in Christ, I *lie not.*" This idiom is especially frequent in 1 John (see chap. i. 5, 6, 8, 10, ii. 4, etc.). (3) The mention of *accompanying circumstances*, as Matt. v. 2 : "he *opened his mouth*, and said" (comp. Acts viii. 35); John xxi. 13 : "Jesus *cometh*, and *taketh* the bread, and *giveth* to them ;" where "every separate act of the wonderful occurrence is designedly specified, and, as it were, placed before the eye."[1] The verbs, *come, arise, take, stretch forth* (the hand), are frequently found in such connection.

b. **An idiom to be especially noticed is that in which an Accusative object and an Object-sentence are both appended to the verb.**

In this case also the double expression conveys an emphasis ; the attention being first called to the Object, and then to that which is said about it. For examples of this idiom, see § 382, *d.* Other instances are John xi. 31 ; Acts iv. 13, ix. 20, xvi. 3 ; 1 Cor. xvi. 15 ; Gal. vi. 1.

412. Anacoloutfion (ἀκολουθέω, *to follow*, with neg. prefix) is literally a breach in the continuity of a sentence, and is a term applied to those numerous instances in which the construction is changed in the course of the same period.

Many so-called *anacoloutha* are, however, to be explained by laws of construction already laid down. The deviations from strict grammatical construction, excepting in the book of Revelation, are *comparatively* few, and are generally to be paralleled from classic authors.

The most frequent cases of anacolouthon may be classed as follows :—

a. The transition from the indirect to the direct form of speech—

---

[1] Winer.

§ 412, e.] PECULIARITIES OF CONSTRUCTION. 353

Luke v. 14: *he charged him to tell no man* (μηδενὶ εἰπεῖν), *but go and show thyself*, etc. (ἀπελθὼν δεῖξον, κ.τ.λ.).

See also Mark vi. 9, xi. 32; Acts i. 4, xvii. 3.

b. The transition from a participial construction to a finite verb—

John v. 44: πῶς δύνασθε ὑμεῖς πιστεῦσαι, δόξαν παρ' ἀλλήλων λαμβάνοντες, καὶ τὴν δόξαν ... οὐ ζητεῖτε; *how can ye believe, receiving glory one of another, and the glory ... ye receive not.*

Eph. i. 20: ἐγείρας αὐτὸν ... καὶ ἐκάθισεν, *having raised him ... and he set him.* (But W. H. and Rev. Text read καθίσας.)

See also 1 Cor. vii. 37; 2 Cor. v. 6, 8; Col. i. 6, 26; 2 John 2.

c. The use of nominative participles in reference to substantives of any case, standing at a distance in the sentence—

Phil. i. 29, 30: ὑμῖν ἐχαρίσθη τὸ ὑπὲρ Χριστοῦ ... πάσχειν, τὸν αὐτὸν ἀγῶνα ἔχοντες, *to you it was granted to suffer for Christ, having the same conflict.* (W. H. by a parenthesis ending at πάσχειν connect the participle with ver. 28, and avoid irregularity).

Compare § 397.

d. A change of structure in the course of the sentence—

Luke xi. 11: τίνα δὲ ἐξ ὑμῶν τὸν πατέρα αἰτήσει ὁ υἱὸς ἰχθύν μὴ ... ὄφιν αὐτῷ ἐπιδώσει; (W. H.); lit., *from which of you, the father, shall his son ask a fish ... will he give him a serpent?*

Compare Mark ix. 20; John vi. 22-24; Acts xix. 34.

e. The non-completion of a compound sentence; the second member of a comparison, for instance, being omitted, or only suggested by the general sense of the passage—

1 Tim. i. 3: καθὼς παρεκάλεσά σε προσμεῖναι ἐν Ἐφέσῳ, *as I exhorted thee to abide in Ephesus* (where the A.V. supplies *so do*, the R.V. *so do I now* at the end of ver. 4, without anything corresponding in the original.)

Rom. v. 12: *as by one man sin entered into the world.* The antithesis, Winer thinks, is completed in sense, though not in form, in ver. 15. Others suppose a long parenthesis from vers. 13-17, inclusive; the parallel being resumed and completed in ver. 18.

See also 2 Pet. ii. 4.

To this head may be referred the frequent occurrence of μέν without the corresponding δέ. (See § 404.)

413. An attention to *sound* and rhythm in the structure of sentences is sometimes observable.

a. **Paronomasia,** or alliteration, was a common ornament of speech with Oriental writers. Hence its employment in the New Testament.

Luke xxi. 11 : λοιμοὶ καὶ λιμοὶ ἔσονται.
Acts xvii. 25 : ζωὴν καὶ πνοήν.
Heb. v. 8 : ἔμαθεν ἀφ' ὧν ἔπαθεν.
Rom. i. 29 : μεστοὺς φθόνου, φόνου.

These are instances of alliteration proper, there being no connection between the words in meaning. Where such a connection exists, the effect of the sentence is rather in the sense than in the sound.

Matt. xvi. 18 : σὺ εἶ Πέτρος, καὶ ἐπὶ ταύτῃ τῇ πέτρᾳ, κ.τ.λ.
Acts viii. 30 : ἆρά γε γινώσκεις ἃ ἀναγινώσκεις ;
Rom. xii. 3 : μὴ ὑπερφρονεῖν παρ' ὃ δεῖ φρονεῖν, ἀλλὰ φρονεῖν εἰς τὸ σωφρονεῖν.
1 Tim. i. 8 : καλὸς ὁ νόμος, ἐάν τις αὐτῷ νομίμως χρῆται.

In the Epistle to Philemon there are probably allusions to the name of Onesimus, ὀνήσιμος, *profitable.* (See ver. 11, and ὀναίμην, ver. 20.)

b. As the characteristic of *Hebrew poetry* is to run in **parallel clauses,** it might naturally be expected that in passages of strong and sustained feeling, the same peculiarity would be found in the New Testament.[1] There are some decided instances, as 1 Tim. iii. 16 :

ἐφανερώθη ἐν σαρκί ... ἐδικαιώθη ἐν πνεύματι.
ὤφθη ἀγγέλοις ... ἐκηρύχθη ἐν ἔθνεσιν.
ἐπιστεύθη ἐν κόσμῳ ... ἀνελήφθη ἐν δόξῃ.[2]

This passage was probably part of a rhythmical creed of the early Church, or of a primitive Christian hymn. For true hymns, see also Luke i. 46-55, 68-79, ii. 29-32 ; Eph. v. 14 ; Jude 24, 25 ; Rev. v. 12-14, etc.

Rom. ix. 2 : λύπη μοι ἐστὶ μεγάλη,
καὶ ἀδιάλειπτος ὀδύνη τῇ καρδίᾳ μου.

Here we have the tone of strong emotion.

---

[1] See Jebb's "Sacred Literature," and especially the versions of the Epistle to the Romans by the Rev. J. H. Hinton, A.M., and by the Rev. Dr. Forbes.
[2] For another arrangement see W. H., *in loc.*

For similar rhythmic constructions, see John xiv. 27 ; Rom. xi. 33 ; 1 Cor. xv. 54-57 ; Col. i. 10-12, and many other passages. The parallel clauses often contain strong contrasts, as John iii. 20, 21 ; Rom. ii. 6-10, where a long series occurs.

Sometimes the construction is more elaborate ; a second series of clauses corresponding with the first, but in reverse order. This is called "**reverted parallelism**," or **chiasmus**,[1] or **epanodos** (ἐπάνοδος). See a simple illustration, § 312, 1. Simpler still is Matt. xii. 22 : "the blind and dumb, both spake and saw." Compare Matt. vii. 6.

So Phil. iii. 10 : "TO KNOW HIM,
  and the power of his resurrection,
  and the fellowship of his sufferings,
  being made conformable unto his death;
  if by any means I might attain to the resurrection of the dead."

John x. 14, 15 : "I am the good shepherd ;
  and I know my own,
  and mine own know me,
  even as the Father knoweth me,
  and I know the Father ;
  and I lay down my life for the sheep."

Other more elaborate harmonies of the kind might easily be traced. The whole subject connects itself with the study of the influence of the Old Testament upon the New—an important field of inquiry, as yet only very partially explored.

c. (1) Three quotations of *Greek poetry* have been found in the New Testament, all by the Apostle Paul.

Acts xvii. 28 : τοῦ γὰρ καὶ γένος ἐσμέν · (the former half of a hexameter), by Aratus, a native of Tarsus, B.C. 270 ; found also with a little variation (ἐκ σοῦ γάρ) in Cleanthes, a poet of Troas, B.C. 300.

1 Cor. xv. 33 : φθείρουσιν ἤθη χρήσθ'[2] ὁμιλίαι κακαί, from Menander, an Athenian comic poet, about B.C. 320. (The measure is iambic trimeter.)

Titus i. 12 : Κρῆτες ἀεὶ ψεῦσται, κακὰ θηρία, γαστέρες ἀργαί (a complete hexameter), by Epimenides, the Cretan bard (see ver. 5), about B.C. 600.

---

[1] From the shape of the letter *chi*, **X**.
[2] W. H. read χρηστὰ.

(2) There are also apparently unconscious verses, such as will sometimes occur in prose style.

Compare the anapæstic line—
"To preach the acceptable year of the Lord."

And the English hexameter—
"Husbands, love your wives, and be not bitter against them."

Also the iambic couplet—
"Her ways are ways of pleasantness,
And all her paths are peace."

The following have been traced:—

Hexameters—

Heb. xii. 13 : καὶ τροχιὰς ὀρθὰς ποιήσατε[1] τοῖς ποσὶν ὑμῶν.

James i. 17 : πᾶσα δόσις ἀγαθὴ καὶ πᾶν δώρημα τέλειον.

Iambic measure—

Acts xxiii. 5 : ἄρχοντα τοῦ λαοῦ σου οὐκ ἐρεῖς κακῶς.

This last is a quotation from the LXX. (Exod. xxii. 28). It is possible that the others may be citations also from some unknown poetic source.

---

[1] W. H. marg., with ποιεῖτε in text.

2 THESSALONIANS I. 1–3. 357

ANALYTICAL EXERCISE ON THE SECOND EPISTLE TO THE THESSALONIANS.

The following Exercise illustrates the application of many of the foregoing rules to an extended portion of the New Testament. The figures refer to the Sections, which the student is recommended to consult.

Verbal analysis is not given, as being unnecessary at the present stage. No word, however, should be left without its stem, declension, conjugation, etc., being accurately known. The verbs of the Epistle have already been taken as material for an Exercise (Ex. 15).

The Epistle is given as in the Text of Westcott and Hort, with their alternative readings. No interpretation of difficult passages is attempted. The first duty of the New Testament student is to ascertain the plain grammatical meaning of the text: the way to its explanation will then be open.

ANALYTICAL EXERCISE.

CHAPTER I.

1 ΠΑΤΛΟΣ καὶ Σιλουανὸς καὶ Τιμόθεος τῇ ἐκκλησίᾳ Θεσσα-
2 λονικέων ἐν Θεῷ πατρὶ ἡμῶν καὶ κυρίῳ Ἰησοῦ Χριστῷ· χάρις

CHAP. I. ver. 1. **Paul, and Silvanus, and Timotheus,** nominatives; the compound subject of the sentence of salutation, some such predicate as "send greeting" being understood, involved in χάρις, ver. 2. (For the proper names, see 159, *c, d.*) **to the church,** dat. of transmission, 278; secondary obj. of the implied verb. **of Thessalonians,** extension of secondary obj.; gen. of material (or origin, 248); article omitted, 233, because only some in Thessalonica belonged to the church. **in God our Father,** further extension of ἐκκλησίᾳ; for ἐν, see 295, 4; πατρί, dat. by apposition, 177; ἡμῶν, unemphatic possessive, 333. **and the Lord Jesus Christ,** κυρίῳ under the same regimen with Θεῷ, without the article, intimating that the union is one and the same with both. See 232, and compare 217, *a, b* (3) *e*, note.

Ver. 2. **Grace unto you, and peace** (the Eastern and Western modes of salutation), subj. of omitted verb, εἴη; comp. 166, 378, *a.* **from God the**

ὑμῖν καὶ εἰρήνη ἀπὸ Θεοῦ πατρὸς καὶ κυρίου Ἰησοῦ Χριστοῦ.

Εὐχαριστεῖν ὀφείλομεν τῷ Θεῷ πάντοτε περὶ ὑμῶν, ἀδελφοί, 3
καθὼς ἄξιόν ἐστιν, ὅτι ὑπεραυξάνει ἡ πίστις ὑμῶν καὶ πλεονάζει ἡ ἀγάπη ἑνὸς ἑκάστου πάντων ὑμῶν εἰς ἀλλήλους, ὥστε 4
αὐτοὺς ἡμᾶς ἐν ὑμῖν ἐνκαυχᾶσθαι ἐν ταῖς ἐκκλησίαις τοῦ Θεοῦ
ὑπὲρ τῆς ὑπομονῆς ὑμῶν καὶ πίστεως ἐν πᾶσιν τοῖς διωγμοῖς
ὑμῶν καὶ ταῖς θλίψεσιν αἷς ⌜ἀνέχεσθε,⌝ ἔνδειγμα τῆς δικαίας 5
κρίσεως τοῦ Θεοῦ, εἰς τὸ καταξιωθῆναι ὑμᾶς τῆς βασιλείας
τοῦ Θεοῦ, ὑπὲρ ἧς καὶ πάσχετε, εἴπερ δίκαιον παρὰ Θεῷ 6

4 ἐνέχεσθε.

Father, extension of subj.; for ἀπό, see 292, 2 (John, in a similar connection, uses παρά, 2 Ep. ver. 3; ἐκ is more usual). **and the Lord Jesus Christ,** prep. not repeated, 314, to show that the source is one.

Ver. 3. **We are bound,** ὀφ. plur., as referring to the three in ver. 1 (some, less probably, understand the Apostle as speaking of himself, see 239); **to thank God,** εὐχ., inf. in its ordinary use, 385; tense as 386; for dat. Θεῷ, see 278, d. **'always,** adv. qualifying εὐχ. **concerning you,** for περί, see 302, a. **brethren,** voc., **as is meet,** ἄξιον, neuter, as referring to the substantivised clause. **because your faith greatly increases** (ὅτι, causal, 407), explanation of the clause immediately preceding. For ὑπέρ in composition, see 147, a; the verb is nowhere else found in the New Testament. **and the love of every one of you all to one another abounds,** ἑνὸς ἑκάστου, possess. gen., 254 (comp. 269); παντ. ὑμ., partitive gen., 261; present tenses as 361, a. For εἰς (dependent upon ἀγάπη), see 298, 3.

Ver. 4. **So that we ourselves boast in you,** ὥστε, 391; ἡμ. αὐτ. (emphatic), subj. of inf., 285, 387; ἐν, 295, 4. **among the churches of God,** for ἐν, see 295, 2; for the art. with Θ, 217, a. **for your endurance and faith,** ὑπέρ, 303, a, 3. For the one article with the two nouns, see 232, a; the endurance and faith combine to form one character. **in all your persecutions, and the afflictions,** the article repeated, 232, b. **which ye endure,** αἷς, dat. by attraction (for ὧν, as the verb governs a gen. in the New Testament, 2 Cor. xi. 1; 2 Tim. iv. 3), 346, b; ἀνέχ, only middle in the New Testament, act., "to hold up;" so mid., "to hold oneself up against," 355, 1.

Ver. 5. (Which is) **a token,** nom. (pred. to an implied relative clause, ὅ ἐστιν); the token being the endurance and faith of the Thessalonians. **of the righteous judgment of God,** genitives of origin or source, 248; article again employed. **in order that ye may be counted worthy,** for inf., see 390, c; tense, 386; ὑμᾶς, 285. The clause expresses the intent of God's righteous judgment; and hence its result, in proving the fitness of the faithful for God's kingdom. **of the kingdom of God,** βασ. gen. after compound of ἄξιος, 272.

Ver. 6. **For the sake of which ye also suffer,** for ὑπέρ, see 303, 2. The καί combines into one the thought of the suffering and the being counted worthy.

7 ἀνταποδοῦναι τοῖς θλίβουσιν ὑμᾶς θλῖψιν καὶ ὑμῖν τοῖς θλιβομένοις ἄνεσιν μεθ' ἡμῶν ἐν τῇ ἀποκαλύψει τοῦ κυρίου
8 Ἰησοῦ ἀπ' οὐρανοῦ μετ' ἀγγέλων δυνάμεως αὐτοῦ ἐν πυρὶ φλογός, διδόντος ἐκδίκησιν τοῖς μὴ εἰδόσι Θεὸν καὶ τοῖς μὴ
9 ὑπακούουσιν τῷ εὐαγγελίῳ τοῦ κυρίου ἡμῶν Ἰησοῦ, οἵτινες δίκην τίσουσιν ὄλεθρον αἰώνιον ἀπὸ προσώπου τοῦ κυρίου καὶ
10 ἀπὸ τῆς δόξης τῆς ἰσχύος αὐτοῦ, ὅταν ἔλθῃ ἐνδοξασθῆναι ἐν

if truly it is righteous (as it is, implied by -περ), copula omitted; δικ. neut., because referring to inf. **with God,** for παρά (dat.), see 306, β, 2. **to repay to those who afflict you, affliction,** in the verb, ἀπό marks the debt, ἀντί the return; for the aorist, see 386. (This verb is used both in a good and a bad sense in the New Testament: to "repay" or to "retaliate," Rom. xii. 19.) For the art. and participle, see 395; dat. secondary object, and acc. primary object after the verb, 278.

Ver. 7. **And to you, the afflicted,** θλιβ. is passive (not middle). **rest with us,** μετά, as 301, α, 1; ἡμῶν, referring to the three, ch. i. 1. **at** (ἐν, 295, 7) **the revelation of the Lord Jesus from heaven,** the time when the recompense shall take place, referred to ἀνταπ., ver. 6; ἀπό, 292, 1; οὐρανοῦ, singular, 240, α, note, and without article, 218. **with the angels of his power,** compare 258. The angels are the ministers of his power. The art. is unnecessary before ἀγγ., as the following gen. defines it, 208.

Ver. 8. **In a fire of flame,** ἐν of investiture, dependent upon κ. Ἰησ., 295, 3; φλογός, gen. of quality or attribute, 257. **allotting vengeance,** διδόντος refers to Ἰησοῦ. (The verb in this connection is unusual.) **to those who know not God,** dat., 278; art. and part., 395; μή, the subjective negative, see 393. **and to those who obey not,** for the repeated article, see 232, b. **the gospel,** dat., 278, d. **of our Lord Jesus,** see 270, note.

Ver. 9. **Who,** the compound relative, denoting character and suggesting the reason, 349. **shall pay** (the) **penalty, eternal destruction,** acc. in apposition with δίκην, 177. (away) **from the presence of the Lord,** art. omitted before προσώπου, 219. The meaning of ἀπό is doubtful. It may either refer to the source of the punishment, 292, 3, "inflicted *by* the presence of the Lord," or to the fact of separation, 292, 1, this being itself the doom. Probably the latter meaning is to be adopted. **and from the glory of his might,** the preposition repeated, to indicate a distinct conception; ἰσχύος is the gen. of origin, 248. The glory is that of God's manifested might, and exclusion from this beatific vision shall be destruction.

Ver. 10. **When he shall have come,** ὅταν with subj., 380; fut. perf. force of subj. aor., 383, β (ὅταν as ἐάν). **to be glorified,** inf. of design, 390, 3, note; for tense, 386. **in** (or *among*, 295, 2) **his saints, and to be admired in** (or *among*) **all who believe,** aor. part., "already believers," compare 364, e; probably ἐν here is to be taken, not as *among* simply, but as showing the *sphere* (295, 4) in which the glory will be displayed, and from which the admiration will

τοῖς ἁγίοις αὐτοῦ καὶ θαυμασθῆναι ἐν πᾶσιν τοῖς πιστεύσασιν, ὅτι ἐπιστεύθη τὸ μαρτύριον ἡμῶν ἐφ' ὑμᾶς, ἐν τῇ ἡμέρᾳ ἐκείνῃ. Εἰς ὃ καὶ προσευχόμεθα πάντοτε περὶ ὑμῶν, ἵνα ὑμᾶς ἀξιώσῃ 11 τῆς κλήσεως ὁ Θεὸς ἡμῶν καὶ πληρώσῃ πᾶσαν εὐδοκίαν ἀγαθωσύνης καὶ ἔργον πίστεως ἐν δυνάμει, ὅπως ἐνδοξασθῇ 12 τὸ ὄνομα τοῦ κυρίου ἡμῶν Ἰησοῦ ἐν ὑμῖν, καὶ ὑμεῖς ἐν αὐτῷ, κατὰ τὴν χάριν τοῦ Θεοῦ ἡμῶν καὶ κυρίου Ἰησοῦ Χριστοῦ.

CHAPTER II.

ἘΡΩΤΩΜΕΝ δὲ ὑμᾶς, ἀδελφοί, ὑπὲρ τῆς παρουσίας τοῦ 1 κυρίου [ἡμῶν] Ἰησοῦ Χριστοῦ, καὶ ἡμῶν ἐπισυναγωγῆς ἐπ'

spring. ' (because our testimony to you was believed), parenthetical expansion of πιστεύσασιν, and the one aor. helps to explain the other: then, belief will have become a fact of the past. ἡμῶν is gen. of origin. For ἐπί, dependent on μαρτύριον, see 305, γ, 4. in that day, clause dependent on ἐνδοξ. καὶ θαυμ., thrown somewhat out of order, compare 409, c. For ἐν, see 295, 7; ἐκείνῃ, the emphatic demonstrative, 340, note.

Ver. 11. Whereto we also pray, εἰς denoting direction, 298, 4; ὅ, rel. pron., acc. neut., antecedent in the entire previous sentence, 344; καί, with reference to the general sentiment of the preceding, "we not only indulge the hope, but also express it in prayer." always concerning you, 313, 2. that (384, note) our God may count you worthy of the calling, gen., as 272, and for art., see 210. The meaning of ἀξιώσῃ is doubtful: *make worthy* would appear best to suit the context, but this sense of the verb in the New Testament is unexampled. and fulfil every good pleasure (see 224, a; 214, c) of goodness, i.e., every voluntary purpose that can spring from (gen. orig.) goodness (R.V., every desire of goodness); not God's goodness, for which ἀγαθωσύνη is never used, but goodness as an element of Christian character, so corresponding with the next clause. and work (also qualified by πᾶσαν, see 318) of faith (248) in power (295, 6), qualifying πληρώσῃ, "powerfully fulfil."

Ver. 12. In order that the name of our Lord Jesus, ὅπως, as distinguished from ἵνα, seems to denote the *how* as contrasted with the *where;* but the line cannot be very clearly drawn. may be glorified (384, a, 1; tense, 374, note) in you (see on ver. 10), and you (understand ἐνδοξασθῆτε) in him (or *in it*, i.e., *the name,* but less probably. See Alford, and 295, 4, note), according to, for κατά, see 300, β, 5. the grace of our God and the Lord Jesus Christ (R.V.) (or *of our God and Lord Jesus Christ*), see 232, a, note on Titus ii. 13, where, however, the phrases are different. Κύριος is so often properly anarthrous (217, b) that the latter of the above renderings is very doubtful. (See Ellicott here.)

CHAP. II. ver. 1. But (δέ transitional, 404; the writer's mind passing from his own prayers to the duty of his readers) we entreat you, brethren, in

2 THESSALONIANS II. 2-4.   361

2 αὐτόν, εἰς τὸ μὴ ταχέως σαλευθῆναι ὑμᾶς ἀπὸ τοῦ νοὸς μηδὲ
    θροεῖσθαι μήτε διὰ πνεύματος μήτε διὰ λόγου μήτε δι' ἐπιστολῆς
3 ὡς δι' ἡμῶν, ὡς ὅτι ἐνέστηκεν ἡ ἡμέρα τοῦ κυρίου. μή τις ὑμᾶς
    ἐξαπατήσῃ κατὰ μηδένα τρόπον· ὅτι ἐὰν μὴ ἔλθῃ ἡ ἀποστασία
    πρῶτον καὶ ἀποκαλυφθῇ ὁ ἄνθρωπος τῆς ⌜ἀνομίας,⌝ ὁ υἱὸς τῆς
4 ἀπωλείας, ὁ ἀντικείμενος καὶ ὑπεραιρόμενος ἐπὶ πάντα λεγό-
    μενον Θεὸν ἢ σέβασμα, ὥστε αὐτὸν εἰς τὸν ναὸν τοῦ Θεοῦ

3 ἁμαρτίας.

---

reference to, 303, *a*, 3 (not *by*, as if in adjuration. See Alf.). **the coming of our Lord Jesus Christ, and our** (gen. obj., 268) **gathering together unto him,** for ἐπί, see 305, γ, 3 (Mark v. 21), not *up to*, although the reference is to the final gathering.

Ver. 2. **That ye be not** (lit., *in order to your not being*) **soon shaken,** for εἰς, see 298, 4. The purpose of the entreaty was to prevent their being shaken. For τό, substantivising the inf., see 390; for μή, 385, *b ;* for ὑμᾶς, 285, and note. **from your mind** (or conviction), ἀπό, as 292, 1 ; the article as an unemphatic possessive, 215. **nor yet be troubled,** for μηδέ, disjunctive (not μήτε, as rec.), see 405 ; θροεῖσθαι, pres. inf., denoting an enduring state, the aor., σαλευθ., referring to a single effect, 386. **neither by spirit nor by word nor by letter, as by us;** the repeated μήτε here breaks up the negation into three parts, and connects them. For διά, see 299, *a*, 2. (*Spirit* no doubt refers to a pretended prophecy ; *word*, to a pretended saying on inspired authority ; *letter*, therefore, according to the parallel, should mean a pretended epistle. That the reference is not to the First Epistle, the ὡς seems further to indicate.) **as that** (2 Cor. v. 19 shows that the ὡς does not in itself imply deceit, but only that the thing was *so represented*—" to the effect that "). **the day of the Lord is already come** (or, *is imminent*, immediately), not simply *is at hand*, for the verb always refers to the present ; the part. ἐνεστώς expressly signifying the present in distinction from the future (Rom. viii. 38 ; 1 Cor. iii. 22); R.V. *is now present*.

Ver. 3. **Let no one deceive you,** ἐξαπ., subj. in imper. sense, 375 ; aor., 373, *b*. **in** (κατά, 300, β, 5) **any way,** the two negatives strengthen the denial, 401. **because, unless the apostasy,** definite, 213. **shall first have come** (383, β, note), **and the man of lawlessness** (*the lawlessness*, 214, *b*) **shall have been revealed,**—the Apostle does not conclude the sentence, see 412, *e*, but passes on to describe the characteristics of the "man of sin." **the son of perdition** (genitives of quality).

Ver. 4. **He that withstands, and exalts himself** (middle, 355, 1). Obs., the single article shows that the two participles refer to the same subject. But ἀντικείμενος cannot take ἐπί following ; an object must, therefore, be understood—*Christ*. On the tense, see 396. **above** (305, γ, 2, R.V. *against*) **every one called God,** observe πάντα, masc. **or an object of worship,** Θεόν and σέβασμα, accus., in apposition with πάντα after copulative verb. **so that**

καθίσαι, ἀποδεικνύντα ἑαυτὸν ὅτι ἔστιν Θεός. Οὐ μνημονεύετε 5
ὅτι ἔτι ὢν πρὸς ὑμᾶς ταῦτα ἔλεγον ὑμῖν; καὶ νῦν τὸ κατέχον 6
οἴδατε, εἰς τὸ ἀποκαλυφθῆναι αὐτὸν ἐν τῷ αὐτοῦ καιρῷ· τὸ 7
γὰρ μυστήριον ἤδη ἐνεργεῖται τῆς ἀνομίας· μόνον ὁ κατέχων
ἄρτι ἕως ἐκ μέσου γένηται. καὶ τότε ἀποκαλυφθήσεται ὁ 8
ἄνομος, ὃν ὁ κύριος ['Ιησοῦς] ⌜ἀνελεῖ⌝ τῷ πνεύματι τοῦ στόματος αὐτοῦ καὶ καταργήσει τῇ ἐπιφανείᾳ τῆς παρουσίας
8 ἀναλοῖ.

he sits, for ὥστε, see 391; καθίσαι, intrans. aor., "he took his seat" **in the temple of God,**—literally, *into—i.e.*, "entered into and sits in," *constructio praegnans*, 298, 8. **exhibiting himself that he is God,** ἀποδεικ., acc. by αὐτόν preced., present, as expressing his habit. For the object and object-sentence, see 411, *b*. ἐστί is emphatic.

Ver. 5. **Remember ye not,** interrog., 369, *b*. **that,** introducing object-sentence, 380. **when yet with you,** ὤν, part. in apposition with subj. of ἔλεγον; for πρός, see 307, γ, 2. **I used to tell you these things,** for imperf., see 362, *b*; ὑμῖν, 278, *h*.

Ver. 6. **And now ye know that which hinders,** νῦν temporal (as *when with you* I gave you the information, so *now* ye know), or logical, without reference to time (Ellicott); τὸ κατέχον, part., substantivised. **in order that he should be revealed in his own time,** for εἰς, see 390, *c*. The hindrance is "in order to" the revelation being made *at the right time*, as a barrier might be said to be for the proper admission of a multitude. For ἐν, see 295, 7; for the position of αὐτοῦ, 229.

Ver. 7. **For,** 407, explanatory of the hindrance. **the mystery of the lawlessness** (or iniquity) **is already at work,** ἀνομίας, definite, gen. either of apposition, 259, "the mystery which is the iniquity;" or of quality, 257, "the mystery characterised by (the) iniquity;" ἤδη, adv. of time, ἐνεργ., middle present, 361, *a*. **only,** μόνον, adv. **he who hinders,** change from neut. to masc. **at present, until he shall have been taken out of the way** (*midst*). This clause may either be read, by a slight inversion of words, as dependent upon the former—"is at work only until he who at present hinders be taken out of the way," the objection to which is the unnatural position of ἕως—or by supposing an ellipsis of a predicate, "only he who hinders (is working, ἐνεργεῖται, or ἔστιν, *there is one who hinders*, R.V.) as yet, until," etc. In this case, the thought which γάρ introduces is in the latter, not the former clause of the verse. Compare the examples in 410, *b*. (*For, although the mystery is even now working, there is as yet a "hinderer."*) For ἐκ μέσου, see 219.

Ver. 8. **And then,** *i.e.*, when the restraining power or person is taken out of the way, τότε emphatic. **shall the lawless one be revealed,** 210. **whom the Lord (Jesus) will consume by the breath** (*Spirit*), 280, *d*. **of his mouth,** 248. **and will destroy by the manifestation of his coming,** 258.

9 αὐτοῦ, οὗ ἐστιν ἡ παρουσία κατ' ἐνέργειαν τοῦ Σατανᾶ ἐν
10 πάσῃ δυνάμει καὶ σημείοις καὶ τέρασιν ψεύδους καὶ ἐν πάσῃ ἀπάτῃ ἀδικίας τοῖς ἀπολλυμένοις, ἀνθ' ὧν τὴν ἀγάπην τῆς
11 ἀληθείας οὐκ ἐδέξαντο εἰς τὸ σωθῆναι αὐτούς· καὶ διὰ τοῦτο πέμπει αὐτοῖς ὁ Θεὸς ἐνέργειαν πλάνης εἰς τὸ πιστεῦσαι αὐτοὺς
12 τῷ ψεύδει, ἵνα κριθῶσιν ⌜πάντες⌝ οἱ μὴ πιστεύσαντες τῇ
13 ἀληθείᾳ ἀλλὰ εὐδοκήσαντες τῇ ἀδικίᾳ. Ἡμεῖς δὲ ὀφείλομεν εὐχαριστεῖν τῷ Θεῷ πάντοτε περὶ ὑμῶν, ἀδελφοὶ ἠγαπημένοι

12 ἅπαντες.

Ver. 9. **Whose coming is**, οὗ, correspondent with ὅν, ver. 8, relative to ἄνομος. **according to the working of Satan**, κατά as 300, 5; ἐνεργ. anarthrous, "such working, in general, as Satan would perform." For the gen., Σατ., see 20, a. **in** (of investiture or accompaniment, 295, 3) **all power and signs and wonders**, πάσῃ in sense belongs to all three nouns, 318, and denotes "every kind of," 224, a. **of falsehood**, prob. gen. of origin, 248 (these things being severally born of falsehood), or perhaps gen. of quality, as A.V., R.V., *lying wonders*.

Ver. 10. **And in all** (*every kind of*, as ver. 9) **deceit**, parallel to the former prepositional clause with ἐν, the two together explanatory of κατ. ἐνεργ. Σατ. **of iniquity**, gen. of quality. **for the perishing**, dat. *incommodi*, 279. For the force of the participle, see 200, note, and 396. **because**, for ἀνθ' ὧν, see 291, note. **they received not**, aorist, viewing their lifetime as past. **the love of the truth**, gen. obj., 268. **in order that they might be saved**, const. as vers. 2, 6.

Ver. 11. **And on this account**, 299, β, *i.e.*, because they received not, etc. **God is sending**, explanatory of the ἀπολλυμένοις. **to them** (dat. of transmission) **a working of delusion**, parallel to ἐνέργειαν above, gen. of characteristic quality, 257. **so that they should believe** (the intent, and so the result, of the *delusion*, 390, c) **the falsehood**, dative, 278, d; article of "renewed mention," 212.

Ver. 12. **That they might all be judged**, a second intentional clause, 384, growing out of the preced. **who believed not the truth**, 396; for negative, see 393. **but took pleasure**, the conduct viewed as past from the point of view of their condemnation. **in the iniquity**, art. as 212; dat., 278, d.

Ver. 13. **But we**, emphatic pron. 169. **are bound to give thanks to God always concerning you**, see on ch. i. 3. **brethren beloved by the Lord** (*i.e.*, by Christ, see 217, b), **because God** (for art., see 217, a) **chose you**, εἵλατο, see 97, b, note; causal sentence; compare the ὅτι in ch. i. 3. **from the beginning**, 219 (alt. reading, *a firstfruit*). **unto salvation**, dependent upon εἵλ.; for εἰς, see 298, 4. **in sanctification of the Spirit**, ἐν denoting the sphere (295, 4) in which the salvation is realised. πνευμ. is gen. of the author, 248; for omitted article, see 217, f. **and belief of truth** (or, *the truth*), πίστει

364 ANALYTICAL EXERCISE.

ὑπὸ Κυρίου, ὅτι εἵλατο ὑμᾶς ὁ Θεὸς ⌜ἀπ' ἀρχῆς⌝ εἰς σωτηρίαν ἐν ἁγιασμῷ πνεύματος καὶ πίστει ἀληθείας, εἰς ὃ ἐκάλεσεν ὑμᾶς 14 διὰ τοῦ εὐαγγελίου ἡμῶν, εἰς περιποίησιν δόξης τοῦ κυρίου ἡμῶν Ἰησοῦ Χριστοῦ. Ἄρα οὖν, ἀδελφοί, στήκετε, καὶ κρα- 15 τεῖτε τὰς παραδόσεις ἃς ἐδιδάχθητε εἴτε διὰ λόγου εἴτε δι' ἐπιστολῆς ἡμῶν. Αὐτὸς δὲ ὁ κύριος ἡμῶν Ἰησοῦς Χριστὸς 16 καὶ [ὁ] Θεὸς ὁ πατὴρ ἡμῶν, ὁ ἀγαπήσας ἡμᾶς καὶ δοὺς παρά-κλησιν αἰωνίαν καὶ ἐλπίδα ἀγαθὴν ἐν χάριτι, παρακαλέσαι 17 ὑμῶν τὰς καρδίας καὶ στηρίξαι ἐν παντὶ ἔργῳ καὶ λόγῳ ἀγαθῷ.

13 ἀπαρχήν.

---

without the art., like ἁγιασμῷ, under the common regimen of ἐν, 314; see also 208. Truth is abstract, 214, and is used in the utmost generality; not so much the specific truth of the Gospel, but the Gospel considered as truth; the disposition given being that of harmony with truth in itself, whatever it might be.

Ver. 14. **Unto which** (state of salvation), the neuter relative referring to the whole object of thought; compare 344. **he called you,** aor., as before, of specific time. **by means of,** 299, *a*, 2. **our gospel,** *i.e.*, the Gospel as preached by us, see 270, note. **for the attainment of the glory,** εἰς, connected with and explanatory of εἰς σωτ.; δοξ., gen. obj., 268. (The glory of Christ is regarded as in a sense the heritage of Christians; compare John xvii. 24.) **of our Lord Jesus Christ,** possess. gen., 254.

Ver. 15. **Accordingly therefore,** for the inferential conjunction, see 406. **brethren, stand fast** (derivative of ἕστηκα, see 108, 4), **and hold fast the instructions,** acc. obj. of κρατ., compare 264. **which ye were taught,** ἅς, secondary object, with pass. ἐδιδάχ., see 284, note, and 356. **whether by word,** 299, *a*, 2. **or by our** (248) **epistle.** For εἴτε, see 405.

Ver. 16. **But our Lord himself,** δέ, as usual, adversative, 404; αὐτός, very emphatic, 335. **Jesus Christ, and God our Father who loved us,** referring to the last antecedent, *God the Father* (aor., as referring to a single and complete act). **and gave eternal consolation and good hope,** abstract, anarthrous; better rendered without indef. art. **in grace,** connected with δούς, 295, 6 and 4.

Ver. 17. **Comfort,** for opt., see 378: sing., indicative of the close union between the Father and the Son; so the following. **your hearts,** plur., see 237. **and establish you,** supply ὑμᾶς from ὑμῶν, or, as R.V., make καρδίας the object of both verbs, *establish them.* **in every good work and word,** ἐν denotes again the element; that in which the confirmation is given.

CHAPTER III.

1 ΤΟ λοιπὸν προσεύχεσθε, ἀδελφοί, περὶ ἡμῶν, ἵνα ὁ λόγος
2 τοῦ κυρίου τρέχῃ καὶ δοξάζηται καθὼς καὶ πρὸς ὑμᾶς, καὶ ἵνα
ῥυσθῶμεν ἀπὸ τῶν ἀτόπων καὶ πονηρῶν ἀνθρώπων, οὐ γὰρ
3 πάντων ἡ πίστις. Πιστὸς δέ ἐστιν ὁ κύριος, ὃς στηρίξει ὑμᾶς
4 καὶ φυλάξει ἀπὸ τοῦ πονηροῦ. πεποίθαμεν δὲ ἐν κυρίῳ ἐφ᾽
5 ὑμᾶς, ὅτι ἃ παραγγέλλομεν [καὶ] ποιεῖτε καὶ ποιήσετε. Ὁ δὲ
κύριος κατευθύναι ὑμῶν τὰς καρδίας εἰς τὴν ἀγάπην τοῦ Θεοῦ
καὶ εἰς τὴν ὑπομονὴν τοῦ χριστοῦ.

CHAP. III. ver. 1. **For the rest** (as to what remains to be said), neut. adj., acc. of time (comp. 286, b, 2; see also 266, and Ellicott on Gal. vi. 17). **pray, brethren, for us,** for περί, see on i. 11; also for ἵνα. **that the word of the Lord may have free course** (*run*) **and be glorified,** passive, not (as some) middle. **even as also** (*it is*) **with you,** καί adds in thought the Thessalonian Church to the other places where the word achieved success. For πρός, see 307, γ, 2.

Ver. 2. **And that we may be delivered,** aor. subj., showing that a *specific* deliverance is desired, 374, note; the pres. subj., ver. 1, suggesting *continuous* success, 374, note. **from the perverse and wicked men,** the article denoting a class, as *the hypocrites*, Matt. vi. 2, probably specifying the Jewish party in Corinth, whence this Ep. was written. **for the faith,** the Christian faith, see 213 (not faith in general, which in this connection would hardly have been definite). **does not belong to all,** lit., "(is) not of all," *i.e.*, is not their possession, see 267, note.

Ver. 3. **But** (although the faith is denied by so many) **faithful is the Lord,** a paronomasia with the preceding clause, 413, *a*. **who will establish you,** ref. to στηρίξαι, ii. 17. **and guard (you) from evil,** or less appropriately (yet see Ellicott), *the Evil One* (R.V.). Comp. the quotations in 316. The neuter sense is sustained by the close connection through στηρίξ. with ἔργῳ in ii. 17. For ἀπό, see 292, 1.

Ver. 4. **But we trust,** the adversative δέ bringing the future just expressed into antithesis with the present (so Ellicott). **in the Lord,** 295, 4 (not simply "in the Lord, who will bring this about by his goodness," but *being* in him, as the element of our life and hope, we trust); for πέποιθα, see 99, *c*, note, also 367. **in reference to you,** for ἐπί, see 305, γ, 4. **that what we command (you)** now, as the verb. is pres. **ye both are doing, and will do,** for καί ... καί, see 403. The whole clause from ὅτι depends on πεποίθ. as an object-sentence, 381.

Ver. 5. **But,** again slightly adversative, "though this is the case, yet as a further blessing." **the Lord,** *i.e.*, Jesus Christ himself, 217, *b*. (As Christ is separately mentioned at the close of the verse, some refer κ. here to the Holy Spirit, quoting 2 Cor. iii. 18; but the argument is very doubtful.) **direct your hearts,** opt.,

ANALYTICAL EXERCISE.

Παραγγέλλομεν δὲ ὑμῖν, ἀδελφοί, ἐν ὀνόματι τοῦ κυρίου 6
ʳ ʼἸησοῦ Χριστοῦ στέλλεσθαι ὑμᾶς ἀπὸ παντὸς ἀδελφοῦ
ἀτάκτως περιπατοῦντος καὶ μὴ κατὰ τὴν παράδοσιν ἣν
ʳπαρελάβετεʼ παρ' ἡμῶν. αὐτοὶ γὰρ οἴδατε πῶς δεῖ μιμεῖσθαι 7
ἡμᾶς, ὅτι οὐκ ἠτακτήσαμεν ἐν ὑμῖν οὐδὲ δωρεὰν ἄρτον ἐφάγομεν 8
παρά τινος, ἀλλ' ἐν κόπῳ καὶ μόχθῳ νυκτὸς καὶ ἡμέρας ἐργαζόμενοι πρὸς τὸ μὴ ἐπιβαρῆσαί τινα ὑμῶν· οὐχ ὅτι οὐκ ἔχομεν 9
ἐξουσίαν, ἀλλ' ἵνα ἑαυτοὺς τύπον δῶμεν ὑμῖν εἰς τὸ μιμεῖσθαι

6 ἡμῶν. παρελάβοσαν.

as in ii. 17; ὑμῶν slightly emphatic from position. **into the love of God,** for εἰς, see 298, 1 ; Θεοῦ objective, 269. **and into the patience of Christ,** prep. repeated, as of a separate object of thought, 314. Χρ. is probably gen. of possession, 254, "such patience as Christ exhibited;" or it may be gen. of author, " the patience that Christ imparts." The objective sense given in A. V., "*patient waiting for,*" is not supported by the meaning of ὑπομονή.

Ver. 6. **Now,** δέ, transitional (404, ii). to the preceptive part. **we command you, brethren,** for παραγ., see ver. 4. **in the name of the Lord Jesus Christ,** ἐν ὀνόμ., dependent upon παρ., 295, 5. **that ye withdraw yourselves,** object. inf., with acc. subject, 285 ; στέλλ., only mid. in the New Testament ; active, *to put together;* mid., *to draw oneself together,* 355, 1 ; hence to shrink from, with acc., as in 2 Cor. viii. 20, or with ἀπό, as here. **from every brother walking disorderly, and not,** subjective neg. **according to,** 300, β, 5. **the instruction** (see ii. 15) **which ye** (var. read *they*) **received,** ἣν, obj. of παρελαβ., 343. **from us,** for παρά, see 306, a.

Ver. 7. **For yourselves know,** emphatic pron. subj. ; γάρ suggests an implied thought : " I need not enter into details, for." **how ye ought to imitate us** (for the impersonal verbs, see 101), "a brachylogy" (Ellicott), implying περιπατεῖν, from preced., "how ye ought to walk—in fact, to imitate us." **because we were not disorderly,** ὅτι gives the reason for μιμεῖσθαι, "we propose our conduct for imitation, because." **among you,** 295, 2.

Ver. 8. **Nor,** slightly ascensive, "nay, and we did not," 404. **did we eat bread,** 306, a, 350 (to eat bread is a quasi-proverbial phrase for "to make a living "). **for nought,** δωρεάν, an old acc. as adv., 126, a ; compare its use in Matt. x. 8, "without an equivalent;" so in other passages. **from any one,** 306, a. **but in** (accompaniment, 295, 3) **toil and travail** (we did so) **labouring night and day,** gen., 266. Both these clauses depend on ἐφάγομεν, implied. **in order not to be burdensome,** for πρός with inf., see 390, c. **to any of you,** for acc., compare 281, a ; ὑμῶν, partitive gen., 262.

Ver. 9. **Not that,** a frequent elliptical formula, correcting a possible misapprehension, "do not suppose me to say that " (see Ellicott on Phil. iii. 12). **we have not a right** (to maintenance), **but** (we do so) **in order that we may present ourselves,** δῶμεν, aor. of one definite determination ; for ἑαυτούς, see 335,

2 THESSALONIANS III. 10–15.

10 ἡμᾶς. καὶ γὰρ ὅτε ἦμεν πρὸς ὑμᾶς, τοῦτο παρηγγέλλομεν
11 ὑμῖν, ὅτι εἴ τις οὐ θέλει ἐργάζεσθαι μηδὲ ἐσθιέτω. ἀκούομεν
γάρ τινας περιπατοῦντας ἐν ὑμῖν ἀτάκτως, μηδὲν ἐργαζομένους
12 ἀλλὰ περιεργαζομένους· τοῖς δὲ τοιούτοις παραγγέλλομεν καὶ
παρακαλοῦμεν ἐν κυρίῳ Ἰησοῦ Χριστῷ ἵνα μετὰ ἡσυχίας
13 ἐργαζόμενοι τὸν ἑαυτῶν ἄρτον ἐσθίωσιν. Ὑμεῖς δέ, ἀδελφοί,
14 μὴ ἐνκακήσητε καλοποιοῦντες. εἰ δέ τις οὐχ ὑπακούει τῷ
λόγῳ ἡμῶν διὰ τῆς ἐπιστολῆς, τοῦτον σημειοῦσθε, μὴ συνανα-
15 μίγνυσθαι αὐτῷ, ἵνα ἐντραπῇ· καὶ μὴ ὡς ἐχθρὸν ἡγεῖσθε,

1, *b*. **an example,** secondary predicate, in apposition with ἑαυτ. **to you, to the end that,** εἰς as in ii. 11, etc. **(ye) should imitate us.**

Ver. 10. **For even,** see 407, note. **when we were among you,** for πρός, compare ii. 5. **we used to enjoin this upon you,** impf., 362, *b*; for παραγγέλλω and its regimen, see ver. 4, 6. **that,** introducing objective sentence explanatory of τοῦτο, but thrown into a quotation form, 382, *a*; hence ἐσθ. imper. "**if any one wills not to work,**" for εἰ, see 383, *a*; for θέλει, 363, *f*. "**neither let him eat,**" neg., 371.

Ver. 11. **For,** introducing the reason of the command. **we hear of some that walk,** predicative participle, 394. **among you,** ἐν as ver. 7. **disorderly, doing no work, but being busybodies,** participles in apposition with περιπ.; for the paronomasia, see 413, *a*. The verb περιεργ. does not again occur in the N.T., although the subst. περίεργος is found, 1 Tim. v. 13.

Ver. 12. **But to such as these,** pron. definite, 220. **we command and exhort,** the dat. obj. belongs grammatically to παραγγ., as in ver. 4, etc.; παρακαλ. takes the acc. **in the Lord Jesus Christ that, working with quietness,** for μετά, see 301, *a*, 2. **they eat,** subj. by ἵνα; tense, 374. Obs. παραγγ. with the inf., ver. 6; with object and obj.-clause, ὅτι, ver. 10, here with the intentional particle. The command is given *in order that* the result may follow. **their own bread,** emphatically, not that of others.

Ver. 13. **But ye,** emphatic, by way of contrast to those just mentioned. **brethren, be not weary,** subj., with imper. force, 375. **in well-doing,** pres. part., adjunct to pred., 394, 3, *b*, "whilst well-doing" being implied; or causal, as *c*.

Ver. 14. **But if any one obeys not,** 383, *a*. **our word,** 278, *d*. **through,** conveyed by, 299, *a*, 2. **the epistle,** *i.e.*, this epistle. **note this man,** for σημ., middle, see 355, 2, "mark for yourselves." **not to keep company with him,** dat. of association, 277, *a*, double object, 411, *b*. The pres. imper. in both cases enjoins the conduct as habitual. **that he be ashamed,** the purpose, again, not simply the result.

Ver. 15. **And,** not adversative, but simply conjunctive; another particular of the conduct to be observed. **esteem** (him) **not as an enemy,** ὡς, a particle of

ἀλλὰ νουθετεῖτε ὡς ἀδελφόν. Αὐτὸς δὲ ὁ κύριος τῆς εἰρήνης 16
δῴη ὑμῖν τὴν εἰρήνην διὰ παντὸς ἐν παντὶ τρόπῳ. ὁ κύριος
μετὰ πάντων ὑμῶν.
Ὁ ἀσπασμὸς τῇ ἐμῇ χειρὶ Παύλου, ὅ ἐστιν σημεῖον ἐν πάσῃ 17
ἐπιστολῇ· οὕτως γράφω. ἡ χάρις τοῦ κυρίου ἡμῶν Ἰησοῦ 18
Χριστοῦ μετὰ πάντων ὑμῶν.

---

apposition connecting ἐχθρ. with τοῦτον, understood from preced. **but admonish (him) as a brother.**

Ver. 16. **But** (the antithesis being between the persons addressed by the Apostle and those just specified, "as for you," "to return to you") **the Lord of** (the) **peace,** gen. of quality. **himself,** emphatic pron. **give** (the) **peace to you,** δῴη, opt. in the usual sense and the ordinary const. of the verb. The article before εἰρ. both times is emphatic, recognising peace as the peculiar and well-understood Christian blessing. **always,** χρόνου understood with παντός, an adverbial adjunct to δῴη. **in every way. The Lord be,** supply εἴη as i. 2. **with,** 301, *a*, 1. **you all.**

Ver. 17. **The salutation,** nominative, in apposition with ver. 18, as a kind of title: "This is the salutation." **of me, Paul, with my own hand,** for const., see 336 ; χειρί, dat. of instr., 280, *d*. **which,** neuter rel. pron., 346, *a*. **is the sign,** pred. omits art., see 206. **in every epistle,** 224, *a*. **so I write,** the other member of the comparison being omitted, as obvious to the orig. readers ; compare examples under 412, *e*. Probably the phrase alludes to some peculiarity in the handwriting. Compare Gal. vi. 11.

Ver. 18. **The grace of our Lord Jesus Christ be,** εἴη, as i. 2. **with** (301, *a*, 1) **you all.**

The subscription to the Epistle, *The second (epistle) to the Thessalonians was written from Athens* (see also subscription to First Epistle), is undoubtedly spurious, and is also incorrect. It arose probably from a careless and mistaken interpretation of 1 Thess. iii. 1. R. V. omits.

NEW TESTAMENT SYNONYMS.

PROBABLY no two words in any language are precisely *synonymous*, although many are *interchangeable*. It has already been shown (§ 290) that words in different languages seldom, if ever, perfectly correspond. Hence arise some of the chief difficulties of translation. It has often been unthinkingly suggested that, in the New Testament for instance, the same Greek word should always be rendered by the same English one. This rule would constantly lead to inaccuracies: although, undoubtedly, capricious or unnecessary variations should be avoided. In the Preface to the R.V., the Revisers note as a fault of the A.V. the intentional and studied avoidance of uniformity in the rendering of the same words, even when occurring in the same context. This fault the R.V. largely rectifies. Greek words which recur several times in one passage, which are found in different books in the same context, or which are characteristic of some particular writer, are rendered by the same English equivalent. Variations involving inconsistency, or suggestive of differences which have no existence in the Greek, have mostly disappeared. Still it will be evident that within these limits there is room for variations which are legitimate and even necessary. The word *suffer*, for instance, covers so great an extent of meaning, that we are hardly surprised to find it employed in the A.V. for ten distinct Greek words, besides various combinations of the same roots. To *provoke*, again, occurs twelve times in the A.V. for eight different Greek words; the R.V. makes a change in one instance only. To *provide* is found eight times, representing six distinct originals; in the R.V. we have a different rendering for three of the six. The verb *ordain* occurs eighteen times, once for ποιέω (not in R.V.), which Greek word has in different places thirty-six English equivalents; once for γίνομαι (not in R.V.), the various equivalents of which are almost innumerable; twice for ὁρίζω, which is translated in four different ways; once for προορίζω, which has three English equivalents (R.V. consistently renders *foreordain* in every case); twice for τίθημι (not in R.V.), a verb translated in fifteen ways; twice for τάσσω, which is rendered by five different words; thrice for διατάσσω, a verb with five renderings; thrice for καθίστημι (not in R.V.), which we find translated in six ways; once for κατασκευάζω (not in R.V.), a verb with four English equivalents; once for κρίνω, which is rendered in fifteen ways; and once for χειροτονέω, a word occurring twice, and in each place differently rendered (R.V. in both cases *appoint*). In addition to these, we have *to ordain before*, for προγράφω and προετοιμάζω (not in R.V.).

Such instances suggest the largeness of the field that is open to the inquirer into the so-called Synonyms, whether of the Greek or the English New Testament. To cover that field, in however perfunctory a manner, would be plainly impossible in the compass of a few pages. All that can be attempted is to point out the main distinctions between some important words in general use, of kindred meaning, and often translated alike in the A.V. The list might be greatly extended, but enough is given to excite the student's inquiries. For further detail, the English reader is referred to Tittmann's "Remarks on the Synonyms of the New Testament," translated in Clark's *Biblical Cabinet*, 1833–37; to Archbishop Trench's "Synonyms of the New Testament;" and to the "Syntax and Synonyms of the New Testament," by the Rev. W. Webster, M.A.

WORDS ILLUSTRATED.

	NO.
ἀγαθός, ἀγαθωσύνη	21
ἀγαπάω, ἀγάπη	19
ἅγιος, ἁγνός	23
ἁγνόημα	39
ἀγοράζω	43
ᾅδης	52
ἄδικος, ἀδικία	22
ἀΐδιος	58
αἰνέω, αἶνος	47
αἰτέω, αἴτημα	9, 38
αἰών, αἰώνιος	58
ἀλείφω	18
ἀληθής, ἀλήθεια, ἀληθινός	24
ἄλλος	76
ἁμαρτάνω, ἁμαρτία, ἁμάρτημα	39
ἀμφίβληστρον	70
ἀνάθημα, ἀνάθεμα, ἀναθεματίζω	51
ἀνακαινόω, ἀνανεόω	26
ἀνήρ	63
ἄνθρωπος	63
ἀνομία	39
ἀνοχή	31
ἀντίλυτρον	43
ἀπολύτρωσις	43
ἅπτομαι	7
ἀρετή	21, 47
ἀρχαῖος	25
αὐλή	72
ἀφίημι, ἄφεσις	42
βάρος	68
βέλτιον	21
βίος	54
βλέπω, βλέμμα	5
βόσκω	16
βούλομαι, βουλή	3
βρέφος	62
βωμός	37
γέεννα	52
γίνομαι	1
γινώσκω	4
γόμος	68

	NO.
δαίμων, δαιμόνιον	53
δακρύω	20
δέησις	38
δεῖ	12
δειλός, δειλία	33
δεισιδαίμων, δεισιδαιμονία	44
δεσπότης	59
δῆμος	73
διάδημα	67
διάκονος, διακονία, διακονέω	36, 60
διαλέγομαι	15
διάνοια	55
διαταγή	49
διδάσκω, διδάσκαλος	14, 59
δίκαιος, δικαιοσύνη, δικαίωμα	21, 49
δίκτυον	70
δίγμα	49
δοκέω, δόξα	6, 47
δοῦλος	60
δύναμαι, δύναμις	45, 57
δῶμα	61
Ἑβραῖος	50
ἔθνος, ἔθνη	73
εἶδον, εἶδος, εἴδωλον	5, 56
εἰκών	56
εἰμί	1
εἶπον, ἔπος	8
ἔλεος	41
Ἕλλην, Ἑλληνιστής	50
ἔνδυμα	66
ἐξουσία	57
ἐντολή	49
ἐπαινέω, ἔπαινος	47
ἐπίσταμαι	4
ἐπιστάτης	59
ἔρχομαι	10
ἐρῶ	8
ἐρωτάω	9, 38
ἐσθής	66
ἕτερος	76
εὐαγγέλιον, εὐαγγελίζω	15
εὐλαβής, εὐλάβεια, εὐλαβέομαι	33, 44
εὐλογητός	28

	NO.		NO.
εὐσεβής, εὐσέβεια	44	λίθος	75
εὔχομαι	38	λόγος	8
		λύτρον, λυτρόω, λύτρωσις	43
ζωή	54	λύχνος, λυχνία	65
ἥκω	10		
ἥττημα	39	μαθητής, μαθητεύω	14
		μακάριος	28
θάνατος, θανατόω	54	μακροθυμία	31
θεάομαι	5	μάντις, μαντεύομαι	15
θέλω	3	μάταιος	29
θεοσεβής, θεοσέβεια	44	μεγαλύνω	47
Θεότης, Θειότης	34	μέλει, μελετάω	11
θεράπων, θεραπεύω	60	μέλλω	3
θεωρέω	5	μεριμνάω, μέριμνα	11
θιγγάνω	7	μεταμέλομαι	40
θνητός	54	μετανοέω, μετάνοια	40
θρῆσκος, θρησκεία	44	μορφή	56
θυμός	32		
θύρα	71	ναός	35
θυσία, θυσιαστήριον	37	νεκρός, νεκρόω	54
		νέος, νεότης	26
ἱερεύς	37	νήπιος	62
ἱερός, ἱερόν	23, 35	νίπτω	17
ἱλάσκομαι, ἱλασμός	43	νοῦς, νόημα	55
ἱμάτιον	66		
Ἰουδαῖος, Ἰσραηλίτης	50	ὄγκος	68
ἰσχύω, ἰσχύς	57	ὀδυρμός	20
		οἶδα	4
καθαρός	23	οἶκος, οἰκία, οἰκέτης	61
καινός, καινότης	26	οἰκουμένη	58
καιρός	64	οἰκτιρμός	41
κακός, κακία	22	ὁλόκληρος, ὁλοτελής	27
καλός	21	ὁράω, ὅραμα, ὄψομαι, ὄψις	5
καρδία	55	ὀργή	32
καταγγέλλω	15	ὅσιος	23
κατηχέω	14	ὀφείλω	12
κενός	29	ὀφείλημα	39
κηρύσσω, κήρυγμα	15	ὄχλος	73
κλαίω	20		
κλέπτης	74	παιδεύω	14
κόφινος	69	παῖς, παιδίον	62
κόσμος	58	παλαιός	25
κράτος, κρείσσων	21, 57	παράβασις, παρακοή, παράπτωμα, παρανομία	39
κτίσις	49	παραβολή, παροιμία	46
κύριος	59	παράδοσις	49
		πάρεσις	42
λαλέω	8, 15	πατριά	61
λαμπάς	65	παροργισμός	32
λαός	73	πένης	30
λατρεύω	36	περιποιέομαι, περιποίησις	43
λέγω, λόγος	8	πέτρα, πέτρος	75
λειτουργός, λειτουργέω, λειτουργία, λειτουργικός	36	πλημμέλεια	39
ληστής	74	πληρόω, πλήρωμα	13

NEW TESTAMENT SYNONYMS. 373

	NO.
πλύνω	17
πνεῦμα	55
ποιέω	2
ποιμαίνω, ποίμνη, ποίμνιον	16, 72
πονηρός, πονηρία	22
πράσσω	2
προσεύχομαι, προσευχή	38
προσκυνέω	36
προσφορά	37
προφήτης, προφητεύω	15
πτωχός	30
πύλη, πυλών	71
πυνθάνομαι	9
ῥαββί	59
ῥέω, ῥῆμα	8
σαγήνη	70
σάρξ, σαρκικός	55
Σατᾶν, Σατανᾶς	53
σέβομαι, σεβάζομαι	36
σημεῖον	45
σκιά	56
σπουδή	11
σπυρίς	69
στέφανος, στέμμα	67
σχῆμα	56
τέκνον	62
τέλος, τελέω, τέλειος, τελειόω	13, 27
τέρας	45
τιμή	43

	NO.
ὕμνος	48
ὑπάρχω	1
ὑπηρέτης	60
ὑπομονή	31
φαίνομαι	6
φαῦλος	22
φέγγος	65
φημί	8
φιλέω, φιλανθρωπία, φιλαδελφία	19
φόβος, φοβέομαι	33
φορτίον	68
φρένες	55
φρονέω, φροντίζω	11
φυλή	61
φῶς, φωστήρ	65
χαρακτήρ, χάραγμα	56
χάρις	41
χιτών	66
χρή	12
χρηστός, χρηστότης	21
χρίω, Χριστός	18
χρόνος	64
ψαλμός	48
ψηλαφάω	7
ψυχή, ψυχικός	54 55
ᾠδή	48

Some groups of Verbs in ordinary use, with their related Substantives.

1. To Be, Exist, Become.

εἰμί is the ordinary verb of existence ; ὑπάρχω implies essential or original condition (Phil. ii. 6), and so is directly contrasted with γίνομαι, *to become* (James i. 22). See further, Acts xvii. 24 ; Heb. xi. 6.

2. To Do, to Make.

ποιέω seems to denote more sustained effort than πράσσω, whence the frequent use of the former for *well-doing*, the latter for *ill-doing*. For other senses of πράσσω, see Eph. vi. 21 ; Luke iii. 13 (this last compared with ποιέω in Luke xii. 33, xix. 18).

3. To Will, to Desire.

βούλομαι denotes the will rather on its intellectual side, "to choose ;" θέλω, will with intent and power to perform. So the latter is used of arbitrary (Luke iv. 6) or absolute (Rom. ix. 18) authority, the former of determinations where the wisdom and justice are apparent (Luke x. 22, xxii. 42). Thus, βουλή is *counsel* ; θέλημα, *will* ; βούλημα, *plan* (only in Acts xxvii. 43 ; Rom. ix. 19). βούλομαι is also used in recommendations backed by reason (1 Tim. ii. 8, v. 14). For a striking instance of distinction between the two verbs, compare Mark xv. 9, 12, with verse 15. So Philemon 13, 14. μέλλω indicates futurity, as the result of predetermination, or of some act or event, "is to be," "is going to," Matt. iii. 7, xi. 14 ; Luke vii. 2 ; Heb. i. 14. So in the phrase τὰ μέλλοντα, *the things to come* (Col. ii. 17).

4. To Know.

οἶδα is properly a perfect, "I have seen," and implies the knowledge which comes from without, *objective* knowledge ; γινώσκω, "I learn," in any way, expresses the knowledge as existing in the mind, *subjective* knowledge. Hence, when knowledge involves experience, γινώσκω is always used (Eph. iii. 19 ; Phil. iii. 10 ; 1 John ii., iii., iv.) ; ἐπίσταμαι (an old dialectic form of the middle of ἐφίστημι), "to set (the mind) upon," may either mean simply *to be aware* of, as in Acts x. 28; xviii. 25, or *to understand* (Mark xiv. 68). The distinction between οἶδα and ἐπίσταμαι may be noted in Jude 10 ; that between γινώσκω and ἐπίσταμαι in Acts xix. 15.

5. To See.

βλέπω denotes the act of seeing, and is referred to the organ ; ὁράω (ὄψομαι, εἶδον) is referred to the thing seen, whether in itself (objectively) or in regard to its impression on the mind (subjectively). The former verb, therefore, may be used without an expressed object (as Matt. xiii. 13). Both verbs are applied to mental vision, the former implying greater vividness (Heb. ii. 8, 9). With μή, they have the sense *beware ;* generally, however, βλέπω is used, occasionally with ἀπό. In accordance with the distinction above mentioned, ὅραμα is a *vision;* βλέμμα, the exercise of the faculty of *sight;* τὰ βλεπόμενα, *the things seen* (2 Cor. iv. 18), *i.e.*, on which the faculty of immediate discernment is exercised ; τὸ ὁρατόν, *the visible* (Col. i. 16), *i.e.*, in itself considered. Tittmann distinguishes ὁράω and its derivatives from εἶδον, in that the former is objective, and the latter subjective, ὄψομαι being a middle term. Compare ὅραμα, εἶδος, ὄψις. It is doubtful, however, if this distinction can be maintained in the use of the verbs. θεάομαι (referred to the *subject*) and θεωρέω (referred to the *object*) are to look at purposely, or attentively to *gaze upon* (Matt. vi. 1, xi. 7 ; John xii. 45 ; Acts vii. 56).

6. To Appear.

δοκέω " expresses the subjective mental estimate or opinion about a matter which men form, their δόξα concerning it, which may be right (Acts xv. 28 ; 1 Cor. iv. 9, vii. 40), but which may be wrong, involving, as it always does, the possibility of error (Matt. vi. 7 ; Mark vi. 49 ; John xvi. 2 ; Acts xxvii. 13) ; " φαίνομαι " expresses how a matter phenomenally shows and presents itself, with no necessary assumption of any beholder at all."—*Trench*. This "phenomenon" may represent a reality (Matt. ii. 7 ; Phil. ii. 15, "appear," not "shine") or a mere show (Matt. xxiii. 27, 28).

7. To Touch.

ἅπτομαι (middle of ἅπτω, *to kindle*) is the usual word ; θιγγάνω denotes a lighter touch (compare the two in Col. ii. 21, where, as Archbishop Trench observes, the order of our translation should be reversed [so R.V.]; and see Heb. xi. 28); ψηλαφάω is to *feel* ("to feel after," Acts xvii. 27), to *handle*. Pres. part. *palpable, material* (Heb. xii. 18).

8. To Speak, Say.

λαλέω is simply to *speak*, to employ the organ of utterance ; λέγω is referred to the *sentiment* of what is spoken (compare βλέπω and ὁράω above) ; φημί, ῥέω, ἐρῶ, εἶπον to the *words;* ῥῆμα is a *word*, in itself considered ; λόγος, a *spoken word*, with reference generally to that which is in the speaker's mind ; ἔπος is only found (Heb. vii. 9) in the phrase ὡς ἔπος εἰπεῖν, *so to speak*. Both λέγω and εἶπον are used for *command;* as in the formula (Sermon on the Mount) ἐγὼ δὲ λέγω ὑμῖν. See also Matt. iv. 3.

9. To Ask.

αἰτέω is to ask for something, *to beg, pray;* ἐρωτάω, *to question, to ask* in general, specifically : "In that day ye shall ask me no questions...whatsoever ye shall ask of the Father in my name." Observe, ἐρωτάω is elsewhere used of Christ's prayers to the Father (John xvii. 9, 15, 20), never of ours. Compare the two in John xvi. 23, and in 1 John v. 16. πυνθάνομαι, to ask for information, to *inquire*.

10. To Come.

ἔρχομαι denotes the act, "I am coming ;" ἥκω, the result, "I am come." John viii. 42: "I came from God, and I am here." See also Heb. x. 9.

11. To Care.

φρονέω, φροντίζω, implies solicitude (Phil. iv. 10; Titus iii. 8); **μελετάω** (and impers. **μέλει**), solicitude expressed in forethought, or the employment of means to the desired result; **μεριμνάω**, anxious or distracting care. So the substantive **μέριμνα**. See especially 1 Peter v. 7. **σπουδή** ("haste") is *earnestness, diligence*, generally.

12. Ought.

δεῖ (impers.) denotes the duty or necessity as existing *in the thing itself*, often used for the *ought* arising from prophecy (Luke xxiv. 26, 46); **ὀφείλω** refers to the obligation *as actually imposed* (John xiii. 14); **χρή** (only once in the New Testament, James iii. 10) is connected with χράομαι, and originally differs from δεῖ as the rule of utility differs from that of abstract right (δεῖ would express Butler's philosophy of morals; χρή, Paley's).

13. To Accomplish, Fulfil, Perfect.

τέλος expresses the end of a course or series: so **τελέω**, to *reach the end*; **τελειόω**, to *complete*; **πληρόω** denotes the accomplishment of a plan or purpose, to *fulfil*; τελέω gives the finishing stroke (John xix. 30); πληρόω adds the completing element: the former brings the topstone, the latter the keystone. Hence they are often interchangeable. Compare Acts xx. 24, where the prominent thought is the completeness of the Apostle's life-work, with 2 Tim. iv. 7, where to this is superadded the thought of its approaching close. The fulfilment of prophecy is expressed by πληρόω, except John xix. 28, which has τελειόω. **πλήρωμα** is generally active, that which brings completeness, fulness, to anything (Matt. ix. 16; 1 Cor. x. 26); but may be used passively, that which is filled (Eph. i. 23), or abstractedly, *fulness* (Col. ii. 9).

14. To Teach, Instruct.

διδάσκω is to *teach* generally; **κατηχέω**, strictly to *teach by word of mouth* (Luke i. 4; Rom. ii. 18). Hence *catechesis, catechise*, of careful, repeated oral instruction; **μαθητεύω** is (actively) to *make*, or (intransitively) to *be a disciple*, in the former sense distinguished from διδάσκω in Matt. xxviii. 19. **παιδεύω** involves the notion of *discipline*, and is often to be rendered *chasten*.

15. To Preach.

κηρύσσω is to *proclaim*, as a herald; **κήρυγμα**, the *proclamation* made; **εὐαγγέλιον** and **εὐαγγελίζω** add the further notion of *glad tidings*; **καταγγέλλω** refers simply to the delivery of the message. Found with εὐαγγελίζω, Acts xv. 35, 36; with κηρύσσω, Phil. i. 15, 16. **λαλέω**, sometimes rendered *preach*, means simply to *talk* (see **8**), and **διαλέγομαι** (Acts xx. 7, 9) implies *conference*; **προφητεύω**, to *forth-tell*, and **προφήτης**, are used for preachers under the New Testament (Eph. iv. 11; 1 Cor. xiv. 1), as for the prophets of the Old, both being set to declare the Divine will; μάντις, a *soothsayer*, is of heathen use, and not found in the New Testament, **μαντεύομαι** occurring only Acts xvi. 16. (See Trench.)

16. To Feed (a flock).

ποιμαίνω is in general to exercise the care of a ποιμήν, to *tend* the flock (Acts xx. 28), hence to *rule, govern* (Matt. ii. 6; Rev. ii. 27); βόσκω refers to the special function of providing food, to *pasture* (Luke xv. 15). Both are included in our Lord's charge to St. Peter (John xxi. 15-17).

17. To Wash, Bathe.

πλύνω is to wash *things*, as garments, etc.; λούω, to wash the *whole body*, "to bathe;" νίπτω, to wash a *part* of the body. See John xiii. 10; and remarks by Archbishop Trench.

18. To Anoint.

χρίω denotes *official* anointing, as of a king or priest, hence Χριστός: ἀλείφω, anointing for *festal* purposes (Luke vii. 46), for *health* (James v. 14), or for embalmment (Mark xvi. 1).

19. Love, to Love.

ἀγαπάω denotes the love of esteem or of kindness, love to character ("diligo"); ἀγάπη, its cognate substantive, "is a word born within the bosom of revealed religion. It occurs in the LXX., but there is no example of its use in any heathen writer whatever; the utmost they attained to here was φιλανθρωπία and φιλαδελφία, and the last, indeed, never in any sense but as the love between brethren in blood." —*Trench.* Wherever "charity" occurs in the A.V., the original is ἀγάπη, but it is more generally and better translated "love" (R.V.). φιλέω expresses the love of the feelings, instinctive, warm affection ("amo"). The force of the two verbs is very beautifully illustrated in John xxi. 15-17.

20. To Weep.

κλαίω is the verb generally employed; δακρύω, "to shed tears," is found but once, John xi. 35: "Jesus wept." In Matt. ii. 18, θρῆνος (reading doubtful; W. H. and R.V. omit), κλαυθμός, ὀδυρμός, form a climax, "(lamentation,) weeping, and mourning."

II.

Some important words, chiefly Adjectives and Substantives, expressive of moral quality.

21. Good.

ἀγαθός is *good*; δίκαιος, *right*. In the former, the notion of beneficence prevails, in the latter that of justice. So with ἀγαθωσύνη, δικαιοσύνη. Still, the two are not opposed. In Rom. vii. 12 both are predicated of the Divine law. In Rom. v. 7 the ἀγαθός is one of the δίκαιοι (as proved by the article and by γάρ); in Matt. vi. 1, *seq.*, δικαιοσύνη[1] refers to almsgiving, prayers, and religious fasting. **καλός** contains the notion of *giving pleasure*, "beautiful," "fair," "honourable." It may be interchanged with ἀγαθός (compare, *e.g.*, 1 Tim. i. 19 with Heb. xiii. 18), or combined with it, as Luke viii. 15. (So in classic Greek, καλοκἀγαθός predicates the highest excellence in morals and manners.) **χρηστός**, *good, gentle* (Matt. xi. 30; 1 Cor. xv. 33), and **χρηστότης**, *goodness, gentleness, benignity*, are connected with χράομαι, χρή. The New Testament comparative of ἀγαθός is usually **κρείσσων, κρείττων**, really akin to κράτος, *force*, and betokening the time when strength and goodness were too closely identified. (Compare ἀρετή, "virtue," really *courage*, found only in the New Testament, Phil. iv. 8; 1 Pet. ii. 9, where see **47**; 2 Pet. i. 3, 5.) **βέλτιον**, as an adverb, is found 2 Tim. i. 18.

22. Evil, Bad.

κακός is *bad*, generically, including every form of evil, physical and moral. So **κακία**, *badness*, especially in its forms of meanness, cowardice, malice; **ἄδικος, ἀδικία** (opposed to δίκαιος, δικαιοσύνη), *wrong*. **πονηρός** expresses the more active form of evil, *malignant* (so ὁ πονηρός, not ὁ κακός, for the Evil one, Satan); **πονηρία**, *malignity*; **φαῦλος** is *worthless*, "good for nothing" like the old Eng. "naughty," from "naught."

23. Holy.

ὅσιος is holy, *intrinsically;* referred once to the Divine purposes (Acts xiii. 34, from Isa. lv. 3), generally to interior purity; predicated both of God and of men ("pious"); **ἅγιος, ἁγνός,** are both derived from a root denoting *separation*, the former, when applied to men, expressing consecration to God (see 1 Pet. ii. 5, 9), the latter, purity, chastity; **ἱερός**, very infrequently (except in its neuter substantival form, ἱερόν, on which see **35**), is "dedicated to God," and is only used in the New Testament of things; **καθαρός**, literally *clean*, free from impure admixture.

24. True.

ἀληθής is "true" morally, and is applied to persons or to declarations; **ἀληθινός** is "genuine," "real." The former epithet, for instance, applied to God, denotes his attribute of faithfulness (John iii. 33); the latter expresses the reality of his Godhead, as distinguished from false deities (John xvii. 3). The use of ἀληθινός in the Revelation is an exception to this rule (see xix. 9, 11). The substantive **ἀλήθεια** includes the idea of both adjectives, though generally correspondent with the former.

25. Old.

παλαιός is "old," as *having existed long;* **ἀρχαῖος**, "old," *as having existed formerly*: ἀρχαῖος μαθητής (Acts xxi. 16), one of the original disciples. Compare 2 Pet. ii. 5; Rev. xii. 9, xx. 2. παλαιός sometimes connotes the idea of decrepitude, decay (opposed to καινός, see **26**), Matt. ix. 16; 1 Cor. v. 7, 8; and for the verb, Heb. viii. 13.

---

[1] Undoubtedly the true reading.

26. New.

νέος is new in reference to *time*, having recently come into existence (young); καινός, new (fresh) in reference to *quality*, different in kind. (See Trench on the words.) So νέα διαθήκη (Heb. xii. 24) is "a covenant recently given;" καινή διαθήκη (Heb. ix. 15), "a covenant new in character;" ἀνανεόω (Eph. iv. 23), to renew in youth; ἀνακαινόω (Col. iii. 10), to renew in character and spirit. So νεότης, youth; καινότης, newness, freshness.

27. Perfect.

τέλειος, "full-grown," applied to character, means that which has attained the moral τέλος—manhood in Christ; "however it may be true that having reached this, other and higher ends will open out before him, to have Christ formed in him more and more."—*Trench.* The attainment of their highest end is expressed by the perfect τετελείωμαι (Phil. iii. 12). ὁλόκληρος is complete in parts, no Christian grace lacking; ὁλοτελής denotes maturity in each separate element of character (1 Thess. v. 23).

28. Blessed.

Two different adjectives are translated *blessed:* μακάριος, *happy*, as in the Beatitudes, and notably 1 Tim. i. 11, vi. 15; and εὐλογητός, verbal adjective of the verb *to bless* (Mark xiv. 61; Rom. i. 25).

29. Void, Vain, Futile.

κενός, literally *empty*, refers to the contents; μάταιος, *purposeless*, to the result. See the two in 1 Cor. xv. 14, 17: "your faith is κενή—there is no substance in it— and ματαία, leads to no happy issue." The latter adjective is also employed (from the LXX.) for *false*, as in the "lying vanities" of heathendom (Acts xiv. 15).

30. Poor.

πένης (only in 2 Cor. ix. 9) may refer to the poverty of *scanty livelihood;* πτωχός implies that of *utter destitution.* See Matt. v. 3, xi. 5.

31. Patience.

ὑπομονή (ὑπομένω) denotes not only the passive, but the active virtue of endurance, and may often be rendered persistence, continuance (Luke viii. 15; Heb. xii. 1; James v. 11); μακροθυμία (μακροθυμέω) seems always to involve the notion of *tolerance*, "long-suffering, bearing with," as God with sinners; ἀνοχή (only in Rom. ii. 4, iii. 25) is *forbearance*, the result and expression of the Divine μακροθυμία.

32. Anger.

θυμός is the impulse and passion; ὀργή, the habit and settled purpose of wrath. Both (as in Rom. ii. 8) are applied to the anger of God against sinners; the latter, however, being the usual word. Both are ranked among the sins of men (as Eph. iv. 31). Still, there may possibly be a righteous human anger (Eph. iv. 26; compare Mark iii. 5), while the exasperation and bitterness of anger, παροργισμός, is utterly forbidden.

33. Fear.

φόβος, φοβέομαι, are words in themselves indifferent, the fear being sinful, or reverent and holy, according to the particular reference; but δειλός, δειλία, are always bad and base, "cowardly, cowardice;" εὐλάβεια, εὐλαβέομαι, denote apprehension generally (see Acts xxiii. 10), but chiefly pious fear (Heb. xii. 28, and perhaps v. 7).

III.

Some words of theological or ecclesiastical meaning.

34. Deity.

Θειότης (Rom. i. 20), Deity, in an abstract sense (Göttlichheit); Θεότης (Col. ii. 9), Deity, personally (Gottheit). See Tittmann.

35. Temple.

ἱερόν, the whole sacred enclosure (Matt. xxvi. 55; John ii. 14); ναός, the shrine itself, the Holy place, and Holy of Holies (Matt. xxvii. 51; John ii. 19; Acts vii. 48; 1 Cor. iii. 16).

36. To Worship.

προσκυνέω is the generic word (primarily expressive of the *act*, "to fawn," from κύων) of homage paid to God, to Christ, and (in the Revelation) to the "dragon" and the "beast;" σέβομαι (σεβάζομαι), of the religious feeling, "to cherish, or to pay devotion;" λατρεύω, of Divine worship, Phil. iii. 3 (idolatrous in Acts vii. 42); λειτουργέω, of solemn, stated observance. So λειτουργία, as Luke i. 23; λειτουργικός, Heb. i. 14; λειτουργός, Heb. viii. 2. But these last words may also apply to the ministry of kindness between fellow-Christians; as διακονέω, but in a more exalted sense. See 60.

37. Altar, Sacrifice.

θυσιαστήριον is the general word, properly an adjective—that on which sacrifices are offered; βωμός, the altar-*structure* (orig., "a raised place"), is only found once, of a heathen altar, Acts xvii. 23; θυσία is a sacrifice offered by a priest (ἱερεύς), either expiatory, in which sense Christ alone is priest, or eucharistic, in which all Christians are priests alike (1 Pet. ii. 5); προσφορά is any offering to God, priestly or otherwise. In Eph. v. 2 some refer προσφοράν to Christ's consecrated *life*, θυσίαν to his atoning death.

38. Prayer, to Pray.

εὐχή is a prayer (James v. 15) or a vow (Acts xviii. 18); εὔχομαι, to pray, or to wish strongly (Rom. ix. 3); προσεύχομαι, προσευχή, are restricted to prayer to God, the latter denoting sometimes a place of prayer, a building below the rank of a synagogue, "proseucha" (Acts xvi. 13); δέησις is in general the expression of *need*, any urgent request, "supplication." For αἰτέω, ἐρωτάω, see 9; αἴτημα is any particular request; in plur., the individual petitions in the προσευχή. See Phil. iv. 6.

39. Sin, to Sin.

"Sin," says Archbishop Trench, "may be contemplated as the missing of a mark or aim ; it is then ἁμαρτία or ἁμάρτημα (ἁμαρτάνω) : the overpassing or transgressing of a line ; it is then παράβασις (παραβαίνω) : the disobedience to a voice ; in which case it is παρακοή (παρακούω) : the falling where one should have stood upright; this will be παράπτωμα : ignorance of what one ought to have known; this will be ἀγνόημα (Heb. ix. 7) : diminishing of that which should have been rendered in full measure ; which is ἥττημα : non-observance of a law ; which is ἀνομία or παρανομία : a discord ; and then it is πλημμέλεια : and in other ways almost out of number." Note also ὀφείλημα, in the Lord's Prayer (Matt. vi. 12), debt to Divine justice. Luke has ἁμαρτία (xi. 4).

40. Repentance, to Repent.

μετάνοια, μετανοέω, express a change of mind, and hence of the whole life ; μεταμέλομαι, a change of feeling, "to regret." Godly sorrow is said to work μετάνοιαν ἀμεταμέλητον, "repentance that leads to no remorse" (2 Cor. vii. 10). Esau found no place of repentance, μετανοίας (Heb. xii. 17), *i.e.*, of changing *his father's* mind with respect to the blessing. See Dr. Campbell's Dissertation, in his "Gospels."

41. Grace, Mercy.

χάρις is free favour, in general, specially of the Divine favour as extended to the *sinful;* ἔλεος is mercy, to the *miserable* (1 Tim. i. 2). The difference between ἔλεος and οἰκτιρμός is that, in the latter, *pity* is the prominent idea ; in the former, *kindness*. For the verbs, see Rom. ix. 15.

42. Forgiveness.

ἄφεσις, ἀφίημι, denote the "remission" of sins, forgiveness, to its full extent, as promised in the Gospel ; πάρεσις, found only Rom. iii. 25, literally, *passing-by*, "prætermission," refers rather to the simple withholding of punishment deserved, a parallel being found in Acts xvii. 30 (ὑπεριδών).

43. Redemption.

"ἀγοράζω, buy, as in a market-place, for a certain price (τιμή) ; λυτρόω, effect deliverance by the payment of ransom and exertion of power ; λύτρον is the price paid for releasing any one from captivity, punishment, or death (λύω, loose), the buying back by paying the price of what had been sold, or the redeeming what had been devoted by substituting something in its place. So ἀντίλυτρον, with the further idea "in room of," denoting exchange, the price paid for procuring the liberation of another by ransom or forfeit ; λύτρωσις, ἀπολύτρωσις, the process of deliverance ; ἱλασμός, ἐξιλασμὸς, are the same as λύτρον, with the leading idea of propitiation."—*Webster*. See the use of ἱλάσκομαι in the publican's prayer, Luke xviii. 13 ; ἱλαστήριον, properly an adjective, "propitiatory" of the mercy-seat, in LXX. and Heb. ix. 5 ; of Christ's sacrifice, Rom. iii. 25 ; περιποιέομαι, περιποίησις, denote acquirements for one's self, purchase, generally (Acts xx. 28 ; 1 Pet. ii. 9 ; Eph. i. 14).

44. Piety, Religion.

εὐσεβής, εὐσέβεια, denote worship or piety *rightly* directed, in human relations as well as Divine; θεοσεβής, θεοσέβεια, worship directed towards *God;* εὐλαβής, εὐλάβεια, denote the devoutness springing from godly *fear;* θρῆσκος, θρησκεία (James i. 26, 27; Acts xxvi. 5; Col. ii. 18, only), refer to external worship, religious service; δεισιδαίμων (Acts xvii. 22), and δεισιδαιμονία (Acts xxv. 19), may have a favourable or unfavourable meaning, "religious" or "superstitious," literally, "devoted to the fear of deities."

45. Miracle, Sign, Wonder.

δύναμις (generally in plur.), applied to Christ's miracles, is a forth-putting of Divine power; τέρας is a prodigy, a wonderful act; σημεῖον, a sign, authenticating Christ's mission, and symbolising heavenly truths (Acts ii. 22).

46. Parable.

παραβολή, a detailed comparison, "parable," as usually understood; παροιμία (literally, a wayside discourse), "a proverb," John xvi. 25, 29; "a comparison," 2 Pet. ii. 22; John x. 6.

47. Praise, to Praise.

αἰνέω, αἶνος (αἴνεσις), are used only of praise offered to God; ἐπαινέω, ἔπαινος, of praise, approbation generally; δόξα, where rendered praise (John ix. 24, xii. 43 : 1 Pet. iv. 11), denotes the recognition of character, "the glory." In 1 Pet. ii. 9 the word is ἀρετάς, *virtues;* μεγαλύνω, *to magnify,* is a yet more exalted word (Luke i. 46).

48. Psalm, Hymn.

ψαλμός is probably used restrictively of the Psalms of the older Scriptures ; ὕμνος (not often used, probably from its associations with heathenism) is an ode of praise to God : "A psalm might be a *de profundis;* a hymn must always be more or less of a *magnificat.*"—*Trench.* ᾠδή is a song that might be either psalm or hymn, or a yet more general expression of Christian feeling (Eph. v. 19 ; Col. iii. 16).

49. Ordinance.

This word is adopted as the rendering of δόγμα, a thing decreed (Eph. ii. 15 ; Col. ii. 14 ; see also Col. ii. 20) ; δικαίωμα, that which it is right to observe (Heb. ix. 1, 10) ; διαταγή, appointment (Rom. xiii. 2) ; παράδοσις (1 Cor. xi. 2 ; R.V., *tradition*), instruction or injunction given, elsewhere translated *tradition* (as 2 Thess. ii. 15) ; and κτίσις, creation, creature (1 Pet. ii. 13). As distinguished from δικαιώματα, the ἐντολαί are moral precepts (Luke i. 6).

50. Hebrew, Israelite, Jew, Greek, Hellenist.

Ἑβραῖος denotes the Hebrew-speaking Jewish community ; Ἑλληνιστής being a Greek-speaking Jew. The latter word is rendered "Grecian" in the A.V., "Grecian Jew" in the R.V., in distinction from Ἕλλην, "Greek," or Gentile (Acts vi. 1, ix. 29; in Acts xi. 20 the reading should probably be Ἕλληνας [R.V.], though W. H.

read 'Ελληνιστάς). 'Ιουδαῖος, Jew, originally referred to the tribe of Judah alone, had come in the New Testament times to designate the whole people; while 'Ισραηλίτης is always a term of honour, "one of the chosen race."

51. Anathema.

ἀνάθημα, a thing devoted in *honour* of God (Luke xxi. 5); ἀνάθεμα (originally the same word), a thing devoted to *destruction*, "accursed." So the verb ἀναθεματίζω. See Acts xxiii. 14. The other occurrences of ἀνάθεμα are Rom. ix. 3; 1 Cor. xii. 3, xvi. 22; Gal. i. 8, 9.

52. Hell, Hades.

ᾅδης (always rendered "Hades" in R.V.) is the unseen world, the place of the departed, generally (compare Luke xvi. 23; Acts ii. 27); by metonymy for death and destruction (Matt. xi. 23); once only rendered "grave," 1 Cor. xv. 55 (where the R.V. reads θάνατε with W. H.); "the gates of Hades" are the powers of destruction (Matt. xvi. 18); γέεννα (Heb. = "Valley of Hinnom" [R.V. always *hell*, with *Gehenna* in marg., except Jas. iii. 6]) is the abode of the lost (Matt. v. 22, 29, 30, x. 28, xviii. 9, xxiii. 15, 33; Mark ix. 43, 45; Luke xii. 5; James iii. 6, only). See Dr. Campbell's Dissertation, in his "Gospels."

53. Devil, Demon.

The almost uniform translation of δαίμων, δαιμόνιον, by "devil" is unfortunate. The word (most usual in the New Testament in the second or diminutive form) classically denotes a subordinate divinity, supernatural being. There were κακοδαίμονες and ἀγαθοδαίμονες. In Scripture the word always has its evil sense, and the *demon* of R.V. marg. might well have been inserted in the text. ὁ διάβολος (Heb., from Σατᾶν, Σατανᾶς) is the one arch-spirit of evil, "the devil." In its sense of calumniator, the word is found (plur.) 1 Tim. iii. 11; 2 Tim. iii. 3; Titus ii. 3.

IV.

Some common words, chiefly Substantives, which present interesting points of distinction.

54. Life, Death.

ζωή is life in its *principle*, life intrinsic; βίος, life in its *manifestations*, life extrinsic. Hence the former is used especially for life spiritual and immortal; the latter may denote the duration or manner of life, livelihood. ψυχή is the principle of animal life, "the soul." (See the next article.) θάνατος is *death*, opposed to ζωή; νεκρός, *dead;* θνητός, *mortal*. The verbs θανατόω (Rom. viii. 13), νεκρόω (Col. iii. 5), are both translated *mortify;* the former, perhaps, referring rather to the *state* "death to sin," the latter to the *deed*, "slay them."

55. Soul, Mind, Spirit.

ψυχή, soul or life, is common to man with the irrational animals (Rev. viii. 9), hence *self* (Matt. xvi. 25, 26), *person* (Rev. xviii. 13), often the soul as the seat of passion or desire, the point of contact between man's bodily and spiritual nature ; ψυχικός, "natural" (1 Cor. ii. 14, xv. 44, 46 ; James iii. 15 ; Jude 19, only) ; σῶμα and ψυχή are jointly elements of what is often called σάρξ, the lower, fleshly nature. So σάρκινος, and the grosser σαρκικός, as 1 Cor. iii. 1, 3 (see § 142 c, note). But σῶμα is sometimes used for *person*, Rom. xii. 1, "your bodies," *i.e.*, the instruments or organs of your entire nature. πνεῦμα, spirit, man's highest nature, the point of contact between the human and the Divine ; πνευματικός, *spiritual*, as 1 Cor. ii. 13, 15 ; φρένες (only in 1 Cor. xiv. 20), the *understanding* ; νοῦς, the mind, percipient and intelligent, the *reason* ; καρδία, the *heart*, is used not only for the seat of the emotions, but for that of the intellectual faculties, αἱ καρδίαι, καὶ τὰ νοήματα (Phil. iv. 7), "thought at its source and in its manifestations ;" διάνοια, the understanding, as exercised, for good or evil, Eph. ii. 3 ; Matt. xxii. 37.

56. Form, Fashion, Likeness.

εἶδος is *appearance*, that may or may not have a basis in reality ; εἴδωλον, a *mere* appearance, "an idol ;" μορφή, the *form* as indicative of the interior nature ; σχῆμα, the form, externally regarded, "the figure, fashion" (see Phil. ii. 6, 7, 8) ; εἰκών denotes the exact representation, "image ;" σκία, the shadowy resemblance (Heb. x. 1) ; χαρακτήρ, the *impress*, as enstamped (Heb. i. 3). Compare χάραγμα. "stamp, engraving."

57. Power.

δύναμις, used also of miracles (see 45), *inherent* power, might ; ἐξουσία, power *employed*, authority ; ἰσχύς, *strength*, as an endowment (so ἰσχύω, to be strong, prevail, more emphatic than δύναμαι) ; κράτος, strength as exerted, "force."

58. World.

κόσμος, the scheme of material things, the world, often in opposition to the kingdom of heaven ; αἰών has reference primarily to duration (probably derived not from ἀεὶ ὤν, but from ἄημι, to *breathe* ; hence *life, duration*), adj., αἰώνιος, belonging to the αἰών : ἀΐδιος is from ἀεί, and means simply *everlasting* (only found Rom. i. 20 ; Jude 6) ; αἰῶνες (Heb. i. 2), "the ages," or, as A.V. and R.V., "the worlds," in respect to their successive ages : οἰκουμένη, the earth as inhabited, the world of men. For κόσμος and οἰκουμένη, interchangeable, compare Matt. iv. 8 with Luke iv. 5.

59. Master.

κύριος expresses lordship in general ; δεσπότης, ownership (correlative with δοῦλος) ; διδάσκαλος (correlative with μαθητής) *is teacher*. In James iii. 1 the meaning seems to be *censors* ; ἐπιστάτης (only in Luke), literally, *superintendent*, is the Greek rendering of the Hebrew ῥαββί, found in its original form in Matt., Mark, John.

60. Servant.

δοῦλος, *slave*, is the lowest word in the scale of servitude (δουλόω, *to enslave*, δουλεύω, *to serve*, as a slave); ὑπηρέτης, "under-rower.' expresses in general subservience to another's will (so ὑπηρετέω); διάκονος, διακονία, διακονέω, imply service, ministry, in every form; θεράπων, is attendant (only in Heb. iii. 5); θεραπεύω θεραπεία have special reference to healing; οἰκέτης, a household servant, Acts x. 7 (so παῖς, see 62).

61. Family, Tribe, House.

φυλή is a *tribe*, as of Israel; πατριά, a *family*, in the wider sense, descendants of a common ancestor (only in Luke ii. 4; Acts iii. 25; Eph. iii. 15; in A.V. a different rendering each time, R.V. consistently *family*); οἶκος, οἰκία, both mean *household*, the former referring to the inmates, the latter to the building and that which it contains (δῶμα always in the New Testament of the building, with ἐπί, "house-top.")

62. Child, Infant.

τέκνον, child by *natural* descent (from τίκτω); παῖς, a *boy* or *girl*, a child in legal relation, also a servant (Luke xv. 26; Matt. xii. 18; Acts iv. 27, 30); παιδίον, a *young child;* βρέφος, a *babe;* νήπιος (from νη, negative, and εἶπον), *infans*, a child in power and character.

63. Man.

ἄνθρωπος, a man, member of the human family (homo); ἀνήρ, a man in sex and age (vir).

64. Time.

χρόνος, time as duration; καιρός, a definite time, with reference to some act or crisis, "opportunity."

65. Lamp, Light.

φῶς, *light*, generally; φωστήρ, *luminary* (Phil. ii. 15); λύχνος, a *lamp* (John v. 35), (λυχνία, a lampstand); λαμπάς, a *torch* (Matt. xxv. 1; Acts xx. 8); φέγγος, light in its splendour, "radiance" (Matt. xxiv. 29).

66. Clothes.

ἱμάτιον, raiment, generally, also an outer garment, opposed to χιτών, an inner vest (Matt. v. 40); ἐσθής, apparel, usually applied to what is ornate or splendid; ἔνδυμα, anything put on (Matt. iii. 4, vi. 28).

67. Crown.

στέφανος, "a garland," a conqueror's or a festal crown (στέμμα, a sacrificial garland, Acts xiv. 13); διάδημα, "a fillet," a royal crown (Rev. xii. 3, xiii. 1, xix. 12, only).

68. Burden.

βάρος denotes the pressure of a weight, which may be relieved or transferred (Gal. vi. 2); φορτίον is specific, the "load" which each must bear for himself (ver. 5); γόμος, the lading of a ship (Acts xxi. 3); ὄγκος, the weight that encumbers (Heb. xii. 1).

69. Basket.

κόφινος, a travelling basket (Matt. xiv. 20); σπυρίς, a large hamper used for storage (Matt. xv. 37; Acts ix. 25). The two miracles of feeding are distinguished in all the accounts by the different word used for basket in each (see Matt. xvi. 9, 10).

70. Net.

δίκτυον, a net, in general; ἀμφίβληστρον, a fishing-net flung from the hand (Matt. iv. 18; Mark i. 16); σαγήνη (Matt. xiii. 47), a large draw-net, "seine."

71. Gate, Door.

θύρα, a *door* (janua): πύλη, a *gate* (porta); πυλών, a great gate, an outer gate, a porch.

72. Fold, Flock.

αὐλή is *fold*; ποίμνη (dim. ποίμνιον) is *flock*. The promise in John x. 16 is, that there shall be "one *flock* and one shepherd" (R.V.), not "one *fold*," as A.V.

73. People.

Four words are so translated: λαός, people, collectively, with a general reference to the Jews as the people of God; ἔθνος, nation (plur., ἔθνη, Gentiles); δῆμος, people, as a municipality; ὄχλος, "irregular crowd, mob."

74. Thief.

κλέπτης, "thief," one who steals by fraud (Lat. *fur*); λῃστής, "robber," one who steals by violence (Lat. *latro*). The crucified malefactor and Barabbas probably belonged to the hordes of banditti which then ravaged the land.

75. Stone.

πέτρα, a rock (Πέτρος, the same word, only with masc. termination to make it a proper name), Lat. *saxum*; λίθος, a stone, detached or hewn, Lat. *lapis*.

76. Other.

ἄλλος denotes numerical, ἕτερος generic distinction, "different." See Gal. i. 6, 7. "to another (ἕτερον) gospel which is not another (ἄλλο)." There may be various kinds of so-called gospels, but there is really no other than that which the apostle preached.

VOCABULARY.

IN the following Vocabulary, the Declension of *Substantives* is marked by the subjoined Genitive termination; their Gender, by the Article.

Of *Adjectives*, the Feminine and Neuter forms are given; in those of two terminations, the Neuter.

To *Verbs*, the Future endings, and, where necessary, other forms, have been generally appended.

The *Hyphen* has been freely used, to indicate the formation, not only of synthetic, but of parathetic compounds. (See §§ 146-148.) For further etymological details, a larger Lexicon must be consulted.

The *Scripture References* are introduced as fully as space would permit. In the case of words of frequent occurrence the references are limited to the illustration of diverse or exceptional usage. But wherever possible, all the passages are quoted where the word is to be found, and this is indicated by an *asterisk*. The Vocabulary thus partially (but only partially) serves the purpose of a Greek Testament Concordance.

The Vocabulary is founded upon the *Received Text*, but indication is given of various readings, orthography, etc., adopted by Westcott and Hort. For words which occur only in the margin of their edition, as well as for some adopted in the text of Tischendorf, the student is referred to the Concordance to the Greek Testament by Moulton and Geden.

VOCABULARY.

A, α, ἄλφα, *alpha; a*, the first letter. Numerally, α΄ = 1 ; α, = 1000. For *a* in composition, see § 147, *b, c*. Fig., τὸ A, or τὸ Ἄλφα (W. H.), *the first principle of all things;* of the Father, Rev. i. 8, xxi. 6; the Son, xxii. 13.*

Ἀαρών, ὁ (Heb.), *Aaron*.

Ἀβαδδών, ὁ (Heb., "destruction"), *Abaddon*, Rev. ix. 11.*

ἀ-βαρής, ές (cf. βάρος), *without weight;* hence, *not burdensome*, 2 Cor. xi. 9.*

Ἀββᾶ, or Ἀββά (W. H.), (Heb. in Aram. form) *Father!* only as an invocation, Mark xiv. 36; Rom. viii. 15; Gal. iv. 6.*

Ἄβελ, ὁ (Heb.), *Abel*.

Ἀβιά, ὁ (Heb.), *Abijah*, the king, Matt. i. 7; the priest, Luke i. 5.*

Ἀβιάθαρ, ὁ (Heb.), *Abiathar*, Mark ii. 26.*

Ἀβιληνή, ῆς, ἡ, *Abilene*, a district in the E. of Anti-Libanus, named from Abila, its chief city, Luke iii. 1.*

Ἀβιούδ, ὁ (Heb.), *Abiud*, Matt. i. 13.*

Ἀβραάμ, ὁ (Heb.), *Abraham*.

ἄ-βυσσος, ου, ἡ (originally adj. *bottomless*), *abyss*, Luke viii. 31; Rom. x. 7; Rev. ix. 1, 2, 11, xi. 7, xvii. 8, xx. 1, 3.*

Ἄγαβος, ου, ὁ, *Agabus*, Acts xi. 28, xxi. 10.*

ἀγαθο-εργέω, ῶ (or ἀγαθουργέω), *to do good*, 1 Tim. vi. 18; Acts xiv. 7 (W. H.).*

ἀγαθο-ποιέω, ῶ, (1) *to do good to*, acc. of pers., Luke vi. 33; (2) *to act well.*

ἀγαθο-ποιΐα, ας, ἡ, *well-doing*, in sense (2) of preceding, 1 Pet. iv. 19.*

ἀγαθο-ποιός, οῦ, ὁ (orig. adj.), *well-doer*, 1 Pet. ii. 14.*

ἀγαθός, ή, όν (κρείσσων, κράτιστος), *good*, intrinsically or beneficially; used of both persons and things. τὸ ἀγαθόν, *the Good*, Matt. xix. 17 (W. H.); τὰ ἀγαθά, *goods, wealth, blessings.*

ἀγαθωσύνη, ης, ἡ, *goodness*.

ἀγαλλίασις, εως, ἡ, *exultation, gladness*.

ἀγαλλιάω, ῶ, άσω, *to leap for joy;* hence, *exult, rejoice;* generally deponent. Followed by ἵνα (subj.), John viii. 56; ἐπί (dat.), Luke i. 47; or ἐν (dat.), John v. 35.

ἄ-γαμος, adj. ὁ, ἡ, *unmarried*, 1 Cor. vii.*

ἀγανακτέω, ῶ, ήσω, *to be indignant, angry, vexed*. With περί (gen.), Matt. xx. 24; or ὅτι, Luke xiii. 14.

ἀγανάκτησις, εως, ἡ, *indignation*, 2 Cor. vii. 11.*

ἀγαπάω, ῶ, ήσω, *to love.* Syn. 19.

ἀγάπη, ης, ἡ, *love.* Syn. 19. Object with εἰς, ἐν, or genitive (§ 269). ἀγάπαι (Jude 12; 2 Pet. ii. 13, R.V.), *love-feasts.*

ἀγαπητός, ή, όν, *beloved.*

Ἄγαρ, ἡ (Heb.), *Hagar*, Gal. iv. 24, 25.*

ἀγγαρεύω, σω (from the Persian), *to impress* into the public service; hence, *to compel*, Matt. v. 41, xxvii. 32; Mark xv. 21.*

ἀγγεῖον, είου, τό, *vessel, utensil*, Matt. xxv. 4.*

ἀγγελία, ας, ἡ, *message*, 1 John i. 5 (W. H.), iii. 11.*

ἄγγελος, ου, ὁ, *messenger;* spec. of God's messengers to men, *angel*. So of fallen spirits. "Angel of a church" (Rev. i. 20, ii., iii.), either *messenger*, or *elder*, or a symbolic representation of the spirit, the *genius* of each church.

ἄγγος, ους, τό, *vessel*, Matt. xiii. 48 (W. H.).*

ἄγε, adv. (see ἄγω), come now, go to, James iv. 13, v. I.*

ἀγέλη, ης, ἡ, a flock or herd.

ἀ-γενεα-λόγητος, ου, adj., of unrecorded genealogy, Heb. vii. 3.*

ἀ-γενής, ές (cf. γένος), low-born, base, I Cor. i. 28.*

ἀγιάζω, σω (see ἅγιος), to set apart from common use. Hence, to hallow, or regard with religious reverence; to consecrate to religious service, whether persons or things; to cleanse for such consecration; so to purify, sanctify. οἱ ἁγιαζόμενοι, those who are being sanctified; οἱ ἡγιασμένοι, those who are sanctified.

ἁγιασμός, οῦ, ὁ, sanctification, holiness.

ἅγιος, α, ον, set apart from common use, spec. to the service of God; hence, hallowed, worthy of veneration, holy, consecrated, whether persons, places, or things. οἱ ἅγιοι, "the Saints;" τὸ ἅγιον, the Temple; τὰ ἅγια, the Sanctuary; ἅγια ἁγίων, the Holy of Holies; πνεῦμα ἅγιον, the Holy Spirit.

ἁγιότης, τητος, ἡ, holiness, Heb. xii. 10; 2 Cor. i. 12 (W. H.).*

ἁγιωσύνη, ης, ἡ, holiness, Rom. i. 4; 2 Cor. vii. I; I Thess. iii. 13.*

ἀγκάλη, ης, ἡ, the (curve of the) arm, only plur., Luke ii. 28.*

ἄγκιστρον, ου, τό, fishhook, Matt. xvii. 27.*

ἄγκυρα, ας, ἡ, an anchor.

ἄ-γναφος, ον, adj. (not fulled or dressed), new, of cloth, Matt. ix. 16; Mark ii. 21.*

ἁγνεία, ας, ἡ, purity, i.e., chastity, I Tim. iv. 12, v. 2.*

ἁγνίζω, σω, to cleanse, purify; lit. as John xi. 55; fig. as James iv. 8.

ἁγνισμός, οῦ, ὁ, ceremonial purification, Acts xxi. 26.*

ἀ-γνοέω, ῶ, ήσω (cf. γιγνώσκω), (1) not to know, to be ignorant (ἀγνοῶν, ignorant; ἀγνοούμενος, unknown personally, Gal. i. 22; ignored, disesteemed, 2 Cor. vi. 9); (2) not to understand, Mark ix. 32; perhaps Acts xiii. 27; I Cor. xiv. 38.

ἀγνόημα, ατος, τό, a sin of ignorance, error, Heb. ix. 7.*

ἄγνοια, ας, ἡ, ignorance, Acts iii. 17, xvii. 30; Eph. iv. 18; I Pet. i. 14.*

ἁγνός, ή, όν, pure, chaste; adv. -ῶς, Phil. i. 17.

ἁγνότης, τητος, ἡ, purity, 2 Cor. vi. 6, xi. 3 (W. H.).*

ἀγνωσία, ας, ἡ, ignorance, spec. wilful ignorance, I Cor. xv. 34; I Pet. ii. 15.*

ἄγνωστος, ον, unknown, Acts xvii. 23.*

ἀγορά, ᾶς, ἡ (ἀγείρω), a place of public resort; hence market place or open street; spec. market, Mark vii. 4; the forum, or place of public assemblies, trials, etc., Acts xvi. 19.*

ἀγοράζω, σω, to purchase, buy, with gen. of price, Mark vi. 37, or ἐκ, Matt. xxvii. 7, once ἐν, Rev. v. 9; fig. to redeem, ransom.

ἀγοραῖος, ον, adj., belonging to the forum; hence (ἡμέραι) court days, Acts xix. 38; (ἄνθρωποι) idlers, of the rabble (R. V.), -xvii. 5.*

ἄγρα, ας, ἡ (hunting), fishing, draught, Luke v. 4, 9.*

ἀ-γράμματος, ον, adj., unlearned, i.e. in Rabbinical lore, Acts iv. 13.*

ἀγρ-αυλέω, ῶ, to remain in the fields, Luke ii. 8.*

ἀγρεύω, σω (to take in hunting), fig. to ensnare, Mark xii. 13.*

ἀγρι-έλαιος, ου, ὁ, wild olive, oleaster, Rom. xi. 17, 24.*

ἄγριος, ία, ιον, wild, of honey, Matt. iii. 4; Mark i. 6; of waves, Jude 13.*

Ἀγρίππας, α, ὁ, Agrippa, i.e., Herod Agrippa II. See Ἡρῴδης.

ἀγρός, οῦ, ὁ, field, spec. the country; plur., country districts, hamlets.

ἀγρυπνέω, ῶ (ὕπνος), "to be sleepless;" hence, met., to watch, to be vigilant, Mark xiii. 33; Luke xxi. 36; Eph. vi. 18; Heb. xiii. 17.*

ἀγρυπνία, ας, ἡ, watching, i.e., assiduous care, 2 Cor. vi. 5, xi. 27.*

ἄγω, ξω, 2 a., ἤγαγον, trans., to lead, bring; with πρός (acc.), ἕως, εἰς, of destination; with ἐπί (acc.), of purpose, as Acts viii. 32; to bring before, for trial, Acts xxv. 17. Also to spend, as of time; to keep, as a particular day, Matt. xiv. 6 (not W. H.); Luke xxiv. 21 (impers.). Fig., to lead the inclination, induce. Mid., to go, depart; intrans. imper., ἄγε, come! subj., ἄγωμεν, let us go! the former being used as an adverb.

ἀγωγή, ῆς, ἡ (ἄγω), manner of life, 2 Tim. iii. 10.*

ἀγών, ῶνος, ὁ, contest, conflict; fig., of the Christian life, as Heb. xii. I.

ἀγωνία, as, ἡ, contest; emphatically, agony, Luke xxii. 44.*
ἀγωνίζομαι, to strive, as in the public games; to contend with an adversary; fig., of Christian effort and endurance.
'Ἀδάμ, ὁ (Heb.), Adam.
ἀ-δάπανος, ον, free of charge, gratuitous, 1 Cor. ix. 18.*
'Ἀδδί, ὁ, Addi, Luke iii. 28 (not mentioned in O.T.).*
ἀδελφή, ῆς, ἡ, a sister, (1) lit., (2) fig. of Christian friendship.
ἀδελφός, οῦ, ὁ, a brother, (1) lit. (see § 256), (2) of more general relations, a fellow-Israelite, Matt. v. 47; a fellow-Christian, Matt. xxiii. 8; a fellow-man, Matt. v. 22-24; also expressing the relation between Christ and believers, Matt. xxv. 40. The "brethren of Christ" (Matt. xiii. 55; John vii. 3; Acts i. 14; Gal. i. 19) are thought by some to have been His cousins or other near relatives.
ἀδελφότης, τητος, ἡ, the brotherhood, i.e., the Christian community, 1 Pet. ii. 17, v. 9.*
ἄ-δηλος, ον, not manifest, uncertain, Luke xi. 44; 1 Cor. xiv. 8*; adv., -ως, uncertainly, 1 Cor. ix. 26.*
ἀ-δηλότης, τητος, uncertainty, 1 Tim. vi. 17.*
ἀδημονέω, ῶ, to be sorely troubled.
ᾅδης, ου, ὁ (ἀ priv. and ῐδ- in ἰδεῖν), the invisible world, Hades; fig. of deep degradation, Matt. xi. 23. Syn. 54, and πύλη.
ἀ-διά-κριτος, ον, either act., not distinguishing, impartial (A.V.), or pass., not distinguishable, unambiguous, without variance (R.V.), James iii. 17.*
ἀ-διά-λειπτος, ον, without intermission, unceasing; adv., -ως, unceasingly.
ἀ-δια-φθορία, as, ἡ, uncorruptness, purity, Tit. ii. 7 (not W. H.).*
ἀδικέω, ῶ, ἤσω (ἄδικος), intrans., to act unjustly, commit a crime; trans., to wrong, injure; hence to hurt, without any notion of wrong, Luke x. 19, and Rev. often; pass., to be wronged.
ἀδίκημα, ατος, τό, a wrong.
ἀδικία, as, ἡ, wrong (towards man or God), injustice, iniquity, unrighteousness, wickedness. In Luke xvi. 9, "the mammon of unrighteousness" (ἀδικίας) denotes riches, which in their nature are deceitful, transitory. Syn. 22.
ἄ-δικος, ον, unjust, wicked generally, opposed to δίκαιος, as Matt. v. 45, or to εὐσεβής, as 2 Pet. ii. 9; adv., -ως, unjustly, undeservedly, 1 Pet. ii. 19.
ἀ-δόκιμος, ον (tested, but not approved), reprobate, rejected, Rom. i. 28; 1 Cor. ix. 27; 2 Cor. xiii. 5, 6, 7; 2 Tim. iii. 8; Tit. i. 16; Heb. vi. 8.*
ἄ-δολος, ον, without fraud, genuine, 1 Pet. ii. 2.*
'Ἀδραμυττηνός, ἡ, όν, of Adramyttium, an Æolian seaport, Acts xxvii. 2.*
'Ἀδρίας, α, ὁ, the Adriatic, embracing the Ionian sea, Acts xxvii. 27.*
ἁδρότης, τητος, ἡ, largeness, abundance, 2 Cor. viii. 20.*
ἀ-δυνατέω, ῶ, to be impossible, with dat. of pers., Matt. xvii. 20; or παρά (gen.), Luke i. 37 (W. H.).*
ἀ-δύνατος, ον, adj., (1) of persons, act., powerless; (2) of things, pass., impossible, Rom. viii. 3.
ᾄδω, ᾄσω (contr. from ἀείδω), to sing, with cognate acc., ᾠδήν, a song, Rev. v. 9, xiv. 3, xv. 3; with dat., to sing (praise) to, Eph. v. 19; Col. iii. 16.*
ἀεί, adv., always; of continuous time, unceasingly; of successive intervals, from time to time, on every occasion.
ἀετός, οῦ, ὁ, an eagle, gen. bird of prey, as Matt. xxiv. 28 (R.V. marg., vultures).
ἄ-ζυμος, ον, unleavened, only in plur., sc. λάγανα, cakes, or ἄρτοι, loaves; met., the paschal feast; fig., incorrupt, sincere, 1 Cor. v. 7, 8.
'Ἀζώρ, ὁ (Heb.), Azor, Matt. i. 13, 14; not mentioned in O.T.*
"Ἀζωτος, ον, ἡ, Azotus or Ashdod, Acts viii. 40.*
ἀήρ, ἀέρος, ἡ, the air, atmosphere; in Eph. ii. 2, the power of the air (ἐξουσία τοῦ ἀέρος) refers to supramundane powers, not earthly and not heavenly.
ἀ-θανασία, as, ἡ (see θάνατος), immortality, 1 Cor. xv. 53, 54; 1 Tim. vi. 16.*
ἀ-θέμιτος, ον (θέμις, law), unlawful, criminal, Acts x. 28; 1 Pet. iv. 3.*
ἄ-θεος, ον, without God, Eph. ii. 12.*
ἄ-θεσμος, ον, adj. (θεσμός, statute), lawless, 2 Pet. ii. 7, iii. 17.*
ἀ-θετέω, ῶ, ήσω (θε- as in τίθημι), to set at nought, i.e., persons, to despise, slight; or things, to nullify, contemn.

ἀ-θέτησις, εως, ἡ, nullification, abrogation, Heb. vii. 18, ix. 26.*
Ἀθῆναι, ὧν, αἱ, Athens.
Ἀθηναῖος, α, ον, Athenian, Acts xvii. 21.
ἀθλέω, ῶ (ἆθλον, prize), to contend in the public games, 2 Tim. ii. 5.*
ἄθλησις, εως, ἡ, contest, as in the public games; only fig. Heb. x. 32.*
ἀθροίζω,, gather together, Luke xxiv. 33 (W. H.).*
ἀ-θυμέω, ῶ, to lose heart, despond, Col. iii. 21.*
ἄθῷος, ον, undeserving of punishment, innocent, Matt. xxvii. 4 (see W. H.); with ἀπό, of the crime, ver. 24.*
αἴγειος, η, ον (αἴξ, goat), of or belonging to a goat, Heb. xi. 37.*
αἰγιαλός, οῦ, ὁ, the shore, beach; in Gospels, of Gennesaret; in Acts, of the Mediterranean.*
Αἰγύπτιος, α, ον, Egyptian.
Αἴγυπτος, ου, ἡ, Egypt.
ἀΐδιος, ον, adj. (ἀεί), eternal, everlasting, Rom. i. 20; Jude 6.*
αἰδώς, οῦς, ἡ, modesty, 1 Tim. ii. 9; reverence, Heb. xii. 28 (not W. H.).*
Αἰθίοψ, οπος, ὁ, an Ethiopian, Acts viii. 27.*
αἷμα, ατος, τό, blood, (1) lit., especially of blood shed, i.e. of animals, victims in sacrifice; so of man, of CHRIST, connected with which latter meaning the word is often used (2) met., of the death of Christ; (3) bloodshed, murder; hence blood-guiltiness, the crime or responsibility of another's destruction; (4) natural life, which was believed to reside in the blood, especially with σάρξ, 1 Cor. xv. 20; so human nature generally; hence (5) natural relationship; (6) in Acts ii. 20, etc., the reference is to the colour of blood.
αἱματ-εκ-χυσία, ας, ἡ, shedding of blood, Heb. ix. 22.*
αἱμορροέω, ῶ, to have a flux or issue of blood, Matt. ix. 20.*
Αἰνέας, α, ὁ, Ænĕas, Acts ix. 33, 34.*
αἴνεσις, εως, ἡ, praise, Heb. xiii. 15.*
αἰνέω, ῶ, έσω and ἤσω, to praise, only of God. Syn. 47.
αἴνιγμα, ατος, τό, an obscure intimation, enigma, riddle, 1 Cor. xiii. 12.*
αἶνος, ου, ὁ, praise, only of God.
Αἰνών, ἡ (Heb.), Ænon, John iii. 23.*
αἵρεσις, εως, ἡ (αἱρέομαι), choice, its act or result; hence a religious sect or party, party spirit, "heresy."
αἱρετίζω, σω, to choose, Matt. xii. 18.*
αἱρετικός, οῦ, ὁ, one who acts from party spirit, a factious person, "heretic," Tit. iii. 10.*
αἱρέω (irreg., § 103, 1), to take, only in mid. in N.T., to choose, prefer.
αἴρω (§ 92), (1) to take up, lift, carry, used of carrying the cross, lit., Matt. xxvii. 32; fig., Matt. xvi. 24; so of raising the eyes, the voice, the mind; hence (with ψυχήν) to keep in suspense, John x. 24; (2) to take away, to abrogate a law, to remove by death; imp., αἶρε, ἆρον, Away with! i.e., to execution; (3) to take away sin, of the redeeming work of Christ, John i. 29; 1 John iii. 5.
αἰσθάνομαι, 2 a. ᾐσθόμην, dep., to perceive, comprehend, Luke ix. 45.*
αἴσθησις, εως, ἡ, perception, accurate judgment, Phil. i. 9.*
αἰσθητήριον, ου, n., organ of perception, faculty of judgment, Heb. v. 14.*
αἰσχρο-κερδής, ές, eager for disgraceful gain, sordid; adv., -ως, sordidly.
αἰσχρο-λογία, ας, ἡ, foul language, scurrility, Col. iii. 8.*
αἰσχρός, ά, όν (orig. deformed, opposed to καλός), base, disgraceful.
αἰσχρότης, τητος, ἡ, obscenity, Eph. v. 4.*
αἰσχύνη, ης, ἡ, shame, in personal feeling or in the estimation of others.
αἰσχύνομαι, οῦμαι, mid., to feel ashamed; pass., to be put to shame, confounded.
αἰτέω, ῶ, ήσω, to ask, pray, require, demand; with two accs., or acc. of thing, and ἀπό or παρά (gen.) of person; mid., to ask for one's self, beg. Syn. 9, 38.
αἴτημα, ατος, τό, petition, request.
αἰτία, ας, ἡ, cause, (1) as the reason or ground of anything; (2) in Matt. xix. 10, the state of the case; (3) forensically, an accusation, a fault.
αἰτίαμα, ατος, τό, accusation, charge, Acts xxv. 7. (W. H. read αἰτίωμα.)*
αἴτιος, ία, ιον, causative of, used as subst., in masc., the cause, author, only Heb. v. 9; in neut., a cause, reason, espec. of punishment; a fault, like αἰτία.
αἰτίωμα. See αἰτίαμα.*
αἰφνίδιος, ον, unexpected, sudden.

αἰχμ-αλωσία, as, ἡ, captivity, Rev. xiii. 10; met., a captivity, i.e., a multitude of captives, Eph. iv. 8.*
αἰχμ-αλωτεύω, σω, to make prisoners of, to take captive, captivate, 2 Tim. iii. 6. (W. H. read the following.)*
αἰχμ-αλωτίζω, σω, to lead captive.
αἰχμ-άλωτος, ου, ὁ, ἡ, a captive, Luke iv. 18 (from Isa. lxi. 1).*
αἰών, -ῶνος, ὁ (ἀεί), continuous duration, (1) time limited, an age, gen. in plural, the ages; before the Messiah (1 Cor. x. 11), or after (Eph. ii. 7); (2) the world, considered under the aspect of time, as Luke i. 70, espec. ὁ αἰὼν οὗτος, this world, in contrast with the world to come (ὁ μέλλων, ὁ ἐρχόμενος); in plur., Heb. i. 2, xi. 3; (3) time unlimited, the age of eternity, past, as Acts xv. 18; future, 2 Pet. iii. 18, especially in the following phrases: εἰς τὸν αἰῶνα, for ever, with negative adv. never; εἰς τοὺς αἰῶνας, a stronger expression, for evermore; εἰς τοὺς αἰῶνας τῶν αἰώνων, stronger still (see § 327, ii.), for ever and ever. Phrase slightly varied, Eph. iii. 21; Heb. i. 8; 2 Pet. iii. 18; Jude 25; Rev. xiv. 11.
αἰώνιος (-ία, only in 2 Thess. ii. 16; Heb. ix. 12; or -ιος), -ιον, perpetual, lasting, (1) of limited duration, with χρόνοι, the times of old, as Rom. xvi. 25; (2) of unlimited duration, eternal, everlasting; mostly with ζωή, eternal life, denoting not so much a future duration as a present quality of life, life which in its character is essentially eternal, see John v. 24, vi. 47, xvii. 3. Neut., used as adv. for ever, Philem. 15.
ἀ-καθαρσία, as, ἡ (καθαίρω), uncleanness, impurity, generally fig.
ἀ-καθάρτης, τητος, ἡ, impurity, Rev. xvii. 4. (W. H. read the following.)*
ἀ-κάθαρτος, ον, adj., unclean, impure, (1) of ceremonial, legal or religious defilement; (2) of evil spirits, with πνεῦμα, Gospels, Acts, Rev.; (3) of human beings, impure, lewd, Eph. v. 5.
ἀ-καιρέομαι, οῦμαι, dep., to lack opportunity, Phil. iv. 10.*
ἀ-καίρως, adv., unseasonably, 2 Tim. iv. 2. See εὐκαίρως.*
ἄ-κακος, ον, adj., guileless, Rom. xvi. 18; Heb. vii. 26.*
ἄκανθα, ης, ἡ, thorn, briar.

ἀκάνθινος, ον, made of thorns, Mark xv. 17; John xix. 5.*
ἄ-καρπος, ον, unfruitful, barren, generally fig.
ἀ-κατά-γνωστος, ον, not to be condemned, Tit. ii. 8.*
ἀ-κατα-κάλυπτος, ον, unveiled, 1 Cor. xi. 5, 13.*
ἀ-κατά-κριτος, ον, uncondemned, Acts xvi. 37, xxii. 25.*
ἀ-κατά-λυτος, ον, indissoluble, Heb. vii. 16.*
ἀ-κατά-παστος, ον, unfed, hungry for (gen.), 2 Pet. ii. 14. (W. H. for the following.)*
ἀ-κατά-παυστος, ον, not to be restrained, with gen., 2 Pet. ii. 14 (see preceding).*
ἀ-κατα-στασία, as, ἡ, instability; hence sedition, tumult, disorder.
ἀ-κατά-στατος, ον, inconstant, unstable, James i. 8, iii. 8 (W. H.).*
ἀ-κατά-σχετος, ον, unruly, untameable, Jas. iii. 8. (W. H. read preceding.)*
Ἀκελ-δαμά (Heb. in Aram. form, field of blood), Aceldama, Acts i. 19. (W. H. read Ἀκελδαμάχ.)*
ἀ-κέραιος, ον (κεράννυμι), unmixed; hence, fig., simple, innocent, guileless, Matt. x. 16; Rom. xvi. 19; Phil. ii. 15.*
ἀ-κλινής, ές, unbending; hence unwavering, steadfast, Heb. x. 23.*
ἀκμάζω, σω, to reach the point of perfection; so, of fruit, to be fully ripe, Rev. xiv. 18.*
ἀκμήν, acc. as adv., up to this point, hitherto, Matt. xv. 16.*
ἀκοή, ῆς, ἡ (ἀκούω), hearing, (1) the sense or faculty, the ear; (2) the act of hearing; (3) the thing heard, a report, speech, doctrine. ἀκοῇ ἀκούειν, "to hear with hearing," i.e., attentively (a Hebraism), Matt. xiii. 14.
ἀκολουθέω, ῶ, ἥσω, (1) to accompany, follow, or attend, with dat., or μετά (gen.), or ὀπίσω (gen.), espec. of the disciples of Christ; so, met., to obey and imitate; (2) to succeed, in order of time, or retribution.
ἀκούω, σω or σομαι, pf., ἀκήκοα, to hear, (1) without object, Mark iv. 3, vii. 37; (2) with object (acc. or gen., § 249, a, 1), to hear, listen to, heed, understand. οἱ ἀκούοντες, hearers or disciples. In pass., to be noised abroad.

ἀ-κρασία, as, ἡ, intemperance, incontinence, Matt. xxiii. 25 ; 1 Cor. vii. 5.*
ἀ-κρατής, ές (κράτος), powerless (over one's self), 2 Tim. iii. 3.*
ἄ-κρατος, ον (κεράννυμι), unmixed, undiluted (of strong wine), Rev. xiv. 10.*
ἀκρίβεια, as, ἡ, precision, strictness, Acts xxii. 3.*
ἀκριβής, ές, accurate, strict, Acts xxvi. 5 ;* -ῶς, adv., diligently, accurately, perfectly.
ἀκριβόω, ῶ, ώσω, to inquire closely, learn carefully (R.V.), Matt. ii. 7, 16.*
ἀκρίς, ίδος, ἡ, a locust.
ἀκροατήριον, ίου, n. (ἀκροάομαι, to hear), the place of (judicial) hearing, Acts xxv. 23.*
ἀκροατής, οῦ, ὁ, a hearer, Rom. ii. 13 ; James i. 22, 23, 25.*
ἀκροβυστία, as, ἡ, the foreskin, uncircumcision; collective for pagans or uncircumcised Gentiles.
ἀκρο-γωνιαῖος, a, ον (with λίθος understood), a corner foundation stone, ref. to Christ, Eph. ii. 20 ; 1 Pet. ii. 6.*
ἀκρο-θίνιον, ίου, τό, firstfruits, i.e., the best of the produce, applied (plur.) to spoils taken in battle, Heb. vii. 4.*
ἄκρος, a, ον, outermost, pointed; neut., τὸ ἄκρον, the end, extremity.
Ἀκύλας, ου, ὁ (Latin), Aquila.
ἀ-κυρόω, ῶ, to deprive of power, set aside (a law), Matt. xv. 6 ; Mark vii. 13 ; Gal. iii. 17.
ἀ-κωλύτως, adv., freely, without hindrance, Acts xxviii. 31.*
ἄκων, ουσα, ον (ἀ, ἑκών), unwilling, 1 Cor. ix. 17.*
ἀλάβαστρον, ου, τό, alabaster, a vessel for perfume, Matt. xxvi. 7 ; Mark xiv. 3 ; Luke vii. 37.*
ἀλαζονία, as, ἡ, boasting, show, ostentation, James iv. 16 ; 1 John ii. 16.*
ἀλαζών, όνος, ὁ, a boaster, Rom. i. 30 ; 2 Tim. iii. 2.*
ἀλαλάζω, άσω, to raise a cry or loud sound; in mourning, Matt. v. 38 ; of cymbals, 1 Cor. xiii. 1.*
ἀ-λάλητος, ον, not to be uttered in words, Rom. viii. 36.*
ἄ-λαλος, ον, dumb, making dumb, Mark vii. 37, ix. 17, 25.*
ἅλας, ατος, τό, salt, lit. and fig., as Matt. v. 13.
ἀλείφω, ψω, to anoint, festally, or in homage ; also medicinally, or in embalming the dead.
ἀλεκτορο-φωνία, as, ἡ, the cock-crowing, between midnight and dawn, Mark xiii. 35.*
ἀλέκτωρ, opos, ὁ, a cock. The name signifies sleepless.
Ἀλεξανδρεύς, έως, ὁ, an Alexandrian.
Ἀλεξανδρινός, ἡ, όν, Alexandrian.
Ἀλέξανδρος, ου, ὁ, Alexander. Four of this name are mentioned, Mark xv. 21 ; Acts iv. 6 ; Acts xix. 33 ; 1 Tim. i. 20.*
ἄλευρον, ου, τό, fine meal or flour, Matt. xiii. 33 ; Luke xiii. 21.*
ἀλήθεια, as, ἡ, truth; generally, as Mark v. 33 ; espec., (1) freedom from error, exactness, as (2) THE TRUTH, or Word of God ; Jesus is called the Truth, John xiv. 6 ; (3) truthfulness, veracity, sincerity, integrity, opposed to ἀδικία, Rom. ii. 8 ; 1 Cor. xiii. 6.
ἀληθεύω, to speak the truth, to deal truly, Gal. iv. 16 ; Eph. iv. 15.*
ἀληθής, ές (ἀ, λαθ- in λανθάνω), unconcealed, true, valid, sure, sincere, upright, just. Syn. 24 for comparison with following. -ῶς, adv., truly ; in truth, really ; in very deed, certainly.
ἀληθινός, ἡ, όν, real, genuine, contrasted with the fictitious, as Luke xvi. 11 ; John i. 9 ; with the typical, as John vi. 32 ; Heb. viii. 2, ix. 24. Syn. 24.
ἀλήθω, ἡσω, to grind with a handmill.
ἁλιεύς, έως, ὁ, a fisherman.
ἁλιεύω, εύσω, to fish, John xxi. 3.*
ἁλίζω, ίσω, to salt.
ἀλίσγημα, ατος, τό, pollution, Acts xv. 20.*
ἀλλά (prop. n. plur. of ἄλλος), but, an adversative particle. See § 404.
ἀλλάσσω, άξω, to alter, exchange.
ἀλλαχόθεν, adv., from elsewhere, John x. 1.*
ἀλλαχοῦ, adv., elsewhere, Mark i. 38 (W. H.).*
ἀλλ-ηγορέω, ῶ, to speak allegorically ; pass. part., Gal. iv. 24.*
Ἀλληλούϊα (Hebrew), HALLELUJAH, Praise ye Jehovah, Rev. xix. 1, 3, 4, 6.*
ἀλλήλων, reciprocal pron., gen. plur. (§ 61, c), one another, each other.
ἀλλο-γενής, ές, of another nation, a stranger, Luke xvii. 18.*

ἅλλομαι (dep.), ἁλοῦμαι, ἡλάμην, to leap up, leap, Acts iii. 8, xiv. 10 ; to bubble up, as water, John iv. 14.*
ἄλλος, η, ο, other, different, another ; οἱ ἄλλοι, the others, the rest. Syn. 76. -ως, adv., otherwise, 1 Tim. v. 25.*
ἀλλοτριο-επίσκοπος, ου, ὁ, one who looks at or busies himself in the things of another, a busybody, 1 Pet. iv. 15. (W. H., ἀλλοτριεπίσκοπος.)*
ἀλλότριος, ία, ιον, belonging to another, foreign, strange, alien ; not of one's own family, hostile.
ἀλλό-φυλος, ον, adj., foreign, of another tribe or race, Acts x. 28.*
ἀλοάω, ῶ, ήσω, to beat or thresh, as corn, 1 Cor. ix. 9, 10 ; 1 Tim. v. 18.*
ἄ-λογος, ον, (1) without speech or reason, irrational, 2 Pet. ii. 12, Jude 10 ; (2) unreasonable, absurd, Acts xxv. 27.*
ἀλόη, ῆς, ἡ, the aloe, John xix. 39.*
ἅλς, ἁλός, ὁ, salt. Rec. only in Luke ix. 49 (dat.), W. H. only in ix. 50 (acc.). See ἅλας.*
ἁλυκός, ή, όν (ἅλς), salt, brackish, James iii. 12.*
ἄ-λυπος, ον, free from sorrow, Phil. ii. 28.*
ἅλυσις, εως, ἡ, a chain or manacle.
ἀ-λυσιτελής, ές, without gain, unprofitable, Heb. xiii. 17.*
Ἀλφαῖος, ου, ὁ, Alphæus. Two of the name are mentioned, Mark ii. 14 ; Mark xv. 4 (the latter being called Κλωπᾶς, John xix. 25 ; another form of the orig. Hebrew name).*
ἅλων, ωνος, ὁ, ἡ, a threshing-floor ; met., the corn of the threshing-floor.
ἀλώπηξ, εκος, ἡ, a fox ; applied to Herod, Luke xiii. 32.
ἅλωσις, εως, ἡ, a taking or catching, 2 Pet. ii. 12.*
ἅμα, adv., at the same time, with or together with (dat.) ; ἅμα πρωΐ, with the dawn, Matt. xx. 1.
ἀ-μαθής, ές, unlearned, rude, 2 Pet. iii. 16.*
ἀ-μαράντινος, ου. adj. (μαραίνομαι), unfading, 1 Pet. v. 4.*
ἀ-μάραντος, ον, adj., unfading, 1 Pet. i. 4.*
ἁμαρτάνω, τήσω, to miss a mark, to err, to sin ; with cogn. acc., ἁμαρτίαν, to sin a sin, 1 John v. 16 ; with εἰς, to sin against. Syn. 39.

ἁμάρτημα, ατος, τό, a sin, error, offence.
ἁμαρτία, ας, ἡ, (1) sin, as a quality of actions or a principle of human nature ; (2) a sin, sing., as Acts vii. 60 ; plur. (more freq.), spec. in the phrase ἀφιέναι τὰς ἁμαρτίας, to forgive sins. In Heb. x. 6, 8, 18, περὶ ἁμαρτίας is sin-offering.
ἀ-μάρτυρος, ον, without witness, Acts xiv. 17.*
ἁμαρτωλός, ον, (1) sinful, espec. habitually and notoriously ; (2) often used substantively, a sinner. The Jews used the word for idolaters, i.e., Gentiles.
ἄ-μαχος, ον, not quarrelsome, 1 Tim. iii. 3 ; Tit. iii. 2.*
ἀμάω, ῶ, ήσω, to reap, James v. 4.*
ἀμέθυστος, ου, m., an amethyst (supposed to be an antidote against drunkenness. Hence the name, from ἀ, μεθύω), Rev. xxi. 20.*
ἀμελέω, ῶ, ήσω, not to care for, to disregard, neglect ; gen. or inf.
ἄ-μεμπτος, ον, without blame, faultless ; adv., -ως, unblameably, faultlessly.
ἀ-μέριμνος, ον, free from solicitude or anxiety, secure, easy.
ἀ-μετά-θετος, ον, unchangeable, Heb. vi. 17, 18.*
ἀ-μετα-κίνητος, ου, adj., immoveable, firm, 1 Cor. xv. 58.*
ἀ-μετα-μέλητος, ον, adj., not to be regretted or repented of ; hence unchangeable, Rom. xi. 29 ; 2 Cor. vii. 10.*
ἀ-μετα-νόητος, ον, adj., unrepentant, impenitent, Rom. ii. 5.*
ἄ-μετρος, ον, beyond measure, immoderate, 2 Cor. x. 13, 15.*
ἀμήν, AMEN, a Hebrew adjective, true, faithful, used (1) as an adverb, at the beginning of a sentence, verily, truly, indeed ; (2) at the end of ascriptions of praise, etc., optatively, as γένοιτο, so be it ; (3) substantively, 2 Cor. i. 20, as a name of Christ, the Amen, the faithful witness, Rev. iii. 14.
ἀ-μήτωρ, ορος, ὁ, ἡ (μήτηρ), without mother, i.e., in the genealogies, Heb. vii. 3.*
ἀ-μίαντος, ου (μιαίνω), undefiled, sincere, pure.
Ἀμιναδάβ, ὁ (Heb.), Aminadab, Matt. i. 4 ; Luke iii. 33.*

ἅμμος, ου, ἡ, *sand*, as of the shore.
ἀμνός, οῦ, ὁ, *a lamb;* fig., of Christ, John i. 29, 36; Acts viii. 32; 1 Pet. i. 19.*
ἀμοιβή, ῆς, ἡ (ἀμείβω), *requital*, 1 Tim. v. 4.*
ἄμπελος, ου, ἡ, *a vine*, (1) lit. ; (2) fig., as John xv. 1.
ἀμπελ-ουργός, οῦ, ὁ, ἡ, *a vine-dresser*, Luke xiii. 7.*
ἀμπελών, ῶνος, ὁ, *a vineyard*.
Ἀμπλίας, ίου, ὁ, *Amplias*, Rom. xvi. 8.*
ἀμύνω, ῶ, only in mid., N.T., *to defend, assist*, Acts vii. 24.*
ἀμφιάζω, *clothe*, Luke xii. 28 (W. H.).*
ἀμφιβάλλω, *cast around*, Mark i. 16 (W. H.).*
ἀμφί-βληστρον, ου, τό, *a fishing net*.
ἀμφι-έννυμι, έσω, *to put on*, as a garment; *to clothe, adorn*.
Ἀμφίπολις, εως, ἡ, *Amphipolis*, a city in the S. of Macedonia, Acts xvii. 1.*
ἄμφ-οδον, ου, n., *a place where two ways meet, a street*, Mark xi. 4.*
ἀμφότεροι, αι, α, *both*.
ἀ-μώμητος, ον, *without blame or fault*, Phil. ii. 15 (W. H., ἄμεμπτοι) ; 2 Pet. iii. 14.*
ἄμωμον, ου, τό, *a spice plant*, Rev. xviii. 13.
ἄ-μωμος, ον, *without spot ;* fig., *blameless*.
Ἀμών, ὁ (Heb.), *Amon*, Matt. i. 10.*
Ἀμώς, ὁ (Heb.), *Amos*, Luke iii. 25.*
ἄν, a particle, expressing *possibility, uncertainty*, or *conditionality*. See §§ 378, b, 380, 383, δ.
ἀνά, prep., lit., *upon ;* in composition, *up, again*. See §§ 297 and 147, a.
ἀνα-βαθμός, οῦ, ὁ (βαίνω), *means of ascent, steps, stairs*, Acts xxi. 35, 40.*
ἀνα-βαίνω, βήσομαι, 2 a. ἀνέβην, (1) *to ascend*, espec. to Jerusalem, on board ship (John xxi. 3), to heaven ; (2) *to spring up*, as plants, etc., used of a rumour, Acts xxi. 31 ; of thoughts coming into mind, Luke xxiv. 38.
ἀνα-βάλλω, mid., *to postpone, defer*, Acts xxiv. 22.*
ἀνα-βιβάζω, *to draw up*, as a net to shore, Matt. xiii. 48.*
ἀνα-βλέπω, (1) *to look up*, as Mark viii. 24; (2) *to look again, to recover sight*, as Matt. xi. 5.
ἀνά-βλεψις, εως, ἡ, *recovery of sight*, Luke iv. 18.*
ἀνα-βοάω, ῶ, *to exclaim, cry aloud* (not in W. H.), Matt. xxvii. 46, Mark xv. 8, Luke ix. 38.*
ἀνα-βολή, ῆς, ἡ, *putting off, delay*, Acts xxv. 17.*
ἀνάγαιον, ου, τό, *upper room*, W. H. in Mark xiv. 15 ; Luke xxii. 12, for Rec. ἀνώγεον.*
ἀν-αγγέλλω, *to tell, to declare openly, to show forth, confess, foretell*.
ἀνα-γεννάω, ῶ, *to beget again*, 1 Pet. i. 3, 23.*
ἀνα-γινώσκω, *to know again, to know well*. N.T., *to read*.
ἀναγκάζω, άσω, *to force, to compel* by force or persuasion.
ἀναγκαῖος, αία, αῖον, *necessary, fit, serviceable ;* also *close* or *near*, as friends, Acts x. 24.
ἀναγκαστῶς, adv., *necessarily* or *by constraint*, 1 Pet. v. 2.*
ἀνάγκη, ης, ἡ, (1) *necessity, constraint ;* followed by inf. (with ἔστι understood), *there is need to ;* (2) *distress*.
ἀνα-γνωρίζω, *to make known*, aor. pass., Acts vii. 13.*
ἀνά-γνωσις, εως, ἡ, *reading*, whether private or public.*
ἀν-άγω, *to bring, lead*, or *take up ; to offer up*, as sacrifices ; pass., *to put to sea, to set sail*.
ἀνα-δείκνυμι, *to show*, as by uplifting, *to show plainly*, Acts i. 24 ; *to appoint*, Luke x. 1.*
ἀνά-δειξις, εως, ἡ, *a showing* or *public appearance*, Luke i. 80.*
ἀνα-δέχομαι, dep., *to receive* with a welcome, guests, Acts xxviii. 7 ; promises, Heb. xi. 17.*
ἀνα-δίδωμι, *to give up, deliver*, as by messengers, Acts xxiii. 33.*
ἀνα-ζάω, ῶ, *to live again, revive* (W. H. only in Rom. vii. 9, and doubtfully Luke xv. 24).
ἀνα-ζητέω, ῶ, *to seek* with diligence.
ἀνα-ζώννυμι, *to gird* or *bind up*, as a loose dress is girded about the loins ; mid. fig., 1 Pet. i. 13.*
ἀνα-ζωπυρέω, ῶ (πῦρ), *to re-kindle* or *rouse up ;* fig., 2 Tim. i. 6.*
ἀνα-θάλλω, *to thrive* or *flourish again*, Phil. iv. 10.*
ἀνά-θεμα, ατος, τό, *a person* or *thing accursed, an execration* or *curse*. Later form for ἀνάθημα (which see).
ἀναθεματίζω, ίσω, *to bind by a curse, to declare on pain of being an anathema*.

ἀνα-θεωρέω, ῶ, to look at attentively, to consider, Acts xvi. 23 ; Heb. xiii. 7.*
ἀνά-θημα, ατος, τό, anything consecrated and laid by, a votive offering, Luke xxi. 5.* See ἀνάθεμα and Syn. 51.
ἀν-αιδεία, as, ἡ, shamelessness, importunity, Luke xi. 8.*
ἀναιρέσις, εως, ἡ, a taking away, i.e., by a violent death, Acts viii. 1.*
ἀν-αίρεω, ῶ (see § 103, 1), to take away, to abolish, to take off, to kill ; mid., to take up, Acts vii. 21.
ἀν-αίτιος, ον, guiltless, Matt. xii. 5, 7.*
ἀνα-καθίζω, to sit up (properly trans. with ἑαυτόν understood).
ἀνα-καινίζω, to renew, restore to a former condition, Heb. vi. 6.*
ἀνα-καινόω, ῶ, to renew, amend, to change the life, 2 Cor. iv. 16 ; Col. iii. 10.*
ἀνα-καίνωσις, εως, ἡ, a renewal or change of heart and life, Rom. xii. 2 ; Tit. iii. 5.*
ἀνα-καλύπτω, to unveil, make manifest; pass., 2 Cor. iii. 14, 18.*
ἀνα-κάμπτω, to bend or turn back, return.
ἀνά-κειμαι, dep., to recline at a meal, to sit at meat ; ὁ ἀνακείμενος, one who reclines at table, a guest. (W. H. omit in Mark v. 40.)
ἀνα-κεφαλαιόω, ῶ, to gather together into one, to sum up under one head ; pass., Rom. xiii. 9 ; mid., Eph. i. 10.*
ἀνα-κλίνω, to lay down an infant, Luke ii. 7 ; to place at table ; mid., to recline, as at a feast, like ἀνάκειμαι.
ἀνα-κόπτω, to hinder (lit., beat back), Gal. v. 7. (W. H., ἐγκόπτω.)*
ἀνα-κράζω, to cry out, to shout aloud.
ἀνα-κρίνω, to investigate, inquire, examine (judicially), to judge of. Only in Luke, Acts, and 1 Cor.
ἀνά-κρισις, εως, ἡ, judicial examination, Acts xxv. 26.*
ἀνα-κυλίω, roll up, Mark xvi. 4. (W. H., for ἀποκ.)*
ἀνα-κύπτω, to raise oneself from a stooping posture ; fig., to be elated.
ἀνα-λαμβάνω, to take up ; pass., of Christ's being taken up to heaven.
ἀνά-ληψις (W. H., -λημψις), εως, ἡ, a being taken up, i.e., into heaven, Luke ix. 51.*
ἀν-αλίσκω, λώσω, to consume, destroy, Luke ix. 54 ; Gal. v. 15 ; 2 Thess. ii. 8 (not W. H.).*

ἀνα-λογία, as, ἡ, proportion, analogy, Rom. xii. 6.*
ἀνα-λογίζομαι, to think upon, consider attentively, Heb. xii. 3.*
ἄν-αλος, ον, without saltness, insipid, Mark ix. 50.*
ἀνά-λυσις, εως, ἡ, a loosening of a ship from her moorings, departure, 2 Tim. iv. 6.*
ἀνα-λύω, to depart, Phil. i. 23 ; to return, Luke xii. 36.*
ἀν-αμάρτητος, ον, without blame, faultless, John viii. 7 (W. H. omit).*
ἀνα-μένω, to await, 1 Thess. i. 10.*
ἀνα-μιμνήσκω, to remind, admonish, two accs., or acc. and inf. ; pass., to remember, to call to mind, gen. or acc.
ἀνά-μνησις, εως, ἡ, remembrance, a memorial.
ἀνα-νεόω, ῶ, to renew ; mid., to renew oneself, to be renewed, Eph. iv. 23.*
ἀνα-νήφω, to recover soberness, 2 Tim. ii. 26.*
Ἀνανίας, α, ὁ (from Heb.), Ananias. Three of the name are mentioned, Acts v. 1-5, ix. 10, xxiii. 2.
ἀν-αντίρ-ρητος, ον, indisputable, not to be contradicted, Acts xix. 36.* Adv., -ως, without hesitation, Acts x. 29.*
ἀν-άξιος, ον, unworthy, inadequate, 1 Cor. vi. 2.* Adv., -ως, unworthily, unbecomingly, 1 Cor. xi. 27 (not in ver. 29, W. H.).*
ἀνά-παυσις, εως, ἡ, rest, refreshment.
ἀνα-παύω, to give rest or refreshment; mid., to take rest. (W. H. read in Rev. xiv. 13, ἀναπαήσονται, 2 fut. pass.)
ἀνα-πείθω, σω, to persuade, in a bad sense, seduce, mislead, Acts xviii. 13.*
ἀνα-πέμπω, to remit, send back.
ἀνα-πηδάω, leap up. (W. H., in Mark x. 50, for rec., ἀνίστημι.)*
ἀνά-πηρος, ον, maimed, having lost a member, Luke xiv. 13, 21.* (W. H., ἀνάπειρος.)
ἀνα-πίπτω, to fall down ; N.T., to recline at table.
ἀνα-πληρόω, ῶ, to fill up ; to fulfil, as a prophecy ; to perform, as a precept ; to occupy or fill a place ; to supply a deficiency.
ἀν-απο-λόγητος, ον, adj., inexcusable, Rom. i. 20, ii. 1.*
ἀνα-πτύσσω, to unroll, as a volume, Luke iv. 17 (not W. H.).*

ἀν-άπτω, to kindle, set on fire.
ἀν-αρίθμητος, ον, innumerable, Heb. xi. 12.*
ἀνα-σείω, to stir up, move, instigate, Mark xv. 11; Luke xxiii. 5.*
ἀνα-σκευάζω, to pervert, unsettle, destroy, Acts xv. 24.*
ἀνα-σπάω, to draw up or back, Luke xiv. 5; Acts xi. 10.*
ἀνά-στασις, εως, ἡ, a rising up, as opposed to falling, Luke ii. 34; rising, as from death or the grave, resurrection, the future state.
ἀνα-στατόω, ῶ, to unsettle, put in commotion, as Acts xvii. 6.
ἀνα-σταυρόω, ῶ, to crucify afresh, Heb. vi. 6.*
ἀνα-στενάζω, to groan or sigh deeply, Mark viii. 12.*
ἀνα-στρέφω, to turn up, overturn, John ii. 15; intrans., to return; mid. (as Lat. versari), to be or to live in a place or state, to move among, to pass one's time or be conversant with persons; generally, to conduct oneself.
ἀνα-στροφή, ῆς, ἡ, behaviour, manner of life.
ἀνα-τάσσομαι, to draw up a narrative (R.V.), Luke i. 1.*
ἀνα-τέλλω, to spring up or rise, as the sun, a star, a cloud; of the Messiah, Heb. vii. 14; trans., to cause to rise, Matt. v. 45.
ἀνα-τίθημι, mid., to place before, declare, Acts xxv. 14; Gal. ii. 2.*
ἀνατολή, ῆς, ἡ, the dawn, dayspring, Luke i. 78; generally, the east, where the sun rises; sing. and plur., see § 240, a.
ἀνα-τρέπω, to subvert, overthrow, 2 Tim. ii. 18; Tit. i. 11.*
ἀνα-τρέφω, to nurse, bring up, educate.
ἀνα-φαίνω, mid., to appear, Luke xix. 11; pass., to be shown a thing (acc.), Acts xxi. 3.* (W. H. read act., in sense to come in sight of.)
ἀνα-φέρω, οἴσω, to bear or lead, to offer, as sacrifice; to bear, as sin.
ἀνα-φωνέω, ῶ, to cry out aloud, Luke i. 42.*
ἀνά-χυσις, εως, ἡ, a pouring out; hence excess, 1 Pet. iv. 4.*
ἀνα-χωρέω, ῶ, to depart, withdraw.
ἀνά-ψυξις, εως, ἡ, refreshment, Acts iii. 20.*

ἀνα-ψύχω, to refresh, to revive, 2 Tim. i. 16.*
Ἀνδρέας, ου, ὁ, Andrew.
ἀνδραποδιστής, οῦ, ὁ, a man-stealer, 1 Tim. i. 10.*
ἀνδρίζω, ίσω, mid., to act like a man, to be brave, 1 Cor. xvi. 13.*
Ἀνδρόνικος, ου, ὁ, Andronicus, Rom. xvi. 7.*
ἀνδρό-φονος, ου, ὁ, a man-slayer, murderer, 1 Tim. i. 9.*
ἀν-έγκλητος, ον, not open to accusation, unblameable.
ἀν-εκ-διήγητος, ον, not to be spoken, inexpressible, 2 Cor. ix. 15.*
ἀν-εκ-λάλητος, unutterable, 1 Pet. i. 8.*
ἀν-έκ-λειπτος, ον, inexhaustible, Luke xii. 33.*
ἀνεκτός, ή, όν, tolerable, supportable; only in comp.
ἀν-ελεήμων, ον, without compassion, cruel, Rom. i. 31.*
ἀνεμίζω, to agitate or drive with wind; pass., James i. 6.*
ἄνεμος, ου, ὁ, the wind; fig., applied to empty doctrines, Eph. iv. 14.
ἀν-ένδεκτος, ον (ἐνδέχομαι), adj., impossible, Luke xvii. 1.*
ἀν-εξ-ερεύνητος (W. H., -ραύ-), ον, adj., inscrutable, Rom. xi. 33.*
ἀνεξί-κακος, ον, patient of injury, 2 Tim. ii. 24.*
ἀν-εξ-ιχνίαστος, ον, that cannot be explored, incomprehensible, Rom. xi. 33; Eph. iii. 8.*
ἀν-επ-αίσχυντος, ον, causing no shame, irreproachable, 2 Tim. ii. 15.*
ἀν-επί-ληπτος (W. H., -λημπ-), ον, adj., never caught doing wrong, blameless, 1 Tim. iii. 2, v. 7, vi. 14.*
ἀν-έρχομαι, to come or go up.
ἄνεσις, εως, ἡ (ἀνίημι), relaxation, remission, as from bonds, burden, etc.
ἀν-ετάζω, to examine by torture, Acts xxii. 24, 29.*
ἄνευ, adv. as prep., with gen., without.
ἀν-εύθετος, ον, inconvenient, Acts xxvii. 12.*
ἀν-ευρίσκω, to find by searching for, Luke ii. 16; Acts xxi. 4.*
ἀν-έχω, mid., to bear with, forbear, have patience with, endure; gen. of pers. or thing.
ἀνεψιός, οῦ, ὁ, a nephew, Col. iv. 10.*
ἄνηθον, ου, τό, anise, dill, Matt. xxiii. 23.*

ἀνήκει, impers., *it is fit* or *proper;* part., τὸ ἀνῆκον, τὰ ἀνήκοντα, *the becoming.*
ἀν-ήμερος, ον, adj., *not gentle, fierce,* 2 Tim. iii. 3.*
ἀνήρ, ἀνδρός, ὁ, (1) *a man,* in sex and age (Lat., *vir*); hence (2) *a husband;* (3) *a person* generally; plur. voc., ἄνδρες, *Sirs!* often in apposition with adjectives and nouns, as ἀνὴρ ἁμαρτωλός, ἀνὴρ προφήτης. Syn. 63.
ἀνθ-ίστημι, *to oppose, withstand, resist,* with dat.
ἀνθ-ομολογέομαι, οῦμαι, *to confess, give thanks to,* dat., Luke ii. 38.*
ἄνθος, ους, τό, *a flower.*
ἀνθρακιά, ᾶς, ἡ, *a heap of live coals,* John xviii. 18, xxi. 9.*
ἄνθραξ, ακος, ὁ, *a coal,* Rom. xii. 20.*
ἀνθρωπ-άρεσκος, ον, *desirous of pleasing men,* Eph. vi. 6, Col. iii. 22.*
ἀνθρώπινος, ίνη, ινον, *human, belonging to man.*
ἀνθρωπο-κτόνος, ου, ὁ, ἡ, *a homicide, a murderer,* John viii. 44; 1 John iii. 15.*
ἄνθρωπος, ου, m., *a man, one of the human race.* Like ἀνήρ, joined in apposition with substantives, as Matt. xviii. 23, xxi. 33. Syn. 63.
ἀνθ-υπατεύω, *to be proconsul,* Acts xviii. 12 (not W. H.).*
ἀνθ-ύπατος, ου, ὁ, *a proconsul.*
ἀν-ίημι, *to unloose, let go, cease from; to leave, neglect.*
ἀν-ίλεως, ων, *without mercy,* James ii. 13. (W. H. read ἀνέλεος.)*
ἄ-νιπτος, ον, adj., *unwashed.*
ἀν-ίστημι, *to raise up* one lying or dead; intrans. (in 2 a., pf. and mid.), *to rise* from a recumbent posture, *to rise again* from the dead; aor. part., often combined with other verbs, as "rising (ἀναστάς) he went."
Ἄννα, ης, ἡ, *Anna,* Luke ii. 36.*
Ἄννας, α, ὁ, *Annas,* Luke iii. 2; John xviii. 13, 24; Acts iv. 6.*
ἀνόητος, ον, *foolish, thoughtless.*
ἄνοια, ας, ἡ, *folly, madness,* Luke vi. 11; 2 Tim. iii. 9.*
ἀνοίγω, ξω, *to open;* intrans. in 2 perf., ἀνέῳγα, *to be open.*
ἀν-οικοδομέω, ῶ, *to build up again,* Acts xv. 16.*
ἄνοιξις, εως, ἡ, *opening* (the act of), Eph. vi. 19.*

ἀ-νομία, ας, ἡ, *transgression of law, lawlessness.*
ἄ-νομος, ον, (1) *without law,* not subject to the law, 1 Cor. ix. 21; met. of Gentiles; (2) *lawless;* as subst., *a malefactor.* ὁ ἄνομος, *the lawless one,* 2 Thess. ii. 8. Adv., -ως, *without law,* Rom. ii. 12.
ἀν-ορθόω, ῶ, *to make upright* or *straight again, to rebuild, make strong,* Luke xiii. 13; Acts xv. 16; Heb. xii. 12.*
ἀνόσιος, ον, *unholy,* 1 Tim. i. 9; 2 Tim. iii. 2.*
ἀνοχή, ῆς, ἡ, *forbearance, patience,* Rom. ii. 4, iii. 25.*
ἀντ-αγωνίζομαι, *to resist, strive against,* Heb. xii. 4.*
ἀντ-άλλαγμα, ατος, τό, *an equivalent, price,* Matt. xvi. 26; Mark viii. 37.*
ἀντ-ανα-πληρόω, ῶ, *to make good* by supplying deficiency, Col. i. 24.*
ἀντ-απο-δίδωμι, *to recompense, requite.*
ἀντ-από-δομα, ατος, τό, *a recompence, requital,* Luke xiv. 12; Rom. xi. 9.*
ἀντ-από-δοσις, εως, ἡ, *a reward, recompence,* Col. iii. 24.*
ἀντ-απο-κρίνομαι, *to reply against, contradict,* Luke xiv. 6; Rom. ix. 20.*
ἀντ-εῖπον (used as 2 aor. of ἀντιλέγω, see φημί), *to contradict, to gainsay,* Luke xxi. 15; Acts iv. 14.*
ἀντ-έχω, mid., *to hold fast, to adhere to* (gen.), Matt. vi. 24; Luke xvi. 13; 1 Thess. v. 14; Tit. i. 9.*
ἀντί, prep., gen., *instead of, for.* See §§ 291, 147, a.
ἀντι-βάλλω, *to throw in turn, exchange* words, Luke xxiv. 17.*
ἀντι-δια-τίθημι, mid., *to set oneself against, oppose,* 2 Tim. ii. 25.*
ἀντί-δικος, ου, ὁ, ἡ (orig. adj.), *an opponent at law, an adversary.*
ἀντί-θεσις, εως, ἡ, *opposition,* 1 Tim. vi. 20.*
ἀντι-καθ-ίστημι, *to resist,* Heb. xii. 4.*
ἀντι-καλέω, *to call* or *invite in turn,* Luke xiv. 12.*
ἀντί-κειμαι, *to oppose, resist* (dat.); ὁ ἀντικείμενος, *the adversary.*
ἀντικρύ (W. H., ἄντικρυς), adv., *over against,* Acts xx. 15.*
ἀντι-λαμβάνω, mid., *to take hold of, help, share in* (gen.).
ἀντι-λέγω, *to speak against, contradict* (dat.); *to oppose, deny* (with μή).

άντί-ληψις (W. H., -λημψ-), εως, help; hence, concrete, a helper, 1 Cor. xii. 28.*
άντι-λογία, as, ή, contradiction, contention, reproach.
άντι-λοιδορέω, to revile or reproach again, 1 Pet. ii. 23.*
άντί-λυτρον, ου, τό, a ransom-price, 1 Tim. ii. 16.*
άντι-μετρέω, ω, to measure in return, Matt. vii. 2 (not W. H.); Luke vi. 38.*
άντι-μισθία, as, ή, recompence, Rom. i. 27; 2 Cor. vi. 13.
'Αντιόχεια, as, ή, Antioch. Two places of the name are mentioned, Acts xi. 26, xiii. 14.
'Αντιοχεύς, έως, ό, a citizen of Antioch, Acts vi. 5.*
άντι-παρ-έρχομαι, to pass by on the other side, Luke x. 31, 32.*
'Αντίπας, a, ό, Antipas, Rev. ii. 13.*
'Αντιπατρίς, ίδος, ή, Antipatris, Acts xxiii. 31.*
άντι-πέραν (W. H.,άντίπερα), adv., on the opposite side or shore, Luke viii. 26.*
άντι-πίπτω, to fall against, resist, Acts vii. 52.*
άντι-στρατεύομαι, dep., to make war against, Rom. vii. 23.*
άντι-τάσσω, mid., to set oneself against, resist (dat.).
άντί-τυπος, ον, corresponding in form, as wax to the seal, antitype, Heb. ix. 24; 1 Pet. iii. 21.*
'Αντί-χριστος, ου, m., opposer of Christ, Antichrist, 1 John ii. 18, 22, iv. 3; 2 John vii.*
άντλέω, ω, to draw from a vessel, John ii. 8, 9, iv. 7, 15.*
άντλημα, ατος, τό, a bucket, John iv. 11.*
άντ-οφθαλμέω, ω, to look in the face; so to meet the wind, Acts xxvii. 15.*
άν-υδρος, ον, without water, dry.
άν-υπό-κριτος, ου, adj., without hypocrisy, unfeigned.
άν-υπό-τακτος, ον, not subject to rule, of things, Heb. ii. 8; unruly, of persons, 1 Tim. i. 9; Tit. i. 6, 10.*
άνω, adv. (άνά), up, above, upwards; τά άνω, heaven or heavenly things, as John viii. 23.
άνώγεον, ον, τό, an upper chamber. See άνάγαιον.*
άνωθεν, adv. (άνω), (1) of place, from above, as John iii. 31, xix. 11; with prepp. άπό, έκ, from the top, as Mark xv. 38; John xix. 23; (2) of time, from the first, only Luke i. 3; Acts xxvi. 5. In John iii. 4, 7, again (see Gal. iv. 9); or, perhaps here also, from above.
άνωτερικός, ή, ον, upper, higher, Acts xix. 1.*
άνώτερος, α, ον (compar. of άνω; only neut. as adv.), higher, to a higher place, Luke xiv. 10; above, before, Heb. x. 8.*
άν-ωφελής, ές, unprofitable, Tit. iii. 9; Heb. vii. 18.*
άξίνη, ης, ή, an axe, Matt. iii. 9; Luke iii. 9.*
άξιος, ία, ιον, adj., worthy, deserving of, suitable to (gen.). Adv., -ως, worthily, suitably to (gen.).
άξιόω, ω, to deem worthy (acc. and gen., or inf.), to desire, think good.
ά-όρατος, adj., invisible, unseen.
άπ-αγγέλλω, to report, relate, make known, declare.
άπ-άγχω, mid., to hang or strangle oneself, Matt. xxvii. 5.*
άπ-άγω, to lead, carry, or take away; pass., to be led away to execution, to lead or tend, as a way.
ά-παίδευτος, ον, adj., uninstructed, ignorant, 2 Tim. ii. 23.*
άπ-αίρω, to take away; in N.T. only, 1 a. pass. (subj.), Matt. ix. 15; Mark ii. 20; Luke v. 35.*
άπ-αιτέω, to ask back, require, reclaim, Luke vi. 30, xii. 20.*
άπ-αλγέω, to be past feeling, Eph. iv. 19.*
άπ-αλλάσσω, mid., to remove oneself from, to depart; pass., to be set free (with άπό).
άπ-αλλοτριόω, to estrange, alienate (gen.), Eph. ii. 12, iv. 18; Col. i. 21.*
άπαλός, ή, όν, tender, as a shoot of a tree, Matt. xxiv. 32; Mark xiii. 28.*
άπ-αντάω, ω, to meet, to encounter (dat.).
άπ-άντησις, εως, ή, a meeting, an encountering; εις άπάντησιν (gen. or dat.), to meet any one.
άπαξ, adv., of time, once.
ά-παρά-βατος, adj., not passing from one to another, not transient, unchangeable, Heb. vii. 24.*
ά-παρα-σκεύαστος, ου, adj., unprepared, 2 Cor. ix. 4.*
άπ-αρνέομαι, ούμαι, to deny, disown.

ἀπ-άρτι, adv., of time (see ἄρτι), henceforth, Rev. xiv. 13. (W. H. read ἀπ' ἄρτι.)*
ἀπ-αρτισμός, οῦ, ὁ, completion, Luke xiv. 28.*
ἀπ-αρχή, ῆς, ἡ, the first fruits, consecrated to God (see W. H., 1 Thess. ii. 13).
ἅ-πας, ασα, αν (like πᾶς, § 37), all, all together, the whole.
ἀπασπάζομαι, see ἀσπάζομαι.*
ἀπατάω, ῶ, ήσω, to deceive, lead into error. (The intensive form ἐξαπατάω is more freq.)
ἀπάτη, ης, ἡ, deceit, fraud.
ἀ-πάτωρ, ορος, ὁ, ἡ (πατήρ), without father, i.e., in the genealogies, Heb. vii. 3.*
ἀπ-αύγασμα, ατος, τό, reflected splendour, effulgence, Heb. i. 3.*
ἀπ-εῖδον (W. H., ἀφεῖδον), 2 aor. of ἀφοράω, which see.
ἀ-πείθεια, ας, ἡ, wilful unbelief, obstinacy, disobedience.
ἀ-πειθέω, ῶ, to refuse belief, be disobedient.
ἀ-πειθής, ές, unbelieving, disobedient.
ἀπειλέω, ῶ, ήσω, to threaten, forbid by threatening, rebuke, Acts iv. 17; 1 Pet. ii. 23.*
ἀπειλή, ῆς, ἡ, threatening, harshness, severity.
ἄπ-ειμι (εἰμί, to be), to be absent, as 1 Cor. v. 3.
ἄπειμι (εἶμι, to go), to go away, to depart, Acts xvii. 10.*
ἀπ-εῖπον (see εἶπον), mid., to renounce, disown, 2 Cor. iv. 2.*
ἀ-πείραστος, ον, adj., incapable of being tempted, James i. 13.*
ἄ-πειρος, ον, adj., inexperienced, unskilful in (gen.), Heb. v. 13.*
ἀπ-εκ-δέχομαι, to wait for, expect earnestly or patiently.
ἀπ-εκ-δύομαι, to strip, divest, renounce, Col. ii. 15, iii. 9.*
ἀπέκδυσις, εως, ἡ, a putting or stripping off, renouncing, Col. ii. 11.*
ἀπ-ελαύνω, to drive away, Acts xviii. 16.*
ἀπ-ελεγμός, οῦ, ὁ (ἐλέγχω), refutation, disgrace, disrepute, scorn, Acts xix. 27.*
ἀπ-ελεύθερος, ον, ὁ, ἡ, made free, 1 Cor. vii. 22.*
'Απελλῆς, οῦ, ὁ, Apelles, Rom. xvi. 10.*
ἀπ-ελπίζω, σω, to despair, Luke vi. 35; A.V., "hoping for nothing again;" R.V. better, "never despairing" (see R.V. marg.).*

ἀπ-έναντι, adv. (gen.), over against, in the presence of, in opposition to.
ἀ-πέραντος, ον (πέρας), interminable, 1 Tim. i. 4.*
ἀ-περισπαστώς, adv. (περισπάω), without distraction, 1 Cor. vii. 37.*
ἀπερίτμητος, ον, uncircumcised; fig., Acts vii. 51.*
ἀπ-έρχομαι, to go or come from one place to another, to go away, depart; to go apart; to go back, to return; to go forth, as a rumour.
ἀπ-έχω, to have in full, Matt. vi. 2; to be far (abs., or ἀπό); impers., ἀπέχει, it is enough; mid., to abstain from (gen., or ἀπό).
ἀπιστέω, ῶ, to disbelieve (dat.); to be unfaithful.
ἀπιστία, ας, ἡ, unbelief, distrust, a state of unbelief, 1 Tim. i. 13; renunciation of faith, apostasy, Heb. iii. 12, 19.
ἄ-πιστος, ον, not believing, incredulous; hence an unbeliever or infidel, faithless, perfidious; pass., incredible, only Acts xxvi. 8.
ἀ-πλόος, οῦς, ῆ, οῦν, simple, sound, Matt. vi. 22; Luke xi. 34.* Adv., -ῶς, sincerely, bountifully, James i. 5.*
ἁπλότης, τητος, ἡ, simplicity, sincerity, purity.
ἀπό, prep. gen., from. See § 292; and for the force of the prep. in composition, § 147, a.
ἀπο-βαίνω (for βαίνω, see § 94, I., 6, d; fut., -βήσομαι), to go or come out of, as from a ship, Luke v. 2; John xxi. 9; to turn out, result, Luke xxi. 13; Phil. i. 19.*
ἀπο-βάλλω, to throw away, Mark x. 50; Heb. x. 35.*
ἀπο-βλέπω, to look away from all besides; hence to look earnestly at (εἰς), Heb. xi. 26.*
ἀπό-βλητος, ον, verbal adj., to be thrown away, refused, 1 Tim. iv. 4.*
ἀπο-βολή, ῆς, ἡ, a casting away, rejection, loss, Acts xxvii. 22; Rom. xi. 15.*
ἀπο-γίνομαι, to die, 1 Pet. ii. 24.*
ἀπο-γραφή, ῆς, ἡ, a record, register, enrolment, Luke ii. 2; Acts v. 37.*
ἀπο-γράφω, to enrol, inscribe in a register, Luke ii. 1, 3, 5; Heb. xii. 23.*
ἀπο-δείκνυμι, to show by proof, demonstrate, set forth.
ἀπό-δειξις, εως, ἡ, demonstration, proof, 1 Cor. ii. 4.*

D D

ἀπο-δεκατόω, ῶ, (1) *to pay the tenth* or *tithe*; (2) *to levy tithes on*, acc.
ἀπό-δεκτος, ον, verbal adj., *acceptable*, 1 Tim. ii. 3, v. 4.*
ἀπο-δέχομαι, *to receive with pleasure, to welcome*.
ἀπο-δημέω, ῶ, *to go from one's own people, to go into another country*; only in the parables of our Lord, as Matt. xxi. 33; Luke xv. 13.
ἀπό-δημος, ον, *gone abroad, sojourning in a far country* (R.V.), Mark xiii. 34.*
ἀπο-δίδωμι, *to give from one's self*, as due, or as reward or testimony; *to give back, render, restore, recompense, pay, reward*; *to yield* (fruit).
ἀπο-δι-ορίζω, *to separate off, i.e., into parties*, Jude 19.*
ἀπο-δοκιμάζω, *to reject*, as disapproved or worthless.
ἀπο-δοχή, ῆς, ἡ, *acceptance, approbation*, 1 Tim. i. 15, iv. 9.*
ἀπό-θεσις, εως, ἡ, *a putting away*, 1 Pet. iii. 21; 2 Pet. i. 14.*
ἀπο-θήκη, ης, ἡ, *a repository, granary, storehouse*.
ἀπο-θησαυρίζω, *to treasure up, lay by in store*, 1 Tim. vi. 19.*
ἀπο-θλίβω, *to press closely*, Luke viii. 45.*
ἀπο-θνήσκω (ἀπό, intensive; the simple θνήσκω is rare), *to die*, (1) of natural death, human, animal, or vegetable; (2) of spiritual death; (3) in Epp. of St. Paul, *to die to* (dat.), as Rom. vi. 2. For tenses see θνήσκω.
ἀπο-καθ-ίστημι, ἀποκαταστήσω (also -καθιστάω and -άνω, see Mark ix. 12; Acts i. 6), *to restore*, e.g., to health, or as a state or kingdom.
ἀπο-καλύπτω, *to uncover, bring to light, reveal*.
ἀπο-κάλυψις, εως, ἡ, *revelation, manifestation, enlightenment;* apocalypse.
ἀπο-καρα-δοκία, ας, ἡ (κάρα, head; ἀπό, intensive), *earnest expectation*, as if looking for with the head outstretched, Rom. viii. 19; Phil. i. 20.*
ἀπο-κατ-αλλάσσω, *to reconcile, change from one state of feeling to another*, Eph. ii. 16; Col. i. 20, 22.*
ἀπο-κατά-στασις, εως, ἡ, *restitution, restoration*, Acts iii. 21.*
ἀπό-κειμαι, *to be laid away, to be reserved for* (dat.).
ἀπο-κεφαλίζω (κεφαλή), *to behead*.

ἀπο-κλείω, *to shut close*, as a door, Luke xiii. 25.*
ἀπο-κόπτω, *to smite* or *cut off*; mid., Gal. v. 12 (see R.V.).
ἀπό-κριμα, ατος, τό, *an answer* (perhaps *sentence*), 2 Cor. i. 9.*
ἀπο-κρίνομαι (for aor., see § 100), *to answer;* often used (like the corresponding Hebrew verb) where the "answer" is not to a distinct question, but to some suggestion of the accompanying circumstances; so especially in the phrase ἀποκριθεὶς εἶπεν, *answered and said*, as Matt. xi. 25; Luke i. 60.
ἀπό-κρισις, εως, ἡ, *an answer, reply*.
ἀπο-κρύπτω, *to hide, conceal*.
ἀπό-κρυφος, ον, *hidden, concealed*.
ἀπο-κτείνω, ενῶ, *to put to death, kill*.
ἀπο-κυέω, ῶ, *to bring forth;* fig., James i. 15, 18.*
ἀπο-κυλίω, ίσω, *to roll away*, Matt. xxviii. 2; Mark xvi. 3; Luke xxiv. 2.*
ἀπο-λαμβάνω, *to receive from* any one; *to receive back*, as requital; *to receive in full, obtain;* mid., *to take aside with one's self*, Mark vii. 33.
ἀπό-λαυσις, εως, ἡ (λαύω, *to enjoy*), *enjoyment*, 1 Tim. vi. 17; Heb. xi. 25.*
ἀπο-λείπω, *to leave, to leave behind, to desert;* pass., *to be reserved*.
ἀπο-λείχω, *to lick*, as a dog, Luke xvi. 21. (W. H., ἐπιλείχω.)
ἀπ-όλλυμι (see § 116, 2), *to destroy, to bring to nought, to put to death; to lose;* mid., pass. (and 2nd perf.), *to perish, die; to be lost*.
Ἀπολλύων, οντος, ὁ (prop. part of ἀπολλύω), *Apollyon, the destroying one*, Rev. ix. 11.*
Ἀπολλωνία, ας, ἡ, *Apollonia*, a city of Macedonia, Acts xvii. 1.*
Ἀπολλώς, ῶ, ὁ, *Apollos*.
ἀπο-λογέομαι, οῦμαι (λόγος), *to defend oneself by speech, to plead, excuse oneself*.
ἀπο-λογία, ας, ἡ, *a verbal defence*, "apology."
ἀπο-λούω, mid., *to wash away*, as sins, Acts xxii. 16; 1 Cor. vi. 11.*
ἀπο-λύτρωσις, εως, ἡ, *redemption, deliverance*.
ἀπο-λύω, *to release, let go, to send away;* spec., *to put away* a wife, *divorce;* mid. and pass., *to depart*.

ἀπο-μάσσω, ξω, to wipe off, as dust from the feet; mid., Luke x. 11.*
ἀπο-νέμω, to assign to, to give, 1 Pet. iii. 7.*
ἀπο-νίπτω, mid., to wash oneself, Matt. xxvii. 24.*
ἀπο-πίπτω, to fall from, Acts ix. 24.*
ἀπο-πλανάω, ῶ, to lead astray, Mark xiii. 22; 1 Tim. vi. 10.*
ἀπο-πλέω, εύσω, to sail away.
ἀπο-πλύνω, to wash or rinse, as nets, Luke v. 2. (W. H., πλύνω.)*
ἀπο-πνίγω, to suffocate, choke, Matt. xiii. 7; Luke viii. 7, 33.*
ἀ-πορέω, ῶ (πόρος, resource), only mid. in N.T., to be in doubt, to be perplexed.
ἀπορία, ας, ἡ, perplexity, disquiet, Luke xxi. 25.*
ἀπορ-ρίπτω, to throw or cast down or off, Acts xxvii. 43; ἑαυτούς understood.*
ἀπ-ορφανίζω (ὀρφανός), "to make orphans of;" to bereave, separate from, pass., 1 Thess. ii. 17.*
ἀπο-σκευάζομαι, to pack away, pack up, Acts xxi. 15. (W. H., ἐπισκευάζομαι.)*
ἀπο-σκίασμα, ατος, τό (σκιάζω), a shade; met., a slight trace, James i. 17.*
ἀπο-σπάω, ῶ, άσω, to draw out, unsheathe; to withdraw, to draw away.
ἀπο-στασία, ας, ἡ, defection, departure, apostasy, Acts xxi. 21; 2 Thess. ii. 3.*
ἀπο-στάσιον, ου, τό, desertion, repudiation, divorce; met., bill of divorce, as Matt. v. 31.
ἀπο-στεγάζω (στέγη), to unroof, Mark ii. 4; probably to remove the awning or covering planks of the court.*
ἀπο-στέλλω, to send away, send forth, send, as a messenger, commission, etc., spoken of prophets, teachers, and other messengers; perhaps in Mark iv. 29, to thrust forth the sickle into corn, but more prob. to send forth the sickle, i.e., the reapers.
ἀπο-στερέω, ῶ, ήσω, to defraud, abs., as Mark x. 19; deprive of by fraud, acc. and gen., 1 Tim. vi. 5.
ἀπο-στολή, ῆς, f., apostleship.
ἀπό-στολος, ου, ὁ, (1) a messenger; (2) an apostle, i.e., a messenger of Christ to the world; used of others beside Paul and the Twelve, Acts xiv. 4, 14; 1 Thess. ii. 6; 2 Cor. viii. 23. Christ himself is so called, Heb. iii. 1.

ἀπο-στοματίζω (στόμα), to provoke to speak, Luke xi. 53.*
ἀπο-στρέφω, to turn away, trans. (with ἀπό, as Acts iii. 26); restore, replace, Matt. xxvi. 52; mid., to desert, reject, acc.
ἀπο-στυγέω, ῶ, to detest, to abhor, Rom. xii. 9.*
ἀπο-συνάγωγος, ον, excluded from the synagogue, excommunicated, John ix. 22, xii. 42, xvi. 2.*
ἀπο-τάσσω, ξω, mid., "to set oneself apart from;" to take leave of, renounce, send away (dat.).
ἀπο-τελέω, ῶ, έσω, to perfect, James i. 15; Luke xiii. 32 (W. H.).*
ἀπο-τίθημι, mid., to lay off or aside, to renounce.
ἀπο-τινάσσω, to shake off, Luke ix. 5; Acts xxviii. 5.*
ἀπο-τίνω (or -τίω), τίσω, to repay, Philemon 19.*
ἀπο-τολμάω, ῶ, to dare boldly, Rom. x. 20.*
ἀπο-τομία, ας, ἡ (τέμνω, to cut), severity, Rom. xi. 22.*
ἀπο-τόμως, adv., severely, sharply, 2 Cor. xiii. 10; Tit. i. 13.*
ἀπο-τρέπω, mid., to turn away from shun, acc., 2 Tim. iii. 5.*
ἀπ-ουσία, ας (ἄπειμι), absence, Phil. ii. 12.*
ἀπο-φέρω, to bear away from one place to another.
ἀπο-φεύγω, to escape, 2 Pet. i. 4, ii. 18, 20.*
ἀπο-φθέγγομαι, to speak out, declare, Acts ii. 4, 14, xxvi. 25.*
ἀπο-φορτίζομαι (φόρτος, a burden), to unlade, Acts xxi. 3.*
ἀπό-χρησις, εως, ἡ (ἀπό, intens.), use, consumption, Col. ii. 22.*
ἀπο-χωρέω, ῶ, to go away, depart, Matt. vii. 23; Luke ix. 39; Acts xiii. 13.*
ἀπο-χωρίζω, to part asunder, Acts xv. 39; Rev. vi. 14.*
ἀπο-ψύχω, "to breathe out," to faint, as from fear, Luke xxi. 26.*
Ἄππιος, ου, ὁ, Appius. Ἀππίου φόρον, the Appian Way, a road from Rome to Brundusium, constructed by Appius Claudius Cæsar, Acts xxviii. 15.*
ἀ-πρόσ-ιτος, adj. (πρός, εἶμι), not to be approached, 1 Tim. vi. 16.*

ά-πρόσ-κοπος, ον (κόπτω), act., *not causing to offend*, 1 Cor. x. 32; pass., *not caused to offend, without offence*, Acts xxiv. 16; Phil. i. 10.*
ά-προσωπο-λήπτως (W. H., -λήμπτ-), adv., *not taken by appearance, impartially*, 1 Pet. i. 17.*
ά-πταιστος, ον (πταίω, *to fall*), *without stumbling* or *falling*, Jude 24.*
άπτω, ψω, *to kindle*, as light or fire; mid., *to touch.* Syn. 7.
'Απφία, ας, ή, *Apphia*, Philemon 2; perhaps Philemon's wife.*
άπωθέω, ῶ, ἀπώσω, mid., *to repulse, to reject.*
άπώλεια, ας, ή (ἀπόλλυμι), *consumption, waste,* of things; *destruction,* of persons; *death* by violence; *perdition.*
ἀρά, ας, ή, *curse, imprecation*, Rom. iii. 14.*
ἄρα, conj., illative, *therefore, thence, since.* See § 406. ἆρα, adv. interrogative, where the answer is negative; only Luke xviii. 8; Acts viii. 30; Gal. ii. 17.
'Αραβία, ας, ή, *Arabia*, Gal. i. 17, iv. 25.*
'Αραμ, ὁ (Heb.), *Aram*, Matt. i. 3; Luke iii. 33.*
'Αραψ, αβος, ὁ, *Arabian*, Acts ii. 11.*
ἀργέω, ῶ, *to linger, to delay*, 2 Pet. ii. 3.*
ἀργός, ον (ἀ, ἔργον), *not working, idle.*
ἀργύρεος, οῦς, ᾶ, οῦν, *made of silver.*
ἀργύριον, ιον, τό, *silver, a piece of silver, a shekel, money* in general.
ἀργυρο-κόπος, ου, ὁ, *one who works in silver, a silversmith*, Acts xix. 24.*
ἄργυρος, ου, ὁ, *silver.*
Ἄρειος πάγος, ου, ὁ, *Areopagus*, or *Mars' Hill*, an open space on a hill in Athens, where the supreme court was held; Acts xvii.* (Ἄρειος is an adj. from Ἄρης, *Mars.*)
'Αρεοπαγίτης, ου, ὁ, *a judge of the Areopagite court*, Acts xvii. 34.*
ἀρέσκεια, ας, ή, *a pleasing, a desire of pleasing*, Col. i. 10.*
ἀρέσκω, ἀρέσω, *to be pleasing to, to seek to please* or *gratify, to accommodate oneself to* (dat.).
ἀρεστός, ή, όν, *acceptable, pleasing to.*
'Αρέτας, α, ὁ, *Aretas*, a king of Arabia Petræa, 2 Cor. xi. 32.*
ἀρετή, ῆς, ή, *virtue, energy, courage*, Phil. iv. 8; 1 Pet. ii. 9; 2 Pet. i. 3, 5.*
(ἄρην) gen., ἀρνός, *a lamb*, Luke x. 3.*

ἀριθμέω, ῶ, *to number.*
ἀριθμός, οῦ, ὁ, *a number.*
'Αριμαθαία, ας, ή, *Arimathæa.*
'Αρίσταρχος, ου, ὁ, *Aristarchus.*
ἀριστάω, ῶ, ἤσω (ἄριστον), *to take the morning meal*, Luke xi. 37; John xxi. 12, 15.*
ἀριστερός, ά, όν, *the left;* ἡ ἀριστερά (χείρ), *the left hand*, Matt. vi. 3; ἐξ ἀριστερῶν, *on the left*, Mark x. 37 (W. H.); Luke xxiii. 33, without ἐξ; 2 Cor. vi. 7. (The more common word is εὐώνυμος.)*
'Αριστόβουλος, ου, ὁ, *Aristobūlus*, Rom. xvi. 10.*
ἄριστον, ου, τό, *the morning meal*, Matt. xxii. 4; Luke xi. 38, xiv. 12.* Cf. δεῖπνον.
ἀρκετός, ή, όν, *sufficient*, Matt. vi. 34, x. 25; 1 Pet. iv. 3.*
ἀρκέω, ῶ, *to be sufficient for;* mid. or pass., *to be satisfied with.*
ἄρκτος (W. H., ἄρκος), ου, ὁ, ή, *a bear*, Rev. xiii. 2.*
ἅρμα, ατος, τό, *a chariot*, Acts viii. 28, 29, 38; Rev. ix. 9.*
'Αρμαγεδδών (Heb., *the mountain of Megiddo,* see Judges v. 19; 2 Kings xxiii. 29), *Armageddon*, Rev. xvi. 16.*
ἁρμόζω, σω, "*to fit together;*" mid., *to espouse, to betroth*, 2 Cor. xi. 2.*
ἁρμός, οῦ, ὁ, *a joint, i.e.,* of limbs in a body, Heb. iv. 12.*
ἀρνέομαι, οῦμαι, *to deny, disclaim, disown.*
ἀρνίον, ου, τό (dimin. of ἀρήν), *a little lamb*, John xxi. 15; freq. in Rev., of Christ.
ἀροτριάω, ῶ, άσω, *to plough*, Luke xvii. 7; 1 Cor. ix. 10.*
ἄροτρον, ου, τό, *a plough*, Luke ix. 62.*
ἁρπαγή, ῆς, ή (ἁρπάζω), *the act of plundering, extortion*, Matt. xxiii. 25; Luke xi. 39; Heb. x. 34.*
ἁρπαγμός, οῦ, ὁ, *spoil, an object of eager desire, a prize* (R. V.), Phil. ii. 6.*
ἁρπάζω, άσω (2 aor. pass., ἡρπάγην), *to snatch, seize violently, take by force; to carry off suddenly.*
ἅρπαξ, αγος, adj., *rapacious, ravening, extortionate.*
ἀρραβών, ῶνος, ὁ (from Heb.), *a pledge, an earnest,* ratifying a contract, 2 Cor i. 22, v. 5; Eph. i. 14.*
ἄρραφος (W. H., ἄραφος), ον, *not seamed* or *sewn*, John xix. 23.*

ἄρρην, εν (W. H., ἄρσην, εν), *of the male sex*, Rom. i. 27 ; Rev. xii. 5, 13.*
ἄρρητος, ον, adj., *unspoken, unspeakable*, 2 Cor. xii. 4.*
ἄρρωστος, ον, adj. (ῥώννυμι), *infirm, sick*.
ἀρσενο-κοίτης, ου, m. (ἄρσην κοίτῃ), *a sodomite*.
Ἀρτεμᾶς, α, ὁ, *Artemas*, Tit. iii. 12.*
Ἄρτεμις, ιδος or ιος, ἡ, *Artemis* (by the Latins called *Diana*), the heathen deity of hunting; also, the goddess of the Moon. She was worshipped at Ephesus as "the personification of the fructifying and all-nourishing powers of nature," Acts xix.*
ἀρτέμων, ονος, m. (ἀρτάω, *to suspend*), prob. *the foresail*, Acts xxvii. 40.*
ἄρτι, adv. of time, *now, already, lately, well-nigh;* with other particles, as ἕως ἄρτι, *till now;* ἀπ' ἄρτι, *from now* or *henceforward*.
ἀρτι-γέννητος, ον, *new-* or *recently born*, 1 Pet. ii. 2.*
ἄρτιος, ου, adj., *perfect, complete*, wanting in nothing, 2 Tim. iii. 17.*
ἄρτος, ου, ὁ, *bread, loaf, food;* fig., *spiritual nutriment;* ἄρτοι τῆς προθέσεως, *shewbread*.
ἀρτύω (ἄρω, *to fit*), *to season, to flavour*, as with salt, Mark ix. 50 ; Luke xiv. 34 ; fig., Col. iv. 6.*
Ἀρφαξάδ, ὁ (Heb.), *Arphaxad*, Luke iii. 36.*
ἀρχ-άγγελος, ου, ὁ, *an arch-* or *chief-angel*, 1 Thess. iv. 16 ; Jude 9.*
ἀρχαῖος, α, ον, *old, ancient*.
Ἀρχέλαος, ου, ὁ, *Archelaus*, Matt. ii. 22.*
ἀρχή, ῆς, f., (1) *a beginning*, of time, space, or series; *the outermost point*, Acts x. 11. Used of Christ, Col. i. 18; Rev. iii. 14, xxi. 6, xxii. 13. Adv. phrases : ἀπ' ἀρχῆς, *from the beginning;* ἐν ἀρχῇ, *in the beginning;* ἐξ ἀρχῆς, *from the beginning or from the first;* κατ' ἀρχάς, *at the beginning;* τὴν ἀρχήν, *originally*. (2) *rule, pre-eminence, principality* (see ἄρχω): espec. in pl., ἀρχαι, *rulers, magistrates*, as Luke xii. 11 ; of supramundane powers, *principalities*, as Eph. iii. 10.
ἀρχ-ηγός, οῦ, ὁ (ἀρχή, ἄγω), *the beginner, author, captain, prince*, Acts iii. 15, v. 31 ; Heb. ii. 10, xii. 2.*
ἀρχ-ιερατικός, ή, όν, *belonging to the office of the high priest, pontifical*, Acts iv. 6.*

ἀρχ-ιερεύς, έως, ὁ, (1) *the high priest;* so of Christ ; (2) *a chief priest, i.e.*, the head priest in his class. See 1 Chron. xxiv. 4-18.
ἀρχι-ποιμήν, ένος, ὁ, *the chief shepherd*, a title of Christ, 1 Pet. v. 4.*
Ἄρχιππος, ου, ὁ, *Archippus*, Col. iv. 17, Philem. 2.*
ἀρχι-συνάγωγος, ου, ὁ, *presiding officer* or *ruler of a synagogue*.
ἀρχι-τέκτων, ανος, ὁ, *a master builder, an architect*, 1 Cor. iii. 10.*
ἀρχι-τελώνης, ου, ὁ, *a chief collector of taxes, a chief publican*, Luke xix. 2.*
ἀρχι-τρίκλινος, ου, ὁ, *a president of a feast*, John ii. 8, 9.*
ἄρχω, *to reign, to rule* (gen.), only Mark v. 42 ; Rom. xv. 12 ; mid., *to begin*, often with infin. ἀρξάμενος ἀπό, *beginning from* (cf. § 287).
ἄρχων, οντος, ὁ, prop. particip., *ruler, chief person, prince, magistrate*.
ἄρωμα, ατος, τό, *spicery, an aromatic*.
Ἀσά (Heb.), *Asa*, Matt. i. 7, 8.*
ἀ-σάλευτος, ον, *unshaken, immovable*, Acts xxvii. 41 ; Heb. xii. 28.*
ἄ-σβεστος, ον, adj. (σβέννυμι), *not to be quenched, inextinguishable*.
ἀσέβεια, ας, ἡ, *impiety, ungodliness, wickedness*. Syn. 36.
ἀσεβέω, ῶ, ήσω, *to act* or *live impiously, wickedly*, 2 Pet. ii. 6 ; Jude 15.*
ἀ-σεβής, ές (σέβομαι), *impious, ungodly, wicked*.
ἀ-σέλγεια, ας, ἡ, *excess, wantonness, lasciviousness*.
ἄ-σημος, *not remarkable, obscure, ignoble*, Acts xxi. 39.*
Ἀσήρ, ὁ, *Asher*, Luke ii. 36 ; Rev. vii. 6.*
ἀσθένεια, ας, ἡ, *weakness, bodily infirmity, sickness;* fig., *mental depression, distress*.
ἀσθενέω, ῶ, *to be weak, sick, faint;* fig., *to be fainthearted*.
ἀσθένημα, ατος, τό, *weakness, infirmity;* fig., Rom. xv. 1.*
ἀ-σθενής, ές (σθένος, *strength*), "without strength," *weak, infirm, sickly;* fig., *fainthearted, afflicted*.
Ἀσία, ας, ἡ, *Asia*, i.e., that district in the west of Asia Minor afterwards called *Proconsular Asia*, with Ephesus its capital.
Ἀσιανός, οῦ, ὁ, *belonging to Asia*, Acts xx. 4.*

Ἀσιάρχης, ου, ὁ, an Asiarch, one of ten appointed to preside over the worship and celebrations in honour of the gods, Acts xix. 31.*
ἀσιτία, as, ἡ (σῖτος, corn), abstinence, a fast, Acts xxvii. 21.*
ἄ-σιτος, ον, fasting, Acts xxvii. 33.*
ἀσκέω, ῶ, ήσω, to exercise oneself, exert diligence in, Acts xxiv. 16.*
ἀσκός, οῦ, ὁ, a bottle of skin, Matt. ix. 17; Mark ii. 22; Luke v. 37, 38.*
ἀσμένως, adv. (from part. of ἤδομαι), with joy, gladly, Acts ii. 41 (W. H. omit); Acts xxi. 17.*
ἄ-σοφος, ον, not wise, Eph. v. 15.*
ἀσπάζομαι, dep., to embrace, salute, to greet (actually or by letter); always of persons, except Heb. xi. 13, "having embraced (R. V., greeted) the promises;" to take leave of (only Acts xx. 1; in xxi. 6, W. H. read ἀπασπάζομαι).
ἀσπασμός, οῦ, ὁ, salutation, greeting.
ἄ-σπιλος, ου, ον (σπίλος), without spot, unblemished.
ἀσπίς, ίδος, ἡ, an asp, a venomous serpent, Rom. iii. 13.*
ἄ-σπονδος, ον (σπονδή), "not to be bound by truce," implacable, 2 Tim. iii. 3; Rom. i. 31 (not W. H.).*
ἀσσάριον, ίου, τό, a small coin equal to the sixteenth part of a denarius, an as. See § 154, a.
ἆσσον, adv. (compar. of ἄγχι), nearer, close by, Acts xxvii. 13.*
Ἆσσος, ου, ἡ, Assos, Acts xx. 13, 14.*
ἀ-στατέω, ῶ, ήσω, to be unsettled, to have no fixed abode, 1 Cor. iv. 11.*
ἀστεῖος, ον (ἄστυ, city, cf. urbane), fair, beautiful, Acts vii. 20; Heb. xi. 23.*
ἀστήρ, έρος, ὁ, a star.
ἀ-στήρικτος, adj. (στηρίζω), unsettled, unstable, 2 Pet. ii. 14, iii. 16.*
ἄ-στοργος, ον (στοργή), without natural affection, Rom. i. 31; 2 Tim. iii. 3.*
ἀ-στοχέω, ῶ (στόχος), to miss in aim, swerve from, 1 Tim. i. 6, vi. 21; 2 Tim. ii. 18.*
ἀστραπή, ῆς, ἡ, lightning, vivid brightness, lustre.
ἀστράπτω, to flash, as lightning, Luke xvii. 24; to be lustrous, xxiv. 4.*
ἄστρον, ου, τό, a constellation, star.
Ἀσύγκριτος, ου, ὁ, Asyncritus, Rom. xvi. 14.*
ἀ-σύμφωνος, ον, dissonant, discordant, Acts xxviii. 25.*
ἀ-σύνετος, ον, without understanding, foolish.
ἀ-σύνθετος, ον, covenant-breaking, treacherous, Rom. i. 31.*
ἀσφάλεια, as, ἡ, security, Acts v. 23; 1 Thess. v. 3; certainty, Luke i. 4.*
ἀ-σφαλής, ές (σφάλλω, fallo), firm, safe, sure, Phil. iii. 1; Heb. vi. 19; certain, Acts xxv. 26. τὸ ἀσφαλές, the certainty, Acts xxi. 34, xxii. 30.* Adv., -ῶς, safely, certainly.
ἀσφαλίζω, σω (mid.), to make fast, to secure, Matt. xxvii. 64, 65, 66; Acts xvi. 24.*
ἀσχημονέω, ῶ, to act improperly or unseemly, 1 Cor. vii. 36, xiii. 5.*
ἀσχημοσύνη, ης, ἡ, unseemliness, shame, Rom. i. 27; Rev. xvi. 15.*
ἀ-σχήμων, ον (σχῆμα), uncomely, indecorous, 1 Cor. xii. 23.*
ἀ-σωτία, as, ἡ (σώζω), an abandoned course, profligacy.
ἀ-σώτως, adv., profligately, dissolutely, Luke xv. 13.*
ἀτακτέω, ῶ, to behave disorderly, 2 Thess. iii. 7.*
ἄ-τακτος, ον (τάσσω), irregular, disorderly, 1 Thess. v. 14.* Adv., -ως, disorderly, irregularly, 2 Thess. iii. 6, 11.*
ἄ-τεκνος, ου, ὁ, ἡ (τέκνον), childless, Luke xx. 28, 29.*
ἀτενίζω, σω, to look intently upon (dat. or εἰς).
ἄτερ, adv., as prep. with gen., without, in the absence of, Luke xxii. 6, 35.*
ἀτιμάζω, σω, to dishonour, contemn, whether persons or things, by word or by deed.
ἀτιμία, as, ἡ, dishonour, ignominy, disgrace, ignoble use.
ἄ-τιμος, ον (τιμή), contemned, despised.
ἀτιμόω, ῶ (or -άω, W. H.), to dishonour, treat with indignity, Mark xii. 4.*
ἀτμίς, ίδος, ἡ, a vapour, Acts ii. 19, James iv. 14.
ἄ-τομον, ου, τό (τέμνω), an atom of time, moment, 1 Cor. xv. 52.*
ἄ-τοπος, ον (τόπος), misplaced, unbecoming, mischievous.
Ἀττάλεια, as, ἡ, Attalia, Acts xiv. 25.
αὐγάζω, to shine upon, to enlighten (dat.), 2 Cor. iv. 4.*

αὐγή, ῆς, ἡ, splendour, daybreak, Acts xx. 11.*
Αὔγουστος, ου, ὁ (Lat.), Augustus, Luke ii. 1.* Compare Σεβαστός.
αὐθάδης, ες (αὐτός, ἥδομαι), self-pleasing, arrogant, Tit. i. 7; 2 Pet. ii. 10.*
αὐθαίρετος, ον (αὐτός, αἱρέομαι), of one's own accord, 2 Cor. viii. 3, 17.*
αὐθεντέω, ῶ, to exercise authority over (gen.), 1 Tim. ii. 12.*
αὐλέω, ῶ, ήσω, to play on a pipe or flute.
αὐλή, ῆς, ἡ (ἄω, to blow), an open space, court or hall of a house, as Luke xi. 21, xxii. 55; a sheepfold, John x. 1, 16.
αὐλητής, οῦ, ὁ, a player on a pipe or flute, Matt. ix. 23; Rev. xviii. 22.*
αὐλίζομαι, (to lodge in the open air,) to lodge, take up a temporary abode, Matt. xxi. 17; Luke xxi. 37.*
αὐλός, οῦ, ὁ (ἄω), a flute, pipe, 1 Cor. xiv. 7.*
αὐξάνω (also αὔξω), αὐξήσω, trans., to make to grow, as 1 Cor. iii. 6, 7; pass., to arrive at maturity; generally intrans., to grow, increase, as Matt. vi. 28.
αὔξησις, εως, ἡ, growth, increase, Eph. iv. 16; Col. ii. 19.*
αὔριον, adv. (αὔρα, morning breeze, ἄω), to-morrow; ἡ (sc., ἡμέρα) αὔριον, the morrow.
αὐστηρός, ά, όν, (dry,) harsh, austere, Luke xix. 21, 22.*
αὐτάρκεια, ας, ἡ, sufficiency, 2 Cor. ix. 8; contentment, 1 Tim. vi. 6.*
αὐτ-άρκης, ες (ἀρκέω, sufficient to self), content, satisfied, Phil. iv. 11.*
αὐτο-κατά-κρῖτος, ον, self-condemned, Tit. iii. 11.*
αὐτόματος, ον, spontaneous, of its own accord, Mark iv. 28; Acts xii. 10.*
αὐτ-όπτης, ου, ὁ, an eye-witness, Luke i. 2.*
αὐτός, ή, ό, pron., he, she, it; in nom. always emphatic. Properly demonstrative, self, very; joined with each of the persons of the verb, with or without a pers. pron.; I myself, thou thyself; with the article, the same; the same with (dat.), 1 Cor. xi. 5. ἐπὶ τὸ αὐτό, at the same place or time, together, κατὰ τὸ αὐτό, together, only Acts xiv. 1. See § 335.
αὐτοῦ, adv. of place, here, there.
αὑτοῦ, ῆς, οῦ, pron. reflex. (contr. for ἑαυτοῦ), of himself, herself, etc. (W. H.

exclude these forms from the N.T., everywhere reading αὐτοῦ, αὐτῷ, etc.)
αὐτό-φωρος, ον (φώρ, a thief), in the very act, John viii. 4, neut. dat. with ἐπί. See W. H.*
αὐτό-χειρ, adj., with one's own hands, Acts xxvii. 19.*
αὐχμηρός, ά, όν, dark, dismal, 2 Pet. i. 19.*
ἀφ-αιρέω, to take away, as Luke x. 42; to take away sin, only Rom. xi. 27; Heb. x. 4; to smite off, as Matt. xxvi. 51, and parallel passages.
ἀ-φανής, ές (φαίνω), not appearing, hidden, Heb. iv. 13.*
ἀ-φανίζω, to put out of sight, to disfigure, Matt. vi. 16, 19, 20; pass., to vanish, perish, Acts xiii. 41; James iv. 14.*
ἀ-φανισμός, οῦ, ὁ, a disappearing, Heb. viii. 13.*
ἄ-φαντος, ον, disappearing, not seen, Luke xxiv. 31.*
ἀφ-εδρών, ῶνος, ὁ, "draught," latrine, Matt. xv. 17; Mark vii. 19.*
ἀ-φειδία, ας, ἡ (φείδομαι), severity, Col. ii. 23.*
ἀφελότης, τητος, simplicity, sincerity, Acts ii. 46.*
ἄφ-εσις, εως, f. (ἀφίημι), deliverance; lit., only Luke iv. 18; elsewhere always of deliverance from sin, remission, forgiveness.
ἀφή, ῆς, ἡ (ἅπτω, to fit), that which connects, a joint, Eph. iv. 16; Col. ii. 19.*
ἀ-φθαρσία, ας, ἡ, incorruption, immortality, 1 Cor. xv.; Rom. ii. 7; 2 Tim. i. 10; perpetuity, uncorruptness (R.V.), Eph. vi. 24; Tit. ii. 7. (W. H., ἀφθορία.)*
ἄ-φθαρτος, ον (φθείρω), incorruptible, immortal, as God, Rom. i. 23; 1 Cor. ix. 25, xv. 52; 1 Tim. i. 17; 1 Pet. i. 4, 23, iii. 4.*
ἀφ-ίημι (see § 112), to send away, as (1) to let go, emit, Matt. xxvii. 50; Mark xv. 37; dismiss, in senses varying according to the obj.; spec., to disregard, pass by, send away, divorce; hence (2) to forgive (dat. pers.), very often; (3) to permit, concede, abs., or with inf., as Mark x. 14; or acc., as Matt. iii. 15 (dat., Matt. v. 40); or ἵνα, subj., Mark xi. 6; or subj. alone, Luke vi. 42; (4) to leave, depart from, abandon, leave behind.

ἀφικνέομαι, οῦμαι (2 aor., ἀφϊκόμην), *to go abroad, to reach*, Rom. xvi. 19.*
ἀ-φιλ-άγαθος, ον, *not loving goodness* (R. V.) or *good men* (A. V.), 2 Tim. iii. 3.*
ἀ-φιλ-άργυρος, ον, *not loving money, not covetous*, 1 Tim. iii. 3; Heb. xiii. 5.*
ἄφιξις, εως, ἡ, "arrival;" *departure*, Acts xx. 29.*
ἀφ-ίστημι, ἀποστήσω, trans. in pres., imperf., 1 aor., fut., *to lead away, to seduce*; intrans. in perf., plup., 2 aor., *to go away, depart, avoid, withdraw from* (often with ἀπό); mid., *to fail, abstain from, absent oneself*.
ἄφνω, adv., *suddenly*, Acts ii. 2, xvi. 26, xxviii. 6.*
ἀ-φόβως, adv., *without fear*.
ἀφ-ομοιόω, ῶ, *to make like*, in pass., Heb. vii. 3.*
ἀφ-οράω, ῶ (2 a., ἀπ- or ἀφ-εῖδον), *to look away from others at* (εἰς) one, *to regard earnestly*, Heb. xii. 2; *to see*, Phil. ii. 23.*
ἀφ-ορίζω, fut. ιῶ, trans., *to separate from* (ἐκ or ἀπό), *to separate for a purpose* (εἰς, Acts xiii. 2; Rom. i. 1; or inf., Gal. i. 15); *to excommunicate*, Luke vi. 22.
ἀφ-ορμή, ῆς, ἡ, *an occasion, opportunity*.
ἀφρίζω, *to foam at the mouth*, Mark ix. 18, 20.*
ἀφρός, οῦ, ὁ, *foam, froth*, Luke ix. 39.*
ἀ-φροσύνη, ης, ἡ, *foolishness*, Mark vii. 22; 2 Cor. xi. 1, 17, 22.*
ἄ-φρων, ονος, ὁ, ἡ (φρήν), *unwise, inconsiderate, foolish*.
ἀφ-υπνόω, ῶ (ἀπό, intensive), *to sleep soundly*, or perhaps simply *fall asleep*, Luke viii. 23.*
ἄ-φωνος, ον, *mute, without the faculty of speech:* of animals, Acts viii. 32; 2 Pet. ii. 16; of idols, 1 Cor. xii. 2. In 1 Cor. xiv. 10 the R.V. marg. is probably the correct rendering.*
Ἄχαζ, ὁ (Heb.), *Achaz*, Matt. i. 9.*
Ἀχαΐα, ας, ἡ, *Achaia*, the Roman province of Greece, including Corinth and its isthmus.
Ἀχαϊκός, οῦ, ὁ, *Achaicus*, 1 Cor. xvi. 17.*
ἀ-χάριστος, ον, *unthankful*, Luke vi. 35; 2 Tim. iii. 2.*
Ἀχείμ, ὁ (Heb.), *Achim*, Matt. i. 14.*
ἀ-χειρο-ποίητος, ον, *not made by hands*, Mark xiv. 58; 2 Cor. v. 1; Col. ii. 11.*
ἀχλύς, ύος, ἡ, *a thick mist, darkness*, Acts xiii. 11.*
ἀ-χρεῖος, ον, *slothful, doing no good, unprofitable*, Matt. xxv. 30; Luke xvii. 10.*
ἀ-χρειόω (W. H., ἀχρεόω), pass., *to become useless*, Rom. iii. 12.*
ἄ-χρηστος, ον, *useless, unprofitable*, Philemon 11.*
ἄχρι and ἄχρις, adv. as prep., with gen., *to, unto, as far as*, whether of place, time, or degree. ἄχρις οὗ or ἄχρις alone, with the force of a conjunction, *until*. See μέχρι.
ἄχυρον, ου, τό, *chaff, straw*, Matt. iii. 12; Luke iii. 17.*
ἀ-ψευδής, ές, *free from falsehood, truthful*, Tit. i. 2.*
ἄψινθος, ου, ἡ, *wormwood* Rev. viii. 11.*
ἄ-ψυχος, ον, *without life, inanimate*, 1 Cor. xiv. 7.*

B.

Β, β, βῆτα, *beta, b*, the second letter. Numerally, β' = 2; β, = 2000.
Βάαλ, ὁ, ἡ (Heb., *Master*), *Baal*, chief deity of the Phœnicians; the Sun, Rom. xi. 4 (fem.), from 1 Kings xix. 18.*
Βαβυλών, ῶνος, ἡ, *Babylon*, lit., Matt. i. 11, 12, 17; Acts vii. 43, and prob. 1 Pet. v. 13; mystically, in Rev.*
βαθμός, οῦ, ὁ (βαίνω, *to step*), *a step* or *degree* in dignity, 1 Tim. iii. 13.*
βάθος, ους, τό, *depth*, lit. or fig. ; 2 Cor. viii. 2, ἡ κατὰ βάθους πτωχεία, *their deep poverty.*
βαθύνω, υνῶ, *to deepen*, Luke vi. 48.*
βαθύς, εῖα, ύ, *deep*, John iv. 11; in Luke xxiv. 1, ὄρθρου βαθέος, in the early dawn (W. H., βαθέως, adv., or perhaps a genit. form).
βαΐον, ου, τό, *branch*, John xii. 13.*
Βαλαάμ, ὁ (Heb.), *Balaam*. A name emblematic of seducing teachers, 2 Pet. ii. 15; Jude 11; Rev. ii. 14.*
Βαλάκ, ὁ (Heb.), *Balak*, Rev. ii. 14.*
βαλάντιον (W. H., -λλ-), ου, τό, *a moneybag* or *purse*.
βάλλω, βαλῶ, βέβληκα, ἔβαλον, *to throw, cast, put* (with more or less force, as

modified by the context); of liquids, *to pour.* Pass. perf., with intrans. force, as Matt. viii. 6 ("has been cast"), *lieth.* The verb is intrans., Acts xxvii. 14, *rushed.* In Mark xiv. 65 the true reading is prob. ἔλαβον. Generally trans. with acc. and dat., or ἐπί (acc., sometimes gen.), εἰς, ἀπό, ἐκ, and other prepp. or advv.

βαπτίζω, σω (in form a frequentative of βάπτω, see § 144, *b*), (1) mid. or pass., reflex., *to bathe* oneself, only in Mark vii. 4; Luke xi. 38; (2) of the Christian ordinance, *to immerse, submerge, to baptise.* The material (water, fire, the Holy Spirit) is expressed by dat., εἰς or ἐν; the purpose or result by εἰς. Pass. or mid., *to be baptised, to receive baptism;* (3) fig., of overwhelming woe, Matt. xx. 22, 23; Luke xii. 50.

βάπτισμα, ατος, τό, *the rite* or *ceremony of baptism;* fig., for overwhelming afflictions, Matt. xx. 22, 23; Luke xii. 50.

βαπτισμός, οῦ, ὁ, *the act of cleansing,* as vessels, Mark vii. 4, 8 (W. H. omit); of Jewish lustrations, *washings* (pl.), Heb. ix. 10. For Heb. vi. 2, see § 260, *b*, 2, (*b*).*

βαπτιστής, οῦ, ὁ, *one who baptises;* the surname of John, Christ's forerunner.

βάπτω, βάψω, *to dip, dye, tinge,* Luke xvi. 24; John xiii. 26; Rev. xix. 13.*

Βαρ-, an Aramaic prefix to many surnames, meaning *son of.*

Βαρ-αββᾶς, ᾶ, ὁ, *Barabbas.* Some ancient MSS. and other authorities give his name as *Jesus* (not W. H.).

Βαράκ, ὁ, *Barak,* Heb. xi. 32.*

Βαρ-αχίας, ου, ἡ, *Barachias,* Matt. xxiii. 35. Some think it a surname of Jehoiada, 2 Chron. xxiv. 20.*

βάρβαρος, ον, ὁ (prob. onomatop., descriptive of unintelligible sounds), properly adj., *a foreigner, barbarian,* as 1 Cor. xiv. 11.

βαρέω, ῶ (cf. βάρος), in N.T. only pass. βαρέομαι, οῦμαι, *to be weighed down, to be oppressed,* as by sleep, Luke ix. 32; mental troubles, 2 Cor. i. 8, v. 4.

βαρέως, adv., *heavily* or *with difficulty,* with ἀκούω, *to be dull of hearing,* Matt. xiii. 15; Acts xxviii. 27.*

Βαρ-θολομαῖος, ου, ὁ, *Bartholomew,* surname (prob.) of Nathanael.

Βαρ-ιησοῦς, οῦ, ὁ, *Bar-jesus,* Acts xiii. 6.*

Βαρ-ιωνᾶς, ᾶ, ὁ, *Bar-jonas,* surname of Peter, Matt. xvi. 17.*

Βαρ-νάβας, α, ὁ, *Barnabas,* "Son of exhortation" or "comfort." See παράκλησις.

βάρος, ους, τό, *weight, burden;* only fig.

Βαρ-σαβᾶς, ᾶ, ὁ, *Barsabas.* Two are mentioned, Acts i. 23, xv. 22.

Βαρ-τίμαιος, ου, ὁ, *Bartimæus.*

βαρύς, εῖα, ύ (cf. βάρος), (1) *heavy,* Matt. xxiii. 4; (2) *weighty, important,* Matt. xxiii. 23; 2 Cor. x. 10; (3) *oppressive* or *grievous,* Acts xx. 29, xxv. 7; 1 John v. 3.*

βαρύ-τιμος, ον, *of great price,* Matt. xxvi. 7.*

βασανίζω (cf. βάσανος), *to examine,* as by torture; hence *to torment, distress, vex, harass;* of waves, *to buffet.*

βασανισμός, οῦ, ὁ, *torture, torment,* Rev.*

βασανιστής, οῦ, ὁ, *one who tortures, a tormentor,* Matt. xviii. 34.*

βάσανος, ου, ἡ (lit., *a touchstone*), *torture, torment,* Matt. iv. 24; Luke xvi. 23, 28.*

βασιλεία, ας, ἡ, *a kingdom, royal power* or *dignity, reign.* ἡ βασιλεία τοῦ Θεοῦ, τοῦ χριστοῦ, τῶν οὐρανῶν (the last form only in Matt.), *the divine, spiritual kingdom,* or *reign* of Messiah, in the world, in the individual, or in the future state. υἱοὶ τῆς βασιλείας, *sons of the kingdom,* Jews, its original possessors, Matt. viii. 12; true believers, Matt. xiii. 38. In Rev. i. 6, v. 10, for βασιλεῖς καὶ, W. H. read βασιλείαν, *a kingdom* consisting of priests (R.V.).

βασίλειος, ον, *royal, regal,* 1 Pet. ii. 9, from Exod. xix. 6. τὰ βασίλεια, as subst., *a regal mansion, palace,* Luke vii. 25.*

βασιλεύς, έως, ὁ, *a leader, ruler, king,* sometimes subordinate to higher authority, as the Herods. Applied to God, always with distinguishing epithets, Matt. v. 35; 1 Tim. i. 17, vi. 15; Rev. xv. 3, xvii. 14; to Christ, Matt. ii. 2; John i. 49, etc.; to Christians, Rev. i. 6, v. 10 (Rec., but see under βασίλεια).

βασιλεύω, εύσω (-εf), to have authority, to reign, or to possess or exercise dominion; to be βασιλεύς generally. With gen. or ἐπί (gen.), of the kingdom; ἐπί (acc.), of the persons governed.
βασιλικός, ή, όν, adj., belonging to a king, royal, John iv. 46, 49 (R.V. marg.); Acts xii. 20, 21; James ii. 8.*
βασίλισσα, ης, ἡ, a queen.
βάσις, εως, ἡ (βαίνω), prop. a going, hence the foot, Acts iii. 7.*
βασκαίνω, ανῶ, to bewitch, bring under malign influence, "fascinate," Gal. iii. 1.*
βαστάζω, άσω, to lift, lift up; often with the sense of bearing away. Thus, (1) to carry, a burden, as Luke xiv. 27; tidings, as Acts ix. 15; (2) to take on oneself, as disease or weaknesses, Rom. xv. 1; condemnation, Gal. v. 10; reproach, Gal. vi. 17; (3) to bear with or endure, Rev. ii. 2; (4) to take away, Matt. viii. 17; John iii. 6.
βάτος, ου, ὁ, ἡ, a thorn-bush or bramble, Luke vi. 44; Acts vii. 30, 35. "The Bush," Mark xii. 26; Luke xx. 37, denotes the section of the O.T. so-called (Exod. iii.).*
βάτος, ου, ὁ (Heb.), a bath, or Jewish measure for liquids containing 7½ gallons, Luke xvi. 6.*
βάτραχος, ου, ὁ, a frog, Rev. xvi. 13.*
βαττο-λογέω, ῶ (prob. from βατ-, an unmeaning sound; cf. βάρβαρος), to babble, talk to no purpose, Matt. vi. 7.*
βδέλυγμα, ατος, τό (cf. βδελύσσω), something unclean and abominable, an object of moral repugnance, Luke xvi. 15; spec. (as often in O.T.) idolatry, Rev. xvii. 4, 5, xxi. 27. "Abomination of desolation," Matt. xxiv. 15; Mark xiii. 14 (from Dan. ix. 27) refers to the pollution of the temple by some idolatrous symbol.*
βδελυκτός, ή, όν, disgusting, abominable, Tit. i. 16.*
βδελύσσω, ξω, to defile, only mid.; to loathe, Rom. ii. 22; and pass. perf. part., defiled, Rev. xxi. 8.*
βέβαιος, α, ον, stedfast, constant, firm.
βεβαιόω, ῶ, to confirm, to establish, whether of persons or things.
βεβαίωσις, εως, ἡ, confirmation, Phil. i. 7; Heb. vi. 16.*

βέβηλος, ον (βα- in βαίνω, "that on which any one may step"), common, unsanctified, profane, of things or persons.
βεβηλόω, ῶ, to make common, to profane, the Sabbath, Matt. xii. 5; the temple, Acts xxiv. 6.*
Βεελ-ζεβούλ, ὁ (Heb.), Beelzebul, "Lord of dung," a contemptuous play upon Beelzebub, "Lord of flies," the Ekronite deity (2 Kings i. 2), applied to Satan, as the ruler of the dæmons.
Βελίαλ, ὁ (Heb., perverseness, malice), or Βελίαρ (W. H.), perhaps "Lord of forests" or "thickets," a name for Satan, 2 Cor. vi. 15.*
βελόνη, ης, ἡ, a needle, Luke xviii. 25 (W. H.).*
βέλος, ους, τό (βάλλω), a missile, such as a javelin or dart, Eph. vi. 16.*
βελτίων, ον, ονος (a compar. of ἀγαθός), better; neut. as adv., 2 Tim. i. 18.*
Βεν-ιαμίν, ὁ (Heb., Ben = son), Benjamin.
Βερνίκη, ης, ἡ, Bernice.
Βέροια, ας, Berœa, Acts xvii. 10, 13.*
Βεροιαῖος, α, ον, Berœan, Acts xx. 4.*
Βηθ-, a Hebrew prefix to many local names, meaning house or abode of.
Βηθ-αβαρά, ᾶς, ἡ, Bethabara, "house of the ford," John i. 28. (W. H. read Bethany.)*
Βηθ-ανία, ας, ἡ, Bethany, "house of dates." There were two places of the name: (1) John xi., etc.; (2) on the Jordan (?), John i. 28. See Βηθαβαρά.
Βηθ εσδά, ᾶς, ἡ, Bethesda, "house of compassion," John v. 2.*
Βηθ-λεέμ, ἡ, Bethlehem, "house of bread."
Βηθ-σαϊδά, ἡ, Bethsaida, "house of hunting" or "fishing." There were two places of the name: one in Galilee, John xii. 21; the other on the east of the Jordan, Luke ix. 10.
Βηθ-φαγή, ἡ, Bethphage, "house of figs."
βῆμα, ατος, τό (βα- in βαίνω), a step, a space; βῆμα ποδός, a space for the foot, Acts vii. 5; a raised space or bench, tribunal, throne, judgment-seat.
βήρυλλος, ου, ὁ, ἡ, a beryl, a gem of greenish hue, Rev. xxi. 20.*
βία, as, ἡ, force, violence, Acts v. 26, xxi. 35, xxiv. 7 (W. H. omit), xxvii. 41.*

βιάζω, *to use violence;* mid., *to enter forcibly,* with εἰς, Luke xvi. 16 ; pass., *to suffer violence, to be assaulted,* Matt. xi. 12.*
βίαιος, α, ον, *violent,* Acts ii. 2.*
βιαστής, οῦ, ὁ, *one who employs force, a man of violence,* Matt. xi. 12.*
βιβλαρίδιον, ου, *a little book,* Rev. x. 2, 8 (not W. H.), 9, 10.*
βιβλίον, ου, τό (dim. of following), *a roll, book, volume,* as Luke iv. 17 ; Rev. v. 1. βιβλίον ἀποστασίου, a bill of divorcement, Matt. xix. 7 ; Mark x. 4.
βίβλος, ου, ὁ, *a written book, roll,* or *volume.* The word means the inner bark or rind, of which ancient books were made.
βιβρώσκω (βρο-), perf. βέβρωκα, *to eat,* John vi. 13.*
Βιθυνία, ας, ἡ, *Bithynia.*
βίος, ου, ὁ, (1) *life,* as Luke viii. 14; (2) *means of life, livelihood,* as Luke viii. 43 ; (3) *goods* or *property,* as Luke xv. 12 ; 1 John iii. 17. **Syn. 54.**
βιόω, ῶ, *to pass one's life,* 1 Pet. iv. 2.*
βίωσις, εως, ἡ, *manner* or *habit of life,* Acts xxvi. 4.*
βιωτικός, ή, όν, *of* or *belonging to* (this) *life,* Luke xxi. 34 ; 1 Cor. vi. 3, 4.*
βλαβερός, adj., *hurtful,* 1 Tim. vi. 9.*
βλάπτω (βλαβ-), βλάψω, *to hurt* or *injure,* Mark xvi. 18 (W. H. omit); Luke iv. 35.*
βλαστάνω (or βλαστάω, Mark iv. 27, W. H.). βλαστήσω, intrans., *to sprout, to spring up, to put forth buds,* Matt. xiii. 26 ; Mark iv. 27 ; Heb. ix. 4 ; trans., *to bring forth* (καρπόν), James v. 18.*
Βλάστος, ου, ὁ, *Blastus,* Acts xii. 20.*
βλασφημέω, ῶ, *to speak abusively, to rail,* abs., as Acts xiii. 45 ; *to calumniate, speak evil of, blaspheme,* with acc., rarely εἰς ; often of men or things. Spec. of God, Rev. xvi. 11 ; the Holy Spirit, Luke xii. 10 ; the Divine name or doctrine, 1 Tim. vi. 1.
βλασφημία, ας, ἡ, *evil-speaking, reviling, blasphemy.*
βλάσφημος, ον, *slanderous;* subst., *a reviler.*
βλέμμα, ατος, τό, *seeing, the thing seen,* 2 Pet. ii. 8.*
βλέπω, ψω, *to see, to have the power of seeing, to look at, behold;* with εἰς, *to look to,* Matt. xxii. 16 ; Mark xii. 14; with ἵνα or μή, *to take care* (once without, Mark xiii. 9) ; with ἀπό, *to beware of;* once with κατά (acc.), geographically, *to look towards,* Acts xxvii. 12. **Syn. 5.**
βλητέος, έα, έον, a verbal adj. (βάλλω), *that ought to be put,* Mark ii. 22 (W. H. omit) ; Luke v. 38.*
Βοανεργές (W.H.,-ηρ-), (Heb.,) *Boanerges,* "Sons of thunder," Mark iii. 17.
βοάω, ῶ (βοή), *to shout* for joy, Gal. iv. 27 ; *to cry* for grief, Acts viii. 7 ; *to publish openly, to cry aloud;* with πρός (acc.), *to appeal to,* Luke xviii. 7, 38.
βοή, ῆς, ἡ, *a loud cry,* James v. 4.*
βοήθεια, ας, ἡ, *help, succour,* Acts xxvii. 17 ; Heb. iv. 16.*
βοηθέω, ῶ, *to go to the help of, to succour* (dat.).
βοηθός, οῦ, ὁ, ἡ (properly adj.), *a helper,* Heb. xiii. 6.*
βόθυνος, ου, ὁ, *a hole, ditch, well.*
βολή, ῆς, ἡ, *a throwing.* λίθου βολή, *a stone's throw,* Luke xxii. 41.*
βολίζω, σω, *to heave the lead, to fathom,* Acts xxvii. 28.*
βολίς, ίδος, ἡ, *a weapon thrown, as a dart* or *javelin,* Heb. xii. 20 (W. H. omit).*
Βοόζ, ὁ (Heb.), *Booz* or *Boaz.*
βόρβορος, ου, ὁ, *dirt, mire, filth,* 2 Pet. ii. 22.*
Βορρᾶς, ᾶ, ὁ (*Boreas,* the north wind), *the North,* Luke xiii. 29 ; Rev. xxi. 13.*
βόσκω, ήσω, *to tend, to tend in feeding,* as Matt. viii. 33 ; John xxi. 15, 17 ; mid., *to feed, graze,* as Mark v. 11.
Βοσόρ, ὁ (Heb., *Beor*), *Bosor,* 2 Pet. ii. 15.*
βοτάνη, ης, ἡ (βόσκω), *herbage, pasturage,* Heb. vi. 7.*
βότρυς, υος, ὁ, *a cluster of grapes,* Rev. xiv. 18.*
βουλευτής, οῦ, ὁ, *a counsellor, a senator,* Mark xv. 43 ; Luke xxiii. 50.*
βουλεύω, σω, *to advise,* N.T. mid. only ; (1) *to consult, to deliberate,* with εἰ, Luke xiv. 31 ; (2) *to resolve on* or *purpose,* with inf., Acts v. 33, xv. 37 (W. H. in both passages read βούλομαι), xxvii. 39 ; ἵνα, John xi. 53 (W. H.), xii. 10 ; acc., 2 Cor. i. 17.*
βουλή, ῆς, ἡ, *a design, decree, purpose, plan.*

βούλημα, ατος, τό (βούλομαι), the thing willed or purposed, Acts xxvii. 43; Rom. ix. 19; 1 Pet. iv. 3 (W. H.).
βούλομαι, 2nd pers. sing. βούλει, aug. with έ or ή, to will, as (1) to be willing, to incline to, Mark xv. 15; (2) to intend, Matt. i. 19; (3) to aim at, 1 Tim. vi. 9. Generally with inf., sometimes understood, as James i. 18; with subj., John xviii. 39. Syn. 3.
βουνός, οῦ, ὁ, a hill, rising ground, Luke iii. 5; xxiii. 30.*
βοῦς, βοός (of-), δ, ή, an animal of the ox kind, male or female.
βραβεῖον, ου, τό, the prize, in the games, 1 Cor. ix. 24; Phil. iii. 14.*
βραβεύω (lit., to act as arbiter in the games), rule, arbitrate, Col. iii. 15.*
βραδύνω, νῶ (βραδύς), to delay, to be slow, 1 Tim. iii. 15; 2 Pet. iii. 9 (gen.).*
βραδυ-πλοέω, ῶ, to sail slowly, Acts xxvii. 7.*
βραδύς, εῖα, ύ, slow; dat. of sphere, Luke xxiv. 25; εἰς, James i. 19.*
βραδυτής, τῆτος, ή, tardiness, 2 Pet. iii. 9.*
βραχίων, ονος, ὁ, the arm; met., strength, Luke i. 51; John xii. 38; Acts xiii. 17.*
βραχύς, εῖα, ύ, short, little; only neut.; of time, Luke xxii. 58; Acts v. 34; place, Acts xxvii. 28. διὰ βραχέων, Heb. xiii. 22, in few words. βραχύ τι, John vi. 7, of quantity, a little; Heb. ii. 7, 9, for a short time, or in a small degree.*
βρέφος, ους, τό, a child unborn, Luke i. 41, 44; a babe, as Luke ii. 12, 16; 2 Tim. iii. 15.
βρέχω, ξω, to moisten, Luke vii. 38, 44; to rain, to send rain, Matt. v. 45; Luke xvii. 29; impers., James v. 17; intrans., Rev. xi. 6.*
βροντή, ῆς, ή, thunder.
βροχή, ῆς, ή (βρέχω), rain, Matt. vii. 25, 27.*
βρόχος, ου, ὁ, a noose or snare, 1 Cor. vii. 35.*
βρυγμός, οῦ, ὁ, a grinding or gnashing, as Matt. viii. 12.
βρύχω, ξω, to grind or gnash, as the teeth, for rage or pain, Acts vii. 54.*
βρύω, σω, to send forth, as a fountain, James iii. 11.*

βρῶμα, ατος, τό (see βιβρώσκω), food of any kind.
βρώσιμος, ον, eatable, Luke xxiv. 41.*
βρῶσις, εως, ή, (1) the act of eating, as 1 Cor. viii. 4; (2) corrosion, Matt. vi. 19, 20; (3) food.
βυθίζω, σω, to drown, trans. and fig., 1 Tim. vi. 9; mid., to sink, Luke v. 7.*
βυθός, οῦ, ὁ, the deep, the sea, 2 Cor. xi. 25.*
βυρσεύς, έως, a skin-dresser, a tanner, Acts ix. 43, x. 6, 32.*
βύσσινος, η, ον, made of byssus, fine linen, Rev. xviii. 12 (W. H.), 16, xix. 8, 14.
βύσσος, ου, ή, byssus, a species of flax, and of linen manufactured from it, highly prized for its softness, whiteness, and delicacy, Luke xvi. 19.*
βωμός, οῦ, ὁ, an altar, Acts xvii. 23.*

Γ.

Γ, γ, γάμμα, gamma, g hard, the third letter of the Greek alphabet. In numeral value, γ´ = 3; γ,= 3000.
Γαββαθᾶ, ή (Heb., Aram. form), Gabbatha; an elevated place or tribunal, John xix. 13. See λιθόστρωτον.*
Γαβριήλ, ὁ (Heb., man of God), the archangel Gabriel, Luke i. 19, 26.*
γάγγραινα, ης, ή, a gangrene, mortification, 2 Tim. ii. 17.*
Γάδ, ὁ (Heb.), Gad, Rev. vii. 5.*
Γαδαρηνός, ή, όν, belonging to Gadara. See Γεργεσηνός.
γάζα, ης, ή (Persian), treasure, as of a government, Acts viii. 27.*
Γάζα, ης, ή (Heb.), Gaza, a strong city of the ancient Philistines in the W. of Palestine, Acts viii. 26. (The adj., ἔρημος, desert, refers to ὁδός.)*
γαζο-φυλάκιον, ου, τό, a place for the guardianship of treasure, treasury; a part of the temple so called, Mark xii. 41, 43; Luke xxi. 1; John viii. 20.*
Γάϊος, ου, ὁ (Lat.), Gaius, or Caius. There are four of the name in N.T., Acts xix. 29, xx. 4; 1 Cor. i. 14; 3 John 1.
γάλα, ακτος, τό, milk, lit., 1 Cor. ix. 7; fig., for the elements of Christian knowledge, 1 Cor. iii. 2; Heb. v. 12, 13; 1 Pet. ii. 2.*

Γαλάτης, ου, ὁ, a *Galatian*, Gal. iii. 1.*
Γαλατία, as, ἡ, *Galatia*, or *Gallogræcia*, a province of Asia Minor.
Γαλατικός, ή, όν, *belonging to Galatia*, Acts xvi. 6; xviii. 23.*
γαλήνη, ης, ἡ, *serenity, calm*, Matt. viii. 26; Mark iv. 39; Luke viii. 24.*
Γαλιλαία, as, ἡ (from Heb.), *Galilee*, the N. division of Palestine.
Γαλιλαῖος, αία, αῖον, *of* or *belonging to Galilee*.
Γαλλίων, ωνος, ὁ, *Gallio*, a proconsul of Achaia, Acts xviii.*
Γαμαλιήλ, ὁ (Heb.), *Gamaliel*, Acts v. 34; xxii. 3.*
γαμέω, ῶ, ήσω, 1st aor. ἐγάμησα and ἔγημα, abs. or trans. (with acc.), *to marry;* active properly of the man; pass. and mid. of the woman, with dat., 1 Cor. vii. 39; Mark x. 12 (W. H., ἄλλον for rec. ἄλλῳ); but in N.T. the act. also is used of the woman, as 1 Cor. vii. 28, 34.
γαμίζω, or γαμίσκω, *to give in marriage* (a daughter), rec. only Mark xii. 25; W. H. add Matt. xxii. 30; Luke xvii. 27, xx. 35; 1 Cor. vii. 38.*
γάμος, ον, ὁ, *marriage*, spec. *a marriage feast*, sing. or plur. See § 240.
γάρ (γε ἄρα), "truly then," a causal particle or conjunction, *for*, introducing a reason for the thing previously said. Used in questions to intensify the inquiry; often with other particles. For the special points of γάρ, see § 407.
γαστήρ, τρός (sync.) ἡ, (1) *the womb*, as Matt. i. 18; (2) *the stomach*, only Tit. i. 12; from Epimenides, "idle bellies," *gluttons*.
γέ, a particle indicating emphasis, *at least, indeed*. Sometimes used alone, as Rom. viii. 32; 1 Cor. iv. 8; generally in connection with other particles, as ἀλλά, ἄρα, εἰ. εἰ δὲ μήγε, *stronger than* εἰ δὲ μή, *if otherwise indeed;* καίγε, *and at least, and even;* καίτοιγε, *though indeed;* μενοῦνγε, *yea, indeed;* μήτιγε, "*to say nothing of*," 1 Cor. vi. 3.
Γεδεών, ὁ (Heb.), *Gideon*, Heb. xi. 32.*
Γε-έννα, ης, ἡ (Heb., *Valley of Hinnom*), met., *place of punishment* in the future world, Matt. x. 28, etc. Sometimes with τοῦ πυρός, as Matt. v. 22. Compare 2 Kings xxiii. 10.

Γεθ-σημανῆ, or -νεί (W. H.), ἡ (Heb., *oil-press*), *Gethsemane*, a small field at the foot of the Mount of Olives, over the brook Cedron; Matt. xxvi. 36; Mark xiv. 32.*
γείτων, ονος, ὁ, ἡ, *a neighbour*, Luke xiv. 12, xv. 6, 9; John ix. 8.*
γελάω, ῶ, άσω, *to laugh, to be merry, rejoice*, Luke vi. 21, 25.*
γέλως, ωτος, ὁ, *laughter, mirth*, James iv. 9.*
γεμίζω, σω, *to fill*, with acc. and gen. (also ἀπό or ἐκ); pass. abs., *to be full*, Mark iv. 37; Luke xiv. 23.
γέμω, only in pres. and impf., *to be full of*, with gen. (ἐκ, Matt. xxiii. 25; perhaps acc., Rev. xvii. 3).
γενεά, ᾶς, ἡ, *generation*, as (1) *offspring, race, descent;* (2) *the people of any given time;* (3) *an age of the world's duration;* εἰς γενεὰς καὶ γενεάς (W.H.), *unto generations and generations* (R.V.), Luke i. 50.
γενεα-λογέω, ῶ, *to reckon a genealogy* or *pedigree*, pass. with ἐκ, Heb. vii. 6.*
γενεα-λογία, as, fem., *genealogy*, N.T. plur., 1 Tim. i. 4; Tit. iii. 9; prob. of Gnostic speculations on the origin of being.*
γενεσία, ῶν, τά, *the festivities of a birthday, a birthday*, Matt. xiv. 6; Mark vi. 21.*
γένεσις, εως, ἡ, *birth, genealogy*, Matt. i. 1. (W. H. add Matt. i. 18, Luke i. 14, for rec. γέννησις). James i. 23: τὸ πρόσωπον τῆς γενέσεως αὐτοῦ, *the countenance of his birth*, or, as A.V., R.V., "his natural face." James iii. 6: τὸν τροχὸν τῆς γενέσεως, *the wheel of nature* (R.V.).*
γενετή, ῆς, ἡ, *birth*, John ix. 1.*
γένημα, ατος, τό. See γέννημα.
γεννάω, ῶ, ήσω, *to beget, give birth to, produce, effect;* pass., *to be begotten, born* (often in John, of spiritual renewal).
γέννημα, ατος, τό, (1) *progeny, generation*, as Matt. iii. 7; (2) *produce* generally, as Matt. xxvi. 29; fig., *fruit, result*, as 2 Cor. ix. 10. In sense (2) W. H. always read γένημα.
Γεννησαρέτ (Heb., in Aram. form), *Gennesareth* (*Chinnereth*, or *Chinneroth*, in O.T.), a region of Galilee, with village or town of the same name. Used of the adjacent lake, as Luke v. 1.

γέννησις, εως, ή. See γένεσις.*
γεννητός, ή, όν, verb. adj., *born, brought forth*, Matt. xi. 11; Luke vii. 28.*
γένος, ους, τό, (1) *offspring;* (2) *lineage;* (3) *nation;* (4) *kind* or *species*.
Γεργεσηνός, ή, όν, or Γερασηνός, *Gergesene, belonging to Gergesa* or *Gerasa*. The copies vary between these forms and Γαδαρηνός, Matt. viii. 28; Mark v. 1; Luke viii. 26, 37.*
γερουσία, as, ἡ (γέρων), *an assembly of elders, senate*, Acts v. 21.*
γέρων, οντος, ὁ, *an old man*, John iii. 4.*
γεύω, *to make to taste*, only mid. in N.T.; *to taste*, as abs., *to take food*, Acts x. 10; or with obj., gen., or acc. See § 249, *a*, (2). Fig., *to experience*, as Matt. xvi. 28; once with ὅτι, 1 Pet. ii. 3.
γεωργέω, ῶ, *to cultivate* or *till the earth*, Heb. vi. 7.*
γεώργιον, ου, τό, *a tilled field*, fig., 1 Cor., iii. 9.*
γεωργός, οῦ, ὁ, *one who tills the ground, a husbandman, a vine-dresser*.
γῆ, γῆς, ἡ, contr. for γέα or γαῖα, *land* or *earth*, as (1) *the material soil;* (2) *the producing soil, the ground;* (3) *land*, as opposed to sea; (4) *earth*, as opposed to heaven, often involving suggestions of human weakness and sin; (5) *region* or *territory*.
γῆρας, (αος), ως, τό, dat. -ᾳ, *old age*, Luke i. 36. (W. H. have γήρει fr. γῆρος).*
γηράσκω, or γηράω, άσω, *to become old*, John xxi. 18; Heb. viii. 13.*
γίνομαι, for γίγνομαι. See § 94, 8, *a*. γενήσομαι, ἐγενόμην and ἐγενήθην, γέγονα (with pres. force) and γεγένημαι, *to become*, as (1) *to begin to be*, used of persons, *to be born*, John v. iii. 58; of the works of creation, *to be made*, John i. 3, 10; and of other works, *to be wrought* or *performed*. So, *to pass out of one state into another, to grow into, to be changed into*, John ii. 9; often with εἰς, Luke xiii. 19. (2) Of ordinary or extraordinary occurrences, *to happen, to take place, to be done;* of the day, the night, Mark vi. 2; of thunder, earthquake, calm, etc.; of feasts or public solemnities, *to be held* or *celebrated;* frequently in the phrase καὶ ἐγένετο,

and it came to pass (with καί, or following verb, or inf.); also, μὴ γένοιτο, *let it never happen!* or *God forbid!* (3) With adj. or predicative subst., *to become*, where quality, character, or condition is specified; often in prohibitions, μὴ γίνου, μὴ γίνεσθε, *become not*, as Matt. vi. 16. (4) With the cases of substantives and the prepositions, the verb forms many phrases, to be interpreted according to the meaning of the case or prep. See SYNTAX. For the distinction between γίνομαι and other copulative verbs, see Syn. 1.
γινώσκω, or γιγνώσκω (see § 94, 8, *b*), γνώσομαι, 2nd aor. ἔγνων (imper. γνῶθι), perf. ἔγνωκα, (1) *to become aware of, to perceive*, with acc., (2) *to know, to perceive, understand*, with acc. or ὅτι, or acc. and inf., or τί interrog.; Ἑλληνιστὶ γ., *to understand Greek*, Acts xxi. 37; *to be conscious of*, by experience, as 2 Cor. v. 21; (3) *to know carnally* (Heb.), Matt. i. 25; Luke i. 34; (4) specially of the fellowship between Christians and the Divine Being, 1 Cor. viii. 3; Matt. vii. 23 (negatively); John xvii. 3; Heb. viii. 11; Phil. iii. 10, etc. Syn. 4.
γλεῦκος, ους, τό, *sweet* or *new wine*, Acts ii. 13.*
γλυκύς, εῖα, ύ, *sweet*, James iii. 11, 12; of water, opposed to "bitter" and "salt," Rev. x. 9, 10.*
γλῶσσα, ης, ἡ, (1) *the tongue;* (2) *a language;* (3) *a nation* or *people* distinguished by their language.
γλωσσό-κομον, ου, neut., *a little box* or *case for money*, John xii. 6, xiii. 29 (orig. from holding the "tongue-pieces" of flutes, etc.).*
γναφεύς, έως, ὁ *a fuller, cloth-dresser*, Mark ix. 3.*
γνήσιος, α, ον (sync. from γενήσιος), *legitimate, genuine, true*, 1 Tim. i. 2; Tit. i. 4; Phil. iv. 3; τὸ γνήσιον, *sincerity*, 2 Cor. viii. 8.* Adv. -ως, *sincerely, naturally*, Phil. ii. 20.*
γνόφος, ου, ὁ, *a dense cloud, darkness*, Heb. xii. 18.*
γνώμη, ης, ἡ (γνο- in γίνωσκω), *opinion, judgment, intention*.
γνωρίζω, ίσω or ιῶ, (1) *to make known, to declare* (with acc. and dat., ὅτι or τί

interrog., Col. i. 27); (2) intrans., *to know*, only Phil. i. 22.
γνῶσις, εως, ἡ, (1) subj., *knowledge*, with gen. of obj. (gen. subj., Rom. xi. 33); (2) obj., *science, doctrine, wisdom*, as Luke xi. 52.
γνώστης, ου, ὁ, *one who knows, an expert*, Acts xxvi. 3.*
γνωστός, ή, όν, verb. adj., *known*, as Acts ii. 14, iv. 10; *knowable*, Rom. i. 19; *notable*, Acts iv. 16. οἱ γνωστοί, *one's acquaintance*, Luke ii. 44; τὸ γνωστόν, *knowledge*, Rom. i. 19.
γογγύζω, ύσω, *to murmur* in a low voice, John xii. 32; discontentedly, *to grumble*, as 1 Cor. x. 10, with acc., or περί, gen., πρός, acc., κατά, gen.
γογγυσμός, οῦ, ὁ, *muttering*, John vii. 12; *murmuring*, Acts vi. 1; Phil. ii. 14; 1 Pet. iv. 9.*
γογγυστής, ου, ὁ, *a murmurer, complainer*, Jude 16.*
γόης, ητος, ὁ (γοάω, *to moan*), *an enchanter, an impostor*, 2 Tim. iii. 13.*
Γολγοθά (Heb. in Aram. form), *Golgotha*, "the place of a skull" (prob. from its shape); *Calvary*. See κρανίον.
Γόμορρα, ας, ἡ, and ων, τά, *Gomorrha*.
γόμος, ου, ὁ (γέμω), (1) *a burden*, e.g., of a ship, Acts xxi. 3; (2) *wares* or *merchandise*, Rev. xviii. 11, 12.*
γονεύς, έως, ὁ (γεν- in γίγνομαι,) *a parent*, only in plural.
γόνυ, ατος, τό, *the knee;* often in plur. after τιθέναι or κάμπτειν, *to put* or *bend the knees, to kneel*, in devotion.
γονυπετέω, ῶ (πίπτω), *to fall down on one's knees, to kneel to* (acc.).
γράμμα, ατος, τό (γράφω), (1) *a letter of the alphabet*. Gal. vi. 11 : *in what large letters*, perhaps noting emphasis; *letter*, as opposed to spirit, Rom. ii. 29, etc.; (2) *a writing*, such as *a bill* or *an epistle*, as Luke xvi. 6, 7; τὰ ἱερὰ γράμματα, 2 Tim. iii. 15, *the holy writings*, or *the Scriptures;* (3) plur., *literature, learning* generally, John vii. 15.
γραμματεύς, έως, ὁ, (1) *a clerk, secretary, a scribe*, Acts xix. 35; (2) one of that class among the Jews who copied and interpreted the O.T. Scriptures (see νομικός); (3) met., *a man of learning generally*, 1 Cor. i. 20; Matt. xiii. 52, etc.

γραπτός, ή, όν, verb. adj., *written, inscribed*, Rom. ii. 15.*
γραφή, ῆς, ἡ, (1) *a writing;* (2) spec., ἡ γραφή or αἱ γραφαί, *the Scriptures, writings* of the O.T.; (3) *a particular passage*.
γράφω, ψω, γέγραφα, *to grave, write, inscribe*. ἐγράφη, γέγραπται, or γεγραμμένον ἐστί, a formula of quotation, *It is written*. Often with dat. of pers., as Mark x. 5.
γραώδης, ες, (γραῦς, ῆδ), *old-womanish, foolish*, 1 Tim. iv. 7.*
γρηγορέω, ῶ (from ἐγρήγορα, perf. of ἐγείρω), *to keep awake, watch, be vigilant*.
γυμνάζω (γυμνός), *to exercise, train*, 1 Tim. iv. 7; Heb. v. 14, xii. 11; 2 Pet. ii. 14.*
γυμνασία, ας, ἡ, *exercise, training*, 1 Tim. iv. 8.*
γυμνητεύω, or -ιτεύω (W. H.), *to be naked* or *poorly clad*, 1 Cor. iv. 11.*
γυμνός, ή, όν, (1) *naked, ill-clad, having only an inner garment;* (2) *bare*, i.e., *open* or *manifest*, Heb. iv. 13; (3) *mere*, 1 Cor. xv. 37.
γυμνότης, τητος, ἡ, (1) *nakedness;* (2) *scanty clothing*.
γυναικάριον, ου, τό (dim.), *a silly woman*, 2 Tim. iii. 6.*
γυναικεῖος, α, ον, *womanish, female;* 1 Pet. iii. 7, *the weaker* vessel.*
γυνή, γυναικός, voc. γύναι, ἡ, (1) *a woman;* (2) *a wife*. The voc. is the form of ordinary address, often used in reverence and honour. Compare John ii. 4 and xix. 26.
Γώγ, ὁ, a proper name, *Gog*. In Ezek. xxxviii. 5, king of Magog, possibly Scandinavia; hence, in Rev. xx. 8, of a people far remote from Palestine, probably in the N.
γωνία, ας, ἡ, *a corner*, as Matt. vi. 5, xxi. 42 (LXX.); met., *a secret place*, Acts xxvi. 26.

Δ.

Δ, δ, δέλτα, *delta, d*, the fourth letter of the Greek alphabet. As a numeral, δ'= 4; δ, = 4000.
Δαβίδ, also Δαυΐδ, Δανείδ (W. H.) ὁ, (Heb.), *David*, king of Israel. Ὁ

υἱὸς Δ., *the Son of David*, an appellation of the Messiah ; ἐν Δ., *in David*, *i.e.*, in the Psalms, Heb. iv. 7.
δαιμονίζομαι (see δαίμων), 1st aor. part., δαιμονισθείς, *to be possessed by a demon*.
δαιμόνιον, ίου, τό (orig. adj.), *a demon* or *evil spirit*. δαιμόνιον ἔχειν, *to have a demon* or *to be a demoniac*. **Syn. 53.**
δαιμονιώδης, ες, *resembling a demon*, *demoniacal*, James iii. 15.*
δαίμων, ονος, ὁ, ἡ, in classic Greek, any spirit superior to man ; hence often of the inferior deities ; in N.T., *an evil spirit*, *a demon*. (W. H. have the word only in one passage, Matt. viii. 31.) δαιμόνιον is generally used. **Syn. 53.**
δάκνω, *to bite*, Gal. v. 15.*
δάκρυ, υος, or δάκρυον, ύου, τό, *a tear*.
δακρύω, σω, *to weep*, John xi. 35.*
δακτύλιος, ου, ὁ (δάκτυλος), *a ring for the finger*, Luke xv. 22.*
δάκτυλος, ου, ὁ, *a finger*. ἐν δακτύλῳ Θεοῦ, met., *by the power of God*, Luke xi. 20. Comp. Matt. xii. 28.
Δαλμανουθά, ἡ, *Dalmanutha*, a town or village near Magdala, Mark viii. 10.*
Δαλματία, ας, ἡ, *Dalmatia*, a part of Illyricum near Macedonia, 2 Tim. iv. 10.*
δαμάζω, σω, *to subdue, tame*, Mark v. 4 ; James iii. 7, 8.*
δάμαλις, εως, ἡ, *a heifer*, Heb. ix. 13.*
Δάμαρις, ιδος, ἡ, *Damaris*, Acts xvii. 34.*
Δαμασκηνός, ή, όν, *belonging to Damascus*, 2 Cor. xi. 32.*
Δαμασκός, οῦ, ἡ, *Damascus*.
δανείζω, *to lend*, Luke vi. 34, 35 ; mid., *to borrow*, Matt. v. 42.*
δάνειον, ου, τό, *a debt*, Matt. xviii. 27.*
δανειστής, οῦ, ὁ, *a lender, a creditor*, Luke vii. 41.*
Δανιήλ, ὁ (Heb.), *Daniel*, Matt. xxiv. 15 ; Mark xiii. 14 (not W. H.).*
δαπανάω, ῶ, ήσω, *to spend*, Mark v. 26 ; trans., *to bear expense for* (ἐπί, dat.), Acts xxi. 24 ; (ὑπέρ, gen.), 2 Cor. xii. 15 ; *to consume in luxury, to waste*, Luke xv. 14 ; James iv. 3.*
δαπάνη, ης, ἡ, *expense, cost*, Luke xiv. 28.*
δέ, an adversative and distinctive particle, *but, now, moreover*, etc. See § 404, ii., and μέν.
δέησις, εως, ἡ, *supplication, prayer*. **Syn. 38.**

δεῖ, impers., see § 101, *it needs, one must, it ought, it is right* or *proper*, with inf. (expressed or implied), as Matt. xvi. 21 ; Acts iv. 12 ; Mark xiii. 14. **Syn. 12.**
δεῖγμα, ατος (δείκνυμι), *an example, a specimen*, Jude 7.*
δειγματίζω, σω, *to make an example* or *spectacle of* (as disgrace), Col. ii. 15, Matt. i. 19 (W. H.).*
δείκνυμι and **δεικνύω** (see § 114), (1) *to present to sight, to show, to teach* (acc. and dat.) ; (2) *to prove* (acc. and ἐκ), *to show by words* (ὅτι), Matt. xvi. 21 ; inf., Acts x. 28.
δειλία, ας, ἡ, *timidity*, 2 Tim. i. 7.*
δειλιάω, ῶ, *to shrink for fear, to be afraid*, John xiv. 27.*
δειλός, ἡ, όν, *timid, cowardly*, Matt. viii. 26 ; Mark iv. 40 ; Rev. xxi. 8.* **Syn. 33.**
δεῖνα, ὁ, ἡ, τό, gen. δεῖνος, pron., *a certain person, such a one*, Matt. xxvi. 18.*
δεινῶς, adv. (δεινός, *vehement*), *greatly, vehemently*, Matt. viii. 6 ; Luke xi. 53.*
δειπνέω, ῶ, *to take the* δεῖπνον, *to banquet*, Luke xvii. 8, xxii. 20 ; 1 Cor. xi. 25 ; met., of familiar intercourse, Rev. iii. 20.*
δεῖπνον, ου, τό, *the chief* or *evening meal, supper* (cf. ἄριστον) ; κυριακὸν δεῖπνον, *the Lord's Supper*, 1 Cor. xi. 20.
δεισιδαιμονία, ας, ἡ, *religion*, prob. *superstition*, Acts xxv. 19.*
δεισιδαίμων, ονος (δείδω, *to fear*), adj., *devoutly disposed, addicted to worship*. Acts xvii. 22. See § 323, c.*
δέκα, οἱ, αἱ, τά, *ten;* in Rev. ii. 10, *a ten days' tribulation*, *i.e.*, brief.
δεκα-δύο (not in W. H.), more frequently δώδεκα, *twelve*, Acts xix. 7, xxiv. 11.*
δεκα-πέντε, *fifteen*.
Δεκά-πολις, εως, ἡ, *Decapolis*, a district E. of Jordan comprising ten towns. It is uncertain what they all were, but they included Gadara, Hippo, Pella, and Scythopolis.
δεκα-τέσσαρες, α, ων, *fourteen*.
δεκάτη, ης, ἡ, *a tenth part, the tithe*, Heb. vii. 2, 4, 8, 9.*
δέκατος, η, ον, ordinal, *tenth*. τὸ δέκατον, Rev. xi. 13, *the tenth part*.
δεκατόω, ῶ, *to receive tithe of*, acc., Heb. vii. 6 ; pass., *to pay tithe*, Heb. vii. 9.*

δεκτός, ή, όν (verbal adj. from δέχομαι), *accepted, acceptable,* Luke iv. 19, 24; Acts x. 35; 2 Cor. vi. 2; Phil. iv. 18.*
δελεάζω (δέλεαρ, *a bait*), *to take* or *entice,* as with a bait, James i. 14; 2 Pet. ii. 14, 18.*
δένδρον, ου, τό, *a tree.*
δεξιό-λαβος, ου, ὁ, "holding in the right hand;" plur., *spearmen,* Acts xxiii. 23.*
δεξιός, ά, όν, *the right,* opp. to ἀριστερός, *the left.* ἡ δεξιά, *the right hand;* τὰ δεξιά, *the right-hand side;* ἐκ δεξιῶν, *on the right* (see § **293,** 1); δεξιὰς διδόναι, *to give the right hand,* i.e., *to receive to friendship* or *fellowship.*
δέομαι, 1st aor. ἐδεήθην, *to have need of* (gen.), as mid. of δέω (see δεῖ); *to make request of* (gen.); *to beseech, pray,* abs., or with εἰ, ἵνα, or ὅπως, of purpose.
δέον, οντος, τό (particip. of δεῖ, as subst.), *the becoming* or *needful;* with ἐστί = δεῖ. Plur., 1 Tim. v. 13.
δέος, ους, τό (W. H.), *awe,* Heb. xii. 28.*
Δερβαῖος, ου, ὁ, *of Derbe,* Acts xx. 4.*
Δέρβη, ης, ἡ, *Derbe,* a city of Lycaonia, Acts xiv. 6, 20, xvi. 1.*
δέρμα, ατος, τό (δέρω), *an animal's skin,* Heb. xi. 37.*
δερμάτινος, η, ον, *made of skin, leathern,* Matt. iii. 4; Mark i. 6.*
δέρω, 1st aor. ἔδειρα, 2nd fut. pass. δαρήσομαι, *to scourge, to beat,* so as to flay off the skin. ἀέρα δέρων, 1 Cor. ix. 26, *beating air.*
δεσμεύω, σω, *to bind,* as a prisoner, Acts xxii. 4; as a bundle, Matt. xxiii. 4.*
δεσμέω, ῶ, *to bind,* Luke viii. 29.*
δέσμη, ης, ἡ, *a bundle,* Matt. xiii. 30.*
δέσμιος, ίου, ὁ, *one bound, a prisoner.*
δεσμός, οῦ, ὁ (δέω), *a bond,* sing. only in Mark vii. 35, ὁ δεσμὸς τῆς γλώσσης, and Luke xiii. 16; plur., δεσμοί or (τὰ) δεσμά, *bonds* or *imprisonment.*
δεσμο-φύλαξ, ακος, ὁ, *a jailor,* Acts xvi. 23, 27, 36.*
δεσμωτήριον, ίου, τό, *a prison,* Matt. xi. 2; Acts v. 21, 23, xvi. 26.*
δεσμώτης, ου, ὁ, *a prisoner,* Acts xxvii. 1, 42.*
δεσπότης, ου, ὁ, *a foreign lord* or *prince, a master,* as 1 Tim. vi. 1; applied to God, Luke ii. 29; Acts iv. 24; Jude 4; Rev. vi. 10; to Christ, 2 Pet. ii. 1. **Syn. 59.**
δεῦρο, adv., (1) of place, *here, hither;* used only as an imperative, *come hither,* as Matt. xix. 21; (2) of time, only Rom. i. 13.
δεῦτε, adv., as if plur. of δεῦρο (or contr. from δεῦρ' ἴτε), *come, come hither,* as Matt. iv. 19, xi. 28.
δευτεραῖος, αία, αῖον, *on the second day,* Acts xxviii. 13. See § **319.***
δευτερό-πρωτος, adj., *the second-first,* Luke vi. 1. See § **148,** and note.*
δεύτερος, α, ον, ordinal, *second* in number, as Matt. xxii. 26; in order, Matt. xxii. 39. τὸ δεύτερον or δεύτερον, adverbially, *the second time, again,* as 2 Cor. xiii. 2. So ἐκ δευτέρου, as Mark xiv. 72; ἐν τῷ δευτέρῳ, Acts vii. 13.
δέχομαι, 1st aor. ἐδεξάμην, dep., *to take, receive, accept, to receive* kindly, *to welcome,* persons, as Mark vi. 11; things (a doctrine, the kingdom of heaven), as Mark x. 15; 2 Cor. xi. 4.
δέω, *to want.* See δεῖ and δέομαι.
δέω, 1st aor., ἐδησα; perf., δέδεκα; pass., δέδεμαι; 1st aor. pass. inf., δεθῆναι, *to bind together,* bundles, as Acts x. 11; *to swathe* dead bodies for burial, as John xi. 44; *to bind* persons in bondage, as Matt. xxii. 13; Mark vi. 17; 2 Tim. ii. 9; fig., Matt. xviii. 18. δεδεμένος τῷ πνεύματι, Acts xx. 22, *bound in the spirit,* under an irresistible impulse.
δή, a particle indicating *certainty* or *reality,* and so augmenting the vivacity of a clause or sentence; *truly, indeed, by all means, therefore.* Used with other particles, δήποτε, δήπου, which see.
δῆλος, η, ον, *manifest, evident,* Matt. xxvi. 73; neut. sc., ἐστί, *it is plain,* with ὅτι, 1 Cor. xv. 27; Gal. iii. 11; 1 Tim. vi. 7 (W. H., R. V. omit).*
δηλόω, ῶ, *to manifest, to reveal, to bring to light; to imply* or *signify,* 1 Cor. i. 11, iii. 13; Col. i. 8; Heb. ix. 8, iii. 27; 1 Pet. i. 11; 2 Pet. i. 14.*
Δημᾶς, ᾶ, ὁ. *Demas,* Col. iv. 14; Philem. 24: 2 Tim. iv. 10.*
δημ-ηγορέω, ῶ, *to deliver a public oration* or *harangue;* with πρός, Acts xii. 21.*

Δημήτριος, ου, ὁ, *Demetrius*. Two of the name are mentioned, Acts xix. 24, 38; 3 John 12.*

δημι-ουργός, οῦ, ὁ ("a public worker"), *one who makes* or *is the author of* anything, Heb. xi. 10.*

δῆμος, ου, ὁ, *the people*, a multitude publicly convened, Acts xii. 22, xvii. 5, xix. 30, 33.* Syn. 73.

δημόσιος, α, ον, *public, common*, Acts v. 18. Dat. fem., as adv., δημοσίᾳ, *publicly*, Acts xvi. 37, xviii. 28, xx. 20.*

δηνάριον, ίου, τό, properly a Latin word (see § 154, *a*), *denarius*.

δή-ποτε, adv. with ᾧ, *at whatsoever time*, John v. 4 (W. H. omit).

δή-που, adv., *indeed, truly, verily*, Heb. ii. 16.*

διά, prep. (cognate with δύο, *two*; δίς, *twice*), *through*; (1) with gen., *through, during, by means of*; (2) with acc., *through, on account of, for the sake of*. See §§ 147, *a*, 299.

δια-βαίνω, *to pass through*, trans., Heb. xi. 29; or intrans., with πρός (person), Luke xvi. 26; εἰς (place), Acts xvi. 9.*

δια-βάλλω, *to accuse*, Luke xvi. 1.*

δια-βεβαιόω, ῶ, in mid., *to affirm, assert strongly*, 1 Tim. i. 7; Tit. iii. 8.*

δια-βλέπω, *to see through, to see clearly*, Matt. vii. 5; Luke vi. 42; Mark viii. 25 (W. H.).*

διάβολος, ου, ὁ (διαβάλλω, orig. adj.), *an accuser, a slanderer, an adversary*, 1 Tim. iii. 11; 2 Tim. iii. 3; Tit. ii. 3. ὁ διάβολος, *the accuser, the devil*, equivalent to the Hebrew *Satan*.

δι-αγγέλλω, *to tell, publish abroad, divulge*, Luke ix. 60; Acts xxi. 26; Rom. ix. 17.*

διά-γε, or διά γε (W. H.), *yet on account of*, Luke xi. 8.*

δια-γίνομαι, *to pass, elapse*, of time; in N.T. only 2nd aor. part., gen. abs., *having elapsed*, Mark xvi. 1; Acts xxv. 13, xxvii. 9.*

δια-γινώσκω, *to examine and know thoroughly*, judicially, Acts xxiii. 15, xxiv. 22.*

δια-γνωρίζω, *to publish abroad*, Luke ii. 17. (W. H., γνωρίζω.)*

διά-γνωσις, εως, ἡ, *judicial hearing, accurate knowledge*, Acts xxv. 21.*

δια-γογγύζω, *to murmur greatly*, Luke xv. 2, xix. 7.*

δια-γρηγορέω, ῶ, *to be fully* or *thoroughly awake*, Luke ix. 32.*

δι-άγω, *to lead* or *pass*, as time, life, 1 Tim. ii. 2 (βίον); Tit. iii. 3 (βίον omitted).*

δια-δέχομαι, *to succeed to*, Acts vii. 45.*

διά-δημα, ατος, τό (δέω), *a diadem, tiara*, or *crown*, Rev. xii. 3, xiii. 1, xix. 12.* Syn. 67.

δια-δίδωμι, *to distribute, divide*, Luke xi. 22, xviii. 22; John vi. 11; Acts iv. 35; Rev. xvii. 13 (W. H., δίδωμι).*

διά-δοχος, ου, ὁ, ἡ, *a successor*, Acts xxiv. 27.*

δια-ζώννυμι, *to gird, to gird up*, John xiii. 4, 5, xxi. 7.*

δια-θήκη, ης, ἡ (διατίθημι), (1) *a will* or *testament, a disposition*, as of property, *a dispensation*, Gal. iii. 15; Heb. ix. 16, 17; (2) *a compact* or *covenant* between God and man (cf. Gen. vi., ix., xv., xvii.; Exod. xxiv.; Deut. v., xxviii.). The two covenants mentioned, Gal. iv. 24; that of the O.T. is termed ἡ πρώτη δ., Heb. ix. 15; that of the N.T., ἡ καινὴ δ., Luke xxii. 20. The O.T. itself (ἡ παλαιὰ δ., 2 Cor. iii. 14) as containing the first, and the N.T. as containing the second, are each called διαθήκη.

δι-αίρεσις, εως, fem., *difference, diversity*, as the result of distribution, 1 Cor. xii. 4, 5, 6.*

δι-αιρέω, ῶ, *to divide, distribute*, Luke xv. 12; 1 Cor. xii. 11.*

δια-καθαρίζω, f. ιῶ, *to cleanse thoroughly*, Matt. iii. 12; Luke iii. 17.*

δια-κατ-ελέγχομαι, *to confute entirely*, Acts xviii. 28.*

διακονέω, ῶ, *to serve* or *wait upon*, especially at table; *to supply wants, to administer* or *distribute alms*, etc. (dat., pers.; acc., thing; occasionally abs.). Of prophets and apostles who *ministered* the Divine will, 1 Pet. i. 12; 2 Cor. iii. 3.

διακονία, ας, ἡ, *management*, as of a household, Luke x. 40; *ministering relief*, or *the relief ministered*, Acts xii. 25; 2 Cor. viii. 4; *ministry* or *service in the church of Christ*, frequently.

διάκονος, ου, ὁ, ἡ, a servant, specially at table, as Matt. xxiii. 11; Mark x. 43; one in God's service, a minister, as Rom. xiii. 4, xv. 8; one who serves in the church, deacon or deaconess, Phil. i. 1; 1 Tim. iii. 8, 12; Rom. xvi. 1. Syn. 60.
διακόσιοι, αι, α, card. numb., two hundred.
δι-ακούω, to hear thoroughly, Acts xxiii. 35.*
δια-κρίνω, to discern, to distinguish, make a distinction, as Acts xv. 9; 1 Cor. xi. 29. Mid. (aor., pass.), (1) to doubt, to hesitate, as Matt. xxi. 21; James i. 6; prob. Jude 22; (2) to dispute with, Acts xi. 2; Jude 9.
διά-κρισις, εως, ἡ, the act of distinction, discrimination, Rom. xiv. 1; 1 Cor. xii. 10; Heb. v. 14.*
δια-κωλύω, to forbid, to hinder, Matt. iii. 14.*
δια-λαλέω, ῶ, to discuss, Luke vi. 11; to spread abroad by speaking of, Luke i. 65.*
δια-λέγω, in mid., to discourse, to reason, to dispute, as Mark ix. 34; Acts xx. 7; Jude 9.
δια-λείπω, to cease, to intermit, Luke vii. 45.*
διά-λεκτος, ου, ἡ, speech, dialect, language, Acts i. 19, ii. 6, 8, xxi. 40, xxii. 2, xxvi. 14.*
δι-αλλάσσω, to change, as the disposition; pass., to be reconciled to, Matt. v. 24.*
δια-λογίζομαι, to reason, to discourse, to ponder, to reflect, to deliberate, to debate, as Mark ii. 6, 8, viii. 16, ix. 33.
δια-λογισμός, οῦ, ὁ, reflection, thought, as Luke ii. 35; reasoning, opinion, as Rom. i. 21, xiv. 1; dispute, debate, as Phil. ii. 14; 1 Tim. ii. 8.
δια-λύω, to disperse, to break up, Acts v. 36.*
δια-μαρτύρομαι, dep. mid., to testify earnestly, witness solemnly, as Acts ii. 40, viii. 25; 1 Tim. v. 21 (A.V.; R.V., charge).
δια-μάχομαι, dep. mid., to contend or dispute warmly, Acts xxiii. 9.*
δια-μένω, to remain, continue, endure, Luke i. 22, xxii. 28; Gal. ii. 5; Heb. i. 11; 2 Pet. iii. 4.*
δια-μερίζω, (1) to divide or separate into parts, as Matt. xxvii. 35, etc.; to distribute, as Luke xxii. 17; (2) pass. with ἐπί, to be divided against, be at discord with; acc., Luke xi. 17; dat., xii. 52.
δια-μερισμός, οῦ, ὁ, dissension, Luke xii. 51.*
δια-νέμω, to divulge, to spread abroad, Acts iv. 17.*
δια-νεύω, to make signs, prop. by nodding, Luke i. 22.*
δια-νόημα, ατος, τό, a thought, imagination, device, Luke xi. 17.*
διά-νοια, ας, ἡ, the mind, the intellect, or thinking faculty, as Mark xii. 30; the understanding, 1 John v. 20; the feelings, disposition, affections, as Col. i. 21; plur., the thoughts, as wilful, depraved, Eph. ii. 3. (In Eph. i. 8, A.V., the eyes of your understanding (διανοίας), W.H. and R.V. read καρδίας, the eyes of your heart.)
δι-ανοίγω, to open fully, i.e., the ears, Mark vii. 34; the eyes, Luke xxiv. 31; the heart, Acts xvi. 14; the Scriptures, Acts xvii. 3.
δια-νυκτερεύω, to pass the night through, Luke vi. 12.*
δι-ανύω, to perform to the end, complete, Acts xxi. 7.*
δια-παντός, adv., always, continually. (W. H. always read διὰ παντός.)
δια-παρα-τριβή, ῆς, ἡ, contention, fierce dispute to no purpose, 1 Tim. vi. 5. (W. H.; rec. has παραδιατριβή.)*
δια-περάω, ῶ, άσω, to pass, to pass through, to pass over, as Matt. ix. 1.
δια-πλέω, εύσω, to sail through or over, Acts xxvii. 5.*
δια-πονέω, ῶ, mid., aor. pass., to grieve oneself, to be indignant, Acts iv. 2, xvi. 18.*
δια-πορεύομαι, to go or pass through, as Luke xiii. 22.
δι-απορέω, ῶ, to be in great doubt or perplexity, Luke ix. 7, xxiv. 4 (W. H., ἀπορέω); Acts ii. 12, v. 24, x. 17.*
δια-πραγματεύομαι, to gain by business or trading, Luke xix. 15.*
δια-πρίω (πρίω, to saw), in pass., to be sawn right through, to be enraged, to be greatly moved with anger, Acts v. 33, vii. 54.*
δι-αρπάζω, to plunder, to spoil by robbery, etc., Matt. xii. 29; Mark iii. 27.*

διαῤ-ῥήγνυμι and διαρρήσσω, ξω, *to tear,* as garments, in grief or indignation, Matt. xxvi. 65; Mark xiv. 63; Acts xiv. 14; *to break asunder,* as a net, Luke v. 6; as bonds, Luke viii. 29.*

δια-σαφέω, ῶ, *to make fully manifest, to tell all,* Matt. xviii. 31, xiii. 36 (W. H.).

δια-σείω, *to treat with violence, so as to extort anything,* Luke iii. 14.*

δια-σκορπίζω, *to strew or scatter,* as Matt. xxv. 24; *to disperse* in conquest, as Luke i. 51; *to waste or squander,* Luke xv. 13, xvi. 1.

δια-σπάω, 1st aor. pass. διεσπάσθην, *to pull or pluck asunder or in pieces,* Mark v. 4; Acts xxiii. 10.*

δια-σπείρω, 2nd aor. pass. διεσπάρην, *to scatter abroad,* as seed; so of Christians dispersed by persecution, Acts viii. 1, 4, xi. 19.*

δια-σπορά, ᾶς, ἡ, *dispersion, state of being dispersed.* Used of the Jews as scattered among the Gentiles, John vii. 35; James i. 1; 1 Pet. i. 1.*

δια-στέλλω, in mid., *to give in charge, to command expressly,* Mark viii. 15; Acts xv. 24; with negative words, *to forbid, to prohibit,* Matt. xvi. 20 (W. H. marg.); Mark v. 43, vii. 36, ix. 9. pass. part., τὸ διαστελλόμενον, Heb. xii. 20, *the command.*

διά-στημα, ατος, τό, *an interval* of time, Acts v. 7.*

δια-στολή, ῆς, ἡ, *distinction, difference,* Rom. iii. 22, x. 12; 1 Cor. xiv. 7.*

δια-στρέφω, *to seduce, turn away,* Luke xxiii. 2; Acts xiii. 8; *to pervert,* Acts xiii. 10. Perf. part., pass., διεστραμμένος, *perverse, vicious,* Matt. xvii. 17; Luke ix. 41; Acts xx. 30; Phil. ii. 15.*

διασώζω, σω, *to save, to convey safe through,* Acts xxiii. 24, xxvii. 43; 1 Pet. iii. 20; pass., *to reach a place in safety,* Acts xxvii. 44, xxviii. 1, 4; *to heal perfectly,* Matt. xiv. 36; Luke vii. 3.*

δια-ταγή, ῆς, ἡ, *a disposing of, ordinance, appointment,* Acts vii. 53; Rom. xiii. 2.*

διά-ταγμα, ατος, τό, *a mandate, a decree,* Heb. xi. 23.*

δια-ταράσσω, *to trouble greatly, to agitate,* Luke i. 29.*

δια-τάσσω, *to dispose, to give orders to* (dat.), *arrange, constitute;* mid., *to appoint, to ordain,* as 1 Cor. vii. 17 (also with dat. pers.; acc., thing).

δια-τελέω, ῶ, *to continue, to remain through a certain time,* Acts xxvii. 33.*

δια-τηρέω, *to guard or keep with care,* as in the heart, Luke ii. 51; with ἑαυτόν, etc., *to guard oneself from, to abstain* (ἐκ or ἀπό), Acts xv. 29.*

δια-τί or διὰ τι; (W. H.) *wherefore?*

δια-τίθημι, only mid. in N.T., *to dispose,* as (1) *to commit to, appoint,* Luke xxii. 29; (2) with cog. acc., διαθήκην, *make* a covenant with (dat. or πρός, acc.), Acts iii. 25; Heb. viii. 10, x. 16; *make* a will, Heb. ix. 16, 17. See διαθήκη.*

δια-τρίβω, *to spend* (χρόνον or ἡμέρας), *tarry,* as Acts xiv. 3, 28; abs., *to sojourn,* as John iii. 22.

δια-τροφή, ῆς, ἡ, *food, nourishment,* 1 Tim. vi. 8.*

δι-αυγάζω, *to shine through, to dawn,* 2 Pet. i. 19.*

δια-φανής, ές, *shining through, transparent,* Rev. xxi. 21. (W. H., διαυγής in same signif.)

δια-φέρω, (1) *to carry through,* Mark xi. 16; (2) *to bear abroad,* Acts xiii. 49, xxvii. 27; (3) *to differ from* (gen.), 1 Cor. xv. 41; Gal. iv. 1; hence (4) *to be better than, to surpass,* as Matt. vi. 26; (5) impers., διαφέρει, with οὐδέν, *it makes no difference to* (dat.), *matters nothing* to, Gal. ii. 6.

δια-φεύγω, *to escape by flight,* Acts xxvii. 42.*

δια-φημίζω, *to report, publish abroad, divulge,* Matt. ix. 31, xxviii. 15; Mark i. 45.*

δια-φθείρω, *to destroy utterly,* Luke xii. 33; Rev. viii. 9, xi. 18; pass., *to decay, to perish,* 2 Cor. iv. 16; 1 Tim. vi. 5.* Opp. to ἀνακαινόω, *to renew.*

δια-φθορά, ᾶς, ἡ, *decay, corruption, i.e.,* of the grave, Acts ii. 27, 31, xiii. 34-37 (LXX.).*

διά-φορος, ον, (1) *diverse, of different kinds,* Rom. xii. 6; Heb. ix. 10; (2) compar., *more excellent* than, Heb. i. 4, viii. 6.*

δια-φυλάσσω—δικαίωμα] VOCABULARY. 421

δια-φυλάσσω, to guard carefully, protect, defend, Luke iv. 10 (LXX.).*
δια-χειρίζω, mid. N.T., to lay hands on, put to death, Acts v. 30, xxvi. 21.*
δια-χλευάζω, see χλευάζω.
δια-χωρίζω, pass. N.T., "to be separated," to leave, to depart from (ἀπό), Luke ix. 33.*
διδακτικός, ή, όν, apt at teaching, 1 Tim. iii. 2; 2 Tim. ii. 24.*
διδακτός, ή, όν, taught, instructed, John vi. 45; 1 Cor. ii. 13.
διδασκαλία, as, ή, teaching, i.e., (1) the manner or art of teaching, as Rom. xii. 7; or (2) the doctrine taught, precept, instruction, as Matt. xv. 9, etc.
διδάσκαλος, ου, ὁ, a teacher, especially of the Jewish law, master, doctor, as Luke ii. 49; often in voc. as a title of address to Christ, Master, Teacher.
διδάσκω, f. διδάξω, to teach, to be a teacher, abs.; to teach, with acc. of pers., generally also acc. of thing; also with inf. or ὅτι.
διδαχή, ῆς, ἡ, doctrine, teaching, i.e., (1) the act, (2) the mode, or (3) the thing taught. With obj. gen., perhaps, in Heb. vi. 2, see § 260, b, note.
δί-δραχμον, ου, τό (prop. adj., sc. νόμισμα, coin), a double drachma, or silver half-shekel (in LXX., the shekel), Matt. xvii. 24.
Δίδυμος, η, ον, double, or twin; a surname of Thomas the apostle, John xi. 16, xx. 24, xxi. 2.*
δίδωμι, to give (acc. and dat.). Hence, in various connections, to yield, deliver, supply, commit, etc. When used in a general sense, the dat. of pers. may be omitted, as Matt. xiii. 8. The thing given may be expressed by ἐκ or ἀπό, with gen. in a partitive sense instead of acc. So Matt. xxv. 8; Luke xx. 10. The purpose of a gift may be expressed by inf., as Matt. xiv. 16; John iv. 7; Luke i. 73.
δι-εγείρω, to wake up thoroughly, as Luke viii. 24; to excite, John vi. 18; fig., to stir up, arouse, 2 Pet. i. 13.
δι-ενθυμέομαι, οὖμαι (W. H.), to reflect, Acts x. 19.*
δι-έξ-οδος, ου, ἡ, lit., " a crossway of exit;" so, a meeting-place of roads, a public spot in a city, Matt. xxii. 9.*

δι-ερμηνευτής, οὗ, ὁ, an interpreter, 1 Cor. xiv. 28.*
δι-ερμηνεύω, to interpret, explain, Luke xxiv. 27; Acts ix. 36; 1 Cor. xii. 30, xiv. 5, 13, 27.*
δί-ερχομαι, to pass through, acc. or διά (gen.), destination expressed by εἰς or ἕως; to pass over or travel, abs., Acts viii. 4; to spread, as a report, Luke v. 15.
δι-ερωτάω, ῶ, to find by inquiry, Acts x. 17.*
δι-ετής, ές (δίς), of two years, Matt. ii. 16.*
δι-ετία, as, ἡ, the space of two years, Acts xxiv. 27, xxviii. 30.*
δι-ηγέομαι, οὖμαι, to lead through, to recount perfectly, to declare the whole of a matter.
διήγησις, εως, ἡ, narrative or history, Luke i. 1.*
δι-ηνεκής, ές, continuous, perpetual, εἰς τὸ διηνεκές, adverbial, for ever, Heb. vii. 3, x. 1, 12, 14.*
δι-θάλασσος, ον (δίς), washed by the sea on two sides, Acts xxvii. 41.*
δι-ικνέομαι, οὖμαι, to pass through, as a sword piercing, Heb. iv. 12.*
δι-ίστημι, to put apart, to interpose, Acts xxvii. 28, lit., having interposed a little (space), i.e., having gone a little further; 2 aor., intrans., Luke xxii. 59, one hour having intervened; xxiv. 51, he was parted from them.*
δι-ισχυρίζομαι, to affirm strongly, Luke xxii. 59; Acts xii. 15.*
δικαιο-κρισία, as, ἡ, just judgment, Rom. ii. 5.*
δίκαιος, αία, ον, just, right, upright, righteous, impartial; applied to things, to persons, to Christ, to God. Adv., -ως, justly, deservedly. Syn. 21.
δικαιοσύνη, ης, ἡ, righteousness, justice, rectitude, goodness generally.
δικαιόω, ῶ, to make just, make righteous; also in N.T. in the declarative sense, to hold guiltless, to justify, to pronounce or treat as righteous, as Matt. xii. 37; 1 Cor. iv. 4.
δικαίωμα, ατος, τό, a righteous decree or statute, an ordinance, Luke i. 6; Rom. i. 32, ii. 26; Heb. ix. 1, 10; especially a decree of acquittal, justification (opp. to κατάκριμα, condemnation), Rom. v. 16; a righteous act, Rom. v. 18; Rev. xv. 4, xix. 8.*

δικαίωσις, εως, ἡ, *acquittal, justification*, Rom. iv. 25, v. 18.*
δικαστής, οῦ, ὁ, *a judge*, Luke xii. 14 (W. H., κριτής); Acts vii. 27, 35.*
δίκη, ης, ἡ, *a judicial sentence*, Acts xxv. 15 (W. H., καταδίκη); *τίω* or *ὑπέχω δίκην*, *to suffer punishment*, 2 Thess. i. 9; Jude 7; *Vengeance, the name of a heathen deity*, Acts xxviii. 4.*
δίκτυον, ου, τό, *a fishing-net*.
δί-λογος, ον (δίς), *double-tongued, deceitful*, 1 Tim. iii. 8.*
διό, conj. (διά and ὅ), *therefore, on which account, wherefore*.
δι-οδεύω, *to journey* or *pass through*, Luke viii. 1; Acts xvii. 1.*
Διονύσιος, ιου, ὁ, *Dionysius*, Acts xvii. 34.*
διό-περ, conj., *for which very reason*, 1 Cor. viii. 13, x. 14, xiv. 13.*
Διο-πετής, ές, *fallen from Zeus* or *Jupiter*, Acts xix. 35.*
δι-όρθωμα, see κατόρθωμά.
δι-όρθωσις, εως, ἡ, *an amendment, reformation*, Heb. ix. 10.*
δι-ορύσσω, ξω, *to dig through*, Matt. vi. 19, 20, xxiv. 43; Luke xii. 39.*
Διόσ-κουροι, ων, οἱ (children of Zeus), *Castor* and *Pollux*, Acts xxviii. 11.*
δι-ότι, conj. (= διὰ τοῦτο, ὅτι), *wherefore, on this account, because, for*.
Διο-τρεφής, οῦς, ὁ, *Diotrephes*, 3 John 9.*
διπλόος, οῦς, ῆ, οῦν, *double, twofold*, 1 Tim. v. 17; Rev. xviii. 6; comp., *διπλότερος* with gen., Matt. xxiii. 15.*
διπλόω, ῶ, *to double*, Rev. xviii. 6.*
δίς, adv., *twice*.
(Δίς), obsolete nom. for Ζεύς, gen. Διός, acc. Δία, *Zeus* or *Jupiter*.
διστάζω, σω (δίς), *to waver, to doubt*, Matt. xiv. 31, xxviii. 17.*
δί-στομος, ον (δίς), *two-edged*, Heb. iv. 12; Rev. i. 16, ii. 12.*
δισ-χίλιοι, αι, α, num., *two thousand*, Mark v. 13.
δι-υλίζω, *to strain off, filter through a sieve*, Matt. xxiii. 24.*
διχάζω, σω, *to set at variance, divide*, Matt. x. 35.*
διχο-στασία, ας, ἡ, *a faction, division, separation*, Rom. xvi. 17; 1 Cor. iii. 3 (not W. H.); Gal. v. 20.*
διχο-τομέω, ῶ, *to cut in two* or *asunder*, Matt. xxiv. 51; Luke xii. 46.*
διψάω, ῶ, ήσω, *to thirst for, to desire earnestly*, acc.; or abs., *to thirst*.

δίψος, ους, τό, *thirst*, 2 Cor. xi. 27.*
δί-ψυχος, ον (δίς), *double-minded*, James i. 8, iv. 8.*
διωγμός, οῦ, ὁ, *persecution*.
διώκτης, ου, ὁ, *a persecutor*, 1 Tim. i. 13.*
διώκω, ξω, *to pursue*, in various senses according to context; *to follow, follow after, press forward; to persecute*.
δόγμα, ατος, τό (δοκέω), *that which seems good to some one, a decree, edict, ordinance*, Luke ii. 1; Acts xvi. 4, xvii. 7; Eph. ii. 15; Col. ii. 14.*
δογματίζω, σω, *to make a decree, to impose an ordinance;* mid., *to submit to ordinances*, Col. ii. 20.*
δοκέω, ῶ, δόξω, (1) *to think*, acc. and inf.; (2) *to seem, appear, be evident;* (3) δοκεῖ, impers., *it seems; it seems good to* or *pleases*, dat.
δοκιμάζω, σω, *to try, put to the proof, prove*, as 2 Cor. viii. 22; *to discern, interpret*, Luke xii. 56; *to judge fit, approve*, as 1 Cor. xvi. 3.
δοκιμασία, ἡ, *the act of proving*, Heb. iii. 9 (W. H.).*
δοκιμή, ῆς, ἡ, *proof, knowledge acquired by proof, experience*.
δοκίμιον, ου, τό, *a test, a means of trying, a criterion*, 1 Pet. i. 7; Jas. i. 3.*
δόκιμος, ον (δέχομαι), *approved, genuine, acceptable*, as Rom. xvi. 10, xiv. 18.
δοκός, οῦ, ἡ, *a beam of timber*, Matt. vii. 3, 4, 5; Luke vi. 41, 42.*
δόλιος, ία, ιον, *deceitful*, 2 Cor. xi. 13.*
δολιόω, ῶ, *to deceive*. Impf., 3rd pers. plur., ἐδολιοῦσαν, an Alexandrian form from LXX., Rom. iii. 13.*
δόλος, ου, ὁ, *fraud, deceit, craft*.
δολόω, ῶ, *to falsify, adulterate*, 2 Cor. iv. 2.*
δόμα, ατος, τό (δίδωμι), *a gift*, Matt. vii. 11; Luke xi. 13; Eph. iv. 8; Phil. iv. 17.*
δόξα, ας, ἡ, from δοκέω, in two main significations: (1) *favourable recognition* or *estimation, honour, renown*, as John v. 41, 44; 2 Cor. vi. 8; Luke xvii. 18; and very frequently (2) *a seeming, appearance, the manifestation of that which calls forth praise;* so especially in the freq. phrase ἡ δόξα τοῦ Θεοῦ, *glory, splendour*. Concrete plur. δόξαι, in 2 Pet. ii. 10; Jude 8, *dignities*, angelic powers.

δοξάζω—δῶρον] VOCABULARY. 423

δοξάζω, σω, *to ascribe glory to, to honour, glorify.*
Δορκάς, άδος, ἡ, *Dorcas,* Acts ix. 36, 39.*
δόσις, εως, ἡ, *a giving,* Phil. iv. 15; *a gift,* James i. 17.*
δότης, ου, ὁ, *a giver,* 2 Cor. ix. 7.*
δουλ-αγωγέω, ῶ, *to bring into subjection,* 1 Cor. ix. 27.*
δουλεία, ας, ἡ, *slavery, bondage.*
δουλεύω, σω, (1) *to be a slave,* absolutely; (2) *to be subject to, to obey,* dat.
δούλη, ης, ἡ, *a handmaid, a female slave.*
δοῦλος, ου, ὁ, (once as adj., Rom. vi. 19), *a slave, bondman* (opp. to ἐλεύθερος); *a servant* (opp. to κύριος, δεσπότης), so in the freq. phrases δοῦλος τοῦ Θεοῦ, δοῦλος Χριστοῦ. **Syn.** 60.
δουλόω, ῶ, ώσω, *to reduce to bondage* (acc. and dat.); pass., *to be held subject to, be in bondage.*
δοχή, ῆς, ἡ (δέχομαι), "*a receiving of guests,*" *a banquet,* Luke xiv. 13.*
δράκων, οντος, ὁ, *a dragon* or *huge serpent;* symb. for Satan, Rev.*
δράσσομαι, dep., *to grasp, take, catch;* acc., 1 Cor. iii. 19.*
δραχμή, ῆς, ἡ, *a drachma,* an Attic silver coin equal to the Roman denarius, or worth between sevenpence and eightpence of our money, Luke xv. 8, 9.*
(δρέμω), obs. (see τρέχω), *to run.*
δρέπανον, ου, τό, *a sickle* or *pruning-hook,* Mark iv. 29; Rev. xiv.*
δρόμος, ου, ὁ, *a running;* fig., *course, career,* Acts xiii. 25, xx. 24; 2 Tim. iv. 7.*
Δρούσιλλα, ης, ἡ, *Drusilla,* Acts xxiv. 24.*
δύναμαι, dep. (see § 109, *b*, 1), *to be able,* abs., or with inf. (sometimes omitted) or acc.; *to have a capacity for; to be strong,* as 1 Cor. iii. 2; *to have power to do,* whether through ability, disposition, permission, or opportunity.
δύναμις, εως, ἡ, (1) *power, might,* absolutely or as an attribute; (2) *power over,* expressed by εἰς or ἐπί (acc.), *ability to do;* (3) *exercise of power, mighty work, miracle,* as Matt. xi. 20; (4) *forces,* as of an army, spoken of the heavenly hosts, as Matt. xxiv. 29; (5) *force,* as of a word, *i.e., significance,* 1 Cor. xiv. 11. **Synn.** 45, 57.

δυναμόω, ῶ, *to strengthen, confirm,* Col. i. 11; Heb. xi. 34 (W. H.).*
δυνάστης, ου, ὁ, (1) *a potentate, prince,* Luke i. 52; 1 Tim. vi. 15; (2) *one in authority,* Acts viii. 27.*
δυνατέω, ῶ, *to be powerful, have power to* (inf.), 2 Cor. xiii. 3; Rom. xiv. 4 (W. H.); 2 Cor. ix. 8 (W. H.).*
δυνατός, ἡ, όν, *able, having power, mighty.* ὁ δυνατός, THE ALMIGHTY, Luke i. 49. δυνατόν, *possible.*
δύνω or **δύω**, 2nd aor. ἔδυν, *to sink; to set,* as the sun, Mark i. 32; Luke iv. 40.*
δύο, num., indecl., except dat., δυσί, *two.*
δυσ-, an inseparable prefix, implying *adverse, difficult,* or *grievous.*
δυσ-βάστακτος, ον, *oppressive, difficult to be borne,* Matt. xxiii. 4 (not W. H.); Luke xi. 46.*
δυσ-εντερία, ας, ἡ (W. H., -ιον τό), *a dysentery, a flux,* Acts xxviii. 8.*
δυσ-ερμήνευτος, ον, *hard to be explained,* Heb. v. 11.*
δύσ-κολος, ον (lit., "difficult about food"), *difficult, hard to accomplish,* Mark x. 24.* Adv., -ως, *with difficulty, hardly,* Matt. xix. 23; Mark x. 23; Luke xviii. 24.*
δυσμή, ῆς, ἡ (only plur., δυσμαί), *the setting of the sun, the west.*
δυσ-νόητος, ον, *hard* or *difficult to be understood,* 2 Pet. iii. 16.*
δυσ-φημέω, *to speak evil, defame,* 1 Cor. iv. 13 (W. H.).*
δυσ-φημία, ας, ἡ, *evil report, infamy.*
δώδεκα, indecl., num., *twelve.* οἱ δώδεκα, *the twelve, i.e., the Apostles.*
δωδέκατος, η, ον, num., ord., *twelfth,* Rev. xxi. 20.*
δωδεκά-φυλον, ου, τό, *the twelve tribes, Israel,* Acts xxvi. 7.
δῶμα, ατος, τό, *a house, a house-top.* **Syn.** 61.
δωρεά, ᾶς, ἡ, *a free gift.*
δωρεάν, accus. of preced., as an adv., *freely,* as 2 Cor. xi. 7; *without cause, groundlessly,* John xv. 25; Gal. ii. 21.
δωρέομαι, οῦμαι, *to give freely,* Mark xv. 45; pass., 2 Pet. i. 3, 4.*
δώρημα, ατος, τό, *a free gift,* Rom. v. 16; James i. 17.*
δῶρον, ου, τό, *a gift.*

E.

Ε, ε, ἐψῖλον, epsilon, ὄ, the fifth letter. As a numeral, ε' = 5 ; ε,= 5000.
ἔα, interj., expressing surprise or complaint, *oh ! alas!* Mark i. 24 (W. H. omit); Luke iv. 34.*
ἐάν, or **ἄν,** conj. (for εἰ ἄν), *if,* usually construed with subjunctive verb. See § 383. W. H. have the indic. fut. in Luke xix. 40; Acts viii. 31 ; pres. in 1 Thess. iii. 8 ; 1 John v. 15 (rec. also). Sometimes equivalent to a particle of time, John xii. 32, *when;* after the relative, with an indefinite force, ὅς ἐάν, *whosoever,* as Matt. v. 19, viii. 19 ; 1 Cor. xvi. 6. ἐὰν δὲ καί, *and if also;* ἐὰν μή, *except, unless,* Matt. v. 20; *but that,* Mark iv. 22 ; ἐὰν πέρ, *if indeed,* Heb. vi. 3.
ἑαυτοῦ, pron., reflex., 3rd pers., *of oneself;* used also in 1st (plur.) and 2nd persons. See § 335. Genitive often for possess. pron. λέγειν or εἰπεῖν ἐν ἑαυτῷ, *to say within oneself;* γίνεσθαι or ἔρχεσθαι ἐν ἑαυτῷ, *to come to oneself;* πρὸς ἑαυτόν, *to one's home,* John xx. 10, or *privately,* as Luke xviii. 11 ; ἐν ἑαυτοῖς, *among yourselves,* i.e., one with another ; καθ' ἑαυτόν, *apart;* παρ' ἑαυτόν, *at home.*
ἐάω, ῶ, ἐάσω ; impf., εἴων ; 1st aor., εἴασα, (1) *to permit,* inf., or acc. and inf. ; (2) *to leave,* Acts xxiii. 32, and prob. (R.V.) Acts xxvii. 40.
ἑβδομήκοντα, indecl., num., *seventy.* οἱ ἑβδομήκοντα, *the seventy disciples,* Luke x. 1, 17.
ἑβδομηκοντάκις, num. adv., *seventy times,* Matt. xviii. 22.*
ἕβδομος, η, ον, ord. num., *seventh.*
Ἕβερ, ὁ, *Eber* or *Heber,* Luke iii. 35.*
Ἑβραϊκός, ή, όν, *Hebrew.*
Ἑβραῖος (W. H.,'E.), αία, αῖον, also subst., ὁ, ἡ, *a Hebrew;* a Jew of Palestine, in distinction from οἱ Ἑλληνισταί, or Jews born out of Palestine, and using the Greek language.
Ἑβραΐς (W. H.,'E.), ίδος, ἡ, *the Hebrew* or *Aramæan language,* vernacular in the time of Christ and the Apostles. See § 150.
Ἑβραϊστί (W. H.,'E.), adv., *in the Hebrew language.* See preceding,

ἐγγίζω, fut. att., ἐγγιῶ; pf., ἤγγικα, *to approach, to draw near, to be near,* abs., or with dat. or εἰς, or ἐπί (acc.).
ἐγ-γράφω (W. H., ἐνγ-), *to inscribe, infix,* 2 Cor. iii. 2 ; Luke x. 20 (W. H.).*
ἔγγυος, ον, ὁ, ἡ, *a surety, sponsor,* Heb. vii. 22.*
ἐγγύς, adv., *near;* used of both place and time, with gen. or dat.
ἐγγύτερον, comp. of preceding, *nearer;* Rom. xiii. 11.*
ἐγείρω, ἐγερῶ, pass. perf., ἐγήγερμαι, *to arouse, to awaken; to raise up,* as a Saviour ; *to erect,* as a building; mid., *to rise up,* as from sleep, or from a recumbent posture, as at table. Applied to raising the dead ; used also of *rising up against,* as an adversary, or in judgment.
ἔγερσις, εως, ἡ, *a waking up;* of the resurrection, Matt. xxvii. 53.*
ἐγκ-. In words beginning thus, W. H. generally write ἐνκ-.
ἐγ-κάθ-ετος, ον, adj. (ἐγκαθίημι), *a spy, an insidious foe,* Luke xx. 20.*
ἐγκαίνια, ίων, τά, *a dedication,* John x. 22 ; of the feast commemorating the dedicating or purifying of the temple, after its pollution by Antiochus Epiphanes, 25 Chisleu, answering to mid-December.
ἐγ-καινίζω, *to dedicate,* Heb. ix. 18. x. 20.*
ἐγ-κακέω, ῶ, *to grow weary, to faint* (W.H.).*
ἐγ-καλέω, ῶ, έσω, impf., ἐνεκάλουν, *to summon to a court for trial, to indict,* pers. dat., or κατά (gen.) ; *crime,* in gen.
ἐγ-κατα-λείπω, ψω, (1) *to desert, to abandon ;* (2) *to leave remaining,* Rom. ix. 29.
ἐγ-κατ-οικέω, ῶ, *to dwell among* (ἐν), 2 Pet. ii. 8.*
ἐγ-καυχάομαι, *to boast in,* 2 Thess. i. 4 (W. H.).*
ἐγ-κεντρίζω, *to insert,* as a bud or graft ; fig., Rom. xi.*
ἔγ-κλημα, ατος, τό, *a charge* or *accusation,* Acts xxiii. 29, xxv. 16.*
ἐγ-κομβόομαι, οῦμαι, *to clothe,* as with an outer garment tied closely with knots, 1 Pet. v. 5.*
ἐγ-κοπή, ῆς, ἡ, *an impediment,* 1 Cor. ix. 12.*
ἐγ-κόπτω, ψω, *to interrupt, to hinder* (acc., or inf. with τοῦ).

ἐγ-κράτεια, as, ἡ, self-control, temperance, continence, Acts xxiv. 25; Gal. v. 23; 2 Pet. i. 6.*

ἐγ-κρατεύομαι, dep., to restrain oneself in sensual pleasures; to be temperate, 1 Cor. vii. 9, ix. 25.*

ἐγ-κρατής, ές, having power over, self-controlled, temperate, abstinent, Tit. i. 8.*

ἐγ-κρίνω, to adjudge or reckon, to a particular rank (acc. and dat.), 2 Cor. x. 12.*

ἐγ-κρύπτω, to hide in, to mix with, Matt. xiii. 33; Luke xiii. 2 (W. H., κρύπτω).*

ἔγ-κυος, ον, pregnant, Luke ii. 5.*

ἐγ-χρίω, to rub in, anoint, Rev. iii. 18.*

ἐγώ, pron., pers., I; plur., ἡμεῖς, we. See § 53.

ἐδαφίζω, fut. (Attic), -ιῶ, to lay level with the ground, to raze, Luke xix. 44.*

ἔδαφος, ους, τό, the ground, Acts xxii. 7.*

ἑδραῖος, αία, αῖον, stedfast, firm, fixed, 1 Cor. vii. 37, xv. 58; Col. i. 23.*

ἑδραίωμα, ατος, τό, a basis, stay, support, 1 Tim. iii. 15.*

Ἐζεκίας, ου, ὁ, Hezekiah, Matt. i. 9, 10.*

ἐθελο-θρησκεία, ας, ἡ, will-worship, Col. ii. 23.*

ἐθέλω. See θέλω.

ἐθίζω, to accustom; pass., perf. part., neut., τὸ εἰθισμένον, the accustomed practice, the custom, Luke ii. 27.*

ἐθνάρχης, ου, ὁ, a prefect, lieutenant-governor, ethnarch, 2 Cor. xi. 32.*

ἐθνικός, ή, όν, national, of Gentile race, heathen, Matt. v. 47 (W. H.), vi. 7, xviii. 17; 3 John 7 (W. H.).* Adv., -ῶς, heathenly, after the manner of heathens, Gal. ii. 14.*

ἔθνος, ους, τό, the people of any country, a nation. τὰ ἔθνη, the nations, the heathen world, the Gentiles.

ἔθος, ους, τό, a usage, custom, manner.

ἔθω, obs., pf. εἴωθα, in pres. signif. to be accustomed, Matt. xxvii. 15; Mark x. 1. τὸ εἰωθὸς αὐτῷ, his custom, Luke iv. 16; Acts xvii. 2.*

εἰ, a conditional conjunction (see § 383), if, since, though. After verbs indicating emotion, εἰ is equivalent to ὅτι, Mark xv. 44. As an interrogative particle, εἰ occurs in both indirect and direct questions, Mark xv. 45; Acts i. 6. In oaths and solemn assertions, it may be rendered by that ... not. εἰ μή and εἰ μήτι, unless, except. εἰ δὲ μή, but if not, otherwise, John xiv. 2. εἴ περ, if so be. εἴ πως, if possibly. εἴτε ... εἴτε, whether ... or.

εἶδον. See ὁράω, οἶδα.

εἶδος, ους, τό, outward appearance, form, aspect, Luke iii. 22, ix. 29; John v. 37; 2 Cor. v. 7; perhaps species, kind, 1 Thess. v. 22.*

εἰδωλεῖον, ου, τό, an idol-temple, 1 Cor. viii. 10.*

εἰδωλό-θυτος, ον, sacrificed to idols; used of meats, as Acts xv. 29.

εἰδωλο-λατρεία, ας, ἡ, idolatry.

εἰδωλο-λάτρης, ου, ὁ, an idolater.

εἴδωλον, ου, τό, an idol, a false god worshipped in an image.

εἰκῇ or εἰκῆ (W. H.), adv., to no purpose, in vain, as Rom. xiii. 4; 1 Cor. xv. 2. (W. H. and R.V. omit in Matt. v. 22.)

εἴκοσι, indecl., num., twenty.

εἴκω, to give way, to yield, Gal. ii. 5.*

(εἴκω), obs., whence 2nd perf. ἔοικα, to resemble; with dat., James i. 6, 23.*

εἰκών, όνος, ἡ, an image, copy, representation, likeness.

εἰλικρίνεια, as, ἡ, clearness, sincerity, 1 Cor. v. 8; 2 Cor. i. 12, ii. 17.*

εἰλικρινής, ές, sincere, pure, without spot or blemish (perhaps from εἴλη, sunlight, and κρίνω, to judge, "capable of being judged in the light," but doubtful, for εἴλη is rather the sun's warmth), Phil. i. 10; 2 Pet. iii. 1.*

εἱλίσσω (W. H., ἑλίσσω), to roll together, as a scroll, Rev. vi. 14.*

εἰμί (see § 110), a verb of existence, (1) used as a predicate, to be, to exist, to happen, to come to pass; with an infin. following, ἔστι, it is convenient, proper, etc., as Heb. ix. 5; (2) as the copula of subject and predicate, simply to be, or in the sense of to be like, to represent, John vi. 35; Matt. xxvi. 26; 1 Cor. x. 4. With participles, it is used to form the "resolved tenses," as Luke i. 22, iv. 16; Matt. xvi. 19, etc. With gen., as predicate, it marks quality, possession, participation, etc.; with dat., property, possession, destination, etc. For its force with a prep. and its case, see Syntax of Prepositions. The verb,

when copula, is often omitted. Participle, ὤν, being; τὸ ὄν, that which is; οἱ ὄντες, τὰ ὄντα, persons or things, that are.
εἶμι, to go, in some copies for εἰμί, in John vii. 34, 36 (not W. H.).*
εἵνεκα, -εν. See ἕνεκα, -εν.
εἴπερ, **εἴπως**. See under εἰ.
εἶπον (see § 103, 7), (W. H., εἶπα,) from obs. ἔπω, or εἴπω, to say; in reply, to answer; in narration, to tell; in authoritative directions, to bid or command, as Luke vii. 7.
εἰρηνεύω, to have peace, to be at peace, Mark ix. 50; Rom. xii. 18; 2 Cor. xiii. 11; 2 Thess. v. 13.*
εἰρήνη, ης, ἡ, peace, the opposite of strife; peace of mind, arising from reconciliation with God. In N.T. (like the corresponding Heb. word in O.T.), εἰρήνη generally denotes a perfect wellbeing. Often employed in salutations, as in Heb.
εἰρηνικός, ή, όν, peaceable, James iii. 17; peaceful, Heb. xii. 11.*
εἰρηνοποιέω, ῶ, to make peace, reconcile, Col. i. 20.*
εἰρηνοποιός, οῦ, ὁ, a peacemaker, Matt. v. 9.*
εἰς, prep. governing acc., into, to (the interior). See §§ 124, 298. In composition, it implies motion into or towards.
εἷς, μία, ἕν, a card. num., one; used distributively, as Matt. xx. 21; by way of emphasis, as Mark ii. 7; and indefinitely, as Matt. viii. 19; Mark xii. 42. As an ordinal, the first, Matt. xxviii. 1; Rev. ix. 12.
εἰσ-άγω, 2nd aor. εἰσήγαγον, to bring in, introduce.
εἰσ-ακούω, to listen to, to hear prayer, Matt. vi. 7; Luke i. 13; Acts x. 31; Heb. v. 7; to hear so as to obey (gen.), 1 Cor. xiv. 21.*
εἰσ-δέχομαι, to receive into favour (acc.), 2 Cor. vi. 17; from LXX.*
εἴσ-ειμι, impf. εἰσῄειν, inf. εἰσιέναι (εἶμι), to go in, to enter (with εἰς), Acts iii. 3, xxi. 18, 26; Heb. ix. 6.*
εἰσ-έρχομαι, 2nd aor. εἰσῆλθον, to come in, to enter (chiefly with εἰς). εἰσέρχομαι καὶ ἐξέρχομαι, to come and go in and out, spoken of daily life and intercourse, Acts i. 21. Fig., of entrance upon a state.

εἰσ-καλέω, ῶ, only mid. in N.T., to call or invite in, Acts x. 23.*
εἴσ-οδος, ου, ἡ, an entrance, a first coming, an admission.
εἰσ-πηδάω, ῶ, to leap in, to spring in Acts xiv. 14 (W. H., ἐκπ-), xvi. 29.*
εἰσ-πορεύομαι, dep., to go in, to enter; spoken of persons, as Mark i. 21; of things, as Matt. xv. 17. εἰσπορεύομαι καὶ ἐκπορεύομαι, to go in and out in daily duties, Acts ix. 28.
εἰσ-τρέχω, 2nd aor. εἰσέδραμον, to run in or into, Acts xii. 14.*
εἰσ-φέρω (see § 103, 6), to lead into (with εἰς), e.g., temptation, as Luke xi. 4; to bring to the ears of, Acts xvii. 20.
εἶτα, adv., then, afterwards.
εἴτε, conj. See εἰ.
ἐκ, or, before a vowel, **ἐξ**, a prep. gov. gen., from, out of (the interior). See § 293. In composition, ἐκ implies removal, continuance, completion, or is of intensive force.
ἕκαστος, each, every one (with partitive gen.). εἷς ἕκαστος, every one soever.
ἑκάστοτε, adv., each time, always, 2 Pet. i. 15.*
ἑκατόν, card. num., a hundred.
ἑκατονταέτης, ες, a hundred years old, Rom. iv. 9.*
ἑκατονταπλασίων, ον, a hundredfold, acc., -ονα, Matt. xix. 29 (not W. H.); Mark x. 30; Luke viii. 8.*
ἑκατοντάρχης (or -ος), ου, ὁ, captain over a hundred men, a centurion.
ἐκ-βαίνω, 2nd aor. ἐξέβην (W. H.), to go out, Heb. xi. 15.*
ἐκ-βάλλω, to cast out, send out, as labourers into a field; to send away, dismiss, reject; to extract or take out.
ἔκ-βασις, εως, ἡ, a way out, event, end, 1 Cor. x. 13; Heb. xiii. 7.*
ἐκ-βολή, ῆς, ἡ, a casting out, as lading from a ship, Acts xxvii. 18.*
ἐκ-γαμίζω or -ίσκω, to give in marriage.
ἔκ-γονος, ον, sprung from; neut. plur., descendants, 1 Tim. v. 4.*
ἐκ-δαπανάω, ῶ, to spend entirely; pass. reflex., to expend one's energies for (ὑπέρ), 2 Cor. xii. 15.*
ἐκ-δέχομαι, to look out for, to expect (ἕως), to wait for (acc.).
ἔκδηλος, ον, quite plain, conspicuous, manifest, 2 Tim. iii. 9.*

ἐκ-δημέω, ῶ, to be away from, absent from, 2 Cor. v. 6-9.*
ἐκ-δίδωμι, N.T. mid., to let out to farm, Matt. xxi. 33, 41; Mark xii. 1; Luke xx. 9.*
ἐκ-δι-ηγέομαι, οῦμαι, dep. mid., to rehearse particularly, tell fully, Acts xiii. 41, xv. 3.*
ἐκ-δικέω, ῶ, to do justice to, avenge a person (acc. and ἀπό), Luke xviii. 3, 5; Rom. xii. 19; to demand requital for, avenge a deed (acc.), 2 Cor. x. 6; Rev. vi. 10, xix. 2.*
ἐκ-δίκησις, εως, ἡ, an avenging, vindication, punishment.
ἔκ-δικος, ον, ὁ, ἡ, an avenger, one who adjudges a culprit (dat.) to punishment for (περί) a crime, Rom. xiii. 4; 1 Thess. iv. 6.*
ἐκ-διώκω, to persecute, to expel by persecuting, Luke xi. 49; 1 Thess. ii. 15.*
ἐκ-δότος, ον, delivered up, Acts ii. 23.*
ἐκ-δοχή, ῆς, ἡ, a waiting for, expectation, Heb. x. 27.*
ἐκ-δύω, to unclothe, to strip off (two accs.).
ἐκεῖ, adv., there, thither.
ἐκεῖθεν, adv., from that place, thence.
ἐκεῖνος, η, ο, pron., demonst., that, that one there; used antithetically, Mark xvi. 20, and by way of emphasis, Matt. xxii. 23. See §§ 338, 340.
ἐκεῖσε, adv., thither, in const. praeg., Acts xxi. 3, xxii. 5.*
ἐκ-ζητέω, ῶ, to seek out with diligence, Heb. xii. 17; 1 Pet. i. 10; to seek after God, Acts xv. 17; Rom. iii. 11; Heb. xi. 6; to require, judicially, Luke xi. 50, 51.*
ἐκ-θαμβέω, ῶ, N.T. pass., to be amazed, greatly astonished, Mark ix. 15, xiv. 33, xvi. 5, 6.*
ἔκ-θαμβος, ον, surprised, greatly amazed, Acts iii. 11.*
ἔκ-θετος, ον, cast out, exposed to perish, Acts vii. 19.*
ἐκ-καθαίρω, 1st aor. ἐξεκάθαρα, to purge out, to cleanse, 1 Cor. v. 7; 2 Tim. ii. 4.*
ἐκ-καίω, to burn vehemently, as with lust, Rom. i. 27.*
ἐκ-κακέω, ῶ, to faint, to despond through fear. (W. H. exclude the word, reading in every case ἐνκ-.)
ἐκ-κεντέω, ῶ, to pierce through, to transfix, John xix. 37; Rev. i. 7.*

ἐκ-κλάω, to break off, as branches from a stem, Rom. xi. 17, 19, 20.*
ἐκ-κλείω, σω, to shut out, Rom. iii. 27; Gal. iv. 27.*
ἐκκλησία, ας, ἡ (ἐκκαλέω), an assembly of the people, Acts xix. 32, 39, 41; legally or tumultuously gathered. Espec. in N.T., the assembly of believers, the Church as a whole, or a church in one place, 1 Cor. xii. 28; Acts xi. 26. So, often plural, as Acts xv. 41.
ἐκ-κλίνω, to decline, turn away from (ἀπό), Rom. iii. 12, xvi. 17; 1 Pet. iii. 11.*
ἐκ-κολυμβάω, ῶ, to swim out or away, Acts xxvii. 42.*
ἐκ-κομίζω, to carry out to burial, Luke vii. 12.*
ἐκ-κόπτω, to cut off or down, as a tree, branch, or limb. (In 1 Pet. iii. 7, to hinder, W. H. read ἐν-κόπτω.)
ἐκ-κρέμαμαι (mid. of ἐκκρεμάννυμι), to hang upon, or to be earnestly attentive to, Luke xix. 48.*
ἐκ-λαλέω, ῶ, to speak out, to disclose, Acts xxiii. 22.*
ἐκ-λάμπω, to shine out or brightly, Matt. xiii. 43.*
ἐκ-λανθάνω, in mid., to forget entirely, Heb. xii. 5.*
ἐκ-λέγω, mid. in N.T., 1st aor. ἐξελεξάμην, to choose out for oneself, to elect.
ἐκ-λείπω, 2nd aor. ἐξέλιπον, to fail, to cease, to die, Luke xvi. 9, xxii. 32; Heb. i. 12.*
ἐκλεκτός, ή, όν, (1) chosen, elect; (2) choice, approved.
ἐκλογή, ῆς, ἡ, a choice, selection, as Acts ix. 15 (a vessel of choice, i.e., a chosen vessel); concr., the chosen ones, Rom. xi. 7.
ἐκ-λύω, in pass. or mid., to become weary in body, or despondent in mind.
ἐκ-μάσσω, ξω, to wipe, to wipe dry, Luke vii. 38, 44; John xi. 2, xii. 3, xiii. 5.*
ἐκ-μυκτηρίζω, to deride, scoff at (acc.), Luke xvi. 14, xxiii. 35.*
ἐκ-νέω (lit., swim out), or ἐκνεύω (lit., turn by a side motion), to withdraw, John v. 13.*
ἐκνήφω, to awake, as from a drunken sleep, 1 Cor. xv. 34.*
ἑκούσιος, ον (ἑκών), voluntary, spon-

taneous, Philem. 14.* Adv., *-ως, willingly, of one's own accord*, Heb. x. 26; I Pet. v. 2.*
ἐκ-πάλαι, adv., *of old, of long standing*, 2 Pet. ii. 3, iii. 5.*
ἐκ-πειράζω, σω, *to put to the test, to make trial of, to tempt*, Matt. iv. 7; Luke iv. 12, x. 25; I Cor. x. 9.*
ἐκ-πέμπω, *to send out* or *forth*, Acts xiii. 4, xvii. 10.*
ἐκ-περισσῶs, *exceedingly*, Mark xiv. 31 (W. H.).
ἐκ-πετάννυμι, 1st aor. ἐξεπέτασα, *to stretch forth*, Rom. x. 21.*
ἐκ-πηδάω, ῶ, 1st aor. ἐξεπήδησα (W. H.), *to spring forth*, Acts xiv. 14.
ἐκ-πίπτω, (1) *to fall from* (ἐκ), Mark xiii. 25; abs., *to fall*, James i. 11; of a ship driven from its course, Acts xxvii. 17; of love, *to fail*, I Cor. xiii. 8; (2), of moral lapse, Gal. v. 4.
ἐκ-πλέω, εύσω, *to sail out, to sail from*, Acts xv. 39, xviii. 18, xx. 6.*
ἐκ-πληρόω, *to fulfil entirely*, Acts xiii. 32.*
ἐκ-πλήρωσις, εως, ἡ, *entire fulfilment*, Acts xxi. 26.*
ἐκ-πλήσσω, 2nd aor. pass. ἐξεπλάγην, *to strike with astonishment*.
ἐκ-πνέω, εύσω, *to breathe out, to expire, to die*, Mark xv. 37, 39; Luke xxiii. 46.*
ἐκ-πορεύομαι, dep., *to go out* (ἀπό, ἐκ, παρά, and εἰς, ἐπί, πρός); *to proceed from*, as from the heart; or as a river from its source, etc.
ἐκ-πορνεύω, *to be given up to lewdness*, Jude 7.
ἐκ-πτύω, *to reject as distasteful, to loathe*, Gal. iv. 14.*
ἐκ-ριζόω, ῶ, *to root out* or *root up*, Matt. xiii. 29, xv. 13; Luke xvii. 6; Jude 12.*
ἔκ-στασις, εως, ἡ, "ecstasy," (1) *trance*, as Acts x. 10; (2) *amazement*, as Mark v. 42.
ἐκ-στρέφω, perf. pass. ἐξέστραμμαι, *to turn out of a place, to corrupt, to pervert*, Tit. iii. 11.*
ἐκ-ταράσσω, ξω, *to agitate greatly*, Acts xvi. 20.*
ἐκ-τείνω, νῶ, 1st aor. ἐξέτεινα, *to stretch out* the hand, as Luke v. 13; *to throw out*, as anchors from a vessel, as Acts xxvii. 30.
ἐκ-τελέω, ῶ, έσω, *to complete*, Luke xiv. 29, 30.*

ἐκ-τένεια, as, ἡ, *intentness*, Acts xxvi. 7.*
ἐκ-τενής, ές, *intense, vehement, fervent*, I Pet. iv. 8; Acts xii. 5 (W. H., -ῶς).* Adv., *-ῶς, intensely, earnestly*, I Pet. i. 22. ἐκτενέστερον, comp. as adv., *more earnestly*, Luke xxii. 44.*
ἐκ-τίθημι (see § 107), (1) *to put out* or *expose*, as the infant Moses, Acts vii. 21; (2) *to expound*, Acts xi. 4, xviii. 26, xxviii. 23.*
ἐκ-τινάσσω, ξω, *to shake off* dust from the feet, Matt. x. 14; Mark vi. 11; Acts xiii. 51; *to shake out*, Acts xviii. 6.*
ἕκτος, η, ον, ord. num., *sixth*.
ἐκτός, adv., generally as prep., with gen., *without, besides, except*. ἐκτὸς εἰ μή, *except*, I Cor. xiv. 5. τὸ ἐκτός, *the outside*, Matt. xxiii. 26.
ἐκ-τρέπω, mid., *to turn from, to forsake*, I Tim. i. 6, v. 15, vi. 20; 2 Tim. iv. 4; Heb. xii. 13.*
ἐκ-τρέφω, *to nourish, nurture, train up*, Eph. v. 29, vi. 4; Rev. xii. 6 (W. H.).*
ἔκ-τρωμα, ατος, τό, *an abortive birth, an abortion*, I Cor. xv. 8.*
ἐκ-φέρω, *to bring forth, carry out*; espec. to burial, Acts v. 6, 9; *to produce*, of the earth, Heb. vi. 8.
ἐκ-φεύγω, *to flee out from, escape* (abs., or with ἐκ); *to avoid* (acc.).
ἐκ-φοβέω, ῶ, *to terrify greatly*, 2 Cor. x. 9.*
ἔκ-φοβος, ον, *terrified*, Mark ix. 6; Heb. xii. 21.*
ἐκ-φύω, 2nd aor. pass. ἐξεφύην, *to put forth*, as a tree its leaves, Matt. xxiv. 32; Mark xiii. 28.*
ἐκ-χέω, also ἐκχύνω; fut. ἐκχεῶ, 1st aor. ἐξέχεα (see § 96, c), *to pour out*, as Rev. xvi. 1-17; money, John ii. 15; *to shed* blood; fig., *to shed abroad*, love, Rom. v. 5; pass., *to run riotously* (R.V.), Jude 11.
ἐκ-χωρέω, ῶ, *to depart from, to go out*, Luke xxi. 21.*
ἐκ-ψύχω, *to expire, to die*, Acts v. 5, 10, xii. 23.*
ἑκών, οῦσα, όν, *willing*; used adverbially, Rom. viii. 20; I Cor. ix. 17.*
ἐλαία, as, ἡ, *an olive tree*; its fruit, *the olive*. τὸ ὄρος τῶν ἐλαιῶν, *the Mount of Olives*.
ἔλαιον, ου, τό, *olive oil*.

ἐλαιών, ῶνος, ὁ, *an olive grove, Olivet,* Acts i. 12.*

Ἐλαμίτης, ου, ὁ, *an Elamite,* or *inhabitant of Elam,* a region of Persia, Acts ii. 9.*

ἐλάσσων or -ττων, ον, compar. of ἐλαχύς for μικρός, *less;* in quality, John ii. 10 (acc., -ω contracted for -ονα); in age, Rom. ix. 12; in dignity, Heb. vii. 7. ἔλαττον, adv., *less,* 1 Tim. v. 9.*

ἐλαττονέω, ῶ, *to have too little, to lack,* 2 Cor. viii. 15.*

ἐλαττόω, ῶ, *to make lower* or *inferior,* Heb. ii. 7, 9; pass., *to decrease,* John iii. 30.*

ἐλαύνω (tenses from ἐλάω), ἐλάσω, ἐλήλακα, *to drive,* Luke viii. 29; James iii. 4; 2 Pet. ii. 17; *to drive* a ship, *to row,* Mark vi. 48; John vi. 19.*

ἐλαφρία, ας, ἡ, *levity, inconstancy,* 2 Cor. i. 17.*

ἐλαφρός, ά, όν, *light,* as a burden easily borne, Matt. xi. 30; 2 Cor. iv. 17.*

ἐλάχιστος, η, ον, adj. (superl. of ἐλαχύς for μικρός), *least, very little,* in number, magnitude, importance.

ἐλαχιστότερος, α, ον, a double comparison, *less than the least,* Eph. iii. 8.*

ἐλάω. See ἐλαύνω.

Ἐλεάζαρ, ὁ, *Eleazar,* Matt. i. 15.*

ἐλεγμός, οῦ, ὁ, *reproof* (W. H.), 2 Tim. iii. 16.*

ἔλεγξις, εως, ἡ, *reproof,* 2 Pet. ii. 16.*

ἔλεγχος, ου, ὁ, *evident demonstration, proof,* Heb. xi. 1; 2 Tim. iii. 16.*

ἐλέγχω, ξω, *to convict, reprove, rebuke.*

ἐλεεινός, ή, όν, *pitiable, miserable,* 1 Cor. xv. 19; Rev. iii. 17.*

ἐλεέω, ῶ, *to have compassion on, succour* (acc.), *to show mercy;* pass., *to obtain mercy.*

ἐλεημοσύνη, ης, ἡ, *pity, compassion;* in N.T., *alms,* sometimes plur.

ἐλεήμων, ον, *full of pity, merciful, compassionate,* Matt. v. 7; Heb. ii. 17.*

ἔλεος, ους, τό (and ου, ὁ, see § 32, *a*), *pity, mercy, act of compassion.*

ἐλευθερία, ας, ἡ, *liberty, freedom,* from the Mosaic yoke, as 1 Cor. x. 29; Gal. ii. 4; from evil, as James ii. 12; Rom. viii. 21.

ἐλεύθερος, α, ον, *free,* as opposed to the condition of a slave; *delivered from obligation* (often with ἐκ, ἀπό); *at liberty to* (inf.). Once with dat. of reference, Rom. vi. 20.

ἐλευθερόω, ῶ, *to set free* (generally with acc. and ἀπό); with modal dative, Gal. v. 1.

ἔλευσις, εως, ἡ (ἔρχομαι), *a coming, an advent,* Acts vii. 52.*

ἐλεφάντινος, η, ον, *made of ivory,* Rev. xviii. 12.*

Ἐλιακίμ, ὁ (Heb.), *Eliakim,* Matt. i. 13; Luke iii. 30.*

Ἐλιέζερ, ὁ (Heb.), *Eliezer,* Luke iii. 29.*

Ἐλιούδ, ὁ (Heb.), *Eliud,* Matt. i. 14, 15.*

Ἐλισάβετ, ἡ (Heb., *Elisheba*), *Elizabeth,* Luke i.*

Ἐλισσαῖος, ου, ὁ, *Elisha,* Luke iv. 27.*

ἑλίσσω, ἕξω, as εἱλίσσω, *to roll up,* Heb. i. 12; Rev. vi. 14 (W. H.).*

ἕλκος, ους, τό, *a wound, an ulcer, a sore,* Luke xvi. 21; Rev. xvi. 2, 11.*

ἑλκόω, ῶ, *to make a sore;* pass., *to be full of sores,* Luke xvi. 20.*

ἑλκύω, σω, *to drag,* Acts xvi. 19; *to draw,* a net, John xxi. 6, 11; a sword, John xviii. 10; *to draw over, to persuade,* John vi. 42, xii. 32.*

ἕλκω (old form of foregoing), impf. εἷλκον, James ii. 6; Acts xxi. 30.*

Ἑλλάς, άδος, ἡ, *Hellas, Greece* = Ἀχαΐα, Acts xx. 2.*

Ἕλλην, ηνος, ὁ, *a Greek,* as distinguished (1) from βάρβαρος, barbarian, Rom. i. 14, and (2) from Ἰουδαῖος, *Jew,* as John vii. 35. Used for Greek proselytes to Judaism, John xii. 20; Acts xvii. 4.

Ἑλληνικός, ή, όν, *Grecian,* Luke xxiii. 38; Rev. ix. 11.*

Ἑλληνίς, ίδος, *a Greek* or *Gentile woman,* Mark vii. 26; Acts xvii. 12.*

Ἑλληνιστής, οῦ (ἑλληνίζω, *to Hellenise,* or *adopt Greek manners and language*), *a Hellenist, Grecian Jew* (R.V.); a Jew by parentage and religion, but born in a Gentile country and speaking Greek, Acts vi. 1, ix. 29, xi. 20.*

Ἑλληνιστί, adv., *in the Greek language,* John xix. 20; Acts xxi. 37.*

ἐλ-λογέω (ἐν; W. H., -άω), *to charge to, to put to one's account,* Rom. v. 13; Philem. 18.*

Ἐλμωδάμ, ὁ, *Elmodam,* Luke iii. 28.*

ἐλπίζω, att. fut. ἐλπιῶ, 1st aor. ἤλπισα, *to expect* (acc. or inf., or ὅτι); *to hope for* (acc.); *to trust in* (ἐπί, dat.; ἐν, once dat. only); *to direct hope towards* (εἰς, ἐπί, acc.).

ἐλπίς, ίδος, ἡ, *expectation, hope, secure confidence;* especially of the Christian hope. Met., (1) *the author,* as 1 Tim. i. 1 ; (2) *the object of hope,* as Tit. ii. 13. (In Rom. viii. 20 W. H. read ἐφ' ἐλπίδι.)
Ἐλύμας, α, ὁ (from Arabic), *Elymas, i.e.,* a magus or sorcerer, Acts xiii. 8.*
Ἐλωΐ, *My God!* Mark xv. 34. The word is Hebrew (Ps. xxii. 2), pronounced in that language ἠλί, and so written, Matt. xxvii. 46 (W. H., ἐλωί).
ἐμαυτοῦ, ῆς, οῦ, *of myself,* a reflexive pron., found only in the gen., dat., and accus. cases : ἀπ' ἐμαυτοῦ, *from myself,* John v. 30.
ἐμ-βαίνω, 2nd aor. ἐνέβην, part. ἐμβάς, *to go upon, into* (εἰς), always of entering a ship except John v. 4 (W. H. omit).
ἐμ-βάλλω, *to cast into,* Luke xii. 5.*
ἐμ-βάπτω, *to dip into,* Matt. xxvi. 23 ; Mark xiv. 20 ; John xiii. 26. (W. H., βάπτω.)*
ἐμ-βατεύω, *to enter, to intrude, to pry into,* Col. ii. 18.*
ἐμ-βιβάζω, *to cause to enter, to put on board,* Acts xxvii. 6.*
ἐμ-βλέπω, *to direct the eyes to anything, to look fixedly, to consider, to know by inspection* (acc., dat., or εἰς).
ἐμ-βριμάομαι, ῶμαι, dep., *to be moved with indignation,* Mark xiv. 5 ; John xi. 33, 38 (R.V. marg.); *to charge sternly* (dat.), Matt. ix. 30 ; Mark i. 43.*
ἐμέω, ῶ, 1st aor., inf. ἐμέσαι, *to vomit, to spue out,* Rev. iii. 16.*
ἐμ-μαίνομαι, *to be mad against* (dat.), Acts xxvi. 11.*
Ἐμμανουήλ, ὁ, *Emmanuel,* a Hebrew word signifying "God with us;" a name of Christ, Matt. i. 23.*
Ἐμμαούς, ἡ, *Emmaus,* a village a short distance from Jerusalem, Luke xxiv. 13.*
ἐμ-μένω, *to remain* or *persevere in* (dat. or ἐν).
Ἐμμόρ, ὁ, *Emmor,* or *Hamor,* Acts vii. 16.*
ἐμός, ή, όν, *mine,* denoting possession, power over, authorship, right, etc. See § 336.
ἐμπαιγμονή, *mockery,* 2 Pet. iii. 3 (W.H.).
ἐμ-παιγμός, οῦ, ὁ, *a being mocked* or *derided,* Heb. xi. 36.*
ἐμ-παίζω, ξω, *to mock, deride, scoff at* (abs. or dat.).

ἐμ-παίκτης, ου, ὁ, *a scoffer, deceiver,* 2 Pet. iii. 13 ; Jude 18.*
ἐμ-περιπατέω, ῶ, ήσω, *to walk about in, to dwell among* (ἐν), 2 Cor. vi. 16.*
ἐμ-πίμπλημι and -πλάω, ἐμπλήσω, ἐνέπλησα, part. pres. ἐμπιπλῶν, *to fill up, to satisfy,* as with food, etc. (gen.).
ἐμ-πίπτω, *to fall into* or *among* (εἰς) ; fig., *to incur,* as condemnation or punishment, 1 Tim. iii. 6 ; Heb. x. 31.
ἐμ-πλέκω, 2nd aor. pass. ἐνεπλάκην, *to entangle, implicate,* 2 Tim. ii. 4 ; 2 Pet. ii. 20 (dat. of thing).*
ἐμ-πλοκή, ῆς, ἡ, *a plaiting, braiding,* of hair, 1 Pet. iii. 3.*
ἐμ-πνέω (W. H., ἐνπ-), *to breathe out* (gen.), Acts ix. 1.*
ἐμ-πορεύομαι, dep., *to go about ;* hence *to trade, to traffic,* abs., James iv. 13 ; *to make gain of* (acc.), 2 Pet. ii. 3.*
ἐμ-πορία, ας, ἡ, *trade, merchandise,* Matt. xxii. 5.*
ἐμ-πόριον, ου, τό, *emporium, a place for trading,* John ii. 16.*
ἔμ-πορος, ου, ὁ, *a traveller, merchant, trader,* Matt. xiii. 45 ; Rev. xviii.*
ἐμ-πρήθω, σω, *to set on fire, to burn,* Matt. xxii. 7.*
ἔμ-προσθεν, adv., *before* (ἔμπροσθεν καὶ ὄπισθεν, *in front and behind,* Rev. iv. 6); as prep. (gen.), *before,* in presence of, Matt. x. 32 ; *before,* in dignity, John i. 15, 27.
ἐμ-πτύω, σω, *to spit upon* (dat. or εἰς).
ἐμ-φανής, ές, *manifest* (dat.), Acts x. 40 ; Rom. x. 20.*
ἐμ-φανίζω, ίσω, *to make manifest* (acc. and dat.) ; *to show plainly* (ὅτι, or prepp. πρός, περί, etc.).
ἔμ-φοβος, ον, *terrified, afraid.*
ἐμ-φυσάω, ῶ, *to breathe upon,* acc., John xx. 22.*
ἔμ-φυτος, ον, *engrafted,* James i. 21.*
ἐν, prep. gov. dat., *in,* generally as being or resting in ; *within, among.* See § 295. ἐν- in composition has the force of *in, upon, into.* It is changed before γ, κ, and χ, into ἐγ- ; before β, π, φ, and μ, into ἐμ- ; and before λ, into ἐλ- (but W. H. prefer the unassimilated forms). The ν is, however, restored before the augment in verbs.
ἐν-αγκαλίζομαι, *to take up into one's arms,* Mark ix. 36, x. 16.*

ἐν-άλιος, ον (ἅλς), *being* or *living in the sea, marine*, James iii. 7.*

ἔν-αντι, adv., as prep. with gen., *in the presence of, before*, Luke i. 8; Acts viii. 21 (W. H.).*

ἐν-αντίος, α, ον, *over against, contrary*, of the wind, as Acts xxvii. 4; *adverse, hostile*, as Acts xxvi. 9; ἐξ ἐναντίας, *over against*, Mark xv. 39. Neut., ἐναντίον, adv. as prep. with gen., *in the presence of*, as Luke xxiv. 16; Acts vii. 10.

ἐν-άρχομαι, *to begin*, Gal. iii. 3; Phil. i. 6.*

ἔνατος. See ἔννατος.

ἐν-δεής, ές, *in want, destitute, needy*, Acts iv. 34.*

ἔν-δειγμα, ατος, τό, *an indication, proof, manifest token*, 2 Thess. i. 5.*

ἐν-δείκνυμι, N.T. mid., *to show, to manifest*.

ἔνδειξις, εως, ἡ, *a showing, declaration*, Rom. iii. 25; 2 Cor. viii. 24; *an evident token*, Phil. i. 28.*

ἕνδεκα, οἱ, αἱ, τά, *eleven*. οἱ ἕνδεκα, *the Eleven, i.e., apostles*.

ἑνδέκατος, η, ον, *eleventh*.

ἐν-δέχομαι, dep., *to admit;* only impersonally, οὐκ ἐνδέχεται, *it is not admissible* or *possible*, Luke xiii. 33.*

ἐν-δημέω, ῶ, *to be at home*, 2 Cor. v. 6, 8, 9.*

ἐν-διδύσκω, mid., *to clothe oneself with* (acc.), Luke viii. 27, xvi. 19; Mark xv. 17 (W. H.).* See ἐνδύω.

ἔν-δικος, ον, *agreeable to justice, right, righteous*, Rom. iii. 8; Heb. ii. 3.*

ἐν-δόμησις, εως, ἡ, *a structure, a building*, Rev. xxi. 18.*

ἐν-δοξάζω, σω, *to glorify, to honour*, 2 Thess. i. 10, 12.*

ἔν-δοξος, ον, *adorned with honour, glorious*, Luke xiii. 17; Eph. v. 27; of persons, *had in honour*, 1 Cor. iv. 10; of external appearance, *splendid*, Luke vii. 25.*

ἔν-δυμα, ατος, τό, *a garment, raiment*.

ἐν-δυναμόω, ῶ, *to strengthen, to furnish with power;* pass., *to acquire strength, be strong*.

ἐν-δύνω (2 Tim. iii. 6) and ἐνδύω, *to clothe* or *to invest with* (two accs.); mid., *to enter, insinuate oneself into* (2 Tim. iii. 6), *to put on, to clothe oneself with* (acc.); often fig., *to invest with*.

ἔν-δυσις, εως, ἡ, *a putting on* or *wearing of clothes*, 1 Pet. iii. 3.*

ἐν-έδρα, ας, ἡ, *an ambush, a snare*, Acts xxiii. 16 (W. H.), xxv. 3.*

ἐν-εδρεύω, *to watch, to entrap, to lie in ambush for* (acc.), Luke xi. 54; Acts xxiii. 21.*

ἐν-ειλέω, ῶ, 1st aor. ἐνείλησα, *to roll up, to wrap in* (acc. and dat.), Mark xv. 46.*

ἔν-ειμι, *to be in, to have a place in*, Luke xi. 41, τὰ ἐνόντα, *such things as are in* [*the platter*, ver. 39], or *such as ye have, i.e., according to your ability*. For ἔνεστι impers., see ἔνι.

ἕνεκα or ἕνεκεν, sometimes εἵνεκεν, prep. adv., gen., *because of, by reason of, on account of*. οὗ ἕνεκεν, *because*, Luke iv. 18; τίνος ἕνεκεν; *to what end?* Acts xix. 32.

ἐν-έργεια, ας, ἡ, *energy, efficacy, effectual operation*.

ἐν-εργέω, ῶ, *to exert one's power, to work in one*, as Gal. ii. 8; trans., *to accomplish*, as 1 Cor. xii. 11; mid., *to be effective, to be in action*. Part., ἐνεργουμένη, James v. 16 (see R.V.).

ἐν-έργημα, ατος, τό, *working, effect;* plur. with gen., 1 Cor. xii. 6, 10.*

ἐν-εργής, ές, *effectual, energetic*, 1 Cor. xvi. 9; Heb. iv. 12; Philem. 6.*

ἐν-εστώς, perf. participle of ἐνίστημι.

ἐν-ευ-λογέω, ῶ, *to bless, to distinguish by blessings*, Acts iii. 25; Gal. iii. 8.*

ἐν-έχω, (1) *to hold in, entangle*, only in pass. (dat.), Gal. v. 1; (2) *to set oneself against* (dat.), Mark vi. 19; Luke xi. 53.*

ἐνθάδε, adv., (1) *hither, to this place;* (2) *here, in this place*.

ἐν-θυμέομαι, οῦμαι, dep. pass., *to revolve in mind, to think upon*, Matt. i. 20, ix. 4; Acts x. 19 (W. H., διεν-).*

ἐν-θύμησις, εως, ἡ, *thought, reflection, contrivance*.

ἔνι, elliptical for ἔνεστι, impers., *there is in*, 1 Cor. vi. 5 (W. H.); Gal. iii. 28; Col. iii. 11; James i. 17.*

ἐνιαυτός, οῦ, ὁ, *a year*.

ἐν-ίστημι, *to be present, to be at hand*, 2 Thess. ii. 2; 2 Tim. iii. 1; perf. part. ἐνεστηκώς, sync. ἐνεστώς, *impending*, or *present*, 1 Cor. vii. 26; Gal. i. 4; Heb. ix. 9. τὰ ἐνεστῶτα, *present things*, opposed to τὰ μέλλοντα,

things to come, Rom. viii. 38 ; 1 Cor. iii. 22.*
ἐν-ισχύω, *to invigorate, to strengthen*, Luke xxii. 43; Acts ix. 19 (see W. H.).*
ἔννατος, η, ον (W. H., ἔνατος), *ninth*.
ἐννέα, οἱ, αἱ, τά, *nine*, Luke xvii. 17.*
ἐννενηκοντα-εννέα, *ninety-nine*, Matt. xviii. 12, 13 ; Luke xv. 4, 7 (see W. H.).*
ἐννεός, ον (W. H., ἐνεός), *dumb, speechless*, as with amazement, Acts ix. 7.*
ἐν-νεύω, *to ask* or *signify by beckoning* (dat.), Luke i. 62 ; Heb. iv. 12 ; 1 Pet. iv. 1.*
ἔν-νοια, ας, ἡ (νοῦς), *intention, purpose*.
ἔν-νομος, ον, *under law*, 1 Cor. ix. 21 ; *according to law*, Acts xix. 39.*
ἔν-νυχος, ον (νύξ), *in the night*, neut. as adv., Mark i. 35. (W. H., ἔννυχα.)*
ἐν-οικέω, ῶ, *to dwell in, to inhabit* (ἐν).
ἑνότης, τητος, ἡ (εἷς), *unity, concord*, Eph. iv. 3, 13.*
ἐν-οχλέω, ῶ, *to disturb, to occasion tumult*, Heb. xii. 15 ; Luke vi. 18 (W. H.).*
ἔν-οχος, ον, *guilty of* (gen. of the crime, or of that which is violated); *subject to* (dat. of court, gen. of punishment, εἰς of the place of punishment).
ἔν-ταλμα, ατος, τό, *a commandment, an institute*, Matt. xv. 9 ; Mark vii. 7 ; Col. ii. 22.*
ἐν-ταφιάζω, *to prepare for burial*, as by washing, swathing, adorning, anointing the corpse, Matt. xxvi. 12 ; John xix. 40.*
ἐν-ταφιασμός, οῦ, ὁ, *the preparation of a corpse for burial*, Mark xiv. 8 ; John xii. 7.
ἐν-τέλλω, in N.T. only mid. and pass.; fut. mid., ἐντελοῦμαι ; perf., ἐντέταλμαι, *to charge, to command, to commit* (dat. of pers., or πρός with acc.).
ἐντεῦθεν, adv., *hence ; from this place or cause ;* repeated John xix. 18, *on this side and that*.
ἔν-τευξις, εως, ἡ, *prayer, intercession*, 1 Tim. ii. 1, iv. 5.*
ἔν-τιμος, ον, *held in renown ; precious, highly esteemed*, Luke vii. 2, xiv. 8 ; Phil. ii. 29 ; 1 Pet. ii. 4, 6.*
ἐντολή, ῆς, ἡ, *a divine precept or prohibition: of God's commands*, 1 Cor. vii. 19; *Christ's precepts or teachings*, 1 Cor. xiv. 37 ; 1 Tim. vi. 14 ; *traditions of the Rabbis*, Tit. i. 14. αἱ

ἐντολαί, *the commandments, i.e.*, the ten.
ἐν-τόπιος, ον, ὁ (prop. adj.), *an inhabitant*, Acts xxi. 12.*
ἐντός, adv. as prep., with gen., *within*, Luke xvii. 21. τὸ ἐντός, *the interior*, Matt. xxiii. 26.*
ἐν-τρέπω, ψω, 2nd fut. pass., ἐντραπήσομαι ; 2nd aor. pass., ἐνετράπην ; *to put to shame*, as 1 Cor. iv. 14 ; Tit. ii. 8 ; mid., *to reverence, to be in awe of*, as Matt. xxi. 37.
ἐν-τρέφω, *to nourish in* (dat.) ; pass., fig., 1 Tim. iv. 6.*
ἔν-τρομος, ον, *terrified, trembling through fear*, Acts vii. 32, xvi. 29 ; Heb. xii. 21.*
ἐν-τροπή, ῆς, ἡ, *a putting to shame*, 1 Cor. vi. 5, xv. 34.*
ἐν-τρυφάω, ῶ, *to live luxuriously, to banquet, to revel* (with ἐν), 2 Pet. ii. 13.*
ἐν-τυγχάνω, *to come to, to address*, Acts xxv. 24 ; with ὑπέρ (gen.), *to intercede for*, Rom. viii. 27, 34 ; Heb. vii. 25 ; with κατά (gen.), *to plead against*, Rom. xi. 2.*
ἐν-τυλίσσω, ξω, *to wrap in, to wrap up*, Matt. xxvii. 59 ; Luke xxiii. 53 ; John xx. 7.*
ἐν-τυπόω, ῶ, *to engrave, sculpture*, 2 Cor. iii. 7.*
ἐν-υβρίζω, σω. *to treat contemptuously or in despite*, Heb. x. 29.*
ἐν-υπνιάζομαι, dep. pass., *to dream* (cognate acc.), Acts ii. 17 ; *to conceive wild or impure thoughts*, Jude 8.*
ἐν-ύπνιον, ου, τό, *a dream*, Acts ii. 17.*
ἐνώπιον (neut. of ἐνώπιος, from ἐν ὠπί, *in view*), as prep., with gen., *before, in sight or presence of*, Luke i. 17 ; Rev. iii. 9. ἐνώπιον τοῦ Θεοῦ, *in the sight of God*, Rom. xiv. 22 ; used in obtestation, 1 Tim. v. 21. χάρις ἐνώπιον τοῦ Θεοῦ (Acts vii. 4), *favour with God*.
Ἐνώς, ὁ, *Enos*, Luke iii. 38.*
ἐν-ωτίζομαι, dep. mid. (ἐν ὠτίοις, *in the ears*), *to listen to*, Acts ii. 14.*
Ἐνώχ, ὁ, *Enoch*, Luke iii. 37 ; Jude 14.*
ἐξ, prep. See ἐκ.
ἕξ, οἱ, αἱ, τά, card. num., *six*.
ἐξ-αγγέλλω, *to declare abroad, celebrate*, 1 Pet. ii. 9.*
ἐξ-αγοράζω, *to buy from, buy back, redeem*, Gal. iii. 13 (ἐκ), iv. 5. τὸν καιρόν, *to*

redeem the opportunity from being lost, Eph. v. 16; Col. iv. 5.*
ἐξ-άγω, 2nd aor. ἐξήγαγον, *to lead out, to send forth* (with ἔξω, ἐκ, εἰς).
ἐξαιρέω, ῶ (see § 103, 1), *to take* or *pluck out*, Matt. v. 29, xviii. 9; mid., *to rescue, deliver*, Acts vii. 10, 34, xii. 11, xxiii. 27, xxvi. 17; Gal. i. 4.*
ἐξ-αίρω (see § 92), *to take out* or *away; to expel* or *excommunicate*, 1 Cor. v. 2 (W. H., αἴρω), 13.*
ἐξ-αιτέω, ῶ, N.T., mid., *to require, to ask for*, Luke xxii. 31.*
ἐξ-αίφνης, adv., *suddenly, unexpectedly*.
ἐξ-ακολουθέω, ῶ, *to follow, to persist in following* (dat.), 2 Pet. i. 16, ii. 2, 15.*
ἐξακόσιοι, αι, α, *six hundred*.
ἐξ-αλείφω, *to wipe out, obliterate*, Rev. iii. 5; Col. ii. 14; Acts iii. 19; *to wipe away*, Rev. vii. 17, xxi. 4 (ἀπό or ἐκ).*
ἐξ-άλλομαι, *to leap forth* or *up*, Acts iii. 8.*
ἐξ-ανά-στασις, εως, ἡ, *a resurrection*, Phil. iii. 11 (followed by ἐκ, W. H.).*
ἐξ-ανα-τέλλω, *to spring up, to shoot forth*, as plants or corn, Matt. xiii. 5; Mark iv. 5.*
ἐξ-αν-ίστημι, (1) trans., *to raise up* offspring, Mark xii. 19; Luke xx. 28; (2) 2nd aor. intrans., *to rise up, to stand forth*, Acts xv. 5.*
ἐξ-απατάω, ῶ, *to deceive utterly, to seduce* from truth.
ἐξάπινα, adv. (= ἐξαίφνης), *unexpectedly*, Mark ix. 8.*
ἐξ-α-πορέομαι, οῦμαι, dep., *to be utterly without resource, to be in utmost perplexity*, 2 Cor. i. 8, iv. 8.*
ἐξ-απο-στέλλω, *to send forth, send away*.
ἐξ-αρτίζω, (1) *to complete*, Acts xxi. 5; (2) *to furnish thoroughly for* (πρός, acc.), 2 Tim. iii. 17.*
ἐξ-αστράπτω, *to gleam*, as lightning; of raiment, Luke ix. 29.*
ἐξ-αυτῆς, adv. (sc. ὥρας), *from that very time, instantly*, as Mark vi. 25; Acts x. 33.
ἐξ-εγείρω, *to raise up*, as from death, Rom. ix. 17; 1 Cor. vi. 14.*
ἐξ-ειμι, (εἶμι, see § 111), *to go out*, Acts xiii. 42, xvii. 15, xx. 7, xxvii. 43.*
ἐξ-ειμι (εἰμί). See ἔξεστι.
ἐξ-ελέγχω, *to convict, to rebuke sternly, to punish*, Jude 15 (W. H., ἐλέγχω).*

ἐξ-έλκω, *to draw out* from the right way, James i. 14.*
ἐξ-έραμα, ατος, τό, *that which is vomited*, 2 Pet. ii. 22.*
ἐξερευνάω (W. H., -ραυ-), *to search diligently*, 1 Pet. i. 10.*
ἐξ-έρχομαι (see § 103, 2), *to go* or *to come out of* (with gen. or ἐκ, ἀπό, ἔξω, παρά); *to go away, to depart, to issue* or *to spring from; to go forth;* of a rumour, *to be divulged* or *spread abroad; to emanate*, as thoughts from the heart, healing power from the Saviour; *to go out*, i.e., vanish, as expiring hope, Acts xvi. 19.
ἔξεστι, part. neut. ἐξόν (impers. from ἔξειμι), *it is lawful*, as Matt. xiv. 4; *it is becoming*, as Acts xvi. 21; *it is possible*, as Matt. xx. 15. The part. is used in the same sense, with or without subst. verb, Matt. xii. 4; 2 Cor. xii. 4 (dat. and inf.).
ἐξ-ετάζω, *to inquire, to ask, to examine strictly*, Matt. ii. 8, x. 11; John xxi. 12.*
ἐξ-ηγέομαι, οῦμαι, dep. mid., *to narrate fully and accurately*, as Luke xxiv. 35; *to expound*, as a teacher, as John i. 18.
ἑξήκοντα, οἱ, αἱ, τά, *sixty*.
ἑξῆς, adv. (ἔχω) *next in order*, only in the phrase τῇ ἑξῆς (sc. ἡμέρᾳ), *on the next day.* (ἡμέρᾳ is expressed, Luke ix. 37.)
ἐξ-ηχέω, ῶ, only in pass., N.T., *to be sounded forth, propagated widely*, 1 Thess. i. 8.*
ἕξις, εως, ἡ (ἔχω), *habit, use*, Heb. v. 14.*
ἐξ-ίστημι, -ιστάω and -ιστάνω (see § 107), "to remove from the natural state," (1) trans., *to astonish*, Luke xxiv. 22; Acts viii. 9, 11; (2) 2nd aor., perf. and mid., intrans., *to be astonished, confounded, to be beside oneself*, as 2 Cor. v. 13.
ἐξ-ισχύω, *to be perfectly able*, Eph. iii. 18.*
ἔξ-οδος, ου, ἡ, "*exodus*," *a going out*, Heb. xi. 22; *departure*, as from life, Luke ix. 31; 2 Pet. i. 15.*
ἐξ-ολοθρεύω, *to destroy utterly*, Acts iii. 23.*
ἐξ-ομολογέω, ῶ, *to confess fully, to make acknowledgment of*, as of sins, etc.; in mid., *to acknowledge benefits conferred, to praise* (with dat.). Once, *to promise*, Luke xxii. 6.

F F

ἐξ-ορκίζω, to adjure, put to oath, Matt. xxvi. 63.*
ἐξ-ορκιστής, οῦ, ὁ, one who puts to oath or adjures, "exorcist," Acts xix. 13.*
ἐξ-ορύσσω, ξω, to dig out, Gal. iv. 15; hence, to break up, Mark ii. 4.*
ἐξ-ουδενέω, or ἐξουθενέω, ῶ (οὐδείς), to set at nought, to treat with contempt. Perf. pass. part. ἐξουθενημένος, contemned, disesteemed, 1 Cor. i. 28, vi. 4.
ἐξ-ουδενόω, ῶ, as preceding, Mark ix. 12 (W. H., -έω).*
ἐξ-ουσία, as, ἡ (ἔξεστι), (1) power, ability, as John xix. 11; (2) liberty, licence, privilege, right, as Rom. ix. 21; (3) commission, authority, as Matt. xxi. 23; (4) αἱ ἐξουσίαι, the powers, i.e., rulers, magistrates, Luke xii. 11; angels, good and bad, Eph. i. 21, vi. 12. In 1 Cor. xi. 10, ἐξουσίαν, emblem of power, or subjection to the power of a husband, i.e., the veil.
ἐξ-ουσιάζω, to have right over, to exercise authority over (gen.), Luke xxii. 25; 1 Cor. vii. 4; pass., to be under the power of (ὑπό), 1 Cor vi. 12.*
ἐξ-οχή, ῆς, ἡ, eminence, distinction; only in the phrase κατ' ἐξοχήν, by way of distinction, Acts xxv. 23 (§ 300, β, 5).*
ἐξ-υπνίζω, σω, to wake from sleep, John xi. 11.*
ἐξ-υπνος, ον, roused out of sleep, Acts xvi. 27.*
ἔξω, adv., abs., or as prep. with gen., without, outside. οἱ ἔξω, those without, as Mark iv. 11; 1 Cor. v. 12, 13. Used often after verbs of motion compounded with ἐκ.
ἔξωθεν, adv. of place, from without. τὸ ἔξωθεν, the outside, as Luke xi. 39. οἱ ἔξωθεν, those from without, as 1 Tim. iii. 7. As prep. gen., Mark vii. 15; Rev. xi. 2.
ἐξ-ωθέω, ῶ, ώσω, to drive out, expel, Acts vii. 45; to propel, as a vessel, Acts xxvii. 39 (see W. H. and marg.).*
ἐξώτερος, α, ον (comp. of ἔξω), outer, in the phrase "outer darkness," Matt. viii. 12, xxii. 13, xxv. 30.*
ἔοικα. See εἴκω.
ἑορτάζω, to keep or celebrate a feast, 1 Cor. v. 8.*
ἑορτή, ῆς, ἡ, a solemn feast or festival. Used of Jewish feasts, especially of the Passover, with its accompanying feast of unleavened bread, as Luke ii. 41, xxii. 1.
ἐπ-αγγελία, ας, ἡ, (1) a message, commission, Acts xxiii. 21; (2) a promise, as 2 Cor. i. 20, generally plur.; the promises, specially, e.g., to Abraham, or those of the Gospel, as 2 Tim. i. 1; (3) met., the thing promised, as Acts ii. 33; Heb. xi. 13, 33, 39.
ἐπ-αγγέλλω, mid. in N.T., except pass., Gal. iii. 19, (1) to promise, with dat., or acc. and dat., or inf., once cognate acc., 1 John ii. 25; (2) to make profession or avowal of (acc.), 1 Tim. ii. 10, vi. 21.
ἐπ-άγγελμα, ατος, τό, a promise, 2 Pet. i. 4, iii. 13.*
ἐπ-άγω, to bring upon, Acts v. 28; 2 Pet. ii. 1, 5.*
ἐπ-αγωνίζομαι, to contend or strive earnestly for (dat.), Jude 3.*
ἐπ-αθροίζω, pass., to gather together, to crowd, Luke xi. 29.*
Ἐπ-αίνετος, ου, ὁ, Epœnĕtus, Rom. xvi. 5.*
ἐπ-αινέω, ῶ, έσω, 1st aor. ἐπῄνεσα, to commend, to praise, Luke xvi. 8; Rom. xv. 11; 1 Cor. xi. 2, 17, 22.*
ἔπ-αινος, ου, ὁ, commendation, as Rom. ii. 29; praise, as Eph. i. 6, 12, 14; Phil. i. 11.
ἐπ-αίρω (see § 92), to raise up, as hoisting a sail, Acts xxvii. 40; to lift up, as the eyes, the hands in prayer, the head in courage, the heel against, or in opposition; pass., to be lifted up, to become elated, 2 Cor. xi. 20. Of the ascension of Christ, Acts i. 9.
ἐπ-αισχύνομαι, to be ashamed, abs.; to be ashamed of (acc. or ἐπί, dat.).
ἐπ-αιτέω, ῶ, to beg, to ask alms, Luke xvi. 3, xviii. 35 (W. H.).
ἐπ-ακολουθέω, ῶ, to follow after (dat.); fig., 1 Tim. v. 10, 24; 1 Pet. ii. 21; part., attendant, Mark xvi. 20 (see W. H.).*
ἐπ-ακούω, to hearken to favourably (gen. pers.); 2 Cor. vi. 2.*
ἐπ-ακροάομαι, ῶμαι, to hear, listen to (gen. pers.), Acts xvi. 25.*
ἐπάν, conj. (ἐπεὶ ἄν), if, after that, when, (subj.), Matt. ii. 8; Luke xi. 22, 34.*
ἐπ-άναγκες, adv., of necessity, necessarily (with art.), Acts xv. 28.*

ἐπ-αν-άγω, trans., *to put* (a vessel) *out to sea*, Luke v. 3, 4 ; intrans., *to return*, Matt. xxi. 18.*

ἐπ-ανα-μιμνήσκω, *to remind, put in remembrance* (acc.), Rom. xv. 15.*

ἐπ-ανα-παύομαι, *to rest upon* (ἐπί, acc.), Luke x. 6 ; *to rely, to trust in* (dat.), Rom. ii. 17.*

ἐπ-αν-έρχομαι, *to come back, return*, Luke x. 35 ; xix. 15.*

ἐπ-αν-ίστημι, N.T., mid., *to rise up against* (ἐπί, acc.), Matt. x. 21 ; Mark xiii. 12.*

ἐπ-αν-όρθωσις, εως, ἡ, *correction, reformation*, 2 Tim. iii. 16.*

ἐπ-άνω, adv. abs., or as prep. gen., *above, upon ; more than*, in price or number ; *superior to*, in authority.

ἐπ-αρκέω, ῶ, ἔσω, *to suffice for, to relieve, support* (dat.), 1 Tim. v. 10, 16.*

ἐπ-αρχία, as, ἡ, *a province*, division of the Roman Empire, Acts xxiii. 34, xxv. 1.*

ἔπ-αυλις, εως, ἡ, *a dwelling, a habitation*, Acts i. 20.*

ἐπ-αύριον, adv., *on the morrow.* τῇ (ἡμέρᾳ) ἐπαύριον, *on the next day.*

ἐπ-αυτο-φώρῳ. See αὐτό-φωρος.

'Επαφρᾶς, ᾶ, ὁ, *Epaphras* of Colossæ, Col. i. 7, iv. 12 ; Philem. 23 (contr. from *Epaphroditus*, but different from St. Paul's companion of that name).*

ἐπ-αφρίζω, *to foam up or out* (acc.), Jude 13.*

'Επαφρόδιτος, ον, ὁ, *Epaphroditus*, a Macedonian, Phil. ii. 25, iv. 18.*

ἐπ-εγείρω, *to raise up, to excite against* (ἐπί, acc., or κατά, gen.), Acts xiii. 50, xiv. 2.*

ἐπεί, conj., (1) of time, *when*, only Luke vii. 1 (W. H., ἐπειδή); (2) of reason, *since, because, seeing that.*

ἐπει-δή, conj., *since truly, inasmuch as*, as Matt. xxi. 46 ; Phil. ii. 26 ; of time, *when*, only Luke vii. 1 (W. H.).

ἐπει-δή-περ, conj., *since verily, forasmuch as*, Luke i. 1.*

ἐπ-είδον. See ἐφοράω.

ἔπ-ειμι (εἶμι, § 111), *to come after, to follow ;* only in part., ἐπιών, οὖσα, ὀν, *following*, Acts vii. 26, xxiii. 11. τῇ ἐπιούσῃ (sc. ἡμέρᾳ), *on the following day*, Acts xvi. 11, xx. 15, xxi. 18.*

ἐπεί-περ, conj., *since indeed*, Rom. iii. 30. (W. H., εἴπερ.)*

ἐπ-εισ-αγωγή, ῆς, ἡ, *a bringing in, introduction*, Heb. vii. 9.*

ἔπ-ειτα, adv., *thereupon, thereafter ;* marking succession of time, as Gal. i. 18 ; also of order, as 1 Cor. xv. 46 ; 1 Thess. iv. 17.

ἐπ-έκεινα (μέρη), adv. with gen., *beyond*, as to place, Acts vii. 43.*

ἐπ-εκ-τείνω, in mid., *to stretch forwards to* (dat.), Phil. iii. 14.*

ἐπ-εν-δύτης, ου, *an upper garment*, John xxi. 7.*

ἐπ-εν-δύω, in mid., *to put on*, as an upper garment, 2 Cor. v. 2, 4.*

ἐπ-έρχομαι, *to come upon, approach, arrive at, befall, happen ; to attack*, Luke xi. 22. τὰ ἐπερχόμενα, *the things that are coming on* (dat.), Luke xxi. 26.

ἐπ-ερωτάω, ῶ, (1) *to interrogate, to question* (two accs., or acc. and περί, gen., or with εἰ, τίς ; etc.) ; *to question judicially*, John xviii. 21 ; *to inquire after* God, Rom. x. 20 ; (2) *to request of* (acc. and inf.), Matt. xvi. 1.

ἐπ-ερώτημα, ατος, τό (1 Pet. iii. 21), probably *inquiry after* God ; "the seeking after God in a good and pure conscience" (Alford). See R.V.*

ἐπ-έχω, (1) *to apply* (the mind) *to* (dat.), *take heed to*, Luke xiv. 7 ; Acts iii. 5 ; 1 Tim. iv. 16 ; (2) *to hold out, to exhibit*, Phil. ii. 16 ; (3) "*to detain* (oneself)," *to tarry*, Acts xix. 22.*

ἐπ-ηρεάζω, *to injure, to treat despitefully*, Matt. v. 44 (not W. H.), Luke vi. 28 ; *to traduce, to accuse falsely* (acc. of charge), 1 Pet. iii. 16.*

ἐπί, a preposition governing gen., dat., or acc. General signification, *upon.* For its various applications, see § 305. ἐπι-, in composition, signifies *motion upon, towards*, or *against ; rest on, over*, or *at ; addition, succession, repetition, renewal ;* and it is often intensive.

ἐπι-βαίνω, *to go upon* a ship, *to mount* a horse or ass, *to come to* or *into* a country (ἐπί, acc., εἰς, or simple dat.), Matt. xxi. 5 ; Acts xxi. 2, 6 (W. H., ἐμβ.), xxv. 1, xxvii. 2.*

ἐπι-βάλλω, (1) trans., *to cast on* or *over*, as Mark xi. 7 ; *to put on*, as a patch on a garment, Luke v. 36 ; (2) intrans., *to rush violently* on, Mark iv. 37 ; *to fix the mind stedfastly* on anything, Mark xiv. 72 ; (3) part., ἐπιβάλλων, *falling to* his share, Luke xv 12.

ἐπι-βαρέω, ῶ, to burden; fig., 2 Cor. ii. 5; 1 Thess. ii. 9; 2 Thess. iii. 8.*
ἐπι-βιβάζω, to put or to set upon, as on a beast to ride, Luke x. 34, xix. 35; Acts xxiii. 24.*
ἐπι-βλέπω, to look upon with favour (with ἐπί), Luke i. 48, ix. 38; James ii. 3.*
ἐπί-βλημα, ατος, τό, a patch on a garment, Matt. ix. 16; Mark ii. 21; Luke v. 36.*
ἐπι-βοάω, ῶ, to cry aloud, Acts xxv. 24. (W. H., βοάω.)*
ἐπι-βουλή, ῆς, ἡ, a design against, a plot, an ambush, Acts ix. 24, xx. 3, 19 (plur.), xxiii. 30.*
ἐπι-γαμβρεύω, to marry by right of affinity (acc.), Matt. xxii. 24.*
ἐπί-γειος, ον, earthly, belonging to the earth. τὰ ἐπίγεια, earthly things.
ἐπι-γίνομαι, to arise or spring up, as a wind, Acts xxviii. 13.*
ἐπι-γινώσκω, (1) to know clearly, understand, discern; (2) to acknowledge; (3) to recognise; (4) to learn (ὅτι), become acquainted with (acc.).
ἐπί-γνωσις, εως, ἡ, knowledge, acknowledgment.
ἐπι-γραφή, ῆς, ἡ, an inscription, a superscription, as Luke xx. 24, xxiii. 38.
ἐπι-γράφω, to inscribe, engrave, write upon, as Mark xv. 26; Rev. xxi. 12.
ἐπι-δείκνυμι (see § 114), (1) to show, exhibit; (2) to demonstrate, prove by argument.
ἐπι-δέχομαι, to receive kindly, 3 John 9, 10.*
ἐπι-δημέω, ῶ, to sojourn, as foreigners in a country, Acts ii. 10, xvii. 21.*
ἐπι-δια-τάσσομαι, to superadd, Gal. iii. 15.*
ἐπι-δίδωμι, to deliver, to give up (acc. and dat.), as Matt. vii. 9; Acts xv. 30; to give way to the wind, Acts xxvii. 15.
ἐπι-δι-ορθόω, to set or bring into order, Tit. i. 5.*
ἐπι-δύω, to set, as the sun, Eph. iv. 26.*
ἐπι-είκεια, as, ἡ, clemency, gentleness, Acts xxiv. 4; 2 Cor. x. 1.*
ἐπι-εικής, ές, gentle, mild, kind, Phil. iv. 5; 1 Tim. iii. 2, 3; James iii. 17; 1 Pet. ii. 18.*
ἐπι-ζητέω, ῶ, to seek earnestly or continuously (acc. of pers. or thing; also

περί, gen. or inf.); to beg earnestly, to desire.
ἐπι-θανάτιος, ον, appointed to death, 1 Cor. iv. 9.*
ἐπί-θεσις, εως, ἡ, a laying on of hands, Acts viii. 18; 1 Tim. iv. 14; 2 Tim. i. 6; Heb. vi. 2.*
ἐπι-θυμέω, ῶ, to desire, to long for, to covet, to lust after. (On Luke xxii. 15, see § 280, b.)
ἐπι-θυμητής, οῦ, ὁ, an eager desirer of, 1 Cor. x. 6.*
ἐπι-θυμία, ας, ἡ, desire, eagerness for; generally in a bad sense, inordinate desire, lust, cupidity.
ἐπι-καθίζω, to seat upon or sit upon, Matt. xxi. 7 (rec., ἐπεκάθισαν, trans., they seated [him]; W. H., -εν, intrans., he sat).*
ἐπι-καλέω, ῶ, έσω, to call upon, to call by name, to invoke in prayer, Acts vii. 59 (abs.); Rom. x. 12, 14 (acc.); mid., to appeal to (acc.), Acts xxv. 11; pass., to be called or surnamed, Luke xxii. 3; Acts xv. 17.
ἐπι-κάλυμμα, ατος, τό, a covering, a cloak, a pretext, 1 Pet. ii. 16.*
ἐπι-καλύπτω, to cover, of sins; to hide, to give over to oblivion, Rom. iv. 7 (LXX.).*
ἐπι-κατάρατος, ον, accursed, doomed to punishment or destruction, John vii. 49 (W. H., ἐπάρατος); Gal. iii. 10, 13 (LXX.).*
ἐπί-κειμαι, to lie upon (dat.), John xi. 38, xxi. 9; so to press upon, as the multitude upon Christ, Luke v. 1; as a tempest on a ship, Acts xxvii. 20; fig., to be laid on, as necessity, 1 Cor. ix. 16; to be laid or imposed upon, as by a law, Heb. ix. 10; to be urgent with entreaties, Luke xxiii. 23.*
Ἐπικούρειος, ον, ὁ, an Epicurean, a follower of Epicurus, Acts xvii. 18.*
ἐπι-κουρία, ας, ἡ (κοῦρος, help), assistance, help, aid, Acts xxvi. 22.*
ἐπι-κρίνω, to decide, to give judgment (acc. and inf.), Luke xxiii. 24.*
ἐπι-λαμβάνω, N.T., mid., to take hold of (gen.), in kindness, as Luke ix. 47; Acts ix. 27; Heb. ii. 16; to seize, as a prisoner, Acts xxi. 30, 33; met., to lay hold of, so as to possess, 1 Tim. vi. 12, 19.

ἐπι-λανθάνομαι, dep., *to forget* (inf., gen. or acc.); part. perf. pass., ἐπιλελησμένον, *forgotten*, Luke xii. 6.
ἐπι-λέγω, in pass., *to be named* or *called*, John v. 2; mid., *to choose*, Acts xv. 40.*
ἐπι-λείπω, *not to suffice, to fail*, Heb. xi. 32.*
ἐπι-λησμονή, ῆς, ἡ, *forgetfulness*, James i. 25. See § 257.*
ἐπί-λοιπος, ον, *remaining*, 1 Pet. iv. 2.*
ἐπί-λυσις, εως, ἡ, *solution, interpretation*, 2 Pet. i. 20. (See ἴδιος.)*
ἐπι-λύω, *to solve, explain, interpret*, Mark iv. 34; *to determine on*, as a debated question, Acts xix. 39.*
ἐπι-μαρτυρέω, ῶ, *to testify earnestly*, 1 Pet. v. 12.*
ἐπι-μέλεια, ας, ἡ, *care for, study, attention*, Acts xxvii. 3.*
ἐπι-μέλομαι and έομαι, οῦμαι, *to take care of* (gen.), Luke x. 34, 35; 1 Tim. iii. 5.*
ἐπι-μελῶς, adv., *carefully, diligently*, Luke xv. 8.*
ἐπι-μένω, (1) *to remain, abide, continue;* (2) met., *to be constant, or persevering in* (dat.).
ἐπι-νεύω, *to nod, to assent by nodding, to consent*, Acts xviii. 20.*
ἐπί-νοια, as, ἡ, *thought, device, purpose of mind*, Acts viii. 22.*
ἐπι-ορκέω, ῶ, *to swear falsely*, Matt. v. 33.*
ἐπί-ορκος, ον, *perjured*, 1 Tim. i. 10.*
ἐπι-ούσιος, ον, adj. (οὐσία, either in the sense of subsistence or existence), *pertaining to subsistence* or *existence, sufficient for support, daily*. (Cf. the Heb. phrase, Prov. xxx. 8, "the food that is needful for me," R.V.) Others with less probability connect the word with ἔπειμι (εἶμι) (which see), the bread *which belongs to the following day*, Matt. vi. 11; Luke xi. 3.*
ἐπι-πίπτω, *to fall upon* (ἐπί, acc.), *rush upon*, Mark iii. 10 (dat.); fig., *to come upon* (dat., or ἐπί, acc. or dat.), as an emotion, etc., Luke i. 12; Acts viii. 16.
ἐπι-πλήσσω, *to rebuke, to chide*, 1 Tim. v. 1.*
ἐπι-ποθέω, ῶ, *to desire earnestly, to long for* or *after* (inf. or acc.), as 2 Cor. v. 2; *to lust*, abs., James iv. 5.

ἐπι-πόθησις, εως, ἡ, *vehement desire, strong affection*, 2 Cor. vii. 7, 11.*
ἐπι-πόθητος, ον, *greatly desired, longed for*, Phil. iv. 1.*
ἐπι-ποθία, ας, ἡ, like ἐπιπόθησις, *strong desire*, Rom. xv. 23.*
ἐπι-πορεύομαι, dep., mid., *to come to* (πρός), Luke viii. 4.*
ἐπιρ-ράπτω, *to sew to*, or *upon*, Mark ii. 21 (ἐπί, dat.).*
ἐπιρ-ρίπτω, *to cast*, or *fling upon*, Luke xix. 35; of care *cast upon* God, 1 Pet. v. 7 (ἐπί, acc.).*
ἐπί-σημος, ον, *remarkable, distinguished*, in either a bad or good sense, Matt. xxvii. 16; Rom. xvi. 7.*
ἐπι-σιτισμός, οῦ, ὁ, *victuals, food, provision*, Luke ix. 12.*
ἐπι-σκέπτομαι, dep., *to look upon, to visit*, as Acts vii. 23; Matt. xxv. 36, 43; of God, Acts xv. 14; *to look out*, for selection, Acts vi. 3.
ἐπι-σκευάζομαι. See ἀποσκ.
ἐπι-σκηνόω, ῶ, *to fix one's tabernacle upon, to dwell*, or *remain on* (ἐπί, acc.), 2 Cor. xii. 9.*
ἐπι-σκιάζω, *to overshadow* (acc. or dat.), Matt. xvii. 5; Mark ix. 7; Luke i. 35, ix. 34; Acts v. 15.*
ἐπι-σκοπέω, ῶ, *to act as*, ἐπίσκοπος, *to take diligent care, to superintend*, 1 Pet. v. 2; μή, *lest*, Heb. xii. 15.*
ἐπι-σκοπή, ῆς, ἡ, (1) *office, charge*, Acts i. 20; LXX.; (2) *the office*, or *work*, of one who oversees a church, 1 Tim. iii. 1; (3) *visitation* for kind and gracious purposes, Luke xix. 44; 1 Pet. ii. 12.*
ἐπί-σκοπος, ον, ὁ, (1) *one who inspects*, or *takes care of*, of Christ, 1 Pet. ii. 25; *an overseer of a church*, "*bishop*," Acts xx. 28; Phil. i. 1; 1 Tim. iii. 2; Tit. i. 7.*
ἐπι-σπάω, ῶ, *to become uncircumcised*, 1 Cor. vii. 18.*
ἐπί-σταμαι, dep., *to know well, to understand* (acc.), *to know*, with ὅτι, ὡς, etc.). Syn. 4.
ἐπι-στάτης, ου, ὁ, *master*, only in Luke, in voc., ἐπιστάτα, addressed to Jesus, *Rabbi*, v. 5, viii. 24, 45, ix. 33, 49, xvii. 13.* Syn. 59.
ἐπι-στέλλω, *to send by letter to, to give directions by letter, to write*, Acts xv. 20, xxi. 25 (W. H. ἀποστ); Heb. xiii. 22.*

ἐπι-στήμων, ον, *skilful, knowing*, James iii. 13.*
ἐπι-στηρίζω, *to establish, confirm*, Acts xiv. 22, xv. 32, 41, xviii. 23 (not W. H.).*
ἐπι-στολή, ῆς, ἡ, *an epistle, a letter.*
ἐπι-στομίζω, *to stop the mouth of*, Tit. i. 11.*
ἐπι-στρέφω, (1) trans., *to cause to turn* (acc. and ἐπί), as to God, or to the worship of God, Acts ix. 35; (2) intrans., *to return, to turn back*, either to good or evil, Acts xxvi. 18; 2 Pet. ii. 21; *to return upon*, as a refused salutation, Matt. x. 13 (ἐπ, εἰς, πρός).
ἐπι-στροφή, ῆς, ἡ, *a turning, conversion*, Acts xv. 3.*
ἐπι-συν-άγω, *to gather together*, into one place, as Matt. xxiii. 37.
ἐπι-συν-αγωγή, ῆς, ἡ, *a gathering together*, 2 Thess. ii. 1; Heb. x. 25.*
ἐπι-συν-τρέχω, *to run together*, to a place, Mark ix. 25.*
ἐπι-σύ-στασις, εως, ἡ (ἐπίστασις, W. H.), (1) *a seditious concourse*, Acts xxiv. 12; (2) *pressure of business*, 2 Cor. xi. 28.*
ἐπι-σφαλής, ές, "*likely to fall*," *dangerous*, Acts xxvii. 9.*
ἐπ-ισχύω, *to be the more urgent*, Luke xxiii. 5.*
ἐπι-σωρεύω, *to heap up, to obtain a multitude of*, 2 Tim. iv. 3.*
ἐπι-ταγή, ῆς, ἡ, *a command, an injunction*, 2 Cor. viii. 8; Titus ii. 15.
ἐπι-τάσσω, ξω, *to command* (abs.), *enjoin upon* (dat. of pers., thing in acc. or inf.), Mark ix. 25.
ἐπι-τελέω, ῶ, έσω, *to finish, to bring to an end, to perform*, as a service, Heb. ix. 6; mid., *to come to an end, to leave off*, Gal. iii. 3; pass., of sufferings, *to be accomplished*, 1 Pet. v. 9.
ἐπιτήδειος, α, ον, *fit, needful*, James ii. 16.*
ἐπι-τίθημι, *to put, place*, or *lay upon* (with acc. and dat., or ἐπί, acc. or gen.), as the hands (to heal), as stripes, etc.; of gifts, *to load with*, Acts xxviii. 10; mid., *to rush upon in hostility, to oppose*, Acts xviii. 10.
ἐπι-τιμάω, ῶ, (1) *to rebuke* (dat.); (2) *to charge strictly*, or *enjoin* (ἵνα), Matt. xii. 16, *to admonish, to exhort*.

ἐπι-τιμία, as, ἡ, *censure, penalty*, 2 Cor. ii. 6.*
ἐπι-τρέπω, *to allow, permit*, Matt. viii. 21; Heb. vi. 3.
ἐπι-τροπή, ῆς, ἡ, *commission, full power*, Acts xxvi. 12.*
ἐπί-τροπος, ου, ὁ, "one who is charged with," (1) *a steward*, Matt. xx. 8, Luke viii. 3; (2) *a tutor*, Gal. iv. 2.*
ἐπι-τυγχάνω, *to attain, acquire* (gen. or acc.), Rom. xi. 7; Heb. vi. 15, xi. 33; James iv. 2.*
ἐπι-φαίνω, 1 aor. inf., ἐπιφᾶναι, 2 aor. pass., ἐπεφάνην; (1) *to appear*, as stars in the night, Acts xxvii. 20; (2) *to shine upon* (dat.), Luke i. 79; (3) met., *to be known*, or *manifest*, Tit. ii. 11, iii. 4.*
ἐπι-φάνεια, as, ἡ, *appearance*, 1 Tim. vi. 14; *manifestation*, 2 Thess. ii. 8; 2 Tim. i. 10, iv. 1, 8; Tit. ii. 13.*
ἐπι-φανής, ές, *glorious, illustrious*, Acts ii. 20.*
ἐπι-φαύω, or -φαύσκω, fut. σω, *to shine upon, give light to* (dat.), Eph. v. 14.*
ἐπι-φέρω (see § 103, 6), *to bring to* (ἐπί, acc.), Acts xix. 12; *to superadd* (to, by dat.), Phil. i. 16; *to bring upon, inflict*, as punishment, Rom. iii. 5; *to bring against*, as an accusation, Acts xxv. 18; Jude 9.*
ἐπι-φωνέω, ῶ, *to cry out*, or *aloud, to cry against*, Luke xxiii. 21; Acts xii. 22, xxii. 24 (xxi. 34, W. H.).*
ἐπι-φώσκω, *to shine upon, to dawn*, Matt. xxviii. 1; Luke xxiii. 54.*
ἐπι-χειρέω, ῶ, *to take in hand, undertake*, Luke i. 1; Acts ix. 29, xix. 13.*
ἐπι-χέω, *to pour upon*, as medicaments on wounds, Luke x. 34.*
ἐπι-χορηγέω, ῶ, *to supply*, 2 Pet. i. 5; 2 Cor. ix. 10; Gal. iii. 5; pass., *to be furnished* or *supplied*, Col. ii. 19; 2 Pet. i. 11.*
ἐπι-χορηγία, as, ἡ, *a supply, ministration*, Phil. i. 19; Eph. iv. 16.*
ἐπι-χρίω, *to rub*, or *smear upon* (ἐπί, acc.), John ix. 6, 11.*
ἐπ-οικοδομέω, ῶ, *to build upon* (ἐπί, acc. or dat.), fig., 1 Cor. iii. 10–14; Eph. ii. 20; *to build up, edify*, Acts xx. 32 (not W. H.); Col. ii. 7; Jude 20.*
ἐπ-οκέλλω, *to force forward, to run* (a ship) *aground*, Acts xxvii. 41 (ἐπικέλλω, W. H.).*
ἐπ-ονομάζω, *to name*, or *call by a name of honour*, pass. only, Rom. ii. 17.*

ἐπ-οπτεύω, *to be witness of,* 1 Pet. ii. 12, iii. 2.*
ἐπ-όπτης, ου, ὁ, *an eye-witness, a beholder,* 2 Pet. i. 16.*
ἔπος, ους, τό, *a word;* ὡς ἔπος εἰπεῖν, *as I may say,* Heb. vii. 9.*
ἐπουράνιος, ιον, *heavenly, celestial,* of God, Matt. xviii. 35 (οὐράνιος, W. H.) ; of intelligent beings, Phil. ii. 10 ; of the starry bodies, 1 Cor. xv. 40. So of kingdom, country, etc. Neut. plur., τὰ ἐπουράνια, *heavenly things,* or *places,* John iii. 12; Eph. i. 3, 20, ii. 6, iii. 10; Heb. viii. 5, ix. 23.
ἑπτά, οἱ, αἱ, τά, card. num., *seven,* "the perfect number." So often symbol. in Revelation. οἱ ἑπτά, *the seven* deacons, Acts xxi. 8.
ἑπτάκις, num., adv., *seven times,* Matt. xviii. 21, 22 ; Luke xvii. 4.*
ἑπτακισχίλιοι, αι, α, card. num., *seven thousand,* Rom. xi. 4.*
ἔπω. See εἶπον and § 103, 7.
Ἔραστος, ου, ὁ, *Erastus,* Acts xix. 22.
ἐργάζομαι, σομαι, dep., perf. εἴργασμαι, pass., (1) abs., *to work, to labour, to trade;* (2) *to accomplish, perform, do;* (3) *to practise,* as virtues, *to commit,* as sin; (4) *to acquire by labour,* John vi. 27.
ἐργασία, ας, ἡ, (1) *effort, diligent labour,* Luke xii. 58 ; (2) *working, doing, i.e.,* the practice or performance of, Eph. iv. 19 ; (3) *work, gain by work,* Acts xvi. 16, 19 ; Acts xix. 24 ; (4) *trade, craft,* Acts xix. 25.*
ἐργάτης, ου, ὁ, *a worker, labourer,* Matt. ix. 37 ; applied to workers in the church, 2 Tim. ii. 15 ; *a doer,* of iniquity, Luke xiii. 27.
ἔργον, ου, τό (Ϝεργ-; so Germ., *werk*), *a work, a deed, an enterprise,* Acts v. 38 ; *a miracle,* John vii. 3, 21 ; *act,* contrasted with λόγος, speech, Luke xxiv. 19 ; *any action,* good or bad, Acts ix. 36 ; John iii. 19 ; *a thing wrought,* by God, Acts xv. 18 ; by men, Acts vii. 41 ; by the devil, 1 John iii. 8.
ἐρεθίζω (ἔρις), *to provoke, to excite, to exasperate,* 2 Cor. ix. 2 ; Col. iii. 21.*
ἐρείδω, σω, *to stick in, to stick fast,* Acts xxvii. 41.*
ἐρεύγομαι, ξομαι, *to utter,* Matt. xiii. 35.*
ἐρευνάω, ῶ, ήσω (ἐραυνάω, W. H.), *to search diligently,* John v. 39 ; Rom. viii. 27; Rev. ii. 23.

ἐρέω, obsolete. See φημί, εἶπον, and § 103, 7.
ἐρημία, ας, ἡ, *an uninhabited tract, a desert.*
ἔρημος, ον, *deserted, desolate, waste, barren,* Acts i. 20; Gal. iv. 27 ; used in the fem., as a subst., for a *desert,* Luke i. 80; ἔρημος τῆς Ἰουδαίας, *the wilderness of Judæa,* the tract west of the Dead Sea, Matt. iii. 12 ; ἡ ἔρημος, the desert in which the Israelites wandered.
ἐρημόω, ῶ, *to make desolate,* Matt. xii. 25 ; Luke xi. 17 ; *to reduce to nought,* Rev. xvii. 16, xviii. 17, 19.*
ἐρήμωσις, εως, ἡ, *desolation, a laying waste,* Matt. xxiv. 15 ; Luke xxi. 20 ; Mark xiii. 14.*
ἐρίζω (ἔρις), *to contend, dispute,* Matt. xii. 19.*
ἐριθεία, ας, ἡ (ἔριθος, *a worker for wages,* perhaps connected with ἔριον), ἐριθία, W. H., "the spirit of a mercenary," *self-seeking,* or *party-spirit,* Rom. ii. 8; Phil. i. 16, ii. 3 ; James iii. 14, 16 ; plur. in 2 Cor. xii. 20 ; Gal. v. 20.*
ἔριον, ου, τό, *wool,* Heb. ix. 19 ; Rev. i. 14.*
ἔρις, ιδος, ἡ, *contention, strife, quarrel, love of contention.*
ἐρίφιον, ου, τό, and ἔριφος, ου, ὁ, *a goat, kid,* Matt. xxv. 32, 33 ; Luke xv. 29.*
Ἑρμᾶς, ᾶ, ὁ, *Hermas* (sometimes written Ἑρμῆς), Rom. xvi. 14.*
ἑρμηνεία, ας, ἡ, *interpretation, explanation,* 1 Cor. xii. 10, xiv. 26.*
ἑρμηνεύω, *to interpret, translate,* John i. 39, 43, ix. 7 ; Heb. vii. 2.*
Ἑρμῆς, ου, ὁ, the Greek deity *Hermes* (in Latin, *Mercury*), Acts xiv. 12.*
Ἑρμογένης, ους, ὁ, *Hermogenes,* 2 Tim. i. 15.*
ἑρπετόν, οῦ, τό, *a creeping creature, a reptile,* Acts x. 12, xi. 6 : Rom. i. 23.*
ἐρυθρός, ά, όν, *red.* ἐρυθρὰ θάλασσα, *the Red Sea,* Acts vii. 36 ; Heb. xi. 29.*
ἔρχομαι (see § 103, 2), *to come, to go,* of persons or of things ; ὁ ἐρχόμενος, *the coming one, i.e.,* the Messiah, Matt. xi. 3 ; Heb. x. 37; in Rev. i. 4, 8, iv. 8 ; *He who is to come : to come,* after, before, to, against, etc., as determined by the preposition which follows ; *to come forth,* as from the grave, 1 Cor. xv. 35; *to come back,* as the prodigal, Luke xv. 30.

ἐρωτάω, ῶ, to interrogate, Matt. xxi. 24, to ask, to request, to beseech. Syn. 9.
ἐσθής, ῆτος, ἡ (ἕννυμι, 1 aor., ἔσθην), a robe, raiment, Luke xxiii. 11; Acts xii. 21. Syn. 66.
ἔσθησις, εως, ἡ, raiment, Luke xxiv. 4. (ἐσθής, W.H.)*
ἐσθίω, 2nd aor., ἔφαγον (see § 103, 3), to eat, to partake of food, used abs. or with acc. of food, or ἐκ, a word like some being understood; with μετά, gen., to eat with; with dat. (as Rom. xiv. 6), to eat to the honour of; met., to devour, to consume, as rust does, James v. 3; or fire, Heb. x. 27.
Ἐσλί, ὁ, Esli, Luke iii. 25.*
ἔσ-οπτρον, ου, τό, a mirror (of polished metal) James i. 23; δι' ἐσόπτρου, 1 Cor. xiii. 12, lit. through a mirror, as the image appears on the opposite side.*
ἑσπέρα, ας, ἡ (prop. adj. with ὥρα), Luke xxiv. 29; the evening, Acts iv. 3, xxviii. 23.*
Ἐσρώμ, ὁ, Esrom, Matt. i. 3; Luke iii. 33.*
ἔσχατος, η, ον, (1) the last, remotest, in situation, dignity, or time, τὸ ἔσχατον, τὰ ἔσχατα, as subst., the extremity, last state; (2) used predicatively as an adverb, Mark xii. 6, 22; absolutely, 1 Cor. xv. 8; (3) the end of what is spoken of, e.g., the feast, John vii. 37; the world, John vi. 39, 40; (4) spec. of the Christian dispensation as the last, or latter (days), Heb. i. 2; (5) the last (day), i.e., the day of judgment, (6) the phrase ὁ πρῶτος καὶ ὁ ἔσχατος, Rev. i. 11, 17, ii. 8, the first and the last, describes the eternity of God; adv. -ως, extremely, i.e., in extremity, ἐσχάτως ἔχει, is at the last extremity, Mark v. 23.
ἔσω, adv. of place, within, abs., as Matt. xxvi. 58; with gen., Mark xv. 16; with an article preced., the inner; οἱ ἔσω, those within the Christian pale, opp. to οἱ ἔξω, 1 Cor. v. 12.
ἔσωθεν, adv. of place, from within, within; τὸ ἔσωθεν, the interior, i.e., the mind or heart, 2 Cor. iv. 16.
ἐσώτερος, α, ον (comp. of ἔσω), inner, interior, Acts xvi. 24; Heb. vi. 19.*
ἑταῖρος, ου, ὁ, a companion, comrade, Matt. xi. 16 (ἕτερος, W.H.); ἑταῖρε, voc., as in English, my good friend, Matt. xx. 13, xxii. 12, xxvi. 50.*

ἑτερό-γλωσσος, ον, ὁ, one of another tongue, or language, 1 Cor. xiv. 21.*
ἑτερο-διδασκαλέω, ῶ, to teach otherwise, to teach a different doctrine, from that of the apostle, 1 Tim. i. 3, vi. 3.*
ἑτερο-ζυγέω, ῶ, to be yoked unfitly, or heterogeneously, 2 Cor. vi. 14.*
ἕτερος, distrib. pron., other, another; indefinitely, any other; definitely, the other; diverse, different from; adv. -ως, otherwise, differently. Syn. 76.
ἔτι, adv., any more, any longer, yet, still, even, Luke i. 15; also, Heb. xi. 36; implying accession or addition, besides.
ἑτοιμάζω, άσω, to prepare, make ready.
ἑτοιμασία, ας, ἡ, preparation, promptitude, Eph. vi. 15.*
ἕτοιμος, η or ος, ον, prompt, prepared, of things or persons; ἐν ἑτοίμῳ ἔχειν, to be in readiness, 2 Cor. x. 6; adv. -ως, in readiness, with ἔχω, Acts xxi. 13; 2 Cor. xii. 14; 1 Pet. iv. 5.
ἔτος, ους, τό, a year, Luke iv. 25; κατ' ἔτος, yearly, Luke ii. 41.
εὖ, adv. (old neuter, from εὖς), well; Luke xix. 17, Eph. vi. 3; εὖ ποιεῖν (acc.), Mark xiv. 7, to do good to; εὖ πράσσειν, to fare well, to prosper, Acts xv. 29; used in commendation, well! well done! Matt. xxv. 21, 23.*
Εὖα, ας, ἡ, Eve, 2 Cor. xi. 3; 1 Tim. ii. 13.*
εὐ-αγγελίζω, σω, εὐηγγέλισα, εὐηγγέλισμαι (1) act., to bring glad tidings to (acc. or dat.), Rev. x. 7, xiv. 6; (2) mid., to announce, to publish (acc. of message), to announce the gospel (abs.), to preach to, evangelise (acc. pers.); pass., to be announced, to have glad tidings announced to one. See Matt. xi. 5; Heb. iv. 2.
εὐ-αγγέλιον, ου, τό, the good tidings, the gospel. In the epistles, (1) the announcing of the tidings, (2) the gospel scheme, (3) the work of evangelisation.
εὐ-αγγελιστής, οῦ, ὁ, a messenger of good tidings, of the gospel, an evangelist, Acts xxi. 8; Eph. iv. 11; 2 Tim. iv. 5.*
εὐ-αρεστέω, ῶ, to be well-pleasing to (dat.), Heb. xi. 5, 6; pass., to be pleased with, Heb. xiii. 16.*
εὐ-άρεστος, ον, acceptable, well-pleasing, Rom. xii. 1; adv. -ως, acceptably, Heb. xii. 28.

Εὔβουλος, ου, ὁ, *Eubūlus*, 2 Tim. iv. 2:.*
εὐγενής, ές, *well-born, noble, ingenuous, generous*, Luke xix. 12; Acts xvii. 11; 1 Cor. i. 26.*
εὐδία, as, ἡ (from Ζεύς, gen. Διός), *fair weather, a serene sky*, Matt. xvi. 2.*
εὐ-δοκέω, ῶ, σω, εὐδόκησα and ηὐδόκησα, *to think well of, to be pleased with*, Matt. xvii. 5; 2 Pet. i. 17; *to resolve benevolently*, Luke xii. 32.
εὐδοκία, as, ἡ, *pleasure, good-will, favour*, Phil. ii. 13; 2 Thess. i. 11; Matt. xi. 26.
εὐ-εργεσία, as, ἡ, *a good work done to* (gen.), *a benefit bestowed*, Acts iv. 9; 1 Tim. vi. 2.*
εὐ-εργετέω, *to do good, to confer kindness*, Acts x. 38.*
εὐ-εργέτης, ου, ὁ, *a benefactor, a patron*, Luke xxii. 25.*
εὔ-θετος, ον, *well-placed, fit, useful*, Luke ix. 62, xiv. 35; Heb. vi. 7.*
εὐθέως, adv., *immediately, soon, speedily, forthwith*, see εὐθύς.
εὐθυ-δρομέω, ῶ, *to run in a straight course*, Acts xvi. 11, xxi. 1.*
εὐ-θυμέω, ῶ, *to be in good spirits, to be cheerful*, Acts xxvii. 22, 25; James v. 13.*
εὔ-θυμος, ον, *cheerful, having good courage*, Acts xxvii. 36*; adv., -ως, *with alacrity, cheerfully*, Acts xxiv. 10.*
εὐθύνω, νῶ, *to make straight*, John i. 23; *to guide, to steer*, as a ship, James iii. 4.*
εὐθύς, εῖα, ύ, adj., *straight;* met., *right, true;* also adv., of time, *straight*, i.e., *immediately, forthwith*, as εὐθέως. (The editions vary much between the two forms of the adverb.)
εὐθύτης, τητος, ἡ, *rightness, rectitude, equity*, Heb. i. 8 (LXX.).*
εὐ-καιρέω, ῶ, *to have leisure* or *opportunity*, Mark vi. 31; Acts xvii. 21; 1 Cor. xvi. 12.*
εὐ-καιρία, as, ἡ, *convenient time* or *opportunity*, Luke xxii. 6.*
εὔ-καιρος, ον, *well-timed, timely, opportune*, Mark vi. 21; Heb. iv. 16*; adv., -ως, *opportunely*, Mark xiv. 11; opposed to ἀκαίρως, 2 Tim. iv. 2.*
εὔ-κοπος, ον, *easy*, neut. compar. only; εὐκοπώτερον, *easier*, as Matt. ix. 5.
εὐ-λάβεια, as, ἡ, *reverence, fear of God, piety*, Heb. v. 7, xii. 28.* Syn. 33, 44.

εὐ-λαβέομαι, οῦμαι, dep. pass., *to fear*, Acts xxiii. 10 (φοβέω, W. H.); *with μή, to take precaution*, Heb. xi. 7.*
εὐ-λαβής, ές, *cautious, God-fearing, devout*, Luke ii. 25; Acts ii. 5, viii. 2, xxii. 12 (W. H.).*
εὐ-λογέω, ῶ, ήσω, *to bless, speak well to, to praise*, i.e., God; *to invoke blessings on*, i.e., men; *to bless* or *to ask blessing on*, i.e., food, Luke ix. 16. So of the Lord's Supper, Matt. xxvi. 26; 1 Cor. x. 16. *Used of what God does, to bless*, to distinguish *with favour*. Hence pass. part. εὐλογημένος, *blessed, favoured of God*, Matt. xxv. 34. Syn. 28.
εὐ-λογητός, όν (verbal adj. from preced.), *worthy of praise, of blessing*, used only of God, Mark xiv. 61; Luke i. 68; Rom. i. 25, ix. 5; 2 Cor. i. 3, xi. 31; Eph. i. 3; 1 Pet. i. 3.*
εὐ-λογία, as, ἡ, "*eulogy*," *commendation*, in a good sense, and in a bad sense *adulation*, Rom. xvi. 18; *blessing, praise*, to God, Rev. vii. 12; *benediction*, i.e., *wishing* or *conferring good upon*, Heb. xii. 17; *bounty*, 2 Cor. ix. 5; *the blessing which the Gospel secures*, 1 Pet. iii. 9.
εὐ-μετά-δοτος, ον, *ready to distribute*, 1 Tim. vi. 18.*
Εὐνίκη, ης, η, *Eunīce*, 2 Tim. i. 5.*
εὐ-νοέω, ῶ, *to be well affected to, to be reconciled to*, Matt. v. 25.*
εὔ-νοια, as, ἡ, *good-will, benevolence*, 1 Cor. vii. 3; Eph. vi. 7.*
εὐνουχίζω, σω, εὐνουχίσθην, pass., *to live as a eunuch*, Matt. xix. 12.*
εὐνοῦχος, ου, ἡ, *a eunuch*, Matt. xix. 12; Acts viii. 27–39.*
Εὐοδία, as, *Euodia*, Phil. iv. 2.*
εὐ-οδόω, ῶ, pass. only, *to be led in a good way, to be made prosperous*, Rom. i. 10; 1 Cor. xvi. 2; 3 John 2.*
εὐ-πάρεδρος, ον. See εὐπρόσεδρος.
εὐ-πειθής, ές, *easily entreated, compliant*, James iii. 17.*
εὐ-περί-στατος, ον, *easily besetting*, or *well circumstanced, closely clinging;* or *admired of many* (R.V. marg.), Heb. xii. 1.*
εὐ-ποιΐα, as, ἡ, *well-doing, beneficence*, Heb. xiii. 16.*
εὐ-πορέω, ῶ, mid., *to be well-to-do, to be prosperous*, Acts xi. 29.*

εὐ-πορία, ας, ἡ, *wealth, prosperity*, Acts xix. 25.*
εὐ-πρέπεια, ας, ἡ, *beauty, gracefulness*, James i. 11.*
εὐ-πρόσ-δεκτος, ον, *well received, acceptable*, Rom. xv. 16, 31; 2 Cor. vi. 2, viii. 12; 1 Pet. ii. 5.*
εὐ-πρόσ-εδρος, ον, *assiduous, constantly attending on*, 1 Cor. vii. 35 (εὐπάρεδρος, W. H.).*
εὐ-προσωπέω, ῶ, *to make a fair appearance*, Gal. vi. 12.*
εὑρίσκω, εὑρήσω, εὕρηκα, εὗρον, εὑρέθην, (1) *to find, to discover, to light upon;* (2) *to ascertain, to find by computation, or by examination, as a judge;* (3) *to obtain, to get*, Heb. ix. 12; (4) *to find how, to be able;* (5) *to contrive or find out how, by thought and inventing*, Luke xix. 48.
εὐρο-κλύδων, ωνος, ὁ (from εὖρος, *the east wind*, and κλύδων, *wave*), *euroclydon, a stormy wind, a hurricane*, Acts xxvii. 14. (W. H. give εὐρακύλων, Lat. *euraquilo, a north-east gale*.)
εὐρύ-χωρος, ον, *broad, spacious*, Matt. vii. 13.*
εὐ-σέβεια, ας, ἡ, *piety, godliness, devotion*, Acts iii. 12; 2 Tim. iii. 5. Syn. 44.
εὐ-σεβέω, ῶ, *to exercise piety, to worship, to reverence*, Acts xvii. 23; 1 Tim. v. 4.*
εὐ-σεβής, ές, *religious, devout*, Acts x. 2, 7, xxii. 12 (W. H., εὐλαβής); 2 Pet. ii. 9*; adv., -ως, *devoutly, religiously*, 2 Tim. iii. 12; Tit. ii. 12.*
εὔ-σημος, ον, *significant, distinct, easy to be understood*, 1 Cor. xiv. 9.*
εὔ-σπλαγχνος, ον, *full of pity, tenderhearted*, Eph. iv. 32; 1 Pet. iii. 8.*
εὐ-σχημόνως, adv., *honourably, becomingly, gracefully*, Rom. xiii. 13; 1 Cor. xiv. 14; 1 Thess. iv. 12.*
εὐ-σχημοσύνη, ης, ἡ, *decorum, becomingness*, 1 Cor. ii. 23.*
εὐ-σχήμων, ον, *reputable, decorous, of good standing*, Mark xv. 43; Acts xiii. 50, xvii. 12; 1 Cor. xii. 24, τὸ εὐσχῆμον, *seemliness.*
εὐ-τόνως, adv., *strenuously, earnestly*, Luke xxiii. 10; Acts xviii. 28.*
εὐ-τραπελία, ας, ἡ, *jesting, frivolous and indecent talk*, Eph. v. 4.*
Εὔτυχος, ου, ὁ, *Eutychus*, Acts xx. 9.*
εὐ-φημία, ας, ἡ, *commendation, good report*, 2 Cor. vi. 8.*

εὔ-φημος, ον, *praiseworthy, of good report*, Phil. iv. 8.*
εὐ-φορέω, ῶ, *to bear plentifully*, Luke xii. 16.*
εὐ-φραίνω, νῶ, εὐφράνθην and ηὐφράνθην, act., *to make glad*, 2 Cor. ii. 2; pass., *to be joyful, to rejoice*, Luke xii. 19; Acts. ii. 26; Rev. xviii. 20.
Εὐφράτης, ου, ὁ, *the Euphrates*, Rev. ix. 14, xvi. 12.*
εὐφροσύνη, ης, ἡ, *joy, gladness*, Acts ii. 28, xiv. 17.*
εὐ-χαριστέω, ῶ, *to thank, give thanks, to be thankful*.
εὐ-χαριστία, ας, ἡ, *gratitude, thanksgiving*, as 2 Cor. ix. 11, 12.
εὐ-χάριστος, ον, *thankful, grateful*, Col. iii. 15.*
εὐχή, ῆς, ἡ, (1) *prayer*, James v. 15; (2) *a vow*, Acts xviii. 18, xxi. 23.*
εὔχομαι, *to pray*, 2 Cor. xiii. 9; James v. 16 (*for* with ὑπέρ or περί, gen.); *to wish earnestly*, Acts xxvi. 29, xxvii. 29; Rom. ix. 3; 2 Cor. xiii. 9; 3 John 2.*
εὔ-χρηστος, ον, *useful, very useful*, 2 Tim. iv. 11; Philemon 11.*
εὐ-ψυχέω, ῶ, *to be in good spirits, to be animated*, Phil. ii. 19.*
εὐ-ωδία, ας, ἡ, *fragrance, good odour*, 2 Cor. ii. 15; Eph. v. 2; Phil. iv. 18.*
εὐώνυμος, ον, *left*, hand, Acts xxi. 3; foot, Rev. x. 2; ἐξ εὐωνύμων (neut. plur.), *on the left*.
ἐφ-άλλομαι, *to leap upon*, ἐπί, acc., Acts xix. 16.*
ἐφ-άπαξ, adv., *once for all*, Rom. vi. 10; Heb. vii. 27, x. 10; *at once*, 1 Cor. xv. 6.*
Ἐφεσῖνος, ον, *Ephesian, i.e., church*, Rev. ii. 1.*
Ἐφέσιος, ον, *Ephesian, belonging to Ephesus*, Acts xix. 28, xxi. 29.*
Ἔφεσος, ου, ἡ, *Ephesus*.
ἐφ-ευρετής, οῦ, ὁ, *an inventor, one who finds out*, Rom. i. 30.*
ἐφ-ημερία, ας, ἡ, *a course, a division of priests for interchange of service*, Luke i. 5, 8.*
ἐφ-ήμερος, ον, *daily, sufficient for the day*, James ii. 15.*
ἐφ-ικνέομαι, dep., 2nd aor. ἐφικόμην, *to come to, arrive at*, ἄχρι or εἰς, 2 Cor. x. 13, 14.*
ἐφ-ίστημι, 2nd aor., ἐπέστην; perf.

part., ἐφεστώς ; always intrans. or mid. in N.T. (1) *to stand by* or *near, to come in* or *near ;* (2) *to come upon*, with hostile intent ; (3) *to be earnest*, 2 Tim. iv. 2 ; (4) *to befall one*, as evil ; (5) *to be at hand, to be present, i.e.*, suddenly, unexpectedly, 2 Tim. iv. 6.

ἐφ-οράω, ῶ, 2nd aor. ἐπεῖδον, *to look upon*, Luke i. 25 ; Acts iv. 29.*

Ἐφραίμ, ὁ, *Ephraim*, a place, John xi. 54.*

ἐφφαθά, an Aramaic verb, imperative, *be opened*, Mark vii. 34.*

ἔχθρα, as, ἡ, *enmity, hatred*, Gal. v. 20 ; Eph. ii. 15, 17.

ἐχθρός, ά, όν, (1) *hated, odious to*, Rom. xi. 28 ; used as subst., *an enemy ; ὁ ἐχθρός*, Luke x. 19, *the enemy, i.e.*, Satan.

ἔχιδνα, ης, ἡ, *a viper*, lit., Acts xxviii. 3 ; fig., as Matt. iii. 7.

ἔχω, ἕξω, impf., εἶχον ; 2nd aor., ἔσχον ; perf., ἔσχηκα ; (1) *to have* or *possess*, in general, physically or mentally, temporarily or permanently ; *μὴ ἔχειν, to lack, to be poor*, Luke viii. 6 ; 1 Cor. xi. 22 ; (2) *to be able*, Mark xiv. 8 ; Heb. vi. 13 ; 2 Pet. i. 15 ; (3) with adverbs, or adverbial phrases, elliptically, "to have (oneself) in any manner ;" *to be*, as *κακῶς ἔχειν, to be ill ; ἐσχάτως ἔχειν, to be at the last extremity ;* (4) *to hold*, 1 Tim. iii. 9, 2 Tim. i. 13 ; *to esteem*, Matt. xiv. 5 ; Phil. ii. 29 ; (5) mid., ἔχομαι, *to be near* or *next to*, Mark i. 38 ; used of time, Acts xxi. 26, *the day coming, the next day ; τὰ ἐχόμενα σωτηρίας, things joined to* or *pertaining to salvation*, Heb. vi. 9.

ἕως, adv., (1) of time, *till, until*, used as conj., also as prep. with gen. *ἕως οὗ*, or *ἕως ὅτου, until when*, Luke xiii. 8 ; (2) of place, *up to*, or *as far as*, also with gen., sometimes with εἰς or πρός (acc.), Matt. xxvi. 58 ; Luke xxiv. 50 ; Acts xxvi. 11 ; (3) spoken of a limit or term to anything, *up to the point of*, Matt. xxvi. 38 ; Luke xxii. 51 ; Rom. ii. 12 ; (4) with particles, *ἕως ἄρτι, ἕως τοῦ νῦν, until now ; ἕως ὧδε, to this place ; ἕως πότε ; how long ? ἕως ἑπτάκις, until seven times ; ἕως ἄνω, up to the brim*, etc.

Z.

Z, ζ, Ζῆτα, *zeta*, the sixth letter, orig. of a mixed or compound sound, as if δs, now generally pronounced *z* or *ts*. As a numeral, ζ´ = 7 ; ͵ζ, = 7,000.

Ζαβουλών, ὁ (Heb.), *Zebulon*, Matt. iv. 13, 15 ; Rev. vii. 8.*

Ζακχαῖος, ου, ὁ, *Zacchæus*, Luke xix.*

Ζαρά, ὁ (Heb.), *Zara* or *Zerah*, Matt. i. 3.*

Ζαχαρίας, ου, ὁ, (1) *Zacharias*, the father of John the Baptist, Luke i. ; (2) *Zechariah*, the son of Jehoiada (2 Chron. xxiv. 20), or of Barachiah (Matt. xxiii. 35), slain in the temple, Luke xi. 51.* (The prophet of the same name, not mentioned in the N.T., though repeatedly quoted, was also the son of a Barachiah.)

ζάω, ῶ, ζῆς, ζῇ, inf., ζῆν (W. H., ζῆν) ; fut., ζήσω or -ομαι ; 1st aor., ἔζησα ; *to live*, as (1) *to be alive ;* part., ὁ ζῶν, *the Living One*, a description of God, as Matt. xvi. 16 ; (2) *to receive* or *regain life*, John iv. 50 ; (3) *to spend life* in any way, Gal. ii. 14 ; 2 Tim. iii. 12 ; (4) *to live*, in the highest sense, to possess spiritual and eternal life ; (5) met., as of water, *living* or *fresh*, opposed to stagnant, as John iv. 10.

Ζεβεδαῖος, ου, ὁ, *Zebedee*.

ζεστός, ή, όν (ζέω), *boiling, hot*, fig., Rev. iii. 15, 16.*

ζεῦγος, ους, τό, (1) *a yoke* (ζεύγνυμι, *to join*), Luke xiv. 19 ; (2) *a pair*, Luke ii. 24.*

ζευκτηρία, as, ἡ, *a band, a fastening, a chain*, Acts xxvii. 40.*

Ζεύς, Διός, acc. Δία, *Zeus* (Lat., *Jupiter*), the chief of the heathen deities, Acts xiv. 12, 13.*

ζέω, part. ζέων, *to boil ;* fig., *to be fervent* or *earnest*, Acts xviii. 25 ; Rom. xii. 11.*

ζηλεύω, *to be zealous*, in a good sense, Rev. iii. 19 (W. H.).*

ζῆλος, ου, ὁ, (1) *fervour, zeal*, in a good sense, John ii. 17 ; (2) *heartburning, jealousy*, in a bad sense ; Acts xiii. 45 ; *anger*, Acts v. 17.

ζηλόω, ῶ, ώσω, (1) *to have zeal for* or *against, to desire earnestly* (acc.), 1 Cor. xii. 31 ; 2 Cor. xi. 2 ; Gal. iv. 17 ; (2) *to be envious* or *jealous*, Acts vii. 9 ; 1 Cor. xiii. 4 ; James iv. 2.

ζηλωτής, οῦ, (1) *a zealot, one very zealous for* (gen.), Acts xxi. 20; (2) as a surname, *Zelotes*, Luke vi. 15; Acts i. 13. See Κανανίτης.
ζημία, ας, ἡ, *damage, loss*, Acts xxvii. 10, 21; Phil. iii. 7, 8.*
ζημιόω, ῶ, pass., *to be endamaged, to suffer loss of* (acc.), Matt. xvi. 26; Phil. iii. 8.
Ζηνᾶς, ᾶ, *Zenas*, Titus iii. 13.*
ζητέω, ῶ, ήσω, (1) *to seek*, absolutely, as Matt. vii. 7; (2) *to endeavour after, to seek for* (acc.), Matt. vi. 33; John v. 30; (3) *to desire, to wish for*, Matt. xii. 46, 47; Col. iii. 1.
ζήτημα, ατος, τό, *a question, dispute, controversy* (gen., or περί, gen.); Acts xv. 2, xviii. 15, xxiii. 29, xxv. 19, xxvi. 3.*
ζήτησις, εως, *question, debate, altercation*, John iii. 25; Acts xxv. 20.
ζιζάνιον, ου, τό (A.V., R.V., "tares"), *darnel*, a kind of bastard wheat; Matt. xiii. 25-40.*
Ζοροβάβελ, ὁ (Heb.), *Zerubbabel*, Matt. i. 12; Luke iii. 27.*
ζόφος, ου, ὁ, *darkness, thick gloom*, 2 Pet. ii. 4, 17; Jude 6, 13 (Heb. xii. 18, W. H.).*
ζυγός, οῦ, ὁ, *a yoke*, (1) met., of servitude, 1 Tim. vi. 1; (2) fig., of any imposition by authority, Matt. xi. 29, 30; Acts xv. 10; Gal. v. 1; (3) *the beam of a pair of scales*, Rev. vi. 5.*
ζύμη, ης, ἡ, *leaven*, Matt. xvi. 6; fig., *corruptness*, 1 Cor. v. 6, 7, 8.
ζυμόω, ῶ, *to ferment, to leaven*, Matt. xiii. 33; Luke xiii. 21; 1 Cor. v. 6; Gal. v. 9.*
ζωγρέω, ῶ (ζωός, ἀγρέω), "to take alive," *to catch, take captive*, Luke v. 10; 2 Tim. ii. 26.*
ζωή, ῆς (cf. ζάω), (1) *life*, literal, spiritual, eternal. ζωὴ αἰώνιος, *eternal life*; (2) a title of Christ, as *the source of life*, John v. 26. **Syn. 54.**
ζώνη, ης, ἡ, *a girdle*, Acts xxi. 11; *a purse*, for which the girdle usually served, Mark vi. 8.
ζώννυμι or -ννύω, see § 114, *to gird*, John xxi. 18; Acts xii. 8.*
ζωο-γονέω, ῶ, ήσω, *to preserve alive*, Luke xvii. 33; Acts vii. 19; 1 Tim. vi. 13, (W. H.).*
ζῷον, ου, τό, *a living creature, animal, beast.*

ζωο-ποιέω, ῶ, ήσω, *to make alive, to cause to live, to quicken*, John v. 21, vi. 63; 1 Cor. xv. 22, 36, 45; 2 Cor. iii. 6; Gal. iii. 21; Rom. iv. 17, viii. 11; 1 Pet. iii. 18.*

H.

Η, η, Ἦτα, *Eta*, ē, the seventh letter. As a numeral, η' = 8; η, = 8,000.
ἤ, a particle, disjunctive, *or*; interrogative, *whether* (see § 405); or comparative, *than* (see § 320). With other particles, ἀλλ' ἤ, *except*; ἢ καί, *or else*; ἤπερ, *than at all*, John xii. 43; ἤτοι ... ἤ, *whether ... or* (excluding any other alternative), Rom. vi. 16; ἤ, particle with μήν, *surely*, Heb. vi. 14 (W. H., εἰ).
ἡγεμονεύω, *to be governor*, as proconsul, Luke ii. 2; procurator, Luke iii. 1.*
ἡγεμονία, ας, ἡ, *rule*, as of an emperor, Luke iii. 1.*
ἡγεμών, όνος, *governor*, as the head of a district, Matt. ii. 6; especially the procurator of Judæa, as Pilate, Felix, Festus.
ἡγέομαι, οῦμαι, dep. mid., (1) *to be leader*, in N.T. only participle, ὁ ἡγούμενος, *the leader or chief* (gen.), as Acts xiv. 12; Heb. xiii. 7, 17, 24; (2) *to deem, regard, reckon, count*, as Phil. iii. 7, 8.
ἡδέως, adv. (ἡδύς. *sweet*), *gladly, with good-will*; superlative, ἥδιστα.
ἤδη, adv. of time, *now, already*, as Matt. iii. 10; of the immediate future, Rom. i. 10.
ἡδονή, ῆς, ἡ, *pleasure*, *i.e.*, sensual; *lust, strong desire*, Luke viii. 14; Tit. ii. 3; James iv. 1, 3; 2 Pet. ii. 13.*
ἡδύοσμον, ου, τό (ἡδὺς ὀσμή), *mint*, Matt. xxiii. 23; Luke xi. 42.*
ἦθος, ους, τό, as ἔθος, *manner, custom*; plur., ἤθη, *morals*, 1 Cor. xv. 33.*
ἥκω, ξω (perf., ἥκα, only Mark viii. 3), *to be come, to be present* (see § 361, *d*, note).
Ἠλί, ὁ (Heb.), *Heli*, Luke iii. 23.*
Ἠλί (W. H., Ἐλωΐ), a Hebrew word, *my God*, Matt. xxvii. 46.*
Ἠλίας, ου, ὁ, *Elias*, i.e., *Elijah*.
ἡλικία, ας, ἡ, (1) *stature, size*, Luke xix. 3; (2) *age, full age, vigour*; ἡλικίαν ἔχει, *he is of age*, John ix. 21. So, prob., Matt. vi. 27 (R.V. marg.).

ἡλίκος, η, ον, how great, how much, how little, Col. ii. 1 ; James iii. 5.*
ἥλιος, ου, ὁ, the sun, the light of the sun.
ἧλος, ου, ὁ, a nail, John xx. 25.*
ἡμεῖς, gen. ἡμῶν, dat. ἡμῖν, acc. ἡμᾶς, plur. of ἐγώ.
ἡμέρα, ας, ἡ, a day, i.e., the time from sunrise to sunset.
ἡμέτερος, α, ον, our, our own.
ἡμιθανής, ές, half dead, Luke x. 30.*
ἥμισυς, εια, υ, gen., ἡμίσους, half; in neut. only, the half of, (gen.) plur. (ἡμίση, W. H. ἡμίσια), Luke xix. 8; sing., Mark vi. 23; Rev. xi. 9, 11, xii. 14.*
ἡμιώριον, ου, τό, a half-hour, Rev. viii. 1.*
ἡνίκα, adv., when, whenever, with ἄν (ἐάν, W. H.), 2 Cor. iii. 15, 16.*
ἤπερ, see ἤ.
ἤπιος, α, ον, placid, gentle, 1 Thess. ii. 7; 2 Tim. ii. 24.*
Ἤρ, ὁ (Heb.), Er, Luke iii. 28.*
ἤρεμος, ον, quiet, tranquil, 1 Tim. ii. 2.*
Ἡρῴδης (W. H., -ῴ-), ου, ὁ, Herod. Four of the name are mentioned : (1) Herod the Great, Matt. ii. ; (2) Herod Antipas, or H. the tetrarch, Matt. xiv.; Luke xxiii.; (3) H. Agrippa, Acts xii.; (4) H. Agrippa the younger, called only Agrippa, Acts xxv.
Ἡρῳδιανοί (W. H., -ῳ-), ῶν, οἱ, Herodians, partisans of Herod Antipas, Matt. xxii. 16 ; Mark iii. 6, xii. 13.*
Ἡρῳδιάς (W. H., -ῳ-), άδος, ἡ, Herodias. Matt. xiv. 3, 6.
Ἡρῳδίων (W. H., -ῳ-), ωνος, ὁ, Herodion, Rom. xvi. 11.*
Ἡσαΐας, ου, ὁ, Esaias, i.e., Isaiah.
Ἡσαῦ, ὁ (Heb.), Esau, Rom. ix. 13 ; Heb. xi. 20, xii. 16.*
ἡσυχάζω, σω, (1) to rest from work, Luke xxiii. 56 ; (2) to cease from altercation, to be silent, Luke xiv. 4 ; Acts xi. 18 ; (3) to live quietly, 1 Thess. iv. 11.*
ἡσυχία, ας, ἡ, (1) quiet, silence, Acts xxii. 2 ; 1 Tim. ii. 11 ; (2) tranquillity, quiet, modesty, 2 Thess. iii. 12.*
ἡσύχιος, ία, ιον, quiet, gentle, 1 Tim. ii. 2 ; 1 Pet. iii. 4.*
ἤτοι, see ἤ.
ἡττάομαι, pass., (1) to be inferior (abs.), 2 Cor. xii. 13 ; (2) to be overcome by (dat.); 2 Pet. ii. 19, 20.*
ἥττημα, ατος, τό, inferiority, diminution, Rom. xi. 12 ; loss, 1 Cor. vi. 7.*

ἥττων or ἥσσων (W. H.), irreg., compar. of κακός, inferior, neut. as adv., 2 Cor. xii. 15 ; τὸ ἧττον, as subst., the worse, 1 Cor. xi. 17.*
ἠχέω, ῶ, to sound, as the sea, Luke xxi. 25 ; as brass, 1 Cor. xiii. 1.*
ἦχος, ου, ὁ, sound, Heb. xii. 19 ; Acts ii. 2, fame or report, Luke iv. 37.*
ἦχος, ους, τό, sound, noise, Luke xxi. 25 (W. H.).*

Θ.

Θ, θ, and ϑ, Θῆτα, theta, th, the eighth letter. Numerically, θ′ = 9 ; θ, = 9,000.
Θαδδαῖος, ου, ὁ, Thaddaeus, a surname of the apostle Jude (also called Lebbaeus), Matt. x. 3 ; Mark iii. 18.*
θάλασσα, ης, ἡ, (1) the sea ; (2) sea, as the Mediterranean, the Red Sea ; (3) Hebraistically, for the lake Gennesaret, Matt. viii. 24.
θάλπω, to cherish, nourish, Eph. v. 29 ; 1 Thess. ii. 7.*
Θάμαρ, ἡ, Tamar, Matt. i. 3.*
θαμβέω, ῶ, to be astonished, amazed, Acts ix. 6 (W. H. omit). So pass., Mark i. 27, x. 32; with ἐπί (dat.), Mark x. 24.*
θάμβος, ους, τό, astonishment, Luke iv. 36, v. 9 ; Acts iii. 10.*
θανάσιμος, ον, deadly, mortal, Mark xvi. 18.*
θανατη-φόρος, ον, death-bringing, James iii. 8.*
θάνατος, ου, ὁ, death, lit. or fig.; the cause of death, Rom. vii. 13.
θανατόω, ῶ, ώσω, to put to death, pass., to be in danger of death, Rom. viii. 36 ; fig., to mortify, subdue, as evil passions, Rom. viii. 13 ; pass., to become dead to (dat.), Rom. vii. 4.
θάπτω, ψω, 2nd aor. ἔταφον, to bury.
Θάρα, ὁ, Terah, Luke iii. 34.*
θαρρέω, ῶ, ήσω, to be of good cheer, to have confidence in, εἰς or ἐν. In imperative, forms from θαρσέω are used, θάρσει, θαρσεῖτε, take courage.
θάρσος, ους, τό, courage, Acts xxviii. 15.*
θαῦμα, ατος, τό, wonder, amazement, 2 Cor. xi. 14 (W. H.) ; Rev. xvii. 6.*
θαυμάζω, σω, or σομαι, to wonder, abs., with διά, acc.; ἐπί, dat.; περί, gen., or

ὅτι, εἰ; *to wonder at, admire,* acc.; pass., *to be admired or honoured.*
θαυμάσιος, ία, ιον, *wonderful,* Matt. xxi. 15.*
θαυμαστός, ή, όν, *wonderful, marvellous,* Matt. xxi. 42; Mark xii. 11; John ix. 30; 1 Pet. ii. 9; Rev. xv. 1, 3.*
θεά, ᾶς, ἡ, *a goddess,* Acts xix. 27.
θεάομαι, ῶμαι, dep., 1st aor. ἐθεασάμην, pass. ἐθεάθην, *to behold, to contemplate earnestly, to see, to visit.*
θεατρίζω, *to make a spectacle of, so to expose to contempt,* Heb. x. 33.*
θέατρον, ου, τό, (1) *a place for public shows, a theatre,* Acts xix. 29, 31; (2) *spectacle,* 1 Cor. iv. 9.*
θεῖος, εία, εῖον, *divine,* 2 Pet. i. 3, 4; τὸ θεῖον, perhaps *the Deity,* Acts xvii. 29.*
θεῖον, ου, τό, *sulphur* (from the preceding, "a magic fume").
θειότης, τητος, ἡ, *godhead, deity,* Rom. i. 20.* **Syn. 34.**
θειώδης, ες, *sulphureous,* Rev. ix. 17.*
θέλημα, ατος, τό, *will, desire, a lust;* plur., Acts xiii. 22; Eph. ii. 3.
θέλησις, εως, ἡ, *will, pleasure,* Heb. ii. 4.*
θέλω, impf., ἤθελον; 1st aor., ἐθέλησα; *to wish, delight in, prefer, to will,* in the sense of assent, determination, or requirement. **Syn. 3.**
θεμέλιος, ον, *belonging to a foundation, fundamental.* Hence, masc. (sc. λίθος), *a foundation,* or τὸ θεμέλιον (Luke), in the same sense. Fig. for the elements of sound doctrine.
θεμελιόω, ῶ, ώσω, *to lay a foundation, to found;* fig., pass., *to be firm and stable.*
θεο-δίδακτος, ον, *taught of God,* 1 Thess. iv. 9.*
θεό-λογος, ου, ὁ, *the divine,* or *the theologian,* of the apostle John in the title to Rev. (W. H. omit).*
θεο-μαχέω, ῶ, *to fight against God,* Acts xxiii. 9.*
θεο-μάχος, ου, ὁ, *a fighter against God,* Acts v. 39.*
θεό-πνευστος, ον (πνέω), *God-breathed, inspired by God,* 2 Tim. iii. 16.*
Θεός, οῦ, ὁ, voc. once Θεέ, Matt. xxvii. 46; (1) GOD; ὁ Θεός, *the revealed God,* John i. 1; Acts xvii. 24, etc.; (2) *a god,* generically, Acts vii. 43; xii. 22; 2 Cor. iv. 4; Phil. iii. 19; John x. 34 (quoted from LXX.).

θεο-σέβεια, ας, ἡ, *piety,* towards God, 1 Tim. ii. 10.*
θεο-σεβής, ές, *God-worshipping, devout,* John ix. 31.*
θεο-στυγής, ές, *God-hating,* or *God-hated,* Rom. i. 30.*
θεότης, τητος, ἡ, *deity, godhead, the divine nature,* Col. ii. 9.* **Syn. 34.**
Θεό-φιλος, ου, ὁ, *Theophilus,* Luke i. 3; Acts i. 1.*
θεραπεία, ας, ἡ, (1) *service;* hence (abs. for concrete) *servants, household,* Luke xii. 42; Matt. xxiv. 45 (not W. H.); (2) *healing,* as the service which brings health and cure, Luke ix. 11; Rev. xxii. 2.*
θεραπεύω, εύσω, (1) *to serve, minister to,* only Acts xvii. 25; (2) *to heal;* acc. of pers., and ἀπό or acc. of disease.
θεράπων, οντος, ὁ, *a servant,* Heb. iii. 5.*
θερίζω, ίσω, *to reap* or *gather,* as corn, lit. or fig.
θερισμός, οῦ, ὁ, *harvest, the gathering-time,* lit. or fig.
θεριστής, οῦ, ὁ, *a reaper,* Matt. xii. 30, 39.*
θερμαίνω, ανῶ, only mid. in N.T., *to warm oneself,* Mark xiv. 54, 67; John xviii. 18, 25; James ii. 16.*
θέρμη, ης, ἡ, *heat, burning,* Acts xxviii. 3.*
θέρος, ους, τό, *summer, harvest-time,* Matt. xxiv. 32; Mark xiii. 28; Luke xxi. 30.*
Θεσσαλονικεύς, έως, ὁ, *a Thessalonian.*
Θεσσαλονίκη, ης, ἡ, *Thessalonica.*
Θευδᾶς, ᾶ, ὁ, *Theudas,* Acts v. 36.*
θεωρέω, ῶ, *to be a spectator of, to behold, to see, to know by seeing, to experience;* abs., or with acc. or obj. clause.
θεωρία, ας, ἡ, *a sight, a spectacle,* Luke xxiii. 48.*
θήκη, ης (τίθημι), *a receptacle,* as a scabbard, John xviii. 11.*
θηλάζω, (1) *to give suck,* Matt. xxiv. 19; (2) *to suck at the breast,* Matt. xxi. 16.
θῆλυς, εια, υ, *female,* fem., Rom. i. 26, 27; neut., Matt. xix. 4; Mark x. 6; Gal. iii. 28.*
θήρα, ας, ἡ, *hunting,* hence *a snare,* Rom. xi. 9.*
θηρεύω, σω, *to hunt, to catch,* Luke xi. 54.*
θηριο-μαχέω, ῶ, *to fight with wild beasts,* 1 Cor. xv. 32.*

θηρίον, ου, τό, a wild beast, as Acts xi. 6; freq. in Rev.
θησαυρίζω, σω, to treasure up, reserve, lit. and fig.
θησαυρός, οῦ, ὁ, treasure, wealth.
θιγγάνω, 2nd aor. ἔθιγον, to touch, handle, abs., Col. ii. 21; with gen., Heb. xi. 28, xii. 20.*
θλίβω, ψω, to press, to throng, Mark iii. 9; fig., to afflict, press with trouble, 2 Cor. i. 6; pass., perf. part., τεθλιμμένος, contracted, narrow, Matt. vii. 14.
θλῖψις, εως, ἡ, pressure, affliction, tribulation.
θνήσκω, 2nd aor. ἔθανον, to die; in N.T. only, perf. τέθνηκα, to be dead.
θνητός, ή, όν, mortal, dying, Rom. vi. 12, viii. 11; 1 Cor. xv. 53, 54; 2 Cor. iv. 11, v. 4.*
θορυβάζω, to disturb, trouble, Luke x. 41 (W. H.).*
θορυβέω, ῶ, to disturb, Acts xvii. 5; mid., to make a noise, as of lamentation over the dead, Matt. ix. 23; Mark v. 39; Acts xx. 10.*
θόρυβος, ου, ὁ, noise, uproar.
θραύω, σω, to break, bruise, Luke iv. 18.*
θρέμμα, ατος, το (τρέφω), the young of cattle, sheep, etc., John iv. 12.*
θρηνέω, ῶ, abs., to wail, lament, to raise a funeral cry, Matt. xi. 17; Luke vii. 32; John xvi. 20; to bewail, acc., Luke xxiii. 27.*
θρῆνος, ου, ὁ, a wailing, Matt. ii. 18 (not W. H.).*
θρησκεία, ας, ἡ, external worship, religious homage, ritual, Acts xxvi. 5; Col. ii. 18; James i. 26, 27.*
θρῆσκος, ου (prop. adj.), a devotee, religious person, James i. 26.*
θριαμβεύω, σω, to triumph over, to lead in triumph, 2 Cor. ii. 14; Col. ii. 15.*
θρίξ, τριχός, dat. plur. θριξί, ἡ, a hair, human or animal.
θροέω, ῶ, to disturb, terrify by clamour; only pass. in N.T., Matt. xxiv. 6; Mark xiii. 7; 2 Thess. ii. 2.*
θρόμβος, ου, ὁ, a clot, large drop, as of blood, Luke xxii. 44.*
θρόνος, ου, ὁ, a seat, as of judgment, Matt. xix. 28; a throne, or seat of power, Rev. iii. 21; met., of dominion, Rev. xiii. 2; concrete, of the ruler, or occupant of the throne, Col. i. 16.
Θυάτειρα, ων, τά, Thyatira.

θυγάτηρ, τρός, ἡ, a daughter, a female descendant, Luke xiii. 16; met., of the inhabitants of a place, collectively, Matt. xxi. 5.
θυγάτριον, ου, τό (dim. of θυγάτηρ), a little daughter, Mark v. 23, vii. 25.*
θύελλα, ης, ἡ, a tempest, whirlwind, Heb. xii. 18.*
θύϊνος, η, ον, made of the thyine tree, a strongly aromatic and hard-wooded tree of Africa, Rev. xviii. 12.*
θυμίαμα, ατος, τό, incense, Luke i. 10, 11; Rev. v. 8, viii. 3, 4, xviii. 13.*
θυμιατήριον, ου, τό, the censer, or vessel in which the materials of incense were burned, the altar on which the incense was placed to burn, Heb. ix. 4.*
θυμιάω, ῶ, to burn incense, Luke i. 9.*
θυμομαχέω, ῶ, to be greatly displeased with (dat.), Acts xii. 20.*
θυμός, οῦ, ὁ, passion, or violent commotion of mind, great anger, wrath.
θυμόω, ῶ, to provoke to great anger; pass., to be greatly angry with, Matt. ii. 16.*
θύρα, ας, ἡ, a door, Luke xi. 7; Matt. xxvii. 60; met., John x. 7, 9.
θυρεός, οῦ, ὁ, a (door-shaped) shield, Eph. vi. 16.*
θυρίς, ίδος, ἡ, an opening, used for a window or wicket, Acts xx. 9; 2 Cor. xi. 33.*
θυρωρός, οῦ, ὁ, ἡ, a door-keeper, porter, Mark xiii. 34; John x. 3, xviii. 16, 17.*
θυσία, ας, ἡ, (1) the act of sacrificing; (2) the victim sacrificed, a sacrifice.
θυσιαστήριον, ου, τό, an altar, for sacrifices.
θύω, σω, (1) to slay in sacrifice, Acts xiv. 13; (2) to kill animals, for feasting, Matt. xxii. 4; (3) to slay, generally, John x. 10.
Θωμᾶς, ᾶ (from Heb. = δίδυμος), Thomas.
θώραξ, ακος, masc., a breast-plate, Eph. vi. 14; 1 Thess. v. 8; Rev. ix. 9, 17.*

I.

I, ι, Ἰῶτα, Iōta, the ninth letter. As a numeral, ι´ = 10; ι, = 10,000.
Ἰάειρος, ου, ὁ, Jairus.
Ἰακώβ, ὁ (Heb.), Jacob, (1) the patriarch; (2) the father-in-law of Mary, Matt. i. 15.

Ἰάκωβος, ου, ὁ, Greek form of preced., *James*, (1) the son of Zebedee; (2) the son of Alphæus; (3) the Lord's brother. Some identify (2) and (3).
ἴαμα, ατος, τό, *healing, cure*, plur., 1 Cor. xii. 9, 28, 30.*
Ἰαμβρῆς, οῦ, ὁ, *Jambres*, with Ἰαννῆς, 2 Tim. iii. 8.*
Ἰαννά, ὁ (Heb.), *Janna*, Luke iii. 24.*
Ἰαννῆς, οῦ, ὁ. See Ἰαμβρῆς.
ἰάομαι, ῶμαι, ἰάσομαι, dep., mid. aor., but passive in aor., perf. and fut., *to heal, to restore to health*, of body or mind; with ἀπό, of malady.
Ἰαρέδ, ὁ (Heb.), *Jared*, Luke iii. 37.*
ἴασις, εως, ἡ, *a cure, healing*, Luke xiii. 32; Acts iv. 22, 30.*
ἴασπις, ιδος, ἡ, *jasper, a precious stone*, Rev. iv. 3, xxi. 11, 18, 19.*
Ἰάσων, ονος, ὁ, *Jason*, Acts xvii. 5; Rom. xvi. 21; perhaps two persons.*
ἰατρός, οῦ, ὁ, *a physician*.
ἴδε, or ἰδέ (εἶδον), imper. act. as interj., *behold!* often followed by nominative.
ἰδέα, ας, ἡ, *form, aspect*, Matt. xxviii. 3.*
ἴδιος, ία, ον, (1) *one's own*, denoting ownership, Matt. xxii. 5; John x. 12; also what is peculiar to, Acts i. 19. Hence, τὰ ἴδια, *one's own things, home, nation* or *people, business* or *duty;* οἱ ἴδιοι, *one's own people, friends, companions*, neut. and masc. contrasted in John i. 11; (2) *that which specially pertains to, and is proper for*, as 1 Cor. iii. 8; Gal. vi. 9; (3) adverbially, κατ' ἰδίαν, *privately;* ἰδίᾳ, *individually*.
ἰδιώτης, ου, ὁ, *a private person, one of the vulgar, an unlettered one*, Acts iv. 13; 1 Cor. xiv. 16, 23, 24; 2 Cor. xi. 6.*
ἰδού (comp. ἴδε), imper. mid. as interj., *lo! behold!* used to call attention not only to that which may be seen, but also heard, or apprehended in any way.
Ἰδουμαία, ας, ἡ, *Idumea*, the O.T. Edom, Mark iii. 8.*
ἱδρώς, ῶτος, ὁ, *sweat*, Luke xxii. 44.*
Ἰεζαβήλ, ἡ (Heb.), *Jezebel*, symbolically used, Rev. ii. 20.*
Ἱεράπολις, εως, ἡ, *Hierapolis*, in Phrygia, Col. iv. 13.*
ἱερατεία, ας, ἡ, *the office of a priest, priesthood*, Luke i. 9; Heb. vii. 5.*
ἱεράτευμα, ατος, τό, *the assembly* or *society of priests*, a title applied to Christians, 1 Pet. ii. 5, 9.*
ἱερατεύω, σω, *to officiate as a priest, to perform the priest's office*, Luke i. 8.*
Ἰερεμίας, ιου, ὁ, *Jeremiah*. (In Matt. xxvii. 9, the quotation is from Zechariah.)
ἱερεύς, έως, *a priest*, sometimes *the High Priest*, Acts v. 24; of Christ, Heb. v. 6 (Ps. cx. 4); of Christians generally, Rev. i. 6, v. 10.
Ἰεριχώ, ἡ (Heb.), *Jericho*.
ἱερόν, οῦ, τό (prop. neut. of ἱερός), *a place consecrated to God, a fane* or *temple*, used of a heathen temple, as Acts xix. 27; of the temple at Jerusalem, as Matt. xxiv. 1; and of parts of the temple, as Matt. xii. 5. Syn. 35.
ἱερο-πρεπής, οῦς, adj., *becoming* or *suitable to a sacred character (reverent, R. V.)*, Tit. ii. 3.*
ἱερός, ά, όν, *consecrated, holy*, of the Scriptures, 2 Tim. iii. 15; τὰ ἱερά, *sacred things*, 1 Cor. ix. 13.*
Ἱεροσόλυμα (W. H., ʼI.), ων, τά. See Ἱερουσαλήμ.
Ἱεροσολυμίτης, ου, ὁ, *one of Jerusalem*, Mark i. 5; John vii. 25.*
ἱερο-συλέω, ῶ, *to commit sacrilege*, Rom. ii. 22.*
ἱερό-συλος, ον, *robbing temples, sacrilegious*, Acts xix. 37.*
ἱερουργέω, ῶ (ἱερόν, ἔργον), *to minister in holy things*, Rom. xv. 16.*
Ἱερουσαλήμ (W. H., ʼI.), ἡ (Heb.), (for form, see § 156), *Jerusalem*, (1) the city; (2) the inhabitants. In Gal. iv. 25, 26, ἡ νῦν ʼI. is the Jewish dispensation, and is contrasted with ἡ ἄνω ʼI., the ideal Christian community; also called ʼI. ἐπουράνιος, Heb. xii. 22; ἡ καινή ʼI., Rev. iii. 12, xxi. 2.
ἱερωσύνη, ης, ἡ, *the priestly office*, Heb. vii. 11, 12, 24.*
Ἰεσσαί, ὁ (Heb.), *Jesse*.
Ἰεφθάε, ὁ (Heb.), *Jephthah*.
Ἰεχονίας, ου, ὁ, *Jechonias*, or *Jehoiachin*.
Ἰησοῦς, οῦ (see § 25), (1) JESUS, the Saviour; (2) *Joshua*, Acts vii. 45; Heb. iv. 8; (3) *a fellow-labourer of Paul*, so named, Col. iv. 11; (4) *Barabbas* is so named in some early MSS., Matt. xxvii. 16; (5) *an ancestor of Joseph*, Luke iii. 29 (W. H.).

ἱκανός, ή, όν, (1) sufficient, competent to, inf., πρός (acc.) or ἵνα ; (2) many, much, of number or time.
ἱκανότης, ητος, ἡ, sufficiency, ability, 2 Cor. iii. 5.*
ἱκανόω, ῶ, to make sufficient or competent, 2 Cor. iii. 6 ; Col. i. 12.*
ἱκετηρία, ας, ἡ, supplication, Heb. v. 7.*
ἰκμάς, άδος, ἡ, moisture, Luke viii. 6.*
Ἰκόνιον, ου, τό, Iconium.
ἱλαρός, ά, όν, joyous, cheerful, "hilarious," 2 Cor. ix. 7.*
ἱλαρότης, τητος, ἡ, cheerfulness, alacrity, Rom. xii. 8.*
ἱλάσκομαι, άσομαι, 1st aor. ἱλάσθην, (1) to be propitious to, dat., Luke xviii. 13 ; (2) to make propitiation or atonement for, expiate, acc., Heb. ii. 17.*
ἱλασμός, οῦ, ὁ, a propitiation, atoning sacrifice, 1 John ii. 2, iv. 10.*
ἱλαστήριος, ία, ον, atoning, neut., propitiation, Rom. iii. 25 ; (sc. ἐπίθεμα, covering), the mercy-seat, Heb. ix. 5.*
ἵλεως, ων (Attic form), propitious, favourable, merciful, Heb. viii. 12 ; Matt. xvi. 22, ἵλεώς σοι (God be) merciful to thee ! God forbid !*
Ἰλλυρικόν, οῦ, τό, Illyricum.
ἱμάς, άντος, ὁ, a thong for scourging, Acts xxii. 25 ; thong, latchet of a shoe, Mark i. 7 ; Luke iii. 16 ; John i. 27.*
ἱματίζω, perf., pass., part., ἱματισμένος, to clothe, Mark v. 15 ; Luke viii. 35.*
ἱμάτιον, ίου, τό (dim of ἵμα=εἷμα, from ἕννυμι), (1) clothing ; (2) the outer garment, disting. from χιτών.
ἱματισμός, οῦ, ὁ, clothes, raiment.
ἱμείρομαι, to have a strong affection for, to love earnestly, 1 Thess. ii. 8. (W. H., ὁμείρομαι.)*
ἵνα, conj., that, to the end that ; ἵνα μή, that not, lest. See § 384.
ἱνατί ; or ἵνα τί ; (W. H.,) conj., in order that what (may happen ? sc. γενήται), to what end?
Ἰόππη, ης, ἡ, Joppa.
Ἰορδάνης, ου, ὁ, the Jordan.
ἰός, οῦ, ὁ, (1) poison, Rom. iii. 13 ; James iii. 8 ; (2) rust, James v. 3.*
Ἰουδαία, ας, ἡ (really adj., fem., sc. γῆ), Judæa.
Ἰουδαΐζω, to conform to Jewish practice, to "Judaise," in life or ritual, Gal. ii. 14.*

Ἰουδαϊκός, ή, όν, Jewish, or Judaical, Tit. i. 14* ; -ῶς, adv., Jewishly, in Jewish style, Gal. ii. 14.*
Ἰουδαῖος, αία, ον, belonging to Judah, Jewish. Often in plur., with subst. understood, οἱ Ἰουδαῖοι, the Jews.
Ἰουδαϊσμός, οῦ, ὁ, Judaism, the Jewish system, Gal. i. 13, 14.*
Ἰούδας, α, ὁ, Judah, (1) Son of Jacob ; (2, 3) other ancestors of Christ, Luke iii. 26, 30 ; (4) Jude, the apostle ; (5) Judas Iscariot ; (6) Judas Barsabas, Acts xv. 22 ; (7) a Jew living in Damascus, Acts ix. 11 ; (8) a leader of sedition, Acts v. 37 ; (9) a brother of our Lord, Matt. xiii. 55 ; perhaps identical with (4). See Ἰάκωβος.
Ἰουλία, ας, ἡ, Julia, Rom. xvi. 15.*
Ἰούλιος, ου, ὁ, Julius, Acts xxvii. 1, 3.*
Ἰουνίας, α, ὁ, Junias, Rom. xvi. 7.*
Ἰοῦστος, ου, ὁ, Justus. Three of the name are mentioned, Acts i. 23, xviii. 7 ; Col. iv. 11.*
ἱππεύς, έως, ὁ, a horse-soldier, Acts xxiii. 23, 32.*
ἱππικόν (prop. neut. adj.), cavalry, Rev. ix. 16.*
ἵππος, ου, ὁ, a horse.
ἶρις, ἴριδος, ἡ, the rainbow, Rev. iv. 3, x. 1.*
Ἰσαάκ, ὁ (Heb.), Isaac.
ἰσ-άγγελος, ον, like or equal to angels, Luke xx. 36.*
ἴσασι. See οἶδα.
Ἰσαχάρ and Ἰσασχάρ (Heb.), Issachar.
Ἰσκαριώτης, ου, ὁ, Iscariot, i.e., a man of Kerioth. See Joshua xv. 25.
ἴσος, η, ον (or ἴσος), like, equal to (dat.), Matt. xx. 12 ; Luke vi. 34 ; John v. 18 ; Acts xi. 17 ; Rev. xxi. 16 ; alike, consistent, as truthful witnesses, Mark xiv. 56, 59 ; ἴσα, adverbially, on an equality, Phil. ii. 6 ; ἴσως, adv., perhaps, Luke xx. 13.*
ἰσότης, τητος, ἡ, equality, 2 Cor. viii. 14 ; equity, Col. iv. 1.*
ἰσό-τιμος, ον, prized equally, of like value, 2 Pet. i. 1.*
ἰσό-ψυχος, ον, like-minded, Phil. ii. 20.*
Ἰσραήλ, ὁ (Heb.), Israel, met., for the whole nation of the Israelites.
Ἰσραηλίτης, ου, ὁ, an Israelite. Syn. 50.
ἴστε. See οἶδα.
ἵστημι (in Rom. iii. 31, Rec. has ἱστάω, W. H. ἱστάνω, § 107), trans. in pres.,

G G

imperf., fut., 1st aor.; *to cause to stand, to set up, to place, to fix a time, to confirm, to establish, to put in the balance, to weigh;* intrans. in perf., plup., and 2nd aor., *to stand, to stand still* or *firm, to endure, to be confirmed* or *established, to come to a stand, to cease.*

ἱστορέω, ῶ, *to know, ascertain by examination,* Gal. i. 18.*

ἰσχυρός, ά, όν, *strong, mighty, powerful, vehement.*

ἰσχύς, ύος, ἡ, *strength, might, power, ability.*

ἰσχύω, ύσω, *to be strong, sound, whole, to prevail, to be able* (inf.), *to have ability* for (acc.).

Ἰταλία, ας, *Italy.*

Ἰταλικός, ή, όν, *Italian,* Acts x. 1.*

Ἰτουραία, ας, ἡ, *Iturea,* Luke iii. 1.*

ἰχθύδιον, ου, τό (dim. of ἰχθύς), *a little fish,* Matt. xv. 34; Mark viii. 7.*

ἰχθύς, ύος, ὁ, *a fish.*

ἴχνος, ους, τό, ' *a footstep,* fig., Rom. iv. 12; 2 Cor. xii. 18; 1 Pet. ii. 21.*

Ἰωάθαμ, ὁ (Heb.), *Jotham,* Matt. i. 9.*

Ἰωάννα, ης, ἡ, *Joanna,* Luke viii. 3, xxiv. 10.*

Ἰωαννᾶς, α, ὁ, *Joannas,* Luke iii. 27.*

Ἰωάννης, ου, ὁ, *John,* (1) the Baptist; (2) the Apostle; (3) a member of the Sanhedrin, Acts iv. 6; (4) John Mark, Acts xii. 12.

Ἰώβ, ὁ (Heb.), *Job,* the patriarch, James v. 11.*

Ἰωήλ, ὁ (Heb.), *Joel,* the prophet, Acts ii. 16.*

Ἰωνάν, ὁ (Heb.), *Jonan,* Luke iii. 30.*

Ἰωνᾶς, ᾶ, ὁ, *Jonas,* or *Jonah,* (1) the prophet, Matt. xii. 39–41; (2) the father of Peter, John i. 42.

Ἰωράμ, ὁ (Heb.), *Joram,* or *Jehoram,* son of Jehoshaphat, Matt. i. 8.

Ἰωρείμ, ὁ (Heb.) *Jorim,* Luke iii. 29.*

Ἰωσαφάτ, ὁ (Heb.), *Jehoshaphat,* Matt. i. 8.*

Ἰωσῆς, ῆ (or -ῆτος, W. H.), *Joses.* Four are mentioned: (1) Luke iii. 29 (W. H., Ἰησοῦ); (2) Mark vi. 3; Matt. xiii. 55 (W. H., Ἰωσήφ); (3) Matt. xxvii. 56 (W. H. marg.), Mark xv. 40, 47; (4) Acts iv. 36 (W. H., Ἰωσήφ). Some think (2) and (3) identical.

Ἰωσήφ, ὁ (Heb.), *Joseph,* (1) the patriarch, (2, 3, 4) three among the ancestors of Jesus, Luke iii. 24, 26 (W. H., Ἰωσήχ), 30; (5) Mary's husband; (6) Joseph of Arimathæa; (7) Joseph, called also Barsabas, Acts i. 23. See also under Ἰωσῆς.

Ἰωσίας, ου, ὁ, *Josiah,* Matt. i. 10, 11.*

ἰῶτα, τό, *iota, yod,* the smallest letter of the Hebrew alphabet, Matt. v. 18.*

K.

Κ, κ, κάππα, *kappa, k,* the tenth letter. As a numeral, κ′ = 20; κ, = 20,000.

κἀγώ (κἀμοί, κἀμέ), contr. for καὶ ἐγώ (καὶ ἐμοί, καὶ ἐμέ), *and I, I also, even I.*

καθά, adv., contr. from καθ' ἅ, *according as,* Matt. xxvii. 10.*

καθ-αίρεσις, εως, ἡ, *demolition, destruction* (opp. to οἰκοδομή, which see), 2 Cor. x. 4, 8, xiii. 10.*

καθ-αιρέω, καθελῶ, καθεῖλον, (1) *to take down* or *away,* Acts xiii. 29; (2) *demolish, destroy,* lit., Luke xii. 18, or fig., 2 Cor. x. 5.

καθ-αίρω, αρῶ, *to cleanse, to clear by pruning,* John xv. 2; Heb. x. 2. (W. H., καθαρίζω.)*

καθ-άπερ, adv., *even as, truly as.*

καθ-άπτω, άψω, *to fasten upon,* intrans., Acts xxviii. 3 (gen.).*

καθαρίζω, att. fut. καθαριῶ, *to cleanse, e.g.,* a leper, by healing his disease, Matt. viii. 2, 3; from moral pollution, Heb. ix. 22, 23; *to declare clean, i.e.,* from ceremonial pollution, Acts x. 15.

καθαρισμός, οῦ, ὁ, *cleansing,* physical, moral, or ceremonial, Mark i. 44; Luke ii. 22, v. 14; John ii. 6, iii. 25; Heb. i. 3; 2 Pet. i. 9.*

καθαρός, ά, όν, *clean, pure,* physically, morally, or ceremonially.

καθαρότης, ητος, ἡ, *purity, i.e.,* ceremonial, Heb. ix. 13.*

καθ-έδρα, ας, ἡ, *a seat,* lit., Matt. xxi. 12; Mark xi. 15; met., *a chair* of authority, Matt. xxiii. 2.*

καθέζομαι, *to sit down;* ἐν or ἐπί, dat.

καθ-εῖς, adv. (see § 300, β, 4), *one by one.* (W. H., καθ' εἷς.)

καθ-εξῆς, adv. (see § 126, d), *in orderly succession,* Luke i. 3; Acts xi. 4, xviii. 23. With art., Luke viii. 1, ἐν τῷ κ., *soon afterwards;* Acts iii. 24, οἱ κ., *those that come after.*

καθ-εύδω, to sleep, to be asleep; fig., 1 Thess. v. 6.
καθηγητής, οῦ, ὁ, a leader, teacher, master, Matt. xxiii. 8 (not W. H.), 10.*
καθ-ήκω, used only impers., it is fit, it is becoming (acc., inf.), Acts xxii. 22 ; τὸ καθῆκον, the becoming, duty, Rom. i. 28.*
κάθ-ημαι, 2 p. κάθη for κάθησαι, imper., κάθου (see § 367), to be seated, to sit down, to sit, to be settled, to abide; with εἰς, ἐν, ἐπί (gen., dat., acc.).
καθ-ημερινός, ή, όν, daily, Acts vi. 1.*
καθίζω, ίσω, (1) trans., to cause to sit down, to set ; (2) intrans., to seat oneself, preps. as κάθημαι ; to sit down, to be sitting, to tarry ; mid. in Matt. xix. 28 ; Luke xxii. 30.
καθ-ίημι, 1st aor. καθῆκα (comp. § 112), to send or let down, Luke v. 19 ; Acts ix. 25, x. 11, xi. 5.*
καθ-ίστημι (and καθιστάω or -ανω), to appoint, constitute, make, ordain, to conduct, Acts xvii. 15 ; to appoint as ruler over (ἐπί, gen., dat., acc.).
καθ-ό, adv. (for καθ' ὅ), as, according as, Rom. viii. 26 ; 2 Cor. viii. 12 ; 1 Pet. iv. 13.*
καθολικός, ή, όν, general, universal, "catholic" (found in the inscriptions of seven Epistles, but omitted by W. H.)*
καθ-όλου, adv., entirely ; καθόλου μή, Acts iv. 18, not at all.*
καθ-οπλίζω, to arm fully, pass., Luke xi. 21.*
καθ-οράω, ῶ, to see clearly, pass., Rom. i. 20.*
καθ-ότι, adv., as, according as, Acts ii. 45, iv. 35 ; because that, for, Luke i. 7, xix. 9 ; Acts ii. 24, xvii. 31 (W. H.).*
καθ-ώς, adv., according as, even as, as.
καί, conj., and, also, even. For the various uses of this conjunction, see § 403.
Καιάφας, α, ὁ, Caiaphas.
Καΐν, ὁ (Heb.), Cain.
Καϊνάν, ὁ (Heb.), Cainan. Two are mentioned, Luke iii. 36, 37.*
καινός, ή, όν, new. Syn. 26.
καινότης, ητος, ἡ, newness, renovation (moral and spiritual), Rom. vi. 4, vii. 6.*
καί-περ, conj., although.
καιρός, οῦ, ὁ, the fit or critical time, season, opportunity ; time that is in any way limited or defined. Syn. 64.
Καῖσαρ, αρος, ὁ, Cæsar, a title assumed by Roman emperors, after the dictator Julius Cæsar, as Luke ii. 1, xx. 22 ; Acts xi. 28 ; Phil. iv. 22.
Καισαρεία, ας, ἡ, Cæsarea. Two cities of Palestine, one in Galilee (Cæsarea Philippi), Matt. xvi. 13 ; the other on the coast of the Mediterranean, Acts viii. 40.
καί-τοι, conj., nevertheless, though indeed; so καίτοιγε.
καίω (αί), pf., pass., κέκαυμαι, to burn, to kindle ; pass., to be on fire ; fig., Luke xxiv. 32.
κἀκεῖ (καὶ ἐκεῖ), and there.
κἀκεῖθεν (καὶ ἐκεῖθεν), and thence, and from that.
κἀκεῖνος, η, ο (καὶ ἐκεῖνος), and he, she, it.
κακία, ας, ἡ, badness, (1) of character, wickedness, Acts viii. 22 ; (2) of disposition, malice, ill-will, 1 Cor. v. 8 ; (3) of condition, affliction, evil, Matt. vi. 34.
κακο-ήθεια, ας, ἡ, malevolence, Rom. i. 29.*
κακο-λογέω, ῶ, to revile, to speak evil of (acc.), Matt. xv. 4 ; Mark vii. 10, ix. 39 ; Acts xix. 9.*
κακο-πάθεια, ας, ἡ, a suffering of evil, James v. 10.*
κακο-παθέω, ῶ, to suffer evil, to endure affliction, 2 Tim. ii. 3 (W. H., συνκακ-), 9, iv. 5 ; James v. 13.*
κακο-ποιέω, ῶ, abs., to do injury, Mark iii. 4 ; Luke vi. 9 ; to do evil, 1 Pet. iii. 17 ; 3 John 11.*
κακο-ποιός, όν, as subst., an evildoer, malefactor, John xviii. 30 ; 1 Pet. ii. 12, 14, iii. 16, iv. 15.*
κακός, ή, όν, evil, wicked, malignant ; τὸ κακόν, wickedness, Matt. xxvii. 23 ; also calamity, affliction. Syn. 22. Adv. -ῶς, wickedly ; κακῶς ἔχειν, to be ill, or in trouble.
κακ-οῦργος, ον, as subst., an evil-worker, malefactor, Luke xxiii. 32, 33, 39 ; 2 Tim. ii. 9.*
κακ-ουχέω, ῶ, only in pass., part., treated ill, harassed, Heb. xi. 37, xiii. 3.*
κακόω, ῶ, ώσω, to ill-treat, Acts vii. 6, 19, xii. 1, xviii. 10 ; 1 Pet. iii. 13 ; to exasperate, Acts xiv. 2.*

κάκωσις, εως, ἡ, evil condition, affliction, ill-treatment, Acts vii. 34.*
καλάμη, ης, ἡ, stubble, 1 Cor. iii. 12.*
κάλαμος, ου, ὁ, a stalk, as (1) a reed, growing, Matt. xi. 7; (2) a reed, as a mock sceptre, Matt. xxvii. 29; (3) a pen, 3 John 13; (4) a measuring-rod, Rev. xxi. 15.
καλέω, ῶ, ἐσω, κέκληκα, to call; hence, (1) to summon, Luke xix. 13; (2) to name, Matt. i. 21, x. 25; (3) to invite, John ii. 2; (4) to appoint, or select, for an office, Heb. v. 4; (5) pass., to be called, or accounted, i.e., to be, Matt. v. 9, 19; James ii. 23.
καλλι-έλαιος, ου, ἡ, a good olive tree, Rom. xi. 24.*
καλλίων (compar. of καλός), better; adv., κάλλιον, Acts xxv. 10.*
καλο-διδάσκαλος, ου, ὁ, ἡ, a teacher of what is good, Tit. ii. 3.*
Καλοὶ Λιμένες, Fair Havens, a place of good harbourage in the island of Crete, Acts xxvii. 8.
καλο-ποιέω, ῶ, to act well or honourably, 2 Thess. iii. 13.*
καλός, ἡ, όν, fair; hence, (1) physically beautiful, goodly; (2) morally beautiful, good, honourable, noble; (3) excellent, advantageous: adv., -ῶς, well, fairly.
κάλυμμα, ατος, τό, a covering, veil, 2 Cor. iii. 13-16.*
καλύπτω, ψω, to cover, veil.
κάμέ. See κἀγώ.
κάμηλος, ου, ὁ, ἡ, a camel.
κάμινος, ου, ἡ, a furnace, Matt. xiii. 42, 50; Rev. i. 15, ix. 2.*
καμ-μύω (κατά and μύω), to shut, close the eyes, Matt.xiii. 15; Acts xxviii. 27.*
κάμνω, καμῶ, pf. κέκμηκα, to be weary, faint, to be sick, Heb. xii. 3; James v. 15; Rev. ii. 3 (W. H. omit).*
κάμοί. See κἀγώ.
κάμπτω, ψω, to bend the knee, Rom. xi. 4, xiv. 11; Eph. iii. 14; Phil. ii. 10.*
κἄν (καὶ ἐάν), and if, Luke xiii. 9; even if, though, Matt. xxvi. 35; if even, Heb. xii. 20; elliptically, if only, Mark v. 28; Acts v. 15.
Κανᾶ, ἡ (Heb.), Cana.
Κανανίτης, ου, ὁ, a Canaanite (from the Hebrew, meaning the same as Zelotes), Matt. x. 4; Mark iii. 18.* (W. H. read Καναναῖος; Cananaean, R. V.)

Κανδάκη, ης, ἡ, Candace, Acts viii. 27.*
κανών, όνος, ὁ, prep., a measuring rod; hence, (1) a rule of conduct, "canon," Gal. vi. 16; Phil. iii. 16: (2) a limit or sphere of duty, province (R.V.), 2 Cor. x. 13, 15, 16.*
Καπερ-ναούμ, or Καφαρ-ναούμ (W. H.), ἡ (Heb.), Capernaum.
καπηλεύω, to be a petty trader: hence (with acc.), to make merchandise of (R.V. marg.), or perhaps adulterate, corrupt, 2 Cor. ii. 17.*
καπνός, οῦ, ὁ, a smoke, a vapour.
Καππαδοκία, ας, ἡ, Cappadocia, Acts ii. 9; 1 Pet. i. 1.*
καρδία, ας, ἡ, the heart, met., as the seat of the affections, but chiefly of the understanding. Syn. 55. Fig., the heart or bowels of the earth, Matt. xii. 40.
καρδιο-γνώστης, ου, ὁ, one who knows the heart, Acts i. 24, xv. 8.*
καρπός, οῦ, ὁ, fruit, produce, Luke xii. 17; met., for children, Acts ii. 30; deeds, conduct, the fruit of the hands, Matt. iii. 8; effect, result, emolument, Rom. vi. 21. Praise is called the fruit of the lips, Heb. xiii. 15.
Κάρπος, ου, ὁ, Carpus, 2 Tim. iv. 13.*
καρπο-φορέω, ῶ, ήσω, to bring forth fruit, Mark iv. 28; mid., to bear fruit to oneself, to increase, Col. i. 6.
καρπο-φόρος, ον, bringing forth fruit, fruitful, Acts xiv. 17.*
καρτερέω, ῶ, ήσω, to be strong, to endure, Heb. xi. 27.*
κάρφος, ους, τό, a mote, a splinter, Matt. vii. 3, 4, 5; Luke vi. 41, 42.*
κατά, prep., gov. the gen. and accus. cases, down; hence, gen., down from, against, etc.; acc., according to, against, etc. (see §§ 124, 147, a). In composition, κατά may import descent, subjection, opposition, distribution, and with certain verbs (as of destruction, diminution, and the like) is intensive = "utterly."
κατα-βαίνω, βήσομαι, βέβηκα, 2nd aor. κατέβην, to go or come down, descend, used of persons and of things, as gifts from heaven, of the clouds, storms, lightnings; also of anything that falls, Luke xxii. 44; Rev. xvi. 21.
κατα-βάλλω, 1st aor., pass., κατεβλήθην, to cast down, Rev. xii. 10 (W. H.;

βάλλω), mid., *to lay*, as a foundation, Heb. vi. 1.*
κατα-βαρέω, ῶ, *to weigh down, to oppress*, 2 Cor. xii. 16.*
κατα-βαρύνω, *oppress*, Mark xiv. 40 (W. H.).*
κατά-βασις, εως, ή, *descent, declivity*, Luke xix. 37.*
κατα-βιβάζω, *to bring down, cast down*, Matt. xi. 23 (W. H., καταβαίνω), Luke x. 15 (Rec., W. H. marg.).*
κατα-βολή, ῆς, ή, *a founding, laying the foundation of*, Matt. xiii. 35 ; Heb. xi. 11.
κατα-βραβεύω, *to give judgment against as umpire of the games, to deprive of due reward*, Col. ii. 18.*
κατ-αγγελεύς, έως, ό, *a proclaimer, a herald*, Acts xvii. 18.*
κατ-αγγέλλω, *to declare openly, to proclaim, to preach.* Syn. 15.
κατα-γελάω, ῶ, *to laugh at, deride*, gen., Matt. ix. 24 ; Mark v. 40 ; Luke viii. 53.*
κατα-γινώσκω, *to condemn, blame*, gen. of pers., Gal. ii. 11 ; 1 John iii. 20, 21.*
κατ-άγνυμι, fut. κατεάξω, *to break down, to break in pieces*, Matt. xii. 20 ; John xix. 31-33.*
κατ-άγω, *to bring down*, as Acts ix. 30 ; Rom. x. 6 ; as a naval term, *to bring to land*, Luke v. 11 ; pass., *to come to land*, Acts xxi. 3, xxvii. 3.
κατ-αγωνίζομαι, dep., *to contend against, subdue* (acc.), Heb. xi. 33.*
κατα-δέω, ῶ, *to bind up*, as wounds, Luke x. 34.*
κατά-δηλος, ον, *quite evident*, Heb. vii. 15.*
κατα-δικάζω, *to condemn, to pronounce sentence against*, Matt. xii. 7, 37 ; Luke vi. 37 ; James v. 6.*
κατα-δίκη, ης, ή, *condemnation*, Acts xxv. 15 (W. H.).*
κατα-διώκω, *to follow closely, to pursue intently*, Mark i. 36.*
κατα-δουλόω, ῶ, ώσω, *to bring into slavery*, 2 Cor. xi. 20 ; Gal. ii. 4.*
κατα-δυναστεύω, *to exercise power over, to oppress*, Acts x. 38 ; James ii. 6.*
κατά-θεμα, W. H. for κατανάθεμα, Rev. xxii. 3.*
κατα-θεματίζω, W. H. for καταναθεματίζω, Matt. xxvi. 74.*

κατ-αισχύνω, *to put to shame*, as 1 Cor. i. 27 ; *to dishonour*, 1 Cor. xi. 4, 5 ; *to shame*, as with disappointed expectation, 1 Pet. ii. 6 ; pass., *to be ashamed*, as Luke xiii. 17.
κατα-καίω (αϝ), αύσω, *to burn up, to consume entirely*, as Matt. iii. 12 ; Heb. xiii. 11.
κατα-καλύπτω, in mid., *to wear a veil*, 1 Cor. xi. 6, 7.*
κατα-καυχάομαι, ῶμαι, *to glory, to rejoice against, to glory over* (gen.), Rom. xi. 18 ; James ii. 13, iii. 14.*
κατά-κειμαι, *to lie down*, as the sick, Mark i. 30 ; *to recline* at table, Mark xiv. 3.
κατα-κλάω, ῶ, *to break in pieces*, Mark vi. 41 ; Luke ix. 16.*
κατα-κλείω, *to shut up, confine*, Luke iii. 20 ; Acts xxvi. 10.*
κατα-κληρο-δοτέω, ῶ, *to give by lot, to distribute an inheritance by lot*, Acts xiii. 19. (W. H. read the following.)*
κατα-κληρο-νομέω, *to assign by lot*, Acts xiii. 19 (W. H.).*
κατα-κλίνω, νῶ, *to cause to recline* at table, *make sit down*, Luke ix. 14, 15 (W. H.) ; mid., *to recline* at table, Luke vii. 36 (W. H.), xiv. 8, xxiv. 30.*
κατα-κλύζω, σω, *to inundate, deluge*, pass., 2 Pet. iii. 6.*
κατα-κλυσμός, οῦ, ό, *a deluge, flood*, Matt. xxiv. 38, 39 ; Luke xvii. 27 ; 2 Pet. ii. 5.*
κατ-ακολουθέω, ῶ, *to follow closely* (abs. or dat.), Luke xxiii. 55 ; Acts xvi. 17.*
κατα-κόπτω, ψω, *to wound*, Mark v. 5.*
κατα-κρημνίζω, σω, *to cast down headlong*, Luke iv. 29.*
κατά-κριμα, ατος, τό, *condemnation*, Rom. v. 16, 18 ; viii. 1.*
κατα-κρίνω, νῶ, *to give judgment against, to adjudge worthy of punishment* (gen. and dat.), *to condemn*, as Matt. xx. 18 ; Rom. ii. 1, viii. 3.
κατά-κρισις, εως, ή, *the act of condemnation*, 2 Cor. iii. 9, vii. 3.*
κατα-κυριεύω, *to exercise authority over*, as Matt. xx. 25 ; *to get the mastery of*, Acts xix. 16 (gen.).
κατα-λαλέω, ῶ, *to speak against* (gen.), James iv. 11 ; 1 Pet. ii. 12, iii. 16.*
κατα-λαλία, as, fem., *evil-speaking, obloquy, reproach*, 2 Cor. xii. 20, 1 Pet. ii. 1.*

κατά-λαλος, ον, ὁ, ἡ, a calumniator, detractor, Rom. i. 30.*
κατα-λαμβάνω, λήψομαι, to seize or lay hold of, as Mark ix. 18 ; to grasp, as the prize in public games, Phil. iii. 12, 13 ; to overtake, 1 Thess. v. 4 ; mid., to comprehend, i.e., to hold, with the mind ; to perceive, to apprehend, ὅτι, or acc. and inf., Eph. iii. 18.
κατα-λέγω, to reckon among, pass., 1 Tim. v. 9.*
κατά-λειμμα, ατος, τό, a remnant, a residue, Rom. ix. 27 (W. H., ὑπόλιμμα).*
κατα-λείπω, ψω, to leave utterly, to depart from, to forsake, to leave remaining, to reserve, Rom. xi. 4.
κατα-λιθάζω, σω, to stone, to destroy by stoning, Luke xx. 6.*
κατ-αλλαγή, ῆς, ἡ, reconciliation, Rom. v. 11, xi. 15 ; 2 Cor. v. 18, 19.*
κατ-αλλάσσω, ξω, to reconcile (acc. and dat.), Rom. v. 10 ; 1 Cor. vii. 11 ; 2 Cor. v. 18, 19, 20.*
κατά-λοιπος, ον, plur., the rest, the residue, Acts xv. 17.*
κατά-λυμα, ατος, τό, a lodging-place, an inn, Luke ii. 7 ; a guest-chamber, Mark xiv. 14 ; Luke xxii. 11.*
κατα-λύω, ύσω, to loosen down, (1) lit., of a building, to destroy, Mark xiv. 58 ; (2) fig., of law or command, to render void, Matt. v. 17 ; (3) met., of beasts of burden, to unbind ; hence, to halt, to lodge, Luke ix. 12, xix. 7.
κατα-μανθάνω, 2nd aor. κατέμαθον, to consider, to note accurately, Matt. vi. 28.*
κατα-μαρτυρέω, ῶ, to bear testimony against (acc. of thing, gen. of pers.), Matt. xxvi. 62, xxvii. 13 ; Mark xiv. 60, xv. 4 (not W. H.).*
κατα-μένω, to remain, abide, Acts i. 13.*
κατα-μόνας (W. H., κατὰ μόνας), adv., separately, by oneself, privately, Mark iv. 10 ; Luke ix. 18.*
κατ-ανά-θεμα, ατος, τό, curse, Rev. xxii. 3. See κατάθεμα.*
κατ-ανα-θεματίζω, to curse, devote to destruction, Matt. xxvi. 74. See καταθεματίζω.*
κατ-αν-αλίσκω, to consume, to devour, as fire, Heb. xii. 29.*
κατα-ναρκάω, ῶ, ήσω, to be idly burdensome to (gen.), 2 Cor. xi. 9, xii. 13, 14.*

κατα-νεύω, to nod, to make signs to, dat., Luke v. 7.*
κατα-νοέω, ῶ, (1) to observe carefully, remark, consider ; (2) to have respect to, to regard (acc.).
κατ-αντάω, ῶ, to come to, to arrive at, to attain to, with εἰς, as Acts xvi. 1 ; Phil. iii. 11 ; once with ἀντικρύ, Acts xx. 15.
κατά-νυξις, εως, ἡ, stupor, deep sleep, Rom. xi. 8.*
κατα-νύσσω, ξω, 2nd aor., pass., κατενύγην, to prick through, to move greatly, pass., Acts ii. 37.*
κατ-αξιόω, ῶ, ώσω, to count worthy of (gen.), pass., Luke xx. 35, xxi. 36 ; Acts v. 41 ; 2 Thess. i. 5.*
κατα-πατέω, ῶ, to trample on, to tread under foot (acc.), as Luke viii. 5.
κατά-παυσις, εως, ἡ, rest, place of rest, Acts vii. 49 ; Heb. iii. 11, 18, iv. 1, 3, 5, 10, 11.*
κατα-παύω, (1) trans., to hold back, restrain, acc. (also τοῦ μή, and inf.), Acts xiv. 18 ; to give rest, to cause to rest, Heb. iv. 8 ; (2) intrans., to rest from, ἀπό, Heb. iv. 4, 10.*
κατα-πέτασμα (πετάννυμι), ατος, τό, a veil or curtain, as Luke xxiii. 45.
κατα-πίνω, 2nd aor., κατέπιον ; 1st aor., pass., κατεπόθην ; to drink up, swallow, Matt. xxiii. 24 ; fig. to overwhelm, destroy, 1 Cor. xv. 54 ; 2 Cor. ii. 7, v. 4 ; Heb. xi. 29 ; 1 Pet. v. 4 ; Rev. xii. 16.*
κατα-πίπτω, 2nd aor. κατέπεσον, to fall down, Luke viii. 6 (W. H.) ; Acts xxvi. 14, xxviii. 6.*
κατα-πλέω (εῖ), εύσομαι, 1st aor. κατέπλευσα, to sail to, Luke viii. 26.*
κατα-πονέω, ῶ, in pass., to be oppressed; distressed, Acts vii. 24 ; 2 Pet. ii. 7.*
κατα-ποντίζω, mid. or pass., to sink down, to be drowned, Matt. xiv. 30, xviii. 6.*
κατ-άρα, ας, ἡ, a curse, cursing, Gal. iii. 10, 13 ; Heb. vi. 8 ; 2 Pet. ii. 14 ; James iii. 10.*
κατ-αράομαι, ῶμαι, to imprecate, to devote to destruction, Matt. v. 44 (W. H. omit) ; Mark xi. 21 ; Luke vi. 28 ; Rom. xii. 14 ; James iii. 9 ; pass., perf. part., accursed, Matt. xxv. 41.*
κατ-αργέω, ῶ, ήσω, to render useless, Luke xiii. 7 ; to bring to nought, make to cease, abolish, as Rom. iii. 3, 31, and frequently in Paul ; to make to

κατ-αριθμέω—κατ-εξουσιάζω] VOCABULARY. 455

cease from, *sever* from (ἀπό), Rom. vii. 2; Gal. v. 4.
κατ-αριθμέω, ῶ, *to number among*, Acts i. 17.*
κατ-αρτίζω, ίσω, *to refit, to repair*, Matt. iv. 21 ; *to restore from error or sin*, Gal. vi. 1 ; *to perfect, to complete*, 1 Thess. iii. 10 ; 1 Pet. v, 10 ; pass., *to be thoroughly united*, 1 Cor. i. 10.
κατ-άρτισις, εως, ἡ, *a perfecting*, 2 Cor. xiii. 9.*
κατ-αρτισμός, οῦ, ὁ, *a perfecting*, Eph. iv. 12.*
κατα-σείω, σω, *to wave the hand, to beckon*, Acts xii. 17, xiii. 16, xix. 33, xxi. 40.*
κατα-σκάπτω, ψω, *to demolish* by digging under, *to overthrow, to raze*, Rom. xi. 3 ; perf. part., pass., *ruins*, Acts xv. 16.*
κατα-σκευάζω, άσω, *to prepare fully, to build, to adjust*, as Matt. xi. 10 ; Luke i. 17 ; Heb. iii. 3, 4.
κατα-σκηνόω, ῶ, ώσω, *to dwell, lodge*, Matt. xiii. 32 ; Mark iv. 32 ; Luke xiii. 19 ; Acts ii. 26.*
κατα-σκήνωσις, εως, ἡ, *a dwelling-place, a haunt*, as of birds, Matt. viii. 20 ; Luke ix. 58.*
κατα-σκιάζω, σω, *to overshadow*, Heb. ix. 5.*
κατα-σκοπέω, ῶ, *to inspect narrowly, to plot against*, Gal. ii. 4.*
κατα-σκοπός, *a scout, a spy*, Heb. xi. 31.*
κατα-σοφίζομαι, σομαι, *to deal deceitfully with*, Acts vii. 19.*
κατα-στέλλω, λῶ, 1st aor. κατέστειλα, *to appease, restrain*, Acts xix. 35, 36.*
κατά-στημα, ατος, τό, *behaviour, conduct*, Tit. ii. 3.*
κατα-στολή, ῆς, ἡ, *raiment, outer clothing*, 1 Tim. ii. 9.*
κατα-στρέφω, ψω, *to overthrow*, Matt. xxi. 12 ; Mark xi. 15.*
κατα-στρηνιάω, ῶ, άσω, *to grow wanton against* (gen.), 1 Tim. v. 11.*
κατα-στροφή, ῆς, ἡ, *an overthrow*, "catastrophe," 2 Tim. ii. 14 ; 2 Pet. ii. 6.*
κατα-στρώννυμι, στρώσω, *to strew down, scatter, to overthrow*, 1 Cor. x. 5.*
κατα-σύρω, *to drag along*, Luke xii. 58.*
κατα-σφάζω, ξω, *to slay, to slaughter*, Luke xix. 27.*

κατα-σφραγίζω, σω, *to close, to seal up*, as a book, Rev. v. 1.*
κατά-σχεσις, εως, ἡ, *a possession*, Acts vii. 5, 45.*
κατα-τίθημι, θήσω, 1st aor. κατέθηκα, *to deposit*, as a body in a tomb, Mark xv. 46 (W. H., τίθημι) ; mid. κατα τίθεσθαι χάριν, *to gain favour* with (dat.), Acts xxiv. 27, xxv. 9.*
κατα-τομή, ῆς, ἡ, paronomasia with περιτομή, *mutilation*, Phil. iii. 2.*
κατα-τοξεύω, *to transfix*, Heb. xii. 20 (W. H. omit).*
κατα-τρέχω, 2nd aor. κατέδραμον, *to run down* (ἐπί, acc.), Acts xxi. 32.*
κατα-φάγω. See κατεσθίω.
κατα-φέρω, κατοίσω, 1st aor. κατήνεγκα, pass. κατηνέχθην, *to throw down*, as an adverse vote, Acts xxvi. 10, xxv. 7 (W. H.) ; pass., *to be borne down, to fall*, Acts xx. 9.*
κατα-φεύγω, 2nd aor. κατέφυγον, *to flee for refuge*, with εἰς, Acts xiv. 6 ; with inf., Heb. vi. 18.*
κατα-φθείρω, pass., perf., κατέφθαρμαι ; 2nd aor., κατεφθάρην, *to corrupt utterly*, 2 Tim. iii. 8 ; *to destroy*, 2 Pet. ii. 12 (W. H., φθείρω.)*
κατα-φιλέω, ῶ, *to kiss affectionately*, or repeatedly (acc.), as Matt. xxvi. 49 ; Luke xx. 20.
κατα-φρονέω, ῶ, *to think lightly of, neglect, despise* (gen.), as Matt. vi. 24.
κατα-φρονητής, οῦ, ὁ, *a despiser, a scorner*, Acts xiii. 41.*
κατα-χέω (εf), εύσω, 1st aor. κατέχεα, *to pour down upon*, Matt. xxvi. 7 ; Mark xiv. 3.*
κατα-χθόνιος, ον, *subterranean*, Phil. ii. 10.*
κατα-χράομαι, ῶμαι, *to use overmuch, to abuse*, 1 Cor. vii. 31, ix. 18 (dat.).*
κατα-ψύχω, *to cool, to refresh*, Luke xvi. 24.*
κατ-είδωλος, ον, *full of idols* (R.V.), Acts xvii. 16.*
κατ-έναντι, adv., or as prep. with gen., *over against, before, in presence* or *in sight of*.
κατ-ενώπιον, adv., *in the very presence of* (gen.).
κατ-εξουσιάζω, *to exercise authority against* or *over* (gen.), Matt. xx. 25 ; Mark x. 42.*

κατ-εργάζομαι, άσομαι, with mid. and pass., aor. (augm., εἰ-), to work out, to do fully, Rom. iv. 15; Eph. vi. 13; to work, to practise.

κατ-έρχομαι, 2nd aor. κατῆλθον, to descend, come down to.

κατ-εσθίω and -έσθω (Mark xii. 40, W. H.), fut. καταφάγομαι (John ii. 17, W. H.); 2nd aor. κατέφαγον, to eat up, to devour entirely, lit. or fig., Matt. xiii. 4; John ii. 17; Gal. v. 15.

κατ-ευθύνω, νῶ, to direct well, to guide successfully, Luke i. 79; 1 Thess. iii. 11; 2 Thess. iii. 5.*

κατ-ευλογέω, to bless much, Mark x. 16 (W. H.).

κατ-εφ-ίστημι, 2nd aor. κατεπέστην, to rise up against, Acts xviii. 12.*

κατ-έχω, κατασχήσω, to seize on, to hold fast, to retain, possess, to prevent from doing a thing (τοῦ μή, with inf.), to repress, Rom. i. 18; τὸ κάτεχον, the hindrance, 2 Thess. ii. 6, 7; κατεῖχον εἰς τὸν αἰγιαλόν, they held for the shore, Acts xxvii. 40.

κατ-ηγορέω, ῶ, ήσω, to accuse, to speak against, abs., or with person in gen.; charge in gen. alone or after περί or κατά; pass., to be accused; with ὑπό or παρά, of the accuser.

κατ-ηγορία, as, ή, an accusation, a charge, pers. in gen. alone, or after κατά; charge also in gen.

κατ-ήγορος, ου, ό, an accuser.

κατ-ήγωρ, ό, an accuser, Rev. xii. 10 (W. H.).

κατήφεια, as, ή, dejection, sorrow, James iv. 9.*

κατηχέω, ῶ, ήσω, perf., pass., κατήχημαι (ἦχος), to instruct orally, to teach, "catechise;" Luke i. 4; Acts xviii. 25, xxi. 21, 24; Rom. ii. 18; 1 Cor. xiv. 19; Gal. vi. 6.* Syn. 14.

κατ' ἰδίαν, separately, privately, by oneself (see ἴδιος).

κατ-ιόω, ῶ (ιός), to consume by rust, James v. 3.*

κατ-ισχύω, to prevail, prevail against (gen.), Matt. xvi. 18; Luke xxi. 36 (W. H.), xxiii. 23.*

κατ-οικέω, ῶ, (1) intrans., to dwell, with ἐν, εἰς (const. praeg.), ἐπί, gen. or adverbs of place; (2) trans., to dwell in, to inhabit, acc.; fig., of qualities or attributes, to abide.

κατ-οίκησις, εως, ή, a dwelling, habitation, Mark v. 3.*

κατ-οικητήριον, ου, τό, a dwelling-place, Eph. ii. 22; Rev. xviii. 2.*

κατ-οικία, as, ή, a dwelling, a habitation, Acts xvii. 26.*

κατ-οικίζω, to make to dwell, James iv. 5 (W. H.).*

κατ-οπτρίζω, mid., to behold, as in a mirror, 2 Cor. iii. 18.*

κατ-όρθωμα, ατος, τό, an honourable act well performed, Acts xxiv. 3 (W. H., διόρθωμα).*

κάτω, adv., downwards, down, Matt. iv. 6; beneath, Mark xiv. 66; with relation to age, comparat., κατωτέρω, under, Matt. ii. 16.

κατώτερος, α, ον (κάτω), lower, Eph. iv. 9 (on which see § 259).*

καῦμα, ατός, τό (καίω), heat, scorching heat, burning, Rev. vii. 16, xvi. 9.*

καυματίζω, σω, to scorch, burn, torture by fire, Matt. xiii. 6; Mark iv. 6; Rev. xvi. 8, 9.*

καῦσις, εως, ή, a burning, burning up, Heb. vi. 8.*

καυσόω, ῶ, to burn with intense heat, pass., 2 Pet. iii. 10, 12.*

καύσων, ωνος, ὁ, scorching heat; perhaps a hot wind from the E., Matt. xx. 12; Luke xii. 55; James i. 11 (see Hos. xii. 1, etc.).*

καυτηριάζω, to brand or sear, as with a hot iron; fig., pass., 1 Tim. iv. 2.*

καυχάομαι, ῶμαι, 2nd pers. καυχᾶσαι, fut. ήσομαι, to glory, to boast, to exult, both in a good sense and in a bad, 1 Cor. i. 29; Eph. ii. 9; followed with prep., ἐν, περί, gen.; ὑπέρ, gen.; ἐπί, dat.

καύχημα, ατος, τό, glorying, boasting; met., the object or ground of boasting, as Rom. iv. 2.

καύχησις, εως, ή, the act of boasting, glorying.

Καφαρναούμ (see Καπερναούμ), Capernaum.

Κεγχρεαί, ῶν, αί, Cenchreae, the port of Corinth, Acts xviii. 18; Rom. xvi. 1.*

κέδρος, ου, ή, a cedar, John xviii. 1 (not W. H.); probably a mistaken reading for following.*

Κεδρών, ὁ (Heb., dark or turbid), Cedron, a turbid brook between the Mount of Olives and Jerusalem, John xviii. 1.*

κεῖμαι, σαι, ται ; impf., ἐκείμην, σο, το ; to lie, to recline, to be laid, Luke xxiii. 53 ; 1 John v. 19 ; met., to be given, as laws, 1 Tim. i. 9.

κειρία, ας, ἡ, a band or a roller of linen, John xi. 44.*

κείρω, κερῶ, to shear, as sheep, Acts viii. 32 ; mid., to shave the head, Acts xviii. 18 ; 1 Cor. xi. 6.*

κέλευσμα, ατος, τό, a shout, a crying out, 1 Thess. iv. 16.*

κελεύω, σω, to command, to bid.

κενο-δοξία, ας, ἡ, vainglory, inordinate desire for praise, Phil. ii. 3.*

κενό-δοξος, ον, vainglorious, Gal. v. 26.*

κενός, ή, όν, empty : hence, destitute, Mark xii. 3 ; fruitless, Acts iv. 25 ; fallacious, Eph. v. 6 ; foolish, James ii. 20 ; adv., -ῶς, in vain, to no purpose, only James iv. 5. Syn. 29.

κενο-φωνία, ας, ἡ, empty disputing, useless babbling, 1 Tim. vi. 20 ; 2 Tim. ii. 16.*

κενόω, ῶ, ώσω, to empty oneself, divest oneself of rightful dignity, Phil. ii. 7 ; to make void, render useless, Rom. iv. 14 ; 1 Cor. i. 17, ix. 15 ; 2 Cor. ix. 3.*

κέντρον, ου, τό, a goad, a spike, a sting, Acts ix. 5 ; 1 Cor. xv. 55, 56.*

κεντυρίων, ωνος, ὁ, Latin (see § 154, c), a centurion, the commander of a hundred foot-soldiers.

κεραία, ας, ἡ, a little horn (the small projecting stroke by which certain similar Hebrew letters are distinguished, as ר and ד) ; met., the minutest part, Matt. v. 18 ; Luke xvi. 17.*

κεραμεύς, έως, ὁ, a potter, Matt. xxvii. 7, 10 ; Rom. ix. 21.*

κεραμικός, ή, όν, made of potter's clay, earthen, Rev. ii. 27.*

κεράμιον, ίου, τό, an earthen vessel, a pitcher, Mark xiv. 13 ; Luke xxii. 10.*

κέραμος, ου, ὁ, a tile, of potter's clay, Luke v. 19.*

κεράννυμι (see §§ 113, 114), to mix, to prepare a draught, Rev. xiv. 10, xviii. 6.*

κέρας, ατος, τό, a horn, as Rev. v. 6 ; fig., for strength, only Luke i. 69 ; a projecting point, horn of the altar, only Rev. ix. 13.

κεράτιον, ίου, τό, a pod, a kind of sweet broad bean, Luke xv. 16.*

κερδαίνω, ανῶ, 1st aor. ἐκέρδησα, to gain by trading, Matt. xxv. 16 (W. H.)–22 ; to get gain, James iv. 13 ; to gain, win, Phil. iii. 8 ; to gain over to a cause, 1 Cor. ix. 19–22.

κέρδος, ους, τό, gain, profit, Phil. i. 21, iii. 7 ; Tit. i. 11.*

κέρμα, ατος, τό (κείρω), a small piece of money, John ii. 15.*

κερματιστής, οῦ, ὁ, a money-changer, John ii. 14.*

κεφάλαιον, αίου, τό, a sum of money, Acts xxii. 28 ; the sum of an argument, Heb. viii. 1 (see R.V. and marg.).*

κεφαλαιόω, ῶ, ώσω, to smite on the head, Mark xii. 4.*

κεφαλή, ῆς, ἡ, the head, of human beings or animals ; for the whole person, Acts xviii. 6 ; the summit, or copestone, of a building, Luke xx. 17 ; met., implying authority, head, lord, 1 Cor. xi. 3 ; Eph. i. 22 ; Col. i. 18.

κεφαλίς, ίδος, ἡ, the top of anything, the top or knob of the roll on which Hebrew manuscripts were rolled ; hence, the roll itself, Heb. x. 7.*

κημόω, to muzzle, 1 Cor. ix. 9 (W. H. marg.).*

κῆνσος, ου, ὁ, Latin (§ 154, d), a tax, a poll-tax, Matt. xvii. 25, xxii. 17, 19 ; Mark xii. 14.*

κῆπος, ου, ὁ, a garden Luke xiii. 19 ; John xviii. 1, 26, xix. 41.*

κηπουρός, οῦ, ὁ, a gardener, John xx. 15.*

κηρίον, ου, τό, a honeycomb, Luke xxiv. 42 (W. H. omit).*

κήρυγμα, ατος, τό, a proclaiming, preaching, as Matt. xii. 41 ; 1 Cor. i. 21 ; 2 Tim. iv. 17. Syn. 15.

κῆρυξ, ὕκος, ὁ, a herald, a preacher, 1 Tim. ii. 7 ; 2 Tim. i. 11 ; 2 Pet. ii. 5.*

κηρύσσω, ξω, (1) to proclaim, to publish, Mark vii. 36 ; (2) specially, to preach the Gospel, abs., or acc. and dat. Syn. 15.

κῆτος, ους, τό, a large fish, a sea monster, Matt. xii. 40.*

Κηφᾶς, ᾶ, ὁ (Aramaic, a rock or stone), Cephas, i.e., Peter.

κιβωτός, οῦ, ἡ, a hollow vessel, an ark, of Noah, or the ark of the covenant.

κιθάρα, ας, ἡ, a harp, a lyre, " guitar."

κιθαρίζω, to play upon a harp or lyre, 1 Cor. xiv. 7 ; Rev. xiv. 2.*

κιθαρῳδός, οῦ, ὁ, a harper, lyrist, singer to the harp, Rev. xiv. 2, xviii. 22.*

Κιλικία, ας, ἡ, Cilicia.

κινάμωμον (W. H., κιννά.), ου, τό, *cinnamon*, Rev. xviii. 13.*
κινδυνεύω, σω, *to be in danger*, Luke viii. 23 ; Acts xix. 27, 40 ; I Cor. xv. 30.*
κίνδυνος, ου, ὁ, *danger, peril*, Rom. viii. 35 ; 2 Cor. xi. 26.*
κινέω, ῶ, ήσω, *to move, to stir*, Matt. xxiii. 4 ; *to shake* the head in mockery, Matt. xxvii. 39 ; Mark xv. 29 ; *to remove*, Rev. ii. 5, vi. 14 ; *to excite*, Acts xvii. 28, xxi. 30, xxiv. 5.*
κίνησις, εως, ἡ, *motion, commotion*, John v. 3 (W. H. omit).*
Κίς (W. H., Κείς), ὁ (Heb.), *Kish*, father of Saul, Acts xiii. 21.*
κλάδος, ου, ὁ, *a branch*, as Matt. xiii. 32 ; met., Rom. xi. 16-19.
κλαίω (αf), αύσω, (1) abs., *to wail, to lament, weep* for (ἐπί dat. [W. H., acc.]), Luke xix. 41 ; (2) trans., *to weep for* (acc.), Matt. ii. 18. **Syn. 20**.
κλάσις, εως, ἡ, *a breaking*, Luke xxiv. 35 ; Acts ii. 42.*
κλάσμα, ατος, τό, *a piece broken off, a fragment*, as Matt. xiv. 20.
Κλαύδη, ης, ἡ, *Clauda* or *Claude*, a small island off Crete, Acts xxvii. 16.*
Κλαυδία, ας, ἡ, *Claudia*, 2 Tim. iv. 21.*
Κλαύδιος, ου, ὁ, *Claudius*, the Emperor, Acts xi. 28, xviii. 2 ; a military tribune (Lysias), Acts xxiii. 26.*
κλαυθμός, οῦ, ὁ (κλαίω), *weeping, lamentation*, as Matt. ii. 18.
κλάω, άσω, only with ἄρτον, *to break bread*, in the ordinary meal, Matt. xiv. 19 ; or in the Lord's Supper, xxvi. 26 ; fig., of the body of Christ, I Cor. xi. 24.
κλείς, κλειδός, acc. sing. κλεῖδα or κλεῖν, acc. plur. κλεῖδας or κλεῖς, ἡ, *a key*, the emblem of power, Matt. xvi. 19 ; Rev. i.18,iii. 7,ix. 1,xx. 1; met., Luke xi. 52.*
κλείω, σω, *to shut, shut up, close*.
κλέμμα, ατος, τό (κλέπτω), *theft*, Rev. xi. 21.*
Κλεόπας, α, ὁ, *Cleopas*, Luke xxiv. 18.*
κλέος, ους, τό, *good report, glory*, I Pet. ii. 20.*
κλέπτης, ου, ὁ, *a thief*, as Matt. vi. 19 ; met., of false teachers, John x. 8. **Syn. 74**.
κλέπτω, ψω, *to steal*, abs., Matt. xix. 18 ; or trans. (acc.), Matt. xxvii. 64.
κλῆμα, ατος, τό (κλάω), *a branch, a shoot, a tendril*, of a vine, etc., John xv. 2, 4, 5, 6.*

Κλήμης, εντος, ὁ, *Clement*, Phil. iv. 3.*
κληρονομέω, ω, ήσω, *to obtain by inheritance, to inherit*, Gal. iv. 30 ; *to obtain*, generally.
κληρονομία, ας, ἡ, *an inheritance*.
κληρονόμος, *an heir, one who obtains an inheritance;* applied to Christ, Heb. i. 2.
κλῆρος, ου, ὁ, (1) *a lot*, Matt. xxvii. 35 ; hence (2) *that which is allotted, a portion*, Acts viii. 21 ; *an office*, Acts i. 17, 25 ; plur., *persons assigned to one's care*, I Pet. v. 3.*
κληρόω, ῶ, in mid., *to obtain by lot*, Eph. i. 11.*
κλῆσις, εως, ἡ, *a calling*, in N.T. always of the Divine *call*, as Rom. xi. 29; Eph. iv. 4.
κλητός, όν, verbal adj. (καλέω), *called, invited*, Matt. xxii. 14 ; of Christians, *the called*, Rom. i. 6, 7, viii. 28 ; of the apostolic vocation, Rom. i. 1; I Cor. i. 1.
κλίβανος, ου, ὁ, *an oven, a furnace*, Matt. vi. 30 ; Luke xii. 28.*
κλίμα, ατος, τό, *a climate ; a tract of country, a region*, Rom. xv. 23 ; 2 Cor. xi. 10 ; Gal. i. 21.*
κλινάριον, τό, *a small bed*, Acts v. 15 (W. H.).
κλίνη, ης, ἡ, *a bed*, Mark vii. 30 ; *a portable bed*, Matt. ix. 2, 6 ; *a couch for reclining at meals*, Mark iv. 21.
κλινίδιον, ου, τό (dim.), *a little bed* or *couch*, Luke v. 19, 24.*
κλίνω, νῶ, perf. κέκλικα, (1) trans., *to bow*, in reverence, Luke xxiv. 5 ; in death, John xix. 30 ; *to lay down*, as the head, to rest, Matt. viii. 20 ; *to turn to flight*, Heb. xi. 34 ; (2) intrans., *to decline*, as the day, Luke ix. 12.
κλισία, ας, ἡ, *a table party, a company*, Luke ix. 14.*
κλοπή, ῆς, ἡ, *theft*, Matt. xv. 19 ; Mark vii. 22.*
κλύδων, ωνος, ὁ, *the raging* of the sea ; *a wave, a surge*, Luke viii. 24 ; James i. 6.*
κλυδωνίζομαι, *to be tossed*, as waves by the wind, Eph. iv. 14.*
Κλωπᾶς, ᾶ, ὁ, *Clopas*, John xix. 25.*
κνήθω, *to tickle ;* pass., *to be tickled, to itch*, 2 Tim. iv. 3.
Κνίδος, ου, ἡ, *Cnidus*, Acts xxvii. 7.*
κοδράντης, ου, ὁ, Lat. (see § 154, a), *a farthing*, the smallest coin in use, Matt. v. 26 ; Mark xii. 42.*

κοιλία, as, ἡ, (1) *the belly*, Matt. xv. 17; (2) *the womb*, Matt. xix. 12; (3) fig., *the inner man, the heart*, John vii. 38.

κοιμάω, ῶ, in mid., *to fall asleep*, Luke xxii. 45; pass., *to be asleep, to be asleep in death*, John xi. 12.

κοίμησις, εως, ἡ, *sleep, repose*, John xi. 13.*

κοινός, ή, όν, *common*, *i.e.*, shared by all, Acts iv. 32; *unclean, ceremonially*, Acts x. 15; *unconsecrated*, Heb. x. 29.

κοινόω, ῶ, ώσω, *to make common* or *unclean*, Matt. xv. 11; *to profane, to desecrate*, Acts xxi. 28.

κοινωνέω, ῶ, ήσω, *to have common share in, to partake in*, Rom. xv. 27; *to share with*, Gal. vi. 6.

κοινωνία, as, ἡ, *participation, communion, fellowship*, as 2 Cor. x. 16; 2 Cor. xiii. 13; 1 John i. 3, 6, 7; *contribution*, as of alms, Rom. xv. 26; Heb. xiii. 16.

κοινωνικός, ή, όν, *ready to communicate, liberal*, 1 Tim. vi. 18.*

κοινωνός, ή, όν, as subst., *a partner, a sharer with*, gen. obj.

κοίτη, ης, ἡ, *a bed*, Luke xi. 7; met., *marriage bed*, Heb. xiii. 4; *sexual intercourse* (as illicit), Rom. xiii. 13; κοίτην ἔχειν, *to conceive*, Rom. ix. 10.*

κοιτών, ῶνος, ὁ, *a bed-chamber*, Acts xii. 20.*

κόκκινος, η, ον, *dyed from the* κόκκος, *crimson*.

κόκκος, ου, ὁ, *a kernel, a grain* or *seed*.

κολάζω, σω, mid., *to chastise, to punish*, Acts iv. 21; pass., 2 Pet. ii. 9.*

κολακεία, as, ἡ, *flattery, adulation*, 1 Thess. ii. 5.*

κόλασις, εως, ἡ, *chastisement, punishment*, Matt. xxv. 46; 1 John iv. 18.*

Κολασσαί, ῶν, αἱ. See Κολοσσαί.

κολαφίζω, σω, *to strike with the fist, to buffet, to maltreat*, Mark xiv. 65.

κολλάω, ῶ, ήσω, mid. and pass., *to cleave to, to be joined with, to adhere*.

κολλούριον, or κολλύριον, ίου, τό, *eyesalve*, "collyrium," Rev. iii. 18.*

κολλυβιστής, οῦ, ὁ (κόλλυβος, *small coin*), *a money-changer*, Matt. xxi. 12; Mark xi. 15; John ii. 15.*

κολοβόω, ώσω, *to cut off, to shorten*, Matt. xxiv. 22; Mark xiii. 20.*

Κολοσσαεύς, εως, plur. Κολοσσαεῖς (W. H., Κολασσαεῖς), *Colossians*, only in the subscription to the Epistle.

Κολοσσαί, ῶν, αἱ, *Colossæ*, Col. i. 2.*

κόλπος, ου, ὁ, *the bosom, the chest*, (1) of the body; ἐν τῷ κόλπῳ (or τοῖς κόλποις) εἶναι, ἀνακεῖσθαι, *to be in the bosom of*, *i.e.*, recline next to, at table; Luke xvi. 22, 23 (of the heavenly banquet); John xiii. 23. The phrase in John i. 18 implies a still closer fellowship. (2) of the dress, used as a bag or pocket, Luke vi. 38; (3) *a bay, a gulf, an inlet of the sea*, Acts xxvii. 39.*

κολυμβάω, ῶ, ήσω, *to swim*, Acts xxvii. 43.*

κολυμβήθρα, as, ἡ, *a pool, a swimming-place, a bath*.

κολώνια, as, ἡ, or κολωνία, *a colony*; Philippi is so called, Acts xvi. 12.*

κομάω, ῶ, *to nourish the hair, to wear the hair long*, 1 Cor. xi. 14, 15.*

κόμη, ης, ἡ, *hair of the head*, 1 Cor. xi. 15.*

κομίζω, σω, mid. fut. κομίσομαι or κομοῦμαι, *to bear, to bring*, Luke vii. 37; mid., *to bring to oneself*, *i.e.*, *to acquire, to obtain*, as a recompense, Heb. x. 36; *to receive again, to recover*, Heb. xi. 19.

κομψότερον (comp. of κόμψος), *better, of convalescence*, adverbially with ἔχω, John iv. 52.*

κονιάω, *to whitewash*, Matt. xxiii. 27; pass., Acts xxiii. 3.*

κονι-ορτός, οῦ, ὁ (ὄρνυμι), *dust*.

κοπάζω, σω, *to be quieted, to cease*, of the wind, Matt. xiv. 32; Mark iv. 39, vi. 51.*

κοπετός, οῦ, ὁ (κόπτω), *vehement lamentation*, Acts viii. 2.*

κοπή, ῆς, ἡ, *smiting, slaughter*, Heb. vii. 1.*

κοπιάω, ῶ, άσω, *to toil*, Luke v. 5; *to be fatigued*, or *spent*, with labour, Matt. xi. 28; *to labour*, in the gospel, Rom. xvi. 6, 12; 1 Cor. xv. 10.

κόπος, ου, ὁ, *labour, toil, trouble, uneasiness*.

κοπρία, as, ἡ, *filth, a dunghill*, Luke xiii. 8 (not W. H.), xiv. 35.*

κόπριον, ου, τό, *dung, manure*, Luke xiii. 8 (W. H.).*

κόπτω, mid. fut. κόψομαι, *to cut down*, as branches, trees, etc.; mid., *to beat*

or *cut oneself in grief, to bewail*, as Matt. xi. 17.
κόραξ, ακος, ὁ, *a raven*, Luke xii. 24.*
κοράσιον, ιον, τό (dim. from κόρη), *a girl, a damsel*, as Mark vi. 22, 28.
κορβᾶν (W. H., κορβάν), (indecl.) and κορβανᾶς, ᾶ, ὁ (from Heb.), (1) *a gift, something offered to God*, Mark vii. 11; (2) *the sacred treasury*, Matt. xxvii. 6.*
Κορέ, ὁ (Heb.), *Korah*, Jude 11.*
κορέννυμι, έσω, pass. perf. κεκόρεσμαι, *to satiate*; pass., *to be full*, Acts xxvii. 38; 1 Cor. iv. 8.*
Κορίνθιος, ιον, *Corinthian, a Corinthian*, Acts xviii. 8; 2 Cor. vi. 11.*
Κόρινθος, ου, ἡ, *Corinth*.
Κορνήλιος, ιον, ὁ, *Cornelius*, Acts x.*
κόρος, ου, ὁ (from Heb.), *a cor*, the largest dry measure, equal to ten βάτοι, or nearly fifteen English bushels, Luke xvi. 7.*
κοσμέω, ῶ, ήσω, *to set in order, to garnish*, Matt. xxiii. 29; 1 Tim. ii. 9; *to trim*, as lamps, Matt. xxv. 7; met., *to adorn*, with honour, Tit. ii. 10; 1 Pet. iii. 5.
κοσμικός, ή, όν, (1) *terrestrial*, opp. to ἐπουράνιος, Heb. ix. 1; (2) *worldly*, i.e., *vicious*, Tit. ii. 12.*
κόσμιος, ον, *orderly, decorous*, 1 Tim. ii. 9, iii. 2.*
κοσμο-κράτωρ, ορος, ὁ, *prince of the world, world-ruler* (R.V.), Eph. vi. 12.*
κόσμος, ου, ὁ, (1) *ornament, decoration*, only 1 Pet. iii. 3; hence (2) *the material universe*, Luke xi. 50, as well ordered and beautiful; (3) *the world*, John xi. 9; *the world*, in opposition to the heavenly and the good, John viii. 23; (4) *the inhabitants of the world*, 1 Cor. iv. 9; (5) *the present life*, as distinguished from life eternal; (6) *a vast collection*, of anything, James iii. 6; 2 Pet. ii. 5. Syn. 58.
Κούαρτος, ου, ὁ (Latin, see § 159), *Quartus*, Rom. xvi. 23.*
κοῦμι (a Hebrew imperative fem., in Greek form), *arise*, Mark v. 41 (W. H. read κούμ, the masc. form).
κουστωδία, ας, ἡ' (Latin, see § 154, c), *a guard*, Matt. xxvii. 65, 66, xxviii. 11.*
κουφίζω, *to lighten*, as a ship, Acts xxvii. 38.*

κόφινος, ου, ὁ, *a basket, a travelling basket*, as Matt. xiv. 20. Syn. 69.
κράββατος (W. H., κράβαττος), ου, ὁ, *a couch, a light bed*, as Mark ii. 12.
κράζω, ξω, *to cry out*, hoarsely, or urgently, or in anguish.
κραιπάλη, ης, *surfeiting*, Luke xxi. 34.*
κρανίον, ου, τό, *a skull*; Κρανίου Τόπος, Greek for Γολγοθά, which see, Matt. xxvii. 33. Lat., *Calvaria*, whence our *Calvary*.
κράσπεδον, ου, τό, *the fringe, border*, e.g., of a garment, as Matt. xxiii. 5.
κραταιός, ά, όν, *strong, mighty*, 1 Pet. v. 6.*
κραταιόω, ῶ, in pass. only, *to be strong, to grow strong*, Luke i. 80, ii. 40; 1 Cor. xvi. 13; Eph. iii. 16.*
κρατέω, ῶ, ήσω, *to lay strong hold on, to detain*, acc. or gen., or acc. and gen. (see § 264); *to attain to*, Heb. iv. 14; Matt. ix. 25; *to have power over*, Matt. xiv. 3; *to be master of*, Rev. ii. 1; Acts ii. 24; *to cleave to*, Acts iii. 11, Mark vii. 3; *to retain*, of sins, John xx. 23.
κράτιστος, η, ον (properly superlative of κρατύς, see κράτος), *most excellent, most noble*, a title of honour, Luke i. 3; Acts xxiii. 26, xxiv. 3, xxvi. 25.*
κράτος, ους, τό, *strength, power, dominion*, 1 Pet.iv.11; Heb.ii.14; κατὰ κράτος, Acts xix. 20, *greatly, mightily*. Syn. 57.
κραυγάζω, σω, *to cry out, to clamour*, as Matt. xii. 19.
κραυγή, ῆς, ἡ, *a cry, clamour*, as Heb. v. 7.
κρέας (ατος, αος, contr., κρέως), τό, plur. κρέατα, κρέα, *flesh, flesh-meat*, Rom. xiv. 21; 1 Cor. viii. 13.*
κρείσσων, ον, ττών, ονος, adj. (properly compar. of κρατύς, see κράτος), *stronger, more powerful, better*, as Heb. vii. 7, xii. 24. Syn. 21.
κρεμάννυμι or κρεμάω, ῶ, fut. άσω, *to hang*, trans., Acts v. 30; mid., *to be suspended, to depend*, Matt. xxii. 40; Acts xxviii. 4.
κρημνός, οῦ, ὁ (κρεμάννυμι), *a precipice*, from its overhanging, Matt. viii. 32; Mark v. 13; Luke viii. 33.*
Κρής, ητός, ὁ, *a Cretan*, Acts ii. 11; Tit. i. 12.*
Κρήσκης, εντος, ὁ (Latin), *Crescens*, 2 Tim. iv. 10.*

Κρήτη, ης, ἡ, Crete, now Candia.
κριθή, ῆς, fem., *barley,* Rev. vi. 6.*
κρίθινος, η, ον, *made of barley;* ἄρτοι κρίθινοι, *barley loaves,* John vi. 9, 13.*
κρίμα, ατος, τό, *a judgment, a sentence, condemnation,* as 1 Cor. xi. 29.
κρίνον, ου, τό, *a lily,* Matt. vi. 28; Luke xii. 27.*
κρίνω, νῶ, κέκρικα, 1st aor., pass., ἐκρίθην, (1) *to judge, to deem, to determine,* Acts xiii. 46, xv. 19; Rom. xiv. 5; (2) *to form or express an opinion of,* usually unfavourable, Rom. ii. 1, 3; (3) *to try, to sit in judgment on,* John xviii. 31; pass., *to be on trial, to be judged;* mid., *to appeal to trial,* i.e., *to have a law-suit,* 1 Cor. vi. 6.
κρίσις, εως, ἡ, (1) *opinion,* formed and expressed; (2) *judgment,* the act or result of; (3) *condemnation;* (4) *a tribunal,* Matt. v. 21, 22; (5) *justice,* Matt. xxiii. 23; (6) *the divine law,* Matt. xii. 18, 20.
Κρίσπος, ου, ὁ, *Crispus,* Acts xviii. 8; 1 Cor. i. 14.*
κριτήριον, ου, τό, (1) *a tribunal, a court of justice,* 1 Cor. vi. 2, 4 (see R.V.); James ii. 6.*
κριτής, ου, τό, *a judge;* of the O.T. "Judges," Acts xiii. 20.
κριτικός, ή, όν, *apt at judging, quick to discern,* gen. obj., Heb. iv. 12.*
κρούω, σω, *to knock* at a door for entrance, Luke xiii. 25.
κρύπτη, ης, ἡ, "crypt," *an underground cell, a vault,* Luke xi. 33.*
κρυπτός, ή, όν, verbal adj. (κρύπτω), *hidden, secret, unknown,* Matt. x. 26; Rom. ii. 16.
κρύπτω, ψω, 2nd aor., pass., ἐκρύβην, *to hide, conceal, to lay up, to reserve,* as Col. iii. 3.
κρυσταλλίζω, *to be clear,* like crystal, Rev. xxi. 11.*
κρύσταλλος, ου, ὁ, *crystal,* Rev. iv. 6, xxii. 1.*
κρυφαῖος, α, ον, *hidden, secret,* Matt. vi. 18 (W. H.).*
κρυφῇ, adv., *in secret, secretly,* Eph. v. 12.
κτάομαι, ῶμαι, fut. ἤσομαι, ἐκτησάμην, dep., *to acquire, procure* (price, gen., or ἐκ), (see § **273**,) Matt. x. 9; Luke xviii. 12, xxi. 19; Acts i. 18, viii. 20, xxii. 28; 1 Thess. iv. 4.*
κτῆμα, ατος, τό, *anything acquired, a possession,* Matt. xix. 22; Mark x. 22; Acts ii. 45, v. 1.
κτῆνος, ους, τό, *a beast of burden* (as representing property), Luke x. 34; Acts xxiii. 24; 1 Cor. xv. 39; Rev. xviii. 13.*
κτήτωρ, ορος, ὁ, *a possessor, an owner,* Acts iv. 34.*
κτίζω, σω, perf., pass., ἔκτισμαι, *to create, form, compose,* physically or spiritually, as Rom. i. 25; Eph. ii. 10.
κτίσις, εως, ἡ, *creation,* (1) the act, Rom. i. 20; (2) the thing created, *creature,* Rom. i. 25; *creation,* generally, Rom. viii. 19-22; (3) met., *institution,* 1 Pet. ii. 13.
κτίσμα, ατος, τό, *a thing created, a creature,* 1 Tim. iv. 4; James i. 18; Rev. v. 13, viii. 9.*
κτιστής, οῦ, ὁ, *one who makes or founds, the Creator,* 1 Pet. iv. 19.*
κυβεία, ας, ἡ, *gambling, fraud,* Eph. iv. 14.*
κυβέρνησις, εως, ἡ, *governing, direction,* 1 Cor. xii. 28.*
κυβερνήτης, ου, ὁ, *a steersman, a pilot,* Acts xxvii. 11; Rev. xviii. 17.*
κυκλεύω, *encircle, surround,* Rev. xx. 9 (W. H.).*
κυκλόθεν, adv. (κύκλος), *from around, round about,* gen., Rev. iv. 3, 4, 8, v. 11 (not W. H.).*
κύκλος, ου, ὁ, *a circle.* Only in dat., κύκλῳ, as adv., abs., or with gen., *round about, around.*
κυκλόω, ῶ, *to encircle, surround, besiege,* Luke xxi. 20; John x. 24; Acts xiv. 20; Heb. xi. 30; Rev. xx. 9 (see κυκλεύω).*
κύλισμα, ατος, τό (W. H., κυλισμός, ὁ), *a place for wallowing,* 2 Pet. ii. 22.*
κυλίω (for κυλίνδω), *to wallow or roll,* Mark ix. 20.*
κυλλός, ή, όν, *crippled, lame,* especially in the hands, Matt. xv. 30, 31, xviii. 8; Mark ix. 43.*
κῦμα, ατος, neut., *a wave, a billow,* as Matt. viii. 24; Acts xxvii. 41; Jude 13.
κύμβαλον, ου, τό (κύμβος, *hollow*), *a cymbal,* 1 Cor. xiii. 1.*

κύμινον, ου, τό (from Heb.), *cumin*, Matt. xxiii. 23.*
κυνάριον, ου, τό (dim. of κύων), *a little dog, a cur*, Matt. xv. 26, 27; Mark vii. 27, 28.*
Κύπριος, ου, ό, *a Cyprian or Cypriot*.
Κύπρος, ου, ή, *Cyprus*.
κύπτω, ψω, *to bend, to stoop down*, Mark i. 7; John viii. 6, 8 (W. H. omit).
Κυρηναίος, ου, ό, *a Cyrenian*.
Κυρήνη, ης, ή, a prop. name, *Cyrene*, a city of Africa, Acts ii. 10.*
Κυρήνιος, ου, ό, a prop. name, *Cyrenius or Quirinus*, Luke ii. 2.*
κυρία, ας, ή, *a lady*, 2 John i. 5. (W. H., Κυρία, *Cyria*, a proper name.)*
κυριακός, ή, όν, *of or pertaining to the Lord Christ*, as the supper, 1 Cor. xi. 20; the day, Rev. i. 10.*
κυριεύω, εύσω, *to have authority*, abs., 1 Tim. vi. 15; *to rule over* (gen.), Luke xxii. 25.
Κύριος, ίου, ό, (1) *a lord, possessor of, and having power over*, a title of honour, *Sir*, 1 Pet. iii. 6; (2) The LORD (Heb., JEHOVAH); (3) *The Lord* (employed in the Epp. constantly of Christ [see § 217, b]).
κυριότης, ητος, ή, *lordship, dominion*; collective concr., *lords, princes*, Eph. i. 21; Col. i. 16; 2 Pet. ii. 10; Jude 8.*
κυρόω, ω, *to confirm, ratify*, 2 Cor. ii. 8; Gal. iii. 15.*
κύων, κυνός, ό, ή, *a dog*, Luke xvi. 21; fig., of *shameless persons*, Phil. iii. 2.
κώλον, ου, τό, *a limb*, N.T. plur. only, Heb. iii. 17, *the carcases*.*
κωλύω, σω, *to restrain, forbid, hinder, withhold*, Mark ix. 38.
κώμη, ης, ή, *a village*, unwalled, or lying open, Matt. ix. 35.
κωμόπολις, εως, ή, *a large, city-like village*, without walls, Mark i. 38.*
κώμος, ου, ό, *a feasting, a revelling*, among the heathen, in honour of Bacchus, Rom. xiii. 13; Gal. v. 21; 1 Pet. iv. 3.
κώνωψ, ωπος, ό, *a gnat*, Matt. xxiii. 24.*
Κώς, ώ, ή, *Cos*, Acts xxi. 1.*
Κωσάμ, ό (Heb.), *Cosam*, Luke iii. 28.*
κωφός, ή, όν (κόπτω, lit., *blunted*), *dumb*, Matt. ix. 32, 33; *deaf*, Matt. xi. 5.

Δ.

Δ, λ, Λάμβδα, *Lambda, l*, the eleventh letter. As a numeral, λ' = 30; λ, = 30,000.
λαγχάνω, 2nd aor. έλαχον, trans., *to obtain by lot, to obtain*, acc. or gen., Luke i. 9; Acts i. 17; 2 Pet. i. 1; abs., *to cast lots, to draw lots, περί*, gen., John xix. 24.*
Λάζαρος, ου, ό, *Lazarus*, (1) of Bethany, (2) in the parable, Luke xvi. 20-25.
λάθρα (W. H., λάθρᾳ), (λανθάνω,) *secretly*, as John xi. 28.
λαίλαψ, απος, ή, *a whirlwind, a violent storm*, Mark iv. 37; Luke viii. 23; 2 Pet. ii. 17.*
λακέω, ληκέω, and λάσκω, *to burst with a loud report*, Acts i. 18.*
λακτίζω (λαξ, adv., *with the heel*), *to kick*, Acts ix. 5 (W. H. omit), xxvi. 14.*
λαλέω, ώ, ήσω, (1) *to speak*, absolutely; (2) *to speak, to talk*, with acc. of thing spoken, also with modal dat. and dat. of person addressed. Hence, according to the nature of the case, met., *to declare*, by other methods than *vivâ voce*, as Rom. vii. 1; *to preach, to publish, to announce*. **Synn. 8, 15.**
λαλιά, ᾶς, ή, (1) *speech, talk*, John viii. 43; hence, (2) *report*, John iv. 42; (3) *manner of speech, dialect*, Matt. xxvi. 73; Mark xiv. 70 (W. H. omit).*
λαμά, or λαμμᾶ (Heb.), *why*, Matt. xxvii. 46 (W. H., λεμά); Mark xv. 34 (Ps. xxii. 1).*
λαμβάνω, λήψομαι (W. H., λήμψομαι), είληφα, έλαβον, (1) *to take*, as in the hand, Matt. xiv. 19; hence, (2) *to receive, obtain*, of things material or spiritual, *to accept*, "take up," Matt. x. 38; (3) *to take by force, seize*, Matt. xxi. 35; (4) *to take away*, by violence or fraud, Matt. v. 40; (5) *to choose*, Acts xv. 14; (6) *to receive* or *accept*, as a friend, and as a teacher; (7) in certain periphrastic expressions—λαμβάνειν αρχήν, *to begin*; λ. λήθην, *to forget*; λ. ὑπόμνησιν, *to remember*; λ. πεῖραν, *to experience*; λ. πρόσωπον, "*to accept the person*," *i.e.*, *to be partial*. The preposition "from," after this verb, is expressed by ἐκ, ἀπό, παρά (ὑπό, 2 Cor. xi. 24).

Λάμεχ, ὁ (Heb.), *Lamech*, Luke iii. 36.*

λαμπάς, άδος, ἡ, *a lamp, a torch*. Syn. 65.

λαμπρός, ά, όν, *resplendent, shining, gorgeous;* adv., -ῶς, *gorgeously, sumptuously,* only Luke xvi. 19.

λαμπρότης, τητος, ἡ, *splendour, brightness,* Acts xxvi. 13.*

λάμπω, ψω, *to give light, to shine,* Matt. v. 15, 16, xvii. 2.

λανθάνω, 2nd aor. ἔλαθον, (1) *to be concealed,* abs., Mark vii. 24 ; Luke viii. 47 ; (2) *to be concealed from, unknown to* (acc.), Acts xxvi. 26 ; 2 Pet. iii. 5, 8 ; (3) for particip. constr., see § 394, 2 ; Heb. xiii. 2.*

λα-ξευτός, ή, όν, *hewn out of a rock,* Luke xxiii. 53.*

Λαοδικεία, ας, ἡ, *Laodicea.*

Λαοδικεύς, έως, ὁ, *a Laodicean.*

λαός, οῦ, ὁ, (1) *a people,* spec. of the people of God ; (2) *the common people.* Syn. 73.

λάρυγξ, υγγος, ὁ, *the throat,* "larynx," Rom. iii. 13.*

Λασαία, as (W. H., Λασέα), ἡ, *Lasæa,* Acts xxvii. 8.*

λάσκω. See λακέω.

λα-τομέω, ῶ, *to hew stones, to cut stone,* Matt. xxvii. 60 ; Mark xv. 46.*

λατρεία, ας, ἡ, *worship, service rendered to God,* John xvi. 2 ; Rom. ix. 4, xii. 1 ; Heb. ix. 1, 6.*

λατρεύω, σω, (1) *to worship, to serve ;* (2) *to officiate as a priest.* Syn. 36.

λάχανον, ου, τό, *a herb, a garden plant,* Matt. xiii. 32.

Λεββαῖος, ου, ὁ, *Lebbæus,* Matt. x. 3 (not W. H.). See Θαδδαῖος.*

λεγεών (W. H., λεγιών), ῶνος, ὁ (Lat., see § 154, c), *a legion,* Matt. xxvi. 53 ; Mark v. 9, 15 ; Luke viii. 30 ; in N.T. times containing probably 6,826 men.*

λέγω, only pres. and impf. in N.T., (1) *to speak,* used also of writings, as John xix. 37 ; (2) *to say, to discourse ;* (3) *to relate, to tell,* Luke ix. 31, xviii. 1 ; (4) *to call,* pass., *to be called* or *named ;* (5) pass., *to be chosen* or *appointed.* Dat. of person addressed. Syn. 8.

λεῖμμα, ατος, τό (λείπω), *a remnant,* Rom. xi. 5.*

λεῖος, εία, εῖον, *smooth, plain, level,* Luke iii. 5 (LXX.).*

λείπω, ψω, *to leave, to be wanting,* Luke xviii. 22 ; Tit. i. 5, iii. 13 ; pass., *to be left, to be lacking, to be destitute of,* James i. 4, 5, ii. 15.*

λειτουργέω, ῶ, (1) *to serve publicly in sacred things,* Acts xiii. 2 ; Heb. x. 11 ; (2) *to minister to,* pecuniarily, Rom. xv. 27.* Syn. 36.

λειτουργία, as, ἡ, (1) *a public ministration* or *service,* Luke i. 23 ; Phil. ii. 17 ; Heb. viii. 6, ix. 21 ; (2) *a friendly service,* as rendering aid or alms to, Phil. ii. 30 ; 2 Cor. ix. 12.* Syn. 36.

λειτουργικός, ή, όν, *rendering service to,* Heb. i. 14.* Syn. 36.

λειτουργός, οῦ, ὁ, *a minister* or *servant to,* gen. obj., Rom. xiii. 6, xv. 16 ; Phil. ii. 25 ; Heb. i. 7, viii. 2.* Syn. 36.

λέντιον, ου, τό (Lat., see § 154, e), *a napkin* or *towel,* John xiii. 4, 5.*

λεπίς, ίδος, ἡ, *a scale* or *crust,* Acts ix. 18.*

λέπρα, as, ἡ, *the leprosy.*

λεπρός, οῦ, ὁ, *a leper.*

λεπτόν, οῦ, prop. verb. adj. (sc. νόμισμα), from λέπω (*to strip off, pare down*), *a mite,* one eighth of an *as,* the smallest Jewish coin, Mark xii. 42 ; Luke xii. 59, xxi. 2.*

Λευΐ or **Λευΐς**, ὁ, *Levi.* Four are mentioned : (1) son of Jacob, ancestor of the priestly tribe ; (2, 3) ancestors of Jesus, Luke iii. 24, 29 ; (4) the apostle, also called *Matthew* (W. H., 1, 2 and 3, Λευεί, 4, Λευείς).

Λευΐτης, ου, ὁ, *a Levite.*

Λευϊτικός, ή, όν, *Levitical,* Heb. vii. 11.*

λευκαίνω, ανῶ, 1st aor. ἐλεύκανα, *to make white,* Mark ix. 3 ; Rev. vii. 14.*

λευκός, ή, όν, (1) *white,* as Matt. v. 36 ; John iv. 35 ; (2) *bright,* as Matt. xvii. 2.

λέων, οντος, ὁ, *a lion ;* fig., for a tyrant, 2 Tim. iv. 17 ; of Christ, Rev. v. 5.

λήθη, ης, ἡ, *forgetfulness,* 2 Pet. i. 9.*

ληκέω. See λακέω.

ληνός, οῦ, ὁ, ἡ, *a wine-press,* Matt. xxi. 33 ; fig. in Rev. xiv. 19, 20, xix. 15.*

λῆρος, ου, ὁ, *idle talk,* Luke xxiv. 11.*

ληστής, οῦ, ὁ, *a robber,* Mark xi. 17 ; John x. 1, 8. Syn. 74.

λῆψις (W. H., λῆμψις), εως, ἡ (λαμβάνω), *a receiving,* Phil. iv. 15.*

λίαν, adv., *very much ;* with adj. or adv., *very,* Matt. iv. 8 ; Mark xvi. 2.

λίβανος, οῦ, ὁ, *frankincense,* Matt. ii. 11 ; Rev. xviii. 13.*

λιβανωτός, οῦ, ὁ, *a censer for burning frankincense*, Rev. viii. 3, 5.*
Διβερτῖνος, ου, ὁ (Lat., *a freed-man*), *Libertine*, Acts vi. 9. Probably Jews who had been slaves at Rome, afterwards freed.*
Διβύη, ης, ἡ, *Libya*, Acts ii. 10.*
λιθάζω, σω, *to stone, to execute by stoning*.
λίθινος, η, ον, *made of stone*, John ii. 6; 2 Cor. iii. 3; Rev. ix. 20.*
λιθο-βολέω, ῶ, ήσω, *to throw stones at, so as to wound or kill, to stone*, Matt. xxiii. 37; Mark xii. 4 (W. H. omit).
λίθος, ου, ὁ, *a stone, i.e.*, (1) *loose and lying about*, Matt. iv. 3, 6; (2) *built into a wall*, etc., Mark xiii. 2; (4) *a precious stone*, Rev. iv. 3, xv. 6 (R.V.); (5) *a statue or idol of stone*, Acts xvii. 29. Syn. 75.
Λιθό-στρωτον, ου, τό (prop. adj., *strewed with stones*), *the Pavement*, part of a Roman court of justice, John xix. 13.*
λικμάω, ω, ήσω, *to scatter*, as corn in winnowing, *to reduce to particles* that may be scattered, Matt. xxi. 44; Luke xx. 18.*
λιμήν, ένος, ὁ, *harbour, haven*, Acts xxvii. 8, 12.*
λίμνη, ης, ἡ, *a lake, e.g.*, Gennesareth, Luke v. 1.
λιμός, οῦ, ὁ, (1) *hunger*, 2 Cor. xi. 27; (2) *a famine*, Matt. xxiv. 7.
λίνον, ου, τό, *flax, linen made of flax*, Rev. xv. 6 (W. H., λίθος); *a lampwick*, Matt. xii. 20.*
Δῖνος (W. H., Λίνος), ου, ὁ, *Linus*, 2 Tim. iv. 21.*
λιπαρός, ά, όν, *sumptuous, precious, delicate*, Rev. xviii. 14.*
λίτρα, ας, ἡ, *a pound weight*, John xii. 3, xix. 39.*
λίψ, λιβός, ὁ, *the S. W. wind*, Acts xxvii. 12. (To look "*down the S. W. wind*" is to look *toward the north-east*.)*
λογία, ας, ἡ, *a collection, i.e.*, of money, 1 Cor. xvi. 1, 2.*
λογίζομαι, σομαι, dep. with mid. and pass. aor., (1) *to reckon*; (2) *to place to the account of, to charge with*, acc. and dat., or with εἰς (see § 298, 6); (3) *to reason, argue, to infer, conclude, compute*, from reasoning; (4) *to think, suppose*.
λογικός, ή, όν, *rational, i.e.*, belonging to the sphere of the reason, Rom. xii. 1; 1 Pet. ii. 2.*

λόγιον, ου, τό, *something spoken*, in N.T., of *divine communications, e.g.*, the Old Testament, Acts vii. 38; Rom. iii. 2; and the doctrines of Christ, Heb. v. 12; 1 Pet. iv. 11.*
λόγιος, ον, *eloquent*, Acts xviii. 24.*
λογισμός, οῦ, ὁ, *reasoning, thought, imagination*, Rom. ii. 15; 2 Cor. x. 5.*
λογο-μαχέω, ῶ, *to strive about words*, 2 Tim. ii. 14.*
λογομαχία, ας, ἡ, *contention about words*, "logomachy," 1 Tim. vi. 4.*
λόγος, ου, ὁ, (1) *a speaking, a saying, a word*, as the expression of thought (whereas ἔπος, ὄνομα, ῥῆμα refer to words in their outward form, as parts of speech), Matt. viii. 8; (2) *the thing spoken*, Matt. vii. 24, 26—whether *doctrine*, 1 Tim. iv. 6; *prophecy*, 2 Pet. i. 19; *question*, Matt. xxi. 24; *a common saying* or *proverb*, John iv. 37; *a precept, a command*, John viii. 55; *the truth*, Mark viii. 38; *conversation*, Luke xxiv. 17; *teaching*, 1 Cor. ii. 4; *a narrative*, Acts i. 1; *a public rumour*, Matt. xxviii. 15; *an argument*, Acts ii. 40; *a charge or accusation*, Acts xix. 38; (3) *reason*, Acts xviii. 14; (4) *account, reckoning*, Heb. iv. 13; Acts xx. 24; Matt. xviii. 23; Acts x. 29. Λόγος is used by John as a name of Christ, the WORD of God, *i.e.*, the expression or manifestation of his thoughts to man, John i. 1, etc. Syn. 8.
λόγχη, ης, ἡ, *a lance, a spear*, John xix. 34.*
λοιδορέω, ῶ, *to revile, to rail at, to reproach*, John ix. 28; Acts xxiii. 4; 1 Cor. iv. 12; 1 Pet. ii. 23.*
λοιδορία, ας, ἡ, *reproach, reviling*, 1 Tim. v. 14; 1 Pet. iii. 9.*
λοίδορος, ου, ὁ, *one who rails at, a reviler*, 1 Cor. v. 11, vi. 10.*
λοιμός, οῦ, ὁ, *a plague, pestilence*, Matt. xxiv. 7 (W. H. omit), Luke xxi. 11; Paul so called, Acts xxiv. 5.*
λοιπός, ή, όν, *remaining, the rest*, Matt. xxv. 11; adv., τὸ λοιπόν, *as for the rest, moreover, finally, henceforth*, 1 Cor. i. 16; Heb. x. 13; τοῦ λοιποῦ, *from henceforth*, Gal. vi. 17.
Δουκᾶς, ᾶ, ὁ (from Λουκανός, see § 159, d), *Luke*.

Λούκιος, ίου, ὁ (Latin), *Lucius*, Acts xiii. 1; Rom. xvi. 21.*
λουτρόν, οῦ, τό, *a bath, a washing*, Eph. v. 26; Tit. iii. 5.*
λούω, σω, *to bathe, to wash*, Acts ix. 37, xvi. 33; *to cleanse, to purify*, Rev. i. 5. Syn. 17.
Λύδδα, ης, ἡ, *Lydda*, Acts ix. 32, 53.*
Λυδία, ας, ἡ, *Lydia*, Acts xvi. 14, 40.*
Λυκαονία, ας, ἡ, *Lycaonia*, Acts xiv. 6.*
Λυκαονιστί, adv., *in the speech of Lycaonia*, Acts xiv. 11.*
Λυκία, ας, ἡ, *Lycia*, Acts xxvii. 5.*
λύκος, ου, ὁ, *a wolf*; fig., Acts xx. 29.
λυμαίνομαι, *to ravage*, Acts viii. 3.*
λυπέω, ῶ, *to grieve*; pass., *to be grieved, saddened*, Matt. xxvi. 22, 37; 1 Pet. i. 6; *to be aggrieved* or *offended*, Matt. xiv. 9; Rom. xiv. 15.
λύπη, ης, ἡ, *grief, sorrow, aversion*, 2 Cor. ix. 7; *cause of grief*, 1 Pet. ii. 19.
Λυσανίας, ου, ὁ, *Lysanias*, Luke iii. 1.*
Λυσίας, ου, ὁ, *Lysias*.
λύσις, εως, ἡ, *a loosening, divorce*, 1 Cor. vii. 27.*
λυσι-τελέω, ῶ (lit., *to pay taxes*), impers., -εῖ, *it is profitable* or *preferable* (dat. and ἤ), Luke xvii. 2.*
Λύστρα, ας, ἡ, or ων, τά, *Lystra*, Acts xiv. 6, 8.
λύτρον, ου, τό, *a ransom price*, Matt. xx. 28; Mark x. 45.* Syn. 43.
λυτρόω, ώσω, in N.T. only, mid. and pass., *to ransom, to deliver* by paying a ransom, Luke xxiv. 21; Tit. ii. 14; 1 Pet. i. 18 (acc., pers.; dat., price, and ἀπό or ἐκ).* Syn. 43.
λύτρωσις, εως, ἡ, *deliverance, redemption*, Luke i. 68, ii. 38; Heb. ix. 12.*
λυτρωτής, οῦ, ὁ, *a redeemer, a deliverer*, Acts vii. 35.*
λυχνία, ας, ἡ, *a lamp-stand*, Matt. v. 15; fig., of a church, Rev. ii. 1, 5; of a Christian teacher, Rev. xi. 4. Syn. 65.
λύχνος, ου, ὁ, *a lamp*, Matt. v. 15, vi. 22. Used of John the Baptist, John v. 35; of Christ, Rev. xxi. 23. Syn. 65.
λύω, σω, *to loosen*, as (1) lit., *to unbind*, Mark i. 7; Rev. v. 2; (2) *to set at liberty*; (3) *to pronounce not binding*, e.g., a law, Matt. xviii. 18; (4) *to disobey* or *nullify* the Divine word, John vii. 23, x. 35; (5) *to destroy, e.g., the temple*, John ii. 19; (6) *to dismiss, i.e., an assembly*, Acts xiii. 43.

Λωΐς, ίδος, ἡ, *Lois*, 2 T:m. i. 5.*
Λώτ, ὁ (Heb.), *Lot*, Luke xvii. 28-32; 2 Pet. ii. 7.*

M.

M, μ, μῦ, *mu, m, the twelfth letter*. As a numeral, μ'=40 μι̃; =40,000.
Μαάθ, ὁ (Heb.), *Maath*, Luke iii. 26.*
Μαγδαλά, ἡ (Heb., Aram.), *Magdala*, Matt. xv. 39 (W. H. and R.V., Μαγαδάν).*
Μαγδαληνή, ῆς, ἡ, *Magdalene, i.e., a woman of Magdala*, as Matt. xxvii. 56, 61.
μαγεία (W. H., μαγία), ας, ἡ, *magic*, plur., *magic arts*, Acts viii. 11.*
μαγεύω, σω, *to practise magic arts*, Acts viii. 9.*
μάγος, ου, ὁ, (1) *magus*, Persian astrologer, Matt. ii. 1, 7, 16; (2) *a sorcerer*, Acts xiii. 6, 8.*
Μαγώγ, ὁ (Heb.), *Magog*. See Γώγ.
Μαδιάν (W. H., Μαδιάμ), ὁ (Heb.), *Madian* or *Midian*, Acts vii. 29.*
μαθητεύω, σω, (1) trans., *to make a disciple of* (acc.), *to instruct*, Matt. xiii. 52; xxviii. 19; Acts xiv. 21; (2) intrans., *to be a disciple*, Matt. xxvii. 57 (W. H., however, read the passive, with active in margin).* Syn. 14.
μαθητής, οῦ, ὁ (μανθάνω), *a disciple*, Matt. ix. 14, x. 24, xxii. 16; οἱ μαθηταί, specially, *the twelve*, Matt. ix. 19.
μαθήτρια, ας, ἡ, *a female disciple*, Acts ix. 36.*
Μαθουσάλα, ὁ (Heb.), *Methuselah*, Luke iii. 37.*
Μαϊνάν, ὁ (Heb.), *Mainan*, Luke iii. 31.*
μαίνομαι, dep., *to be mad, to rave*, John x. 20; Acts xii. 15, xxvi. 24, 25; 1 Cor. xiv. 23.*
μακαρίζω, fut. -ιῶ, *to pronounce happy, congratulate*, Luke i. 48; James v. 11.*
μακάριος, ία, ιον, *happy, blessed*, Matt. v. 3-11; Luke i. 45, vi. 20; 1 Cor. vii. 40. Syn. 28.
μακαρισμός, οῦ, ὁ, *congratulation, a pronouncing happy*, Rom. iv. 6, 9; Gal. iv. 15.*
Μακεδονία, ας, ἡ, *Macedonia*.
Μακεδών, όνος, ὁ, *a Macedonian*.
μάκελλον, ου, τό, *a slaughter-house, shambles*, 1 Cor. x. 25.*
μακράν, adv. (acc. of μακρός, sc. ὁδόν),

afar, afar off, Luke xv. 20; εἰς preceding, Acts ii. 39; ἀπό following, Acts xvii. 27.
μακρόθεν, adv., *from afar,* Mark viii. 3; with ἀπό, as Matt. xxvi. 58.
μακροθυμέω, ῶ, ήσω, *to suffer long, to have patience, to be forbearing,* 1 Cor. xiii. 4; *to delay,* Luke xviii. 7; *to wait patiently* for, εἰς or ἐπί, dat., Heb. vi. 15.
μακροθυμία, ας, ή, *forbearance, longsuffering, patience.* **Syn. 31.**
μακροθύμως, adv., *patiently, indulgently,* Acts xxvi. 3.*
μακρός, ά, όν, *long;* of place, *distant,* Luke xv. 13, xix. 12; of time, *prolix,* only in the phrase μακρὰ προσεύχεσθαι, *to make long prayers,* Matt. xxiii. 14 (W. H. omit); Mark xii. 40; Luke xx. 47.*
μακροχρόνιος, ον, *long-lived,* Eph. vi. 3.*
μαλακία, ας, ή, *softness, weakness, infirmity,* Matt. iv. 23, ix. 35, x. 1.*
μαλακός, ή, όν, *soft,* of garments, Matt. xi. 8; Luke vii. 25; *disgracefully effeminate,* 1 Cor. vi. 10.*
Μαλελεήλ, ὁ (Heb.), *Maleleel,* or Mahalaleel, Luke iii. 37.*
μάλιστα, adv. (superl. of μάλα, *very*), *most of all, especially.*
μᾶλλον, adv. (comp. of μάλα), *more, rather;* πολλῷ μᾶλλον, *much more,* Matt. vi. 30; πόσῳ μᾶλλον, *how much more,* Matt. vii. 11; μᾶλλον ἤ, *more than,* Matt. xviii. 13. μᾶλλον is often of intensive force, *e.g.,* Matt. xxvii. 24; Rom. viii. 34. See § 321.
Μάλχος, ου, ὁ, *Malchus,* John xviii. 10.*
μάμμη, ης, ή, *a grandmother,* 2 Tim. i. 5.*
μαμμωνᾶς (W. H., μαμωνᾶς), ᾶ, ὁ, *mammon, gain, wealth* (from Chald.), Matt. vi. 24; Luke xvi. 9, 11, 13.*
Μαναήν, ὁ (Heb.), *Manaen,* Acts xiii. 1.*
Μανασσῆς, gen. and acc., ῆ, ὁ, *Manasseh,* (1) Son of Joseph, Rev. vii. 6; (2) Matt. i. 10.*
μανθάνω, μαθήσομαι, 2nd aor. ἔμαθον, perf. μεμάθηκα, *to learn, to understand, to know, to be informed, to comprehend.* Used abs., or with acc. (ἀπό, παρά [gen.], with the teacher, ἐν with example, 1 Cor. iv. 6).
μανία, ας, ή, *madness, insanity,* Acts xxvi. 24.*
μάννα, τό (Heb., deriv. uncertain), *manna, the food of the Israelites in the desert.*

μαντεύομαι, dep., *to utter responses, prophesy,* Acts xvi. 16.* **Syn. 15.**
μαραίνω, ανῶ, fut. pass. μαρανθήσομαι, *to wither, to fade away,* James i. 11.*
μαρὰν ἀθά (two Aramaic words), *our Lord cometh* (R.V. marg.), 1 Cor. xvi. 22.*
μαργαρίτης, ου, ὁ, *a pearl,* Matt. xiii. 45, 46.
Μαρθά, ης, ή, *Martha.*
Μαρία, ας, or Μαριάμ (indecl., Heb., *Miriam*), ή, *Mary.* Six of the name are mentioned: (1) the mother of Jesus; (2) the Magdalen; (3) the sister of Martha and Lazarus; (4) the wife of Cleopas; (5) the mother of John Mark; (6) a Christian woman in Rome, Rom. xvi. 6.
Μάρκος, ου, ὁ, *Mark.*
μάρμαρος, ου, ὁ, ή, *marble,* Rev. xviii. 12.*
μαρτυρέω, ῶ, ήσω, *to be a witness,* abs., *to testify* (περί, gen.), *to give testimony* (to, dat. of pers. or thing), *to commend;* pass., *to be attested,* i.e., honourably, *to be of good report.*
μαρτυρία, ας, ή, *testimony borne,* i.e., judicially, Mark xiv. 56, 59, or generally, *honourable attestation,* John v. 34. With obj. gen., as Rev. xix. 10.
μαρτύριον, ου, τό, *testimony,* Matt. viii. 4 (*to,* dat.; *against,* ἐπί, acc.).
μαρτύρομαι, dep., *to call to witness,* Acts xx. 26; Gal. v. 3; *to exhort solemnly,* Eph. iv. 17; 1 Thess. ii. 11 (W. H.).*
μάρτυς, υρος, dat. plur. μάρτυσι, ὁ, *a witness,* i.e., judicially, Matt. xviii. 16; *one who testifies* from what he has seen and known, 1 Thess. ii. 10; Luke xxiv. 48; *a martyr,* witnessing by his death, Acts xxii. 20; Rev. ii. 13, xvii. 6.
μασσάομαι, ῶμαι, *to bite, to gnaw,* Rev. xvi. 10.*
μαστιγόω, ῶ, ώσω, *to scourge,* Matt. x. 17; fig., Heb. xii. 6.
μαστίζω, *to scourge,* Acts xxii. 25.*
μάστιξ, ιγος, ή, *a whip, a scourge,* Acts xxii. 24; Heb. xi. 36; fig., *sharp pain, disease, affliction,* Mark iii. 10, v. 29, 34; Luke vii. 21.*
μαστός, οῦ, ὁ, *the breast, the paps,* Luke xi. 27, xxiii. 29; Rev. i. 13.*
ματαιολογία, ας, ή, *vain talk, empty, fruitless conversation,* 1 Tim. i. 6.*

ματαιο-λόγος, ου, ὁ, *a vain, empty talker,* Tit. i. 10.*
μάταιος (αία), αιον, *vain, fruitless, empty,* 1 Cor. xv. 17; James i. 26; τὰ μάταια, *vanities,* spec. of heathen deities, Acts xiv. 15 (and O.T.). **Syn. 29.**
ματαιότης, τητος, ἡ, (1) *vanity,* 2 Pet. ii. 18; (2) *perverseness,* Eph. iv. 17; (3) *frailty,* Rom. viii. 20.*
ματαιόω, ῶ, *to render vain or foolish, to deprave;* pass., Rom. i. 21.*
μάτην, adv., *in vain, fruitlessly,* Matt. xv. 9; Mark vii. 7.*
Ματθαῖος, ου, ὁ (W. H., Μαθθαῖος), *Matthew,* the apostle and evangelist; also Λευΐ.
Ματθάν, ὁ (Heb.) (W. H., Μαθθάν,) *Matthan,* Matt. i. 15.*
Ματθάτ, ὁ (Heb.), (W. H., Μαθθάθ,) *Matthat,* Luke iii. 24, 29.*
Ματθίας, α (ὁ), (W. H., Μαθθίας,) *Matthias,* Acts i. 23, 26.*
Ματταθά, ὁ (Heb.), *Mattatha,* Luke iii. 31.*
Ματταθίας, ου, ὁ, *Mattathias,* Luke iii. 25, 26.*
μάχαιρα, as and ης, ἡ, *a sword;* met., for *strife,* Matt. x. 34; fig., of spiritual weapons, Eph. vi. 17.
μάχη, ης, ἡ, *contention, strife, dispute,* 2 Cor. vii. 5; 2 Tim. ii. 23; Tit. iii. 9; James iv. 1.*
μάχομαι, *to fight, contend, dispute,* John vi. 52; Acts vii. 26; 2 Tim. ii. 24; James iv. 2.*
μεγαλ-αυχέω, ῶ, *to boast great things, to be arrogant,* James iii. 5. (W. H., μεγάλα αὐχεῖ.)†
μεγαλεῖος, εία, εῖον, *grand, magnificent, wondrous,* Luke i. 49 (W. H., μεγάλα); Acts ii. 11.*
μεγαλειότης, τητος, ἡ, *greatness, majesty, magnificence,* Luke ix. 43; Acts xix. 27; 2 Pet. i. 16.*
μεγαλο-πρεπής, ές, gen. οῦς, *fitting for a great man, magnificent, excellent,* 2 Pet. i. 17.*
μεγαλύνω, νῶ, (1) *to enlarge,* Matt. xxiii. 5; (2) *to magnify, extol, celebrate with praise,* Luke i. 58; Acts v. 13. **Syn. 47.**
μεγάλως, adv., *greatly,* Phil. iv. 10.*
μεγαλωσύνη, ης, ἡ, *magnificence, majesty,* Heb. i. 3, viii. 1; Jude 25.*
μέγας, μεγάλη, μέγα (see § 39), comp. μείζων, sup. μέγιστος, *great,* in size,

full-grown, intense, Matt. ii. 10, xxviii. 8; *wonderful,* 2 Cor. xi. 15; *noble, of high rank,* Rev. xi. 18, xiii. 16; applied to age, ὁ μείζων, *the elder,* Rom. ix. 12. μέγας indicates the *size* of things, their *measure, number, cost,* and *estimation;* μεγάλη ἡμέρα, *a high day,* John xix. 31.
μέγεθος, ους, τό, *greatness, vastness, immensity,* Eph. i. 19.*
μεγιστᾶνες, άνων, οἱ, *princes, great men* (sing., μεγιστάν, only in LXX., Sirach iv. 7), *lords,* Mark vi. 21; Rev. vi. 15, xviii. 23.*
μεθ-ερμηνεύω, *to translate, to interpret,* pass. only, Mark v. 41; John i. 42.
μέθη, ης, ἡ, *drunkenness, drunken frolic or riot,* Luke xxi. 34; Rom. xiii. 13; Gal. v. 21.*
μεθ-ίστημι (and μεθ-ιστάνω, 1 Cor. xiii. 2, W. H.), μεταστήσω, 1st aor., pass., μετεστάθην, lit., *to change the place of;* hence, *to remove, translate,* 1 Cor. xiii. 2; Col. i. 13; *to seduce or draw over,* Acts xix. 26; *to remove from office, e.g.,* a king, Acts xiii. 22; or a steward, Luke xvi. 4.*
μεθ-οδεία (-οδία, W. H.), as, ἡ, *fraudulent artifice, a trick, a stratagem,* Eph. iv. 14, vi. 11.*
μεθ-όριος, *bordering on;* τὰ μεθόρια, *borders, confines,* Mark vii. 24 (W. H., ὅρια).*
μεθύσκω, *to make drunk;* pass., *to be drunk,* Luke xii. 45; Eph. v. 18; 1 Thess. v. 7.*
μέθυσος, ου, ὁ (prop. adj.), *a drunkard,* 1 Cor. v. 11, vi. 10.*
μεθύω, *to be drunken,* Matt. xxiv. 49; Acts ii. 15; met., Rev. xvii. 6.
μείζων, comp. of μέγας, which see. It has itself a comparative, μειζότερος, 3 John 4 (see § 47).
μέλαν, ανος, τό (μέλας), *ink,* 2 Cor. iii. 3; 2 John 12; 3 John 13.*
μέλας, αινα, αν, *black,* Matt. v. 36; Rev. vi. 5, 12.*
Μελεᾶς, ᾶ, ὁ, *Melea,* Luke iii. 31.*
μέλει, impers. (see § 101), *it concerns,* dat. of pers., with gen. of object, as 1 Cor. ix. 9; or περί, as John x. 13; or ὅτι, as Mark iv. 38. **Syn. 11.**
μελετάω, ῶ, ἥσω, *to think upon, to revolve in mind, to premeditate,* Mark xiii. 11 (not W. H.); Acts iv. 25; 1 Tim. iv. 15.*

μέλι, ιτος, τό, honey, Matt. iii. 4 ; Mark i. 6 ; Rev. x. 9, 10.*

μελίσσιος, α, ον, made of honey, Luke xxiv. 42 (W. H. omit).*

Μελίτη, ης, ἡ, Melita, now Malta, Acts xxviii. 1.*

μέλλω, ήσω, to be about to do, to be on the point of doing, with infin., generally the present infin., rarely aor. ; the fut. infin. (the regular classical use) occurs only in the phrase μέλλειν ἔσεσθαι (only in Acts) ; the verb may often be adequately rendered by our auxiliaries, will, shall, must; to delay, only Acts xxii. 16. The participle is used absolutely: τὸ μέλλον, the future, Luke xiii. 9 ; τὰ μέλλοντα, things to come, Rom. viii. 38. See § 363, f, and Syn. 3.

μέλος, ους, τό, a member of the body, a limb, as Matt. v. 29, 30 ; Rom. xii. 4; fig., 1 Cor. vi. 15.

Μελχί (W. H., -εί), ὁ (Heb.), Melchi. Two are mentioned, Luke iii. 24, 28.*

Μελχισεδέκ, ὁ (Heb., king of righteousness), Melchizedek, Heb. v., vi., vii.*

μεμβράνα, ης, ἡ, parchment, 2 Tim. iv. 13.*

μέμφομαι, ψομαι, dep., to complain, to censure, abs., Mark vii. 2 (W. H. omit); Rom. ix. 19 ; abs. or dat., Heb. viii. 8 (W. H., acc., with dat. marg.).*

μεμψί-μοιρος, ον, adj., discontented, complaining, Jude 16.*

μέν, antithetic particle, truly, indeed (see § 136).

μεν-οῦν, conj., moreover, therefore, but.

μεν-οῦν-γε, conj., yea rather, yea truly, nay but, Luke xi. 28 (W. H., μενοῦν); Rom. ix. 20, x. 18 ; Phil. iii. 8 (W. H., μὲν οὖν). See § 406.*

μέν-τοι, conj., yet truly, certainly, nevertheless, however, John iv. 27.

μένω, μενῶ, ἔμεινα, (1) intrans., to remain, to abide. So (a) of place, to dwell, Matt. x. 11 ; to lodge, Luke xix. 5 ; (b) of state, as Acts v. 4 ; to continue firm and constant in, John xv. 4 ; to endure, to last, to be permanent, 1 Cor. iii. 14 ; (2) trans., to await, wait for, to expect, only Acts xx. 5.

μερίζω, σω, (1) to divide, separate, mid., to share (μετά, gen.), Luke xii. 13 ; pass., to be divided, to be at variance, Matt. xii. 25, 26 ; 1 Cor. i. 13 ; (2) to distinguish, pass., to differ, 1 Cor. vii. 34 ; (3) to distribute, Mark vi. 41, acc. and dat.

μέριμνα, ης, ἡ, care, anxiety, as dividing, distracting the mind, Matt. xiii. 22 ; Luke viii. 14.

μεριμνάω, ῶ, to be anxious, distracted ; abs., with dat., περί (gen.), acc. The various constructions may be illustrated from Matt. vi. : abs., vers. 27, 31 ; acc., ver. 34 (Rec. ; see also 1 Cor. vii. 32-34) ; gen., ver. 34 (W. H.) ; dat., ver. 25 ; εἰς, ver. 34 ; περί, ver. 28. Syn. 11.

μερίς, ίδος, ἡ, a part or division of a country, Acts xvi. 12 ; a share, portion, Luke x. 42 ; Acts viii. 21 ; 2 Cor. vi. 15 ; Col. i. 12.*

μερισμός, οῦ, ὁ, a dividing, the act of dividing, Heb. iv. 12 ; distribution, gifts distributed, Heb. ii. 4.*

μεριστής, οῦ, ὁ, a divider, an arbiter, Luke xii. 14.*

μέρος, ους, τό, a part ; hence, (1) a part, as assigned, share, Rev. xxii. 19 ; fellowship, John xiii. 8 ; a business or calling, Acts xix. 27 ; (2) a part, as the result of division, John xix. 23. In adverbial phrases, μέρος τι, partly, in some part ; ἀνὰ μέρος, alternately ; ἀπὸ μέρους, partly ; ἐκ μέρους, individually, of persons, partially, imperfectly, of things ; κατὰ μέρος, particularly, in detail, Heb. ix. 5.

μεσ-ημβρία, ας, ἡ, midday, noon, the south, Acts viii. 26, xxii. 6.*

μεσιτεύω, σω, to mediate, to interpose, Heb. vi. 17.*

μεσίτης, ου, ὁ, a mediator, i.e., one who interposes between parties and reconciles them, Gal. iii. 19, 20 ; 1 Tim. ii. 5 ; mediator, or perhaps guarantee, in the phrase μεσίτης διαθήκης, mediator of a covenant, Heb. viii. 6, ix. 15, xii. 24.*

μεσο-νύκτιον, ίου, τό, midnight, as Luke xi. 5.

Μεσο-ποταμία, ας, ἡ, Mesopotamia, the region between the Euphrates and the Tigris.

μέσος, η, ον, middle, of time or place, in the midst of (gen.), as Matt. xxv. 6 ; John i. 26, xix. 18 ; Acts i. 18, xxvi. 13 ; neut., τὸ μέσον, the middle part, used chiefly in adverbial phrases, with prepositions (art. generally om.), ἐκ μέσου, *from among, away*; ἐν μέσῳ, *among*; ἀνὰ μέσον, *through the midst, among, between*; also with διά and εἰς.

μεσό-τοιχον, ου, τό, *a middle wall, a separation*, Eph. ii. 14.*

μεσ-ουράνημα, ατος, τό, *mid-heaven*, Rev. viii. 13, xiv. 6, xix. 17.*

μεσόω, ῶ, *to be in the middle* or *midst*, John vii. 14.*

Μεσσίας, ου (from Heb., *anointed*), *Messiah*, the same as Gr. Χριστός, John i. 41, iv. 25.*

μεστός, ή, όν, *full, filled with*, gen.

μεστόω, ῶ, *to fill*; pass., *to be full of*, gen., Acts ii. 13.*

μετά (akin to μέσος), prep., gov. the gen. and accus. Gen., *with, among*; acc., *after* (see § 301). In composition, μετά denotes *participation, nearness, change*, or *succession* (often like the Latin prefix *trans-*, as in the words *transfer, translate*).

μετα-βαίνω, *to go* or *pass over, to pass away, to depart*, Luke x. 7; Matt. xi. 1.

μετα-βάλλω, in mid., *to change one's mind*, Acts xxviii. 6.*

μετ-άγω, *to move* or *turn about*, as horses, ships, James iii. 3, 4.*

μετα-δίδωμι, *to impart, to communicate*, Luke iii. 11; Rom. i. 11; 1 Thess. ii. 8; Eph. iv. 28; ὁ μεταδιδούς, *a distributor of alms*, Rom. xii. 8.*

μετά-θεσις, εως, ἡ, (1) *a removal, a translation*, Heb. xi. 5, xii. 27; (2) *a change*, or *substitution*, Heb. xii. 12.*

μετ-αίρω, *to remove*, intrans., *to depart*, Matt. xiii. 53, xix. 1.*

μετα-καλέω, ῶ, in mid., *to call* or *send for, to invite to oneself*, Acts vii. 14, x. 32, xx. 17, xxiv. 25.*

μετα-κινέω, ῶ, *to move away*, pass., *to be removed*, Col. i. 23.*

μετα-λαμβάνω, *to take a share of*, Acts ii. 46; *partake*, gen., 2 Tim. ii. 6; *to obtain* (acc.), Acts xxiv. 25.

μετά-ληψις (W. H., -λημψις), εως, ἡ, *participation*; εἰς μ., *to be received*, 1 Tim. iv. 3.*

μετ-αλλάσσω, *to change* one thing (acc.) for (ἐν, εἰς) another, Rom. i. 25, 26.*

μετα-μέλομαι, μελήσομαι, 1st aor. μετεμελήθην, dep., pass., *to change one's mind*, Matt. xxi. 29, 32; Heb. vii. 21; *to repent, to feel sorrow for, regret*, Matt. xxvii. 3; 2 Cor. vii. 8. **Syn. 40.***

μετα-μορφόω, ῶ, *to change the form*, mid., *to alter one's form* or *aspect*, Matt. xvii. 2; Mark ix. 2; 2 Cor. iii. 18; fig., *to be changed in mind*, Rom. xii. 2.*

μετα-νοέω, ῶ, ήσω, *to change one's views* and *purpose, to repent*, as Matt. iii. 2; Acts viii. 22. **Syn. 40.**

μετά-νοια, ας, ἡ, *change of mind, repentance*, as Matt. iii. 8. **Syn. 40.**

μετα-ξύ (σύν or ξύν), adv. of time, *meanwhile*, John iv. 31; *afterwards*, perh., Acts xiii. 42 (see § **298, 7, b**). As prep., with gen., *between, of place*, Matt. xxiii. 35.

μετα-πέμπω, in mid., *to send for to oneself, to summon*, Acts x. 5, 22, 29, xi. 13; xxiv. 24, 26, xxv. 3; pass., x. 29.*

μετα-στρέφω (with 2nd fut. and 2nd aor. pass.), *to turn, to change*, James iv. 9; Acts ii. 20; *to pervert, to corrupt*, Gal. i. 7.*

μετα-σχηματίζω, ίσω, *to transform*, Phil. iii. 21; mid., *to assume the appearance of any one*, 2 Cor. xi. 13, 14, 15; fig., *to transfer*, i.e., *to speak by way of accommodation*, 1 Cor. iv. 6.*

μετα-τίθημι, *to transpose*, Acts vii. 16; *to transfer, to translate*, Heb. vii. 12, xi. 5; mid., *to transfer oneself*, i.e., *to go over* or *to fall away*, Gal. i. 6; *to pervert*, Jude 4.*

μετ-έπειτα, adv., *afterwards*, Heb. xii. 17.*

μετ-έχω, μετασχήσω, 2nd aor. μέτεσχον, *to be partaker of, to share in, to enjoy*, 1 Cor. ix. 10, 12, x. 17, 21, 30; Heb. ii. 14, v. 13, vii. 13.*

μετεωρίζω, in mid., *to be in suspense, to be of doubtful mind*, Luke xii. 29.*

μετ-οικεσία, ας, ἡ, *change of abode, migration* (of the Babylonian exile), Matt. i. 11, 12, 17.*

μετ-οικίζω, *to change one's habitation, to migrate*, Acts vii. 4, 43.*

μετοχή, ῆς, ἡ, *a partaking, a consorting with, communion*, 2 Cor. vi. 14.*

μέτοχος, ου, ὁ, ἡ, *a partner, a companion, an associate*, Heb. i. 9; Luke v. 7; *a partaker*, Heb. iii. 1, 14, vi. 4, xii. 8.*

μετρέω, ῶ, *to measure,* Matt. vii. 2; met., *to estimate, to judge of,* 2 Cor. x. 12.

μετρητής, οῦ, ὁ, *"a measurer,"* a liquid measure (72 sextarii) containing nearly eight and a half English gallons, *firkin* (A. V., R. V.), John ii. 6.*

μετριο-παθέω, ῶ, *to treat with gentleness, bear gently with* (R. V.), Heb. v. 2.*

μετρίως, adv., *moderately, a little,* Acts xx. 12.*

μέτρον. ου, τό *a measure,* of capacity, Mark iv. 24; of length, Rev. xxi. 15; *a measure assigned,* Matt. xxiii. 32; adv. phrases, ἐκ μέτρου *by measure, sparingly,* John iii. 34; ἐν μέτρῳ, *in due measure,* Eph. iv. 16.

μέτ-ωπον, ου, τό (ὤψ), *the forehead,* Rev.*

μέχρι or μέχρις, adv., as prep. with gen., *unto,* time, Matt. xiii. 30; Mark xiii. 30; place, Rom. xv. 19; degree, 2 Tim. ii. 9; Heb. xii. 4. As conj., *until,* Eph. iv. 13.

μή, a negative particle, *not.* For distinction between μή, οὐ, see § 401; elliptically, *lest,* see § 384; interrogatively, see § 369. For the combination οὐ μή, see § 377.

μή-γε, in the phrase εἰ δὲ μήγε, *but if not,* emphatic.

μηδαμῶς, adv., *by no means,* Acts x. 14, xi. 8.*

μηδέ, compare οὐδέ, and see § 401; *not even,* Mark ii. 2; 1 Cor. v. 11; generally used after a preceding μή, *and not, neither, but not, nor yet,* as Matt. vi. 25, vii. 6.

μηδείς, μηδεμία, μηδέν (εἷς), differing from οὐδείς as μή from οὐ (see § 401); *not one, no one, no person* or *thing, nothing,* Matt. viii. 4; Mark v. 26; Gal. vi. 3.

μηδέ-ποτε, adv., *never,* 2 Tim. iii. 7.*

μηδέ-πω, adv., *not yet,* Heb. xi. 7.*

Μῆδος, ου, ὁ, *a Mede,* Acts ii. 9.*

μηκέτι, adv. (ἔτι), *no more, no longer, lest further.*

μῆκος, ους, τό, *length,* Eph. iii. 18; Rev. xxi. 16.*

μηκύνω, *to make long;* mid., *to grow up,* as plants, Mark iv. 27.*

μηλωτή, ῆς, ἡ, *a fleece, a sheep's skin,* Heb. xi. 37.*

μήν, a part. of strong affirmation, N.T., only in the combination ἦ μήν, *assuredly, certainly,* Heb. vi. 14 (W. H., εἰ μήν).*

μήν, μηνός, ὁ, (1) *a month,* as Acts vii. 20; (2) *the new moon,* as a festival, Gal. iv. 10.

μηνύω, *to show, declare,* Luke xx. 37; John xi. 57; Acts xxiii. 30; 1 Cor. x. 28.*

μὴ οὐκ, an interrogative formula, expecting the answer *"yes,"* Rom. x. 18, 19; 1 Cor. ix. 4, 5.*

μή-ποτε, adv., *no longer,* Heb. ix. 17. As conj., *lest ever, lest perhaps, whether indeed, if so be,* Luke iii. 15; John vii. 26.

μή που, *lest anywhere,* Acts xxvii. 29 (W. H., for Rec. μήπως).

μή-πω, adv., *not as yet, not yet,* Rom. ix. 11; Heb. ix. 8.*

μήπως, conj., *lest in any way, lest perhaps,* as Acts xxvii. 29 (W. H., μή που), 1 Thess. iii. 5.

μηρός, οῦ, ὁ, *the thigh,* Rev. xix. 16.*

μήτε, conj., differing from οὔτε as μή from οὐ (see § 401); *and not,* used after a preceding μή or μήτε, *neither...nor;* in Mark iii. 20, *not even,* W. H. read μηδέ.

μήτηρ, τρός, ἡ, *a mother;* met., *a mother city,* Gal. iv. 26.

μήτι, adv., interrogatively used, *is it? whether at all?* generally expecting a negative answer; μήτιγε; *not to say then?* 1 Cor. vi. 3.

μήτις (W. H., μή τις), pron. interrog., *has* or *is any one? whether any one?* John iv. 33.

μήτρα, ας, ἡ, *the womb,* Luke ii. 23; Rom. iv. 19.*

μητρ-αλῴας (W. H., -ολῴας), ου, ὁ, *a matricide,* 1 Tim. i. 9.*

μία, fem. of εἷς, *one.*

μιαίνω, ανῶ, perf. pass. μεμίασμαι, *to stain, pollute, defile,* John xviii. 28; Tit. i. 15; Heb. xii. 15; Jude 8.*

μίασμα, ατος, τό, *pollution, defilement,* 2 Pet. ii. 20; *"miasma."*

μιασμός, οῦ, ὁ, *pollution, defilement,* 2 Pet. ii. 10.*

μίγμα, ατος, τό, *a mixture,* John xix. 39.*

μίγνυμι, μίξω, ἔμιξα, perf. pass. μέμιγμαι, *to mix, to mingle,* Matt. xxvii. 34; Luke xiii. 1; Rev. viii. 7, xv. 2.*

μικρός, ά, όν, *little, small,* i.e., in size, Matt. xiii. 32; quantity, 1 Cor. v. 6; number, Luke xii. 32; time, John vii. 33; dignity, Matt. x. 42.

Μίλητος, ου, ή, *Miletus.*
μίλιον, ίου, τό (Latin, *mille* passuum, 1,000 paces), *a mile* (about 80 yards less than our mile), Matt. v. 41.*
μιμέομαι, οῦμαι, dep. mid., *to imitate, to follow the example of,* 2 Thess. iii. 7, 9; Heb. xiii. 7; 3 John 11.*
μιμητής, οῦ, ὁ, *an imitator, a follower,* as 1 Cor. iv. 16.
μιμνήσκω (μνα-), mid., with fut. in pass. form μνησθήσομαι, 1 aor. ἐμνήσθην, perf. μέμνημαι, *to call to mind, to remember,* gen. pers. or thing, Matt. xxvi. 75; Luke xxiii. 42; pass., *to be remembered, to be had in mind,* only Acts x. 31; Rev. xvi. 16.
μισέω, ῶ, ήσω, *to hate, to detest, to abhor.* Used in antith. with ἀγαπάω, *to love less, not to love, to slight,* Matt. vi. 24; John xii. 25.
μισθ-απο-δοσία, ας, ἡ, *recompense,* as (1) *reward,* Heb. x. 35, xi. 26; (2) *punishment,* Heb. ii. 2.*
μισθ-απο-δότης, ου, ὁ, *a rewarder,* Heb. xi. 6.*
μίσθιος, ον, *hired,* as subst., *a hired servant, a hireling,* Luke xv. 17, 19.*
μισθός, οῦ, ὁ, *hire, wages, recompense, requital,* Matt. xx. 8. Used of *reward,* Matt. v. 12, 46; of *punishment,* 2 Pet. ii. 13.
μισθόω, ῶ, ώσω, *to hire out;* mid., *to hire, to engage to labour for wages,* Matt. xx. 1, 7.*
μίσθωμα, ατος, τό, *hire, rent;* met., *anything rented,* as a house, Acts xxviii. 30.*
μισθωτός, οῦ, ὁ, *a hired servant, one who serves for wages,* Mark i. 20; John x. 12, 13.*
Μιτυλήνη, ης, ἡ, *Mitylene,* the capital of Lesbos, Acts xx. 14.*
Μιχαήλ, ὁ (Heb., *who is like God?*), *Michael,* an archangel, Jude 9; Rev. xii. 7.*
μνᾶ, ᾶς, ἡ, *a mina,* silver money = 100 δράχμαι, or about 3*l.* 15*s.*; rendered *pound,* Luke xix. 13-25.*
μνάομαι. See μιμνήσκω.
Μνάσων, ωνος, ὁ, *Mnason,* Acts xxi. 16.*
μνεία, ας, ἡ, *remembrance, recollection,* Phil. i. 3; 1 Thess. iii. 6; μνείαν ποιεῖσθαι, *to mention, to bear in mind,* Rom. i. 9.

μνῆμα, ατος, τό, *a memorial, a monument, a tomb,* Mark v. 5; Luke xxiii. 53; less frequent than the following.
μνημεῖον, ου, τό, *a tomb, a grave,* Matt. viii. 28; John xi. 31.
μνήμη, ης, ἡ, *remembrance, mention;* μνήμην ποιεῖσθαι, *to make mention,* 2 Pet. i. 15.*
μνημονεύω, *to remember* (ὅτι), *recollect, call to mind* (gen. or acc.), Matt. xvi. 9; Acts xx. 31; *to be mindful of,* Heb. xi. 15; *to make mention of* (gen., or περί, gen.), Heb. xi. 22.
μνημόσυνον, ου, τό, *a memorial, honourable remembrance, fame,* Matt. xxvi. 13; Mark xiv. 9; Acts x. 4.*
μνηστεύω, *to ask in marriage;* mid., *to woo;* pass., *to be betrothed,* Matt. i. 18; Luke i. 27, ii. 5.*
μογι-λάλος, ου, *one who can scarcely speak, a stammerer,* Mark vii. 32.*
μόγις, adv. (like μόλις), *with difficulty, scarcely, hardly,* Luke ix. 39.*
μόδιος, ου, ὁ, *a dry measure* (16 sextarii), containing about a peck; *a modius, bushel,* Matt. v. 15; Mark iv. 21; Luke xi. 33.*
μοιχαλίς, ίδος, ἡ, *an adulteress,* Rom. vii. 3; fig. for departure from God, Matt. xvi. 4; James iv. 4.
μοιχάομαι, ῶμαι, *to commit adultery, to be guilty of adultery,* Matt. v. 32.
μοιχεία, ας, ἡ, *adultery,* Matt. xv. 19.
μοιχεύω, σω, *to commit adultery,* abs. (acc., Matt. v. 28); fig. of forsaking God, Rev. ii. 22.
μοιχός, οῦ, ὁ, *an adulterer,* Luke xviii. 11; 1 Cor. vi. 9; Heb. xiii. 4; James iv. 4 (not W. H.).*
μόλις, adv. (like μόγις), *with difficulty, scarcely, hardly,* Acts xiv. 18, xxvii. 7, 8, 16; Rom. v. 7; 1 Pet. iv.
Μολόχ, ὁ (Heb.), *Moloch,* Acts vii. 43, LXX.*
μολύνω, υνῶ, *to pollute, to defile,* 1 Cor. viii. 7; Rev. iii. 4, xiv. 4.*
μολυσμός, οῦ, ὁ, *pollution, defilement,* 2 Cor. vii. 1.*
μομφή, ῆς, ἡ, *complaint, ground of complaint,* Col. iii. 13.*
μονή, ῆς, ἡ, *a place of abode, a dwelling-place,* John xiv. 2, 23.*
μονο-γενής, ές, gen. οῦς, *only begotten,* Luke vii. 12, viii. 42, ix. 38; Heb.

xi. 17; of CHRIST, John i. 14, 18, iii. 16, 18; 1 John iv. 9.*

μόνος, η, ον, *only, alone, single*, Luke xxiv. 12, 18; *solitary, without company* or *help*, Mark vi. 47; *forsaken, desolate*, John viii. 29; adv., μόνον, *only*.

μον-όφθαλμος, *having but one eye*, Matt. xviii. 9; Mark ix. 47.*

μονόω, ῶ, *to leave alone;* pass., *to be left alone* or *desolate*, 1 Tim. v. 5.*

μορφή, ῆς, ἡ, *outward appearance, form, shape*, Mark xvi. 12; Phil. ii. 6, 7. Syn. 56.*

μορφόω, ῶ, ώσω, *to form, to fashion*, Gal. iv. 19.*

μόρφωσις, εως, ἡ, *formation, external appearance*, 2 Tim. iii. 5; *form, rule, system*, Rom. ii. 20.*

μοσχο-ποιέω, ῶ, *to form the image of a calf*, Acts vii. 41.*

μόσχος, ου, ὁ, ἡ, *a calf, a young bullock*, Luke xv. 23, 27, 30; Heb. ix. 12, 19; Rev. iv. 7.*

μουσικός, ή, όν, *skilled in music, a musician*, Rev. xviii. 22.*

μόχθος, ου, ὁ, *wearisome labour, toil*, with pain and sorrow, 2 Cor. xi. 27; 1 Thess. ii. 9; 2 Thess. iii. 8.*

μυελός, οῦ, ὁ, *the marrow,* Heb. iv. 12.*

μυέω, ῶ, *to instruct, to initiate into*, Phil. iv. 12.*

μῦθος, ου, ὁ, *a word;* hence, *a tale, fable*, "myth," 1 Tim. i. 4, iv. 7; 2 Tim. iv. 4; Tit. i. 14; 2 Pet. i. 16.*

μυκάομαι, ῶμαι, *to low, to bellow*, as a bull; *to roar*, as a lion, Rev. x. 3.*

μυκτηρίζω, *to contract the nostrils in contempt*, *to mock, sneer*, or *deride*, Gal. vi. 7.*

μυλικός, ή, όν, *pertaining to a mill;* with λίθος, *millstone*, Mark ix. 42 (not W. H.); Luke xvii. 2 (W. H.).*

μύλινος, in sense of foregoing, Rev. xviii. 21 (W. H.).*

μύλος, ου, ὁ, *a millstone*, as Matt. xviii. 6.

μυλών, ῶνος, ὁ, *a mill-house,* the place where corn was ground, Matt. xxiv. 41 (W. H., μύλος).*

μυριάς, άδος, ἡ, *a myriad, ten thousand, a vast multitude*, Luke xii. 1; Acts xix. 19, xxi. 20; Heb. xii. 22; Jude 14; Rev. v. 11, ix. 16.*

μυρίζω, σω, *to anoint* for burial, Mark xiv. 8.*

μύριοι, αι, α, *ten thousand*, Matt. xviii. 24; μυρίοι, ίαι, ία, *innumerable*, 1 Cor. iv. 15, xiv. 19.*

μύρον, ου, τό, *a perfumed ointment*, Matt. xxvi. 7.

Μυσία, ας, ἡ, *Mysia*, Acts xvi. 7, 8.*

μυστήριον, ίον, τό, *a mystery, anything hidden, a secret*, Matt. xiii. 11; Rom. xi. 25. In classical Greek, τὰ μυστήρια are *hidden rites and knowledge*, revealed only to the initiated (like the Masonic secrets); hence the word is used in N.T. of the truths of the Gospel as *mysteries* partly hidden, partly revealed, Eph. iii. 9; Col. i. 26, iv. 3; 1 Tim. iii. 16.

μυωπάζω, *to wink, to be dim-sighted*, 2 Pet. i. 9.*

μώλωψ, ωπος, ὁ, *the mark of a stripe;* met., *pain, anguish*, 1 Pet. ii. 24.*

μωμάομαι, ῶμαι, dep., aor., mid. and pass., *to blame, to find fault with*, 2 Cor. vi. 3, viii. 20.*

μῶμος, ου, ὁ, *a spot, a blemish;* met., *disgrace*, 2 Pet. ii. 13.*

μωραίνω, ανῶ, *to infatuate, to make foolish*, 1 Cor. i. 20; pass., *to become foolish*, Rom. i. 22; *to become insipid, tasteless*, like spoiled salt, Matt. v. 13; Luke xiv. 34.*

μωρία, ας, ἡ, *folly, absurdity, contemptibleness*, 1 Cor. i. 18, 21, 23, ii. 14, iii. 19.*

μωρο-λογία, ας, ἡ, *foolish talking, babble*, Eph. v. 4.*

μωρός, ά, όν, *stupid, foolish*, Matt. vii. 26, xxiii. 17, 19 (on Matt. v. 22, see § 153, ii.); τὸ μωρόν, *foolishness, foolish thing*, 1 Cor. i. 25, 27.

Μωσῆς (W. H., Μωυσῆς), έως, dat. εἶ or ῇ; acc. ἦν (once έα, Luke xvi. 29; W. H., ῆν), ὁ, *Moses*, met., the books of Moses, the *Pentateuch*, Luke xvi. 29; 2 Cor. iii. 15.

N.

N, ν, Nῦ, *Nu, n*, the thirteenth letter. As a numeral, ν' = 50; ,ν = 50,000.

Ναασσών, ὁ (Heb.), *Naasson*, Matt. i. 4; Luke iii. 31.*

Ναγγαί, ὁ (Heb.), *Naggœ*, Luke iii. 25.*

Ναζαρέτ, -ρέτ or -ρά (W. H. have all the forms), ἡ, *Nazareth*.

Ναζαρηνός, οῦ, ὁ, a *Nazarene*, as Mark i. 24.
Ναζωραῖος, ου, ὁ, a *Nazarene*, an appellation of Christ. Christians are called οἱ Ναζωραῖοι, Acts xxiv. 5.
Ναθάν, ὁ (Heb.), *Nathan*, Luke iii. 31.*
Ναθαναήλ, ὁ, *Nathanael*, probably the same as *Bartholomew*.
ναί, adv., affirming, *yes*, Matt. ix. 28; *even so*, Matt. xi. 26; Luke x. 21; Rev. xxii. 20; *yea*, strongly affirming, Luke vii. 26.
Ναΐν, ἡ, *Nain*, Luke vii. 11.*
ναός, οῦ, ὁ (ναίω), a *temple, a shrine*, or small model of a temple, the abode of deity, pretended, Acts xix. 24; *the temple*, Matt. xxiii. 16; used of Jesus Christ, John ii. 19, 20; of Christians generally, 1 Cor. iii. 16; 2 Cor. vi. 16. Syn. 35.
Ναούμ, ὁ (Heb.), *Nahum*, Luke iii. 25 (not the prophet).*
νάρδος, ου, ἡ, *nard, spikenard*, a costly ointment, Mark xiv. 3; John xii. 3.*
Νάρκισσος, ου, ὁ, *Narcissus*, Rom. xvi. 11.*
ναυ-αγέω, ῶ (ἄγνυμι), *to make shipwreck, to be shipwrecked*, 2 Cor. xi. 25; fig., 1 Tim. i. 19.*
ναύ-κληρος, ου, ὁ, a *ship-master*, or *owner*, Acts xxvii. 11.*
ναῦς, νέως, acc. ναῦν, ἡ, a *ship*, Acts xxvii. 41.*
ναύτης, ου, ὁ, a *sailor*, Acts xxvii. 27, 30; Rev. xviii. 17.*
Ναχώρ, ὁ (Heb.), *Nahor*, Luke iii. 34.*
νεανίας, ου, ὁ, a *young man, a youth*, Acts vii. 58, xx. 9, xxiii. 17, 18, 22 (not W. H.).*
νεανίσκος, ου, ὁ, a *young man*, Matt. xix. 20; plur., of soldiers, Mark xiv. 51; of the middle stage in the divine life, 1 John ii. 13, 14.
Νεάπολις, εως, ἡ, *Neapolis*, Acts xvi. 11.*
Νεεμάν (W. H., Ναιμάν), ὁ (Heb.), *Naaman*, Luke iv. 27.*
νεκρός, ά, όν, *dead*, (1) lit., as Matt. xi. 5; οἱ νεκροί, *the dead*, generally; (2) fig., *dead*, spiritually, Eph. ii. 1; *dead* to (dat.), Rom. vi. 11; *inactive, inoperative*, Rom. vii. 8. Syn. 54.
νεκρόω, ῶ, *to put to death;* fig., *to mortify, to deprive of power, to render weak and impotent*, Rom. iv. 19; Col. iii. 5; Heb. xi. 12. Syn. 54.*

νέκρωσις, εως, ἡ, *death, a being put to death*, 2 Cor. iv. 10; *deadness, impotency*, Rom. iv. 19.*
νεομηνία. See νουμηνία.
νέος, α, ον, (1) *new, fresh*, Matt. ix. 17; *new*, in disposition and character; (2) *young*, of persons, Tit. ii. 4. Compar., νεώτερος, *younger*, Luke xv. 12, 13. Syn. 26.
νεοσσός, οῦ, ὁ, *the young of birds, a youngling, a chicken*, Luke ii. 24.*
νεότης, ητος, ἡ, *youth, youthfulness*, Luke xviii. 21; 1 Tim. iv. 12.
νεό-φυτος, ον, *newly planted;* fig., a *recent convert, novice*, " neophyte," 1 Tim. iii. 6.*
νεύω, σω, *to nod;* so, *to beckon, to signify*, John xiii. 24; Acts xxiv. 10.*
νεφέλη, ης, ἡ, a *cloud*.
Νεφθαλείμ, ὁ (Heb.), *Naphthali*, Matt. iv. 14; Rev. vii. 6.*
νέφος, ους, τό, a *cloud;* met., a *multitude, a great company*, Heb. xii. 1.*
νεφρός, οῦ, ὁ, *the kidney*, plur., *the reins*, used (as Heb.) for the secret thoughts, desires, and affections, Rev. ii. 23.*
νεω-κόρος, ου, ὁ, ἡ (ναός and κορέω, *to sweep*), " temple-sweeper," a *temple-keeper*, a designation of the people of Ephesus, Acts xix. 35.*
νεωτερικός, ή, όν, *youthful, juvenile*, 2 Tim. ii. 22.*
νεώτερος, α, ον (comp. of νέος, which see), *younger, inferior in rank, more humble*, Luke xxii. 26.
νή, adv., of affirmative swearing, *by*, with acc., 1 Cor. xv. 31.*
νήθω, *to spin*, Matt. vi. 28; Luke xii. 27.*
νηπιάζω, *to be like a child*, 1 Cor. xiv. 20.*
νήπιος, ία, ιον, *infantile;* as subst., an *infant, a babe, a child*, Matt. xxi. 16; 1 Cor. xiii. 11; used of an age below manhood, Gal. iv. 1; fig., of *unlearned, unenlightened* persons, Matt. xi. 25; Rom. ii. 20. Syn. 62.
Νηρεύς, έως, ὁ, *Nereus*, Rom. xvi. 15.*
Νηρί, ὁ (Heb.), *Neri*, Luke iii. 27.*
νησίον, ου, τό (dim. of νῆσος), a *small island, an islet*, Acts xxvii. 16.*
νῆσος, ου, ἡ (νέω, *to swim*), an *island*.
νηστεία, ας, ἡ, *fasting, a fast*, Matt. xvii. 21 (W. H. omit); Acts xiv. 23; *the day of atonement, the chief Jewish fast-day*, Acts xxvii. 9.

νηστεύω, σω, *to abstain from food, to fast*, Matt. vi. 16-18.
νῆστις, ιος, plur. νήστεις, ὁ, ἡ, *fasting*, Matt. xv. 32; Mark viii. 3.*
νηφάλιος or -λεος, ον, *sober-minded, temperate*; 1 Tim. iii. 2, 11; Tit. ii. 2.*
νήφω, ψω, *to be sober, temperate*, fig., 1 Thess. v. 6, 8.
Νίγερ, ὁ (Lat.), *Niger*, Acts xiii. 1.*
Νικάνωρ, ορος, ὁ, *Nicanor*, Acts vi. 5.*
νικάω, ῶ, ήσω, *to prevail*, abs., Rev. iii. 21; *to conquer, overcome* (acc.), Luke xi. 22; John xvi. 33.
νίκη, ης, ἡ, *victory*, 1 John v. 4.*
Νικόδημος, ου, ὁ, *Nicodemus*, John iii. 1.
Νικολαΐτης, ου, ὁ, *a follower of Nicolaus, Nicolaitan* (probably a Greek equivalent for *Balaam*), Rev. ii. 6, 15.*
Νικόλαος, ου, ὁ, *Nicolaus*, Acts vi. 5 (not to be confounded with preced.).*
Νικόπολις, εως, ἡ, *Nicopolis*, Tit. iii. 12. Several cities of the name existed; this was probably in Macedonia.*
νῖκος, ους, τό, *victory*; εἰς νῖκος, from LXX., *to a victorious consummation, utterly*, Matt. xii. 20; 1 Cor. xv. 54, 55, 57.*
Νινευΐ, ἡ (Heb.), *Nineveh*, Luke xi. 32 (W. H. read following).*
Νινευΐτης (W. H.,-είτης), ου, ὁ, *a Ninevite*, Matt. xii. 41; Luke xi. 30, 32 (W. H.).*
νιπτήρ, ῆρος, ὁ, *a basin for washing*, hands or feet, John xiii. 5.*
νίπτω, ψω, *to wash* (acc.), mid., *to wash oneself*, acc. of part, as Mark vii. 3. Syn. 17.
νοέω, ῶ, ήσω, *to understand, to perceive*, abs., or with acc., or ὅτι.
νόημα, ατος, τό, (1) *a thought, purpose, device*, 2 Cor. ii. 11, x. 5; Phil. iv. 7; (2) *the mind*, i.e., *the understanding or intellect*, 2 Cor. iii. 14, iv. 4, xi. 3.*
νόθος, η, ον, *bastard, spurious*, Heb. xii. 8.*
νομή, ῆς, ἡ (νέμω, *to apportion*, as pasture to cattle), (1) *pasturage*, John x. 9; (2) met., *a feeding, spreading*, as of a gangrene, 2 Tim. ii. 17.*
νομίζω, σω (νόμος), (1) *to be wont, to do by custom*, only Acts xvi. 13 (but see W. H. and R. V.); (2) *to think, to reckon, to expect*, as the result of thinking, Matt. v. 17, xx. 10.
νομικός, ή, όν, *pertaining to law, legal*, Tit. iii. 9; as subst., *a person skilled in law*, Tit. iii. 13; *a teacher of the Mosaic law*, Matt. xxii. 35.
νομίμως, adv., *lawfully, agreeably to rule*, 1 Tim. i. 8; 2 Tim. ii. 5.*
νόμισμα, ατος, τό, *money, coin*, whose value is settled by law, Matt. xxii. 19.*
νομο-διδάσκαλος, ου, ὁ, *a teacher or interpreter of the law*, Luke v. 17; Acts v. 34; 1 Tim. i. 7.*
νομο-θεσία, ας, ἡ, *legislation, the laws given*, i.e., *the Mosaic law*, Rom. ix. 4.*
νομο-θετέω, ω, *to sanction, to establish for a law*, Heb. viii. 6; pass., *to have a law established*, Heb. vii. 11.*
νομο-θέτης, ου, ὁ (τίθημι), *a law-giver, legislator*, James iv. 12.*
νόμος, ου, ὁ (νέμω, *to apportion*), *a law, an edict, a decree, a statute*, Luke ii. 22; *a standard of acting* or *judging*, Rom. iii. 27; *a written law*, Rom. ii. 14; *the Mosaic economy*, Matt. v. 18; Rom. x. 4; *the Christian dispensation* or *doctrines*, Gal. vi. 2; Rom. xiii. 8; met., for the books containing the Mosaic law, i.e., the five books of Moses, Matt. xii. 5; and for the Old Testament generally, John x. 34. On the article with νόμος, see § 234.
νόος. See νοῦς.
νοσέω, ῶ, *to be sick*; fig., *to have a diseased appetite* or *craving for*, περί (acc.), 1 Tim. vi. 4.*
νόσημα, ατος, τό, *a disease, a sickness*, John v. 4 (W. H. omit).*
νόσος, ου, ἡ, *a sickness, a disease, a distemper*, Matt. iv. 23, 24.
νοσσιά, ᾶς, ἡ, *a brood of young birds*, Luke xiii. 34.*
νοσσίον, ου, τό, *a young bird*, Matt. xxiii. 37.*
νοσσός. See νεοσσός.*
νοσφίζω, in mid., *to secrete for oneself, to purloin*, Acts v. 2, 3; Tit. ii. 10.*
νότος, ου, ὁ, *the south wind*, Luke xii. 55; *the southern quarter*, Luke xi. 31.
νου-θεσία, ας, ἡ, *a warning, admonition, counsel*, 1 Cor. x. 11; Eph. vi. 4; Tit. iii. 10.*
νου-θετέω, ῶ, *to warn, to admonish, to counsel*, Acts xx. 31.
νου-μηνία (W. H., νεο-), ας, ἡ, *the new moon*, or *month*, as a festival, Col. ii. 16.*

νουν-εχῶς, adv., *understandingly, wisely, judiciously*, Mark xii. 34.*

νοῦς, or *νοός, νοῦ, νοΐ, νοῦν, ὁ, the mind*, i.e., *the understanding* or *intellect*, Luke xxiv. 45; Rom. xii. 2; Phil. iv. 7. Hence, *any affection of the mind*—as modes of thought—*inclinations*, or *dispositions*, Rom. xiv. 5; 1 Cor. i. 10; 2 Thess. ii. 2; more widely, *the rational soul*, with its powers and affections, Rom. vii. 25. Syn. 55.

Νυμφᾶς, ᾶ, ὁ, *Nymphas*, Col. iv. 15.*

νύμφη, ης, ἡ, *a bride*, Rev. xviii. 23; *a daughter-in-law*, Matt. x. 35.

νυμφίος, ου, ὁ, *a bridegroom*, John iii. 29.

νυμφών, ῶνος, ὁ, *a bridal chamber*; οἱ υἱοὶ τοῦ νυμφῶνος, *the sons of the bridal chamber, bridesmen*, Matt. ix. 15; Mark ii. 19; Luke v. 34.*

νῦν and **νυνί**, adv., (1) of time, *now*, i.e., the actually present; *now*, in relation to time just past, *just now, even now*; *now*, in relation to future time, *just at hand, even now, immediately*; ὁ, ἡ, τό, νῦν, *the present*, with subst. or (neut.) without; (2) of logical connection, *now*, i.e., "seeing that things are so," 2 Cor. vii. 9; *now then*, i.e., implying the rise of one thing from another, 1 Cor. xiv. 6. (3) In commands and appeals, *νῦν* is emphatic, Matt. xxvii. 42; James iv. 13, *at this instant*.

νύξ, νυκτός, ἡ, *the night, night-time*, lit.; often fig., *a time of darkness and ignorance*, Rom. xiii. 12; 1 Thess. v. 5.

νύσσω, ξω, *to stab, to pierce*, John xix. 34.*

νυστάζω, ξω, *to nod*, as asleep, *to be drowsy*, Matt. xxv. 5; fig., *to delay*, 2 Pet. ii. 3.*

νυχθ-ήμερον, ου, τό, *a day and a night, twenty-four hours*, 2 Cor. xi. 25.*

Νῶε, ὁ (Heb.), *Noah*.

νωθρός, ά, όν, *slow, dull, stupid*, Heb. v. 11, vi. 12.*

νῶτος, ου, ὁ, *the back* of men or animals, Rom. xi. 10.*

Ξ.

Ξ, ξ, ξῖ, *xi*, the double letter *x* (=γς, κς, or χς), the fourteenth letter. As numeral, ξ' = 60; ξ͵ = 60,000.

ξενία, ας, ἡ, *hospitality, entertainment, a lodging*, Acts xxviii. 23; Philem. 22.*

ξενίζω, σω, (1) *to receive as a guest* (acc.), Acts x. 18, 23, 32, xxviii. 7; Heb. xiii. 2; pass., *to be entertained, to lodge as a guest with*, Acts x. 6. xxi. 16; (2) *to appear strange to* (acc.), Acts xvii. 20; pass., *to think strangely of, to be surprised at* (dat.), 1 Pet. iv. 4, 12.*

ξενο-δοχέω, ῶ, *to entertain guests, to practise hospitality*, 1 Tim. v. 10.*

ξένος, η, ον, *strange, foreign*, Acts xvii. 18; 1 Pet. iv. 12; with gen., Eph. ii. 12; as subst., *a stranger, a guest, a host*, Matt. xxv. 35-44; Rom. xvi. 23.

ξέστης, ου, ὁ (the Latin *sextarius*), *a measure*, about a pint and a half English; met., *a cup* or *pitcher*, of any size, Mark vii. 4, 8.*

ξηραίνω, ανῶ, 1st aor., act., ἐξήρανα; 1 aor., pass., ἐξηράνθην; perf., pass., εξήραμμαι (3 s., ἐξήρανται, Mark xi. 21), *to dry, to make dry, to wither*, James i. 11; pass., *to be* or *become dry, withered*, Matt. xiii. 6; *to be dried up*, Rev. xvi. 12; *to be ripened*, as corn, Rev. xiv. 15; *to pine away*, Mark ix. 18.

ξηρός, ά, όν, *dry, withered*, of a tree, Luke xxiii. 31; of a useless limb, Matt. xii. 10; Mark iii. 3 (W. H.); Luke vi. 6, 8; John v. 3; of land, Heb. xi. 29; ἡ ξηρά (sc. γῆ), *dry land*, Matt. xxiii. 15.*

ξύλινος, ίνη, ινον, *wooden*, 2 Tim. ii. 20; Rev. ix. 20.*

ξύλον, ου, τό, *wood*, e.g., *timber* in building, 1 Cor. iii. 12; or for burning; *anything made of wood*, e.g., *the stocks*, Acts xvi. 24; *a staff*, Matt. xxvi. 47, 55; *a cross* or *gibbet*, Acts xiii. 29; Gal. iii. 13; *a living tree*, Rev. ii. 7.

ξυράω, ῶ, ήσω, perf. pass. ἐξύρημαι, *to shear* or *shave*, e.g., the locks and the beard, Acts xxi. 24; 1 Cor. xi. 5, 6.*

O.

Ο, ο, ὂ μικρόν, *omicron*, short *o*, the fifteenth letter. As a numeral, ο' = 70; ο͵ = 70,000.

ὁ, ἡ, τό, the definite article, *the*, originally demonstrative. For its uses, see §§ 193-234.

ὀγδοήκοντα, num., indecl., *eighty.*
ὄγδοος, η, ον, ord., *eighth;* on 2 Pet. ii. 5, see § 331.
ὄγκος, ου, ὁ, *a weight, an impediment,* Heb. xii. 1. Syn. 68.*
ὅδε, ἥδε, τόδε, demon. pron., *this, that* (here). See § 339.
ὁδεύω, *to pass along a way, to journey,* Luke x. 33.*
ὁδ-ηγέω, ῶ, ήσω, *to lead along a way, to conduct, to guide,* Matt. xv. 14; Luke vi. 39; John xvi. 13; Acts viii. 31; Rev. vii. 17.*
ὁδ-ηγός, οῦ, ὁ, *a leader,* Acts i. 16; fig., of instructors, Matt. xv. 14, xxiii. 16, 24; Rom. ii. 19.*
ὁδοι-πορέω, ῶ, *to travel, to pursue a way,* Acts x. 9.*
ὁδοι-πορία, ας, ἡ, *a journey, a journeying,* John iv. 6; 2 Cor. xi. 26.*
ὁδός, οῦ, ἡ, (1) *a way, a road, a highway,* Matt. ii. 12; (2) *a going, a progress,* Mark vi. 8; (3) *a journey,* a day's or a Sabbath day's, Luke ii. 44; Acts i. 12; (4) fig., *manner of action, method of proceeding,* Acts xiii. 10; Matt. xxi. 32; especially (5) *the Christian way,* Acts ix. 2; 2 Pet. ii. 2; (6) used of Christ himself, *the Way,* John xiv. 6.
ὁδούς, ὀδόντος, ὁ, *a tooth,* Matt. v. 38.
ὀδυνάω, ῶ, in mid. and pass., *to be in an agony, to be tormented, to be greatly grieved* or *distressed,* Luke ii. 48, xvi. 24, 25; Acts xx. 38.*
ὀδύνη, ης, ἡ, *pain, distress,* of body or mind, Rom. ix. 2; 1 Tim. vi. 10.*
ὀδυρμός, οῦ, ὁ, *lamentation, wailing,* Matt. ii. 18; 2 Cor. vii. 7. Syn. 20.*
Ὀζίας, ου, *Uzziah,* Matt. i. 8.*
ὄζω, intrans., *to stink, be offensive,* John xi. 39.*
ὅθεν, adv., *whence,* of place or source.
ὀθόνη, ης, ἡ, *a linen cloth;* hence, *a sheet,* Acts x. 11, xi. 5.*
ὀθόνιον, ου, τό (dim. of ὀθόνη), *a linen swathe, a bandage,* Luke xxiv. 12.
οἶδα (ϝιδ-), Attic plur. (ἴσμεν) ἴστε (Heb. xii. 17*), ἴσασι (Acts xxvi. 4*), *I know* (see § 103, 4, and Syn. 4).
οἰκειακός. See οἰκιακός.
οἰκεῖος, α, ον, *domestic, belonging to a house,* Gal. vi. 10; Eph. ii. 19; 1 Tim. v. 8.*
οἰκέτεια, ας, ἡ, *household* (W. H.), Matt. xxiv. 45.*
οἰκέτης, ου, ὁ, *a domestic,* Luke xvi. 13;
Acts x. 7; Rom. xiv. 4; 1 Pet. ii. 18. Syn. 61.*
οἰκέω, ῶ, ήσω, *to inhabit, to dwell in,* Rom. viii. 9; 1 Tim. vi. 16.
οἴκημα, ατος, τό, *a dwelling,* used of *a prison,* Acts xii. 7.*
οἰκητήριον, ου, τό, *a domicile, habitation,* 2 Cor. v. 2; Jude 6.*
οἰκία, ας, ἡ, (1) *a house;* (2) met., *a household, a family, goods, i.e.,* a house and all that is in it. Syn. 61.
οἰκιακός, οῦ, ὁ, *one of a family,* whether child, relative, or servant, Matt. x. 25, 36.*
οἰκο-δεσποτέω, ῶ, *to govern a household,* 1 Tim. v. 14.*
οἰκο-δεσπότης, ου, ὁ, *a householder, a head of a family,* Matt. x. 25.
οἰκο-δομέω, ῶ, *to erect a building, build,* Luke xiv. 30; fig., of the building up of character, *to build up, edify,* 1 Cor. x. 23; *to embolden,* 1 Cor. viii. 10.
οἰκο-δομή, ῆς, ἡ (δέμω), *the act of building; a building, structure,* lit., Matt. xxiv. 1; of the spiritual body, 2 Cor. v. 1; of the church, Eph. ii. 21; met., *edification, spiritual advancement,* Rom. xiv. 19, xv. 2.
οἰκο-δομία, ας, ἡ, *edification,* 1 Tim. i. 4 (W. H., οἰκονομία).*
οἰκο-δόμος, ου, ὁ, *a builder,* Acts iv. 11 (W. H.).*
οἰκο-νομέω, ῶ, *to be steward,* Luke xvi. 2.
οἰκονομία, ας, *management of family affairs, stewardship,* Luke xvi. 2-4; *dispensation,* 1 Cor. x. 17.
οἰκο-νόμος, ου (νέμω), *a house-manager, a steward,* Luke xvi. 1-8; of the Christian stewardship, 1 Cor. iv. 1, 2; 1 Pet. iv. 10; Tit. i. 7.
οἶκος, ου, ὁ, *a house, a building,* for any purpose (gen.); met., *a family* resident in one house, *a family* perpetuated by succession, *the house* of God, i.e., the temple; *the family* of God, i.e., the church. Syn. 61.
οἰκουμένη, ης, pres. part., pass., fem. of οἰκέω (sc. γῆ), *the inhabited land,* or *world;* (1) *the Roman empire;* (2) prob. *the Syrian province,* Luke ii. 1; (3) *the world at large;* (4) met., *the inhabitants of the world;* (5) *a state,* or *economy,* Heb. ii. 5. Syn. 58.
οἰκ-ουρός, οῦ, ὁ, ἡ (οὖρος, *keeper*), *a house-manager,* Tit. ii. 5 (W. H., οἰκουργός).*

οἰκτείρω, ήσω, *to pity, to have compassion*, Rom. ix. 15; LXX.*
οἰκτιρμός, οῦ, ὁ, *compassion, mercy*, Rom. xii. 1; 2 Cor. i. 3; Phil. ii. 1; Col. iii. 12; Heb. x. 28. **Syn. 41.***
οἰκτίρμων, ονος, ὁ, ἡ, *pitiful, compassionate, merciful*, Luke vi. 36; James v. 11.*
οἶμαι. See οἴομαι.
οἰνο-πότης, ου, ὁ, *a wine-bibber, one who drinks to excess*, Matt. xi. 19; Luke vii. 34.*
οἶνος, ου, ὁ, *wine*, Mark ii. 22; met., *the vine*, Rev. vi. 6; fig., *of that which excites or inflames*, Rev. xiv. 10, xvii. 2.
οἰνο-φλυγία, ας, ἡ (φλύω, *to be hot*), *the state of being heated with wine, drunkenness*, 1 Pet. iv. 3.*
οἴομαι and **οἶμαι**, *to think, to suppose*, acc. and inf., or ὅτι, John xxi. 25; Phil. i. 16; James i. 7.*
οἷος, α, ον, rel. pron., correl. to τοιοῦτος, *of what kind, such as*.
οἴω. See φέρω.
ὀκνέω, ῶ, ήσω, *to be slothful, to delay, to be loth*, Acts ix. 38.*
ὀκνηρύς, ά, όν, *slothful, indolent, tedious*, Matt. xxv. 26; Rom. xii. 11; Phil. iii. 1.*
ὀκτα-ήμερος, ου, ὁ, ἡ, *of or belonging to the eighth day*, Phil. iii. 5.*
ὀκτώ, num., indecl., *eight*.
ὄλεθρος, ου, ὁ, *destruction, perdition, misery*, 1 Cor. v. 5; 1 Thess. v. 3; 2 Thess. i. 9; 1 Tim. vi. 9.*
ὀλιγο-πιστία, ἡ, *little faith*, Matt. xvii. 20 (W. H.).*
ὀλιγό-πιστος, ου, ὁ, ἡ, *of little faith*, Matt. vi. 30.
ὀλίγος, η, ον, (1) *little, small, brief;* (2) in plur., *few*, sometimes with gen.; (3) neut. as adv., ὀλίγον, *of time, soon;* of space, *a little way;* (3) with prepositions preced. in various phrases, as ἐν ὀλίγῳ, *in a short time*, or *with little trouble*, Acts xxvi. 28.
ὀλιγό-ψυχος, adv., *small-souled, fainthearted*, 1 Thess. v. 14.*
ὀλιγ-ωρέω, ῶ, *to make little of, to despise* (gen.), Heb. xii. 5; LXX.*
ὀλοθρευτής, οῦ, ὁ, *a destroyer*, 1 Cor. x. 10.*
ὀλοθρεύω, *to destroy, cause to perish*, Heb. xi. 28.*

ὁλο-καύτωμα, ατος, τό (καίω), *a whole burnt-offering, the whole being consumed,* "holocaust," Mark xii. 33; Heb. x. 6, 8.*
ὁλο-κληρία, ας, ἡ, *perfect soundness*, Acts iii. 16.*
ὁλό-κληρος, ον, *whole in every part, sound, perfect*, 1 Thess. v. 23; James i. 4. **Syn. 27.***
ὀλολύζω, as from the cry, ὀλ-ὀλ ! *to howl, to yell, to lament aloud*, James v. 1.*
ὅλος, η, ον, *all, the whole* (see § 225); adv.,-ως, *wholly, altogether;* with neg. preced., *not at all*.
ὁλο-τελής, ές, *perfect, complete*, 1 Thess. v. 23. **Syn. 27.***
Ὀλυμπᾶς, ᾶ, ὁ, *Olympas*, Rom. xvi. 15.*
ὄλυνθος, ου, ὁ, *an unseasonable fig* (one which, not ripening in due time, hangs till nearly winter), Rev. vi. 13.*
ὄμβρος, ου, ὁ, *a heavy rain*, Luke xii. 54.*
ὁμείρομαι, *to long for*, 1 Thess. ii. 8 (W. H.).*
ὁμιλέω, ῶ, ήσω, *to be in company with, to associate with* (dat.), *to talk with* (πρός, acc.), Luke xxiv. 14, 15; Acts xx. 11, xxiv. 26.*
ὁμιλία, ας, ἡ, *intercourse, converse, discourse*, 1 Cor. xv. 33; "homily."*
ὅμιλος, ου, ὁ, *a crowd, company*, Rev. xviii. 17 (not W. H.).*
ὁμίχλη, ης, ἡ, *a mist*, 2 Pet. ii. 17 (W. H.).*
ὄμμα, ατος, τό, *an eye*, Matt. xx. 34 (W. H.); Mark viii. 23.*
ὄμνυμι and **ὀμνύω**, ὀμόσω (see § 116, 3), *to swear, to take an oath*, Mark xiv. 71; *to promise with an oath*, Mark vi. 23.
ὁμο-θυμαδόν, adv., *with one mind, unanimously, with one accord*, only in Acts and Rom. xv. 6.
ὁμοιάζω, σω, *to be like*, Mark xiv. 70 (not W. H.).*
ὁμοιο-παθής, οῦς, ὁ, ἡ, *being affected like another* (dat.), *having like passions or feelings*, Acts xiv. 15; James v. 17.*
ὅμοιος, οία, οιον, *like, similar to, resembling* (dat.), *of equal rank*, Matt. xxii. 39. Once with gen., John viii. 55. Adv., -ως, *in like manner, likewise*.
ὁμοιότης, ητος, ἡ, *likeness, similitude*, Heb. iv. 15, vii. 15.*

ὁμοιόω, ῶ, (1) *to render like;* pass., *to be like,* or *to resemble,* Matt. vi. 8, xiii. 24; Acts xiv. 11; (2) *to liken, to compare,* Matt. vii. 24; Mark iv. 30; with acc. and dat.

ὁμοίωμα, ατος, τό, *likeness, similitude,* Rom. i. 23, v. 14, v 5, viii. 3; Phil. ii. 7; Rev. ix. 7.*

ὁμοίωσις, εως, ἡ, *likeness, resemblance,* James iii. 9.*

ὁμο-λογέω, ῶ, ήσω, 1st aor. ὡμολόγησα, *to speak the same thing;* hence, (1) *to confess,* in the sense of conceding or admitting, generally with ὅτι; (2) *to profess,* or *acknowledge openly,* acc., or with ἐν, Matt. x. 32; Luke xii. 8; John ix. 22; (3) as ἐξομολογέω, *to praise, to give thanks* (dat.), Heb. xiii. 15.

ὁμολογία, ας, ἡ, *a profession,* 2 Cor. ix. 13; 1 Tim. vi. 12, 13; Heb. iii. 1, iv. 14, x. 23.*

ὁμολογουμένως, adv., *by consent of all, confessedly, without controversy,* 1 Tim. iii. 16.*

ὁμό-τεχνος, ον, *of the same art* or *craft,* Acts xviii. 3.*

ὁμοῦ, adv., *together, at the same place* or *time.*

ὁμό-φρων, ονος (φρήν), *of the same mind,* 1 Pet. iii. 8.*

ὁμόω. See ὄμνυμι.

ὅμως, adv., *yet, nevertheless,* 1 Cor. xiv. 7; Gal. iii. 15; with μέντοι, *notwithstanding,* John xii. 42.*

ὄναρ, τό, indecl., *a dream;* κατ' ὄναρ, *in a dream,* Matt. i. 20, ii. 12, 13, 19, 22, xxvii. 19.*

ὀνάριον, ἰον, τό (dim. of ὄνος), *a young ass, an ass's colt,* John xii. 14.*

ὀνειδίζω, σω, *to reproach, revile, upbraid,* Matt. xi. 20; Mark xvi. 14.

ὀνειδισμός, οῦ, ὁ, *reproach, reviling, contumely,* Rom. xv. 3; 1 Tim. iii. 7; Heb. x. 33, xi. 26, xiii. 13.*

ὄνειδος, ους, τό, *reproach,* Luke i. 25.*

'Ονήσιμος, ου (*profitable*), *Onesimus,* Col. iv. 9; Philem. 10.*

'Ονησί-φορος, ου, ὁ, *Onesiphorus,* 2 Tim. i. 16, iv. 19.*

ὀνικός, ή, όν, *pertaining to an ass;* μύλος ὀνικός, *a millstone turned by an ass, i.e.,* the large upper millstone, Matt. xviii. 6; Luke xvii. 2 (not W. H.); Mark ix. 42 (W. H.).*

ὀνίνημι, *to be of use to;* mid. aor., opt., ὀναίμην, *may I have help* or *joy from,* Philem. 20.*

ὄνομα, ατος, τό, *a name,* almost always of persons; in N.T., as in O.T., the *name* of a person is a mark of what he himself is; the name expresses the character, Matt. i. 21; Mark iii. 16, v. 9; Luke i. 31: hence the expressions ποιεῖν τι ἐπὶ τῷ ὀνόματι, ἐν τῷ ὀνόματι, διὰ τοῦ ὀνόματος; the name is often introduced by ὀνόματι, *by name,* once by τοὔνομα [τὸ ὄνομα], Matt. xxvii. 57; *fame, reputation,* Eph. i. 21; Phil. ii. 9.

ὀνομάζω, σω, *to give a name to,* Luke vi. 13, 14; *to mention,* Eph. v. 3; *to call upon* or *profess the name of,* 2 Tim. ii. 19.

ὄνος, ου, ὁ, ἡ, *an ass.*

ὄντως, adv. (ὄν, neut. part. of εἰμί), *really, in very deed.*

ὄξος, ους, τό, *vinegar;* in N.T., *a poor wine,* mixed with water, a common drink of Roman soldiers.

ὀξύς, εῖα, ύ, (1) *sharp,* as a weapon, Rev.; (2) *swift, eager,* Rom. iii. 15.*

ὀπή, ῆς, ἡ, *an opening, a cavern,* James iii. 11; Heb. xi. 38.*

ὄπισθεν, adv., *behind, after, at the back of.*

ὀπίσω, adv., *behind, after,* of place, Luke vii. 38; of time, Matt. iii. 11; abs., or with gen.; τὰ ὀπίσω, *those things that are behind,* Phil. iii. 13; εἰς τὰ ὀπίσω, *backward,* John xviii. 6. ι

ὁπλίζω, σω, N.T., mid., *to arm oneself* with, acc., fig., 1 Pet. iv. 1.*

ὅπλον, ον, τό, *an instrument,* perhaps Rom. vi. 13 (see R.V. and marg.); hence, plur., *arms, armour,* John xviii. 3; Rom. xiii. 12; 2 Cor. vi. 7, x. 4.*

ὁποῖος, οἵα, οἵον, relat. pron., *of what kind* or *manner,* correl. to τοιοῦτος, Acts xxvi. 29; 1 Cor. iii. 13; Gal. ii. 6; 1 Thess. i. 9; James i. 24.*

ὁπότε, adv. of time, *when,* Luke vi. 3 (W. H., ὅτε).*

ὅπου, adv. of place, *where, whither; where,* referring to state, Col. iii. 11; *whereas,* 1 Cor. iii. 3.

ὀπτάνω, in pass., *to appear,* Acts i. 3. See ὁράω.*

ὀπτασία, ας, ἡ, *a vision, a supernatural appearance,* Luke i. 22, xxiv. 23; Acts xxvi. 19; 2 Cor. xii. 1.*

ὀπτός, ή, όν, roasted, broiled, Luke xxiv. 42.*
ὅπτω, ὅπτομαι. See ὁράω.
ὀπ-ώρα, ας, ἡ (perhaps ὀπός, juice), the autumn, autumnal fruits, Rev. xviii. 14.*
ὅπως, rel. adv., how, Luke xxiv. 20. As conj., in such manner that, to the end that, so that; with ἄν, Acts iii. 19 (see § 384, 2). After verbs of beseeching, and the like, with demonstrative force, that, Matt. ix. 38; Mark iii. 6.
ὅραμα, ατος, τό, (1) a spectacle, Acts vii. 31; (2) a vision, Acts ix. 10, 12.
ὅρασις, εως, ἡ, appearance, aspect, Acts ii. 17; Rev. iv. 3, ix. 17.*
ὁρατός, ή, όν, visible, seen, plur., neut., Col. i. 16.*
ὁράω, ῶ, ὄψομαι, ἑώρακα, εἶδον (see § 103, 4), (1) to see, generally; (2) to look upon or contemplate; (3) to see, and so to participate in, Luke xvii. 22; John iii. 36; (4) to take heed, Heb. viii. 5; Matt. viii. 4; with μή or equiv., to beware, Matt. xvi. 6; (5) pass., to be seen, to appear to, to present oneself to (dat.). Syn. 5.
ὀργή, ῆς, ἡ, anger, indignation. Often of the wrath of God, and its manifestation. Syn. 32.
ὀργίζω, σω, to irritate; pass., to be angry, abs.; to be enraged with, dat., or ἐπί, dat.
ὀργίλος, η, ον, prone to anger, Tit. i. 7.*
ὀργυιά, ᾶς, ἡ, a fathom, the length from finger's end to finger's end with both arms stretched outwards, Acts xxvii. 28.*
ὀρέγω, to stretch out; mid., to reach after, to desire or long eagerly for, gen., 1 Tim. iii. 1, vi. 10; Heb. xi. 16.*
ὀρεινός, ή, όν, mountainous, hilly, Luke i. 39, 65.*
ὄρεξις, εως, ἡ, strong desire, lust, Rom. i. 27.*
ὀρθο-ποδέω, ῶ, to walk in a straight course, fig., to walk uprightly, Gal. ii. 14.*
ὀρθός, ή, όν, upright, Acts xiv. 10; straight, Heb. xii. 13;* adv., -ῶς, rightly, Mark vii. 35; Luke vii. 43, x. 28, xx. 21.*
ὀρθο-τομέω, ῶ (τέμνω), to cut straight or rightly, to manage or administer rightly, 2 Tim. ii. 15.*

ὀρθρίζω, to rise early, to do anything n early morning, Luke xxi. 38.*
ὀρθρινός, ή, όν, belonging to early morning, Luke xxiv. 22 (W. H.); Rev. xxii. 16 (not W. H.).*
ὄρθριος, ία, ιον, adj., early in the morning, Luke xxiv. 22 (W. H. read preceding).*
ὄρθρος, ου, masc., morning twilight, early dawn, daybreak, Luke xxiv. 1; John viii. (W. H. omit); Acts v. 21.*
ὁρίζω, σω (comp. "horizon"), to define, determine, Rom. i. 4; Heb. iv. 7; to appoint, to decree, as Acts xvii. 26; pass., perf., part., ὡρισμένος, decreed, Acts ii. 23; neut., decree, Luke xxii. 22.
ὅριον, ίου, τό, plur., the borders of a place; hence, districts, territory.
ὁρκίζω, to adjure by, to charge solemnly by, with double acc., Mark v. 7; Acts xix. 13; 1 Thess. v. 27 (W. H., ἐνορκίζω).*
ὅρκος, ου, ὁ, an oath, Matt. xiv. 7, 9; a promise with an oath, Matt. v. 33.
ὁρκ-ωμοσία, ας, ἡ, an oath, Heb. vii. 20, 21, 28.*
ὁρμάω, ῶ, σω, N.T., intrans., to rush, Matt. viii. 32; Acts vii. 57 (εἰς, or ἐπί, acc.).
ὁρμή, ῆς, ἡ, a rush, a violent assault, Acts v. 5; James iii. 4.*
ὅρμημα, ατος, τό, a rushing on, violence, Rev. xviii. 21.*
ὄρνεον, ου, τό, a bird of prey, a fowl, Rev. xviii. 2, xix. 17, 21.*
ὄρνις, ιθος, ὁ, ἡ, a fowl, Matt. xxiii. 37; Luke xiii. 34.*
ὁρο-θεσία, ας, ἡ, a setting bounds or limits, Acts xvii. 26.*
ὄρος, ους, τό, a mountain, highland.
ὀρύσσω, ξω, to dig, to dig out, Matt. xxi. 33, xxv. 18; Mark xii. 1.*
ὀρφανός, ή, όν, bereaved, "orphan," John xiv. 18; as subst., James i. 27.*
ὀρχέομαι, οῦμαι, ήσομαι, dep., mid., to leap, to dance, Matt. xi. 17, xiv. 6; Mark vi. 22; Luke vii. 32.*
ὅς, ἥ, ὅ, relative pronoun, who, which (see §§ 58, 343–348; for ὃς ἄν, ὃς ἐάν, whoever, see § 380). As demonst. in the phrase, ὃς μέν...ὃς δέ, that one... this one, as 2 Cor. ii. 16.
ὁσάκις, rel. adv., how many times, as often as, always with ἐάν, 1 Cor. xi. 25, 26; Rev. xi. 6.*

ὅσιος (ία), ιον, *holy*, of human beings, of Christ, and of God ; τὰ ὅσια, *the holy promises*, Acts xiii. 34 ; adv., -ως, *holily*, only 1 Thess. ii. 10. **Syn. 23.**

ὁσιότης, ητος, ἡ, *holiness, godliness*, Luke i. 75 ; Eph. iv. 24.*

ὀσμή, ῆς, ἡ, *an odour, savour*, lit., John xii. 3 ; fig., 2 Cor. ii. 14, 16 ; Eph. v. 2 ; Phil. iv. 18.*

ὅσος, η, ον, relat. pron., *how much, how great*, (1) of time, *how long, as long as*, Rom. vii. 1. Repeated, the meaning is intensified, Heb. x. 37 : ἔπι μικρὸν ὅσον ὅσον, *yet a little, a very, very little;* (2) of quantity, of number, *how much*, plur., *how many*, Mark iii. 8 ; John vi. 11 ; Acts ix. 13 ; *as many as*, Matt. xiv. 36 ; with ἄν, ἐάν, *as many as, whatsoever*, Matt. vii. 12, xxi. 22 ; (3) of measure, degree, Heb. vii. 20.

ὅσ-περ, ἥ-περ, ὅ-περ, *the very one who*, Mark xv. 6.*

ὀστέον, contr. ὀστοῦν, ου, τό, *a bone*, John xix. 36.

ὅσ-τις, ἥ-τις, ὅτι, compound relat., *whosoever, whichsoever, whatsoever* (see §§ 58, c, 349) ; the addition of ἄν, ἐάν, gives indefiniteness.

ὀστράκινος, η, ον, *made of earth, earthen*, 2 Cor. iv. 7 ; 2 Tim. ii. 20.*

ὄσφρησις, εως, *the sense of smell, the organ of smell*, 1 Cor. xii. 17.*

ὀσφύς, ύος, ἡ, *the loins*, Matt. iii. 4 ; Acts ii. 30; to "have the loins girded" was to have the robes gathered up so as to be ready for work, Luke xii. 35 ; fig., 1 Pet. i. 13.

ὅταν (ὅτε, ἄν), rel. adv., *when, whensoever;* always with subj. except Mark iii. 11 ; Rev. iv. 9, viii. 1 (W.H.).

ὅτε, rel. adv., *when.*

ὅτι, conj., (1) *that*, after verbs of declaring, etc., introducing the object-sentence ; sometimes as a mere quotation mark, Matt. ii. 23 ; (2) *because* (see § 136, 6).

ὅτου (gen. of ὅστις), ἕως ὅτου, *until, whilst*, as Luke xxii. 16.

οὗ, adv. (gen. of ὅς), *where, whither;* οὗ ἐάν, *whithersoever;* also used of time, *when*, in the phrases, ἀφ᾽ οὗ, *since*, ἄχρις, ἕως, μέχρις οὗ, *until.*

οὐ (οὐκ before a vowel, οὐχ if the vowel is aspirated), *no, not* (see §§ 134, 401).

οὐά, interj., *ah! aha!* derisive, Mark xv. 29.*

οὐαί, interj., *woe! alas!* uttered in grief or indignation, Matt. xi. 21 ; 1 Cor. ix. 16 ; ἡ οὐαί, as subst., Rev. ix. 12, *the woe, the calamity.*

οὐδαμῶς, adv., *by no means, not in anywise*, Matt. ii. 6.*

οὐ-δέ, conj., disj. neg., *but not, nor yet* (cf. μηδέ), *neither, nor, not even* (see § 401).

οὐδ-είς, οὐδε-μία, οὐδ-έν (οὐδὲ εἷς), neg. adj., *not one, no one, none, nothing, of no moment, of no value, vain.*

οὐδέ-ποτε, adv., *not ever, never*, 1 Cor. xiii. 8, Matt. vii. 23.

οὐδέ-πω, adv., *not ever yet, not yet, never*, Luke xxiii. 53.

οὐθείς, οὐθέν (οὔτε εἷς), *no one, nothing*, Acts xxvi. 26 (W. H.) ; 1 Cor. xiii. 2, 2 Cor. xi. 9 (W. H.).*

οὐκ-έτι, adv., *no further, no more, no longer.*

οὐκ-οῦν ; adv., *not so then?* hence, in ordinary classic usage, an affirmative adverb, *therefore* (whereas οὔκουν retains its negative force, *not therefore*) ; interrogative, John xviii. 37, *art thou then a king?*

οὐ μή, an emphatic negative (see § 377).

οὖν, conj., *therefore, then*, Matt. xii. 12. Employed espec. (1) in arguing, 1 Cor. iv. 16 ; (2) in exhortation, Matt. xxii. 9, 17, 21 ; (3) in interrogation, Matt. xiii. 27 ; Gal. iii. 19, 21 ; (4) to resume an interrupted subject, Mark iii. 31 ; John xi. 6 ; (5) to indicate mere transition from one point to another, most frequently in John, as viii. 13.

οὔ-πω, adv., *not yet.*

οὐρά, ᾶς, ἡ, *the tail* of an animal.

οὐράνιος, ον, *heavenly, celestial, in* or *pertaining to heaven*, as Luke ii. 13 ; Acts xxvi. 19.

οὐρανόθεν, adv., *from heaven*, Acts xiv. 17, xxvi. 13.*

οὐρανός, οῦ, ὁ, *heaven*, (1) *the visible heavens* (both sing. and plur.), through their whole extent, *the atmosphere, the sky, the starry heavens;* (2) *the spiritual heavens*, the abode of God and holy beings, Matt. vi. 10 ; 2 Cor. xii. 2 ; "the third heaven," above the atmospheric and the sidereal ; met., for the inhabitants of heaven, Rev.

xviii. 20; especially for God, Luke xv. 18.

Οὐρβανός, οῦ, ὁ, *Urban*, Rom. xvi. 9.*

Οὐρίας, ου, ὁ, *Uriah*, Matt. i. 6.*

οὖς, ὠτός, τό, (1) *the ear*, Matt. x. 27; (2) met., *the faculty of apprehension*, Matt. xi. 15.

οὐσία, ας, ἡ (ὤν, partic. εἰμί), *substance, wealth*, Luke xv. 12, 13.*

οὔ-τε, conj., *and not; neither, nor*, with a negative preced.; οὔτε ... οὔτε, *neither ... nor*. (The readings often vary between οὔτε and οὐδέ.)

οὗτος, αὔτη, τοῦτο, demonstr. pron., *this* (near), appl. to persons and things, sometimes emphatic, Matt. v. 19; sometimes contemptuous, *this fellow*, Matt. xiii. 55 (see §§ 338-342; also ἐκεῖνος and ὅδε).

οὔτως (and before a consonant sometimes οὔτω), adv., *thus, in this wise, so*, (1) in reference to antecedent or following statement; (2) correlative with ὡς or καθώς, *so ... as*; (3) qualifying adjectives, adverbs, or verbs, *so*, Heb. xii. 21; Matt. ix. 33; οὔτως ... οὔτως, 1 Cor. vii. 7, *in this manner ... in that*.

οὐχί, adv., (1) an intensive form of οὐ, John xiii. 10, *by no means, no, nay*; (2) mostly interrog., as Matt. v. 46, expecting an affirmative answer.

ὀφειλέτης, ου, *a debtor*, Matt. xviii. 24; *one who owes morally*, i.e., obedience to the law, Gal. v. 3; *a delinquent, sinner*, Luke xiii. 4.

ὀφειλή, ῆς, ἡ, *a debt, a duty*, Matt. xviii. 32; Rom. xiii. 7; 1 Cor. vii. 3 (W. H.).*

ὀφείλημα, ατος, τό, *a debt, what is justly due*, Rom. iv. 4; fig., *an offence, a fault, a failure in duty*, Matt. vi. 12. **Syn. 39.***

ὀφείλω, (1) *to owe* (acc. and dat.), Matt. xviii. 28; τὸ ὀφειλόμενον, *the due*, Matt. xviii. 30; (2) *to be under obligation*, Matt. xxiii. 16; hence, *to sin against*, Luke xi. 4. **Syn. 39.**

ὄφελον (see § 378), interj., *O that! I wish! would that!* followed by indicative, 1 Cor. iv. 8; Gal. v. 12; Rev. iii. 15.*

ὄφελος, ους, τό (ὀφέλλω, *to increase*), *profit, utility*, 1 Cor. xv. 32; James ii. 14, 16.*

ὀφθαλμο-δουλεία, ας, ἡ, *eye-service*, Eph. vi. 6; Col. iii. 22.*

ὀφθαλμός, οῦ, ὁ, *an eye;* fig., of the eye as the receptive channel into mind and heart, Matt. vi. 23 (comp. Mark vii. 22; Matt. xx. 15); fig., *the eye of the mind*, i.e., *the understanding*, Acts xxvi. 18.

ὄφις, εως, ὁ, *a serpent*, Matt. vii. 10; an emblem of wisdom, Matt. x. 16; of cunning, Matt. xxiii. 33; used symbol. for Satan, 2 Cor. xi. 3.

ὀφρύς, ύος, ἡ, *the eyebrow; the brow* of a mountain or hill, Luke iv. 29.*

ὀχλέω, ῶ, *to disturb, to vex*, only in pass., Luke vi. 18 (W. H., ἐνοχλέω), Acts v. 16.*

ὀχλο-ποιέω, ῶ, *to gather a crowd*, Acts xvii. 5.*

ὄχλος, ου, ὁ, *a crowd, the common people, the multitude*, plur., *crowds*. **Syn. 73.**

ὀχύρωμα, ατος, τό, *a fortress, a strong place of defence*, 2 Cor. x. 4.*

ὀψάριον, ου, τό (a relish with bread), *a little fish*, John vi. 9, 11, xxi. 9, 10, 13.*

ὀψέ, adv., *late, in the evening*, Mark xi. 11 (W. H.), 19, xiii. 35; *at the end of, after*, gen., Matt. xxviii. 1.*

ὄψιμος, ον, *latter*, of the rain, James v. 7.*

ὄψιος, ία, ιον, *late*, Mark xi. 11 (not W. H.; see marg.); as subst., ἡ ὀψία, *evening*, i.e., the former of the two evenings reckoned among the Jews, Matt. viii. 16; the latter evening is mentioned, Matt. xiv. 23; comp. ver. 15.

ὄψις, εως, ἡ, *the aspect, the countenance*, John xi. 44; Rev. i. 16; *external appearance*, John vii. 24.*

ὀψώνιον, ου, τό, lit., *relish, sauce*, like ὀψάριον, (1) plur., the *rations* of soldiers, their *wages*, Luke iii. 14; 1 Cor. ix. 7. Hence, (2) *recompense*, generally, Rom. vi. 23; 2 Cor. xi. 8.*

Π.

Π, π, πῖ, *pi, p*, the sixteenth letter. As a numeral, π′ = 80; π͵ = 80,000.

παγιδεύω, σω, *to ensnare, to lie in wait for*, fig., Matt. xxii. 15.*

παγίς, ίδος, ἡ, *a snare, a trap*, Luke xxi. 35; Rom. xi. 9; 1 Tim. iii. 7, vi. 9; 2 Tim. ii. 26.*

πάγος, ου, ὁ, a hill; only with the adj. Ἄρειος, Mars' Hill, Areopagus, Acts xvii. 19, 22.*
πάθημα, ατος, τό, (1) suffering, affliction, Rom. viii. 18; (2) affection of mind, passion, Rom. vii. 5; Gal. v. 24.
παθητός, ή, όν, destined to suffer, Acts xxvi. 23.*
πάθος, ους, τό, suffering, emotion, in N.T., of an evil kind, concupiscence, Rom. i. 26; 1 Thess. iv. 5; Col. iii. 5.*
παιδ-αγωγός, οῦ, ὁ, a boys' leader or guardian, a slave who had the charge of the boys of a family during their nonage, 1 Cor. iv. 15; Gal. iii. 24, 25; "paedagogue."*
παιδάριον, ίου, τό (dim. of παῖς), a boy, a lad, Matt. xi. 16 (W. H., παιδίον); John vi. 9.*
παιδεία, ας, ἡ, training, of children and youth, Eph. vi. 4; hence, instruction, 2 Tim. iii. 16; chastisement, correction, Heb. xii. 5–11.*
παιδευτής, οῦ, ὁ, (1) an instructor, a preceptor, Rom. ii. 20; (2) a corrector, a chastiser, Heb. xii. 9.*
παιδεύω, σω, to train a child; hence, (1) to instruct, to admonish; (2) to correct, to chasten. Syn. 14.
παιδιόθεν, adv., from childhood, Mark ix. 21.*
παιδίον, ίου, τό (dim. of παῖς), a little child, an infant, Matt. ii. 8; a child more advanced, Matt. xiv. 21; fig., 1 Cor. xiv. 20. Syn. 62.
παιδίσκη, ης, ἡ (fem. dim. of παῖς), a young girl, a female slave, a bondmaid.
παίζω, ξομαι, to play, as a child, to dance, as in idolatrous worship, 1 Cor. x. 7.*
παῖς, παιδός, ὁ, ἡ, (1) a child, a boy or girl; (2) a servant, a slave, as Acts iv. 27 (R.V.); ὁ παῖς τοῦ Θεοῦ, the servant of God, used of any servant, Luke i. 69; of the Messiah, Matt. xii. 18. Syn. 62.
παίω, σω, to strike, to smite, with the fist, Matt. xxvi. 68; Luke xxii. 64; with a sword, Mark xiv. 47; John xviii. 10; as a scorpion with its sting, Rev. ix. 5.*
πάλαι, adv., of old, formerly, long ago, Heb. i. 1.
παλαιός, ά, όν, (1) old, former, ancient; ὁ παλαιὸς ἄνθρωπος, the old or former man, i.e., man in his old, unrenewed nature, Rom. vi. 6; (2) worn out, as a garment, Matt. ix. 16; corrupt, vitiated. Syn. 25.
παλαιότης, ητος, ἡ, age, oldness, Rom. vii. 6.*
παλαιόω, ῶ, ώσω, to make old, Heb. viii. 13; pass., to grow old, to become obsolete, Luke xii. 33; Heb. i. 11, viii. 13.*
πάλη, ης, ἡ, a wrestling, a struggle, Eph. vi. 12.*
παλιγ-γενεσία (W. H., παλινγ-), ᾶς, ἡ, a new birth, renovation, regeneration, Matt. xix. 28; Tit. iii. 5.*
πάλιν, adv., again, back, used of place or of time; a particle of continuation, again, once more, further; and of antithesis, as 2 Cor. x. 7, on the other hand.
παμ-πληθεί, adv., all at once, the whole crowd together, Luke xxiii. 18.*
πάμ-πολυς, παμπόλλη, πάμπολυ, very great, vast, Mark viii. 1 (not W. H.).*
Παμφυλία, ας, ἡ, Pamphylia.
παν-δοχεῖον, ου, τό, a khan, a caravanserai, or Eastern inn, Luke x. 34.*
παν-δοχεύς, έως, ὁ (δέχομαι), the keeper of a khan or caravanserai, a host, Luke x. 35.*
παν-ήγυρις, ιδος, ἡ (ἀγείρω), a general assembly, a public convocation, Heb. xii. 23.*
παν-οικί, adv., with one's whole household or family, Acts xvi. 34.*
πανοπλία, ας, ἡ, complete armour, "panoply," Luke xi. 22; Eph. vi. 11, 13.*
παν-ουργία, ας, ἡ, shrewdness, skill; hence, cunning, craftiness, Luke xx. 23; 1 Cor. iii. 19; 2 Cor. iv. 2, xi. 3; Eph. iv. 14.*
παν-οῦργος, ον (ἔργον, ϝεργ-), doing everything, cunning, crafty, 2 Cor. xii. 16.*
πανταχῇ, adv., everywhere, Acts xxi. 28 (W. H.).*
πανταχόθεν, adv., from all sides, Mark i. 45 (W. H., πάντοθεν).*
πανταχοῦ, adv., in every place, everywhere.
παντελής, ές, gen. οῦς, complete; εἰς τὸ παντελές, perfectly, to the uttermost, Heb. vii. 25; the same phrase, with μή, in no wise, Luke xiii. 11.*
πάντῃ, adv., in every way, Acts xxiv. 3.*

πάντοθεν, adv., *from every place*, Mark i. 45 (W. H.); Luke xix. 43; Heb. ix. 4.*
παντο-κράτωρ, ορος, ὁ, *the Almighty*.
πάντοτε, adv., *always, at all times, ever*, Matt. xxvi. 11.
πάντως, adv., *wholly, entirely*, 1 Cor. v. 10; *in every way, by all means*, Rom. iii. 9; *assuredly, certainly*, Acts xviii. 21.
παρά, prep., gov. the gen., the dat., and accus., *beside*. With a gen. (of person), it indicates *source* or *origin*; with a dat., it denotes *presence with*; with an accus., it indicates motion *towards*, or *alongside*, and is employed in comparisons, *beyond*. For details see § 306. IN COMPOSITION, παρά retains its general meaning, *besides*, sometimes denoting *nearness*, sometimes *motion by* or *past*, so as to miss or fail; occasionally also stealthiness (*by the way*), as in παρεισάγω.
παρα-βαίνω, 2nd aor. παρέβην, *to go aside from, to desert*, Acts i. 25; *to transgress*, Matt. xv. 2, 3; 2 John 9 (W. H., προάγω).*
παρα-βάλλω, "*to place side by side*," (1) *to compare*, Mark iv. 30 (not W. H.); (2) *to betake oneself any whither, arrive*, Acts xx. 15.*
παρά-βασις, εως, ἡ, *a transgression*, Rom. ii. 23. Syn. 39.
παρα-βάτης, ου, ὁ, *a transgressor*, Rom. ii. 25, 27; Gal. ii. 18; James ii. 9, 11.*
παρα-βιάζομαι, *to constrain by persuasion*, Luke xxiv. 29; Acts xvi. 15.*
παρα-βολεύομαι, *to expose oneself to peril, to be regardless of life*, Phil. ii. 30 (W. H.).*
παρα-βολή, ῆς, ἡ, "*a placing side by side*," (1) *a comparison*, Heb. ix. 9; (2) *a parable*, often of those uttered by our Lord; (3) *a proverb, an adage*, Luke iv. 23; (4) possibly in Heb. xi. 19; *a crisis of danger* (see παραβολεύομαι). Syn. 46.
παρ-αγγελία, ας, ἡ, *a command, a charge*, Acts v. 28, xvi. 24; 1 Thess. iv. 2; 1 Tim. i. 5, 18.*
παρ-αγγέλλω, *to notify, to command, to charge*, Luke ix. 21; 2 Thess. iii. 4; dat. of pers., acc. of thing, or ὅτι, ἵνα or inf., 1 Tim. vi. 13.

παρα-γίνομαι, *to come beside, come near, come, come against* (ἐπί, πρός), Luke xii. 51, xxii. 52; John iii. 23; Heb. ix. 11.
παρ-άγω, *to pass by*, Matt. xx. 30; *to depart*, Matt. ix. 27; *to pass away*, act. 1 Cor. vii. 31; mid., only 1 John ii. 8, 17.
παρα-δειγματίζω, *to make a public example of, to expose to ignominy*, Matt. i. 19 (W. H., δειγματίζω); Heb. vi. 6.*
παράδεισος, ου, ὁ (a Persian word, "garden," "park"), *Paradise*, Luke xxiii. 43; 2 Cor. xii. 4; Rev. ii. 7.*
παρα-δέχομαι, dep., mid., *to receive, admit, approve*, Mark iv. 20; Acts xv. 4 (W. H.), xvi. 21, xxii. 18; 1 Tim. v. 19; Heb. xii. 6:*
παρα-δια-τριβή, ῆς, ἡ, *useless occupation*, or *agitation about trifles*, 1 Tim. vi. 5 (W. H., διαπαρατριβή).*
παρα-δίδωμι, acc. and dat., (1) *to deliver over*, as to prison, judgment, or punishment, Matt. iv. 12; *to betray*, spec. of the betrayal by Judas; (2) *to surrender, abandon* oneself, Eph. iv. 19; (3) *to hand over, entrust, commit, deliver*, as Matt. xxv. 14; Luke i. 2; Acts vi. 14; (4) *to commend* to kindness, Acts xiv. 26; (5) *to give* or *prescribe*, as laws, etc., Acts vi. 14; (6) prob. *to permit*, in Mark iv. 29, *when the fruit permits* or *allows*.
παρά-δοξος, ον, *strange, wonderful*, Luke v. 26; "*paradox*."*
παρά-δοσις, εως, ἡ, *an instruction*, or *tradition*, Matt. xv. 2; 1 Cor. xi. 2; 2 Thess. ii. 15, iii. 6. Syn. 49.
παρα-ζηλόω, ῶ, *to excite to emulation*, Rom. xi. 11, 14; *to jealousy*, Rom. x. 19; *to anger*, 1 Cor. x. 22.*
παρα-θαλάσσιος, ία, ιον, *by the seaside*, Matt. iv. 13.*
παρα-θεωρέω, ῶ, *to overlook, neglect*, Acts vi. 1.*
παρα-θήκη, ης, ἡ. *a deposit, anything committed to one's charge*, 1 Tim. vi. 20 (W. H.); 2 Tim. i. 12, 14 (W. H.).*
παρ-αινέω, ῶ, *to exhort, admonish*, Acts xxvii. 9, 22.*
παρ-αιτέομαι, οῦμαι, dep., mid., *to beg off, make excuse, refuse, reject*, Luke xiv. 18, 19; Acts xxv. 11; 1 Tim. iv. 7, v. 11; 2 Tim. ii. 23; Tit. iii. 10; Heb. xii. 19, 25.*

παρα-καθίζω, intrans., to sit by the side of, Luke x. 39.*
παρα-καλέω, ῶ, έσω, (1) to send for, invite, Acts xxviii. 20; (2) to beseech, entreat, Mark i. 40; (3) to exhort, admonish, Acts xv. 32; 1 Tim. vi. 2; (4) to comfort, 2 Cor. i. 4; pass., to be comforted, Luke xvi. 25.
παρα-καλύπτω, to veil, to hide, Luke ix. 45.*
παρα-κατα-θήκη, ης, ἡ, a trust, a deposit, 1 Tim. vi. 20; 2 Tim. i. 14 (in both passages W. H. read παραθήκη).*
παρά-κειμαι, to be at hand, be present with (dat.), Rom. vii. 18, 21.*
παρά-κλησις, εως, ἡ, a calling for, "a summons to one's side." Hence, (1) exhortation, Heb. xii. 5; (2) entreaty, 2 Cor. viii. 4; (3) encouragement, Phil. ii. 1; (4) consolation, Rom. xv. 4; met., of the Consoler, Luke ii. 25; (5) generally, of the power of imparting all these, Acts iv. 36.
παρά-κλητος, ου, ὁ, (1) an advocate, intercessor, 1 John ii. 1; (2) a consoler, comforter, helper, John xiv. 16, 26, xv. 26, xvi. 7; "paraclete."*
παρ-ακοή, ῆς, ἡ, disobedience, Rom. v. 19; 2 Cor. x. 6; Heb. ii. 2.*
παρ-ακολουθέω, ῶ, ήσω, to follow closely, to accompany (dat.), Mark xvi. 17 (not W. H.; see marg.); to follow so as to trace out, to examine, Luke i. 3; to follow teaching, 1 Tim. iv. 6; 2 Tim. iii. 10.*
παρ-ακούω, to hear negligently, to disregard, Matt. xviii. 17; Mark v. 36 (W. H.).*
παρα-κύπτω, ψω, to stoop, Luke xxiv. 12, John xx. 5, 11; fig., with εἰς, to search into. James i. 25; 1 Pet. i. 12.*
παρα-λαμβάνω, λήψομαι (W. H., -λήμψ-), (1) to take to oneself, to take with one, to assume, obtain; (2) to take upon oneself, to engage in; fig., to receive intellectually, to learn, Mark vii. 4; to assent to, to acknowledge, to seize, to take, to carry captive.
παρα-λέγω, N.T., in mid., to lay one's course near, in sailing, to coast along, Acts xxvii. 8, 13.*
παρ-άλιος, ον, adjacent to the sea, on the coast, Luke vi. 17.*
παρ-αλλαγή, ῆς, ἡ, change, variableness, James i. 17.*

παρα-λογίζομαι, dep., to impose upon, to delude, acc., Col. ii. 4; James i. 22.*
παρα-λυτικός, ή, όν, palsied, "paralytic," in the whole or a part of the body.
παρα-λύω, to relax, to enfeeble, only perf., part., pass., παραλελυμένος, enfeebled, "paralysed."
παρα-μένω, μενῶ, to remain by (dat., or πρός, acc.), to abide with, 1 Cor. xvi. 6 (W. H., καταμένω); Phil. i. 25 (W. H.); fig., to remain constant in, James i. 25; to continue, Heb. vii. 23.*
παρα-μυθέομαι, οῦμαι, dep., mid., to speak kindly to, to cheer, to comfort, John ix. 19, 31; 1 Thess. ii. 11, v. 14.*
παρα-μυθία, as, ἡ, encouragement, comfort, 1 Cor. xiv. 3.*
παρα-μύθιον, ιου, τό, comfort, Phil. ii. 1.*
παρα-νομέω, ῶ, abs., to act contrary to law, Acts xxiii. 3.*
παρα-νομία, as, ἡ, violation of law, transgression, 2 Pet. ii. 16.*
παρα-πικραίνω, ανῶ, 1st aor. παρεπίκρᾱνα, to provoke (God) to anger; so, to rebel, Heb. iii. 16.*
παρα-πικρασμός, οῦ, ὁ, provocation (of God); so, rebellion, Heb. iii. 8, 15.*
παρα-πίπτω, 2nd aor. παρέπεσον, to fall away, Heb. vi. 6.*
παρα-πλέω, ῶ (Ϝ), εύσομαι, to sail past, acc., Acts xx. 16.*
παραπλήσιον, adv., near to (gen.), Phil. ii. 27.*
παραπλησίως, adv., likewise, in like manner, Heb. ii. 14.*
παρα-πορεύομαι, dep., mid., to pass by, to pass along by.
παρά-πτωμα, ατος, τό (πίπτω), a falling away or aside, a transgression. Syn. 39.
παραρ-ρέω (Ϝ), ῥεύσομαι, 2nd aor., pass., παρερρύην, pass., to drift away from (R. V.), to lose, Heb. ii. 1.*
παρά-σημος, ον, marked on the side (with, dat.), Acts xxviii. 11.*
παρα-σκευάζω, σω, perf., mid., παρεσκεύασμαι, to prepare, to make ready, Acts x. 10; mid., to prepare oneself, 1 Cor. xiv. 8; to be in readiness, 2 Cor. ix. 2, 3.*
παρα-σκευή, ῆς, ἡ, a preparation, i.e., the time immediately before a Sabbath or other festival, the eve, the Preparation (R.V.), Matt. xxvii. 62; Mark

xv. 42 ; Luke xxiii. 54 ; John xix. 14, 31, 42.*
παρα-τείνω, to ex.end to prolong, Acts xx. 7.*
παρα-ηρέω, ῶ, ήσω, (1) to observe narrowly, watch, Mark iii. 2; (2) to observe scrupulously, Gal. iv. 10.
παρα-τήρησις, εως, ἡ, a close watching, observation, Luke xvii. 20.*
παρα-τίθημι (see § 107), (1) to place near or by the side of, as food, Luke xi. 6 ; (2) to set or lay before, as instruction, spec. to propound, to deliver, as a parable, Matt. xiii. 24 ; mid., to give in charge to, to entrust, Luke xii. 48 ; to commend, to recommend (acc. and dat., or εἰς), Acts xiv. 23.
παρα-τυγχάνω, to fall in with, chance to meet, Acts xvii. 17.*
παρ-αυτίκα, adv., instantly, immediately; τὸ παραυτίκα ἐλαφρὸν τῆς θλίψεως, the momentary lightness of our affliction, 2 Cor. iv. 17.*
παρα-φέρω (see § 103, 6), to remove (acc. and ἀπό), Mark xiv. 36 ; Luke xxii. 42 ; pass., to be driven about, agitated, Heb. xiii. 9 (W. H.) ; Jude 12 (W. H.).*
παρα-φρονέω, ῶ, to be beside oneself, 2 Cor. xi. 23.*
παρα-φρονία, as, ἡ, being beside oneself, madness, folly, 2 Pet. ii. 16.*
παρα-χειμάζω, άσω, to winter, to spend the winter, Acts xxvii. 12, xxviii. 11 ; 1 Cor. xvi. 6 ; Tit. iii. 12.*
παρα-χειμασία, as, ἡ, a wintering, a spending the winter, Acts xxvii. 12.*
παρα-χρῆμα, adv. (lit., in the very thing), instantly, immediately.
πάρδαλις, εως, ἡ, a leopard, a panther, Rev. xiii. 2.*
παρ-εδρεύω, to wait upon (dat.), 1 Cor. ix. 13 (W. H.).*
πάρ-ειμι (εἰμί), to be near, to be present ; part., παρών, present ; τὸ παρόν, the present time ; τὰ παρόντα, possessions.
παρ-εισ-άγω, ξω, to introduce, to bring in clandestinely, 2 Pet. ii. 1.*
παρ-είσ-ακτος, ον, brought in clandestinely, surreptitious, Gal. ii. 4.*
παρ-εισ-δύω, or -ύνω, ύσω, to come in by stealth, to enter secretly, Jude 4.*
παρ-εισ-έρχομαι (see § 103, 2), (1) to enter clandestinely, Gal. ii. 4 ; (2) to come in addition, to be superadded, Rom. v. 20.*

παρ-εισ-φέρω, to bring in besides, add, 2 Pet. i. 5.*
παρ-εκτός, adv., on the outside, besides ; τὰ παρεκτός, things in addition, the things that are without, 2 Cor. xi. 28 (see R.V. marg.). With a gen. following, except, Matt. v. 32 ; Acts xxvi. 29 ; see also Matt. xix. 9, W. H. marg.*
παρ-εμ-βολή, ῆς, ἡ (βάλλω), (1) a camp, Heb. xiii. 11, 13 ; (2) soldiers' quarters, Acts xxi. 34, 37 ; (3) the encampments of Israel in the wilderness, Heb. xiii. 11 ; (4) an army in array, Heb. xi. 34.
παρ-εν-οχλέω, ῶ, to cause disturbance to, to disquiet (dat.), Acts xv. 19.*
παρ-επί-δημος, ον, residing in a strange country ; as subst., a stranger, foreigner, Heb. xi. 13 ; 1 Pet. i. 1, ii. 11.*
παρ-έρχομαι (see § 103, 2), (1) to pass by, with acc. of pers. or place ; (2) to pass, elapse, as time ; (3) to pass away or perish, become nugatory ; (4) to pass from any one ; (5) to pass carelessly, i.e., to disregard, neglect, transgress.
πάρ-εσις, εως, ἡ (ἵημι), passing over, prætermission, Rom. iii. 25. Syn. 42.*
παρ-έχω, έξω, 2nd aor. παρέσχον (dat. and acc.), (1) to exhibit, to present, afford, Luke vi. 29 ; Acts xxii. 2 ; espec. the phrase παρέχω κόπους, to cause trouble, Matt. xxvi. 10 ; (2) in mid., to present, manifest, Tit. ii. 7 ; to bestow, Col. iv. 1.
παρ-ηγορία, as, ἡ, solace, Col. iv. 11.*
παρθενία, as, ἡ, virginity, Luke ii. 36.*
παρθένος, ον, ἡ, a virgin, a maid ; hence one who is chaste, Rev. xiv. 4, applied to the male sex.
Πάρθος, ου, ὁ, a Parthian, Acts ii. 9.*
παρ-ίημι, to pass by or over, to relax ; pass., perf., part., παρειμένος, weary, Heb. xii. 12.*
παρ-ίστημι or παρ-ιστάνω (Rom. vi. 13, 16 ; see § 107), (1) trans. in act., pres., imp., fut., and 1st aor., to place near or at hand, to have in readiness, provide, Acts xxiii. 24 ; to present, to offer, Rom. vi. 13, 16 ; specially, to dedicate, consecrate, devote, Luke ii. 22; to cause to appear, to demonstrate, Acts xxiv. 13 ; (2) intrans., perf., plup., 2nd aor., and mid., to stand by, Mark xiv. 47, 69, 70 ; Luke xix. 24 ;

to have come, Mark iv. 29 ; *to stand by*, i.e., *for aid or support*, Rom. xvi. 2 ; *to stand in hostile array*, Acts iv. 26.
Παρμενᾶς, ᾶ, ὁ, *Parmenas*, Acts vi. 5.*
πάρ-οδος, ου, ἡ, *a passing by or through*, 1 Cor. xvi. 7.*
παρ-οικέω, ῶ, *to dwell in* (ἐν or εἰς, const. præg.) *as a stranger*, Luke xxiv. 18 ; Heb. xi. 9.*
παρ-οικία, ας, ἡ, *a sojourning, a temporary dwelling*, Acts xiii. 17 ; 1 Pet. i. 17.*
πάρ-οικος, ον, *sojourning, temporarily resident*, generally as subst., Acts vii. 6, 29 ; Eph. ii. 19 ; 1 Pet. ii. 11.*
παρ-οιμία, ας, ἡ (οἶμος, *a way*), (1) *a common or trite saying, a proverb*, 2 Pet. ii. 22 ; (2) *an obscure saying, an enigma*, John xvi. 25, 29 ; (3) *a parable, a comparative discourse*, John x. 6. Syn. 46.*
πάρ-οινος, ον, *given to wine, intemperate*, 1 Tim. iii. 3 ; Tit. i. 7.*
παρ-οίχομαι, *to pass away*, of time, Acts xiv. 16.*
παρ-ομοιάζω, *to resemble*, Matt. xxiii. 27.*
παρ-όμοιος, ον, *similar*, Mark vii. 8 (W. H. omit), 13.*
παρ-οξύνω, *to stir up, to irritate*, in pass., Acts xvii. 16 ; 1 Cor. xiii. 5.*
παρ-οξυσμός, οῦ, ὁ, (1) *incitement*, Heb. x. 24 ; (2) *sharp contention*, Acts xv. 39, "paroxysm."*
παρ-οργίζω, ιῶ, *to provoke greatly, exasperate*, Rom. x. 19 ; Eph. vi. 4.*
παρ-οργισμός, οῦ, ὁ, *exasperation, wrath*, Eph. iv. 26. Syn. 32.*
παρ-οτρύνω, *to stir up, to instigate*, Acts xiii. 50.*
παρ-ουσία, ας, ἡ (εἰμί), (1) *presence*, only 2 Cor. x. 10, Phil. ii. 20 ; elsewhere, (2) *a coming, an arrival, advent*, often of the second coming of Christ.
παρ-οψίς, ίδος, ἡ, *a dish for food or sauce*, Matt. xxiii. 25, 26.*
παρ-ρησία, ας, ἡ, *freedom, openness*, especially in speaking, *boldness, confidence ;* παρρησίᾳ, ἐν παρρησίᾳ, or μετὰ παρρησίας, *boldly, openly*.
παρ-ρησιάζομαι, dep., mid., 1st aor. ἐπαρρησιασάμην, *to speak freely, boldly, plainly, to be confident*.
πᾶς, πᾶσα, πᾶν (see § 37), *all, the whole, every kind of*. (See § 224, and for negative in phrases, § 328, iii.) Adverbial phrases are διαπαντός (which see), *always ;* ἐν παντί, ἐν πᾶσιν, *in everything ;* and πάντα (acc., neut., plur.), *altogether*.
πάσχα, τό (Heb., in Chald. form), *the paschal lamb, the passover feast ;* appl. to Christ, 1 Cor. v. 7.
πάσχω (παθ-, see § 94, i. 7), *to be affected with* anything, good or bad ; so, *to enjoy good*, Gal. iii. 4 ; more commonly, *to endure suffering*, Matt. xvii. 15 ; *to suffer* (acc. of that suffered, ἀπό or ὑπό, gen., of persons inflicting).
Πάταρα, άρων, τά, *Patara*, Acts xxi. 1.*
πατάσσω, ξω, *to smite, to strike, to smite to death, to afflict*, Matt. xxvi. 31 ; Acts xii. 23.
πατέω, ῶ, ήσω, *to tread, to trample on*, Luke x. 19 ; *to press by treading*, as grapes, Rev. xiv. 20, xix. 15 ; fig., *to tread down*, Luke xxi. 24 ; Rev. xi. 2.*
πατήρ, τρός, ὁ (see § 30, ii.), *a father ;* often of God as the Father of men, Matt. v. 16, 45 ; as the Father of the Lord Jesus Christ, Matt. vii. 21 ; as the First Person in the Trinity, Matt. xxviii. 19 ; as the Source of manifold blessings, 2 Cor. i. 3. Secondary meanings are : (1) *a remote progenitor, the founder of a race, an ancestor ;* (2) *a senior, a father in age*, 1 John ii. 13, 14 ; (3) *the author, or cause, or source of anything*, John viii. 44 ; Heb. xii. 9 ; (4) *a spiritual father*, or means of converting any one to Christ, 1 Cor. iv. 15 ; (5) *one to whom resemblance is borne*, John viii. 38, 41, 44.
Πάτμος, ου, ἡ, *Patmos*, Rev. i. 9.*
πατρ-αλῴας (W. H. -ολῴας), ου, ὁ, *a parricide*, 1 Tim. i. 9.*
πατριά, ᾶς, ἡ, *a family* (in O.T., mediate between the tribe and the household), Luke ii. 4 ; Acts iii. 25 ; Eph. iii. 15 (on which see § 224). Syn. 61.*
πατρι-άρχης, ου, ὁ, *head or founder of a family*, "patriarch," Acts ii. 29, vii. 8, 9 ; Heb. vii. 4.*
πατρικός, ή, όν, *paternal, ancestral*, Gal. i. 14.*
πατρίς, ίδος, ἡ, *one's native place, fatherland*, Matt. xiii. 54 ; Heb. xi. 14.
Πατρόβας, ᾶ, ὁ, *Patrobas*, Rom. xvi. 14.*
πατρο-παρά-δοτος, ον, *handed down, obtained by tradition from ancestors*, 1 Pet. i. 18.*

πατρῷος, α, ον, *paternal, hereditary*, Acts xxii. 3, xxiv. 14, xxviii. 17.*

Παῦλος, ου, ὁ, *Paul*, (1) Sergius Paulus, Acts xiii. 7; (2) the Apostle of the Gentiles. (See § 159, c.)

παύω, σω, *to cause to cease, to restrain,* 1 Pet. iii. 10; *generally* mid., *to cease, desist, refrain,* Luke v. 4, viii. 24.

Πάφος, ου, ἡ, *Paphos,* Acts xiii. 6, 13.*

παχύνω (παχύς), *to fatten, to make gross;* pass., fig., *to become gross or stupid,* Matt. xiii. 15; Acts xxviii. 27.*

πέδη, ης, ἡ, *a shackle, a fetter for the feet,* Mark v. 4; Luke viii. 29.*

πεδινός, ἡ, όν, *level, open,* Luke vi. 17.*

πεζεύω (πεζός), *to travel on foot or on land,* Acts xx. 13.*

πεζῇ, adv., *on foot, or by land,* Matt. xiv. 13; Mark vi. 33.*

πειθ-αρχέω, ῶ, (1) *to obey a ruler or one in authority,* Acts v. 29, 32; Tit. iii. 1; (2) *to obey, or conform to advice,* Acts xxvii. 21.*

πειθός (W. H., πιθός), ἡ, όν, *persuasive, winning,* 1 Cor. ii. 4.*

πείθω, πείσω, *to persuade,* but in the pres. and imperf. rather *to be persuading,* i.e., *to endeavour to convince,* Acts xviii. 4; *to influence by persuasion,* Matt. xxvii. 20; *to incite, to instigate,* Acts xiv. 29; *to appease, to render tranquil,* 1 John iii. 19; *to conciliate, to aspire to the favour of,* Gal. i. 10; pass., *to be confident of, to yield to persuasion, to assent, to listen to, to obey, to follow,* Acts v. 36, 37; the 2nd perf., πέποιθα, is intrans., *to be confident of, to trust, to rely on, to place hope in,* Matt. xxvii. 43; Rom. ii. 19.

πεινάω, ῶ, άσω, inf. πεινᾶν, (1) *to be hungry;* hence, (2) *to be needy;* (3) *to desire earnestly, to long for,* acc., "to pine."

πεῖρα, ας, ἡ, *trial, experiment;* with λαμβάνω, *to make trial of, attempt,* Heb. xi. 29, 36.*

πειράζω, σω, (1) *to attempt* (inf.); (2) *to tempt, to make trial of, to prove, to put to the proof* (acc.); (3) *to tempt to sin;* ὁ πειράζων, *the tempter,* i.e., *the devil.*

πειρασμός, οῦ, ὁ, *a trying, proving,* 1 Pet. iv. 12; Heb. iii. 8; *a tempting to sin,* Matt. vi. 13; *calamity, sore affliction,* as trying men, Acts xx. 19.

πειράω, ῶ, *only in* mid., *to attempt, essay,* Acts ix. 26 (W. H., πειράζω), xxvi. 21.*

πεισμονή, ῆς, ἡ, *persuasion, conviction,* Gal. v. 8.*

πέλαγος, ους, τό, *the sea, the deep,* Matt. xviii. 6; Acts xxvii. 5.*

πελεκίζω (πέλεκυς, *an axe*), *to behead,* Rev. xx. 4.*

πέμπτος, ἡ, όν, num., ord., *the fifth.*

πέμπω, ψω, (1) *to send,* of persons, *to despatch on a message,* spoken of teachers, as John Baptist, John i. 33; of Jesus, John iv. 34; of the Spirit, John xiv. 26; of apostles, John xiii. 20; (2) *to send,* of things, *to transmit,* Rev. xi. 10; *to send among or upon,* 2 Thess. ii. 11; perhaps *to thrust in the sickle,* Rev. xiv. 15, 18 (but probably to "send the sickle" is to "send forth the reapers").

πένης, ητος, ὁ, ἡ, *poor, needy,* 2 Cor. ix. 9. Syn. 30.*

πενθερά, ᾶς, ἡ, *a mother-in-law,* i.e., a wife's mother.

πενθερός, οῦ, ὁ, *a father-in-law,* i.e., a wife's father, John xviii. 13.*

πενθέω, ῶ, ήσω, (1) *to mourn,* intrans.; (2) *to mourn for,* trans., 2 Cor. xii. 21.

πένθος, ους, τό, *mourning, sorrow,* James iv. 9; Rev. xviii. 7, 8, xxi. 4.*

πενιχρός, ά, όν, *poor, needy,* Luke xxi. 2.*

πεντάκις, adv., num., *five times,* 2 Cor. xi. 24.*

πεντακισ-χίλιοι, αι, α, num., *five thousand.*

πεντακόσιοι, αι, α, num., *five hundred,* Luke vii. 41; 1 Cor. xv. 6.*

πέντε, num., indecl., *five.*

πεντε-και-δέκατος, num., ord., *fifteenth,* Luke iii. 1.*

πεντήκοντα, num., indecl., *fifty.*

Πεντηκοστή, ῆς, ἡ (lit., *fiftieth*), *Pentecost,* the feast beginning the fiftieth day after the second day of the Passover, i.e., from the sixteenth day of the month Nisan, Acts ii. 1, xx. 16; 1 Cor. xvi. 8.*

πέποιθα. See πείθω.

πεποίθησις, εως, ἡ, *trust, confidence,* with εἰς or ἐν.

περ, an enclitic particle, cognate with περί, only found joined to pronouns or particles for intensity of meaning, as

ἐάνπερ, εἴπερ, *if indeed;* ἐπείπερ, *since indeed;* καίπερ, *and really;* ὅσπερ, *the very one who.*
πέραν, adv., *over, on the other side, beyond,* with article prefixed or genitive following.
πέρας, ατος, τό, *a limit, the extremity,* in space, as Matt. xii. 42; or time, Heb. vi. 16.
Πέργαμος, ου, ἡ, *Pergamus* or *Pergamum,* Rev. i. 11, ii. 12.*
Πέργη, ης, ἡ, a prop. name, *Perga,* Acts xiii. 13.
περί, a prep., governing the gen. and accus. With gen., *about, i.e.,* concerning or respecting a thing; with accus., *about, around,* in reference to (see § 302). In composition, περί denotes *round about, on account of, above, beyond.*
περι-άγω, trans., *to lead* or *take about,* 1 Cor. ix. 5; intrans., *to go about* (acc., or περί, acc.), Matt. iv. 23, ix. 35, xxiii. 15; Mark vi. 6; Acts xiii. 11.*
περι-αιρέω, ῶ (see § 103, 2), *to take from around, take entirely away,* lit., Acts xxvii. 20, 40 (*to cast off* anchors, R. V.); fig., of the removal of sin, 2 Cor. iii. 16; Heb. x. 11.
περι-άπτω, *to kindle,* Luke xxii. 55 (W. H.).*
περι-αστράπτω, *to lighten around, to flash around* (acc., or περί, acc.), Acts ix. 3, xxii. 6.*
περι-βάλλω, βαλῶ, βέβληκα, *to cast around* (acc. and dat.), Luke xix. 43; *to clothe,* Matt. xxv. 36; for const., see § 284; mid., *to clothe oneself, to be clothed,* Matt. vi. 29.
περι-βλέπω, N.T., in mid., *to look around,* abs., Mark v. 32, ix. 8, x. 23; *to look round upon,* acc., Mark iii. 5, 34, xi. 11; Luke vi. 10.*
περι-βόλαιον, ου, τό, (1) *clothing, vesture,* Heb. i. 12; (2) *a veil,* 1 Cor. xi. 15.*
περι-δέω, *to bind round about,* pass., plup., John xi. 44.*
περι-δρέμω. See περιτρέχω.
περι-εργάζομαι, *to overdo, to be a busybody,* 2 Thess. iii. 11.*
περί-εργος, ον, act., *overdoing, intermeddling,* 1 Tim. v. 13; pass., τὰ περίεργα, *curious arts,* Acts xix. 19.*

περι-έρχομαι (see § 103, 2), *to go about,* Acts xix. 13; 1 Tim. v. 13; Heb. xi. 37; *to tack,* as a ship, Acts xxviii. 13.*
περι-έχω, *to encompass;* so, *to contain,* as a writing, Acts xxiii. 25 (W. H., ἔχω); intrans., *to be contained,* 1 Pet. ii. 6; *to seize,* as astonishment, Luke v. 9.*
περι-ζώννυμι (see § 114), *to gird oneself around,* mid. or pass.; pass., perf., part., *girt,* Luke xii. 35.
περί-θεσις, εως, ἡ, *a putting around, i.e., ornaments,* 1 Pet. iii. 3.*
περι-ίστημι (see § 107), in intrans. tenses of act., *to stand around,* John xi. 42; Acts xxv. 7; mid., *to stand aloof from* (acc.), 2 Tim. ii. 16; Tit. iii. 9.*
περι-κάθαρμα, ατος, τό, *refuse, offscouring,* 1 Cor. iv. 13.*
περι-καλύπτω, *to cover round about, to cover,* as the face, Mark xiv. 65; Luke xxii. 64; Heb. ix. 4.*
περί-κειμαι, *to lie about, surround,* dat., or περί, acc., Mark ix. 42; Luke xvii. 2; *to be encompassed* or *surrounded with,* acc., Acts xxviii. 20; Heb. v. 2, xii. 1.*
περι-κεφαλαία, ας, ἡ, *a helmet,* Eph. vi. 17; 1 Thess. v. 8.*
περι-κρατής, ές, *being entire master of,* Acts xxvii. 16.*
περι-κρύπτω, *to hide entirely,* Luke i. 24.*
περι-κυκλόω, ῶ, *to encircle, surround,* Luke xix. 43.*
περι-λάμπω, *to shine around,* Luke ii. 9; Acts xxvi. 13.*
περι-λείπω, *to leave;* pass., *to be left,* 1 Thess. iv. 15, 17.*
περί-λυπος, ον, *greatly sorrowful,* Matt. xxvi. 38; Mark vi. 26, xiv. 34; Luke xviii. 23, 24 (W. H. omit).*
περι-μένω, *to await* (acc.), Acts i. 4.*
πέριξ, adv., *round about,* Acts␣v. 16.*
περι-οικέω, ῶ, *to dwell around, to be neighbouring to* (acc.), Luke i. 65.*
περί-οικος, ον, *neighbouring,* Luke i. 58.*
περι-ούσιος, ον, *superabundant, costly, treasured;* hence, *specially chosen,* Tit. ii. 14 (LXX.); "*a people for his own possession,*" R. V.*
περι-οχή, ῆς, ἡ (see περιέχω), *a section* or *passage* of Scripture, Acts viii. 32.*
περι-πατέω, ῶ, ήσω, *to walk, to walk about, to roam;* fig., as Heb., *to pass*

one's life, to conduct oneself (adv. or nom. pred.), to live according to (ἐν, dat. ; κατά, acc.).

περι-πείρω, to pierce through, transfix, fig., 1 Tim. vi. 10.*

περι-πίπτω, to fall into the midst of (dat.), robbers, Luke x. 30; temptations, James i. 2; to light upon a place, Acts xxvii. 41.*

περι-ποιέω, ῶ, N.T., in mid., to get for oneself, acquire, gain, purchase, Luke xvii. 33 (W. H.); Acts xx. 28; 1 Tim. iii. 13. Syn. 43.*

περι-ποίησις, εως, ἡ, (1) a gaining, a possessing, 1 Thess. v. 9; 2 Thess. ii. 14; Heb. x. 39; 1 Pet. ii. 9; (2) a possession, Eph. i. 14. Syn. 43.

περιρ-ρήγνυμι, to tear off, as garments, Acts xvi. 22.*

περι-σπάω, ῶ, to drag around; hence, fig., pass., to be distracted in mind, Luke x. 40.*

περισσεία, ας, ἡ, abundance, superfluity, Rom. v. 17 ; 2 Cor. viii. 2; James i. 21 ; εἰς περισσείαν, as adv., abundantly, 2 Cor. x. 15.*

περίσσευμα, ατος, τό, abundance, affluence, superfluity, Matt. xii. 34 ; Mark viii. 8; Luke vi. 45 ; 2 Cor. viii. 14.*

περισσεύω, (1) to be more than enough, to be left over, to abound richly ; τὸ περισσεῦον, Matt. xiv. 20, the residue ; (2) to redound to, εἰς, 2 Cor. viii. 2 ; pass., to be in abundance, to be augmented, Matt. xiii. 12 ; 2 Cor. iv. 15.

περισσός, ή, όν, abundant, remaining over and above ; τὸ περισσόν, excellence, pre-eminence, Rom. iii. 1 ; adv., -ῶς, exceedingly, vehemently.

περισσοτέρως, adv. (compar. of περισσῶς), more abundantly, more earnestly, more vehemently.

περιστερά, ᾶς, ἡ, a dove, a pigeon.

περι-τέμνω, to cut around, to circumcise ; mid., to undergo circumcision, to cause oneself to be circumcised.

περι-τίθημι, to place, or put about or around (dat. and acc.) ; fig., to bestow, to attribute, 1 Cor. xii. 23.

περι-τομή, ῆς, ἡ, circumcision, i.e., the act, the custom, or state ; with art., the circumcision, i.e., the Jews ; fig., for spiritual purity, Rom. ii. 28, 29 ; Col. ii. 11.

περι-τρέπω, to turn about, to convert to (εἰς) madness, Acts xxvi. 24.*

περι-τρέχω, 2nd aor. περιέδραμον, to run around (acc.), Mark vi. 55.*

περι-φέρω, to bear or carry around, to carry about in oneself, Mark vi. 55 ; 2 Cor. iv. 10 ; pass., fig., to be carried about, carried away by false teaching, Eph. iv. 14 ; Heb. xiii. 9 ; Jude 12 (W. H., παραφέρω).*

περι-φρονέω, ῶ, to look down upon, to contemn, to despise, Tit. ii. 15.*

περί-χωρος, ον, circumjacent ; only as subst. (ἡ, sc. γῆ), the region round about ; the inhabitants of such a region, Matt. iii. 5.

περί-ψημα, ατος, τό, scrapings, offscourings, 1 Cor. iv. 13.*

περπερεύομαι, dep., intrans., to vaunt, 1 Cor. xiii. 4.*

Περσίς, ίδος, ἡ, Persis, Rom. xvi. 12.*

πέρυσι, adv., during the year just passed; ἀπὸ πέρυσι, a year ago, 2 Cor. viii. 10, ix. 2.*

πετάομαι, ῶμαι, or πέτομαι (W. H.), to fly, as a bird, Rev.*

πετεινόν, οῦ, τό, a bird, a fowl ; only in plur., the birds.

πέτομαι. See πετάομαι.

πέτρα, ας, ἡ, a rock, any large block of stone ; with art., the rock, i.e., the rocky substratum of the soil ; met., for caverns, Rev. vi. 15 ; fig., Rom. ix. 33 ; see also Matt. xvi. 18. Syn. 75.

Πέτρος, ου, ὁ, Peter, Greek for the Heb. (Chald.) kēpha, rock. Same with πέτρα, but with the termination of a masc. name.

πετρώδης, ες, rocky, stony, Matt. xiii. 5, 20 ; Mark iv. 5, 16.*

πήγανον, ου, τό, rue, Luke xi. 42.*

πηγή, ῆς, ἡ, a fountain, source, well ; fig. of "the water of life"; a flow of blood, Mark v. 29.

πήγνυμι, πήξω, to fix, as a tent, Heb. viii. 2.*

πηδάλιον, ίου, τό, the rudder of a ship, Acts xxvii. 40 ; James iii. 4.*

πηλίκος, η, ον, how great, Heb. vii. 4 ; how large, Gal. vi. 7 (see γράμμα).*

πηλός, οῦ, ὁ, clay, mire, mortar, John ix. 6-15 ; Rom. ix. 21.*

πήρα, ας, ἡ, a bag, wallet, for carrying provisions, Matt. x. 10 ; Mark vi. 8 ; Luke ix. 3, x. 4, xxii. 35, 36.*

πῆχυς, εως, ὁ, a cubit, the length from the elbow to the tip of the middle finger, Matt. vi. 27; Luke xii. 25; John xxi. 8; Rev. xxi. 17.*
πιάζω, σω, to lay hold of, Acts iii. 7; to take, as in fishing or in hunting; to arrest, John vii. 30.
πιέζω, to press down, as in a measure, Luke vi. 38.*
πιθανο-λογία, as, ἡ, persuasive or plausible speech, Col. ii. 4.*
πικραίνω, ανῶ, to render bitter, fit., Rev. viii. 11, x. 9, 10; to embitter, fig., Col. iii. 19.*
πικρία, as, ἡ, bitterness, fig., Acts viii. 23; Rom. iii. 14; Eph. iv. 31; Heb. xii. 15.*
πικρός, ά, όν, bitter, acrid, malignant, James iii. 11, 14;* adv., -ῶς, bitterly, of weeping, Matt. xxvi. 75; Luke xxii. 12.*
Πιλᾶτος or Πιλᾶτος (W. H., Πειλᾶτος), ου, ὁ (Lat., pilatus, "armed with javelin"), Pilate.
πίμπλημι (πλε-). See πλήθω.
πίμπρημι (πρα-), pass., inf., πίμπρασθαι, to be inflamed, to swell, Acts xxviii. 6.*
πινακίδιον, ιου, τό (dim. of πίναξ), a tablet for writing, Luke i. 63.*
πίναξ, ακος, ὁ, a plate, platter, dish.
πίνω, fut., πίομαι, -εσαι, -εται; perf., πέπωκα; 2nd aor., ἔπιον (inf., πεῖν, W. H.), to drink, abs., or with acc. of thing drunk (sometimes ἐκ or ἀπό), to imbibe, as the earth imbibes rain; fig., to receive into the soul, to partake of.
πιότης, τητος, ἡ, fatness, richness, as of the olive, Rom. xi. 17.*
πιπράσκω (πρα-), perf., πέπρακα; 1st aor. pass., ἐπράθην; perf. pass., πέπραμαι, to sell, Matt. xiii. 46; pass., with ὑπό, to be sold under, to be a slave to.
πίπτω (πετ-, see § 94, i. 8, d), (1) to fall (whence, by ἀπό or ἐκ; whither, by ἐπί or εἰς, acc.); hence, (2) to fall prostrate, as of persons, to die, to perish; of structures, to fall in ruins; of institutions, to fail; (3) to fall to, as a lot; (4) to fall into or under, as condemnation.
Πισιδία, as, ἡ, Pisidia, Acts xiv. 24, xiii. 14, where W. H. have adj. form.*
πιστεύω (see § 74), to believe, be persuaded of a thing (acc. or ὅτι); to give credit to, dat.; to have confidence in, to trust, believe, dat., εἰς, ἐν, ἐπί (dat.) or ἐπί (acc.), often of Christian faith, in God, in Christ; to entrust something (acc.) to any one (dat.); pass., to be entrusted with (acc.).
πιστικός, ή, όν, genuine, pure, of ointment, Mark xiv. 3; John xii. 3.*
πίστις, εως, ἡ, (1) faith, generally, as 2 Thess. ii. 13; Heb. xi. 1; the object of the faith is expressed by obj. gen., or by εἰς, ἐν, πρός (acc.); (2) fidelity, good faith, Rom. iii. 3; 2 Tim. ii. 22; (3) a pledge, a promise given, 2 Tim. iv. 7; (4) met., for the whole of the Christian character, and (generally with art.) for the Christian religion.
πιστός, ή, όν, (1) trustworthy, faithful, in any relation or to any promise, of things or (generally) persons; (2) believing, abs., as οἱ πιστοί, the followers of Christ, or with dat.
πιστόω, ῶ, to make faithful; N.T., only in pass., to be assured of, 2 Tim. iii. 14.*
πλανάω, ῶ, ήσω, to lead astray, to cause to wander; fig., to deceive; pass., to be misled, to err, to mistake.
πλάνη, ης, ἡ, wandering; only fig., deceit, delusion, error.
πλανήτης, ου, ὁ, wandering; ἀστὴρ πλανήτης, a wandering star, Jude 13 ("planet").*
πλάνος, ον, causing to wander, deceitful, 1 Tim. iv. 1; as subst., an impostor, Matt. xxvii. 63; 2 Cor. vi. 8; 2 John 7.*
πλάξ, ακός, ἡ, a tablet to write on, 2 Cor. iii. 3; Heb. ix. 4.*
πλάσμα, ατος, τό, a thing formed or fashioned, Rom. ix. 20.*
πλάσσω, άσω, to form, fashion, mould, as a potter his clay, Rom. ix. 20; 1 Tim. ii. 13.*
πλαστός, ή, όν, formed, moulded; fig., deceitful, 2 Pet. ii. 3.*
πλατεῖα, as, ἡ (fem. of πλατύς, broad, sc. ὁδός), a street.
πλάτος, ους, τό, breadth, Eph. iii. 18; Rev. xx. 9, xxi. 16.*
πλατύνω, νῶ, to make broad, to enlarge, Matt. xxiii. 5; pass., fig., to be enlarged, in mind or heart, 2 Cor. vi. 11, 13.*
πλατύς, εῖα, ύ, broad, Matt. vii. 13.*

πλέγμα, ατος, τό (πλέκω), *anything interwoven, braided hair*, 1 Tim. ii. 9.*

πλεῖστος, η, ον, superl. of πολύς, *the greatest, the most, very great;* τό πλεῖστον, adv., *mostly, at most*, 1 Cor. xiv. 27.

πλείων, εῖον (for declension see § 44), compar. of πολύς, *more, greater*, in number—magnitude—comparison; οἱ πλείονες, οἱ πλείους, *the more, the most, the many*, majority, 2 Cor. ii. 6; πλεῖον or πλέον, as adv., *more*, John xxi. 15; ἐπὶ πλεῖον, *further, longer*, Acts iv. 17.

πλέκω, ξω, *to weave together, to plait*, Matt. xxvii. 29; Mark xv. 17; John xix. 2.*

πλέον. See πλείων.

πλεονάζω, σω, intrans., *to have more than enough, to superabound;* trans., *to increase, to cause to abound*, 1 Thess. iii. 12.

πλεον-εκτέω, ῶ (ἔχω), *to have more than another, to desire to have more;* hence, *to overreach, take advantage of* (R.V.), 2 Cor. vii. 2, xii. 17, 18; 1 Thess. iv. 6; pass., *to be taken advantage of*, 2 Cor. ii. 11.*

πλεον-έκτης, ου, ὁ, *a covetous* or *avaricious person*, 1 Cor. v. 10, 11, vi. 10; Eph. v. 5.*

πλεον-εξία, as, ἡ, *covetousness, avarice.*

πλευρά, ᾶς, ἡ, *the side of the human body*, John xix. 34.

πλέω. See πλήθω.

πλέω (ƒ), impf. ἔπλεον, fut. πλεύσομαι, *to sail*, Luke viii. 23; Acts xxi. 3, xxvii. 6, 24; Rev. xviii. 17 (W. H.); with acc. of direction, Acts xxvii. 2 (but W. H. read εἰς).*

πληγή, ῆς, ἡ (πλήσσω), *a stroke, a stripe, a wound*, Acts xvi. 33; Rev. xiii. 14; *an affliction*, Rev. ix. 20.

πλῆθος, ους, τό, *a multitude, crowd, throng;* with art., *the multitude, the whole number, population*, Acts xiv. 4; *a quantity*, Acts xxviii. 3.

πληθύνω, νῶ, (1) intrans., *to increase;* (2) trans., *to multiply, augment;* pass., *to be increased.*

πλήθω (or πίμπλημι), πλήσω; 1st aor. pass., ἐπλήσθην; (1) *to fill* with (gen.); fig., of emotions, as Luke iv. 28; or of the Holy Spirit, Acts ii. 4; (2) pass., *to be fulfilled*, of time, Luke i. 23, 57.

πλήκτης, ου, ὁ, *a striker, a contentious person*, 1 Tim. iii. 3; Tit. i. 7.*

πλημμύρα, as (W. H., -ης), ἡ, *a flood, an inundation*, Luke vi. 48.*

πλήν, adv. (akin to πλέον, hence it *adds* a thought, generally adversative, sometimes partly confirmatory), *besides, but, nevertheless, howbeit, of a truth*, Matt. xi. 22, xviii. 7, xxvi. 39, 64; πλὴν ὅτι, *except that*, Acts xx. 23; as prep. with gen., *besides, excepting*, Mark xii. 32; Acts viii. 1.

πλήρης, ες, (1) *full*, abs., Mark iv. 28; (2) *full of* (gen.), *abounding in*.

πληρο-φορέω, ῶ (φέρω), *to bring to the full, to fulfil*, 2 Tim. iv. 5; pass., of things, *to be fulfilled*, Luke i. 1, "the things fulfilled among us," *i.e.*, fully accomplished; 2 Tim. iv. 17, "that the proclamation may be fulfilled," *i.e.*, made everywhere known; of persons, *to be fully assured*, Rom. iv. 21, xiv. 5; Col. iv. 12 (W. H.).*

πληρο-φορία, as, ἡ, *fulness, entire possession, full assurance*, Col. ii. 2; 1 Thess. i. 5; Heb. vi. 11, x. 22.*

πληρόω, ῶ, ώσω, *to fill* with (gen.), *to fill up, to pervade, to complete*, either time or number; *to bestow abundantly, to furnish liberally*, Phil. iv. 18; Eph. iii. 19; *to accomplish, to perform fully*, as prophecies, etc.; pass., *to be full of*, 2 Cor. vii. 4; Eph. v. 18; *to be made full, complete*, or *perfect*, John iii. 29; Col. iv. 12 (W. H. read preceding). Syn. 13.

πλήρωμα, ατος, τό, *fulness, plenitude, i.e., that which fills*, 1 Cor. x. 26, 28; so, *the full number*, Rom. xi. 25; *the completion, i.e., that which makes full, the fulfilment*, Matt. xvi. 16; Rom. xiii. 10; *the fulness of time*, Gal. iv. 4, is the completion of an era; *the fulness of Christ*, Eph. i. 23, that which is filled by Christ, *i.e.*, the Church; *the fulness of the Godhead*, Col. ii. 19 (see Lightfoot's note), all Divine attributes.

πλησίον, adv., *near, near by*, with gen., John iv. 5; with the art., ὁ πλησίον, *a neighbour*.

πλησμονή, ῆς, ἡ, *full satisfying, indulgence*, Col. ii. 23.*

πλήσσω, ξω, 2nd aor. pass. ἐπλήγην, *to smite*, Rev. viii. 12.*

πλοιάριον, ίου, τό (dim. of πλοῖον), a small boat, as the fishing-boats on the lake of Galilee.
πλοῖον, ου, τό, a ship, a vessel, large or small.
πλόος, οῦς, gen. οῦ or οός, sailing, voyage, Acts xxi. 7, xxvii. 9, 10.*
πλούσιος, ία, ιον, rich, abounding in (ἐν); adv., -ως, richly, abundantly, Col. iii. 16.
πλουτέω, ῶ, ἥσω, to become rich, to be rich, to abound in.
πλουτίζω, to make rich, to enrich, to cause to abound in, 1 Cor. i. 5; 2 Cor. vi. 10, ix. 11.*
πλοῦτος, ου, ὁ (see § 32, a), riches, wealth, abundance; spiritually, enrichment, Rom. xi. 12.
πλύνω, νῶ, to wash, as garments, Luke v. 2 (W. H.); Rev. vii. 14, xxii. 14 (W. H.). Syn. 17.*
πνεῦμα, ατος, τό, (1) properly, the wind, or the air in motion, John iii. 8; hence, (2) the human spirit, dist. from σῶμα and ψυχή, 1 Thess. v. 23; (3) a temper or disposition of the soul, Luke ix. 55; Rom. viii. 15; (4) any intelligent, incorporeal being, as (a) the human spirit, separated from the body, the undying soul; (b) angels, good and bad; (c) GOD, the immaterial One, John iv. 24; (d) THE HOLY SPIRIT (see § 217, f). Used of the influence of which the Holy Spirit is the author, in respect of Jesus, Luke iv. 1; Acts x. 38, in respect of prophets and apostles; and in respect of saints generally, Eph. i. 17. Syn. 55.
πνευματικός, ή, όν, spiritual, relating to that which is imparted by the Spirit, or is allied to the spiritual world, 1 Cor. ii. 13 (see § 316), 15, xv. 44; τὰ πνευματικά, spiritual things, Rom. xv. 27; spiritual gifts, 1 Cor. xii. 1; adv., -ῶς, spiritually, i.e., (1) mystically, Rev. xi. 8; (2) by the spiritual faculty (opposed to ψυχικός), 1 Cor. ii. 14.
πνέω (Ϝ), εὔσω, to blow, as the wind.
πνίγω, to choke, to seize by the throat, Matt. xviii. 28; Mark v. 13.*
πνικτός, ή, όν, strangled.
πνοή, ῆς, ἡ, (1) breath, Acts xvii. 25; (2) a breeze or blast, Acts ii. 2.*
ποδήρης, ες, reaching to the feet; as subst. (sc. χιτών), a long robe. Rev. i. 13.*
ποθέν, adv., interrog., whence, of place, Matt. xv. 33; suggestive of cause, how, Matt. xiii. 27; of surprise, or admiration, as Luke i. 43; also of strong negation, Mark xii. 37.
ποία, as, ἡ, grass, herbage, according to some, in James iv. 14; but more probably the word here is the fem. of ποῖος, "of what nature is your life?"*
ποιέω, ῶ, ἥσω, (1) to make, i.e., to form, to bring about, to cause; spoken of religious festivals, etc., to observe, to celebrate; of trees and plants, to germinate, to produce; to cause to be or to become, Matt. xxi. 13; to declare to be, John viii. 53; to assume, Matt. xii. 33; (2) to do, generally; to do, i.e., habitually, to perform, to execute, to exercise, to practise, i.e., to pursue a course of action, to be active, to work, to spend, to pass, i.e., time or life, Acts xv. 33. Syn. 2.
ποίημα, ατος, τό, a thing made, workmanship, Rom. i. 20; Eph. ii. 10.*
ποίησις, εως, ἡ, a doing, James i. 25.*
ποιητής, οῦ, ὁ, (1) a maker, doer, Rom. ii. 13; James i. 22, 23, 25, iv. 11; (2) a poet, Acts xvii. 28.*
ποικίλος, η, ον, various, of different colours, diverse.
ποιμαίνω, ανῶ, (1) to feed a flock, Luke xvii. 7; hence, fig., (2) to be shepherd of, to tend, to feed, cherish, Matt. ii. 6; John xxi. 16; Acts xx. 28; 1 Cor. ix. 7; 1 Pet. v. 2; Jude 12; Rev. vii. 17; (3) in Rev., "to be shepherd of, with a rod of iron," i.e., to rule, ii. 27, xii. 5, xix. 15. Syn. 16.*
ποιμήν, ένος, ὁ, (1) a shepherd; (2) fig., of CHRIST as the Shepherd, Heb. xiii. 20; 1 Pet. ii. 25; and of his ministers as pastors, Eph. iv. 11.
ποίμνη, ης, ἡ, (1) a flock of sheep or goats, Luke ii. 8; 1 Cor. ix. 7; (2) fig., of Christ's followers, Matt. xxvi. 35; John x. 16. Syn. 72.*
ποίμνιον, ίου, τό (dim. of ποίμνη), a little flock; only fig., Luke xii. 32; Acts xx. 28, 29; 1 Pet. v. 2, 3.*
ποῖος, ποία, ποῖον, an interrog. pron. corresponding with οἷος and τοῖος, of what kind, sort, species? what? what one? which? In Luke v. 19, sc. ὁδοῦ.

πολεμέω, ῶ, ήσω, to make war, to contend with (μετά, gen.).
πόλεμος, ου, ὁ, (1) war, a war; (2) a battle; (3) strife.
πόλις, εως, ἡ, a city, a walled town; met., the inhabitants of a city; with art., the city Jerusalem, the heavenly city, of which Jerusalem was a symbol.
πολιτ-άρχης, ου, ὁ, the ruler of a city, a city magistrate, "politarch," Acts xvii. 6, 8.*
πολιτεία, as, ἡ, (1) citizenship, Acts xxii. 28; (2) a state or commonwealth, Eph. ii. 12.*
πολίτευμα, ατος, τό, a community, as of a city, a commonwealth, Phil. iii. 20.*
πολιτεύω, in mid., to be a citizen; hence, to live, i.e., to order one's life, Acts xxiii. 1; Phil. i. 27.*
πολίτης, ου, ὁ, a citizen, Luke xv. 15, Acts xxi. 39; with gen., αὐτοῦ, a fellow-citizen, Luke xix. 14; Heb. viii. 11 (W. H.).*
πολλάκις, adv., many times, often.
πολλα-πλασίων, ον, gen. ονος, manifold, many times more, Matt. xix. 29 (W. H.); Luke xviii. 30.*
πολυ-λογία, ας, ἡ, much speaking, loquacity, Matt. vi. 7.*
πολυ-μερῶς, adv., in many parts, by divers portions (R. V.), Heb. i. 1.*
πολυ-ποίκιλος, ον, very varied, manifold, Eph. iii. 10.*
πολύς, πολλή, πολύ (see § 39, 2), many, numerous; πολύ, much, greatly, as adv.; πολλοί, many, often with partitive genitive, or ἐκ; οἱ πολλοί, the many (see § 227); πολλά, in like manner, much, very much, often, many times; πολλῷ, by much, joined with comparatives; ἐπὶ πολύ, for a great while, Acts xxviii. 6; ἐν πολλῷ, altogether, Acts xxvi. 29.
πολύ-σπλαγχνος, ον, very compassionate, of great mercy, James v. 11.*
πολυ-τελής, ές, very costly, very precious, Mark xiv. 3; 1 Tim. ii. 9; 1 Pet. iii. 4.*
πολύ-τῖμος, ου, ὁ, ἡ, of great value, very costly, Matt. xiii. 46; John xii. 3; compar., 1 Pet. i. 7 (W. H.).*
πολυ-τρόπως, adv., in various ways, Heb. i. 1.*

πόμα, ατος, τό, drink, 1 Cor. x. 4; Heb. ix. 10.*
πονηρία, ας, ἡ, evil disposition, wickedness, Matt. xxii. 18; Luke xi. 39; Rom. i. 29; 1 Cor. v. 8; Eph. vi. 12; plur., malignant passions, iniquities, Mark vii. 22; Acts iii. 26. Syn. 22.*
πονηρός, ά, όν (πόνος), evil, bad, of things or persons; wicked, depraved, spec. malignant, opp. to ἀγαθός. ὁ πονηρός, the Wicked One, i.e., Satan; τὸ πονηρόν, evil. Syn. 22.
πόνος, ου, ὁ, (1) labour, Col. iv. 13 (W. H.); (2) pain, sorrow, anguish, Rev. xvi. 10, 11, xxi. 4.*
Ποντικός, ή, όν, belonging to Pontus, Acts xviii. 2.*
Πόντιος, ίου, ὁ, Pontius, the praenomen of Pilate.
Πόντος, ου, ὁ, Pontus, Acts ii. 9; 1 Pet. i. 1.*
Πόπλιος, ου, ὁ, Publius, Acts xxviii. 7, 8.*
πορεία, ας, ἡ, a way, a journey, Luke xiii. 22; way or course of life, James i. 11.*
πορεύομαι, σομαι, dep., with pass. aor., ἐπορεύθην, to go, to go away, to depart, to journey, to travel, often (as Heb.) to take a course in life.
πορθέω, ήσω, to lay waste, harass, persecute, Acts ix. 21; Gal. i. 13, 23.*
πορισμός, οῦ, ὁ, gain, 1 Tim. vi. 5, 6.*
Πόρκιος, ου, ὁ, Porcius, the praenomen of Festus, Acts xxiv. 27.*
πορνεία, ας, ἡ, fornication, lewdness; fig. in Rev., idolatry.
πορνεύω, σω, to commit fornication; fig. in Rev., to worship idols.
πόρνη, ης, ἡ, a harlot, a prostitute; fig. in Rev., an idolatrous community.
πόρνος, ου, ὁ, one who prostitutes himself, a fornicator.
πόρρω, adv., far, far off, Matt. xv. 8; Mark vii. 6; Luke xiv. 32; comp., πορρωτέρω (or -τερον, W. H.), Luke xxiv. 28.*
πόρρωθεν, adv., further, from afar, far off, Luke xvii. 12; Heb. xi. 13.*
πορφύρα, ας, ἡ, a purple or crimson garment, indicating wealth or rank, Mark xv. 17, 20; Luke xvi. 19; Rev. xvii. 4 (W. H. read following), xviii. 12.*
πορφύρεος, οῦς, ᾶ, οῦν, purple or crimson, John xix. 2, 5; Rev. xvii. 4 (W. H.), xviii. 16.*

πορφυρό-πωλις, εως, ή, a seller of purple or crimson cloth, Acts xvi. 14.*
ποσάκις, adv., interrog., how many times? how often? Matt. xviii. 21, xxiii. 37; Luke xiii. 34.*
πόσις, εως, ή, drink, John vi. 55; Rom. xiv. 17; Col. ii. 16.*
πόσος, η, ov, pron., interrog., how much? how great? plur., how many? πόσῳ, as adv. with comparatives, by how much?
ποταμός, οῦ, ὁ, a river, torrent, flood.
ποταμο-φόρητος, ον, carried away by a flood, Rev. xii. 15.*
ποταπός, ή, όν, adj., interrog., of what kind? of what manner? how great?
πότε, adv., interrog., when? at what time? till when? how long? ποτέ, enclitic, at some time, at one time or other (see § 129).
πότερος, pron., interrog., which of the two? N.T. only neut. as adv., whether, correlating with ἤ, or, John vii. 17.*
ποτήριον, ίου, τό, a drinking-cup, the contents of the cup; fig., the portion which God allots, whether of good or ill, commonly of the latter.
ποτίζω, σω, to cause to drink (two accs.); to give drink to (acc.); fig., to minister to, generally, 1 Cor. iii. 2; to water or irrigate, as plants, 1 Cor. iii. 6–8.
Ποτίολοι, ων, οἱ, Puteoli, Acts xxviii. 13.*
πότος, ου, ὁ (see πίνω), a drinking bout, drunkenness, 1 Pet. iv. 3.*
ποῦ, adv., interrog., where? whither? Matt. ii. 4; John vii. 35.
που, enclitic, an indef. particle of place or degree, somewhere, somewhere about, Heb. ii. 6, 16 (W. H., see δήπου), iv. 4; Rom. iv. 19 (see § 129).*
Πούδης, δεντος, ὁ, Pudens, 2 Tim. iv. 21.*
πούς, ποδός, ὁ, the foot; met., for the person journeying, Luke i. 79; ὑπὸ τοὺς πόδας, under the feet, i.e., entirely subdued, as Rom. xvi. 20.
πρᾶγμα, ατος, τό, a thing done, a fact, a thing, a business, a suit, as at law.
πραγματεία (W. H., -τία), as, ή, a business, an affair, 2 Tim. ii. 4.*
πραγματεύομαι, σομαι, dep., to transact business, to trade, Luke xix. 13.*
πραιτώριον, ίου, τό (from Lat., prætor), the palace at Jerusalem occupied by the Roman governor, Matt. xxvii. 27;

Mark xv. 16; John xviii. 28, 33, xix. 9; so at Cæsarea, Acts xxiii. 35; the quarters of the prætorian army in Rome, Phil. i. 13.*
πράκτωρ, ορος, ὁ, an officer employed to execute judicial sentences, Luke xii. 58.*
πρᾶξις, εως, ή, (1) a doing, action, mode of action, Matt. xvi. 27; Luke xxiii. 51; plur., deeds, acts, Acts xix. 18; Rom. viii. 13; Col. iii. 9; and in inscription to the Acts of the Apostles; (2) function, office, Rom. xii. 4.*
πρᾷος, α, ον, rec. in Matt. xi. 29 for πραΰς (W. H.).*
πραότης, rec. for πραΰτης (W. H.) in 1 Cor. iv. 21; 2 Cor. x. 1; Gal. v. 23, vi. 1; Eph. iv. 2; Col. iii. 12; 1 Tim. vi. 11 (W. H., πραϋπάθια); 2 Tim. ii. 25; Tit. iii. 2.*
πρασιά, ᾶς, ή, a company formed into square, Mark vi. 40. For constr., see § 242.*
πράσσω or πράττω, ξω, pf. πέπραχα, πέπραγμαι, (1) to do, perform, accomplish, with acc.; (2) with advs., to be in any condition, i.e., to fare, Acts xv. 29; Eph. vi. 21; (3) to exact, to require, Luke xix. 23.
πραϋ-παθεία (or ία), ας, ή (W. H.), meekness, 1 Tim. vi. 11.*
πραΰς, gen. -έος or -έως (W. H.), pl. -εῖς, meek, gentle, Matt. v. 5, xi. 29 (see πρᾷος), xxi. 5; 1 Pet. iii. 4. The form πραΰς (with iota subscript) has little or no authority.*
πραΰτης, τητος, ή, meekness, gentleness, James i. 21, iii. 13; 1 Pet. iii. 15; and W. H. in the passage quoted under πραότης.*
πρέπω, to become, be fitting to (dat.), 1 Tim. ii. 10; Tit. ii. 1; Heb. vii. 26; impers. (see § 101), it becomes, it is fitting to, Matt. iii. 15; 1 Cor. xi. 13; Eph. v. 3; Heb. ii. 10.*
πρεσβεία, ας, ή, an embassy, ambassadors, Luke xiv. 32, xix. 14.*
πρεσβεύω, σω (lit., to be aged), elder men being chosen for the office), to act as ambassador, 2 Cor. v. 20; Eph. vi. 20.*
πρεσβυτέριον, ίου, τό, an assembly of elders, the Sanhedrin, Luke xxii. 66; Acts xxii. 5; officers of the church assembled, presbytery, 1 Tim. iv. 14.*
πρεσβύτερος, τέρα, τερον (compar. of πρέσβυς, old), generally used as subst.

elder, (1) in age, Acts ii. 17 ; 1 Tim. v. 1; plur., often, ancestors, as Heb. xi. 2 ; (2) as subst.,*an elder*, in dignity and office, whether of the Jewish community, Matt. xvi. 21 ; or the Christian, Acts xx. 17, 28; "presbyter"; in Rev., of the twenty-four *elders*.
πρεσβύτης, ου, ὁ, *an old man*, Luke i. 18 ; Tit. ii. 2 ; Philem. 9.*
πρεσβῦτις, ιδος, ἡ, *an old woman*, Tit. ii. 3.*
πρηνής, ές, *prone, falling headlong*, Acts i. 18.*
πρίζω or πρίω, 1st aor. pass. ἐπρίσθην, *to saw, to saw asunder*, Heb. xi. 37.*
πρίν, adv., of time, *before*, as conj. in N.T., with or without ἤ, *sooner than;* generally with acc. and inf., Matt. xxvi. 34 ; but after a negative we find πρὶν ἄν with subj. where the principal verb is in a primary tense, Luke ii. 26 ; πρίν with opt. where it is in a historical tense, Acts xxv. 16.
Πρίσκα, ης, ἡ, and dim. Πρισκίλλα, ας, a proper name, *Prisca* or *Priscilla*.
πρό, prep., gov. the gen., *before, i.e.*, of place, time, or superiority (see § **294**). In composition, it retains the same meanings.
προ-άγω, *to bring out*, Acts xvi. 30 ; gen. intrans., *to go before, to lead the way, to precede*, in place, Matt. ii. 9 ; in time, Mark vi. 45; part., προάγων, *preceding, previous*, 1 Tim. i. 18; Heb. vii. 18.
προ-αιρέω, ῶ, N.T., in mid., *to propose to oneself, resolve*, 2 Cor. ix. 7.*
προ-αιτιάομαι, ῶμαι, *to lay to one's charge beforehand*, Rom. iii. 9.*
προ-ακούω, *to hear before*, Col. i. 5.*
προ-αμαρτάνω, *to sin before*, 2 Cor. xii. 21, xiii. 2.*
προ-αύλιον, ου, τό, *the court before a building, the porch*, Mark xiv. 68.*
προ-βαίνω, *to go forward*, Matt. iv. 21 ; Mark i. 19 ; pf. part., προβεβηκὼς ἐν ἡμέραις, *advanced in life*, Luke i. 7, 18, ii. 36.*
προ-βάλλω, *to put forth*, as trees their leaves, Luke xxi. 30; *to thrust forward*, Acts xix. 33.*
προβατικός, ή, όν, *pertaining to sheep*, John v. 2.*
προβάτιον, ου, τό, dim. of following, John xxi. 16-17 (W. H.).*

πρόβατον, ου, τό (προβαίνω), *a sheep;* fig., *a follower of Christ*.
προ-βιβάζω, σω, *to put forward*, Matt. xiv. 8 ; Acts xix. 33.*
προ-βλέπω, N.T., in mid., *to foresee* or *provide*, Heb. xi. 40.*
προ-γίνομαι, *to be* or *be done before*, Rom. iii. 25.*
προ-γινώσκω, *to know beforehand*, Acts xxvi. 5 ; 2 Pet. iii. 17 ; of the Divine foreknowledge, Rom. viii. 29, xi. 2 ; 1 Pet. i. 20.*
πρό-γνωσις, εως, ἡ, *foreknowledge*, Acts ii. 23; 1 Pet. i. 2.*
πρό-γονος, ου, ὁ, *a progenitor*, plur., *ancestors*, 1 Tim. v. 4 ; 2 Tim. i. 3.*
προ-γράφω, ψω, *to write before*, in time, Rom. xv. 4 ; Eph. iii. 3 ; *to write up, exhibit before any one*, Gal. iii. 1 ; *to pre-ordain*, Jude 4.*
πρό-δηλος, ον, *manifest to all, evident*, 1 Tim. v. 24, 25; Heb. xii. 14.*
προ-δίδωμι, (1) *to give before*, Rom. xi. 35 : (2) *to give forth, betray;* see following word.*
προ-δότης, ου, ὁ, *a betrayer*, Luke vi. 16; Acts vii. 52 ; 2 Tim. iii. 4.*
πρό-δρομος, ου, ὁ, ἡ (see προτρέχω), *a precursor, forerunner*, Heb. vi. 20.*
προ-εῖδον, 2nd aor. of προοράω.
προ-εῖπον, 2nd aor. of πρόφημι, perf. προείρηκα.
προ-ελπίζω, *to hope before*, Eph. i. 12.*
προ-εν-άρχομαι, *to begin before*, 2 Cor. viii. 10, 10.*
προ-επ-αγγέλλω, in mid., *to promise before*, Rom. i. 2 ; 2 Cor. ix. 5 (W. H.).*
προ-έρχομαι (see § 103, 2), (1) *to go forward, advance ;* (2) *to go before, precede*, in time or place (gen. or acc.).
προ-ετοιμάζω, σω, *to appoint beforehand, to predestine*, Rom. ix. 23 ; Eph. ii. 10.*
προ-ευ-αγγελίζομαι, *to foretell good tidings, preach the gospel beforehand*, Gal. iii. 8.*
προ-έχω, in mid., *to hold oneself before, to be superior*, Rom. iii. 9 (see § 358).*
προ-ηγέομαι, οῦμαι, *to lead onward by example*, or *to consider before, prefer*, Rom. xii. 10.*
πρό-θεσις, εως, ἡ (τίθημι), (1) *a setting before ;* οἱ ἄρτοι τῆς προθέσεως, *the loaves*

of the presentation, or *the shewbread,* compare Heb. ix. 2; (2) *a predetermination, purpose,* Acts xi. 23.
προ-θέσμιος, ία, ιον, *set beforehand, appointed before,* Gal. iv. 2.*
προ-θυμία, ας, ἡ, *alacrity, willingness,* Acts xvii. 11; 2 Cor. viii. 11, 12, 19, ix. 2.*
πρό-θυμος, ον, *eager, ready, willing,* Matt. xxvi. 41; Mark xiv. 38; τὸ πρόθυμον, *alacrity,* Rom. i. 15; adv., -ως, *readily, with alacrity,* 1 Pet. v. 2.*
πρόϊμος (W. H., for πρώϊμος).
προ-ίστημι, N.T. only intrans., act., 2nd aor. and perf., and mid., (1) *to preside over, to rule,* gen., Rom. xii. 8; 1 Thess. v. 12; 1 Tim. iii. 4, 5, 12, v. 17; (2) *maintain* or *profess,* gen., Tit. iii. 8.*
προ-καλέω, ῶ, in mid., *to provoke, stimulate,* Gal. v. 26.*
προ-κατ-αγγέλλω, *to announce beforehand, to promise,* Acts iii. 18, 24 (not W. H.), vii. 52; 2 Cor. ix. 5 (not W. H.).*
προ-κατ-αρτίζω, *to make ready beforehand,* 2 Cor. ix. 5.*
πρό-κειμαι, *to lie* or *be placed before, to be proposed,* as duty, example, reward, etc., Heb. vi. 18, xii. 1, 2; Jude 7; *to be at hand, to be present,* 2 Cor. viii. 12.*
προ-κηρύσσω, ξω, *to announce* or *preach beforehand,* Acts iii. 20 (not W. H.), xiii. 24.*
προ-κοπή, ῆς, ἡ, *urging forward, furtherance, progress,* Phil. i. 12, 25; 1 Tim. iv. 15.*
προ-κόπτω, *to make progress in* (dat. or ἐν); *to advance to* (ἐπί, acc.); of time, *to be advanced* or *far spent,* Rom. xiii. 12.
πρό-κριμα, ατος, τό, *a forejudging, prejudice;* or perhaps a *judging* one thing *before* another, *preference,* 1 Tim. v. 21.*
προ-κυρόω, ῶ, *to establish* or *ratify before,* Gal. iii. 17.*
προ-λαμβάνω, *to take before, anticipate,* Mark xiv. 8 ("she hath anticipated the anointing," *i.e.,* hath anointed beforehand); 1 Cor. xi. 21; pass., *to be overtaken* or *caught,* Gal. vi. 1.*
προ-λέγω, *to tell beforehand, forewarn,* 2 Cor. xiii. 2: Gal. v. 2: 1 Thess. iii. 4.*

προ-μαρτύρομαι, *to testify beforehand, to predict,* 1 Pet. i. 11.*
προ-μελετάω, ῶ, *to care for beforehand, to premeditate,* Luke xxi. 14.*
προ-μεριμνάω, ῶ, *to be anxious* or *solicitous beforehand,* Mark xiii. 11.*
προ-νοέω, ῶ, *to perceive beforehand, to provide for,* gen., 1 Tim. v. 8; in mid., *to provide for oneself, to practise,* acc., Rom. xii. 17; 2 Cor. viii. 21.*
πρό-νοια, ας, ἡ, *providence,* Acts xxiv. 3; *care for* (gen.), Rom. xiii. 14.*
προ-οράω, ῶ, 2nd aor. προεῖδον, *to see beforehand,* Acts ii. 31, xxi. 29; Gal. iii. 8; mid., *to have before one's eyes,* Acts ii. 25 (LXX.).*
προ-ορίζω, *to predetermine, to pre-ordain,* Acts iv. 28; Rom. viii. 29, 30; 1 Cor. ii. 7; Eph. i. 5, 11.*
προ-πάσχω, *to suffer beforehand,* 1 Thess. ii. 2.*
προ-πάτωρ, ορος, ὁ, *a forefather,* Rom. iv. 1 (W. H.).*
προ-πέμπω, *to send forward, to accompany, to bring one on his way.*
προ-πετής, ές (πίπτω), *precipitate, headlong, rash,* Acts xix. 36; 2 Tim. iii. 4.*
προ-πορεύομαι, σομαι, in mid., *to precede, to pass on before* (gen.), Luke i. 76; Acts vii. 40.*
πρός (see § 307), prep., gov. gen., dat., and accus. cases, general signif., *towards.* IN COMPOSITION, it denotes motion, direction, reference, nearness, addition.
προ-σάββατον, ον, τό, *the day before the sabbath,* Mark xv. 42.*
προσ-αγορεύω, *to address by name, to designate,* Heb. v. 10.*
προσ-άγω, (1) trans., *to bring to, to bring near,* Matt. xviii. 24 (W. H.); Luke ix. 41; Acts xvi. 20; 1 Pet. iii. 18; (2) intrans., *to come to* or *towards, to approach,* Acts xxvii. 27.*
προσ-αγωγή, ῆς, ἡ, *approach, access,* Rom. v. 2; Eph. ii. 18, iii. 12 (εἰς, πρός, acc.).*
προσ-αιτέω, ῶ, *to beg, to ask earnestly,* Mark x. 46 (not W. H.); Luke xviii. 35 (not W. H.); John ix. 8.*
προσ-αίτης, ου, ὁ, *a beggar,* Mark x. 46 (W. H.); John ix. 8 (W. H.).*
προσ-ανα-βαίνω, *to go up to* (a more honourable place), Luke xiv. 10.*
προσ-αναλίσκω, *to spend in addition,* Luke viii. 43.*

προσ-ανα-πληρόω, ῶ, to fill up by adding to, to supply, 2 Cor. ix. 12, xi. 9.*
προσ-ανα-τίθημι, to lay up over and above; in mid., (1) to communicate or impart in addition (acc. and dat.), Gal. ii. 6; (2) to confer with (dat.), Gal. i. 16.*
προσ-απειλέω, ῶ, to utter additional threats, Acts iv. 21.*
προσ-δαπανάω, ῶ, ήσω, to spend in addition, Luke x. 35.*
προσ-δέομαι, to want more, to stand in need of (gen.), Acts xvii. 25.*
προσ-δέχομαι, dep. mid., (1) to receive to one's company, Luke xv. 2; (2) to admit, allow, accept, Heb. xi. 35; (3) to await, to expect (acc.), Mark xv. 43.
προσ-δοκάω, ῶ, to look for, expect, anticipate, whether with hope or fear.
προσ-δοκία, as, ἡ, a looking for, expectation, anticipation, Luke xxi. 26; Acts xii. 11.*
προσ-εάω, ῶ, to permit or suffer further, Acts xxvii. 7.*
προσ-εγγίζω, to approach, to come near to (dat.), Mark ii. 4.*
προσ-εδρεύω, to wait upon, to minister to (dat.), 1 Cor. ix. 13 (W. H., παρεδρεύω).
προσ-εργάζομαι, dep. mid., to gain by labour in addition, Luke xix. 16.*
προσ-έρχομαι (see § 103, 2), (1) generally, to come or to go to, abs., or dat. of place or person, to visit, to have intercourse with; (2) specially, to approach, to draw near to, GOD or CHRIST, Heb. vii. 25; (3) to assent to, concur in, 1 Tim. vi. 3.
προσ-ευχή, ῆς, ἡ, (1) prayer to God; (2) a place where prayer is offered, an oratory, only Acts xvi. 13, 16 (see § 268, note). Syn. 38.
προσ-εύχομαι, dep. mid., to pray to God (dat.), to offer prayer, to pray for (acc. of thing, ὑπέρ or περί, of person, ἵνα or ὅπως, of object, occasionally inf). Syn. 38.
προσ-έχω, to apply, with νοῦν expressed or understood, to apply the mind, to attend to, dat.; with ἀπό, to beware of; also, to give heed to, inf. with μή.
προσ-ηλόω, ῶ, to affix with nails, nail to, Col. ii. 14.*
προσ-ήλυτος, ου, ὁ, ἡ (ἔρχομαι), a "proselyte," a convert to Judaism, Matt. xxiii. 15; Acts ii. 10, vi. 5, xiii. 43.*

πρόσ-καιρος, ον, for a season, temporary, transient, Matt. xiii. 21; Mark iv. 17; 2 Cor. iv. 18; Heb. xi. 25.*
προσ-καλέω, ῶ, N.T., mid., to call to oneself, to call for, to summon; fig., to call to an office, to call to the Christian faith.
προσ-καρτερέω, ῶ, to persevere in, to continue stedfast in (dat.), Acts i. 14, ii. 42; to wait upon (dat.), Mark iii. 9; Acts x. 7.
προσ-καρτέρησις, εως, ἡ, perseverance, Eph. vi. 18.*
προσ-κεφάλαιον, ου, a cushion for the head, a pillow, Mark iv. 38.*
προσ-κληρόω, ῶ, to adjoin by lot or choice; pass., to consort with (dat.), Acts xvii. 4.*
προσ-κλίνω, to incline towards, Acts v. 36 (W. H.).*
πρόσ-κλισις, εως, ἡ (κλίνω), a leaning towards, partiality, 1 Tim. v. 21.*
προσ-κολλάω, ῶ, ήσω, pass., to join oneself to (dat.), as a companion, Acts v. 36 (W. H., προσκλίνω); to cleave to (πρός, acc.), as husband to wife, Matt. xix. 5 (W. H., κολλάω); Mark x. 7; Eph. v. 31.*
πρόσ-κομμα, τος, τό, a stumbling-block, offence, an occasion of falling, Rom. xiv. 13, 20; 1 Cor. viii. 9; 1 Pet. ii. 8; with λίθος, a stone of stumbling (R.V.), Rom. ix. 32, 33.*
προσ-κοπή, ῆς, ἡ, offence, an occasion of offence or stumbling, 2 Cor. vi. 3.*
προσ-κόπτω, to strike the foot against, Matt. iv. 6; so, to stumble, to take offence, 1 Pet. ii. 8.
προσ-κυλίω, to roll to, or upon (ἐπί, acc.), Matt. xxvii. 60; Mark xv. 46.*
προσ-κυνέω, to bow down, to prostrate oneself to, to worship, God or inferior beings, to adore (dat. or acc.). Syn. 36.
προσ-κυνητής, οῦ, ὁ, a worshipper, John iv. 23.*
προσ-λαλέω, ῶ, to speak to, to converse with (dat.), Acts xiii. 43, xxviii. 20.*
προσ-λαμβάνω, N.T., mid., to take to oneself, i.e., food, companions, to receive to fellowship, Rom. xiv. 1.
πρόσ-ληψις (W. H., -λημψις, εως, ἡ, a taking to oneself, a receiving, Rom. xi. 15.*
προσ-μένω, to continue with or in, to

adhere to (dat.), to stay in (ἐν) a place.
προσ-ορμίζω (ὅρμος), mid., to come to anchor, to draw to shore, Mark vi. 53.*
προσ-οφείλω, to owe besides or in addition, Philem. 19.*
προσ-οχθίζω (ὀχθέω), to be grieved or offended with (dat.), Heb. iii. 10, 17 (LXX.).*
πρόσ-πεινος, ον (πεῖνα), very hungry, Acts x. 10.*
προσ-πήγνυμι, to affix, to fasten, applied to Christ's being fastened to the cross, Acts ii. 23.*
προσ-πίπτω, (1) to fall down before (dat., or πρός, acc.); (2) to beat against (dat.), Matt. vii. 25.
προσ-ποιέω, ῶ, in mid., to fashion oneself to; hence, to pretend (inf.), Luke xxiv. 28; in John viii. 6, perhaps, to regard (W. H. omit).*
προσ-πορεύομαι, to come to, approach (dat.), Mark x. 35.*
προσ-ρήγνυμι, to dash against, as waves, Luke vi. 48, 49.*
προσ-τάσσω, ξω, abs. or acc., and inf., to enjoin (acc.) upon (dat.).
προ-στάτις, ιδος, ἡ, a patroness, succourer, Rom. xvi. 2.*
προσ-τίθημι, to place near or by the side of, to add to (dat., or ἐπί, dat. or acc.); mid., with inf., to go on to do a thing, i.e., to do again, Acts xii. 3; Luke xx. 11, 12; so 1st aor., pass., part., Luke xix. 11, προσθεὶς εἶπεν, he spake again (see § 399, d).
προσ-τρέχω, 2nd aor. προσέδραμον, to run to, Mark ix. 15, x. 17; Acts viii. 30.*
προσ-φάγιον, ου, τό, anything eaten with bread, as fish, meat, etc., John xxi. 5.*
πρόσ-φατος, ον (from φένω, perf. pass. πέφαμαι, see Westcott on Heb. x. 20), lit. "just slain," recent, new, Heb. x. 20;* adv., -ως, recently, Acts xviii. 2.*
προσ-φέρω, to bring to, dat.; to offer, to present, as money, Acts viii. 18; specially, to offer sacrifice; mid., to bear oneself towards, to deal with, Heb. xii. 7.
προσ-φιλής, ές, pleasing, loveable, Phil. iv. 8.*
προσ-φορά, ᾶς, ἡ, an offering, a sacrifice, an oblation. Syn. 37.

προσ-φωνέω, ῶ, to call to (dat.), to cry aloud, to call to oneself (acc.).
πρόσ-χυσις, εως, ἡ (χέω), an affusion, a sprinkling, Heb. xi. 28.*
προσ-ψαύω, to touch lightly, Luke xi. 46.*
προσωπο-ληπτέω (W. H., -λημπτ-), ῶ, to accept the person of any one, to show partiality, James ii. 9.*
προσωπο-λήπτης (W. H., -λημπτ-), ου, ὁ, a respecter of persons, a partial one, Acts x. 34.*
προσωπο-ληψία (W. H., -λημψ-), ας, ἡ, respect of persons, partiality, Rom. ii. 11; Eph. vi. 9; Col. iii. 25; James ii. 1.*
πρόσωπον, ου, τό (ὤψ), (1) the face, the countenance; in antithesis with καρδία, mere appearance; (2) the surface, as of the earth, Luke xxi. 35; of the heaven, Matt. xvi. 3.
προ-τάσσω, ξω, to appoint before, Acts xvii. 26 (W. H., προστάσσω).*
προ-τείνω, to stretch out, to tie up for scourging, Acts xxii. 25.*
πρότερος, έρα, ερον (comparative of πρό), former, Eph. iv. 22; πρότερον or τὸ πρότερον, as adv., before, formerly.
προ-τίθημι, N.T., mid., to set forth, perhaps Rom. iii. 25; to purpose, to design beforehand, Rom. i. 13; Eph. i. 9.*
προ-τρέπω, in mid., to exhort, Acts xviii. 27.*
προ-τρέχω, 2nd aor. προέδραμον, to run before, Luke xix. 4; John xx. 4.*
προ-υπάρχω, to be formerly, with participle, Luke xxiii. 12; Acts viii. 9.*
πρό-φασις, εως, ἡ, a pretext, an excuse; dat., adverbially, in appearance, pretence.*
προ-φέρω, to bring forth, Luke vi. 45.*
πρό-φημι, fut. προερῶ, perf. προείρηκα, 2nd aor. προεῖπον, to say before, i.e., at an earlier time, Gal. i. 9; in an earlier part of the discourse, 2 Cor. vii. 3; or prophetically, Mark xiii. 23.
προ-φητεία, ας, ἡ, (1) the gift of prophecy; (2) the exercise of the gift; plur., prophecies.
προ-φητεύω, σω, to be a prophet, to prophesy, to forth-tell, or speak of Divine things; (the meaning foretell is secondary and accidental); of false prophets, Matt. vii. 22; to divine,

used in mockery, Matt. xxvi. 68. Syn. 15.

προ-φήτης, ου, ὁ, (1) *a prophet*, i.e., one who has insight into Divine things and speaks them forth to others; plur., *the prophetic books of the O.T.;* (2) *a poet, a minstrel*, Tit. i. 12. Syn. 15.

προ-φητικός, ή, όν, *prophetic, uttered by prophets*, Rom. xvi. 26; 2 Pet. i. 19.*

προ-φῆτις, ιδος, ἡ, *a prophetess*. Luke ii. 36; Rev. ii. 20.*

προ-φθάνω, *to anticipate, to be beforehand*, with participle, Matt. xvii. 25.*

προ-χειρίζομαι, *to appoint, to choose, to destine*, Acts iii. 20 (W. H.), xxii. 14, xxvi. 16.*

προ-χειρο-τονέω, ῶ, *to fore-appoint, to choose beforehand*, Acts x. 41.*

Πρόχορος, ου, ὁ, *Prochorus*, Acts vi. 5.*

πρύμνα, ας, ἡ, *the hindmost part of a ship, the stern*, Mark iv. 38; Acts xxvii. 29, 41.*

πρωΐ, adv., *early in the morning, at dawn;* with advs., ἅμα πρωΐ, λίαν πρωΐ, *very early in the morning*.

πρωΐμος, η, ον, *early, of the early rain*, James v. 7 (W. H., πρώϊμος).*

πρωϊνός, adj., *belonging to the morning, of the morning star*, Rev. ii. 28, xxii. 16.*

πρῶτος, ία, ον, *of the morning;* fem. (sc. ὥρα), *morning*, Matt. xxvii. 1, xxi. 18 (W. H., πρωΐ); John xviii. 28 (W. H., πρωΐ), xxi. 4.*

πρῷρα, ας, ἡ, *the forward part of a ship, the prow*, Acts xxvii. 30, 41.*

πρωτεύω, *to have pre-eminence, to be chief*, Col. i. 18.*

πρωτο-καθ-εδρία, ας, ἡ, *a chief* or *uppermost seat*.

πρωτο-κλισία, ας, ἡ, *the chief place at a banquet*.

πρῶτος, η, ον (superlative of πρό), *first*, in place, time, or order; like πρότερος with following gen., *before*, only John i. 15, 30; πρῶτον, as adverb, *first*, Mark iv. 28; with gen., *before*, John xv. 18; τὸ πρῶτον, *at the first*, John x. 40.

πρωτο-στάτης, ου, ὁ, *a leader, a ringleader*, Acts xxiv. 5.*

πρωτο-τόκια, ίων, τά, *the rights of the first-born, the birthright*, Heb. xii. 16.*

πρωτό-τοκος, ον, *first-born;* ὁ πρωτότοκος, specially a title of Christ. Plur., *the first-born*, Heb. xii. 23, *of saints who died before Christ's coming*.

πταίω, σω, intrans., *to stumble, to fall, to err*, Rom. xi. 11; 2 Pet. i. 10; James ii. 10, iii. 2.*

πτέρνα, ας, ἡ, *the heel*, John xiii. 18.*

πτερύγιον, ου, τό (dim. πτέρυξ), *the extremity*, as *a battlement* or *parapet*, Matt. iv. 5; Luke iv. 9.*

πτέρυξ, υγος, ἡ, *a wing, a pinion*.

πτηνός, ή, όν (πέτομαι), *winged*, τὰ πτηνά, *birds, fowls*, 1 Cor. xv. 39.*

πτοέω, ῶ, *to terrify*, Luke xxi. 9, xxiv. 37.*

πτόησις, εως, ἡ, *terror, consternation*, 1 Pet. iii. 6.*

Πτολεμαΐς, ΐδος, ἡ, *Ptolemais*, Acts xxi. 7.*

πτύον, ου, τό, *a fan, a winnowing-shovel*, Matt. iii. 12; Luke iii. 17.*

πτύρω, *to terrify*, Phil. i. 28.*

πτύσμα, ατος, τό, *spittle, saliva*, John ix. 6.*

πτύσσω, ξω, *to fold, to roll up*, as a scroll, Luke iv. 20.*

πτύω, σω, *to spit*, Mark vii. 33, viii. 23; John ix. 6.*

πτῶμα, ατος, τό (πίπτω), *a body fallen in death, a carcase*, Matt. xxiv. 28.

πτῶσις, εως, ἡ, *a fall*, lit. or fig., Matt. vii. 27; Luke ii. 34.*

πτωχεία, ας, ἡ, *poverty, want*, 2 Cor. viii. 2, 9; Rev. ii. 9.*

πτωχεύω, σω, *to be in poverty*, 2 Cor. viii. 9.*

πτωχός, ή, όν, *reduced to beggary, poor, destitute, spiritually poor*, in a good sense, Matt. v. 3; in a bad sense, Rev. iii. 17. Syn. 30.

πυγμή, ῆς, ἡ (πύξ), *the fist*, Mark vii. 3 (see R.V. and marg.).*

Πύθων (W. H., Πύθων), ωνος, ὁ, *Python, a divining demon;* called after a name of the heathen deity Apollo, Acts xvi. 16 (see R.V.).*

πυκνός, ή, όν, *frequent*, 1 Tim. v. 23; neut. plur. πυκνά, as adverb, *often*, Luke v. 33; so πυκνότερον, *more frequently*, Acts xxiv. 26.*

πυκτεύω (πύξ), *to box, fight*, 1 Cor. ix 26.*

πύλη, ης, ἡ, *a door* or *gate* πύλαι ᾄδου, *the gates of Hades*, i.e., the powers of the unseen world, Matt. xvi. 18. Syn 71.

πυλών, ῶνος, ὁ, *the entrance to a house*, Acts x. 17; *a gateway, porch*, Matt. xxvi. 71. Syn. 71.

πυνθάνομαι, 2nd aor. ἐπυθόμην, (1) *to ask, ask* from (παρά, gen.), *to inquire;* (2) *to ascertain by inquiry*, only Acts xxiii. 34. Syn. 9.

πῦρ, πυρός, τό, *fire* generally; *of the heat of the sun*, Rev. xvi. 8; *of lightning*, Luke ix. 54; GOD is so called, Heb. xii. 29; fig. for *strife*, Luke xii. 49; *trials*, 1 Cor. iii. 13; *of the eternal fire*, or *future punishment*, Matt. xviii. 8.

πυρά, ᾶς, ἡ, *a heap of fuel burning, a fire*, Acts xxviii. 2, 3.*

πύργος, ου, ὁ, *a tower, a lofty building, a fortress* (comp. *burgh*).

πύρεσσω, *to be sick of a fever*, Matt. viii. 14; Mark i. 30.*

πυρετός, οῦ, ὁ, *a fever*.

πύρινος, η, ον, *fiery, glittering*, Rev. ix. 17.*

πυρόω, ῶ, N.T., pass., *to be set on fire, to burn, to be inflamed, to glow with heat*, as metal in a furnace, *to be tried with fire*.

πυρράζω, *to be fire-coloured, to be red*, Matt. xvi. 2, 3.*

πυρρός, ά, όν, *fiery-red, fire-coloured*, Rev. vi. 4, xii. 3.*

πύρωσις, εως, ἡ, *a burning, a conflagration*, Rev. xviii. 9, 18; *severe trial*, as by fire, 1 Pet. iv. 12.*

πω, an enclitic particle, *even, yet*, used only in composition; see μήπω, μηδέπω, οὔπω, οὐδέπω.

πωλέω, ῶ, ἤσω, *to sell, to trade*, Matt. xxi. 12.

πῶλος, ου, ὁ, *a youngling, a foal* or *colt*, as Matt. xxi. 2.

πώ-ποτε, adv., *at any time*, used only after a negative, *not at any time, never*.

πωρόω, ῶ, σω, *to harden, to render callous*, fig.

πώρωσις, εως, ἡ, *hardness of heart, callousness*, Mark iii. 5; Rom. xi. 25; Eph. iv. 18.*

πως, an enclitic particle, *in a manner, by any means*.

πῶς, adv., interrog., *how? in what manner? by what means?* Also in exclamations, as Luke xii. 50; John xi. 36; with subj. or opt. (ἄν),

implying a strong negative, Matt. xxvi. 54; Acts viii. 31. Often (N.T.) in indirect interrogations (classical, ὅπως), Matt. vi. 28, etc.

P.

P, ρ, ῥῶ, *rho, r*, and as an initial always, ῥ, *rh*, the seventeenth letter. As a numeral, ρ′ = 100; ρ, = 100,000.

'Ραάβ, or 'Ραχάβ, ἡ (Heb.), *Rahab*.

'Ραββί (W. H., 'Ραββεί), (Heb.,) "*Rabbi*," *my master*, a title of respect in Jewish schools of learning; often applied to CHRIST. Syn. 59.

'Ραββονί or 'Ραββουνί (W. H., 'Ραββουνεί) (Heb.,) like 'Ραββί, but of higher honour, *my great master*, Mark x. 51; John xx. 16.*

ῥαβδίζω, ίσω, *to scourge, to beat with rods*, Acts xvi. 22; 2 Cor. xi. 25.*

ῥάβδος, ου, ἡ, *a wand, rod, staff*, Matt. x. 10; 1 Cor. iv. 21; Rev. xi. 1; *a rod of authority, a sceptre*, Heb. i. 8.

ῥαβδ-οῦχος, ου, ὁ (ἔχω), *the holder of the rods*, a Roman officer, *lictor*, Acts xvi. 35, 38.*

'Ραγαῦ, ὁ (Heb.), *Ragau*, Luke iii. 35.*

ῥᾳδι-ούργημα, ατος, τό (ῥᾴδιος, *easy*, and ἔργον, "*an easy or careless deed*"), *an act of villany*, Acts xviii. 14.*

ῥᾳδι-ουργία, ας, ἡ, *craftiness, villany*, Acts xiii. 10.*

'Ρακά (Heb., Aram. form), *Raca!* a term of contempt, Matt. v. 22 (see § 153, ii.).*

ῥάκος, ους, τό (ῥήγνυμι), *a remnant torn off, a piece*, Matt. ix. 16; Mark ii. 21.*

'Ραμᾶ, ἡ (Heb.), *Rama*, Matt. ii. 18.*

ῥαντίζω, ίσω, *to sprinkle, to cleanse ceremonially* (acc.) *by sprinkling, to purify from* (ἀπό), Heb. ix. 13, 19, 21, x. 22.*

ῥαντισμός, οῦ, ὁ, *sprinkling, purification*, Heb. xii. 24; 1 Pet. i. 2.*

ῥαπίζω, ίσω, *to smite with the hand* (as distinguished from ῥαβδίζω), Matt. v. 39, xxvi. 67.*

ῥάπισμα, ατος, τό, *a blow with the open hand*, Mark xiv. 65; John xviii. 22, xix. 3.*

ῥαφίς, ίδος, ἡ, *a needle*, Matt. xix. 24;

Mark x. 25; Luke xviii. 25 (W. H., βελόνη).*
'Ραχάβ. See 'Ραάβ.
'Ραχήλ, ή (Heb.), *Rachel*, Matt. ii. 18.*
'Ρεβέκκα, ης, ή, *Rebekah*, Rom. ix. 10.*
ῥέδα or ῥέδη, ης, ή, *a chariot*, Rev. xviii. 13.*
'Ρεμφάν or 'Ρεφάν (W. H., 'Ρομφά), ὁ, a Coptic word, *Remphan*, the *Saturn* of later mythology, Acts vii. 43 (Heb., *Chiun*, Amos v. 26).*
ῥέω (*F*), ῥεύσω, *to flow*, John vii. 38.*
ῥέω (see φημί, εἶπον). From this obs. root, *to say*, are derived: act. perf., εἴρηκα; pass., εἴρημαι; 1st aor. pass., ἐρρέθην or ἐρρήθην; part., ῥηθείς; espec. the neut. τὸ ῥηθέν, *that which was spoken* by (ὑπό, gen.).
'Ρήγιον, ου, τό, *Rhegium*, now Rheggio, Acts xxviii. 13.*
ῥῆγμα, ατος, τό (ῥήγνυμι), *what is broken, a crash, a ruin*, Luke vi. 49.*
ῥήγνυμι (or ῥήσσω, as Mark ix. 18), ῥήξω, *to break, to rend, to burst, to dash against the ground, to break forth*, as into praise, Matt. vii. 6, ix. 17; Mark ii. 22, ix. 18; Luke v. 37, ix. 42; Gal. iv. 27.*
ῥῆμα, ατος, τό, *a thing spoken;* (1) *a word* or *saying* of any kind, as *command, report, promise;* (2) *a thing, a matter, a business.* Syn. 8.
'Ρησά, ὁ (Heb.), *Rhesa*, Luke iii. 27.*
ῥήσσω. See ῥίγνυμι.
ῥήτωρ, ορος, ὁ, *an orator*, Acts xxiv. 1.*
ῥητῶς, adv., *expressly, in so many words*, 1 Tim. iv. 1.*
ῥίζα, ης, ή, (1) *a root of a tree* or *a plant;* met., *the origin* or *source of anything;* fig., *constancy, perseverance;* (2) that which comes from the root, *a descendant*, Rom. xv. 12; Rev. v. 5.
ῥιζόω, ῶ, ώσω, *to root;* perf., pass., part., ἐρριζωμένος, *firmly rooted*, fig., Eph. iii. 17; Col. ii. 7.*
ῥιπή, ῆς, ή (ῥίπτω), *a jerk, a twinkle*, as of the eye, 1 Cor. xv. 52.*
ῥιπίζω, ίσω, *to move*, as waves by the wind, James i. 6.*
ῥιπτέω, ῶ, *to throw off* or *away*, Acts xxii. 23.*
ῥίπτω, ψω, 1st aor., ἔρριψα; part., ῥῖψας; *to throw, throw down, throw out, throw apart, scatter*, Matt. ix. 36, xv. 30, xxvii. 5; Luke iv. 35, xvii. 2; Acts xxvii. 19, 29.*
'Ροβοάμ, ὁ (Heb.), *Rehoboam*, Matt. i. 7.*
'Ρόδη, ης, ή (*Rose*), *Rhoda*, Acts xii. 13.*
'Ρόδος, ου, ή, *Rhodes*, Acts xxi. 2.*
ῥοιζηδόν, adv. (ῥοῖζος, *roaring*, as of waves), *with a great noise*, 2 Pet. iii. 10.*
ῥομφαία, ας, ή, *a sword*, as Rev. i. 16; fig., *piercing grief*, Luke ii. 35.
'Ρουβήν, ὁ (Heb.), *Reuben*, Rev. vii. 5.*
'Ρούθ, ή (Heb.), *Ruth*, Mark i. 5.*
'Ροῦφος, ου (Lat.), *Rufus*, (1) Mark xv. 21; (2) Rom. xvi. 13, perhaps the same person.*
ῥύμη, ης, ή, *a narrow street, a lane*, Matt. vi. 2; Luke xiv. 21; Acts ix. 11, xii. 10.*
ῥύομαι, σομαι, dep. mid., 1st aor., pass., ἐρρύσθην, *to draw* or *snatch from danger, to deliver;* ὁ ῥυόμενος, *the Deliverer.*
ῥυπαίνω, *to defile*, Rev. xxii. 11 (W. H.).*
ῥυπαρεύομαι, *to be filthy*, Rev. xxii. 11 (W. H. marg.).*
ῥυπαρία, ας, ή, *filth, pollution*, James i. 21.*
ῥυπαρός, ά, όν, *sordid, filthy, defiled*, James ii. 2; Rev. xxii. 11 (W. H.).*
ῥύπος, ου, ὁ, *filth, filthiness*, 1 Pet. iii. 21.*
ῥυπόω, ῶ, *to be filthy*, Rev. xxii. 11 (not W. H.).*
ῥύσις, εως, ή (ῥέω), *a flux, issue*, Mark v. 25; Luke viii. 43, 44.*
ῥυτίς, ίδος, ή, *a wrinkle;* fig., *a spiritual defect*, Eph. v. 27.*
'Ρωμαϊκός, ή, όν, *Roman*, Luke xxiii. 38.*
'Ρωμαῖος, ου, ὁ, *a Roman, a citizen of Rome.*
'Ρωμαϊστί, adv., *in the Roman* or *Latin tongue*, John xix. 10.*
'Ρώμη, ης, ή, *Rome.*
ῥώννυμι, ῥώσω, *to strengthen;* only perf., pass., imper., ἔρρωσο, ἔρρωσθε, *farewell*, Acts xv. 29, xxiii. 30 (W. H. omit).*

Σ.

Σ, σ, final **s,** σίγμα, *sigma*, **s**, the eighteenth letter. As a numeral, σ´ = 200; σ, = 200,000.

σαβαχθανί (W. H., -εί), (Aram.), sabachthani, thou hast or hast thou forsaken me? Matt. xxvii. 46; Mark xv. 34; from the Aram. rendering of Ps. xxii. 1.*
σαβαώθ (Heb.), sabaoth, hosts, armies, in the phrase, "the LORD (Jehovah) of hosts," Rom. ix. 29; James v. 4.*
σαββατισμός, οῦ, ὁ, a keeping of sabbath, a sabbath rest (R.V.), Heb. iv. 9.*
σάββατον, ου, τό (from Heb.), dat., plur., σάββασι(ν), (1) the sabbath; (2) a period of seven days, a week. In both senses the plural is sometimes used.
σαγήνη, ης, ἡ, a drag-net, Matt. xiii. 47. Syn. 70.*
Σαδδουκαῖος, ου, ὁ, a Sadducee. Plur., of the sect in general. Prob. derived from the Heb. word for just, righteous.
Σαδώκ, ὁ (Heb.), Sadok, Matt. i. 13.*
σαίνω, to move, disturb, pass., 1 Thess. iii. 3.*
σάκκος, ου, ὁ, sackcloth, a sign of mourning, Matt. xi. 21; Luke x. 13; Rev. vi. 12, xi. 3.*
Σαλά, ὁ (Heb.), Sala, Luke iii. 35.*
Σαλαθιήλ, ὁ (Heb.), Salathiel, Matt. i. 12.*
Σαλαμίς, ῖνος, ἡ, Salamis, Acts xiii. 5.*
Σαλείμ, ἡ, Salim, John iii. 23.*
σαλεύω, σω, to shake, to cause to shake, as Matt. xi. 7; Heb. xii. 27; so, to excite, as the populace, Acts xvii. 13; fig., to disturb in mind, 2 Thess. ii. 2.
Σαλήμ, ἡ (Heb.), Salem, Heb. vii. 1.*
Σαλμών, ὁ (Heb.), Salmon, Matt. i. 4.*
Σαλμώνη, ης, ἡ, Salmone, Acts xxvii. 7.*
σάλος, ου, ὁ, the rolling of the sea in a tempest, Luke xxi. 25.*
σάλπιγξ, ιγγος, ἡ, a trumpet.
σαλπίζω, ίσω (class., -ίγξω), to sound a trumpet. For impers. use, 1 Cor. xv. 52 (see § 171).
σαλπιστής, οῦ, ὁ (class., -ιγκτής), a trumpeter, Rev. xviii. 22.*
Σαλώμη, ης, ἡ, Salome, wife of Zebedee, Mark xv. 40, xvi. 1.*
Σαμάρεια, ας, ἡ, Samaria, either (1) the district, or (2) the city, afterwards called Sebaste.
Σαμαρείτης, ου, ὁ, a Samaritan.
Σαμαρεῖτις, ιδος, ἡ, a Samaritan woman, John iv. 9.*
Σαμο-θράκη, ης. ἡ. Samothrace, Acts xvi. 11.*

Σάμος, ου, ἡ, Samos, Acts xx. 15.*
Σαμουήλ, ὁ (Heb.), Samuel.
Σαμψών, ὁ (Heb.), Samson, Heb. xi. 32.*
σανδάλιον, ου, τό, a sandal, Mark vi. 9; Acts xii. 8.*
σανίς, ίδος, ἡ, a plank, a board, Acts xxvii. 44.*
Σαούλ, ὁ (Heb.), Saul, (1) the king of Israel; (2) the apostle, only in direct address (see Σαῦλος).
σαπρός, ά, όν, rotten, hence useless; fig., corrupt.
Σαπφείρη, ης, ἡ, Sapphira, Acts v. 1.*
σάπφειρος, ου, ὁ, a sapphire, Rev. xxi. 19.*
σαργάνη, ης, ἡ, a basket, generally of twisted cords, 2 Cor. xi. 33.*
Σάρδεις, ων, dat. εσι(ν), αἱ, Sardis, Rev. i. 11, iii. 1, 4.*
σάρδινος, ου, ὁ (Rec. in Rev. iv. 3 for following).
σάρδιον, ίου, τό, a sardine stone, blood or fresh coloured; or carnelian, Rev. iv. 3 (W. H.), xxi. 20.*
σαρδ-όνυξ, υχος, ἡ, a sardonyx, a precious stone, white streaked with red, Rev. xxi. 20.*
Σάρεπτα, ων, τά, Sarepta, Luke iv. 26.*
σαρκικός, ή, όν, fleshly, carnal, whether (1) belonging to human nature in its bodily manifestation, or (2) belonging to human nature as sinful, Rom. xv. 27; 1 Cor. iii. 3, ix. 11; 2 Cor. i. 12, x. 4; 1 Pet. ii. 11; for Rec. σαρκικός, W. H. substitute σάρκινος, in Rom. vii. 14; 1 Cor. iii. 1; Heb. vii. 16; and ἄνθρωπος in 1 Cor. iii. 4. Syn. 55.*
σάρκινος, η, ον, (1) fleshy, constituted of flesh, opp. to λίθινος, 2 Cor. iii. 3; (2) fleshly, carnal (W. H. in the passages quoted under σαρκικός). Syn. 55.*
σάρξ, σαρκός, ἡ, flesh, sing., Luke xxiv. 39; plur., James v. 3; the human body, man; the human nature of man as distinguished from his divine nature (πνεῦμα); human nature, as sinful; πᾶσα σάρξ, every man, all men; κατὰ σάρκα, as a man; σάρξ καὶ αἷμα, flesh and blood, i.e., man as frail and simple; ζῆν, περιπατεῖν κατὰ σάρκα, to live, to walk after flesh, of a carnal, unspiritual life. The word also denotes kinship, Rom. xi. 14. Syn. 55.
Σαρούχ, ὁ (Heb.), (W. H., Σερούχ,) Saruch or Seruch (Serug), Luke iii. 35.*

σαρόω—Σίμων]   VOCABULARY.   503

σαρόω, ῶ, ώσω, to sweep, to cleanse with a broom, Matt. xii. 44; Luke xi. 25, xv. 8.*
Σάρρα, ας, ἡ, Sarah.
Σάρων, ωνος, ὁ, Saron, Acts ix. 35.*
Σατᾶν, ὁ (Heb.), and Σατανᾶς, ᾶ, the Adversary, Satan, the Heb. proper name for the Devil, διάβολος; met., for one who would do (consciously or unconsciously) the work of the Adversary, Matt. xvi. 23; Mark viii. 33. Syn. 53.
σάτον, ου, τό (see μόδιος), a seah, a measure equal to a modius and a half, Matt. xiii. 33; Luke xiii. 21.*
Σαῦλος, ου, ὁ, Saul, the apostle, generally in this form (see Σαούλ).
σβέννυμι, σβέσω, (1) to extinguish, to quench; (2) fig., to restrain.
σεαυτοῦ, ῆς, οῦ (only masc. in N.T.), a reflex. pron., of thyself; dat., σεαυτῷ, to thyself; acc., σεαυτόν, thyself.
σεβάζομαι, dep., pass., to stand in awe of, to worship. Syn. 36.
σέβασμα, ατος, τό, an object of religious worship, Acts xvii. 23; 2 Thess. ii. 4.*
σεβαστός, ή, όν, venerated, august, a title of the Cæsars, Augustus, Acts xxv. 21, 25. Hence, secondarily, Augustan, imperial, Acts xxvii. 1.*
σέβομαι, dep., to reverence, to worship God, Mark vii. 7; οἱ σεβόμενοι, the devout, "proselytes of the gate," Acts xvii. 17. Syn. 36.
σειρά, ᾶς, ἡ, a chain, 2 Pet. ii. 4 (W. H. read following).*
σειρός, ὸν, ὁ, a pit, 2 Pet. ii. 4 (W. H.).*
σεισμός, οῦ, ὁ, a shaking, as an earthquake, Matt. xxiv. 7; a storm at sea, Matt. viii. 24.
σείω, σω, to shake; fig., to agitate.
Σεκοῦνδος, ου, ὁ (Lat.), Secundus, Acts xx. 4.*
Σελεύκεια, ας, ἡ, Seleucia, Acts xiii. 4.*
σελήνη, ης, ἡ, the moon.
σεληνιάζομαι, to be lunatic, to suffer from periodical disease, as epilepsy, Matt. iv. 24, xvii. 15.*
Σεμεΐ, ὁ (Heb.), Shimei, Luke iii. 26.*
σεμίδαλις, εως, ἡ, flour, Rev. xviii. 13.*
σεμνός, ή, όν, (1) venerable, serious, of men, 1 Tim. iii. 8, 11; Tit. ii. 2; (2) honourable, of acts, Phil. iv. 8.*
σεμνότης, τητος, ἡ, dignity, seriousness, 1 Tim. ii. 2, iii. 4; Tit. ii. 7.*
Σέργιος, ου, ὁ, Sergius, Acts xiii. 7.*

Σήθ, ὁ (Heb.), Seth, Luke iii. 38.*
Σήμ, ὁ (Heb.), Shem, Luke iii. 36.*
σημαίνω, ανῶ, 1st aor. ἐσήμανα, to signify, intimate.
σημεῖον, ου, τό, a sign, that by which a thing is known, a token, an indication, of Divine presence and power, 1 Cor. xiv. 22; Luke xxi. 7, 11. Hence, especially, a miracle, whether real or unreal. Syn. 54.
σημειόω, ῶ, in mid., to mark for oneself, to note, 2 Thess. iii. 14.*
σήμερον, adv., to-day, at this time, now; ἡ (ἡμέρα) σήμερον, this very day, Acts xix. 40.
σήπω, to make rotten; 2nd perf. σέσηπα, to become rotten, perish, James v. 2.*
σηρικός, ή, όν (W. H., σιρικός), adj., silken, neut. as subst., silk, Rev. xviii. 12.*
σής, σητός, ὁ, a moth, Matt. vi. 19, 20; Luke xii. 33.*
σητόβρωτος, ον, moth-eaten, James v. 2.*
σθενόω, ῶ, to strengthen, to confirm, 1 Pet. v. 10.*
σιαγών, όνος, ἡ, the cheek or jawbone, Matt. v. 39; Luke vi. 29.*
σιγάω, ῶ, ήσω, to keep silence; to keep secret, Luke ix. 36; pass., to be concealed, Rom. xvi. 25.
σιγή, ῆς, ἡ, silence, Acts xxi. 40; Rev. viii. 1.*
σιδήρεος, έα, εον, contr., οῦς, ᾶ, οῦν, made of iron, Acts xii. 10, Rev.*
σίδηρος, ου, ὁ, iron, Rev. xviii. 12.*
Σιδών, ῶνος, ἡ, Sidon.
Σιδώνιος, ία, όν, Sidonian, inhabitant of Sidon.
σικάριος, ίου, ὁ (Lat.), an assassin, Acts xxi. 38.*
σίκερα, τό (Heb., Aram. form), strong drink, Luke i. 15.*
Σίλας, dat. ᾳ, acc. αν, ὁ, Silas, contr. from Silvanus.
Σιλουανός, οῦ, ὁ, Silvanus.
Σιλωάμ, ὁ, Siloam or Siloah, Luke xiii. 4; John ix. 7, 11.*
σιμικίνθιον, ίου, τό (Lat., semicinctium), an apron, worn by artisans, Acts xix. 12.*
Σίμων, ωνος, ὁ, Simon. Nine persons of the name appear to be mentioned: (1) the Apostle Peter; (2) the Apostle Zelotes; (3) brother of Jesus, Mark vi. 3; (4) Simon of Cyrene; (5) father of

Judas Iscariot; (6) a "certain Pharisee," Luke vii. 40; (7) Simon the leper, Matt. xxvi. 6; (8) Simon Magus, Acts viii. 9; (9) Simon the tanner, Acts ix. 43. Possibly (2) and (3) were identical; see also (6) and (7).
Σινά, τό (Heb.), *Sinai.*
σίναπι, εως, τό, *mustard, mustard-seed.*
σινδών, όνος, ή, *linen, a linen cloth.*
σ.νιάζω, *to sift,* as corn, *to prove by trials* and *afflictions,* Luke xxii. 31.*
σιρικός. See σηρικός.
σιτευτός, ή, όν, *fed with corn, fatted,* Luke xv. 23, 27, 30.*
σιτίον, ου, τό, *grain, corn,* Acts vii. 12 (W. H.).*
σιτιστός, ή, όν, *fed, nourished;* τὰ σιτιστά, *fatlings,* Matt. xxii. 4.*
σιτο-μέτριον, ίου, τό, *a corn-ration,* Luke xii. 42.*
σῖτος, ου, ὁ, *wheat, corn;* τὰ σῖτα, *grain.*
Σιχάρ. See Συχάρ.
Σιών, ὁ or τό, *Sion,* the mountain; met. (fem.), for the *city* Jerusalem; and fig., for the *church,* the spiritual Jerusalem.
σιωπάω, ῶ, ήσω, *to be silent,* whether voluntarily or from dumbness; *to become still,* as the sea, Mark iv. 39.
σκανδαλίζω, ίσω, *to cause to stumble, pervert, to grieve* (acc.); pass., *to stumble, to be provoked, to be indignant.*
σκάνδαλον, ου, τό, *a snare, a stumbling-block;* fig., *a cause of offence or perversion.*
σκάπτω, ψω, *to dig,* Luke vi. 48, xiii. 8, xvi. 3.*
σκάφη, ης, ή, *a boat, a skiff* (as excavated from a tree), Acts xxvii. 16, 30, 32.*
σκέλος, ους, τό, *the leg,* John xix. 31, 32, 33.*
σκέπασμα, ατος, τό, *clothing,* 1 Tim. vi. 8.*
Σκευᾶς, ᾶ, ὁ, *Scéva,* Acts xix. 14.*
σκευή, ῆς, ή, *furniture, fittings,* Acts xxvii. 19.*
σκεῦος, ους, τό, (1) *a vessel* or *utensil,* to contain a liquid, or for any other purpose; fig., of recipients generally, *a vessel* of mercy, of wrath, Rom. ix. 23, 32; *an instrument* by which anything is done; domestic *goods,* Matt. xii. 29; of a ship, *the gear,* Acts xxvii. 17; fig., of God's servants, Acts ix. 15; 2 Cor. iv. 7.

σκηνή, ῆς, ή, *a tent, an abode* or *dwelling, the tabernacle reared in the wilderness, an idolatrous tabernacle.*
σκηνο-πηγία, ας, ή (lit., *tent-fixing*), *the feast of tabernacles,* John vii. 2.*
σκηνο-ποιός, οῦ, ὁ, *a tent-maker,* Acts xviii. 3.*
σκῆνος, ους, τό, *a tent;* fig., of the human body, 2 Cor. v. 1, 4.*
σκηνόω, ῶ, ώσω, *to frame* or *spread a tent,* Rev. vii. 15; met., *to dwell,* John i. 14; Rev. xii. 12, xiii. 6, xxi. 3.*
σκήνωμα, ατος, τό, *a tent pitched, a dwelling,* Acts vii. 46; fig., of the body, 2 Pet. i. 13, 14.*
σκιά, ᾶς, ή, (1) *a shadow, a thick darkness,* Matt. iv. 16 (LXX.); (2) *a faint delineation,* Col. ii. 17. Syn. 56.
σκιρτάω, ῶ, ήσω, *to leap* for joy, *exult,* Luke i. 41, 44, vi. 23.*
σκληρο-καρδία, ας, ή, *hardness of heart, perverseness,* Matt. xix. 8; Mark x. 5; xvi. 14.*
σκληρός, ά, όν, *hard, violent,* as the wind, James iii. 4; fig., *grievous, painful,* Acts ix. 5 (W. H. omit), xxvi. 14; Jude 15; *stern, severe,* Matt. xxv. 24; John vi. 60.*
σκληρότης, τητος, ή, fig., *hardness* of heart, *obstinacy,* Rom. ii. 5.*
σκληρο-τράχηλος, ον, *hard-* or *stiff-necked;* fig., *perverse,* Acts vii. 51.*
σκληρύνω, υνῶ, fig., *to make hard, to harden,* as the heart, Rom. ix. 18; Heb. iii. 8, 15, iv. 7; mid., *to harden oneself, to become obdurate,* Acts xix. 9; Heb. iii. 13.*
σκολιός, ά, όν, *crooked,* Luke iii. 5; fig., *perverse, morose,* Acts ii. 40; Phil. ii. 15; 1 Pet. ii. 18.*
σκόλοψ, οπος, ὁ, *a thorn;* fig., *a sharp infliction,* 2 Cor. xii. 7.*
σκοπέω, ῶ, (1) *to look at, to regard attentively;* (2) *to take heed* (acc.), *beware*(μή).
σκοπός, οῦ, ὁ, *a mark aimed at, a goal;* κατὰ σκοπόν, *in accordance with the goal, i.e.,* aiming straight at it, Phil. iii. 14.*
σκορπίζω, σω, *to disperse, to scatter abroad,* as frightened sheep, John x. 12; *to distribute alms,* 2 Cor. ix. 9.
σκορπίος, ίου, ὁ, *a scorpion.*
σκοτεινός, ή, όν, *dark,* Mark vi. 23; Luke xi. 34, 36.*

σκοτία, ας, ἡ, darkness, Matt. x. 27; fig., spiritual darkness.
σκοτίζω, σω, in pass., to be darkened, as the sun, Matt. xiii. 24; fig., as the mind, Rom. i. 21.
σκότος, ους, τό (masc. only in Heb. xii. 18, where W. H. read ζόφος), darkness, physical, Matt. xxvii. 45; moral, John iii. 19.
σκοτόω, ῶ, pass. only, to be darkened, Eph. iv. 18; Rev. ix. 2 (W. H.), xvi. 10.*
σκύβαλον, ου, τό (perhaps from κυσὶ βάλλειν, to cast to the dogs), refuse, dregs, Phil. iii. 8.*
Σκύθης, ου, ὁ, a Scythian, as typical of the uncivilised, Col. iii. 11.*
σκυθρ-ωπός, όν, sad-countenanced, stern, grim, Matt. vi. 16; Luke xxiv. 17.*
σκύλλω, λῶ, pass., perf., ἔσκυλμαι, to trouble, harass, tire, Matt. ix. 36 (W. H.); Mark v. 35; Luke vii. 6, viii. 29.*
σκῦλον, ου, τό, spoil taken from a foe, Luke xi. 22.*
σκωληκό-βρωτος, ον, eaten by worms, Acts xii. 23.*
σκώληξ, ηκος, ὁ, a gnawing worm, Mark ix. 44 (W. H. omit), 46 (W. H. omit), 48.*
σμαράγδινος, ίνη, ινον, made of emerald, Rev. iv. 3.*
σμάραγδος, ου, ὁ, an emerald, Rev. xxi. 19.*
σμύρνα, ης, ἡ, myrrh, Matt. ii. 11; John xix. 39.*
Σμύρνα, ης, ἡ, Smyrna.
Σμυρναῖος, ου, ὁ, ἡ, one of Smyrna, a Smyrnæan, Rev. ii. 8 (not W. H.).*
σμυρνίζω, to mingle with myrrh, Mark xv. 23.*
Σόδομα, ων, τά, Sodom.
Σολομών or -μῶν, ῶντος or ῶνος, Solomon.
σορός, οῦ, ὁ, a bier, an open coffin, Luke vii. 14.*
σός, σή, σόν, a poss. pron., thy, thine (see §§ 56, 255).
σουδάριον, ίου, τό (Lat.), a napkin, handkerchief.
Σουσάννα, ης, ἡ, Susanna, Luke viii. 3.*
σοφία, ας, ἡ, wisdom, insight, skill, human, Luke xi. 31; or divine, 1 Cor. i. 21, 24.

σοφίζω, ίσω, to make wise, to enlighten, 2 Tim. iii. 15; pass., to be devised skilfully, 2 Pet. i. 16.*
σοφός, ή, όν, wise, either (1) in action, (2) in acquirement, learned, skilful, able; (3) in philosophy, profound.
Σπανία, ας, ἡ, Spain, Rom. xv. 24, 28.*
σπαράσσω, ξω, to tear, to convulse, to throw into spasms, Mark i. 26, ix. 20 (not W. H.), 26; Luke ix. 39.*
σπαργανόω, ῶ, ώσω, perf., pass., part., ἐσπαργανωμένος, to swathe, to wrap in swaddling clothes, Luke ii. 7, 12.*
σπαταλάω, ῶ, ήσω, to live extravagantly or luxuriously, 1 Tim. v. 6; James v. 5.*
σπάω, ῶ, άσω, mid., to draw, to draw out, as a sword, Mark xiv. 47; Acts xvi. 27.*
σπεῖρα, ης, ἡ, (1) a band or cohort of soldiers, the tenth part of a legion, Acts x. 1; (2) a military guard, John xviii. 3, 12.
σπείρω, σπερῶ, 1st aor., ἔσπειρα; perf., pass., ἔσπαρμαι; 2nd aor., pass., ἐσπάρην, to sow or scatter, as seed; to spread or scatter, as the word of God. Applied to giving alms, 2 Cor. ix. 6; to burial, 1 Cor. xv. 42, 43; and to spiritual effort generally, Gal. vi. 8.
σπεκουλάτωρ, ορος, ὁ (Lat.), a body-guardsman, a soldier in attendance upon royalty, Mark vi. 27. (See § 154, c.)*
σπένδω, σω, to pour out, as a drink offering, to offer in sacrifice, Phil. ii. 17; 2 Tim. iv. 6.*
σπέρμα, ατος, τό, a seed, produce, Matt. xiii. 24-38; children, offspring, posterity, John vii. 42; a remnant, Rom. ix. 29.
σπερμο-λόγος, ου, ὁ, ἡ, a trifler, Acts xvii. 18; i.e., one who picks up trifles, as birds do seed.*
σπεύδω, σω, (1) to hasten, intrans., often adding to another verb the notion of speed, Luke xix. 5, 6; (2) to desire earnestly (acc.), 2 Pet. iii. 12.
σπήλαιον, ου, τό, a cave, a den, Heb. xi. 38.
σπιλάς, άδος, ἡ, a rock, occasioning shipwreck; of false teachers, a hidden rock (R. V.), Jude 12.*
σπίλος, ου, a spot; fig., a blot, Eph v. 27; 2 Pet. ii. 13.*

σπιλόω, ῶ, to stain, to contaminate, James iii. 6; Jude 23.*
σπλάγχνα, ων, τά, bowels, only Acts i. 18; elsewhere, fig., the affections, compassion, the heart, as Col. iii. 12; 1 John iii. 17.
σπλαγχνίζομαι, dep., with 1st aor., pass., ἐσπλαγχνίσθην, to feel compassion, to have pity on (gen., or ἐπί, dat. or acc., once περί, Matt. ix. 36).
σπόγγος, ου, ὁ, a sponge, Matt. xxvii. 48; Mark xv. 36; John xix. 29.*
σποδός, οῦ, ἡ, ashes, Matt. xi. 21; Luke x. 13; Heb. xi. 13.*
σπορά, ᾶς, ἡ, seed, 1 Pet. i. 23.*
σπόριμος, ον, sown; neut. plur., τὰ σπόριμα, cornfields, Matt. xii. 1; Mark ii. 23; Luke vi. 1.*
σπόρος, ου, ὁ, seed for sowing.
σπουδάζω, άσω, to hasten, to give diligence, to be in earnest (with inf.).
σπουδαῖος, αία, αῖον, diligent, earnest, 2 Cor. viii. 17, 22;* adv., -ως, earnestly, Luke vii. 4; 2 Tim. i. 17 (W. H.); Tit. iii. 13;* compar. advs., σπουδαιότερον, 2 Tim. i. 17 (not W. H.), and -τέρως, Phil. ii. 28.*
σπουδή, ῆς, ἡ, (1) speed, haste; (2) diligence, earnestness. Syn. 11.
σπυρίς (W. H., σφυρίς), ίδος, ἡ, a basket. Syn. 69.
στάδιον, ου, τό, plur. στάδιοι, οἱ, (1) a stadium, the eighth part of a Roman mile, John xi. 18; (2) a racecourse, for public games, 1 Cor. ix. 24.
στάμνος, ου, ὁ, ἡ, an urn or vase, for the manna, Heb. ix. 4.*
στασιαστής, οῦ, ὁ, an insurgent, Mark xv. 7 (W. H.).*
στάσις, εως, ἡ (ἵστημι), a standing, lit. only Heb. ix. 8; elsewhere, a riot, sedition, contention, Mark xv. 7; Acts xv. 2.
στατήρ, ἐρος, masc., a stater, a silver coin equal to the δίδραχμον (which see), Matt. xvii. 27.*
σταυρός, οῦ, ὁ, a cross; met., often of Christ's death.
σταυρόω, ῶ, ώσω, to fix to the cross, to crucify; fig., to mortify, destroy, the corrupt nature.
σταφυλή, ῆς, ἡ, a grape, a cluster or bunch of grapes, Matt. vii. 16 (W. H. plur.); Luke vi. 44; Rev. xiv. 18.*
στάχυς, υος, ὁ, an ear of corn, Matt. xii. 1; Mark ii. 23, iv. 28; Luke vi. 1.*
Στάχυς, υος, ὁ, Stachys, Rom. xvi. 9.*
στέγη, ης, ἡ (lit., a cover), a flat roof of a house, Matt. viii. 8; Mark ii. 4; Luke vii. 6.*
στέγω, to cover, to conceal, to bear with, 1 Cor. ix. 12, xiii. 7; 1 Thess. iii. 1, 5.*
στεῖρος, α, ον, barren, not bearing children, Luke i. 7, 36, xxiii. 29; Gal. iv. 27.*
στέλλω, to set, arrange; hence, to set close together, repress, check; and so in mid., to avoid, 2 Cor. viii. 20; to withdraw from (ἀπό), 2 Thess. iii. 6.*
στέμμα, ατος, τό, a crown, a garland, Acts xiv. 13. Syn. 67.*
στεναγμός, οῦ, ὁ, a groaning, Acts vii. 34; Rom. viii. 26.*
στενάζω, ξω, to groan, expressing grief, anger, or desire.
στενός, ἡ, όν, narrow, strait, Matt. vii. 13, 14; Luke xiii. 24.*
στενο-χωρέω, ῶ, in pass., to be straitened, to be distressed, 2 Cor. iv. 8, vi. 12.*
στενο-χωρία, ας, ἡ, great distress or straits, Rom. ii. 9, viii. 35; 2 Cor. vi. 4, xii. 10.*
στερεός, ά, όν, solid, as food, Heb. v. 12, 14; fig., firm, stedfast, 1 Pet. v. 9; 2 Tim. ii. 19.*
στερεόω, ῶ, ώσω, to strengthen, confirm, establish, Acts iii. 7, 16, xvi. 5.*
στερέωμα, ατος, τό, firmness, constancy, Col. ii. 5.*
Στεφανᾶς, ᾶ, ὁ, Stephanas.
στέφανος, ου, ὁ, a crown, a garland, of royalty, of victory in the games, of festal joy; often used fig. Syn. 67.
Στέφανος, ου, ὁ, Stephen, Acts vi. vii.
στεφανόω, ῶ, ώσω, to crown, to adorn, to decorate, 2 Tim. ii. 5; Heb. ii. 7, 9.*
στῆθος, ους, τό, the breast.
στήκω (ἵστημι, ἔστηκα), to stand, in the attitude of prayer, Mark xi. 25; generally, to stand firm, stand fast, as Rom. xiv. 4; 1 Cor. xvi. 13; Gal. v. 1.
στηριγμός, οῦ, ὁ, firmness, fixedness, 2 Pet. iii. 17.*
στηρίζω, ίξω or ίσω, pass., perf., ἐστήριγμαι, (1) to fix, to set firmly, Luke ix. 51, xvi. 26; (2) to strengthen, to confirm, to support, as Luke xxii. 32; Rom. i. 11.

στιβάς. See στοιβάς.
στίγμα, ατος, τό, a mark or brand, Gal. vi. 17 ; of the tokens of the Apostle's sufferings for Christ.*
στιγμή, ῆς, ἡ, a point of time, an instant, Luke iv. 5.*
στίλβω, to shine, to glisten, to be resplendent, Mark ix. 3.*
στοά, ᾶς, ἡ, a colonnade, a portico, a porch, John v. 2, x. 23 ; Acts iii. 11, v. 12.*
στοιβάς, άδος, ἡ (W. H., στιβάς), a bough, a branch of a tree, Mark xi. 8.*
στοιχεῖα, ων, τά, elements, rudiments, Gal. iv. 3, 9 ; Col. ii. 8, 20 ; Heb. v. 12 ; 2 Pet. iii. 10, 12.*
στοιχέω, ῶ, ήσω, to walk, always fig. of conduct ; to walk in (local dat.), Acts xxi. 24 ; Rom. iv. 21 ; Gal. v. 25, vi. 16 ; Phil. iii. 16.*
στολή, ῆς, ἡ, a robe, i.e., the long outer garment which was a mark of distinction, Luke xv. 22.
στόμα, ατος, τό, (1) the mouth, generally ; hence, (2) speech, speaking ; used of testimony, Matt. xviii. 16 ; eloquence or power in speaking, Luke xxi. 15 ; (3) applied to an opening in the parched earth, Rev. xii. 16 ; (4) the edge or point of a sword, Luke xxi. 24.
στόμαχος, ου, ὁ, the stomach, 1 Tim. v. 23.*
στρατεία, ας, ἡ, warfare, military service ; of Christian warfare, 2 Cor. x. 4 ; 1 Tim. i. 18.*
στράτευμα, ατος, τό, (1) an army ; (2) a detachment of troops, Acts xxiii. 10, 27 ; plur., Luke xxiii. 11.
στρατεύομαι, σομαι, dep. mid., to wage war ; fig., of the warring of lusts against the soul, James iv. 1 ; to serve as a soldier, of Christian work, 1 Tim. i. 18 ; 2 Tim. ii. 4.
στρατ-ηγός, οῦ, ὁ (ἄγω), (1) a leader of an army, a general ; (2) a magistrate or ruler, Acts xvi. 20-38 ; (3) the captain of the temple, Luke xxii. 4, 52 ; Acts iv. 1, v. 24, 26.*
στρατιά, ᾶς, ἡ, an army ; met., a host of angels, Luke ii. 13 ; the host of heaven, Acts vii. 42.*
στρατιώτης, ου, ὁ, a soldier, as Matt. viii. 9 ; fig., of Christian teachers, 2 Tim. ii. 3.
στρατο-λογέω, ῶ, ήσω, to collect or levy an army, to enlist troops, 2 Tim. ii. 4.*

στρατοπεδ-άρχης, ου, ὁ, the prefect, or commander of the emperor's guards, Acts xxviii. 16 (W. H. omit).*
στρατόπεδον, ου, τό, an encamped army, a host, Luke xxi. 20.*
στρεβλόω, ῶ, to rack, to pervert, to wrest, as words from their proper meaning, 2 Pet. iii. 16.*
στρέφω, ψω, 2nd aor. pass. ἐστράφην, to turn, trans., Matt. v. 39 ; Rev. xi. 6 (to change into, εἰς); intrans., Acts vii. 42; mostly in pass., to turn oneself, John xx. 14 ; to be converted, to be changed in mind and conduct, Matt. xviii. 3.
στρηνιάω, ῶ, άσω, to live voluptuously, Rev. xviii. 7, 9.*
στρῆνος, ους, τό, profligate luxury, voluptuousness, revel, riot, Rev. xviii. 3.*
στρουθίον, ίου, τό (dim. of στρουθός), a small bird, a sparrow, Matt. x. 29, 31 ; Luke xii. 6, 7.*
στρωννύω or -ννυμι, στρώσω, pass., perf., ἔστρωμαι, to strew, Matt. xxi. 8 ; to make a bed, Acts ix. 34 ; pass., to be strewed or covered, i.e., the couches at table with the usual tapestries ; hence, ἀνάγαιον ἐστρωμένον, an upper room furnished, Mark xiv. 15 ; Luke xxii. 12.
στυγητός, όν, hateful, odious, Tit. iii. 3.*
στυγνάζω, άσω, to become gloomy, Mark x. 22 ; of the sky, Matt. xvi. 3.*
στύλος, ου, ὁ, a pillar, Gal. ii. 9 ; 1 Tim. iii. 15 ; Rev. iii. 12, x. 1.*
στωϊκός, ή, όν, stoic, plur., the Stoics (philosophers of the Porch, στοά), Acts xvii. 18.*
σύ, σοῦ, σοί, σέ, plur., ὑμεῖς, thou, ye, the pers. pron. of second person (see § 53).
συγγ-. In some words commencing thus, W. H. prefer the unassimilated form συνγ-.
συγ-γένεια, ας, ἡ, kindred, family, Luke i. 61 ; Acts vii. 3, 14.*
συγ-γενής, ές, akin to as subst., a kinsman, relative, a fellow-countryman, Rom. ix. 3.
συγ-γενίς, ίδος, ἡ, a kinswoman, Luke i. 36 (W. H.).*
συγ-γνώμη, ης, ἡ, permission, leave, 1 Cor. vii. 6.*
συγκ-. In words commencing thus, W. H. prefer the unassimilated form συνκ-.
συγ-κάθ-ημαι, to be seated with (dat. or μετά, gen.), Mark xiv. 54 ; Acts xxvi. 30.*

συγ-καθίζω, σω, (1) *to cause to sit down with*, Eph. ii. 6; (2) *to sit down together*, Luke xxii. 55.*
συγ-κακο-παθέω, ῶ, *to suffer evil or hardship with, to be partaker of hardship*, 2 Tim. i. 8, ii. 3 (W. H.).*
συγ-κακουχέω, *to suffer hardship with*, Heb. xi. 25.*
συγ-καλέω, ῶ, έσω, *to call together;* mid., *to call together to oneself.*
συγ-καλύπτω, ψω, *to conceal closely, to hide wholly*, Luke xii. 2.*
συγ-κάμπτω, ψω, *to bow down wholly, to oppress*, Rom. xi. 10 (LXX.).*
συγ-κατα-βαίνω, *to go down with any one*, as from Jerusalem to Cæsarea, Acts xxv. 5.*
συγ-κατά-θεσις, εως, ἡ, *consent, agreement*, 2 Cor. vi. 16.*
συγ-κατα-τίθημι, in mid., *to give a vote with, to assent to* (dat.), Luke xxiii. 51.*
συγ-κατα-ψηφίζω, in pass., *to be voted or classed with* (μετά), Acts i. 26.*
συγ-κεράννυμι, άσω, 1st aor., συνεκέρασα; pass., perf., συγκέκραμαι, *to mix with, to temper*, 1 Cor. xii. 24; pass., *to be mixed with*, Heb. iv. 2.*
συγ-κινέω, ῶ, ἡσω, *to move together, to put into commotion, stir up*, Acts vi. 12.*
συγ-κλείω, σω, *to inclose, to shut in*, as fishes in a net, Luke v. 6; *to shut one up into* (εἰς) *or under* (ὑπό, acc.) something, *to make subject to*, Rom. xi. 32; Gal. iii. 22, 23.*
συγ-κληρονόμος, ου, ὁ, *a joint-heir, i.e., a joint possessor or co-partner*, Rom. viii. 17; Eph. iii. 6; Heb. xi. 9; 1 Pet. iii. 7.*
συγ-κοινωνέω, ῶ, *to be a joint partaker with, have fellowship with*, Eph. v. 11; Phil. iv. 14; Rev. xviii. 4.*
συγ-κοινωνός, οῦ, ὁ, ἡ, *a partaker with, a co-partner, an associate.*
συγ-κομίζω, *to bear away together*, as in burying a corpse, Acts viii. 2.*
συγ-κρίνω, ινῶ, *to place together in order to judge of, to compare* (acc., dat.), *to estimate or explain by comparison*, 1 Cor. ii. 13; 2 Cor. x. 12.*
συγ-κύπτω, *to be bowed together or bent double*, Luke xiii. 11.*
συγκυρία, ας, ἡ, *a coincidence, a concurrence;* κατὰ συγκυρίαν, *by chance*, Luke x. 31.*

συγ-χαίρω, 2nd aor. in pass. form, συνεχάρην, *to rejoice with* (dat.), Luke i. 58, xv. 6, 9; 1 Cor. xii. 26, xiii. 6; Phil. ii. 17, 18.*
συγ-χέω(ϝ), also συγχύω and συγχύνω, perf., pass., συγκέχυμαι, *to confound, confuse, i.e.*, (1) *to startle, amaze*, Acts ii. 6; (2) *to stir up, to throw into confusion*, Acts xix. 32, xxi. 27, 31; (3) *to confute in argument*, Acts ix. 22.*
συγ-χράομαι, ῶμαι, *to have fellowship or dealings with* (dat.), John iv. 9.*
σύγ-χυσις, εως, ἡ, *confusion, commotion, uproar*, Acts xix. 29.*
συ-ζάω, ῶ, ἡσω, *to live together with* (dat.), Rom. vi. 8; 2 Cor. vii. 3; 2 Tim. ii. 11.*
συ-ζεύγνυμι, 1st aor. συνέζευξα, *to conjoin* (acc.), *to unite*, as man and wife, Matt. xix. 6; Mark x. 9.*
συ-ζητέω, ῶ, ἡσω, *to ask one another, to discuss, dispute*, with dat., or πρός, acc.
συ-ζήτησις, εως, ἡ, *questioning, disputation*, Acts xv. 2 (W. H., ζήτησις), 7 (W. H., ζήτησις), xxviii. 29 (W. H. omit).*
συ-ζητητής, οῦ, ὁ, *a disputer*, as the Greek sophists, 1 Cor. i. 20.*
σύ-ζυγος, ου, ὁ, ἡ, *a yoke-fellow, a co-adjutor*, Phil. iv. 3 (possibly a proper name, *Syzygus*).*
συ-ζωο-ποιέω, ῶ, 1st aor. συνεζωοποίησα, *to make alive with, to quicken together with*, Eph. ii. 5; Col. ii. 13.*
συκάμινος, ου, ἡ, *a sycamore-tree*, Luke xvii. 6.*
συκῆ, ῆς, ἡ (contr. from -έα), *a fig-tree.*
συκο-μωραία, ας, ἡ (W. H., -έα), *a sycamore-tree*, Luke xix. 4.*
σῦκον, ου, τό, *a fig.*
συκο-φαντέω, ῶ, ἡσω, *to accuse falsely, to defraud*, Luke iii. 14, xix. 8 (gen. pers., acc. thing).*
συλ-αγωγέω, ῶ, *to plunder, to make a prey of*, Col. ii. 8.*
συλάω, ῶ, ἡσω, *to rob, to plunder*, 2 Cor. xi. 8.*
συλλ-. In words commencing thus, W. H. prefer the unassimilated form συνλ-.
συλ-λαλέω, 1st aor. συνελάλησα, *to converse with*(dat.), μετά(gen.), πρός(acc.), Matt. xvii. 2; Mark ix. 4; Luke iv. 36, ix. 30, xxii. 4; Acts xxv. 12.*
συλ-λαμβάνω, συλλήψομαι, συνείληφα, συνέλαβον, (1) *to take together, to catch, to seize;* (2) *to conceive*, as a female;

(3) mid., *apprehend* (acc.), *to help* (dat.).

συλ-λέγω, ξω, *to collect, to gather.*

συλ-λογίζομαι, σομαι, *to reckon together, to deliberate*, Luke xx. 5.*

συλ-λυπέομαι, οῦμαι, pass., *to be greatly grieved* (ἐπί, dat.), Mark iii. 5.*

συμβ-, συμμ-, συμπ-, συμφ-. In some words commencing thus, W. H. prefer the unassimilated form συνβ-, συνμ-, συνπ-, συνφ-.

συμ-βαίνω, -βήσομαι, 2nd aor. συνέβην, *to happen, to befall, to occur;* perf., part., τὸ συμβεβηκός, *an event.*

συμ-βάλλω, 2nd aor. συνέβαλον, *to put together,* hence, *to ponder,* Luke ii. 19; *to come up with, to encounter,* with or without hostile intent (dat.), Luke xiv. 31; Acts xvii. 18, xx. 14; mid., *to confer, consult with,* Acts iv. 15; *to contribute, help to* (dat.), Acts xviii. 27.*

συμ-βασιλεύω, σω, *to reign with*, 1 Cor. iv. 8; 2 Tim. ii. 12.*

συμ-βιβάζω, άσω, (1) *to unite,* or *knit together* Col. ii. 2, 19; (2) *to put together in reasoning,* and so, *to conclude, prove,* Acts ix. 22; (3) *to teach, instruct,* 1 Cor. ii. 16.

συμ-βουλεύω, *to advise* (dat.), John xviii. 14; Rev. iii. 18; mid., *to take counsel together* (ἵνα or inf.), Matt. xxvi. 4; John xi. 53 (W. H., βουλεύομαι); Acts ix. 23.*

συμ-βούλιον, ίου, τό, (1) *mutual consultation, united counsel;* λαμβάνω, ποιέω συμβούλιον, *to take counsel together,* Matt. xii. 14, xxii. 15, xxvii. 1, 7, xxviii. 12; Mark iii. 6, xv. 1; (2) *a council, a gathering of counsellors,* Acts xxv. 12.*

σύμ-βουλος, ου, ὁ, *a counsellor,* Rom. xi. 34.*

Συμεών, ὁ (Heb.), *Simeon* or *Simon* (see Σίμων). The Apostle Peter is so called, Acts xv. 14; 2 Pet. i. 1; and four others are mentioned: (1) Luke ii. 25, 34; (2) Luke iii. 30; (3) Acts xiii. 1; (4) Rev. vii. 7.*

συμ-μαθητής, οῦ, ὁ, *a fellow-disciple,* John xi. 16.*

συμ-μαρτυρέω, ῶ, *to bear witness together with, to testify along with,* Rom. ii. 15, viii. 16, ix. 1; Rev. xxii. 18 (not W. H.).*

συμ-μερίζω, in mid., *to divide with, partake with* (dat.), 1 Cor. ix. 13.*

συμ-μέτοχος, ον, *jointly partaking,* Eph. iii. 6, v. 7.*

συμ-μιμητής, οῦ, ὁ, *a joint-imitator, a co-follower,* Phil. iii. 17.*

συμ-μορφίζω. See συμμορφόω.

σύμ-μορφος, ον, *conformed to,* gen., Rom. viii. 29; dat., Phil. iii. 21.*

συμ-μορφόω, ῶ, *to conform to* (dat.), Phil. iii. 10 (W. H., συμμορφίζω, in same sense).*

συμ-παθέω, ῶ, ήσω, *to sympathise with* (dat.), Heb. iv. 15, x. 34.*

συμ-παθής, ές, *sympathising, compassionate,* 1 Pet. iii. 8.*

συμ-παρα-γίνομαι, *to come together* (to, ἐπί, acc.), Luke xxiii. 48; *to stand by one, to support* (dat.), 2 Tim. iv. 16 (W. H., παραγίνομαι).*

συμ-παρα-καλέω, ῶ, in pass., *to be comforted together,* Rom. i. 12.*

συμ-παρα-λαμβάνω, 2nd aor. συμπαρέλαβον, *to take with oneself,* as companion, Acts xii. 25, xv. 37, 38; Gal. ii. 1.*

συμ-παρα-μένω, *to remain* or *continue with* (dat.), Phil. i. 25 (W. H., παραμένω).*

συμ-πάρ-ειμι, *to be present with,* Acts xxv. 24.*

συμ-πάσχω, *to suffer together with,* Rom. viii. 17; 1 Cor. xii. 26.*

συμ-πέμπω, *to send with,* 2 Cor. viii. 18, 22.*

συμ-περι-λαμβάνω, Acts xx. 10.*

συμ-πίνω, 2nd aor. συνέπιον, *to drink with,* Acts x. 41.*

συμ-πίπτω, *to fall together,* Luke vi. 49 (W. H.).*

συμ-πληρόω, ῶ, *to fill, to fill up, to fill fully,* Luke viii. 23; pass., *to be fully come,* Luke ix. 51; Acts ii. 1.*

συμ-πνίγω, *to choke,* as weeds do plants, Matt. xiii. 22; Mark iv. 7; Luke viii. 14; *to throng, to suffocate by crowding, to throng upon* (acc.), Luke viii. 42.*

συμ-πολίτης, ου, ὁ, *a fellow-citizen,* Eph. ii. 19.*

συμ-πορεύομαι, (1) *to accompany, to go with* (dat.), Luke vii. 11, xiv. 25, xxiv. 15; (2) intrans., *to come together, to assemble,* Mark x. 1.*

συμ-πόσιον, ου, τό (πίνω), *a table party, a festive company, a feast;* Mark vi. 39, συμπόσια συμπόσια, *by companies.*

συμ-πρεσβύτερος, ου, ὁ, *a fellow-elder,* 1 Pet. v. 1.*

συμ-φάγω. See συνεσθίω.
συμ-φέρω, 1st aor., συνήνεγκα, to bring together, to collect, only Acts xix. 19; generally intrans., and often impers., to conduce to, to be profitable to, 1 Cor. x. 23; 2 Cor. xii. 1; part., τὸ συμφέρον, good, profit, advantage, 1 Cor. vii. 35.
σύμ-φημι, to assent to, Rom. vii. 16.*
σύμ-φορος, α, ον, profitable, 1 Cor. vii. 35, x. 33 (W. H., for συμφέρον).*
συμ-φυλέτης, ου, ὁ, one of the same tribe, a fellow-countryman, 1 Thess. ii. 14.*
σύμ-φυτος, ον, grown together, planted together, united with (R. V.), Rom. vi. 5.*
συμ-φύω, pass., 2nd aor., part., συμφυείς, pass., to grow at the same time, Luke viii. 7.*
συμ-φωνέω, ῶ, ήσω, to agree with, agree together, arrange with (dat., or μετά, gen.), of persons, Matt. xviii. 19, xx. 2, 13; Acts v. 9; of things, to be in accord with, Luke v. 36; Acts xv. 15.*
συμ-φώνησις, εως, ἡ, accord, unison, 2 Cor. vi. 15.*
συμ-φωνία, ας, ἡ, a concert, or symphony, of instruments, music, Luke xv. 25.*
σύμ-φωνος, ον, harmonious, agreeing with; ἐκ συμφώνου, by agreement, 1 Cor. vii. 5.*
συμ-ψηφίζω, to compute, reckon up, Acts xix. 19.*
σύμ-ψυχος, adj., like-minded, Phil. ii. 2.*
σύν, a prep. gov. dative, with (see § 296). In composition, σύν denotes association with, or is intensive. The final ν changes to γ, λ, or μ, or is dropped, according to the initial letter of the word with which it is compounded (see § 4, d, 5); but W. H. prefer the unassimilated forms.
συν-άγω, άξω, (1) to bring together, to gather, to assemble; pass., to be assembled, to come together; (2) to receive hospitably, only Matt. xxv. 35, 38, 43.
συναγωγή, ῆς, ἡ, an assembly, a congregation, synagogue, either the place, or the people gathered in the place.
συν-αγωνίζομαι, σομαι, to strive together with another, to aid (dat.), Rom. xv. 30.*
συν-αθλέω, ῶ, ήσω, to strive together for

(dat. of thing), Phil. i. 27; or with (dat. of person), Phil. iv. 3.*
συν-αθροίζω, σω, to gather or collect together, Acts xii. 12, xix. 25; pass., to throng together, Luke xxiv. 33 (W. H., ἀθροίζω).*
συν-αίρω, to reckon together, to take account with, Matt. xviii. 23, 24; xxv. 19.*
συν-αιχμάλωτος, ου, ὁ, a fellow-captive or prisoner, Rom. xvi. 7; Col. iv. 10; Philem. 23.*
συν-ακολουθέω, ῶ, ήσω, to follow with, to accompany, Mark v. 37, xiv. 51 (W. H.); Luke xxiii. 49.*
συν-αλίζω, in pass., to be assembled together with (dat.), Acts i. 4.*
συν-αλλάσσω, to reconcile. See συνελαύνω.
συν-ανα-βαίνω, to go up with (dat.), Mark xv. 41; Acts xiii. 31.*
συν-ανά-κειμαι, to recline with, as at a meal, to sup with (dat.); part., οἱ συνανακείμενοι, the guests, Mark vi. 22, 26.
συν-ανα-μίγνυμι, pass., to mingle together with, to keep company with (dat.), 1 Cor. v. 9, 11; 2 Thess. iii. 14.*
συν-ανα-παύομαι, σομαι, to find rest or refreshment together with (dat.), Rom. xv. 32.*
συν-αντάω, ῶ, ήσω, (1) to meet with, to encounter (dat.), Luke ix. 37, xxii. 10; Acts x. 25; Heb. vii. 1, 10; (2) of things, to happen to, to befall; τὰ συναντήσοντα, the things that shall befall, Acts xx. 22.*
συν-άντησις, εως, ἡ, a meeting with, an encountering, Matt. viii. 34 (W. H., ὑπάντησις).*
συν-αντι-λαμβάνω, mid., lit., to take hold on the other side together with; to assist, help (dat.), Luke x. 40; Rom. viii. 26.*
συν-απ-άγω, in pass., to be led or carried away in mind, Rom. xii. 16 (see R.V. marg.); Gal. ii. 13; 2 Pet. iii. 17.*
συν-απο-θνήσκω, to die together with (dat.), Mark xiv. 31; 2 Cor. vii. 3; 2 Tim. ii. 11.*
συν-απ-όλλυμι, in mid., to perish with (dat.), Heb. xi. 31.*
συν-απο-στέλλω, to send together (acc.), 2 Cor. xii. 18.*

συν-αρμο-λογέω, ῶ, in pass., to be joined fitly or harmoniously together, Eph. ii. 21, iv. 16.*

συν-αρπάζω, σω, to seize, or drag by force (dat.), Luke viii. 29 ; Acts vi. 12, xix. 29, xxvii. 15.*

συν-αυξάνω, in mid., to grow together, Matt. xiii. 30.*

σύν-δεσμος, ου, ὁ, that which binds together, a band, a bond, Acts viii. 23; Eph. iv. 3 ; Col. ii. 19, iii. 14.*

συν-δέω, in pass., to be bound with any one, as fellow-prisoners, Heb. xiii. 3.*

συν-δοξάζω, άσω, to glorify with (σύν), pass., Rom. viii. 17.*

σύν-δουλος, ου, ὁ, a fellow-slave, a fellow-servant, Matt. xviii. 28-33 ; of ministers, the fellow-servants of Christ, a colleague, Col. i. 7.

συν-δρομή, ῆς, ἡ, a running together, a concourse, Acts xxi. 30.*

συν-εγείρω, ερῶ, 1st aor., συνήγειρα ; pass., συνηγέρθην ; to raise together, to raise with, Eph. ii. 6; Col. ii. 12, iii. 1.*

συν-έδριον, ου, τό, a council, a tribunal, Matt. x. 17 ; specially, the Sanhedrin, the Jewish council of seventy members, presided over by the high priest ; the council-hall, where the Sanhedrin met, Acts iv. 15.

συν-είδησις, εως, ἡ, prop., self-consciousness, the consciousness man has of himself in his relation to God ; the conscience, Rom. ii. 15 ; 1 Pet. ii. 19 ; the sentence pronounced by the conscience, 2 Cor. iv. 2, v. 11.

σύν-είδον, 2nd aor. of obs., present, to be conscious or aware of, to consider, Acts xii. 12, xiv. 6 ; perf., σύνοιδα, part., συνειδώς, to be privy to a design, Acts v. 2 ; to be conscious to oneself (dat.) of guilt (acc.), 1 Cor. v. 4.*

σύν-ειμι, to be with (dat.), Luke ix. 18 ; Acts xxii. 11.*

σύν-ειμι (εἶμι), part., συνιών, to go or come with, to assemble, Luke viii. 4.*

συν-εισ-έρχομαι, to go in, or come in, with any one (dat.), John xviii. 15 ; to embark with, John vi. 22.*

συν-έκ-δημος, ου, ὁ, ἡ, a fellow-traveller, Acts xix. 29 ; 2 Cor. viii. 19.*

συν-εκλεκτός, ἡ, όν, elected together with, 1 Pet. v. 13.*

συν-ελαύνω, -ελάσω, to compel, to persuade (acc. and εἰς), Acts vii. 26 (W. H., συναλλάσσω).*

συν-επι-μαρτυρέω, ῶ, to bear joint witness, Heb. ii. 4.*

συν-επι-τίθημι, mid., to join in assailing, Acts xxiv. 9 (W. H., for συντίθημι).*

συν-έπομαι, to attend, to accompany (dat.), Acts xx. 4.*

συν-εργέω, ῶ, to co-operate with (dat.), to work together, 1 Cor. xvi. 16 ; Rom. viii. 28.

συν-εργός, όν, co-working, helping ; as a subst., a joint-helper, a co-worker, gen. of person, obj. with εἰς, or dat., or (met.) gen., 2 Cor. i. 24.

συν-έρχομαι (see § 103, 2), to come or go with, to accompany ; to come together, to assemble ; used also of conjugal intercourse, to come or live together.

συν-εσθίω, 2nd aor. συνέφαγον, to eat with, to live in familiar intercourse with (dat., or μετά, gen.), Luke xv. 2 ; Acts x. 41, xi. 3 ; 1 Cor. v. 11 ; Gal. ii. 12,*

σύν-εσις, εως, ἡ (ἵημι), a putting together, in mind, hence discernment ; met., the understanding, the source of discernment.

συν-ετός, ή, όν (ἵημι), intelligent, prudent, wise, Matt. xi. 25 ; Luke x. 21 ; Acts xiii. 7 ; 1 Cor. i. 19.*

συν-ευ-δοκέω, ῶ, to approve together ; to consent to (dat.), Luke xi. 48 ; Acts viii. 1, xxii. 20 ; to be of one mind with (dat.), Rom. i. 32; to be content to (inf.), 1 Cor. vii. 12, 13.*

συν-ευωχέω, ῶ, in mid., to feast with, to revel with, 2 Pet. ii. 13 ; Jude 12.*

συν-εφ-ίστημι, to rise together against (κατά), to attack, Acts xvi. 22.*

συν-έχω, ξω, (1) to press together, constrain ; (2) to hold fast, as a prisoner, to stop, as the ears, the mouth ; (3) to hem in, Luke viii. 45 ; (4) pass., to be straitened, or repressed, as by an unaccomplished purpose, Luke xii. 50 ; (5) to be pressed or occupied with a work, Acts xviii. 5 ; (6) to be held fast by sickness, Luke iv. 38.

συν-ήδομαι, to delight in (dat.), Rom. vii. 22.*

συν-ήθεια, as, ἡ, a custom, a usage. John xviii. 39 ; 1 Cor. viii. 7 (W. H.), xi, 16.*

συν-ηλικιώτης, ου, ὁ, *one of the same age*, Gal. i. 14.*
συν-θάπτω, ψω, 2nd aor., pass., συνετάφην, in. pass., *to be buried with*, Rom. vi. 4; Col. ii. 12.*
συν-θλάω, ῶ, fut., pass., συνθλασθήσομαι, *to break, to break in pieces*, Matt. xxi. 44; Luke xx. 18.*
συν-θλίβω, *to throng, to press closely upon*, Mark v. 24, 31.*
συν-θρύπτω, *to break down ;* fig., with καρδίαν, *to take away one's fortitude*, Acts xxi. 13.*
συν-ίημι, inf., συνιέναι, part., συνιῶν or συνιείς; fut., συνήσω; 1st aor., συνῆκα; *to put together*, in mind ; hence, *to consider, understand* (acc.), *to be aware* (ὅτι), *to be wise, to attend to* (ἐπί, dat.).
συν-ίστημι, also συνιστάνω and συνιστάω, *to place together; to constitute, prove, approve, commend*, Gal. ii. 18 ; Rom. iii. 5, v. 8; perf. and 2nd aor., intrans., *to stand together, stand with*, Luke ix. 32 ; Col. i. 17 ; 2 Pet. iii. 5.
συν-οδεύω, *to journey with, to accompany* (dat.), Acts ix. 7.*
συν-οδία, as, ἡ, *a company travelling together, a caravan*, Luke ii. 44.*
συνοικέω, ῶ, ήσω, *to dwell together*, as in marriage, 1 Pet. iii. 7.*
συν-οικο-δομέω, in pass., *to be built up together*, Eph. ii. 22.*
συν-ομιλέω, ῶ, *to talk with* (dat.), Acts x. 27.*
συν-ομορέω, ῶ, *to adjoin* (dat.), Acts xviii. 7.*
συν-οχή, ῆς, ἡ, *constraint* of mind ; hence, *distress, disquiet*, Luke xxi. 25 ; 2 Cor. ii. 4.*
συν-τάσσω, ξω, *to arrange with, to charge, command*, Matt. xxi. 6 (W. H.), xxvi. 19, xxvii. 10.*
συν-τέλεια, as, ἡ, *a finishing, a consummation, an end*, Matt. xiii. 39, 40, 49, xxiv. 3, xxviii. 20 ; Heb. ix. 26.*
συν-τελέω, ῶ, έσω, (1) *to bring completely to an end*, Matt. vii. 28 (W. H., τελέω); Luke iv. 2, 13 ; Acts xxi. 27 ; (2) *to fulfil, to accomplish*, Rom. ix. 28 ; Mark xiii. 4 ; Heb. viii. 8.*
συν-τέμνω, *to cut short, to bring to swift fulfilment*, Rom. ix. 28.*
συν-τηρέω, ῶ, (1) *to preserve safely, to keep safe*, Matt. ix. 17 ; Mark vi. 20 ;

Luke v. 38 (W. H. omit) ; (2) *to lay up in mind*, Luke ii. 19.*
συν-τίθημι, in mid., *to set or place together*, as in agreement between two or more persons, *to agree*, Luke xxii. 5 ; John ix. 22 ; Acts xxiii. 20; *to assent*, Acts xxiv. 9 (W. H., συνεπιτίθημι).*
συν-τόμως, adv., *concisely, briefly*, Acts xxiv. 4.*
συν-τρέχω, 2nd aor. συνέδραμον, *to run together*, as a multitude, Mark vi. 33 ; Acts iii. 11 ; *to run with*, (fig.), 1 Pet. iv. 4.*
συν-τρίβω, ψω, 2nd aor., pass., συνετρίβην, *to break by crushing, to break in pieces*, Luke ix. 39 ; Rom. xvi. 20 ; pass., perf., part., συντετριμμένος, *bruised*, Matt. xii. 20.
σύν-τριμμα, ατος, τό, *crushing;* fig., *destruction*, Rom. iii. 16 (LXX.).*
σύν-τροφος, ου, ὁ, *one brought up with, a foster-brother*, Acts xiii. 1.*
συν-τυγχάνω, 2nd aor. συνέτυχον, *to fall in with* (dat.), Luke viii. 19.*
Συντύχη, ης, ἡ, *Syntyche*, Phil. iv. 2.*
συν-υπο-κρίνομαι, dep., 1st aor., συνυπεκρίθην, *to dissemble with*, Gal. ii. 13.*
συν-υπ-ουργέω, ῶ, *to help together with*, 2 Cor. i. 11.*
συν-ωδίνω, *to travail in pain together*, Rom. viii. 22.*
συν-ωμοσία, as, ἡ, *a conspiracy by oath*, Acts xxiii. 13.*
Συράκουσαι, ῶν, αἱ, *Syracuse*, Acts xxviii. 12.*
Συρία, ας, ἡ, *Syria*.
Σύρος, ου, ὁ, *a Syrian*, Luke iv. 27.*
Συρο-φοίνισσα (W. H., Συρο-φοινίκισσα marg., Σύρα Φοινίκισσα), as, ἡ, an appellative, *a Syrophenician woman*, Mark vii. 26.*
Σύρτις, εως, acc. ιν, ἡ, (*a quicksand*) *the Syrtis Major*, Acts xxvii. 17.*
σύρω, *to draw, to drag*, John xxi. 8 ; Acts viii. 3, xiv. 19, xvii. 6 ; Rev. xii. 4.*
συσ-. In some words commencing thus, W. H. prefer the uncontracted form συνσ-.
συ-σπαράσσω, ξω, *to convulse violently* (acc.), Mark ix. 20 (W. H.) ; Luke ix. 42.*
σύσ-σημον, ου, τό, *a concerted signal, a token agreed upon*, Mark xiv. 44.*

σύσ-σωμος—σωματικός] VOCABULARY. 513

σύσ-σωμος (W. H., σύνσωμος), ον, *united in the same body;* fig., of Jews and Gentiles, in one church, Eph. iii. 6.*
συ-στασιαστής, ον, ὁ, *a fellow-insurgent* (W. H., στασιαστής), Mark xv. 7.*
συ-στατικός, ή, όν, *commendatory,* 2 Cor. iii. 1.*
συ-σταυρόω, ῶ, *to crucify together with* (acc. and dat.); lit., as Matt. xxvii. 44; fig., as Gal. ii. 19.
συ-στέλλω (see στέλλω),(1) *to wrap round, to swathe,* as a dead body, Acts v. 6; (2) *to contract,* perf., pass., part., *contracted, shortened,* 1 Cor. vii. 29.*
συ-στενάζω, *to groan together,* Rom. viii. 22.*
συ-στοιχέω, ῶ, *to be in the same rank with; to answer to* (dat.), Gal. iv. 25.*
συ-στρατιώτης, ον, ὁ, *a fellow-soldier,* i.e., in the Christian service, Phil. ii. 25; Philem. 2.*
συ-στρέφω, ψω, *to roll* or *gather together,* Matt. xvii. 22 (W. H.); Acts xxviii. 3.*
συ-στροφή, ῆς, ή, *a gathering together, a concourse,* Acts xix. 40; *a conspiracy,* Acts xxiii. 12.*
συ-σχηματίζω, in mid. or pass., *to conform oneself,* or *to be assimilated to* (dat.), Rom. xii. 2; 1 Pet. i. 14.*
Συχάρ (W. H.), or Σιχάρ, ή, *Sychar,* John iv. 5.*
Συχέμ, (1) ὁ, *Shechem,* the prince, Acts vii. 16 (W. H. and R. V. read ἐν Συχέμ, *in Shechem,* for the Rec. τοῦ Συχέμ, *the father of Shechem);* (2) ή, *Shechem,* the city, Acts vii. 16.*
σφαγή, ῆς, ή, (1) *slaughter,* Acts viii. 32; Rom. viii. 36 (LXX.); (2) perhaps met., *a feast,* or *feasting,* James v. 5, but the meaning (1) is more probable.*
σφάγιον, ον, τό, *a slaughtered victim in sacrifice,* Acts vii. 42.*
σφάζω, ξω, pass., perf., ἔσφαγμαι; 2nd aor., ἐσφάγην, *to kill by violence, to slay,* 1 John iii. 12, and Rev.*
σφόδρα, adv., *exceedingly, greatly, vehemently,* as Matt. ii. 10.
σφοδρῶς, adv., *vehemently,* Acts xxvii. 18.*
σφραγίζω, ίσω, *to seal, to set a seal upon,* (1) for security, Matt. xxvii. 66; (2) for secrecy, Rev. xxii. 10; (3) for designation, Eph. i. 13; or (4) for confirmation, Rom. xv. 28.

σφραγίς, ῖδος, ή, (1) *a seal,* the instrument, Rev. vii. 2; (2) *the impression,* whether for security and secrecy, as Rev. v. 1; or for designation, Rev. ix. 4; (3) *the motto of a seal,* 2 Tim. ii. 19; (4) *that which the seal attests, the proof,* 1 Cor. ix. 2.
σφυρίς. See σπυρίς.
σφυρόν, ον, τό, *the ankle-bone.*
σχεδόν, adv., *nearly, almost,* Acts xiii. 44, xix. 26; Heb. ix. 22.*
σχῆμα, ατος, τό, *fashion, habit,* 1 Cor. vii. 31; *form, appearance,* Phil. ii. 8. Syn. 56.*
σχίζω, ίσω, *to rend, to divide asunder,* i.e., rocks, Matt. xxvii. 51; pass., *to be divided into parties,* Acts xiv. 4.
σχίσμα, ατος, τό, *a rent,* as in a garment, Mark ii. 21; *a division, a dissension,* "schism," 1 Cor. i. 10.
σχοινίον, ου, τό (σχοῖνος, *a rush*), *a cord, a rope,* John ii. 15; Acts xxvii. 32.*
σχολάζω, άσω, *to be at leisure; to be empty* or *unoccupied,* Matt. xii. 44; *to be at leisure for* (dat.), *give oneself to,* 1 Cor. vii. 6.*
σχολή, ῆς, ή, *leisure;* the studies of one's leisure, espec. philosophy; the place where such studies were carried on; hence, *a school,* Acts xix. 9.*
σώζω, σώσω, perf., σέσωκα; pass., σέσωσμαι; 1st aor., pass., ἐσώθην; (1) *to save,* from evil or danger, Matt. viii. 25, xvi. 25; (2) *to heal,* Matt. ix. 21, 22; John xi. 12; (3) *to save,* i.e., from eternal death, 1 Tim. i. 15; part., pass., οἱ σωζόμενοι, *those who are being saved,* Acts ii. 47, i.e., who are in the way of salvation.
σῶμα, ατος, τό, *a body,* i.e., (1) *any material body,* plants, sun, moon, etc.; (2) *the living body* of an animal, James iii. 3; or of a man, as 1 Cor. xii. 12, espec. as the medium of human life, and of human life as sinful; the *body* of CHRIST, as the medium and witness of his humanity; σώματα, Rev. xviii. 13, *slaves;* (3) *a dead body, a corpse,* Acts ix. 40; (4) fig., *a community,* the church, *the mystic body of Christ,* Col. i. 24; (5) met., for the entire man, *the self,* Rom. xii. 1; (6) *substance,* opp. to shadow, Col. ii. 17.
σωματικός, ή, όν, *of* or *pertaining to the body,* 1 Tim. iv. 8; *bodily corporeal,*

LL

Luke iii. 22 ; adv., -ως, corporeally, in bodily manifestation, Col. ii. 9.*
Σώπατρος, ου, ὁ, Sopater or Sosipater, Acts xx. 4 (cf. Rom. xvi. 21).*
σωρεύω, σω, to heap up, to load, Rom. xii. 20 ; 2 Tim. iii. 16.*
Σωσθένης, ου, ὁ, Sosthenes, Acts xviii. 17 ; 1 Cor. i. 1. It is uncertain whether the reference is to the same person.*
Σωσίπατρος, ου, ὁ, Sosipater or Sopater, Rom. xvi. 21 (cf. Acts xx. 4).*
σωτήρ, ῆρος, ὁ, a saviour, deliverer, preserver; a name given to GOD, Luke i. 47 ; 1 Tim. i. 1, ii. 3, iv. 10 ; Tit. i. 3, ii. 10, iii. 4 ; Jude 25 ; elsewhere always of CHRIST.
σωτηρία, ας, ἡ, welfare, prosperity, deliverance, preservation, from temporal evils, Acts xxvii. 34; Heb. xi. 7 ; Acts vii. 25 ; 2 Pet. iii. 15 ; specially salvation, i.e., deliverance from spiritual and eternal evils, and the attainment of a perfect well-being, the realisation of the highest and completest life.
σωτήριος, ον, saving, healthful, bringing salvation, Tit. ii. 11 ; neut., τὸ σωτήριον, salvation, Luke ii. 30, iii. 6; Acts xxviii. 28 ; Eph. vi. 17.*
σωφρονέω, ῶ, ήσω, (1) to be of sound mind, Mark v. 15 ; (2) to be soberminded, Rom. xii. 3 ; Tit. ii. 6.
σωφρονίζω, to make sober-minded, to teach, to train, Tit. ii. 4.*
σωφρονισμός, οῦ, ὁ, soundness of mind, sobriety, 2 Tim. i. 7.*
σωφρόνως, adv., soberly, with prudence, moderation, Tit. ii. 12.*
σωφροσύνη, ης, ἡ, soundness of mind, sobriety, moderation, discretion, Acts xxvi. 25 ; 1 Tim. ii. 9, 15.*
σώφρων, ον (σάος, σῶς [sound], and φρήν), of sound mind, sober-minded, discreet, modest, 1 Tim. iii. 2 ; Tit. i. 8, ii. 2, 5.*

T.

Τ, τ, ταῦ, tau, t, the nineteenth letter. As a numeral, τʹ = 300 ; ͵τ = 300,000.
ταβέρναι, ῶν, αἱ (Lat.), taverns; Acts xxviii. 15, Tres Tabernœ, the three Taverns, a place on the Appian Way.*
Ταβιθά, ἡ (Aram.), Tabitha, Acts ix. 36, 40.*

τάγμα, ατος, τό, an order or series, a regular method, 1 Cor. xv. 23.*
τακτός, ή, όν, appointed, set, Acts xii. 21.*
ταλαιπωρέω, ῶ, ήσω, to be distressed, to be in affliction, to be miserable, James iv. 9.*
ταλαιπωρία, ας, ἡ, affliction, distress, misery, Rom. iii. 16 ; James v. 1.*
ταλαίπωρος, ον, distressed, miserable, Rom. vii. 24 ; Rev. iii. 17.*
ταλαντιαῖος, αία, αῖον, of a talent weight, Rev. xvi. 21.*
τάλαντον, ου, τό, a talent, of silver or gold. The Jewish talent weighed 3,000 shekels (Ex. xxxviii. 25, 26), the shekel being about ½ oz. avoirdupois.
ταλιθά, ἡ (Aram.), a damsel, Mark v. 41.*
ταμεῖον, ου, τό, a storehouse, a secret chamber, Matt. vi. 6, xxiv. 26 ; Luke xii. 3, 24.*
τανῦν, adv. (τὰ νῦν, the things that now are), now, or in present circumstances, according to present necessity; only in Acts. (W. H. always write τὰ νῦν.)
τάξις, εως, ἡ, order, i.e., (1) regular arrangement, Col. ii. 5 ; (2) appointed succession, Luke i. 8 ; (3) rank, Heb. v. 6.
ταπεινός, ή, όν (down-trodden), humble, lowly, in condition or in spirit; in N.T. in a good sense.
ταπεινο-φροσύνη, ης, ἡ, lowliness of mind, humility, real, as Phil. ii. 3 ; or affected, as Col. ii. 18.
ταπεινό-φρων, ον, humble, 1 Pet. iii. 8 (W. H. for φιλόφρων).*
ταπεινόω, ῶ, ώσω, to make or bring low, Luke iii. 5 ; to humble, humiliate, to lower in esteem, 2 Cor. xii. 21 ; pass., to be humbled, Luke xviii. 14 ; mid., to humble oneself, to make oneself lowly, James iv. 10.
ταπείνωσις, εως, ἡ, humiliation, in circumstances, Luke i. 48 ; in spirit, James i. 10.
ταράσσω, ξω, to agitate, as water in a pool, John v. 4 (W. H. omit), 7 ; to stir up, to disturb in mind, with fear, grief, anxiety, doubt.
ταραχή, ῆς, ἡ, a stirring, John v. 4 (W. H. omit) ; a commotion or tumult, Mark xiii. 8 (W. H. omit).*

τάραχος, ου, ὁ, a disturbance, Acts xix. 23 ; consternation, Acts xii. 18.*
Ταρσεύς, έως, ὁ, one of Tarsus, Acts ix. 11, xxi. 39.*
Τάρσος, οῦ, ἡ, Tarsus, Acts ix. 30.
ταρταρόω, ῶ, ώσω, to thrust down to Tartarus, 2 Pet. ii. 4.*
τάσσω, ξω, (1) to constitute, arrange ; (2) to determine ; mid., to appoint.
ταῦρος, ου, ὁ, a bull, a bullock.
ταὐτά, by crasis for τὰ αὐτά, the same things.
ταῦτα. See οὗτος.
ταφή, ῆς, ἡ (θάπτω), a burial, a sepulture, Matt. xxvii. 7.*
τάφος, ου, ὁ, a burial-place, a sepulchre, as Matt. xxiii. 27.
τάχα, adv., quickly ; perhaps, Rom. v. 7 ; Philem. 15.*
ταχέως, adv. (ταχύς), soon, shortly, Gal. i. 6 ; hastily, Luke xiv. 21 ; John xi. 31.
ταχινός, ή, όν, swift, shortly to happen, 2 Pet. i. 14 ; ii. 1.*
τάχος, ους, τό, quickness, speed, only in the phrase ἐν τάχει ; quickly, speedily, shortly.
ταχύς, εῖα, ύ, quick, swift, only James i. 19 ; ταχύ, compar. τάχιον (W. H., τάχειον), superl. τάχιστα, adverbially, swiftly ; more, most, speedily.
τε, conj. of annexation, and, both (see § 403).
τεῖχος, ους, τό, a wall of a city, Acts ix. 25.
τεκμήριον, ου, τό, a sign, a certain proof, Acts i. 3.*
τεκνίον, ου, τό (dim. of τέκνον), a little child, John xiii. 33 ; Gal. iv. 19 ; 1 John ii. 1, 12, 28, iii. 7, 18, iv. 4, v. 21.*
τεκνο-γονέω, ῶ, to bear children, 1 Tim. v. 14.*
τεκνο-γονία, ας, ἡ, child-bearing, 1 Tim. ii. 15.*
τέκνον, ου, τό (τίκτω), a child, a descendant ; fig. of various forms of intimate union and relationship, a disciple, a follower, Philem. 10 ; hence such phrases as τέκνα τῆς σοφίας, τέκνα ὑπακοῆς, τέκνα τοῦ φωτός, children of wisdom, obedience, the light, and espec. τέκνα τοῦ Θεοῦ, children of God, Rom. viii. 16, 17, 21 ; 1 John ; an inhabitant, Luke xiii. 34. Syn. 62.

τεκνο-τροφέω, ῶ, to bring up children, 1 Tim. v. 10.*
τέκτων, ονος τό (compare τέχνη), an artificer, a carpenter, Matt. xiii. 55, Mark vi. 3.*
τέλειος, εία, εῖον, perfect, as (1) complete in all its parts ; (2) full grown, of full age ; (3) specially of the completeness of Christian character, perfect ; adv., -ως, perfectly, only 1 Pet. i. 13. Syn. 27.
τελειότης, τητος, ἡ, perfectness, perfection, Col. iii. 14 ; Heb. vi. 1.*
τελειόω, ῶ, ώσω, (1) to complete, to finish, as a course, a race, or the like ; (2) to accomplish, as time, or prediction, Luke ii. 43 ; John xix. 28 ; (3) to make perfect, Heb. vii. 19 ; pass., be perfected, Luke xiii. 32 ; to reach the perfect state, Phil. iii. 12. Syn. 13.
τελείωσις, εως, ἡ, complexion, fulfilment, Luke i. 45 ; perfection, Heb. vii. 11.*
τελειωτής, οῦ, ὁ, one who makes perfect, a finisher, Heb. xii. 2 (comp. Heb. ii. 10).*
τελεσ-φορέω, ῶ, to bring to maturity, as grain, Luke viii. 14.*
τελευτάω, ῶ, to end, to finish, e.g., life ; so, to die, Matt. ix. 18 ; to be put to death, Mark vii. 10.
τελευτή, ῆς, ἡ, end of life, death, Matt. ii. 15.*
τελέω, ῶ, έσω, τετέλεκα, τετέλεσμαι, ἐτελέσθην, (1) to end, to finish ; (2) to fulfil, to accomplish, to go through ; (3) to pay off in full. Syn. 13.
τέλος, ους, τό, (1) an end ; (2) an accomplishment, Luke xxii. 37 ; (3) event or issue, Matt. xxvi. 58 ; (4) the sum, the principal end or scope ; (5) an impost or tax [see τελέω (3)], Matt. xvii. 25 ; Rom. xiii. 7. Syn. 13.
τελώνης, ου, ὁ, a toll-gatherer, a collector of customs, one who farms taxes, a "publican."
τελώνιον, ου, τό, a toll-house, a tax-collector's office, Matt. ix. 9 ; Mark ii. 14 ; Luke v. 27.*
τέρας, ατος, τό, a wonder, a portent ; in N.T. only in plur., and joined with σημεῖα, signs and wonders, Acts vii. 36 ; John iv. 48. Syn. 45.
Τέρτιος, ου, ὁ (Lat.), Tertius, Rom. xvi. 22.*
Τέρτυλλος, ου, ὁ, Tertullus, Acts xxiv. 1, 2.*

τεσσαράκοντα, forty.
τεσσαρακοντα-ετής, ές, of forty years, age or time, Acts vii. 23, xiii. 18.*
τέσσαρες, τέσσαρα, gen., ων, four.
τεσσαρες-και-δέκατος, ord. num., fourteenth, Acts xxvii. 27, 33.*
τεταρταίος, αία, αίον, of the fourth (day); τεταρταίος έστιν, he hath been dead four days, John xi. 39.*
τέταρτος, η, ον, ord. num., fourth.
τετρά-γωνος, ον, four-cornered, Rev. xxi. 16.*
τετράδιον, ίου, τό, a quaternion, or guard of four soldiers, Acts xii. 2.*
τετρακισ-χίλιοι, αι, α, four thousand.
τετρακόσιοι, αι, α, four hundred.
τετρά-μηνος, ον, of four months; sc. χρόνος, a period of four months, John iv. 35.*
τετρα-πλόος, ούς, ή, ούν, fourfold, Luke xix. 8.*
τετρά-πους, ουν, οδος, four-footed, Acts x. 12, xi. 6; Rom. i. 23.*
τετρ-αρχέω (W. H., τετρααρχέω), ώ, to rule over as a tetrarch (gen.), Luke iii. 1.*
τετρ-άρχης (W. H., τετραάρχης), ου, ό, a ruler over a fourth part of a kingdom, a tetrarch, applied to rulers over any part, Matt. xiv. 1.
τεύχω. See τυγχάνω.
τεφρόω, ώ, ώσω (τέφρα, ashes), to reduce to ashes, 2 Pet. ii. 6.*
τέχνη, ης, ή, (1) art, skill, Acts xvii. 29; (2) an art, craft, a trade, Acts xviii. 3; Rev. xviii. 22.*
τεχνίτης, ου, ό, an artificer, craftsman, Acts xix. 24, 38; Rev. xviii. 22; of the Divine artificer, Heb. xi. 10.*
τήκω, to melt, pass., 2 Pet. iii. 13.*
τηλ-αυγώς, adv. (τήλε, afar, αύγέω, to shine), brilliantly, clearly, Mark viii. 25.*
τηλικούτος, αύτη, ούτο, dem. pron., so great, 2 Cor. i. 10; Heb. ii. 3; James iii. 4; Rev. xvi. 18.*
τηρέω, ώ, ήσω, (1) to watch carefully, with good or evil design; (2) to guard; (3) to keep or reserve; (4) to observe, keep, enactments or ordinances.
τήρησις, εως, ή, (1) a place of ward, a prison, Acts iv. 3, v. 18; (2) observance, as of precepts, 1 Cor. vii. 19.*
Τιβεριάς, άδος, ή, Tiberias, John vi. 1, 23, xxi. 1.*
Τιβέριος, ου, ό, Tiberius, Luke iii. 1.*

τίθημι (see § 107), (1) to place, set, lay, put forth, put down, put away, put aside; mid., to cause to put, or to put for oneself; (2) to constitute, to make, to render; mid., to assign, determine.
τίκτω, τέξομαι, 2nd aor., έτεκον; 1st aor., pass., ετέχθην; to bear, to bring forth, of women; to produce, of the earth; to be in travail, John xvi. 21.
τίλλω, to pluck, to pluck off, Matt. xii. 1; Mark ii. 23; Luke vi. 1.*
Τιμαίος, ου, ό, Timæus, Mark x. 46.*
τιμάω, ώ, ήσω, (1) to estimate, to value at a price, Matt. xxvii. 9; (2) to honour, to reverence.
τιμή, ής, ή, (1) a price, value, Matt. xxvii. 6, 9; preciousness, i.e., great value, 1 Pet. ii. 7; (2) honour, a state of honour, Rom. ix. 21; an honourable office, Heb. v. 4; an honourable use, 2 Tim. ii. 20, 21.
τίμιος, ία, ιον, of great price, precious, honoured.
τιμιότης, τητος, ή, preciousness, costliness, Rev. xviii. 19.*
Τιμό-θεος, ου, ό, Timotheus or Timothy.
Τίμων, ωνος, Timon, Acts vi. 5.*
τιμωρέω, ώ, to punish (acc.), Acts xxii. 5, xxvi. 11.*
τιμωρία, ας, ή, punishment, retribution, Heb. x. 29.*
τίνω. See τίω.
τις, τι, gen. τινός (enclitic), indef. pron., any one, some one (see § 352).
τίς; τί; gen. τίνος; an interrogative pron., who? which? what? (see § 350).
τίτλος, ου, ό (Lat.), title, superscription, John xix. 19, 20.*
Τίτος, ου, ό Titus.
τίω or τίνω, τίσω, to pay; in N.T. only in the phrase τίω δίκην, to pay justice, i.e., to suffer punishment, 2 Thess. i. 9.*
τοι, an enclitic part., truly, indeed. See καιτοίγε, μέντοι, τοιγαρούν, τοίνυν.
τοι-γαρ-ούν, consequently, therefore, 1 Thess. iv. 8; Heb. xii. 1.*
τοί-γε, although (in καιτοίγε).
τοί-νυν, indeed now, therefore, Luke xx. 25; 1 Cor. ix. 26; Heb. xiii. 13; James ii. 24.*
τοιόσ-δε, τοιάδε, τοιόνδε, demonst. pron., of this kind, such, 2 Pet. i. 17.*
τοιούτος, τοιαύτη, τοιούτο, demonst. denoting quality (as τοσούτος denotes

quantity, and οὗτος simply determines), *of such a kind, such, so,* used either with or without a noun.. (The corresponding relative is οἶος, *as,* only Mark xiii. 19 ; 1 Cor. xv. 48 ; 2 Cor. x. 11 ; once ὁποῖος, Acts xxvi. 29.) For τοιοῦτος with the article, see § 220.

τοῖχος, ου, ὁ, *a wall* of a house, Acts xxiii. 3 ; disting. from τεῖχος, *a wall of a city.**

τόκος, ου, ὁ (*a bringing forth*), *interest, usury,* Matt. xxv. 27 ; Luke xix. 23.*

τολμάω, ῶ, ήσω, (1) *to dare, to venture* (inf.); (2) *to have courage.*

τολμηρότερον (comp. of τολμηρῶς, adv., *boldly*), *the more boldly,* Rom. xv. 15.*

τολμητής, οῦ, ὁ, *a daring one, one overbold* or *presumptuous,* 2 Pet. ii. 10.*

τομός, ή, όν, *sharp, keen,* comp., τομώτερος, Heb. iv. 12.*

τόξον, ου, τό, *a bow,* Rev. vi. 2.*

τοπάζιον, ίου, τό, *the topaz,* Rev. xxi. 20.*

τόπος, ου, ὁ, (1) *a place,* i.e., *a district* or *region,* or *a particular spot in a region ;* (2) *the place one occupies, the room, an abode, a seat, a sheath for a sword ;* (3) *a passage in a book ;* (4) *state, condition ;* (5) *opportunity, possibility.* (See under κρανίον.)

τοσοῦτος, τοσαύτη, τοσοῦτο, demonst. pron. denoting quantity (cf. τοιοῦτος), *so great, so much, so long ;* plur., *so many.*

τότε, demonst. adv., *then.*

τοὐναντίον, for τὸ ἐναντίον, *on the contrary,* 2 Cor. ii. 7 ; Gal. ii. 7 ; 1 Pet. iii. 9.*

τοὔνομα, for τὸ ὄνομα, *by name,* Matt. xxvii. 57.*

τουτέστι, for τοῦτ᾽ ἔστιν (W. H. prefer the uncontracted form), *that is; "i.e.,"* Acts i. 19 ; Rom. x. 6, 7, 8.

τοῦτο, neut. of οὗτος, which see.

τράγος, ου, ὁ, *a he-goat,* Heb. ix. 12, 13, 19, x. 4.*

τράπεζα, ης, ἡ, *a table,* (1) *for food and banqueting ;* (2) *for money-changing* or *business.*

τραπεζίτης, ου, ὁ, *a money-changer, a banker,* Matt. xxv. 27.*

τραῦμα, ατος, τό, *a wound,* Luke x. 34.*

τραυματίζω, ίσω, *to wound,* Luke xx. 12; Acts xix. 16.*

τραχηλίζω, ίσω, in pass., *to be laid bare, to be laid open,* Heb. iv. 13.*

τράχηλος, ου, ὁ, *the neck,* as Luke xv. 20; met. for *life,* Rom. xvi. 4.

τραχύς, εῖα, ύ, *rough, uneven,* as *ways,* Luke iii. 5 ; as rocks in the sea, Acts xxvii. 29.*

Τραχωνῖτις, ιδος, ἡ, *Trachonitis,* the N.E. of the territory beyond Jordan, Luke iii. 1.*

τρεῖς, τρία, *three.*

τρέμω, *to tremble, to be afraid,* Mark v. 33 ; Luke viii. 47 ; Acts ix. 6 (W. H. omit) ; 2 Pet. ii. 10.*

τρέφω θρέψω, perf., pass., τέθραμμαι, *to feed, to nourish, to sustain,* Matt. vi. 26 ; Acts xii. 20 ; James v. 5 ; *to bring up, rear,* Luke iv. 16.

τρέχω, 2nd aor. ἔδραμον, (1) *to run,* as in a race, 1 Cor. ix. 24 ; Rom. ix. 16 ; (2) *to run,* or *spread,* as a rumour, 2 Thess. iii. 1.

τρῆμα, ατος, τό, *a hole, the eye of a needle.* See τρυμαλιά.*

τριάκοντα, indecl., *thirty.*

τρια-κόσιοι, αι, α, *three hundred,* Mark xiv. 5 ; John xii. 5.*

τρίβολος, ου, ὁ, *a triple-thorned shrub, a thistle,* Matt. vii. 16 ; Heb. vi. 8.*

τρίβος, ου, ἡ, *a path worn, a road, a beaten way,* Matt. iii. 3 ; Mark i. 3 ; Luke iii. 4.*

τρι-ετία, ας, ἡ, *a space of three years,* Acts xx. 31.*

τρίζω, *to grate, to gnash,* as the teeth, Mark ix. 18.*

τρί-μηνος, ον, *of three months,* neut. as subst., Heb. xi. 23.*

τρίς, num. adv., *thrice.*

τρί-στεγος, ον, *having three floors;* neut., *the third floor* or *storey,* Acts xx. 9.*

τρισ-χίλιοι, αι, α, *three thousand,* Acts ii. 41.*

τρίτος, η, ον, ord. num., *third ;* neut., τὸ τρίτον, *the third part,* Rev. viii. 7 ; *the third time,* Mark xiv. 41 ; ἐκ τρίτου, *the third time,* Matt. xxvi. 44; τῇ τρίτῃ (sc. ἡμέρᾳ), *on the third day,* Luke xiii. 32.

τρίχες, plur. of θρίξ, which see.

τρίχινος, η, ον, *made of hair,* Rev. vi. 12.*

τρόμος, ου, ὁ, *a trembling, e.g.,* from fear.

τροπή, ῆς, ἡ, *a turning,* James i. 17 (see R.V.).*

τρόπος, ου, ὁ, (1) *manner ;* ὃν τρόπον, *in like manner as, as,* Matt. xxiii. 37 ; (2) *course of life, disposition,* Heb. xiii. 5.

τροπο-φορέω, ῶ, ήσω, to bear with the disposition or character of others, Acts xiii. 18, where perhaps the true reading is ἐτροποφόρησεν, he bare them as a nurse.*

τροφή, ῆς, ἡ, food, nourishment, maintenance.

Τρόφιμος, ου, ὁ, Trophimus.

τροφός, ου, ἡ, a nurse, 1 Thess. ii. 7.*

τροφο-φορέω. See τροποφορέω (not W. H.).*

τροχιά, ᾶς, ἡ, the track of a wheel, a path, fig., Heb. xii. 13.*

τροχός, ου, ὁ, a track of a wheel, a circle, a course, James iii. 6.*

τρύβλιον, ίου, τό, a dish, a platter, Matt. xxvi. 23; Mark xiv. 20.*

τρυγάω, ῶ, ήσω, to gather, as the vintage, Luke vi. 44; Rev. xiv. 18, 19.*

τρυγών, όνος, ἡ (τρύζω), a turtle-dove, Luke ii. 24.*

τρυμαλιά, ᾶς, ἡ, the eye of a needle, Mark x. 25; Luke xviii. 25 (W. H., τρῆμα).*

τρύπημα, ατος, τό, a hole, the eye of a needle, Matt. xix. 24.*

Τρύφαινα, ης, ἡ, Tryphæna, Rom. xvi. 12.*

τρυφάω, ῶ, ήσω, to live luxuriously, to take one's fill of pleasure, James v. 5.*

τρυφή, ῆς, ἡ, luxury, Luke vii. 25; 2 Pet. ii. 13.*

Τρυφῶσα, ης, ἡ, Tryphosa, Rom. xvi. 12.*

Τρωάς, άδος, ἡ, Troas, a city of Mysia, properly Alexandria Troas.

Τρωγύλλιον, ου, τό, Trogyllium, Acts xx. 15 (W. H. omit).*

τρώγω, to eat, Matt. xxiv. 38; John vi. 54-58, xiii. 18.*

τυγχάνω (τυχ- or τευχ-), fut., τεύξομαι; 2nd aor., ἔτυχον; perf., τέτυχα; (1) to obtain, to get possession of, enjoy (gen.), Luke xx. 35; Acts xxiv. 3; (2) to fall out, to happen, to happen to be; εἰ τύχοι, if it should chance, it may be, perhaps, 1 Cor. xiv. 10; 2nd aor., part., τυχών, ordinary, commonplace, Acts xix. 11; neut., τυχόν, what may be, perhaps, 1 Cor. xvi. 6.

τυμπανίζω, ίσω, to beat or scourge to death when stretched on a wheel, Heb. xi. 35.*

τυπικῶς, adv., typically, in figures, 1 Cor. x. 11 (W. H.).*

τύπος, ου, ὁ, (1) a mark, an impression, produced by a blow; (2) the figure of a thing, a pattern, "type"; (3) an emblem, an example; (4) the form or contents of a letter; (5) a form, a rule of doctrine.

τύπτω, ψω, to beat, to strike, as the breast in grief, Luke xviii. 13; to inflict punishment, Acts xxiii. 3; to wound or offend the conscience, 1 Cor. viii. 12.

Τύραννος, ου, ὁ, Tyrannus, Acts xix. 9.*

τυρβάζω, to agitate or disturb in mind, Luke x. 41 (W. H., θορυβάζω).*

Τύριος, ον, of Tyre, Tyrian, Acts xii. 20.*

Τύρος, ου, ἡ, Tyre, a city of Phenicia.

τυφλός, ή, όν, blind, (1) physically, (2) mentally, i.e., ignorant, stupid, dull of apprehension.

τυφλόω, ῶ, ώσω, fig., to make blind or dull of apprehension, John xii. 40; 2 Cor. iv. 4; 1 John ii. 11.*

τυφόω, ῶ, ώσω, to raise a smoke; pass., fig., to be proud, to be arrogant and conceited, 1 Tim. iii. 6, vi. 4; 2 Tim. iii. 4.*

τύφω, in pass., part., smoking, dimly burning, Matt. xii. 20.*

τυφωνικός, ή, όν, violent, tempestuous, like a whirlwind, Acts xxvii. 14.*

Τύχικος, ου, ὁ (or Τυχικός), Tychichus.

τυχόν. See τυγχάνω.

Υ.

Υ, υ, ὔψιλον, upsilon, u, the twentieth letter. As a numeral, υ' = 400; ͵υ = 400,000. At the commencement of a word, υ is always aspirated.

ὑακίνθινος, η, ον, "hyacinthine," of the colour of the hyacinth, dark purple, Rev. ix. 17.*

ὑάκινθος, ου, ὁ, "hyacinth," a purple or blue gem, "jacinth," perhaps sapphire, Rev. xxi. 20.*

ὑάλινος, η, ον, glassy, transparent, Rev. iv. 6.*

ὕαλος, ου, ἡ, a transparent stone like glass, crystal, Rev. xxi. 21.*

ὑβρίζω, σω, to treat with insolence or contumely, to abuse.

ὕβρις, εως, ἡ, (1) insolence, injury, 2 Cor. xii. 10; (2) damage, loss, Acts xxvii. 10, 21.*

ὑβριστής, οῦ, ὁ, *an insolent, injurious man*, Rom. i. 30; 1 Tim. i. 13.*

ὑγιαίνω, *to be well, to be in health*, Luke v. 31, xv. 27; fig., *to be sound*, in (ἐν) faith, doctrine, etc., Tit. i. 13; part., ὑγιαίνων, *healthful, wholesome*, of instruction, 1 Tim. i. 10.

ὑγιής, ές, (1) *sound, whole*, in health; (2) fig., *wholesome*, of teaching, Tit. ii. 8.

ὑγρός, ά, όν, *moist*, of a tree; *green*, i.e., full of sap, Luke xxiii. 31.*

ὑδρία, ας, ἡ, *a water-pot*, John ii. 6, 7, iv. 28.*

ὑδρο-ποτέω, ῶ, *to be a water-drinker*, 1 Tim. v. 23.*

ὑδρωπικός, ή, όν, *dropsical*, Luke xiv. 2.*

ὕδωρ, ὕδατος, τό, *water*; ὕδατα, *waters, streams*, also *a body of water*, as Matt. xiv. 28; ὕδωρ ζῶν, *living* or *running water*; fig., of spiritual truth, John iv. 14.

ὑετός, οῦ, ὁ (ὕω, *to rain*), *rain*.

υἱο-θεσία, ας, ἡ, *adoption, sonship*, into the Divine family, Rom. viii. 15, 23, ix. 4; Gal. iv. 5; Eph. i. 5.*

υἱός, οῦ, ὁ, *a son, a child*, Matt. xvii. 25; *a descendant; the offspring* or *young of an animal*, Matt. xxi. 5; *an adopted son*, Heb. xi. 24; of various forms of close union and relationship (cf. τέκνον); *a disciple* or *follower*, Matt. xii. 27; *one who resembles* (gen.), Matt. v. 45; *one who partakes of any quality* or *character*, Luke x. 6; John xii. 36; ὁ υἱὸς τοῦ ἀνθρώπου, *Son of man* (once only without art., John v. 27), very often used by our Lord of himself (only once by another of him, Acts vii. 56); in reference to Dan. vii. 13 (*sons of men* denote *men generally* in Mark iii. 28, Eph. iii. 5, only). For υἱὸς Θεοῦ, *Son of God*, see § 217, c.

ὕλη, ης, ἡ, *wood, fuel*, James iii. 5.*

ὑμεῖς, plur. of σύ, which see.

Ὑμεναῖος, ου, ὁ, *Hymenæus*, 1 Tim. i. 20; 2 Tim. ii. 17.*

ὑμέτερος, possess. pron., *your*, as belonging to, or as proceeding from. (For the use of the article with the word, see § 223.)

ὑμνέω, ῶ, ήσω, (1) *to sing* or *recite hymns to* (acc.); *to sing praise*, Matt. xxvi.

30; Mark xiv. 26; Acts xvi. 25; Heb. ii. 12.*

ὕμνος, ου, ὁ, *a hymn, a sacred song*, Eph. v. 19; Col. iii. 16. Syn. 48.*

ὑπ-άγω, *to go away, to take oneself away;* imperat., sometimes an expression of aversion, *begone*, Matt. iv. 10; sometimes a farewell only, Matt. viii. 13, 32; *to die*, Matt. xxvi. 24.

ὑπ-ακοή, ῆς, ἡ, *obedience*, Rom. vi. 16.

ὑπ-ακούω, σω, (1) *to listen*, as at a door, to find who seeks admission, only Acts xii. 13; (2) *to hearken to*, hence *to obey* (dat.).

ὕπ-ανδρος, ον, *under a husband, married*, Rom. vii. 2.*

ὑπ-αντάω, ῶ, ήσω, *to meet* (dat.), Matt. viii. 28.

ὑπ-άντησις, εως, ἡ, *a meeting*, Matt. viii. 34 (W. H.), xxv. 1 (W. H.); John xii. 13.*

ὕπαρξις, εως, ἡ, *goods, substance, property*, Acts ii. 45; Heb. x. 34.*

ὑπ-άρχω, *to begin to be; to be originally, to subsist;* hence generally, *to be*, Luke viii. 41; Acts iii. 6; with dat. of pers., *to have, to possess;* part., neut., pl., τὰ ὑπάρχοντα, *things which one possesses, goods, property*, Matt. xix. 21. Syn. 1.

ὑπ-είκω, *to yield, to submit to authority*, Heb. xiii. 17.*

ὑπ-εναντίος, ία, ίον, *opposite to, adverse*, Col. ii. 14; as subst., *an adversary*, Heb. x. 27.*

ὑπέρ, prep., gov. gen. and accus: with gen., *over, for, on behalf of;* with accus., *above, superior to* (see § 303). Adverbially, *above, more*, 2 Cor. xi. 23. IN COMPOSITION, ὑπέρ denotes *superiority* (above), or *aid* (on behalf of).

ὑπερ-αίρω, in mid., *to lift up oneself, to exalt oneself, to be arrogant*, 2 Cor. xii. 7; 2 Thess. ii. 4.*

ὑπέρ-ακμος, ον, *past the acme* or *flower of life*, 1 Cor. vii. 36.*

ὑπερ-άνω, adv. (gen.), *above*, Eph. i. 21, iv. 10; Heb. ix. 5.*

ὑπερ-αυξάνω, *to increase exceedingly*, 2 Thess. i. 3.*

ὑπερ-βαίνω, *to go beyond, to over-reach*, 1 Thess. iv. 6.*

ὑπερ-βαλλόντως, adv., *beyond measure*, 2 Cor. xi. 23.*

ὑπερ-βάλλω, intrans., *to surpass;* N.T.,

only pres. participle, *surpassing exceeding*, 2 Cor. iii. 10, ix. 14 ; Eph. i. 19, ii. 7, iii. 19.*
ὑπερ-βολή, ῆς, ἡ, *excess, exuberance, surpassing excellence, pre-eminence*, 2 Cor. iv. 7, xii. 7 ; καθ' ὑπερβολήν, as adv., *exceedingly*, Rom. vii. 13 ; 1 Cor. xii. 31 ; 2 Cor. i. 8 ; Gal. i. 13 ; καθ' ὑπερβολὴν εἰς ὑπερβολήν, *more and more exceedingly* (R.V.), 2 Cor. iv. 17.*
ὑπερ-είδον (see εἴδον), *to overlook, to bear with*, Acts xvii. 30.*
ὑπερ-έκεινα, adv., *beyond, farther*, 2 Cor. x. 16.*
ὑπερ-εκ-περισσοῦ, adv., *beyond all measure, in the highest possible degree*, Eph. iii. 20 ; 1 Thess. iii. 10, v. 13.*
ὑπερ-εκ-τείνω, *to stretch out overmuch*, 2 Cor. x. 14.*
ὑπερ-εκ-χύνω, pass., *to be poured out over, to overflow*, Luke vi. 38.*
ὑπερ-εν-τυγχάνω, *to intercede for*, Rom. viii. 26.*
ὑπερ-έχω, *to excel, to surpass* (gen.), *to be supreme;* N.T. only participle, Rom. xiii. 1 ; Phil. ii. 3, iv. 7 ; 1 Pet. ii. 13 ; part. neut., τὸ ὑπερέχον, *excellency, super-eminence*, Phil. iii. 8.*
ὑπερ-ηφανία, ας, ἡ, *pride, arrogance*, Mark vii. 22.*
ὑπερ-ήφανος, ον (φαίνω, η connective), *proud, arrogant*, James iv. 6.
ὑπερ-λίαν, adv., *very much, pre-eminently*, 2 Cor. xi. 5, xii. 11.*
ὑπερ-νικάω, ῶ, *to be more than conqueror*, Rom. viii. 37.*
ὑπέρ-ογκος, *tumid, boastful*, of language, 2 Pet. ii. 18 ; Jude 16.*
ὑπερ-οχή, ῆς, ἡ, *eminence, superiority*, 1 Cor. ii. 1 ; 1 Tim. ii. 2.*
ὑπερ-περισσεύω, *to superabound*, Rom. v. 20 ; pass., *to be very abundant in* (dat.), 2 Cor. vii. 4.*
ὑπερ-περισσῶς, adv., *superabundantly, above measure*, Mark vii. 37.*
ὑπερ-πλεονάζω, *to superabound*, 1 Tim. i. 14.*
ὑπερ-υψόω, ῶ, *to highly exalt*, Phil. ii. 9.*
ὑπερ-φρονέω, ῶ, *to think over-highly of oneself*, Rom. xii. 3.*
ὑπερῷον, ου, τό, *the upper part of a house, an upper chamber*, Acts i. 13, ix. 37, 39, xx. 8.*
ὑπ-έχω, *to submit to, to undergo* (acc.), Jude 7.*

ὑπ-ήκοος, ον, *listening to, obedient to* (dat.), *submissive*, Acts vii. 39 ; 2 Cor. ii. 9 ; Phil. ii. 8.*
ὑπ-ηρετέω, ῶ, *to minister to, to serve* (dat.), Acts xiii. 36, xx. 34, xxiv. 23.*
ὑπ-ηρέτης, ου, ὁ (ἐρέτης, *a rower*), *a servant, attendant*, specially (1) *an officer, a lictor;* (2) *an attendant in a synagogue;* (3) *a minister of the Gospel*. Syn. 60.
ὕπνος, ου, ὁ, *sleep;* fig., *spiritual sleep*.
ὑπό, prep., gov. gen. and accus., *under*: with gen., *by*, generally signifying the agent ; with accus., *under, beneath*, of place, of time, or of subjection to authority (see § 304). IN COMPOSITION, ὑπό denotes *subjection, diminution, concealment*.
ὑπο-βάλλω, *to suborn, to suggest* what is false, Acts vi. 11.*
ὑπο-γραμμός, οῦ, ὁ, *a pattern, an example*, 1 Pet. ii. 21.*
ὑπό-δειγμα, ατος, τό, (1) *an example* for imitation, or for warning, John xiii. 15 ; Heb. iv. 11 ; 2 Pet. ii. 6 ; James v. 10 ; (2) *a typical representation, pattern, copy*, Heb. viii. 5, ix. 23.*
ὑπο-δείκνυμι, *to show plainly*, as by placing under the eyes, *to warn* (dat.), Matt. iii. 7 ; Luke iii. 7, 'vi. 47, xii. 5 ; Acts ix. 16, xx. 35.*
ὑπο-δέχομαι, *to receive as a guest, to entertain* (acc.), Luke x. 38, xix. 6 ; Acts xvii. 7 ; James ii. 25.*
ὑπο-δέω, ῶ, ἥσω, in mid., *to bind on one's sandals, be shod with* (acc.), Mark vi. 9 ; Acts xii. 8 ; Eph. vi. 15 (lit., *shod as to your feet*).*
ὑπό-δημα, ατος, τό, *a sandal, shoe*.
ὑπό-δικος, ον, *subject to judgment, under penalty to* (dat.), Rom. iii. 19.*
ὑπο-ζύγιον, ου, τό, *an animal under yoke, an ass*, Matt. xxi. 5 ; 2 Pet. ii. 16.*
ὑπο-ζώννυμι, *to undergird*, as a ship for strength against the waves, Acts xxvii. 17.*
ὑπο-κάτω, adv., *underneath* (as prep. with gen.).
ὑπο-κρίνομαι, dep., *to act under a mask, to personate, to feign* (acc., inf.), Luke xx. 20.*
ὑπό-κρισις, εως, ἡ, lit., *stage playing; hypocrisy, dissembling*, 1 Tim. .

ὑπο-κριτής, οῦ, ὁ, lit., *a stage player ; a hypocrite, a dissembler*, Matt. xvi. 3.
ὑπο-λαμβάνω, 2nd aor. ὑπέλαβον, (1) *to take from under, to receive up*, Acts i. 9 ; (2) *to take up a discourse, to answer*, Luke x. 30 ; (3) *to think, to judge, to suppose*, Luke vii. 43 ; Acts ii. 15 ; (4) *to receive, welcome*, 3 John 8 (W. H.).*
ὑπό-λειμμα (or -λιμμα), ατος, τό, *a remnant*, Rom. ix. 27 (W. H.).*
ὑπο-λείπω, *to leave behind*, pass., Rom. xi. 3.*
ὑπο-λήνιον, ου, τό (ληνός), *a wine-vat, wine-press*, dug in the ground, Mark xii. 1.*
ὑπο-λιμπάνω, *to leave, to leave behind*, 1 Pet. ii. 21.*
ὑπο-μένω, (1) *to bear up under, to endure* (acc.) ; (2) *to persevere, to remain constant*, Matt. x. 22 ; (3) *to remain or stay behind*, Luke ii. 43.
ὑπο-μιμνήσκω, ὑπομνήσω, 1st aor. pass. ὑπεμνήσθην, *to remind* (acc. of pers.), John xiv. 26 ; mid., *to call to mind, to remember*, only Luke xxii. 61.
ὑπό-μνησις, εως, ἡ, (1) *remembrance, recollection*, 2 Tim. i. 5 ; (2) *a putting in mind*, 2 Pet. i. 13, iii. 1.*
ὑπο-μονή, ῆς, ἡ, *a bearing up under, endurance, perseverance, patient waiting for* (gen.).
ὑπο-νοέω, ῶ, *to conjecture, to suspect*, Acts xiii. 25, xxv. 18, xxvii. 27.*
ὑπό-νοια, ας, ἡ, *a surmising, suspicion*, 1 Tim. vi. 4.*
ὑπο-πλέω (F), 1st aor. ὑπέπλευσα, *to sail under shelter of* (acc.), Acts xxvii. 4, 7.*
ὑπο-πνέω (F), 1st aor. ὑπέπνευσα, *to blow gently*, of the wind, Acts xxvii. 13.*
ὑπο-πόδιον, ου, τό, *a footstool*.
ὑπό-στασις, εως, ἡ, *that which underlies ;* hence (1), *the substance, the reality* underlying mere appearance, Heb. i. 3, perhaps, Heb. xi. 1 (R.V. marg.) ; (2) *support, confidence, assurance*, 2 Cor. ix. 4, xi. 17 ; Heb. iii. 14 ; perhaps Heb. xi. 1 (R.V.).*
ὑπο-στέλλω, ελῶ, 1st aor. ὑπέστειλα, *to draw back*, Gal. ii. 12 ; mid., *to shrink, to draw oneself back* from (τοῦ μή, with inf.), Acts xx. 27 ; Heb. x. 38.*
ὑπο-στολή, ῆς, ἡ, *a shrinking, a drawing back*, Heb. x. 39.*

ὑπο-στρέφω, ψω, *to turn back, to return*, intrans.
ὑπο-στρώννυμι or -ωννύω, *to strew under*, Luke xix. 36.*
ὑπο-ταγή, ῆς, ἡ, *subjection, submission*, 2 Cor. ix. 13 ; Gal. ii. 5 ; 1 Tim. ii. 11, iii. 4.*
ὑπο-τάσσω, ξω, 2nd aor., pass., ὑπετάγην, *to place under, to subject ;* mid., *to submit oneself, to be obedient*.
ὑπο-τίθημι, *to set or put under, to lay down*, Rom. xvi. 4 ; mid., *to suggest to, put in mind* ; 1 Tim. iv. 6.*
ὑπο-τρέχω, 2nd aor. ὑπέδραμον, *to run under lee or shelter of*, Acts xxvii. 16.*
ὑπο-τύπωσις, εως, ἡ, *pattern, example*, 1 Tim. i. 16 ; 2 Tim. i. 13.*
ὑπο-φέρω, 1st aor. ὑπήνεγκα, *to bear up under, to sustain, to endure*, 1 Cor. x. 13 ; 2 Tim. iii. 11 ; 1 Pet. ii. 19.*
ὑπο-χωρέω, ῶ, ήσω, *to withdraw quietly, to retire*, Luke v. 16, ix. 10.*
ὑπ-ωπιάζω, *to strike under the eye ;* hence, (1) *to bruise ;* fig., *to buffet*, 1 Cor. ix. 27 ; (2) *to weary out*, by repeated application, Luke xviii. 5.*
ὗς, ὑός, ὁ, ἡ, *a hog, boar*, or *sow*, 2 Pet. ii. 22.*
ὕσσωπος, ου, ἡ, *hyssop, a stalk* or *stem of hyssop*, John xix. 29 ; *a bunch of hyssop for sprinkling*, Heb. ix. 19.*
ὑστερέω, ῶ, ήσω, *to be behind ;* abs., *to be lacking, to fall short*, John ii. 3 ; with obj., *to be lacking in, to fall short of*, acc., Matt. xix. 20 ; gen., Luke xxii. 35 ; ἀπό, Heb. xii. 15 ; *to be lacking to*, acc., Mark x. 21 ; pass., *to lack, to come short*, 1 Cor. i. 7, viii. 8 ; *to suffer need*, Luke xv. 14.
ὑστέρημα, ματος, τό, (1) *that which is lacking* from (gen.), Col. i. 24 ; 1 Thess. iii. 10 ; (2) *need, poverty*, Luke xxi. 4.
ὑστέρησις, εως, ἡ, *poverty, penury*, Mark xii. 44 ; Phil. iv. 11.*
ὕστερος, α, ον, compar., *latter*, only, Tim. iv. 1 and Matt. xxi. 31 (W. H.) ; neut. as an adv., *last, afterwards*, with gen., Matt. xxii. 27 ; Luke xx. 32.
ὑφαντός, ή, όν (ὑφαίνω, *to weave*), *woven*, John xix. 23.*
ὑψηλός, ή, όν, *high, lofty*, lit. or fig., τα ὑψηλά, *things that are high*, Rom. xii. 16 : ἐν ὑψηλοῖς, *on high*, Heb. i. 3.
ὑψηλο-φρονέω, ῶ, *to be high-minded*,

proud, assuming, Rom. xi. 20 (W. H., ὑψηλὰ φρόνει); 1 Tim. vi. 17.*
ὕψιστος, η, ον (superlat. of ὕψι, *highly*), *highest, most elevated*; neut., plur., *the highest places, the heights, i.e.*, the heavens, Luke ii. 14; ὁ ὕψιστος, *the Most High*, i.e., *God*, Luke i. 32, 35, 76.
ὕψος, ους, τό, *height*, opp. to βάθος, Eph. iii. 18; Rev. xxi. 16; ἐξ ὕψους, *from on high, i.e.*, from God, Luke i. 78, xxiv. 49; so εἰς ὕψος, *to God*, Eph. iv. 8; fig., *exaltation*, James i. 9.*
ὑψόω, ῶ, ώσω, (1) *to raise on high, to elevate*, as the brazen serpent, and Jesus on the cross; (2) *to exalt, to set on high*, Acts ii. 33; (3) *to elevate, i.e., to raise from a lowly to a dignified condition*; (4) *to exalt in estimation*, Matt. xxiii. 12.
ὕψωμα, ατος, τό, *height*, Rom. viii. 39; *citadel* (fig.), 2 Cor. x. 5.*

Φ.

Φ, φ, φῖ, *phi, ph*, the twenty-first letter. As a numeral, φ′ = 500; φ, = 500,000.
φάγος, ον, ὁ, *a glutton*, Matt. xi. 19; Luke vii. 34.*
φάγω, only used in fut., φάγομαι, and 2nd aor., ἔφαγον. See ἐσθίω.
φαιλόνης, ου, ὁ (W. H., φελόνης), (Lat., paenula,) *a cloak*, 2 Tim. iv. 13.*
φαίνω, φανῶ, 2nd aor., pass., ἐφανήν, (1) trans., *to show*, in N.T. only mid. or pass., *to appear, to be seen, to seem*; τὰ φαινόμενα, *things which can be seen*, Heb. xi. 3; (2) intrans., *to shine, to give light*, John i. 5, v. 35. **Syn. 6.**
Φάλεκ, ὁ (Heb.), *Peleg*, Luke iii. 35.*
φανερός, ά, όν, *apparent, manifest*; ἐν τῷ φανερῷ, as adv., *manifestly, openly*, Matt. vi. 4, 6; *externally, outwardly*, Rom. ii. 28; adv., -ῶς, *clearly*, Acts x. 3; *publicly*, Mark i. 45.
φανερόω, ῶ, ώσω, *to make apparent, to manifest, to disclose*; pass., *to be manifested, made manifest*, 1 Tim. iii. 16; 2 Cor. v. 11.
φανέρωσις, εως, ἡ, *a manifestation* (gen. obj.), 1 Cor xii. 7; 2 Cor. iv. 2.*
φανός, οῦ, ὁ, *a torch, a lantern*, John xviii. 3.*

Φανουήλ, ὁ (Heb.), *Phanuel*, Luke ii. 36.*
φαντάζω, *to cause to appear*; pass., part., τὸ φανταζόμενον, *the spectacle*, Heb. xii. 21.*
φαντασία, ας, ἡ, *show, pomp*, Acts xxv. 23.*
φάντασμα, ατος, τό, *a phantom, an apparition*, Matt. xiv. 26; Mark vi. 49.*
φάραγξ, αγγος, ἡ, *a valley, dell*, or *gorge*, Luke iii. 5.*
Φαραώ, ὁ, *Pharaoh*, the title of ancient Egyptian kings.
Φαρές, ὁ (Heb.), *Phares*, Matt. i. 3; Luke iii. 33.*
Φαρισαῖος, ου, ὁ, (from the Heb. verb, *to separate*), *a Pharisee*, one of the Jewish sect so called.
φαρμακεία (W. H., -κία), ας, ἡ, *magic, art, sorcery, enchantment*, Gal. v. 20; Rev. ix. 21 (W. H., φαρμακός), xviii. 23.*
φαρμακεύς, έως, ὁ, *a magician, sorcerer, enchanter*, Rev. xxi. 8 (W. H. read following).*
φαρμακός, οῦ, ὁ, *a magician, sorcerer, enchanter*, Rev. xxi. 8 (W. H.), xxii. 15.*
φάσις, εως, ἡ, *report, tidings*, Acts xxi. 31.*
φάσκω (freq. of φημί), *to assert, to affirm, to profess*, Acts xxiv. 9, xxv. 19; Rom. i. 22; Rev. ii. 2 (W. H. omit).*
φάτνη, ης, ἡ, *a manger, a crib*, Luke ii. 7; *a stable*, Luke xiii. 15.
φαῦλος, η, ον, *vile, wicked, base*, John iii. 20, v. 29; Rom. ix. 11 (W. H.); 2 Cor. v. 10 (W. H.); Tit. ii. 8; James iii. 16. **Syn. 22.***
φέγγος, ους, τό, *brightness, splendour*, Matt. xxiv. 29; Mark xiii. 24; Luke xi. 33 (W. H., φῶς). **Syn. 65.***
φείδομαι, φείσομαι, dep., (1) *to spare* (gen.), Acts xx. 29; (2) *to forbear* (inf.), 2 Cor. xii. 6.
φειδομένως, adv., *sparingly, parsimoniously*, 2 Cor. ix. 6.*
φελόνης. See φαιλόνης.
φέρω, οἴσω, ἤνεγκα, ἠνέχθην (see § 103), *to bear*, as (1) *to produce* fruit; (2) *to carry*, as a burden; (3) *to bring*; (4) *to endure, to bear with*, Rom. ix. 22; (5) *to bring forward*, as charges, John xviii. 29; (6) *to uphold*, Heb. i. 3; (7) pass., as nautical term, *to be*

driven, Acts xxvii. 15, 17; (8) mid., *to rush* (bear itself on), Acts ii. 2; *to go on* or *advance*, in learning, Heb. vi. 1.
φεύγω, ξομαι, έφυγον, *to flee, to escape, to shun* (acc. or από).
Φῆλιξ, ικος, ὁ, *Felix*.
φήμη, ης, ἡ, *a rumour, fame*, Matt. ix. 26; Luke iv. 14.*
φημί, impf. and 2nd aor. ἔφην (for other tenses, see εἶπον, ἐρέω), *to say*, with ὅτι, dat. of pers., πρός (acc.), with pers., acc. of thing (once acc., inf., Rom. iii. 8). Syn. 8.
Φῆστος, ου, ὁ, *Festus*.
φθάνω, φθάσω, perf. ἔφθακα, (1) *to be before, to precede*, 1 Thess. iv. 15; *to come sooner than expected*, Matt. xii. 28; Luke xi. 20; 2 Cor. x. 14; 1 Thess. ii. 16; (2) *to arrive, attain to* (εἰς, ἄχρι), Rom. ix. 31; Phil. iii. 16.*
φθαρτός, ή, όν (φθείρω), *corruptible, perishable*, Rom. i. 23; 1 Cor. ix. 25; xv. 53, 54; 1 Pet. i. 18, 23.*
φθέγγομαι, γξομαι, dep., *to speak aloud, to utter*, Acts iv. 18; 2 Pet. ii. 16, 18.*
φθείρω, φθερῶ, 2nd aor., pass., ἐφθάρην, *to corrupt*, physically or morally, *to spoil, to destroy*.
φθινο-πωρινός, *autumnal*, Jude 12.*
φθόγγος, ου, ὁ (φθέγγομαι), *a sound*, Rom. x. 18; 1 Cor. xiv. 7.*
φθονέω, ῶ, ήσω, *to envy* (dat.), Gal. v. 26.*
φθόνος, ου, ὁ, *envy*.
φθορά, ᾶς, ἡ (φθείρω), *corruption, destruction*, physical or spiritual.
φιάλη, ης, ἡ, *a bowl*, broad and flat, Rev.*
φιλ-άγαθος, ον, *loving goodness* (R.V.) or *loving good men* (A.V.), Tit. i. 8.*
Φιλ-αδέλφεια, ας, ἡ, *Philadelphia*, Rev. i. 11, iii. 7.*
φιλ-αδελφία, ας, ἡ, *brotherly love, love of Christian brethren*, Rom. xii. 10; 1 Thess. iv. 9; Heb. xiii. 1; 1 Pet. i. 22; 2 Pet. i. 7.*
φιλ-άδελφος, ον, *loving the brethren*, 1 Pet. iii. 8.*
φίλ-ανδρος, ον, *loving one's husband*, Tit. ii. 4.*
φιλ-ανθρωπία, ας, ἡ, *love of man, benevolence*, "philanthropy," Acts xxviii. 2; Tit. iii. 4.*

φιλ-ανθρώπως, adv., *kindly*, Acts xxvii. 3.*
φιλ-αργυρία, ας, ἡ, *love of money, covetousness*, 1 Tim. vi. 10.*
φιλ-άργυρος, ον, *money-loving, covetous*, Luke xvi. 14; 2 Tim. iii. 2.*
φίλ-αυτος, ον, *self-loving, selfish*, 2 Tim. iii. 2.*
φιλέω, ῶ, ήσω, (1) *to love*; (2) with inf., *to be wont*, a classical usage perhaps found in Matt. vi. 5; (3) *to kiss*, Matt. xxvi. 48. Syn. 19.
φίλη, ης, ἡ, *a female friend* (see φίλος), Luke xv. 9.*
φιλ-ήδονος, ον, *pleasure-loving*; as subst., 2 Tim. iii. 4.*
φίλημα, ατος, τό, *a kiss*.
Φιλήμων, ονος, ὁ, *Philemon*, Philem. 1.*
Φίλητος or **Φιλητός,** *Philetus*, 2 Tim. ii. 17.*
φιλία, ας, ἡ, *friendship, love*, James iv. 4 (gen. obj.).*
Φιλιππήσιος, ου, ὁ, *a Philippian*, Phil. iv. 15.*
Φίλιπποι, ων, οἱ, *Philippi*.
Φίλιππος, ου, ὁ, *Philip*. Four of the name are mentioned: (1) John i. 44-47; (2) Acts vi. 5; (3) Luke iii. 1; (4) Matt. xiv. 3.
Φιλό-θεος, ου, ὁ, ἡ, *a lover of God*, 2 Tim. iii. 4.*
Φιλό-λογος, ου, ὁ, *Philologus*, Rom. xvi. 15.*
φιλο-νεικία, ας, ἡ, *love of dispute, contention, strife*, Luke xxii. 24.*
φιλό-νεικος, ον, *strife-loving, contentious*, 1 Cor. xi. 16.*
φιλο-ξενία, ας, ἡ, *hospitality, love of strangers*, Rom. xii. 13; Heb. xiii. 2.*
φιλό-ξενος, ον, ὁ, *hospitable*, 1 Tim. iii. 2; Tit. i. 8; 1 Pet. iv. 9.*
φιλο-πρωτεύω, *to love the first place, to affect pre-eminence*, 3 John 9.*
φίλος, η, ον, either act. *loving*, or pass. *dear*; in N.T. as subst., *a friend, a loved companion* or *associate* with (gen. or dat.).
φιλο-σοφία, ας, ἡ, *philosophy*, in N.T. of the Jewish traditional theology, Col. ii. 8.*
φιλό-σοφος, ου, ὁ (prop. adj.), *wisdom-loving*, in N.T. of Greek philosophers, Acts xvii. 18.*
φιλό-στοργος, ον, *tenderly loving, kindly affectionate to* (εἰς), Rom. xii. 10.*

φιλό-τεκνος, ον, child-loving, Tit. ii. 4.*
φιλο-τιμέομαι, οῦμαι, dep., to make a thing one's ambition, to desire very strongly (inf.), Rom. xv. 20; 2 Cor. v. 9; 1 Thess. iv. 11.*
φιλο-φρόνως, adv., in a friendly or hospitable manner, courteously, Acts xxviii. 7.*
φιλό-φρων, ον, friendly-minded, hospitable, courteous, 1 Pet. iii. 8 (W. H., ταπεινόφρων).*
φιμόω, ῶ, ώσω, to muzzle, 1 Cor. ix. 9; to reduce to silence, Matt. xxii. 34; pass., to be reduced to silence, to be silent, Matt. xxii. 12; of a storm, Mark iv. 39.
Φλέγων, οντος, ὁ, Phlegon, Rom. xvi. 14.*
φλογίζω, to inflame, to fire with passion, James iii. 6.*
φλόξ, φλογός, ἡ, a flame.
φλυαρέω, ῶ, to prate, to talk idly against any one (acc.), 3 John 10.*
φλύαρος, ον, prating; as subst., an idle talker, 1 Tim. v. 13.*
φοβερός, ά, όν, fearful, dreadful, Heb. x. 27, 31, xii. 21.*
φοβέω, ῶ, ήσω, to make afraid, to terrify; in N.T. only passive, to be afraid, to be terrified, sometimes with cognate acc., Mark iv. 41; to fear (acc.), Matt. x. 26; to reverence, Mark vi. 20; met., to cherish piety towards (acc.), Luke i. 50. **Syn. 33.**
φόβητρον (W. H., -θρον), ου, τό, a terrible sight, a portent, Luke xxi. 11.*
φόβος, ου, ὁ, (1) fear, terror, alarm, Matt. xiv. 26; (2) the object or cause of fear, Rom. xiii. 3; (3) reverence, awe, respect; (4) met. for piety, Rom. iii. 18; 1 Pet. i. 17. **Syn. 33.**
Φοίβη, ης, ἡ, Phœbe, Rom. xvi. 1.*
Φοινίκη, ης, ἡ, Phenice or Phenicia.
φοῖνιξ, ικος, ὁ, a palm-tree, a palm branch, John xii. 13; Rev. vii. 9.*
Φοῖνιξ, ικος, ἡ, a proper name, Phenice, a city of Crete, Acts xxvii. 12.*
φονεύς, έως, ὁ, a murderer, a manslayer.
φονεύω, σω, to murder, to kill.
φόνος, ου, ὁ, murder, bloodthirstiness.
φορέω, ῶ, έσω, to bear about, to wear, Matt. xi. 8; John xix. 5; Rom. xiii. 4; 1 Cor. xv. 49; James ii. 3.*
φόρον, ου, τό (Latin), the forum (see Ἄππιος), Acts xxviii. 15.*

φόρος, ου, ὁ (φέρω), a tax on persons (distinguished from τέλος, a tax on merchandise), Luke xx. 22, xxiii. 2; Rom. xiii. 6, 7.*
φορτίζω, pass., perf., part., πεφορτισμένος, to load, to burden, to afflict, Matt. xi. 28; Luke xi. 46.*
φορτίον, ου, τό, a burden, Matt. xi. 30; the freight of a ship, Acts xxvii. 10 (W. H.); the burden of ceremonial observances, Matt. xxiii. 4; Luke xi. 46; the burden of responsibility, Gal. vi. 5. **Syn. 68.***
φόρτος, ου, ὁ, load, a ship's cargo, Acts xxvii. 10 (W. H. read φορτίον).*
Φορτουνᾶτος, ου (Lat.), Fortunatus, 1 Cor. xvi. 17.*
φραγέλλιον, ίου, τό (Lat.), a scourge, a whip, John ii. 15.*
φραγελλόω, ῶ, to flagellate, to scourge with whips, Matt. xxvii. 26; Mark xv. 15.*
φραγμός, οῦ, ὁ, a hedge, Matt. xxi. 33; Mark xii. 1; Luke xiv. 23; fig., partition, Eph. ii. 14.*
φράζω, άσω, to tell, explain, interpret, Matt. xiii. 36 (not W. H.), xv. 15.*
φράσσω, ξω, 2nd aor., pass., ἐφράγην, to stop, to stay, Rom. iii. 19; 2 Cor. xi. 10; Heb. xi. 33.*
φρέαρ, φρέατος, τό, a pit, a well, John iv. 11, 12.
φρεν-απατάω, ῶ, to deceive the mind, to impose upon (acc.), Gal. vi. 3.*
φρεν-απάτης, ου, ὁ, a deceiver, impostor, Tit. i. 10.*
φρήν, φρενός, ἡ (lit., diaphragm), plur., αἱ φρένες, the intellect, 1 Cor. xiv. 20. **Syn. 55.***
φρίσσω, ξω, to shudder, James ii. 19.*
φρονέω, ῶ, ήσω (φρήν), (1) to mind, to think (abs.); (2) to think, judge (acc.); (3) to set the mind and affections on (acc.); (4) to observe, a time as sacred, Rom. xiv. 6; (5) with ὑπέρ, to care for, Phil. iv. 10. **Syn. 11.**
φρόνημα, ατος, τό, thought, regard, care for, Rom. viii. 6, 7, 27, vii. 27.*
φρόνησις, εως, ἡ, understanding, wisdom, Luke i. 17; Eph. i. 8.*
φρόνιμος, ον, intelligent, wise, prudent; adv., -ως, prudently, only Luke xvi. 8.
φροντίζω, to take care, to be anxious, inf., Tit. iii. 8. **Syn. 11.***
φρουρέω, ῶ, to watch, to keep, as by a

military guard, lit., 2 Cor. xi. 32; fig., Gal. iii. 23 (as if in custody); Phil. iv. 7 (in security); 1 Pet. i. 5 (in reserve).*

φρυάσσω, ξω, to rage, as in a tumult, Acts iv. 25 (LXX.).*

φρύγανον, ου, τό, a dry stick, a faggot stick, for burning, Acts xxviii. 3.*

Φρυγία, as, ἡ, Phrygia.

Φύγελλος (W. H., -ελος), ου, ὁ, Phygellus, 2 Tim. i. 15.*

φυγή, ῆς, ἡ, flight, Matt. xxiv. 20; Mark xiii. 18 (W. H. omit).*

φυλακή, ῆς, ἡ, (1) a keeping guard, a watching, Luke ii. 8; espec. of the four watches into which the night was divided, Matt. xiv. 25, Luke xii. 38; (2) a guard, or men on guard, a watch, Acts xii. 10; (3) a prison, Matt. v. 25; (4) an imprisonment, 2 Cor. vi. 5.

φυλακίζω, to imprison, to deliver into custody, Acts xxii. 19.*

φυλακτήρια, ων, τά (plur. of adj.), a safeguard, amulet, or charm, a phylactery, or slip of parchment, with Scripture words thereon, and worn by some of the Jews as protective, Matt. xxiii. 5.*

φύλαξ, ακος, ὁ, a keeper, sentinel, Acts v. 23, xii. 6, 19.*

φυλάσσω, ξω, (1) to keep guard, or watch over; (2) to keep in safety; (3) to observe, as a precept; (4) mid., to keep oneself from (acc. or ἀπό), Luke xii. 15; Acts xxi. 25.

φυλή, ῆς, ἡ, (1) a tribe, of Israel; (2) race, or people. Syn. 61.

φύλλον, ου, τό, a leaf.

φύραμα, ατος, τό, a mass kneaded into consistency, a lump, as of dough or clay, Rom. ix. 21, xi. 16; 1 Cor. v. 6, 7; Gal. v. 9.*

φυσικός, ή, όν, natural, as (1) according to nature, Rom. i. 26, 27; (2) merely animal, 2 Pet. ii. 12; adv., -ως, physically, naturally, Jude 10.*

φυσιόω, ῶ, to inflate, to puff up, 1 Cor. viii. 1.; pass., to be inflated, arrogant, 1 Cor. iv. 6, 18, 19, v. 2, xiii. 4; Col. ii. 18.*

φύσις, εως, ἡ, generally, nature; specially, (1) natural birth, Gal. ii. 15; (2) natural disposition, instinct, propensity, Eph. ii. 3; (3) long-established custom, 1 Cor. xi. 14; (4) native qualities, or properties, Gal. iv. 8.

φυσίωσις, εως, ἡ, inflation of mind, boasting, 2 Cor. xii. 20.*

φυτεία, as, ἡ, a plant, Matt. xv. 13.*

φυτεύω, σω, to plant, to set, abs., or with acc.; fig., of introducing the Gospel, 1 Cor. iii. 6, 8.

φύω, σω, 2nd aor., pass., ἐφύην; part., φυείς; to produce; N. T. only intrans., to spring up, Heb. xii. 15; pass., to grow, Luke viii. 6, 8.*

φωλεός, οῦ, ὁ, a burrow, a hole, Matt. viii. 20.*

φωνέω, ῶ, ήσω, (1) to sound, to utter a sound or cry; espec. of cocks, to crow; (2) to call to, to invite (acc.); (3) to name, to denominate, acc. (nom. of title), John xiii. 13.

φωνή, ῆς, ἡ, (1) a sound, musical or otherwise, freq. in this sense in Rev.; (2) an articulate sound, a voice, a cry; (3) a language, dialect, 1 Cor. xiv. 10.

φῶς, φωτός, τό, contr. from φάος (φα-, to show, whence φαίνω, φημί), (1) lit., light; a source of light; plur., torches, Acts xvi. 29; ἐν τῷ φωτί, publicly, Matt. x. 27; (2) fig., light, as the symbol of truth, righteousness, purity, the element or medium of the Divine life; so applied to Christ as the source of this Divine life, John i. 4, 5; and to God as Himself the Light, 1 John i. 5. Syn. 65.

φωστήρ, ῆρος, ὁ, (1) a luminary, Phil. ii. 15; (2) brightness, splendour, Rev. xxi. 11. Syn. 65.*

φωσ-φόρος, ον, light-bearing, radiant; the name of the morning star, Phosphorus (Lat., Lucifer), the day-star, 2 Pet. i. 19.*

φωτεινός (W. H., -τινός), ή, όν, bright, luminous, full of light, lit., Matt. xvii. 5; fig., Matt. vi. 22; Luke xi. 34, 36.*

φωτίζω, ίσω, pass., perf., πεφώτισμαι; 1st aor., ἐφωτίσθην; (1) to enlighten, to shed light upon, lit. or fig. (acc., but ἐπί in Rev. xxii. 5); (2) to bring to light.

φωτισμός, οῦ, ὁ, light, lustre, illumination, 2 Cor. iv. 4, 6.*

X.

Χ, χ, χί, *chi, ch,* guttural, the twenty-second letter. As a numeral, χ' = 600; χ = 600,000.
χαίρω, χαρήσομαι, 2nd aor., ἐχάρην, *to rejoice, to be joyful, to be glad;* imp., χαῖρε, χαίρετε, *hail! farewell!* inf., χαίρειν, *greeting,* Acts xv. 23.
χάλαζα, ας, ἡ, *hail,* Rev.*
χαλάω, ῶ, άσω, 1st aor., pass., ἐχαλάσθην, *to let down, to lower,* Mark ii. 4; Luke v. 4, 5; Acts ix. 25, xxvii. 17, 30; 2 Cor. xi. 33.*
Χαλδαῖος, ου, ὁ, *a Chaldæan,* Acts vii. 4.*
χαλεπός, ή, όν,(1) *hard, difficult, grievous,* 2 Tim. iii. 1; (2) *harsh, fierce,* Matt. viii. 28.*
χαλιν-αγωγέω, ῶ, *to bridle, to curb,* James i. 26, iii. 2.*
χαλινός, οῦ, ὁ, *a bridle, a curb,* James iii. 3; Rev. xiv. 20.*
χάλκεος, οῦς, ῆ, οῦν, *made of brass or copper,* Rev. ix. 20.*
χαλκεύς, έως, ὁ, *a worker in brass or copper, a coppersmith,* 2 Tim. iv. 14.*
χαλκηδών, όνος, ὁ, *a gem,* including several varieties, *a chalcedony,* Rev. xxi. 19.*
χαλκίον, ου, τό, *a brazen vessel,* Mark vii. 4.*
χαλκο-λίβανον, ου, τό, meaning uncertain, perhaps *fine brass, burnished brass,* or *frankincense* (λίβανος) *of a gold colour,* Rev. i. 15, ii. 8.*
χαλκός, οῦ, ὁ, *copper, brass; money.*
χαμαί, adv. *on* or *to the ground,* John ix. 6, xviii. 6 *
Χαναάν, ἡ, *Canaan.*
Χαναναῖος, αία, αῖον, *Canaanitish,* Matt. xv. 22.*
χαρά, ᾶς, ἡ, *joy, gladness; a source of joy,* 1 Thess. ii. 19, 20.
χάραγμα, ατος, τό, *sculpture,* Acts xvii. 29; *engraving, a stamp, a sign,* Rev. **Syn. 56.***
χαρακτήρ, ῆρος, ὁ, *an impress, a perfect likeness,* Heb. i. 3. **Syn. 56.***
χάραξ, ακος, ὁ, *a palisade, a mound for besieging,* Luke xix. 43.*
χαρίζομαι, ίσομαι, dep., mid., pass. fut., χαρισθήσομαι, (1) *to give freely,* Luke vii. 21; 1 Cor. ii. 12; (2) *to show favour to* (dat.), Gal. iii. 18; (3) *to forgive* (dat., pers., acc. thing), 2 Cor. xii. 10; Eph. iv. 32; Col. ii. 13.
χάρις, ιτος, acc. χάριν and χάριτα (W. H., in Acts xxiv. 27; Jude 4), ἡ, (1) objectively, *agreeableness, acceptableness,* Luke iv. 22; (2) subjectively, *inclination towards, favour, kindness, liberality, thanks,* Luke i. 30, ii. 40, 52; Acts ii. 47, xxiv. 27; χάριν ἔχειν, *to thank;* χάριν ἔχειν πρός, *to be in favour with;* χάριν, adverbially used, with gen. (lit. *with inclination towards, for the sake of, on account of;* espec. of the *grace* of GOD or of CHRIST, *i.e.,* the spontaneous unrestrained kindness shown to men. **Syn 41.**
χάρισμα, ατος, τό, *a gift* from God to man, Rom. i. 11, v. 15, 16, vi. 23, xi. 29, xii. 6; 1 Cor. i. 7, vii. 7, xii. 4, 9, 28, 30, 31; 2 Cor. i. 11; 1 Tim. iv. 14; 2 Tim. i. 6; 1 Pet. iv. 10.*
χαριτόω, ῶ, *to favour, bestow freely on* (acc.), Eph. i. 6; pass., *to be favoured,* Luke i. 28.*
Χαρράν, ἡ (Heb.), *Charran* or *Haran,* Acts vii. 2, 4.*
χάρτης, ου, ὁ (Lat., charta), *paper,* 2 John 12.*
χάσμα, ατος, τό, *a gap, a gulf, "chasm,"* Luke xvi. 26.*
χεῖλος, ους, τό, *a lip;* plur., *language, dialect,* 1 Cor. xiv. 21; fig., *shore,* Heb. xi. 12.
χειμάζω, in pass., *to be storm-beaten,* or *tempest-tossed,* Acts xxvii. 18.*
χείμαρρος, ου, ὁ, *a storm-brook, a wintry torrent,* John xviii. 1.*
χειμών, ῶνος, ὁ, (1) *a storm, a tempest, foul weather,* Acts xxvii. 20; (2) *winter, the rainy season,* Matt. xxiv. 20.
χείρ, ός, ἡ, *a hand;* met., for any exertion of *power;* espec. in the phrases *the hand of God, the hand of the Lord* for help, Acts iv. 30, xi. 21; for punishment, Heb. x. 31.
χειρ-αγωγέω, ῶ, *to lead by the hand,* Acts ix. 8, xxii. 11.*
χειρ-αγωγός, οῦ, ὁ, *one who leads by the hand,* Acts xiii. 11.*
χειρό-γραφον, ου, τό (*hand-writing*), *a bond;* fig., of the Mosaic law, Col. ii. 14.*
χειρο-ποίητος, ον, *made with hands,* Mark xiv. 58; Acts vii. 48, xvii. 24; Eph. ii. 11; Heb. ix. 11, 24.*

χειρο-τονέω, ῶ (τείνω), to elect by stretching out the hand, to choose by vote, to appoint, Acts xiv. 23 ; 2 Cor. viii. 19.*
χείρων, ον, compar. of κακός (which see), worse, Matt. xii. 45 ; worse, severer, Heb. x. 29 ; εἰς τὸ χεῖρον, worse, Mark v. 26, ἐπὶ τὸ χεῖρον, worse and worse, 2 Tim. iii. 13.
χερουβίμ (W. H., Χερουβείν), Hebrew plural of cherub, the cherubim, the golden figures on the mercy-seat, Heb. ix. 5.*
χήρα, as, ἡ, a widow.
χθές (W. H. ἐχθές), adv., yesterday.
χιλί-αρχος, ου, ὁ, a commander of a thousand men, a military tribune, Acts xxi.-xxv.
χιλιάς, άδος, ἡ, a thousand (subst.).
χίλιοι, αι, α, a thousand (adj.).
Χίος, ου, ἡ, Chios, Acts xx. 15.*
χιτών, ῶνος, ὁ, a vest, an inner garment. Syn. 66.
χιών, όνος, ἡ, snow, Matt. xxviii. 3 ; Mark ix. 3 (W. H. omit); Rev. i. 14.*
χλαμύς, ύδος, ἡ, a cloak worn by Roman officers and magistrates, most frequently scarlet, Matt. xxvii. 28, 31.*
χλευάζω, to mock, scoff (abs.), Acts ii. 13 (W. H., διαχλευάζω), xvii. 32.*
χλιαρός, ά, όν, warm, lukewarm, Rev. iii. 16.*
Χλόη, ης, Chloe, 1 Cor. i. 11.*
χλωρός, ά, όν, (1) green, verdant; Mark vi. 39 ; Rev. viii. 7, ix. 4 ; (2) pale, Rev. vi. 8.*
χξϛ', six hundred and sixty-six, Rev. xiii. 18 (W. H. write in full).*
χοϊκός, ή, όν, earthy, made of earth, 1 Cor. xv. 47-49.*
χοῖνιξ, ικος, ἡ, a chœnix, measure containing two sextarii (see ξέστης), Rev. vi. 6.*
χοῖρος, ου, ὁ, a pig ; plur., swine.
χολάω, ῶ, to be angry, to be incensed at (dat.), John vii. 23.*
χολή, ῆς, (1) gall, fig., Acts viii. 23 ; (2) bitter herbs, such as wormwood, Matt. xxvii. 34.*
χόος, see χοῦς.
Χοραζίν (W. H., Χοραζείν), ἡ, Chorazin, Matt. xi. 21 ; Luke x. 13.*
χορ-ηγέω, ῶ (ἄγω) (properly, to supply or furnish a chorus for the Gk. games), hence, to furnish, to supply, to give, 2 Cor. ix. 10 ; 1 Pet. iv. 11.*

χορός, οῦ, ὁ, a dance with singing, "chorus," plur., Luke xv. 25.*
χορτάζω, to feed, to satisfy with (gen. or ἀπό).
χόρτασμα, ατος, τό, food, sustenance, Acts vii. 11.*
χόρτος, ου, ὁ, grass, herbage, Matt. vi. 30 ; springing grain, Matt. xiii. 26.
Χουζᾶς, ᾶ, ὁ, Chuza, Luke viii. 3.*
χοῦς, οός, ὁ, acc. χοῦν, dust, Mark vi. 11 ; Rev. xviii. 19.*
χράομαι, ῶμαι, χρῆσθαι, dep. (prop. mid. of χράω), to use (dat.), to make use of, to treat, Acts xxvii. 3 ; 2 Cor. xiii. 10 (dat. om.).
χράω, or κίχρημι, χρήσω, to lend, Luke xi. 5.*
χρεία, ας, ἡ, (1) use, necessity, need, plur., necessities ; ἔχω χρείαν, to need ; (2) business, Acts vi. 3.
χρε-ωφειλέτης (W. H., χρε-οφιλέτης), ου, ὁ, a debtor, Luke vii. 41, xvi. 5.*
χρή, impers., it needs, it behoves (acc. and inf.), James iii. 10. Syn. 12.*
χρῄζω, to have need of, to need (gen.).
χρῆμα, ατος, τό, "a thing of use," money, sing., only Acts iv. 37 ; plur., riches, wealth.
χρηματίζω, ίσω, to transact business ; hence, (1) to utter an oracle, to give a Divine warning, Heb. xii. 25 ; pass., to receive a Divine response, be warned of God, Matt. ii. 12, 22 ; Luke ii. 26 ; Acts x. 22 ; Heb. viii. 5, xi. 7 ; (2) to bear or take a name, to be called, Acts xi. 26 ; Rom. vii. 3.*
χρηματισμός, οῦ, ὁ, an oracle, Rom. xi. 4.*
χρήσιμος, η, ον, useful, profitable, 2 Tim. ii. 14.*
χρῆσις, εως, ἡ, use, manner of using, Rom. i. 26, 27.*
χρηστεύομαι, dep., to be kind, 1 Cor. xiii. 4.*
χρηστο-λογία, ας, ἡ, a kind address ; in a bad sense, fair speaking, Rom. xvi. 18.*
χρηστός, ή, όν, useful, good, gentle, kind ; τὸ χρηστόν, goodness, kindness. Syn. 21.
χρηστότης, τητος, ἡ, (1) goodness, generally, Rom. iii. 12 ; (2) specially, benignity, gentleness.
χρίσμα, ατος τό, an anointing, an unction, 1 John ii. 20, 27.*

Χριστιανός, οῦ, ὁ, *a Christian*, Acts xi. 26, xxvi. 28 : 1 Pet. iv. 16.*
Χριστός, οῦ, ὁ (prop. verbal. adj. from χρίω), *the Anointed, the Messiah*, THE CHRIST (see § 217, *e*).
χρίω, σω, *to anoint, to consecrate by anointing*, as Jesus, the Christ, Luke iv. 18 ; Acts iv. 27, x. 38 ; Heb. i. 9 ; applied also to Christians, 2 Cor. i. 21. Syn. 18.*
χρονίζω, *to delay, to defer, to tarry*, Matt. xxiv. 48, xxv. 5 ; Luke i. 21, xii. 45 ; Heb. x. 37.*
χρόνος, ου, (1) *time*, generally; (2) *a particular time*, or *season*, Matt. ii. 7 ; Acts i. 7. Syn. 64.
χρονο-τριβέω, ῶ, *to spend time, to wear away time*, Acts xx. 16.*
χρύσεος, οῦς, ῆ, οῦν, *golden*.
χρυσίον, ου, τό (dim. of χρυσός), *a piece of gold, gold, a golden ornament*.
χρυσο-δακτύλιος, ον, *gold-ringed on the fingers*, James ii. 2.*
χρυσό-λιθος, ου, ὁ, *a golden stone*, a gem of a bright yellow colour, "a chrysolite," or topaz, Rev. xxi. 20.*
χρυσό-πρασος, ου, ὁ, *a gem*, of a greenish, golden colour, "a chrysoprase," Rev. xxi. 20.*
χρυσός, οῦ, ὁ, *gold, anything made of gold, gold coin*, or *money*.
χρυσόω, ῶ, *to deck with gold, to gild,* Rev. xvii. 4, xviii. 16.*
χρώς, χρωτός, ὁ, *the skin* · met., *the body*, Acts xix. 12.*
χωλός, ή, όν, *lame, crippled in the feet*.
χώρα, ας, ἡ, (1) *a country*, or *region ;* (2) *the land*, opposed to the sea ; (3) *the country*, dist. from town ; (4) - plur., *fields*, John iv. 35.
χωρέω, ῶ, lit., *to make room ;* hence, (1) *to make room for, receive, contain*, Matt. xix. 11, 12; John ii. 6, xxi. 25 ; 2 Cor. vii. 2 ; impers., *to be room for*, Mark ii. 2 ; (2) *to make room by departing, to go*, Matt. xv. 17, *to have free course*, John viii. 37 (see R. V. and marg.) ; *to come*, 2 Pet. iii. 9.*
χωρίζω, ίσω, *to put apart, to separate*, Matt. xix. 6 ; mid. (1st aor. pass.), *to separate oneself, to depart, to go away* (ἀπό or ἐκ), Acts i. 4, xviii. 1.
χωρίον, ου, τό, *a place, a field, a farm, a possession ;* plur., *possessions*, Acts iv. 34.

χωρίς, adv., *separately, by itself*, only John xx. 7 ; as prep. gov. gen., *apart from, without*, John xv. 5 ; Rom. iii. 21 ; *besides, exclusive of*, Matt. xiv. 21.
Χῶρος, ου, ὁ (Latin, "Caurus"), *the N. W. wind ;* met., *of that quarter of the heavens*, Acts xxvii. 12.*

Ψ.

Ψ, ψ, ψῖ, *psi, ps*, the twenty-third letter. As a numeral, $\psi = 700$; $\psi = 700{,}000$.
ψάλλω, ψαλῶ, *to sing, to chant*, accompanied with instruments, *to sing psalms*, Rom. xv. 9 ; 1 Cor. xiv. 15 ; Eph. v. 19 ; James v. 13.*
ψαλμός, οῦ, *a psalm, a song of praise ;* plur., *the book of Psalms in the Old Testament, the Hagiographa*, or division of the Scriptures in which this book stands first, Luke xxiv. 44. Syn. 48.
ψευδ-άδελφος, ου, ὁ, *a false brother, a pretended Christian*, 2 Cor. xi. 26 ; Gal. ii. 4.*
ψευδ-απόστολος, ου, ὁ, *a false* or *pretended apostle*, 2 Cor. xi. 13.*
ψευδής, ές, *false, deceiving, lying*, Acts vi. 13 ; Rev. ii. 2, xxi. 8.*
ψευδο-διδάσκαλος, ου, *a false teacher, a teacher of false doctrines*, 2 Pet. ii. 1.*
ψευδο-λόγος, ον, *false-speaking*, 1 Tim. iv. 2.*
ψεύδομαι, dep., σομαι, 1st aor., ἐψευσάμην, *to deceive, to lie, to speak falsely, to lie to* (acc.), Acts v. 3.
ψευδο-μάρτυρ, or -υς, υρος, ὁ, *a false witness*, Matt. xxvi. 60 ; 1 Cor. xv. 15.*
ψευδο-μαρτυρέω, ῶ, *to bear false witness*.
ψευδο-μαρτυρία, ας, ἡ, *false testimony*, Matt. xv. 19, xxvi. 59.*
ψευδο-προφήτης, ου, ὁ, *a false prophet*, one who in God's name teaches what is false.
ψεῦδος, ους, τό, *falsehood, lying, a lie*.
ψευδό-χριστος, ου, ὁ, *a false Christ, a pretended Messiah*, Matt. xxiv. 24.
ψεύδω. See ψεύδομαι.
ψευδ-ώνυμος, ου, *falsely named, falsely called*, 1 Tim. vi. 20.*
ψεῦσμα, ατος, τό, *falsehood, perfidy*, Rom. iii. 7.*
ψεύστης, ου, ὁ, *a deceiver, liar*.
ψηλαφάω, ῶ, *touch, to feel, to handle*

(acc.), Luke xxiv. 39; Heb. xii. 18; 1 John i. 1; *to feel after,* as persons blind, or in the dark, fig., Acts xvii. 27. **Syn. 7.***

ψηφίζω, ίσω, *to reckon, to compute,* Luke xiv. 28; Rev. xiii. 18.*

ψῆφος, ου, ἡ, *a small stone, a pebble,* used as a counter, and for voting; hence, *a vote,* Acts xxvi. 10; *a token,* Rev. ii. 17.*

ψιθυρισμός, οῦ, ὁ, *a whispering, a detraction,* 2 Cor. xii. 20.*

ψιθυριστής, οῦ, ὁ, *a whisperer, a slanderer, a detractor,* Rom. i. 30.*

ψιχίον, ου, τό, *a crumb,* Matt. xv. 27; Mark vii. 28; Luke xvi. 21 (W. H. omit).*

ψυχή, ῆς, ἡ, (1) *the vital breath, the animal life,* of animals, Rev. viii. 9, xvi. 3; elsewhere only of man; (2) *the human soul,* as distinguished from the body; (3) *the soul* as the seat of the affections, the will, etc.; (4) *the self* (like Heb.), Matt. x. 39; (5) *a human person, an individual.* **Synn. 54, 55.**

ψυχικός, ή, όν, *animal, natural, sensual,* 1 Cor. ii. 14, xv. 44, 46; James iii. 15; Jude 19.*

ψῦχος, ους, τό, *cold.*

ψυχρός, ά, όν, *cold, cool,* Matt. x. 42, (sc., ὕδατος); fig., *cold-hearted,* Rev. iii. 15, 16.*

ψύχω, 2nd fut. pass., ψυγήσομαι, *to cool;* pass., fig., *to be cooled, to grow cold,* Matt. xxiv. 12.*

ψωμίζω, *to feed,* Rom. xii. 20; *to spend in feeding,* 1 Cor. xiii. 3.*

ψωμίον, ίου, *a bit, a morsel,* John xiii. 26-30.*

ψώχω, *to rub, to break in pieces,* as ears of corn, Luke vi. 1.*

Ω.

Ω, ω, ὦ μέγα, *ōmega, ō,* the twenty-fourth letter. As a numeral, ω′ = 800; ͵ω = 800,000. τὸ Ὦ, a name of the Eternal (cf. under Ἀ), Rev. i. 8, 11 (W. H. omit), xxi. 6, xxii. 13.

ὦ, interj., used before the vocative where the appeal is emphatic: sometimes in simple address, and once in admiration, Rom. xi. 33.

Ὠβήδ, ὁ, *Obed,* Matt. i. 5; Luke iii. 32.*

ὧδε, adv., of place, *hither, here.* So *in this life,* Heb. xiii. 14; *herein, in this matter,* Rev. xiii. 10; ὧδε ἢ ὧδε, *here or there,* Matt. xxiv. 23.

ᾠδή, ῆς, ἡ, *an ode, a song, a hymn.* **Syn. 48.**

ὠδίν, ῖνος, ἡ, *the pain of childbirth, acute pain, severe calamity,* Matt. xxiv. 8; Mark xiii. 8; Acts ii. 24; 1 Thess. v. 3.*

ὠδίνω, ινῶ, *to be in the throes,* or *pains of childbirth,* Rev. xii. 2; fig., Gal. iv. 19, 27.*

ὦμος, ου, ὁ, *a shoulder,* Matt. xxiii. 4; Luke xv. 5.

ὠνέομαι, οῦμαι, ἥσομαι, *to buy* (gen. of price), Acts vii. 16.

ὠόν (W. H., ᾠόν), οῦ, τό, *an egg,* Luke xii. 12.*

ὥρα, ας, ἡ, (1) *a definite space of time, a season;* (2) *an hour;* (3) *the particular time for anything,* Luke xiv. 17; Matt. xxvi. 45.

ὡραῖος, αία, αῖον, *fair, comely, beautiful,* Matt. xxiii. 27; Acts iii. 2, 10; Rom. x. 15.*

ὠρύομαι, dep., mid., *to roar, to howl,* as a beast, 1 Pet. v. 8.*

ὡς, an adv. of comparison, *as, like as, about, as it were, according as,* 2 Pet. i. 3; *to wit,* 2 Cor. v. 19; *how,* Luke viii. 47; *how!* Rom. x. 15; as particle of time, *when, whilst, as soon as;* as consecutive particle, *so that* (inf.), Acts xx. 24; ὡς ἔπος εἰπεῖν, *so to speak,* Heb. vii. 9.

Ὡσαννά, interj., *Hosanna!* (Heb., Ps. cxviii. 25) *Save now!* a word of joyful acclamation, Matt. xxi. 9, 13; Mark xi. 9, 10; John xii. 13.*

ὡσ-αύτως, adv., *in the same way, in like manner as, likewise.*

ὡσ-εί, adv., *as if, as though like, as,* with numerals, *about.*

Ὡσηέ, ὁ, *Hosea,* Rom. ix. 25.*

ὥσ-περ, adv., *just as, as,* Matt. xii. 40; 1 Cor. viii. 5.

ὡσ-περ-εί, adv., *just as if, as it were,* 1 Cor. xv. 8.*

ὥσ-τε, conj., *so that* (inf., see § 391), *therefore.*

ὠτάριον, ίου, τό (dim. of οὖς; cf. παιδάριον), an ear, Mark xiv. 47 (W. H.); John xviii. 10 (W. H.).*

ὠτίον, ίου, τό (dim. of οὖς, an ear), an ear, Matt. xxvi. 51; Luke xxii. 51; John xviii. 26; see also the passages under ὠτάριον (rec.).*

ὠφέλεια, as, ἡ, profit, advantage, gain, Rom. iii. 1; Jude 16.*

ὠφελέω, ῶ, ήσω, to profit, to benefit, to help (acc., also acc. of definition); pass., to be profited, to have advantage, Matt. xvi. 26.

ὠφέλιμος, ον, profitable, beneficial, dat. of pers., Tit. iii. 8; πρός (acc.), of obj., 1 Tim. iv. 8; 2 Tim. iii. 16.*

ALPHABETICAL INDEX.

[The references are to the *Pages*, not to the Sections.
For convenience, each letter in Greek is placed under the corresponding one in English.
K and X are under C; Φ, Ψ, with Π, under P; and Θ, with T, under T.]

ABLATION, by the genitive . . 210
Abstract nouns, in connection with the article, 183; in the plural number, 202; in the genitive, to express quality 213
Accents, the, 7. Accentuation of the several classes of words, and of the forms of declension and conjugation, *under the proper sections.*
Accessory clauses 172
Accessory circumstance, by dative, 226; by participle 332
Accusative, like nominative in neuter nouns, 16; its general senses, 229; case of the object, 15, 229; subject of the infinitive verb, 232, 325; double accusative (nearer and remoter object), 231; accusative, with passive verbs, 295; cognate accusative, 230; accusative of definition, 231; adverbial, 135; in elliptical constructions, 233; accusative of the infinitive verb, 327. *For other uses of the case, see* 229, *sq., and under Prepositions.*
"Accusative middle" . . . 292
Active voice, the, 55, 291; not always distinguishable in sense from the middle 293
Adjectives, in three forms, 34; of two terminations, 35; comparison of, 40; classes of, 146; agreement of, with substantive, 267; usually placed after substantives, 350; with omitted substantive, 267; with several substantives, 269; adjective, with article, 176, 268; of plenty, etc., with genitive, 210; of worthiness, etc., with genitive, 220; adjective, with genitive

of relation, 220; with infinitive, 326; adverbially used, 269; comparative, with genitive 211
Adverbs, the cases of nouns as, 135; derivative, 136; negative, 139, 338; in composition, 151; preceded by article, 175; of time, with genitive, 217; used as prepositions, 138, 338; adverbs after ἔχω, 292; adverbial phrases and combinations, 241, 249, 269, 337
Adversative conjunction, δέ . . 344
Affirmative answers . . . 308
Agent, after passive verbs, 295; by ὑπό, 253; apparently expressed by dative. 227
Alexander's conquests, their effect on language 155
Alexandrian, or compound aorist . 97
Alexandrian version of Old Testament 156
Alford, Dean, 191, 209, 219, 272, 273, 297, 305, 311, 338, 344, 347
Alliteration 354
Alphabet, the Greek, 1; meaning of the word 2
Also, even, by καί 341
Alternative expressions, 290; questions 288
Angus's "Handbook of the English Language," 55, 218; "Bible Handbook". 204
Anacolouthon. . . . 336, 352
Annexation, conjunctions of . . 340
Antecedent, attraction of the, 285; omission of the . . . 317
Antithesis, conjunctions of, 342; omitted 348

ALPHABETICAL INDEX.

Aorist, the first and second generally identical in meaning, 81; first, act. and mid., 96; first and second, pass., 98; second, 81, 94; aorists of deponent verbs, 100; force of the aorist, 303; distinguished from imperfect, 299; distinguished from perfect, 304; aorist imperative, 310; subjunctive (and optative), 303, 311, 312; as future perfect, 318; infinitive, 324; participle, 334; indicative, with ἄν, in conditional sentences. . 318
Apiece, how expressed in Greek . 242
Apocalypse, grammatical anomalies in, 156, 352
Apodosis 317
Aposiopēsis 351
Apostrophe, the 3
Apposition, 170; by genitive . . 214
Appropriative middle . . . 293
Aramaic dialect, 155; words in the New Testament 156
Aratus (or Cleanthes), quoted by St. Paul 355
Arrangement of words . . . 350
Article, the, 15; declined, 16; syntax of the, 174, sq.; originally a demonstrative pronoun, 174; always significant, 178; often neglected in E.V., 181; with the Divine names, 186; position of article, 195; repetition of the, 196; article in enumerations, 198; omission of the, 199; article with infinitive, 326; with participles 334
Aspirate, the 3
Association, by dative . . . 223
Asyndeton 348
Attic Greek contrasted with that of the New Testament . . . 156
Attic augment . . . 94, 97
Attic future 95
Attraction, of the relative to the predicate, 284; to the antecedent, 284; of the antecedent to the relative 285
Attributive use of participles, 330, 334
Augment, 58; Attic or double, 94, 97; irregularities in 98
Augustus, in Latin and Greek . . 163
Author or source, by genitive . . 208

A- declension, the (first) . . . 19
ἀ-, intensive in composition . . 151
ἀ-, negative in composition . . 151

ἁ-, *together* in composition . . 151
ἀγαθός, comparison of . . . 42
ἀγάπη, with genitive in different relations 219
ἀγγέλλω, conjugated . . . 87
ἄγε, ἄγωμεν, intransitive . . . 292
ἄγνυμι, augment of 97
ἄγω, conjugated . . . 78, 94
ἀδελφός, ellipsis of 213
ᾅδης (ᾅδου, with εἰς) 213
ἄδικος, with infinitive . . . 326
-ἄζω, verbs in 148
αἰδώς, declined 27
αἷμα, plural 19
-αίνω, verbs in 148
αἱρέω, defective 102
αἴρω, conjugated 87
αἰσχρός, comparison of . . . 41
αἰών, declined 25
αἰῶνες, plural use of . . . 203
ἀκούω, future of, 96; perfect, 99; with genitive 208
ἀληθής, ές, declined 39
ἀλλά 342
ἄλλος and ἕτερος, 54; with article . 194
ἁμαρτάνω 93
ἄν, potential with optative, 314; with relatives or conjunctions, requires subjunctive, 314; in conditional sentences, with indicative . . 319
ἀνά 242
ἀνατέλλω, transitive use of . . 291
ἀνήρ, declined 27
ἄνθρωπος, declined 18
ἀνθ' ὧν 236, 347
ἀνοίγω, augment of 98
ἀντί, 236; with infinitive . . 328
ἄξιος, with genitive, 220; with infinitive 327
ἀπό, 237; and διά, 262; and ἐκ, 262; adverbial phrases with . . 337
ἀποδίδωμι, active and middle . . 294
'Απολλώς, declined 24
ἄρα and ἆρα, and οὖν . . . 346
ἄραγε 346
Ἄραψ, declined 26
ἀρκέω, future of 95
ἄρνας 32
ἀρτι-, in composition . . . 151
ἀρχήν, adverbial 337
αὐξάνω, transitive use of . . 291
αὐτός, ή, ό, declined, 49; used for third personal pronoun, 277; emphatic nominative, 166; meaning *self*, 278; with article, *the same*, 192; comple-

ALPHABETICAL INDEX 533

mentary to the relative, 286; αὐτὸς
τρίτος 276
αὐτοῦ and αὑτοῦ 50
ἀφίημι, conjugated 118
ἀφικνέομαι 93
ἀφορίζω, future of 96
-άω, verbs in 148

B.

Benefit or injury, by dative . . 225
Bengel, Dr. J. A. 209
Both ... and, how expressed . . 340
Breathings, the 2
Burgon, Rev. J. W., "Inspiration and Interpretation " 204

βαίνω 93, 94
βάλλω, transposition of stem-letters in, 98
βαπτισμῶν διδαχῆς 215
βαπτίζω, future of 96
βασιλεύς, declined 28
βασιλεύω, transitive in the Old Testament 291
βουλεύω, why not chosen as a paradigm 61
βούλομαι, augment of . . . 97
βοῦς, declined 29
βρέχει (called impersonal), true subject of 167

C.

"Canaanite," surname of Simon . 161
Cardinal numbers, the . . . 44
Cases of nouns, 15, 234; as used with prepositions, 131, 234; cases of the infinitive, 326; case-endings, old, with adverbial force 135
Causal conjunctions, 347; omitted . 351
Causal use of participles . . . 333
Causal middle 293
Causative verbs 148
Cause or motive by dative . . 226
Chiasmus 355
Cities, plural names of . . . 186
Cleanthes (or Aratus), quoted by St. Paul 355
Climax, the rising 342
Coins, Latin names of . . . 158
Coins, measures, etc., with numerals 276
Collective nouns, with plural adjective, 170; with plural verb . . 168
Combination of consonants . . 5

Commands by future tense . . 301
Common gender 7
Comparative in -ων, paradigm, 41; comparative with genitive, 211, 270; elliptical, 271; emphatic comparative, 42, 272; comparative notion, by prepositions 271
Comparison of adjectives. . . 40
Comparisons, καί in . . . 342
Complements of the simple sentence 171
Completeness, marked by aorist . 305
Compound imperfect, 301; future, 302; perfect and pluperfect . . . 330
Compound relative 53
Compound sentences . . 172, 173
Compound words 150
Concessive use of participles . . 333
Concord, the first, 167; the second, 170, 267; the third . . . 283
Concord, rational. See Synesis.
Conditional sentences . . 317, 343
Conditional use of participles . . 333
Conjugations of verbs, the, 58; the second conjugation . . . 104
Conjunctions, or pronominal adverbs, 137; the conjunctions classified, 140; with ἄν followed by subjunctive, 314; syntax of the 340
Consonants, division of, 4; changes in, 5, 6; changes in mute verbs . 73
Constructio ad sensum. See Synesis.
Constructio prægnans, 241, 245, 255, 256, 257, 264
Constructions, unusual, for emphasis, 351
Contracted substantives, 23; adjectives, 35; pure verbs . . . 71, sq.
Contraction of vowels . . . 3
Contrast, emphatic, by negative . 339
Copula, the, 164; omission of . 165
Copulative verbs 171
Coronis, the 4, 51
Correlative pronouns, 54; adverbs . 137
Crasis 4
Creeds, rhythmical, in the early church 354
Customary actions by imperfect tense. 298

-κ-, in the first aorist . . . 114
κ.τ.λ. 10
καθαρίζω, future 96
κάθημαι 115
καθ' ὑπερβολὴν εἰς ὑπερβολήν . . 264
καί, 340; with τε, 340; with δέ, 344; καὶ γάρ, 348; καί omitted . . 348

Καῖσαρ, Cæsar, to whom applied in the New Testament 163
καίω, stem and future . . . 96
κακός, comparison of 42
καλέω, future of, 95 ; transposition of stem-letters 98
καλός, comparison of . . . 41
κάμνω, stem and second aorist. . 93
κατά, 248, sq.; sometimes supposed with accusative of definition, 231 ; adverbial combinations with . . . 337
κατηγορέω, with genitive . . . 210
κατώτερα 42, 214
κεῖμαι 115
κεράννυμι 125
κέρας, κρέας, stems and declension of 32
κερδαίνω, future and first aorist of . 97
κῆρυξ, declined 26
κλαίω, stem and future . . . 96
κλάω, future 95
κομίζω, future 96
κορέννυμι 125
κρέμαμαι 115
κρίνω, conjugated, 87 ; its root, derivatives, and compounds . . 153
κρίνομαι, middle force of . . . 294
Κύριος, with the article . . . 187
κύων, irregular 32

χαίρειν, as imperative . . . 329
χαλάω, future 95
χείρ, omitted with adjective . . 267
χέω, stem, future, and aorist . . 96
χράομαι, future of, 95 ; governs dative, 227
χρή 101
Χριστός, with article . . . 188
χρυσοῦς (εος), ῆ, οῦν, declined . . 35

D.

Dative case, the (singular always in -ι), 16 ; its general senses, 15, 222 ; obsolete forms of, as adverbs, 135 ; dative of association, 223 ; of transmission, 223 ; of reference, 225 ; of accessory, 226 ; of time, 228 ; may be interchanged with ἐν (dat.), 263 ; with εἰς (acc.), 264 ; usually placed after governing word 350
"Dative middle" 293
Dativus commodi vel incommodi . 225
Death of Christ, prepositions respecting, 252, 265

Declensions, of substantives, the three, 15 ; similarity of the first and second, 19 ; nouns of variable . . . 32
Defective verbs 101
Deliberative subjunctive . . . 312
Demonstrative pronouns, 51, 281 ; with the article, 191 ; as equivalent to a clause 282
Dependent clauses 314
Deponent verbs . . 75, note, 100
Design, expressed by genitive of infinitive, 327 ; by infinitive with εἰς, πρός, 328. See Intentional.
Derivation 149
De Wette, Dr. 231
Diæresis 4
Difficulties of interpretation, 173, 218
Digamma, the, 44 ; in substantives, 31 ; in verbs, 96. See under V.
Diminutives 17
Diphthongs, 2 ; regularly long, but often counted short for accentuation, 20, 22, 97
Disjunctives, the 345
Distributive numerals, 47 ; pronouns, 54
Divine names, with the article . 186
Donaldson, Dr. . 207, 222, 229, 232
Double names of persons . . 161
Dress, Latin names of, in the New Testament 159
Dual number, the 15

δάκνω, stem 93
δανείζω, active and middle . . 294
δέ, conjunction of antithesis . . 344
δεῖ, impersonal 101
δείκνυμι, conjugated . . . 121
δευτερόπρωτος 153
δηλόω, conjugated 72
διά, 245 ; and ἐκ, 261 ; and ἀπό, 261; and εἰς, 262 ; and ἐν, 262 ; and περί, 265 ; with genitive and accusative distinguished 247
διδάσκω, future 93
δίδωμι, conjugated 106
δίκαιος, αία, αιον, declined . . 34
Διοπετής 268
Διός, Δία 32
διότι, relative causal particle . . 347
δοκεῖ, impersonal 101
δοκέω, future of 93
δόξα, declined 19
δύναμαι 115
δυνατός, with infinitive . . . 326
δύνω, stem and second aorist . . 94

ALPHABETICAL INDEX. 535

δύο, declined 45
δυσ-, in composition . . . 152
δωδεκάφυλον 153
δῶμα (or οἶκος, οἰκία), ellipsis of . 213

E.

Ecbatic and final particles . 321, 328
Elision of vowels 4
Ellicott, Bishop, 193, 198, 211, 220, 230, 234, 278, 298, 304, 321, 329, 339, 348
Ellipsis, with nominative, 206; with accusative, 233; of words of kindred before genitive, 212; of substantives, with adjective, 267; of measures and coins, with numerals, 276; of the antecedent, with relative, 285; with the subjunctive, 311; with the optative, 313; before ἵνα . . . 312
Elliptical questions, 308; constructions 351
Emphasis, by particles, 141; by insertion of pronominal subject, 166; by the article, 180; by the order of words, 350; by repetition or pleonasm 352
Emphatic comparison of adjectives, 42; verbs, 148; indefinite pronoun, 289; negatives, 302, 312; future . 303
Enclitics 8
English rendering of Greek letters . 9
Enumerations, with article, 198; by καί ... τε 340
Epanodos 355
Epexegetic, καί, 341; omitted . 341
Epicœne gender 17
Epimenides, quoted by St. Paul . 355
Epistolary aorist, the . . . 304
Ethical future, the 302
Even, also, by καί 341
Exhortations, substituted for statements by New Testament transcribers 311

ἐάν, for ἄν, 314; for εἰ ἄν . . 318
ἑαυτοῦ, -ῆς, declined . . . 50
ἐάω, future of 95
ἐγένετο 325
ἔγραψα, epistolary aorist . . 304
ἐγώ, ἡμεῖς, declined . . . 49
εἰ, in conditional sentences, 317; interrogative use of . . . 308
-εια and -εία, terminations of nouns, 144

εἰμί, conjugated, 116; as copula, 165; as predicate, 165; with genitive, 217; with dative 223
εἶμι, *to go* 117
εἶπον 102
εἰς, 242; compared with ἐν and διά, 262, 263; with πρός, 265; with ἐπί, 264; with simple dative, 264; with infinitive, 328; adverbial combinations 337
εἷς, μία, ἕν, declined, 44; as indefinite pronoun, 275; for πρῶτος . . 275
ἐκ, ἐξ, 237; compared with διά, 261; with ἀπό, 262; adverbial combinations 337
εἴτε ... εἴτε 345
ἕκαστος, anarthrous . . . 192
ἐκεῖνος, with article, 191; refers to remoter antecedent, 281; may refer to the nearer, 282; the emphatic demonstrative 282
ἑκών, ἑκοῦσα, ἑκόν, declined . . 37
ἐλαύνω, stem and future . . . 93
ἐλαχιστότερος, double comparative . 43
ἔλεος, of variable declension . . 32
ἐλεύθερος, with dative, 226; with infinitive 326
ἐλπίζω, future of 96
ἐμαυτοῦ, -ῆς, declined . . . 50
ἐν, 239; compared with εἰς, διά, 262, 264; interchanged with dative, 263; adverbial combinations, 337; with infinitive 328
ἕννυμι 125
ἔξεστι, impersonal 101
-εος, -ους, adjectives in . . . 147
ἐπαινέω, future of 95
ἐπεί, temporal or causal . . 347
ἐπειδή 347
ἐπειδήπερ 347
ἐπείπερ 347
ἐπί, 254; compared with εἰς, 264; in adverbial combinations . . 337
ἐπίσταμαι 115
ἔρχομαι, 102; and ἥκω . . 298
ἐσθίω 102
ἑστώς, ὧσα, ὥς, participle for ἑστηκώς, declined 38
ἕτερος and ἄλλος . . 54, 194
ἕτοιμος, with infinitive . . 326
εὐ-, as prefix, 151; how augmented 97
εὑρίσκω, stem 93
-ευς, substantives in . . . 145
-εύω, verbs in 148
ἐφ᾽ ᾧ 347

ἔχω, alternative stem, 93 ; construction of, with adverbs 292
-έω, verbs in 159
ἕως, in combination with other adverbs, 338 ; with infinitive . . . 328

ἤ, particle of comparison, 270; interchanged with καὶ οὐ, 339 ; disjunctive, 345 ; interrogative . . 346
ἥκω and ἔρχομαι 298
ἧμαι 115
ἡμέρα, declined, 20 ; ellipsis of . 267
ἡμι-, in composition . . . 151
-ης, -ές, adjectives in . . 147, 148

F.

Festivals, names of, in plural . . 203
Final, or intentional clauses . . 320
First declension, paradigms . . 19
Forbes, Rev. Dr., on the Romans . 354
Foreign elements in New Testament Greek 155
Forgetting, verbs of, with genitive . 210
Frequentative verbs . . . 148
Fulness, want, etc., by genitive. 210 ; by dative or εἰς 227
Future time, tenses expressing . 57
Future tense, its characteristic, 60 ; in liquid verbs, 86; in pure verbs, 95 ; Attic future, 95 ; second future, 84 ; future imperfect, 302 ; future perfect (paulo-post future), 79, 100 ; *see also* 318 ; force of the future, 301, *sq.*; with οὐ μή, 302 ; indicative, with ἵνα, 323 ; infinitive, 324 ; participle, 333 ; future auxiliary verbs . . . 302
Futurity, certain, by present . . 298

G.

Galilee, or Tiberias, the lake of . 221
Gender of nouns, 15 ; rules for determining, 17 ; variable in some substantives 32
General for particular statements . 204
Genitive case, the (plural always in -ων), 16 ; exhibits the stem in the third declension, 25 ; adverbially used, 135 ; of personal pronouns for possessive, 277 ; genitive after the article, 175 ; different uses of the, 207, *sq.* ; usual position of the, 215,

350 ; genitives in different relations with the same noun, 221 ; genitive absolute, the, 222, 330 ; prepositions governing the genitive, 236 ; genitive after διά, compared with accusative, 247 ; objective genitive, by possessive pronoun, 277 ; genitive in apposition with possessive pronoun, 280 ; genitive of infinitive, 326 ; expressing design or result . . 327
Goodwin, Dr., "Greek Grammar," 133, 143
Gospel, with genitive in different senses 219
Greek in Palestine 155
Greek names in the New Testament 162
Greek poetry, quoted by St. Paul . 355
Green, Rev. T. S. . . 205, 305, 321
Grotius on fulfilment of prophecy . 322

γάρ . . . . . 347, *sq.*
γέγραπται 305
γελάω, future of 95
γένος, declined 29
γεύομαι, with genitive or accusative 209
γῆ, ellipsis of 267
γίνομαι, stem and forms . . 94, 101
γινώσκω, stem and forms . . . 94
γόνυ, irregular substantive . . 32
γρηγορέω 149
γυνή, irregular substantive, 32 ; ellipsis of 213, 267

H.

Hackett, Dr., on the Acts . . 218
Hamilton, Sir W., "Logic" . . 179
Hebraisms, so-called, often to be rejected 275
Hebraistic use of plural of *blood*, 203 ; superlative, 274 ; use of εἰς, 276 ; of relative and αὐτός, 286 ; causal sense in intransitive verbs, 291 ; use of participles, 333 ; combination of verbs 338
Hebrew, as spoken in Palestine, 155 ; words, 33 ; names in the New Testament, 160 ; poetry, parallelism . 354
Hendiadys (ἓν διὰ δυοῖν, *one idea in two words*), unnecessary, 214 (§ 258) . 338
Hiatus 4
Hinton, Rev. J. H., on the Romans 354
Historic present, the . . . 297
Historical and principal tenses, 57, 297

ALPHABETICAL INDEX. 537

Hort. *See* Westcott.
Hymns in the New Testament . 354
Hyperbaton 351
Hypothesis, fourfold form of . . 317

I.

Imparisyllabic declension, the . 19
Imperative mood, the, 55, 309; tenses in, 309; subjunctive used for, 311; infinitive, 329; future indicative in prohibitions 301
Imperfect tense, the, 94, 298; distinguished from aorist, 299; in conditional sentences, with ἄν . . 319
Imperfect tenses, properly so called. 57
Impersonal verbs, 101; singular and plural, 166; often improperly so called 167
Improper prepositions, the . 138, 253
Inchoative acts, by imperfect . . 300
Inchoative or inceptive verbs . 93, 148
Indeclinable proper names . . 33
Indefinite article, the . . . 275
Indefinite pronouns, the . 54, 286, 288
Indefinite tenses, the . . . 57
Indefiniteness by omission of article, 199
Indicative mood, 55; the objective part of the verb, 298; in indirect interrogation, 315; interchanged with optative, 316; in conditional sentences, 318; *apparent* in intentional clauses, 323; with ὥστε, 328; compared with infinitive . . . 329
Indirect form changed to direct . 352
Indirect interrogation . . . 315
Indirect quotation 315
Individual acts in plural expressions 204
Inferential conjunctions . . . 346
Infinitive mood, the, 56; a verbal substantive, 324; with article, 177; with accusative subject, 232; as subject, 325; as object, 325; expressing result, 326; oblique cases of, 326; with ὥστε, 328; for imperative, 329; in modern Greek. . . . 321
Inseparable declensions, the . . 19
Instrument, by dative . . 227, 253
Instrumental, ἐν 240
Intensive use of participles . . 333
Intentional or final clauses, 320; particles 321, 322
Interjections 142
Interrogative, its sign, 10; pronouns,

53, 287; particles, 139, 141; forms, 307; ἦ, 346; γάρ . . . 347
Interrupted statements, by ἀλλά . 342
Investiture, by ἐν 240
Irregular substantives . . 21, 32
Irregular comparisons . . . 42

-ία, substantives in 144
Ἰάομαι, future of 95
Ἱεροσόλυμα, or Ἱερουσαλήμ . . 33
-ίζω, verbs in 148
Ἵημι, conjugated (in ἀφίημι) . . 118
Ἰησοῦς, declined, 24; with article . 188
ἱκανός, with infinitive . . . 326
-ικός, -ική, -ικόν, adjectives in . . 147
-ιμος, -ον, adjectives in . . . 147
-ίνα, with subjunctive for imperative, 312; intentional, 320; explanatory, 320; is it ever ecbatic? 321; distinguished from ὅτι, 320; from ὅπως, 320
ἵνα τι, or ἱνατί 287
ἵνα πληρωθῇ 322
-ινος, -ίνη, -ινον, adjectives in . . 147
-ιον (-άριον, -ίδιον), substantives in . 144
-ιος, -ία, -ιον, adjectives in . . 146
-ισκος (-ίσκη), substantives in . . 145
Ἵστημι, conjugated, 106; its two aorists, 114; transitive and intransitive tenses, 292; its compounds . . . 307
ἰχθύς, declined 27

J.

Jacob, Rev. Dr. 231
Jebb's "Sacred Literature" . . 354
JEHOVAH, equivalent of the term in the Apocalypse 206
Judicial words, Latin, in the New Testament 159

K.

Kühner's "Greek Grammar," ed. by Jelf 209

L.

Lachmann 307, 316
Languages of Palestine . . . 155
Languages not verbally coincident . 235
Latin influences on New Testament Greek, 156; words in the New Testament, 158; names in the New Testament 162

538   ALPHABETICAL INDEX.

Lee, Dr., on "Inspiration" . . 204
Letters, names of the, neuter, 33; as numeral signs 44
Lightfoot, Bishop 321
Likeness, unlikeness, etc., by dative, 223
Linus, possibly a Briton . . . 162
Liquid verbs, 86, *sq.*; change of short vowel in the stem . . . 98
Local genitive, 217; dative, 228; accusative 233
Luther's version of the New Testament 305

λαμβάνω, stem and present, 93; future, 96; perfect 99
λανθάνω, with participle . . . 331
λείπω, second aorist of . . . 84
λευκαίνω, future and first aorist of . 97
λέων, declined 27
λύω, why not chosen as paradigm . 61

M.

Madvig's "Greek Syntax" . . 313
Measures, coins, etc., with numerals, 276
Mediation, expressed by διά . . 246
Menander, quoted by St. Paul . 355
Mental affection, verbs of, with genitive, 208; with dative . . 224
Meyer, Dr. 218, 321
Middle voice, the, 55; its meaning, 292, *sq.*; not always distinguishable in sense from active, 293; often indistinguishable in form from passive, 297
Middleton, on the article with names of Christ, 188; on 2 Tim. iii. 16 . 193
Military terms, Latin, in the New Testament 159
Minister of another's will, by διά . 253
Modal dative, 226; participle . . 332
Monadic substantives . . 179, 190
Moods, the . . . 55, 60, 298
"Most highest," corresponding idiom to 43
Motive or cause, by διά, with accusative 253
Mutes, the, classified . . ▸. 5
Müller, Max, Professor . 59, 207, 212

-μα (-ματ-), substantives in . . 145
μαθητεύω, transitive and intransitive 291
μαθητής, declined 20
μᾶλλον, in comparisons . . 42, 271
μαμμωνᾶς 157

μανθάνω, stem of 93
μάρτυς, irregular in declension. . 32
μέγας, declined, 38; comparison of . 41
μείζων, comparative, declined, 41; double comparative from . . . 43
μέλει, impersonal 101
μέλλω, auxiliary future verb . . 302
μέν and δέ, 344; without δέ . . 345
μενοῦνγε 346
μένω, stems and forms of . . 93
Μεσσίας 157
μετά, 250, *sq.*; distinguished from σύν, 250; with infinitive (accusative) . 328
μή and οὐ, 139; μή in questions, 139, 308; with imperative, 309; with optative, 313; negative intentional particle, 322; after verbs of fearing 323
μὴ γένοιτο 313
μήτηρ, ellipsis of 213
μήτι, interrogative 308
-μι, verbs in 104
μίγνυμι 124
μικρός, ά, όν, declined, 34; comparison of 42
μιμνήσκομαι, stem of . . . 94
-μός, substantives in . . . 144
-μων, -μον, adjectives in . . . 148
Μωσῆς, declined 33
μυστήριον, predicated of Christ . 284

N.

Names, proper, in the New Testament, of various languages, 160; use of the article with 185
Neander on προσευχή . . . 218
Negative adverbs, 139, 338; joined to predicate, 275; emphatic, 302, 312; with infinitive, 324; with participle, 330; followed by ἀλλά, 342; combination of negatives . . . 339
Negative indefinite pronoun . . 290
Negative questions 308
Neuter, forms alike in, 16; plural subject, with singular verb, 167; predicate, with masculine or feminine subjunctive 171
Neuter verbs, 55. *See* Intransitive.
Nominative, the case of the subject, 167, 205; of personal pronouns omitted, 277; predicate after copulative verbs, 171; for vocative, with article, 195, 206; suspended, 206; elliptic . 206

Number of nouns, 15, 202; of verbs 57
Numbers, compound and distributive, 47
Numerals, the, 44, 275; with genitive, 216; adverbs 137

ν ἐφελκυστικόν 4
ν, inserted in stems . . 93, 104
νά, in the modern Greek infinitive 321
νεανίας, declined 20
νόμος, with and without article . 200
νοῦς, declined, 23; irregularities in 32

O.

Object of verbs, direct (or nearer, primary), indirect (or remoter, secondary), by different cases, 224, 231; direct object of a transitive verb in accusative, 229; may be omitted, 230; "internal," 230; object (direct or indirect) of active the subject of passive, 294; object usually placed after governing verb 350
Object of comparison in genitive, 211, 270; or by ἤ, 270; may be omitted, 271
Object-sentences, 314, sq.; sometimes found with accusative object, 317, 352
Objective genitive . . . 218, sq.
Oblique cases, why so called . . 15
Occasion, the, sometimes by ἀπό, 237, 253
Old Testament, its influence on the New, 355. See Hebrew, Hebraistic.
Olshausen on fulfilment of prophecy, 322
Omission of article in defined phrases, 179; to mark indefiniteness, 199; of logical links between clauses, 352. See Ellipsis.
Opposition, by ἀλλά . . . 342
Optative mood, the 56; subjective, 298; in independent sentences, 312; in indirect interrogation, 315; optative and indicative combined, 316; in conditional sentences . . . 318
Oratio obliqua 315
Ordinal numbers, the, 45; cardinal used for 275
Origin, by genitive . . . 207
Ostervald's version quoted . . 231
Oxytone words 8

Ὁ, ἡ, τό. See Article.
O- declension, the (second) . . 19

ὅδε 51, 191, 281
οἴκειοι, ellipsis of 213
οἶκος, ellipsis of (or οἰκία) . . 213
ὄλλυμι 124
ὅλος, with article 194
ὄμνυμι 125
ὀνίνημι 114
ὄνομα, use of 206
ὀξύς, -εῖα, -ύ, declined . . . 36
ὅπως and ἵνα, distinction of . 320
ὁράω, defective, 102; augment of . 94
ὅς, ἥ, ὅ, declined, 52. See Relative.
-ος, neuter (stem, -ες), substantives in 145
ὅστ(εον), οὖν, declined . . 23
ὅστις, ἥτις, ὅ,τι, declined, 52, 286. See Compound relative.
-οσύνη, substantives in . . 144
ὅτι, particle introducing object-sentences, 314; relative causal particle . 347
οὐ, the objective negative particle, in questions, 308; distinguished from μή, 139, 338; οὐ μή, 302, 312; οὐ μόνον ... ἀλλὰ καί 342
οὖν and ἄρα 346
οὐρανοί, plural 204
οὗτος, declined, 51; with article, 191; demonstrative force, 281; may refer to the more distant antecedent . 281
οὗτος ... ἵνα 320
ὄφελον, as particle . . . 314
-όω, verbs in 148

ὦ, interjection, with vocative . . 207
ὡς, a particle of comparison, with predicative participles . . . 333
ὡσεί 276
ὥστε, ecbatic, with infinitive, 328; with indicative 329

P.

Parallelism, Hebrew . . . 354
Parathetic compounds . . . 150
Parisyllabic declension . . 19
Paronomasia 354
Paroxytone 8
Partaking, verbs of, with genitive . 216
Participial constructions changed for the finite verb 353
Participles, the, 56; in -ων, declension of, 37; in -ως, 36; tenses of, 56, 334; with article, 176; as relative and finite verb, 176, 197, 334; general use

ALPHABETICAL INDEX.

of 329, *sq.;* predicative, 330 ; adjunct to predicate, 332 ; attributive, 330 ; adverbial, 332 ; in broken constructions, 335, 337
Particles, the, 140 ; emphatic suffixes, 53 ; separable in composition, 151 ; inseparable, 151. *See* Conjunctions.
Partitive genitive . . . 215, *sq.*
Partitive plural 203
Parts of speech 14
Passive voice, the, 55, 294 ; sometimes difficult to distinguish from the middle, 295
Past time, tenses expressing . . 57
Paul and *Saul* . . . 161, 163
Paul, St., his name, with the article, 185
Perfect state, tenses expressing . 57
Perfect tense, the, 99 ; of liquid verbs, 87 ; second perfect, 85, 99 ; third person plural in -αν, 99 ; perfect passive, 100 ; force of the perfect, 309 ; distinguished from aorist, 305 ; aorist may sometimes be rendered by, 303 ; "present-perfect," 306 ; perfect imperative 309
Perispōmenon 8
Permission, by imperative . . 309
Person, in verbs 57
Personal endings, in verbs, origin of 59
Personal pronouns, 49, 277 ; nominative subject, when unemphatic, omitted, 277 ; genitive of, for possessive pronoun, 212, 277 ; pleonastic use, 278 ; αὐτός for third person . . 278
Peter, St., his name, with the article 185
Place, by genitive, 217 ; by dative, 228 ; by accusative 233
Pluperfect tense, the, 99, 306 ; its notion expressed by aorist . . 304
Plural verb in general expressions, 166 ; neuter nominative with singular verb, 167 ; verb with collective subject, 168 ; with several subjects, 169 ; of substantives, how used, 202, *sq.;* plural forms with singular force . . 203
Political terms, Latin, in the New Testament 159
Possessive genitive . . 212, *sq.*
Possessive pronouns, the, 50, 280 ; unemphatic, by article, 185 ; with the article, 192 ; for objective genitive, 277
Postpositive particles . . . 340
Potential by imperfect . . . 300
Prayer, its object, by περί or ὑπέρ, 265 ; by ἵνα 320

Predicate, the, 164 ; anarthrous, 178 ; with article, 178 ; participles with, 330, *sq.*
Predicative verbs 165
Prepositions, use of, 131, 234 ; table of, 236 ; with genitive, 131, 236 ; with dative, 132, 239 ; with accusative, 132, 242 ; with genitive and accusative, 131, 245 ; with genitive, dative, and accusative, 132, 254 ; table of, 133 ; in composition, 151 ; combined, 152 ; preposition and case, after article, 175 ; adverbially used, 135, 337 ; interchange of prepositions, 235, 261, *sq.;* governing several words, 265 ; with infinitive, 327 ; corresponding adverbs, 138 ; adverbs as "improper prepositions" 138
Prepositional phrases, without article, 190
Present time, tenses expressing . 57
Present tense, its stem, as modified, 82, 86, 92 ; force of the tense, 297, *sq.;* aorist rendered by, 303 ; present-perfect, 306 ; present and aorist distinguished in imperative, 309 ; in subjunctive, 311 ; in infinitive . 324
Price equivalent, etc., by genitive . 221
Principal and historical tenses 57, 297
Proclitics, the 8
Prohibitions, by future indicative, with οὐ, 301 ; by subjunctive aorist, with μή 311
Pronominal subject, its omission and insertion 166, 277
Pronouns, the, 49, 277 ; personal, 49, 277 ; possessive, 50, 280 ; demonstrative, 281 ; relative, 283 ; interrogative, 287 ; indefinite, 16, 287 ; distributive pronouns, with genitive 216
Proparoxytone 8
Proper names, with article . 185, *sq.*
Properispōmenon 8
Prophecy, Old Testament . . 322
Punctuation 10
Pure verbs, uncontracted, 70 ; contracted 71

παῖς, declined 8
παλιν-, in composition . . . 151
παρά . . . . . 259, *sq.*
πᾶς, declined, 37 ; its use with article, 192 ; in Hebraistic negative, 275 ; παν- in composition . . . 151

ALPHABETICAL INDEX. 541

πατήρ, declined, 27 ; ellipsis of . 213
παύομαι, perfect passive of, 100 ; with
   participle 331
πείθω conjugated 78
πεινάω, future of 95
πειράομαι, future of. . . . 95
περί, 250 ; compared with διά, 265 ; with
   ὑπέρ 265
πῆχυς, genitive plural πηχῶν . . 37
πίμπρημι 114
πίνω, present and second aorist of, 92 ;
   future, 96 ; first aorist passive . 98
πίπτω, stem of, and second aorist . 94
πιστεύω, conjugated . . . 61
πλέω, stem of, and future . . 96
πλήσσω, second aorist passive . . 98
πλοῦτος, of variable declension . 32
πνεῦμα ἅγιον, with article . . 190
πνέω, stem of, and future . . 96
ποιμήν, declined 27
πόλις, declined 27
πολύς, declined, 38 ; comparison of, 42 ;
   with article. 195
πότερος 288
πράσσω, second perfect of . . 85
πραΰς, or πρᾶος (or ᾳ) . . . 38
πρέπει, impersonal 101
πρό, 239 ; with infinitive . . 328
πρός, 260, sq. ; compared with εἰς, 266 ;
   with infinitive (accusative) . . 328
πρὸς φθόνον, adverbial . . . 337
προσευχή, special sense of . . 218
προσέχω, elliptical use of . . 230
προφητεύω, augment of . . . 97
πύλη, declined 7

φαίνομαι, with participle . . . 331
φέρω, defective 102
φεύγω, future of 96
φημί 114
φθάνω, stem of 93
φιλέω, conjugated 72
φορέω, future of 95
ψηλαφάω 209

Q.

"Quarterly Review," the, January,
   1863 189
Quirinus, governor of Syria . . 269
Quotations, with article prefixed . 177
Quotation, direct and indirect. . 315

R.

Rational Concord. *See* Synesis.
Reciprocal force of middle . . 293
Redundancy, apparent . 278, 282, 352
Reduplicated stems, 94 ; of verbs in -μι,
   105
Reduplication, 58 ; varieties of . 99
Reflexive middle 292
Reflexive pronouns . . . 49, 278
Regimen, combined . . . 265
Relation, by genitive . . . 219
Relative pronoun, the, 52 ; compound or
   indefinite, 286 ; relative and antece-
   dent, 283 ; case of relative, how deter-
   mined, 283 ; relative in apposition
   with a clause, 283 ; relative and ἄν, 314
Remembrance, verbs of, with genitive,
   210
Renewed mention, by article . . 181
Repetition for emphasis . . 352
Resolved tenses . . 301, 302, 330
Result, by genitive of infinitive, 327 ;
   by ὥστε 328
Revelation, the Book of, anomalous
   forms and constructions in, 156, 352
Revised Version . . . *passim*
Rhetorical *we* 202
Rhythm in sentences . . . 354
Roberts, Dr., "Discussions on the Gos-
   pels" 155
Romans, Epistle to the, expounded by
   parallelism 357

ῥέω, stem and future . . . 96
ῥήγνυμι 125
ῥῆμα, declined 25
-ρος, -ρα, -ρον, adjectives in . . 147
ῥύομαι, augment of . . . 94, 98
ῥώννυμι 125

S.

Saul and *Paul* . . . 161, 163
Second declension, paradigms . 22, *sq.*
Second tenses, the, 83. *See* Aorist,
   Future, Perfect.
Sentences, simple and compound, 164,
   172 ; how to analyse, 173 ; qualified
   by article, 177 ; objective, 314 ; conditional, 317 ; intentional, 320 ;
   changed structure in, 353 ; non-completion of compound . . . 353
Separable declension . . . 19

Separation, verbs of, with genitive . 210
Septuagint version of the Old Testament 156
Shakespeare 43
Singular number, the, 202; singular verb, with neuter plural nominative, 167; singular for collective, by article. 180
Smith's "Dictionary of the Bible" 269
Source or author, by genitive . . 208
Space by accusative . . . 233
Speaker using the plural of himself, 202
"Sphere," the, by dative, 228; by ἐν, 240
Stem, the, 14; verbal, 58; modifications of . . 81, 92, 105, 143, 144
Stier, Dr. 335
Stuart, Dr. M., "New Testament Syntax" 204
Subject, the (nominative), 164; with article, 178; of the infinitive (accusative), 232, 325; of passive verbs . 294
Subjunctive mood, the, 55; anomalous, from verbs in -όω, 323; strictly subjective, 298; in independent clauses, 311; after relatives or particles with ἄν, 314; in indirect interrogations, 315; aorist as future perfect, 318; in conditional sentences, 317; in intentional clauses 320
Substantives, genders of, classified, 144; declensions of, 17, sq.; syntax of, 202, sq.; number, 202; case, 205; with prepositions, 234; followed by infinitive, 326; adverbially used. . 337
Substantive verb, the, as copula, 164; as predicate, 165; with genitive, 217; with dative 223
Substantivised phrases . . 178, 334
Superlative degree, the, 40; with genitive, 216; use of, 273; Hebraistic, 274
Synesis, or Rational Concord (*constructio ad sensum*), in verbs, 168; in adjectives, 171, 268; in αὐτός, 279; in the relative. 283
Synthetic compounds . . 150, 152
Syro-Chaldaic dialect . . . 155

-s, appended to οὕτω, μέχρι, ἄχρι . 4
σάββατον, of variable declension . 32
σαλπίζω, future of, 96; elliptical use of, 166
σάρκινος and σαρκικός . . . 147
σεαυτοῦ, ἧς, declined, 50; ἑαυτοῦ used for 279
σημαίνω, first aorist of . . . 97

-σις, substantives in . . . 145
σκία, declined 20
σκότος, of variable declension . . 32
σπείρω, stem and forms . . 94, 97
στήκω 114, 149, 307
στρέφω, transitive and intransitive . 291
στρώννυμι 126
σύ, ὑμεῖς, declined 49
σὺ λέγεις, formula of affirmation . 308
σύν, 241; distinguished from μετά . 242
σώζω, first aorist and perfect passive of 98
σώφρων, declined 40

T.

"Taxing," the, in Luke ii. 2 . . 269
Telic and ecbatic particles . 321, 328
Temporal augment, the . . . 59
Temporal use of participles . . 332
Tenses, scheme of, 56; principal and historical, 57; characteristic letters, 60; expressive of time and state, 296; tenses of the indicative, 296, sq.; of the imperative, 309; of the subjunctive, 311; of the infinitive, 324; of the participles 330
Than, by genitive after comparative, 211, 270; by ἤ 270
Third declension, paradigms, 25, sq.; terminations of nominatives. . 26
Time, by genitive, 217; by dative, 228; by accusative 233
Tischendorf 311, 316
Transition, particles of . . 341, 343
Trench, Archbishop . . 204, 304

ταὐτά and ταῦτα . . . 51, 192
ταχύς, comparison of . . . 41
τε, with καί, ascensive . . . 341
τελέω, future of, 95; with participles 332
τέρας 32
τέσσαρες, -α, declined . . . 45
τηλε-, in composition . . . 151
-τήρ and -τωρ, substantives in . 145
-της, -τητος, substantives in . . 145
-της, -του, substantives in . . 144
τίθημι, conjugated . . . 106
τιμάω, conjugated 72
τιμή, declined 20
τίς; τί; interrogative . . . 287
τις, τι, indefinite 289
τοιγαροῦν 346

ALPHABETICAL INDEX. 543

τοίνυν 346
τοσοῦτος 192
τρεῖς, τρία, declined . . 45
τρέφω, perfect, active and passive . 100
τρέχω, defective 103
τρίβω, conjugated 78
-τρον, substantives in . . . 144
τύπτω, second aorist forms . . 84

θαυμάζω, future of 96
θέλω, how augmented, 93 ; emphatic future. 302
Θεός, with and without article. . 186
θιγγάνω, with genitive . . . 209
θνήσκω, stem and forms . . . 93
θραύω, perfect passive . . . 100

U.

Unconscious versification . . 356

ὕδωρ, omitted after certain adjectives 267
υἱός, ellipsis of 212
υἱὸς Θεοῦ, with article . . . 187
-ύνω, verbs in 148
ὑπέρ, 251, sq. ; distinguished from ἀντί, 252 ; from περί 265
ὑπό. . . . . . 253, sq.

V.

Vaughan, Dr. C. J. . . 214, 297
Verb, the, 55, 291 ; verbal stem, the, 58 ; denominative verbs, 148 ; classes of verbs, 148 ; verbal predicate, 165 ; concord of, 167, sq.; transitive, with accusative object, 229 ; some verbs both transitive and intransitive, 229 ; verbs with modal dative, 226 ; with cognate accusative, 230 ; with double accusative object, 231 ; verbs with genitive of secondary object, 208, sq., 216 ; with dative, 223, sq.; compounded with prepositions, 266 ; complemented by participles, 331 ; followed by infinitive, 325 ; combined with adverbial force, 338 ; verbal forms as adverbs . 137
Verbal adjectives in τός, τέος . . 61
Vocative case, the 206
Voice, the distinction of . , 55, 291
Vowels, the 2
Vowel aorist, the 94

Vau, v, a lost letter of the Greek alphabet, called, from its shape, F, Digamma, Ϝ being an old form of the gamma 44
F, as influencing the declension of nouns, 31 ; the conjugation of verbs . 96

W.

Want, fulness, etc., by genitive . 210
Watts, Dr. 186
Webster, Rev. W. . . 234, 300, 321
Webster and Wilkinson's "New Testament" 180
Westcott, Bishop, and Dr. Hort's edition of the Greek Testament passim
Wilderness of the temptation . . 180
Winer's "New Testament Grammar," 181, 199, 203, 220, 236, 247, 249, 270, 272, 273, 278, 294, 300, 301, 339, 345, 347, 352
Wish, expressed by optative . . 313
Words, formation of . . . 143
Words of one language not precisely coincident with those of another . 235

Z.

Zeugma 351
Zumpt, Dr. A. W., on Quirinus . 269
ζάω, infinitive ζῆν, future . . 96
Ζεύς, genitive, Διός . . . 32
ζώννυμι, conjugated . . . 121

INDEX OF SCRIPTURE PASSAGES.

[The letter *s* prefixed denotes the number of the paragraph in the chapter on Synonyms.]

I.—OLD TESTAMENT, CHIEFLY THE SEPTUAGINT.

Genesis.

CH. VER.	PAGE
2. 7	244
24	244
9. 24	274n
25	274
22. 17	333

Exodus.

4. 19	204
16. 15	157
22. 28	356

Leviticus.

7. 1	220n
14. 2	220n
15. 32	220n
19. 18	279

Numbers.

6. 13	220n
21	220n
31. 12	231n

Deuteronomy.

6. 5	263

Joshua.

15. 25	161

1 Kings.

CH. VER.	PAGE
1. 43	291n
18. 44	183
45	183

2 Kings.

1. 2	157
3	157
23. 10	157

1 Chronicles.

23. 31	32

Nehemiah.

5. 18	242

Psalms.

9. 2	43
16. 10	213, 245
22. 1	158
25. 11	347
51. 4	294
68. 18	231
103. 2	276
118. 5	237n
22	244, 285
23	258, 269
25	158

Proverbs.

CH. VER.	PAGE
30. 30	274

Isaiah.

6. 10	321
7. 14	182
9. 1	234
14. 14	214
30. 33	157
40. 4	244
8	203
41. 4	165
61. 1	224
65. 1	227

Jeremiah.

7. 22	339
31	157

Hosea.

6. 6	339

Amos.

5. 26	157
9. 12	286, 296

Jonah.

4. 8	183

Micah.

5. 2	239

INDEX OF SCRIPTURE PASSAGES.

II.—NEW TESTAMENT.

Matthew.

CH.	VER.	PAGE
1.	1	. . . 179, 189
	6	 213
	11	 255
	16	 334
	17	 46
	18	. . 191n, 222, 331, 347
	20	. . . 222, 249
	21	. 166, 237, 279, 301, 347
	22	. 176, 246, 322n
	23	. . . 182, 250
2.	1	. 181, 190, 222, 239, 241
	2	. 225, 326, 347
	3	. 33, 160n, 193
	4	. 205, 258, 299
	5	. . . 175, 347
	6	. 239, 347, s16
	7	. . . 181, s6
	8	 320
	9	 383
	10	 231
	11	 242
	12	 324
	13	. . 222, 302, 327, 347
	14	 217
	15	 322
	18	. . . . s20
	20	. 204, 305, 347
	23	 322
3.	1	 297
	2	 347
	3	 347
	4	. . . s66, 251
	5	. . . . 160n
	7	. s3, 216, 257, 287, s6
	8	. . . 220, 347
	9	. . . 238, 347
	10	 297
	11	. . . 263, 265
	12	. . . 227, 286
	13	. . . 237, 327
	14	. . . 300, 340
	15	 347
	16	 225
	17	. 206, 237, 305
4.	1	. . 180n, 253
	3	. 187, 318, 320

Matthew.

CH.	VER.	PAGE
4.	4	. . . 241, 255
	7	 301
	8	. . . . s58
	10	 225
	11	. . 224, 299
	14	 322
	15	 234
	17	 237
	18	. . s70, 264
	21	. . 212, 229
	23	. . 219n, 280
	24	. . 269, 292
5.	1	. . . 182, 242
	1–16	 12
	2	. . 332, 352
	3	. s30, 228, 301
	3–11	 350
	4	 176
	4–8	 166
	5	. 165, 178, 301
	6	 184
	8	 228
	9	 171
	10	. . 184, 301
	11	 166
	13	. . 179, 240, 253, 287
	15	. 159, 175, 182, 253, 256
	16	. . 197, 310
	17	. 312, 343, 345
	18	. . 33, 166, 275, 312
	19	 314
	20	. . 166, 270, 312, 314
	21	. . 166, 228, 264, 301
	22	s52, 158, 166, 225, 264
	25	 52
	26	 158
	27	 301
	28	 166
	29	. . s52, 216
	30	. . . s52
	32	 166
	33	 301
	34	. 166, 241, 324
	37	 268
	38	 236

Matthew.

CH.	VER.	PAGE
5.	39	. . 166, 268, 286, 342
	40	. s55, 294, 303
	41	 159
	42	 294
	44	. 166, 252, 309
	45	 291
	46	 287
	47	 287
	48	 301
6.	1	s5, s21, 261, 328
	2	. 297, 312, 314
	3	 312
	4	 230
	5	 301
	6	 310
	7	. . . s6, 332
	8	 328
	9	 277
	9–11	 310
	10	. 254, 277, 342
	12	. . . . s39
	13	. 237, 242, 268
	16	. . 320, 331
	17	 293
	18	. . 241, 331
	22	 178
	24	. 157, 194, 217, 275, 326
	25	. . 224, 316
	26	. 211, 243, 340
	27	 333
	28	. s66, 224, 251, 288, 291
	34	. . 175, 245
7.	1	 309
	2	 263
	3	. . 196, 230, 277, 288
	6	. 176, 224, 355
	7	 224
	8	 297
	9	. . 232, 308
	11	 324
	13	 350
	13–15	 350
	14	 288
	15	. . 230, 286
	16	. . 262, 308
	20	 346
	21	 276

INDEX OF SCRIPTURE PASSAGES.

Matthew.

CH.	VER.	PAGE
7.	22	308
	23	206
	24	208, 256, 286
	25	99
	26	286
	28	314
	29	170
8.	1	278
	3	315
	4	243, 312
	8	341
	9	348
	10	166
	11	166, 190
	16	166
	17	322
	18	251
	19	275
	24	328
	25	292, 309
	26	288
	28	237, 324
	29	226
	32	248
9.	1	281
	3	216
	4	287
	5	288
	6	191
	8	204
	9	223
	11	287
	13	305, 339, 339n
	15	258
	16	s13, s25, 256
	17	125
	22	237
	28	307, 315
	29	249
	34	241
	35	219n, 269
	36	251
	37	344
10.	1	218
	2	175
	3	161
	4	161
	10	220
	15	241, 271
	18	243, 344, 344n
	20	339
	21	167
	22	247, 282, 302

Matthew.

CH.	VER.	PAGE
10.	24	253
	25	321
	26	330
	27	285
	28	s52, 230
	29	275
	31	211
	42	205, 267
11.	1	331
	2	188
	3	176, 180
	5	s30, 267, 295
	7	s5, 180
	8	125, 232, 343
	9	343
	10	239
	11	272
	12	338
	14	s3, 303
	16	194n
	21	319
	23	s52
	25	332, 352
	26	195
	28	260
	29	237
	30	s21
12.	3	169, 250
	7	319
	10	210, 308
	12	211
	13	98
	17	322
	18	s62
	20	97
	22	355
	23	309
	24	157
	26	318
	29	180
	33	345
	35	180
	36	205, 241
	41, 42	186, 199, 250
13.	3	176, 224
	4	177, 233, 241, 259
	5	328
	8	299
	13	s5
	14	333
	15	321
	20	208

Matthew.

CH.	VER.	PAGE
13.	20–23	282
	24	305
	25	181, 242, 328
	25–40	159
	26	181
	29	139
	30	328
	31	170
	32	211, 328
	35	322
	38	165, 282
	39	178
	47	s70
	52	291
	56	260
14.	3	216, 304
	6	203
	13	249
	17	204
	21	276
	22	324
	26	237
	27	165
	29	256
	31	217, 288
15.	1	204
	4	226
	11	282, 180
	12	204
	16	135
	24	215
	25	224
	26	182
	28	207
	32	205, 257
	37	216
16.	3	344
	8	288
	9, 10	s69
	14	275
	16	179, 187
	18	s52, 165, 344, 354
	19	27
	22	302, 313
	24	303
	25	s55, 303
	26	s55, 194
	28	314
17.	1	198
	4	225, 325
	5	196
	9	190, 222

INDEX OF SCRIPTURE PASSAGES. 547

Matthew.

CH.	VER.	PAGE	CH.	VER.	PAGE	CH.	VER.	PAGE
17.	11	298	21.	8–11	299	24.	45	327
	12	302		9	158, 180	25.	1	s65, 287
	17	338		12	182		4	250
	20	318		16	293		5	299
	22	302		18	344		8	297
	24	182		19	203		14	281n
	25	159		23	297, 345		15	281
	26	346		26	225		37	307
	27	236, 243		31	288		40	258
18.	1	272		32	327	26.	2	243, 259, 298
	6	251		40	312		8	204
	7	237		42	244, 258,		12	255, 328
	8	271, 325			268, 285		16	276
	9	s52, 271	22.	2	305		17	203
	10	323		5	174, 281n		22	308
	12	47, 223		8	344		23	241, 282
	13	271		10	340		25	308, 309
	17	180		16	337		26	106n, 179
	21	338		17	159		28	179, 335
	22	137, 338		20	287		32	233, 328
	23	305		23	297		33	318
	24	275		29	180		35	241
	26–34	294		35	275		41	344
	28	158		37	s55, 263,		45	309
19.	4	190			265, 301		46	292
	5	167, 244		39	301		50	266
	8	190, 260		42	188		53	159, 271
	11	276		43	240		54	312
	13	280, 299, 320	23.	2	303		55	s35, 249, 257
	14	191		7	158		56	322
	16	275		15	s52, 176		59	194n
	17	268, 318		17	288		61	247
	18	177		19	288		63	248
	19	279		24	182		64	308
	22	332		27	s6, 223, 344		69	275
	23	344		28	s6, 344		73	156, 348
	26	258		31	225	27.	4	301
	28	151, 254, 257		33	s52		5	292
20.	3	239, 251		34	260		6	157
	6	233		37	176		8	338
	8	344		39	180, 237		11	308
	9	242	24.	1	204		12	233, 328
	10	242		2	256, 312		17	288
	12	183, 223		6	302		21	288
	19	229, 328		9	302		23	347
	21	237, 275		12	195, 247, 328		24	301
	22	288, 293, 302		16	264		26	159
	23	177, 344		18	245, 264		27	159
	28	236, 326		21	175, 338		29	238
	30–34	204		22	276		33	157
21.	3	344		27	190		37	204
	4	322		29	s65, 330		38	275
	8	168, 264		40	275, 297		40	335

INDEX OF SCRIPTURE PASSAGES.

Matthew.

CH.	VER.	PAGE
27.	44	204
	46	158, 287
	48	204, 275
	51	835
	54	187
	57	85, 291
	62	175
	65	159
	66	159, 250
28.	1	139, 217, 276, 344
	2	304
	6	306
	7	306
	9	342
	11	159
	19	814, 244, 256, 279, 291, 332

Mark.

CH.	VER.	PAGE
1.	1	189
	2	239
	4	219
	7	286, 326
	13	180n
	16	870, 265
	24	176
	27	344
	29	212
	33	194n
	36	175
2.	1	247
	4	159
	15	328
	19	241
	23	325
3.	2	316
	5	832
	13–26	341
	17	157
	18	161
	21	258, 315
4.	12	321
	19	251
	21	309
	24	230
	28	269
	31	211
	39	310
5.	4	328
	7	226

Mark.

CH.	VER.	PAGE
5.	9	159, 170
	11	260
	13	248, 276
	14	297
	15	159, 297
	21	257
	22	275
	23	292, 312
	29	315
	33	182
	35	213
	41	158, 279
	42	226, 347
6.	2	334
	4	265
	7	47, 218
	9	353
	11	253
	16	285
	21	203, 228
	25	250
	27	159
	38	204
	40	206, 242
	45	166
	49	86
	50	165
	56	314
7.	4	159, 292, 294
	11	157
	17	204
	22	202
	25	286
	27	182
	31	242
	34	158
	35	299
	36	42
8.	2	205
	10–18	341
	15	230
	25	151
	34	303
	35	303
	36	194n
	38	229
9.	1	209
	7	208
	12	257, 345
	19	338
	20	353
	21	135
	34	272

Mark.

CH.	VER.	PAGE
9.	37	256, 339
	40	252
	41	189, 311
	42	42, 271
	43	852
	43–47	271
	45	852
	50	240
10.	8	244
	13	166, 280, 300
	17	275
	18	268
	37	275
	45	348
	46–52	204
	51	158
11.	2	216
	7	307
	8	265
	9	158
	10	158
	14	313
	18	299
	22	218
	25	248
	27	297
	32	317, 353
12.	4	338
	5	174
	10	244
	14	254, 312
	17	175
	18	297
	26	255
	28	274
	30	263, 265
	31	279
	34	317
	38	230
	42	158, 275
13.	1	204, 269
	4	302
	8	249
	9	279
	14	264
	16	245, 265, 312
	20	276, 319
	22	328
	25	302, 330
14.	3	248
	4	287
	5	276
	6	241

INDEX OF SCRIPTURE PASSAGES.   549

Mark.

CH. VER.	PAGE
14. 19	47, 139, 249
25	312
28	177
31	302, 313
35	255
36	157, 206
49	322
54	338
55	328
58	247, 331
60	308
61	175
68	s4
71	125
15. 1	199
6	298
9	s3
12	s3
15	159
16	284
17	232
21	190
22	157
24	316
29	142
34	158
36	204
39	159, 187
44	159, 305, 316
45	159
47	213
16. 1	213
2	276
4	347
5	295
6	306
9	48, 266, 276
12	190

Luke.

CH. VER.	PAGE
1. 1	141, 303, 347
2	190
3	274
4	s14
5	289
6	s49
9	327
13	301
15	33, 158, 189, 275

Luke.

CH. VER.	PAGE
1. 19	260, 297n, 303
20	236, 302
21	328
23	s36
29	316
31	301
33	203, 257
35	187n
37	275
41	189
42	274
46	s47
46–55	354
50	244
51	240, 305
53	210, 305
57	327
59	300
62	177
64	351
67	189
68–79	354
74	233
76	239
79	97
2. 1	163
2	269, 274
4	287, 328
5	294
6	326
8	231
10	193, 297n
12	199
13	268
18	251
20	285
21	326, 328, 342
25	189, 191
29–32	354
31	193, 249
37	47
39	175, 248, 304
41	248
48	98, 303
49	213, 288
3. 1	163
2	255
5	244
13	s2, 259
16	263, 286
18	224, 269, 297n
19	285
4. 2	339

Luke.

CH. VER.	PAGE
4. 5	s58
6	s3
13	192
14	248
16	330
18	100, 297n, 306
23	331
25	254
34	142
42	327
43	194, 297n
5. 1	165
4	331
5	247, 255
6	300
10	175, 302
14	353
17	328
19	217
27	250
32	305
33	293
6. 1	153, 325
6	325
12	182, 218
15	161
16	213
20	243
23	192
25	96
26	192
27	343
32	348
34	294, 320, 348
35	257, 294
37	313
38	263
43	330
44	263, 281
47	288
48	338
7. 2	s2, 302
13	257
19	290
25	343
39	319
45	331
46	s18
47	195, 286
8. 1	249
6	98
8	98
10	321

INDEX OF SCRIPTURE PASSAGES.

Luke.

CH. VER.	PAGE
8. 13	 254
15	. . . s21, s31
23	 299
29	 228
30	. . . 159, 168
33	 248
39	 248
41	 341
45	 242
49	 315
54	. . . 195, 216
9. 3	 242
7	 290
8	 290
13	. 181, 270, 318n
14	 242
16	 181
23	 303
24	 303
25	. . . . 194n
27	 209
28	 205
30	 287
31	 302
35	 208
41	 338
44	 302
45	 321
46	. . . 177, 272
52	 329
10. 1	. . 47, 242, 269, 302
7	 180
14	 180
19	. 302, 313, 326
20	 339
22	. . . . s3
23	 166
24	 166
27	 279
29	 341
35	. . . 258, 286
36	 216
37	 250
39	 281
40	. . . 152, 251
41	 251
42	. . 274n, 293
11. 4	. . . . s39
8	 328
11	 353
13	 189
28	 346

Luke.

CH. VER.	PAGE
11. 35	 323
36	. . . . 194n
42	 343
12. 1	. . 241, 279
3	 236
5	. . . s52, 328
6	. . 158, 275
7	 211
10	. . 205, 243
11	 198
20	. . 207, 287
22	. . 224, 316
24	 211
26	 224
33	. . . . s2
39	 319
44	 255
47	 261
48	 285
51	 343
54	. 182, 190, 298
55	 183
13. 2	 259
4	 46
9	 351
11	 337
16	 47
18	 223
19	 244
22	 293
29	. . 190, 292
32	. . . . 7n
14. 3	 229
6	 154
7	. . 230, 299
17	 170
18	. . 304, 337
19	 304
24	 209
30	 191
31	 239
15. 4	 47
7	 271
15	. . . s16, 223
19	 326
25	. . 190, 208
26	. . . . s62
27	 298
29	 233
16. 1	 334
3	 332
8	. . 213, 253
9	. 157, 278, 293

Luke.

CH. VER.	PAGE
16. 10	 196
11	. . . 157, 350
13	 157
16	. . . . 298n
19	 232
22	 203
23	. . . s52, 203
25	. . . 176, 281
26	 256
30	 289
17. 2	. . 271, 321
3	. . 230, 279
4	 217
8	 96
12	 289
15	 315
23	 166
30	 192
32	 210
34	 298
35	. . . 258, 302
18. 1	 328
4	 258
7	 217
8	. . 141, 307
11	 345
12	. . 217, 306
13	. . . . s43
14	. . 271, 281
17	 313
26	 341
35–43	 204
35	 307
19. 3	. . 237n, 317
8	. . 216, 297
11	 338
18	. . . . s2
20	 159
37	. 168, 260, 268
40	. . 81, 100
42	 351
44	. . 236, 255
48	 316
20. 2	 345
11	 338
12	 338
16	 313
17	. . 244, 285
20	. . 154, 233
21	 204
25	 346
35	. 197, 216, 324
39	 204

INDEX OF SCRIPTURE PASSAGES. 551

Luke.			Luke.			John.		
CH.	VER.	PAGE	CH.	VER.	PAGE	CH.	VER.	PAGE
21.	5	851	24.	25	327	3.	5	189, 265, 318
	6	255		26	812		6	178
	11	354		27	265, 300		10	181
	12	239		29	327		14	180
	19	306		32	299, 330		15	276
	22	327		34	228, 306		16	276, 329
	24	165		35	228		18	338
	26	265		39	209		19	351
	34	279		41	237n		20	355
	37	334		46	812		21	355
22.	4	177		47	234		28	330
	14	169					29	226
	15	226, 328					33	824
	19	277, 335		John.			36	297
	20	250, 328				4.	4	246
	22	345	1.	1	178, 190		7	238
	24	272			260, 350		11	170, 341
	33	326		2	190		14	285, 313
	35	289		4	179		18	286
	37	177		5	293		19	350
	41	233		6	206		22	182
	42	83, 351		10	340		23	265, 348
	49	240		13	203		24	350
	50	275		14	171, 210, 258		25	157
	57	207		15	270n, 272, 274		27	250
	59	337		16	236, 341		35	317
	66	204		18	282		36	321
	67	313		19	307		40	181
	68	313		20	352		42	278, 311n
	70	308		26	263		43	181
23.	5	248, 338		29	297		44	281
	6	316		30	274		52	233
	12	260		33	263, 282		53	169, 194n
	14	334		40	233	5.	5	233
	15	227, 343		41	281, 281n		6	303
	19	287		42	157, 284		8	311
	24	153		48	328		11	282
	26	190	2.	2	169		13	53
	33	157, 190		4	226, 298		16	299
	41	341		5	286		17	338
	47	187		6	242		18	281
	48	257		7	210		22	193
	49	197		8	311		29	220
	53	241, 339		9	209n		30	280
24.	1	276		10	338		35	865
	5	204		12	169, 233		36	270
	6	306		14	835		40	303
	10	213		15	159		42	219, 317
	11	168		16	311		44	353
	13	206		17	218		46	319
	18	161		20	47, 228		47	307, 318
	21	242		21	214	3.	1	221
	23	233	3.	3	318		2	169, 254

John.

CH.	VER.	PAGE
6.	6	302
	8	204
	9	204, 275
	10	231
	19	233
	20	165, 309
	22	304, 353
	24	188, 353
	27	339
	28	312
	31	157, 180
	37	313
	39	276
	42	191, 282
	45	204
	46	282
	49	157
	51	203, 344
	57	247, 342
	58	157, 203
	60	350
	62	351
	66	238
	71	212
7.	4	318
	6	192
	14	299
	16	339
	17	303
	22	265
	23	194, 321
	24	231
	27	317
	34	117n
	35	220
	36	117n
	38	205
	41	347
	42	263
	45	282
	49	170
8.	4	98
	9	249
	16	344
	17	344
	25	337
	29	304, 305
	40	306
	42	s10, 319
	44	190, 280, 303
	51	313
	52	160, 209
	58	287

John.

CH.	VER.	PAGE
8.	58	165
	59	188
9.	2	321
	3	167
	16	191
	22	294
	24	s47
	30	348
	31	350
	33	319
	36	341
	40	10
	41	319
10.	1	282
	3	208
	4	168
	5	313
	6	s46
	16	s72
	22	203
	24	338
	27	168
	28	313
	30	169
	32	265
	33	265
	35	180
11.	1	263
	4	252
	6	233
	8	204
	11	307
	12	318
	13	300
	15	321
	17	292
	18	46
	21	319
	30	304
	31	352
	32	319
	34	307
	35	s20
	38	243
	44	310
	47	312
	51	188
12.	1	239
	4	204
	13	158
	18	331
	20	335
	23	321

John.

CH.	VER.	PAGE
12.	27	343
	34	188, 331
	40	321
	43	s47, 271
	44	339
	45	s5
	46	276
13.	4	159
	5	159, 182
	6	307
	8	313
	10	s17, 293
	11	335
	14	s12
	16	211
	18	322
	27	272
	28	287
	31	305
14.	3	298
	6	246
	7	320
	13	286
	15	310
	16	152n
	17	190
	22	302
	26	152n, 190, 232
	27	197, 355
	28	319
15.	1	170
	4	239
	6	166
	8	320
	9	278
	16	286
	17	282
	18	274
	20	318
	22	319
	25	322
	26	190
	27	344
16.	2	s6, 321, 343
	4	190
	13	182, 190
	16	298
	20	244, 342
	23	s9
	24	293
	25	s46
	27	258
	29	s46

INDEX OF SCRIPTURE PASSAGES. 553

John.

CH.	VER.	PAGE
16.	32	321
17.	2	111n, 218
	3	s24, 320
	4	304
	7	99
	9	s9
	10	192, 194, 280
	12	322
	15	s9, 268
	17	178
	20	s9
	24	239
18.	3	182
	5	165
	6	165
	8	165, 188
	9	322
	15	169
	16	260
	20	241
	21	288
	24	304
	28	213
	30	319
	32	302
	34	279
	35	309
	37	238, 308
19.	3	196
	11	272
	13	157
	17	157
	19	159, 204
	20	159
	24	311, 322
	25	133, 161, 213, 258
	27	213
	28	s13
	28-30	322
	29	204
	30	s13
	31	97, 168
	32	97, 274
	36	322
	41	181, 339
20.	1	48, 181, 243, 276
	2	166, 265
	3	169, 194, 243
	3-5	300
	4	41n, 136, 243, 269

John.

CH.	VER.	PAGE
20.	5	243
	11	260
	12	260, 275
	14	315
	16	158
	17	298
	19	276
	22	189
	25	194, 313
	28	196
	30	269
21.	6	237n
	8	37
	10	237
	11	47, 210
	13	352
	14	306
	15	211, 212
	15-17	s16, s19
	16	212
	17	212
	18	304
	19	304
	23	298
	25	324

Acts.

CH.	VER.	PAGE
1.	1	207, 274, 285, 293, 341, 345
	2	224
	3	247, 328
	4	208, 353
	5	189, 263
	7	199
	10	342
	13	161, 213
	16	207
	18	167, 229
	19	157
	22	282, 285
2.	1-13	10
	1	258
	2	330
	4	189
	10	249
	11	331
	17	96, 237
	21	296
	22	s45, 285
	24	326
	25	243
	27	s52, 213, 245

Acts.

CH.	VER.	PAGE
2.	29	239, 340
	31	213, 245
	36	193
	38	189, 244, 256
	39	293
	45	314
	46	249
	47	335
3.	1	169
	2	106n, 166, 298, 335
	3	333
	4	333
	5	289
	7	215, 333
	8	332
	10	317
	11	268
	12	327, 333
	13	282
	19	322
	24	344
	25	s61
4.	5	325
	7	266, 269, 333
	8	189, 333
	9	218
	13	333, 352
	15	333
	16	345
	17	226, 257
	18	333
	19	270, 333
	20	166
	21	333
	22	214, 271
	23	333
	25	287
	27	s62
	28	351
	30	s62
	32	289
	35	314
	36	333
	37	333
5.	1	22
	2	293
	4	288, 332, 339
	8	294
	9	288
	13	293
	15	216 289
	16	268

NN2

INDEX OF SCRIPTURE PASSAGES.

Acts.

CH.	VER.	PAGE
5.	19	247
	21	132, 254
	28	226
	30	188
	32	221
	35	279, 302
	36	161, 225, 289
	37	225
	41	252
	42	249, 331
6.	1	$50, 260
	3	189, 254
	5	162
	9	159, 265
	13	331
7.	1	292, 308
	9	294
	12	331
	14	239
	16	212
	19	327
	20	275
	21	244, 278
	26	287
	30	180
	34	333
	35–38	282
	40	205
	42	$36, 292
	43	157
	48	$35
	56	$85
	59	298
8.	1	248
	5	280
	9	289
	11	228
	12	251
	15	189, 287
	17	189
	18	189
	20	313
	21	223
	23	331
	26	281
	27	333
	30	141, 307, 354
	31	314, 347
	35	352
	40	245, 328
9.	3	325
	7	209
	14	296

CH.	VER.	PAGE
9.	16	252
	20	352
	21	296
	29	$50
	31	219, 228, 248
	33	238
	39	293, 332
	42	248
10.	1	22
	3	181, 233
	6	259
	7	$60, 216
	16	258
	18	316
	22	181, 218
	32	171
	37	248
11.	6	300
	10	258
	13	181
	15	190
	16	190, 263
	18	346
	19	256
	20	$50, 187
	23	226
	26	194
	28	163, 255
	29	283
	30	283
12.	2	227
	3	338
	6	239
	7	107n
	14	237n
	15	175
	18	316
	21	254
	23	236
13.	9	162
	10	207, 308, 331
	13	175
	15	207
	20	228
	21	160n, 233
	22	244
	23	188
	31	258
	33	188
	34	$23
	40	204
	42	245
	45	332

CH.	VER.	PAGE
13.	47	327
	50	266
14.	2	248
	4	174
	5	326
	8	228
	9	327
	10	186
	12	32
	13	$67, 32, 239
	16	228
	19	233
	21	229, 291
	23	306
	27	250
15.	1	226
	4	250
	12	169
	14	160n
	17	284, 286, 296
	21	249
	23	281, 329
	28	$6
	35	$15, 230, 269
	36	$15, 284, 289, 292, 317
16.	2	295
	3	171, 352
	4	299
	9	247
	12	159, 287
	13	$38, 218n
	15	318
	16	$15, 293, 325
	25	249
	26	329
	31	169
17.	1	182
	2	64n
	3	188, 353
	4	341
	10	247, 287
	11	316
	12	216
	15	136, 274
	18	266, 303
	21	193n, 272
	22	$44, 272
	23	$37, 199
	25	354
	27	$7, 209, 316, 364
	28	174, 355
	30	$42

INDEX OF SCRIPTURE PASSAGES. 555

Acts.			Acts.			Acts.		
CH.	VER.	PAGE	CH.	VER.	PAGE	CH.	VER.	PAGE
17.	31	240, 302, 337	21.	37	307	26.	4	345
	32	174		38	159, 179, 182		5	s44
18.	3	231	22.	2	155		6	307
	9	352		9	209		7	153, 286, 337
	10	230		11	237n		12	283
	13	259		12	295		14	155
	14	207, 319		16	294, 302		16	282
	15	301		17	325		17	284
	18	s38		20	293		24	185, 195
	25	272, 295		21	243		25	274
	26	272		25	308		29	314
19.	2	308		29	344		30	169
	3	244		30	177, 294		32	324
	7	46, 194	23.	5	301, 356		41	344
	12	159		6	165	27.	3	227
	14	290		9	351		8	273
	15	s4, 165		10	s33, 323		9	32
	17	193n		13	271		10	324
	19	276		14	s51, 226		13	s6, 136, 273
	24	293		15	233, 327		14	248
	25	251		23	290		16	227
	26	191		26	274, 329		17	323
	27	244		30	254		18	293
	29	194n		31	247		20	327
	32	272		32	182		25	207
	34	353	24.	3	135, 274		34	133, 260
	35	268, 347		5	336		37	194
	39	318		6	192		39	319
	40	210, 348		11	271, 284, 333		43	s3, 210
20.	3	327		14	282	28.	4	184
	4	162		17	247, 344		6	114
	6	181		18	283		15	159
	7	s15, 276		19	254, 319		16	249
	8	s65		20	97		18	287
	9	s15, 182, 237n		22	273		20	232
	13	181		23	182		26	313
	18	192n		26	223		27	321
	24	s13, 293	25.	6	254		30	194
	28	s16, 281, 293		7	269			
	31	331		8	163			
	33	209		9	254		Romans.	
	35	271		10	273, 330			
21.	3	s68		17	293	1.	1	212
	5	338		19	s44		2	220n
	11	281		21	163		4	188n, 205
	13	245, 342		22	300		5	218
	16	s25, 285		23	249		7	187
	26	334		25	163		8	194, 345
	28	306, 332		26	154, 254		9	293
	30	194n		27	97		10	255
	31	194	26.	2, 7	199		11	224
	32	331		2	254		13	338
	33	316		3	234, 248		16	202, 229

INDEX OF SCRIPTURE PASSAGES.

Romans.

CH.	VER.	PAGE
1.	17	173
	20	s34, s58
	22	326
	25	s28, 203, 259
	26	213, 259
	29	227, 354
	32	333
2.	1	207
	4	s31, 173
	5	241
	6	283
	6–10	355
	8	s32, 238
	9	202
	10	202
	12	200
	13	259
	14	199
	15	345
	16	220n, 246
	18	s14
	19	233
	21–23	307
	23	200
	25	200
	26	244, 280
	27	333
3.	2	232, 295, 345
	4	294
	9	297
	18	219
	20	200, 276, 302
	22	264
	23	210, 304
	25	s42, s49, 263, 293
	26	s31, 263
	28	200
	29	346
	30	261, 347
	31	200, 343
4.	1–16	11
	1	173
	2	318
	3	167, 180, 244, 344
	5	244
	9	244
	11	214, 262
	13	208
	14	238
	18	259
	19	276

Romans.

CH.	VER.	PAGE
4.	20	226, 332
	22	244
5.	1	238, 246, 311, 311n
	2	311
	3	311
	5	219
	6	249, 252
	7	s21, 252, 267, 347
	8	252
	9	335
	10	262, 311n
	11	335
	12	184, 256, 353
	13	184
	13–17	353
	15–19	195
	15	318, 353
	17	335
	18	220, 346, 353
	19	171
	20	152, 201
6.	2	225, 287, 313
	3	243, 346
	4	243, 306
	5	318, 343
	8	242, 311n
	10	258
	13	310
	14	253, 301
	15	313
	16	345
	17	285, 351
	20	226
7.	1	258, 346
	2	220, 223
	3	327
	7	178, 301, 307
	9	201
	10	282
	12	s21, 345
	13	313
	14	147
	18	325
	24	207, 214
	25	34, 278
8.	3	196, 234, 251
	9	190
	10	240
	11	247
	13	s54, 302
	15	157, 352

Romans.

CH.	VER.	PAGE
8.	18	261, 350
	20	256
	22	338
	23	50, 214n, 333
	24	227
	25	318
	26	152, 177, 192, 316
	27	249
	31	252
	32	53
	33	307
	34	307
	35	219
	36	219
	39	219
9.	1	190, 352
	2	354
	3	300, s38, s51
	5	203, 254
	8	191, 244
	9	217
	11	321
	12	272
	14	308
	15	s41
	18	s3
	19	s3, 307
	20	154, 346
	29	158, 319
	30	197
10.	1	280, 345
	2	218
	4	201
	13	296
	14	296
	16	225, 276
	18	346
	20	227, 338
11.	1	348
	7	184
	9	244
	13	215, 345, 350
	17	318
	18	318
	24	264
	25	337
	31	277, 321
	33	207, 354
	36	262
12.	1	s55
	3	247, 354
	5	195, 249

INDEX OF SCRIPTURE PASSAGES. 557

Romans.			1 Corinthians.			1 Corinthians.		
CH.	VER.	PAGE	CH.	VER.	PAGE	CH.	VER.	PAGE
12.	9	268	1.	29	276	7.	25	334
	15	329	2.	1	166, 186		28	305
	16	243, 259		2	234n, 373		31	227
	19	350		3	166		32–34	224
13.	2	s49, 307		4	190		34	228
	3	220, 303		7	186, 334		37	353
	5	342		8	319		–39	326
	9	177, 279, 301		13	s55, 190, 267		40	s6, 190
	10	201		14	s55	8.	13	313, 318
	11	271, 283		15	s55	9.	1	308
	14	293	3.	1	s55, 147, 166		2	343
14.	1	350		2	351		6	169
	4	307		4	s55, 290		12	218, 227
	5	259		·5	246, 343		14	238
	15	249		6	291, 299		15	227, 241, 304
	20	345		7–9	186		17	232, 294
15.	3	348		7	289, 291		24	309
	4	180, 208, 277		·9	215, 350		26	346
	5	313		10	186, 199	10.	1	193
	6	198		–15	246		2	244, 294
	8	252		16	s35		3	300
	11	310		–20	187, 317		4	300
	13	190		21	217		11	168, 261
	15	247, 272, 304	4.	4	225		13	183
	16	190		5	183, 239		14	230
	22	327		6	323		16	285
	24	233, 325		8	125, 314		17	195, 216
	25	332		9	s6		19	289
	26	293		17	304		21	216
	27	216		21	240, 288		25	159
16.	6	287	5.	4	242		26	s13
	9	162n		5	282		29	287
	12	287		7	s25, 348		30	226
	14	162		8	240		31	345
	15	162		9	183, 224, 304		33	195
	21	162		13	301	11.	1	344
	23	194n	6.	1	254, 289, 294		2	s49, 344
	25	219n, 228		2	221, 318		4	132, 248
				4	282		9	248
1 Corinthians.				5	242		12	248
1.	1	185		6	283		13	325
	2	296, 341		8	283, 341		14	184
	3	187		11	171, 283, 289, 304		18	289, 345
	9	246					22	312
	–10	32		16	167, 244		23	300
	11	213		18	230		24	243, 277, 334
	13	244, 307		19	217		25	137, 250
	17	326	7.	5	258		26	137
	18	215		10	233		27	345
	19	125n		11	233		30	307
	21	183, 262		15	309		31	319
	25	270		16	316	12.	2	314
				19	171		3	s51

558   INDEX OF SCRIPTURE PASSAGES.

1 Corinthians.		1 Corinthians.		2 Corinthians.	
CH. VER.	PAGE	CH. VER.	PAGE	CH. VER.	PAGE
12. 8	262	15. 27	166	2. 17	195, 330
9	262	29	205, 252	3. 1	279
13	244, 348	30	166	3	147, 170, 190
14	348	31	277	5	263
15	259	32	311	6	200
16	259	33	s21, 355	11	262
25	224	34	311	12	227
27	337	37	318	13	106n, 335
31	272	39	276	14	287
13. 1	184, 350	41	211	15	257
2	193	43	349	17	179
4	184	44	s55, 349	18	226
8	292	45	244	4. 2	192
9	337	46	s55	6	214
10	337	49	311n	17	264
11	298	50	169	18	s5
12	246, 260, 337	52	166	5. 1	214, 221
13	212	54–57	355	2	333
14. 1	s15, 344	55	s52	4	321, 348
4	200	16. 2	276	5	157, 214
5	270, 318n	5	298	6	336, 353
9	302	10	312	7	336
10	318	15	352	8	336, 353
11	241	17	277	10	246
13	320	21	280	11	219
15	32, 311n	22	s51, 158	13	225
16	183			14	219, 252
19	190, 272			15	252, 304, 306
20	s55, 228	2 Corinthians.		16	318
22	244			18–21	187
23	194n	1. 3	198	19	240, 280, 330
25	190	4	285	6. 2	167
27	132, 242	5	246	14	223
28	190	8	253, 327	18	244
30	274	9	154, 256, 321	7. 1	219
35	190, 303	10	52	4	227
36	346	12	275	5	336
38	309	13	320, 343, 345	8	183
15. 3	252	14	170, 337	9	249
4	306	16	262	10	s40, 249
6	258, 272, 276	17	227	11	249
8	183	22	157, 214	12	304, 328
9	216	2. 2	342	13	256
10	227, 242	3	257, 304	14	318
12	317	4	238, 304	16	202
14	s29	5	318, 337	8. 2	248
15	248	6	191, 272	7	312
16	318	9	304	9	282
17	s29	10	296	10	135
19	330	12	243, 344	11	327
21	184	13	327	14	244
24	198	14	202	20	323
26	298	15	176, 335	23	252

INDEX OF SCRIPTURE PASSAGES. 559

2 Corinthians.

CH.	VER.	PAGE
9.	2	135
	3	304
	6	256
	9	*830
	10	291
	12	330
10.	2	233, 325
	5	218
	10	167
	12	153
	16	139
11.	1	314
	5	253
	23	138
	26	208
	30	349
	31	198
	33	98
12.	2	239, 247, 282
	3	317
	4	317
	6	208
	11	253
	12	180
	18	228
	19	252, 281
	20	227, 323
	21	323
13.	1	255
	4	219, 348
	5	279, 317
	7	171, 320

Galatians.

CH.	VER.	PAGE
1.	1	246, 261
	4	251, 252, 265
	6	*876, 297
	7	*876
	8	*851
	9	*851, 342
	10	225
	11	298n
	16	240
	22	330
	23	330, 335
2.	1	247
	2	335
	4	323
	6	289
	7	232, 294
	10	283

Galatians.

CH.	VER.	PAGE
2.	11	249
	12	300
	13	154, 329, 329n
	14	148, 343
	16	200, 276
	17	141, 307
	19	201
	20	197, 252
	21	346
3.	1	207, 249
	2	200
	5	200
	6	244
	9	238
	10	200
	13	252
	16	167, 254, 284
	18	201
	21	197, 319
	27	244
4.	1	181, 211
	6	157
	8	330
	10	293
	11	317, 323
	17	323
	19	284
	20	300
	22	174, 275
	24	330
	25	177
	26	287
	31	200
5.	12	314
	14	301
	17	321
	22	348
	24	175
	25	318
6.	1	323, 352
	2	*868
	3	289
	5	*868, 302
	9	281, 331
	11	53, 304, 304n
	12	226
	14	325
	15	289
	17	135, 217

Ephesians.

CH.	VER.	PAGE
1.	1	246

Ephesians.

CH.	VER.	PAGE
1.	3	176, 198
	5	246
	6	214
	10	175
	13	227
	14	*843
	16	331
	20	353
	21	253
	23	*813
2.	1	263
	3	*855, 228
	4	247
	5	227
	8	227, 246, 283, 341
	9	321
	12	210
	15	*849
	20	198
	21	193
3.	8	43, 212
	10	321
	15	*861, 193
	18	198, 278, 293
	19	*84, 219, 227n
4.	1	221
	1-3	336
	6	262
	8	167, 231
	9	177, 214, 273
	10	253
	11	*815, 174
	16	220, 293
	17	268, 282
	18	268
	23	*826
	26	*832
	28	335
	30	245
	31	*832
	32	240
5.	2	*837
	3	223
	5	198
	6	280
	12	280, 325
	14	107n
	16	165, 293
	18	190
	19	*843, 226
	21	219
	22	281n

Ephesians.

CH.	VER.	PAGE
5.	25	252
	31	244, 302
	33	312
6.	2	240
	9	215
	10	296
	14–16	214
	16	268
	18	190
	21	*82
	22	304
	23	187

Philippians.

CH.	VER.	PAGE
1.	2	265
	4	293
	5	338
	9	320
	10	154, 245
	11	231, 246
	12	273
	13	159
	15	*15, 265, 290
	16	*15, 174
	17	174
	18–23	189
	18	226
	21	177
	22	288, 293, 316
	23	42
	27	221
	28	283
	29	353
	30	353
2.	2	321
	4	54
	6	*1, *56, 326
	7	*56
	8	*56
	12	50
	13	252
	15	*6, *65, 138, 284
	25	215
	27	139
	28	272
	30	221
3.	2	230
	3	*36, 165, 184
	5	200, 238
	8	304

Philippians.

CH.	VER.	PAGE
3.	9	280
	10	*84, 355
	12	*27, 304, 318*n*
	13	233
	15	289
	16	329
	20	187, 284
	21	301, 327
4.	2	162
	5	228
	6	*38
	7	*55
	9	220
	10	*11
	13	193
	18	258
	22	163

Colossians.

CH.	VER.	PAGE
1.	6	353
	7	162
	8	190
	9	231, 331
	10	221
	10–12	355
	11	214
	13	214
	14	348
	15	193
	16	*5, 194, 306
	17	239
	23	193, 208
	26	353
	27	284
	28	352
	29	283
2.	1	53
	5	338
	8	323
	9	*13, *34
	12	208, 218
	13	242, 263
	14	*49
	15	279
	18	*44, 218
	19	231, 275
	20	*49, 242
	21	*7
	22	198, 283
	23	260, 330, 345

Colossians.

CH.	VER.	PAGE
3.	1–4	189
	3	242, 306
	5	*54
	16	*43, 336
4.	10	*26
	12	162
	15	162
	17	317, 323
	18	280

1 Thessalonians.

CH.	VER.	PAGE
1.	5	265
	7	199
	8	179, 199
	10	335
2.	1	317
	3	238
	4	232, 294
	6	263
	12	221
	14	192
	15	334
	20	348
3.	3	327
	4	302, 302*n*
	11	313
	12	313
4.	1	177
	5	330
	7	256
	8	339, 346
	9	278
	10	348
	15	179, 241, 313
	16	176, 200
	17	242
5.	3	313
	6	311
	10	242
	14	260
	16–22	309
	23	*27
	24	335
	25	251

2 Thessalonians.

CH.	VER.	PAGE
1.	8	199, 330
	10	232
	11	320

INDEX OF SCRIPTURE PASSAGES.   561

2 Thessalonians.

CH. VER.	PAGE
1. 12	. . . 198, 320
2. 1	 252
2	. . . 246, 307
3	 183
9	 181
10	 236
11	 181
13	 190
15	. s49, 232, 295
3. 1	 320
3	 268
5	. . . 219, 313
10	 348
11	 331
14	 293
17	 280

1 Timothy.

CH. VER.	PAGE
1. 3	. . . 332, 353
2	. . . . s41
4	 353
6	 211
8	. . . 227, 354
10	 334
11	. . s28, 232
13	. . . 332, 351
14	 351
16	. . 192n, 193
17	 244
18	 240
19	. . s21, 251
2. 6	. . . 234, 281
7	 352
8	. . . s3, 232
3. 5	 209
11	. . . . s53
13	 293
14	 273
16	. 228, 284, 354
4. 3	 351
10	 256
14	 250
5. 3	 197
5	 256
8	 211
11	 303
14	. . . . s3
19	 255
21	 154
22	 216
23	. . . 227, 339

1 Timothy.

CH. VER.	PAGE
5. 24	 290
6. 3	 334
4	. . . 169, 251
5	 232
12	. 183, 231, 350
13	. . . 194, 254
14	 350
15	. . . s28, 274

2 Timothy.

CH. VER.	PAGE
1. 12	. . . 245, 326
13	 363
17	 273
18	. . . 136, 273
2. 5	 318
8	. . 220n, 306
11	. . 165, 178, 304, 350
18	 287
19	 187
24	 282
26	 282
3. 3	. . . . s53
9	 282
15	 193
16	 193
4. 3	 334
6	 307
7	. . . . s13
10	 196
13	 159
15	 293
16	 313
17	 98
21	 164

Titus.

CH. VER.	PAGE
1. 3	 281
7	 215
9	 334
11	 194
12	 355
2. 1	 334
3	. . . . s53
4	 176
5	. . . . 281n
9	. . . . 281n
11	 196
13	 198

Titus.

CH. VER.	PAGE
2. 14	 218
3. 5	 151
6	 246
7	. . . 227, 282
8	. . . s11, 209
10	 276
11	 154
12	 162
13	 162

Philemon.

CH. VER.	PAGE
1. 4	 255
5	 263
10	 147
11	. . . 147, 354
13	. . . s3, 252
20	. . 114, 313, 354
22	 320
23	 169
24	. . . 163, 169

Hebrews.

CH. VER.	PAGE
1. 2	s58, 200, 255
3	. . s56, 51, 214, 239, 293
4	. . . 259, 272
5	 244
6	. . . . 193n
8	 196
9	. . . 196, 232
14	. . . s3, s36
2. 1	 272
3	 52
5	 224
7	. . . 257, 289
8	. . . s5, 194
9	. . . s5, 209, 252, 351
10	 248
13	 206
14	. . . 216, 306
15	. . . 247, 328
16	 352
3. 3	 259
5	. . . . s60
12	. . . 220, 323
13	 289
4. 1	 222

INDEX OF SCRIPTURE PASSAGES.

Hebrews.

CH.	VER.	PAGE
4.	2	298n
	3	334
	4	167
	6	298n
	8	319
	9	225
	12	153, 253
5.	1	252
	2	232
	4	181
	7	s33, 237
	8	286, 334, 354
	11	283
	12	247, 348
	13	220
	20	209
6.	1	214
	2	215
	3	311n
	4	209
	5	209
	10	326
	13–16	248
	14	333
	16	350
7.	1	191
	2	263
	4	53, 263, 350
	5	334
	9	s8
	16	147
	20	174
	21	174, 187
	22	215
	24	185
	25	337
	27	258
8.	2	s36
	5	167, 295
	10	336
	11	102, 313
	12	313
	13	s25
9.	1	s49
	3	203, 250, 274
	4	157
	5	s43, 157, 253, 337
	7	s39, 217
	10	s49, 213
	12	97, 203, 258
	15	s26
	21	220

Hebrews.

CH.	VER.	PAGE
9.	23	205, 259
	25	240
10.	1	s56
	2	258, 331
	6	251
	7	196, 289, 327
	8	251
	9	s10, 274, 298
	10	258
	18	251
	19	240
	25	331
	26	251
	27	289
	30	350
	34	348
	37	180
	39	217
11.	2	262, 295
	4	259
	6	s1
	8	302
	9	245
	10	183
	12	283
	13	249
	15	319, 326
	17	300
	20	199
	21	332
	26	209, 218
	28	s7, 335
	35	183
	37	240
	39	262
12.	1	s31, s68, 346
	2	215, 236
	5	209
	10	216
	13	356
	15	323
	16	323
	17	s40, 250
	18	s7, 209
	20	209
	24	s26, 259
	27	177
	28	s33
	29	348
13.	2	331
	5	312
	6	187
	8	165, 203

Hebrews.

CH.	VER.	PAGE
13.	12	240
	13	346
	18	s21
	19	273
	20	196
	21	203
	23	273, 331

James.

CH.	VER.	PAGE
1.	1	329
	5	210
	6	223
	11	183, 304
	13	220
	17	269, 330, 356
	18	289
	22	s1
	24	304
	25	197, 213
	26	s44, 215
	27	s44
2.	1	202
	2	181
	3	181
	4	213
	19	167
	20	303
	22	300
	23	344
	25	228
3.	1	s59
	4	52
	5	53, 350
	6	s52
	10	s12, 115
	11	199, 267
	15	s55, 330
	17	154
	18	225
4.	2	338
	5	337
	8	223
	11	201
	13	138, 191n, 281, 292, 311n
	15	328
5.	1	138, 292
	3	225, 244
	4	158
	6	181

INDEX TO SCRIPTURE PASSAGES. 563

James.

CH. VER.	PAGE
5. 9	239
11	s31
12	239
14	s18
15	s38
17	167, 226

1 Peter.

CH. VER.	PAGE
1. 1	215
2	190
3	194, 198
8	226, 332
9	332
10	197
14	196
17	296, 335
18	227
20	255
23	266
25	187, 197, 203, 298n
2. 1	193n
2	151
5	s23, s37
7	181, 285, 351
9	s21, s23, s43, s47
13	s49
17	335
18	335
19	218
21	252
23	299
24	286, 299
3. 1	281n, 323
5	281n
7	335
10	292, 327
14	231, 319
17	319
19	197
20	197, 215
21	350
4. 1	100, 211, 292
5	292
6	298
8	185, 239
11	s47, 203
12	226
13	216
17	327

1 Peter.

CH. VER.	PAGE
5. 1	239
2	239
7	s11
12	304

2 Peter.

CH. VER.	PAGE
1. 1	160n, 198
2	313
3	227
4	273
5	s21, 344
10	198, 293, 313
12	334
14	304
18	197
19	272, 291, 336
20	281, 336
21	190
2. 1	152
4	353
5	s25, 276
6	214
11	273
15	228
20	167, 318
22	s46, 175
3. 1	154, 284
2	221, 336
3	255, 336
5	261
11	202
14	227
18	244

1 John.

CH. VER.	PAGE
1. 1	190, 209, 306
2	190
3	344
5	352
6	352
8	352
10	352
2. 1	s4, 152n
2	251, 280n
4	352
5	219
13	268
14	268
15	219

1 John.

CH. VER.	PAGE
2. 19	319
21	276, 304
3. 1	s4, 321
2	51
4	179
10	168
12	268
4. 2	s4, 332
8	178, 304
10	184, 251
11	170, 318
16	219
17	250, 321
19	219
5. 3	170, 219, 321
6	262
16	s9
19	194n, 268
20	298

2 John.

VER.	PAGE
1	284
2	353
3	301
7	281
8	279
10	190
11	216
12	159, 260

3 John.

VER.	PAGE
2	132
4	283
5	283
6	221
7	252
9	279, 304
13	246, 303
14	260

Jude.

VER.	PAGE
1	213
6	197
9	273
10	s4

Jude.

CH. VER.	PAGE
14	239
18	255
19	190
24	354
25	354

Revelation.

CH. VER.	PAGE
1. 4	180, 206
8	33, 180
10	190, 240
13	260
18	27, 330
2. 10	183
14	232
16	240
17	157
20	118n
26	205
27	s16
3. 3	233
10	194n, 214
12	205, 278
15	314
21	205, 239
4. 1	99
4	47
8	180, 242
9	254
10	254
11	183
12	183
12-14	354

Revelation.

CH. VER.	PAGE
4. 13	183, 254
6. 1	276
3	276
6	221
8	240
16	254
7. 11	202
12	183
14	170, 183
17	242
8. 3	111n
7	216
8-18	216
9	s55
13	275
9. 12	301
15	245
10. 5	243
11. 2	47, 197
5	318n
15	268
16	202
12. 3	s67
9	s25, 194n
12	204
17	225
13. 1	s67
5	47
10	240
16	111n
18	44
14. 10	125
13	233

Revelation.

CH. VER.	PAGE
14. 15	240, 327
15. 2	275
6	251
16. 9	326
14	194n
18	52
17. 1	195
10	275
18. 4	168
6	125
9	96
13	s55, 159
17	192
21-23	313
22	276
19. 1	158
3	158
4	158
6	158
9	s24
11	s24
12	s67
16	274
20. 2	s25
21. 1	165
13	190
16	258
17	37
21	242
22. 10	349
11	309
14	323
16	304

www.ingramcontent.com/pod-product-compliance
Lightning Source LLC
Chambersburg PA
CBHW071216290426
44108CB00013B/1197